22 MEN AND A BAG OF WIND

The Ultimate History of the World Cup

TIM PARNHAM and STEVE HAINES

First Published 2002
by DSM
The Studio
Denton
Peterborough
Cambs PE7 3SD

British Library Cataloguing in Publication Data
A catalogue record of this book is available from the British Library

ISBN 0 953651 65 7

Produced by
DSM
The Studio
Denton
Peterborough
Cambs PE7 3SD

Cover design by Marc Lowen

Acknowledgements

Obviously a project like this one that has taken 3½ years to come to fruition has not been completed without the help and guidance of a number of important people. We would like to thank Jamie Doran for getting us started and sharing his experience with us, Martin Parsons for introducing us to DSM and Tim's long suffering wife, Sharon, for putting up with us both. We would like to thank all the staff and students at Windsor Girls' School, in particular Emma Easson, Simone Maini, Frank Deakin and the Modern Languages Department - Dawn Basnett, Ann Roderick and Nigel Bass - for their help in translating innumerous foreign language newspapers and articles. We would also like to thank Liz Richards and Julie Sellar for all their help and support and Susan Shephard, Sara Howells and Clive Northover for their useful comments. Peter Markie of the Sheffield Telegraph for our first piece of publicity, Keith Yardley and Justin Whiting for providing some invaluable research materials and Andrew Seal for some helpful suggestions. A big thank you also to all our friends and colleagues who have put up with countless World Cup stories with patience, good grace and a sense of humour. Last of all, we would like to thank those players, commentators and supporters who responded to our letters and for writing with passion about the bag of wind they love so much.

Picture Credits

All pictures courtesy of Popperfoto

About the Authors

TIM PARNHAM was born in 1963 in Dronfield, Derbyshire. He was educated at Dronfield Henry Fanshaw School before spending two years at Teesside University reading Business Studies then moving on to Leeds Metropolitan University to specialize in Hotel and Catering Management. He then took a teaching degree at the University of the West of England at Bristol for two years before taking up his present post as Head of Business Education at Windsor Girls' School. He saw his first game at Bramall Lane, aged seven, a Blades reserve game against Coventry, but because his Grandfather and best friend were Wednesdayites, he started supporting the Owls. He first went to Hillsborough as a ten-year-old on a wet and windy winter's day, the season Wednesday went down to Division Three for the first time in their history. Seeing the 'Boxing Day Massacre' when Wednesday beat United in front of Division Three's largest ever crowd, was something, but perhaps his finest memory came when Wednesday beat the Blades in the 1993 FA Cup semi-final at Wembley. The victory was made even sweeter by the fact that he was sat in the middle of the United fans. Steve was sitting next to him wearing his Rovers scarf.

STEVE HAINES was born in 1955 in Haslingden, Lancashire. He was educated at Accrington Grammar School, before spending six years studying at London (Royal Holloway and Birkbeck Colleges) and Reading universities. He then taught history at St. Crispin's School in Wokingham and later became Head of History at Windsor Girls' School. He played football at a very amateur level regularly until his knees gave way. He has supported Blackburn Rovers from a very young age, attending his first game at Ewood Park against Wolverhampton Wanderers in 1961 and for years after watched the Rovers tailspin into what he thought was terminal decline, until 'Uncle Jack' Walker picked them up and made them champions. That was a great day, but sweeter were the two victories against Burnley in the 2000-01 season and winning the Worthington Cup in 2002.

Preface

This book was conceived on a summer afternoon in June 1998. Steve had been looking around for a book that would guide him comprehensively through the forthcoming World Cup Finals in France, but all he could find was a lot of gloss with very little substance. It was then that we got together and decided to fill the need for such a book ourselves. We had always said that we would write together, but it would be economic history rather than football that would have been the topic - Steve is a history teacher, Tim teaches economics. After several informal meetings over a beer we decided what would go into this encyclopedia of the World Cup. We were looking for something that could be both read and could also be dipped into and used as a reference book. It could therefore be enjoyed by the general reader and by the football nutcase as well. However, neither of us had any experience of writing and getting a publisher was something quite alien to us. Fortunately, we had friends who work in television and related media, and they were able to give us a very helpful kick-start.

We ran our initial synopsis by Jamie Doran, a filmmaker with Atlantic/Celtic Films, and Martin Parsons of Reading University introduced us to his publisher - DSM. In October 1999 the deal was signed and the book is now due for launch in readiness for the Korea/Japan tournament in 2002. Our thanks go DSM for taking us on.

Our book, about the 'bag of wind' and the demented beggars that try to get it between the two sticks, covers a history of the development of football from ancient times to the founding of the English football league in 1888. It gives a history of international football from the first internationals between England and Scotland through to the inception of the World Cup in 1928 and charts the history of each World Cup tournament from 1930 to 1998. Each World Cup has its own section. They include a general historical background, the story of that World Cup, full reports on all the best games, biographical sketches of the stars of each tournament, and all those little but interesting stories that happen around the World Cup that make it the tournament that it is today. It also looks at the build-up to Korea/Japan 2002, including the teams taking part, the characters to look out for, the qualifying tournament and the politics that surround the media frenzy that is the World Cup. We also managed a number of contributions from major personalities in the game. Archie Gemmill recalls his experiences in 1978, the late Bryon Butler talks of the enormity of the World Cup and Alan Green expresses his joys and disappointments in 1982. Kevin Keegan recalls England-Spain in 1982, Brian Labone remembers Mexico in 1970, Sammy McIlroy talks about his experiences with Northern Ireland and John Inverdale paints a picture of what it was like to be in Paris the night France won. David Turner gives a fan's recollection of the 1966 World Cup semi-final between England and Portugal and Marvin Andrews of Trinidad and Tobago expresses his pride in scoring the first World Cup goal of the 2002 series. Finally, there is a full statistical section for each tournament.

The spelling of players' names and use of accents has presented us with enormous difficulty owing to differences that appear in the various sources. We have tried to be as accurate as possible with these and apologize for any inconsistencies.

Contents

Chapter 1

The Origins of Football

"This is the people's passion. It is the common denominator between nations and political and armed antagonism. It is an alternative or an accompaniment to the smile which breaks down barriers. People with no social or cultural connection may suddenly discover that the invocation of magic names such as 'Pelé … Real Madrid… Manchester United' can work a charm or spell.

Kier Radnedge, Encyclopaedia of Soccer, July 1998

The modern game of football (or soccer to some in the world) may have been the invention of the English, but it was not with the English that the game first began. Indeed, variants of the game were being played long before there was a place called England or a race known as the English.

There is plenty of good, hard evidence to suggest that people have been kicking bags of wind for thousands of years. The Ancient Egyptians are thought to have had religious ceremonies and fertility rites that involved aspects which can be linked to the development of the game. What is more certain is that the Chinese of the Ts'in Dynasty (255BC to 206BC) played a form of football as part of military training and that during the Han Dynasty (206BC to 220AD) a type of football called 'tsu chu' was played in which even the emperors took part. 'Tsu' can be roughly translated as 'to kick', whilst 'chu' denotes a stuffed leather ball. By the seventh century AD the Japanese were playing a game involving the use of footballs called 'kemari' or 'askemari'. This was played by eight men kicking a ball on a square ground with trees to mark the corners. The four trees were a willow, a cherry, a pine and a maple, and the ground measured approximately fourteen metres square. It is possible that this Japanese game may have originated in China, especially since there were sporting links between the two cultures and records indicate that they may even have played games, the very first international matches on record.

In other parts of the world, too, games that involved the kicking of footballs developed. The Polynesians of the Pacific are known to have used a ball made either of pigs' bladders or bamboo fibres, whilst the Inuit of Alaska and Northern Canada played a game called "aqseqtuk". This was a sort of football on ice, using a ball stuffed with grass, animal fur or moss. One Inuit legend tells of a game played between two villages, with goals ten miles apart, though quite what the rules were or how games were organised is less clear. One imagines that it had similarities to the rough and tumble football practised in England in the Middle Ages. On a like vein, tribes of North American Indians, in what is now the USA, played a game called "pasuckaukohowog", which means "they gather to play ball with the foot". It was often played on wide beaches, with goals up to a mile apart, and may have been played by as many as a thousand people at one time. The games certainly involved violence, like the ones played in England, and serious injuries were common. It is said that players disguised themselves so that they could not be identified for the purpose of retaliation. Unfinished games were often carried over to the next day, with a celebratory feast being organised for the end of the contest.

The Indians of Mexico and Central America played a football game, in walled courts that were some fifteen metres long, the object of which was to propel a ball through wooden rings or against mounted stones. The balls they used were probably made out of rubber.

In Europe, the Ancient Greeks played a football game called "episkyros", of which Smith's 'Dictionary of Antiquities' says: " It was the game of football, played in much the same way as well as, by a great number of persons divided into parties opposed to one another." Later, the Romans had a game known as "harpastum", which, like the Ts'in Chinese, they encouraged as a form of military training. It was a gymnastic and athletic game, probably often played indoors, and its name comes from the Greek word "arpazo" which means "I seize". This implies that the ball was allowed to be carried and Basil Kennet, in his 'Romae antiquae notitia', described a "larger kind of ball, which they played with" and the players "dividing into two companies and striving to throw it into one another's goal". The Romans seem also to have had another football game, more resembling of modern football, which involved kicking a ball from side to side and over boundaries. As with the other variations of football mentioned so far, there is uncertainty about the rules, but it has been suggested that it survived and developed into a game known as "calcio". This game was played in Tuscany, in Italy, in the Middle Ages and has teams of up to 27-a-side, with 6 umpires. The word "calcio" means "a kick" and clearly the game was a more organised affair than that which was being played in England.

Whilst some Irish antiquarians have asserted that a type of football was being played in Ireland over 2,000 years ago, and that this game spread into Britain to eventually become the modern game, a more widely accepted theory is that it was the Roman legions who introduced the game into Britain. Since the Romans occupied Britain for some four hundred years, there is probably much truth in this, though there is no concrete evidence to connect the game played by Roman soldiers with that played in medieval England, several hundred years later. The link may be a good one - after all, things have to begin somewhere, and then they develop and change - but it is just not possible to prove the point.

What is beyond proof is that by the Middle Ages football was being played in England and that this game was popular among ordinary people. The first historical reference to a game comes from 1175, when William Fitzherbert in his "History of London", speaks of the young men of the city annually going into the fields after dinner to play at the well-known game of ball. The game took place on Shrove Tuesday and it is obvious from the reference that it was not the first time that it had happened. The type of game that it was can be guessed at from other descriptions of what came to be known as "Shrovetide Football".

A description of this Shrovetide football is given in the Victoria County History of Derbyshire and concerns games that took place in Derby. It says: "From very early times Derby was renowned for a most fiercely played game of football which was waged annually on Shrove Tuesday. The contest lay between the parishes of St. Peter and All Saints... The whole of the rougher or more daring portion of the town and the adjacent districts took part in the affray. The ball was tossed up in the market - place at noon, and instantly seized by the strongest and most active of the opposing forces. A dense crowd speedily surrounded the combatants, endeavouring to impel the surging mass towards their particular goal." It was noted that this sport "was in no true sense football, for the ball was chiefly carried and only accidentally kicked." A measure of the popularity of these games can be gauged from the description of its eventual suppression: "Many unavailing attempts were made to put down the pastime, and at last in 1846 the riotous game was stopped, never to be resumed; but it required two troops of dragoons, a large levy of special constables and the reading of the Riot Act to secure the desired result."

The Medieval English game, then, amounted to little more than mob violence, an excuse for a riot. Rules, such as they were, were probably little more than traditions and varied from place to place. In some places the object was to score goals and in others to get the ball back to the team's own village. The goals were often miles apart and hundreds of players, male and female, adult and children might take part. Whatever the case, any means were used to achieve the object. Violence and injury were commonplace, as village fought village through field and river, or street fought street through the towns and cities, in attempts to win the game. Local rivalries could be very strong in the Middle Ages and helped to account for the intensity of the struggles. Utter madness reigned and a broken nose or leg would be counted quite minor mishaps. This remained the nature of the game into the sixteenth and seventeenth centuries, as many historical sources relate. In 1531, Sir Thomas Elyot in his "Boke named the Governour", writes of football being "nothing but beastly fury and extreme violence, whereof proceedeth hurt and consequently rancour and malice do remain with them that be wounded." Elyot recommends that the game should "be put in perpetual silence." Fifty years later things had obviously changed little as, in his book "Anatomie of Abuses", the writer Philip Stubbs describes football as a "devilish pastime... and hereof groweth envy, rancour and malice, and sometimes brawling, murder, homicide, and great effusion of blood, as experience daily teacheth."

In spite of the violence, or maybe because of it, football remained incredibly popular, "a folk custom" as Bryon Butler describes it. Games regularly took place all over England, in London's Cheapside or Smithfield, in Manchester in the North, or Ashbourne in Derbyshire, or in Corfe in the West. This often worried those in authority. King Edward II was concerned by the damage that ensued and "the great noise in the city caused by hustling over large balls", and in 1314 passed a law to ban the game. It failed and in 1365 the more warlike King Edward III tried to put a stop to the game because of the adverse effect it was having on archery practice, so necessary to England's medieval war machine. Other monarchs also tried to outlaw the game, for similar reasons and with similar degrees of failure. Richard II tried in 1388 as did, in Tudor times, both Henry VIII and Elizabeth I. Oli-

The Origins of Football

ver Cromwell, in the republican years of the mid seventeenth century did have more success in preventing the game being played, as he did with several other forms of popular entertainment, but football was revived with the restoration of King Charles II in 1660. It has enjoyed an unbroken history since then.

During the Tudor and Stuart periods, the English game, bloodthirsty as it was, remained largely the preserve of the lower orders in society and involvement in it was frowned upon by many in the gentler classes. King James I, for instance, described football as "meeter for laming than making able the users thereof", and in Shakespeare's "King Lear" we find the Earl of Kent insulting Oswald by calling him a "base foot-ball player". Nonetheless, the thrill of the game did appeal to members of the upper classes and it did have its advocates. King James had to forbid his son from playing, proof in itself that the prince had played and in 1581 Richard Mulcaster, in his book "Positions," said that football could not have "grown to the greatness it is now at… if it had not had great helps, both to health and strength." He clearly saw participation in the sport as bringing physical benefit. Though he too had doubts about the more brutal aspects of the game. He recommended "a training master, a smaller number of players sorted into sides and standings, not meeting with their bodies so boisterously to try their strength", echoes of what was to happen to the game in the nineteenth century.

Whilst the English were allowing the courser elements of human nature to dominate their playing of football, there did exist more refined versions of the game. We have already noted the form of football known as "calcio" being played in Medieval Tuscany and there are references to other varieties of the game being played in parts of Italy in the sixteenth century. There was a game called "pallone" or "balloon", which one contemporary commentator describes as "a strong and moving sport in the open fields, with a great Ball of double Leather filled with Wind, and so driven to and fro with the strength of a man's Arm armed in a Bracer of Wood, either of which actions must be learned by the Eye and practise, not by the Ear or Reading." This must have been a game of some skill, which the players learned from the experience of playing. So too must have been the type of football played at Lent in Padua and described by Antonio Scaino da Sallo in his book "Trattato de Giuocco della Palla" (Treatise on Ball Games") of 1555. He speaks of teams of between twenty and forty players, divided into "anti - guardia" or forwards, "gagliardi" or half-backs and "retroguardia" or full-backs. There were goals into which the ball was driven by any part of the body, while the ball was in movement, though the ball was not allowed to be thrown after being caught. If this occurred, then a "scaramuccia" ensued. The word actually means "a skirmish," but it is easy to imagine a movement of play similar to a modern rugby scrummage, which the Italian word so obviously resembles.

Back in England, in the seventeenth century, developments were taking place that were to have a profound effect on the future of the game. A note in the register of Magdalen College, Cambridge of 1679 gives insight into what this was. It says that "…no scholars give or receive at any time any treat or collation upon account of ye football play, on or about Michaelmass Day, further than College beer or ale in ye open hall to quench their thirsts." The register goes on to describe that season of the year as "that football time", with the implication that the game played in 1679 was no one - off affair. That the game was being taken up more seriously by the young men of England's elite classes was of critical importance because theirs was not to be the violent free-for-all of the Shrovetide football enjoyed by the common folk. Instead, they were to develop a more structured game that stressed the value of strength, skill, sportsmanship and teamwork. The emphasis on such Christian values was to dramatically alter the shape of the game. It is with the young gentlemen of England that the bridge between the medieval and modern game lies.

In the eighteenth century, football flourished in the public schools and colleges of England. The problem was that the schools developed their own individual forms of the game, so much so that it became impossible for schools to play against each other, a fact which in itself meant that no uniform style of play could develop. At Eton, for instance, handling the ball was not allowed, whilst at Rugby it was. At Rugby, also, hacking, or kicking a player's legs, was legal and was not outlawed until 1877. At Westminster and Charterhouse, there were no playing fields and football had to be played in the cloisters and courtyards. A style of play that involved charging, tackling and throwing of balls was too dangerous and so the dribbling game came into existence. Winchester was regarded as having the simplest form of the game, whereas the football played at Harrow was so complicated that few people could understand it without proper explanation. A further complication came through the different terminology used to describe elements of play, often peculiar to individual schools. Expressions such as "piggling", or physically uprooting a player to halt his progress, or "shinning", kicking a player directly on the shins, or "tagging", taking a player out by simply touching him, were all variously used by one school or another.

Rivalry between the schools was another factor that prevented a codification of the game. The footballers of Eton regarded the game played at Rugby as "plebeian", whilst the Etonians were regarded as cowards by the boys of Rugby. By the early nineteenth century, then, the game was a confusion of styles and rules, and this was the next hurdle to be overcome in the development of the modern game.

Meanwhile, as the public schools argued the correct and proper ways to play football, the game that had been so popular with the common people was gradually dying out among them. Eighteenth century English society was brutal and violent, and lacking any effective means of law enforcement other than the army and a few very underpaid and very under–motivated constables, crime was rife in the rapidly expanding towns and cities. By the early nineteenth century, though, attitudes had begun to change and a greater emphasis was placed on law and order. The Bow Street Runners, for example, the first organised, though private police force were set up in 1784, and in 1829 the Metropolitan Police Force was established. Furthermore, the first years of the new century were particularly unstable. The spread of ideas from revolutionary France and a growing discontent among the downtrodden labouring classes, for whom life was extremely hard, meant that gatherings of working men were discouraged. It all spelt the death–knoll of street football, as did the fact that the growing industrialisation of Britain meant life for those who toiled in its mills and factories became increasingly regulated and leisure time restricted. The very harshness of life itself mitigated against football as a popular pastime. By 1830, Shrovetide football had largely died out, except in a few isolated cases, such as in Ashbourne, and it was not until later in the century that interest in the game was rekindled among the working men of Britain. When that interest was eventually reborn, it would have a further profound influence on the development of football.

In the first half of the 19th century, then, football remained in the hands of the English upper classes. The players, as one observer noted, were "a set of harmless lunatics, who amused themselves by kicking one another's shins, but did no great harm to the public at large." Lunacy or not, the game remained popular in the schools and colleges and its popularity brought the growing realisation of a need to codify the rules. After all, when boys move from school to school, or from school to university, they often found themselves facing a game entirely different to the one they had been used to. Further, if any inter-school or inter-college matches were to be played, it would be absolutely necessary to have a common set of rules. In 1846, at Cambridge University, the first effort to standardise the game was begun. Two of the university's football stalwarts, J.C. Thring and H. de Winton met with representatives from the major public schools and two years later an agreement was reached with the publication of the "Cambridge Rules" of 1848. There were ten rules that laid down the basic framework of the game (see appendix one). They laid down when the ball was or was not in play; they allowed for catching the ball, though not running with it; and holding, pushing or tripping players was not legal, although preventing a player from getting to the ball "by any means consistent with this rule" was permissible. This, presumably, did not rule out hacking, which was to become a major controversy, and which would forever split the footballing fraternity into its Association and Rugby codes. As yet the game, as played under the Cambridge Rules, would have more resembled a rugby than a soccer game, but they do mark an important step in a very definite direction.

In 1855 the Sheffield Football Club was founded, the world's oldest football club. It is significant because it shows how football was spreading outside the public school system, though it was far from becoming the mass game of thirty years later. The early football clubs were the creations of young men of the middle classes and above, often ex - public schoolboys, whose love of the game was enough to make them wish to continue playing after their education had ended and who therefore formed themselves into clubs or associations for the purposes of doing so. The Sheffield club published its own set of rules, based very much on the Cambridge Rules, with the stipulation that that different coloured caps should be worn to identify the two teams (see appendix two).

In 1862 the Notts County Football Club was founded, the oldest club in the English football league, and it was one of a number of clubs that were springing up all over the country at the time. These clubs were largely confined to the south east of the country and dominated by ex-public schoolboys, but their emergence brought the need for a much more unified way of playing than the Cambridge Rules allowed for. There was still too much divergence in the ways that the rules were being interpreted. Another attempt was made in 1862 by the evergreen J.C. Thring, the ex-Shrewsbury schoolboy, who had been behind the Cambridge Rules and who was now master at Uppingham School. His was a list of ten rules, known as the Uppingham Rules, and were designed to produce what Thring referred to as "The Simplest Game". They allowed for minimal handling of the ball, for instance to stop it; they outlawed tripping and kicking, except of the ball; and an early form of off-side was enacted, ruling that a player was deemed to be "out of play" when in front of the ball (see appendix three). However, even these regulations failed to provide the strictness needed to bring full unity within the footballing nation and there was still too much diversification. It was a situation that was about to change.

Although it received little notice at the time, an event took place on Monday, 26th October 1863 that was to bring lasting consequences for the game of football. It took place in the evening and happened at the Freemason's Tavern, Great Queen Street, Lincoln's Inn Fields just off Drury Lane in London. It was a meeting of the captains, secretaries and representatives of twelve football clubs from around the London area. The clubs were: Barnes, the WO (War Office) Club, Crusaders, Forest of Leytonstone, No Names Club of Kilburn, Crystal Palace, Blackheath, Kensington School, Percival House (Blackheath), Surbiton, Blackheath Proprietory School and Charterhouse. The outcome of the meeting was the founding of the English Football Association, set up to bring unity to the game, and the oldest football association in the world. At international meetings of the game's rulers, it is still the only association that does not need to be identified by its country's name. It is simply labelled the FA.

The association was the idea of Ebenezer Cobb Morley (1831-1924), one of the founding fathers of the English game. He had been born in Hull, but moved to Barnes, by the Thames, in 1858 and practised as a solicitor. He had not been to public school, but had played football on the green and decided to establish his own club at Barnes. Several ex-public schoolboys joined the club and there ensued several and often heated arguments about how the game should be played. As a consequence Morley, the club's captain, wrote to the press suggesting that there should be a set or rules laid down for football, just as the MCC (Marylebone Cricket Club and headquarters of that game) had done for cricket. Since other people from other clubs were thinking along similar lines, Morley organised the meeting at the Freemason's Tavern and the FA was born. Incidentally, Morley was a player of some style himself, who was once described as "a pretty and most effective dribbler."

At Morley's suggestion, Arthur Pember of the No Names Club, another solicitor, took the chair and the meeting formerly accepted the proposal for an association by eleven votes to one. Only Charterhouse failed to enrol as one of the founding clubs on the grounds that they had to ascertain the views of the other public schools before they could commit themselves.

Having taken this first, momentous step, the association began the process of turning itself into football's dominant authority. Its second meeting laid down the rules of the association itself and, at the third, they began to discuss the rules of the game. It was at this point that differences of opinion began to appear, over the contentious issue of whether to allow hacking. On 24th November, the FA discussed the Cambridge rules and considered them to "embrace the true principles of the game with the greatest simplicity", but behind this apparent concord a fierce argument was raging. The Blackheath Club was all for the adoption of the Rugby code of practice, which allowed for hacking, and felt that the attempt to ban it represented "far more the feelings of those who liked their pipes and grog or schnapps more than the manly game of football". It was the intervention of the Sheffield Club that tipped the balance. The club applied to join the FA and in its letter of application it outlined its own rules and gave its opinion that if carrying the ball or hacking were allowed, then the game would more resemble wrestling than football. Most of the clubs agreed and on 1st December a set of rules were adopted, based on the Cambridge Rules, which allowed handling, but not running with the ball or passing the ball using the hands (see appendix four). Hacking and tripping were finally banned, and the Blackheath Club withdrew from the FA to go on to become one of the founder members of the Rugby Union.

With this vexed issue out of the way, the fledgling FA could go on to oversee the development of the game in its own way. The first game played under the new rules took place on 19th December 1863 between Barnes and Richmond, and was played at Barnes. It was a 0 - 0 draw, but a report of the match which appeared in the sporting paper "The Field" said that "the game was characterised by a great good temper, the rules being so simple and easy of observance that it was difficult for disputes to arise." Over the next few years the game continued to develop. In 1869 goal kicks were introduced and in 1872 so were corner kicks. In 1874 Samuel Widdowson of Nottingham Forest was said to have invented shinguards. By then, though, another more decisive development had occurred, which was to have a defining influence on the future of the game.

22 Men and a Bag of Wind

In 1866, the Sheffield Club, still the only provincial member of the FA, proposed that a representative match be played between players from Sheffield and London. The FA took up the challenge and the game was played at Battersea Park on 31st March. London won easily, with Ebenezer Morley scoring the first goal, but the match set a precedent. Other such matches were arranged and soon the FA began to organise inter-county games, with two important effects. It helped to spread the game and widen its popularity, and it helped to nurture the idea of competitive football. Football clubs began to spring up all over the country: Sheffield Wednesday, for instance, was founded in 1867, Reading in 1871 and Blackburn Rovers in 1875. The game also began to spread outside of England. The Queen's Park Club, in Glasgow, was founded in 1867, Scotland's oldest club, and the Scottish FA was established in 1873. The Welsh FA was set up in 1876 and the Irish in 1880.

The rapid profusion in the number of football clubs coupled with the growing confidence of the FA ensured that it would not be long before some organised competition open to those clubs affiliated to the FA was established. The FA Cup was the idea of Charles William Alcock, an ex-Harrow public schoolboy from Sunderland, and another of the games early pioneering fathers. He had become Secretary of the FA in 1870, a position he held until 1895, and he remembered how there had been an inter-house "sudden-death" football competition at Harrow. Such a thing, he decided, would be ideal for the English game and he suggested it to the FA. The minute book of the association for 20th July, 1871 simply stated: "That it is desirable that a Challenge Cup should be established in connection with the Association for which all clubs belonging to the Association should be invited to compete." So the FA Cup was born.

The first FA Cup competition was launched in October 1872, and 15 clubs entered to play for a silver cup that was bought for £20. The clubs were Barnes, Civil Service, Crystal Palace, Clapham Rovers, Hitchin, Maiden Road, Marlow, Queen's Park (of Glasgow), Donnington Grammar School, Hampton Heathens, Harrow Chequers, Reigate Priory, Royal Engineers, Upton Park and the Wanderers. All the clubs were from the London area, except Donnington School, who were from Spalding in Lincolnshire and Queen's Park, from Scotland, who applied to play in the English cup because Scottish football was in its infancy and it was felt that there would be a higher standard of competition in England. Upton Park would later represent Britain in the football tournament at the 1900 Olympic Games in Paris.

This first FA Cup competition was a loosely organised effort, with three clubs, Harrow Chequers, Reigate Priory and Donnington School, scratching without playing. The Queen's Park club was exempted from playing in any round before the semi-final on account of the cost of the travelling from Scotland to London. Public contributions allowed the club to make it to the Kennington Oval, London's top sporting venue, for the semi-final against the Wanderers, a match which they drew, but their funds ran out and they were unable to stay for the replay. The Wanderers then met the Royal Engineers from Chatham, and the firm favourites to win in the final, which was played at the Oval on 16th March 1872. Two thousand people turned up to watch, but luck was not with the Army team. One of their team, Lieutenant Edmund Cromwell, broke his collarbone within ten minutes and, although he remained on the pitch, it gave the Wanderers a telling advantage. They eventually won 1-0. In their team was Charles Alcock, the founder of the competition, and the goal was scored by Morton Peto Betts, the first man ever to score in an FA Cup final. Betts was listed in the team under the pseudonym "A. H. Chequer", because originally he was playing with the Harrow Chequers. However, when that team scratched he, quite legitimately under the rules, elect to play for the Wanderers and so implanted his name in FA Cup history. He had also been one of the FA committee members that had passed the resolution setting up the cup competition.

From such humble beginnings, the FA Cup soon grew to become England's premier club competition and, although the early cup contests were dominated by the amateur clubs of southern gentlemen, it was not long before its appeal spread. Within ten years the number of clubs entering for it had risen by five times and interest was particularly strong among the expanding number of clubs in England's industrial north and midlands. Here, among the mills and factories spawned by the Industrial Revolution, life was hard and working men sought their pleasure wherever they could find it. Football in general, and the FA Cup in particular, seized the imagination as a passion for the game swept the labouring masses. Interest was particularly raised in 1879 when a club from Darwen, a small Lancashire town of textile workers nestling in the Pennines next to Blackburn, reached the quarter-finals. The team had had to travel to London to play an earlier round and when they were drawn away against the Old Etonians they considered scratching because of the expense. The Darweners, proud of their team's achievements, set up a "London Fund" to raise the money to send their team south again. The

The Origins of Football

Old Etonians were then a major force in English football, having reached the cup final in 1875 and 1876, both of which they lost, and having in their ranks Arthur Fitzgerald Kinnaird, later Baron Kinnaird of Inchture, widely regarded as the greatest player of his day. Darwen eventually lost their quarter-final, though it took two replays to knock them out. The first match was a 5-5 draw, with Darwen scoring 4 goals in the last 15 minutes. The second was a 2-2 draw, and the third saw Darwen go down 6-2. The Old Etonians went on to defeat Clapham Rovers 1-0 in the final.

It had been a remarkable effort by the northern club, but what was controversial about their cup run was the inclusion in the Darwen team of two players by the names of Fergie Suter and Jimmy Love - the world's first two professional footballers. They were Scotsmen, who had originally played for Partick, but had been lured down to Darwen to bolster the club's attempt at the cup. They were set up with better paid jobs than they left behind in Glasgow as inducement and they became regular team members. The rules of the FA was for strict amateurism and since Suter and Love both had paid "jobs", it allowed Darwen to claim that both players were amateur. However, most people saw through the scam and it engendered a debate that dominated the game for the next five years.

J. B. Priestley once wrote about football: "To suggest that people pay money just to see 22 hirelings kick a ball is to say that a violin is merely made of wood and catgut and that Hamlet is so much paper and ink." His words so eloquently express what football became to working people, whose lives were so monotonous, hard and brutal, and in the days before television, the radio or other mass media offered cheap distractions. To the people of the north, the FA Cup had become a fervour and they saw nothing wrong with their clubs paying players to try to win it for them. Suter and Love were soon being followed by dozens of other Scotsmen, who came to play for the clubs of Lancashire and Yorkshire. It rankled with many of the ex-public schoolboys who ran the FA and for whom the Corinthian spirit of amateurism embodied all that was wholesome about sport. Attempts were made to ban professionalism and a rule passed in 1882 stated: "Any member of any club receiving remuneration or consideration of any sort above his actual expenses... shall be debarred from taking part... and any club employing such a player shall be excluded from this Association." Accrington were suspended from the cup in 1883 for paying a player, as were Preston North End in 1884.

Luckily for the northern clubs, though, the FA largely ignored this ruling, but since clubs from the north and midlands came to dominate the FA Cup in the 1880s, the issue of professionalism had to be faced. Blackburn Rovers, with Fergie Suter now playing for the club, reached the final in 1882, only to be defeated 1-0 by the Old Etonians, losing to a goal widely regarded as a fluke. In 1883 the cup did go to Blackburn, though not to the Rovers. Blackburn Olympic were the standard bearers and caused great public joy in the town when they came out 2-1 winners against the Old Etonians. Blackburn Rovers went on to win the cup three times in a row, still the only team to have done so, in 1884, 1885 and 1886, when they defeated West Bromwich Albion in the final. From this point the amateur clubs of the south ceased to have any real influence on the fortunes of the FA Cup. In 1887 Aston Villa beat West Bromich Albion in the final and in the next year West Bromich Albion themselves lifted the trophy when they beat Preston North End.

It was in 1885 that the issue of professionalism was finally resolved by the FA. By now clubs from the north and midlands had become the dominant forces in English football and their use of professional players was widespread. In that year, with the FA committee still in favour of amateurism, the northern clubs threatened to break away and form their own association. It forced the issue. With two of the game's stalwarts, Lord Kinnaird and Charles Alcock, convinced that professionalism was inevitable, but determined that the FA should maintain its control over the game, its committee was persuaded to sanction professionalism. It did so on 20th July, 1885 at Anderton's Hotel in Fleet Street, London,. The love of northern working men for their game of football effected this decisive change of course for the game's history.

The fact that clubs were now paying players meant that they needed regular incomes. For these clubs, seasons that comprised only of a few cup games with the rest being friendlies were not enough to sustain them, especially since friendlies could not be guaranteed fixtures. A club might pull out of an arranged friendly for any number of reasons and without any warning, and it meant that a professional club might not have a game, or an income, for weeks at a time. Something else was needed if the professional game was to be sustained.

22 Men and a Bag of Wind

The Football League was the idea of a Scotsman called William McGregor, who had moved from Perthshire to Birmingham, where he ran a draper's shop. Although he did not play himself, he became interested in football through watching local clubs, in particular Aston Villa, with which he involved himself. The inspiration for his idea came from cricket's county championship, run on a league system with each county playing each other in home and away fixtures, and which had begun in 1873. McGregor became convinced that not only would such a system work for football, but that it was necessary. He set about organising it. In March 1888 he wrote to five clubs "to tender the following suggestion… that ten or twelve of the most prominent clubs in England to combine to arrange home and away fixtures each season." The FA was at first suspicious of the idea, fearing that a league might undermine its authority, but the League was eventually set up on 17 April at a meeting at the Royal Hotel in Manchester.

Twelve clubs were invited to join the new league, six from Lancashire and six from the Midlands. They were Accrington, Aston Villa, Blackburn Rovers, Bolton Wanderers, Burnley, Derby County, Everton, Notts County, Preston North End, Stoke City, West Bromwich Albion, and Wolverhampton Wanderers. The first games in the world's oldest league took place on 8 September, 1888 and the first goal in the league was scored by Preston North End, who went on to beat Burnley 5-2. The man in charge at Preston was a Major William Sudell and he had made it his ambition that his club, founded in 1881, would become the best in the country, to match the dominance of Blackburn Rovers. Preston and Blackburn are towns separated by only a few miles and rivalry was strong between the two. He was as good as his word as Preston dominated that first league season. They won eighteen of their twenty-two games, drawing the other four, scoring 74 goals and conceding only 15. They became the first, undefeated League champions and went on to win the FA Cup as well, beating Bolton Wanderers 3-0 in the final. Preston, therefore, became the first "double" winning team, earning for themselves the nickname of "The Old Invincibles" and the right, should they chose to exercise it, of being able to play all games in their home kit, even for away games. The only other club in the English league with the same right is Reading, because they are the only club to play in the "Royal" county of Berkshire.

With both league and cup competitions now firmly established, the future of professional football in England was secure, but the game had been spreading to other parts of the British Isles. The establishment of the Scottish, Welsh and Irish FAs has already been noted, but in 1872 the English FA took a decision that would develop the game in a new direction, with importance not only for the British game, but for the World Cup as well. The minutes of an F.A. Committee meeting for 3rd October contain the following sentence: "In order to further the interests of the Association in Scotland, it was decided that during the current season, a team should be sent to Glasgow to play a match v Scotland." This was the birth of international football, the birth of the oldest international fixture in football and it was another idea of Charles Alcock, the instigator of the FA Cup.

There had been four "unofficial" internationals played before 1872, the first of which had taken place in London in 1870 at Alcock's suggestion. Three of these games had been won by England and one had been drawn, but the Scots were not satisfied at being represented by teams made up of exiles and largely picked by Alcock himself, an Englishman. Since there was not a Scottish FA at that time, Alcock looked to Glasgow's Queen's Park club to help him organise a full international. They obliged and challenged England to send a team to Glasgow to play a Scottish team that was predominantly comprised of Queen's Park players. The match was played on 30th November at Hamilton Crescent, the home to the West of Scotland Cricket Club, Glasgow's biggest sporting arena and it ended in a 0-0 draw. It was a creditable result for the Scots, for whom rugby had a far wider appeal than the association game, and was described in one newspaper as "one of the jolliest, one of the most spirited and most pleasant matches that have ever been played according to Association rules." The match also served as a springboard for the game in Scotland, with several clubs being formed in its aftermath and the Scottish FA some four months later.

A second England - Scotland international was played in London in March 1873, which England won 4-2, but the Scots were soon to dominate what became a regular feature. Comparison was made between the close passing style of the Scots and the dribbling game favoured by the English, but the value of Scotland's way of playing became obvious when Scotland won ten of the first sixteen matches played between the countries. England won only two. Yet, in spite of England's poor showing against the Scots, further internationals were arranged against other home nations' teams. In 1879 England played their first game against Wales, a 2-1 victory to England, and in 1882 their first match against Ireland, which England won 13-0. A week later Ireland lost 7-1 to Wales at Wrexham in the first international between those countries.

The Origins of Football

At the end of the nineteenth century, as the game became established as part of Britain's social structure, Britons began to export their game overseas, where they found many willing participants. Queen Victoria's citizens were intrepid travellers and wherever they went they played football. They also encouraged the locals to join in. English sailors introduced the game to Brazil in the 1870s, but it was slow to catch on. It was a former Southampton player and son of immigrants into the country, Charles Miller, who did much to popularise the game there through his encouragement of ex-patriot workers to set up football clubs. The first mainly Brazilian club was Associão Athletica Mackenzie College in São Paulo. In 1879 an English football club was set up in Copenhagen and ten years later the Danish FA was founded. It was businessmen, the Charnock brothers from Lancashire, the owners of a cotton mill near Moscow who introduced the game to Russia.

The Dutch FA was established in 1889 and resident British businessmen in Buenos Aires introduced the game to Argentina, whose FA was founded in 1891. In 1895 FAs were set up in Belgium, Switzerland and Chile. In Italy, ex-patriot Englishmen founded the Genoa Football and Cricket Club in 1892 and the Italian FA followed in 1898. Germany's FA was established in 1900 and British railway builders introduced the game to Uruguay, whose own FA dates back to 1900. The FA of Czechoslovakia began in 1901, whilst that of Norway came in 1902. The large British community resident in Austria, some of whom were gardeners on the estate of Baron Rothschild, was responsible for taking football to that country. The Vienna Football and Cricket Club was the first club to be established there and Austria set up its own FA in 1904, the same year as Sweden got theirs, where the game had been introduced by British embassy staff.

Other FAs were created in Paraguay in 1906, Finland in 1907, Luxembourg and Romania in 1908, Spain in 1913 and France in 1918. The game was becoming global, but what was needed was something to pull it together.

Chapter Two

The Origins of the World Cup

"The World Cup is not all things to all people; but nobody on our cosmic speck can be unaware of this regular battle to decide who is cleverest and strongest at putting a ball into a net. Some see it as just a chance to make a quick profit while others are tempted to lock themselves in a closet, especially one at the bottom of the garden, until it goes away. But a cumulative television audience of 37 billion (or, to do full justice to the figure, 37,000,000,000) watched the finals in France in 1998 – which means most of this planet's population paid attention. Many would not have regarded themselves as football fans, at least to begin with, but most probably saw it as a passable substitute for global war. Quite irresistible.

My own view of World Cup football is admittedly biased: it has transported me, on a fraying magic carpet, across all the seven seas. It has also filled the memory bin to overflowing point and, if one match more than another captured the magnetism of the tournament it is the 1978 final between Argentina and Holland in Buenos Aires. The noise hurt, the passion was overwhelming and the atmosphere so tangible it could have been bottled. Sport, yes. Football, of course. But something so much more."

Original contribution by Bryon Butler
(After a distinguished career as a BBC football correspondent, journalist and author, Bryon sadly passed away on 26th April 2001, aged 66)

The rapid spread of football around the world, and particularly in Europe, in the last decades of the nineteenth and early years of the twentieth centuries, and the increasing number of international matches being played, made two developments inevitable. One of these was the establishment of an international organisation to supervise and administer the game. The second was the creation of an international competition to pit nation against nation to determine the best, and matching the inter-club competitions that were being set up as football caught on in individual countries.

Football was played as a demonstration sport in the early stagings of the modern Olympic Games, the first of which was held in Athens in 1896. There were also small-scale competitions at the Games in Paris in 1900, in St. Louis in 1904 and again in Athens in 1906, at an interim running of the Games, but football was not taken seriously. In any case, the select or representatives elevens, few as they were, that competed in these early Olympic competitions could hardly be regarded as international teams in the accepted sense of the term. A structure with greater solidity and permanence would need to be erected, but before this could happen an international organisation devoted purely to football would have to exist.

Since 1872 official teams representing England had regularly played international matches against Scotland. In 1879 England played their first match against Wales and in 1882 against Ireland, the same year that Wales played Ireland for the first time. With international games between the four countries of the British Isles becoming regular features of the British footballing calendar, the need for an umbrella organisation to co-ordinate the functioning of four independent FAs arose and the response was the creation, in 1886, of the International Football Association Board. Its primary purpose was to control the laws of the game and to ensure that each FA played by the same rules. The International Board still exists and still carries out the same duties, and it is still dominated by the British FAs. Of its twenty seats, sixteen are reserved for the British FAs and four for delegates from FIFA, elected for fixed periods on a rotational basis.

The existence of the International Board, however, with its limited function and limited membership, could not satisfy the needs of football's growing international appeal. Something more was required and such an organisation was the idea of a Dutch banker, C.A.W. Hirschman, and Robert Guérin of the Union of French Sports Clubs. Both men clearly saw the benefits that could accrue from such a body, but both men also realised that their notion would be based upon a much more secure foundation if the British FAs, and particularly that of the English, were involved. After all England had been the birthplace of modern football and the British style of play, quite rightly at the time, was regarded as the finest and the one to emulate.

It seems that at around the same time another Dutchman, Count van der Straten Ponthoy, came up with the idea of an international competition. To have any real credibility, such a competition would need the participation of the British and an organisation to oversee it. Accordingly, in 1902, Hirschman wrote to the FA in London to try to enlist its support for his idea of an international governing body. Unfortunately for the immediate future of the game, but sadly and typically in keeping with attitudes that were prevalent within the British establishment, the FA was cool to the idea. Frederick Wall, who had succeeded Charles Alcock as secretary of the FA, a post Wall held until 1934, merely replied that the matter would be discussed at the FA's next meeting. This meeting was not scheduled to be held for another two months and inevitably, given the lukewarm response made to the original request, nothing happened. Hirschman was simply told that the "Council cannot see the advantages of such a federation."

In April 1903 Wall wrote again to Hirschman saying that the latter's proposals would be reconsidered at another meeting of the FA Council, which was to held in June later in the year. Again, the reply was negative and so Guérin travelled to London to try to force the issue. As he later wrote: "His head in his hands, Mr. Wall listened to my story. He said he would report back to his council. I waited a few months. I travelled to London once more and had a meeting with the FA president Lord Kinnaird. However, that, too, was of no avail." The English were just not ready for it and, as Guérin continued in his account: "Tired of the struggle and recognising that the English, true to tradition, wanted to wait and watch. I undertook to invite delegates myself."

Faced with English indifference, continental Europe decided to go it alone and on 21st May 1904 in Paris the Fédération Internationale de Football Association (or FIFA) was born. The countries represented at this inaugural meeting were Belgium, Denmark, France, Holland, Spain, Sweden and Switzerland. The list is indicative of the progress football had made in Europe, but it is also significant and revealing that none of the British FAs were present. It was a stand-off that was to hinder the development of the world game for a few years to come.

In the aftermath of the founding of FIFA, the English FA did appoint a committee to review the development, a rather begrudging gesture, but still turned down an invitation to participate in an international tournament that it was suggested should be organised for the following Easter. In April 1905 an international conference was held in London and it was here that the English FA finally gave its seal of approval to the existence of FIFA. Then, in July, 1906 a British delegation headed by Frederick Wall and Daniel Burley Woolfall, of the Lancashire FA and the treasurer of the English FA from 1901 - 1918, attended a FIFA conference in Berne. To the delight of the other members, the English had finally decided to come aboard. Robert Guérin, who had served as FIFA's president since 1904, stepped down so that Woolfall could take his place. Woolfall held the presidency until 1918 and is recognised for the very good work he did to enable FIFA to establish itself. However, as much the existing FIFA membership may have been pleased with the new attitude coming from London, relations were not fully harmonious. There was a certain amount of suspicion concerning the motives behind the English FA's change of heart and to underline the point, the Scottish and Irish FAs were refused membership. It was felt that they would be too much in the pocket of the English and FIFA did not want to be dominated by the newcomers.

The years after 1906 were years of consolidation for FIFA, but things did not always go smoothly. The period immediately before the outbreak of the First World War in 1914 was a time of much political rivalry in Europe between the countries that eventually ranged against each other in the war. It helped to prevent any real progress towards the establishment of an international competition, which remained a mere pipe dream. Indeed, any such thoughts had to be suspended throughout the years of the war, which lasted from August 1914 to November 1918.

However, this did not mean that attempts to organise such competitions did not go ahead, but it meant that such attempts were not organised under the aegis of FIFA. Football continued to be part of the Olympic Games, and an increasingly important part at that, and in 1909 a wealthy British businessman ran his own tournament. Sir Thomas Lipton had made a fortune as a tea merchant, amongst other things, and had business interests in Britain and Italy. He invited teams from England, Italy, Germany and Switzerland to take part in a competition to be held in Turin in Italy. His original invitation was to the English FA, but with their customary lack of enthusiasm, they turned him down. Lipton, though, was determined that a team representing Great Britain should take part and join Juventus of Turin, FC Winterhour of Switzerland and Stuttgart representing Germany. Since the FA would not cooperate, Lipton set about finding his own team. Details of how this happened are obscure, but it appears that he had an employee who had been a referee in the Northern League

The Origins of the World Cup

in England and it was decided to invite a team from that league. It was an amateur league and so the team that represented England in this first, private "World Cup" was an amateur team.

West Aukland FC, from County Durham in the north east, was a team largely made up of coal miners. They were ordinary working men and struggled to raise the funds needed to get to Italy, which they had to do themselves. Many, in fact, had to pawn possessions to do so. The experience was worth the effort. West Aukland defeated Stuttgart 2-0 and then defeated Winterhour in the final held in the Turin Stadium on 12th April 1909.

The tournament was deemed to have been a success by its organisers and a rerun was held in 1911, again in Turin. As reigning champions, West Aukland were invited back to defend their trophy. Again the team had to fund its own expenses and again it was worth the effort. The Englishmen defeated Red Star of Switzerland 2-0 before going on to meet Juventus in the final on 17th April, a game they won 6-1. Not only had they won the "World Cup" for a second and consecutive time, but it had been laid down in the rules that any team winning the trophy twice would be allowed to keep it. So it was that a team of coal miners became the first outright winners of the "World Cup."

Whilst the Thomas Lipton Trophy may have been, in its own way, a small-scale success, and was certainly revealing of what was possible, FIFA was no nearer organising a tournament of its own. A little over three years after the second Turin final, the limited progress that FIFA had made was disrupted when Europe was plunged into the bloodiest of wars. Many would accept that, at times, life on the Western Front came as close to approximating Dante's "Inferno" as any of the other hell-holes man has created this century. Yet, even in this war, football has become part of the folklore. Amid the horrors of trench fighting, men shared their affection for the game. An entry in the diary of the British war poet William Gibson for 1916 illustrates this perfectly. In it he writes: "We ate our breakfast lying on our backs because the shells were screeching overhead. I bet a rasher to a loaf of bread that Hull United would beat Halifax when Johnny Stainthorpe played full-back instead of Billy Bradford." Then, on Christmas Day of 1914, the first Christmas of the war, in the mud and blood of Flanders Fields, there was the famous incident when men of both sides deliberately put down their weapons in a spontaneous cease-fire. Then, knowing full well that their actions ran counter to general orders and that their actions, if dealt with according to military regulations, would lead to death by firing squad for desertion of post, soldiers from both sides wandered into no-mans land. Fritz met Tommy. They shook hands, exchanged gifts and tokens, and then played football. The next day they went back to killing each other. It was possibly the most unusual international match of all time. It is certainly the most courageously heroic and revealing of the nobility of the human spirit if it allows itself or is allowed free voice.

The end of the war brought FIFA no respite from troubles and dissension. The defeat of Germany and her allies did not end the enmity generated by four years of bitter fighting and ill-feeling was to last into the middle of the 1920s, keeping the defeated nations out of international football competitions. In the aftermath of the war, Britain and her Allies refused to play against countries that they had been at war with. They also decided to boycott games against the international teams of countries who played against countries with whom they had been at war. If the war had divided FIFA, then this decision rent it even further because the Scandinavian countries, which had been neutral in the war and who therefore had no particular bias, claimed the right to play against whoever they wanted. This caused Britain to withdraw from FIFA and the problem was not resolved until 1923, when the well-respected stalwart of Austrian football, Hugo Meisl, intervened. Normality was restored and England played an international against Sweden on 21st May, a game which the English won 4-2. By now, though, a new problem had arisen to bedevil international football, with implications not only for FIFA, but for the Olympic Games also. It was that of professionalism against amateurism.

As has already been noted, football had been part of the modern Olympics from the start, though only as an exhibition sport. Tournaments were always held after the main section of the Games, the track and field events, had taken place, because these sports were regarded as more cultured. Football, in spite of its widening appeal, was not taken seriously, being seen as rather plebeian and, indeed, the tournament records for the 1896 Athens Games have largely disappeared. All that is known is that Denmark beat a select eleven from Izmir 15-0. Izmir, now known as Smyrna, is on the west coast of Turkey and had a large Greek population, which accounts for its Olympic entry. Who won the gold at Athens, or where the matches took place, is unknown.

22 Men and a Bag of Wind

The progress of the football tournament at the 1900 Paris Games is fully documented. Here, in what was one of the most chaotic and disorganised stagings of the Games and which lasted for five months, football was still a demonstration sport and played in September, after the rest of the games had been completed. Three teams entered the competition: a French eleven, a Belgian eleven, a team of students that also contained some British players, and Upton Park FC, an amateur team from London. They were a well known amateur team and worthy of being Britain's representative, having won the London Senior Cup in 1883 and 1884, and the Essex Senior Cup in 1895. Since, at the time, English football was far more advanced than its continental counterpart, the Londoners were the fancied team and they secured automatic qualification for the final. The French and the Belgians played each other in the play-off, a game the French won 6-2, and the final pitted them against the English. The match was played on 2nd September at the Vélodrome Municipal de Vincennes, in Paris, and a modest crowd of 500 turned up to watch. Rugby was the widely played game in France at the turn of the century and the Association code had yet to catch the popular imagination. The English took the gold medal, securing a 4-0 victory, with goals from James Zealley, J Nicholas, who netted twice, and RR Turner. According to surviving match reports, JH Jones, the Upton Park goalkeeper, had an outstanding game. Other players who acquitted themselves well were Alfred Chalk, James Zealley and PG Spakman, who, had the game been played today, would probably have walked off with the "man of the match" award. The team was captained by A Haslam.

The footballing tournament of the 1900 Games may have been a small affair, but its final outcome did at least produce a result that was a reflection of the state of world football at the time. That of 1904 did not. In general, the St. Louis games were a shambolic affair and something of a disaster. The fact that they took place over five months, the remoteness of the venue and its distance from Europe meant that only thirteen countries participated. The number of athletes taking part dropped from 1,330 to 625 and the football tournament, as before, took place when the main games were over, in November. The three teams that entered were all from North America: Galt FC, from Ontario in Canada, the Christian Brothers College, from St. Louis, and St. Rose Kickers, also from St. Louis. Neither were anywhere near the standard of teams that might have come out of Europe.

The competition kicked off on 16th November 1904 when Galt easily defeated the Christian Brothers College 7-0, with goals coming from Taylor, Steep, Hall, who netted a hat trick, and MacDonald, who scored twice. The next day saw Galt beat the St. Rose Kickers 4-0, to secure the gold medal. The scorers were Taylor, with two, Henderson and an own goal. St. Rose, in fact, hold the dubious distinction of only netting once in the tournament, and this an own goal. The silver medal was decided over three matches played between the teams from St. Louis. On 20th November, and then on the 21st, the Christian brothers and the Kickers played out two 0-0 draws, before the Christian Brothers broke the deadlock on 23rd November with a 2-0 victory. It had hardly been the most compelling of football tournaments, but the world game was still in its infancy and it would be a few years yet before it caught on fully.

In 1906, the Greeks held an interim staging of the Olympic Games. Although, they were supposed to be held every four years, the Greek authorities had decided that the birthplace of the Olympics should keep the spirit alive by holding games in between the events proper. As it turned out, the Games were not a major success and the idea was not sustained. These interim games only happened the once, but football was part of the occasion, with all games being played in the Podilatodromio in Athens in April. Four teams entered: Denmark, and representative elevens from Athens, Izmir and Salonika, with the Danes the favourites to win the gold. The Izmir eleven was an international team comprising of players from Great Britain, France and Greece, with the entire forward line being made up of members of one British family, the Whittall family. They had run a trading and shipping company in the Eastern Mediterranean since the Elizabethan days and were very influential in the region. The family members were Albert, Edward and Godfrey, all brothers and the sons of Edward Whittall, and Donald and Harold, who were their first cousins. Denmark opened the tournament on 20th April with a 5-1 victory over Izmir and on 23rd April the Salonika eleven defeated Athens 6-0. Two further matches were played the next day, with Denmark beating Athens 9-0 and Izmir beating Salonika 3-0. Denmark, therefore, took the gold and Izmir the silver.

Football began to come into its own as an international sport at the 1908 London Olympics, when all the games were played at White City. These games were a major success, attracting large crowds, and football, being played in the land of its birth, was recognised as an official Olympic sport for the first time. It was no longer an exhibition sport, though the tournament was still held in October, some three months after the main games, which had been played in July. It also meant that the football section had to compete with the English League programme and it did not receive the press coverage, or the support, that it might otherwise have done.

Due to political problems in the Austro-Hungarian Empire, teams from Hungary and Bohemia, now the Czech Republic, had to withdraw, leaving six teams in the competition. These were Denmark, England, two teams representing France, Holland and Sweden. England, captained by one of the leading amateur international players of the day, Vivian Woodward of Tottenham Hotspur, were favourites to win, but Denmark, where football had made remarkable progress, was seen as England's biggest threat. The Dutch team was coached by Edgar Chadwick, a Lancashire man, who had enjoyed a distinguished career as a professional footballer. He played from the 1880s until 1908, representing Blackburn Olympic, Blackburn Rovers and Everton, before moving to the Netherlands to take up coaching.

In the first round, the French "A" team and Holland were awarded byes into the semi-finals, but England were drawn against Sweden and Denmark against France "B". On 19th October, Denmark had an emphatic 9-0 victory over the French and the following day England secured an even more impressive victory over the Swedes, who were trounced 12-1. Both games attracted crowds of 2,000 spectators. In the semi-finals, which were played on 22nd October, England disposed of Holland with a 4-0 victory played in front of a 6,000 crowd, with all four goals coming from Henry Stapley, who added to the two he had scored against the Swedes in the first round. In the second semi-final Denmark hammered the French "A" team 17-1, with Sophos Neilson scoring ten, a truly remarkable feat. In the third-fourth place play-off Holland won the bronze medal with a 2-0 victory over Sweden and in the final, between the two fancied countries, England eventually came out on top. It was, though, a tight match and, according to a report in the Times, "only the superior shooting of the forwards enabled England to win". In fact "as quite as many openings fell to Denmark, but they were not taken advantage of." England came out 2-0 winners, with goals from Frederick Chapman and Woodward, in front of 8,000 people. The English amateurs may not have been at their best in the final, but overall they were worthy gold medalists. In the tournament Stapley netted six times, to become England's leading scorer, and the goalkeeper, Horace Bailey, conceded only one goal, an own goal scored by Frederick Chapman.

If football had begun to be accepted as a major international sport at the London Olympics, this position was confirmed at the 1912 Stockholm Games, when the number of teams entered almost doubled to eleven, and when football proved to be one of the chief attractions at the Games. The Swedish organisers had been uncertain about the inclusion of a football tournament, doubting its world wide appeal, and the fact that only teams from Europe entered seemed to confirm their views, but the fact that many of the games were well supported dispersed their worries. A new departure at the 1912 Games was the decision to hold a consolation tournament, a separate competition for those teams knocked out in the preliminary and first rounds, so that they did not have to return home having played only one game.

As in the 1908 Games, England, still led by the indomitable Vivian Woodward, and to become the oldest player to win a football gold medal, were favourites to retain their Olympic title, but Holland and Denmark were fancied to be in the running. Football had developed strongly in these countries and they were among the early European footballing powers. Neither England nor Denmark took part in the preliminary rounds, which happened on 29th June, though Holland did. In this round the greatest shock was achieved by Finland, who defeated Italy 3-2 at Stockholm's Traneberg Sportplatz. It was only Finland's third international match, and their previous two had seen them go down to defeats by Sweden (5-2 in 1911 and 7-1 in 1912). The other preliminary games went to form. Holland defeated Sweden 4-3, before a crowd of 14,000, the largest ever seen at an Olympic football match, and Austria scored a 5-1 victory over Germany. Football, at the time, was much more advanced in Austria than it was in Germany.

The first round matches were all played on 30th June and produced no surprises. England defeated Hungary 7-0, with six goals coming from Harold Walden and the other from the inspirational Woodward. Woodward, even though he was an amateur, was regarded as one of the finest centre-forwards of his day and Walden ended up scoring eleven of the fifteen goals his team bagged in the tournament, which is still a British Olympic scoring record. He went on to become a very popular music hall star in West Yorkshire. In the rest of the round Finland knocked out Czarist Russia 2-1, Holland duly defeated Austria 3-1 and Denmark scored seven without reply against Norway. In the semi-final England faced Finland on 2nd July, and an unusual incident demonstrated the spirit of the British amateur game and the sense of fair play prevalent in the English team. The referee awarded a penalty against the Fins, a decision the English regarded as being too harsh, and when the kick was taken, the ball was deliberately hoisted high over the crossbar. The English felt that they did not need such assistance to win, as indeed they did not. They won the match 4-0 and so reached the final without conceding a goal. The second semi-final brought a 4-1 victory for Denmark over Holland and the inevitable final between England and Denmark was reached. It was played on 4th July and, though favoured by fortune, the English ran out worthy 4-2 winners to retain the gold medal place won in 1908. England's fortune, and Denmark's undoing, came when England were 2-1 to the good, but with the Danes making a good game of it. Charles Buchwald of Denmark was forced to leave the field with an injury and, in the days before replacements were allowed, it left the Danes with only ten men. The English made their advantage tell and scored twice in three minutes. The Danes did regroup and change formation, even pulling a goal back, but it was not enough against a resolute English defence. The 3rd/4th place play-off happened on the same day and saw Holland taking the bronze medal with a 9-0 victory over Finland, a team that had defied all expectations in advancing so far in the competition.

Alongside Woodward, Arthur Berry also became a double gold medal winner, having represented England in 1908, when he was a student at Oxford University. He was highly rated as a brilliant amateur, of whom one contempory described his style as "a complete act without tinsel or gaudiness." Two members of the England team, Arthur Knight and Ivan Sharpe, also played in the 1920 Antwerp Olympic Games, with Kenneth Hunt, who had played in the 1908 team, but not in that of 1912. Thomas Burn, another 1912 Olympic champion, sadly died in action on the Western Front in the First World War.

In the consolation tournament, Hungary received a bye and the other three matches took place on 1st July. Austria enjoyed a 1-0 victory over Norway, the same margin by which Italy defeated Sweden. The sensation of the round came when Germany scored sixteen against Czarist Russia without reply, a game in which Gottfried Fuchs scored ten of his country's goals, to equal the scoring feat of Sophos Neilson in 1908. This international scoring record stood until 2001 when Archie Thompson's 13 goals for Australia finally overtook it. Fuchs became one of Germany's big stars in the 1920s, but being Jewish later had to flee to Canada to escape Nazi persecution. The semi-finals, played on 3rd July, saw Hungary beat Germany 3-1 and Austria defeat Italy 5-1. In the final, played on 5th July, Hungary came out on top with a 3-0 victory over Austria.

The Stockholm Games were the last before the First World War caused the suspension of international sporting competitions involving the major European nations. In the pre-war footballing tournaments England had been supreme, but developments were afoot that were to change the face of organised international football forever. The second of these was a phenomenon: the South Americans were coming to challenge the dominance of Europe in the world game. The first, as stated earlier, was the issue of professionalism, which the English had overcome some forty years previously, but which was set to divide seriously international football for the foreseeable future. It was to see FIFA rent by the sort of quarrels that had plagued the English game in the 1880s. Ultimately, it would result in FIFA establishing its own international competition outside the Olympic aegis, the World Cup, but it would also keep the British out of that competition until the 1950s. This was not good for world football, but it was a disaster for the British game. When British teams eventually did participate in the World Cup, they found that some of those to whom they had exported the game had left them behind and some might say that the British have yet to catch up with the best of the rest of the world.

International football resumed after the war at the 1920 Antwerp Olympics. The Games began with a controversy, as the so-called "enemy" teams of Germany, Austria and Turkey were not invited to compete, and they ended controversially. However, the largest issue to cloud the games was that of professionalism. Under Olympic rules all athletes had to be unpaid amateurs, but many of the countries that entered teams for the football tournament were flaunting these rules, and often quite openly. Many of the players who took part were not full professionals in that they had other jobs and did not make their livings by football alone. Yet, their national FAs allowed "broken time" or part-time payments to compensate for the time players took off work to play football. Thus, they were not strictly amateur either. FIFA closed its eye to these payments and allowed such players to be classified as amateur, but for the British this would not do. They referred to it as "shamateurism" and the British decided not to send teams to future Olympic Games unless the matter was resolved. The British had been careful to ensure that teams representing Great Britain were strictly amateur.

The Origins of the World Cup

Fourteen teams entered the football tournament of the Antwerp Games, which was played in August and September of 1920. France and Belgium were awarded byes in the first round and the other teams played their matches on 28th August. One shock came when Spain gained a 1-0 victory over Denmark. It was Spain's first time in the Olympics and it was a notable achievement to take the scalp of old stagers, Denmark, again one of the tournament's favourites. A second shock result came when Norway defeated Britain 3-1. It was ironic that Britain's purely amateur team, whose football authorities were so hostile to the allowed inclusion of part-paid players, should have been knocked out by one of the other purely amateur teams. The result of the round was that of the Swedes, who scored nine against the Greeks without conceding and had all their goals scored by Herbert "Murren" Karlsson. Other results in the first round were: Holland 3 Luxembourg 0; Italy 2 Egypt 0, the first time that an African team had entered the tournament; and Czechoslovakia 7 Yugoslavia 0. The Czechs were to prove one of the better organised of the entries, but, alas, not one of the best disciplined and were to provide the third of the controversies that surrounded the games.

The quarter-finals were all played on 29th August and produced no major upsets, though some high scoring games. Belgium steered their way into the semi-finals with a 3-1 victory over Spain in front of an 18,000 crowd, proof enough that the sport was gaining in popularity. Holland just pipped Sweden with a 5-4 victory and France defeated Italy 3-1. In the last game of the round, Czechoslovakia put four past Norway without reply. The semi-finals were played on 31st August, and saw Czechoslovakia defeat France 4-1 and Belgium defeat Holland 3-0. The final, then, was between Belgium and Czechoslovakia, a game that was to end in fierce controversy when the Belgians were 2-0 up. The Czechs accused the British referee, John Lewis, of bias and walked off the pitch shortly after the Belgians had netted their second goal, six minutes before the half-time break. It is true that Lewis had been strict, but the reaction of the Czechs was very poorly regarded by the authorities and the game was awarded to the Belgians. The Czechs were subsequently banned by FIFA. The Belgian goals had been scored by Robert Coppée and Henrie Larnoe in front of an ecstatic crowd that might have numbered up to 40,000 (some sources quote 35,000). Whatever the true figure, it was further proof of the spread of football's popularity.

The problems surrounding the 1920 final meant that the arrangements made for the allocation of the bronze medal had to be redesignated so that the silver, denied to the Czechs, could be awarded. It had already been arranged that the bronze medal place would be decided by a knockout among the teams who had lost in the quarter-finals and on 1st September Spain beat Sweden 2-1, the same margin by which Italy defeated Norway. In what should have been the match to decide the bronze medal winners, on 2nd September Italy lost 2-0 to Spain, but with the competition ending as it had, Holland were brought back into the reckoning. The French had also been asked to play in this rescheduled part of the tournament, but had refused because most of their best players had gone home. So, on 6th September, Spain took the bronze when they secured a 3-0 victory over Holland. The consolation tournament was also affected by the unusual outcome to the final. On 30th August Egypt defeated Yugoslavia 4-2, but then the competition was abandoned and no further games took place.

The different definitions of amateurism had tarnished the 1920 Olympics, but it was to become a much more burning issue and cause greater damage to international football in the years before the 1924 Paris Olympics. In 1921, Belgium took the decisive step of legitimising "broken time" payments, in effect saying that players so remunerated could still enjoy amateur status. France, Italy, Norway and Switzerland quickly followed suit, moves that ran counter to the strict definition of amateurism favoured by the British, who began to press for the matter to be resolved. In one sense, the British had a fair point. Since they stuck rigidly to the literal definition of what constituted an amateur player and refused to send any paid or partly paid athlete to the games, it meant that its best teams did not represent the country. Such would be a team drawn from among the ranks of its professional players. Britain was plainly disadvantaged by its adherence to the rules, as the result of the game against Norway in 1920 had shown, and was a situation that irked the English FA. In December 1923, the English FA asked FIFA for a definition of amateur status and FIFA had to admit that they had none. They left it to each individual FA to work out its own interpretation. The English then asked FIFA to accept their definition, but the world organisation would not do so and the British promptly withdrew their football team from the 1924 Olympics. Denmark did likewise and for the same reason.

The International Olympic Committee had also been sceptical about FIFA's apparent disregard for the spirit of its amateur ideals and there was a certain amount of friction between the two bodies over the issue. However, it all came down to money and the Olympic fathers were not prepared to press the issue because football had become one of the major attractions of the games. The final of the 1924 football tournament alone was to generate a twelfth of the revenue for the whole games and the IOC was not prepared to lose such a money spinner over a matter of principle. Yet, it was a principle that kept Britain and Denmark, two of the elder statesmen of European football, out of the 1924 Olympic Games and this at the very time when a new footballing sensation was about to explode on to the European stage to shatter its myths for ever. The South Americans took part for the first time in the football tournament of the Olympic Games of 1924, making them much more of a "World Cup" than any previous event. The disappointment was that the principle of amateurism prevented the British and the Danes being there to confront the challenge.

In spite of some poor behaviour from the French home crowds, who often insisted on booing foreign national anthems, the football section of the Paris Games is widely regarded as the finest ever. With twenty two teams, from three continents, it was the most international so far, but it was the Uruguayans, with their dazzling skills, who stole the show. They were, quite frankly, brilliant and, with their short passing style and close ball control, showed the Europeans a new dimension of football. And, they did not have a manager. Instead, the Uruguayans preferred team meetings to thrash out such matters as team selection, tactics and strategy. Almost a peoples' democracy, they were what the Europeans needed to make them stand up and take note.

The first matches in the preliminary round were played on 25th May and produced one shock result: Spain, one of the favoured teams, was surprisingly beaten 1-0 by Italy, a country where football was not the force it was later to become. In the other preliminary round games the USA beat Estonia 2-0 and Czechoslovakia knocked out Turkey with a 5-2 victory. Two further matches were played on 26th May, when Hungary defeated Poland 5-0 and the Uruguayans set out their stall with an emphatic 7-0 drubbing of Yugoslavia. Theirs was a breath-taking display that caught the imagination, set tongues wagging and lit up the tournament. From that moment the Uruguayans were the toasts of Paris, though anybody who had studied the pedigree of the team should not have been surprised. They were the reigning South American champions and had won that title four out of the eight times that it had been contested. This had been in 1916 and 1917, the first two years of that championship, in 1920 and again in 1923. The problem for the Europeans was that few people knew anything about South American football and it allowed them to take the tournament by storm.

The first round proper got underway on 27th May with France putting seven past Latvia and Holland putting six past Romania, with neither victor conceding a goal. The next day the Irish Free State (now the Republic of Ireland), making their first appearance in the Olympics, beat Bulgaria 1-0, whilst Switzerland and Czechoslovakia ground out a 1-1 draw. The 29th May saw the Uruguayans in action again and, once again, they won handsomely. They defeated the USA 3-0, with all three goals being scored by the prolific Pedro Petrone. Also that day, Sweden had an 8-1 victory over Belgium, Egypt beat Hungary 3-0, for the first African victory in a major international football tournament, and Italy defeated Luxembourg 2-0. The Switzerland-Czechoslovakia replay took place on 30th May and produced a 1-0 victory for the Swiss.

The next stage of the competition was that of the quarter-finals, two of which were played on 1st June. Sweden defeated Egypt 5-0, but the telling game of the round was Uruguay's 6-1 victory over France, the host nation. Once more the South Americans were simply devastating and gave the French a lesson in footballing artistry. Their goals came from Héctor Scarone, Pedro Petrone and Angel Romano, names that were to grace international, and especially intercontinental football throughout the decade and into the next. In the other quarter-finals, played on 2nd June, Holland defeated the Irish 2-1 and Switzerland scored a victory over Italy by the same margin.

The semi-finals, played on 5th and 6th June respectively, saw Switzerland defeat Sweden and Uruguay defeat Holland both with 2-1 scorelines. The 3rd/4th play-off took place on 8th June and brought a 1-1 draw between Sweden and Holland, with Sweden winning the replay 3-1 on the following day, which was also that of the final. There was a little controversy surrounding the final because a Dutch referee had been appointed to officiate and since Uruguay had knocked out Holland in the semi-final, the South Americans feared bias. They objected to the choice and a Frenchman was brought in as replacement. A 60,000 crowd turned up for the match, showing just how much the Uruguayans had caught the popular imagination. A further 5,000 people were locked outside the stadium and several were injured in the crush to get in. Those who saw the game were not disappointed and witnessed Uruguay win the gold medal in some style. Goals from Petrone, after 27 minutes, Pedro Ceá, after 63 and Romano, after 81, brought a 3-0 victory for Uruguay. It is worth noting that several of the 1924 team played

The Origins of the World Cup

in the final stages of the inaugural 1930 World Cup: Ceá, Scarone, José Nasazzi and José Leandro Andrade. Ceá, Nasazzi and Andrade played in the final that established Uruguay as the first official world champions, and Ceá scored one of his team's goals that day.

The football section of the 1928 Amsterdam Olympics, the first games at which the Olympic flame was used, was also overshadowed by the question of professionalism. As in 1924, Great Britain did not participate, and this time they were joined in their boycott by the Scandinavian teams. In fact, 1928 was the year that the British FAs finally severed their links with FIFA, because of the world body's indecision on the definition of amateur status, and they did not return to the fold until 1946. It meant that no British home nation was eligible to play in a World Cup until the 1950 tournament, the fourth in the series. Furthermore, Czechoslovakia had introduced full professionalism in 1925, as did Austria and Hungary in 1926, and so neither of these could compete in the Amsterdam Games.

The football competition, which was once again to be dominated by South American teams, got underway on 27th May with a preliminary round game played between two teams making their first foray into the Olympics. In it Portugal ended Chile's involvement in the tournament proper with a 4-2 victory and, on the same day, in a first round match, Belgium put out Luxembourg, defeating them 5-2. The next day saw Germany beat Switzerland 4-0 and Egypt earn a 7-1 victory over Turkey. It was the first time that Germany had been allowed to compete in an Olympic Games since their defeat in World War One and was an indication of the new optimism that was sweeping European international relations in the late 1920s. With the Germans, in particular, seemingly falling over themselves to sign treaties and obligations to confirm their peaceful intentions, the rest of Europe was beginning to feel that Germany was no longer a threat. Acceptance into the Olympic Games was part of their rehabilitation, less than five years before Hitler came to power to alter these flimsy perceptions.

Three further games were played on 29th May. Italy got the better of France with a 4-3 win, Portugal made further progress with a 2-1 victory over Yugoslavia, but the third game was the most telling for the future of the tournament. In it Argentina, making a first appearance in the Games, devastated the USA and blitzed an 11-2 victory, with Tarasconi scoring four of their goals. The round was completed on 30th May when, significantly, Uruguay defeated Holland 2-0 and Spain put out Mexico, another Olympic debutante, with a 7-1 victory.

It was another indication of the popularity of football in the late 1920s that, for the first time, no games were scheduled together in the later stages of the tournament. The quarter-finals were played between 1st and 4th June and got underway with Italy facing Spain. They played out a 1-1 draw, so requiring a replay, which took place on 4th June and was not such an even affair. The Italians ran out 7-1 winners. The second quarter-final was a nine goal thriller and saw Argentina ultimately worthy 6-3 winners over Belgium, with Tarasconi again bagging a four goal tally. The third quarter-final saw Uruguay run Germany ragged and secure a 4-1 victory, with a hat-trick coming from Pedro Petrone, and in the fourth match of the series, the surprise of the round had Egypt defeating Portugal 2-1. Both of these teams had done exceptionally well to get so far, but the Egyptians especially.

Many people expected the South Americans to dominate their respective semi-finals and the Argentinians did. On 6th June they blasted six past the hapless Egyptians, who could find no reply, with Tarasconi weighing in with another two. Argentina, who shone like a footballing beacon, had scored 23 goals in three games, with Tarasconi's personal tally being ten. The next day the Uruguayans did not find things quite so easy against the Italians, but they battled away for a 3-2 victory to set up the inevitable showpiece final. This took place on 10th June, but before it happened, Italy secured the bronze medal with an emphatic 11-3 defeat of the brave Egyptians. The Italian team contained Angelo Schiavio, who would become a World Cup winner in 1934.

With the sideshow over, the main event was a much closer and keenly fought affair, with two games being eventually needed to separate the teams. The first match was a 1-1 draw, the goals coming from Petrone of Uruguay and Manuel Ferreira of Argentina. The replay took place on 13th June and this time Uruguay edged it 2-1 to retain their gold medal and their place as unofficial world Champions. For Uruguay, Roberto Figueroa and Héctor Scarone scored, whilst Argentina's effort came from Luis Monti. Both Scarone and Monti were to play significant parts in their teams' World Cup campaigns in 1930, of which decisions were being taken by FIFA whilst the Olympics were going on.

22 Men and a Bag of Wind

Before discussing how the official World Cup was born out of the muddy waters that surrounded the professional-amateur argument, the 1928 Olympic soccer tournament needs to be brought to its conclusion. As had become a tradition, a consolation tournament was run alongside the later stages of the main event and four countries were involved. The opening matches were played on 5th June, when Holland beat Belgium 3-1 and Chile beat Mexico by the same scoreline, to set up a European and South American "best of the rest" final. It was played on 8th June and ended in a 2-2 draw. Since no arrangements had been made for a replay, the outcome was decided by the drawing of lots. Holland chose the correct straw and so won the contest.

The 1928 Olympics Games were to be the last that contained a football tournament of any significance until more recent times. The sport did not feature at all in the 1932 games, held in Los Angeles and by the time of the 1936 "Hitler" Olympics, the issue of professionalism had finally been worked through. The IOC had finally decided to go with a strict definition of amateurism and few countries could play their best teams. However, long before this, FIFA had decided to organise its own international competition independent of the Olympic movement and Olympic football. It was to replace the Olympics as the premier international event. Having its own tournament, unfettered by Olympic conventions, meant that professional, "broken time" and even amateur players could compete. The only requirement would be that a country be affiliated to FIFA.

The two men most responsible for bringing about the establishment of the World Cup were two Frenchmen. Jules Rimet had become the president of FIFA in 1921 (there had been no president between 1918 and 1921) and had proved himself to have been a gifted administrator. He had been instrumental in bringing the British FAs back into the organisation in 1924, after Hugo Meisl had made the first conciliatory gestures in 1923. It was also Rimet, whom in 1926 stated that: "Soccer could reinforce the ideals of a permanent and real peace", clearly recognising the value of international football in forging ties between nations and reflecting the change of mood in European international affairs in the mid 1920s. This was the gradual improvement in international relations that came after the uncertainties of the years following World War One and which resulted in Germany being readmitted into the Olympic movement. He also fully recognised the significance of the division between the amateur and professional codes, and how this was preventing the unity of the footballing world. He, therefore, suggested a world tournament to be organised within three or four years, outside of the Olympic Games and open to the best teams of all FIFA members, be they amateur or professional.

His vision was supported by Henri Delauney, the secretary of the French FA between 1919 and 1956, when he died. He also recognised the need to resolve the issue of professionalism and to this end, in 1926, he submitted a resolution to FIFA that: "International football can no longer be held within the confines of the Olympics and many countries where professionalism is now recognised and organised cannot any longer be represented by their best teams." His suggestion was not at first taken up, nor was a similar proposal from Hugo Meisl to stage a European international championship, because FIFA had already decided to continue under the Olympic banner, in spite of the division this was creating. Ultimately though, the fact that continuing to run with the Olympics was splitting world football did force the issue, and FIFA discussed the matter in Amsterdam in 1928, where delegates had gathered to watch the Games.

It was the British who inadvertently helped to solve the problem. After the 1924 games, the IOC had decided to adopt Britain's strict definition of amateur status, but FIFA remained unconvinced. Obviously, FIFA had to go with the majority of its members and in 1926 the majority had gone along with Switzerland's proposal that financial compensation for loss of earnings could be paid to amateur footballers without affecting their amateur status. It did cause a rift between the IOC and FIFA, especially when, in 1927, and preparations were underway for the Amsterdam Games, FIFA demanded that the IOC should allow "broken time" payments. The IOC crumbled when FIFA threatened to prevent its members from participating in the forthcoming games. It was all too much for the British, who once again withdrew from the Olympics, and this time from FIFA also. It made FIFA realise that it had to confront the issue that was holding back its progress.

At a meeting in Amsterdam on 26th May 1928 FIFA finally accepted Delauney's 1926 resolution by 25 votes to 5 and the decision to launch the World Cup was made. A commission led by G Bonnet, of the Swiss FA, was set up to look into the practicalities and at FIFA's 1929 Barcelona Convention, the matter was settled. Rudolfe Seeldrayers, of the Belgian FA and FIFA's vice-president (he was president from 1945 to 1955) proposed that the host nation should provide funds for the transport and accommodation of referees, FIFA members and players, in that order. The motion was passed and soon after Uruguay were announced as the first host nation.

The Origins of the World Cup

The World Cup had been born. Meisl, Delauney, Bonnet and Lannemann drew up the regulations and the French sculptor, Abel Lafleur, was commissioned to design the trophy, a "winged victory". It later became known as the Jules Rimet Trophy, in honour of the man who had done so much to make it possible.

Chapter 3

The Winged Goddess Enters
The Uruguay World Cup, 1930

Uruguay 1930

Winners: Uruguay

Runners-up: Argentina

Semi-finalist: Yugoslavia

Semi-finalist: USA

Total Attendance: 447,500

Number of Matches: 18

The world of 1930 was dangerous and depressing. In 1929 the New York Stock Exchange crashed taking the savings and investments of many an American with it. The fall-out sent ripples around the world, plummeting nations into economic and political uncertainty. The result was three million people out of work in the USA and 1.5 million in the UK. In London, there was fighting on the streets as the jobless clashed with the police. In Germany, the recession led to the rise of the Nazis who won 107 seats in the German parliament to become the second largest party. Adolf Hitler was on his way to power. Economic problems in South America had political repercussions too. The price of tin crashed and took Bolivian President Hernando Siles with it and in Argentina, President Hipólito Yrigoyen went down with the falling price of wheat and meat.

Over in the Soviet Union, Stalin was establishing his own brutal dictatorship and his drive to industrialize and collectivize accounted for millions of victims. India was also witnessing major upheaval. The Mahatma Gandhi's demands for independence annoyed the British establishment and threatened such disruption that they put him in jail.

1930 was not all doom and gloom however. It was also a time for new discoveries, new records and new songs. An American astronomer watching the skies from his base at the Lovell Observatory in Arizona noticed a new planet and named it Pluto after the Greek God of the Underworld. Coincidentally, Marlene Dietrich was also having success with a song about the heavens, "Blue Angel", whilst the boogie-woogie was taking American youth by storm. Britain found its own hero when Amy Johnson captured the £10,000 prize from the Daily Mail when she became the first woman to fly solo to Australia. She had with her a bag of tools and patched her plane up as she went along. By the time she reached her destination the plane was so battered that some parts had had to be patched up using sticking plaster.

This was the world that formed the background to the start of a championship that has become the biggest sporting event on earth. Once the decision to run the World Cup had been taken in 1929, a host nation had to be found. Six countries applied for the honour of holding the competition and they were Holland, Hungary, Italy, Spain, Sweden and Uruguay. Holland and Sweden then withdrew their applications in order to support Italy and the other South American FIFA members, notably Argentina, threw their support behind Uruguay. Having won the 1924 and 1928 Olympic football titles, the Uruguayans were de facto unofficial world champions, and this obviously told in their favour, but there were other factors that influenced FIFA's decision to grant the inaugural games to Uruguay. 1930 was the centenary of the country's independence; they announced that they would build a brand new stadium for the tournament; and, possibly more persuasively, the Uruguayans agreed to pay the travel and accommodation expenses of all FIFA delegates, officials and participating teams.

The decision to stage the finals in Uruguay was not popular among the Europeans and those who had aspired to host the show themselves pulled out. The reason, they said, was the long journey of up to a month to South America, but the real reason was pique at not being chosen themselves. Then Austria, Czechoslovakia, Germany and Switzerland announced that they would not be attending and noises from other European countries were decidedly unenthusiastic. The four British nations, of course, were no longer affiliated to FIFA and so were ineligible to participate, and suddenly the whole concept of the World Cup looked like being strangled before it had even been born. The South Americans were, quite understandably, incensed at what they perceived to be European arrogance and threatened to resign, en masse, from FIFA. This prospect triggered a series of

22 Men and a Bag of Wind

The Goddess of Victory and the Eight-sided Chalice

What do you give to soccer's world champions? If the prize is to be worthy, then surely it must have outstanding beauty, and have artistic and cultural merit? After all, such a trophy would be awarded every four years and only a number of very select individuals would ever hold it aloft in triumph.

The task of creating such a prize was given to a French sculptor named Abel Lafleur some two years before FIFA decided to hold an "International Championship", as the minutes of their meeting described it. Lafleur created a trophy 35cm (14 inches) in height and weighing 3.8kg (8.36lbs). The statuette was made of sterling silver and was gold plated, with a blue base made of lapis lazuli. On the base stood a goddess of victory holding aloft an eight-sided chalice. There was a gold plate on each of the four sides of the base, on which have been engraved the name of the trophy as well as the names of the nine champions between 1930 and 1970. It was first presented in 1930 to Uruguay.

Since its creation the trophy had a precarious existence until it finally disappeared in 1983. The "Coupe du Monde de Football Association" lived quite peacefully throughout the 1930s until war broke out in 1939. In order to save the trophy from occupying German troops, the Italian Vice-President of FIFA, Dr. Ottorino Barassi, hid it under his bed in a shoebox. Thankfully, its disguise as the most expensive pair of Italian shoes in the world worked and it emerged to be presented again. In 1946, and in honour of the man who created the World Cup competition, the trophy was renamed "Coupe Jules Rimet". The honour was also in recognition of Rimet's 25 years of service at the helm of FIFA.

For the next twenty years the Goddess of Victory lived the life she was meant to lead, being presented to football's world champions and being admired and coveted by those nations who failed in their quest to possess her. Then, in 1966, the trophy disappeared one day whilst on display as part of the build up to the World Cup finals in England. The hero of the day was a little dog named Pickles, who uncovered the hidden Goddess whilst digging under a tree.

The Jules Rimet Trophy was not so lucky in 1983. The cup, now in permanent possession of three-times winners Brazil, was stolen again. This time the trophy was not to be found and was apparently melted down by the thieves and sold. The Brazilian Football Association ordered a replica to be made. To date the new "FIFA World Cup" trophy has had a much quieter life.

---

behind-the-scenes football diplomacy, which resulted in four European countries being persuaded to send teams: Belgium, France, Romania and Yugoslavia. They were not the best of the crop of European national sides, and many questioned why Belgium and Yugoslavia bothered to go at all, but their participation prevented the first World Cup from being a disaster and they did ensure that it was at least a "world" cup. The snub, though was not lost upon the Uruguayans, who later boycotted the 1934 finals held in Italy.

In Uruguay, too, there were minor teething problems, which cast some slight shadows over the opening of the tournament, most notably surrounding the 100,000 capacity stadium that was being built especially for the event. Torrential rain in Montevideo had prevented its completion in time for the opening game and construction workers had to work in shifts, under floodlights, for twenty four hours a day to get it into a fit enough condition for Uruguay's opening game. This was scheduled to be against Peru on 18th July, the centennial independence day. The stadium was got ready, just, but it was not totally completed and could only admit 80,000 spectators.

Nonetheless, the tournament got underway as planned on 13th July 1930 with Uruguay favourite to win, Argentina, the reigning South American champions, second favourite, and France expected to be the pick of the Europeans. Brazil was not yet the footballing power that it would later become and, whilst the other competitors might be regarded as also-rans, both the USA and Yugoslavia defied the pundits and did remarkably well. Another feature of this opening World Cup was the generally poor standard of refereeing, especially in the face of some robust and often violent play.

> All the games in the 1930 World Cup were played in Montevideo at the Estadio Centenario, the Estadio Pocitos and Central Park.

> Prior to the tournament the Uruguayan team were locked away, incommunicado, in their Montevideo hotel for two months. There was to be no contact with anyone, not even their families. Mazzali, the regular goalkeeper could not however, stand to be away from his loved ones and was caught one morning by the trainer returning to the hotel with his shoes in his hand. He was sent home and never played in the World Cup.

The Winged Goddess Enters - Uruguay 1930

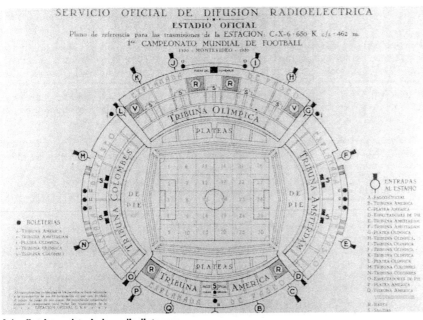

A leaflet issued to help radio listeners enjoy the commentaries with the field marked with numbered boxes.

It had originally been envisaged that the World Cup would be a knock-out tournament, but this idea was rescinded. The prospect of European participants travelling thousands of miles across the Atlantic to possibly play only one match was not very appealing and FIFA needed to encourage reluctant Europeans to attend. Anyway, the low number of entrants made such a format impractical and so it was decided to arrange the teams into groups, with the winners of each of the four groups making up the semi-finalists, thus laying the lines of future World Cups. It would also ensure that each nation would play at twice.

Three of the four competing European nations, France, Belgium and Romania, all travelled together. They sailed on the same boat, the Italian liner Conte Verde, from Villefranche-sur-Mer in France. The trip took two weeks and the teams had to train on-board. The one nation that didn't travel on the same boat was the team that did the best - Yugoslavia.

Another World Cup Mystery

The first goal to be scored in World Cup finals is usually credited to Lucien Laurent of France, but some historians believe it should be Bart McGhee for his goal against Belgium on the same day. The confusion is because no one recorded the time of goals or whether matches kicked off on time then. So, the answer to the question of who scored the first ever World Cup goal is: "We don't know for sure."

Given the influence of Jules Rimet and Henri Delaunay in getting the idea off the ground, it was fitting that France was one of the teams in the first ever World Cup match. This was a Group One game played against Mexico at the Pocitos Stadium, the home of Peñarol, one of Uruguay,s top clubs. It was also appropriate that it should have been a Frenchman who scored one of the first ever World Cup goals. However, before this World Cup milestone was reached, history of a less savoury nature was made when the French goalkeeper, Alex Thépot, had to be taken off after only ten minutes, having been kicked on the jaw. He was the first player to be taken off in a World Cup game. He was replaced by Augustin Chantrel, an outfield player, but in the days before reserves or substitutes were allowed it meant France had to play the rest of the match with ten men. This was no real handicap. The French played confidently and the Mexicans were disappointing. Within minutes of losing Thépot, France took the lead when Lucien Laurent hit a powerful shot passed the Mexican keeper. It was nothing less than France deserved, having dominated the game so far, and further goals from Marcel Langiller and André Maschinot gave them a 3-0 half-time lead. Later, Laurent had this to say: "The stadium we played in was only tiny. About 5,000 people would have filled it. And it was snowing."

The Mexicans made a better show of it in the second half, but the damage had already been done. Juan Carreño pulled a goal back for Mexico, but three minutes from time, Maschinot netted his second goal to secure a 4-1 victory. It had been a good game, though a disappointing crowd of only a thousand had turned up to watch. Yet, it had been a game of historic firsts: the game itself, possibly the first goal, the first player taken off through injury and the first player to score two goals in a World Cup match. It was also a game that saw two brothers play in the same team for the first time in the World Cup, when Manuel and Felipe Rosas represented Mexico. All in all, it had not been a bad advertisement for the new competition, though the event gained little coverage in some of the French press, where leading paper Le Figaro gave it a couple of lines to say that "the French team has been triumphant by 4 goals to 1." In the British press, the games were virtually ignored and when reference was

---

History? We don't have a history.

To most Americans men's soccer does not merit much discussion because they believe they are not very good at it and do not have much of a history. There will be those who can remember the days of the New York Cosmos and the Tampa Bay Rowdies, and there will be a few more who can remember that the World Cup finals took place in the USA in 1994. However, there will be few who can speak about the famous "Shot-putters", who were once a power in world soccer. It is because soccer went into a period of obscurity in the 1940s, 50s and 60s that much of their soccer heritage has been long forgotten. It wasn't even resurrected for analysis at the time of the 1994 World Cup. It will therefore, be a surprise to most Americans that their team once made it to the World Cup semi-finals.

In the 1920s with many European and South American nations in economic decline, people were attracted to the factory, mill and mine work available in the American Midwest and Northeast in search of a better standard of living. There was also money to be had in soccer. Many of the companies fielded their own football teams and there were regular matches. A player could earn up to $50 for an appearance. Added to this was an extra $50 a week if the player also worked for the company. "$100 was a fortune in those days. A packet of cigarettes cost only 11 cents then." So said Jimmy Brown who played for the USA in 1930. He went on to play for Manchester United and Tottenham Hotspur.

It is wrong to presume that the US team that appeared in the 1930 tournament was a bunch of European and South American imports. Teams such as the Ben Miller FC and Brooklyn Wanderers had developed into very good sides and could hold their own against any of the major European teams. In fact, Americans often came to Europe to play exhibition matches and many players were well known. It is true that the American team did contain six ex-British professionals but, as Roger Allaway of the Philadelphia Inquirer established in 1995, they were naturalized American citizens. They earned their places in the US team, not because of where they were from, but because they had done their apprenticeships in the US soccer leagues and had proved themselves capable. Billy Gonsalves from Fall River, Massachusetts, is regarded as the best American soccer player of the 20th century. He was given the nickname the "Babe Ruth of Soccer" to get over to the American public just how good he was. The team was so highly regarded in 1930 that they were made one of the seeds. The coach of the team, Wilfred Cummings, had a very modern way of thinking and his tactics were unlike the norm of the day. Instead of playing a five forward formation he played a defensive game that relied on counter attacks.

Only when the Americans stormed their way to the semi-finals did they begin to get some attention. Before the semi-final the New York Times, which rarely covered soccer, carried the optimistic headline: "US favoured to win world's soccer title". Yet about that match, the Daily Telegraph wrote: "Argentina proved too strong - literally - even for the fit and fast American 'shot putters', who found themselves only one down at half-time but with one player missing (broken leg after 10 minutes), another suffering from a kick in the jaw, and their 'keeper also badly injured. It was not surprising that Argentina put five past them in the second half." The dream was at an end and to this day rreaching the semi-final remains the crowning glory of the American men's soccer team. Four years later in Italy they went down 7-1 in the first round.

However, Americans should remember the names of Jimmy Brown, Billy Gonsalves, Thomas Florie (the captain), Bart McGhee, Jim Douglas (who went on to play for Nottingham Forest) and coach Wilfred Cummings. They can feel proud that their team once reached the semi-finals, though since then little of note has happened in American international soccer except that in 1950, they caused one of the greatest shocks in World Cup history.

---

made to the World Cup, it was usually with derision. The Manchester Guardian made fleeting reference to the "so-called world's Association football championship", whilst the sports journal, the Athletic News scoffed: "This doesn't sound much like a world championship? No, but it is - in title." In an earlier review of the event, the same journal, taking a swipe at its authenticity, predicted that the "title will rest in South America. Judging by reports of the excitable crowds in those parts, there will be trouble if it doesn't."

The second World Cup game, another Old-New World confrontation, also took place on 13th July, at Central Park, the home ground of another of Uruguay's leading clubs, Nacional. It saw the USA take on Belgium in a Group Four game in front of a crowd of around 10,000. The American team was largely made up of British, especially Scottish players, who were, for the most part, ex-professionals and seen as past their best. Few pundits gave them any chance of doing well, regarding them as too old or too fat, and the French team nicknamed them "the shot putters". Marcel Pinel, the French centre-half, later said that they "always amused us when we saw them training, for they were clad in tiny shorts which revealed enormous thighs, like tree trunks, and they would go lapping and slogging round and round a track like long distance runners." It is worth remembering that only two years before, at the 1928 Amsterdam Olympics, Argentina had taken the Americans apart with an 11-2 victory. However, the USA proved to be one of the great surprises of the 1930 World Cup and overcame their first opponents "in decided fashion", as one Argentinian newspaper described it. In doing so, they employed a curious system of eight players in defence and three up front, relying on quick, darting runs to do the damage. It worked and, in the words of the reporter, although "the ground was not conducive to a first class exhibition of form, the public was most favourably impressed, especially in regards the efforts of the winning team." The New York Times thought that "James Brown of New York and William Gonsalves of Fall River, Mass., were the outstanding stars for the Americans", though it was two goals from the Scot, Bart McGhee, and another from centre-forward, Bert Patenaude which gave them a 3-0 victory. It is perhaps indicative of the overall Belgian

U.S.A 3 : Belgium 0
Nicholas Hoydonckx (left) is challenged by U.S.A's Bertram Patenaude.

British 'import' to the USA team, Alec Jackson, had previously helped Huddersfield Town win the English league in 1926. He was also a member of the Scottish 'Wembley Wizards' team that beat England 5-1 in 1928.

There were two player-coaches involved in the first World Cup, Juan Lugue de Serralonga of Mexico and Rudolf Wetzer of Romania. De Serralonga didn't play in the tournament, but Wetzer played in both Romania's games.

performance that the American paper just quoted ended its comment with the remark that "the Belgian goalkeeper starred for the losers."

The next day saw Yugoslavia beat Brazil 2-1 in a Group Two match, described in the local press as "more remarkable for the rough play and fouls principally on the part of the Brazilians... who seemed to suffer from a lack of self-control". It also saw Romania play Peru in Group Three. That the Romanians ever got to Uruguay was down to the intervention of King Carol, who picked the team himself. The squad was made up of part-time players, many of whom worked for a British oil company, and it was reluctant to give them time off work, especially since it would mean them being away for at least three months. The King wrote to the employers and persuaded them to grant his team a three-month leave of absence so that they could take a leisurely return trip that would enable them to visit New York for a spot of sight seeing. They arrived in Montevideo and found themselves involved in the first controversial match of the tournament, one that heralded into World Cup football a problem that has blighted the competition down into modern times, that of poor refereeing. Alberto Warken of Chile, who officiated in only one match of the series, struggled to keep control this very ill tempered and often violent, but action packed game. The excitement began in the first minute when Adalbert Desu scored the quickest goal of the tournament, and then things began to sour, especially after Romania's Adalbert Steiner had his leg broken, and the rest of the game was littered with unsavoury incidents. Peru's Mario de Las Casas was "ordered off the field by the referee for striking an opposing player" and earned notoriety as the first player to be dismissed in a World Cup game. It reduced both teams to ten men, though it is doubtful whether this seriously affected the outcome of the match. Romania were always the better side and their 3-1 victory was fully deserved. Only around 300 people turned up to watch the spectacle, making it the lowest attended match of the finals. This can be explained by the facts that these were not seen as the most attractive teams of the tournament and that it was played on Bastille Day. France's national holiday is also celebrated in Uruguay.

Argentina came into action on 15th July against France in Group One's second game, another game marred by savage play and dreadful refereeing, this time from Almeida Rego of Brazil. When George Orwell wrote, "sport at international level is frankly mimic warfare" he might have had this game in mind. As the New York Times reported: "The game was bitterly contested", the crowd also adding to the atmosphere "voicing their emotions with out particular restraint." For France, Thépot was back in goal, having recovered from the injury he suffered in the opening game, and he and centre-half Pinel played magnificently. Their solid performances were needed against an Argentinian team that showed the two facets of Argentina's national game that have become recognisable to World Cup fans down the years. These are the ability to utilise brain, skill and tempo to such a degree that their football becomes truly beautiful, which they then combine with a petulance and cynicism that can disgust many who only minutes earlier were admiring their brilliance. A more decisive referee might have altered the course of the game, but Rego allowed the Argentinians to get away with a style of play other referees would almost certainly have prevented. After only ten minutes, Argentina's hard man, Luis Monti, scythed down Lucien Laurent, rendering him a passenger for the rest of the game, but Rego took no firm action. It was Monti who scored Argentina's second half goal, after his team had

Yugoslavia 4 : Bolivia 0
Yugoslavia's Alexander Tirnanic (left) causes problems for the Bolivian defence.

been awarded a free kick just outside the French penalty area. Monti, who took the kick, did not allow the French defence to organize itself properly and when Thépot was unsighted by his own defenders, he had no chance against Monti's strike.

The game had been littered with poor refereeing decisions, but the worst came six minutes from time. The French were still 1-0 down, but having the better of the play, when their winger, Langiller, broke through Argentina's defence and was bearing down on goal. Just as it looked as if he might level the game, Rego blew up for time. In delirium, the Argentinian supporters invaded the pitch, whilst the French players, distraught, protested against the blatant injustice. Eventually, the referee admitted his mistake and agreed to restart the game. Cierro, Argentina's inside-right, weighed down with the emotion of the occasion, feinted when he realized that his team had not won and that they had to continue, but he need not have worried. The incident had broken the spirit and concentration of the French and they could not refind their sparkle. They lost the game by Monti's single goal.

The first team to go out of the World Cup was Mexico, who lost their second game on 16th July, when the Chileans gave them a lesson in attacking football. Chile had a player of real power and ability in Guillermo Subiabre, who scored two of his team's goals in their 3-0 victory, a scoreline that flattered the inept Mexicans. The Chileans received a standing ovation at the end of the match in appreciation of their dynamic style of play.

Yugoslavia was the first team to secure a place in the semi-finals when they brushed aside Bolivia on 17th July. They played well throughout the match, but really turned on the style in the second half, scoring all their goals and earning a 4-0 victory. As was said in the Argentinian press, "experience and superior skills ultimately overcame spirit and individual effort.... the Bolivians possessed dash... but the Yugoslavians played a careful, precise game." Soon, they were joined by the USA, whose 3-0 defeat of Paraguay ensured that they would top their group. In preparation for this match, the Americans changed their tactics. Instead of the more defensive formation that they had employed against Belgium, they opted for a more open passing style and the change worked. The Paraguayans, who were clearly not expecting it, were convincingly outplayed in a game in which American centre-half, Patenaude, was outstanding and created that little, but belatedly recognized piece of World Cup history.

The next day was the centenary of Uruguay's independence. It was to be a day of big celebration. The new Centenary Stadium, still only partially completed in spite of the struggle to get it ready, was to be unveiled for the first time and, adding to the sense of the occasion, it was to witness Uruguay's first game of the tournament. To do justice to the day, the event and the venue, two things were needed: a blockbuster of a game and a Uruguayan victory. The crowd of 80,000, by far the biggest of the competition so far, got both. Uruguay's opponents for the day, Peru, had been unconvincing in their previous game against Romania, but they entered this match with an entirely different attitude. As one local newspaper had said of their earlier performance: "The devil was hidden; he had stayed in the Inca's dressing room against Romania without ever appearing on the pitch." He certainly made his appearance against Uruguay, and took the shape of a nippy right-winger called Lavalle, a constant tormentor of the home defence. His runs often threatened a break through, but Uruguay somehow held on, thoroughly grateful for a 0-0 half-time scoreline. The game's only goal came 15 minutes into the second half and was scored by Héctor "Manco" Castro. The crowd went wild but then had to endure another half-hour of intriguing

The Winged Goddess Enters - Uruguay 1930

The First World Cup Hat Trick.

The facts surrounding the first ever hat trick scored in World Cup finals remained a mystery for many years. Prior to 1998 the majority of record books had it down as the three goals scored by Guillermo Stàbile for Argentina in their pool game against Mexico on 19th July. However, those in the USA camp and much of the South American press disputed this. They said the honour went to Bert Patenaude of the USA for his three goals in the victory over Paraguay two days earlier. New evidence has come to light that proves Patenaude should be given the credit. So, why was there a mix up in the first place and why was Stàbile given the credit?

The problem arose because some records gave the USA's third goal to Tom Florie, while others record it as an own goal. However, when the American coach Wilfred Cummings submitted his report to the US Football Association he stated that Patenaude had scored all three. Other members of the US team backed up these claims. Twelve months before he died Arnie Oliver, a member of the squad, in an address to a Soccer History Symposium in New York State, said that Patenaude had scored them. Billy Gonsalves and Jim Brown also claimed Patenaude scored a hat trick.

The most conclusive evidence, however, comes from the South American press of the time. Diagrams that can be found in the Argentinian daily newspaper La Presna, and the match report that goes along with them, clearly show how the goals were scored and that it was Patenaude who scored them. The Brazilian paper Estadio de São Paulo also states that Patenaude got all three. The following are extracts from the Standard, an English language paper published in Buenos Aires, Argentina on 18th July 1930.

Goal One   "After a ten minute period McGhee dribbled down the centre of the field and passed to Patenaude who shot a cannon-like goal."

Goal Two   "Five minutes later Moorehouse and Tracey stopped a Paraguayan advance, and Brown passed to Patenaude, who, finding Denis in the wrong position, shot by Olmedo, scoring the second goal." Denis was the Paraguayan goalkeeper.

Goal Three "From a corner against Paraguay, Patenaude headed the third and last goal for the United States, after five minutes of play." This was five minutes into the second half.

The evidence to award the hat-trick to Patenaude's appears overwhelming. The reason behind the controversy is because of the claim that the third goal was an own one, taking a deflection on the way in. A 'deflected goal' is sometimes credited to the player it came off and sometimes to the player who shot it. Accrediting any goal was difficult, as the players didn't wear numbers in those days. FIFA recognized Patenaude's hat trick in 1998 and record books now give him the credit he deserves.

The opening of the Centenary Stadium in Montivideo on 18th July 1930.

and intensely worrying football as the Peruvians refused to comply with the script and lie down dead. They continued to press, looking for the elusive equalizer and the Uruguayans battled to keep them at bay. They did, but only just and Montevideo was spared further agony when Belgian referee, Jean Langenus, eventually blew for time. The relief was tangible. (See Andrade profile on page 39 and Scarone profile on page 40).

Peru's defeat brought their exit from the World Cup and on 19th July the "fast Chilean team sprang one of the biggest surprises", as one local paper reported, "beating France by one goal to none" to end their World Cup campaign. The French were probably still feeling the effects of their bruising encounter with Argentina and were certainly far from their best against a Chilean team that knew that a semi-final place was still a possibility. It was a victory well deserved for the "steady attack of Chilean forwards and their close defence", and was sealed with another goal from the formidable Subiabre. The 1-0 score did not reflect the dominance of the South Americans and it was France's goalkeeper, Thépot, again at his excellent best and working heroically, who kept the score down.

Argentina took on Mexico later that day in the Centenary Stadium (See Argentina v Mexico profile on page 41) and the two games that were played on the following day were of little more than academic interest, since Yugoslavia had already qualified out of Group Two and the USA out of Group Four. Nonetheless, the formalities had to be gone through. Brazil notched a 4-0 victory over Bolivia and Paraguay defeated Belgium by the only goal of the game. This latter match was a particularly poor one, something that cannot be said of the next day's game between Uruguay and Romania to decide the third semi-finalist. The Uruguayans were desperate to do well in the tournament and at the team meetings that were held to discuss and decide the line-ups and tactics to be employed, they decided to opt for a short passing style of quick movement. They hoped that it would perplex the Romanians and so give the home team the advantage. They were right. Playing what many regarded as the finest displays of football in the competition, the South Americans took the Europeans apart in the first half. Goals by Pablo Dorado, Héctor Scarone, Peregrino Anselmo and Pedro Ceá blasted them to a 4-0 half-time lead. It had been a remarkable show of fast, incisive and totally ruthless football, for which the Romanians had no answer. Having built up such an advantage, Uruguay decided that they could coast through the second period and save themselves for the semi-final place that was rightly theirs. They did and the score remained 4-0.

This left one more semi-final place to be filled and it was decided in the final Group One match played on 22nd July. This was another game that both teams, Argentina and Chile made difficult for referee, Langenus, to control and once again the Argentinians showed both the sublime and the nasty sides of their game. In the first half some subtle and beguiling football brought two goals for Guillermo Stàbile, before Subiabre pulled one back for Chile. Then, just before half-time, the Argentinians unleashed the vicious side of their game and again it was Monti who was behind it. He committed a foul that was regarded as far too dangerous by the Chileans, who, to even things up, set about their opponents with venom. The referee could not prevent the brawl and the police had to be brought on to the pitch to separate the protagonists. It was all so unnecessary, especially since Argentina had been marginally the better team in the first half. In the second half the Chileans were the more resourceful of the two teams, but their frequent attacks could not find away through a solid Argentinian defence. In it, Juan Fuaristo, who had been brought in to the Argentine team for his first World Cup game to give greater strength at the back, played very well and it was he who scored his team's final goal to give them a 3-1 victory and the final place in the semi-finals.

The 1930 World Cup, now reduced to four surviving teams, entered its second and final phase. It paired the winners of Group One, Argentina, with the USA from Group Four, and Uruguay took on Yugoslavia. The first of these semi-finals was played before a near capacity crowd on 26th July. It was a game that people found difficult to predict. Argentina and their record were a known quantity, but the USA had been one of the surprises. In getting this far they had played some attractive football, at times strong in defence and at others skilled and pacey in forward work. They had also reached the semi-finals without conceding a goal and there were those whom fancied them to go all the way, especially in America where the New York Times crooned: "The United States team, because of its splendid showing in the tourney, is favoured to carry off the world's

HECTOR CASTRO

The scorer of Uruguay's first and last goal in the World Cup finals was the one-handed Héctor "Manco" Castro. He had lost his left hand in a childhood accident.

The first penalty in World Cup Finals was awarded by referee Ulysses Saucedo of Bolivia in the game between Argentina and Mexico. He awarded four penalties altogether, three of which were missed. The first player to score from the penalty spot was Manuel Rosas of Mexico in the 38th minute. The first player to miss from the spot was Fernando Paternoster of Argentina. The Mexican goalkeeper, Bonfiglio, also saved two further penalties, probably from Zumelzù.

There were two sets of brothers on show at the 1930 tournament. For Mexico were Filippe and Manuel Rosas and for Argentina Juan and Mario Evaristo. The Evaristo boys were the first to play in a World Cup final.

During the semi-final between the USA and Argentina, in one desperate moment, when Jean Langenus had given a foul to the Argentinians, the US medical attendant ran on to the pitch to remonstrate with the referee. In his disgust, he threw his medical kit onto the ground where it split open and several bottles contained within, broke. One of them contained chloroform, the fumes almost overpowered him and he had to be helped from the field.

Uruguay 4 : Argentina 2
Jose Nasazzi leads out the Uruguayan team for the World Cup final followed by Andrade, Macheroni and Ballesteros.

championship." Sadly for the North Americans, it was not to be and as it turned out, the game was a much more one-sided affair than anybody might have guessed. For one thing, the Americans had a tendency to play as individuals, having a less defined team ethos than did their opponents, and for another the South Americans resorted to the uglier side of their play and it made all the difference. Jimmy Brown later recalled: "They kicked us all over the place. We ended up with six sound men. They really went for us." After only ten minutes American, Raphael Tracey, had his leg broken and other injuries reduced several of his colleagues to the category of walking wounded by half-time. Goalkeeper, Jim Douglas, was hardly able to keep to his feet and Andy Auld was kicked in the face and suffered a terrible mouth injury. Not for the first time referee, Langenus, allowed the Argentinians to get away with appalling play and, in the circumstances, the Americans had done remarkably well to keep the score down to a single Monti goal come the mid-way break. It was a different story in the second half. The Americans were simply in no condition to withstand wave upon wave of Argentinian attacks. Alejandro Scopelli and "Nolo" Ferreira were constant threats and set up Stàbile and Carlos Peucelle with chance after chance. Both netted twice and Scopelli scored another, before Brown grabbed a late consolation two minutes from time. The final score was 6-1 to Argentina. The Uruguayans did not find things so easy against Yugoslavia in their semi-final, played on the next day, but won through anyway. (See Uruguay v Yugoslavia profile on page 42).

There may have been a degree of fortune about how each of the finalists achieved their places, but few could doubt that Argentina, reigning South American champions, and Uruguay, reigning Olympic champions, were there on merit. (See Uruguay v Argentina profile on page 43). They were the tournament's better teams and the fanatical populations of these neighbours and great rivals anticipated the final as if far more than a sporting world championship depended on it. Indeed, the atmosphere that preceded the game was unlike that surrounding any other previous sporting occasion. It unleashed a fervent nationalism in both countries that could easily have turned serious. The night before the final, thousands of Argentinians sailed across the River Plate in hired boats and spent the night on the dockside chanting "Victory or Death". Most of these supporters, of course, would not get in to see the match, but it was a mark of the passions generated that they made the journey at all. The home support was just as fervent, with people travelling from all over the country to see the game or just to be near. The Manchester Guardian reported: "Twenty special trains unloaded thousands of people from up country, and a fleet of aeroplanes brought spectators from remote towns. All the shops and offices in the city were closed, and business was at a standstill. Among the early arrivals were fifty members of Parliament." Security for such an event was very tight. The Argentinian team was given a police escort to the ground and, on the day of the game, armed soldiers with bayonets fixed patrolled the stadium to maintain control. In Buenos Aires things were just as tense and passionate. The match was relayed on loudspeakers and the streets thronged with excitable crowds, which gathered wherever they could get news of the match.

It was an extraordinary occasion and the match provided a spectacle to fit the event with the victory sparking wild celebrations throughout the country. In the capital the night resounded with the noise of car horns, klaxons, sirens and fireworks, and a public holiday was declared for the next day. The celebrations were so furious that one British press correspondent, reporting the event, remarked: "I don't see how soccer can continue in these countries. Surely they will kill off all the referees." In Buenos Aires the mood was quite different. Sadness turned to anger and disappointment, and police had to open fire on a mob that began to stone the Uruguayan embassy. The situation was so dangerous the occupants of the embassy had to barricade themselves in. The first World Cup generated a passion that has echoed down the years and has visited every tournament.

So, how do we assess this first World Cup? As a football pageant, it had its weaknesses. In terms of preparation and organization it had its faults, though these were largely outside the control of FIFA and the Uruguayan authorities. The nations represented, with the obvious exception of the finalists, were not necessarily the strongest in the world, though, again, FIFA cannot be blamed for this. The fact that those countries that did compete were either American or European did not make it a true "world" cup, but in 1930 much of Asia and Africa were dominated by colonialism. Since it would be years before nations from these continents gained their freedom or before football became popular there, the 1930 World Cup was almost as representative as it could have been. Then, the standard of football played was not always scintillating, was sometimes particularly poor and blighted by refereeing that could verge on the dreadful. At times, the quality of football was simply brutal and was matched by some lowly attendances. However, such problems have blighted World Cup tournaments down to the present time.

There were negative features of Uruguay 1930, but FIFA lacked the experience of organizing such an event, and these things have to begin somewhere and at sometime. The organizers of every event learn from their previous experience. The tournament, however, did have some very positive points, which, on balance, outweigh the negative. In footballing terms, the top continents were represented and in this sense it was a "world" cup. There was also some brilliant football played, with games that could thrill and excite, the Uruguay-Peru game, for instance, or the final itself. Furthermore, the contest threw up its genuine star players, like Stàbile, Subiabre, Ceá, Thépot and Paternaude, to name but a few. (See Stàbile profile on page 40). Finally, there was the result. The event may have missed some of the stronger footballing nations, but few would deny that among that elite were Argentina and Uruguay. Had it been a fully representative World Cup, the chances of a similar final ending with a similar result, would have been high. It was a fair assessment of the state of world football in 1930 and, all in all, Uruguay 1930 provided a creditable first effort. It was a firm foundation upon which to stage future events.

FIFA President Jules Rimet presents the Jules Rimet Trophy to Dr. Raul Jude.

Argentinian supporters entering the Centenario Stadium for the final were searched for weapons.

So passionate were the teams that contested the 1930 World Cup final that Uruguay and Argentina both insisted on playing with a ball manufactured in their own country. To settle the dispute the referee decided that they would play with one country's ball in the first half and the other country's in the second.

Uruguay was coached by home grown Alberto Supicci. No World Cup winning team has ever been coached by a foreigner.

The French captain, Alex Villaplane, was executed in 1944 for collaborating with the Nazis.

José Leandro Andrade

Uruguay

Honours: Winner 1930
Played: 1930

Games 4
Goals 0

Early souvenir button badge of José Leandro Andrade used to advertise a garage.

José Andrade was one of the pillars that the world beating Uruguayan team of the 1920s and 30s was built on. He was a rock, a trickster and purveyor of all that was precious in the art of the game, an idol to many. In one game he ran nearly the full length of the pitch with the ball on his head.

Born on 20th November 1898, this towering midfielder plied his trade for the teams Bella Vista and Nacional and was part of the national team that travelled to France for the 1924 Olympic Games. Here he was nicknmaed the "Black Marvel" by the French who fell in love with this charmer. Europe had never seen a black footballer before and he amazed them with his dazzling skills. Uruguayan businessman, Atilio Narancio had raised the money, at great personal expense, to get the team to Europe commenting that: "We are no longer just a tiny spot on the map of the world." The team included Pedro Arispe, a meat packer, José Nasazzi, a marble cutter, "Petrucho" Petrone, a grocer and Pedro Ceá, an ice salesman. Andrade himself was a carnival musician and shoe-shiner. All of them were about 20 years old and they travelled third class to Europe and overland second class by train. They slept on wooden benches at times and at other they played football for bed and board. Prior to the Olympics they took on nine Spanish sides and won every game.

Since it was the first time a South American side played in Europe, their first opponents, Yugoslavia, sent spies to their training sessions. Andrade and his team mates fooled them into thinking they could not kick straight, scuffing the ground and bumping into each other at ever step. The Yugoslavians came in for a real surprise, therefore when they were hammered 7-0 and Uruguay went on to win the Olympic crown. They retained it with much the same side in Amsterdam in 1928.

Andrade himself fast became a celebrity in France after the 1924 Olympic Games and he decided to stick around to "see the sights". Whiskey hemp sandals were replaced by the finest leather shoes and, with a top hat perched on his head, he did the rounds of the cabaret clubs. He cut a dashing figure and the French loved his gay, jaunty style. He had silk handkerchiefs, yellow gloves and a cane with a silver handle. He also had humour and he used it to fool journalists on more than one occasion. The Uruguayan style of play was known as moñas, or ringlets, and was based on the successive figure eights the team drew on the field. When asked about this style a gullible French press was taken in by the story that it had been learned from the shapes made by chickens as they were chased across the ground.

In 1929 his football world so nearly came crashing down around him. He was badly injured and his future looked increasingly uncertain. However, he was always a battler and he fought his way back to fitness to once again become the backbone of the national side. His experience on the field proved invaluable when Uruguay lifted the inaugural World Cup trophy. As Andrade grew older and he retired from the game, his fame left him and poverty assailed a man who had given so much. His friends tried to arrange testimonials for him but they never seemed to take place. He died of tuberculosis in abject poverty. He was a black South American whose mastery of football raised him above the rest, but like so many who came after him, he was put down again. Yet, he was the first all-action, world footballing hero.

Héctor Scarone

Uruguay

Honours: Winner 1930
Played: 1930

Games 3
Goals 1

South America has produced many of the world's outstanding football proponents. However, when memories seem to go back no further than Pelé or Garrincha, it is disappointing that players like Stàbile, Leónidas, Andrade, Ceá and Nasazzi have faded into history. Héctor Scarone is one such player. He was a genius of the game and a member of the Uruguayan team that dazzled the world in the 1920s and early 30s. While conjuring up goals as if they were pennies from behind a child's ear he would sing aloud as he sweetly danced with the ball. He was a songbird; he was the "Magician". According to Eduardo Galeano he "scored goals with a marksmanship he sharpened during practice sessions knocking over bottles at 30 metres" and he was no less deadly with his head. Although only short, a long forehead crowned with a shock of dark curly hair and an ability to stay in the air for so long it was as if he had sprouted wings enabled him to head the ball with grace, power and accuracy.

Born in Montevideo on 21st June 1898, his playing career began at the age of 14 when he signed on to play for Sportsman then in the Uruguayan Third Division. He moved to Nacional and it was here that he earned his nickname, the "Magician", producing some spellbinding performances from the inside-forward position. He made his international debut in 1919 and remained in the side for over 15 years, becoming one of only four players to appear for Uruguay in the Paris and Amsterdam Olympics and in the inaugural World Cup tournament when South American football hit Europe like a hurricane and blasted their way to winner's medals in each competition. Between the two Olympics, Scarone had a spell at Barcelona and was top scorer in the South American championships of both 1926 and 1927. He did not play in Uruguay's opener against Peru in 1930, but commanded a place in the side for the rest of the tournament, scoring in the 4-0 demolition of Romania. His delight in winning the trophy is clear from the expression on his face in pictures from the final.

Following Uruguay's victory offers from Europe were not long in coming but Scarone bided his time, eventually settling on Ambrosiana-Internationale in Italy. After the Second World War, he returned to Spain for a short spell as coach with Real Madrid. However, his time there did not last long and he returned to Nacional back home in Uruguay-as a player. He was now in his 50s but his ability and fitness were such that the club had no qualms about taking him back. He eventually retired in 1953 at the age of 55, a South American record to this day. Héctor Scarone died in 1968. Players of his stature may have faded from popular memory, but this does not diminish his achievement. He was "the Gardel of Football" and merits a place in anyone's Hall of Fame of South American players.

Guillermo Stàbile

Argentina

Honours: Runner-up 1930
Played: 1930

Games 4
Goals 8

Guillermo 'El Filtrador' Stàbile, who did not even make the starting line-up for Argentina's opening game in the 1930 World Cup, earned his nickname for his ability to crack defences and find the net. A prolific striker, he hit an average of two goals a game in 1930, became one of the most successful marksmen in World Cup history and went on to become the tournament's top scorer. Until the records were put straight in the 1990s, he held the honour of scoring the first World Cup hat trick.

Born in Buenos Aires in 1908, Stàbile was the son of an Italian immigrant and the fifth of ten brothers and sisters. He was spotted playing football in the streets of his hometown and was taken on by local club Huracan to play in their youth team. He was given his first team debut at the age of 17 and by 1926 he was playing in the national side. Yet, when the Argentinians arrived in Montevideo in 1930, Stàbile was not the natural choice for the first team. However, after an attack of nerves got the better of Roberto Cierro, the regular striker, Stàbile got his chance. It took him a mere eight minutes to find the net, notching up the first of his eight goals in the tournament against Mexico and Cierro never featured again. He scored twice to gainthat "first" World Cup hat trick, grabbed two in each of the games against Chile and the USA and scored another in the final itself.

His Italian connection made him a natural target for the top Italian league sides. Genoa signed him on Friday, 14th November for a fee of 25,000 pesos, having outbid Juventus. Mass crowds waited to greet his arrival and, because of the demand to see him, he was put in the side to play Bologna on the Sunday. In his first 45 minutes in Italian football he put three past the hapless Bologna goalkeeper making him an instant star and taking him into the hearts of the Genoese people. His initial success in Italy was short lived and he suffered two leg fractures in poor challenges, one against Alessandria goalkeeper Rapetti and another against Galluzzi of Fiorentina. Strangely, the fractures of his fibula were in the same place. He managed only 42 appearances for Genoa, but scored 14 goals, before he was transferred to Napoli. However, he was never the same player and, after a short spell was transferred to Red Star Paris in France. He was capped for the French national side and once scored four goals in a game against Austria.

He returned to Argentina and played in several teams, including Huracan again, until he retired. He became coach of the national side in 1941, a position he held until 1957, and briefly again in 1960. Unfortunately, the fact that Argentina did not appear in the 1950 or 1954 tournaments meant that the World Cup did not get to witness the talents of Guillermo Stàbile the manager. In the 123 games he was in charge of the national team, they triumphed 83 times, a 67% success rate. "El Filtrador" died on 27th November 1966. He was the first prolific goal scoring hero of the World Cup. There will always be arguments as to the standard of teams in the tournament and whether scoring then was easier than now, but this does not alter the fact that here was a man who could carve open defences at will and score eight goals in four World Cup matches - a major feat in anybody's currency.

Argentina 6 : Mexico 3

The 5,000 or so spectators who turned up to watch what one Buenos Aires newspaper described as "one of the most interesting matches of the series" were thrilled by a game that, from start to end, was replete with good football and incident. Previously, the Mexicans had played twice, had disappointed on both occasions and were now playing for pride. With Chile having won earlier in the day, the pressure was on Argentina, playing without their skipper, "Nolo" Ferreira, who had had to return to Buenos Aires to sit the university exams necessary for his graduation. In his place, the captaincy was passed to the fiery mid-fielder, Adolfo Zumelzù, but Ferreira's loss was just one more pressure on the team from across the River Plate.

The match started wonderfully for the Argentinians, who were three goals to the good inside 17 minutes, the result of some swashbuckling forward play. As the local press told it: "The Argentine's quintet of forwards gave a series of best exhibition passing, Stàbile, Spadaro and Peucelle, working smartly throughout, while Varallo tended toward individual play, Zumelzù notably aggressive on the midline". It took just seven minutes for them to crack the Mexican defence, when Zumelzù knocked a ball to Stàbile. Bonfiglio, in the Mexican goal, made the mistake of coming off his line and it opened the way for the Argentinian to open his country's account. The game had barely restarted before the Argentinians were back on the attack and this time Zumelzù drove home himself. Eight minutes later a third was added when Varallo picked out Stàbile in Mexico's area, who made no mistake with his close range effort. The Argentinians dominated the rest of the half without scoring further. The full-backs, Fernando Paternoster and Della Torre kept the Mexican forwards at bay, allowing them little freedom of movement. Their one lapse came seven minutes before half-time, when Paternoster handled the ball in the area. Manuel Rosas took the resulting penalty, the first of the tournament, and gave his team a glimmer of hope.

If Mexico felt that they had any chance of getting back into the game when play resumed, an opening spell of almost total Argentinian pressure, which brought two goals for Varallo, must have shattered them. At 5-1 the game appeared beyond Mexico, but the Argentinians began to relax a little and it allowed their opponents, showing more pluck than at any other time during the competition, to mount a purple patch of their own.

Firstly, Della Torre pulled back Felipe Rosas and he was able to score from the resultant free kick. Then a whole string of Mexican attacks followed, as they began to feel as if there was something in the game for them. Juan Carreño, who "starred for the Mexican forwards", had fired himself up and was ably assisted by López and Olivares. It was Olivares who set up Mexico's third goal in the 75th minute, when he saw Bossio, Argentina's goalkeeper, coming off his line and crossed for Hilário López to head home.

What had been a one-sided affair was now beginning to turn round with the score at 5-3 and still 15 minutes to play. Angelo Bossio, who had been nicknamed the "Elastic Wonder" for his antics at the 1928 Olympic Games, began to crack under the pressure. His game, according to one reporter, "was nervous and irregular" and he has to bear much of the responsible for Mexico's resurgence. However, his team gradually began to reassert themselves again and with just over five minutes to play, they put the game firmly beyond their opponent's reach. Varallo, as nippy as ever, found Stàbile with a pass and he banged in Argentina's sixth.

It had been an excellent game. The Argentinians had played with flashes of real brilliance, but had shown that they had their weaknesses. Bossio was one. He had lost much of the flair that had singled him out in earlier years as an exceptional goalkeeper and he was soon to be dropped from the team. Another was a lack of concentration that allowed the Mexicans to make a comeback out of what should have been an impossible situation. It brought into question Argentina's billing as one of the tournament favourites. The Mexicans, though, had plainly more to offer than they had previously shown. They had fought spiritedly to raise their game, their forwards revealed a cutting edge hitherto hidden and at the back the Rosas "brothers steadily supported Bonfiglio who played a steady game under the heavy fire of the Argentine forwards."

Uruguay 6 : Yugoslavia 1

On 27th July, to the roars of a massive crowd of some 93,000 fans, the Uruguayan team walked out onto the pitch of the Centenary Stadium for their third World Cup game. They had begun their campaign rather nervously against Peru, but had turned on the style in their next game against Romania. Now they were just one step away from a place in the final itself, but standing in their way were the Yugoslavians, a team that had arrived in Montevideo something of an unknown quantity and not well fancied. Yet, they had shown themselves capable of playing very attractive football, having scored six goals in their previous games, one more than Uruguay had managed. In Ivan Beck, who played professional football in France, they had one of the stars of the competition, having scored three of his country's goals.

When the game kicked off, it began to look as if the Europeans might pull off a major upset. They hit the home team hard with a series of attacks and Djordje Vujadinovic scored after only four minutes, the first goal that Uruguay had conceded. Playing in front of such a large, partisan crowd unnerved the home team but they settled and began to turn the game in their favour. They also had three slices of fortune, with a series of key, but controversial refereeing decisions going their way. The first of these came in the 18th minute, when a through ball found Pedro Ceá in free space in a position that appeared offside. He charged in and scored, bringing a tirade of protests from the Yugoslavs, but the referee let it stand. It clearly upset the rhythm of the Yugoslav players and, when the game restarted, they found it difficult to settle. The Uruguayans, now with the wind in their sails, were the team to take full advantage of the disquiet and fall in concentration of their opponents. They quickly gained possession of the ball, rushed it up field with a series of devastating passes and, within two minutes, had taken the lead with a goal from Peregrino Anselmo.

For the rest of the half play was fairly even, with Yugoslavia having slightly the better of it. Both teams defended well, with Stefanovic and Mihalovic steady for Yugoslavia and Mascharoni, Nasazzi and Fernandez keeping things safe for the hosts, keeping goalkeeper "Ballesteros free to maintain a good position throughout the game." With neither attack able to break through, the Uruguayans got their second slice of luck. A Yugoslav goal was disallowed for offside when it was almost certainly legal. It brought further protests from the Yugoslavs, but to no avail and was followed a few minutes later by a third dubious refereeing decision. A Uruguayan attack saw the ball centred into the Yugoslav penalty area, where Anselmo was on hand to score his country's third. The problem was that the ball had crossed the bye line and was out of play before Anselmo put it in the net. It was all too much for Balkan temperaments. The Yugoslavs surrounded the referee in vain protest and even threatened not to continue with the game. Rego would have none of it and when the teams went in at half-time, the 3-1 score line stood, to the great consternation on the Yugoslavs.

It was a disconsolate Yugoslav team that trudged out for the second half and from the start it was clear that their spirits had been broken. They had none of the dash they had shown in the first half and this is shown by the fact that they only mounted three attacks in the whole of the second period. They virtually handed the game to the Uruguayans, who needed no second invitation. Their "forwards utilising short speedy passes swept through the defence of the Europeans with slight difficulty," was how one commentator put it, underplaying somewhat the dominance of the South Americans. He added: "In the forward line Cea, Anselmo and Iriarte took advantage of every scoring opportunity, feeding passes smoothly into the opposing team's area and firing to the net with precision at the most propitious "moments." "Santos Iriarte scored Uruguay's fourth goal on the hour and Ceá added two more, in the 67th and 71st minute to complete his hat trick and produce a final scoreline of 6-1 to Uruguay.

In the end, the poor Yugoslavians were well beaten and with no 3rd/4th play-off, their competition was over. The Uruguayans, however, had swept into the final, their style of play and power of their forwards ultimately triumphant. As one local commentator put it: "To-day's result demonstrated again that the River Plate method and clever managing of the ball, combining short runs and passes with basketball shots over their opponents as the surest way of scoring." It was, he said., "superior to any thing the Old World or the United States has offered." How right he was!

Uruguay 4 : Argentina 2
The World Cup Final

Uruguay's Dorado scores the first goal after 12 minutes.

The 1930 World Cup final was possibly the most remarkable sporting spectacle ever witnessed up to that date. In footballing terms, it put together two of the best teams in the world. In the tournament itself, as in previous Olympic Games, both had demonstrated a quality of football that few other national teams could live with. The Uruguayan team was an experienced and well tuned unit. They had a solid defence, well marshalled by captain José Nasazzi, and up front players like Pedro Ceá and Santos Iriarte could be devastating. They combined movement of vision, both on and off the ball, with a lethal scoring ability. The Argentinians had a similar style of play, a strong defence built around the powerful Luis Monti, and a forward line that could be just as ruthless as that of Uruguay. Men such as Carlos Peucelle, Giullermo Stàbille and Francisco Varallo, known as "El Canonito", "the Little Cannon", because of the power and accuracy of his play, were players of real calibre. They could also utilize a more hardened style when they felt that things were not going their way.

As an occasion, the final was draped in passion and fervour. As one soccer history book tells us: "It was if the entire futures of these neighbouring nations and bitter football rivals depended on the outcome." In Montevideo, crowds roamed the streets and packed any place where they could get news of the game. Thousands of Argentinian fans had arrived, though very few would get into the game. They just wanted to be near and packed the dockside, singing and chanting. Back in Buenos Aires, the atmosphere was just as fervent. Commentary on the game was relayed by loudspeaker and, as one local paper described it: "Every café and balcony were commandeered and even the trees... were climbed by enthusiasts anxious to find points of vantage to hear the loudspeakers better." "It was a wonderful sight - thousands of "soccer" fans of both sexes carrying Argentine flags and "musical" instruments, including "tin cans," anything to make a noise".

The match kicked off at 2.15 and the first half produced a seesaw of attacks, but no goals until the deadlock was broken in the 12th minute. Intercepting a shot from Ferreira, Alvaro Gestido set up the counter attack from which Dorado netted "with a strong low shot that gave no chance to the Argentine goallie." Going behind did not upset Argentina, who went straight back onto the attack and almost equalized when Evaristo's shot was saved. Then it was Uruguay's turn to advance and Botasso, Argentina's goalkeeper, brilliantly saved Scarone's stinger of a shot. Such end to end football was bound to bring further goals and, in the 20th minute, it did. After "splendid combination play on the part of Ferreyra (sic), Arico Suárez and Varallo," it was the latter who fed the ball through to Peucelle to score the equalizer.

As if following a script, Uruguay pelted forward from the restart and it took the best of Botasso to keep Scarone's shot out. The goalkeeper was injured on Uruguay's next attack when Castro came charging in violently to knock him down. Referee, Langenus, had to halt the game whilst he received treatment, but it was more a case of high spirits than deliberate foul play, because the game was never dirty and played in a sporting manner. After the break up of another Uruguayan attack, Della Torre sent the ball to Ferreira, who lobbed the defence for Stàbile to chase. He appeared offside, but the referee allowed him to continue his run and, despite the best efforts of Gestido and the diving Ballesteros, the ball ended up in the net. It brought a storm of protest from the Uruguayan players, but the goal stood and the Argentinians went into the half-time break 2-1 to the better. The Uruguayans needed the interval to settle their nerves and calm their tempers.

The pattern of play in the second half mirrored that of the first, though, as time passed, the Uruguayans gradually gained the ascendancy and their enterprise was rewarded in the 12th minute. Evaristo gave away a free kick, which Gestido knocked over for Ceá to score from close range. Ten minutes later the Uruguayans took when "El Canario" Iriarte let fly a blockbuster shot from 25 metres. It completely caught the Argentinians by surprise, as they never expected him to attempt a shot from that range, let alone score. In 1930 footballs were much heavier than present day types and long distance shooting was more problematical than in the modern game. Had there been a goal of the tournament award in 1930, Iriarte's effort would have taken the prize.

The Argentinians continued to mount their own attacks. The wingers, Evaristo and Peucelle, worked tirelessly in the cause and Stàbile drove a shot against the bar, but Uruguay's defence was getting stronger and was beginning to take the menace out of their opponents. As time wore on, it began to look increasingly like it was going to

be Montevideo's day and the game was finally settled in the last minute of the half. Dorado attacked down the wing, crossed the ball and "Manco" Castro was there to head home. The team went wild, the crowd went wild, Montevideo went wild, but in Buenos Aires news of the score was received "with tears of silence by the multitude."

Years later, José Pedro Damiani, who became the president of Peñarol, described his day at the World Cup final, which he attended as a nine year old boy and through his words can be gauged the passion of the event and its significance for the people of

Jubilant Uruguay players celebrate after winning the Jules Rimet Trophy.

Uruguay. "My family is not well off," he said, "and I couldn't afford a ticket. I walked to the new Centenario Stadium. I joined a big queue. Suddenly, it moved forward and I was swept inside, part of a huge number of gate-crashers. By the end of the first half we were very worried because Argentina was winning two goals to one. The mood was sad. Some people were crying. During the second half Lorenzo Fernandez started running and kicking the ball like crazy. Suddenly "Vasco" Ceá scored an equalizer for Uruguay. Then "Canary" Iriarte scored for us. Finally, another goal by "Manco" Castro and... we'd won, 4-2. The victory was fantastic. The whole of Uruguay was celebrating. We were dancing in the streets. The Argentine team was heartbroken. I finally got home at midnight. My mother had been worried sick about me since sunset. She gave me a massive hiding." One suspects that the "hiding" his mother gave him was a small price to pay for such an unexpectedly wonderful day out.

In the end, it had been a splendid final, well contested by both teams and gripping for the crowd. If the new competition needed a showpiece final to crown its first running, then it got one. Few World Cup finals since have matched this one for pure excitement. It had been a game of committed, open play from the protagonists, largely free of dirty play and generally pursued in a spirit of sportsmanship. Both sides could be proud of their contributions to the first World Cup final. They had done much to get the new tournament off to a solid start.

Statistics - Uruguay 1930

GROUP ONE

Montevideo, July 13th - Estadio Pocitos

4 (3) FRANCE

Laurent, Langiller, Maschinot(2)

Thépot, Mattler, Capelle, Villaplane, Pinel, Chantral, Liberati, Delfour, Maschinot, Laurent, Langellier.

1 (0) MEXICO

Carreño

Bonfiglio, R. Gutiérrez, M.Rosas, F.Rosas, Sánchez, Amezcua, Pérez, Carreño, Mejia, Ruiz, López.

Referee: Domingo Lombardi (Uruguay)
Attendance: 1.000

Montevideo, July 15th - Central Park

1 (0) ARGENTINA

Monti

Bossio, Della Torre, Muttis, Suárez, Monti, J.Evaristo, Perinetti, Varallo, Ferreira, Cierro, M.Evaristo.

0 (0) FRANCE

Thépot, Mattler, Capelle, Villaplane, Pinel, Chantral, Liberati, Delfour, Maschinot, Laurent, Langellier.

Referee: Almeida Rego (Brazil)
Attendance: 3.000

Montevideo, July 16th - Central Park

3 (1) CHILE

Subiabre (2), Vidal

Cortes, Morales, Poirier, A.Torres, Saavedra, Helgueta, Ojeda, Subiabre, Villalobos, Vidal, Schneueberger.

0 (0) MEXICO

Sota, R. Gutiérrez, M.Rosas, F.Rosas, Sánchez, Amezcua, Pérez, Carreño, López, Ruiz, Gayon.

Referee: Henri Chrisophe (Belgium)
Attendance: 500

Montevideo, July 19th - Estadio Centenario

1 (0) CHILE

Subiabre

Cortes, Morales, Ciaparro, A.Torres, Saavedra, C.Torres, Ojeda, Subiabre, Villalobos, Vidal, Schneueberger.

0 (0) FRANCE

Thépot, Mattler, Capelle, Villaplane, Pinel, Chantral, Liberati, Delfour, Delmer, Veinante, Langellier.

Referee: Anibal Tejeda (Uruguay)
Attendance: 2.000

Montevideo, July 19th - Estadio Centenario

6 (3) ARGENTINA

Stàbile (3), Zumelzù (2 pens), Varallo

Bossio, Della Torre, Paternoster, Cividini, Zumelzù, Orlandini, Peucelle, Varallo, Stàbile, Demeria, Spadaro.

3 (1) MEXICO

M.Rosas (2, 1 pen), Gayon

Bonfiglio, R.Gutiérrez, M.Rosas, F.Rosas, Sánchez, Rodríguez, F. Gutiérrez, Carreño, López, Olivares, Gayon.

Referee: Ulysses Saucedo (Bolivia)
Attendance: 5.000

Montevideo, July 22nd - Estadio Centenario

3 (2) ARGENTINA

Stàbile (2), M.Evaristo

Bossio, Della Torre, Paternoster, J.Evaristo, Monti, Orlandini, Peucelle, Varallo, Stàbile, Ferreira, M.Evaristo.

1 (1) CHILE

Subiabre

Cortes, Morales, Ciaparro, A.Torres, Saavedra, C.Torres, Avellano, Subiabre, Villalobos, Vidal, Aguilera.

Referee: Jean Langenus (Belgium)
Attendance: 1.000

	P	W	D	L	F	A	Pts
Argentina	3	3	0	0	10	4	6
Chile	3	2	0	1	5	3	4
France	3	1	0	2	4	3	2
Mexico	3	0	0	3	4	13	0

GROUP TWO

Montevideo, July 14th - Central Park

2 (2) YUGOSLAVIA

Tirnanic, Beck

Jaksic, Ivkovic, Milhailovic, Arsenievic, Stefanovic, Djokic, Tirnanic, Marianovic, Beck, Vujadinovic, Seculic.

1 (0) BRAZIL

Preguinho

Joel, Brilhante, Italia, Hernogenes, Fausto, Fernando, Poly, Nilo, Araken, Preguinho, Teofilo.

Referee: Anibal Tejeda (Uruguay)
Attendance: 5.000

Montevideo, July 17th - Central Park

4 (0) YUGOSLAVIA

Beck (2), Marianovic, Vujadinovic

Yavovic, Ivkovic, Milhailovic, Arsenievic, Stefanovic, Djokic, Tirnanic, Marianovic, Beck, Vujadinovic, Naidanovic.

0 (0) BOLIVIA

Bermudez, Durandal, Civarria, Argote, Lara, Valderama, Gómez, Bustamente, Mendez, Alborta, Fernández.

Referee: Francisco Mateucci (Uruguay)
Attendance: 800

Montevideo, July 20th -
Estadio Centenario

4 (1) BRAZIL

Moderato (2), Preguinho (2)

Veloso, Ze Luis, Italia, Hernogenes, Fausto, Fernando, Benedito, Russinho, Leite, Preguinho, Moderato.

0 (0) BOLIVIA

Bermudez, Durandal, Civarria, Sainz, Lara, Valderama, Ortíz, Bustamente, Mendez, Alborta, Fernández.

Referee: Thomas Balway (France)
Attendance: 1.200

	P	W	D	L	F	A	Pts
Yugoslavia	2	2	0	0	6	1	4
Brazil	2	1	0	1	5	2	2
Bolivia	2	0	0	2	0	8	0

GROUP THREE

Montevideo, July 14th - Estadio Pocitos

3 (1) ROMANIA

Desu, Stanciu, Kovacs

Lapuseanu, Steiner, Bürger, Rafinski, Vogl, Eisembeisser, Kovacs, Desu, Wetzer, Stanciu, Barbu.

1 (0) PERU

Souza

Valdivieso, De Las Casas (RED), Soria, Galindo, Garcia, Valle, Flores, Villanueva, Denegri, Neira, Souza.

Referee: Alberto Warken (Chile)
Attendance: 300

Montevideo, July 18th -
Estadio Centenario

1 (0) URUGUAY

Castro

Ballesteros, Nasazzi, Tejera, Andrade, Fernández, Gestido, Urdinaran, Castro, Petrone, Ceá, Iriarte.

0 (0) PERU

Pardon, De Las Casas, Maquilon, Galindo, Denegri, Astengo, Flores, Villanueva, Lavalle, Neira, Souza.

Referee: Jean Langenus (Belgium)
Attendance: 70.000

Montevideo, July 22nd -
Estadio Centenario

4 (4) URUGUAY

Dorado, Scarone, Anselmo, Ceá

Ballesteros, Nasazzi, Mascheroni, Andrade, Fernández, Gestido, Dorado, Anselmo, Scarone, Ceá, Iriarte.

0 (0) ROMANIA

Lapuseanu, Czako, Bürger, Rafinski, Robe, Vogl, Eisembeisser, Kovacs, Desu, Wetzer, Barbu.

Referee: Almeida Rego (Brazil)
Attendance: 80.000

	P	W	D	L	F	A	Pts
Uruguay	2	2	0	0	5	0	4
Romania	2	1	0	1	3	5	2
Peru	2	0	0	2	1	4	0

GROUP FOUR

Montevideo, July 13th - Central Park

3 (2) UNITED STATES

McGhee(2), Patenaude

Douglas, Wood, Moorhouse, Gallacher, Tracey, Brown, Gonsalvez, Florie, Patenaude, Auld, McGhee.

0 (0) BELGIUM

Badjou, Nouwens, Hoydonckx, Braine, Hellemans, De Clercq, Diddens, Moeschal, Adams, Voorhoof, Versijp.

Referee: José Macias (Argentina)
Attendance: 10.000

Montevideo, July 17th - Central Park

3 (2) UNITED STATES

Patenaude (3)

Douglas, Wood, Moorhouse, Gallacher, Tracey, Brown, Gonsalvez, Florie, Patenaude, Auld, McGhee.

0 (0) PARAGUAY

Denis, Olmedo, Miracca, Etcheverri, Díaz, Aguirre, Nessi, Dominguez, González,

Benitez Caceres, Peña.

Referee: José Macias (Argentina)
Attendance: 800

Montevideo, July 20th -
Estadio Centenario

1 (1) PARAGUAY

Peña

P.Benitez, Olmedo, Flores, S.Benitez, Díaz, Garcete, Nessi, Romero, González,

Benitez Caceres, Peña.

0 (0) BELGIUM

Badjou, De Deken, Hoydonckx, Braine, Hellemans, Delbeke, Diddens, Moeschal, Nouwens, Adams, Versijp.

Referee: Ricardo Vallarino (Uruguay)
Attendance: 900

	P	W	D	L	F	A	Pts
USA	2	2	0	0	6	0	4
Paraguay	2	1	0	1	1	3	2
Belgium	2	0	0	2	0	4	0

SEMI-FINALS

Montevideo, July 26th -
Estadio Centenario

6 (1) ARGENTINA

Monti, Scopelli (2), Stàbile (2), Peucelle

Botasso, Della Torre, Paternoster, J.Evaristo, Monti, Orlandini, Peucelle, Scopelli, Stàbile, Ferreira, M.Evaristo.

1 (0) UNITED STATES

Brown

Douglas, Wood, Moorhouse, Gallacher, Tracey, Auld, Brown, Gonsalvez, Patenaude, Florie, McGhee.

Referee: Jean Langenus (Belgium)
Attendance: 80.000

Montevideo, July 27th -
Estadio Centenario

6 (3) URUGUAY

Ceá (3), Anselmo (2), Iriarte

Ballesteros, Nasazzi, Mascheroni, Andrade, Fernández, Gestido, Dorado, Scarone, Anselmo, Ceá, Iriarte.

1 (1) YUGOSLAVIA

Seculic

Yavovic, Ivkovic, Milhailovic, Arsenievic, Stefanovic, Djokic, Tirnanic, Marianovic, Beck, Vujadinovic, Seculic.

Referee: Almeida Rego (Brazil)
Attendance: 93.000

FINAL

Montevideo, July 30th -
Estadio Centenario

4 (1) URUGUAY

Dorado, Ceá, Iriarte, Castro

Ballesteros, Nasazzi, Mascheroni, Andrade, Fernández, Gestido, Dorado, Scarone, Castro, Ceá, Iriarte.

2 (2) ARGENTINA

Peucelle, Stàbile

Botasso, Della Torre, Paternoster, J.Evaristo, Monti, Suárez, Peucelle, Varallo, Stàbile, Ferreira, M.Evaristo.

Referee: Jean Langenus (Belgium)
Attendance: 93.000

Chapter 4

Fascists, Fights, Knock-outs and Replays
The Italy World Cup, 1934

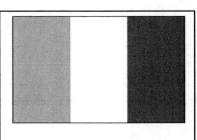

Italy 1934

Winners: Italy

Runners-up: Czechoslovakia

3rd Place: Germany

4th Place: Austria

Total Attendance: 251,000

Number of Matches: 17

As 1934 dawned danger overshadowed the world. The Nazis had taken power in Germany and Jews, Communists and other "enemies of the state" were being thrown into concentration camps. German youngsters were brainwashed by the Hitler Youth movement and citizens were expected to greet each other with the "Heil Hitler" salute. In China, General Chiang Kai-Shek having fought Japan in Manchuria, was now facing a civil war against a peasant by the name of Mao Zedong. His Nationalists had surrounded the Red Army with a ring of concrete blockhouses and barbed-wire fences to starve their opponents out. Meanwhile, Britain and the USA were in economic crisis, but President Roosevelt was offering the Americans a "New Deal" as a cure for their ills.

American gangsters had problems of their own. Al "Scarface" Capone had been jailed for tax fraud, the Louisiana police had caught up with Bonnie and Clyde and in 1934 John Dillinger was shot down in a hail of bullets outside a cinema in Chicago. Dillinger, responsible for the murder of sixteen people, had ironically, been watching a gangster movie at the time. Johnny Weissmuller, the Olympic swimmer, made his celluloid debut as Tarzan, Amelia Earhart had become the first woman to fly the Atlantic solo and Sir Malcolm Campbell had set a new land speed record. At Wimbledon women were allowed to turn out in shorts for the first time, but the decision did not go down well with male officials who argued that shorts were vulgar and unfeminine. The first mass-produced deodorant appeared in the High Street shops and H.G. Wells predicted a second world war would break out in about 1940. Sadly, both Edward Elgar and Marie Curie died in 1934, having both made the world a better place.

At the end of May eyes turned their attention to Mussolini's Italy for the second World Cup. The decision to grant the 1934 World Cup to Italy was taken in October 1932. Given the unsavoury nature of Mussolini's Fascist government, it was a controversial one. FIFA, though, realized that the advantages gained would be greater than any political ramifications. It had been decided that the World Cup was too big a competition to be staged in just one city, as with Montevideo in 1930, and FIFA was searching for a country that had more than one stadium capable of holding big games. FIFA also preferred that it should be a European country to even things out after the previous tournament had gone to South America. When the Italians weighed in with a promise to pick up all of the bills, it proved decisive and, whatever may be said about the authoritarian aspects of the Italian government, the event would almost certainly be well run and well ordered.

That the tournament was to be held in Italy gave Il Duce and his new fascist nation a major propaganda coup. This was not lost on the British press, where the Manchester Guardian noted wryly that "one may perhaps credit Signor Mussolini with following some of the Cæsars in using sport as a distraction for the people." Posters for the tournament showed a picture of Hercules balancing a ball on his foot and throwing out a fascist salute with his right hand. FIFA felt that this was less important than the success of the event itself. Mussolini himself was to be seen at every Italian game surrounded by his Black Shirts and the Italian team dedicated their victories to him. People today may question such judgement, but it must be remembered that it was only the second staging of the World Cup and FIFA officials elected to put safety before politics.

Another good reason for giving the tournament to Italy was that they were one of the best and most consistent contemporary international teams. A look at their record needs no second glance to appreciate the contribution of coach Vittorio Pozzo to Italian football. Between June 1930 and 1948 only one international was lost on Italian soil, a 4-2 defeat by Austria's "Wunderteam" in Turin in 1934, and, during the whole of the 1930s, Italy lost only seven games. Since Uruguay had been granted the 1930 World Cup on the strength of its international success, with a record like this it is difficult to deny that Italy were worthy hosts.

Thirty one countries entered the competition, but there were still no teams from the United Kingdom. Uruguay, the reigning champions, decided to repay what they had seen as Europe's snub in 1930 with one of their own, and refused to take part. They were also in dispute with neighbours, Argentina, who had decided to participate, and so became the only reigning world champions not to defend their title. After the entrants had been divided into twelve groups, representing Europe, South America and Africa-Middle East, that would reduce the number down to sixteen, both Chile and Peru withdrew. This gave automatic qualification to Brazil and Argentina, who had been paired with them. It left 27 teams to play-off for the remaining 14 places in the finals. Even Italy had to qualify, though this was the first and only time that the hosts had to do so. However, to save them the embarrassment of being knocked out of their own tournament, they only had to play one home game, against Greece, which they won 4-0.

The qualification matches got underway on 11th June 1933 when Sweden defeated Estonia 6-2 in Stockholm, making history as the winners of the first ever World Cup game played in Europe. Other firsts were achieved when Egypt beat Palestine in Cairo in March 1934, giving them victory in the first World Cup game played in Africa and the first victory by an African country. The Egyptians also won the return leg in Tel Aviv, a month later, a game that has been described as the first World Cup match played in Asia. In coming top of its qualifying group, Egypt also became the first African nation to reach the World Cup finals. The group game between Belgium and the Irish Free State, now the Republic of Ireland, was the first World Cup game played in the British Isles and Paddy Moore scored all four Irish goals in the 4-4 draw. This made him the first player to score four in a World Cup match.

The surprise of the qualifying stage was the elimination of Yugoslavia, the 1930 semi-finalists, from the group that provided the one big controversy of the stage. The game between Switzerland and Romania, in October 1933, ended in a 2-2 draw, but Romania had fielded an ineligible player, Barotki, and the game was declared a 2-0 victory to Switzerland. FIFA considered throwing the Romanians out of the competition altogether, but their appeal was sustained. Had it not been, Yugoslavia would have gone to Italy in their place.

Perhaps, the most unfortunate elimination from the qualifying stage was that of Mexico. This had been the most complicated of the groups with Haiti and Cuba playing it out over three games in Port au Prince for the right to play Mexico in the group's second phase. The Cubans defeated Haiti, but were then eliminated over three games by Mexico, who believed that they had qualified for the finals. They duly made the long journey to Italy, but found an unexpected and unpleasant surprise when they got there. The United States, who had not originally entered the 1934 World Cup, made a late application and were accepted. However, since their inclusion would have raised the number of finalists to an impractical 17, and since all other finalists had had to qualify, it was decided

When Argentina refused to enter the 1934 tournament, fans attacked the Football Association offices in Buenos Aires. The pressure paid off because a team eventually competed, but it was not the strongest of sides that eventually took the field in Bologna. A number of the best Argentinian players had been poached by the Italians in recent years and the Argentinian authorities were worried that more would follow if they were allowed to go the Italy.

It was just as well that Uruguay didn't defend the trophy as there was a players strike on in the country at the time.

The Egyptian goalkeeper at the 1934 tournament was called Moustafa Kamel.

Complicated isn't it...

In Group Eight of the qualifying tournament the seeded team was Austria. Bulgaria had to play Hungary, home and away, whilst Austria only had to play Bulgaria at home. Both Bulgaria-Hungary games ended in 4-1 home victories, which cancelled each other out. When Bulgaria came up against Austria they lost 6-1 and it was Austria and Hungary that consequently qualified. In Group Nine, the Czech team qualified because Poland withdrew after losing their home game 2-1 to Czechoslovakia. The easiest of qualification routes was from Group 12, which contained France, Germany and the minnows from Luxembourg. France and Germany played one game each, against Luxembourg. Germany won 9-1 and France 6-1 taking both through to the finals.

Eight venues were used for the finals: Rome, Naples, Florence, Bologna, Milan, Trieste, Turin and Genoa.

The Commentary Box.

that the Americans should do likewise. They were pitted against the hapless Mexicans on 24th May, three days before the finals got underway. It ended in a 4-2 victory to the USA and meant that the Americans stayed in Italy. The poor Mexicans had to go home without having played a game in the finals.

Apart from the obvious change of venue, one of the biggest differences between the 1934 finals and those of 1930 was that the Italian tournament was organized as a straight knock-out and this gave rise to a second difference. It is better that the stages of a knock-out competition be played on the same day. FIFA had already decided to use more than one venue for the finals, so the eight first round games took place at the same time in eight different cities. They took place all over Italy, but most were played in the industrial north of the country, where population concentrations were highest and the games would be better attended. FIFA was already learning the lessons of commercialism. It had further been realized that the event's popularity, and its profitability, would be adversely affected if the top nations, especially the hosts, go out of the competition too early. Therefore, the third main difference between the first two World Cups was put in place to avoid this. Seeding the top eight teams - Argentina, Austria, Brazil, Czechoslovakia, Germany, Holland, Hungary and Italy - would prevent them meeting each other in the first round. They were not necessarily the best teams, but it was an important development in the history of professional sport.

Of these teams it was difficult to predict an eventual winner, though one of the more fancied teams was Hugo Meisl's Austrians. Alongside Pozzo, he was one of the giants of European football and one of the finest coaches of his day. (See Hugo Meisl profile on page 55). Closely behind them in the list of those fancied to do well were the Italians, and then the Czechoslovakians and Hungarians, both noted for their clever styles of play. Finally, the Germans, their national pride being restored by the Nazi regime, were also numbered among the favourites. It is telling that all four of the semi-finalists came from this list.

As was the case in 1930, some people, particularly in Britain, doubted the authenticity of the tournament as a world championship, especially without the participation of the British. The decision of the British FAs not to take part gained a fair degree of acceptance and the Manchester Guardian endorsed this in a review of it. "England, Scotland and Wales were wise in abstaining," it said. "It would have been too much to expect our players to maintain top form into the summer or to ask them after the strain of eight months of the most exacting League competition in the world to conserve the qualities which success in this competition will demand." "We would have little to gain," it concluded.

The first round matches all took place on 27th May and the Italians began their campaign very convincingly. Pozzo had shown what a radical coach he was when he took his team on a six week retreat to Lake Maggiore in order to prepare them for the forthcoming tournament and to shield them from the pressures implicit in being the representatives of Mussolini's grand new order. He used the time to relax the players and, as he later wrote, they were "reduced to a state of the purest infantilism." The ploy obviously paid dividends because the Italians were worthy 7-1 winners against a USA team that was a shadow of that which had done so well in 1930. All eight goals were technically scored by Italians because the single US goal was scored by a Neapolitan called Donelli. After the tournament he stayed in Italy to continue his career. Only three members of that team survived into the 1934 squad, including skipper Thomas Florie, whilst Italy's team was brimming with talent, some of it home grown and some of it not. Of uncontestable Italian nationality were Angelo Schiavio, who scored a hat trick that day and who had won a bronze medal at the 1928 Olympic Games, and Giuseppe Meazza, who scored Italy's last. They were two of the finest players in the tournament. More contentious was the inclusion of three Argentinians in the Italian squad: Luis Monti, a losing finalist in 1930, Raimundo Orsi, a right-winger who scored two against the USA, and Enrique Guaita, who did not line up against the USA, but who featured in later games. There were those, particularly in Argentina, who resented their appearance for Italy, but having Italian decent was deemed sufficient justification. Legitimately, it was said, they could be called up to serve in the Italian army and as coach Pozzo maintained: "If they can die for Italy, they can play football for Italy."

Italy 7 : USA 1
The Americans defend their goal.

Other seeded teams did less well in the first round. The Brazilians went out 3-1 to Spain, in a game in which Waldemar de Brito missed a penalty to round off a dismal display from the South Americans. However, de Brito later made a much more telling contribution to the history of football when he discovered and coached the young Pelé. Switzerland surprisingly beat Holland, and Argentina was sent packing by Sweden's amateurs. This game, according to the Sporting Chronicle, "was bitterly fought throughout" and "the crowd was thrilled by the fast open passing of the Argentines." Ernesto Belis opened the scoring after just three minutes with the first goal of the tournament, though the Swedes "took advantage of their opponent's weak defence" and went on to win the game 3-2. The Argentinians could use the excuse that they fielded a weakened team. Holland's excuse could only be that they played badly and from the time they went behind to a 14th minute goal by Leopold Kielholz, they were always chasing the match.

Two other seeded teams were lucky to reach the second round, having won their games despite having played badly. One was Czechoslovakia, who scraped a narrow 2-1 win against Romania, thanks to the brilliance of their captain and goalkeeper, Frantisek Plánicka, whose aerobatics kept his team in the game. The other was Germany, whose 5-2 victory over Belgium sounds much more convincing than it was. Edmund Conen scored a second half hat trick for the Germans, but the

The first European player to score a hat trick in the World Cup finals was Angelo Schiavio of Italy, in the first round tie against the USA.

Spain 3 : Brazil 1
The Brazilians on the team bus
prior to the game.

Spain 3 : Brazil 1
Spanish defenders combine to clear the ball.

The Czech team in 1934 was made of players from only two domestic teams - Sparta and Slavia Prague.

Egypt would have to wait 56 years to put the disappointment of the 1934 World Cup behind them. However, their player Abdel Rahman Fawzi has gone down as the first African to score in the World Cup finals. He scored both goals in the 4-2 defeat by Hungary. There would not be another African finalist until Morocco went to Mexico in 1970. Soccer was still in its infancy on the African continent. The colonial powers had no more desire to see native populations get together to participate in soccer's unruly gatherings than the kings of Medieval England had been when their peasants first discovered the delights of the not so beautiful game.

margin of the scoreline is only explained by the fact that the Belgians played worse football than their opponents. As in 1930, Belgium did not send a strong team to the 1934 World Cup and the Germans were, on the day, the better of two poor teams. Belgium had only qualified out of Group Eleven with Holland because, having conceded eight to the Irish Free State's nine, they had a fractionally better goal difference. The other two seeded teams, Hungary and Austria, went through to the next stage with little difficulty against Egypt and France. (See Austria v France profile on page 57).

It meant that all the non-European teams had been eliminated and the all-European quarter-finals were played on the last day of May. The Germans were again disappointing and played poorly in their 2-1 defeat of Sweden, being rather lucky to win through to the next round. However, lack of excitement or incident could not be said about the game between Austria and their old rivals, Hungary. Putting two of Europe's best teams against each other raised expectations of the game of the competition and, though the attendance was not recorded, a large crowd turned up in anticipation. What they saw was a violent and ill-tempered game, which Meisl described as "a brawl, not an exhibition of football" and which became known as the "Battle of Bologna". The Austrians took an early lead, through Johann Horvath, which they kept until half-time, and then got another early in the second period, when right-winger Karl Zischek netted. Then the trouble began. The game deteriorated as play became more physical and each team sought to exact revenge for the other's misdemeanours. With little over 20 minutes to go, the Hungarians were awarded a penalty, which Sárosi converted and it led to another period of dirty play, which the Italian referee, Francesco Mattea, found difficult to curb. Following one outburst of petulance, Hungary's right-winger, Imre Markos, was sent off. It was unfortunate for his team because it happened at a time when they were beginning to turn the screw and looked as if they might equalize. It naturally worked to Austria's advantage and they were able to hold on against ten men.

The Italians needed two matches to see off a plucky Spain in their quarter-final, two games that were both influenced by some poor refereeing: in the first by the Belgian Louis Baert and in the second by the Swiss Réne Mercet. (See Italy v Spain profile on page 59). After the first game, Pozzo called each of his players to see him in the team hotel and gave each one an individual dressing down. He dropped three of them for the replay, and with Pizziolo injured, it meant four changes in the Italian line up. (See Vittorio Pozzo profile on page 54). Spain's situation was worse. Only four of their players were fit for the rematch and, with a change of referee as well, there were wholesale changes in personnel for the second meeting, which took place the next day. Also, Spain's talisman, Zamora, was missing and the game was another tight, physical contest heavily influenced by poor refereeing. Spain's left-winger, Bosch, was badly injured after only five minutes and was a virtual passenger for the rest of the game. The Spanish also had two goals disallowed for offside, one of which should certainly have stood. Further, the referee seems to have been influenced in Italy's favour by an extremely partisan crowd and he was later suspended by his own FA. In the end it was a 12th minute header from Meazza that took the Italians through to the semi-finals.

The fourth of the quarter-finals, between Czechoslovakia and Switzerland, was the pick of the

Argentinian team in training.

bunch in terms of the quality of football played, and was one of the best matches of the tournament. It was an absorbing seesaw of a contest that could have gone either way and kept the crowd enthralled right until the final whistle. The Swiss took the lead, through Kielholz, only for the Czechs to bring the scores level by half-time. Both scored again to make it 2-2, before Oldrich Nejedlý netted the final strike to ensure victory for the Czechs, but only after they had withstood a final seven minutes of desperate Swiss invasions, as they sought to retrieve the match.

The semi-finals were played on 3rd June and Italy took on Austria in the San Siro Stadium in Milan. Since the Italians had just come through a bruising two-match battle against Spain, and since the "Wunderteam" had enjoyed a break, it was generally assumed that the Austrians would win through to the final. The Italians, however, not showing any of the

> The Spanish team was captained by the legendary Ricardo Zamora. 'The Man in Black' who, in 46 internationals let in only 40 goals, was worshipped by the Spanish. Seven of these goals came in one game, against England in 1931, with the famous Dixie Dean getting one of them. Unusually, two other teams in the finals were also captained by goalkeepers, Italy by Giampero Combi and Czechoslovakia by Frantisek Plánicka. Combi shared the responsibility with full-back Rosetta.

tiredness expected of them, adapted better to conditions made difficult by heavy rain and which inhibited the free flowing style favoured by Austria. All three of Italy's former Argentinian stars played very well and Monti kept Sindelar virtually out of the game, robbing the Austrians of one of their major assets. So out of sorts were the Austrians that it was over 40 minutes into the game before they even registered a shot on goal, by which time Italy had already scored the goal that was to prove the winner. Schiavio had let loose a shot that goalkeeper, Peter Platzer, could only parry. It fell to the feet of Enrique Guaita,

Spain 1 : Italy 1
Italy's Meazza is helped from the field.

who casually slotted home. In the second half the Italians had to hold on as Austria did most of the attacking and Combi, in the Italian goal, played

The Stadio Del P.N.Fon the day of the final.

The introduction of overtime (as extra time used to be known) was another new thing. If scores were tied after ninety minutes, an extra thirty minutes overtime would be played. If the scores were still equal at the end of overtime then a replay would be scheduled.

Whilst the rest of the Czech team celebrated Puc's opening goal in the final, one of their number was unable to join in. Distraught Italian fans, putting their hands through the wire mesh barrier, had grabbed him by the hair and he had to be rescued by police.

The only player to be sent off in 1934 was the Hungarian Imre Markos against Austria.

like his life depended on it. The Austrians almost equalized in the last minute, when Zischek broke through the Italian defence and was bearing down on goal. Looking certain to score, he shot wide and the game was lost. (See Matthias Sindelaar profile on page 56).

In the second semi-final, the Czechoslovakians won through, but not before the Germans, who seemed to finally wake up to the fact that they were involved in a major sporting event, gave them a scare. The opening period of the game was dominated by the superior ball skills of the Czechs, who appeared as if they were about to outclass an overcautious Germany. They fully deserved the lead given them in the 21st minute by Nejedlý, but then the Czechs seemed to decide that it was all going to be so easy and their play became too casual. It might have cost them the game, because the Germans responded with some zeal, especially in the second half. In the 50th minute their enterprise was rewarded when a speculative long shot from Rudolf Noack caught the Czech keeper off guard and rooted to the spot. The ball sailed completely over his head and into the net. Soon after, Ernst Lehner almost scored with a shot that was well saved by Plánicka and then the Czechs almost conceded an own goal. Such sloppiness was needed to re-awaken the Czechs from their stupor and the last period of the game was played as the first, with the Czechs in control. On the hour, a free kick from Antonin Puc came out off the bar and Nejedlý was there to follow in for his second. The victory was made secure nine minutes from the end with a third Nejedlý strike.

A departure from the 1930 World Cup format was the decision to introduce a 3rd/4th place play-off, which took place in Naples on 7th June. Given the respective pedigrees, strengths and previous performances of the two teams, it was a game that the Austrians were expected to win, but, surprisingly, they were just not up for it. Meisl had said that his team was tired before the tournament got underway and perhaps he had been right. In Naples that day they certainly looked it. Their German opponents may have been fortunate to have progressed so far, but were the better team on this day. They struck after only 30 seconds when Lehner scored the fastest goal of the tournament. Inside the half-hour they were 2-0 to the good when Edmund Conen notched their second, but straight from the kick-off, Johann Horvath brought the Austrians back into the game. Just before half-time, Lehner scored his second to give Germany a 3-1 lead at the break. In the second half proceedings were less frenetic and there was only one more score from Austria's Sesta, but it was not enough to deny third place to Germany. The "Wunderteam" went home having never fulfilled their potential.

The final was a gripping affair and for a second time the host nation ended as world champions. (See Italy v Czechoslovakia profile on page 60). Like 1930, Italy 1934 had its faults and weaknesses. Notable absences, like the UK teams and the more powerful South American nations, prevented it from being a truly representative test of contemporary international football. There were also questions to be asked about the standard of refereeing, which although not as big an issue as in 1930, was certainly poor at times. There were claims, with some justification, of referees being intimidated by crowds whipped up by nationalistic fascist propaganda. Without it, some say, Italy might never have won.

Perhaps, the most unfortunate feature of Italy 1934 was the obvious propaganda benefit derived by Mussolini. As one of the event's political organizers said, the purpose was to show "that Fascist sport partakes of a great quality of the ideal", by which he meant that the system brought out the best in its sports people, as it did with all aspects of life. That it had a political organizer at all is indicative of the importance with which the Party viewed the event. For this reason, an Italian victory was highly desirable and, as the Belgian referee, Jean Langenus, later recalled that, "Italy wanted to win, it was natural, but they allowed it to be seen too clearly. It was a sporting fiasco." Pozzo himself was no Fascist, but he was the sort of coach prepared to use any circumstance to achieve his objective and Fascist rabble-rousing propaganda could be as useful a weapon as any other. He was quite prepared to lead his team out onto the field of play waving a flag and lustily singing the Fascist song "Il Piave", "They Shall Not Pass", to lift the fighting spirits of his players.

In passing judgement, we must be careful not to ignore the mood of the day. Whatever sober minds years after the events may think of authoritarian Fascist regimes, they were a reality and mirrored a good part of the political mood of the era. In 1934, the more outwardly evil aspects of such systems had yet to be revealed and there was genuine popular support for Mussolini and his Blackshirts. For many, the suppression of some civil liberties was a small price to pay for good order and restored national pride. To use the World Cup for political ends was expected and many would have seen nothing amiss in so doing.

However, such political considerations need not affect our appraisal of the World Cup as a football occasion and, as such, Italy 1934 had its highlights. There were great games and exceptional players, just as there was mediocrity. There was plenty to excite and talk about, just as there were disappointments. Italy 1934 will not go down in history as the greatest World Cup on record, but it was a very creditable follow up to its predecessor, helping to establish the World Cup as a major sporting fixture. It was not the event that it would later become, in terms of mass appeal, but it was moving towards it. Instant mass media, which does much to promote and market modern day World Cups, was not in place in 1934, but the event still attracted much interest and it made a profit. Its organizers were about a million lire better off as a result of it, not much in today's terms, but impressive by the standards of the day.

Vittorio Pozzo   Italy

Honours: Winner 1934 and 1938
Manager: 1934 and 1938

Vittorio Pozzo was the brain behind the Italian national side that became the first team to retain the world crown. Working under Mussolini's strict regime, he forged teams that were tough and disciplined, like himself. They could hardly be described as artistic, but winning was all that mattered to Pozzo.

Born on 12th March 1886, he studied and worked in Bradford and the Midlands in his student days before World War One. It was here that he studied and learned the game and its intricacies, inspired by the great Manchester United team of 1907-1908. This team, built around the solid defending of Charlie Roberts and the goal scoring talents of Welshman Billy Meredith, had won the English league championship by a clear nine points, a huge margin in the days when a win brought only two points. He never lost his admiration of the English game and became a devotee of Herbert Chapman, the architect of Arsenal's success in the 1920s and 30s. His first stint as a manager was with Italian club Torino, a club he helped to found, before he was drafted in as national team coach to guide the team through the Stockholm Olympics of 1912. It was here that he met a man who was to be-

Italian coach Vittorio Pozzo.

come a rival over the next 25 years - Hugo Meisl of Austria. The Italian team made it through to the semi-finals of the consolation tournament where they came up against Meisl's Austria and were beaten 5-1. He had a second term as national coach in 1924, again being brought in for the Olympic Games in Paris. They got as far as the quarter-finals where they were defeated by the Swiss. He then had a much longer period as national coach between 1929 and 1948.

Pozzo adopted a rugged, martial approach to his team that perhaps reflected the nation's dictatorship in the 1930s. It was a time when players could switch national allegiance with ease and Pozzo, a believer in the "granny rule", employed three Argentinians to boost his team. By 1934 a shrewd Pozzo had put together a talented team that went into the finals as favourites to win. The Austrian "Wunderteam" were there under the tutelage of Hugo Meisl, but it was generally agreed at the time that the Austrians were getting on a bit. Pozzo's time in England had taught him that strength and teamwork were the key to success and he had instilled this in his team. On the opening day of the 1934 tournament his team marched out in front of a partisan home crowd of 30,000 in the Stadio PNF in Rome and promptly dumped the USA out of the competition, the beginning of their successful march to the final. Along the way, he also put his old rival, Meisl, out of the tournament.

Later that year Pozzo took his Italian side to Highbury, London to face England. In what was later to become known as 'The Battle of Highbury' England ran out 3-2 winners. One of the England team remarked after the game that it was "a bit hard to play like a gentleman when somebody closely resembling an enthusiastic member of the Mafia is wiping his studs down your leg." One side suffered a broken toe and the other a broken nose. In 1936 the Italian national side took the Olympic title in Berlin. At the 1938 France World Cup finals the message from Mussolini was perfectly simple - "Win or die". Pozzo didn't have to die however, because his side lifted the World Cup trophy for the second successive time, muscularly brushing aside the Hungarians 4-2. Only Pozzo, Meazza and Ferrari remained from the 1934 winning side, much of the rest of the team being players who had won gold in 1936. After the final Pozzo remarked: "We left aside all flourishes, anything resembling ballet."

Vittorio Pozzo retired from international management in 1948 and died in Turin in 1968. During his time as manager Italy won 64 times. His side of the 1930s still holds the record for the longest run of straight wins in World Cup Finals - seven, between 1934 and 1938. Pozzo himself remains the only manager to manage two World Cup wining sides.

Hugo Meisl   Austria

Honours: 4th 1934
Manager: 1934

Hugo Meisl is regarded as one of the foremost football authorities of the inter-war years. He was the architect of the Austrian "Wunderteam" that took the world by storm in the 1930s.

Born in Czechoslovakia in 1881, Meisl was the son of a wealthy Viennese Jewish banking family. His interest in the game had been stimulated whilst watching English ex-patriots play in Vienna and, becoming a young aficionado of football, he spurned the family business to pursue his interest in the game. He chased his dream as a player for Austrian club side, FK Austria, before taking over the managerial reigns of another Austrian club side, Admira Wacker after he had retired from playing. In 1912 he took over the running of the national side and held the job for 25 years. Only Sepp Herberger of West Germany has had a longer stint as national team manager.

In his first ever test as the national team coach, at the 1912 Olympic Games in Stockholm, his team was knocked out at the first round stage by Holland. However, the Austrians won through to the final of the consolation tournament, beating Norway and Vittorio Pozzo's Italy along the way. In the end, they took the second spot in that competition, going down 3-0 to the Hungarians. After World War One he became Secretary of the Austrian Football Federation, whilst still managing the national team. It was in the inter-war years that his reputation as a great football mind grew and under him the Austrians became a very difficult side to beat. In 1927 he founded the first international club competition, the Mitropa Cup and he was also responsible for co-founding the World Cup itself when he and Henri Delauney were put in charge its early preparations.

Under Meisl the reputation of the "Wunderteam" continued to grow. In 1932 they went to England and, although they lost 4-3, their enthusiastic running and dribbling, and their excellent timing gave their heavier opponents a real scare. One of the English said afterwards: "If only they knew how to finish!" The match became known as the 'Battle of the Bridge'(Stamford Bridge) as there was plenty of kicking and thumping going on from both teams. At Meisl's side, and throughout the 1930s, was a Lancashireman, Jimmy Hogan, his second in command. Hogan had formerly played for Blackpool and Bolton Wanderers and introduced the Austrians to the Scottish style of play of passing the ball and keeping it on the ground.

Meisl's finest moment, and at the same time perhaps his most disappointing, came when his team reached the semi-finals at the 1934 World Cup, which still remains Austria's greatest achievement in world football. Their eventual elimination was at the hands of Pozzo's Italy and the ironic thing was that Austria had beaten the Italians in a friendly match only a few months earlier in Turin.

Hugo Meisl died in 1937 at the age of 56. His involvement in the game had been complete and the roles he played as player, manager, referee, journalist and official make him stand out as a true son of the game. In the 155 games he was in charge of the Austrian national side they won 78 times. No Austrian national team before or since has been as great as Hugo Meisl's "Wunderteam".

Matthias Sindelar   Austria

Honours: 4th 1934   **Games 3**
Played: 1934   **Goals 1**

Matthias "der Papierne" Sindelar was, according to some, technically the best Austrian footballer of all time. His nickname, which means "Paper Man", was a reflection of his slight build, something which never got in the way of a player who could produce inspirational football. The name Matthias Sindelar became synonymous with the "Wunderteam" of the 1930s, when, under the tutelage of Hugo Meisl, the Austrians enjoyed a period of success like no other.

Born in Inglau on 10th March 1903, Sindelar started his footballing career with Hertha Vienna before moving to Austria Vienna in 1924. Whilst there, he was responsible for the greatest period of success in the club's history. Under his leadership, the 'Violets'won the Austrian Championship in the 1925-26 season, won five cup finals and twice won the Mitropa Cup (equivalent to the European Cup, forerunner of the modern Champions League). In 1933 they came up against another of Europe's great teams, Ambrosiana Milan (now Internazionale). They lost the away leg 2-1, but a 3-1 home win gave them a 4-3 aggregate victory. In the 1936 competition the Violets met Sparta Prague in the final and, having drawn the home leg 0-0, no one believed that they could win away. However, amid much celebration, they won 1-0 in Prague, with Sindelar scoring the all-important goal.

Sindelar also enjoyed great success with the Austrian national side. Home and away, the "Wunderteam" beat many of the best national teams in Europe. He made his debut on 16th May 1931 when the Austrians took on Scotland and won 5-0. It is worth noting the other members of the "Wunderteam" who played so brilliantly alongside Sindelar. They were Rudi Hiden the goalkeeper, Schramseis and Blum in defence, Smistik, Braun and Gall in midfield, and Zischek, Gschweidl, Sindelar, Schall and Vogl in attack. The first defeat for Sindelar and the "Wunderteam" following the Scotland game did not occur until they went down 2-1 at home to the Czechoslovakians in April 1933.

Germany's annexation of Austria in March 1938 meant that 1934 was Sindelar's only appearance in the World Cup finals, though he did not appear in the 3rd/4th play-off game, probably due to injury. With the disappearance of his country, Sindelar played only once more for his national side, a game between Austria and Germany staged as a propaganda match to reconcile the Austrians to their loss of national identity. It took place in April 1938 and Sindelar had his revenge on the Germans. Allegedly, the Germans were ordered to play "beautiful, unaggressive football" and the Austrians were warned not to have too many shots on goal. Sindelar, no friend of the Nazis, ignored this command and set about the Germans with gusto. He scored the first goal in a 2-0 victory that was seen as a great humiliation for Germany. His best friend Karl "Schasti" Sesta scored the second, a free kick from 45 metres. Sindelar's joy, however, was only short-lived and he suffered badly under Nazi rule, because they was regarded him as being too "Jew-friendly".

He played his last game for Austria Vienna on 26th December 1938 against Hertha Berlin. He scored one of his widely acclaimed goals, but nobody could have foreseen that it would be his last. On 23rd January 1939, Matthias Sindelar was found dead with his girlfriend, Camilla Castagnola, in his flat in Vienna. The circumstances surrounding the death are shrouded in mystery. The police gave the cause of his death as "Death through carbon monoxide poisoning" though it is possible that he committed suicide to avoid further attention from the Nazis. In all, he had played 44 times for the national team and scored a total of 17 goals.

Sindelar is perhaps one of the few players to have had a song written about him. It was called "Auf den Tod eines Fußballspielers" (On the death of a footballer) and was written by Friedrich Torberg. The first three verses go like this:

Er war ein Kind aus Favoriten	He was a favourite child
Und heiß Matthias Sindelar.	And was called Matthias Sindelar.
Er stand auf grünen Platz in mitten,	He stands in the middle of the green field
Weil er ein Mittelstürmer war.	Because he was a centre-forward.
Er speilte Fußball, und er wußter	He played football, and he knew
Von Leben außer dam nicht viel.	Not much of life besides.
Er lebte, weil er leben mußter	He lived, because he had to live
Vom Fußballspiel fürs Fußballspiel.	From football match to football match.
Er speilte Fußball wie kein Zweiter,	He played football like no other,
Er stak voll Witz und Phantasie.	He played with wit and fantasy.
Er speilte lössig, leicht und heiter,	He played casually, lightly and cheerfully,
Er speilte stets, er kämpfte nie.	He played continually, he never fought.

Austria 3 : France 2

One French newspaper began its coverage of this match with the words: "As was to be expected, the game between France and Austria which took place yesterday in Turin was the occasion of a defeat for France, but a defeat that was the equivalent of a victory." Not many football correspondents would be so cheerful about seeing their national team knocked out of the World Cup finals in the first round, but to the French this was a result of great significance. In 1934, whilst no longer in its infancy, French football was still very much in its youth and had no international credentials to speak of. Indeed, one Vienna newspaper noted that the "French had met strong opposition in recent times... still lacking the best method and technique". Their game was learning quickly and their national squad contained some talented and athletic individuals. Whilst few gave them any realistic chance against the mighty Austrians, they were forced to reassess their judgement when the final whistle blew. The Viennese newspaper quoted earlier was forced to concede that the French "could at any time clear out the toughest opposition with speed, stamina and shooting power."

From the start the Austrians were taken aback by the enterprise and vigorous, hard-hitting football played by the French. It was never a dirty game, but was fast, furious and combative. The French refused to be cowed and committed themselves to throwing everything at their opponents. The Austrians did not expect it and the French made much of the early running, leaving the Viennese sports writer grumbling that "only a few players... played with their usual form" and that the "others were very poor." One of the Austrians who did shine in this early period was goalkeeper, Peter Platzer. He had to be at his best to keep out France's outstanding centre-forward, Jean Nicholas, who put his team in front in the 17th minute and sent the reporter from Le Figaro into delirium. It was a "thing almost impossible", he gloated, "the famous Austrian team held in check", but his team suffered a serious set back moments later. Nicholas collided heavily with the Austrian defender, Smistik, hurt his head badly and spent much of the rest of the game hobbling about the wings, playing "with only half strength." He had to leave the field twice for treatment, but even then the Austrians found it difficult to impose any authority on the game. Alex Thépot in the French goal was in commanding form and, when the Austrians finally contrived a breakthrough, with a goal from Josef Bican in the 33rd minute, it was ruled offside. They had to wait until the last minute of the first half before Matthias Sindelar equalized "with a good shot from 15 metres out."

The second half proceeded much the same way as the first, only without the goals. It had developed into an attractive exhibition of free-flowing, open and attacking football, "end to end stuff" in modern parlance, with both teams contributing greatly to what was widely remembered as one of the best matches of the tournament. The French with "their spirit of initiative, quick attacks, their decisiveness and their pace... brought much trouble to the opposing team." It gave the French supporters something to be proud of, although their players were "unable at any moment, in the normal period of the match, to really impose themselves." The Austrians were equally resolute, equally as inventive and equally unable to find a route to goal. As one of their reporters noted, they "succeeded at nothing and the forwards constantly threw away the best chances." There were chances galore, but with nobody able to make anything of them, this became the first game in the World Cup finals to go into extra time.

When it began again, several of the players were feeling the effects of their previous exertions and the French, with their greater disadvantage, were the first to crack. After only three minutes Anton Schall broke free and ended his run by sliding the ball past Thépot. Many have considered that he was offside when he collected the ball. This was certainly the opinion of the French and they let the referee know in no uncertain terms. It was all in vein. Years later, Schall admitted that he also thought that he had been offside, but having heard no whistle, was happy to carry on and score. The goal clearly affected the French, who momentarily lost their shape and composure. It gave the Austrians another advantage and one they were very quick to seize. Only minutes later, Bican registered his second of the afternoon to give the Austrians an important 3-1 lead.

This third goal was the one that refocused the French. Straining every effort from their tired legs, they redoubled their effort and the match ended as it had begun, with the French bearing down on Austria's goal. Once again, Platzer was called upon to save his team as the Austrians defended "their lead with luck." Six minutes from time, the French were handed a final piece of hope, when Sesta handled the ball in the penalty area and Georges Verriest hammered home the ensuing spot kick. It made for a frantic final few minutes, as the French gallantly pushed in search of the goal that would have forced a replay. Sadly, it would not come and the 3-2 victory saw the "Wunderteam" through to the quarter-final. For the Austrians, there was relief that it was all over and the football reporter from the Neue Freie Presse was left reflecting that "yesterday the strength of play shown by the Austrians was without doubt abnormal and hopefully will never again reach so low." For France, it was defeat with honour, a situation noted by the reporter from Le Temps, who said: "Let them be thanked and let them speak well of themselves that yesterday's match seriously raised the prestige of our national football." It would be some twenty years before French football began to realize its potential, but it had showed that it was on its way.

Italy 1 : Spain 1

When Italy met Spain in this quarter-final in Florence, there was already an element of "history" between the sides to add spice to what promised to be a close encounter. The Italians considered themselves to be the superior football team, but in previous matches between them Spain's legendary goalkeeper and captain, Ricardo Zamora, had always played exceptionally to deprive the Italians of the victories they felt they deserved. It would also be the case in this game, but the Italians had already worked out what they would need to do to neutralize Zamora's presence and it was to stretch the bounds of legality. Pozzo had, as always, prepared his men well, both mentally and tactically.

"The fight began in a wild manner", ran one Austrian account of the match and the reporter had chosen his words aptly. This was a bruising, uncompromizing and often violent occasion, made so by the tactics adopted by Italy. Quite simply, they went for intimidation. They were prepared to use almost any means to win the game and, from the start, the Spanish were subjected to a series of brutal assaults that left seven of their players badly injured. Zamora, in particular, came in for heavy treatment, but the aggression was not all one way. The Spanish were ready to repay like with like and with Louis Baert, the Belgian referee, weakly disregarding any but the most blatant offences, the match quickly deteriorated into a shambles, in which "beside the desire to win, all other sporting considerations were non-existent", as another Belgian official, Jean Langenus, later wrote. It was one of several games in this World Cup that led to referees being criticized for allowing themselves to be swayed by the crowd.

Yet, there was football and some of it quite good. The Italians combined speed with the trusty "W" formation and it gave their forwards the edge over a Spanish side that contained the better players in pure football terms. So whilst both sides created chances in plenty in the first half, the Italians always seemed the more likely to score. That they did not was due to the brilliance of one man - Zamora. Time and again, as Italian forwards brushed aside Spain's defence and bore down on his goal, the valiant keeper stood magnificently to deny them. In spite of the terrible way he was manhandled, they could not get past him and it added to the frustration of a team keenly anxious to please both manager and dictator.

In the 28th minute Italy's defender, Allemandi committed a foul on the centre-forward, Langara. In a rare instance of fairness, the referee awarded a free kick. It was well within shooting range and Regueiro prepared to take it. He completely miskicked the shot, but as it headed goalwards, it swerved unmercifully and totally foxed Giampiero Combi in the goal. Against the odds, the Spanish found themselves one up. It was a situation that, despite mounting Italian pressure, held until half-time.

The second half was even more savage that the first had been. In one swinging retaliatory and unpunished tackle Italy's right-half, Pizziolo, had his leg broken. Meanwhile, with injuries reducing both teams to collections of the "walking wounded", a remarkably high number of scoring chances were created, and spurned by both teams. Reguiero hit a shot against the post, Allemandi cleared a goalbound effort off his line and for Italy Giovanni Ferrari, Raimundo Orsi and Peppino Meazza ran rings round tiring defenders only to see their efforts thwarted by Zamora.

Italy's reprieve from humiliation came in the last minute of the game, in their last piece of attacking action and from another diabolical refereeing decision. As the ball was swung into the Spanish area, Angelo Schiavio clearly obstructed the goalkeeper and prevented him getting to it. It fell nicely to Ferrari, who had the easiest of chances to equalize. Vainly the Spanish protested, but the goal stood and a replay was needed the following day. It was hardly surprising that Pozzo called his men to see him after the game and gave each one an individual dressing down.

Italy 2 : Czechoslovakia 1
The World Cup Final

Goalkeepers and captains Combi of Italy (left) and Czechoslovakia's Plánicka.

The Italians, strong, hard and physical, went into the final clear favourites to win the title. They seemed to have all the advantages, including a passionate crowd of over 50,000 supporters and the presence of Il Duce to keep their minds focused. Yet they were given a tough battle by a remarkably eloquent Czech team and were very fortunate to get the result they did.

Contrasting two differing styles of play - the rugged power of Italy against the subtle artistry of the Czechs - produced a gripping match made more pleasing by the fact that the Italians opted to play football, rather than fight their way to the world crown. Their calmer approach and their obviously greater nervousness allowed the Czechs to show off their skills and for the entire of the first half and most of the second the Italians were plainly second best. The Czechs played some dazzling, short-passing football that often had Italy's defence in knots. Antonin Puc danced on the left-wing, causing no end of problems and had it not been for Luis Monti, so often the anti-hero, and now playing magnificently to hold the line, the home team might have been swamped. When the Italians managed to mount a threat on the Czech goal, they found centre-half Cambal in towering form and goalkeeper Frantisek Plánicka unbeatable.

For over an hour the Czechs hammered at the Italian door, but could not get in. Then, in the 70th minute Puc, who had only recently returned to the pitch after having gone off with cramp, took a corner. Immediately the ball was returned out to him and from an almost impossible angle, he hit a speculative long-range shot. Goalkeeper, Combi seemed to have it covered, but misjudged its trajectory, dived too late and the ball was in the net. It stunned the crowd, but was no less than the Czechs deserved. They ought to have made the result secure as, over the next few minutes, first centre-forward Sobotka missed an open goal and then inside-right Svoboda hit the post.

Going behind put Italy in a desperate situation and their response was to pile on the pressure. For the last period of the game the Czech goal was under constant siege, but Plánicka was as steady as ever and it took a freak shot to level the scores. With eight minutes to go, Orsi collected a pass from fellow Argeninean, Enrique Guaita, and tore through the heart of the Czech defence. With an amazing piece of skill, he feinted with his left foot and fired in a lobbed shot with his right. The ball seemed to come alive as it swerved and dipped in a way that was virtually unsavable. Plánicka managed to get his finger tips to

The victorious Italian team carry coach Vittorio Pozzo.

60

it, but could not keep it out. Revitalized, the Italians went out in search of a winner, but non was forthcoming and so, for the first time, a World Cup final went into extra time.

Three factors combined to defeat the Czechs when the match restarted. They began to tire, their marking got sloppy and Pozzo revealed his tactical nous by switching the positions of his forward players to upset the Czech concentration. Guaita and Schiavio were interchanged and it was when they swapped back again that Italy scored the winner. Meazza had picked up an injury soon after the match restarted. It left him limping on the wing and the Czechs did not give him the attention they ought. With seven minutes having been played he picked up the ball on the right, crossed to Guaita who in turn found Schiavio. He "neatly side-stepped a defender" and fired past Plánicka.

Now it was the turn of Czechoslovakia to seek to salvage the match. Although by now visibly wilting, they went onto the offensive and the last minutes of the game were a succession of attacks from both teams, which kept both goalkeepers busy and on their toes. It provided an exciting finale, but no more goals. By the time the final whistle blew to make Italy the second world champions both sets of players were shattered. A proud Mussolini presented the trophy to his jubilant victors and they lofted Pozzo onto their shoulders to chair him off the field. For the second time the host nation had carried the day.

Statistics - Italy 1934

FIRST ROUND

Rome, May 27th - Stadio PNF

7 (3) ITALY

Schiavio 18,29,64, Orsi 20,69, Ferrari 63, Meazza 90

Combi, Rosetta, Allemandi, Pizziolo, Monti, Bertolini, Guarisi, Meazza, Schiavio, Ferrari, Orsi.

1 (0) UNITED STATES

Donelli 57

Hjulian, Czerkiewicz, Moorhouse, Pietras, Gonsalvez, Florie, Ryan, Nilsen, Donelli, Dick, Maclean.

Referee: Rene Mercet (Switzerland)
Attendance: 30.000

Trieste, May 27th - Stadio Littorio

2 (0) CZECHOSLOVAKIA

Puc 49, Nejedlý 69

Plánicka, Zenisek, Ctyroky, Koštálek, Cambal, Krcil, Junek, Silny, Sobotka, Nejedlý, Puc.

1 (1) ROMANIA

Dobai 10

Zombori, Vogl, Albu, Deheleanu, Kotormani, Moravez, Bindea, Kovacs, Sepi, Bodola, Dobai.

Referee: Jean Langenus (Belgium)
Attendance: Unknown

Florence, May 27th - Stadio Giovanni Berta

5 (1) GERMANY

Kobierski 26, Siffling 47, Conen 67,70,80

Kress, Haringer, Schwartz, Janes, Szepan, Zielinski, Lehner, Hohmann, Conen, Siffling, Kobierski.

2 (2) BELGIUM

Voorhoof 31,43

Van de Weyer, Smellinckx, Joacim, Peeraer, Welkenhuyzen, Klaessens, Devries, Voorhoof, Capelle, Grimmonprez, Heremans.

Referee: Francesco Mattea (Italy)
Attendance: 8.000

Turin, May 27th - Stadio Mussolini

After extra time - 45 mins (1-1), 90 mins (1-1), 120 mins 3-2

3 (1) AUSTRIA

Sindelar 45, Schall 94, Bican 96

Platzer, Cisar, Sesta, Wagner, Smistik, Urbanek, Zischek, Bican, Sindelar, Schall, Viertl.

2 (1) FRANCE

Nicolas 19, Verriest (pen) 114

Thépot, Mairesse, Mattler, Delfour, Verriest, Llense, Keller, Alcazar, Nicolas, Rio, Aston.

Referee: John Van Moorsel (Holland)
Attendance: Unknown

Genoa, May 27th - Stadio Luigi Ferraris

3 (2) SPAIN

Iraragorri (pen)18, Langara 27,77

Zamora, Ciriaco, Quincoces, Cillauren, Muguerza, Lafuente, Iraragorri, Langara, Lecue, Marculeta, Gorostiza.

1 (0) BRAZIL

Leónidas 56

Pedrosa, Silvio, Luz, Tinoco, Martin Silveira, Canalli, Oliviera, de Brito, Leónidas, Armadinho, Bartesko.

Referee: Alfred Birlem (Germany)
Attendance: Unknown

Milan, May 27th - Stadio San Siro

3 (2) SWITZERLAND

Kielholz 14,43, Abegglen III 64

Sechehaye, Minelli, Weiler, Guinchard, Jaccard, Hufschmid, von Känel, Passello, Kielholz, Abegglen III, Bossi.

2 (1) HOLLAND

Smit 22, Vente 87

Van der Meulen, Weber, van Run, Pellikaan, Anderiesen, van Heel, Wels, Vente, Bakhuijs, Smit, van Nellen.

Referee: Ivan Eklind (Sweden)
Attendance: Unknown

Bologna, May 27th - Stadio Littoriale

3 (1) SWEDEN

Jonasson 8,67, Kroon 79

Rydberg, Axelsson, S.Andersson, Carlsson, Rosen, E.Andersson, Dunker, Gustafsson, Jonasson, Keller, Kroon.

2 (1) ARGENTINA

Belis 3, Galeato 47

Freschi, Pedevilla, Belis, Nehin, Sosa-Urbieta, López, Rua, Wilde, De Vincenzi, Galeato, Irañeta.

Referee: M.Braun (Austria)
Attendance: Unknown

Naples, May 27th - Stadio Ascarelli

4 (2) HUNGARY

Teleki 12, Toldi 30,52, Vincze 59

A.Szabó, Futo, Sternberg, Palotas, Szücs, Lazar, Markos, Vincze, Teleki, Toldi, G.Szabó.

2 (1) EGYPT

Fawzi 38,67

Kamel Taha, El Said, Hamidu, El Far, Rafaat, Ragab, Latif, Fawzi, Mokhtar, Kamel Mansour, Hassan.

Referee: Rinaldo Barlassini (Italy)
Attendance: Unknown

SECOND ROUND

Milan, May 31st - Stadio San Siro

2 (0) GERMANY

Hohmann 60,63

Kress, Haringer, Busch, Gramlich, Szepan, Zielinski, Lehner, Hohmann, Conen, Siffling, Kobierski.

1 (0) SWEDEN

Dunker 83

Rydberg, Axelsson, S.Andersson, Carlsson, Rosen, E.Andersson, Dunker, Gustafsson, Jonasson, Keller, Kroon.

Referee: Rinaldo Barlassini (Italy)
Attendance: 3.000

Bologna, May 31st - Stadio Littoriale

2 (1) AUSTRIA

Horvath 5, Zischek 53

Platzer, Cisar, Sesta, Wagner, Smistik, Urbanek, Zischek, Bican, Sindelar, Horvath, Viertl.

1 (0) HUNGARY

Sárosi (pen)67

A.Szabó, Vago, Sternberg, Palotas, Szücs, Szalay, Markos (RED), Avar, Sárosi, Toldi, Kemeny.

Referee: Francesco Mattea (Italy)
Attendance: Unknown

Florence, May 31st - Stadio Giovanni Berta

After extra time - 45 mins (0-1), 90 mins (1-1), 120 mins 1-1

1 (1) ITALY

Ferrari 46

Combi, Monzeglio, Allemandi, Pizziolo, Monti, Castellazzi, Guaita, Meazza, Schiavio, Ferrari, Orsi.

1 (1) SPAIN

Regueiro 31

Zamora, Ciriaco, Quincoces, Cillauren, Muguerza, Lafuente, Iraragorri, Langara, Fede, Regueiro, Gorostiza.

Referee: Louis Baert (Belgium)
Attendance: 35.000

Replay - Florence, June 1st - Stadio Giovanni Berta

1 (1) ITALY

Meazza 12

Combi, Monzeglio, Allemandi, Ferraris IV, Monti, Bertolini, Guaita, Meazza, Borel, De Maria, Orsi.

0 (0) SPAIN

Nogues, Zabalo, Quincoces, Cillauren, Muguerza, Lecue, Vantolra, Regueiro, Campanal, Chacho, Bosch.

Referee: Rene Mercet (Switzerland)
Attendance: 43.000

Turin, May 31st - Stadio Mussolini

3 (1) CZECHOSLOVAKIA

Svoboda 24, Sobotka 48, Nejedlý 83

Plánicka, Zenisek, Ctyroky, Koštálek, Cambal, Krcil, Junek, Svoboda, Sobotka, Nejedlý, Puc.

2 (1) SWITZERLAND

Kielholz 18, Abegglen III 71

Sechehaye, Minelli, Weiler, Guinchard, Jaccard, Hufschmid, von Känel, Jaeggi IV, Kielholz, Abegglen III, Jaeck.

Referee: Alois Beranek (Germany)
Attendance: Unknown

SEMI-FINALS

Milan, June 3rd - Stadio San Siro

1 (1) ITALY

Guaita 19

Combi, Monzeglio, Allemandi, Ferraris IV, Monti, Bertolini, Guaita, Meazza, Schiavio, Ferrari, Orsi.

0 (0) AUSTRIA

Platzer, Cisar, Sesta, Wagner, Smistik, Urbanek, Zischek, Bican, Sindelar, Schall, Viertl.

Referee: Ivan Eklind (Sweden)
Attendance: 60.000

Rome, June 3rd - Stadio PNF

3 (1) CZECHOSLOVAKIA

Nejedlý 21,60,81

Plánicka, Ctyroky, Bürgr, Koštálek, Cambal, Krcil, Junek, Svoboda, Sobotka, Nejedlý, Puc.

1 (0) GERMANY

Noack 50

Kress, Busch, Haringer, Zielinski, Szepan, Bender, Lehner, Siffling, Conen, Noack, Kobierski.

Referee: Rinaldo Barlassini (Italy)
Attendance: 10.000

3RD/4TH PLACE PLAY-OFF

Naples, June 7th - Stadio Ascarelli

3 (3) GERMANY

Lehner 1,42, Conen 29

Jakob, Busch, Janes, Zielinski, Szepan, Münzenberg, Bender, Lehner, Siffling, Conen, Heidemann.

2 (1) AUSTRIA

Horvath 30, Sesta 55

Platzer, Cisar, Sesta, Wagner, Smistik, Urbanek, Zischek, Bican, Braun, Horvath, Viertl.

Referee: Albino Carraro (Italy)
Attendance: 7.000

FINAL

Rome, June 10th - Stadio PNF

After extra time - 45 mins (0-0), 90 mins (1-1), 120 mins 2-1

2 (1) ITALY

Orsi 82, Schiavio 95

Combi, Monzeglio, Allemandi, Ferraris IV, Monti, Guaita, Meazza, Schiavio, Ferrari, Orsi.

1 (1) CZECHOSLOVAKIA

Puc 70

Plánicka, Ctyroky, Zenisek, Koštálek, Cambal, Krcil, Junek, Svoboda, Sobotka, Nejedlý, Puc.

Referee: Ivan Eklind (Sweden)
Attendance: 55.000

QUALIFYING ROUNDS

Europe - Group 1

	P	W	D	L	F	A	Pts
Sweden	2	2	0	0	8	2	4
Lithuania	1	0	0	1	0	2	0
Estonia	1	0	0	1	2	6	0

11-06-1933	Sweden : Estonia	6:2 (4:0)
29-06-1933	Lithuania : Sweden	0:2 (0:0)

Europe - Group 2

	P	W	D	L	F	A	Pts
Spain	2	2	0	0	11	1	4
Portugal	2	0	0	2	1	11	0

11-03-1934	Spain : Portugal	9:0 (3:0)
18-03-1934	Portugal : Spain	1:2 (1:2)

Europe - Group 3

	P	W	D	L	F	A	Pts
Italy	1	1	0	0	4	0	4
Greece	1	0	0	1	0	4	0

25-03-1934	Italy : Greece	4:0 (2:0)

Europe - Group 4

	P	W	D	L	F	A	Pts
Hungary	2	2	0	0	8	2	4
Austria	1	1	0	0	6	1	2
Bulgaria	3	0	0	3	3	14	0

25-03-1934	Bulgaria : Hungary	1:4 (1:1)
25-04-1934	Austria : Bulgaria	6:1 (3:0)
29-04-1934	Hungary : Bulgaria	4:1 (1:0)

Europe - Group 5

	P	W	D	L	F	A	Pts
Czech	2	2	0	0	4	1	4
Poland	2	0	0	2	1	4	0

15-10-1933	Poland : Czechoslovakia	1:2 (0:1)
15-04-1934	Czechoslovakia : Poland	2:0

Europe - Group 6

	P	W	D	L	F	A	Pts
Switzerland	2	1	1	0	4	2	3
Romania	2	1	0	1	2	3	2
Yugoslavia	2	0	1	1	3	4	1

24-09-1933	Yugoslavia : Switzerland	2:2 (0:0)
29-10-1933	Switzerland : Romania	2:0
29-04-1934	Romania : Yugoslavia	2:1 (1:0)

Europe - Group 7

	P	W	D	L	F	A	Pts
Netherlands	2	2	0	0	9	4	4
Belgium	2	0	1	1	6	8	1
Ireland Rep.	2	0	1	1	6	9	1

25-02-1934	Ireland Republic : Belgium	4:4 (1:2)
08-04-1934	Netherlands : Ireland Republic	5:2 (1:1)
29-04-1934	Belgium : Netherlands	2:4 (0:0)

Europe - Group 8

	P	W	D	L	F	A	Pts
Germany	1	1	0	0	9	1	2
France	1	1	0	0	6	1	2
Luxembourg	2	0	0	2	2	15	0

11-03-1934	Luxembourg : Germany	1:9 (1:5)
15-04-1934	Luxembourg : France	1:6 (0:2)

Caribbean/North/Central America Group 11 - Subgroup A - 1st Round

	P	W	D	L	F	A	Pts
Cuba	3	2	1	0	10	2	5
Haiti	3	0	1	2	2	10	1

28-01-1934	Cuba : Haiti	3:1 (1:0)
01-02-1934	Haiti : Cuba	1:1 (0:0)
04-02-1934	Cuba : Haiti	6:0

Caribbean/North/Central America
Group 11 - Subgroup A - 2nd Round

	P	W	D	L	F	A	Pts
Mexico	3	3	0	0	12	3	6
Cuba	3	0	0	3	3	12	0

04-03-1934	Mexico : Cuba	3:2 (3:1)
11-03-1934	Mexico : Cuba	5:0 (3:0)
18-03-1934	Mexico : Cuba	4:1 (2:1)

Caribbean/North/Central America
Group 11 - Play-off

	P	W	D	L	F	A	Pts
USA	1	1	0	0	4	2	2
Mexico	1	0	0	1	2	4	0

24-05-1934	United States : Mexico	4:2 (2:1)

Africa/Asia - Group 12

	P	W	D	L	F	A	Pts
Egypt	2	2	0	0	11	2	4
Palestine	2	0	0	2	2	11	0

16-03-1934	Egypt : Palestine	7:1 (4:0)
06-04-1934	Palestine : Egypt	1:4 (0:4)

Chapter 5

Hitler, Mussolini and the Battle of the Races
The France World Cup, 1938

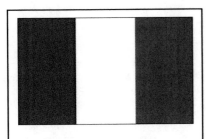

France 1938

Winners: Italy

Runners-up: Hungary

3rd Place: Brazil

4th Place: Sweden

Total Attendance: 748,000

Number of Matches: 18

In the years after the second World Cup, the world had become an even more dangerous place and a general war threatened to escalate from several sources. In China's civil war, Mao's Communists had been forced by Chiang Kai-Shek to make the Long March to safety in the country's remote north, with the loss of about 70,000 men, and in 1937 the Japanese resumed their gradual conquest of that unhappy land, capturing the capital Nanking. With the assistance of his allies in Germany and Italy, General Franco was assuming the upper hand in the Spanish Civil War and, in Central Europe, Hitler was enjoying spectacular success in the field of foreign affairs. The British government was so concerned by the turn of events that Prime Minister Neville Chamberlain ordered 1,000 spitfires to be built and was prepared to seek a deal with Hitler to avoid war.

Yet the Nazis did not have things all their own way. Hitler wanted to use the 1936 Olympic Games to demonstrate the superiority of the Aryan Race over Negroes and other so-called inferior peoples, but was frustrated by the appearance of Jesse Owens. The black American infuriated Germany's rulers by winning four Olympic titles and in 1937 Teutonic pride was further set back when the airship, the Hindenburg, caught fire killing 34 people. Worse was to come when black boxer Joe Louis flattened Germany's champion, Max Schmeling, in a 1938 heavy weight contest in New York.

There were other developments to lighten the darkening world. Max Theiler discovered a vaccine for yellow fever and Walt Disney screened "Snow White and the Seven Dwarves", the first feature-length cartoon. Marvel comic hero, Superman, made his debut in 1938 and an Orson Wells radio broadcast of H G Well's "War of the Worlds" had thousands of gullible Americans fleeing to the hills to escape what they believed was a real invasion from Mars. The recently discovered nylon was being turned into parachutes and stockings for the ladies, Picasso condemned the German bombing of a Basque town with his haunting picture, "Guernica", and in France Jean-Paul Sartre broke new ground with the publication of "Nausea".

France had also been chosen to host the third World Cup, a decision taken at FIFA's 1936 Berlin Congress. It was the most difficult decision to date. Argentina had applied to host the event and felt confident of being granted the honour believing that the tournament would alternate between Europe and South America. Though this had never been officially stated by FIFA, the Argentinian authorities had taken the notion as a convention and were bitterly disappointed when France was chosen over them. They were not going to be given the chance to do what their neighbours and rivals had done in 1930.

It was a combination of factors that prompted the decision. FIFA was mindful of the problems caused by travel difficulties and the withdrawals that had afflicted the 1930 World Cup. They had no desire to risk a repetition. Furthermore, the international situation in 1936 was looking increasingly menacing. Mussolini's Italy had revealed its belligerent tendencies when the dictator ordered the invasion of Abyssinia (now Ethiopia) in 1935. It provoked a major international crisis, which threatened to spill over into a general war after the League of Nations had been called in to settle the dispute. That it failed, and that Italy had its way, cast a long shadow over the prospects of future peace in Europe. In the meantime, Hitler had taken advantage of the distraction presented by the Abyssinian Crisis and had marched his troops into the Rhineland in 1936, the year civil war broke out in Spain. Both were seen as a direct threat to France and merely added to the tension burdening Europe. With all this going on, and wishing for a successful tournament, FIFA elected for safety and chose France, hoping that a neutral choice would offend the fewest. If football was to be a vehicle for promoting international links and better relations, then this was its greatest challenge yet. It could also be claimed that the decision was taken out of loyalty to Jules Rimet for the great service he had given to FIFA and to its World Cup.

Argentina was offended by the decision and promptly withdrew from the competition in anger. They did reapply to enter and were drawn to play Brazil, but pulled out once more and it was not to be for another twenty years that an Argentinian team played in the World Cup. Uruguay, still smarting from the 1930 European snub, also declined to enter and other teams that withdrew included Colombia, Costa Rica, Dutch Guinea, El Salvador, Mexico and the USA. Spain withdrew because of the civil war and only three non-European teams qualified: Brazil, Cuba and the Dutch East Indies, and all because no other teams entered their qualifying groups.

The qualifying stage for France 1938 was, therefore, the shortest in history and reduced the participating nations to the sixteen required for the World Cup to be organized as a knock-out once again. There were no upsets on the way and only one result stood out as anything special, the game between Hungary and Greece, played in Budapest in March 1938. Having beaten Palastine 4-1 on aggregate, the hapless Greeks went down 11-1 and Hungary became the first team to score double figures in a World Cup game.

> There were only four countries that appeared in all three pre-war World Cup finals - Brazil, Belgium, France and Romania.

> Argentina's fans were not only upset by FIFA's rejection of their bid to host the World Cup, they were also angered when their team withdrew for a second time. Once again they vented their frustrations by attacking the offices of their FA.

> For the first time Brazilian fans were able to listen to their heroes play by tuning in to intercontinental radio. In a major technological feat for the day the matches were broadcast over the airways to the South American continent.

Football's Propaganda Value...

Although Austria qualified for the 1938 finals by beating Latvia 2-1, Hitler's aggression ensured that they did not compete. Was the invasion of Austria an attempt by the Germans to win the World Cup? Apparently not. Hitler hated football, preferring motor racing and boxing instead. He only ever attended one football match, the game between Germany and Norway at the 1936 Olympic Games having been persuaded to do so by Josef Goebbels as it was assumed the Germans would win comfortably. Norway took the lead in the sixth minutes and after they netted a second in the 84th minute, the Führer stormed out of the stadium, red faced and furious. Goebbels noted in his diary: "The Führer is incensed. I can hardly bear it. A bag of nerves."

Soon after England went to Berlin to play a friendly against the German national side. The English had already caused a diplomatic row at the Berlin Olympics when they had refused to give the Nazi salute. This time the FA agreed to do so, but some of the players were reluctant and later complained that they had been forced. The seeming propaganda coup did not last long as a superior English side resoundingly beat them 6-3. The English team included Stanley Matthews, Cliff Bastin and Eddie Hapgood. In the crowd were a number of the more powerful Nazis - Goebbels, Hess, Göring and Ribbentrop. Needless to say, the UK press loudly criticized the game.

Hitler, however, like Goebbels, appreciated the propaganda value of football. The Nazi style was to invite the players of the country just occupied to play the German national squad and beat them to emphasize their superiority. It was a ploy that did not work against the Austrians in 1938 and similarly failed in the World Cup finals of that year. One German sports writer had described the problem this way: "This mish mash of players greatly affected Germany's performance over the next few years. It would be the equivalent of suddenly creating a national side by mixing England and Scotland." They didn't get past the first round.

The members of the 'Greater German' squad were expected to attend political training sessions. These included having to learn the date of the Führer's birthday and how to give the correct Nazi salute. Herbert Moll, an international from Bayern Munich recalled: "We had lessons every Tuesday after practice. Those who passed earned a stamp in their 'player passport'. Those who didn't were thrown out." "The whole thing was pure propaganda," said Albert Sing, another German international.

During World War Two the German authorities encouraged international games to keep national morale high. Goebbels tried to capitalize on the propaganda value of football by playing internationals against weaker teams and beating them. However, the Germans tended to do badly against the better teams, such as when they were beaten 5-1 by Hungary in September 1939. In July 1940 they beat Romania 9-3, a game in which Fritz Walter scored his first three international goals. Walter later went on to captain the World Cup winning West German team in 1954. To try to get the team to win every game Goebbels simply commanded the team not to lose. This failed and in 1942 he banned internationals altogether.

Hitler, Mussolini and the Battle of the Races - France 1938

FIFA President Jules Rimet is assisted by a young boy in making the draw for the 1938 World Cup.

By April 1938 the sixteen finalists were in place, but then international politics intervened to upset FIFA's plans. In March 1938 Austria's Nazi Minister of the Interior, Artur Seyss Inquart, invited Hitler to occupy the land of his birth. He duly obliged and Austria ceased to exist. When German troops crossed the border, Austrians became citizens of the Führer's Greater Reich and those members of the Austrian national team deemed good enough were incorporated into the Greater Germany squad. It left FIFA with an organizational difficulty since there were now fifteen entries for the knock-out. The spare place was offered to the English FA, of which Stanley Rous was the secretary, but once again the English disdained to enter. To solve the problem, Sweden was given a bye in the first round.

Informed opinion of the day considered several of the leading teams to be evenly matched. Obviously, the Italians were one of the fancied teams. They were reigning world champions and in Berlin in 1936 the Italian amateur team had added the Olympic gold medal to their country's honours. Vittorio Pozzo was on record for having declared that his 1938 outfit was stronger than that of four years previous. The German team, managed by Sepp Herberger, was also expected to do well and, as the football correspondent of Le Figaro pointed out, with ironic reference to Hitler's most recent territorial acquisition, "the support of the Austrians, which the Germans called upon, must allow the footballers from across the Rhine to carry the day."The Hungarians and the Czechs were also highly regarded and admired for their attractive style of football. The non-European teams were considered weak and not expected to get beyond the first round. Of them, only Brazil was seen as having any realistic chance. That nation's long and happy love affair with the World Cup was about to begin.

As for the chances of the host team, they were tinged with hope and optimism, rather than with realism. One Paris newspaper began its review of the tournament by looking back over previous World Cups and wondered if anything could be concluded that might indicate the possible winner. It said: "If one remembers the preceding competitions, one can see that in 1930 Uruguay carried the day at home, and that Italy won the World Cup at home in 1934. Is it possible that France, the organizer, could win the day?" Having dared to pose the question, the analyst did then plant his feet firmly back on the ground when he added that "in spite of the clear progress of French football, you must expect to see the French team not progressing beyond the first round." He also noted that even if the hosts got past Belgium in the first round, they were likely to meet Italy in the quarter-finals and this would surely be too difficult an obstacle to overcome.

Whilst the majority of the first round games were scheduled for 5th June, the tournament began on 4th June with an opening game between Germany and Switzerland in the Parc des Princes in Paris. It produced one of the shock results of the round. The German population was experiencing a great revival of national pride and were buoyed by incessant Nazi propaganda about German superiority and invincibility. The national mood was reflected in the football team, which entered the Swiss game full of confidence and totally expecting to win. The Swiss, however, refused to be intimidated and showed their mettle by not giving the Nazi salute during the playing of the national anthems. They carried this spirit into the match and completely outplayed the Germans. It was an abysmal performance from the Greater Germans. They had Hans Pesser sent off and were lucky to survive extra time to earn a draw. In the replay the Swiss were reduced to ten men when Aebi had to go off injured and the Germans took full advantage to surge to a 2-0 lead. Justice was done, however, when the Swiss came back strongly. According to one French report, it was because of "its ardour, its spirit, its will to win and, unlike the German team, its good physical condition", that the Swiss team was able to fight their way to a 4-2 victory. It was well earned and well deserved, a famous win that humiliated the Germans. It was certainly a slap in the face for the Führer and sections of the French press could not help having a dig. Le Figaro explained the lack of cohesion in the German team this way: "The Austrian game has not had time to adapt to the German game, or if you prefer, the German game has not had time to adapt to the Austrian game."

Switzerland's defeat of the Greater Germans had been the first real surprise of the competition. An even bigger shock came when the Cubans took on Romania, whose players had all had previous World Cup experience, either in 1930, in 1934 or both. A replay was needed when Cuba secured a remarkable 3-3 draw, the magnitude of which appears even greater when it is appreciated that it was Cuba's first appearance in the World Cup finals. It was hugely humiliating for the Europeans, but worse was to follow. The Cubans replaced their goalkeeper for the replay, bringing in Juan Ayra for Benito Carrajales. It was something of a gamble because Carrajales had played well in the first match, but it was one that paid off. Ayra had an outstanding match and virtually secured Cuba's victory. He was beaten only once, when Stefan Dobai scored the opening goal in the ninth minute, and then he totally defied all that Romania could throw at him. Héctor Socorro, who had scored twice in the first match, equalized in the second half and things began to look ominous for Romania. There was a touch of fortune about Carlos Maquina's winning strike, as he had been flagged offside. The German referee, Alfred Birken, allowed him to play on and Romania's embarrassment was complete.

Other first round results went largely as expected. Czechoslovakia dispatched the Dutch in Le Havre, but not before the game went into extra time. Three late strikes by Josef Košťálek, Oldrich Nejedlý and Josef Zeman sealed the victory. In Paris, France defeated Belgium 3-1 in what was the oldest international football fixture outside the British Isles. For France, captain Etiénne Mattler and Edmond Delfour, and Belgium's Bernard Voorhoof were all appearing in their third World Cup finals, but it was Emile Vienante who made the first mark. He headed home in the first minute as the French took full control of the game and "occupied the opposition's camp", as a local paper put it. Jean Nicholas scored France's second, before Voorhoof grabbed one back. The Belgians came on strongly after the break, but could not score, and Nicholas made it safe for the home team with a breakaway goal.

The most crushing victory of the first round came when Hungary defeated the Dutch East Indies 6-0, ending that team's one and only foray into the World Cup, at least under that name. A hat trick each from Gyula Zsengeller and György Sáros did the damage in an easy victory. However, the best two games in the round were those between Italy and Norway, and Brazil and Poland, the latter being simply a classic and possibly one of the greatest of all World Cup games. (See Leónidas da Silva profile on page 72 and the Brazil v Poland profile on page 75).

The other put one of the best teams in the world against the amateurs of Norway. It was not to be the David and Goliath contest that it at first sight appears and the Italians had good cause to be wary of their opponents. They had met in the semi-finals of the 1936 Olympic Games and the Norwegians had made things very difficult before the Italians had secured a narrow victory. It was to be the same in Marseille in 1938. The Italians

Switzerland 1 : Germany 1 (aet)
The captains shake hands before the match. Switzerland won the replay 4:2.

On the opening day of the 1938 tournament the French President, Albert Lebrun, walked onto the field at the Colombes Stadium in Paris to ceremonially kick the first ball. However, obviously not up to the task, he missed his aim and scuffed the ground.

As the rain lashed down on the two teams battling out for a place in the quarter-finals, the ground turned to mud and the grass of the pitch disappeared. The player entered the box, expectant, playing like the genius of the game that he was. But no, disaster struck. The player stumbled and lost his boot to the quagmire that engulfed his struggling feet. What was he to do? The goal was waiting for his shot, the crowed expecting nothing less than a goal. So the player abandoned his boot, sacrificed in the name of glory, and, now barefoot, he slotted the ball home. This was how Leónidas scored one of his four goals in the 6-5 defeat of Poland. He had wanted to play the whole game bare foot to cope with the conditions but Swedish referee, Ivan Eklind, wouldn't let him.

Hitler, Mussolini and the Battle of the Races - France 1938

For the first time the holders and the hosts of the tournament did not have to qualify. France also has the dubious honour of becoming the first hosts to lose a match in World Cup finals.

Reporting on Sweden's 8-0 victory over Cuba, one French journalist gave up keeping the score, giving as his reason: "Up to five goals is journalism. After that, it becomes statistics."

1938 was the only time only one team represented South America.

Brazil became the first team to use all 22 players in their squad during the 1938 tournament.

took an early lead when, in the second minute, the Norwegian goalkeeper, Johansen, failed to hold on to a shot from Giovanni Ferrari, who followed in to net the loose ball. Then the Norwegians rallied marvellously. In the lugubrious reporting style of Le Figaro: "Big, brave, athletic, fast, the Nordics drove attacks of very great classicism, which often deprived the Italians, who were found lacking." Indeed, the Norwegians hit the bar and the post three times before Arne Brustad rewarded their enterprise with an 82nd minute equalizer. They even had a goal disallowed before the game went into extra time. The Italians were often confined to breakaways and it was one such that brought their winner, in the first period of extra time. Pasinati's shot was stopped by Johansen, but not held, and Silvio Piola, was there to slot home and take Italy through to the quarter-final.

Not surprisingly the biggest crowd in Round Two turn up at the Stade Colombes on 12th June for the Italy-France tie. In its competition preview Le Figaro had anticipated this fixture and the result went as the paper predicted. Italy, who played in Fascist black, took the lead after ten minutes, when the French goalkeeper, Di Lorto, misjudged a cross from Colaussi which sneaked into the net. A minute later the French were back on level terms through a goal from Heisserer, but that was to be the closest they came to getting a result. In the second half the French did much of the attacking, but not for the first time in this World Cup, Italy's defence held firm. It was their commitment to attack that finally undid the French. It allowed the Italian forwards too much room and Piola took full advantage of the freedom he was given to score two more goals and give his team a 3-1 victory.

In Antibes, on the Riviera, the result went with form, as Cuba's World Cup hopes were dashed by the Swedes. Gustav Wetterström, who scored twice in each half, became the third player in the tournament to score four goals in a game, when his team handed the Cubans an 8-0 thrashing. At the other end of the country, in Lille, form also held the key as Hungary defeated Switzerland. Before the game, one Hungarian official, Dr. Diet, had said that he would walk back to Budapest if his team lost, but there was little danger of that. The Swiss were severely weakened by the loss of their influential captain and defender, Severino Muelli, and of the winger Aebi, who had not recovered from the injury he had picked up in the replayed game against Germany. Two goals from Zsengeller gave Hungary passage into the next round and saved Dr. Diet's feet from a bad blistering.

The most sensational game of the second round was the infamous "Battle of Bordeaux", in which the Hungarian referee had struggled to keep any semblance of order and was replaced for the replay by Frenchman, Georges Capdeville. (See Brazil v Czechoslovakia profile on page 76). It took place two days later and turned out to be a totally different game. This is hardly surprising since the Brazilians had made nine changes to their line up and the Czechs five. Only goalkeeper, Walter, and Leónidas survived for Brazil and both had a decisive influence on the game. The Czechs, who were without their most influential players, took the lead in the first half, but Leónidas equalized eleven minutes into the second. Soon after Kopecky had a shot saved by Walter that many said had crossed the line and should have been a goal. It was possibly the defining moment of the game because from the clearance that followed, Brazil broke away and scored the winner. It was unfortunate for the Czechs, but it put Brazil into the semi-finals for the first time in their history.

The Brazilians had been so confident of defeating the Czechs in the replay that most of their party had already left Bordeaux for the semi-final in Marseille before the game even kicked off. They displayed the same over confidence for their semi-final against Italy when they decided to "rest" Leónidas and Tim. It was a strange decision by coach Ademar Pimenta, and it, ultimately, brought about their undoing. A full strength Italian team was always going to be a dif-

Hungary 2 : Switzerland 0. Quarter-final action at Lille.

ficult nut to crack and although both teams played well, Italy's performance was the more complete. Leónidas's replacement, Peracio, squandered two very good chances, when the maestro might not have been so profligate, and the inability of Brazil to convert the few openings that they created allowed the Italians to take charge of the game. Things began to turn in their favour in the second period when, according to one report, they "practised beautiful academic football" and Piola began to harry the Brazilian defence, forcing them to adopt a more physical approach.

Italy's first goal, ten minutes into the second half, came, as one French reporter described, "in the middle of a flow of blows on the whistle". The Brazilians had resorted to foul play to try to stem Italy's increased pressure and the goal scorer, Colaussi, was injured in the process and the game had to be held up temporarily whilst he received treatment. Italy's second strike came from further Brazilian rough stuff when Domingos violently charged down Piola and the referee had no choice but to award a penalty. It was converted by Meazza and, although it brought a more positive response from the South Americans, "who were amusing with the ball," the Italians easily contained their opponents. (See Giuseppe Meazza profile on page 73 and Silvio Piola profile on page 74). Brazil did score, three minutes from time, but it was too late and the Italians went into their second World Cup final deserved 2-1 winners.

In the other semi-final the Hungarians had little trouble seeing off the challenge of the Swedes, even though the Scandinavians opened the scoring with a first minute goal from Arne Nyberg, the fastest of the tournament. After that initial aberration, the game became one way traffic and described by one commentator as "an excellent training match for the Hungarians." In fairness, the Swedes were fortunate to have got that far in the competition, but that is not to deny the brilliance of Hungary or the ease with which they brushed aside their opponents. First half goals by Pál Titkos and Zsengeller, who scored twice, gave them a 3-1 half-time lead, and further strikes by György Sárosi and Zsengeller again after the restart secured a convincing victory. So dominant were the Hungarians that it was reported that a blackbird settled in their half of the field and was hardly troubled by the play.

For the second time in succession the World Cup final was an entirely European affair (See Italy v Hungary profile on page 77), but South America still had an interest in the play-off for the minor positions, which took place in Bordeaux on 19th June, the same day as the final. It was a game which for a time appeared as if it might produce an upset, when the unfancied Swedes found themselves 2-0 to the good inside 40 minutes. Jonasson and Nyberg were the two scorers. However, Romeo pulled a goal back just before half-time, to give his team a platform for the second half. They used it well and took control of the play. Leónidas scored twice and Peracio got another, to give Brazil a 4-2 victory. His goals gave Leónidas a total of eight to make him the tournament's leading scorer and the third place was Brazil's first championship placing, the beginning of their illustrious record in the World Cup.

Hitler, Mussolini and the Battle of the Races - France 1938

Huge crowds greet Brazil in Rio de Janeiro after their 3rd place in France.

The Italian press had a field day when it came to reporting the triumph of the Fascists over their inferiors. Commenting on the final, the sports newspaper La Gazzetta dello Sport spoke about "the apotheosis of Fascist sports symbolized by this victory of the [Italian] race." However, the most racist report came only a few days previously when Italy beat the Brazilians. The Italian press reported: "We salute the triumph of Italic intelligence over the brute force of the Negroes."

Some people have considered that England would have won the World Cup had they accepted FIFA's offer of Austria's place. In that year England beat France 4-2 in Paris, a FIFA XI 3-0 at Highbury, Germany 6-3 in Berlin and Norway 4-0 at Newcastle. However, Switzerland beat them in Zurich, the winning goal being scored by Andre Abegglen III.

When Italy won the Cup in 1938 they set a record of seven successive wins in the finals, a record that still holds.

The Italian team turned up for the victory ceremony on the day after the final in military uniforms. The ceremony was presided over by Il Duce himself.

Neither the final itself nor the tournament of France 1938 were the most exciting on record and, of those played so far, were probably the least interesting. But, in the circumstances in which it was played, this was probably to be expected. In the summer of 1938 war clouds once again cast a bleak shadow over Europe and several of the countries participating in the World Cup were either directly or indirectly threatened by the turn of events. As we have noted, Austria had already disappeared as a country and Hitler's obsessive gaze was already focused on Czechoslovakia, where lived some three million ethnic Germans. He wanted them in his Greater Reich and if war broke out over the dispute, France as a protector of Czechoslovakia and Italy as an ally of Germany, could easily be sucked in. In such a war, the involvement of Britain and Hungary, and on a wider front, Belgium and Holland, was a further distinct possibility. Poland, too, with its own sizeable German minority, could not feel safe and Hitler had frequently spoken, and written, of his ultimate ambitions towards that country. Football should have provided a distraction from such problems, and no doubt France '38 was for many a welcome relief, but the general mood of pessimism that prevailed in Europe was not easy to escape. Footballers cannot be cocooned from the concerns of the wider world.

The tournament can be criticized in other ways. As with previous stagings of the event, France '38 was not a truly representative World Cup. Yet again there was no British participation and of the non-European entrants, only Brazil had any real credibility. We can wonder if the outcome might have been different had Argentina, England or Uruguay competed. Then, there were negative aspects of the football itself. Undoubtedly, some teams did not fulfil their expectations, notably Germany and Romania, and others gave below par performances. Some of the tactics employed and attitudes adopted occasionally adversely affected the quality of football. The Italians have always had the capacity to make too big a virtue of defence, whilst the Brazilians could be downright cynical (to understate the case). The problem of a referee's poor judgement having undue influence on the outcome of games was a feature of the 1938 finals, as it has been in others, before and since.

This said, the French World Cup did have its highlights. Players like Leónidas, Willimowski and Piola are fine testaments to the genuinely world class talent that was on display. Such players were able to contribute to some excellent and on occasion, fantastic, games of football. The match between Brazil and Poland is one that may never be bettered for the sheer exuberance of the soccer played. Attendances were also very encouraging, with plenty of public interest in the spectacle, and, like in Italy in 1934, games were spread around the whole country. It gave wide opportunity for interested people to see games and many took it. Lastly, there can be no question over the fairness of the result. Italy was the best and won deservedly. The 1938 World Cup may not have been the massive success and global event that FIFA might have wished, but in its own modest way France '38 contributed to the gradual metamorphosis that was taking place and would begin again in the 1950s. It was a step, if only such, along a path that was the unfolding history of the World Cup.

France was a tournament played out under the shadow of war. Little over fourteen months and a number of international crises later, Europe was plunged into that war. Whilst some of its causes have been touched upon in this survey, the development of foreign relations is of no more than peripheral concern to a history of World Cup football. However, its effects on the World Cup do need to be noted. Its outbreak ended all possibility of European involvement in international sporting events and it would not be for another twelve years that a fourth World Cup tournament took place.

Ernst Willimowski

Poland's Ernst Willimowski may have narrowly missed out on becoming the first player to score four goals in the finals, but he did not miss out on playing football when the Second World War broke out. The war began when Germany occupied his country. Willimowski, like many Polish citizens, was "Germanized" by the Nazis and therefore became eligible to play for his "new" country. In his international career for Germany he scored 13 goals, including a hat trick against Finland in October 1941 and four against Switzerland in October 1942, one of the last internationals played by Nazi Germany. After the war he played for Poland again.

Leónidas da Silva   Brazil

Honours: 3rd Place 1938   **Games 5**
Played: 1934 and 1938   **Goals 9**

He was as quick and cunning as a fly, untouchable, unstoppable and he tied players' legs into knots. He was the "Black Diamond", he was the "Rubber Man" and he scored goals that were so deliciously graceful that even opposing goalkeepers would get up and applaud. He became so big in South America that he got more letters than movie stars with requests for favours, such as pictures, autographs and even government jobs. At the 1938 World Cup, a Paris Match journalist reported that he had six legs and that this must be due to black magic. Six legs or not, he had an uncanny ability to stretch to heights and lengths in a rubber-like fashion that gave him the advantages of a man of much greater stature.

Leónidas da Silva was born in Rio de Janeiro on 11th November 1913 and began his football career with local sides, making his international debut in 1932 against Uruguay. He scored two goals and prompted the interests of Uruguayan club side Peñarol, where he moved in 1933. He stayed with them for a year before returning to Brazil to help Vasco da Gama win the Rio Championship. At the 1934 World Cup he scored Brazil's only goal in their only game of the tournament. He had travelled 10,000 miles for one game, but he had at least introduced himself to the European public. On his return to Brazil he joined Botafogo who consequently won the 1935 Rio Championship. The following year he signed for Flamenco where he played until 1942.

Among his many honours, Leónidas has been credited with having invented 'la bicicleta' or bicycle kick. He didn't, but he did become the world's foremost exponent of its execution. 'La bicicleta' was invented by the Chilean Ramón Unzaga, on the fields of his hometown, Talcahuano. He performed this sudden snap of the legs, shooting the ball backwards, with body in the air and back to the ground for his club Colo Colo on a tour of Spain in 1927. It was given the name 'chilena' and adopted by 1920s Spanish striker David Arellano. The Brazilians later called it the bicycle kick and Leónidas used it to score goals too numerous to count.

Leónidas's finest moments on the world stage came at the 1938 World Cup when his exploits made sure of his place in the annals of the finest Brazilian players. Unfortunately, circumstances contrived to deny him a place in the final. In 1942, Leónidas moved to São Paulo where he played for eight years before his retirement in 1950. He returned as manager for a short time in 1953, before moving on to become a radio presenter. He later became the owner of a furniture shop in São Paulo. He was capped 23 times for Brazil and was perhaps the most exciting, skilful and extraordinary player of inter-war South America.

Giuseppe Meazza   Italy

Honours: Winner 1934 and 1938   **Games 9**
Played: 1934 and 1938   **Goals 3**

Italy's captain Giuseppe Meazza receives the World Cup from French President Lebrun.

To many Giuseppe Meazza was the greatest European player of his generation. He was a striking figure with classical Italian good looks and slicked-back hair. He was a short man, but handsome, a dandy, a Latin lover, and, as Eduardo Galeano described him, "an elegant artilleryman of penalties." As a player Meazza was a versatile centre-forward, who knew exactly where the goal was and made the ball caress its net on hundreds of occasions.

Born in Milan on 23rd August 1910 "Peppino" Meazza began his career with Internazionale at the age of 17. One year later, in the 1928-29 season, he scored 33 goals. The following season, he became the Italian league's top scorer, a feat he managed to repeat on two further occasions, in 1936 and 1938. In February 1930, he made his debut for the Italian national side against Switzerland and scored two goals. He remained a constant member of the national side until the war in 1939.

At the World Cup of 1934, Vittorio Pozzo brought in Schiavio as the centre-forward and moved Meazza to inside-left. It was a tactic that proved instrumental in winning the cup. His efforts throughout the tournament were massive and his reward was to captain the Azzuri in France in 1938, where he was to score the goal that knocked out arch-rivals Spain. Only he and Ferrari remained from the triumphant 1934 team though they were joined by a number of players from the Italian Olympic Games side that won gold in Berlin in 1936. Meazza was moved back up front to partner centre-forward Silvio Piola at the heart of the Italian attack. His greatest contribution to the team's success, amongst many that year, was perhaps also the funniest moment of the tournament. It was the semi-final and Piola had been "felled" by Brazilian defender Domingos in the penalty area. What happened next has been recorded in a number of different ways but it is Eduardo Galeano's version that we are going to believe. Meazza's had ripped his shorts earlier in the game and it was believed these had fallen away after he had scored the penalty, but Galeano knows better: "His feet, as soft and knowing as hands, never missed. But Walter, the Brazilian goalie, was good at blocking penalty kicks, and felt confident. Meazza began his run up, and just when he was about to execute the kick, he dropped his shorts. The crowd was stupefied and the referee nearly swallowed his whistle. But Meazza, never pausing, grabbed his pants with one hand and sent the goalkeeper, disarmed by laughter, down to defeat."

Shortly after the World Cup, Meazza suffered an injury that was to keep him out of most of the 1938-39 Italian league season. On his return he moved from Internazionale to AC Milan, but he only managed a few games before leaving the club in 1942. He guested for Juventus and Varese, played a season for Atalanta in 1945, before returning to play occasionally for Inter in 1946. He managed the club in the 1947-48 season though with no great success. He died in 1979 at the age of 69. He had made 440 appearances in the Italian league and scored 269 goals. In 53 appearances for Italy he scored 33 goals and was a twice winner of the World Cup. He was so highly esteemed by Inter that their stadium was renamed in his honour. Unfortunately today, most still referred to it by its other name, the San Siro.

Silvio Piola

Italy

Honours: Winner 1938
Played: 1938

Games 4
Goals 5

Italy's Piola beats Brazil's Machado (left) and Domingos in the Italian's 2-1 semi-final victory in Marseille.

Silvio Piola was a prolific goal scorer, an aggressive hardworking centre-forward in the traditional style and he would surely have scored more than his incredible tally of 30 goals in 24 internationals had not World War Two got in the way.

Born on 29th September 1913 at Robbio Lomellini, he began his playing career with Pro Vercelli, where his feat of scoring six goals in a 7-2 defeat of Fiorentina in the 1933-34 season, earned him a considerable reputation. He then moved to Lazio where he stayed for eight years, further developing his reputation as a celebrated striker. Among his achievements he helped the club reach second spot in the 1936-37 season, their best ever inter-war placing, and he was the league's top scorer in 1937 and 1943. In all he scored 143 goals for Lazio, which is still the club record, and 290 in total in Serie A. Leaving Lazio, he had spells with Torino, Juventus and Navara and for all three he continued to find the mark. In 1951 Piola scored his 336th league goal to break the record formerly held by Giuseppe Meazza and by the time he retired in 1955 he had made 566 league appearances.

Piola made his international debut in 1935 and scored both goals in a 2-0 victory over Austria. He also acquired a reputation as something of an actor and two incidents from 1938 illustrate this point well. In the World Cup semi-final against Brazil, when the Italians were one goal to the good, he "suddenly collapsed as if he had been shot, and with the last flutter of life in his finger he pointed at Brazilian defender Domingos. The referee believed him and blew the whistle for a penalty." Piola got up, cleaned himself down and Meazza duly slotted home the penalty to put Italy into the final. Later that year he was picked to play against England in a friendly in Milan. He scored one of the goals in a 2-2 draw, but later admitted that he had punched the ball into the net. It would not be the only time that England fell victim to a "Hand of a God" goal.

He did not feature in Italy's 1950 World Cup teams and played his last international game in 1952, ironically against England. Following his retirement he had spells as manager of Lazio and coach of the Italian Under-23 side. He died on 4th October 1996 age 83.

Brazil 6 : Poland 5

As one football history book says, "the most extraordinary match of the World Cup - and perhaps of any World Cup - was between Poland and Brazil." "One has never seen such!", was one contemporary French newspaper's review of the game and it carried on its adulation this way: "It is more than ever the case for saying it. The Brazilians and Poles offered as prizes to the people of Strasbourg a feast without parallel." Using less showy language, the Gazeta Polska of Warsaw, noted that the match will stand "in the history of Polish football as one of our team's most exciting international meetings."

Quite simply, few expected a game of such enthralling, attractive football from two teams who, to most European followers of the game (and it must be remembered that France 1938 contained very few non-European participants), had no World Cup or recognized international pedigree to speak of. It was Poland's first visit to the World Cup finals and they had only got there on goal difference, above Yugoslavia. This was Brazil's third foray into the finals, but they had yet to show any of the form that would characterize their future involvement. They had hardly distinguished themselves in 1930 or 1934, though significantly, when losing to Spain in 1934, their goal had come from the foot of a young centre-forward by the name of Leónidas da Silva. Since then and unbeknown to the Europeans, the game in Brazil had made exceptional progress and the national team was becoming a power of some repute.

This was the proverbial "game of two halves", with Brazil dominating the earlier period of play. The Poles were a strong, physical side, but were outpaced and outplayed by the nimble, fleet-footed Brazilians. As the Polish correspondent quoted above noted of the forwards: "Szerfke was very slow, Piontek constantly late, you couldn't see Willimowski at all." Not surprisingly, with their goal under sustained pressure, the Poles succumbed and Leónidas gave his country a deserved lead in the 18th minute. So far, the Poles had been restricted to counter-attacks and had hardly presented a serious threat, but Ernst Willimowski grabbed a fortuitous equalizer when he found himself favourably placed in front of goal. The strike came against the run of play and it was not long before it was cancelled out. Two more scores from Leónidas gave Brazil a 3-1 half-time lead and every confidence that the match was already won.

The weather broke at half-time and it had a telling impact on the course of the match. The rain began as a light drizzle, but quickly became a heavy downpour and, as play went on in the second half, the pitch began to cut up. The mud swung the advantage Poland's way and restricted the ability of the Brazilians to practise their silky skills. First Pontiek and then Willimowski found the net to level the scores and, for the first time, the South Americans were looking decidedly vulnerable. This was, however, a game of infinite unpredictability and the renewed optimism of the Polish supporters was dashed when Peracio restored Brazil's lead as the game neared its end. It appeared all up for Poland until, with another dramatic twist of the tale, Willimowski popped up two minutes from the end to equalize once more with the afternoon's second hat trick.

At 4-4, the game went into extra time when the superior fitness of the Brazilians made the difference. The exertions of the second half had been too much and the gallant Poles began to tire. Once more, Brazil became quicker to the ball and from the start forced their opponents into defence. In only the third minute, Leónidas put his team back into the lead and, with the scent of victory in their nostrils, they turned up the pressure to prevent any relapse that might allow the Poles a second chance. When inside-right, Romeo, scored a sixth, the game was virtually secure. Yet, it was not completely dead because Willimowski scored his fourth to become, by 25 minutes, the second man to score four goals in the World Cup finals and provide a final inspirational rallying call to his team mates. They responded, but time was against them and they had little more to give. There were no more goals and the match ended 6-5 to Brazil.

It had been a phenomenal advert for the game and the competition. Totally thrilling from first to last, it had contained almost everything that could be desired from a football game: skill, strength, drama and goals galore. What is more, it had been played out in a thoroughly sporting manner. Afterwards, the Poles sent a telegramme to the Brazilian team congratulating them on the victory and wishing them luck for the rest of the tournament. Brazil had won because they had been the more skilful and, in the end, more resolute of the teams. The Poles had lacked experience, had played falteringly and been unable to sustain their best efforts, and, although Willimowski had played out of his skin in the second half, Poland lacked players of the calibre of Leónidas. They "were mentally too weak", was how the Gazeta Polska described Poland's footballers, an assessment that was echoed by an official from Poland's FA. "They played very nervously and that is why they lost", he said. Perhaps he was being too critical. They had come out of the game with much credit, as acknowledged by the president of Poland's FA, Colonel Glabisz. "We received an honourable result. . . Our boys did what they could. I think that we can consider our appearance in this championship as a success." Indeed, they could.

Brazil 1 : Czechoslovakia 1

This was a game that pitched together two of the more attractive teams in the tournament and was billed as the showcase opening of the new stadium in Bordeaux. It seemed to promise much, but nobody could have guessed at the travesty that awaited the 25,000 spectators who turned up in anticipation of a football festival. Bordeaux was a rugby town and the irony of this was not lost on the reporter from Le Figaro. He noted wryly that if "the city wishes to find in football the same pleasures as it does in rugby" then "it was not yesterday's game that will win for the round ball." Simply put, he was suggesting that the people of Bordeaux might just as well stick with rugby because this game more closely resembled the oval code than it did soccer. "We did not have good football", he lamented after a game "played with brutality like no other."

It has gone down as the "Battle of Bordeaux" and was one of the bloodiest encounters in the history of the World Cup. The trouble began shortly after the kick off. Zezé Precopio, keen to give early indication of his presence to the Czech forwards and warn them off, callously kicked Oldrich Nejedlý and was sent off. The Hungarian referee, Paul Van Hertzka, was also keen to stamp his authority on proceedings, but his action had the reverse effect. Far from nipping trouble in the bud, it precipitated it and from that point on, the match slid relentlessly into the quagmire. Hertzka never regained control.

On balance, the Brazilians played the better football, employing a game of "unstoppable activity" characterized by speed and decisiveness. The Czechs, on the other hand, "played hard, a little too hard, not to say brutally", though violence was never far from the surface in this friable atmosphere. There were outbursts all over the field, with players taking every opportunity to punch, kick or trip each other. Dribbling the ball became something of a lottery and being caught in possession was to risk injury. Understandably, scoring chances were at a premium, but with Brazil holding the slight upper hand, they had the ability to seize what little advantage came out of the carnage. With half an hour gone, Leónidas broke the deadlock with one of his customary strikes and just before the half-time whistle a fight broke out between Ríha and Machado, who had been winding each other up all half. Both were sent off. Brazil now had only nine men and Czechoslovakia ten, but they had a precious and, on balance, deserved lead.

When the players came out for the second half, tempers were still frayed. The Czechs were determined to get back into the game and the Brazilians were equally determined to stop them. The quality of the football deteriorated still further and anarchy continued to reign. In the 64th minute Domingos handled a Czech shot on the line and a penalty was awarded and put away by Nejedlý. It was about the only example of football in the half, the rest being a catalogue of misdemeanour. Not long after Nejedlý had his leg broken in a vicious attack and had to leave the field, whilst in another assault Plánicka had his arm broken. Neither sin received the punishment they deserved, but the Czech goalkeeper bravely played on. It says much about the character of the man. Fortunately, the nature of the game meant that he was not called upon to make any particularly testing saves and when the whistle went to end the period of normal play, scores were still tied.

Both teams began the extra time with only nine men, though several were carrying knocks that severely hindered their effectiveness. It meant that whilst the violence subsided a little, the standard of play saw no improvement. Brazil continued to look the better team, but the Czechs defended in number to protect their injured goalkeeper and nobody was able to find a way to goal. The game ended with a draw and much discredit to both sets of players. A sad indictment of this match is the fact that Brazil was only able to field two of its starting line up, goalkeeper Walter and Leónidas, for the replay two days later.

Italy 4 : Hungary 2
The World Cup Final

Italy 4 : Hungary 2.

Action in the Hungarian goalmouth as an Italian forward hits for goal.

Whilst Italy and Hungary were undoubtedly continental Europe's finest teams, the Italians had the edge in terms of preparation and match toughness. Pozzo had approached his task with his usual single-minded determination, shown by the way his team had negotiated their difficult passage to the final. The Hungarians had hardly had to break sweat to overcome the Dutch East Indies and it was not until the final that they encountered a team in their own class. The Hungarians also had two weaknesses that gave a decided advantage to Italy: an aversion to physical play, an Italian speciality, and a lack of fire power. They had scored 13 goals in reaching the final, but against much weaker opposition.

A pre-match incident serves well to illustrate how Pozzo would allow nothing to unsettle his plans. As the team coach made its way to the Stade Colombes in Paris, the streets became increasingly crowded by fans eager to see the match. When Pozzo realized that they were not going to get through without great difficulty, he ordered the driver to turn round and return to the team hotel. He did not want his team or their concentration upset by having to hang around on a coach in such a crowd. It was far better to have the players relax in the quiet and comfort of the hotel. They would attempt the journey when they could be certain the streets had emptied a little.

The match was not a classic, but it had moments of real inspiration, two of which happened inside the first seven minutes. The first break went to Italy with a move that "swept dazzlingly like lightening from one end of the pitch to the other," as one historian has described it and involving three of Italy's swashbuckling forwards. In the words of Le Figaro's football correspondent, typically in the journalistic style in vogue on the continent at that time, during "a break by right-winger Biatavi, he passed to Piola, who repassed to Colaussi, the left-wing, who with an impeccable shot, beat the goalkeeper, Szabo." The lead lasted a mere two minutes, ending when Hungary's talented centre-forward, György Sárosi, threaded a ball to the unmarked Titkos, who rammed home from a difficult angle.

The equalizer stung the Italians into tightening their game. They "combined Latin flair with Italian muscle, athleticism, and resolute defence", and Giuseppe Meazza, the captain and midfield maestro, began to assert his authority to swing the game in his team's favour. For the rest of the half, the Hungarians played second best and the Italians took full advantage of their dominance. In the 16th minute, Meazza fashioned a goal for Silvio Piola and then some ten minutes before the break he made another opening for Gino Colaussi to net his second.

Given the solid way with which Italy's defence had dealt with anything the Hungarians had been able to throw at them, their 3-1 half-time lead seemed sufficient and not unnaturally, they resorted to a more defensive style for the second half. It allowed the Hungarians back into the match with a series of raids that intensified as time went on. Yet, as Le Figaro's reporter inimically put it, "their initiatives were not happy." Italy's defence proved too rugged and robust, and they gave Hungary's forwards very little room for manoeuvre. The Hungarians

The victorious Italian team celebrate their World Cup victory.

mounted attack upon attack, but could not make them tell, and it was only the result of a mix-up in the Italian defence, "a short black-out" as the French reporter termed it, that they were able to find the target and reduce the deficit. It was Sárosi who was on hand to get the final touch, scoring in the seventieth minute.

Once again, the effect of the strike was to reawaken the attacking instincts of the Italians. They began to push and harry the tiring Hungarians and, with eight minutes to go, got the goal that put the result beyond doubt. It was the goal of the game, one of the finest of the tournament, and involved some devastating interchanges between Biavati and Piola. Together they ripped open the Hungarian defence and a delicate back heel pass to Piola allowed him to hit a hard shot along the ground to secure Italy's fourth goal and the game.

In the four years between 1934 and 1938, Italian football had won two World Cups and an Olympic gold medal, an achievement that few teams have been able to emulate. They had also won this second of their world titles in some style and had never looked like losing. They were always in control and were too powerful, too quick, too well organized, too clever and too determined for the Hungarians. Yet the magnitude of their victory only becomes apparent when set in its proper context. The Hungarians were a great team and their contribution to the game must not be ignored. As Le Figaro said: "One must... pay homage to the courage of the Hungarian players. Taken by speed and dominated from the start of the meeting, they never admitted to being beaten and sought goals whenever they could." That they only scored twice is testament to Italy's defensive qualities, but that they did score twice is testament to the merit of their forwards.

Statistics - France 1938

FIRST ROUND

Paris, June 4th - Parc de Princes

After extra time - 45 mins (1-1), 90 mins (1-1), 120 mins 1-1

1 (1) GERMANY

Gauchel 29

Raftl, Janes, Schmaus, Kupfer, Mock, Kitzinger, Lehner, Gellesch, Gauchel, Hahnemann, Pesser (RED).

1 (1) SWITZERLAND

Abegglen III 43

Huber, Minelli, Lehmann, Springer, Vernati, Lörtscher, Amado, Walaschek, Bickel, Abegglen III, Aebi.

Referee: Jean Langenus (Belgium)
Attendance: 30.000

Replay - Paris, June 9th - Parc de Princes

4 (1) SWITZERLAND

Walaschek 41, Bickel 64, Abegglen III 75,78

Huber, Minelli, Lehmann, Springer, Vernati, Lörtscher, Amado, Walaschek, Bickel, Abegglen III, Aebi.

2 (2) GERMANY

Hahnemann 8, Lörtscher (og) 22

Raftl, Janes, Streitle, Kupfer, Goldbrunner, Skoumal, Lehner, Stroh, Szepan, Hahnemann, Neumer.

Referee: Ivan Eklind (Sweden)
Attendance: 22.000

Toulouse, June 5th - Stade Chapou

After extra time - 45 mins (1-1), 90 mins (2-2), 120 mins 3-3

3 (2) CUBA

Socorro 45,103, Maquina 69

Carvajeles, Barquin, Chorens, Arias, Rodríguez, Berges, Maquina, Fernández, Socorro, Tunas, Sosa.

3 (2) ROMANIA

Bindea 35, Baratki 59, Dobai 105

Pavlovici, Bürger, Cossini, Chiroiu, Rasinaru, Rafinski, Bindea, Kovacs, Baratki, Bodola, Dobai.

Referee: Giovanni Scarpi (Italy)
Attendance: 6.000

Replay - Toulouse, June 9th - Stade Chapou

2 (0) CUBA

Socorro 68, Maquina 80

Ayra, Barquin, Chorens, Arias, Rodríguez, Berges, Maquina, Fernández, Socorro, Tunas, Sosa.

1 (1) ROMANIA

Dobai 9

Sadowski, Bürger, Felecan, Barbulescu, Rasinaru, Rafinski, Bogden, Moldoveanu, Baratki, Prassler, Dobai.

Referee: Alfred Birlem (Germany)
Attendance: 5.000

Le Havre, June 5th - Stade de la Cavée Verte

After extra time - 45 mins (0-0), 90 mins (0-0), 120 mins 3-0

3 (0) CZECHOSLOVAKIA

Koštálek 96, Nejedlý 111, Zeman 119

Plánicka, Bürgr, Daucik, Koštálek, Boucek, Kopecky, Riha, Simunek, Zeman, Nejedlý, Puc.

0 (0) HOLLAND

Van Male, Weber, Caldenhove, Paawe, Anderiesen, Van Heel, Wels, Van der Veen, Smit, Vente, De Harder.

Referee: Lucien Leclercq (France)
Attendance: Unknown

Paris, June 5th - Stade Colombes

3 (2) FRANCE

Veinante 1, Nicolas 12,69

Di Lorto, Cazenave, Mattler, Bastien, Jordan, Diagne, Aston, Heisserer, Nicolas, Delfour, Veinante.

1 (1) BELGIUM

Isemborghs 38

Badjou, Paverick, Seys, Van Alphen, Stijnen, De Winter, Van de Wouwer, Voorhoof, Isemborghs, Braine, Buyle.

Referee: Hans Wuthrich (Switzerland)
Attendance: Unknown

Reims, June 5th - Stade Velodrome Municipal

6 (4) HUNGARY

Kohut 18, Toldi 23, Sárosi 28,77, Zsengeller 38,52

Hada, Koranyi, Biro, Lazar, Turai, Balogh, Sas, Zsengeller, Sárosi, Toldi, Kohut.

0 (0) DUTCH EAST INDIES

Mo Heng, Hu Kom, Samuels, Nawir, Meng, Anwar, Hong Dijen, Soedarmadji, Sommers, Pattiwael, Taihuttu.

Referee: M.Conrie (France)
Attendance: Unknown

Marseilles, June 5th - Stade Velodrome

After extra time - 45 mins (1-0), 90 mins (1-1), 120 mins 2-1

2 (1) ITALY

Ferrari 2, Piola 94

Olivieri, Monzeglio, Rava, Serantoni, Andreolo, Locatelli, Pasinati, Meazza, Piola, Ferrari, Ferraris II.

1 (1) NORWAY

Brustad 83

Johansen, Johannesen, Holmsen, Henriksen, Eriksen, Holmberg, Frantzen, Kvammen, Brynildsen, Isaksen, Brustad.

Referee: Alois Beranek (Germany)
Attendance: Unknown

Strasbourg, June 5th - Stade de la Meinau

After extra time - 45 mins (3-1), 90 mins (4-4), 120 mins 6-5

6 (4) BRAZIL

Leónidas 18,25,44,93, Peracio 72, Romeo 102

Batatais, Domingos, Machado, Zezé Procopio, Martim Silveira, Alfonsinho, López, Romeo, Leónidas, Peracio, Hercules.

5 (4) POLAND

Willimowski 22,60,88,118, Piontek 50

Madejski, Szczepaniak, Galecki, Gora, Nyc, Dytko, Piec I, Piontek, Szerfke, Willimowski, Wodarz.

Referee: Ivan Eklind (Sweden)
Attendance: Unknown

SECOND ROUND

Paris, June 12th - Stade Colombes

3 (1) ITALY

Colaussi 10, Piola 52,72

Olivieri, Foni, Rava, Serantoni, Andreolo, Locatelli, Biavati, Meazza, Piola, Ferrari, Colaussi.

1 (1) FRANCE

Heisserer 11

Di Lorto, Cazenave, Mattler, Bastien, Jordan, Diagne, Aston, Heisserer, Nicolas, Delfour, Veinante.

Referee: Louis Baert (Belgium)
Attendance: 58.000

Antibes, June 12th - Stade du Fort Carré

8 (4) SWEDEN

H.Andersson 15, Jonasson 32, Wetterström 37,44,52,90, Keller 54, Nyberg 60

Abrahamsson, Eriksson, Källgren, Almgren, Jacobsson, Svanström, Wetterström, Keller, H.Andersson, Jonasson, Nyberg.

0 (0) CUBA

Carvajeles, Barquin, Chorens, Arias, Rodríguez, Berges, Ferrer, Fernández, Socorro, Tunas, Alonzo.

Referee: M.Kirst (Czechoslovakia)
Attendance: Unknown

Lille, June 12th - Stade Victor Boucquey

2 (1) HUNGARY

Zsengeller 42,68

Szabó, Koranyi, Biro, Lazar, Turai, Szalay, Sas, Zsengeller, Sárosi, Vincze, Kohut.

0 (0) SWITZERLAND

Huber, Stelzer, Lehmann, Springer, Vernati, Lörtscher, Amado, Walaschek, Bickel, Abegglen III, Grassi.

Referee: Rinaldo Barlassina (Italy)
Attendance: Unknown

Bordeaux, June 12th - Parc de Lescure

After extra time - 45 mins (1-0), 90 mins (1-1), 120 mins 1-1

1 (1) BRAZIL

Leónidas 31

Walter, Domingos, Machado (RED), Zezé Procopio (RED), Martim Silveira, Alfonsinho, López, Romeo, Leónidas, Peracio, Hercules.

1 (1) CZECHOSLOVAKIA

Nejedlý (pen)64

Plánicka, Bürgr, Daucik, Koštálek, Boucek, Kopecky, Riha (RED), Simunek, Ludl, Nejedlý, Puc.

Referee: Paul Van Hertzka (Hungary)
Attendance: 25.000

Replay - Bordeaux, June 14th - Parc de Lescure

2 (0) BRAZIL

Leónidas 56, Roberto 62

Walter, Jau, Nariz, Brito, Brandao, Argemiro, Roberto, Luizinho, Leónidas, Tim, Patesko.

1 (1) CZECHOSLOVAKIA

Kopecky 30

Burket, Bürgr, Daucik, Koštálek, Boucek, Kopecky, Kreutz, Horak, Ludl, Senecky, Rulc.

Referee: Georges Capdeville (France)
Attendance: Unknown

SEMI-FINALS

Marseilles, June 16th - Stade Velodrome

2 (0) ITALY

Colaussi 55, Meazza (pen)60

Olivieri, Foni, Rava, Serantoni, Andreolo, Locatelli, Biavati, Meazza, Piola, Ferrari, Colaussi.

1 (0) BRAZIL

Romeo 87

Walter, Domingos, Machado, Zezé Procopi, Martim Silveira, Alfonsinho, López, Luizinho, Peracio, Romeo, Patesko.

Referee: Hans Wuthrich (Switzerland)
Attendance: 35.000

Paris, June 16th - Parc de Princes

5 (3) HUNGARY

Zsengeller 18,38,77, Titkos 26, Sárosi 61

Szabó, Koranyi, Biro, Szalay, Turai, Lazar, Sas, Zsengeller, Sárosi, Toldi, Titkos.

1 (1) SWEDEN

Nyberg 1

Abrahamsson, Eriksson, Källgren, Almgren, Jacobsson, Svanström, Wetterström, Keller, H.Andersson, Jonasson, Nyberg.

Referee: Lucien Leclercq (France)
Attendance: 17.000

3RD/4TH PLACE PLAY-OFF

Bordeaux, June 19th - Parc de Lescure

4 (1) BRAZIL

Romeo 43, Leónidas 63,73, Peracio 80

Batatais, Domingos, Machado, Zezé Procopio, Brandao, Alfonsinho, Roberto, Leónidas, Peracio, Romeo, Patesko.

2 (2) SWEDEN

Jonasson 18, Nyberg 38

Abrahamsson, Eriksson, Nilsson, Almgren, Linderholm, Svanström, Perssen, A.Andersson, H.Andersson, Jonasson, Nyberg.

Referee: Jean Langenus (Belgium)
Attendance: Unknown

FINAL

Paris, June 19th - Stade Colombes

4 (3) ITALY

Colaussi 6,35, Piola 15,80

Olivieri, Foni, Rava, Serantoni, Andreolo, Locatelli, Biavati, Meazza, Piola, Ferrari, Colaussi.

2 (1) HUNGARY

Titkos 8, Sárosi 70

Szabó, Polgar, Biro, Szalay, Szücs, Lazar, Sas, Zsengeller, Sárosi, Vincze, Titkos.

Referee: Georges Capdeville (France)
Attendance: 55.000

QUALIFICATION ROUNDS

Europe - Group 1

	P	W	D	L	F	A	Pts
Germany	3	3	0	0	11	1	6
Sweden	3	2	0	1	11	7	4
Estonia	3	1	0	2	4	11	2
Finland	3	0	0	3	0	7	0

16-06-1937	Sweden : Finland	4:0 (0:0)
20-06-1937	Sweden : Estonia	7:2 (3:2)
29-06-1937	Finland : Germany	0:2 (0:2)
19-08-1937	Finland : Estonia	0:1 (0:0)
29-08-1937	Germany : Estonia	4:1 (0:1)
21-11-1937	Germany : Sweden	5:0 (2:0)

Europe - Group 2

	P	W	D	L	F	A	Pts
Norway	2	1	1	0	6	5	3
Ireland Rep.	2	0	1	2	5	6	1

| 10-10-1937 | Norway : Ireland Republic | 3:2 (2:1) |
| 07-11-1937 | Ireland Republic : Norway | 3:3 (1:2) |

Europe - Group 3

	P	W	D	L	F	A	Pts
Poland	2	1	0	1	4	1	2
Yugoslavia	2	1	0	1	1	4	2

| 10-10-1937 | Poland : Yugoslavia | 4:0 (2:0) |
| 03-04-1938 | Yugoslavia : Poland | 1:0 (0:0) |

Europe - Group 4

	P	W	D	L	F	A	Pts
Switzerland	1	1	0	0	2	1	2
Portugal	1	0	0	1	1	2	0

| 01-05-1938 | Switzerland : Portugal | 2:1 (2:0) |
| Played in Milan |

Europe - Group 5

	P	W	D	L	F	A	Pts
Greece	3	2	0	1	5	12	4
Hungary	1	1	0	0	11	1	2
Palestine	2	0	0	2	1	4	0

22-01-1938	Palestine : Greece	1:3 (1:2)
20-02-1938	Greece : Palestine	1:0 (0:0)
25-03-1938	Hungary : Greece	11:1 (7:1)

Europe - Group 6

	P	W	D	L	F	A	Pts
Czech	2	1	1	0	7	1	3
Bulgaria	2	0	1	1	1	7	1

| 07-11-1937 | Bulgaria : Czechoslovakia | 1:1 (0:1) |
| 24-04-1938 | Czechoslovakia : Bulgaria | 6:0 (1:0) |

Europe - Group 7

	P	W	D	L	F	A	Pts
Latvia	3	2	0	1	10	5	4
Austria	1	1	0	0	2	1	2
Lithuania	2	0	0	2	3	9	0

29-07-1937	Latvia : Lithuania	4:2 (2:0)
03-09-1937	Lithuania : Latvia	1:5 (0:4)
05-10-1937	Austria : Latvia	2:1 (2:1)

Europe - Group 8

	P	W	D	L	F	A	Pts
Netherlands	2	1	1	0	5	1	3
Belgium	2	1	1	0	4	3	3
Luxembourg	2	0	0	2	2	7	0

28-11-1937	Netherlands : Luxembourg	4:0 (1:0)
13-03-1938	Luxembourg : Belgium	2:3 (2:1)
03-04-1938	Belgium : Netherlands	1:1 (0:1)

Chapter 6

Pride comes before a Fall for the Mighty
The Brazil World Cup, 1950

Brazil 1950

Winners: Uruguay

Runners-up: Brazil

3rd Place: Sweden

4th Place: Spain

Total Attendance: 1,091,230

Number of Matches: 22

The 1950 World Cup was played under the shadow of the Korean War, which broke out when Communist North Korea invaded the South on 25th June, only hours after the tournament kicked off. The victory of Mao's Communists in China in 1949 and the anti-Communist "witch hunts" of Senator Joseph McCarthy, which accused hundreds of un-American activities, ensured that American troops would play a decisive roll in the war, as their footballers would in the World Cup. In China, Mao rang the changes by outlawing polygamy and the sale of children and in Britain a blow was struck for Scottish national pride when the Stone of Scone disappeared from Westminster Abbey. It had been used to crown the monarchs of England since Edward I had stolen it from the Scots some 650 years before and the police naturally began their search for it in Scotland.

The war in Korea was not the only development that would bring irreversible changes to the world. The colour television had been invented and scientists were experimenting with computers the size of houses. On the cultural front, Marilyn Monroe was about to make her Big Screen debut, whilst Frank Sinatra was wooing audiences across the world with his silky Italian-American charms. Dan Dare made his first appearance when the Eagle comic hit the shelves of British newsagents in April and motor racing crowds were being thrilled by the exploits Argentinian Juan Manuel Fangio. Another Latin to hit the headlines that year was legendary Italian bandit Salvatore Giuliano, who was betrayed and gunned down by police and in Brazil the players gathered to celebrate FIFA's fourth world Cup.

It had been on the opening day of the 1938 World Cup finals that FIFA met in Paris to discuss the venue of the next tournament. Brazil and Germany had applied to host the competition and it presented the world body with a dilemma. Germany could present a strong case, having recently, with seeming success, overseen the running of the 1936 Olympic Games. Bombastic Nazi propaganda, presenting an image of a nascent people, living happily and harmoniously with its new order, and proud of its achievements, reinforced this claim. Many in 1938, among them some of the most influential people, went along with this myth. Ignoring the nastier features of Nazism and chosing to see only the positive, they were anxious to appease Germany to undo the wrongs that had been inflicted upon her after World War One. The award of the World Cup would be one such step, especially since France and Italy had recently been so honoured. Such people were keen that Hitler should be not insulted by a refusal of Germany's offer.

However, Brazil's claim was also a good one. The country was becoming recognized as one of the great football powers and, with Europe having hosted the second and third tournaments, many felt that South America should be the venue of the fourth. Furthermore, Brazil's application was not tainted by the political considerations that surrounded that of Germany. Hitler may have had his defenders and apologists, but he had his critics too. The savage treatment of the Jews and political opponents in Germany could be cited against him, and Germany's foreign policy was becoming increasingly alarming. His large-scale rearmament programme, in clear breach of international obligations; his tacit support of Mussolini's invasion and conquest of Abyssinia in 1935; and his remilitarisation of the Rhineland in 1936, all pointed to a greater adventurousness on the part of Hitler. Yet, these could be presented as Germany breaking free from the unfair and irksome restrictions imposed after World War One. More sinister, though, were the Rome-Berlin Axis alliance with Italy, his invasion of Austria in March of that year, and his more recent threats against Czechoslovakia. To reward such militarism with the World Cup would, it was felt, send out the wrong signals. No such baggage accompanied Brazil's offer.

Being unable to resolve the dilemma in 1938, and facing a worrying and uncertain international situation, FIFA decided to put off its decision. It was agreed that the hosts would be chosen at the 1940 FIFA Congress scheduled to be held in Luxembourg. In the meantime, Argentina put in an application to stage the event, but then the Second World War broke out, forcing an indefinite postponement of plans for the next World Cup.

The next FIFA Congress did not open until 1st July 1946, a year after the war in Europe had ended. Much of continental Europe had been shattered by the conflict and, not only did this prohibit any chance of a European country hosting the World Cup, but also seriously limited the probable number of European entrants. It was decided that the next tournament would go ahead in 1949 and, since by now only Brazil was still prepared to serve as host nation, the award was uncontested. It was also decided to give the next tournament to Switzerland.

The decision to go to Brazil was a logical one, even though in the end it was to prove something of a mistake. Europe was in disarray, whilst South American football had been largely unaffected by the devastating events going on elsewhere. The South American championship had been business as usual and with Brazil winning the title in 1949, the country seemed to be going football crazy. Then, there was the promise of a spectacular new stadium. In 1946, Brazil appeared to be a wise choice and FIFA could feel satisfied with the award.

They also had other reasons for feeling optimistic about the future. The four British FAs had opted to rejoin the fold earlier in the year and had therefore become eligible to compete in the World Cup for the first time. To celebrate the occasion a representative international match was played at Hampden Park in Glasgow between Great Britain and the rest of Europe, a scratch team that was skippered by Johnny Carey, Manchester United's Irish international. In a Britain keen to forget the rigours of the war years and starved of first class football for the duration, 135,000 people turned up to see Great Britain run out easy 6-1 victors. Everton's Tommy Lawton and Middlesbrough's Wilf Mannion, two of the great contemporary names in British football, both scored twice, but far more significantly for FIFA, it was granted the gate receipts. For the first time in its history, the world organization was financially secure. Out of gratefulness, and happy that the British were back, FIFA designated the home championship, the annual competition between the four British nations as qualifying Group One. It was also at the 1946 Congress that the trophy was renamed the Jules Rimet Trophy, in recognition of the great man's contribution to the world game.

Although scheduled for 1949, it was decided to use the South American championships of that year as a dress rehearsal for the World Cup and the tournament was put back to 1950. The qualifying stage got underway in June 1949, but long before a ball was kicked, problems began to bedevil its smooth running. Almost as if to presage the main event itself, the qualifying rounds turned into little short of a farce as team after team withdrew, some without playing a game and some after reaching the finals.

The chilly wind of international politics was one of the factors that plagued FIFA and its competition. By 1949, Europe had become divided into Communist Eastern Europe, controlled by Stalin's USSR, and democratic Western Europe, supported by the USA. There seemed to be no

One of the nicest stories to come out of the build-up to the 1950 tournament concerned Jimmy Taylor of Fulham and England. Prior to the tournament his wife, Marguerite, had given birth to a son Robert, but the only time Taylor had seen him was when he had peered over the cot side to see his little face poking out from under the blankets. Soon after the birth, Taylor had gone off on a FA tour of Canada before joining his England team mates in Rio. Marguerite did not want her husband to have to wait three months before seeing the baby again so she took pictures of him and had them flown out to Brazil. Helpfully, the Daily Herald, now the Sun, kindly flew them to Canada so he did not have to wait until Rio. As it turned out, Taylor did not play in a World Cup match until Switzerland in 1954.

The Maracana Stadium

On 2nd August 1948 football mad Brazil decided it was time to build what they hoped would be the biggest and finest football stadium in the world in readiness for the World Cup. After all, they were convinced they would win it and needed a fitting venue for the occasion. The Maracana Stadium was to be built in the suburbs of Rio de Janeiro and have a capacity of 220,000. However, the deadline for completion proved a little to ambitious, schedules were not met and, five weeks before the opening game of the tournament the organizers began to panic. FIFA decided to send someone to help them out and he was Ottorino Barrasi who had so effectively organized the second World Cup Finals in Italy in 1934.

On 24th June 1950 the Maracana Stadium was inaugurated although for the most part it still resembled a building site. It certainly wasn't going to hold 220,00 people and there was no press stand. However, it was ready to hold the World Cup finals and to witness some fine matches.

Pride comes before a Fall for the Mighty - Brazil 1950

Indian Team Withdraw

The draw for the 1950 World Cup finals was made on 23rd May. Group Three was to be contested between the teams from Italy, Sweden, Paraguay and India. On 24th May however, India withdrew. The reason for the withdrawal is not fully clear. The English press reported that the All-Indian Football Federation would not send a team and gave as the reason that Brazil's offer of air transport to the Indians had come too late, having arrived only a week before the draw was made. This would not give the players enough time to prepare adequately for the tournament. Their qualification had been because the other members of the group had withdrawn earlier. The favoured reason for the Indian team's withdrawal, given by most books, is that FIFA would not allow the team to compete barefoot.

The first World Cup match in the post-war era was that between Yugoslavia and Israel, on 18th August, 1949. The Yugoslavs won 11-2 on aggregate.

---

middle ground as both sides glared at each other across the Iron Curtain. Its effect on international football was damaging and almost immediate. Two of Europe's finest teams, Hungary and Czechoslovakia, both suffered the steely fist of hard-line Stalinist regimes and refused to enter. When the USSR itself decided to do the same, other Eastern European Communist countries followed suit leaving only Yugoslavia from the region in the tournament. Its leader, Marshall Tito, was in dispute with Stalin, who had unsuccessfully tried to dictate policy there. Tito would have none of it and his stand of independence was reflected in Yugoslavia's decision to compete for a place in Brazil.

Other teams that withdrew without kicking a ball were Indonesia, Burma and the Philippines, who pulled out before the qualifying draw was made. They were followed by Argentina, whose FA was in dispute with that of Brazil, Ecuador and Peru. This meant that Bolivia, Chile, Paraguay and Uruguay qualified for the finals without playing a match. In Group Two, Turkey defeated Syria to win the right to play Austria for a place in the finals, only for Austria to withdraw. Their excuse was that the team was too young and inexperienced to have any chance of mounting a viable challenge for the trophy. Then Turkey also withdrew. A similar story occurred in Group Four where Switzerland and Luxembourg played off over two legs to see who would meet Belgium in a head-to-head. Switzerland won through only for Belgium to withdraw, handing the group's place to the Swiss. It was an incredible list of self-inflicted wounds, such as would never happen today, but it was not the end of it.

Qualifying Group One was the British home championship, the first ever World Cup matches on United Kingdom soil and involving United Kingdom teams. Generously, FIFA had declared that places in Brazil would go to the top two teams, but the Scottish FA, in an inexplicable outburst of ill-placed national pride, stated that they would only travel to South America as British champions. The championship went down to the last game of the series, played at Hampden Park on 15th April 1950 and Scotland, the reigning champions, only needed a draw to secure top spot. They were unlucky not to take the lead when a shot from Willie Bauld bounced off the bar and on to the goal line. It did not go in and Roy Bentley scored to give England a narrow 1-0 victory and the championship. With Scotland in second place, their FA stubbornly stuck to its misguided principles and, in spite of pleas from both English and Scottish players alike, would not reverse its decision. So it was that Scotland qualified for its first World Cup finals, but did not take its place.

With so many teams deciding not to compete, FIFA began anxiously to look around for countries to fill vacant places and make up the numbers. France and Portugal were both invited to fill the spots left empty by Scot-

England captain Billy Wright (centre) and Stan Mortensen (left) before they fly to Rio de Janeiro.

land and Turkey. The Portuguese, who had been defeated by Spain in Group Six declined, but the French accepted. The FFF then looked at the schedule their team would have to face in Brazil and the thousands of miles that would have to be travelled to fulfil the commitment, and decided that it was simply too much to ask. They also withdrew and, since there was not enough time to organize any replacements, it left just thirteen nations in the finals.

The Brazilian World Cup has been described as "the most chaotic, disorganized and ramshackle tournament in the event's history", and the peculiar number of teams competing gives one reason to explain this. The knock-out format used previously could not be repeated and FIFA reverted to the group system first used in Uruguay in 1930, though with one significant difference. In Uruguay, the organizers had at least tried to create groups of roughly equal size out of the thirteen competitors, but this did not happen in Brazil. Absurdly, the teams were organized into two groups of four, one group of three and another of two. It was a most illogical formula and certainly did not give equal opportunity to each side. It was as if the confidence of the Brazilian organizers was such that they felt the others were merely there to make up the numbers and that the format was an irrelevance.

The grouping of teams was one organizational fault of Brazil 1950. Another was the playing schedule. Little thought seems to have been given to this aspect and teams were not based in particular areas to play their matches in that region. Instead, fixtures were allocated all over the country, one of the largest in the world, and each team could expect to travel thousands of miles, and none too easily, to meet their commitments. In such circumstances, it is difficult to keep players in top physical and mental condition, another factor that plagued this World Cup.

In spite of the non-completion of the Maracana Stadium, things got underway as expected on 24th June with a fanfare opening before 81,000 adoring fans. It was a spectacular occasion that involved a 21-gun salute, a fireworks display and the release of 5,000 pigeons. The Pool One game, for which all of this was merely the hors d'ouvres, was something of a one-sided affair and saw Brazil defeat Mexico very comfortably. The Brazilians were one of the teams which, alongside England, were felt to have any realistic chance of winning the championship. They were the only nation to have played in each World Cup so far and the 1950 team was capable of producing dashing, charismatic football that, at its best, few could live with. The style with which they won the 1949 South American championship had been as decisive as any seen in an international tournament and they had scored 46 goals in 8 matches. Along the way, they had beaten Ecuador 9-1, Bolivia 10-1, Colombia 5-0 and Peru 7-1 and in Ademir Marques de Menezes and Jair Pinto, they had players of truly devastating class. Yet, the Brazilians were also capable of woeful underperformance as their final South American championship game against Paraguay in Rio illustrated. They lost it 2-1 and the result meant that both teams tied the championship with twelve points each. A play-off was needed to decide the title and the Brazilians won it 7-0. It was the ridiculous to the sublime, revealing an unpredictability brought about by their carefree, yet zestful approach to the game.

As one book has said, "the winning of the World Cup has become an obsession for everybody involved in Brazilian football", and this obsession

---

The First World Cup Goal scored in the United Kingdom

The honour for the first World Cup goal to be scored on United Kingdom soil was taken by Henry Morris in Belfast on 11th October 1949. Scotland defeated Northern Ireland 8-2 and Morris, in his first full international, scored a hat trick. It was the first World Cup game to be played on UK soil. The first World Cup game to be played in Great Britain (which excludes Northern Ireland) was in Cardiff on 15th October 1949 when England beat Wales 4-1. The first World Cup game to be played in England happened in Manchester on 16th November 1949 and saw England defeat Northern Ireland 9-0.

Prior to the World Cup finals there was a heatwave in Rio de Janeiro and temperatures reached 84°F, even though it was winter.

To get into the Municipal Stadium in Rio cost the general public 30 pence a ticket. Soldiers and boys were charged 20 pence.

The win bonus for a Brazilian player in 1950 was £200. They would receive £1000 if they won the final.

Pride comes before a Fall for the Mighty - Brazil 1950

The Brazilian team that lost to Uruguay 2-1 in the final pool match.

can be traced back to 1950. A world championship was nothing less than their fanatical supporters demanded and it was what they expected, so much so that overconfidence is probably the best description of the Brazilian mood. It was a mood that was not dimmed by their display against Mexico in that opening game. One of the busiest men on the field was Antonio Carbajal, the Mexican goalkeeper, who was to make World Cup history by appearing in five consecutive World Cups between 1950 and 1966. From the start, Brazil had the Mexicans on the ropes, though it was 30 minutes before they broke through with a goal from Ademir, one of the finest

players in the world and another in the growing list of brilliant Brazilians who have illuminated the world stage. It was fitting that he should have scored the tournament's opening goal. Three more second half goals, from Jair, Baltazar and a second from Ademir, gave Brazil a 4-0 victory. It had been very easy and convincing for the home team.

Four games were played on the following day and with one of these came England's debut in the finals of a World Cup. The English had a team brimming with talent from back to front. In goal was Bert Williams of Wolverhampton Wanderers, in defence there was Tottenham Hotspur's Alf Ramsey, whilst the front line was replete with names that have become legends of British football - Wilf Mannion, Tom Finney, Stan Mortensen and, of course, the incomparable Stanley Matthews. Many people saw this as the finest national side in the world and justly they were hailed as one of the favourites to win the title. (See Stanley Matthews profile on page 91, Tom Finney profile on page 92 and Alf Ramsey profile on page 93).

However, the England team lacked World Cup experience and were not well prepared physically or mentally for what they would encounter. As Preston's Tom Finney later recalled: "When I think back now to the World Cup, we had a three - or - four day get together in London after a hard season, and hard grounds at that time of year, and we went off then and stopped in Rio right on the Copacabana beach, in a hotel where you were very fortunate to get any sleep with the noise that was going on. It was early hours and there were car horns blaring away...." Then there was the heat, a new factor for many English players and Wilf Mannion later noted its effects. "You got out there," he said, "into a climate where you needed to be a few weeks, after having had a hard season, just walking about maybe, but he had you training in the heat.... It was all against us."

Much was amiss, then, in the English camp and it told in their opening game against Chile, was a team made up largely of amateurs and containing only one professional, the centre-forward George Robledo, who was to enjoy much success at Newcastle United. It was a match that England were expected to win, and this they did. Playing in the rain, Blackpool's Stan Mortensen put his team ahead in the 38th minute with a header from a Jimmy Mullen cross. However, the English were far from confident and, as the Times reporter said, "the England attack never really settled down and the defence found the Chilean forwards fast and tricky." Chile might easily have taken the lead before half time when first Carvalho hit the crossbar and then Robledo hit the post, but the English held on to their slender advantage. They were more creative in the second period, when the English themselves hit the crossbar twice and both Bentley and Mortensen came close with headers. However, the game was not secured until seven minutes from time. Mortensen passed the ball out to Finney on the wing. He then picked out Mannion, who "placed a low shot neatly inside the post." Admittedly, Matthews was not playing, but this does not excuse a below par performance from a team of such star quality. Warning bells should have been sounded, but they were not, and things were to get much worse for England's World Cup party.

22 Men and a Bag of Wind

Whilst the English were making things difficult for themselves in Rio, about 200 miles to the north, on a ground that was to be of a decisive significance for England's World Cup challenge, the Yugoslavians were finding the going much easier. Theirs, too, was a team of much ability and had won the silver medal at the 1948 London Olympic Games, losing 3-1 to Sweden in the final after having defeated Luxembourg, Turkey and Great Britain to get there. Only weeks before this World Cup clash, they had defeated their opponents, Switzerland, 4-0 in an international in Berne and they had no difficulty dispatching the Swiss a second time in this Pool One game. Two first half goals in quick succession from Kosta Tomasevic set the victory up and a third from Ognjanov near the end of the match secured it.

In this game, the Swiss skipper, Alfred Bickel, made history for being one of only two players to have appeared in World Cup finals before and after the war, having also played in 1938. The other was Nilsson of Sweden, who was playing in São Paulo against Italy in a Pool Three game that was as significant as any played that day. Italy's Hungarian-born coach, Lajos Czeizler, had struggled to rebuild the team after Superga and his was a team lacking in confidence. They had even gone to Brazil by sea to avoid flying. The Swedes, on the other hand, were a team of fighters. Their English coach, George Raynor, had built a solid outfit and though purely amateur, they had some pedigree. They had won gold in the 1948 Olympic Games and had played some excellent football, scoring 22 goals in 4 matches. The only cloud on their horizon was that some of their best players had been poached by Italian clubs and were ineligible to play in Brazil. They went behind to a 7th minute goal from Italy's captain, Carapellese, but made a good response through Hans Jeppson and Sune Andersson to take a 2-1 half time lead. Some 15 minutes after the interval, Jeppson scored again and it was now Italy's turn to fight back. Seven minutes later, Muccinelli scored for Italy, but try as they might, they could not do it again. Their 3-2 defeat was the first World Cup game Italy had lost.

The fourth match played on 25th June was another Pool Two confrontation, between Spain and the USA. American football had waned since 1930, but they took a surprising first half lead, through a John Souza goal, and they valiantly defended it for the next hour or so. They had to soak up an enormous amount of Spanish pressure and their Belgian-born half-back, Joe Macca, had an exceptional game. Eventually they buckled and Spain scored three times in the last ten minutes to take the victory. It was the first of these goals, scored by Basora in the 80th minute that did the real damage. The Americans lost their composure, and two minutes later Basora scored his second. Three minutes after that the game was well and truly lost when Zarra netted Spain's third. The Americans had given a gritty performance against a technically more gifted side, but the end result was fair given the degree of Spain's dominance.

For their second game, against Switzerland, Brazil's coach Flavio Costa made a tactical blunder, which almost backfired and brought the wrath of the crowd about his head. Since the match was to be played in São Paulo, he opted away from his usual team and promoted several local players into the starting line up to make the expected victory even sweeter. Although, they took the lead early in the game, when Alfredo Ramos de Santos scored the tournament's fastest goal, the Swiss rallied strongly and after just a quarter of an hour equalized through Jacques Fatton. It was a

Floodlights were only to be used at a game if both teams agreed. When England faced Chile in Rio on 24th June England disagreed and the kick-off time was brought forward to 3.00pm. It went dark at 5.30pm, the set kick-off time.

One of the rules for the tournament stated that, should a team be more than one minute late onto the pitch for the start of a game, they would be disqualified.

The Superga Disaster

Although the Italians went to Brazil in 1950 as reigning world champions, few serious pundits gave them any realistic chance of retaining the title. On 4th May 1949 Italian football had suffered a major tragedy when an aircraft carrying the Torino Football Club crashed into the Superga Basillica in the suburbs of Turin, killing all 31 passengers. The team was returning home from Lisbon, having undertaken a tour of Portugal, when the plane encountered bad weather above Turin. Low cloud and rain caused poor visibility and the pilot accidently approached the city too low. He caught a wing against the Superga Hill and the craft cashed into the gardens of the historic basillica that lies there. According to the Times: "Flames immediately spurted from the wing and none of the occupants could be saved." In all 31 people were killed, including all 17 of the players, 4 team attendants, 3 journalists and 7 crew members. Of the players, 8 of them were internationals, 7 of whom had played against England in Italy's 4-0 defeat in Turin the previous May.

Among those killed was Valentin Mazzola, the father of Alessandro Mazzola, who represented his country in the 1966 World Cup finals. Another was Leslie Lievesley, the British team trainer, who had played professional football at Manchester United. Such a heavy death toll devastated both club and national team and it would be years before either fully recovered from the tragedy.

Pride comes before a Fall for the Mighty - Brazil 1950

total shock to the home supporters and it was not until just before the break that Baltazar restored the lead. Brazil dominated the second half, but could not score and two minutes from the end, on a rare attack, the Swiss equalized again. A draw was all too much for the São Paulo crowd, who blamed Costa for the mini disaster. He was assaulted as he left the field and was fortunate not to suffer serious injury.

Yugoslavia and Mexico were the next Pool One teams in action and the Europeans showed, once again, what a fine side they were. They played well throughout the game, controlling the pace from the start, and Zeliko Caikowski, on the left-wing, had an outstanding match. Stepjan Bobek was the first to score, inside twenty minutes, and three minutes later Caikowski got his first to give his team a 2-0 half time lead. Two more goals in the second half, one from Caikowski, saw Yugoslavia take a 4-0 lead before the Mexicans scored a consolation from the penalty spot. It had been another exhilarating display by the Yugoslavs and the result meant that Mexico and Switzerland were now unable to reach the second phase of the tournament. Whoever went through from Pool One would be decided by its next game, between Yugoslavia and Brazil.

That game was two days away and other matches were played in the meantime. In Pool Three, Sweden took on Paraguay, a game in which the Europeans only needed a draw to qualify for the next stage. They looked to be heading towards a handsome victory when Sundqvist and Palmer shot them into a 2-0 lead inside half an hour, but the Paraguayans came back. Atilo López got one back to give a 2-1 half time scoreline and then Fretes López equalized ten minutes from the end.

In Pool Two, Spain had no problems in dispatching Chile in the Maracana. Basora and Zarra were their scorers in the 2-0 victory, but the other Pool Two game played that day brought the greatest of World Cup shocks as England unbelievably crashed to the USA. It left the Belo Horizonte crowd celebrating wildly, not from any anti-English feeling, but from the shock at having witnessed a football miracle. Back home, the reaction was much different. When the score came through, the editor of one newspaper assumed that it was a typing error and published it as a 10-1 victory. Another bordered its page with black and headlined it "The Impossible Result." Excuses were sought. Some blamed the pitch, which was small, uneven and made playing quality football difficult and others talked up the Americans. It was, though, just one of those freak results that occasionally happen in football and which all supporters love, except when it happens to their team. As the England captain, Billy Wright, said: "We didn't play brilliantly, we didn't play badly, but we just couldn't hit the target." After the game, Wilf Mannion said: "Bloody ridiculous. Can't we play them again tomorrow?" (See England v USA profile on page 96).

Perhaps the real reason for England's defeat and generally poor showing in their first World Cup can be discerned in a remark manager Walter Winterbottom once made. "We were so insular that we couldn't believe that other methods could be used for doing things, other ways of playing the game could be better than ours." The Americans had employed strategy to counter the strengths of the English and had refused to bow to the inevitable. They had put their faith in hard tackling to prevent the English from playing their usual game, and the English had not the flexibility to adapt to a situation they had not expected. The country that had given football to the world, had turned its footballing back on that world so that it did not notice the world catch it up and pass it by. It was now the English that had the catching up to do. The teacher had to learn from its pupil.

On 1st July, the game to decide who would go through to the next stage out of Pool One was played in the Maracana. The Yugoslavs were severely handicapped from the start and began the match with only ten men after inside-right, Rajko Mitic, ran into a beam when leaving the changing room. He suffered a serious head injury and needed medical attention. He did not get onto the pitch until after Ademir had given Brazil the lead and was unable to play any meaningful part in the game. It made things very difficult for the Europeans and their exit from the tournament was sealed in the second half when Zizinho, on his international debut, scored a magnificent solo goal.

The rest of the qualifiers were decided the next day. In Pool One, bottom spot went to Mexico, who were defeated 2-1 by Switzerland and in the Maracana, England compounded their dismal World Cup. Both Stanley Matthews and Jackie Milburn were brought into the game against Spain, but it was as if they were fated to lose. The Italian referee, Giovani Galeati, was exceptionally lenient and allowed the Spanish to get away with some cynical and obstructive football, but was harsh on the English. Milburn had what looked like a perfectly good goal disallowed for off side in the twelfth minute and just after half time Zarra headed Spain into the lead. The

22 Men and a Bag of Wind

Spanish then took to defence, or "rough tactics and time wasting" as the Times described it, and the ploy succeeded. England failed to score, but so negative were the Spaniards that the crowd booed them off at the end. The victory saw Spain through to the next stage, but for England it was the boat back home.

The final Pool Two game produced another unusual result, given the context of the other scores in the group. As one historian had noted: "What a strange pool this turned out to be. England lost to the United States and Spain. The Americans surprised both England and Spain. And then Chile, outplayed by the two fancied teams, beat the USA in the last game." Chile's "Englishman", Robledo, opened the scoring after 20 minutes and a second goal, ten minutes later, from Atilio Cremaschi, gave Chile a 2-0 half time lead. Within four minutes of the restart, the Americans were level, but three more goals from Chile, including two more from Cremaschi to achieve his hat trick, gave Chile the 5-2 victory.

Italy met Paraguay in Pool Three's final game. The Italians had no chance of making further progress in the tournament, but Paraguay could. They were, however, completely outplayed by the Italians, who were much more convincing than the 2-0 scoreline might suggest and it meant that the Swedes went through as top of the pool. The final match was the only Pool Four game played, since this was the pool that contained only two teams. It was the most one-sided game so far, with the possible exception of the England-USA match, and the Uruguayans stuck eight past their opponents without reply. Juan Alberto Schiaffino of Peñarol scored four of his country's goals, thus becoming the fourth player to score four goals in a World Cup match. It had been Bolivia's second appearance in the World Cup finals and on neither occasion had they needed to qualify. (See Juan Alberto Schiaffino profile on page 95).

The four qualifiers for the final pool were Brazil, Spain, Sweden and Uruguay, with the home team everybody's favourite to win. They certainly began their final push for the cup in some style when they took on Sweden

So convinced were they that they would lose against the English in their pool game, that many of the American players spent much of the previous night carousing.

Candidate for the World Cup's Bravest Referee No. 1 Bert Griffith

Our first nomination for the World Cup's bravest referee has got to go to Bert Griffith of Newport, Wales.

Refereeing has never been an easy occupation in Brazil, where players are prone to gamesmanship and referees to attack from players or be pelted with missiles by crowds when controversial decisions are made. In preparation for the first post-war World Cup British referees went to Brazil to help bring a steadying influence and offer their expertise to the game there.

Bert Griffith had been chosen to take charge of the Group One match between Brazil and Yugoslavia played in front of the world's largest ever crowd -142,409. Brazil won the match 2-0 but not before Griffith had made what could have been a potentially suicidal decision by disallowing a Brazilian goal. However, the riots that might have taken place on another day, didn't happen, despite rumours before the tournament that fans would severely punish bad refereeing. The crowd took the decision quite well!

The Fate of Joe Gaetjens

The tiny Caribbean country of Haiti has never had much World Cup success having only ever made it to the final stages of the World Cup once, in 1974 when they failed to distinguish themselves. However, one Haitian-born player caused one of the greatest World Cup shocks in 1950. His name was Joe Gaetjens and he scored the winning goal in the USA's humiliating 1-0 defeat of England. Seven years later François Duvalier was elected president of Haiti. Better known by his nickname, "Papa Doc", he became one of the most brutal dictators in history and in 1964 he declared himself president for life, where he remained until his death in 1979. Papa Doc employed a curious mixture of terror and superstition to maintain his grip on power, and one of the instruments of this savage repression was his dreaded secret police force, the "Tontons Macoutes".

Whilst the people of Haiti are nominally Roman Catholic, the vast majority of the population also adhere to Voodoo, a religion that has its origins in the beliefs of their African ancestors, who arrived on the island as Negro slaves. Like many pagan religions Voodoo had its good and dark sides, and one of its most feared beliefs is in the ability of its practitioners to bring back the dead as zombies. These living dead then eke out a nightmarish existence as the slave workers of whoever revives them. In the 1960s Haiti's government encouraged the belief that Papa Doc and his cronies practiced the evil arts of Voodoo. As opponents of the regime began to disappear into the prisons of the Tontons Macoutes, rumours began to circulate that they were being ritually turned into zombies. Gradually, Haiti became an island of fear, where the power of the Tontons Macoutes was unlimited.

In July 1964, Joe Gaetjens, living in the United States at the time, made a visit to the land of his birth. That month, whilst walking through the streets of Port au Prince, the country's capital, he was arrested by the Tontons Macoutes and disappeared into one of their prisons, never to be seen again. No explanation was given and no charges were ever made. Such legal niceties are disregarded by regimes such as that of Papa Doc, where arbitrary arrest is one of the ways of keeping a population cowed. Joe's brother, Jean, who lived on the US Virgin Islands, took up the case. For years, Jean pursued a virtual one-man campaign to find out what happened. He pressed the Haitian authorities to either release his brother, admit that he had been murdered or that he had died in prison. He met with a wall of silence and maybe we will never know the fate of Joe Gaetjens.

Pride comes before a Fall for the Mighty - Brazil 1950

Spain 1 : England 0
The English Team.

George Robledo was a Chilean player having been born in the Andes. However, his mother was from Yorkshire in England and Robledo had been brought up in Barnsley. In the game between Chile and the USA Robledo was subject to very rough treatment by the US defender Colombo. Throughout the game Robledo kept his thoughts to himself and so Colombo was under the impression that he did not speak English. At the end of the game however, Colombo got a shock when Robledo walked up to him and gave him a piece of his mind using choice broad Yorkshire expletives.

In 1950 Uruguay still had the same coach who had led them to success in the 1930 tournament, Juan López.

A total of 715,570 watched Brazil's five games at the Maracana Stadium.

on 3rd July. Nearly 140,000 expectant fans turned up to witness a 7-1 rout. It was a devastating display of fast, non-stop football that left the Swedes reeling. In the first half, two goals from Ademir and another from Chico gave Brazil a 3-0 half time lead. After the break, Ademir got another two before the Swedes had some consolation with an Andersson penalty. The rampant Brazilians then added two more to their tally in the last five minutes to round off a display that had the words "world champions" running right through it.

Two days later, Spain took on Uruguay in what turned out to be a very dirty game, full of vicious, nasty tackling from both sides. The scoring was opened by Elcides Ghiggia, Uruguay's right-winger, but by half time the Spaniards had got their noses in front, the result of two goals by Basora. In the second period, the Uruguayans went all out to try to win the game, but resolute and often brutal defending kept the South Americans at bay. It was not until the 73rd minute that Uruguay's captain, Obdulio Varela, broke Spain's resolve and secured a draw.

The result gave Uruguay a point, but it meant that Brazil, with two points, headed the final pool and were seemingly on course for the title. This situation was reinforced on 13th July when Brazil took on Spain in the Maracana. This time, over 150,000 people thronged into the stadium and they were treated to another vintage display from their idols. The home team was in sparkling form and in spite of the Spaniards detailing two men to look after Ademir, he still managed to score twice. Brazil were 3-0 up after the first half-hour, with goals from Ademir, Jair and Chico. They added three more within 22 minutes of the restart and then slowed down to save themselves for their final game against Uruguay, which allowed the Spanish to grab a late consolation. Victory gave Brazil two more points and a seemingly unassailable lead at the top of the pool. With the European teams fading rapidly, it was only Uruguay who could catch them. They had narrowly defeated Sweden that afternoon by three goals to two to keep in touch with the hosts, but they had had to struggle to achieve the win. The Swedes had twice taken the lead, but two second half goals from Oscar Míguez gave his team the victory they needed.

On 16th July Sweden defeated Spain 3-1 to secure the third place, but it was the last match of the pool that people were waiting for, the so-called final between Brazil and Uruguay. That it did not go to Brazil's plan left the crowd stunned in instantaneous mourning. Thousands, men and women alike, wept openly whilst others fell into fits of hysterics. It was not, perhaps, the defeat alone that produced this effect, but the totally unexpected shock of it. The Uruguayans understandably went wild. (See Uruguay v Brazil profile on page 98).

So the fourth World Cup finals, a tournament so replete with surprises, ended with one of the biggest of all. Yet, the tournament came in for much criticism. The generally poor organization, the nightmarish logistics of transporting football teams across such a vast country and the crazy format adopted were far from adequate. It could easily have brought disaster and might have done so had more teams voted with their feet and stayed away. FIFA was fortunate that sufficient countries stayed loyal to keep it afloat, but never again would they allow such problems to blight the game's showpiece.

However, it would be unfair to close the story of Brazil's World Cup without highlighting some of its more positive features, especially since it was the most interesting of the tournaments held so far. For one thing, it produced some of the most scintillating football ever seen on the world stage. The Brazilians, in particular, were outstanding and few, outside of Uruguay, would deny that they deserved to have won it. They contributed greatly to the entertainment and helped to produce some first class games of football. There were also some brilliant footballers on view. Players of the quality of Ademir and Jair of Brazil, Varela of Uruguay, Caikowski of Yugoslavia, or Mortensen and Matthews of England would find their way into many a critic's list of all-time greats. The English contingent may not have played at their best, but their presence was appreciated by the Brazilian public and they brought an air of expectancy with them. It also helped to produce another intriguing aspect of this World Cup, the element of shock and surprise, greater than in any previous competition. The final itself was such an example, but England's defeat by the USA has become one of international football's great legends.

Though the large number of withdrawals reduces the claim that Brazil 1950 was a World Cup in the literal sense, the fact that the British took part made it more representative of world football than any of the previous events. This fact, too, added to the air of expectancy that surrounded it and helped to create the wonderful atmosphere in which it was played. At times, Brazil 1950 resembled a massive sporting carnival and the local public's love affair with the game of football was apparent everywhere. This was certainly one of the more memorable features of the tournament. It may also account for the generally sporting way in which the games were played. There were no "battles" in this World Cup and, for the first time, there were no players sent off. It would be in Mexico, twenty years later that this would happen again. In conclusion, there was much to be unhappy with in the Brazilian World Cup, but there was far more to be positive about. After the ravages of World War Two, the World Cup had re-established itself as a major international sporting fixture.

Sweden 2 : Uruguay 3
Sweden's captain Erik Nilsson (right) meets Uruguay's Varela before their final pool match.

The "Eat My Own Words" Award for the 1950 World Cup Finals goes to...

The State Governor of Rio for his address before the kick-off of the deciding match of the series. "You Brazilians," he said, "whom I consider victors of the tournament, you players who in less than a few hours will be crowned champions, you who have no equals in the terrestrial hemisphere, you who are so superior to every other competitor, you whom I already salute as conquerors." His words probably haunted his every waking moment.

For the final of the 1950 World Cup oranges and bottled drinks were banned from the stadium as they might have been used as missiles to throw at the English referee George Reader, who had already demanded life insurance. Fireworks and rockets were also banned. However, tears were not. Doctors in Rio reported 169 cases of treatment for fits and hysteria, of which six were very serious.

Sir Stanley Matthews   England

Honours: Quarter-finals 1954   **Games 3**
Played: 1950 and 1954   **Goals 0**

Stanley Matthews only ever played at two speeds - dawdling and quick time. He was the demon of the right-wing and haunted the dreams of many an unfortunate full-back when he had inevitably burnt them alive. They would hold onto his shirt or shorts in the faint hope that he would not get past, they would wrestle him to the ground or give him a kick that would today land them in court for grievous bodily harm, but he still did it. Matthews was the fastest man over ten yards, and those yards happened to be the most important on the pitch. He was both a winger who flew down the touchline and goal maker and it was for this reason that he was nicknamed the "Wizard of Dribble". He is regarded by many as the best dribbler of the ball the game has ever seen.

Matthews was born on 1st February 1915 over a barber's shop in Hanley, Stoke-on-Trent. He joined the ground staff of Stoke City at the age of 15 and was paid £1 a week. Six weeks after his 17th birthday, he made his debut for the club and between 1930 and 1947 he made 203 pre-war and 24 post-war appearances for Stoke City, helping them to the first of their Division Two championships. In 1934 he drew average attendances of over 66,000 to six consecutive games and, when he asked for a transfer in 1938, 1,000 fans demonstrated outside the Victoria Ground to persuade him to stay. A transfer to Blackpool eventually arrived in 1947 and they paid a mere £11,500 for him. His new team won the FA Cup in 1953 and were beaten finalists in 1948 and 1951. They were also league runners-up in 1956.

Perhaps his greatest moment came in the FA Cup Final of 1953 against Bolton Wanderers, now famously known as the 'Matthews Final'. With three minutes to play Blackpool were 3-1 down. Matthews centred for Mortensen, who slotted home his second goal. With less than a minute to go, Mortensen completed his hat trick. During injury time, Matthews found himself on the wing with the ball at his feet and promptly took it past the full-back and raced for the bye line. The Bolton centre-half, staring despair in the face, abandoned all hope of stopping the "Wizard of the Wing" and, expecting a cross, opted to mark Mortensen instead. However, Matthews did not do as expected and pulled the ball back behind Mortensen before centring for the left-winger, Perry who had now arrived in the box. At 4-3, the cup was won. It was one of the greatest comebacks in a Cup final and one of Matthew's greatest displays.

He had been like a god at the Victoria Ground and it was no surprise that in 1961, even though he was slowing down, Stoke took him back. He was 46 years old and feeling that life in the top flight was getting too much. Stoke had to pay Blackpool £3,500 for the privilege and offered him the highest wage he had ever known in his career - £50 a week, plus a £25 match fee. Stoke went on to win the Second Division Championship again in 1963 when Matthews was 48. Two weeks before his move back to Stoke their home attendance had been 8,409. Two weeks after he had returned, there was a crowd of 32,288 for a game against Huddersfield Town. He later said: "People told me I should have asked for £100. But the money doesn't make you play better does it? I was happy there. They were nice people. I had a lot of friends, thousands of them, on the other side of the touchline." He finally hung up his boots as a player five days after his fiftieth birthday in 1965 having never been booked or sent off. His final league appearance was played out in front of a 35,000 crowd. In 1941 he had became the first European Player of the Year, in 1957 he received the CBE and in 1965 he was knighted, the first active footballer to receive the honour. On his retirement as a player he managed Port Vale between 1965 and 1968. He also had a short stint as manager of Hibernian in Malta in 1970 and made several appearances for them aged 55.

He made his England debut in 1934 at the age of 1934. In a playing career that spanned almost 33 years, he made 84 appearances for his country, including two for Great Britain, scoring 11 goals, the first of which was on his debut. His last international was in 1957 at the age of 42. He was expected to play a major part when England returned to the world stage for the 1950 World Cup, but missed the first two games through injury, including the shambles against the USA. He played against Spain but the team's performance was a demoralized one and England went out. He made two further World Cup appearances, in the 1954 finals, against Belgium and Uruguay. There were many stars in both tournaments, but Matthews was not to go down in history as one of them. However, there were good times in his international career. At the end of 1954, when he was two months short of his fortieth birthday, West Germany came to Wembley. He destroyed the German left-back, prompting the Daily Telegraph reporter to write: "Through the changing scenes of international football, the genius of Stanley Matthews remains a radiant beacon. He won this match for England just as nearly 20 years ago he inspired the 3-0 defeat of Germany at Tottenham."

Matthews never took his genius lightly and always knew he had to work at it. He never smoked, never drank, ate salads and fruit, starved on Mondays and got up at six every morning to exercise, even after his playing career ended. At 50 he was still as fit as any young man in the game. His feet did the talking and he took great care of them, even designing his own style of boot based on those he saw in use in Brazil. He once said: "The Co-op used to pay me £20 a week to wear their boots, and pretty early on I realised I didn't need these great stiff things with their rigid toecaps. So I went to the factory and got them to take the sole plate out and the toecap off and make me a really soft pair. It was the first time anybody had done that, and they were beautiful. I could fold them up and put them in my pocket. I got them to make me a white pair once, but I never wore them, too embarrassed."

David Miller's biography of Matthews rightly portrays him as the great man he was. However, he never read the book through. He read the first page and put it down feeling too embarrassed to go on. He claimed, in his interview with David Hunn of the Times that, "I can't take people going on about how good I was. You just do your best, don't you." When it came to dancing with the bag of wind, to many, Sir Stanley Matthews was the best. He died on 23rd February 2000 at the age of 85.

Sir Tom Finney   England

Honours: Quarter-finals 1954   **Games 6**
Played: 1950 and 1954   **Goals 1**

England's Tom Finney evades Chile's Roldan in the 2-0 English victory.

Tom Finney has been described as being three players in one. He was a whippet-quick player and was once described by Bill Shankley as being "so grizzly good he could have played in an overcoat." Shankly and Finney played together at Preston North End, where Finney spent his whole career. In 1987 Shankley, was asked whether he thought Kevin Keegan was anywhere near as good as Finney. He said: "At the present time, he probably is, but you have to remember that Tommy is 65." In the days when pitches were like ploughed fields, footballs were like cannonballs, boots as heavy as lead and shirts and shorts only came in one size, large, he played for the fun of it.

The fact that his wages were never higher than £20 per week and a win bonus was a mere £2, didn't make a blind bit of difference. In an interview with Len Capeling for the Evertonian magazine, Finney said: "That was the way I played. I wanted to be happy and make the supporters happy." Another reporter once recalled Finney and Stanley Matthews running out onto the pitch for England "laughing like children who'd discovered they were going to the party after all."

Finney was born on 5th April 1922 and made his league debut for Preston on 31st August 1946 against Leeds United at the age of 24. He had already played representative games and had taken part in war time competitions, including the Cup Final of 1941 against Arsenal. In his first league game, he gave notice that he would become one of the best players England has ever known. He scored one goal and made the other two in Preston's 3-2 victory. His approach to wing play was dazzling. He was speedy, direct and deadly when shooting at goal, he could dribble and swerve, making him a defender's nightmare. In 433 league games for Preston between 1946 and 1960, he scored 187 goals. During the 1950s Preston were twice runners-up in the league, once losing out to Arsenal on goal difference and were runners up in the 1954 FA Cup final. The previous final had been dubbed the 'Matthews Final' and 1954 was supposed to be the 'Finney Final'. However, on his own admittance, he did not have a good game. Consolation came with of the Player of the Year Award, which he won again in 1957, but surprisingly, he won no major honours with Preston. A chance to make his fortune came in June 1952 when Prince Roberto Lanza di Trabia of Palermo offered him £10,000 to sign for the Italian club on a salary of £140 per week. The offer was taken to the then Chairman of Preston who told him: "Tha'll play for us, or tha'll play for nobody."

Finney made his England debut in September 1946 and went on to win 76 caps, scoring 30 goals. His international career was studded with highlights, including scoring a spectacular goal against Portugal in 1949, when he carried the ball from the halfway line, taking it past three players before slotting the ball home. England won the game 10-0. England only lost 12 times when Finney was in the team and unfortunately one of those was the shock defeat by the USA in 1950. He did not have a spectacular tournament, but neither did any England player. However, in the Switzerland World Cup, England made a better showing, and, in a much-improved performance, Finney scored one of England's two goals. He did not appear in the 1958 tournament and in 1960 he retired from the game at the age of 38. He had been injured and it was slowing him down. He made one swansong appearance when he was asked to appear for Distillery of Ireland in the European Cup against Benfica of Portugal. He only played in the home leg, a 3-3 draw.

Finney was originally a plumber by trade and on leaving the game started his own successful business. He also spent time as a football reporter, a magistrate, was chairman of Preston Health Authority and president of Preston North End. He received an OBE in 1961 and was knighted in 1998. Many things have obviously been written and said about Sir Tom Finney, but two of the best tributes came from his fellow professionals. Tommy Lawton, who played along side him for England said: "Tom was a wonder. An absolute wonder. He could play anywhere, left-wing, right-wing, centre-forward. And he never let you down. A great man and a great player." However, the finest comment was the one made by Scotland's Tommy Docherty who commented that: "Tom Finney was the greatest footballer in the world. Di Stéfano and Puskás were not fit to lace Finney's boots. And he was way out in front of Stanley Matthews too." Many commentators may not agree with this, but it's not far from the truth. However, let us leave the last words to Finney himself. When talking about footballers today, he remarked: "I don't think they get the fun out of the game we got. I always looked upon it as a game to be enjoyed, irrespective of the result. They make a lot of money these days, but many of them don't seem to enjoy it. I don't see much laughter anymore. I used to think when you came down the tunnel it was a bit of fun. It was a question of going out onto the field to entertain the crowd. I still think that's what football is all about, but now results are so important…"

Sir Alfred Ernest Ramsey   England

Honours: Winner 1966; Quarter-finals 1970 (both as manager)   **Games 3**
Played: 1950 and 1954; Manager: 1966 and 1970   **Goals 0**

Alf Ramsey's career as an England player did not bring him much fame and fortune. He was a defender of some note, but because England had not played on the world stage since the British amateur side had participated in the Olympic Games in the early part of the century, his experiences were to bring lessons rather than trophies. However, as manager at both club and national level in the 1960s and 70s, it was to be a different matter altogether.

Sir Alf Ramsey prior to the 1970 World Cup game against Czechoslovakia.

Ramsey was born on 22nd January 1920 in Dagenham. He learnt to play football, along side his three brothers, Albert, Len and Cyril, in the lanes and fields that surrounded his house, an area that is now covered by the Becontree housing estate. He went to Becontree Heath School and was later picked to play for Dagenham Schools and Five Elms FC. He left school at the age of 14 to take a job with the local Co-op store, where he spent six years, finally ending up as a counter hand at the Oxlow Road store, also in Dagenham. At the age of 20 he joined the army and represented them until he was discharged in 1942, by which time he had been spotted by Southampton, who gave him his first professional appointment. Between 1942 and 1949 he made 90 appearances for the club and scored 8 goals before being transferred to Tottenham Hotspur. Over the next seven years he made 226 first team appearances, scoring 24 goals. In 1955, his playing days ended, his more successful management career was about to start. He was given the job of transforming Ipswich Town and took the side to the second and first division titles in successive years. It weighed heavily in his favour when he was appointed to manage the national team in 1963.

Whilst at Spurs he was picked to play for England and was a member of the party that flew to the World Cup finals in Brazil in 1950. Sadly, the most noteworthy thing about his appearances was a mistake against Spain. Gaínza, the Spanish winger, went on the rampage and left-half of the English team for dead. He lobbed toward the hapless Ramsey, who only managed to graze the ball as it went past. It was at this point that Telmo Zarra stormed into the fray to slam the ball home off the left post. It was Ramsey's last appearance for his country in the World Cup finals.

By 1966, the national side was beginning to gain back some of the respectability that it had lost in the lean years of Walter Winterbottom. Ramsey put together a team of class players, including Bobby Moore, the Charlton brothers and the inspired Jimmy Greaves, but the build-up to the tournament did not begin well, when England lost to Austria 3-2 at Wembley in October 1965. Greaves, out of the side suffering from jaundice, did not get game until May 1966, an obvious worry for Ramsey. He experimented with the side, opting for a 4-3-3 formation and promptly won 2-0 against Spain in December in Madrid. With the exception of a 1-1 draw with Poland, the next few results went well and included, notably, the 1-0 defeat of West Germany at Wembley in February 1966 and the 4-3 win over arch rivals Scotland at Hampden Park. Geoff Hurst had made his debut against West Germany and retained his place against Scotland when he scored the opening goal. Ramsey then made wholesale changes and experimented with formations, intent on trying to bring together the right blend that would be flexible enough to face any country in the world. He studied the nature of his opponents and the problems they might throw up and at an intensive, military style training camp at Lilleshall it was a well motivated squad that embarked on a whirlwind four-match tour of Europe. England won every game.

From the outset Ramsey insisted on being in charge of team selection, the first England manager to have this power. He made it very clear that his intention was to win the World Cup and he was going to do it his way, but his approach did not make him many friends. The English press were bewildered by his ideas and attacked him incessantly, claiming that his team would never win the World Cup. He had the audacity to dismantle the historical cornerstones of English football and his hard running, hard working approach dispensed with wingers. Problems with the press and the FA were not helped by the fact that he was not a good communicator. He did not let this bother him. He was quoted in the Daily Mail as saying: "I care for nobody or anything other than my wife, my country and my football. We are of course the greatest nation in the world." The FA often treated their national coach disrespectfully and it was rumoured that this was because he refused to endorse a clothing company wishing to sponsor England for financial gain. It incensed Ramsey, who declared that he would never sell the shirt of his country.

He was vindicated when his "Wingless Wonders" became a world-beating team. Ramsey had blended a side that probably had more skill than any other England team, past or present. He was knighted soon after and his critics had to eat their words. He had less success in Mexico and his sacking in 1974, after England failed to qualify for the World Cup finals that year was a major disappointment. He had served his nation well. Adding insult to injury, the FA's appalling treatment did not stop there. The organizers of the 1996 European Championships decided to reassemble the team of 1966 to parade before a packed Wembley crowed prior to England's opening game against Switzerland. The man who had created that team was not invited.

Ramsey suffered a stroke in 1998 and finally passed away on 28th April 1999 at the age of 79. People tend to remember the Hurst hat trick, the Nobby Stiles jig or the "They think it's all over" television quote when they think of England and the 1966 World Cup final. However it is the man who had spent three years of his life dedicated to bringing about the proudest moment in English soccer history that should be remembered most. He knew what he wanted and how he was going to get it and that's exactly what he did. He was a football man through and through, a master tactician with an innate genius for the game. Terry Paine once commented on the 'Soccernet' web site that: "He had a great sense of loyalty toward his players who responded accordingly by lifting their performances for Alf's beloved England. A nice touch for me was that after every game, win, lose or draw, he would shake every players hand and thank them for their efforts."

Juan Alberto Schiaffino   Uruguay

Honours: Winner 1950; 4th Place 1954   **Games 9**
Played: 1950 and 1954   **Goals 7**

Schiaffino scores Uruguay's first goal past Barbosa in their 2-1 victory over Brazil.

Not put off by his size and the comments made about it, Juan Alberto Schiaffino became one of the most celebrated inside forwards of the 1950s and early 1960s. Born in Montevideo on 28th July 1925 of Italian parentage he became a youth team player for Peñarol at the age of 17 and a first team player a year later. Nicknamed "Pepe" and, playing at inside-left, he formed a formidable partnership with his older brother, Raúl, in the centre and Walter Gómez at inside-right. Despite the criticism, his stature was offset by his ability to take on the world's best defenders and not fail. With a grace and agility that larger players found difficult to cope with, he traversed the pitch and scored many goals. He always seemed to be in the right place at the right time and his intelligence, speed and distribution skills got him noticed.

It was therefore, no surprise that an international call up was just around the corner, but his debut at the age of 19 came in a rather unusual way. There was a professional player strike in Uruguay at the time of the 1949 South American Cup but because the FA did not want to withdraw they sent their best amateur team, which included Schiaffino. On the way to taking fourth spot, Uruguay were beaten 5-1 by Brazil but, for the young Schiaffino there were lessons to be learned from that game and, one year later, revenge came in the most emphatic way. At the 1950 World Cup finals, Schiaffino and his team mates snatched the winged goddess from the hands of a host nation who believe they had a divine right to football's greatest prize. He also became the second highest scorer in the tournament with six goals. The most important of these was undoubtedly the equalizer he slammed home in the final. It was a 66th minute bombshell that silenced a whole nation, and on their home soil. He then helped to conjure up the winner and afterwards described the victory as "a miracle". The reception the team received when they arrived home was out of this world.

Four years on in Switzerland, the triumph was not to be repeated. Schiaffino was injured in the semi-final against Hungary and they lost 4-2. However, his play had impressed watching European club presidents, so much that AC Milan paid a then world record transfer fee of £72,000 for him. He was 29 years old. He repaid them by helping the team to three Italian championships and a European Cup final in 1958 where they lost 3-2 to Real Madrid. Six months after his transfer, Schiaffino surprisingly switched his national allegiances and was picked for Italy, who did not make the Sweden World Cup and the world stage was not to be graced by his presence again. He had played for Uruguay 45 times and made four appearances for Italy.

He retired in 1962 at the age of 35, the last two seasons of his career having been with AC Roma. For the next 14 years his involvement in the game was minimal and when he was tempted back in 1976 as manager of Peñarol he stayed only six months. He also served a brief spell as the national coach, manager for two games, but his business interests took over and they were to keep him out of the full-time game.

England 0 : USA 1

When the Daily Mirror carried its report of the game between England and the USA, it began with the words: "English Soccer was humiliated as it has never been before". They were sentiments that permeated right through the British press as the reality of what had happened in Belo Horizonte sank in and sportswriters sought to explain what is still one of the greatest upsets in World Cup history.

Putting the game in context is relatively easy, explaining the result is not. As fathers of the game, the English were rightly recognized and respected throughout the football world. It was naturally assumed, at home and abroad, that since the English had taught the world to play the game, they were masters of it, a notion that had never been put to a realistic test. The English had arrogantly disdained FIFA membership for years and, whilst international matches had been played, the English had never played in the World Cup. The international opposition that had been encountered had not been a true reflection of the proper state of the world game and, anyway, much of this international football had been played before the Second World War, when things were much different. The English had never, for instance, played a South American team. The plain truth is that in 1950 English soccer existed in a reality vacuum. Since nothing had ever shaken the myth of its superiority, there was nothing to suggest that the conventional belief be anything but true. Why, then, should the English football establishment think any different? Theirs was the proper way to do things, and that was that. It was a way of thinking that ran right through England's preparations for this World Cup, if that is the correct word to use. This attitude may have stemmed from arrogance or it may have come from ignorance, but it was to prove costly.

The English authorities learned nothing from the unconvincing performance against Chile and totally failed to take account of the fact that it had taken Spain 80 minutes to crack a resolute American defence. They were clearly no team of also-rans, but the English went into this game choosing to treat it as little more than a practice match. Typical of this complacency was the decision to leave out Matthews, one which amazed the USA's Scots-born coach, Bill Jeffrey.

The local press had dubbed the English the "kings of football" and rightly it seemed as, after a sluggish start, they began what became a procession of assaults on the American goal. In a series of attacks, Billy Wright began a move that ended with Wilf Mannion shooing against the post and soon after, Jimmy Mullen presented an excellent chance to Tom Finney, who blasted over the bar. The ball, it seemed, did not want to go into the net. In the 30th minute Finney set up Mannion unmarked and close to goal with "a golden opportunity", but he failed to find the target. Five minutes later, Finney himself hit the post with the goalkeeper well beaten.

The passage of time and their failure to score began to affect the English forwards. "Over anxiety was England's worst enemy", which led to "exasperating fiddling in front of goal", wrote the discerning football correspondent of the Daily Herald. "The English forwards were particularly at fault, blazing the ball wide or over the bar and hesitating in front of goal for the nippy American defenders to rob them before they could get in a shot", was

Pride comes before a Fall for the Mighty - Brazil 1950

Gaetjens deflects the ball pasts Englands'Bert Williams for the shock USA winner.

how the Daily Telegraph described it, revealing one of the neglected features of this game. A poor English performance has often been the verdict of historians, but this has ignored the excellent defending of the Americans. They had done it against Spain, and they were now doing it against England. Their tackling was sharp, quick and effective, and the fact that the English, too confident in their possession, held on to the ball for too long, gave plenty of opportunity for those tackles to go in and make their mark. Charles Colombo, the American centre-half, and Frank Borghi, in goal, both had outstanding games and contributed much to their team's ultimate victory.

For most of the first half, the Americans hardly threatened England's goal, but in the 37th minute, on a rare breakaway, Walter Bahr lofted a speculative cross into the English penalty area. What happened next has been the subject of much debate. Certainly, Bert Williams in goal seemed to have it covered, but he misread the situation and the ball ended up in the net off the head of Joe "Larry" Gaetjens, the Haitian-born centre-forward (and not Argentinian-born, as many reporters of the day describe him). Some reporters describe a glancing header, carefully steered into the goal, whilst others feel that it simply hit him and went in. Sadly, Gaetjens disappeared and so the truth will probably never be known. Whatever happened, it placed the English in the embarrassing position of trailing to a team made up of Mickey Mouse and Donald Duck, as one writer contemptuously described the Americans.

Not surprisingly, the crowd went wild at this unexpected reversal. They danced, lit bonfires, set off firecrackers and, throughout the rest of the match, whistled and cheered at the discomfort of the English. This may have affected the concentration and morale of the English players, but they went straight back onto the attack from the restart and the game resumed its previous course. So did the precession of near misses, mis-kicked shots and saves. Despite their lack of success, the English made no change in tactics and they continued with "the mistake of trying to walk the ball into the net, instead of having a crack". Meanwhile, in the stands, grim faced, sat Stanley Matthews, the one man who might have made a difference to the whole sorry show.

The English changed the forward combination at half time and it did bring some slight improvement in performance, but no goal. At times there were as many as nine English players in the American penalty area, such was the one-sided flow of the game, but such overcrowding did not improve England's chance of scoring. The Americans packed as many behind the ball as the English put in front of it. As the game went on, the Americans visibly tired, but they stuck to their task doggedly. If anything, their tackling got more ferocious and at one point, towards the end of the match, Mortensen was rugby tackled just outside the area. Alf Ramsey took the free kick and Mortensen's header was well saved. Jimmy Mullen did get a header into the net, but was adjudged off side by the Italian referee. For the English, nothing went right and when the whistle went to end the game, a dispirited team trudged off the field. They left the jubilant Americans and their new-found supporters celebrating on the pitch, the players lofted shoulder high.

Uruguay 2 : Brazil 1
The World Cup Final

Technically, this game was not a final at all. Since there was no knock-out stages none had been scheduled for this World Cup. The peculiar arrangements of Brazil 1950 with its final pool decreed that a league system would decide the world champions. It happened that the last game of the series featured the only two teams who could win and historians have tended to describe it as the final. There is no reason to diverge from this convention.

Brazil went into the game top of the final group, a point ahead of Uruguay, and only needing a draw to win the title. Given the way they had been playing and improving as the tournament progressed, they were clear favourites to obtain the result they needed. Having scored thirteen goals and conceding only two in their two previous games, it was world beating form indeed. They were a team playing at the height of their potential and confidence, their football full of raw passion and extravagance, and nobody in Brazil expected them to lose. The preparations that had already been made for the victory celebrations testify to this belief, yet they also underscore the one problem that could emerge to spoil the party - that of overconfidence. "Had the Brazilians the mental toughness and discipline?" was the question that Costa should have been addressing, rather than considering what was to happen once the job had been completed. Uruguay's progress to the "final" had been an altogether quieter affair, disposing of Bolivia easily and hardly distinguishing themselves in the final pool.

On the day of the match, a world record crowd of 199,854 packed the stadium to witness the inevitable, about 20,000 of whom got in without paying. They saw a series of blistering attacks that did nothing to diminish their optimism. Under a constant barrage, it seemed only a matter of time before they would score, but Uruguay matched Brazilian endeavour with not a little of their own. They defended resolutely, with captain, Obdulio Varela particularly outstanding. His workrate was prodigious and his leadership inspirational, as he rallied his men to keep out the Brazilians. The goal that long threatened did not materialise and by half time, with the score resting at 0-0, the Uruguayans were still hanging in there.

When the game restarted in the second half, the Brazilians took up where they had left off and after three minutes of play got the breakthrough they were seeking. Ademir, who had been his usual tantalizing self all game, finally set Friaça free with a rakish through pass that got behind the defence and the ball ended up in the net. It was more than was needed for the title, but what followed can only described as tactical naïvety, for which many have blamed the Brazilian coach. The criticism is unfair because Costa sent a message to Jair to drop back and strengthen the defence, but the message seems not to have reached him. If it did, he disobeyed because he continued to play up front and his team continued to attack. Such top experienced players ought to have known better, but overconfidence got the better of their judgement. Their self-belief and faith in their invincibility would not allow for any other strategy and it brought their downfall. Continued pressure allowed the Uruguayans to make openings of their own and when they did, they took them gleefully.

Uruguay, 1950 World Champions.

Uruguay's equalizer came in the 66th minute and was set up when Varela sent the ball out to Elcides Ghiggia on the right-wing. The man who put the ball in the net, Juan Schiaffino, years later described what happened: "I'd say that it was a very strange goal and it seems even funnier looking back after all these years. Ghiggia came hurtling down the wing and he centred. Well, I was unmarked and I shot at goal. It wasn't the shot that I meant it to be, it didn't go where I wanted it to go at all and, even now, it seems unbelievable. I went for one side of the goal, the ball went for the other, but, luckily for us, it hit the post and went in. We'd equalized."

The goal may have been fortuitous, but it gave the Uruguayans the heart to push themselves further. Inexplicably, the Brazilians still made no move to close the game down and from the restart went in search of a winner. However, now there was a greater sense of authority about the Uruguayans and they began to assert themselves with increasing force. With Varela commanding at the back and Victor Andrade, nephew of José, growing ever more influential in midfield, the Uruguayans began to look the more menacing. With a little over ten minutes of play left, Ghiggia again picked up the ball on the wing. He turned Bigode, in Brazil's defence, and instead of crossing the ball, as was expected of him, he ran in on goal himself. Nearing the target, he let go a low shot, which evaded Barbosa and landed in the corner of the net.

The Uruguayans were now in front and there was no way that Varela would allow them to make the same mistake as the Brazilians. He knew the importance of tight defence and immediately organized his men to close everything down at the back. Total concentration was vital and his troops did not disappoint. They ferociously stopped everything the home team could throw at them and stood firm as Brazilian heads began to drop. When the whistle went, the unthinkable had happened - Brazil had lost the match and the championship. It had been Uruguay's second World Cup campaign and their second victory.

Whilst the Uruguayan team went wild, the Maracana crowd stood transfixed with shock. People wept, others collapsed and were taken to hospital and an entire nation went into grieving. So great was the surprise that it even merited editorial comment from the Times, in 1950 a newspaper not noted for its interest in association football. "And yet many not normally soft-hearted people must have felt truly sorry for the swift and skilful Brazilian football players who have just lost to Uruguay in the final of the World Cup", it said. "Let us hope that the victors of Uruguay will likewise not rub it in too fiercely: they can afford to be generous", it continued and, in conclusion, remarked: "As to poor Brazil, we can, in Mr. Michael Finsbury's words, do nothing but sympathize - sincerely. It is 'just too bad.'"

Statistics - Brazil 1950

POOL ONE

Rio de Janeiro, June 24th - Estadio Maracana

4 (1) BRAZIL

Ademir 30,79, Jair 66, Baltazar 71

Barbosa, Augusto, Juvenal, Eli, Danilo, Bigode, Maneca, Ademir, Baltazar, Jair, Friaça.

0 (0) MEXICO

Carbajal, Zetter, Montemajor, Ruiz, Ochoa, Roca, Septien, Ortíz, Casarin, Pérez, Velásquez.

Referee: George Reader (England)
Attendance: 81.649

Belo Horizonte, June 25th - Estadio Sete de Setembro

3 (2) YUGOSLAVIA

Tomasevic 19,25, Ognjanov 82

Mrkusic, Horvat, Stankovic, Zlatko Caikowski, Jovanovic, Djajic, Ognjanov, Mitic, Tomasevic, Bobek, Vukas.

0 (0) SWITZERLAND

Stuber, Neury, Bocquet, Lusenti, Eggimann, Quinche, Bickel, Antenen, Tamini, Bader, Fatton.

Referee: Giovanni Galeati (Italy)
Attendance: 7.336

Sao Paulo, June 28th - Estadio Pacaembu

2 (2) BRAZIL

Alfredo 2, Baltazar 44

Barbosa, Augusto, Juvenal, Bauer, Ruy, Noronha, Maneca, Ademir, Baltazar, Alfredo, Friaça.

2 (1) SWITZERLAND

Fatton 16,88

Stuber, Neury, Bocquet, Lusenti, Eggimann, Quinche, Bickel, Friedländer, Tamini, Bader, Fatton.

Referee: Ramon Azon Roma (Spain)
Attendance: 42.032

Porto Alegre, June 29th - Estadio Beira-Rio

4 (2) YUGOSLAVIA

Bobek 19, Zeliko Ciakowski 22,62, Tomasevic 81

Mrkusic, Horvat, Stankovic, Zlatko Caikowski, Jovanovic, Djajic, Mihalovic, Mitic, Tomasevic, Bobek, Zeliko Caikowski.

1 (0) MEXICO

Casarin (pen)88

Carbajal, Gutiérrez, Gómez, Ruiz, Ochoa, Flores, Naranjo, Ortíz, Casarin, Pérez, Velásquez.

Referee: Reg Leafe (England)
Attendance: 11.078

Rio de Janeiro, July 1st - Estadio Maracana

2 (1) BRAZIL

Ademir 3, Zizinho 89

Barbosa, Augusto, Juvenal, Bauer, Danilo, Bigode, Maneca, Ademir, Jair, Zizinho, Chico.

0 (0) YUGOSLAVIA

Mrkusic, Horvat, Brokela, Zlatko Caikowski, Jovanovic, Djajic, Vukas, Mitic, Tomasevic, Bobek, Zeliko Caikowski.

Referee: Mervyn Griffiths (Wales)
Attendance: 142.409

Porto Alegre, July 2nd - Estadio Beira-Rio

2 (2) SWITZERLAND

Bader 12, Antenen 45

Hug, Neury, Bocquet, Lusenti, Eggimann, Quinche, Antenen, Friedländer, Tamini, Bader, Fatton.

1 (0) MEXICO

Casarin 88

Carbajal, Gutiérrez, Gómez, Guevara, Ochoa, Flores, Roca, Ortíz, Casarin, Borbolla, Velásquez.

Referee: Ivan Eklind (Sweden)
Attendance: 3.580

	P	W	D	L	F	A	Pts
Brazil	3	2	1	0	8	2	5
Yugoslavia	3	2	0	1	7	3	4
Switzerland	3	1	1	1	4	6	3
Mexico	3	0	0	3	2	10	0

POOL TWO

Rio de Janeiro, June 25th - Estadio Maracana

2 (1) ENGLAND

Mortensen 27, Mannion 52

Williams, Ramsey, Aston, Wright, Hughes, Dickinson, Finney, Mortensen, Bentley, Mannion, Mullen.

0 (0) CHILE

Livingstone, Farias, Roldan, Alvarez, Busquet, Carvalho, Mayanes, Cremaschi, Robledo, Muñoz, Díaz.

Referee: Karel Van Der Meer (Holland)
Attendance: 29.703

Curitiba, June 25th - Estadio Brito

3 (0) SPAIN

Basora 80,82, Zarra 85

Eizaguirre, Alonzo, Antuñez, J.Gonzalvo, M.Gonzalvo, Puchades, Basora, Hernández, Zarra, Igoa, Gaínza.

1 (1) UNITED STATES

J.Souza 18

Borghi, Keough, Maca, McIlvenny, Colombo, Bahr, Craddock, J.Souza, Gaetjens, Pariani, Valentini.

Referee: Mario Viana (Brazil)
Attendance: 9.511

Rio de Janeiro, June 29th - Estadio Maracana

2 (2) SPAIN

Basora 19, Zarra 35

Ramallets, Alonzo, Parra, J.Gonzalvo, M.Gonzalvo, Puchades, Basora, Panizo, Zarra, Igoa, Gaínza.

0 (0) CHILE

Livingstone, Farias, Roldan, Alvarez, Busquet, Carvalho, Prieto, Cremaschi, Robledo, Muñoz, Díaz.

Referee: Alberto Gama Malcher (Brazil)
Attendance: 19.790

Belo Horizonte, June 29th - Estadio Mineiro

1 (1) UNITED STATES

Gaetjens 37

Borghi, Keough, Maca, McIlvenny, Colombo, Bahr, Wallace, J.Souza, Gaetjens, Pariani, E.Souza.

0 (0) ENGLAND

Williams, Ramsey, Aston, Wright, Hughes, Dickinson, Finney, Mortensen, Bentley, Mannion, Mullen.

Referee: Generoso Dattilo (Italy)
Attendance: 10.151

Rio de Janeiro, July 2nd - Estadio Maracana

1 (0) SPAIN

Zarra 49

Ramallets, Alonzo, Parra, J.Gonzalvo, M.Gonzalvo, Puchades, Basora, Panizo, Zarra, Igoa, Gaínza.

0 (0) ENGLAND

Williams, Ramsey, Eckersley, Wright, Hughes, Dickinson, Finney, Mortensen, Matthews, Baily, Milburn.

Referee: Giovanni Galeati (Italy)
Attendance: 74.462

Recife, July 2nd - Estadio Ilha do Retiro

5 (2) CHILE

Robledo 20, Cremaschi 30,54,89, Prieto 59

Livingstone, Farias, Machuca, Alvarez, Busquet, Rojas, Prieto, Cremaschi, Robledo, Riera, Ibañez.

2 (0) UNITED STATES

Pariani 46, E.Souza (pen)49

Borghi, Keough, Maca, McIlvenny, Colombo, Bahr, Wallace, J.Souza, Gaetjens, Pariani, E.Souza.

Referee: Mario Gardelli (Brazil)
Attendance: 8.501

	P	W	D	L	F	A	Pts
Spain	3	3	0	0	6	1	6
England	3	1	0	2	2	2	2
Chile	3	1	0	2	5	6	2
USA	3	1	0	2	4	8	2

POOL THREE

Sao Paulo, June 25th - Estadio Pacaembu

3 (2) SWEDEN

Jeppson 25,69, Andersson 34

Svensson, Samuelsson, E.Nilsson, Andersson, Nordahl, Gärd, Sundqvist, Palmer, Jeppson, Skoglund, S.Nilsson.

2 (1) ITALY

Carapellese 7, Muccinelli 76

Sentimenti IV, Giovannini, Furiassi, Annovazzi, Parola, Magli, Muccinelli, Boniperti, Cappello, Campatelli, Carapellese.

Referee: M.Lutz (Switzerland)
Attendance: 56.502

Curitiba, June 29th - Estadio Brito

2 (2) SWEDEN

Sundqvist 23, Palmer 25

Svensson, Samuelsson, E.Nilsson, Andersson, Nordahl, Gärd, Sundqvist, Palmer, Jeppson, Skoglund, Jönsson.

2 (1) PARAGUAY

López A 35, López F 80

Vargas, González, Cespedes, Gavilan, Lequizamon, Cantero, Avalos, López A, Saguir, López F, Unzain.

Referee: Bobby Mitchell (Scotland)
Attendance: 7.903

Sao Paulo, July 2nd - Estadio Pacaembu

2 (1) ITALY

Carapellese 12, Pandolfini 62

Moro, Blason, Fattori, Furiassi, Remondini, Mari, Pandolfini, Muccinelli, Cappello, Amadei, Carapellese.

0 (0) PARAGUAY

Vargas, González, Cespedes, Gavilan, Lequizamon, Cantero, Avalos, López A, Saguir, López F, Unzain.

Referee: Arthur Ellis (England)
Attendance: 25.811

	P	W	D	L	F	A	Pts
Sweden	2	1	1	0	5	4	3
Italy	2	1	0	1	4	3	2
Paraguay	2	0	1	1	2	4	1

POOL FOUR

Belo Horizonte, July 2nd - Estadio Mineiro

8 (4) URUGUAY

Schiaffino 12,20,37,54, Vidal 18, Míguez 51,78, Ghiggia 83

Maspoli, M.González, Tejera, J-C Gonzáles, Varela, Andrade, Ghiggia, Pérez, Míguez, Schiaffino, Vidal.

0 (0) BOLIVIA

B.Gutiérrez, Acha, Bustamente, Greco, Valencia, Ferrel, Algarañaz, Ugarte, Caparelli, E. Gutiérrez, Maldonado.

Referee: George Reader (England)
Attendance: 5.284

	P	W	D	L	F	A	Pts
Uruguay	1	1	0	0	8	0	2
Bolivia	1	0	0	1	0	8	0

FINAL POOL

Rio de Janeiro, July 3rd - Estadio Maracana

7 (3) BRAZIL

Ademir 17,36,51,64, Chico 39,87, Maneca 65

Barbosa, Augusto, Juvenal, Bauer, Danilo, Bigode, Maneca, Zizinho, Ademir, Jair, Chico.

1 (0) SWEDEN

Andersson (pen)57

Svensson, Samuelsson, E.Nilsson, Andersson, Nordahl, Gärd, Sundqvist, Palmer, Jeppson, Skoglund, S.Nilsson.

Referee: Arthur Ellis (England)
Attendance: 138.886

Sao Paulo, July 9th - Estadio Pacaembu

2 (2) SPAIN

Basora 39,41

Ramallets, Alonzo, Parra, J.Gonzalvo, M.Gonzalvo, Puchades, Basora, Igoa, Zarra, Molowny, Gaínza.

2 (1) URUGUAY

Ghiggia 29, Varela 73

Maspoli, M.González, Tejera, J-C González, Varela, Andrade, Ghiggia, Pérez, Míguez, Schiaffino, Vidal.

Referee: George Reader (England)
Attendance: 44.802

Pride comes before a Fall for the Mighty - Brazil 1950

Rio de Janeiro, July 13th -
Estadio Maracana

6 (3) BRAZIL

Ademir 15,57, Jair 21, Chico 29,55, Zizinho 67

Barbosa, Augusto, Juvenal, Bauer, Danilo, Bigode,
Friaça, Zizinho, Ademir, Jair, Chico.

1 (0) SPAIN

Igoa 70

Ramallets, Alonzo, Parra, J.Gonzalvo, M.Gonzalvo,
Puchades, Basora, Igoa, Zarra, Panizo, Gaínza.

Referee: Reg Leafe (England)
Attendance: 152.772

Sao Paulo, July 13th - Estadio Pacaembu

3 (1) URUGUAY

Ghiggia 39, Míguez 77,85

Paz, M.González, Tejera, Gambetta, Varela, Andrade,
Ghiggia, Pérez, Míguez, Schiaffino, Vidal.

2 (2) SWEDEN

Palmer 5, Sundqvist 40

Svensson, Samuelsson, E.Nilsson, Andersson,
Johansson, Gärd, Sundqvist, Palmer, Mellberg,
Skoglund, Jönsson.

Referee: Giovanni Galeati (Italy)
Attendance: 7.987

Sao Paulo, July 16th -
Estadio Pacaembu

3 (2) SWEDEN

Sundqvist 15, Mellberg 34, Palmer 80

Svensson, Samuelsson, E.Nilsson, Andersson,
Johansson, Gärd, Sundqvist, Palmer, Mellberg, Rydell,
Jönsson.

1 (0) SPAIN

Zarra 82

Eizaguirre, Asensi, Parra, Alonzo, Silva, Puchades,
Basora, Hernández, Zarra, Panizo, Juncosa.

Referee: Karel Van Der Meer (Holland)
Attendance: 11.227

	P	W	D	L	F	A	Pts
Brazil	2	2	0	0	13	2	4
Uruguay	2	1	1	0	5	4	3
Sweden	3	1	0	2	6	11	2
Spain	3	0	1	2	4	11	1

FINAL POOL MATCH

Rio de Janeiro, July 16th -
Estadio Maracana

2 (0) URUGUAY

Schiaffino 66, Ghiggia 79

Maspoli, M.González, Tejera, Gambetta, Varela,
Andrade, Ghiggia, Pérez, Míguez, Schiaffino, Moran.

1 (0) BRAZIL

Friaça 47

Barbosa, Augusto, Juvenal, Bauer, Danilo, Bigode,
Friaça, Zizinho, Ademir, Jair, Chico.

Referee: George Reader (England)
Attendance: 199.854

QUALIFICATION ROUNDS

Europe - Group 1

	P	W	D	L	F	A	Pts
England	3	3	0	0	14	3	6
Scotland	3	2	0	1	10	3	4
Wales	3	0	1	2	1	6	1
N. Ireland	3	0	1	2	4	17	1

01-10-1949	Northern Ireland : Scotland	2:8 (0:5)
15-10-1949	Wales : England	1:4 (0:3)
09-11-1949	Scotland : Wales	2:0 (1:0)
16-11-1949	England : Northern Ireland	9:2 (4:0)
08-03-1950	Wales : Northern Ireland	0:0
15-04-1950	Scotland : England	0:1 (0:0)

Europe - Group 2

	P	W	D	L	F	A	Pts
Turkey	1	1	0	0	7	0	2
Syria	1	0	0	1	0	7	0

20-11-1949	Turkey : Syria	7:0 (3:0)

Europe - Group 3

	P	W	D	L	F	A	Pts
Yugoslavia	4	2	2	0	13	4	6
France	2	0	2	0	2	2	2
Israel	2	0	0	2	2	11	0

21-08-1949	Yugoslavia : Israel	6:0 (4:0)
18-09-1949	Israel : Yugoslavia	2:5 (0:3)
09-10-1949	Yugoslavia : France	1:1 (1:0)
30-10-1949	France : Yugoslavia	1:1 (1:1)

Europe - Group 3 Play-off

	P	W	D	L	F	A	Pts
Yugoslavia	1	1	0	0	3	2	2
France	1	0	0	1	2	3	0

11-12-1949	Yugoslavia : France	3:2 a.e.t. (2:2, 1:1)

Played in Florence

Europe - Group 4

	P	W	D	L	F	A	Pts
Switzerland	2	2	0	0	8	4	4
Luxembourg	2	0	0	2	4	8	0

26-06-1949	Switzerland : Luxembourg	5:2 (3:1)
18-09-1949	Luxembourg : Switzerland	2:3 (2:1)

Europe - Group 5

	P	W	D	L	F	A	Pts
Sweden	2	2	0	0	6	2	4
Ireland Rep.	4	1	1	2	6	7	3
Finland	2	0	1	1	1	4	1

02-06-1949	Sweden : Ireland Republic	3:1 (2:1)
08-09-1949	Ireland Republic : Finland	3:0 (2:0)
09-10-1949	Finland : Ireland Republic	1:1 (0:0)
13-11-1949	Ireland Republic : Sweden	1:3 (0:2)

Europe - Group 6

	P	W	D	L	F	A	Pts
Spain	2	1	1	0	7	3	3
Portugal	2	0	1	1	3	7	1

02-04-1950	Spain : Portugal	5:1 (3:1)
09-04-1950	Portugal : Spain	2:2 (0:1)

Caribbean/North/Central America - Group 10

	P	W	D	L	F	A	Pts
Mexico	4	4	0	0	17	2	8
USA	4	1	1	2	8	15	3
Cuba	4	0	1	3	3	11	1

04-09-1949	Mexico : United States	6:0 (3:0)
11-09-1949	Mexico : Cuba	2:0 (1:0)
14-09-1949	United States : Cuba	1:1 (1:1)
18-09-1949	Mexico : United States	6:2 (3:0)
21-09-1949	Cuba : United States	2:5 (1:4)
25-09-1949	Cuba : Mexico	0:3 (0:1)

All games played in Mexico City

Chapter 7

A Heatwave, a Punch-up and the Armchair Fan
The Switzerland World Cup, 1954

Switzerland 1954

Winners: West Germany

Runners-up: Hungary

3rd Place: Austria

4th Place: Uruguay

Total Attendance: 762,000

Number of Matches: 26

By 1954 the Korean War had ended and the Vietnam War was about to begin. Ho Chi Minh, the leader of the Communist guerrillas had out-foxed the armies of France, the colonial power, and was demanding independence. So, in July the United Nations ruled that Vietnam should be divided in two at the 17th parallel. The north of the country was to be ruled by Ho Chi Minh, whilst the south was put under the control of the corrupt and unpopular Ngo Dinh Diem supported by the French and Americans. The Algerians were also tired of France's presence and were starting their own war of independence. The USA, becoming concerned about Communist support for such independence movements, were keen to put out the leftist fires, particularly when they came too close to their own doorstep. They sided with those Guatemalans opposed to left-wing President Arbenz and bombed the country. However, in the US itself, the career of Communist-hating Senator McCarthy was at an end. His friends in Congress turned against him because he had taken his accusations too far. Even presidents had been implicated.

In Britain citizens were told they could burn their ration books. Food was back in plentiful supply though people were turning to foods designed for a healthier lifestyle. In the countryside, however, ill-health was decimating one species of native animal. For years farmers, who had hated the damage done by rabbits to their property, introduced the lethal myxomatosis virus that killed thousands of fluffy bunnies. In the sporting world, Roger Bannister became the first man to run a sub-four minute mile in May with a time of 3 minutes 59.4 seconds at an Oxford track. Fangio won a second World Motor Racing Championship and sixteen of the world's best soccer teams were gathering in Switzerland for the fifth World Cup. It has been generally accepted that the decision to stage it there was the right one. The country had stayed neutral in World War Two and, with much of the continent still recovering from the effects of the war, it was one of the few European countries capable of hosting the event. 1954 also marked FIFA's 50th birthday and, with its headquarters in Zurich, Switzerland seemed the obvious venue for the celebratory party that the World Cup would provide.

A record number of 41 countries applied to enter the tournament, but this number was soon whittled down. India withdrew before the qualifying draw was made and then Bolivia, Costa Rica, Cuba, Iceland, Peru and Vietnam were refused entry because their applications were either received late or had been made on the wrong forms. China and Poland both subsequently withdrew after the draw had been made, but the Cold War had less effect on this World Cup than previously and, of the Communist countries, only the Soviet Union did not apply to enter. Poland's decision to pull out meant that Hungary qualified with out playing a match and the hosts and reigning champions also received automatic qualification. The rest had to play it out in the usual group system.

The qualifying rounds got underway on 9th May 1953 when Yugoslavia took on Greece in Belgrade in Group Ten. The Yugoslavs, who eventually went on to the finals, won the match 1-0, but the scoreline set a benchmark that was followed by the rest of the group. It was one of the lowest scoring qualifying groups in World Cup history, six games producing only seven goals, a remarkable tally considering that there were no draws in the group. The highest score was Greece's 2-0 defeat of Israel.

Most of the interest in 1954 came from European states, which made up the large majority of those who contested the qualifying stages. In the European sections there was only one newcomer and it was the only World Cup appearance as a separate entity of the Saar, which had been and is now part of Germany. Since the rest of

Germany had become politically divided into Communist East Germany and West Germany, this was also West Germany's first appearance in the World Cup. They qualified easily. Group Six was the only European Group to produce an upset when Turkey qualified in controversial circumstances.

Sweden was another team that might have been expected to make it through to the finals. They had an impressive international record, especially in Olympic competitions, having taken the gold medal in London in 1948 and the bronze in Helsinki in 1952. Their Olympic success, however, was the key to their World Cup failure. The insatiable quest of Italian clubs for success lured Sweden's best players abroad and the Swedish FA at that time would not include foreign-based players.

Of the other European countries, the French proved the free-scorers of the tournament. Theirs was a talented team and included players of the calibre of Raymond Kopa, Jean Vincent and Roger Piantoni, who went on to become some of the greatest players of the decade and genuine household names among football fans. They hit 20 goals in just four matches, putting 14 past Luxembourg over two legs and six past the Irish. Their opponents may not have been the most accomplished sides in the tournament, but France's strike rate was impressive and indicated what was to come later in the decade.

Considering the football culture that existed there, South America's representation in the qualifying stages was paltry. Uruguay, as reigning champions, enjoyed automatic qualification, but only three other teams from the continent applied to enter the 1954 World Cup. Paraguay, Chile and Brazil fought it out in Group Eleven, with undefeated Brazil the eventual winners. Argentina, with its "continued persecution complex", once again refused to enter, whilst the only other group that had American teams in it saw Mexico qualify for its third World Cup finals above Haiti and the USA.

Since 12 nations would take part in the football section of the Asian Games in May, it is surprising that so few Asian teams showed any interest in the World Cup. Only South Korea, whom Taiwan defeated in the final of those games, Japan and China entered. China then withdrew leaving the others to play it out over two legs in Group Thirteen. The South Koreans came out on top and so became the first sovereign Asian country to appear in the World Cup finals. (The Dutch East Indies had appeared in 1938, but not as an independent country.) Africa's lone entry into the competition was Egypt, the only independent country on the continent to have organized football. Much of the rest of Africa was under the aegis of European imperialism and, as such, ineligible to enter. Egypt was knocked out by Italy in Group Nine.

By April of 1954, the original entrants had been reduced down to the requisite sixteen and, mindful of the problems that had attended the organization of previous World Cups, FIFA opted for a more sensible four-pool format, with a straight knock-out for the later stages. The formula seemed to provide the fairest and most practical alternative, but then a strange twist was added. It was decided that two teams in each group would be seeded and that the seeded teams would only play the non-seeded teams. They would not play each other. It meant that each team played only two games in the first stage and that the strongest teams

The Germans Play Themselves
Group 1 (W. Germany, Saar, Norway)

Today, the Saar is a state in Germany on the Franco-German border, with Saarbrücken as its capital and large coal and iron deposits giving it it's prosperity. Before World War One it belonged to Germany, but control of its coal mines and steel mills went to the French in 1919 as payment for damages suffered during the war. It was governed by the League of Nations. A German protest in 1930 brought an end to allied interference and in 1935 its people voted in favour of becoming part of Germany again.

After World War Two, the French were back in control. They directed the region's defences and foreign relations, and controlled its heavy industry. In 1947, the Saar was allowed partial self-government and because this was still the case in 1953, it was allowed to enter a team in the World Cup. Hence Germans played each other in international football. The Saar's sojourn into the World Cup was successful for a small state. They failed to qualify, but achieved some creditable results, beating Norway 3-2 away and drawing 0-0 at home. Their fellow Germans beat them both times, but they still finished second in the group.

In October 1955 the people rejected a proposal to transfer responsibilities for defence and foreign affairs to the Western European Union and in December they elected a government committed to re-unification with West Germany. It happened on 1st January 1957 after France and W. Germany agreed terms.

Spain's bad luck in the World Cup appeared again in the 1954 qualifiers. Under today's rules their results against Turkey would have seen them through, but then a toss of a coin was needed. A blind Italian boy was asked to do the honours and the coin fell in Turkey's favour to put them in the finals for the first time. The Spanish press lamented that "Spain had been struck out of the World Football Cup by the hand of an Innocent Child."

Gate money at the finals was expected to be £900,000. It also gave the Swiss the opportunity to show off their wealth. The world's best-paid hotel porters got paid a massive 1s 8d (8p) for each suitcase they carried and there were no cut rates for anybody.

A Heatwave, a Punch-up and the Armchair Fan - Switzerland 1954

FIFA President Jules Rimet opens the 1954 tournament.

France 0 : Yugoslavia 1
France's Vincent (left) chases Nitic of Yugoslavia.

The firm favourites for the 1954 tournament were Hungary and Brazil. Brazil had shown what they could do in 1950 and Hungary had thrashed the English 7-1 in Budapest that year. Oddly, both teams tipped England as a good outside bet. One Hungarian, Gyula Mandis, said: "They may pull off a surprise."

only played the weakest. The idea was to try to ensure that the best nations made it through to the knock out stage to maintain its commercial viability, but it made the system open to abuse.

The opening day of the finals was 16th June and two games from each of Pools One and Three were featured. The day also produced the first shock of the tournament when the unseeded Yugoslavia defeated France 1-0 in Lausanne. The Yugoslavs were known to be a useful side, but were given no chance against a French team noted for its dashing, free-scoring forwards. On this occasion, though, those forwards were kept quiet and things began to look ominous when the Yugoslavs snatched the lead after only 15 minutes with a goal from Milos Milutinovic, the right-winger. Having got in front, the Yugoslavs looked to the value of solid defence to maintain it. Both Stepjan Bobek and Zlatko Caikowski, the captain, played excellently to keep the French forwards at bay and, try as they might, the French were unable to pierce the well organized back line. The Yugoslavs held on for a worthy 1-0 victory, though the French did take something from the match: Milutinovic later joined Racing Club de Paris and became one of the club's star players.

Other matches played that day went, more or less, to form. In Pool One, Brazil took on Mexico in Geneva and, for the third World Cup in succession, unveiled a team of considerable ability. After what was regarded in Brazil as a debacle in 1950, the side had a new coach, Zezé Moreira, who had rebuilt the national team in the hope of going further than his predecessor. Only three players, Francisco Rodríguez, Baltazar and Bauer, remained from the 1950 squad and a new array of talent had been brought into the team, including Didí, Julinho and Pinga. In the first half against Mexico, they were to show their potential as they tore the unfortunate Mexicans apart. Strikes from Didí, Julinho and two from Pinga blasted them into a 4-0 half-time lead. It was breathtaking football and the Mexicans were powerless to hold back the tide. Brazil slowed down in the second period and a lone goal from Julinho, on the hour, ensured a 5-0 win. It was a result that made the other teams who fancied their chances take note. (See Djalma Santos profile on page 114).

The games in Pool Three saw Scotland make its debut in the World Cup finals. Having accepted its mistake in not attending the 1950 finals, the Scottish FA willingly accepted its place in Switzerland, even though, once again, the Scots had come second in the home championship. However, there were serious problems in the Scottish camp, which were to have dramatic effect. The Scots had gone on a shoestring budget and had taken only 13 players, but because of the attitude of Glasgow Rangers, they were not necessarily Andy Beattie's first choice. It is not surprising, then, that the Scots did not have a particularly auspicious first foray into the World Cup finals, although, it must be said, they were unlucky to lose their first match against Austria who employed an unusual defensive formation, known as the "Bolt" system. It was an early version of the sweeper system, in which full-backs served as central defenders and half-backs dropped to the flanks. It allowed the centre-half freedom to move up and support the forwards, giving the team greater flexibility, but made it difficult for British teams who still favoured the more rigid 2-3-5 formation. Against the Scots, though, Austria's "delicate, well-oiled machine was shaken and disturbed long before the end", to use the words of a contemporary reporter. They took the lead in the 33rd minute with a goal from old war-horse, Erich Probst, but then had to struggle to hold on to it. The Scots were courageous fighters, who "not only beat the Austrians for pace but also kept the ball moving quickly along the ground." Schmied, in the Austrian goal, was certainly the busier of the two keepers, but he was not to be beaten. Probst's single strike was enough to secure the victory, though the defeat seems to have confirmed everything that manager Beattie had been struggling against and his resignation followed soon after.

Fewer histrionics accompanied the other Pool Three game played on 16th June. This saw reigning champions, Uruguay, take on Czechoslovakia, now coached by Oldrich Nejedlý, in Berne's Wankdorf Stadium. The Uruguayans had a gifted team, with several players who had won the title in 1950, among them Juan Schiaffino and captain, Obdulio Varela, at 39 years old the oldest man to appear in the World Cup finals so far. The Czechoslovaks, on the other hand, were disappointing and failed to emulate the reputation of former Czech teams. They were lucky to keep the South Americans out for as long as they did, but eventually the superior Uruguayans got their desserts. Oscar Míguez scored in the 70th minute and Schiaffino added a second eight minutes from the end to give his country a 2-0 victory.

Pool Two was the high scoring group whose five games produced 41 of the tournament's 140 goals and kicked off on 17th June. In the pool were the Hungarians, seeded and everybody's favourite to win the championship. The South Koreans were the first to be on the receiving end of their wizardry. (See Ferenc Puskás profile on page 115). "The Galloping Major", Puskás, was the first Hungarian to register a goal and then strikes by Mihaly Lantos and two from Kocsis gave them a 4-0 half-time lead. The South Koreans played with guts and enthusiasm, and no little skill themselves, but they were no match for the "uncrowned" world champions. Five more goals in the second half, including three in the last 15 minutes, ensured a 9-0 victory and a new scoring record for the World Cup finals. The men who appeared in that team put their success down to commitment, experience and team work. Hidegkúti once said: "We knew each other's dreams, every movement. The more unified a team is, the more chances it has to win. If I went forward, Puskás immediately came into my place. If Kocsis went to the side then Bozsic went to the centre. We always found a way to have an empty space in the field to where we can pass the ball." Walter Winterbottom, England's manager, explained their tactical inventiveness when he said that: "Hidegkúti was creating the problem because he was the centre-forward, so called, and came 20 yards further back, drawing the centre-half (if the centre-half was going with him) out of position so that people could slot into the gap." It created delightfully innovative football that was far ahead of anything the rest of the world could muster.

On the same day, the West Germans faced Turkey, the other seeded team in the group. It seems unusual to think that the Germans were not seeded, but in 1954 West Germany was a new country, having only come into existence in 1949, after the four years of Allied occupation that followed the defeat of the Nazis in 1945. For several years after that defeat, the Germans had not competed in international sport. With the establishment of West Germany, the country had been readmitted into international sporting circles, but remained relatively unknown as a football nation. The game against Turkey provided the perfect springboard from which to begin rebuilding a reputation, though it did not begin particularly well. After only two minutes they fell behind to a goal from Mamet Suat. However, the Germans quickly regained their composure and equalized twelve minutes later, when Hans Schäfer was on target. In the second half, the Germans took control of the game and scored three times to run out eventual 4-1 winners.

Two Pool Four games were also played on 17th June. One of them was England's first game, against Belgium, a team the English had beaten 5-0 at Wembley just over a year previously. The Belgians, though, were an improved side and were able to take advantage of England's defensive frailties and especially of the edginess of their goalkeeper, Birmingham City's Gil Merrick. It took the Belgians only five minutes to take the lead, when Léopold Anoul hit the back of the net, but England's response was spirited and to the point. In the words of the Times's reporter, "after shaking that opening cloud off their shoulders they dominated the central hour with some pure cultured football to take a lead that should have given them victory." In the 25th minute, Ivor Broadis equalized and ten minutes later, Nat Lofthouse put the team in front. England were playing well and "their football wore an elegance not seen from them for two or three seasons." Driving England on was wingman, Stanley Matthews, "once more the entertainer supreme, the magician who brought the crowd to a tiptoe of expectancy with the maze of his dribbling." He was the constant torment of Belgium's defence. The English increased their lead in the second half, when Broadis added his second, but the Belgian goalkeeper pulled off a string of excellent saves to keep the England tally down to three. It was in the last 20 minutes that things began to fall apart for England. First, Anoul scored his second and seven minutes later Henri Coppens found the net to level the scores. New FIFA rules said that drawn games should go in to extra time and England dominated the extra period. Lofthouse scored his second goal to regain the lead, but the game still ended as a 4-4 draw. It was an unlucky Jimmy Dickinson who headed into his own net to deny England victory and give Belgium a point.

The other Pool Two match saw the home team defeat Italy in a violent and brutal confrontation, over which Brazilian referee, Mario Viana, had little control. Both teams were responsible for some ugly tackling and, since the Swiss proved marginally "better" at it than did the Italians, they had the advantage that enabled them to go on to win the game. Robert Ballaman opened the scoring for the Swiss in the 17th minute, only for Giampiero Boniperti to equalize shortly before half-time. By this time, though, the game had long deteriorated and the nastiness continued after the restart. A stronger, less tolerant referee would have sent players off for the sort of conduct that was on show and one man who should certainly have walked was Italy's left-winger, Benito Lorenzi. His team mates had nicknamed him "Poison" and, no doubt, the referee would have concurred with this judgement. Constantly throughout the match, Lorenzi subjected him to a string of verbal abuse, questioning his decisions. He was not the only Italian to show dissent, but he was the worst and after the game, the enraged Italians chased the referee off the field, though their claims of injustice were hardly convincing. They had been just as violent as the Swiss.

The second batch of pool games took place on 19th June, one of which saw Brazil take on Yugoslavia in the most entertaining game in Pool One. Both teams played clean, attractive football and both committed themselves to attack from the start. Numerous chances were fashioned by both teams and, after a goalless first half, the Yugoslavs made a tactical switch. Left-wing, Branko Zebec was moved inside to play centre-forward and the effect was almost immediate. Within three minutes he had scored and the Europeans held on to their lead until the 70th minute, when Didí equalized. Both sides continued to attack and both created further openings, but neither could make them tell. So, with the scores tied extra time had to be played. A draw was enough to see both teams into the next stage and the extra time proved an anti-climax. Neither pressed for a victory and there was no further score. It meant that the final Pool One game, between France and Mexico, was a mere formality. The French took a two goal lead, with a first half score from Jean Vincent and a second half own goal from Raúl Cardeñas, then the Mexicans staged a fight back. They brought the scores back level and seemed to be heading for their first World Cup point, when the referee, Manuel Asensi of Spain, awarded a highly controversial penalty to the French. It was converted by Vincent to secure a victory. It was the end of France's World Cup campaign, but they were a team of much promise. It would mature and reveal its brilliance in Sweden in 1958. It was Mexico's third appearance in the World Cup finals and they had lost all of the eight games they had played.

The Austrians had begun unconvincingly, but were about to blossom and reveal just what a fine and high scoring team they were. The Czechoslovaks, one of the disappointments of 1954, were to be the first to feel the force of Austria's power in their clash on 19th June. The Austrians hit form from the first whistle and were two goals up inside four minutes, Ernst Stojaspal and Erich Probst doing the damage. Probst netted twice more before the half-hour was over to score a hat trick. These four first half goals demoralized the Czechs and took the fight out of them, so that the Austrians could slow their assault in the second half, knowing that their passage into the next stage was certain. Stojaspal added a fifth to make sure and rounded off a superb individual and collective team performance.

The last Pool Three game saw the Scots taken apart by Uruguay. Admittedly, the Scots had been deflated by the resignation of their manager and it left them in some disarray, but this only partly explains the nature of their defeat. The other reason is that the Uruguayans, once they had found their flow, were electrifying and the Scots could find no answer, especially in the savage temperature in which the game was played. Scotland did reasonably well in the first half, keeping the score down to 2-0, but the second half was entirely different. The Uruguayans lifted their game and the Scottish defence collapsed. Two goals in the first twelve minutes by Carlos Borges gave him his hat trick. Then Julio César Abbadie made it 5-0. Two late goals, one from Míguez adding to the one he scored in the first half, and another from Abbadie, who rounded the Scottish goalkeeper to slot into an empty net, ended the humiliation. It had been exhibition football from the South Americans, but for the Scots, it was a salutary lesson in how to play the game. The football correspondent of the Scottish Daily Record did not hold back in his analysis of why the Scots were so convincingly beaten and in his praise of the Uruguayans. "I was made to realise more than ever before that... we are at the bow and arrow stage, while the Uruguayans were employing the H-Bomb or... we have been content with the mud-hut of soccer while the South Americans have been building marble palaces." Partick Thistle's George Davidson remarked rather sombrely: "We could not raise a gallop."

So far Austria, Brazil, Uruguay and Yugoslavia had qualified for the quarter-finals. The four countries who would join them would be decided the next day and West Germany's manager, Sepp Herberger, gambled on being able to play the system to his team's advantage. For some, his ploy was a case of cheating, whilst for others it was a tactical masterpiece. The situation was that if the Germans lost to Hungary, as seemed likely, then they would have to play-off against either Turkey or South Korea for the pool's second place. Herberger was confident that his team could beat either. Coming second in the pool would bring added advantage in that Germany would avoid Brazil in the quarter-final and would, instead, meet Yugoslavia, who had come second in Pool One. Herberger reckoned that his team had a greater chance of making further progress against the weaker Yugoslavs than against the much-fancied Brazilians. So, he fielded a deliberately weakened team to fail knowing that it would improve his chance of future success. His team was made up almost entirely of reserves, including a debutante goalkeeper and Helmut Rahn, who had been dropped from international duty and was now recalled. He was brought back from a club tour of Uruguay for the match and a very propitious return it was to be - both in 1954 and, again, in 1958.

Herberger's decision did not win him many friends in the short term. Some 30,000 Germans had travelled to Basle to watch their team take on the "Mighty Magyars" and most of them stood in disbelief when the team was announced. They had come to see a battle, and instead witnessed a surrender. They showed their displeasure by whistling throughout, as the Hungarians gave "a splendid exhibition of the game", as one British reporter wrote. "Puskas, Kocsis and Hidegkúti, with their speedy wingers Toth and Czibor in close support, tore the German defence to shreds", he continued. Within 20 minutes the rampant Hungarians were three goals up, as Kocsis netted twice and Puskás once. (See Sandor Kocsis profile on page 118). Pfaff made a single reply for the Germans before half-time, but on the

Uruguay 7 : Scotland 0
The Scottish defence fail to clear the ball and Uruguay score.

In the programme for England's opening game against Belgium on 17th June at St Jakob Stadium, Basle, Stanley Matthews was listed as "St. Matthews". As it happened he had an angelic game. A quote from the Times said: "He certainly was a football saint this evening, the man who softened up Belgium to the point of defeat."

The circumstances surrounding Scotland's first World Cup campaign were not to manager Andy Beattie's liking. Beattie, also manager of Huddersfield Town, was not happy with the way the Scottish FA had handled the arrangements and had differences with the selectors, especially since he had not been allowed to take the players he wanted. Glasgow Rangers were on a tour of North America at the same time and refused to release their players, including national team captain, George Young. By Friday, 18th June it had got too much. "Tomorrow, after we meet Uruguay, win, lose or draw I am going home", he announced. Officially, his reason was that he was spending too much time away from his family, but the real reasons went much deeper.

A Heatwave, a Punch-up and the Armchair Fan - Switzerland 1954

Hungary 8 : Germany 3
Hungary's Kocsis shoots past Kwiatkowski to score. Note the train in the background that has been halted to use as a stand.

restart the onslaught began again. Hidegkúti scored twice within two minutes of the whistle and Kocsis made it 6-1 to in the 67th minute to become the first player to score two hat tricks in the World Cup finals. József Tóth was the next to score and then Rahn hit a withering shot from a very difficult angle to give the Germans a second. Kocsis netted his fourth and finally, Richard Hermann got in on the act to make the final scoreline 8-3 to the Hungarians. One sour note in what was a brilliant game of football came when Puskás was deliberately kicked by Germany's centre-half, Werner Liebrich. He was badly injured, needing treatment for over an hour and did not play again until the final. The Germans had again shown a cynical disregard for the spirit of the game.

The final game in Pool Two, between Turkey and South Korea, would decide whom Herberger's Germans would meet in the play-off. It quickly became apparent that this would be Turkey. They surged to a rapid 3-0 lead within half an hour, with goals from Suat, Kucuandoniadis Lefter and Suat again, before Sargun Burhan gave them a 4-0 half-time advantage. He scored twice early in the second half to achieve his hat trick and Keksin Erol finished the job in the 76th minute, making the final result 7-0 to the Turks.

In the "baking oven of the Wankdorf Stadium" England's second game, against the hosts, was described in the Times as one of "extreme mediocrity." Matthews was injured and could not play and the only other point of interest was captain Billy Wright's switch to centre-half to replace the injured Syd Owen. It proved to be Wright's natural position and he played there for the rest of his international career. England won it 2-0 to secure a place in the quarter-finals. Just before half-time, Taylor headed Dickinson's long pass down to Jimmy Mullen, who rounded the goalkeeper and slid the ball into an open net. The second, after the break, was a solo effort from Dennis Wilshaw, who dribbled through the Swiss defence, beating three players before shooting into the goal.

Italy's approach to their final pool game against Belgium was entirely different from that they had adopted against the Swiss. It was a game that they had to win if they were to have a chance of making further progress and they decided to put the emphasis on skill, rather than brute force. Though the change of heart brought only one first half goal, from Egito Pandofini, it paid off in the second when the Italians went on the rampage. Carlo Galli, Amleto Frignani and "Poison" Lorenzi all scored in the first 13 minutes of the half before the Italians, confident of victory, slowed it down. The Belgians grabbed a late consolation, through Anoul, but the 4-1 result meant that Italy had earned a play-off against Switzerland to see who would reach the quarter-finals.

This was played on 23rd June at the St. Jakob Stadium in Basle and the Swiss came out worthy winners against an Italian side that had been strangely messed about by Italy's Hungarian-born coach, Lajos Czeizler. Surprisingly, he dropped several players and played others out of position. It seriously weakened the team, which proved far less troublesome than that which had fouled its way through their first meeting. The violent nature of this first encounter had seen experienced Welsh referee, Mervyn Griffiths, brought in to officiate and he did well. He kept the players focused on the football and his judgement contributed to an entertaining match. The Swiss were the first to show, when Josef Hügi scored in the 14th minute and this remained the situation until half-time. When the game resumed, the Swiss again had the early advantage when Robert Ballaman hit the net after only three minutes. Fulvio Nesti pulled one back for Italy mid way through the half, but the Swiss sealed their victory with two goals in the last five minutes, through Hügi with his second and Jacques Fatton.

Sepp Herberger's scheming brought a play-off against Turkey and, as he anticipated, the Germans won through with little difficulty. He restored his best players and they were soon in control, going two up in 12 minutes, through Ottmar Walter and Hans Schäfer. Ertan Mustafa pulled one back to give his team a faint glimmer of hope, but it was dashed when Max Morlock fired home to give the Germans a two goal half-time advantage. The flow of German goals continued after the restart. Morlock netted again in the 60th minute and two minutes later captain, Fritz Walter, brother of Ottmar, made the score 5-1. Morlock then completed his hat trick and Schäfer got his second, before Lefter scored a late goal to bring a final scoreline of 7-2 in Germany's favour.

Turkey 7 : Korea 0
Ismail Suat scores Turkey's third goal past Korean goalkeeper Hong Duk-yung.

The quarter-finals produced some high scoring matches, beginning when Austria and Switzerland set a new scoring record in the finals with a 12 goal thriller. (See Austria v Switzerland profile on page 120). The other quarter-final tie staged that day was that between Uruguay and England, in which the South Americans achieved a British double. Both teams played very well and the two centre-half captains, Wright and Varela, were outstanding. Matthews also had a good game for England, but his team were let down by some wayward goalkeeping from Merrick, who should have saved two of Uruguay's goals. The first was taken by Carlos Borges after only five minutes, but the early set back did not upset the English, who responded positively with some penetrating attacks of their own. On one of them, Matthews created space for himself to send a pass through to Dennis Wilshaw. He, in turn picked out Lofthouse, whose strike levelled the score. It was 1-1, with minutes to go in the half, when Varela hit a searching shot from outside the area that seemed to catch Merrick totally unprepared. He misjudged it completely and the Uruguayans were back in front. Unfortunately, soon after scoring Varela pulled a muscle and had to leave the field. When he returned, after the break, his leg was heavily bandaged. Shortly after the restart Lofthouse failed to convert a good chance and when Varela's free kick was misread by Merrick, Schiaffino punished the error. At 3-1 down, England resumed the attack and Finney found the net in the 67th minute to bring his team back into the game. However, a series of misses by the English forwards, including one where Matthews hit the post, cost them dearly. Uruguay killed the game off 12 minutes from the end with a score by Javier Ambrois, but the English could take heart from some of their best international performances in over two years.

The England-Uruguay game had been super fare. The so-called Battle of Berne between Hungary and Brazil (See Hungary v Brazil profile on page 119) the next day was not and it was left to West Germany and Yugoslavia

The match between England and the Swiss was hot stuff in more ways than one. The English team was passed cotton wool soaked in iced water during the match when temperatures reached over 100 degrees Fahrenheit as Switzerland went through a mini heatwave. They also took cold showers before and after the game. Similar temperatures afflicted the Scots when they faced Uruguay, but they hadn't come prepared and had to turn out in energy-sapping long sleeved woollen jerseys. The prospect unsettled them more than that of facing the world champions.

The result of the Group 4 match between England and Switzerland was mistakenly cabled to the UK as a 9-2 victory to the Swiss. England had in fact won the game 2-0.

A Heatwave, a Punch-up and the Armchair Fan - Switzerland 1954

An Architect of Success - Sepp Herberger...

Born on 28th March 1897, Sepp Herberger was the man responsible for putting German football on the map and for regaining the nation a degree of respectability that it had lost in the 1930s and 40s. He was the first of the great German managers and a fine exponent of the game. His management style and the type of play he encouraged had been learnt from watching matches all over the world in preparation for glory. He was appointed assistant manager of the national side in 1932 and took full control in 1936 even though he had never managed a German club side

Herberger's approach to the 1954 tournament was a little bewildering at first, though tactically very astute. By fielding a deliberately weakened team against Hungary in the pool game, he eased his team's passage to the final and ensured that that they would not meet the Hungarians until the final. He also hid from the Hungarians the true strength of his squad. The fans were not convinced by his ploy, but it worked. It was the hour of Herberger's greatest triumph. He was in charge of the German side for 27 years between 1936 and 1963 and they won 92 of the 162 games played.

The "Eat My Own Words" Award for 1954 goes to...

Clifford Webb of the Daily Herald for his comments on 3rd July, the day before the final. He wrote: "There is not enough skill in the German team to counteract the Magyar magic. There is much speed and grand determination, but this is not likely to be enough."

to restore sanity to the competition. The talented Yugoslavs played some delightful football, showing much more flair and ball skill than their opponents and put the German defence under far more pressure than they suffered. Herberger, though, had prepared his team carefully and the defence, in particular, was well organized. It combined discipline with muscle, and a little luck - Kohlmeyer cleared several Yugoslav efforts off the line. Two goals won the game for Germany, the first in the first half when Ivan Horvat put through his own net the second when Helmuth Rahn broke free.

Both semi-finals were played on the last day of June and that between Hungary and Uruguay produced "one of the most keenly contested matches ever witnessed in the World Cup finals". Some "people have called it the finest game of football ever played." The Swiss authorities had expected trouble and had surrounded the pitch with police, but they need not have worried since both sides knew that here were the best in the world and they were determined to let their football do the talking. Both were, as one book describes it, "at their brilliant, mercurial best and the match swung like a pendulum." It was played in heavy rain and both sides were missing important, key players - Puskás for Hungary; Varela, Míguez and Abbadie for Uruguay - but neither factor affected the entertainment. The Magyars went ahead in the 13th minute when Kocsis headed down a cross for Czibor to volley into the net, but no further score was registered in the first half. Soon after the break, Hidegkúti headed his team into a 2-0 lead and things looked to be going their way. The South Americans, though, had mounted some pacey attacks of their own without success and were unlucky not to have had something to show for all their skill and élan. They staged a spirited comeback in the final quarter of an hour to take the game into extra time. Firstly, Schiaffino sent a clever through pass for Juan Hohberg to chase, pull under control and score the type of goal that had earned him the nickname "the executioner" by his Peñarol team mates. Then, four minutes from the end, Schiaffino again found a pass that split the Hungarian defence and, again, Hohberg latched on to it. This time he almost lost the ball as he raced into the penalty area, but in the midst of a knot of defenders, regained control and placed the ball neatly into the net. His team mates celebrated so hard that he needed treatment before he could continue.

In extra time the Uruguayans visibly tired. Hohberg could have bagged his hat trick in the first period, when a shot hit the post, but two problems combined to give Hungary the advantage. Schiaffino, who had played brilliantly, was badly injured and was a passenger for the rest of the match. Then, with about ten minutes to go, Victor Andrade, who had also played a solid game, went down with cramp. It was at this point, with Uruguay effectively reduced to nine men, that Kocsis headed Hungary into the lead. Four minutes from time, he headed his second to secure a 4-2 victory. It was his 11th goal of the tournament and set a new record for the finals, overtaking that set by Ademir in 1950.

The Austrians made one unfortunate change of personnel for their semi-final against West Germany. Mindful of having conceded five in the quarter-final, they changed goalkeepers. Walter Zeman, who had been out of form, was brought back to replace Schmied. The problem was that Zeman had not regained his form and he contributed greatly to an emphatic German victory. The only first half goal came from Schäfer, who side footed the ball into the net from close range, but in the second half

---

A World Cup brawl (otherwise known as "The Battle of Berne")

At the infamous quarter-final between Hungary and Brazil the fighting that had gone on during the match continued after the final whistle. As the Times's reporter noted: "At the end a minor revolution broke out" and the press dubbed the whole affair the "Battle of Berne". Such was the chaos at the entrance to the tunnel, with the photographers and spectators pushing and shoving, eager to get a glimpse of what was going on, that the police struggled to maintain order. There was hooliganism, running battles, flying bottles and football boots brandished as weapons, but none of it to do with the supporters. One Brazilian reserve, dressed in ordinary clothes, ran onto the pitch and attacked two policemen, one of whom he floored "with a perfect foul tackle."

No one knows who began the trouble in the tunnel, but Ferenc Puskás, and Gusztav Sebes, the team coach and Deputy Sports Minister, were waiting to congratulate their team as they came off the field. Whilst the Hungarians were getting their bouquets for winning, the Brazilians gathered in the tunnel and took off their boots, with which they prepared to ambush their opponents. All hell broke loose when Puskás and Sebes, on seeing this, got involved and were joined by the rest of the team as they came off the pitch. In the ensuing brawl, Puskás received a crack on the head, Sebes a gash under the eye and the Brazilian, Pinheiro, ended with his head swathed in bandages that concealed a five-inch wound. He later claimed that Puskás had hit him with a bottle.

Fighting also broke out in the stands, involving well dressed Brazilian supporters and their wives, and in the confusion Mrs. Ellis, wife of the referee, and their two children were rescued from the trouble by the Scots referee, Charlie Faultless, who was sitting nearby. They were taken into the stadium for safety, but things were worse down in the players' area. The Police tried to hustle the teams into their respective changing rooms and seal the entrances, but the fighting continued. The disturbances went on for a further half-hour and 30 minutes more passed before the teams were smuggled out of the ground. It was a dreadful ending to a shameful exhibition of how the game should not be played. Describing the scene in the players area after they had gone, Faultless said: "There were boots and broken bottles all over the shop and one dressing room was totally wrecked." Later that day, Sandor Baros, president of the Hungarian FA and who was himself hurt in the fray, announced the cancellation of a proposed tour of South America. The central figure in the whole incident had been British referee Arthur Ellis of Halifax, who was given a police escort back to his hotel after the match. Later he was to say: "It was the sort of game I knew was going to be tough and I decided that the only thing to do was to be firm."

---

the floodgates opened. After only two minutes, Morlock headed in Fritz Walter's corner and a short time later, Probst pulled a goal back for the Austrians, with their last touch of any significance. From that point the game belonged exclusively to the Germans. In the 54th minute, Fritz Walter struck from the penalty spot and six minutes later he provided the cross for his brother, Ottmar, to score with a back header. Both brothers struck again, Fritz with another penalty and Ottmar with another header, to bring a final score of 6-1.

The 1954 World Cup finals had now come down to two teams, but before Hungary could meet West Germany in the final, Austria took on Uruguay in the now customary 3rd/4th place play-off. In it the usually classy Uruguayans for once looked dispirited and out of sorts. The semi-final, three days earlier, had taken a lot out of them, physically and mentally, and they found it difficult to pick themselves up for what must have seemed like a "B" movie to a team so used to top billing. The Austrians, though, were in a more buoyant mood and took the lead in the 16th minute, when Ernst Stojaspal, who played superbly throughout, converted a penalty. Five minutes later, Hohberg equalized with what was to be Uruguay's last major contribution to the game. Their play became increasingly less influential and an injury to Schiaffino soon after seriously added to their decline. This was un-

---

A Wizard in the Making - Gusztav Sebes

Born on 21st June 1906, Gusztav Sebes, affectionately known as "Uncle Guszhi" by his players, was the wizard who created the "Mighty Magyars", as they were christened by the British press. As a player, he gained a respectable reputation with club sides Vasas and MTK Budapest. However, it was his Hungarian national side that made him famous. The post-war Communist Hungarian government heavily invested in football, recognizing its great propaganda value. This allowed Sebes to mould the finest of Hungarian talent into what became one of the most exciting sides to kick a football. Names such as Ferenc Puskás, Nandor Hidegkúti, Sandor Kocsis, to name but three, became world famous. Their game was "a blend of artistry, intelligence and athleticism that neither Europe nor the world had ever seen."

Going into the 1954 series they had not lost a game since May 1950 when Austria had defeated them 5-3 in Vienna. They had won the Olympic title in 1952 and then had stunned the football world in November 1953 when they defeated England 6-3 at Wembley. They had become the first team from outside the British Isles to beat England beneath the "twin towers" and did even better in the return match in Budapest, when the score was 7-1. Simple statistics reveal the power of that team. Between their defeat by Austria and the World Cup finals of 1954, they had played 27 international fixtures. Of these they had drawn four and had won 23, a phenomenal record.

Following the 1956 Hungarian Uprising, many of the top players defected to the West and in 1957 Sebes resigned because of it. He had combined his job as national coach with that of Deputy Sports Minister and, although remaining in the game for a while, he retired soon after. He died in 1986. He had been in charge of the national side for 68 games between 1949 and 1957. They lost only seven of those games but won 49, a success rate of 74.24%.

Uruguay 2 : Hungary 4
Hidegkúti heads Hungary's second goal.

The wives of the Hungarian players had been escorted to the Switzerland World Cup by Communist plain clothed guards so that they could watch their husbands play in the final. Having been kept isolated at their hotel until an hour before kick-off, they set off laden with the flowers they hoped to present to their victorious heroes. They sat and watched the game in the rain only to be disappointed by the final outcome. When it was over, the wives were escorted back their hotel, the flowers remained unpresented and were thrown away. The week's holiday the players hoped to spend with their wives in Switzerland if they won never materialized.

The phenomenon of the "armchair supporter" made its World Cup debut in Switzerland. Television was now widely watched by many in Europe and highlights of matches were transmitted to all those who could receive them. At one stage in the tournament crowds were down so much that the organizers feared it would not pay its own way. In the end the crowds did pick up and the tournament was a financial success.

derlined in the second half when Luis Cruz, a normally reliable defender, put through his own net and the Uruguayan discomfort was completed eleven minutes from time, when Ernst Ocwirk lashed home a fine shot from 25 yards.

The end of the tournament came with the final that refused to go with form and it is no disrespect to the Germans to say that the best team in the world had lost the World Cup. (See W. Germany v Hungary profile on page 121). It was Hungary's first defeat in 32 internationals and, as if to underline their brilliance, they had scored 27 goals in just five World Cup games. Theirs was a defeat as unpredictable as any in World Cup history and it was, of course, the beginning of Germany's own fine World Cup tradition. The Germans may have been fortunate, but they had also played with resolute determination and not a little flair of their own. Fortune favours the brave and this time it favoured the Germans and their valiant goalkeeper.

The presentation of the trophy that bore his name by Jules Rimet to Fritz Walter brought the curtain down on Switzerland '54. (See Fritz Walter profile on page 116). The 1950 finals gave a sense of the World Cup moving away from the more staid events of the 1930s and into the modern era of keen interest, high expectation, heavy media coverage and lucrative rewards. The trend was confirmed by the Swiss World Cup. The tournament's appeal was widening, the number of countries wishing to take part expanding with every event, and the stars of other nations were becoming as well known outside their own countries as in them. Matches could be easily followed, in the press, on cinema newsreels and on the radio, and it signified a massive difference between the World Cup of 1934 and that of 1954. Four years later that difference would be even wider, when television became an important factor.

In only five tournaments, the World Cup had come a long way and as long as fans continued to be served with football of the calibre of that played by Hungary, Brazil, Uruguay and Yugoslavia; whilst they could be entertained by the genius of Hidegkúti, Puskás, Vincent, Militunovic, Matthews, Didí et al; and whilst they could be thrilled by games like Hungary against Brazil, England against Uruguay or Austria against Switzerland; the World Cup would continue to grow. Hardly had the cheering died down in the Wankdorf Stadium, than people were anticipating the next tournament, four years away.

Djalma Santos (Dejalma dos Santos)   Brazil

**Honours: Winner 1958 and 1962; Quarter-finals 1954   Games 12
Played: 1954, 1958, 1962 and 1966   Goals 1**

Brazilian full backs, Nilton Santos (left) and Djalma Santos (right).

Today he would be referred to as a wing-back, but, in the 1950s and 60s he was simply a good old-fashioned defender with a flair for attack. His admirable creative qualities made him one of the greatest exponents of the Brazilian right-back position. His talent was such that it kept him in the Brazilian side for four consecutive World Cup tournaments and made him a twice winner of the championships. Knowing exactly when to tackle, he would draw his opponents into a false sense of security, holding back on committing a challenge before racing in to dispossess the luckless attacker.

Born at São Paulo, Brazil on 27th February 1929 Santos made a late start in the professional game. At the age of 17 he made a mistake that prevented him playing the game for two years. He was caught playing truant from school and his father banned him from football until his studies were complete. However, at the age of 19 it was with his parents' approval that he signed for Brazilian club side, Portuguesa, where he spent the next 11 years of his career, developing into a tough, stylish central defender. He also made a big impression with his ability to attack and it was not long before he took on a more flexible role linking forwards to back with excellent results. By 1952 he had caught the eye of enough people to be granted his first place in the international side at the Pan-American Games that year. He played in all three games and following a 0-0 draw with Peru and 5-0 and 4-2 victories over Paraguay and Uruguay respectively, he ended the tournament with a gold medal.

His performances in the tournament and subsequently, made him the natural choice for the national side that was to go to Switzerland in 1954. In the qualifying tournament Santos played in all four of Brazil's games, all of them victories and making Brazil one of the pre-tournament favourites. His finals debut came in the team's 5-0 thrashing of Mexico and he was ever present until Brazil were eventually knocked out by the Hungarians. Santos was a dead-ball specialist and also Brazil's designated penalty taker and it was from the penalty spot in that he scored his one and only goal of the series in the quarter-final. Throughout the tournament he had forged a fine understanding with his namesake (but white and no relation) Nilton Santos that was to develop magnificently over the years.

The years between the '54 and '58 tournaments brought mixed fortunes for Santos. He played only one game for Brazil, in 1955, but this did not diminish his desire to appear for his country. Portuguesa picked up the Rio-São Paulo Cup in 1955, two years after an earlier success, and the fact that Santos had become the most outstanding defender in the league meant that he could not be ignored for too long. However, positional changes needed to be made and, when Bauer, the Brazilian wing-half in the 1950 World Cup series and captain in 1954, was eventually switched to the left side of midfield Santos was back in. He once again became the regular choice at right-back, playing 19 games in 1956.

It was between World Cup tournaments that Santos began to learn the role of overlapping full-back, a tactic that became instrumental to the Brazilian 4-2-4 formation. However, in 1956, while he could perhaps claim he was still learning the job, he was taught a valuable lesson at Wembley by a 41 year old Stanley Matthews who ran him ragged. The Brazilians were swept aside, 4-2, by a devastating Matthews-led performance. Not disheartened however, Santos went on to perfect his cautious, but clever approach to defensive work and his excellent positional sense, a technique that was in stark contrast to his attacking game, which he took to with a gung-ho style that played havoc down the wings.

Santos appeared in both qualifying matches for the 1958 series against Peru, though coach, Feola, was still not certain about his way forward in the finals themselves. Santos lost his place to De Sordi and he was not to figure in the tournament until the final itself. The Brazilians overran the Swedes and Santos was instrumental in neutralizing the attacking threat of the Swedish winger Skoglund, and forwards Hamrin and Liedholm. Santos did not allow himself to be caught out and his 'wait and see' defensive policy was to confuse and confound the Swedish attack at every turn. And, due to the miracle of television, the world could witness one of the best defenders in the game at work. The following year he moved to Palmeiros where he achieved honours in three São Paulo Championships and another Rio-São Paulo Cup. At the 1962 World Cup finals and, at the age of 33, Santos was still in the national side. He was as good as he had ever been. The understanding he developed with right-winger, and player of the tournament, Garrincha, was to prove the combination that took Brazil to their second successive World Cup title, this and the inspired performances of Amarildo. In the final itself he made the cross that lead to Brazil's third goal and he was named the championship's best all round defender. He was an obvious choice for the Rest of the World team that played England in 1963.

The World Cup in 1966 proved to be a tournament too far for the Brazilians and, at the age of 37, Santos was a surprise selection in the side. He was past his best and he could only stand and watch as Farkas's volley hit the back of the net in Hungary's 3-1 victory. He was made one of the scapegoats for this defeat and he was consequently dropped for the final game against Portugal. It signalled the end of his international career. In 1968, he was given one last outing as a farewell gesture, a friendly against Uruguay in front of his home supporters in São Paulo. Brazil won the game 2-0 but Santos was replaced by Carlos Alberto before its end.

Ferenc Puskás   Hungary

Honours: Runner-up 1954 (with Hungary)   **Games 6**
Played: 1954 and 1962 (with Spain)   **Goals 4**

Ferenc Puskás (right) takes on West German Horst Eckel in the 1954 World Cup Final.

Ferenc Puskás was the most feared striker of the 1950s and early 1960s and this was despite the fact that he was squat and tubby, not very good in the air and decidedly one footed. However, his left foot caused countless problems for anyone who played against him and guided him to captain of one of the greatest international sides ever put together. He was a man with many nicknames, but is perhaps most famously known as "The Galloping Major". Born in Budapest on 2nd April 1927, he played his club football for Hungarian sides Kispest and Honved. He took over the captaincy of the national side in 1950, and led them to an overwhelming triumph at the 1952 Olympic Games. Under his generalship, the "Mighty Magyars" lost only once before the Hungarian Uprising in 1956. Ironically, this one defeat was in a game when Puskás was not at his best due to an earlier injury. It was the World Cup final of 1954.

In 1954 the public eagerly awaited the arrival of Puskás and his team in Switzerland. Puskás was the greatest player in the world and the smart money was on the Hungarians to win the trophy. They did not disappoint in their opening game, demolishing South Korea with Puskás scoring twice. The public did not blink an eye as they cruised past West Germany in their second. Unfortunately a foul, deliberate or otherwise, caused Puskás to limp out of the tournament, not to reappear until the final itself. He later claimed that West German man-marker, Liebrich, had intentionally fouled him as he drew back to release another powerful shot. After the final, Puskás remarked that the German dressing room smelled like a garden of poppies and perhaps this was the reason why the winners ran like trains.

In 1958, Puskás did not appear at the World Cup finals and a somewhat second rate Hungarian side did not make it past the first round. The Russian suppression of the 1956 Uprising led many of Hungary's top players to flee the country. Puskás, who was on tour with Honved in Spain, did not return home and went to Austria before moving back to Spain where he joined Real Madrid. During his time there Puskás helped form an "Hungarian team in exile". For his efforts he was suspended by FIFA along with other former international team mates who made up the squad. The years at Real proved to be some of the best Puskás ever had in club football. Along with Frenchman Raymond Kopa, the two Argentinians Di Stefano and Rial, and Uruguayan Santamaría, Real Madrid ruled the world. They won four Spanish titles, five European cups and one Intercontinental Championship. Puskás became known in Spain as "Little Cannon Boom" for the amazing power and the suppleness of his left leg. His finest moment came in the 1960 European Cup final when Real amazingly destroyed Eintracht Frankfurt 7-3. Puskás scored four goals that night.

In 1962, at the age of 35 and now a naturalized Spaniard, Puskás turned out for his adopted nation at the World Cup finals in Chile. He took the place of Di Stefano who was allegedly injured. In the vital game against Brazil he made the goal that put Spain ahead, but a repeat of 1954 was not on the cards. Brazil eventually won the game and Spain went home. Puskás certainly became one of the most exciting and exhilarating players of the 20th Century. In an international career that spanned 84 games, he scored an amazing 83 goals. Only Pelé has ever done better.

Fritz Walter   # West Germany

Honours: Winner 1954; 4th Place 1958   **Games 11**
Played:1954 and 1958   **Goals 3**

Fritz Walter was the mid-filed inspiration who, along with manager Sepp Herberger, brought West Germany back into the international fold and captained them to their first World Cup triumph in 1954. He was a general and an organizer who directed, coached and coaxed his team mates to victory. He would have also been Germany's first player to achieve 100 caps had not World War Two got in the way. He was a minimalist when it came to contact with the ball, preferring to make the players around him do the work while he directed the play. However, he could play the ball when needed and take on defenders with clinical precision.

Born on 31st October 1920 in Kaiserslauten, he made his international debut at the age of 19 at a time when Germany was already at war. In one of Goebbels's so called 'friendlies' against Romania, in July 1940, he scored a hat trick in a 9-3 victory to the Germans. He was also to play in Germany's last international against the satellite state of Slovakia in 1942 before the demands of war, put paid to further internationals until 1950. In his position as an inside-left, he had made 24 appearances, scoring 19 goals. Walter missed the first post-war international in November 1949 and did not restart his international career until April 1951 against Switzerland. Long before, in Walter's youth, Herberger had recognized in him the ability to lead and read the game. It was not surprising therefore, that Herberger made him captain against the Swiss.

Having had his football career curtailed in 1942, Walter became a paratrooper in the German army. This had a profound affect on the young man, so much so that, in later years his fear of flying made him refuse to travel with his team mates to matches by air. When the war ended Walter found himself in a prisoner of war camp in Romania. It is only because the guards recognized who he was that he was given false travel papers and not whisked off

A Heatwave, a Punch-up and the Armchair Fan - Switzerland 1954

German captain Fritz Walter (left) with Ferenc Puskás.

to a forced labour camp in the USSR. He made his way home to play football once again and he returned to his only club, Kaiserslauten. A rebuilt team, inspired by Walter, made it to the final of the West German Championships in 1948, being beaten by Nurnberg. However, they did return as winners in 1951 and 1953. With his younger brother, Ottmar, at centre-forward, and with Walter's strategical know-how in mid-field, Kaiserslauten became a force to be reckoned with in German club football.

The relationship that Walter built up with Herberger, both during and after the war, was crucial to the success of West Germany, and Herberger knew that the physical and mental well-being of his captain was vital if they were going to bring the Jules Rimet Trophy back to Germany in 1954. Herberger knew of Walter's nervous fragility and tried to protect him from the stresses and strains of the competitive game. However, the best-laid plans can always come unstuck in a game that often shows no pity to a wounded animal. In the weeks before the 1954 tournament, Kaiserslauten went to Hanover in the West German Championship and were thumped 5-1. The Kaiserslauten team contained five players destined for Switzerland, while Hanover had none. So, with his morale down around his knees, Walter set off for the first World Cup to feature a team from West Germany. In a move to lighten his captain's mood, Herberger billeted Walter in a room with the enigmatic and playful winger Helmuth Rahn. He needn't have worried as the Germans opened the tournament with an emphatic 4-1 win over Turkey.

From then on it was the "Herberger and Walter Show". As a somewhat unknown quantity in world football, the West Germans had not been seeded, but they made it through to the quarter-finals. With Walter now in inspirational form the West Germans disposed of Yugoslavia and then destroyed Austria in the semi-final. Spurred on by his prompting, the German wingers and attackers had a field day, and Walter even grabbed two goals himself, both from the penalty spot.

In the final the West Germans once again came up against Hungary, who had already thumped a tactically weakened German side. It was no surprise to most that Hungary went into an early lead, but Walter who became the driving force behind one of the World Cup's greatest ever comebacks. He stopped playing his usual minimalist game and set about the Hungarians with all the skill and determination he could muster. He produced a performance of exceptional quality, managing to turn the game and lead West Germany to victory. Herberger and Walter had done it. With Rimet stood behind him, the trophy in his left hand and his winners' medal tucked under his arm, he shook the hand of the man most thought would lift the trophy that day, Puskás.

In Sweden in 1958, Walter led the West Germans to the semi-finals, where Walter was crucially injured, leaving the German team without its rudder. After the tournament he went back to playing for Kaiserslauten and continued to do so until he was 40. However, he had long retired from the international scene having played 61 times for West Germany, scoring 33 goals. With Herberger at the helm and Fritz Walter steering the ship, West Germany sailed back into the post-war international waters and became champions of the world. In January 2001, Fritz Walter enjoyed his eightieth birthday party with the help of Franz Beckenbauer, Uwe Seeler and three of the surviving members the 1954 Mighty Magyars - Gyula Grosics, Nandor Hidegkúti and Jenó Buzánsky. Beckenbauer has called him "the most important German footballer of the century."He was the first of the German greats.

Sandor Kocsis

Hungary

Honours: Runner-up 1954
Played: 1954

Games 5
Goals 11

Sandor Kocsis was known as the "Man with the Golden Head" for his amazing ability as one of the best headers the game has ever known. He could rise to such heights that it made him seem as though he was being carried on the wings of an angel. The nickname "Golden Head" was his long before Uwe Seeler of West Germany inherited the mantle in the 1960s. Kocsis was one of the "Magic Magyars" and his devastating partnership with Ferenc Puskás literally demolished some of the best teams in the world. In 68 internationals for Hungary he scored a staggering 75 goals.

Kocsis was born in Budapest on 30th September 1929. He served his footballing apprenticeship with club side, KTC, before mov-

Sandor Kocsis (2nd from right) looks on as Brazilian goalkeeper Castilho throws himself at the feet of Hungarian forward Czibor.

ing to Ferencvaros where, at the age of only 19, he helped them win the Hungarian title in 1949. Shortly after this the Ferencvaros team were amalgamated into the new Honved team, where Kocsis came across Ferenc Puskás and the deadly partnership was born. In fact, Kocsis was the Hungarian league's top scorer three times in the early 1950s. Gusztav Sebes, the national team coach, obviously saw something special in Kocsis and he was soon to realize the damage that could be done if he played Kocsis and Puskás together. Kocsis was given his international debut in 1949 and he was to become fundamental to the national side's success. He was a constant member during the four year unbeaten run the team had from 1950 until the World Cup final in 1954. And, like Puskás, he was instrumental in bringing down England at Wembley in 1953.

In Switzerland in 1954, he showed what a scoring machine he was by setting the record for the most goals scored in a World Cup tournament at 11. The record lasted four years, but he still remains the fourth highest scorer in World Cup tournament history. It is unlikely that anyone will score more even though teams play more games, testament to his fine ability. Kocsis opened his account in the 1954 finals with three goals against the hapless South Koreans and went one better in the 8-3 victory over West Germany. He bagged another two in the infamous Battle of Berne, for one of which he sailed into the air as if he was as light as a feather, floating on the breeze, before heading the ball into the corner of the goal. It was an incredible moment. His finest hour however, came in the semi-final against Uruguay. The Magyars stormed into a 2-0 lead, but they were then pegged back to 2-2 by the final whistle. In extra-time, it was time for Kocsis to pounce and he scored two exquisitely taken goals to inflict the first ever World Cup defeat on the South Americans. Fortune did not smile on the Hungarians in the final however, and it was with a runners-up medal that Kocsis returned home.

In 1956 Honved were on tour in Spain when the Hungarian Uprising took place. Kocsis was amongst a number of players who decided to stay abroad and he continued his career as player-coach with Young Fellows Berne, before moving to Spain to play for Barcelona in 1957. Here he enjoyed massive success playing alongside fellow Hungarians Laszlo Kubala and Zoltan Czibor. It was said that the Nou Camp Stadium, whose cornerstone was laid in 1954, was built for Kubala and the like, and the numerous Kocsis goals were greeted by the mass waving of thousands of white handkerchiefs. Kocsis was also one of the "Hungarian Team in Exile" that were banned from playing football shortly after the Soviet Army swarmed into Budapest. However, with Barcelona life became much sweeter and, in 1961 his team reached the European Cup final. Kocsis scored in a game that was ultimately lost to Benfica.

Sandor Kocsis retired from the game in 1966 at the age of 37 and he died in 1980. Of the 75 goals he scored in his international career there were an amazing 7 hat tricks. His aerial ability was so fantastic that it was claimed he had the best head in Europe after Winston Churchill.

Brazil 2 : Hungary 4

The so-called "Battle of Berne" played out on 27th June at the Wankdorf Stadium was one of the most violent and brutal games ever to disgrace the World Cup. It was all the more terrible because it involved "two sides more renowned for their skills on the ball than their fouls off it." "Here were two of the greatest sides in the world," reported the Times, " finally destroying their own superb artistry by the barefaced and attempted annihilation of each other by unethical tactics."

It is difficult to explain how a game between two such outstanding teams could have deteriorated into the travesty it became, except through sheer competitiveness on the part of both. Certainly, they were teams not noted for their foul play. Yet, they were teams from whom much was expected and were given every chance by experts of going on to win the title. The best of South America was playing the best of Europe and both knowing that only a win was good enough - defeat would put the loser out of the tournament. After failure in 1950, domestic pressure on the Brazilians was immense, but equally the Magyars carried the expectation, if not necessarily the hopes, of most of Europe. It was a heady combination and, in the end, neither could resist the slide into cynicism, as each sought, by any means, the semi-final spot that was the prize. It was just not possible to contemplate failure.

The general consensus of opinion is that it was the Brazilians who must take the blame for starting the rot and, indeed, one of the first incidents of misbehaviour took place in the opening exchanges of the game. As Nandor Hidegkúti tried to round his man, he almost had his shorts ripped off as the defender tried to hold him back. However, the Hungarians were not averse to retaliatory rough stuff of their own and soon after, their centre-half, Lóránt, fouled badly and was booked for his sin. He ought to have been dealt with more severely because, showing blatant disregard for the authority of Arthur Ellis, the English referee, he laughed at the decision. The lack of firmness shown in that instant was another cause of what ensued.

Both teams were quite capable of loftier play and the Hungarians were the first to show what they could do. After only four minutes, from close range, Hidegkúti "slashed a rising shot into the roof of the Brazilian net," and, three minutes after that, they struck again. This time Hidegkúti was the supplier, sending in a perfect diagonal cross "which Kocsis, always brilliant with his head, nodded in as clean as a whistle." It was at this point that the Brazilians seemed to wake up to the plight they were in and began to ply their own brand of attack. They mounted a series of assaults on the Hungarian goal, which elicited a host of niggling fouls from the defenders and which angered the South Americans. One such foul, in the 18th minute, resulted in a penalty, when Buzánsky bundled Indio down in the area. Djalma Santos stepped up to convert it and though the Brazilians had the best of the play during the rest of the half, they could not score further. The Hungarians defended well, but seemed to lack penetration up front. They clearly missed Puskás and were further hindered when, in the last minute of the half, József Tóth, their left-winger, pulled a muscle and limped for the rest of the match.

The first half ended with the Hungarians marginally in front, but with tempers on both sides frayed. In the second half the situation got worse and some of the tackling can only be described as dangerous. For a referee as experienced as Ellis not to have taken a tighter grip is inexplicable, but he did not and the atmosphere grew more volatile by the minute. Serious trouble erupted some 15 minutes into the half. Pinheiro handled a cross sent in by Czibor and intended for Kocsis. Ellis awarded a penalty, but the decision infuriated the Brazilians, whose fierce protests were all in vein, and it was several minutes before Lantos was able to take the kick. The game continued to deteriorate and over the next few minutes both Humberto of Brazil and Czibor of Hungary were lucky

Brazilian defender Nilton Santos and Hungarian captain József Bozsic leave the field after being sent off for fighting.

to remain on the pitch for fouls that were well over the bounds of acceptability. Twice during the half, the police had to be called onto the pitch by the referee. The first time was to remove to Brazilian trainers, who had run on to remonstrate with the referee and refused to leave, and the second time was to remove two photographers.

In the 20th minute a little bit of football broke out. Julinho found himself with the ball in a little space. He "picked his spot from 20 yards and shot a flaming arrow past Grosiks (sic) at full pace" - the words are those of the Times's reporter, as is the spelling! However, not five minutes after this, mayhem broke out as Nilton Santos and József Bozsic began punching each other. Both were dismissed and both should have known better, but we might single out Bozsic for particular disapprobation. He was not only the team's captain, he was also a member of Hungary's parliament.

In the last ten minutes of the game, Brazil had two presentable chances to draw level, but both were missed. First Didí and then Maurinho shot

Swiss Police go into the dressing room as fighting breaks out between players and fans after the match.

narrowly wide in quick succession, but the game was wrapped up with less than five minutes on the clock. Humberto launched a horrible kick at Lóránt and was deservedly sent off, and then, with less than three minutes remaining, Hidegkúti sent Czibor on a run down the right. He sent across into the Brazilian penalty area and there was Kocsis, ever ready, to head the ball into the net. The Brazilian goalkeeper, Castilho, wept as he pulled the ball out of the net and his side crashed out of the World Cup, but on the balance of things, good and bad, the Magyars went through on merit. However, the action in this game was far from over when the final whistle blew.

Austria 7 : Switzerland 5

Swiss goalkeeper Parlier dives at the feet of Austrian forward Wagner.

Almost every World Cup tournament throws up high scoring matches, but few have been as remarkable as this record-breaking quarter-final duel between Austria and Switzerland in Lausanne. It was made to appear more so by the fact that neither were among the tournament's more fancied teams. The initial performances of both in the pool stage had been unspectacular and had done little to enhance their reputations, but both had then given far more convincing shows that left spectators feeling that here were two teams who could turn on the heat when they wanted. This was to be the match that brought the best out of both, a real classic in the best traditions of the World Cup.

The Swiss were handicapped from the start by their captain, Bocquet, who was suffering a serious bout of illness, but who had ignored the advice of his doctor and opted to play. It was to prove a costly error of judgement, though one that was not immediately apparent as his team romped to an early and seemingly impregnable lead. The first to register was the ever reliable Robert Ballaman, who found the target in the 16th minute and only seconds later Josef Hügi made it 2-0. Hügi struck again in the 23rd minute and it appeared to be all up for the Austrians. There then happened one of the greatest and fastest reversals of fortunes in World Cup history as the Austrians battered down the door to turn this match on its head. With Alfred and Robert Körner, the two wingers wreaking havoc, in an amazing three minutes of quick-fire action, first Theodore Wagner found the back of the net. Switzerland kicked off again, immediately lost possession and with lightening precision, Alfred Körner rammed the ball home to reduce the deficit further. Inside a minute Wagner bagged his second and the scores were level. A stunned crowd wondered what had hit them, but it was not over. In the 32nd minute Austria's captain, Ernst Ocwirk, scored to put his team ahead and two minutes later Körner scored his second. In a ten minute spell Austria had scored five goals to go from 3-0 down to 5-3 in front. Eight strikes inside 35 minutes is the greatest goal feast the World Cup finals has ever witnessed. For a few minutes the Swiss were reeling and could make no response to what had been a devastating turn of fortune, but they steadied their nerves and just before half-time Ballaman netted his second to give a half-time scoreline of 5-4 to Austria.

The air temperature had been steadily rising throughout the first half and with conditions becoming increasingly difficult, play naturally slowed down in the second. Bocquet, in particular, began to suffer and it gave the Swiss a decided disadvantage, though they valiantly battled on in the hope of retrieving the situation. They would dearly have loved to secure a place in the semi-finals, but their ambitions received another set back in the 52nd minute when Wagner's goal completed his hat trick. A second two goal deficit was a severe test of Switzerland's mental reserves and once again they dragged themselves out of the mire to get back into it. In the 58th minute Hügi broke through to score his third of the afternoon and it was now 6-5 to Austria. There was still enough time and in a game like this anything can happen, but the heat and their exertions were taking their toll. Legs were tiring rapidly and forward momentum was difficult to sustain. The action was rounded off in the 76th minute when Erich Probst fired in the game's final goal and secure Austria's place in the semi-finals.

Quite understandably, the final 15 minutes were played out at what was a snail's pace in comparison to how the first half had gone, but this does not detract from what had been stupendous piece of football action. It had ebbed and flowed unpredictably, first one way then the other, and had tested the emotions of both players and fans alike. Putting away 12 goals in under an hour of play speaks volumes of the players involved and their desire to both win and entertain. It is almost certainly something that the World Cup will never see again, especially given the way the game has developed since those glorious days of the 1950s.

West Germany 3 : Hungary 2
The World Cup Final

People would have staked their livelihoods on the outcome of this game: unseeded and unfancied West Germany against the "Mighty Magyars", the greatest team in the world and restored to full strength with the "Galloping Major", Ferenc Puskás, back. There was only ever going to be one team in this game, and one result. And it was not going to be the Germans!!

After an early bout of German pressure, the Hungarians found their touch. In the sixth minute, József Bozsic sent Kocsis through with a glorious, defence-splitting pass along the ground. Kocsis changed direction to gain possession and drove in a fierce shot that was charged down by Toni Turek in the German goal. Following in was Puskás, who hit a low, left foot shot into the corner of the net and the Hungarians had the lead. Two minutes later, the Magyars attacked down the middle. Kohlmeyer and Turek seemed to have the situation under control, especially when the goalkeeper stopped to gather the back pass from his defender that would have broken up the attack. However, in a moment of indecision, Turek lost possession of the ball and the nippy winger, Zoltan Czibor, like a flash, stole the ball, side stepped into space and tapped into an open net. Only eight minutes had gone and even the most ardent of German supporters must have felt the sense of doom.

Yet, the Hungarians were too cock-sure and their over-confidence affected the way they played. They saw much more of the ball than the Germans, mounted attack after attack, but were unable to make them count. Commentators noted that they held the ball too long and tried to be too clever. Their play, consequently, lacked the fluidity and penetration normally associated with it and heavy German tackling often broke down their attacks. They were becoming the authors of their own ignominy. The danger signs were there and, showing "tremendous enthusiasm, drive, stamina, strength and will power," the Germans came back immediately. Within two minutes of Czibor's strike, captain Fritz Walter sent a low, angled cross that skidded across the turf, into the heart of the Hungarian penalty area. It eluded the waiting defenders, but not Max Morlock, who lunged and just got a foot to the ball. It was enough to steer it into the net and eight minutes after that came a second. Grosics seemed to misjudge a corner and the ball fell to Helmuth Rahn, lurking by the far post. His half volley went crashing into the net and the scores were level. "From that time," noted the Times's correspondent, "the tide flowed more steadily against the defiant German defence, but time after time, by some miracle or other, the Hungarians were held at bay." Hidegkúti hit the post, other forwards came close, but Turek made saves "that bordered on the miraculous", including one that denied Hidegkúti's ferocious volley from only feet out.

When the teams came out for the second half the Hungarians resumed their pattern of play. Their confidence was undented and they seemed to believe that they only had to go forward for their endeavour to be rewarded. If this was the plan, it failed to take account of German resolve and their excellent goalkeeper. On one attack, Kocsis whipped in a demon of a header from six yards out to force a magnificent reflex save from Turek. Twice more he denied Puskás when the ball appeared to be going in and later, "a brilliant, penetrating move that strung the whole Hungarian forward line together in a poetry of movement", saw Tóth beat Turek, only for Kohlmeyer to clear off the line. As time went on, the crowd began to sense that the game was slipping from the Hungarians. The Germans, whose tackling was timely and hard, grew stronger. Puskás was not fully fit and became less influential as Eckel got the measure of him. Fritz Walter "kept prodding his forward line into swift counter attack", and their menace increased with their frequency. Fifteen minutes before the end, Rahn hammered in a shot that had Grosics scrambling to save under the angle of the left post and with only six minutes to go another German attack brought the telling breakthrough. Bozsik was guilty of holding the ball too long and was robbed by Schäfer, who passed it to Walter. Lantos, failed to deal with his cross and it was picked up by Rahn, sprinting to the edge of the area. With no defenders near him, his low shot found the corner of the net.

West Germany's captain Fritz Walter and coach Sepp Herberger carried aloft after victory over the Hungarians.

The Hungarians were behind for the first time in the tournament, but they did not lose their confidence. With minutes to go, Tóth sent in a low diagonal cross for Puskás to run on to. He gathered the ball and fired it into the net. Everyone thought he had scored, but controversially, Welsh linesman, Mervyn Griffiths, did not. Up went his flag for offside and a goal that many still feel should have counted was disallowed. Then, in the dying seconds, Turek "miraculously leaped to punch away" Czibor's rasping shot and the game was lost. The "impossible has happened", was the Daily Mirror's summary. The West Germans had "stolen" the World Cup. It was a severe disappointment for Hungary. On the balance of play and on the chances that went "spinning away, the victory ought to have been theirs." Yet, the Germans had given a momentous performance. They "played classic football", said the Austrian Ernst Stojaspal, whilst Vittorio Pozzo described it as "one of the finest cup finals ever played. The Germans deserved their victory." They had harried and held firm when they needed to, but had shown the strength and enterprise to fashion chances of their own.

The principal difference between the teams had been that the Germans had put theirs away and the Hungarians had not. So "amidst surging closing scenes, with the Deutschland banners forming a rich backcloth, the precious golden trophy was presented by Mr J. Rimet". There was jubilation among the travelling German supporters and back in Berlin, those who had been listening on radios congregated on the streets, dancing, singing and making merry. At the little town of Singen, on the border between Switzerland and Germany, where the team first stopped on its homeward progress, the mayor and officials wheeled out a metre high cake that had been baked in honour of the world champions. At Lindar, a few kilometres away, they were mobbed amid scenes that were repeated wherever they stopped.

Statistics - Switzerland 1954

POOL ONE

Lausanne, June 16th - La Pontaise

1 (1) YUGOSLAVIA

Milutinovic 15

Beara, Stankovic, Crnkovic, Caikowski, Horvat, Boskov, Milutinovic, Mitic, Vukas, Bobek, Zebek.

0 (0) FRANCE

Remetter, Gianessi, Kaelbel, Penverne, Jonquet, Marcel, Kopa, Glovacki, Strappe, Dereuddre, Vincent.

Referee: Mervyn Griffiths (Wales)
Attendance: 16.000

Geneva, June 16th - Les Charmilles

5 (4) BRAZIL

Baltazar 23, Didí 29, Pinga 34,42, Julinho 60

Castilho, D.Santos, N.Santos, Brandãozinho, Pinheiro, Bauer, Julinho, Didí, Baltazar, Pinga, Rodríguez.

0 (0) MEXICO

Mota, López, Gómez, Cardeñas, Romo, Avalos, Torres, Naranjo, Lamadrid, Balcazar, Arellano.

Referee: Raymon Wyssling (Switzerland)
Attendance: 12.500

Lausanne, June 19th - La Pontaise

After extra time - 45mins (0-0), 90 mins (1-1), 120 mins 1-1

1 (1) BRAZIL

Didí 70

Castilho, D.Santos, N.Santos, Brandãozinho, Pinheiro, Bauer, Julinho, Didí, Baltazar, Pinga, Rodríguez.

1 (1) YUGOSLAVIA

Zebek 48

Beara, Stankovic, Crnkovic, Caikowski, Horvat, Boskov, Milutinovic, Mitic, Vukas, Dvornic, Zebek.

Referee: Edward Faultless (Scotland)
Attendance: 21.000

Geneva, June 19th - Les Charmilles

3 (1) FRANCE

Vincent 19, Cardeñas (og)49, Kopa (pen)88

Remetter, Gianessi, Kaelbel, Marche, Ben Tifour, Marcel, Kopa, Mahjoub, Strappe, Dereuddre, Vincent.

2 (0) MEXICO

Naranjo 54, Balcazar 85

Carbajal, López, Martínez, Cardeñas, Romo, Avalos, Torres, Naranjo, Lamadrid, Balcazar, Arellano.

Referee: Manuel Asensi (Spain)
Attendance: 19.000

	P	W	D	L	F	A	Pts
Brazil	2	1	1	0	6	1	3
Yugoslavia	2	1	1	0	2	1	3
France	2	1	0	1	3	3	2
Mexico	2	0	0	2	2	8	0

POOL TWO

Zurich, June 17th - Sportzplatz Hardturm

9 (4) HUNGARY

Puskás 11,90, Lantos 16, Kocsis 24,31,50, Czibor 60, Palotas 76,83

Grosics, Buzánszky, Lantos, Bozsik, Lóránt, Szojka, Budai, Kocsis, Palotas, Puskás, Czibor.

0 (0) SOUTH KOREA

Hong Duk-yung, Park Kyu-jong, Kang Chang-chi, Min Byung-dai, Park Yae-sung, Chu Young-kwang, Chung Hae-won, Park Il-kap, Sung Nak-woon, Woo Sang-kwon, Choi Yung-kuen.

Referee: Raymond Vincenti (France)
Attendance: 13.000

Berne, June 17th - Wankdorf Stadion

4 (1) WEST GERMANY

Schäfer 14, Klodt 52, O.Walter 60, Morlock 81

Turek, Laband, Kohlmeyer, Eckel, Posipal, Mai, Klodt, Morlock, O.Walter, F.Walter, Schäfer.

1 (1) TURKEY

Suat 2

Turgay, Ridvan, Basri, Mustafa, Cetin, Rober, Erol, Suat, Feridun, Burhan, Lefter.

Referee: José Da Costa (Portugal)
Attendance: 28.000

Basle, June 20th - St Jakob Stadion

8 (3) HUNGARY

Kocsis 3,20,67,78, Puskás 18, Hidegkúti 52,56, J.Tóth 73

Grosics, Buzánszky, Lantos, Bozsik, Lóránt, Zakarias, J.Tóth, Kocsis, Hidegkúti, Puskás, Czibor.

3 (1) WEST GERMANY

Pfaff 28, Rahn 77, Herrmann 81

Kwiatkowski, Bauer, Kohlmeyer, Posipal, Liebrich, Mebus, Rahn, Eckel, F.Walter, Pfaff, Herrmann.

Referee: Bill Ling (England)
Attendance: 56.000

Geneva, June 20th - Les Charmilles

7 (4) TURKEY

Suat 10,30, Lefter 24, Burhan 37,64,70, Erol 76

Turgay, Ridvan, Basri, Mustafa, Cetin, Rober, Erol, Suat, Necmi, Burhan, Lefter.

0 (0) SOUTH KOREA

Hong Duk-yung, Park Kyu-jong, Kang Chang-chi, Han Chong-wha, Lee Chong-kap, Kim Chi-sung, Choi Yung-keun, Lee Soo-nam, Lee Gi-choo, Woo Sang-kwan, Chung Kook-chin.

Referee: Esteban Marino (Uruguay)
Attendance: 4.000

Play-off - Zurich, June 23rd - Sportzplatz Hardturm

7 (3) WEST GERMANY

O.Walter 7, Schäfer 12,79, Morlock 31,60,71, F.Walter 62

Turek, Laband, Bauer, Eckel, Posipal, Mai, Klodt, Morlock, O.Walter, F.Walter, Schäfer.

2 (1) TURKEY

Mustafa 22, Lefter 82

Sükrü, Ridvan, Basri, Naci, Mustafa, Cetin, Rober, Erol, Necmi, Coskun, Lefter.

Referee: Raymond Vincent (France)
Attendance: 17.000

	P	W	D	L	F	A	Pts
Hungary	2	2	0	0	17	3	4
W. Germany	2	1	0	1	7	9	2
Turkey	2	1	0	1	8	4	2
S. Korea	2	1	0	2	0	16	0

POOL THREE

Zurich, June 16th - Sportzplatz Hardturm

1 (1) AUSTRIA

Probst 33

Schmied, Hanappi, Barschandt, Ocwirk, Happel, Koller, R.Körner, Schleger, Dienst, Probst, A.Körner.

0 (0) SCOTLAND

Martin, Cunningham, Aird, Docherty, Davidson, Cowie, McKenzie, Fernie, Mochan, Brown, Ormond.

Referee: Laurent Franken (Belgium)
Attendance: 25.000

22 Men and a Bag of Wind

Berne, June 16th - Wankdorf Stadion

2 (0) URUGUAY

Míguez 70, Schiaffino 82

Maspoli, Santamaria, Martínez, Andrade, Varela, Cruz, Abbadie, Ambrois, Míguez, Schiaffino, Borges.

0 (0) CZECHOSLOVAKIA

Reiman, Safranek, Novak, Trnka, Hledik, Hertl, Hlavacek, Hemele, Kacany, Pazicky, Kraus.

Referee: Arthur Ellis (England)
Attendance: 20.500

Zurich, June 19th - Sportzplatz Hardturm

5 (4) AUSTRIA

Stojaspal 2,65, Probst 4,21,24

Schmied, Hanappi, Barschandt, Ocwirk, Happel, Koller, R.Körner, Wagner, Stojaspal, Probst, A.Körner.

0 (0) CZECHOSLOVAKIA

Stacho, Safranek, Novak, Trnka, Pluskal, Hertl, Hlavacek, Hemele, Kacany, Pazicky, Kraus.

Referee: Vasa Stefanovic (Yugoslavia)
Attendance: 21.000

Basle, June 19th - St Jakob Stadion

7 (2) URUGUAY

Borges 17,48,58, Míguez 31,82, Abbadie 55,84

Maspoli, Santamaria, Martínez, Andrade, Varela, Cruz, Abbadie, Ambrois, Míguez, Schiaffino, Borges.

0 (0) SCOTLAND

Martin, Cunningham, Aird, Docherty, Davidson, Cowie, McKenzie, Fernie, Mochan, Brown, Ormond.

Referee: Vincenzo Orlandini (Italy)
Attendance: 34.000

	P	W	D	L	F	A	Pts
Uruguay	2	2	0	0	9	0	4
Austria	2	2	0	0	6	0	4
Czech	2	0	0	2	0	7	0
Scotland	2	0	0	2	0	8	0

POOL FOUR

Basle, June 17th - St Jakob Stadion

After extra time - 45mins (2-1), 90 mins (3-3), 120 mins 4-4

4 (3) ENGLAND

Broadis 25,63, Lofthouse 35,91

Merrick, Staniforth, Byrne, Wright, Owen, Dickinson, Matthews, Broadis, Lofthouse, Taylor, Finney.

4 (3) BELGIUM

Anoul 5,71, Coppens 78, Dickinson (og) 94

Gerneay, Dries, Van Brandt, Huysmans, Carre, Mees, Mermans, Houf, Coppens, Anoul, P.Van Den Bosch.

Referee: Emil Schmetzer (West Germany)
Attendance: 14.000

Lausanne, June 17th - La Pontaise

2 (1) SWITZERLAND

Ballaman 17, Hügi 78

Parlier, Neury, Kernen, Flückiger, Bocquet, Casali, Ballaman, Vonlanthen, Hügi, Meier, Fatton.

1 (1) ITALY

Boniperti 44

Ghezzi, Vincenzi, Giacomazzi, Neri, Tognon, Nesti, Muccinelli, Boniperti, Galli, Pandolfini, Lorenzi.

Referee: Mario Viana (Brazil)
Attendance: 40.500

Berne, June 20th - Wankdorf Stadion

2 (1) ENGLAND

Mullen 43, Wilshaw 69

Merrick, Staniforth, Byrne, Wright, McGarry, Dickinson, Wilshaw, Broadis, Mullen, Taylor, Finney.

0 (0) SWITZERLAND

Parlier, Neury, Kernen, Eggimann, Bocquet, Bigler, Ballaman, Vonlanthen, Antenen, Meier, Fatton.

Referee: Istvan Zsolt (Hungary)
Attendance: 43.500

Lugano, June 20th - Comunale di Cornaredo

4 (1) ITALY

Pandolfini 40, Galli 49, Frignani 58, Lorenzi 73

Ghezzi, Magnini, Giacomazzi, Neri, Tognon, Nesti, Frignani, Cappello, Galli, Pandolfini, Lorenzi.

1 (0) BELGIUM

Anoul 81

Gerneay, Dries, Van Brandt, Huysmans, Carre, Mees, Mermans, H.Van Den Bosch, Coppens, Anoul, P.Van Den Bosch.

Referee: Erich Steiner (Austria)
Attendance: 24.000

Play-off - Basle, June 23rd - St Jakob Stadion

4 (1) SWITZERLAND

Hügi 14,85, Ballaman 48, Fatton 90

Parlier, Neury, Kernen, Eggimann, Bocquet, Casali, Ballaman, Vonlanthen, Hügi, Antenen, Fatton.

1 (0) ITALY

Nesti 67

Viola, Magnini, Giacomazzi, Mari, Tognon, Nesti, Muccinelli, Segato, Frignani, Pandolfini, Lorenzi.

Referee: Mervyn Griffiths (Wales)
Attendance: 29.000

	P	W	D	L	F	A	Pts
England	2	1	1	0	6	4	3
Switzerland	2	1	0	1	2	3	2
Italy	2	1	0	1	5	3	2
Belgium	2	0	1	1	5	8	1

QUARTER-FINALS

Lausanne, June 26th - La Pontaise

7 (5) AUSTRIA

Wagner 25,28,52, A.Körner 27,34, Ocwirk 32, Probst 76

Schmied, Hanappi, Barschandt, Ocwirk, Happel, Koller, R.Körner, Wagner, Stojaspal, Probst, A.Körner.

5 (4) SWITZERLAND

Ballaman 16,41, Hügi 17,23,58

Parlier, Neury, Kernen, Eggimann, Bocquet, Casali, Antenen, Vonlanthen, Hügi, Ballaman, Fatton.

Referee: Edward Faultless (Scotland)
Attendance: 31.000

Basle, June 26th - St Jakob Stadion

4 (2) URUGUAY

Borges 5, Varela 44, Schiaffino 47, Ambrois 78

Maspoli, Martínez, Santamaria, Andrade, Varela, Cruz, Abbadie, Ambrois, Míguez, Schiaffino, Borges.

2 (1) ENGLAND

Lofthouse 16, Finney 67

Merrick, Staniforth, Byrne, McGarry, Wright, Dickinson, Matthews, Broadis, Lofthouse, Wilshaw, Finney.

Referee: Erich Steiner (Austria)
Attendance: 50.000

Berne, June 27th - Wankdorf Stadion

4 (2) HUNGARY

Hidegkúti 4, Kocsis 7,90, Lantos (pen)53

Grosics, Buzánszky, Lantos, Bozsik (RED), Lóránt, Zakarias, M. Tóth, Kocsis, Hidegkúti, Czibor, J. Tóth.

2 (1) BRAZIL

D.Santos (pen)18, Julinho 65

Castilho, D.Santos, N.Santos (RED), Brandãozinho, Pinheiro, Bauer, Julinho, Didí, Indio, Humberto Tozzi (RED), Maurinho.

Referee: Arthur Ellis (England)
Attendance: 40.000

Geneva, June 27th - Les Charmilles

2 (1) WEST GERMANY

Horvat (og) 9, Rahn 85

Turek, Laband, Kohlmeyer, Eckel, Liebrich, Mai, Rahn, Morlock, O.Walter, F.Walter, Schäfer.

0 (0) YUGOSLAVIA

Beara, Stankovic, Crnkovic, Caikowski, Horvat, Boskov, Milutinovic, Mitic, Vukas, Bobek, Zebek.

Referee: Istvan Zsolt (Hungary)
Attendance: 17.000

A Heatwave, a Punch-up and the Armchair Fan - Switzerland 1954

SEMI-FINALS

Lausanne, June 30th - La Pontaise

After extra time - 45mins (1-0), 90 mins (2-2), 120 mins (4-2)

4 (2) HUNGARY

Czibor 13, Hidegkúti 46, Kocsis 111,116

Grosics, Buzánszky, Lantos, Bozsik, Lóránt, Zakarias, Budai, Kocsis, Hidegkúti, Czibor, Palotas.

2 (2) URUGUAY

Hohberg 75,86

Maspoli, Martínez, Santamaria, Andrade, Carballo, Cruz, Souto, Ambrois, Hohberg, Schiaffino, Borges.

Referee: Mervyn Griffiths (Wales)
Attendance: 37.000

Basle, June 30th - St Jakob Stadion

6 (1) WEST GERMANY

Schäfer 32, Morlock 47, F.Walter (pen)54,(pen)65, O.Walter 60,90

Turek, Posipal, Kohlmeyer, Eckel, Liebrich, Mai, Rahn, Morlock, O.Walter, F.Walter, Schäfer.

1 (0) AUSTRIA

Probst 51

Zeman, Hanappi, Schleger, Ocwirk, Happel, Koller, R.Körner, Wagner, Stojaspal, Probst, A.Körner.

Referee: Vincenzo Orlandini (Italy)
Attendance: 58.000

3rd/4th PLACE PLAY-OFF

Zurich, July 3rd - Sportzplatz Hardturm

3 (1) AUSTRIA

Stojaspal (pen) 16, Cruz (og)59, Ocwirk 79

Schmied, Hanappi, Barschandt, Ocwirk, Kollmann, Koller, R.Körner, Wagner, Stojaspal, Probst, Dienst.

1 (1) URUGUAY

Hohberg 21

Maspoli, Martínez, Santamaria, Andrade, Carballo, Cruz, Abbadie, Mendez, Hohberg, Schiaffino, Borges.

Referee: Raymon Wyssling (Switzerland)
Attendance: 31.000

FINAL

Berne, July 4th - Wankdorf Stadion

3 (2) WEST GERMANY

Morlock 10, Rahn 18,84

Turek, Posipal, Kohlmeyer, Eckel, Liebrich, Mai, Rahn, Morlock, O.Walter, F.Walter, Schäfer.

2 (2) HUNGARY

Puskás 6, Czibor 8

Grosics, Buzánszky, Lantos, Bozsik, Lóránt, Zakarias, Puskás, Kocsis, Hidegkúti, Czibor, J. Tóth.

Referee: Bill Ling (England)
Attendance: 60.000

QUALIFYING ROUNDS

Europe and the Near East - Group 1

	P	W	D	L	F	A	Pts
Germany FR	4	3	1	0	12	3	7
Saar	4	1	1	2	4	8	3
Norway	4	0	2	2	4	9	2

24-06-53	Norway : Saar	2:3 (2:2)
19-08-53	Norway : Germany FR	1:1 (1:1)
11-10-53	Germany FR : Saar	3:0 (1:0)
08-11-53	Saar : Norway	0:0
22-11-53	Germany FR : Norway	5:1 (1:1)
28-03-54	Saar : Germany FR	1:3 (0:1)

Europe and the Near East - Group 2

	P	W	D	L	F	A	Pts
Belgium	4	3	1	0	11	6	7
Sweden	4	1	1	2	9	8	3
Finland	4	0	2	2	7	13	2

25-05-53	Finland : Belgium	2:4 (0:3)
28-05-53	Sweden : Belgium	2:3 (2:3)
05-08-53	Finland : Sweden	3:3 (0:2)
16-08-53	Sweden : Finland	4:0 (2:0)
23-09-53	Belgium : Finland	2:2 (2:0)
08-10-53	Belgium : Sweden	2:0 (1:0)

Europe and the Near East - Group 3

	P	W	D	L	F	A	Pts
England	3	3	0	0	11	4	6
Scotland	3	1	1	1	8	8	3
N. Ireland	3	1	0	2	4	7	2
Wales	3	0	1	2	5	9	1

03-10-53	Northern Ireland : Scotland	1:3 (0:0)
10-10-53	Wales : England	1:4 (1:1)
04-11-53	Scotland : Wales	3:3 (2:0)
11-11-53	England : Northern Ireland	3:1 (1:0)
31-03-54	Wales : Northern Ireland	1:2 (0:1)
03-04-54	Scotland : England	2:4 (1:1)

Europe and the Near East - Group 4

	P	W	D	L	F	A	Pts
France	4	4	0	0	20	4	8
Rep. Ireland	4	2	0	2	8	6	4
Luxembourg	4	0	0	4	1	19	0

20-09-53	Luxembourg : France	1:6 (1:4)
04-10-53	Ireland Republic : France	3:5 (0:2)
28-10-53	Ireland Republic : Luxembourg	4:0 (1:0)
25-11-53	France : Ireland Republic	1:0 (0:0)
27-12-53	France : Luxembourg	8:0 (4:0)
07-03-54	Luxembourg : Ireland Republic	0:1 (0:0)

Europe and the Near East - Group 5

	P	W	D	L	F	A	Pts
Austria	2	1	1	0	9	1	3
Portugal	2	0	1	1	1	9	1

27-09-53	Austria : Portugal	9:1 (4:0)
29-11-53	Portugal : Austria	0:0

Europe and the Near East - Group 6

	P	W	D	L	F	A	Pts
Spain	2	1	0	1	4	2	2
Turkey	2	1	0	1	2	4	2

06-01-54	Spain : Turkey	4:1 (1:1)
14-03-54	Turkey : Spain	1:0 (1:0)

Play-off

17-03-54	Turkey : Spain	2:2 (1:1)

Played in Rome

Europe and the Near East - Group 8

	P	W	D	L	F	A	Pts
Czech	4	3	1	0	5	1	7
Romania	4	2	0	2	5	5	4
Bulgaria	4	0	1	3	3	7	1

28-06-53	Romania : Bulgaria	3:1 (2:0)
14-07-53	Czechoslovakia : Romania	2:0 (0:0)
06-09-53	Bulgaria : Czechoslovakia	1:2 (0:2)
11-10-53	Bulgaria : Romania	1:2 (1:1)
25-10-53	Romania : Czechoslovakia	0:1 (0:1)
08-11-53	Czechoslovakia : Bulgaria	0:0

Europe and the Near East - Group 9

	P	W	D	L	F	A	Pts
Italy	2	2	0	0	7	2	4
Egypt	2	0	0	2	2	7	0

13-11-53	Egypt : Italy	1:2 (1:0)
24-01-54	Italy : Egypt	5:1 (1:1)

Europe and the Near East - Group 10

	P	W	D	L	F	A	Pts
Yugoslavia	4	4	0	0	4	0	8
Greece	4	2	0	2	3	2	4
Israel	4	0	0	4	0	5	0

09-05-53	Yugoslavia : Greece	1:0 (1:0)
01-11-53	Greece : Israel	1:0 (0:0)
08-11-53	Yugoslavia : Israel	1:0 (1:0)
08-03-54	Israel : Greece	0:2 (0:0)
21-03-54	Israel : Yugoslavia	0:1 (0:0)
28-03-54	Greece : Yugoslavia	0:1 (0:0)

South America - Group 11

	P	W	D	L	F	A	Pts
Brazil	4	4	0	0	8	1	8
Paraguay	4	2	0	2	8	6	4
Chile	4	0	0	4	1	10	0

14-02-54	Paraguay : Chile	4:0 (1:0)
21-02-54	Chile : Paraguay	1:3 (1:1)
28-02-54	Chile : Brazil	0:2 (0:1)
07-03-54	Paraguay : Brazil	0:1 (0:0)
14-03-54	Brazil : Chile	1:0 (1:0)
21-04-54	Brazil : Paraguay	4:1 (0:0)

**Caribbean/North & Central America
Group 12**

	P	W	D	L	F	A	Pts
Mexico	4	4	0	0	19	1	8
USA	4	2	0	2	7	9	4
Haiti	4	0	0	4	2	18	0

19-07-53	Mexico : Haiti	8:0 (5:0)
27-12-53	Haiti : Mexico	0:4 (0:2)
10-01-54	Mexico : United States	4:0 (2:0)
14-01-54	United States : Mexico	1:3 (1:0)

Both USA v Mexico games played in Mexico City

03-04-54	United States : Haiti	3:2 (1:0)
04-04-54	United States : Haiti	3:0 (0:2)

Both USA v Haiti games played in Port-au Prince

Asia - Group 13

	P	W	D	L	F	A	Pts
Korea Rep.	2	1	1	0	7	3	3
Japan	2	0	1	1	3	7	1

07-03-54	Japan : Korea Republic	1:5 (1:2)
14-03-54	Korea Republic : Japan	2:2 (2:1)

Both games played in Tokyo

Chapter 8

Love, Losses and the Boys from Brazil
The Sweden World Cup, 1958

Sweden1958

Winners: Brazil

Runners-up: Sweden

3rd Place: France

4th Place: West Germany

Total Attendance: 823,426

Number of Matches: 35

By 1958 the space age had arrived. The previous year the USSR had launched the world's first artificial satellite, Sputnik, and the USA had responded with the foundation of NASA to action its own space programme. While this was happening in the skies, the fires of unrest burned on the ground. Vietnam was sliding into its own tragedy and Algeria was still in the throws of its war with France. The French caused international outrage when they bombed a village just over the boarder in Tunisia claiming that members of the independence movement, the National Liberation Front (FLN) were hiding there. In consequence, the Tunisian Prime Minister asked French troops to leave Algeria. In Cuba, Fidel Castro's struggle against the Batista dictatorship was gaining momentum. The USSR had re-established it's dictatorship in Hungary following the unsuccessful 1956 Uprising and had executed its leader, Imre Nagy. Another dictator establishing himself was "Papa Doc" Duvalier in Haiti. The countries of Western Europe were attempting to put aside the differences of the past by attempting peaceful co-operation. 1957 had seen the Treaty of Rome and the beginning of the European Economic Community.

In Britain, the Campaign for Nuclear Disarmament (CND) headed by philosopher, Bertrand Russell, made Aldermaston the focus of its campaigning against the development of new nuclear weapons. In America, military matters also grabbed the headlines when Elvis Presley was called up for his national service. The eye make-up and pink jacket were replaced by a short haircut. Barbie became the queen of plastic dolls and Boris Pasternak was awarded the Nobel Prize for Literature for his book Dr Zhivago. Regarding him as a dissident voice, the Soviet authorities refused him permission to collect his prize and his work was only published abroad. Jet planes took off for the first time between London and New York and also flying high were the sixteen teams winging their way to Sweden.

The 1958 World Cup has been remembered in several ways: the "Friendly World Cup", the "Brazilian World Cup", the "Pelé World Cup"; but this fascinating competition threw up intriguing surprises long before the finals began. It mixed stories of endeavour, of fortitude, of defying the odds, of sadness and of fortunate escape with global and domestic politics, the full range of the human experience.

Forty eight countries entered the tournament, the highest number to date, though this was still less than half of FIFA's membership. The qualifying stage got underway on 30th September 1956 in Vienna when Austria took on Luxembourg in European Group Five. It is, perhaps, time to spare a thought for the footballers of the tiny Grand Duchy and give them the recognition their effort deserves. Apart from the inaugural World Cup, Luxembourg had entered the qualifying stage of every tournament since and had not only failed to get to the finals, they had failed to win a game. Between 1934, when they played their first qualifier against Germany, and 1957, they had played 10 games, lost 10, scored 9 goals and conceded 49. This World Cup would bring no change in their fortune. They lost 7-0 to the Austrians and were defeated in other games. To their credit is their determination against the odds.

Under pressure from other members, FIFA stopped using the British home championship as a qualifying group. It was considered unfair that the four British nations should be guaranteed two places in the finals and so they were placed in qualifying groups like the rest. Ironically, through an unlikely series of events, all four qualified, the first and only time this has happened. The English qualified out of Group One and did so with a team of real promise, containing players of the quality of Roger Byrne, Tommy Taylor and Duncan Edwards, who many regarded as the most gifted of his generation. All three played for Manchester United and all three, tragically lost their lives in the Munich Air Disaster. The aircraft that was taking the United team home from a 3-3 draw against Red Star Belgrade in a European Cup match stopped to refuel at Munich. As the plane tried to take off, for the third time in the snow and ice, it ran into difficulty and 23 people died in the crash that followed. It ripped the heart out of the Manchester United team, the famous "Busby Babes", but it also decimated the England squad.

Scotland's qualification out of Group Nine was one of the surprises of the phase, not because of the Scots, but because the Spanish were considered to be the stars of the group. Spanish football, particularly at club level, was going through a purple patch. Real Madrid, Europe's premier club, won the European Cup in 1956, 1957 and 1958, the first years it was played, and Barcelona won the new Inter-Cities Fairs Cup in 1958. The national team was brimming with stars from these two clubs and included the Argentine-born, Alfredo Di Stefano, one of the world's greats. The Spanish were expected to qualify easily, but when they drew with Switzerland in the group's opening game and lost to Scotland in Glasgow, they never recovered the momentum. The Spaniards beat Scotland in Madrid, but it was the Scots that went to Sweden.

The Northern Irish were the recipients of some good fortune on their journey to the finals. The Italians were the team fancied to qualify from their group, but they were the victims of their own pettiness. It proved to be a very tight group, but by the time the Italians went to Belfast to play the Irish in December 1957 they only needed a draw to see them through. The Hungarian referee, Istvan Zsolt, had been chosen to officiate. However, his plane was delayed at London's fog-bound Heathrow airport. The Irish suggested using another referee, but the Italians refused and the match had to be rescheduled. They agreed to play a friendly, though this is hardly the word to describe it, as the Italians allowed the more brutal aspects of their game to resurface. The so-called "Battle of Belfast" ended in a 2-2 draw, which would have seen Italy through to the finals. The qualifying game was played in January 1958 and a 2-1 victory took the Irish to the finals.

The French, once again, were the qualifying stage's free scorers, netting 19 times in four games, though some sympathy must go to Iceland in their first World Cup, who conceded 26 goals in four games. Also making a debut in the World Cup was the Soviet Union, a rather unknown, but nonetheless skilful team. They finished joint top of Group Six with Poland, above Finland against whom the Soviets had scored ten, and with six points apiece a play-off was required. It was played in Leipzig, in neutral East Germany, and the Soviets won 2-0 to secure a place in the finals at the first attempt.

The South American entrants were drawn into three groups for the three places on offer to that continent. Argentina entered a team for the first time since 1934, in spite of the fact that, once again, several of the country's top players had been poached by Italian clubs, following Argentina's victory in the 1957 South American championship, and played for Italy's national side. With the loss of the cream of their team, the Argentinians did not find qualification easy, but getting there indirectly cost Uruguay a place. Argentina went into a group with Chile and Bolivia, displacing Paraguay, which went into a group with Colombia and Uruguay. Paraguay qualified at the expense of both.

The CONCACAF countries, of North and Central America, were divided into two groups, the winners of each to play-off in a two-legged final for the one spot allocated. Mexico qualified easily out of Group Two, above the USA and newcomers, Canada, but political problems upset the free flow of Group One, though not the eventual outcome. Costa Rica won all of its four matches and so topped the group. However, the game between Curaçao and Guatemala, due to be played in Willemstad, did not take place because the unpopular military ruler of Guatemala had been assassinated. In the disturbed political circumstances that followed his death, the national team were refused permission to leave the country. The Mexicans eventually won the place in Sweden.

Political problems also beset the Asia-Africa group and the unlikely beneficiary of it was Wales. The thorny problem of Israel's quarrel with its Arab neighbours has long bedevilled international affairs and it now bedevilled the World Cup. Before 1947, the area known as Palestine had been under British control and its Jewish and Arab communities had lived mostly at peace. For years Jews had been calling for a homeland and these intensified after the full horrors of wartime Nazi persecution of the Jews was revealed. The influx of Jewish immigrants that followed the war angered the Palestinian Arabs and trouble erupted. With the country sliding

Love, Losses and the Boys from Brazil - Sweden 1958

All the British players were to get a £2-a-day spending allowance from their FAs. Previously FIFA had decided that, since players could earn up to £150 a week for their clubs, they should not get any allowance at all. It was only when Northern Ireland protested that the FAs, in conference, decided to allow the £2.

At the 1958 World Cup there were to be no substitutes, "not even if the goalkeeper gets injured", said Arthur Drewry, the FIFA President.

into civil war, the British pulled out and Palestine's Jewish population declared the independence of the state of Israel. It was immediately attacked by neighbouring Arab states, but survived and the region has been a source of danger ever since. Israel had entered the 1950 and 1954 World Cups and had always been paired with European teams in the qualifying stages. For the 1958 tournament, in an act of pure stupidity, Israel was placed in the Asia-Africa group.

Group One contained its own political time bomb, that of a quarrel between Taiwan (Formosa) and China, which had once been part of the same country. However, Mao's Communists had seized power in 1949 and Chiang's Nationalists had fled to Taiwan. Both claimed to be the sole legitimate authority in China and neither accepted the independent existence of the other. When they were grouped together in the World Cup, Taiwan refused to play China and promptly withdrew. It left Indonesia and China to play a three match stalemate before Indonesia went through on goal average.

Group Two contained Israel and Turkey, but Moslem Turkey refused to play Israel and withdrew. In Group Three Egypt and Cyprus were paired, but Cyprus withdrew, and in Group Four the Sudan qualified above Syria. Then politics reared its ugly head when Indonesia and Egypt, both Islamic countries, withdrew refusing to play Israel. Their departure left Israel to play the Sudan in the final, but the Islamic Sudan also pulled out. It meant that Israel had qualified without playing a game, but this was now against FIFA rules. Lots were therefore drawn among the runners up in the European groups to decide who would meet Israel in a two-legged play-off for the final place in Sweden. The Welsh won the right and then the play-off.

There is a final twist to this story. The Welsh were managed by Jimmy Murphy, who was also Matt Busby's second in command at Manchester United. He was meant to have travelled to Belgrade for United's game against Red Star, but because Wales's second game against Israel had been scheduled for the 5th February 1958, the club had given him dispensation to be with them. It meant he was not on the plane that killed so many of his friends and colleagues in Munich and it must have been with a heavy heart that Murphy took his team to the World Cup finals.

Quite by chance, the sixteen finalists came from four geographic zones and, conveniently, each zone supplied four teams: from South America, the British Isles, Eastern Europe and Western Europe. In consequence, FIFA decided that each of the four pools would consist of one team from each zone. There were no seeded teams. The new system produced pools of varying strengths, but this was not seen as a problem and, undoubtedly, the strongest group was Pool Four, which contained Austria, Brazil, England and the Soviet Union. It was also decided that there would no longer be extra time in the pool games, but there would be play-offs if teams finishing in second and third spots tied with equal points.

The tournament got underway on 8th June, with an opening ceremony in the Råsunda Stadium in Stockholm and the Pool Three game between Sweden and Mexico. In that opening game, Sweden easily brushed aside Mexico's challenge. Before the World Cup had started, Sweden's coach, George Raynor, had said that his team would get to the final, though few had taken him seriously. His prediction was based on a change of circumstance that greatly affected Swedish national football. Their FA had accepted professionalism and it made players who had gone abroad eligible to represent their country. The team was immeasurably strengthened and the Mexicans were the first to feel its force. Centre-forward, Agne Simonsson scored his country's first two goals, one in each half, and the third was a penalty. It was converted by Nils Liedholm of AC Milan, "one of the real artists of the contemporary game".

There were seven other games played that day and in Pool One, Northern Ireland met Czechoslovakia, and West Germany played Argentina. Northern Ireland may have been one of the smaller nations, but they had reached their first finals on merit. Manager Peter Doherty had blended a team of real quality, containing men like Manchester United's Harry Gregg in goal, Tottenham's Danny Blanchflower and Burnley's Jimmy McIlroy, who were among the finest practitioners in the English league. Their enthusiasm can be gauged from a remark made by captain Blanchflower when asked about team tactics: "Our tactics are to equalize before the other team scores," he jibbed. If they had a point to prove, it was that they were not just there to make up the numbers, as Czechoslovakia discovered on that opening day. The more fancied Czechs did most of the attacking, but "playing their typical do-or-die brand of football", as one analyst described it, the Irish went in front in the 20th minute. McIlroy crossed the ball and Leeds United's Wilbur Cush headed it in. Stunned, the Czechs were spurred to exert even more pressure, but with Gregg in sparkling form and Blanchflower a tower in defence, there was no way through for the East Europeans. The game ended 1-0 to the Irish. It was one of the first shocks of the tournament and, curiously, the Irish would not have been in Sweden but for a change of rules by their FA. In a land where religion is a major determinant in peoples' lives, the Northern Irish FA did not allow football to be played on Sunday. Some of the World Cup games were scheduled for Sundays and the Irish had to change their rules to accommodate this.

The surprise in the other Pool One game was not the score, but how mediocrely the Argentinians played. They were managed by their former goal ace, Guillermo Stàbile and he had assembled a strong team that had won the 1957 South American championship. Since then the insatiable appetites of Italian clubs denuded it of its finest players and it was a weakened team that crossed the seas to Sweden. It showed in the game against Germany, whose team was, if anything, stronger than the one that had won the cup in 1954. Four of that team, Hans Schäfer, Fritz Walter, Horst Eckel and Helmuth Rahn survived from Switzerland, but the Germans could boast new talent, like the young Uwe Seeler, soon to make his own unique contribution to World Cup history. The Germans were the stronger of the two sides, but it was the Argentinians who took an early lead, when Orestes Omar Corbatta found the net. The Germans are notoriously slow World Cup starters, and it took half an hour before they found their feet with Rahn's first goal of the tournament. Three minutes before half-time, Seeler got his and in the last minute of the game scored his second for a 3-1 victory.

The French were the obvious favourites to progress out of Pool Two. This was arguably the finest French team ever, managed by former international Paul Nicholas, and awash with dazzling individuals, many of whom played for Stade de Reims, the most successful French club of the era. Among the names that illuminated this team were Jean Vincent,

Brazil's Belllini and Vavá with the Jules Rimet Trophy.

In Argentina's opening game against West Germany British referee, Reg Leafe of Nottingham, judged that the Argentine shirts were too close in colour to those of the Germans and made them change into yellow ones.

The Argentinians started fighting amongst themselves before the tournament had even started. Frederico Vairo, the reserve team goalkeeper, turned up late for training and insisted on taking his place on the pitch. When he was pushed away by stand-in full-back, Guillio Mesimessi, fighting broke out and coach Guillermo Stàbile, threatened to send everyone home if anything like it happened again.

Due to a bad winter that year, the pitches were in a particularly poor condition and the stadium at Norrköping, where Scotland played their games, was still incomplete with only six days to go. The changing rooms were not finished on time and teams would have had to change in rather primitive looking buildings in another part of the stadium. However, this was not acceptable to one FIFA official, Kurt Gassman, who said, "This was out of the question. Teams will use the facilities at the Sports Palace and go to and from the stadium in their kits."

Hungary's top sports chef, Antal Keruez, had turned up for the tournament with nearly four cwt (200 kilos) of kitchen equipment and two pans of special Hungarian pancakes.

Love, Losses and the Boys from Brazil - Sweden 1958

Roger Piantoni and Maryan Wisnieski. There was also Raymond Kopa of Real Madrid, a midfield powerhouse and European Player of the Year in 1957. And there was Juste Fontaine, whose 13 goals in the tournament is still a record and after whom this World Cup might have been remembered had it not been for a 17 year old wonder boy by the name of Pelé.

France's opening game was against Paraguay, a team "compounded largely of Guarani Indians, farm boys from the plains and backwoods" and one to be respected, though they were outshone on this day by vintage French performance. The Paraguayans took the lead when, in the 20th minute, Florencio Amarilla scored. Fontaine, however, equalized soon after. Six minutes later, he notched his second, and the French seemed well in control. In the last minute of the first half Paraguay won a penalty, which Amarilla converted and soon after the restart Jorgelino Romero scored to see Paraguay in front for the second time. The rest of the game, though, belonged to the French and their powerful, tricky forwards. Two minutes after Romero's goal, Piantoni equalized. Then came three goals in seven minutes, from Wisnieski, Fontaine and Kopa, before Vincent rounded proceedings off in the 84th minute to give a final scoreline of 7-3 to France.

The other team in Pool Two given a realistic chance of doing well was Yugoslavia, who entertained Scotland on the opening day. The Scots got off to the worst possible start when after only five minutes of play, Todor Vaselinovic got the better of his marker and set up Aleksander Petakovic, whose shot "flashed by Younger just inside the post." The Scots found it tough throughout the game and their "small forwards were usually outpaced or outweighted", but they fought on manfully. They had a better second half, with Hibernian's Eddie Turnbull playing particularly well and setting up the equalizer. He picked the up ball on the right, whipped in a first time cross and Jim Murray of Hearts leaped up with the Yugoslav goalkeeper, Beara. Murray's challenge was the stronger and he headed the ball through the keeper's hands and "a dozen Scotsmen did a jig", as the Times noted. It was Scotland's first point in the World Cup finals and it would be 1974 before they got another.

The Hungarians, who opened their campaign against Wales, were not the force they had been four years earlier. In 1956, with the country experiencing economic decline, a series of political developments resulted in the ruling Communist Party falling under the control of a reformist, less repressive faction, headed by Imre Nagy. Their desire to make the system more responsive to popular needs met with hearty approval from the public, but the new leadership lost control of events. Pressed on by the aspirations of a beleaguered people, promises were made that threatened to undo the Communist system erected after World War Two. The response of the Soviet Union was to send in the tanks and amid scenes of slaughter, hard-line Communist authority was restored in Budapest. Tens of thousands lost their lives and tens of thousands fled abroad, among them many of the "Mighty Magyars." Gone were the likes of Puskás, Czibor and Kocsis, defected to the West, and their loss was much felt, typically in the game against Wales.

Like the Irish, the Welsh were a team of battlers. In John Charles of Juventus they had one of the big names of European soccer, but there were many in the side capable of holding their own against more famed opposition. Against the Hungarians, they needed to show their spirit because they went behind to a Bozsik goal after only five minutes. That the Magyars were a more skilful side was plain, but every Welshman put "his heart into every minute of the game in spite of some rugged tactics by the Hungarians." Their bravado paid dividends in the 27th minute when Charles headed home a Cliff Jones cross to level the scores. From then on the Welsh defended stoutly to maintain the situation and pull off another of the day's surprises.

Whatever challenges came out of Europe, there were few in 1958 who did not recognize the potency of the Brazilian team, whose revolutionary 4-2-4 formation "neatly expounded the artistry of their players while confounding their opponents." Their's was a team full of masters of the football, resounding with players of the quality of Garrincha, Vavá and Zagalo and, though by the standards they later expounded, they made a slow start, in the end they easily overcame the Austrians in their first game. A lone first half goal and two in the second, the last being an excellent effort from Mazzola, was to get their campaign off to a solid start.

England's game against the Soviet Union was one of those "games of two halves." The Soviets were a "superior, more cultured side" and deserved the two goal lead they took. McDonald, in the England goal, was only able to parry a first half shot from Valentin Ivanov that rebounded to Nikita Simoneon and he flicked it into the net. Ivanov himself scored after the break to confirm his team's dominance, though it could have been worse for the English had the Soviets taken any of the many chances they created. With the English not having recovered from the Munich Air Disaster, their problems were compounded by the failure to include Matthews and Lofthouse in the squad and the refusal to play the superbly talented Bobby Charlton. They were serious errors of judgement by the management. However, they fought back, inspired by the ebullient Tom Finney and "one minute were Russia cruising to an assured win, and the next they were thrown back as if in retreat across the wide Steppes." England's recovery began with a Billy Wright free kick taken from inside his own half and which the head of Derek Kevan steered into the net. It was completed five minutes from time when Finney scored a penalty after Haynes had been brought down.

The second lot of pool matches got underway on 11th June, a day on which Argentina exposed the frailties of the Northern Irish. Things began well enough when Aston Villa's Peter McParland, one of the stars of the tournament, put the Irish ahead, but they made the tactical error of trying to defend their lead from too early in the game. They "struggled on gallantly", though "were outplayed by clever ball players whose passing was admirable." A penalty, given when Keith Dick handled in the area seven minutes before the break and stroked home by Corbatta, started Argentina's recovery. Ten minutes into the second period, Norberto Menendez's goal gave them the lead and Ludovico Avio sealed the win on the hour with a third. It had been a brave effort from the Irish, but a stronger, more technically proficient team had overcome them.

Against the Germans, the Czechs made changes to their attack and it seemed to work. A Milan Dvorak penalty and a goal from Zdenek Zikan gave them a 2-0 half-time lead, but things can never be taken for granted against Germany. They came back strongly in the second half and goals from Schäfer and Rahn, in the 60th and 70th minutes respectively, earned them the draw that took them to the top of the pool.

Both Pool Two games played that day brought 3-2 scorelines. Paraguay's victory over Scotland "was a triumph for speed and shooting power against more methodical football," noted the Times and it was achieved because, disappointed by their display against the French, the Paraguayans made important changes to their team. They made changes to the defence and it brought about a greater determination that got the better of a lacklustre Scottish side. The South Americans took the lead in the fourth minute, through Juan Bautisto Aquero, only for Blackpool's Jackie Mudie to equalize some twenty minutes later. Just before half-time Cayetano Re restored his country's lead and they grew stronger after the break, controlling much of the flow of the play. José Parado extended their lead, before Bobby Collins pulled one back late in the game.

It was a similar story when France took on Yugoslavia, a game in which the French seemed strangely nervous and made things difficult for themselves. They allowed the Yugoslavs to dominate whole patches of the play, a dangerous ploy because, whilst the French forwards were among the best on show, their defence was prone to lapses. The Yugoslavs were always good enough to exploit any particular weakness. So, although Fontaine shot France into an early lead, Petakovic equalized in the first half and Vaselinovic put his team in front in the second. Five minutes before full time the French appeared to have salvaged a draw, when Fontaine scored his second, but the Yugoslavs pressed on and Vaselinovic won the match with a late strike.

The whole of the Welsh team had to be treated for knocks and bruises after their crunching game against the 'push-about' Hungarians on the opening day.

Hungarian Uprising remembered…

17th June 1958 was a very sad day for all Hungarians in more ways than one. Not only did they lose their play-off match against Wales, but they also lost one of their national heroes, Imre Nagy. The Russians had arrested the former Hungarian leader at the time of the 1956 Uprising. He was executed on the morning of the game and it must have affected the players. Hungarian supporters at the game unfurled their red, white and green flags with the Kossuth, the symbol of the revolt. They also waved black streamers. Just before the game kicked off the Swedish authorities ordered them to remove their flags and banners on the grounds that political demonstrations were not allowed in the stadium. The supporters complied, but just before half time, two of the flag bearers unfurled their banners again and were promptly ejected from the ground. They burst into tears shouting: "Why don't you leave us alone; we love our flags and our country." Ironically, one of the flags flying over the ground was the Soviet flag as the referee for the game was a Russian, Nikolai Latychev. After the game and, having just kicked lumps out of the Welsh, the Hungarian Captain József Bozsic went over to Ivor Allchurch, scorer of one of the goals, to say: "We are sorry for what happened. Please forgive us."

The referee for England's opener against the USSR, Istvan Zsolt, was a theatre manager from Budapest.

Love, Losses and the Boys from Brazil - Sweden 1958

Young lovers in a Swedish summertime - The Billy Wright/Joy Beverley Story

As the World Cup was about to get under way there was some concern that England captain, Billy Wright, had his mind on other things. One of the chart-topping groups of the day was the singing trio, the Beverley Sisters, whose best known hit, "Sisters", contained the line - "Lord help the mister who comes between me and my sisters". The speculation was that the "mister" that might come between Joy and the other two sisters, was Billy himself. Like the girls, this teen idol had classic good looks and for weeks the press had been following the story closely.

Wright played for one of England's premier club, Wolverhampton Wanderers, and it was while the girls were performing in the town that the couple first met. Cupid was Vincent, Joy's nine-year son from her first marriage. He had gone with his mother to see the Wolves play Arsenal and after the game they went to meet the players. They met for a second time when Vincent and Joy were invited to Billy's home to see his trophies.

Wright had the press on his tail throughout the World Cup but he remained steadfast, saying that he would make a statement about his relationship with Joy after the competition was over. However, when England went out and Wright returned home, all three Beverley sisters were waiting for him at the airport. Embarrassingly red, he walked the gauntlet of flash guns to where they were, kissed them all lightly on the cheek, swallowed hard and said: "Hello, lets get out of here." Even then he remained coy about his intentions. As the pair sat outside the Beverley Sisters' home in Highgate, London Wright said: "I want time to think things through. People keep asking me when I'm going to marry Joy. Well, I've only known her eight weeks. I come back from two weeks hard soccer and I want some rest. I shall spend it thinking about Joy and me. But I don't like rushing into things. I'm all right on the soccer field, but this sort of thing puts me right out of my depth."

Joy Beverley and Billy Wright were "secretly" married on 27th July 1958 in Poole, Dorset. However, word had leaked out that the event was about to take place and the scenes outside the register office were chaotic. Holiday traffic and buses were held up and Teddie Beverley, another of the girls, lost a shoe. At the wedding the sisters wore identical sack-style dresses of turquoise with white spots. Unfortunately there was not to be a honeymoon. Wright had to be in Wolverhampton the next day because the Wolves were off on a pre-season tour of Sweden of all places. As for Billy and Joy, they remained together until he died in 1994. Joy is still belting out the hits with her sisters.

Arthur Ellis who had refereed the notorious 'Battle of Berne' in 1954 was causing more controversy in 1958. On 11th June the Czechs played West Germany and were leading 2-0 when goalkeeper, Bretislav Dolejsi, was bundled over his own goal line with the ball by Hans Schäfer. Ellis awarded a goal and the Germans went on to equalize ten minutes later. Pictures of the game published in newspapers the next day clearly showed that the ball had never crossed the line. The Czechs promptly stated that they would not accept Ellis as referee in any more of their matches, something they were entitled to do, if they did it on time. When he saw the pictures Ellis said: "Good pictures, no doubt - but what proves it was a goal? I had a very good position twelve feet from the post. The ball was over the line." The Czech coach, Harel Kolsky said, "It was not a goal. Mr Ellis was good in the first half but bad in the second."

If it wasn't bad enough that the Scots ended their opener against Yugoslavia with ten injured players, Alex Scot, the reserve right-winger, also got himself hurt. On 10th July he slipped and fell while getting out of the bath after training, injuring his hip. They managed to pull themselves together for their game against Paraguay and there were only three remaining doubts before kick off.

The only Pool Three game played that day featured Mexico and Wales. It was a good match, which gave the Welsh their second draw of the tournament and the Mexicans their first World Cup point at their tenth attempt. Always finely balanced, there was a clear contrast in style between "the exuberance of Mexico's ball play, the interchanging and improvisation of their forwards" against the more dour, workmanlike Welsh. The Welsh got the breakthrough in the first half after John Charles won them a corner. The ball landed at the feet of Ivor Allchurch, lurking near the penalty spot, and he smashed it into the net. For the rest of the game the Welsh had to keep their wits about them as the Mexicans "in their exotic emerald" swarmed "around a desperate, panicking Wales at the end." "Baker had to limp off near the end, reducing his gallant team to ten men and the Mexicans took their chance. In the last minute a ball was floated into the Welsh goalmouth and Jaime Belmonte " timed his header to perfection."

In Pool Four, the Soviet Union proved much too strong for the Austrians and goals in each half, from Anatoli Ilyin and Valentin Ivanov, brought a 2-0 victory that was more comfortable than the scoreline suggested. The best game played that day was the 0-0 draw fought out between England and Brazil. It was the first ever no score draw in the World Cup finals, but was exciting from first to last. It "throbbed with near misses at each end; it tingled with poetic movement; and if most of the poetry and the tingle was created by the dark ability of the New World, England answered in her own open and often deviously subtle ways", as one contemporary waxed. On another day, the game would have seen a myriad of goals, but posts, crossbars and excellent goalkeeping served to deny both sets of forwards.

The only game played on 12th June was that between Sweden and Hungary, with both teams seemingly out of sorts. The Hungarians had dropped Hidegkúti and played Bozsic up front as a deep lying

133

centre-forward, reverting to the style of play that had been so successful earlier in the decade. On this occasion, it brought no dividend and the Swedes took the lead some ten minutes before half-time when Kurt Hamrin scored a goal that seemed off-side. The Scottish referee, Jack Mowatt, allowed it to stand and he advantaged the Swedes a second time when he disallowed a seemingly good goal from the Hungarians. A shot by Lajos Tichy, one of Hungary's new stars, went in off Svensson, the goalkeeper, onto the bar and rebounded onto the goal line before coming out. Many people said that it had crossed the line, but Mowatt disagreed. It summed up Hungary's day and within a minute Hamrin, with a darting run, had scored his second. Tichy blasted a thundering 25 yard drive into the Swedish goal, but it was not enough and the Swedes held out for a 2-1 victory.

West Germany 2 : Czechoslovakia 2
The controversial moment when referee Arthur Ellis ruled that West German Hans Schäfer had scored by charging the Czech goalkeeper over the goal line.

Northern Ireland's draw against West Germany (See N. Ireland v W. Germany profile on page 146) gave them three points, but their fate rested on the result of the game between Argentina and Czechoslovakia. It went favourably for the Irish because the South Americans were completely overwhelmed by the Czechs. They conceded three goals in the first half, before Corbatta replied with a penalty, but three more Czech goals after the interval gave an emphatic 6-1 victory. The Czechs and the Irish would need to play-off to decide who would progress, whilst the Argentinians went home to be pelted with fruit on their arrival. One of the reasons for their demise was that the players had spent too much time carousing the Swedish nightspots and their pleasurable excesses had got the better of them.

With Yugoslavia on top of Pool Two, France took on Scotland in the final pool game. It was a match the French had to win to be sure of making the next phase and they made changes to shore up their leaky defence. The Scots gave a good account of themselves and "more than matched the Frenchmen for skill but they made the mistake of passing the ball too squarely and too slowly." The French were tactically more aware and were given a half-time lead by Kopa and Fontaine, who had now scored six times in three matches. Sammy Baird got Scotland's reply in the second half, but the French held on for the win. It could have been so different had Hewie not missed a penalty. The result put Scotland out of the tournament and it was between Yugoslavia and Paraguay to see who would go through with the French. The Paraguayans gave their best performance of the World Cup to match the Yugoslavs move for move. They fell behind three times and three times they levelled the scores, but a draw was not good enough. The Yugoslavs were in the quarter-finals.

The Swedish press were so unimpressed by 'King' John Charles' performance for Wales against Mexico that they offered him for sale at 5 Crowns, about £5, as a joke. Juventus had bought Charles the year before for £75,000 making him one of the world's most expensive players. Wales were due to play Sweden in their final group match and they were just trying to put him off.

It wasn't until the 1958 World Cup finals that the world got to see the 'Golden Boy' of Welsh football, Ivor Allchurch. He was a sublime, elegant player who caressed the ball with grace. He was a goal scorer who belongs with those others who were prolific at the art. He remains the record holder for the most goals score by any Swansea City player with 160. However, most of his football was played with other clubs, including Newcastle United, Cardiff City and Swansea City again, and his audience of adoring and appreciative fans is relatively small.

Love, Losses and the Boys from Brazil - Sweden 1958

W. Germany 2 : N. Ireland 2
N. Ireland's McIlroy leaps over Erhardt of W. Germany.

The Swedes went into their final pool game with Wales, knowing that they had already qualified for the next phase. George Raynor had decided to rest his players and fielded an understrength team. The Welsh, though, whose play had witnessed a steady deterioration through all of their games, were unable to capitalize and this dull game ended scoreless. It gave Wales three points, though whether this would mean automatic qualification depended on the game between Hungary and Mexico. That game kicked off later than the Swedish game and by half-time the Hungarians had taken a one goal lead, scored by Tichy. During the break, the result of the earlier game became known and both teams realized that a win would secure a play-off with Wales. It fired the Magyars up and they hit the Mexicans hard. Almost straight away, Tichy scored his second and eight minutes later Karoly Sándor made the score 3-0. The poor Mexicans went crashing out of another World Cup and when Juan Gómez Gonzáles put the ball into his own net, to register the tournament's only own goal, their fate was sealed.

When the final Pool Four games kicked off, only the Austrians had no chance of qualification. The others had all to play for and the English began their game against Austria in determined mood. They applied plenty of early pressure, but when Karl Koller unleashed a "flaming 25-yard rocket" to take the lead, things began to fall apart. "From that moment to the interval England went from muddled bad to muddled worse", as one reporter noted. Two more shots from Koller that were well saved and a bad miss in front of an open goal, had they gone in, would have put the situation beyond England's reach, but they were reprieved to give a better second half display. In the 60th minute, Szanwald, in Austria's goal, failed to hold on to a shot from Alan A'Court and Johnny Haynes drove in the rebound. Alfred Körner restored Austria's lead with another long range strike that McDonald seemed to see late, but the closing stages brought much England pressure. It was rewarded when Haynes sent Derek Kevan through on goal to score the equalizer.

For the game against the Soviet Union, Brazil's coach, Vincente Feola, had been persuaded to give World Cup debuts to three of his rising stars, Zito, Garrincha and Pelé. They slotted into and complemented the team perfectly and Brazil produced a very polished performance to see off the Soviets with a 2-0 win. Garrincha and Didí, in particular were outstanding, though it was Vavá who scored both the goals. His first came in the third minute and whilst the team had to wait until late in the second half for his second, it was a game the Brazilians never looked like losing. Their defeat left the Soviets with three points and a play-off with England was needed for the quarter-final place. (See Didí profile on page 140 and Garrincha profile on page 141).

Unusually, three of the four pools required play-off games and all three were played on 17th June. The Northern Irish were clearly the underdogs in their game against Czechoslovakia and they got off to a poor start. The Czechs, the better team, "were yards faster in defence, their physique was superior and their heading was at times domineering." They had much of the early pressure and could have taken the lead several times before they did. Their goal came in the 19th minute when Feureisl and Uprichard, Ireland's goalkeeper, both went for the same high ball. Both missed and Zikan nipped in to head his team in front. It was not until late in the half that the Irish began to assert themselves. Towards the end of the half Cush had three shots blocked in quick succession before the last fell to McParland, who scored the equalizer. The goal unnerved the Czechs, whose play grew increasingly vicious. The Irish suffered some costly injuries, but when Titus Bubernik was sent off, the beleaguered Irish found some respite and they took the opportunity presented by their numeric superiority.

McParland got onto the end of a Blanchflower free kick to thump the ball home and take the Irish into the quarter-finals. It was a proud moment for a team that had done far better than anybody could have imagined.

Much the same can be said of the Welsh, who had not played well in their last two matches and were given no chance against Hungary. Like the Czechs, the Magyars resorted to rough tactics to intimidate their opponents and the Soviet referee, Nikolai Latychev, afforded them little protection. They held out until the 33rd minute, when Tichy nudged his team in front. It might have began a rout, but the Welsh showed plenty of character and, though the rest of the half saw much Hungarian activity, there were no further goals. In the second half things got better for the Welsh, particularly after Ferenc Sipos was sent off for foul play. Allchurch equalized with a thumping 35-yard volley some ten minutes after the restart and, with a little under 15 minutes to go Grosics made the mistake that gave Wales the victory. He miskicked a short out pass to one of his defenders and Terry Medwin stole the ball to score.

On the balance of play, England should have won their play-off against the Soviet Union. They dominated much of the game, but could not find the telling blow against an opposition who "were at times like a heavyweight boxer stumbling on his knees and holding on for dear life." New caps, Peter Broadbent and Peter Brabrook both played well and created enough chances to have put the game beyond the Soviets, but they were profligate and there was always the woodwork or Lev Yashin to deny those shots that were on target. The English also defended well when they had to, especially in the first half when the Soviets looked more dangerous, though it was a defensive error that cost them the match. McDonald's throw out, in the 63rd minute, was a poor one and the ball fell to Ilyin. He hit a shot that went in off the post and for the rest of the game, his team was able to soak up the massive English pressure to uphold their slender lead. Oddly, then, of the four British teams, the more fancied

Sweden 0 : Wales 0
John Charles of Wales (left) with Sweden's Julle Gustafsson.

When Brazil played the USSR, two-goal hero Vavá was hugged and slapped on the back so much after scoring his second that he had to leave the pitch to recover

---

An Englishman abroad - George Raynor...

In 1958, George Raynor, a miner's son from South Yorkshire in England took Sweden to the World Cup final. They didn't win, but this should not detract from the enormity of the achievement. Few English people know the man who revolutionized Swedish football and became a national hero there.

Raynor was born in 1907 and as a boy won a scholarship to Barnsley Grammar School. He did not shine academically and began his working life as a butcher's apprentice. His career in football began as a winger with Sheffield United and continued with stints at Mansfield Town and Bury before the Second World War interrupted it. He became an Army PT instructor in Iraq enabling him to indulge his passion for the game and he became an accomplished soccer coach. It was while coaching Aldershot reserves in 1946 that he came to the attention of the FA secretary, Stanley Rous, who recommended him to the then-managerless Swedes. They took him on and within two years were Olympic Champions. Following the 1950 World Cup finals Raynor spent two years in Italy managing Lazio and then Juventus before returning home. He had grown disillusioned by the changing attitudes of players who were becoming too full of their own self-importance as their wages crept higher and higher and he cut short his time in Italy.

Sweden's success in the Olympics and the 1958 World Cup was down to the tactics he employed both on and off the field. His first move was to take time to watch Swedish club sides to assess their strengths and weaknesses. He then introduced the tactic that was to revolutionize their play, that of using the centre-forward in a deep lying position, one that was later refined by the Hungarians who used it to such devastating affect in the 1950s. He had been briefly unemployed when recalled to take charge of Sweden's national team once again. Before the final, he said in his strong Yorkshire accent: "If Brazil go a goal down they'll panic all over t'shop." It didn't quite happen like that, but his great achievement was recognized by the Swedish King who knighted him. Raynor then had the audacity to bring his side to England and beat them on their own ground, only the second overseas team to do it

Is it a sad indictment of the FA, English football in general and the suspicion of his methods that the only job Raynor could get on his return to England was in the stores at Butlin's Holiday Camp in Skegness? He achieved more than Walter Winterbottom ever did, but the dinosaur-like manner of the English FA was always going to be against him. Raynor did get back into the game with Doncaster Rovers for a short while before he retired to live in Armthorpe.

Wales 2 : Hungary 1
Hungarian goalkeeper Grosics can't stop Medwin (left) scoring the second Welsh goal.

English and Scots had gone out of the tournament, whilst the Irish and the Welsh had survived.

West Germany's quarter-final against Yugoslavia turned out to be a "dour defensive battle", the stakes now being too high to risk mistakes. The Yugoslavs were the better team, launching frequent attacks against the German goal, but, as always, the Germans were well organized and dogged in their wish to give nothing away. It was never going to be a high scoring game and so it proved. The Germans took a 12th minute lead, through Rahn, and spent the rest of the game protecting it.

A far more attractive spectacle was France's encounter with the Northern Irish. The French had had a decent break since their last game, allowing them to recuperate, but the Irish were still suffering the effects of their tough game only two days before. Several of the Irish were carrying knocks, including Tom Casey, who had four stitches in his leg, and Gregg, who only played because Uprichard, the replacement goalkeeper, was more badly injured than he was. Furthermore, a long coach journey to Norrköping only added to their discomfort and, in the circumstances, they did well to hold the French at bay for as long as they did. It was not until the last two minutes of the first half that Maryan Wisnieski put the French in front, but, once it had happened, the French opened up to make their superiority tell. Taking control of the midfield, Raymond Kopa initiated a barrage of French attacks and the Irish began to crack. Goals came regularly. Fontaine scored twice and Piantoni added the fourth, whilst at the other end, Abbès's goal was hardly threatened.

Soviet Union 1 : England 0
Ilyin of the Soviet Union shoots for goal.

The Soviets also appeared tired for their quarter-final - it is significant that none of the three quarter-finalists who had come through the play-offs survived the round and FIFA dropped the idea of group play-offs for the 1962 World Cup. The Swedes, playing "neatly and much superior in their mid-field work", dominated large periods of the match, though the Soviets kept a clean sheet for the whole of the first half. Swedish pressure told early in the second, when Inter Milan's "Nacka" Skoglund set up a goal for the other winger, Hamrin. From that point on it was virtually all Sweden. The Soviets had to defend valiantly against an almost non-stop bombardment. It was not until two minutes from the end that Agne Simonsson, with a very powerful strike, scored his country's second.

The pluckiest of the play-off survivors proved to be the Welsh, whose sturdy defence kept the dancing Brazilians out for 73 minutes of the game. It was 73 minutes of almost total Brazilian pressure, but it could not breach the Welsh back line. As one reporter put it, "the impression remained that Garrincha, Didí, Mazzola, Pelé, Zagalo (sic) and company hated to hurt the ball with some strong blow. They wanted to walk it into the net." When the goal finally came, it was of great significance. It was Pelé's first World Cup goal and one he later described as "the most important goal of my career." He

Sweden's Liedholm(left) and Svensson with crew cut hair, a bet for reaching the final.

took advantage of Welsh hesitancy, picking the ball up on the six yard line with his back to goal. He cleverly flicked it goalwards, turned into the space between two defenders and stuck the ball into the net. It was an excellent goal, worthy of a victory, though the Welsh pushed the Brazilians hard to the end. (See Pelé profile on page 143).

It was only when their team reached the semi-finals that the Swedish public began to take notice of the dramatic events unfolding around them. Just one step away from the final and with the Germans to overcome, special cheerleaders were brought in to Gothenburg's Nya Ullevi Stadium to whip up the crowd and get them behind Raynor's team. They did the job well and never before had such scenes of patriotism been witnessed on a Swedish football ground. The team responded well and from the start took the game to the Germans. Although, it was the Germans who scored first against the run of play. Seeler broke down the left to the bye line and angled a reverse cross back into the area, where Schäfer was waiting to volley into the net. Not long after the home team were level, though there was an element of luck about the goal. Liedholm, who appeared to handle the ball as he controlled it, sent it across the face of the German goal and found Skoglund unmarked on the edge of the six yard box. He had little trouble dispatching it into the net to a torrent of noise from the excitable crowd. A defining moment of the match came with the sending off of Erich Justowick for an altercation with Hamrin and when Fritz Walter had to leave the pitch for treatment, the Swedes had the chance to press their advantage. They won the game in the last ten minutes, with goals by Gunnar Gren and Hamrin, who dribbled the ball along the bye line to fire it into the net.

The second semi-final had gone to Brazil (see Brazil v France profile on page 145), but before the hosts met them in the final, France and West Germany played out one of the most entertaining of 3rd/4th play-offs. The semi-final had been Pelé's: this game was the stage upon which Juste Fontaine stamped his brand of genius. He gave France the lead in the 14th minute, only for the Germans to equalize soon after. Less than a minute later, Kopa restored the lead and ten minutes after that Fontaine extended it with his second of the match. The next player to find the net, early in the second half, was Yvon Douis, on his World Cup debut and then Rahn made the score 4-2. In the last twelve minutes Fontaine netted twice, either side of a Schäfer goal, and the game ended 6-3 to France. His four goals took Fontaine's tally for the tournament to 13, a remarkable achievement - the next highest scorers were Pelé and Rahn with six. (See Juste Fontaine profile on page 142). It set a new competition record and one that is going to be very difficult to better. Since then, only Gerhard Müller with ten in 1970 and Eusébio with nine in 1966 have come anywhere near it.

Love, Losses and the Boys from Brazil - Sweden 1958

Sweden 2 : Brazil 5.
Brazil go on a lap of honour.

In winning the championship the Brazilian team became national heroes. The people in Rio de Janeiro went mad and every goal scored by the Brazilians was greeted with fireworks over Copaccabana Beach. The President of Brazil, Dr Juscellino Kubitschek was so impressed he sent his own presidential airliner to bring the team the last 1200 miles from Recife, Pernambuco. The day they arrived home was declared a public holiday.

Like both semi-finals, the final itself had been a classic and gave Brazil their first world championship. (See Brazil v Sweden profile on page 147). They had been the only team to have played in all six World Cup tournaments and, at last, had gained the title they awaited. Their football had got better as the series went on and the nature of their achievement, with its pulsating, mesmerizing football, was justly and widely hailed. The Swedes had been good, the French magnificent, but the Brazilians hit another dimension and, with one of the finest displays ever seen in the World Cup, they brought one of the best tournaments on record to a fitting close.

After being presented with the trophy by Arthur Drewry, the English president of FIFA, the jubilant Brazilians grabbed a Swedish flag and lapped the pitch in honour and salutation of their hosts. It was a magnanimous gesture, warmly applauded and a grand reflection of the spirit of 1958. Sweden had not been as high scoring a tournament as that in Switzerland, but it surpassed it, for the quality of its football and the atmosphere in which it was played. There were no "battles" to mar Sweden 1958, only the football, the Brazilians and their Pelé. Fans would have to wait until 1970, in Mexico, for a show as clean and as good.

If the 1930s had created the World Cup, the 1950s had established it as the major event on the world's sporting calendar. They were the tournament's halcyon days, of football innocence, when teams played for the love of it. Of course, they wanted to win, but there was also a pride in the manner of the victory. Teams like the Hungarians, the French and the Brazilians knew that they were good, but in winning they wanted to celebrate and expound their art form and develop it to its fullest. They were craftsmen as well as sportsmen. Sweden 1958 marks the apex of this era and attitude. By the time the 1960s dawned, a different way of thinking was penetrating the game. The rewards were getting greater, mass media was placing greater pressure on the players and the victory, not the game, was becoming the overriding concern. Football was losing its innocence. In this respect, Sweden 1958 was the last World Cup of its kind. An era was coming to an end.

Waldyr Pereira (Didí)   **Brazil**

Honours: Winner 1958 and 1962; Quarter-finals 1954   **Games 15**
Played: 1954, 1958 and 1962   **Goals 3**

Waldyr Pereira (Didí).

Didí overcame early adversity and fought back to become a midfield maestro, a magnificent all-rounder, who practised for hours and was at the heart of two consecutive World Cup victories. Whilst Pelé and Garrincha got the lion's share of the acclaim, Didí went about his business linking defence to attack with inspirational tenacity. He is remembered with affection and one admirer wrote: "Didí could drop the ball on a coin from any angle, any distance"

Born in Campos on 8th October 1928, his career almost ended before it began when, aged 14 and playing in an amateur game, he was brutally kicked on his right knee. An abscess formed and the doctors considered amputation. Fortunately, good care prevented it coming to that, though the road to recovery was long. He spent six months in a wheelchair and was left with a permanent limp. His love of the game drove him on and at 18 he was chosen to play for local team, Americano of Campos. It was a special moment in his life. He had spent hours alone working on his skills, neglecting no aspect of his game and in 1949, and after a spell at Lencoense of São Paulo, moved to Madureira. By the age of 21 he had drawn the attention of the bigger clubs, but it was Fluminense of the Rio League that secured his services. It was there he perfected his ability to bend the ball and make it fade at the end, a shot known as the "banana kick", or "folha seca" (dry leaf) to Brazilians. He also played his first representative game when a team of young professionals was brought together in 1950 to play a game to commemorate the opening of the Maracana. The "deformed" boy from Campos christened it with its first goal. As he recalled: "I played for the Carioca youth team against the Paulista youth team. After about six or seven minutes I played a one-two in the penalty area and there I was with only the goalkeeper in front of me. It was simple. We lost 3-1 but I'm pleased that nobody remembers the result, only the first goal."

In 1951, Didí's excellence helped Fluminense to the Rio Championship and national team coach, Zezé Moreira, took note. He was given his international debut at the 1952 Pan American Championships in Chile in a 2-0 victory over Mexico, and from then on he became a permanent fixture, taking the place of his boyhood hero, Zizinho. His tactical awareness and creativity became invaluable to the Brazilian midfield and he scored the first of his three World Cup goals in his tournament debut, also against Mexico. In Switzerland in 1954 he had a magnificent World Cup, scoring twice and helping Brazil to the quarter-finals.

In 1956 a move to Botafogo had a profound effect on his game. His coach did not like him training alone and his dipping, swerving free kicks suffered. However, the skill did not leave him and in the qualifying tournament for the Sweden World Cup, he produced a "folha seca" to secure a vital 1-0 victory against Peru that took them to the finals. Didí's place was still not assured as some felt he was too old and demotivated to play in the 4-2-4 formation. Coach Feola, however, stuck with him and his faith paid off. He scored only once, but his midfield play was critical to Brazil's final victory. His performance also attracted the attention of Real Madrid who paid £30,000 for him in October 1959. It was the beginning of the worst time of his career. Didí was 31 and the quality of his football caused many in the press to hail him the best in the world. It was an accolade that did not endear him to Real's other star, Di Stefano, and the club atmosphere became decidedly frosty. Di Stefano's influence led to Didí being virtually ignored and after a short loan spell with Valencia, he asked Real to terminate his contract. He returned to Botafogo, having played only 85 times for Real, scoring 35 goals.

Firing on all cylinders, he helped Botafogo win the Rio Championship in 1961 and 1962, but his place in the national side was threatened by new boy, Cinesinho. Experience prevailed over youth and Didí went to Chile to compete in his third World Cup tournament. Aged 34, he was not as dominant as he had been in 1958 and shortly after his international playing career ended. He had made 72 appearances and scored 21 goals. He then enjoyed a spell as player-coach with Peruvian club side, Sporting Cristal, who he led to a second place in the league and by 1970 was coach of the Peruvian national side, taking them to the World Cup finals. He described disciplined approach to managerial philosophy this way: "Without discipline we cannot get anywhere, we cannot construct. Teamwork is what counts in football and that depends on every player giving himself for the sake of the team. I am an enemy of the individual." It was successful and took Peru to the quarter-finals, but it was not without its tensions. He once fined star centre-forward Pedro Leon £160 for being late for training and caused a public outcry. Didí dug in and had his way.

Didí was still involved in the game, making appearances at big occasions, until his death from pneumonia on 12th May 2001. Having had a back operation that left him walking with the aide of a stick, he looked physically frail as he accepted his induction into the FIFA Hall of Fame at the 1999 World Player of the Year Awards. It was a fitting honour for one so important to the game of the 1950s and 60s. He never tried to hide the fact that he not only wanted to be a star in the game, he also wanted to earn as much money as he could. Coming from such humble beginnings this is no disgrace. "As a kid I had to work as a peanut seller to help my parents. A man can speak lightly of poverty only if he has never experienced its terrors."

Manoel dos Santos Francisco (Garrincha)   Brazil

Honours: Winner 1958 and 1962   Games 12
Played:1958, 1962 and 1966   Goals 5

Manoel dos Santos Francisco
(Garrincha).

Manoel dos Santos Francisco was born a cripple at Pau Grande on 28th October, 1933 and his nickname "Garrincha", an ugly, useless little bird, was given to him by one of his many brothers. He had a body ravaged by hunger and polio, an S-shaped spine and legs that bowed to the same side. Dumb and lame, he had the mental capacity of an infant and had to undergo an operation to enable him to walk. His left leg was permanently deformed and his doctors, not believing that such a child could ever make it in the world of football, made the sign of the cross every time he played. However, he went on to win two World Cup Winners medals, he was the best right-winger in the 1958 World Cup and was named Player of the Tournament in 1962.

Garrnicha joined Botafogo in 1953. Botafogo means "firelighter" and it was said that he gave them their name. His domain was the right-wing, a position he had learned in the shantytowns of his home and there was never a player so happy to get out into the arena to entertain with his delicate skills and rascal moves. To the delight of the crowd, he humiliated and tied defenders in knots. He loved to dance and not just on the pitch. He loved to chase the girls as well as the ball.

He made his international debut in 1957 in the South American Championship and settled effortlessly into the side. Prior to the 1958 World Cup Brazil warmed-up by playing matches in Europe. In a game against Fiorentina of Italy, Garrincha, leaving one player sitting on his backside, and two others floundering and bewildered, raced into the penalty area. He casually stepped round the advancing goalkeeper only to find yet another defender on the goal line. Feinting to one side as if to shoot, then appearing to change his mind before changing it again, he left the poor defender confused. A feigned shot to the near corner sent the defender flying head first into the post. By this time the goalkeeper had returned, but to no avail. Garrincha placed the ball between his legs and followed it into the net. Eduardo Galeano continues the story: "Afterwards, with the ball under his arm, he slowly returned to the field. He walked with his gaze lowered, Chaplin in slow motion, as if asking forgiveness for that goal which had all Florence on its feet."

Coach Feola had always recognized that Garrincha was a potential match winner and it was strange that he kept him out of the first two games in the 1958 tournament. When a rebellion led by Nilton Santos demanded that he be restored to the side, Feola conceded and Garrincha linked up with Pelé for their third game against the USSR. The results of the change were spectacular, especially in the final when Garrincha created the first two goals. His partnership with Pelé was to cap one of the most exciting performances of any Brazilian side in World Cup finals. The fact that Sweden had gone one up in the final did not dampen Garrincha's spirit and he set about tormenting the Swedish defence. With swerves of his body and the ball glued to his feet, he teased defenders into mistakes. Accelerating past them, his slight build too much for the bigger, clumsier Swedes, he would send crosses high and low into the area. Two such moves found Vavá and the inevitable goals followed.

Despite being sent off in the semi-final, he helped the side to another final in 1962. This time his partnership with Pelé was dissolved through injury and Garrincha had to do it all by himself. It was perhaps his crowning glory. He made goal after goal for his team mates and scored four himself, two in the quarter-final against England and two in the semi-final against the hosts. Inspiring his new striking partner, Amarildo, the Brazilians were devastating and it was little wonder that they came out on top. He was also joint top-scorer. Garrincha had shown the world that football could be a mythical game and in 1962 he was the subject of many legends.

It was from that point that things began to turn sour. He had a cartilage operation in 1963 and caused a scandal when he left his wife and eight children to run off with a local singer. He fell into dispute with Botafogo over his pay and was also fighting the authorities over income tax irregularities. After Hungary knocked Brazil out of the 1966 World Cup, he bowed out of international football, but not before he produced an immaculate free kick to score against Bulgaria. He played on in club football for a number of teams in South America, France and Italy, but a knee injury led to his eventual retirement. His luck was running out and, as they say in Brazil, "if shit was worth anything, the poor would be born without arses."He died penniless, drunk and alone in January 1983 at the age of 50.

Juste Fontaine   France

Honours: 3rd Place 1958
Played: 1958

Games 6
Goals 13

Juste Fontaine after scoring 4 goals in the 3rd/4th place play-off.

The most prolific goal scorer in the history of the World Cup finals was an African. Juste Fontaine was born in Marrakesh in Morocco on 18th August 1933. He began his career with AC Marrakesh before moving to USM Casablanca and then, on his "discovery" by the French, to OGC Nice where he turned professional. An impressive first season included 17 goals as Nice finished eighth in the league. They also won the French Cup, beating Marseille 2-1. Finishing ninth the following year, Fontaine increased his tally to 20. OGC Nice won the French league in 1955-56 for the first time, but it wasn't the celebration it should have been for Fontaine, whose season was dogged by injury. In the few appearances he made he scored only six times. He moved to Stade de Reims at the end of the 1956 season when Nice accepted a £12,000 offer. He replaced Raymond Kopa, who had moved on to Real Madrid. The move was to totally rejuvenate the Moroccan and he opened his Reims account with 30 goals. The following season Reims won the domestic double for the first time in their history, with Fontaine scoring in the 3-1 cup victory over Nîmes. His 34 league goals had already made him the leading scorer that season. It had been a momentous year.

Fontaine made his international debut in a World Cup qualifier on 17th December 1953 against Luxembourg in Paris. The oddity about the occasion was that the French fielded an Under 23 side and to this day do not regard the match as a "full" international. Fontaine scored a hat trick in the 8-0 victory. He was "recalled" to the full national side in 1956 at the age of 23 and got his first official outing when France played Hungary in October, a 2-1 defeat. He then had to wait another year before he got another chance, the return leg against Hungary in Budapest. After another defeat, Fontaine lost his place again. His international career was back in the doldrums despite the fantastic performances he was putting in for Reims and it was not until March 1958 at the Parc de Princes that he was given another outing, this time in a friendly against Spain. He scored in the 2-2 draw and managed to keep his place for the next game against Switzerland.

He made the squad for the 1958 World Cup in Sweden, but only as a last minute replacement. René Bliard, a Reims team mate, had been injured and did not travel. Bliard's misfortune was Fontaine's opportunity. Teaming up with Raymond Kopa in attack, the pair became known as "le tandem terrible" and a force to be reckoned with. Fontaine ended the tournament scoring in every game, including a hat trick in the first round against Paraguay and four against West Germany in the 3rd/4th play-off.

In the 1958-59 season Fontaine netted another 24 goals as Reims made it through to the European Cup final, ironically against Raymond Kopa and Real Madrid. The Spanish won 2-0. The following season Reims won the French title again, but the season ended in tragedy. Fontaine suffered a broken leg in February 1960 while playing at Sochaux. He had scored 28 goals and was leading scorer in the league at the time, a position he maintained even though he did not complete the season. The injury was a double blow in that his career was reaching its peak and was performing magnificently for the national side. In three consecutive post-World Cup matches he scored eight goals, including two hat tricks against Austria and Spain, and two goals against Chile. Despite much pain and discomfort, he made a comeback in December in a World Cup qualifier against Bulgaria, but it was all too much and, following a second leg fracture suffered early in 1961, the curtain came down on his career. He was only 28 years old.

Fontaine later became a sports writer, studied for a coaching diploma and had brief spells as manager of Paris St. Germain and the national side. He also had a spell as President of the French Football Union, but it will always be for his feats in 1958 that he will be remembered. Gerd Müller may hold the record for most goals scored in World Cup finals with 14, but it took two tournaments to do it. Fontaine got his 13 in just one blissful and dynamic performance, a record that is unlikely to be broken.

Edson Arantes do Nascimento (Pelé)   Brazil

Honours: Winner 1958, 1962 and 1970   **Games 14**
Played: 1958, 1962, 1966 and 1970   **Goals 12**

So much has been written about Pelé that it is difficult to begin a profile of this genius of the game. We could write endlessly about his World Cup debut in 1958 and his magnificent goal against Wales. We could talk about the disappointments of both the 1962 and 1966 tournament or we could concentrate on his most famous moments in 1970, such as when he tried to lob the Czech goalkeeper from inside his own half and brilliantly dummied the Uruguayan keeper only to miss the target. We could highlight incidents from his club career and the game between Santos and Fluminense in the Maracana when he started from his own penalty area, took on seven players and scored. There are the 97 goals he scored for Brazil or the 1,281st career goal he scored in his last game for the New York Cosmos on 1st October 1977, against Santos, of all teams. In that match he played

22 Men and a Bag of Wind

Edson Arantes do Nascimento (Pelé) holds the Jules Rimet Trophy after the 1970 World Cup final.

for both sides in front of a crowd of 75,646. We could go on about his enigmatic smile and the delight in seeing him dismiss opponents with a flick of his boot or a shimmy of his hips. We could concentrate on his life after he finished playing and the excellent work he has done as an ambassador for the game in both Brazil and worldwide. But, we won't. Our own insight will look at the boy before he became the king of world football, and we will hear what he had to say about life and the beautiful game in an interview he did in the build up to his second World Cup finals.

Pelé was born on 23rd October 1940 at Tres Coracoes. No one is quite sure where he got the nickname Pelé (it has no meaning in Portuguese) as his family always refers to him as Dico. He was born into a footballing family, his father Joao Ramos, or Dondinho, being a professional. When Dondinho was offered a public service job and a place in the FC Bauru team the family moved to the town in the state of São Paulo. "My first real memory begins with the train ride to Bauru when I was about four years old. I vaguely recall being taken to the railway station in an old wagon drawn by a pony." However, when they arrived they found that the football club had been restructured, was now called Bauru Athletic Club and the new director, while honouring his commitment to take on Dondinho as a player, denied all knowledge of the job. It was, therefore, a life of poverty that faced the family in the early years of the 1940s.

By the age of ten Pelé was playing in a team formed by the older boys of the neighbourhood. They called themselves September 7 after the country's Independence Day, but a total lack of money meant they had to beg, steal and borrow simply to get a ball. It was only when they decided to enter a local tournament that a businessman took pity on them and paid for their entry, a kit and second hand boots in return for becoming their coach. The boys renamed the team, Ameriquinha (Little America), made to the final of the tournament and Pelé, at 12 the youngest boy on the pitch and playing in front of a crowd of 5,000, scored in the victory. "Of all the memories I have of that glorious day, two things stand out. The crowd calling my name, Pelé, Pelé, in a constantly crowing chant, until I found myself no longer hating the name but actually beginning to like it, and my father holding me tightly after the match and saying, 'You played a beautiful game, Dico. I couldn't have played any better myself.' When we got home and Dondinho triumphantly reported the news, my mother smiled for the first time at something involving football."

His breakthrough into club football came when he was chosen to play for Baquinho, the junior side of Bauru Athletic Club. The new coach of BAC juniors was Waldemar de Brito, a friend of his father and member of the 1934 Brazilian World Cup team. He was to have a lasting impact on the young Pelé. Waldemar could see the inherent ability in the youngster and never tried to stifle it. Not only did Waldemar teach him all he knew, he tried to work more on the weaknesses in Pelé's game, developing him into one of the most outstanding players the game has known. Waldemar's friendship with Pelé's father was such that, when Bangu tried to sign him at the age of 15, he persuaded him to wait in the hope that Santos would come in with a better offer. They did and Pelé made his debut for the club at the age 16 in a friendly against AIK Stockholm, won with a late goal. He was not on the score sheet that day and his first club goal came on 7th September 1956 in a 7-1 drubbing of Corinthians. In 1957 he was the São Paulo league's top scorer with 36 goals and the following year he netted a record 53 times.

Pelé had not quite reached 17 when he was selected to play for the national side against Argentina in the first leg of the Roca Cup. Within ten minutes of coming on as a substitute he scored his first international goal, but Brazil lost 2-1. In the second leg he played from the start and scored one of the two goals that gave Brazil a 3-2 aggregate win. A knee injury in 1958 almost kept him out of the World Cup finals and the coach was on the verge of leaving him behind, but better counsel prevailed. After a player protest, he was selected to play against the USSR and from then on never looked back.

Without doubt, Pelé's influence on the game has been enormous and his attitude put the "beautiful" in the "beautiful game". In an interview with Peter Lorenzo of the Daily Herald prior to the 1962 tournament, when asked about the game, life in Brazil and his training regime, he replied: "Why be frightened in football. Always three, sometimes five, men mark me. It makes it more difficult but I am not angry or worried. I like to play for my team, not for myself. Many clubs all over the world want me but why should I leave my home, my football, my life. My father, brother and sister are here. All my friends are here. I enjoy my home, my football, my life. I will never leave. On Monday I rest. Every other day I train, always with a ball. No one tells me how to play these days! I don't drink, smoke or go out with girls. Sometimes I go out with a girl... but we always talk about football." When his friends were asked about him they replied: "He has always remained the friendly one, the sincere one." Say no more!

Brazil 5 : France 2

To many, this game ought to have been the final. Fate, however, conspired to throw together at the semi-final stage the two teams of the tournament. They were teams of very similar outlooks: the point of the game of football was to win and to do this a team needed to score goals. The logic of this plain deduction was simple and compelling: football teams attacked and both did it with artistry, flair and vision. It was the perfect recipe for exciting, eminently watchable football and there were few teams that could play the game like these. Indeed, things "hardly could have started at a more furious pace," as the correspondent of the Manchester Guardian panted. The Brazilians went straight onto the attack. One was repulsed, when Garrincha was halted in midfield, but Zito pounced onto the ensuing loose ball. Centre-forward, Vavá, "who roared round an uncertain defence", chested his pass, let it drop and volleyed fiercely into the net. Within 75 seconds, the Brazilians were 1-0 up.

Undaunted, sky high on confidence and nurturing ambition of their own, the French responded with great determination. In close succession, Piantoni had a shot blocked by centre-half, Bellini, and Fontaine was clearly obstructed whilst running through on goal, though nothing was given. Only seven minutes after Vavá had taken the lead, Fontaine profited from a brilliant interchange between Kopa and Vincent, and raced in on goal. He was checked, recovered and scored with a piece of pure genius. "He seemed to have gone too far out and too near the goal line, but somehow he screwed back the ball into the net." The momentum of his effort left him sprawled on the grass, but it had produced the all-important equalizer.

The next phase of the game up until half-time was the most even, with both sides revealing their mastery of the sport and their differing styles of playing. The French, more systematic in approach, "led finely by Kopa, now were moving the ball beautifully", one reporter narrated, "although they hardly could match the unorthodoxy and jugglery of the Brazilians." The better chances fell to Brazil, but the French kept their defence tight. They smothered out Vavá when he looked like he might score, though had to rely on the good offices of the referee when Zagalo crashed a vicious shot against the underside of the crossbar, which bounced madly around the goal line before an anxious defence was able to clear the danger. The Brazilians turned pleadingly to Welsh referee, Mervyn Griffiths, to signal that it had crossed the line, but a consultation with English linesman, Reg Leafe, saw their appeal turned down.

It was soon after this that the French suffered a blow from which they would not recover. In the 35th minute, Robert Jonquet, the captain and centre-half, was injured by a foul by Vavá. He had to leave the field to receive treatment and within minutes of him going off Didí had restored Brazil's lead. He picked up a lose ball some 35 yards from goal and unleashed one of his "folha secas" that appeared to be swerving wide. Suddenly, it turned and went inside the far post, leaving the Guardian's reporter, switching sports, to declare that "any off-spinner would have been proud of it." The combination of both incidents proved to be the turning point of the game, although the French stubbornly refused to surrender or bow to their disadvantage at any stage. Only minutes later, Fontaine produced a piece of excellence to dribble through the Brazilian defence and force a superb save out of Gilmar. More ominous, perhaps, was the fact that Brazil had a goal disallowed shortly before half-time, when Garrincha hit what seemed a perfectly legal 30 yard drive in to the French goal only to see it cancelled by linesman, Leafe.

Jonquet returned in the second half, but was able to take no further meaningful part in the game. As the Daily Mirror reported, he "hobbled gamely on the right-wing" - though, it was the left-wing he positioned himself on, so as not to interfere too much with what his colleagues might create. However, it was the Brazilians, with Pelé the prime mover, that did most of the creating. They "put on an intriguing exhibition of their own particular brand of magic, and it was appreciated even by the disconsolate French supporters." With a quite outstanding display of football's finer arts, Pelé produced a 20 minute hat trick that launched his indomitable World Cup career. His first came from a goalkeeping error, after Abbès misjudged a Vavá cross and the ball fell to Pelé's feet to give him "the lightest of taps." His second was thumped in from the edge of the six yard box following a defensive mix-up and his third, the best of the bunch, was pure Pelé magic, a brilliant, striding volley hit from the edge of the penalty area. So dominant were the Brazilians in this second period of play that Gilmar was hardly troubled. He merely watched from a distance as his backs went up field to join the fun.

As the game entered its last ten minutes, the crowd became increasingly excitable and, in this rather strange atmosphere, the French grabbed their second goal. Its scorer, Piantoni must have felt flattered as he acknowledged the reaction of the spectators, but his strike was not the cause of the ferment. News was beginning to circulate that Sweden had beaten West Germany and had reached the World Cup final. The crowd were not cheering the French, but their gritty performance was worthy of its plaudits. They had been well beaten by the Brazilians, superior on the day, but they had given good account of themselves in the face of adverse odds. They were blighted by Jonquet's injury and the Brazilians were more than capable of destroying most full strength teams. They were both magnificent and ruthless, but there was no disgrace to the French. As the Daily Herald invoked: "give full marks to the ten fighting Frenchmen. They never tossed in the towel."

Northern Ireland 2 : West Germany 2

Northern Ireland were one of the surprise packages of the 1958 finals. Coming from a small nation on Europe's fringe, with no great football tradition they were expected to have no significant influence on its outcome. Yet, their impact was bigger than any of their near neighbours and they went into the game against the fancied West Germans knowing that the pool was wide open and that a favourable result would bring qualification for the next stage. They had all to play for and the determination of both teams was apparent from the start in this "hard-hitting match", as one paper described it. Ireland's "man of the match" was undoubtedly the goalkeeper, Harry Gregg, whose superb display was in spite of the problems that afflicted him from the start. In the first half he had the sun in his eyes and had to pull his cap deep down over them to protect his vision. He also twisted his ankle in the third minute and from then on carried a limp, leaving goalkicks to his full-backs. Yet, he could not afford to let such hindrances affect his concentration because the Germans put his goal under considerable pressure in the early stages. In the opening minutes, Rahn flashed a shot over the bar and twice Gregg had to dive courageously at Seeler's feet after the German had broken through and looked like scoring.

The Germans may have exerted much of the early pressure, but the Irish carried threats of their own. Up front, Casey, "playing a busy, deep-lying game", and Bingham, always a menace on the right-wing, were troubling German defenders and it was the Irish who took the lead before 20 minutes were up. Receiving a ball from Casey, Bingham whipped a cross into the German area, which reached McParland via Cush's head. The Aston Villa man smashed the ball into the net, but worryingly, Casey was injured in the attack and had to leave the field for treatment. It was whilst the Irish were down to ten men that the Germans equalized through Rahn, their World Cup evergreen. Advancing on goal, he drew Gregg out and cleverly lobbed him. The Irish had been in front for just two minutes and, their confidence restored, the Germans ended the first half the stronger and forcing the best out of the hobbling Gregg.

The Germans resumed their offensive when the second half began. Under enormous pressure, the Irish were "living on their courage" and just about hanging on. More then once, Gregg kept his team's hopes alive with a series of "superlative and often daring saves." McMichael cleared one German effort off the line and a particularly splendid save saw Gregg spring himself backwards to stop a Seeler header that looked certain to go in. Yet, the Irish were able to claw their way out of the mire and begin to mount promising attacks of their own. Close to the hour, Casey forced a corner that he took himself. McIlroy headed the ball on to McParland, who dispatched it into the net to restore his coutry's lead.

Once again, Ireland's goal drew a spirited response from the Germans, and especially from Seeler and Rahn, who were outstanding. More than once, either singly or together, they threatened to undo Ireland's endeavour and it required both complete concentration from the defenders and Gregg's magnificence to keep the marauding Germans at bay. This they did for most of the second half until Seeler, ten minutes from the end, struck a pile driver of a shot, his hardest of the match, which beat the diving Gregg for pace. In the last minutes of the game, the Irish streamed forward to try to take the match and with just five minutes to go, McParland narrowly missed when he volleyed a Cunningham free kick over the bar. The game ended with "the Germans hanging on for the final whistle."

The draw put the Germans through to the quarter-finals and earned the Irish the right to a play-off against Czechoslovakia to decide that group's other place in the knock-out stage. It had been a totally gripping game and one from which the Irish deserved at least a draw for all their work and initiative. Play had swung first one way, then the other and had thrilled the crowd of almost 22,000. Most of these were applauding Gregg, as he limped off the field at the end, a real Irish hero.

Brazil 5 : Sweden 2
The World Cup Final

Nobody with an eye for football would have denied Brazil's right to contest the final, though the Swedes had rather crept up on the tournament, to the surprise of virtually everybody. Equally surprising was the way that they opened the match. It had rained overnight and the pitch was greasy and easily cut up. The Brazilians had also changed their back line, bringing in Djalma Santos, now recovered from injury, to replace Di Sordi and Brazil did not settle immediately. The defence looked jittery in the initial salvos and the Swedes took an early and unexpected lead. Gunnar Gren initiated the move when he took possession of the ball in his own penalty area. He swept it upfield to Agne Simonsson. His pass set up AC Milan's Nils Liedholm, who "danced through a closing ring of defenders" to set up his shot. He had Simonsson free and unmarked to his right, but he chose to go it alone and "swung his own lethal right foot, and flashed the ball into the far corner with goalkeeper Gylmar (sic) groping the air", to use the words of the Daily Mirror.

It was just what the Brazilians needed to get the sap rising and, soon after, a dynamic run down the right saw Garrincha fire into the side netting. It was an ominous sign for the Swedes whose lead was cancelled four minutes after they had taken it. Garrincha cut in from the right and sent a low pass across the face of the Swedish goal, which defender, Axböm, missed. It travelled perfectly to Vavá, who, with only the goalkeeper to beat, knocked it in from close range. Seconds later Pelé hit the post and then Vavá had another shot, this time well saved. The South Americans were beginning to look dangerous. They often caught the home defence off balance with cleverly punctuated attacks that began deep and employed long passes, from wing to wing, to keep the Swedes wondering where the next sortie was coming from. Yet, the Swedes also had their moments and it was far from one-way football. "Nacka" Skoglund had one cross headed off the Brazilian goal line and other half chances were created, but not taken. The Brazilians always looked more likely to score and in the 30th minute they did. A Swedish attack was broken up, Pelé passed the ball forwards to Zito and he sent it on to Garrincha, flying down the wing. Once again, he cut inside, sent the ball across the goal face and Vavá popped up to net his second. It was an almost identical goal to his first and during the whole move, from back to front, the ball had barely risen an inch above the ground. It was pure class and served notice to the Swedes that their opponents had warmed up. In his next raid, Garrincha tried it again, but his touch let him down and the Swedes cleared. Then, just before half-time, Pelé teed himself up. He jinked and juggled in front of goal, but missed with his final effort and the Brazilians went into the break 2-1 up. The balance of first half play had been fairly even, but a widening difference in technique and ball control was very evident. As one newspaper noted "the writing was on the wall."

Brazilian goalkeeper Gilmar on the ground as he tries in vain to stop Sweden's first goal.

As they had in the semi-final, Brazil upped the tempo in the second half and "established their superiority in all departments to such a marked degree... that at times the play was almost boring." They " sauntered along almost contemptuously" and "by the end the mesmerised home defence hardly seemed to know whether it was Christmas or Easter." The Swedes had clearly understood the lesson of the first half and tried to lift their game to hold the gathering storm. However, their play became tense and hesitant and they made mistakes. Passes went astray, their touch deserted them and it handed Brazil the opportunity to turn the screw. They did it with relish. Within 10 minutes of the restart, Pelé, outstanding in the second half, "a wriggling shadow of black lightening with the ball jugglery of a circus star, volleyed a superb goal." He trapped a high pass from Nilton Santos effortlessly on his chest, whilst weaving his way through the defenders around him and unleashed a shot into the net to score the sort of goal that would make him a legend. Less than 15 minutes later, Brazil struck again. This time Zagalo profited from some careless defence when his corner was only half cleared by Boerjesson and quickly returned into the penalty area. Zagalo followed in and picked up the ball to squeeze it through the goalkeeper's legs from a narrow angle. He was almost injured in the celebrations, when his team mates hammered him to the ground and fell all over him.

This fourth goal sealed the game for Brazil and they began to ease up, particularly at the back. Garrincha was unlucky not to get a penalty when he was brought down by Boerjesson, but the next goal went to the Swedes. A fine move, with a hint of offside, was finished by Simonsson for a goal that did nothing to diminish Brazil's complete mastery of the pitch. To emphasize this control, as the match neared its conclusion, Nilton Santos crossed a "high, hovering ball and, leaping like a jungle cat, Pelé soared over two yellow-shirted defenders to nod into the empty net."

In the end it had been all too easy, though it still evoked celebrations. Pelé, the youngest player to appear in a World Cup final, burst into tears, as his fellows jumped, sambaed and embraced each other across the pitch. Back in Brazil, where winning the World Cup had the import of winning a war, the scenes were even more jubilant. Crowds of thousands had gathered to listen to the game relayed on public address systems and each goal had been greeted with hails of rockets and fireworks. The final

Brazil's Garrincha shoots across the Swedish goal for Vavá (20) to score the first goal.

result brought an eruption of spontaneous acclaim and joy, and festivities went well into the next day. The Copacabana Beach was a mass of swaying, dancing, singing bodies. The president captured the mood when he sent his own jet to bring the team back and declared the day of their return a public holiday. The victory had brought the fulfilment of a national obsession to the people of Brazil. It also created history with Brazil becoming the first country to win outside its own continent. In presenting the trophy FIFA's president, Arthur Drewry, described the final as "an exhibition of football so fittingly worthy of the world's greatest football competition." To Brazil this was entirely true.

Statistics - Sweden 1958

GROUP ONE

Halmstad, June 8th - Örjans Vall

1 (1) NORTHERN IRELAND

Cush 20

Gregg, Keith, McMichael, Blanchflower, Cunningham, Peacock, Bingham, Cush, Dougan, McIlroy, McParland.

0 (0) CZECHOSLOVAKIA

Dolejsi, Mraz, Novak, Pluskal, Cadek, Masopust, Hovorka, Dvorak, Borovicka, Hartl, Kraus.

Referee: Eric Seipelt (Austria)
Attendance: 10.647

Malmö, June 8th - Malmö Stadion

3 (2) WEST GERMANY

Rahn 32,89, Seeler 42

Herkenrath, Stollenwerk, Juskowiak, Eckel, Erhardt, Szymaniak, Rahn, Walter, Seeler, Schmidt, Schäfer.

1 (1) ARGENTINA

Corbatta 3

Carrizo, Lombardo, Vairo, Rossi, Dellacha, Varacka, Corbatta, Prado, Menendez, Rojas, Cruz.

Referee: Reg Leafe (England)
Attendance: 31.156

Halmstad, June 11th - Örjans Vall

3 (1) ARGENTINA

Corbatta (pen)38, Menendez 55, Avio 60

Carrizo, Lombardo, Vairo, Rossi, Dellacha, Varacka, Corbatta, Avio, Menendez, Labruna, Boggio.

1 (1) NORTHERN IRELAND

McParland 3

Gregg, Keith, McMichael, Blanchflower, Cunningham, Peacock, Bingham, Cush, Coyle, McIlroy, McParland.

Referee: Sten Ahlner (Sweden)
Attendance: 14.174

Hälsingborg, June 11th - Olympia

2 (0) WEST GERMANY

Schäfer 60, Rahn 70

Herkenrath, Stollenwerk, Juskowiak, Schnellinger, Erhardt, Szymaniak, Rahn, Walter, Seeler, Klodt, Schäfer.

2 (2) CZECHOSLOVAKIA

Dvorak (pen)22, Zikan 43

Dolejsi, Mraz, Novak, Pluskal, Popluhár, Masopust, Hovorka, Dvorak, Molnar, Feureisl, Zikan.

Referee: Arthur Ellis (England)
Attendance: 25.000

Malmö, June 15th - Malmö Stadion

2 (1) WEST GERMANY

Rahn 20, Seeler 80

Herkenrath, Stollenwerk, Juskowiak, Eckel, Erhardt, Szymaniak, Rahn, Walter, Seeler, Klodt, Schäfer.

2 (1) NORTHERN IRELAND

McParland 17,58

Gregg, Keith, McMichael, Blanchflower, Cunningham, Peacock, Bingham, Cush, Casey, McIlroy, McParland.

Referee: Joaquim Campos (Portugal)
Attendance: 21.990

Hälsingborg, June 15th - Olympia

6 (3) CZECHOSLOVAKIA

Dvorak 8, Zikan 17,40, Feureisl 69, Hovorka 82,89

Dolejsi, Mraz, Novak, Popluhár, Masopust, Hovorka, Dvorak, Borovicka, Molnar, Feureisl, Zikan.

1 (0) ARGENTINA

Corbatta (pen)65

Carrizo, Lombardo, Vairo, Rossi, Dellacha, Varacka, Corbatta, Avio, Menendez, Labruna, Cruz.

Referee: Arthur Ellis (England)
Attendance: 16.418

Play-off - Malmö, June 17th - Malmö Stadion

After extra time. Half-time (1-1), full-time (1-1)

2 (1) NORTHERN IRELAND

McParland 44,110

Uprichard, Keith, McMichael, Blanchflower, Cunningham, Peacock, Bingham, Cush, Scott, McIlroy, McParland.

1 (1) CZECHOSLOVAKIA

Zikan 19

Dolejsi, Mraz, Novak, Bubernik (RED), Popluhár, Masopust, Zikan, Dvorak, Borovicka, Feureisl, Molnar.

Referee: Maurice Guigue (France)
Attendance: 6.196

	P	W	D	L	F	A	Pts
W. Germany	3	1	2	0	7	5	4
N. Ireland	3	1	1	1	4	5	3
Czech	3	1	1	1	8	4	3
Argentina	3	1	0	2	5	10	2

GROUP TWO

Västerås, June 8th - Arosvallen

1 (0) SCOTLAND

Murray 48

Younger, Caldow, Hewie, Turnbull, Evans, Cowie, Leggat, Murray, Mudie, Collins, Imlach.

1 (1) YUGOSLAVIA

Petakovic 6

Beara, Sijakovic, Crnkovic, Krstic, Zebek, Boskov, Petakovic, Veselinovic, Milutinovic Sekularac, Rajkov.

Referee: Paul Wyssling (Switzerland)
Attendance: 9.591

Norrköping, June 8th - Idrottsparken

7 (2) FRANCE

Fontaine 24,30,67, Piantoni 52, Kopa 68, Wisnieski 61, Vincent 84

Remetter, Kaelbel, Lerond, Penverne, Jonquet, Marcel, Wisnieski, Fontaine, Kopa, Piantoni, Vincent.

3 (2) PARAGUAY

Amarilla 20,(pen)45, Romero 50

Mageregger, Arevalo, Miranda, Achucaro, Lezcano, Villalba, Aguero, Parodi, Romero, Re, Amarilla.

Referee: Juan Gardeazabal Garay (Spain)
Attendance: 16.518

Norrköping, June 11th - Idrottsparken

3 (2) PARAGUAY

Aguero 4, Re 45, Parodi 71

Aguilar, Arevalo, Echague, Achucaro, Lezcano, Villalba, Aguero, Parodi, Romero, Re, Amarilla.

2 (1) SCOTLAND

Mudie 24, Collins 72

Younger, Caldow, Parker, Turnbull, Evans, Cowie, Leggat, Robertson, Mudie, Collins, Fernie.

Referee: Vincenzo Orlandini (Italy)
Attendance: 11.665

Västerås, June 11th - Arosvallen

3 (1) YUGOSLAVIA

Petakovic 15, Veselinovic 61,90

Beara, Tomic, Crnkovic, Krstic, Zebek, Boskov, Petakovic, Veselinovic, Milutinovic Sekularac, Rajkov.

2 (1) FRANCE

Fontaine 4,85

Remetter, Kaelbel, Lerond, Penverne, Jonquet, March, Wisnieski, Fontaine, Kopa, Piantoni, Vincent.

Referee: Mervyn Griffiths (Wales)
Attendance: 12.217

Örebro, June 15th - Eyravallen

2 (2) FRANCE

Kopa 23, Fontaine 44

Abbès, Kaelbel, Lerond, Penverne, Jonquet, Marcel, Wisnieski, Fontaine, Kopa, Piantoni, Vincent.

1 (0) SCOTLAND

Baird 58

Brown, Caldow, Hewie, Turnbull, Evans, Mackay, Imlach, Murray, Mudie, Collins, Baird.

Referee: Juan Brozzi (Argentina)
Attendance: 13.554

Eskilstuna, June 15th - Tunavallen

3 (1) PARAGUAY

Parodi 20, Aguero 52, Romero 80

Aguilar, Arevalo, Echague, Achucaro, Lezcano, Villalba, Aguero, Parodi, Romero, Re, Amarilla.

3 (2) YUGOSLAVIA

Ognjanovic 12, Veselinovic 28, Rajkov 73

Beara, Tomic, Crnkovic, Krstic, Zebek, Boskov, Petakovic, Veselinovic, Ognjanovic Sekularac, Rajkov.

Referee: Martin Macko (Czechoslovakia)
Attendance: 13.103

	P	W	D	L	F	A	Pts
France	3	2	0	1	11	7	4
Yugoslavia	3	1	2	0	7	6	4
Paraguay	3	1	1	1	9	12	3
Scotland	3	0	1	2	4	6	1

GROUP THREE

Solna, June 8th - Råsunda Stadion

3 (1) SWEDEN

Simonsson 17,64, Liedholm (pen)58

Svensson, Bergmark, Axbom, Liedholm, Gustavsson, Parling, Hamrin, Mellberg, Simonsson, Gren, Skoglund.

0 (0) MEXICO

Carbajal, Del Muro, Villegas, Portugal, Romo, Flores, Hernández, Reyes, Calderón, Gutiérrez, Sesma.

Referee: Nikolai Latychev (Soviet Union)
Attendance: 34.107

Sandviken, June 8th - Jernvallen

1 (1) HUNGARY

Bozsik 5

Grosics, Matrai, Sárosi, Bozsik, Sipos, Berendi, Sándor, Hidegkúti, Tichy, Bundzsak, Fenyvesi.

1 (1) WALES

J.Charles 27

Kelsey, Williams, Hopkins, Sullivan, M.Charles, Bowen, Webster, Medwin, J.Charles, Allchurch, Jones.

Referee: José Maria Codesal (Uruguay)
Attendance: 15.343

Solna, June 11th - Råsunda Stadion

1 (0) MEXICO

Belmonte 90

Carbajal, Del Muro, Cardeñas, Belmonte, Romo, Flores, González, Reyes, Blanco, Gutiérrez, Sesma.

1 (1) WALES

Allchurch 30

Kelsey, Williams, Hopkins, Baker, M.Charles, Bowen, Webster, Medwin, J.Charles, Allchurch, Jones.

Referee: Leo Lemesic (Yugoslavia)
Attendance: 15.150

Solna, June 12th - Råsunda Stadion

2 (1) SWEDEN

Hamrin 34,56

Svensson, Bergmark, Axbom, Liedholm, Gustavsson, Parling, Hamrin, Mellberg, Simonsson, Gren, Skoglund.

1 (0) HUNGARY

Tichy 77

Grosics, Matrai, Sárosi, Bozsik, Sipos, Berendi, Sándor, Szojka, Tichy, Bundzsak, Fenyvesi.

Referee: Jack Mowat (Scotland)
Attendance: 38.850

Solna, June 15th - Råsunda Stadion

0 (0) SWEDEN

Svensson, Bergmark, Axbom, Börjesson, Gustavsson, Parling, Berndtsson, Selmonsson, Källgren, Löfgren, Skoglund.

0 (0) WALES

Kelsey, Williams, Hopkins, Sullivan, M.Charles, Bowen, Vernon, Hewitt, J.Charles, Allchurch, Jones.

Referee: Lucien Van Nuffel (Belgium)
Attendance: 29.800

Sandviken, June 15th - Jernvallen

4 (1) HUNGARY

Tichy 19,46, Sándor 54, Gonzalez (og)60

Ilku, Matrai, Sárosi, Kotasz, Sipos, Budai, Hidegkúti, Szojka, Tichy, Bencsics, Sándor.

0 (0) MEXICO

Carbajal, Del Muro, Cardeñas, Belmonte, Sepulveda, Flores, González, Reyes, Blanco, Gutiérrez, Sesma.

Referee: A.Eriksson (Finland)
Attendance: 13.310

Play-off - Malmö, June 17th - Malmö Stadion

2 (0) WALES

Allchurch 55, Medwin 76

Kelsey, Williams, Hopkins, Sullivan, M.Charles, Bowen, Medwin, Hewitt, J.Charles, Allchurch, Jones.

1 (1) HUNGARY

Tichy 33

Grosics, Matrai, Sárosi, Bozsik, Sipos (RED), Bencsics, Kotasz, Budai, Tichy, Bundzsak, Fenyvesi.

Referee: Nikolai Latychev (Soviet Union)
Attendance: 2.832

	P	W	D	L	F	A	Pts
Sweden	3	2	1	0	5	1	5
Wales	3	0	3	0	2	2	3
Hungary	3	1	1	1	6	3	3
Mexico	3	0	1	2	1	8	1

GROUP FOUR

Uddevalla, June 8th - Rimnersvallen

3 (1) BRAZIL

Mazola 38,90, N.Santos 49

Gilmar, De Sordi, N.Santos, Dino, Bellini, Orlando, Joel, Didí, Mazola, Dida, Zagalo.

0 (0) AUSTRIA

Szanwald, Halla, Swoboda, Hanappi, Happel, Koller, Horak, Senekowitsch, Buzek, Körner, Schleger.

Referee: Maurice Guigue (France)
Attendance: 21.000

Gothenburg, June 8th - Nya Ullevi Stadion

2 (0) ENGLAND

Kevan 65, Finney (pen)86

McDonald, Howe, Banks, Clamp, Wright, Slater, Douglas, Robson, Kevan, Haynes, Finney.

2 (1) SOVIET UNION

Simonian 13, A.Ivanov 55

Yashin, Kesarev, Kuznetsov, Voinov, Krijevski, Tsarev, A.Ivanov, V.Ivanov, Simonian, Salnikov, Ilyin.

Referee: Istvan Zsolt (Hungary)
Attendance: 49.348

Borås, June 11th - Ryavallen

2 (1) SOVIET UNION

Ilyin 15, V.Ivanov 62

Yashin, Kesarev, Kuznetsov, Voinov, Krijevski, Tsarev, A.Ivanov, V.Ivanov, Simonian, Salnikov, Ilyin.

0 (0) AUSTRIA

Schmied, E.Kozlicek, Swoboda, Hanappi, Stotz, Koller, Horak, P.Kozlicek, Buzek, Körner, Senekowitsch.

Referee: Carl Jørgensen (Denmark)
Attendance: 21.239

Gothenburg, June 11th - Nya Ullevi Stadion

0 (0) BRAZIL

Gilmar, De Sordi, N.Santos, Dino, Bellini, Orlando, Joel, Didí, Mazola, Vavá, Zagalo.

0 (0) ENGLAND

McDonald, Howe, Banks, Clamp, Wright, Slater, Douglas, Robson, Kevan, Haynes, A'Court.

Referee: Albert Dusch (West Germany)
Attendance: 40.895

Borås, June 15th - Ryavallen

2 (1) AUSTRIA

Koller 16, Körner 70

Szanwald, Kollmann, Swoboda, Hanappi, Happel, Koller, E.Kozlicek, Senekowitsch, Buzek, Körner, P.Kozlicek.

2 (1) ENGLAND

Haynes 60, Kevan 78

McDonald, Howe, Banks, Clamp, Wright, Slater, Douglas, Robson, Kevan, Haynes, A'Court.

Referee: A.Asmussen (Denmark)
Attendance: 16.800

**Gothenburg, June 15th -
Nya Ullevi Stadion**

2 (1) BRAZIL

Vavá 3,77

Gilmar, De Sordi, N.Santos, Zito, Bellini, Orlando,
Garrincha, Didí, Pelé, Vavá, Zagalo.

0 (0) SOVIET UNION

Yashin, Kesarev, Kuznetsov, Voinov, Krijevski,
Tsarev, A.Ivanov, V.Ivanov, Simonian, Netto, Ilyin.

Referee: Maurice Guigue (France)
Attendance: 50.928

**Play-off - Gothenburg, June 17th -
Nya Ullevi Stadion**

1 (0) SOVIET UNION

Ilyin 63

Yashin, Kesarev, Kuznetsov, Voinov, Krijevski,
Tsarev, Apoukhtin, V.Ivanov, Simonian, Falin, Ilyin.

0 (0) ENGLAND

McDonald, Howe, Banks, Clayton, Wright, Slater,
Brabrook, Broadbent, Kevan, Haynes, A'Court.

Referee: Albert Dusch (West Germany)
Attendance: 23.182

	P	W	D	L	F	A	Pts
Brazil	3	2	1	0	5	0	5
USSR	3	1	1	1	4	4	3
England	3	0	3	0	4	4	3
Austria	3	0	1	2	2	7	1

QUARTER-FINALS

Malmö, June 19th - Malmö Stadion

1 (1) WEST GERMANY

Rahn 12

Herkenrath, Stollenwerk, Juskowiak, Eckel, Erhardt,
Szymaniak, Rahn, Walter, Seeler, Schmidt, Schäfer.

0 (0) YUGOSLAVIA

Krivokuca, Sijakovic, Crnkovic, Krstic, Zebek, Boskov,
Petakovic, Ognjanovic, Veselinovic, Milutinovic,
Rajkov.

Referee: Paul Wyssling (Switzerland)
Attendance: 20.000

Solna, June 19th - Råsunda Stadion

2 (0) SWEDEN

Hamrin 49, Simonsson 88

Svensson, Bergmark, Axbom, Börjesson, Gustavsson,
Parling, Hamrin, Gren, Simonsson, Liedholm,
Skoglund.

0 (0) SOVIET UNION

Yashin, Kesarev, Kuznetsov, Voinov, Krijevski,
Tsarev, A.Ivanov, V.Ivanov, Simonian, Salnikov, Ilyin.

Referee: Reg Leafe (England)
Attendance: 31.900

Norrköping, June 19th - Idrottsparken

4 (1) FRANCE

Fontaine 55,63, Wisnieski 43, Piantoni 70

Abbès, Kaelbel, Lerond, Penverne, Jonquet, Marcel,
Wisnieski, Fontaine, Kopa, Piantoni, Vincent.

0 (0) NORTHERN IRELAND

Gregg, Keith, McMichael, Blanchflower, Cunningham,
Cush, Bingham, Casey, Scott, McIlroy, McParland.

Referee: Juan Gardeazabal Garay (Spain)
Attendance: 11.800

**Gothenburg, June 19th -
Nya Ullevi Stadion**

1 (0) BRAZIL

Pelé 73

Gilmar, De Sordi, N.Santos, Zito, Bellini, Orlando,
Garrincha, Didí, Mazola, Pelé, Zagalo.

0 (0) WALES

Kelsey, Williams, Hopkins, Sullivan, M.Charles,
Bowen, Medwin, Hewitt, Webster, Allchurch, Jones.

Referee: Erich Seipelt (Austria)
Attendance: 25.923

SEMI-FINALS

**Gothenburg, June 24th -
Nya Ullevi Stadion**

3 (1) SWEDEN

Skoglund 33, Gren 81, Hamrin 88

Svensson, Bergmark, Axbom, Börjesson, Gustavsson,
Parling, Hamrin, Gren, Simonsson, Liedholm,
Skoglund.

1 (1) WEST GERMANY

Schäfer 23

Herkenrath, Stollenwerk, Juskowiak (RED), Eckel,
Erhardt, Szymaniak, Rahn, Walter, Seeler, Cieslarczyk,
Schäfer.

Referee: Istvan Zsolt (Hungary)
Attendance: 49.471

Solna, June 24th - Råsunda Stadion

5 (2) BRAZIL

Vavá 1, Didí 39, Pelé 53,58,74

Gilmar, De Sordi, N.Santos, Zito, Bellini, Orlando,
Garrincha, Didí, Vavá, Pelé, Zagalo.

2 (1) FRANCE

Fontaine 9, Piantoni 83

Abbès, Kaelbel, Lerond, Penverne, Jonquet, Marcel,
Wisnieski, Fontaine, Kopa, Piantoni, Vincent.

Referee: Mervyn Griffiths (Wales)
Attendance: 27.100

3RD/4TH PLACE PLAY-OFF

**Gothenburg, June 28th - Nya Ullevi
Stadion**

6 (3) FRANCE

Fontaine 14,36,78,90, Kopa (pen)26, Douis 47

Abbès, Kaelbel, Lerond, Penverne, Lafont, Marcel,
Wisnieski, Fontaine, Kopa, Douis, Vincent.

3 (1) WEST GERMANY

Cieslarczyk 17, Rahn 51, Schäfer 84

Kwiatkowski, Stollenwerk, Schnellinger, Wewers,
Erhardt, Szymaniak, Rahn, Sturm, Kelbassa,
Cieslarczyk, Schäfer.

Referee: Juan Brozzi (Argentina)
Attendance: 32.482

FINAL

Solna, June 29th - Råsunda Stadion

5 (2) BRAZIL

Vavá 9,30, Pelé 55,89, Zagalo 68

Gilmar, D.Santos, N.Santos, Zito, Bellini, Orlando,
Garrincha, Didí, Vavá, Pelé, Zagalo.

2 (1) SWEDEN

Liedholm 4, Simonsson 80

Svensson, Bergmark, Axbom, Börjesson, Gustavsson,
Parling, Hamrin, Gren, Simonsson, Liedholm,
Skoglund.

Referee: Maurice Guigue (France)
Attendance: 49.737

QUALIFYING ROUNDS

Africa/Asia - Group 1 CAF/AFC

	P	W	D	L	F	A	Pts
Indonesia	3	1	1	1	5	4	3
China PR	3	1	1	1	4	5	3

12-05-57	Indonesia : China PR	2:0 (0:0)
02-06-57	China PR : Indonesia	4:3 (2:1)
23-06-57	China PR : Indonesia	0:0

Africa/Asia - Group 4 CAF/AFC

	P	W	D	L	F	A	Pts
Sudan	2	1	1	0	2	1	3
Syria	2	0	1	1	1	2	1

| 08-03-57 | Sudan : Syria | 1:0 (0:0) |
| 24-05-57 | Syria : Sudan | 1:1 (0:1) |

Europe - Group 1

	P	W	D	L	F	A	Pts
England	4	3	1	0	15	5	7
Rep. Ireland	4	2	1	1	6	7	5
Denmark	4	0	0	4	4	13	0

03-10-56	Ireland Republic : Denmark	2:1 (2:0)
05-12-56	England : Denmark	5:2 (2:1)
08-05-57	England : Ireland Republic	5:1 (4:0)
15-05-57	Denmark : England	1:4 (1:1)
19-05-57	Ireland Republic : England	1:1 (1:0)
02-10-57	Denmark : Ireland Republic	0:2 (0:0)

Europe - Group 2

	P	W	D	L	F	A	Pts
France	4	3	1	0	19	4	7
Belgium	4	2	1	1	16	11	5
Iceland	4	0	0	4	6	26	0

11-11-56	France : Belgium	6:3 (4:1)
02-06-57	France : Iceland	8:0 (5:0)
05-06-57	Belgium : Iceland	8:3 (7:1)
01-09-57	Iceland : France	1:5 (0:2)
04-09-57	Iceland : Belgium	2:5 (1:2)
27-10-57	Belgium : France	0:0

Europe - Group 3

	P	W	D	L	F	A	Pts
Hungary	4	3	0	1	12	4	6
Bulgaria	4	2	0	2	11	7	4
Norway	4	1	0	3	3	15	2

22-05-57	Norway : Bulgaria	1:2 (0:1)
12-06-57	Norway : Hungary	2:1 (1:1)
23-06-57	Hungary : Bulgaria	4:1 (3:0)
15-09-57	Bulgaria : Hungary	1:2 (1:2)
03-11-57	Bulgaria : Norway	7:0 (3:0)
10-11-57	Hungary : Norway	5:0 (2:0)

Europe - Group 4

	P	W	D	L	F	A	Pts
Czech	4	3	0	1	9	3	6
Wales	4	2	0	2	6	5	4
German DR	4	1	0	3	5	12	2

01-05-57	Wales : Czechoslovakia	1:0 (0:0)
19-05-57	Germany DR : Wales	2:1 (1:1)
26-05-57	Czechoslovakia : Wales	2:0 (1:0)
16-06-57	Czechoslovakia : Germany DR	3:1 (0:1)
25-09-57	Wales : Germany DR	4:1 (3:0)
27-10-57	Germany DR : Czechoslovakia	1:4 (1:3)

Europe - Group 5

	P	W	D	L	F	A	Pts
Austria	4	3	1	0	14	3	7
Netherlands	4	2	1	1	12	7	5
Luxembourg	4	0	0	4	3	19	0

30-09-56	Austria : Luxembourg	7:0 (2:0)
20-03-57	Netherlands : Luxembourg	4:1 (2:1)
26-05-57	Austria : Netherlands	3:2 (0:2)
11-09-57	Luxembourg : Netherlands	2:5 (1:4)
25-09-57	Netherlands : Austria	1:1 (0:1)
29-09-57	Luxembourg : Austria	0:3 (0:1)

Europe - Group 6

	P	W	D	L	F	A	Pts
USSR	4	3	0	1	16	3	6
Poland	4	3	0	1	9	5	6
Finland	4	0	0	4	2	19	0

23-06-57	USSR : Poland	3:0 (1:0)
05-07-57	Finland : Poland	1:3 (0:1)
27-07-57	USSR : Finland	2:1 (1:1)
15-08-57	Finland : USSR	0:10 (0:7)
20-10-57	Poland : USSR	2:1 (1:0)
03-11-57	Poland : Finland	4:0 (2:0)

Europe - Group 6 Play-off

24-11-57	USSR : Poland	2:0 (1:0)

Played in Leipzig

Europe - Group 7

	P	W	D	L	F	A	Pts
Yugoslavia	4	2	2	0	7	2	6
Romania	4	2	1	1	6	4	5
Greece	4	0	1	3	2	9	1

05-05-57	Greece : Yugoslavia	0:0
16-06-57	Greece : Romania	1:2 (1:1)
29-09-57	Romania : Yugoslavia	1:1 (0:0)
03-11-57	Romania : Greece	3:0 (0:0)
10-11-57	Yugoslavia : Greece	4:1 (2:1)
17-11-57	Yugoslavia : Romania	2:0 (0:0)

Europe - Group 8

	P	W	D	L	F	A	Pts
N. Ireland	4	2	1	1	6	3	5
Italy	4	2	0	2	5	5	4
Portugal	4	1	1	2	4	7	3

16-01-57	Portugal : Northern Ireland	1:1 (1:1)
25-04-57	Italy : Northern Ireland	1:0 (1:0)
01-05-57	Northern Ireland : Portugal	3:0 (1:0)
26-05-57	Portugal : Italy	3:0 (1:0)
22-12-57	Italy : Portugal	3:0 (1:0)
15-01-58	Northern Ireland : Italy	2:1 (2:0)

Europe - Group 9

	P	W	D	L	F	A	Pts
Scotland	4	3	0	1	10	9	6
Spain	4	2	1	1	12	8	5
Switzerland	4	0	1	3	6	11	1

10-03-57	Spain : Switzerland	2:2 (2:1)
08-05-57	Scotland : Spain	4:2 (2:2)
19-05-57	Switzerland : Scotland	1:2 (1:1)
26-05-57	Spain : Scotland	4:1 (2:0)
06-11-57	Scotland : Switzerland	3:2 (1:1)
24-11-57	Switzerland : Spain	1:4 (0:2)

Play-off

	P	W	D	L	F	A	Pts
Wales	2	2	0	0	4	0	4
Israel	2	0	0	2	0	4	0

15-01-58	Israel : Wales	0:2 (0:1)
05-02-58	Wales : Israel	2:0 (0:0)

North/Central America - Group 1

	P	W	D	L	F	A	Pts
Costa Rica	4	4	0	0	15	4	8
N. Antilles	3	1	0	2	4	7	2
Guatemala	3	0	0	3	4	12	0

0-02-57	Guatemala : Costa Rica	2:6 (1:4)
17-02-57	Costa Rica : Guatemala	3:1 (2:0)
03-03-57	Costa Rica : Neth. Antilles	4:0 (2:0)
10-03-57	Guatemala : Neth. Antilles	1:3 (1:2)
04-08-57	Neth. Antilles : Costa Rica	1:2 (0:1)

North/Central America - Group 2

	P	W	D	L	F	A	Pts
Mexico	4	4	0	0	18	2	8
Canada	4	2	0	2	8	8	4
USA	4	0	0	4	5	21	0

07-04-57	Mexico : United States	6:0 (3:0)
28-04-57	United States : Mexico	2:7 (2:3)
22-06-57	Canada : United States	5:1 (2:1)
30-06-57	Canada : Mexico	0:3 (0:1)
03-07-57	Mexico : Canada	2:0 (2:0)
06-07-57	United States : Canada	2:3 (1:3)

North/Central America - Group Winners

	P	W	D	L	F	A	Pts
Mexico	2	1	1	0	3	1	3
Costa Rica	2	0	1	1	1	3	1

20-10-57	Mexico : Costa Rica	2:0 (0:0)
27-10-57	Costa Rica : Mexico	1:1 (1:1)

South America - Group 1

	P	W	D	L	F	A	Pts
Brazil	4	1	1	0	2	1	3
Peru	4	0	1	1	1	2	1

13-04-57	Peru : Brazil	1:1 (1:0)
21-04-57	Brazil : Peru	1:0 (1:0)

South America - Group 2

	P	W	D	L	F	A	Pts
Argentina	4	3	0	1	10	2	6
Bolivia	4	2	0	2	6	6	4
Chile	4	1	0	3	2	10	2

22-09-57	Chile : Bolivia	2:1 (1:1)
29-09-57	Bolivia : Chile	3:0 (1:0)
06-10-57	Bolivia : Argentina	2:0 (1:0)
13-10-57	Chile : Argentina	0:2 (0:1)
20-10-57	Argentina : Chile	4:0 (4:0)
27-10-57	Argentina : Bolivia	4:0 (1:0)

South America - Group 3

	P	W	D	L	F	A	Pts
Paraguay	4	3	0	1	11	4	6
Uruguay	4	2	1	1	4	6	5
Colombia	4	0	1	3	3	8	1

16-06-57	Colombia : Uruguay	1:1 (1:0)
20-06-57	Colombia : Paraguay	2:3 (1:1)
30-06-57	Uruguay : Colombia	1:0 (0:0)
07-07-57	Paraguay : Colombia	3:0 (1:0)
14-07-57	Paraguay : Uruguay	5:0 (1:0)
28-07-57	Uruguay : Paraguay	2:0 (1:0)

Chapter 9

Drink, Drugs and a Goal Drought
The Chile World Cup, 1962

Chile 1962

Winners: Brazil

Runners-up: Czechoslovakia

3rd Place: Chile

4th Place: Yugoslavia

Total Attendance: 893,536

Number of Matches: 32

Although in India and Malaysia the end of the world was being predicted, it managed to keep revolving and the unpredictability of world affairs kept everyone on their toes. Algeria's seven year war with the French came to an end, though President de Gaulle almost lost his life when disgruntled Frenchmen blamed him for what they regarded as a national disgrace. Three members of the OAS, secret forces operating in Algeria, made an attempt on the President's life in May while he addressed a crowd from the town hall steps in Limoges. More successfully the Israelis convicted and executed Nazi war criminal, Adolf Eichmann, for his part in the genocide of Hungary's Jews in 1944. Further east thousands of American military advisors were being sent to Vietnam in President Kennedy's desperate attempt to stem the tide of the Communist advance there. The year before he had sanctioned an unsuccessful attempt to overthrow Cuba's Communist leader, Castro, in the "Bay of Pigs" fiasco. Castro turned to the Soviet Union for military assistance and its leader, Khrushchev spent the summer of 1962 installing nuclear missiles on the island. Later that year it would erupt into the most dangerous crisis of the Cold War.

In Britain, in 1962 the Beatles dropped Pete Best and replaced him with Ringo Starr and had their first taste of chart success later in the year when "Love Me Do" reached number 17 in the hit parade. Decca had refused them a record deal, but they were snapped up EMI Parlaphone who made a fortune. It was a defining moment at a time when the country was beginning to swing. The show business world was stunned by the death of screen sex goddess, Marilyn Monroe, who failed to see the point of life anymore, Elvis Presley announced his retirement, though it was short lived, and the sporting world once again turned its attentions to South America for the sixth World Cup.

When FIFA's 1956 Congress met in Lisbon, three countries had applied to host the 1962 World Cup finals: West Germany, Argentina and Chile. The two strongest bids were those of Argentina and the Germans, but since the last two tournaments had been staged in Europe, it was wisely felt that the next should be held elsewhere. It left Argentina as the obvious favourite. It had the grounds with the capacity to accommodate the crowds, a fine football tradition and the game had a mass appeal there. Since, Chile could claim none of this, the Argentinians naturally assumed that the 1962 World Cup would be theirs by right.

There was much surprise, then, when FIFA announced that the World Cup would go to Chile. The poor country from the far side of South America pledged that it had the means to stage the tournament and some powerful pleading from the President of Chile's FA, Carlos Dittborn, swung the decision. However, in May 1960 Chile was devastated by a terrible series of earthquakes. Whole areas were flattened, 5,000 people lost their lives and the economic consequences were astronomical. In the aftermath of the disaster, and in full sympathy with Chile's plight, FIFA offered to re-allocate its showpiece, but once again Dittborn was adamant: "We have nothing, that is why we must have the World Cup." His call from the heart that has resounded down the years, was enough to persuade FIFA. Chile kept the World Cup and made titanic efforts to meet its responsibilities. New stadia were erected, including the impressive Estadio Nacional in Santiago, and the tournament went off without any hitches. The Chilean authorities had to charge high admission prices and hotel costs were greater than might have been expected, but this was understandable in the circumstances. The sad note that cast a shadow over the event was the death, a month before it opened, of Dittborn, whose drive had made it possible. Aged only 41, he had suffered a heart attack, not unrelated, one suspects, to the massive effort he had given to the organization of the World Cup.

Once again, the World Cup attracted a record number of applicants, though of the 57 countries that entered, only 52 eventually took part. The first game, between Costa Rica and Guatemala, kicked off on 21st August 1960 in the city of San José, the home team's capital. The arrangements for the CONCACAF region placed the participating countries into three sub-groups. The winner of each then went into a second phase group of three teams and the team that came top was to play Paraguay in a two-legged final. Eventually, Mexico emerged out of this organizational maze, having played eight games, the most any team had to play to reach the finals.

Only Costa Rica played more qualifying games than Mexico. They had been placed in Sub-Group Two and by September 1960 had played all their four group games and had accumulated five points putting them top of the group. Guatemala, who had played three games and had three points, lay second. However, the last group match between Guatemala and Honduras was abandoned and never replayed. Had Honduras won this game, they would also have had five points and be joint top. It was decided that Costa Rica and Honduras should play-off for the right to go through to the next phase. The Costa Ricans won the game 1-0. In the next phase they played four more games to add to the five already played in the first round. Nine games were the most any team had played in a World Cup qualifying tournament to date.

Two of the biggest shocks of the European qualifying stages came with the elimination of Sweden and France. The Swedes and the Swiss both ended their group matches with six points each. Neither goal average nor goal difference were used to differentiate teams with the same points and a play-off was required. It was won by the Swiss. (Had goal average been used to determine the group winner, the Swiss would have qualified, but had goal difference been used, the Swedes would have gone through.) France's qualification for the finals depended on their last game, against Bulgaria, from which they only needed a draw. They played for it and with the score tied at 0-0 they were only seconds away from qualification. Then the Bulgarians scored a last minute winner, which put them on equal points with France. A play-off was needed and a 1-0 victory took the Bulgarians to their first World Cup finals.

Whilst the other European groups went more or less with form, one produced a notable first, whilst another had its course disrupted by politics. Luxembourg's first ever World Cup victory came on 8th October 1961, on home soil. Their 4-2 defeat of Portugal, in which Eusébio made his international debut, ended a losing sequence that had begun on 11th March, 1934 with a 9-1 drubbing at the hands of Hitler's Germany. It ended a sequence of 17 consecutive World Cup defeats. Luxembourg still finished bottom of Group Six, but it was a milestone for a country with a long, if not necessarily distinguished World Cup history. In Group Four, in which Hungary were clearly the best team, Holland and East Germany fought out a 1-1 draw in May in Leipzig. The Dutch authorities then refused to grant visas to the East German players, the return match did not take place and the Hungarians went through.

The way that countries from Africa and Asia were grouped meant that no country from either continent qualified for Chile, at a time when more of them wished to take part. In the late 1950s, as the era of decolonization developed and the former colonies gained their independence from the European empires, they were anxious to emphasize their new status by participation in international sport. It was part of the process of gaining recognition and establishing their identities. Ghana, Morocco, Nigeria and Tunisia were all countries who made their World Cup debuts in the qualifying stages. However, in a move that showed a distinct lack of sympathy with the prevailing "wind of change", as Britain's Prime Minister, Harold Macmillan described the decolonization process, the countries of Africa and Asia were each placed in groups that contained European opposition. Inevitability, the strength of European football meant that the system was biased against African and Asian teams.

In Group Nine, Spain and Wales played each other twice with Spain emerging victorious to await the outcome of the African section of the group. In this the African nations were paired into three sub-groups though the withdrawal of Egypt and Sudan reduced this to two. The winners of the two sub-groups, Ghana and Morocco, then played each other twice with Morocco winning through to play Spain in the group final. In spite of a very good showing they narrowly lost both legs. A similar story occurred in the Asia-Europe group, in which Japan and South Korea were paired in one sub-group and Poland and Yugoslavia in the other. Yugoslavia eventually

Drink, Drugs and a Goal Drought - Chile 1962

Argentinian players training prior to their opening game against Bulgaria.

At all stages in 1962 the toss of a coin in a Santiago restaurant could be used to decide the outcome of games. In the groups, it would be used if goal difference could not separate the teams; in the knock-out stage it would be used if teams were level after extra time; and in the final after a replay. Walter Winterbottom called it: "a devilishly unsatisfactory way to end four years work by going out of the World Cup by the toss of a coin."

Being a superstitious lot the Brazilian team insisted that they be flown to Chile in a plane crewed by the same men who flew them back from the World Cup in Sweden. Yet, superstition was not the sole property of the team. A group of Brazilian businessmen cancelled their trip to the World Cup finals when a Brazilian radio reporter predicted earthquakes in the region in May and June.

Referees were treated like second class citizens when they arrived in Chile. They were put up in second class hotels, received a mere £3.50-a-day expenses and there were no match fees, not even for the final.

saw off the South Koreans in the final and eliminating the last survivor from the two continents.

Argentina, Colombia and Uruguay qualified from South America, joining Chile, Brazil and Mexico as the only non-European competitors in the finals. FIFA had yet to find a formula capable of ensuring adequate representation for countries outside the recognized football power blocks of Europe and the Americas. It could be argued that this situation was a fair reflection of the state of the world game in 1962 because teams from outside these regions would have little chance of doing well unless there was a major upset. Yet FIFA's membership was increasing and changes to the qualifying tournament were needed to reflect this. The lack of concern for its Asian and African members and their growing demands for representation in the finals was to have a major impact on the 1966 tournament.

The tournament kicked off on 30th May in the brand new Estadio Nacional in Santiago. It began with a ceremony that culminated with the emotional sight of Dittborn's two sons raising the national flags of Chile and Switzerland, the two countries competing in the opening game, his real children getting his spiritual child underway. For the first time the people of Chile had the full stare of the world's gaze upon them and the aspirations of these embattled people rested on the shoulders of their footballers. Over 65,000 fans turned out to support them that day, with millions of others listening on radios or watching on television sets, and they were not disappointed by the opening salvos. The Swiss took an early and spectacular lead, when Rolf Wüthrich drove home a 30 yard rocket, but the Chileans were not unduly troubled and began to claw their way back into the match. Leonel Sánchez scored an equalizer in the last minute of the first half and victory was set up ten minutes into the second, when Jaime Ramírez put Chile in front. It was secured some 14 minutes from time when Sánchez converted a penalty.

The opening game had been well attended, but gates at games played away from Santiago were much smaller. This is partly because the grounds used had lower capacities, but also because, by and large, the Chilean public was less interested in the World Cup than in Chile's part in it. The opening game in Group One (from 1962 the term "group" and not "pool" was used) between Uruguay and Colombia was watched by less than 8,000 people. It was played in the Carlos Dittborn Stadium in Arica, Dittborn's home town, situated in the very north of the country, near the border with Peru. The game they saw featured a Uruguayan team much weaker than those of the past and, although the Uruguayans won easily, it was more owing to the impotence of their opponents, than to their own virtues. Notwithstanding, it was Colombia that took the lead through a 20 minute penalty converted by Francisco Zuluago, and held on to it for nearly 40 minutes more. Eventually, Uruguay's pressure began to tell and in the 57th minute Luís Cubilla equalized. Just over a quarter of an hour later, José Sacia cored his country's second to give a final score of 2-1 to Uruguay.

The Group Three games were played in the picturesque Estadio Sausalito in the seaside town of Viña del Mar, about 100 miles west of Santiago. This pretty little ground had woods on two sides and the Pacific Ocean on the other two, but neither the setting nor the mighty Brazilians could tempt more than 10,500 specta-

Chilean players Conpas and Tabar relax.

tors for their opening game against Mexico. This low turnout was not due to a shortage of publicity, because the Brazilians had attracted this in plenty since their victory in 1958. Now managed by Aimoré Moreira, whose brother Zezé had managed the team in 1954, their camp was the focus of crowds of journalists and camp followers, avid for photographs, news or interviews. Many of the squad were happy to oblige, to capitalize on the interest they aroused and on the lucrative advertising deals with which they were contracted. At times, it seemed as if almost every article worn or used by the team, including the minibuses they travelled in, were emblazoned with some corporate logo or name. It was indicative of a new trend in football, the start of the long road to commercialism that many football lovers have come to regret. The game itself went to form and left the Mexicans, whose evergreen goalkeeper, Antonio Carbajal, was in his fourth World Cup, still seeking their first victory in the tournament's final stages. The Brazilian performance was not as fluid as might have been expected, with less of the cavalier showiness that hallmarked their victory in 1958. Their 4-3-3 formation reflected an approach to the game that lacked adventurousness, but it was enough to get the win. Their two goals came in the second half, from Zagalo and Pelé, whose brilliant effort saw him beat four players before placing the ball in the net. (See Zagalo profile on page 167). It was comfortable, but lacked the zest normally associated with Brazilian football.

The fact that Chile was so poorly off for first class grounds of the size and quality FIFA would normally require for the staging of the World Cup, was exemplified by that used for the Group Four games. These took place in Rancagua, about 100 miles south of Santiago, in a tiny stadium owned by the Bradon Copper Company. The small crowd that turned out to see Argentina play Bulgaria on the opening day were not treated to anything special. The Bulgarians had brought a young team, more with the object of gaining experience than in any hope of doing well. The Argentinians, revealing that they were fully-fledged believers in the philosophy that was

Chilean President, George Alesandri opened the tournament by saying: "Chile is not a big power in world sport. But our people admire the skill and ability of these sportsmen who make sport so important."

With only nine days to go ticket sales were worryingly low. The public seemed reluctant to part with their hard-earned escudos. Only 9,000 tickets had been sold at Rancagua where England, Hungary, Argentina and Bulgaria were to play.

A group of 500 school children were let in to see the Brazilian team at their training camp at Quilpue after they threatened to burn down their school if they were kept out.

The Brazilian team turned up in Chile accompanied by twenty three officials and 200 press and radiomen. Their party also included a doctor, a dentist, three trainers, a masseur and a chiropodist.

Drink, Drugs and a Goal Drought - Chile 1962

becoming more widespread in football, were there to gain results and were less interested in how they did it. They went ahead with an early, fourth-minute strike by Héctor Facundo, the first goal of the tournament, and were then content to sit back and defend their lead. The Bulgarians did not have the tactical awareness to breach a packed and rugged defence and the single goal was sufficient to take the points.

The second batch of opening group games was played on the last day of May and that in Group One produced a nasty, bad tempered match between the USSR and Yugoslavia. Poor relations had existed between these countries since the 1940s and the propaganda generated during their quarrel influenced attitudes in both countries. Of greater consequence, though, was the fact that the Soviet Union had defeated Yugoslavia 2-1 in the final of the first European championships in the Parc des Princes, in Paris in July 1960. Both sets of players felt they had a point to prove and it added to the tension that began to build once the match got underway. There was some good football to be seen in the first half, when both showed a desire to go forwards. Things began to deteriorate after the break, when Valentin Ivanov followed in a shot that rebounded off the post and swept the ball home to give the Soviets the lead. The response of the Yugoslavs was to resort to strong-arm tactics and the atmosphere darkened considerably. It got worse when the Soviet full-back, Eduard Dubinski had his leg broken in a particularly vicious tackle. The culprit, Mujic, was subsequently sent home by Yugoslavia's team management in an act of some contrition. It prompted the Soviets to give back as good as they got and what had the potential to have been the match of the group became a parody. Viktor Ponedelnik secured victory for the Soviet Union by scoring their second in the last five minutes.

Another ill-tempered affair was the Group Two game between Italy and West Germany, in which the large Santiago crowd had a great bearing on attitudes on the pitch. The Italians were not popular in Chile and had a reputation for "stealing" South American players. They numbered in their current squad José Altafini, who had played for Brazil in 1958 under the name of Mazzola and Omar Sivori and Humberto Maschia, both of whom were Argentine-born and had played in 1957 side that had won the South American championship. This feeling was exacerbated by two recent articles written by Italian journalists that described life in Chile, and in Santiago particularly, as being awful. It had inflamed the locals and, not surprisingly, the Italians came out onto the pitch to a chorus of boos and catcalls, which hardly let up throughout the match. Maybe the crowd needed something to amuse them because the fare on the pitch was not at all attractive. Before the tournament former coach, Vittorio Pozzo, had indicated that the Italians had not the right attitude to go on to win the championship. "Our football is too riddled with a defensive mentality to allow the necessary switch to free attack", he said and so it proved. Neither team was prepared to take risks and the match became bogged down in a defensive stalemate. The players prefered to kick each other than kick at goal. A goalless draw was no advert for the game, but all too typical of the approach of some teams to this World Cup.

A much better game was the seaside clash between Czechoslovakia and Spain. Much was expected from the Spaniards, with their quota of Real Madrid stars and foreign imports, like Ferenc Puskás, an exile from the 1956 Hungarian uprising, and the Argentine-born, Alfredo Di Stefano. One of the most highly rated forwards of his day, Di Stefano now finally had the World Cup stage upon which to weave his magic. However, he had not been seeing eye to eye with the national coach, Helenio Herrera, and in a fit of pique used the excuse of a pulled muscle to refuse to play. His decision was one of the tournament's great disappointments and his absence was felt by his team mates. The Spanish had much of the play, certainly in the early stages of the game, but were unable to break through a tight and well disciplined Czech defence. As time wore on, the Spanish began to fade and the Czechs, a useful side in their own right, began to show more of their attacking capability. They broke the deadlock in the 80th minute, with a goal from Josef Štibrányi and it was enough to take the points needed to keep up with Brazil.

Going into their opening game against Hungary, the English had been training well, "particularly in attack," noted one observer, "where Charlton, Greaves, Hitchens, and Peacock have been in powerful finishing mood." However, the Hungarians had assembled a team that was getting close to the standard of the "Mighty Magyars" of the early 1950s and they revealed plenty of flair and imagination against an English team that was out of sorts with those reports of the training sessions. Bryan Douglas and Gerry Hitchens both flunked innumerable chances, whilst Hungary's first goal spotlighted the difference in guile between the teams. In the 15th minute, Tichy "made an aimless drifting run, then scored with a superb, unexpected shot", from 30 yards. England equalized with a second half penalty, taken by Ron Flowers after Jimmy Greaves's shot had been handled on the line, but the Hungarians were always the more creative. Fifteen minutes later, they were back in front after Flowers slipped on the wet turf and allowed Florian Albert in on goal. The often one-dimensional nature of England's football had been astutely surmised in a remark made by the Yugoslav manager before the tournament, alluding to the influence of captain, Johnny Haynes. "Number 10 takes the corners. Number 10 takes the throw ins", he said. "So what do we do? We put a man on Number 10. Goodbye England." His strictures had fallen on deaf ears.

In their game against the Soviet Union, the Yugoslavs had not been given the opportunity to reveal the potential or quality of their football. Against Uruguay, on 2nd June, they were and took it willingly. Before they found their stride they had the worst of the opening quarter of the game, during which Rubens Cabrera put the South Americans in front. The goal, however, revitalized Yugoslavia and, in particular Milan Galic, whose fine performance underlay much of what his team achieved that day. In the 27th minute a penalty, taken by Josip Skoblar, levelled the scores and within a minute Galic had given Yugoslavia the

With too many players switching nations and representing more than one country, the rules governing qualification for international matches were cleared up in 1962. From then on a player must have been born in "the area of the national association." For players born abroad, their nationality would be decided by that of their fathers.

England had their base at the Coya Camp, a first class retreat owned by the Bradon Copper Company. Top company executives usually used it for rest and relaxation, where facilities included a golf course, ten-pin bowling, a gym, a cinema, tennis, billiards and table tennis. Their stay had been arranged by George Robledo, who had played for Chile in the 1950 World Cup finals. He was now a liaison officer with the company, which provided the facilities free of charge. A British-born cook, Mrs Bertha Lewis, who had been flown in from Conception in Southern Chile, catered for the squad. She said: "I have brought up five big sons of my own on the sort of food I am giving these lovely young gentlemen. Steak and kidney puds, roast beef, Cornish pasties, ham and egg, Irish stew and home-made cakes. They are going to get all they want four times daily unless Mr Winterbottom tells me they are getting too fat."

Sunday morning golf for the English team at Coya. Johnny Haynes drives off watched by (right to left) Don Howe, Ron Flowers, Bobby Charlton and Ray Wilson.

Drink, Drugs and a Goal Drought - Chile 1962

lead. They were now in complete control and a third goal, scored just after half-time by Drazan Jerkovic, gave them a well-deserved 3-1 victory.

There were three other games played that day: the notorious "Battle of Santiago" (See Italy v Chile profile on page 170), the scoreless draw between Brazil and Czechoslovakia and England returning to winning ways against Argentina. In their match, Brazil suffered a major setback when, as he set up to shoot, Pelé tore a thigh muscle and had to limp off. He returned, but as a mere bystander and without him the Brazilians were unable to crack a Czech defence that often contained eight men. England's forwards, however, rekindled the vigour that had been apparent in training and exposed the weakness of Argentina's defence. Their first goal was a 17th minute penalty, scored by Flowers after Navarro had handled Peacock's header on the line. Bobby Charlton's cross had set up the chance on that occasion and just before half-time he scored his first World Cup goal when he "made a typical drift inside and then suddenly released an explosive right foot shot." Jimmy Greaves got England's third goal and a late consolation scored by Francisco Sanfilippo made a 3-1 final score. Making his debut for Argentina that day was Antonio Ráttin, who was to earn notoriety in the 1966 finals, in a match against England.

The next day, Colombia made their remarkable comeback against the USSR (See USSR v Colombia profile on page 171 and Lev Yashin profile on page 165) and in their game against West Germany, the Swiss suffered an early set back when Eschmann broke his ankle. Bravely, he stayed on the field, but could do nothing to help his team, who went behind, just before half-time, to a goal by Albert Brülls. Uwe Seeler put the Germans further ahead in the 60th minute and, although Heinz Schneiter got a late reply for Switzerland, it was not enough to knock the Germans off course.

Both Hungary and Spain dominated their group games, against Bulgaria and Mexico respectively. Albert and Tichy were outstanding as the Magyars outclassed the hapless Bulgarians, with a display that came as close as anything yet to recapturing the splendour of the pre-1956 team. They scored four goals in the first twelve rampaging minutes, with Albert grabbing two in the first six, Tichy adding another after eight and Ernö Solymosi scoring the fourth. Further goals from Albert and Tichy merely confirmed their dominance. The Spanish were equally dominant in their game, though more profligate in front of goal. Their forwards squandered countless chances before Joaquin Piéro finally made their superiority tell with a last minute goal that they so richly deserved.

The domination of the defences was one of the less attractive features of the 1962 World Cup finals and defence was the defining influence in two of the games played on 6th June. The match between the USSR and Uruguay was one in which neither side had any desire to give anything away and the contest was decided by breakaway goals. Alexei Mamikin got the first for the Soviets shortly before half-time and José Sacia replied eight minutes after the break. The winner came in the last minute, when Ivanov scored to take his tally to four and make him one of the tournament's joint top goal scorers. There were no such goals to lighten the day's other defensive battle between Argentina and Hungary. The Argentinians showed more commitment to going forward than did their opponents, but the Hungarians were determined to hang on for a draw that was sufficient to see them through to the next phase. When the South

Following England's defeat against Hungary, ex-Juventus star Giampiero Boniperti asked: "What has happened to England? They're going backwards instead of forwards." Less critical was Hungary's veteran goalkeeper Gyula Grosics, who played in the game. He said: "This is the best England side I have faced in four matches since Wembley in 1953. But they still do not shoot." Since 1953 Hungary had won all four meetings between the two nations, but this time the English really thought they would win.

Candidate for "The World's Bravest Referee" Award: Ken Aston (England)

The issue of drugs cropped up after the "Battle of Santiago" when the President of the Chilean technical Committee, Jorge Pica, made the statement: "I think all the Italians were doped because they lost all control. It was abnormal. Now I can see the necessity for lab tests and a specialist to examine players after the game." At half-time the Chilean Medical Officer, Dr Sergio Reyes, had gone into the Italian dressing room and was spat at by the Milan centre-forward Salvadore. Ironically, referee Ken Aston had been scheduled to take the Hungary-Bulgaria game, but Hungary had objected because England was in the same group. On being switched to Santiago, Aston remarked that "One game is the same as another to me. I don't mind." Afterwards, he changed his mind. "It wasn't my most difficult match because it was never at any time a match", he said. One British newspaper described the match as a bloodbath and warned parents not to let their children watch when it was re-run on television.

Alan Peacock, England's centre-half against Argentina, remarked after the two teams met: "I knew I was going to get a lot of stick from tough guy Navarro - and got it. I was punched in the eye, pushed, kicked and hacked - but that was nothing to the stick I would have got back home if I hadn't done well." When asked why his team had performed so much better than in their opening game, Walter Winterbottom simply said: "I just don't know. That's football isn't it."

Americans did penetrate, they were let down by poor shooting and the game remained goalless.

The best game played that day was that between West Germany and Chile, which produced clean, attacking football from both sides. The first goal came from a penalty, after Navarro had been adjudged to have caught Seeler with his elbow. Horst Szymaniak converted it. The Chileans suffered a further set back when an injury to Landa reduced the potency of their attack and the Germans were able to capitalize with a second from Seeler. The win took the Germans through to the next phase, as did Brazil's victory over Spain, which they struggled to

England 3 : Argentina 1
(Left to right) England's Bobby Moore, Maurice Norman and Ron Flowers fend off an Argentinian attack.

achieve. The Spaniards knew that they had to win and they went on to the offensive from the beginning, often outplaying their opponents, "switching the ball quickly from man to man." Adelardo Sánchez gave them a 35th minute lead, but they were unable to gain greater advantage from their possession. It was costly because the Brazilians had a better second half and in Amarildo had a more than adequate replacement for Pelé. He struck twice in the last twenty minutes to give Brazil the victory.

In their final group game, against Colombia, the Yugoslavs really turned on the style. Technically, either team could have gone through to the next stage, and Yugoslavia only needed a draw, but they hit the South Americans hard. Admittedly, the Colombians were tired following their classic encounter with the Soviet Union, but they were shown no mercy by Yugoslavia's speedy and incisive forwards. Two goals in a five minute spell from Drazan Jerkovic got the scoring underway and three more in the second half brought an emphatic 5-0 victory.

Once again, defence proved to be the shaping influence in England's 0-0 draw with Bulgaria, the first international between the two countries. England only needed a draw to qualify and the Bulgarians were already confined to the group's bottom spot, but, curiously, they opted to play a defensive game. They must have been determined to come away from Chile with at least one point. It made for a "feeble, insipid match", "played under sullen grey skies, and in bitter cold." Such conditions should have suited the English, but they were unable to find any sparkle, causing one reporter to complain about the "formlessness and unpredictability" of their football being "slightly exasperating", and bordering "on the ridiculous." Greaves forced one shot against the post early in the first half, but there was little else to occupy the attention of the fewer than 6,000 crowd who bothered to turn up.

Two more games were played that day to complete the group stage of the tournament. There was no possibility of further progress for either of the teams in the match between Italy and Switzerland and the Italians made

One player who disgraced himself in 1962 was the giant of Russian football, Lev Yashin. At half-time in the game against Colombia, he hit the bottle too hard and came out onto the pitch drunk. Not surprisingly his team squandered a 3-1 lead.

Jean Eskenagi, a French journalist commenting on the forthcoming tournament remarked that: "The Bulgarians are the worst team in the championship. They play in circles." What this was supposed to mean is anybody's guess.

For Spain's final Group Three game against Brazil, tough-guy coach, Helenio Herrera, dropped the £1.2 million trio of stars Suárez, Del Sol and Santamaria, stating that "I want players who will work and fight. It's our only hope."

A group of Soviet scientists in Moscow programmed a computer to try to forecast the winners of the series. Naturally it predicted that the USSR would win.

England 0 : Bulgaria 0
England's Jimmy Greaves (left) battles with Ivan Dimitrov of Bulgaria.

In 1962 the Daily Herald, ran a column under the heading "Under 25" where young people were asked for their opinions on issues of the day. On 9th June the question was "Do you think winning has become too important in international sport?" Peter Wadsley of Christchurch in Hampshire answered: "In general no. But in international football, definitely yes." Malcolm Binks of Nottingham said: "Short of inflicting injury on opponents, players should be free to employ any tactics to win." On 15th June the question posed was "In view of England's World Cup failure should we in future enter one British Isles team?" Mandy Williams of Swansea said: "No - we are four separate countries", while Gillian Hill of Shoreham, Sussex replied: "England is England and the team should stay like that."

wholesale changes to the line up that had fought against Chile five days previously. They eventually came out 3-0 winners, but this was more down to a second half injury to Charles Elsner in the Swiss goal than to anything the Italians did. The other game, between Mexico and Czechoslovakia, did produce a noteworthy first. The Czechs were looking for a win that would take them to the top of the group and seemed to be heading for it when Vaclav Musek scored the fastest goal of the tournament, in only 15 seconds to set a new World Cup record. However, this did not cow the Mexicans. It was, after all, goalkeeper Antonio Carbajal's 33rd birthday and his fourth World Cup and they obviously wanted to give him something to celebrate. In the tenth minute Isidoro Díaz equalized and some twenty minutes later Alfredo Del Aguila grabbed a second to give the Mexicans a half-time lead. After the break, the Czechs put the Mexican defence under considerable pressure as they grafted to find the win, but the Mexicans held out. Their victory was assured when Héctor Hernández converted a penalty in the dying stages of the game. It was Mexico's first ever win in the World Cup finals, at their 14th attempt, and it can be truthfully said that they deserved it. The postscript to this game was Carbajal's decision to retire from international football. He plainly wanted to go out on a high note, but the doughty campaigner was later persuaded to change his mind. (See Antonio Carbajal profile on page 168).

The quarter-finals were all played on 10th June, the day that Dittborn's widow gave birth to his posthumous son and, thankfully, the quality of the football improved now that the knock-out stage had been reached. The largest crowd was that in Santiago, which went to see Yugoslavia take on the West Germans, though it was one of the most oddly behaved crowds ever to have attended a football match. At least the players must have thought so because the reactions of the crowd bore little resemblance to the shape of play on the field. They were treated to a good game, with both teams playing crisply, but the mass attention was in far away Arica, where Chile were playing the Soviet Union. With thousands of radios tuned in to the commentary of that game, it was that to which the crowd reacted. What the spectators missed (or saw) was Petar Radocovic score a late winner to steer Yugoslavia into the semi-finals. It had been the third tournament in a row that the two teams had met at this stage of the knock-out and it was the first time that Yugoslavia had won.

Up in Arica, where the thoughts of much of Chile's population were that afternoon, the host nation battled gallantly against a more highly rated Soviet team. The Chileans took a lead in the 11th minute, when Leonel Sánchez blasted in a brilliant free kick from the edge of the penalty area, and then were forced to defend deeply as the Soviets searched for an equalizer. They got it just before the half-hour mark, when Chislenko took advantage of some poor defending. The Chileans failed to clear a loose ball from their penalty area and it fell to Chislenko, who made no mistake with his shot. Within a minute, though, the home team were back in front when Eliado Rojas scored with a spectacular 30 yard drive that many people thought Lev Yashin should have stopped. The crowd went wild, invaded the pitch and it was a while before order was restored. The next hour was full of nervous tension, as the Chileans dug deep into their reserves to defend their slender lead and go further in the World Cup than any other Chilean team has since.

22 Men and a Bag of Wind

Another tense, though completely absorbing game was that between Czechoslovakia and Hungary. The Czechs had been the surprise package of this World Cup and had outdone most predictions by getting this far. They were certainly not expected to get past the Hungarians. Yet, they had been gradually growing in confidence and this is what probably gave them the edge in their quarter-final. They took an early lead, when Adolf Scherer blasted home a 20 yard pile driver of a shot and then had to summon every vestige of courage and commitment to maintain it. Just like the Chileans, the well organized Czech defence proved equal to the task, though there was an element of good fortune about their victory. Tichy had the ball in the net, but it was disallowed for offside and Viliam Schrojf, in the Czech goal, played one of the best games of his career. He produced a whole series of tremendous saves and Czechoslovakia's semi-final place was more down to him than of any other player. "Schrojf's virtuosity was as vital to Czechoslovakia as was Garrincha's to Brazil", one historian has stated.

With Pelé out of the team, attention was given to some of the other Brazilian players and to what fine footballers they were. Garrincha and Amarildo, in particular, shone out as two world class players in the game against England. It was a "first-class and immensely thrilling" encounter, with England giving what many saw as their finest World Cup performance to date. Both teams were committed to attack and chances were set up at both ends. Greaves rattled the bar in one of England's first moves, Jimmy Armfield scrambled a Garrincha effort off the line, Springett made some excellent saves and Gilmar just got a hand to a Greaves shot to force it over the bar. Greaves even caught a stray dog that had wandered onto the pitch. The Brazilians got the first break when Garrincha headed in a corner, but the English did not trail for long. In the 38th minute, Greaves headed a free kick onto the bar and Gerry Hitchens followed in to score from the rebound. With Garrincha seeming to grow in stature by the minute, Brazil began to take control of the game in the second half. In the 53rd minute it was his free kick that came off Springett's chest on to the head of Vavá and into the net. Not long after that, he hit a beautiful, swerving shot from outside the penalty area, which completely wrong-footed Springett. The English were never going to make good a two goal deficit against a Brazilian team that had found its natural rhythm and the game ended 3-1 to the South Americans. (See Vavá profile on page 169).

The World Cup had now come down to its last four teams and both semi-finals saw the South American and the European sides paired off. Czechoslovakia and Yugoslavia played their

Many Hungarian players who have appeared in World Cup finals have had unusual occupations. The Hungarian inside-left Lajos Tichy was a cameraman.

The "Eat My Own Words" Award for 1962 goes to...

Bobby Robson of England. Before the quarter-final match with Brazil he said that the opposition were "nowhere near the side they were in Sweden and surely we have a better team this time. Brazil still have tremendous potential but they are not playing well. I fancy our chances more this time than I did before Gothenburg."

Walter Winterbottom, was coach of England for 17 years and 130 games, between 1946 and 1963. He took England to four consecutive World Cups, but never got further than the quarter-finals. On arriving home from Chile and anticipating the next tournament, he said: "We have got to keep working. Whether we can produce a world beating team for 1966 remains to be seen.

Brazil 3 : England 1

The England team (back row l-r): Armfield, Flowers, Springett, Norman, Charlton, Moore
(front row l-r): Douglas, Greaves, Haynes, Wilson, Hitchens.

Drink, Drugs and a Goal Drought - Chile 1962

Brazil 3 : England 1

English defender Ray Wilson attempts to tackle Brazil's Garrincha.

When a stray dog wandered onto the field during the England-Brazil game several players tried and failed to grab it. Jimmy Greaves managed to sweet talk it into his arms but the dog then proceeded to pee down the front of his shirt, leaving a nasty yellow stain. The dog was nicknamed Garrincha and the player of the same name took pity and adopted it.

When the hosts reached the semi-finals the whole of Santiago went mad. From dawn until dusk, and from dusk until dawn, the streets were crowded with people of all ages chanting "Chile, Chile, Chile." Car horns and sirens sounded non-stop, usually coming from stolen vehicles that were raced around the streets. The danger was immense and accidents common, sometimes fatally. It was unusual from a people not noted for great shows of emotion.

game in Viña del Mar on 13th June and, for the first time, the Czechs opened up and showed their real attacking potential. Although goalless, the first half had its moments of excitement, as both teams worked hard to create an opening. Once again, Schrojf was on top form and a string of superb saves was the foundation upon which the Czechs built their second half dominance. They took the lead soon after the restart through Josef Kadraba, but the Yugoslavs equalized in the 69th minute, when Drazan Jerkovic headed in a long ball down the middle. From that moment the game belonged almost exclusively to the Czechs. They mounted raid upon raid and were rewarded with two goals in the last ten minutes, both from the boot of Adolf Scherer. For the second time the Czechs had reached a World Cup final.

In the second semi-final, played in Santiago, the Brazilians, and Garrincha, again shone like the beacons they were. They played "as if they were in a different class" and it took the "Little Bird" just nine minutes to crack the Chilean defence. An overhead kick rebounded off a Chilean defender into his path, on the edge of the area, and he released a 20 yard drive that gave the goalkeeper no chance. With a little over half an hour gone, he struck again, this time with a powerful header from a corner. Though clearly playing second fiddle and roared on by their partisan following, the home team were not out of it yet and about four minutes from the end of the half, Jorge Toro scored to give them a crumb of hope. However, the Brazilians again stamped their authority on the tie soon after the break when Garrincha floated over a corner and Vavá headed it home. By now, the Chileans were looking ragged and their attacks less and less convincing. They scored once more, in the 61st minute, when Sánchez converted a penalty, but their front line lacked Brazil's sharpness and free kicks appeared their only way to goal. The Brazilians rounded off the scoring with a goal that did not involve Garrincha. Zagalo provided the cross that gave Vavá his second headed goal and his team the 4-2 victory.

It had been a good game, and was generally a cleanly contested, though there was some unpleasantness, especially near the end. Chile's Honorino Landa was sent off for a foul on Zito and as the game drew towards its close Garrincha received his marching orders from the Peruvian referee, Arturo Yamasaki, for retaliation after Eladio Rojas had kicked him. As he left he field he was hit by a bottle thrown from the crowd. For his offence, Landa was suspended for a game and could not take part in the 3rd/4th place play-off. When dealing with Garrincha, FIFA took into account the fact the he had been provoked several times during the match and decided that his was the lesser offence. To the relief of his team mates, he got away with a reprimand and was allowed to play in the final.

For the people of Chile, the 3rd/4th play-off was the World Cup final. Very few had expected to see the tournament in Chile at all; they had certainly not expected to see their team reach the semi-finals. In eager anticipation, over 66,000 people crowded into the Estadio Nacional to see them battle against Yugoslavia for that important third spot. Yugoslavia was definitely the more fancied team, but the Chileans played with heart, determined to give their supporters a little piece of World Cup glory. However, they had to wait a full, tense ninety minutes before they achieved it. Eladio Rojas won it for them with the last kick of the game and triggered off scenes of wild jubilation that went on throughout the night. For the Chileans, taking that third place was a seismic achievement and one of which Carlos Dittborn would have been extremely proud.

Brazil 4 : Chile 2
Brazil's Garrincha holds his head after a being hit by a bottle thrown from the crowd following his sending-off.

The final took place on 17th June and gave Brazil their second world title. (See Brazil v Czechoslovakia profile on page 172). It provided a fitting end to a tournament that, like all others, had its high and low points and its fair share of surprise and incident. There was much to admire about the football played. Players like Schrojf of Czechoslovakia, Albert of Hungary, or Amarildo and Garrincha of Brazil buzzed with the excellence. Games like the quarter-final between Chile and the USSR or the group match between the USSR and Colombia, and the surprising progress of Chile and Czechoslovakia epitomized what the World Cup is all about.

In anticipating the final Daily Herald commentator, Peter Lorenzo, reported that: "Sunday's final without Garrincha, the great, and Pelé would be like water without whiskey." Pelé would not play, but FIFA held back from suspending Garrincha following his dismissal against Chile after he apologized. "I'm terribly sorry it happened," he said. "It was involuntary reaction - probably as a consequence of some kicks I had taken previously. But there is no justification for the way I behaved. I apologise to the Chilean public."

In 1962 referees needed to be tough. It was widely agreed that Russian, Nikolai Latychev, was the right choice for the final. He had a reputation for keeping games under tight control.

Brazil impressively won the tournament using only twelve players, a record that still stands.

The Czechoslovakian team before their Quarter-final match against Hungary.

The Santiago public had responded to the spectacle with enthusiasm.

Yet there can be no hiding the often negative attitude of some teams, which mitigated against the quality of football played. Pozzo's comments about Italian negativity could equally apply to several other teams. The Bulgarians and Argentinians were particularly guilty of this mentality, though not exclusively. It led, naturally, to some boring games of football as in the group games between Argentina and Hungary or Bulgaria against England. Defence-mindedness led to petulance and ill temper, and several games were marred by misbehaviour. The low point was, of course, the "Battle of Santiago" and FIFA and its referees should shoulder some of the responsibility for this through a lack of resolute action. It was also, though, symptomatic of a culture that was beginning to pervade the world of football, fuelled by media pressure and financial reward. The beneficiaries of this were, of course, the footballers themselves; the losers were football and its growing band of followers.

Loyova Ivanovich Yashin   USSR

Honours: 4th Place 1966; Quarter-finals 1958/62   Games 12
Played: 1958, 1962 and 1966

Lev Yashin in action in the 1966 World Cup.

If not the best goalkeeper the game has known, Lev Yashin was certainly one of its greatest characters. His match preparation was always a little eccentric and he once explained: "The trick was to have a smoke to calm your nerves, then toss back a strong drink to tone your muscles." He believed this gave the qualities needed to be the best in the world and to many Russians this is what he will always be. His contribution to the modern game cannot be denied. He was the first goalkeeper to venture out of the penalty area with regularity and reliability. He rejected the traditional notion that goalkeepers should always catch the ball and employed various ways of clearing the ball from his area. He had many nicknames, but the Russians knew him as the "Black Spider", not only for the colour of his kit, but because he could cover every inch of his goal with the agility of a spider. He would build a web of defence across his goalmouth, impenetrable to all but the mightiest of attackers. His reaction times and flexibility made him a superb shot-stopper and he stopped over 150 penalties in his career.

Yashin was born on 22nd October 1929 into a family of industrial workers and he got his first job in 1942 as a turner at the Krasnyi Bogatyr tool factory in Moscow. It was here in 1944 that he started playing football and was picked to play for the works youth team. Yashin claimed that he always wanted to be a centre-forward, but because he was so tall and strong, and the fact that Lev is Russian for "lion", his coach put him between the posts. He later spent some time as a police officer and it was because of this that A. I. Chernyshov, a football and ice hockey coach invited him to play for Dinamo Moscow in 1949. Dinamo represented the Interior Ministry. He spent the next 22 seasons with the Moscow club, a faithfulness that was highly creditable, though it was not uncommon in the USSR for a player to spend their entire career with just one club. Transfers between the top Russian clubs were severely discouraged, particularly for an Interior Ministry team and one that wished to hold on to such a promising talent. However, his early career did not run smoothly and after making his club debut on 6th July 1950, he could not command a regular first team place and, in 1953 was on the verge of changing to ice hockey when fortune smiled on him. Dinamo's regular 'keeper, Aleksi "The Tiger" Khomich suffered an injury that kept him out of the game for a long time and inadvertently heralded the start of Yashin's glorious career.

Rivalry between the top Moscow clubs, Spartak and Dinamo, was intense at the time and derby games always sold out. Between 1949 and 1970 Spartak were the most successful of the two, winning six championships to Dinamo's five and four Soviet Cup finals to Dinamo's three, but Yashin was crucial to Dinamo's defence. He managed it with force, always shouting and commanding, so much so that his wife accused him of yelling too much. Yet, he rarely captained the team. Making a goalkeeper captain was a rare concept in the 1950s and 60s.

As his reputation for athleticism and courage grew, Yashin was soon in the national side and the USSR went on to enjoy its most successful period in international football. To many he was "the greatest goalkeeper" in the world, but his performances were not always flawless. In 78 games for his country he conceded 70 goals, many more than today's keepers would be allowed to get away with. At that time defences were not the strongest aspect of Soviet football and it was not unusual for teams to field three strikers in the hope that more goals would be scored than conceded. Yashin's ability and strength were beyond question and the team coach's confidence in him never wavered. With his ability to help teams win games, it was better to be with Yashin than without.

In 1956 the Soviet team travelled to Melbourne, Australia to compete in the Olympic Games. They returned home triumphant and Yashin had his first international honour. Alongside him in the team that would qualify for the World Cup in Sweden were two other legends of Soviet football, Eduard Streltsov and Igor Netto. Unfortunately, Netto only played once in Sweden because a severe knee injury in the first game kept him out for the rest of the tournament and Streltsov never made it to the finals at all. He was sentenced to seven years in a Labour Camp for an alleged sexual assault just before it started. In the finals, the USSR made it to the quarter-finals, but failed to live up to the promise they had shown in Australia. Two years later, however, the USSR roared back to international stardom, winning the European Nations Cup. Yashin performed brilliantly and it was not surprising that they travelled to Chile in 1962 with high hopes.

For Yashin, the 1962 World Cup finals were a little embarrassing. He made several uncharacteristic blunders and he let in some easy goals. The team topped their group in the first round but were beaten by the hosts in the quarter-finals. In one group game the unfancied Colombians held them to a surprising draw, not unusual in the heat of a World Cup tournament but there were rumours that Yashin had had one too many of his "muscle toners" at half-time. Despite this, Yashin's fame continued to grow and, in 1963 he was awarded the Best Player Award by the prestigious France Football Magazine. He was the only goalkeeper to have been so recognized. In 1966, the English eagerly awaited the arrival of Yashin so they too could see the great man perform. As he walked through the airport on his arrival, fishing rods in hand, he said: "Not for football I come, but for fishing. I prefer to catch trout but I will take anything that comes." Commenting on the tournament he said: "We shall have plenty to do to come out on top. As for myself, despite my age [35] I am in top form, better than I was in Chile." He did not disappoint and the USSR had their best tournament to date, though Yashin appeared only once in the group stage against Italy. As their quarter-final approached the coach then decided that Yashin was too important to leave out any more and he was first choice for the USSR's further three games which ended in defeat in the 3rd/4th place play-off.

Although his international career soon came to a close, Yashin played on for Dinamo Moscow until 1970 winning two further runners-up prizes in the Soviet League and two more cups in 1967 and 1970. His final club game was in 1971 when Dinamo played a European All Stars team to honour the USSR's most famous goalkeeper. He played 326 times for Dinamo, a club record. In later life he suffered much ill health and in 1986 had a leg amputated, the consequence of a knee injury suffered during his playing days. He died at the age of 61 on 20th March 1990, from complications incurred during surgery. It was a sad ending to a life that had turned goalkeeping into an art form. In 1968, he was awarded the USSR's highest honour, the Order of Lenin.

Mario Jorge Lubo Zagalo   **Brazil**

Honours:
Player: Winner 1958 and 1962   **Games 12**
Manager: Winner 1970; Runner-up 1998; 4th 1974   **Goals 2**
Technical Advisor: Winner 1994
Played: 1958 and 1962
Manager: 1970,1974 and 1998

"One simple, if astonishing, truth is that Brazil have never won a World Cup without the involvement of Zagalo." This is what soccer journalist, Michael Walker, had to say about the man who is undoubtedly one of the most important participants the World Cup has known. Both as a player and as an intelligent, but much maligned, manager, Mario Zagalo achieved more in the world game than anyone else and his record is unlikely to be matched. He is the only person to have won the World Cup four times and he was the first to win the trophy both as a player and as a manager. He was also responsible for creating one of the greatest teams the game has ever seen, that of 1970.

Born on 2nd July 1932, Zagalo was a very successful player with Botafogo and Flamenco. He was a fit and versatile winger who covered much ground and created chances galore for his fellow strikers. Although he didn't possess the flair that has characterized many Brazilians, he was thoughtful, could play in midfield or defence and his consistency brought him to the attention of the national team manager prior to the 1958 World Cup. Yet, before success, he had to face adversity and he was not the natural first choice in the team. He got his chance through injury to other players and it earned him the nickname "Lucky".

In 1958 Zagalo was picked to play on the left-wing, with the more exotic Garrincha on the right. Their styles of play were very different but it did not stop them turning over opposition with such ease. The Brazilian team and Zagalo both got better as the tournament progressed. By the final, he was in top form and played brilliantly, scoring his team's fourth goal and creating the fifth for Pelé. By 1962 the game had become more defensive and few national sides afforded themselves the luxury of two wingers. For Brazil, the picture also had to be redrawn. With Didí well into his 30s, Zagalo was moved into midfield where his influence was such that the transition from 4-2-4 to 4-3-3 was smooth and ultimately successful. With Zagalo directing, Garrincha thrilling and Vavá popping them in the Brazilians were unstoppable. Zagalo scored the second of his two World Cup goals against Mexico.

His playing career came to an end shortly after the 1966 tournament and he became national team manager. Brazil had travelled to England as world champions and returned home in ridicule for performing so badly. It was now down to Zagalo to turn them into a world-beating outfit and one the nation could be proud of. The result of his work was one of the most thrilling and gifted sides the game has ever seen. Putting Rivelino on the left side of midfield was an inspired decision, and allowing talented individuals such as Pelé, Gérson, Jairzinho and Tostão to express themselves as they wished led to some of the most outstanding moments in World Cup history. A decision to play so adventurously was one many managers would have scorned, but to Zagalo it was natural and paid off. He was held up as a shining example of positive thinking at a time when Italian catenaccio tactics had embedded themselves in the international game. It was, therefore, out of character that Zagalo took a more physical and defensive team to the World Cup in 1974. He was criticized for his approach and the 1974 series was one of the low points of his career. Brazil was comprehensively beaten by the "total football" of the Dutch, a side full of flair and imagination.

He then spent time as manager of Kuwait and the United Arab Emirates, before returning as technical advisor to Brazilian manager, Carlos Alberto Perreiro for the 1994 finals. Brazil won the World Cup for a fourth time, but it did not bring Zagalo the joy it should have done. Brazil's tactics were exceptionally cautious and produced some often forgettable safety-first performances that brought much criticism from fans and media alike. The "win at all cost" approach did not wash with Brazilian fans, who believe implicitly in the spirit of the game and after the 1994 victory the hand of fate struck once again. He was put back in charge of the national team and once again his methods were the cause of much comment. He hit back by taking the side to the final, where with the enigmatic Ronaldo on board, they were favourites. Yet, the events that took place only hours before kick-off have gone down as some of the most incredible and constitute Zagalo's greatest mistake that cost him his job.

The poor performances of 1974 and strange events of 1998 do not change the fact that Mario Zagalo is the most successful man in the game at international level. In the 140 games he was in charge between 1968 and 1998 Brazil won 99 and lost only 12. In 1996 he took Brazil to third place in the Olympic Games and in 1997 his team won the Copa America and the Confederation Cup. He was a good player, but a fabulous manager, with a genius that has brought him unequalled honours.

Antonio Carbajal   Mexico

Played: 1950, 1954, 1958, 1962 and 1966   Games 11

Antonio Carbajal is one of the best and most enduring goalkeepers the game has known. In the qualifying tournaments for five consecutive World Cup finals between 1949 and 1966, with Carbajal in goal, Mexico played 18 qualifying games conceding only ten goals. They never lost a game, drew only twice and in 13 of the games didn't concede at all. A supplement published by the France Football Magazine, "Les 100 Héros de la Coupe de Monde" ranked players that had appeared in the World Cup finals between 1930 and 1990. Carbajal was ranked 27. Only two other goalkeepers appeared higher up the list - Gordon Banks at 14 and Dino Zoff at 22. Surprisingly, one name missing from the list was that of Lev Yashin who was considered not to have achieved at World Cup level.

Carbajal was born on 7th June 1929. His father was a baseball fan and wanted him to be a pitcher, but Carbajal was much more interested in football. He formed his own team and, with Raúl Cardeñas at his side, would skip school to practice twice a week. His schoolwork naturally suffered and when he was told he would have to give up the game he ran away from home. He was determined to be a goalkeeper, a brave decision in the days when goalkeepers were little protected by the rules of the game. In one match he had 12 goals put past him and in another he had his front four teeth kicked out, which caused him to grow his famous moustache. Aged 16, he was given a trial by the club, America, but the coach's report read: "He is a player with no future." Instead he joined España and never looked back. He made such excellent progress that he was chosen to play for the national amateur side at the 1948 Olympic Games in London and although Mexico only played once, a 3-2 defeat to South Korea, on his return home he signed professional forms with top side, Léon, and remained with them until his retirement in 1966.

He made his World Cup debut in 1950, aged 22, but the tournament was a disaster. Brazil and Yugoslavia destroyed Mexico in their first two games and things were little better against Switzerland in their last. It was a massive blow to the self-esteem of the young keeper, who had conceded ten goals in three games, but his character was strong and he picked himself up to become the greatest player in Mexico. The 1958 tournament similarly brought little joy for Mexico, though Carbajal produced some fine displays in spite of the sloppy defence in front of him. Ironically, it was on his 29th birthday that Mexico secured their first World Cup point against Wales.

Although Mexico went out in the first round, the 1962 finals proved their best tournament to date. It was Carbajal's a record breaking fourth appearance and his team was only narrowly beaten in their first game. In their second Carbajal came up against the much vaunted Spanish front line of Puskás, Gento, Suárez and Del Sol. He was in exceptional form and conceding only one goal says much about the 32 year old goalkeeper and his importance to the Mexican side. The final game, on Carbajal's 33rd birthday, brought Mexico's first ever win in World Cup finals and the poignancy of the moment was not lost. It was meant to be his last international and he burst into tears at the final whistle, but four years later, in England, he was still in the squad. His good club form could not be ignored. He did not feature in Mexico's first two games, but with progress to the next round in jeopardy, he was brought back to face Uruguay in the final group game. It was his fifth World Cup finals and, as a mark of respect for the great man, the English FA moved the game to Wembley. It was both his last international and World Cup game. A 0-0 draw was not enough to save the team from another first round exit, but it was a minor triumph for Carbajal. His international career fittingly ended with a clean sheet.

Carbajal went on to become president of the Mexican Football Association. He is still widely regarded as the best player to come out of Mexican football and is was one of the most respected goalkeepers in the world. Although Lothar Matthäus has now equalled his record of five consecutive World Cup finals appearances, it is highly unlikely that this will be matched.

Edvaldo Isídìo Neto (Vavá)   Brazil

Honours: Winner 1958 and 1962   **Games 10**
Played: 1958 and 1962   **Goals 9**

Vavá (right) watches as Amarildo (out of picture) scores Brazil's second goal in the 2-1 victory over Spain.

Soccer journalist, Richard Henshaw, once said that: "Vavá ranked close to Pelé as an intuitive goal scorer." Yet, though Vavá has a strike-rate of almost one goal for every game in the World Cup finals he played in, he is remembered far less than his more celebrated team mates Pelé and Garrincha. It was because his international career was far shorter and his place in the national side was not always guaranteed.

The Brazilian public expect to see football that is theatrical, skilful, and played by wizards whose every gesture, trick and spell is performed as if their lives depend on it. Young men and boys spill out of the favelas on to the beaches, onto the streets and into the clubs with the single hope that they may be spotted and whisked away to perform their art in front of the world. In the 1940s and 50s one such person was Edvaldo Isídìo Neto. Born on 12th November 1934, Vavá wanted to be the spearhead of the Brazilian attack, ready to grab the glory by deftly putting the ball past hapless goalkeepers. In those days the Brazilian public cared more about attack than defence and competition to get to the top was fierce. Vavá's determination to play at the highest level drew him on and with fine performances in the league with Recife and then Vasco da Gama, he found his way into the national side in 1952, but was only picked sporadically over the next six years.

He was in the squad that travelled to the 1958 World Cup finals, but was passed over in favour of Mazzola and Didí in the attack. His prospects seemed even bleaker when Mazzola netted twice the opening game, but he was given his chance in the next game when he replaced Didí. Although he failed to find the target, events were moving favourably. Mazzola was not on form and his replacement by Pelé meant that Vavá was switched to centre-forward. Against the USSR, he responded with a magnificent performance that laid his reputation as the scorer of crucial World Cup goals. He beat the "Black Spider" twice as his team progressed to the next stage when, strangely, he was again replaced by Mazzola. In another twist of fate he was chosen to partner Pelé in the semi-final and again in the final. He combined brilliantly with Didí and Garrincha, converting the chances they made for him and he ended the tournament with five goals from four appearances.

Like many of that Brazilian team he became a target for European clubs and Athletico Madrid secured his services. His appearances for the Spanish side were successful, he became a firm favourite with the fans, but his family were homesick and his exile was affecting his international career. Coutinho of Santos was forging a very successful club partnership with Pelé and it was Coutinho who was in line for selection for the 1962 Brazilian World Cup squad. Eager not to miss out and ambitious to be with the defending champions he returned to Brazil, to Botafogo, and ultimately, back to his place at the forefront of the national side.

In the 1962 finals, Vavá appeared in every game, but took time to form a partnership with new boy Amarildo. It was not until the second round that he found the net, but he had not lost his knack of getting goals at critical moments and, linking up with Garrincha, got one such goal against England. He pounced twice in the semi-final and in the final, when the Czech goalkeeper had an uncharacteristic nightmare, Vavá leapt to score Brazil's third goal. He had become a World Cup winner for the second time and ended the tournament joint top scorer with four goals. He may not have been the most renowned player in the world, but was vital to the winning side. In all Vavá made only 22 appearances for his country, scoring 12 goals, but he was still the first player to score in consecutive World Cup finals.

Italy 0 : Chile 2

Referee Ken Ashton sends off an Italian as two Chileans lie injured after fighting in the infamous "Battle of Santiago".

The World Cup has had its history littered with violent matches, but none have been worse than that played on 2nd June, 1962 between Italy and Chile in the Estadio Nacional. The notorious "Battle of Santiago", as it has become known, has even eclipsed the infamy generated by the "Battle of Bordeaux" of 1938 or the "Battle of Berne" of 1954. After the game, Jorge Pica of the Chilean FA said: "The Italians seemed to go on the field only with the intention of injuring the Chileans. It was a rodeo." He was right in part, but the Chileans were far from being the innocent victims of Italian brutality. They easily gave as good as they received.

There was a conspicuous nasty atmosphere before the match kicked off and the crowd hurled a torrent of vindictive against the Italians as soon as their arrival in the arena was announced. It set the tone for what followed and, as the Sunday Times lamented: "In this fracas football was a secondary consideration." From the whistle, both sides set about each other with a passion, often "ignoring the ball to kick each other." It took only five minutes for the first fighting to break out, with Georgio Ferrini exchanging blows with Chile's Eladio Rojas and Leonel Sánchez and Altafini trying to kick lumps out of each other's legs. In the middle was poor Mr. Aston attempting to separate the assailants. He managed to restore order, but no sooner had play resumed when mayhem erupted again. In the eighth minute Honorino Landa fouled Ferrini and the Italian turned round and kicked him back. It left the referee with little option. The Italian had to go, but, enraged to the point of bluster, he refused to leave the field. Aston's decision sparked off fighting all over the pitch, with disgruntled Italians registering their protests in violent set-tos against Chileans only too willing to accept the challenge. It put the referee in an impossible position and gave him little option than to seek assistance. FIFA officials and police officers came on to the pitch to sort out the sorry mess and, even then, it was some ten minutes before Ferrini could be persuaded to leave and sanity restored to the point where the "game" could restart. P70

In the meantime, Aston had summoned the accompanying Italian officials and warned them against the future conduct of their players. Satisfied that he had done his best, Aston let play recommence, but "peace did not reign for long." "There was almost no football during the first half... just rough and tumble with referee Aston attempting to put an end to the battles." The game was constantly interrupted by misbehaviour, as tempers refused to settle down and malice ruled the intentions of both teams. Intimidation was the order of the day and, what little football did occur, the best of it went to Chile.

The worst incident of the game happened some five minutes before the end of the first half. It occurred as Sánchez was trying to create an opening in the forward left position and was viciously hacked by Maschio. Sánchez had obviously paid childhood attention to the skills shown by his father, a professional boxer, and he planted a firm left hook into the Italian's face, breaking his nose. The referee did not see the incident, but it happened right in front of the linesman who, amazingly, did not report it to Aston. Had he done so, Sánchez would certainly have been ordered off. A couple of minutes later, in an act of seeming retaliation for the punch, Mario David kicked Sánchez on the head, leaving him dazed. The referee saw this and David became the second Italian to be sent off. Both incidents were outrageous and it is deplorable that only one had been punished, though the referee cannot be blamed for what he did not see. The linesman should have been more fastidious.

The Italians began the second half greatly disadvantaged, with nine men on the field and only two forwards, Altafini and Maschio. Taking anything from this game was going to be extremely difficult, especially when the quality of play did not improve and the emphasis continued to remain on hurting the opposition. As the game wore on the balance of play fell more and more to Chile and they made it tell in the last 15 minutes. That it took the home team so long to crack Italy's defence is proof enough of Italy's implacable tactics. Chile's first goal, scored by Jaime Ramírez, precipitated further fighting which saw Mr. Aston on his knees trying to physically force apart two battling players. A few minutes later, Jorge Toro scored Chile's second, to put the game beyond reach, and a few minutes later a much relieved Ken Aston blew time to bring the shambles to an end.

The police escorted both teams from the pitch to prevent further trouble and FIFA could only ponder what had just taken place. On more than one occasion, the referee had contemplated abandoning the game, but had not done so for fear for the safety of all concerned. Something would have to be done. FIFA, however, has hardly an impressive record when it has come to taking decisive, disciplinary action and, in this instance, they failed once again to grasp the nettle firmly and take the sort of action that might deter future transgressions. True enough, the managers of all 16 competing teams were summoned to a meeting and lectured about the conduct of their teams, but the players were treated very leniently, considering the gravity of their sins. Ferrini was suspended for one game, whilst David and Sánchez were merely given a "severe admonition". This was tantamount to a whitewash, especially in the case of Sánchez, whose assault on Maschio had been captured on film and seen by millions around the world.

USSR 4 : Colombia 4

One of the strangest matches of any World Cup series has to be that between the USSR and Colombia, played in Arica. It was "like a script from Roy of the Rovers", as one historian has described it and it featured one of the greatest come backs in the tournament's history. Since taking up participation in international sport in the 1950s, the Soviet Union had been quietly making a name for themselves and the team they sent to Chile was highly regarded by many in the know. They arrived having already won the European championship and had made a solid start to this campaign. The Colombians had also performed well in their opening match, though they had made several changes for the meeting with the USSR.

The match began like a maelstrom. The Soviet forwards set about their opponents with the speed of a sprinter out of the blocks and the deadly precision of a blitzkrieg. In the opening quarter of the game they were so over-whelmingly superior that it seemed as if the South Americans would sink without trace. They literally ran rings round the dazed Colombian full-backs and inside eleven minutes had rushed to a three goal lead. The first came when Valentin Ivanov picked up a poor defensive clearance on the edge of the area and scored with a strong shot. Igor Chislenko then started and finished a devastating move down the right that tore through the Colombian defence and, with Ivanov netting his second minutes later, there appeared to be no way back. However, after that initial onslaught, the Colombian ship began to steady a little and the team began to see more of the ball. Having possession and finding more time to knock the ball around restored some of their battered confidence. In the 20th minute they worked the ball down the middle and a stabbing pass into the Soviet area found German Aceros unmarked. His angle was not easy, but he was able to turn and chip over the advancing Yashin in goal.

The second half began as had the first, with a period of Soviet pressure that saw them extend their lead with a goal from Viktor Ponedelnik ten minutes into the half. The score was now 4-1 and, apart from the occasional flash, there was little to indicate that Colombia had the ability to make anything but the slightest impression on the game. Yet, they "showed magnificent spirit, took control as the second half advanced, while the Russians seemed unable to get back on top", as the Guardian noted. They struck again in the 67th minute with the most curious of goals. They won a corner on the left and Ignacio Coll took it. The ball looped over, took a couple of bounces on the edge of the six yard box and, with Yashin standing towards the back of the goal, evaded the sleeping defender on the near post and went in. Yashin was furious, but worse was to come. The Colombians were spurred into a series of blistering attacks as they realized there might be something for them. Four minutes later "Klinger, Gonzalez (sic) and Rada took part in a fine move" that saw the ball dribbled into the area from the left. It was passed across the face of the goal and Antonio Rada got to it before the Soviet defender to beat Yashin from close range. The goalkeeper was well placed to have saved the shot, but dived late. Marino Klinger was now the dominant figure on the park and, fittingly, he scored the goal that levelled the scores. It was made by Rada, who knocked a telling pass down the middle and through a gap in the Soviet defence. As Klinger chased it into the area, Yashin came racing off his line to try to clear the danger. He made a terrible mess of it and completely failed to remove the ball from the Colombian's feet. He fell and was left stranded, leaving Klinger with the easiest of chances.

Scoring three times in eight minutes, the Colombians had staged one of the most impressive come backs in the World Cup. In the final period of the game the roles were totally reversed and the demoralized Soviets were the players who were reeling. Colombia pressed on with their attacks and more than once came close to stealing the unlikeliest of results. Desperately, though, the Soviets held on and managed to salvage a draw. They were lucky and mightily relieved to hear the final whistle. It had been tense, it had been exciting and the whole curious encounter had stretched the nerves of both sets of players. However, the oddest aspect of it was he inexplicable collapse of the Soviet Union and the uncharacteristic mistakes of goalkeeper Yashin, the "Man in Black".

Brazil 3 : Czechoslovakia 1
The World Cup Final

Brazil's appearance in the 1962 World Cup final was as inevitable as it was predictable. With a squad that contained many of the men who had played so brilliantly to lift the trophy in 1958, the 1962 version was just as irresistible as its predecessor. The team may have lost Pelé to injury on their march to the final, but they had come up with a more than adequate replacement in Amarildo, the "White Pelé". He slotted perfectly into the great man's boots to uphold the devastating traditions set by the more established forwards around him. Those forwards had often displayed the ruthless cutting quality that singled them out as the best in the world, although they needed more time to get into their stride this time around. The Czechs, on the other hand, "had surprised everybody, including themselves" in getting to the final. That they had done so was in no small way due to the agility and bravery of their goalkeeper, Viliam Schrojf, though this is not to deny the quality of some of their outfield players. Josef Masopust was "a very inventive and cunning left-half", whilst Adolf Scherer was stylish, hard working and in possession of a keen eye for the game. The Czechs were a disciplined unit and, if a little defensively-minded, were also capable of rapid and piercing attacks that often caught unwary defences by surprise. A

Drink, Drugs and a Goal Drought - Chile 1962

Brazil 3 : Czechoslovakia 1
Brazil's Zozimo wins the ball under pressure from Kadraba of Czechoslovakia.

final that put together teams of contrasting styles, the "intricate and methodical short-passing by the highly drilled Czechs" and "the freedom and improvisation of the Brazilians", promised to be an intriguing affair.

It opened with a flurry of attacks from both teams and either could have taken an early lead. Inside the first five minutes, Kadraba had a shot saved on the line by Gilmar and Kvašnák hit another over the bar, whilst Zito saw two shots sail wide of the post. In the fifth minute, the Czechs had a lucky escape when Garrincha swept past Tichy and crossed the ball into the penalty area. Schrojf came out for it, but Vavá got in first and crashed the ball against the post before the danger was cleared. Not long after, Schrojf was called into action again, as this time Zagalo beat the defence to send in a cross. Garrincha met it with a powerful header which the goalkeeper had to fling himself to the left to stop. It was excellent football.

With both sides showing full commitment to the cause, the crowd did not have long to wait for the first goal and in the 15th minute, it went to the Czechs. In the words of the Daily Telegraph, "Scherer and Pospichal caught the defence on the wrong foot with a quick move." Scherer then threaded an intelligent long ball right through that defence and Masopust, showing great anticipation, ran on to score from six yards. It was a lovely goal, but it drew immediate response from the Brazilians, not used to going behind. Within two minutes, "Amarildo, standing on the edge of the penalty area, accepted a pass from Zagalo, dribbled past two defenders and beat Schroif (sic) with a swerving drive." It was a goal that typified the two styles of play. The Czechs had expected a cross from the difficult angle the Brazilian had made for himself, and in opting to shoot, Amarildo forced an untypical error from the Czech keeper, who was guarding the wrong post. It was the first of three mistakes from Schrojf that were to cost his team the world title.

The goal took some of the confidence out of the Czechs and it allowed the Brazilians to make more of a showing. They began to look "much more dangerous with their quick raids" and the Czechs had to tackle strongly to keep their opponents out. When the line was breached, Schrojf stood firmly. He made three superb saves in quick succession, once to stop a sharp shot from Zagalo, another "grabbing a ball from Vavá's toes and then pushing a tremendous free-kick from Didí just wide of the inrushing Garrincha." Yet, the Czechs also had their moments in what had become a fascinating, totally absorbing game and on the half hour Masopust let loose "a hard drive which brought Gylmar (sic) to his knees." When the teams trudged in at half-time, the 1-1 scoreline was a fair reflection of the balance of play. The Czechs, especially, had "played better than had been expected and deserved to be level at half-time."

The second half began with a series of furious onslaughts from the Brazilians. Within the first couple of minutes, Vavá had two shots well saved, but it was the turn of the Brazilians to get anxious as they failed to find a breakthrough. Garrincha was being tightly marked by the Czech skipper, Novák, and was becoming increasingly frustrated by his inability to influence proceedings. At times the crowd whistled and jeered his mistakes and miskicks and it added to his discomfort. Brazil's disquiet gave the Czechs the opportunity to reassert themselves and they gradually gained the ascendancy, "building carefully in mid-field and then thrusting long through passes to Pospichal and Scherer." Then, in the 68th minute, against the run of play, disaster struck. Zagalo broke free on the left and passed the ball forward to Amarildo. He sent in a stunning cross that was completely misread by both Popluhár and Schrojf, who had come off his line in a vain attempt to get the ball. Seeing what was happening, and as quick as lightening, Zito nipped in to chest the ball into the empty net. It was Schrojf's second mistake.

It was now Brazil's turn to dictate the pace of play and watch the Czechs grow increasingly disheartened. Their mood worsened not long after Zito's goal, when Djalma Santos appeared to handle the ball in his area and the referee turned down Czechoslovakia's appeals for a penalty. It was as if nothing would go their way and less than ten minutes after they had taken the lead, Brazil scored again to reinforce Czech dejection. Again, the goal came from a goalkeeping error, as Schrojf dropped a Djalma Santos lob straight into the path of Vavá's incoming charge. He made no mistake and the game was beyond the Europeans.

Brazil had become the second team to have retained the World Cup and the first to have done so since the war. In the end, it had been down to the superiority of their forwards and their ability to overcome a regimented defence with imagination and originality. When the situation demanded the unexpected, the Brazilians had the flair to produce it and when they sensed that advantage was turning their way, they had the ruthlessness to turn the screw. It was the decisive difference between the teams. The approach of the Europeans was more formal, relying on hard work and discipline to grind out a result. Against many teams such a formula was sufficient, but against the Brazilians its limitations were all too starkly revealed. It was prose against poetry and the poetry stole the prize. Yet, the Czechs should be applauded for their bravery and doggedness. They had, in the words of the Guardian, "put up a magnificent fight and made a big contribution to a splendid game."

Statistics - Chile 1962

GROUP ONE

Arica, May 30th - Estadio Carlos Dittborn

2 (0) URUGUAY

Cubilla 57, Sacia 73

Sosa, Troche, Emilia Alvarez, Eliseo Alvarez, Mendez, Gonsalves, Cubilla, Rocha, Langon, Sacia, Pérez.

1 (1) COLOMBIA

Zuluaga (pen)20

Sánchez, Zuluaga, J.González, López, Echeverri, Silva, Coll, Aceros, Klinger, Gamboa, Arias.

Referee: Albert Dorogy (Hungary)
Attendance: 7.908

Arica, May 31st - Estadio Carlos Dittborn

2 (0) SOVIET UNION

Ivanov 60, Ponedelnik 85

Yashin, Dubinski, Ostrovski, Voronin, Maslenkin, Netto, Metreveli, Ivanov, Ponedelnik, Kanevski, Meschki.

0 (0) YUGOSLAVIA

Soskic, Durkovic, Jusufi, Matus, Markovic, Popovic, Mujic, Sekularac, Jerkovic, Galic, Skoblar.

Referee: Albert Dusch (West Germany)
Attendance: 9.622

Arica, June 2nd - Estadio Carlos Dittborn

3 (2) YUGOSLAVIA

Skoblar (pen)25, Galic 28, Jerkovic 47

Soski, Durkovic, Jusufi, Radakovic, Markovic, Popovic, Melic, Sekularac, Jerkovic, Galic, Skoblar.

1 (1) URUGUAY

Cabrera 18

Sosa, Troche, Emilia Alvarez, Eliseo Alvarez, Mendez, Gonsalves, Bergara, Rocha, Cabrera (RED), Sacia, Pérez.

Referee: Karol Galba (Czechoslovakia)
Attendance: 8.829

Arica, June 3rd - Estadio Carlos Dittborn

4 (3) SOVIET UNION

Ivanov 8,12, Chislenko 10, Ponedelnik 55

Yashin, Dubinski, Ostrovski, Voronin, Maslenkin, Netto, Metreveli, Ivanov, Ponedelnik, Kanevski, Meschki.

4 (1) COLOMBIA

Aceros 20, Coll 67, Rada 71, Klinger 77

Sánchez, Alzate, J. González, López, Echeverri, Serrano, Coll, Aceros, Klinger, Rada, H. González.

Referee: José Etzel Filho (Brazil)
Attendance: 8.040

Arica, June 6th - Estadio Carlos Dittborn

2 (1) SOVIET UNION

Mamikin 37, Ivanov 90

Yashin, Tchokelli, Ostrovski, Voronin, Maslenkin, Netto, Khussainov, Ivanov, Ponedelnik, Chislenko, Mamikin.

1 (0) URUGUAY

Sacia 53

Sosa, Troche, Emilia Alvarez, Eliseo Alvarez, Mendez, Gonsalves, Cortés, Cubilla, Cabrera, Sacia, Pérez.

Referee: Cesare Jonni (Italy)
Attendance: 9.973

Arica, June 7th - Estadio Carlos Dittborn

5 (2) YUGOSLAVIA

Jerkovic 21,25, Galic 62,87, Melic 73

Soskic, Durkovic, Jusufi, Radakovic, Markovic, Popovic, Melic, Sekularac, Jerkovic, Galic, Ankovic.

0 (0) COLOMBIA

Sánchez, Alzate, J. González, López, Echeverri, Serrano, Coll, Aceros, Klinger, Rada, H.González.

Referee: Carlos Robles (Chile)
Attendance: 7.167

	P	W	D	L	F	A	Pts
Soviet Union	3	2	1	0	8	5	5
Yugoslavia	3	2	0	1	8	3	4
Uruguay	3	1	0	2	4	6	2
Colombia	3	0	1	2	5	11	1

GROUP TWO

Santiago, May 30th - Estadio Nacional

3 (1) CHILE

L. Sánchez 45,(pen)59, Ramírez 55

Escuti, Eyzaguirre, R. Sánchez, Contreras, Navarro, Toro, Rojas, Ramírez, Landa, Fouilloux, L. Sánchez.

1 (1) SWITZERLAND

Wüthrich 8

Elsener, Morf, Schneiter, Tacchella, Grobety, Weber, Allemann, Pottier, Eschmann, Wüthrich, Antenen.

Referee: Ken Aston (England)
Attendance: 65.006

Santiago, May 31st - Estadio Nacional

0 (0) ITALY

Buffon, Losi, Robotti, Salvadore, Maldini, Radice, Ferrini, Rivera, Altafini, Sivori, Menichelli.

0 (0) WEST GERMANY

Fahrian, Nowak, Schnellinger, Schulz, Erhardt, Szymaniak, Sturm, Haller, Seeler, Brülls, Schäfer.

Referee: Bob Davidson (Scotland)
Attendance: 65.440

Santiago, June 2nd - Estadio Nacional

2 (0) CHILE

Ramírez 74, Toro 88

Escuti, Eyzaguirre, R. Sánchez, Contreras, Navarro, Toro, Rojas, Ramírez, Landa, Fouilloux, L. Sánchez.

0 (0) ITALY

Mattrel, David (RED), Robotti, Salvadore, Janich, Tumburus, Ferrini (RED), Maschio, Altafini, Sivori, Menichelli.

Referee: Ken Aston (England)
Attendance: 66.057

Santiago, June 3rd - Estadio Nacional

2 (1) WEST GERMANY

Brülls 45, Seeler 60

Fahrian, Nowak, Schnellinger, Schulz, Erhardt, Szymaniak, Koslowski, Haller, Seeler, Brülls, Schäfer.

1 (0) SWITZERLAND

Schneiter 75

Elsener, Schneiter, Tacchella, Grobety, Weber, Allemann, Vonlanthen, Dürr, Eschmann, Wüthrich, Antenen.

Referee: Leo Horn (Holland)
Attendance: 64.922

Drink, Drugs and a Goal Drought - Chile 1962

Santiago, June 6th - Estadio Nacional

2 (1) WEST GERMANY

Szymaniak (pen)23, Seeler 82

Fahrian, Nowak, Schnellinger, Schulz, Erhardt, Szymaniak, Giesemann, Kraus, Seeler, Brülls, Schäfer.

0 (0) CHILE

Escuti, Eyzaguirre, R. Sánchez, Contreras, Navarro, Tobar, Rojas, Ramírez, Landa, Moreno, L. Sánchez.

Referee: Bob Davidson (Scotland)
Attendance: 67.224

Santiago, June 7th - Estadio Nacional

3 (1) ITALY

Mora 3, Bulgarelli 65,67

Buffon, Losi, Robotti, Salvadore, Maldini, Radice, Mora, Bulgarelli, Sormani, Sivori, Pascutti.

0 (0) SWITZERLAND

Elsener, Schneiter, Tacchella, Grobety, Meier, Weber, Allemann, Vonlanthen, Dürr, Wüthrich, Antenen.

Referee: Nikolai Latychev (Soviet Union)
Attendance: 59.828

	P	W	D	L	F	A	Pts
W. Germany	3	2	1	0	4	1	5
Chile	3	2	0	1	5	3	4
Italy	3	1	1	1	3	2	3
Switzerland	3	0	0	3	2	8	0

GROUP THREE

Viña del Mar, May 30th - Estadio Sausalito

2 (0) BRAZIL

Zagalo 56, Pelé 72

Gilmar, D.Santos, Mauro, Zozimo, N.Santos, Zito, Garrincha, Didí, Vavá, Pelé, Zagalo.

0 (0) MEXICO

Carbajal, Del Muro, Cardeñas, Sepulveda, Villegas, Reyes, Najera, Del Aguila, H.Hernández, Jasso, Díaz.

Referee: Gottfried Dienst (Switzerland)
Attendance: 10.484

Viña del Mar, May 31st - Estadio Sausalito

1 (0) CZECHOSLOVAKIA

Štibranyi 80

Schrojf, Lala, Novak, Pluskal, Poplukár, Masopust, Štibranyi, Scherer, Kvašnák, Adamec, Jelinek.

0 (0) SPAIN

Carmelo, Rivilla, Reija, Segarra, Santamaria, Garay, Del Sol, Martínez, Puskás, Suárez, Gento.

Referee: Erich Steiner (Austria)
Attendance: 12.700

Viña del Mar, June 2nd - Estadio Sausalito

0 (0) BRAZIL

Gilmar, D.Santos, Mauro, Zozimo, N.Santos, Zito, Garrincha, Didí, Vavá, Pelé, Zagalo.

0 (0) CZECHOSLOVAKIA

Schrojf, Lala, Novak, Pluskal, Poplukár, Masopust, Štibranyi, Scherer, Kvašnák, Adamec, Jelinek.

Referee: Pierre Schwinte (France)
Attendance: 14.903

Viña del Mar, June 3rd - Estadio Sausalito

1 (0) SPAIN

Peiro 89

Carmelo, Rodri, Gracia, Verges, Santamaria, Pachin, Del Sol, Peiro, Puskás, Suárez, Gento.

0 (0) MEXICO

Carbajal, Del Muro, Cardeñas, Sepulveda, Jauregui, Reyes, Najera, Del Aguila, H. Hernández, Jasso, Díaz.

Referee: Branko Tesanic (Yugoslavia)
Attendance: 11.875

Viña del Mar, June 6th - Estadio Sausalito

2 (0) BRAZIL

Amarildo 71,90

Gilmar, D.Santos, Mauro, Zozimo, N.Santos, Zito, Garrincha, Didí, Vavá, Amarildo, Zagalo.

1 (1) SPAIN

Adelardo 35

Araguistain, Rodri, Gracia, Verges, Echevarria, Pachin, Collar, Peiro, Puskás, Adelardo, Gento.

Referee: Salvador Gonzáles Bustamente (Chile)
Attendance: 18.715

Viña del Mar, June 7th - Estadio Sausalito

3 (2) MEXICO

Díaz 10, Del Aguila 29, H. Hernández (pen)89

Carbajal, Del Muro, Cardeñas, Sepulveda, Jauregui, Reyes, Najera, Del Aguila, H. Hernández, A. Hernández, Díaz.

1 (1) CZECHOSLOVAKIA

Masek 1

Schrojf, Lala, Novak, Pluskal, Poplukár, Masopust, Štibranyi, Scherer, Kvašnák, Adamec, Masek.

Referee: Gottfried Dienst (Switzerland)
Attendance: 10.648

	P	W	D	L	F	A	Pts
Brazil	3	2	1	0	4	1	5
Czech	3	1	1	1	2	3	3
Mexico	3	1	0	2	3	4	2
Spain	3	1	0	2	2	3	2

GROUP FOUR

Rancagua, May 30th - Estadio Braden

1 (1) ARGENTINA

Facundo 4

Roma, Navarro, Paez, Sainz, Marzolini, Sacchi, Rossi, Facundo, Pagani, Sanfilippo, Belen.

0 (0) BULGARIA

Naidenov, Rakarov, Kitov, A.Kostov, Dimitrov, Kovatchev, Diev, Velitchkov, Iliev, Yakimov, Kolev.

Referee: Juan Gardeazabal Garay (Spain)
Attendance: 7.134

Rancagua, May 31st - Estadio Braden

2 (1) HUNGARY

Tichy 15, Albert 75

Grosics, Matrai, Sárosi, Solymosi, Meszöly, Sipos, Sándor, Rákosi, Albert, Tichy, Fenyvesi.

1 (0) ENGLAND

Flowers (pen)60

Springett, Armfield, Wilson, Moore, Norman, Flowers, Douglas, Greaves, Hitchens, Haynes, Charlton.

Referee: Leo Horn (Holland)
Attendance: 7.938

Rancagua, June 2nd - Estadio Braden

3 (2) ENGLAND

Flowers (pen)17, Charlton 42, Greaves 65

Springett, Armfield, Wilson, Moore, Norman, Flowers, Douglas, Greaves, Peacock, Haynes, Charlton.

1 (0) ARGENTINA

Sanfilippo 87

Roma, Navarro, Paez, Capp, Marzolini, Sacchi, Ráttin, Oleniak, Sosa, Sanfilippo, Belen.

Referee: Nikolai Latychev (Soviet Union)
Attendance: 9.794

Rancagua, June 3rd - Estadio Braden

6 (4) HUNGARY

Albert 1,6,58, Tichy 8,70, Solymosi 12

Ilku, Matrai, Sárosi, Solymosi, Meszöly, Sipos, Sándor, Göröcs, Albert, Tichy, Fenyvesi.

1 (0) BULGARIA

Sokolov 64

Naidenov, Rakarov, Kitov, A.Kostov, Dimitrov, Kovatchev, Sokolov, Velitchkov, Asparoukhov, Dermendiev, Kolev.

Referee: Juan Gardeazabal Garay (Spain)
Attendance: 7.442

Rancagua, June 6th - Estadio Braden

0 (0) ARGENTINA

Dominguez, Sainz, Delgado, Capp, Marzolini, Sacchi, Pando, Oleniak, Facundo, Pagani, González.

0 (0) HUNGARY

Grosics, Matrai, Sárosi, Solymosi, Meszöly, Sipos, Kuharszki, Göröcs, Monostroi, Tichy, Rákosi.

Referee: Arturo Maldonado Yamasaki (Peru)
Attendance: 7.945

Rancagua, June 7th - Estadio Braden

0 (0) BULGARIA

Naidenov, Pentchev, Zechev, A.Kostov, D.Kostov, Dimitrov, Kovatchev, Sokolov, Velitchkov, Dermendiev, Kolev.

0 (0) ENGLAND

Springett, Armfield, Wilson, Moore, Norman, Flowers, Douglas, Greaves, Peacock, Haynes, Charlton.

Referee: Antoine Blavier (Belgium)
Attendance: 5.700

	P	W	D	L	F	A	Pts
Hungary	3	2	1	0	8	2	5
England	3	1	1	1	4	3	3
Argentina	3	1	1	1	2	3	3
Bulgaria	3	0	1	2	1	7	1

QUARTER-FINALS

Arica, June 10th - Estadio Carlos Dittborn

2 (2) CHILE

L. Sánchez 11, Rojas 27

Escuti, Eyzaguirre, Contreras, R. Sánchez, Navarro, Toro, Rojas, Ramírez, Landa, Tobar, L. Sánchez.

1 (1) SOVIET UNION

Chislenko 26

Yashin, Tchokelli, Ostrovski, Voronin, Maslenkin, Netto, Chislenko, Ivanov, Ponedelnik, Mamikin, Meschki.

Referee: Leo Horn (Holland)
Attendance: 17.268

Santiago, June 10th - Estadio Nacional

1 (0) YUGOSLAVIA

Radakovic 87

Soskic, Durkovic, Jusufi, Radakovic, Markovic, Popovic, Kovacevic, Sekularac, Jerkovic, Galic, Skoblar.

0 (0) WEST GERMANY

Fahrian, Nowak, Schnellinger, Schulz, Erhardt, Giesemann, Brülls, Haller, Seeler, Szymaniak, Schäfer.

Referee: Arturo Maldonado Yamasaki (Peru)
Attendance: 63.324

Viña del Mar, June 10th - Estadio Sausalito

3 (1) BRAZIL

Garrincha 30,59, Vavá 53

Gilmar, D.Santos, Mauro, Zozimo, N.Santos, Zito, Garrincha, Didí, Vavá, Amarildo, Zagalo.

1 (1) ENGLAND

Hitchens 38

Springett, Armfield, Wilson, Moore, Norman, Flowers, Douglas, Greaves, Hitchens, Haynes, Charlton.

Referee: Pierre Schwinte (France)
Attendance: 17.736

Rancagua, June 10th - Estadio Braden

1 (1) CZECHOSLOVAKIA

Scherer 12

Schrojf, Lala, Novak, Pluskal, Popluhár, Masopust, Pospichal, Scherer, Kvašnák, Kadraba, Jelinek.

0 (0) HUNGARY

Grosics, Matrai, Sárosi, Solymosi, Meszöly, Sipos, Sándor, Rákosi, Albert, Tichy, Fenyvesi.

Referee: Nikolai Latychev (Soviet Union)
Attendance: 11.690

SEMI-FINALS

Santiago, June 13th - Estadio Nacional

4 (2) BRAZIL

Garrincha 9,31, Vavá 48,77

Gilmar, D.Santos, Mauro, Zozimo, N.Santos, Zito, Garrincha (RED), Didí, Vavá, Amarildo, Zagalo.

2 (1) CHILE

Toro 41, L. Sánchez (pen)61

Escuti, Eyzaguirre, Contreras, R. Sánchez, Rodríguez, Toro, Rojas, Ramírez, Landa (RED), Tobar, L. Sánchez.

Referee: Arturo Maldonado Yamasaki (Peru)
Attendance: 76.594

Viña del Mar, June 13th - Estadio Sausalito

3 (0) CZECHOSLOVAKIA

Kadraba 49, Scherer 80,(pen)87

Schrojf, Lala, Novak, Pluskal, Popluhár, Masopust, Pospichal, Scherer, Kvašnák, Kadraba, Jelinek.

1 (0) YUGOSLAVIA

Jerkovic 69

Soskic, Durkovic, Jusufi, Radakovic, Markovic, Popovic, Sijakovic, Sekularac, Jerkovic, Galic, Skoblar.

Referee: Gottfried Dienst (Switzerland)
Attendance: 5.890

3RD/4TH PLACE PLAY-OFF

Santiago, June 16th - Estadio Nacional

1 (0) CHILE

Rojas 90

Godoy, Eyzaguirre, Cruz, R. Sánchez, Rodríguez, Toro, Rojas, Ramírez, Campos, Tobar, L. Sánchez.

0 (0) YUGOSLAVIA

Soskic, Durkovic, Svinjarevic, Radakovic, Markovic, Popovic, Kovacevic, Sekularac, Jerkovic, Galic, Skoblar.

Referee: Juan Gardeazabal Garay (Spain)
Attendance: 66.697

FINAL

Santiago, June 17th - Estadio Nacional

3 (1) BRAZIL

Amarildo 17, Zito 68, Vavá 77

Gilmar, D.Santos, Mauro, Zozimo, N.Santos, Zito, Garrincha, Didí, Vavá, Amarildo, Zagalo.

1 (1) CZECHOSLOVAKIA

Masopust 15

Schrojf, Tichy, Novak, Pluskal, Popluhár, Masopust, Pospichal, Scherer, Kvašnák, Kadraba, Jelinek.

Referee: Nikolai Latychev (Soviet Union)
Attendance: 68.679

QUALIFYING ROUND

Europe/Africa/Asia - Phase 1

Group 1

	P	W	D	L	F	A	Pts
Sweden	4	3	0	1	10	3	6
Switzerland	4	3	0	1	9	9	6
Belgium	4	0	0	4	3	10	0

19-10-60	Sweden : Belgium	2:0 (0:0)
20-11-60	Belgium : Switzerland	2:4 (1:2)
20-05-61	Switzerland : Belgium	2:1 (2:0)
28-05-61	Sweden : Switzerland	4:0 (2:0)
04-10-61	Belgium : Sweden	0:2 (0:0)
29-10-61	Switzerland : Sweden	3:2 (1:1)

Group 1 - Play-off

| 12-11-61 | Switzerland : Sweden | 2:1 (0:1) |

Played in Berlin

Group 2

	P	W	D	L	F	A	Pts
France	4	3	0	1	10	3	6
Bulgaria	4	3	0	1	6	4	6
Finland	4	0	0	4	3	12	0

25-09-60	Finland : France	1:2 (1:0)
11-12-60	France : Bulgaria	3:0 (0:0)
16-06-61	Finland : Bulgaria	0:2 (0:1)
28-09-61	France : Finland	5:1 (3:1)
29-10-61	Bulgaria : Finland	3:1 (2:1)
12-11-61	Bulgaria : France	1:0 (0:0)

Group 2 - Play-off

| 16-12-61 | Bulgaria : France | 1:0 (0:0) |

Played in Milan

Group 3

	P	W	D	L	F	A	Pts
Germany FR	4	4	0	0	11	5	8
N. Ireland	4	1	0	3	7	8	2
Greece	4	1	0	3	3	8	2

26-10-60	Northern Ireland : Germany FR	3:4 (1:1)
20-11-60	Greece : Germany FR	0:3 (0:3)
03-05-61	Greece : Northern Ireland	2:1 (1:0)
10-05-61	Germany FR : Northern Ireland	2:1 (1:0)
17-10-61	Northern Ireland : Greece	2:0 (1:0)
22-10-61	Germany FR : Greece	2:1 (2:0)

Group 4

	P	W	D	L	F	A	Pts
Hungary	4	3	1	0	11	5	7
Netherlands	3	0	2	1	4	7	2
Germany DR	3	0	1	2	3	6	1

16-04-61	Hungary : Germany DR	2:0 (1:0)
30-04-61	Netherlands : Hungary	0:3 (0:3)
14-05-61	Germany DR : Netherlands	1:1 (0:0)
10-09-61	Germany DR : Hungary	2:3 (1:1)
22-10-61	Hungary : Netherlands	3:3 (2:2)

Group 5

	P	W	D	L	F	A	Pts
USSR	4	4	0	0	11	3	8
Turkey	4	2	0	2	4	4	4
Norway	4	0	0	4	3	11	0

01-06-61	Norway : Turkey	0:1 (0:1)
18-06-61	USSR : Turkey	1:0 (1:0)
01-07-61	USSR : Norway	5:2 (3:0)
23-08-61	Norway : USSR	0:3 (0:0)
29-10-61	Turkey : Norway	2:1 (0:0)
12-11-61	Turkey : USSR	1:2 (1:2)

Group 6

	P	W	D	L	F	A	Pts
England	4	3	1	0	16	2	7
Portugal	4	1	1	2	9	7	3
Luxembourg	4	1	0	3	5	21	2

19-10-60	Luxembourg : England	0:9 (0:4)
19-03-61	Portugal : Luxembourg	6:0 (1:0)
21-05-61	Portugal : England	1:1 (0:0)
28-09-61	England : Luxembourg	4:1 (1:0)
08-10-61	Luxembourg : Portugal	4:2 (1:0)
25-10-61	England : Portugal	2:0 (2:0)

Drink, Drugs and a Goal Drought - Chile 1962

Group 7 - 1st Round

	P	W	D	L	F	A	Pts
Israel	2	1	1	0	7	2	3
Cyprus	2	0	1	1	2	7	1

| 13-11-60 | Cyprus : Israel | 1:1 (1:1) |
| 27-11-60 | Israel : Cyprus | 6:1 (3:0) |

Group 7 - 2nd Round

	P	W	D	L	F	A	Pts
Israel	2	2	0	0	4	2	4
Ethiopia	2	0	0	2	2	4	0

| 14-03-61 | Israel : Ethiopia | 1:0 (0:0) |
| 19-03-61 | Ethiopia : Israel | 2:3 (1:1) |
| Played in Tel Aviv |

Group 7 - 3rd Round

	P	W	D	L	F	A	Pts
Italy	2	2	0	0	10	2	4
Israel	2	0	0	2	2	10	0

| 15-10-61 | Israel : Italy | 2:4 (2:0) |
| 04-11-61 | Italy : Israel | 6:0 (1:0) |

Group 8

	P	W	D	L	F	A	Pts
Czech	4	3	0	1	16	5	6
Scotland	4	3	0	1	10	7	6
Rep. Ireland	4	0	0	4	3	17	0

03-05-61	Scotland : Ireland Republic	4:1 (2:0)
07-05-61	Ireland Republic : Scotland	0:3 (0:2)
14-05-61	Czechoslovakia : Scotland	4:0 (3:0)
26-09-61	Scotland : Czechoslovakia	3:2 (1:1)
08-10-61	Ireland Republic : Czechoslovakia	1:3 (1:1)
29-10-61	Czechoslovakia : Ireland Republic	7:1 (4:0)

Group 8 - Play-off

| 29-11-61 | Czechoslovakia : Scotland | 4:2 a.e.t. |
| Played in Brussels | | (2:2, 0:1) |

Europe/Africa/Asia - Phase 2

UEFA/CAF Sub-Group 1

	P	W	D	L	F	A	Pts
Tunisia	3	1	1	1	4	4	3
Morocco	3	1	1	1	4	4	3

| 30-10-60 | Morocco : Tunisia | 2:1 (1:1) |
| Played in Casablanca |
| 13-11-60 | Tunisia : Morocco | 2:1 (0:0) |
| Played in Tunis |
| 22-02-61 | Morocco : Tunisia | 1:1 (1:0) |
| Palyed in Palermo |

UEFA/CAF Sub-Group 2

	P	W	D	L	F	A	Pts
Ghana	2	1	1	0	6	3	3
Nigeria	2	0	1	1	3	6	1

| 28-08-60 | Ghana : Nigeria | 4:1 (2:0) |
| 10-09-60 | Nigeria : Ghana | 2:2 (1:1) |

UEFA/CAF Sub-Group 3

	P	W	D	L	F	A	Pts
Spain	2	1	1	0	3	2	3
Wales	2	0	1	1	2	3	1

| 19-04-61 | Wales : Spain | 1:2 (1:1) |
| 18-05-61 | Spain : Wales | 1:1 (0:0) |

UEFA/CAF Semi-final

| 02-04-61 | Ghana : Morocco | 0:0 |
| 28-05-61 | Morocco : Ghana | 1:0 (1:0) |

UEFA/CAF Final

| 12-11-61 | Morocco : Spain | 0:1 (0:0) |
| 23-11-61 | Spain : Morocco | 3:2 (2:1) |

Europe/Africa/Asia - Phase 3

UEFA/AFC Sub-Group 1

	P	W	D	L	F	A	Pts
Korea Rep.	2	2	0	0	4	1	4
Japan	2	0	0	2	1	4	0

| 06-11-60 | Korea Republic : Japan | 2:1 (2:1) |
| 11-06-61 | Japan : Korea Republic | 0:2 (0:1) |

UEFA/AFC Sub-Group 2

	P	W	D	L	F	A	Pts
Yugoslavia	2	1	1	0	3	2	3
Poland	2	0	1	1	2	3	1

| 04-06-61 | Yugoslavia : Poland | 2:1 (1:0) |
| 25-06-61 | Poland : Yugoslavia | 1:1 (1:1) |

UEFA/AFC Final

| 08-10-61 | Yugoslavia : Korea Republic | 5:1 |
| 26-11-61 | Korea Republic : Yugoslavia | 1:3 (0:2) |

North/Central America - Phase 1

Group 1

	P	W	D	L	F	A	Pts
Mexico	2	1	1	0	6	3	3
USA	2	0	1	1	3	6	1

| 06-11-60 | United States : Mexico | 3:3 (1:3) |
| 13-11-60 | Mexico : United States | 3:0 (3:0) |

Group 2

	P	W	D	L	F	A	Pts
Costa Rica	4	2	1	1	13	8	5
Honduras	4	2	1	1	5	7	5
Guatemala	4	0	2	2	7	10	2

21-08-60	Costa Rica : Guatemala	3:2 (1:2)
28-08-60	Guatemala : Costa Rica	4:4 (1:2)
04-09-60	Honduras : Costa Rica	2:1 (2:0)
11-09-60	Costa Rica : Honduras	5:0 (3:0)
25-09-60	Honduras : Guatemala	1:1 (0:1)
02-10-60	Guatemala : Honduras	0:2

Group 2 - Play-off

| 14-01-61 | Costa Rica : Honduras | 1:0 (1:0) |
| Played in Guatemala City |

Group 3

	P	W	D	L	F	A	Pts
Nth. Antilles	2	1	1	0	2	1	3
Surinam	2	0	1	1	1	2	1

| 02-10-60 | Surinam : Neth. Antilles | 1:2 (1:1) |
| 27-11-60 | Neth. Antilles : Surinam | 0:0 |

North/Central America - Phase 2

Group Winners

	P	W	D	L	F	A	Pts
Mexico	4	2	1	1	11	2	5
Costa Rica	4	2	0	2	8	6	4
Nth. Antilles	4	1	1	2	2	13	3

22-03-61	Costa Rica : Mexico	1:0 (0:0)
29-03-61	Costa Rica : Neth. Antilles	6:0 (4:0)
05-04-61	Mexico : Neth. Antilles	7:0 (2:0)
12-04-61	Mexico : Costa Rica	4:1 (2:0)
23-04-61	Neth. Antilles : Costa Rica	2:0 (2:0)
21-05-61	Neth. Antilles : Mexico	0:0

North/Central America - Phase 3

CONCACAF/CONMEBOL Play-off

	P	W	D	L	F	A	Pts
Mexico	2	1	1	0	1	0	3
Paraguay	2	0	1	1	0	1	1

| 29-10-61 | Mexico : Paraguay | 1:0 (0:0) |
| 05-11-61 | Paraguay : Mexico | 0:0 |

South America - Group 1

	P	W	D	L	F	A	Pts
Argentina	2	2	0	0	11	3	4
Ecuador	2	0	0	2	3	11	0

| 04-12-60 | Ecuador : Argentina | 3:6 (0:4) |
| 17-12-60 | Argentina : Ecuador | 5:0 (1:0) |

South America - Group 2

	P	W	D	L	F	A	Pts
Uruguay	2	1	1	0	3	2	3
Bolivia	2	0	1	1	2	3	1

| 15-07-61 | Bolivia : Uruguay | 1:1 (0:0) |
| 30-07-61 | Uruguay : Bolivia | 2:1 (2:0) |

South America - Group 3

	P	W	D	L	F	A	Pts
Colombia	2	1	1	0	2	1	3
Peru	2	0	1	1	1	2	1

| 30-04-61 | Colombia : Peru | 1:0 (1:0) |
| 07-05-61 | Peru : Colombia | 1:1 (1:1) |

Chapter 10

Ramsey, Ráttin and the Boy from Mozambique
The England World Cup, 1966

England 1966

Winners: England

Runners-up: West Germany

3rd Place: Portugal

4th Place: Soviet Union

Total Attendance: 1,610,919

Number of Matches: 32

I was 17 at the time of the World Cup of 1966 and was attending Grammar School in Bakewell in Derbyshire. My father, mother and I had attended the four matches at Hillsborough and we now looked forward to watching the semi-final and final on TV. However, I came home from school of the afternoon of Monday July 25th to be told by my father that a friend of his had rang up to say that he had a spare ticket for the England v Portugal semi-final on the following evening, and would I like it. Well, there was no doubt about the response so the arrangements were quickly finalised and these included me being reported as "sick" to school.

Two companions and myself travelled from the Hope Valley on the Tuesday morning in an old Ford Prefect to Sheffield to catch the train to London. We arrived at Wembley and took up our three Guinea (£3.15p) seats. The atmosphere was absolutely amazing - everyone was absorbed into a frenzy of national passion and hysteria. It's something I will never forget and of course, the result was right. It had healed some very deep wounds for me because I had been at the Cup Final earlier in the year when my team, Sheffield Wednesday, had thrown away a 2-0 lead. As a football supporter, 1966 will always be the year for me - it represents the lowest and highest points of my football viewing life and experiences.

Anyway, after the semi-final was over, we returned to Sheffield on a very slow "milk train", arriving about 3.30am in Sheffield. As we drove up Eccleshall Road in that dodgy-looking Ford Prefect, we were apprehended by the police who enquired of our activities at this unusual hour. When told that we had been to the World Cup semi-final, their suspicions increased and incredulity set in. However, I reached in my pocket and produced the stub of the ticket to Row 4 Seat 2 of the North Stand of Wembley. With expressions of envy and admiration, the police allowed us to continue. I still have the stub - it shows a value of £3.3 shillings but it's priceless to me!

Original contribution by David J Turner of Hope Valley, Derbyshire

The world of 1966 was one of revolution, dictatorship and profound change. Millions of Chinese students were waving their little red books as Mao launched his "Cultural Revolution" in an attempt to stay on top of the political ladder. Che Guevare was exporting the Cuban revolution to the peasants of Bolivia in the hope that revolutionaries everywhere would take up his call to arms. His "ultimate goal" was to "destroy imperialism" and bring down capitalism. However, Communism was not to everyone's liking and the philosophy suffered a serious reversal in Indonesia where General Suharto painted the country red with the blood of thousands of political undesirables and removed President Sukarno from office. Other leaders suffering a similar fate were presidents Illia of Argentina and Nkruma of Ghana, the "father" of African independence, at the hands of their generals. In India history was made when they acquired their first female Prime Minister, Indira Gandhi. She was not the world's first, but it was a major step forward for feminism. In Vietnam, the Communist insurrection had met with a more vigorous response from President Johnson. The USA was now fully involved in the Vietnam War and using the most extreme methods to destroy the Vietcong and their North Vietnam allies. "Charlie" took to hiding in tunnels and led the Americans a merry dance down the Ho Chi Minh Trail. Growing resentment at the rising body count led to calls in America to bring the boys back home.

The Vietnam War had torn American society apart, as did another of the day's burning issues. Black American civil rights leader Martin Luther King was making his thoughts clear on the situation in Vietnam and on racial and economic discrimination. King, one of the world's greatest civil rights activists and public orators, had won the Nobel Prize for Peace in 1964 for his campaign, but his strive for equity and equality eventually led to his assassination in 1968, allegedly by James Earl Ray.

By 1966 Britain had become one of the cultural centres of the world. London was the "coolest" place to be and was swinging to the sound of the Beatles, the Rolling Stones and The Who. British pop music and fashion were breaking new ground, with the mini-skirt and Mary Quant making the King's Road and Carnaby Street the hippest streets in town. Meanwhile, with his campaign receiving an unexpected boost from the English football squad, the pipe smoking Harold Wilson was on his way to a second term in office.

The venue for the 1966 World Cup finals was decided at FIFA's Rome congress in 1962. England, Spain and West Germany had all applied to host the event, but the Spanish withdrew their bid at the last minute. Both of the remaining applications were strong ones and a close vote narrowly decided in England's favour. The fact that 1963 marked the centenary of the FA and that England had been the birthplace of the game appear to have been the decisive influences.

The qualifying tournament kicked off in Rotterdam on 24th May 1964 when the Dutch took on World Cup newcomers, Albania. The Dutch were not yet the football force that they would become, but a 2-0 victory that day came as no surprise. As expected, the end of that series of group matches found Albania at the bottom of the pile, although they secured their first World Cup point when, in their last game in November 1965, they held Northern Ireland to a 1-1 draw in Tiranë. Only three teams in the European qualifying groups failed to take any points: Luxembourg, who conceded 20 goals, Cyprus who conceded 19, and Israel who let in 12. In losing 4-2 to Norway in May 1965 in Trondheim, Norway's fourth was the 100th World Cup goal conceded by Luxembourg, the first team to "achieve" this landmark. Finland, whose own World Cup history stretched as far back as June 1937, made its own piece of history by beating Poland 2-0 in May 1965. It was the country's 22nd World Cup game and the first they had won. The previous 21 games had produced 18 defeats and three draws.

Little of any note came out of the qualifying rounds for the Americas. Argentina, Chile and Uruguay topped their respective groups to join holders, Brazil in the finals. The competition for the place allotted to the CONCACAF countries of North and Central America was organized in a similar way to that used for the 1962 tournament. The entrants were divided into three sub-groups, each of which sent one team to the group final. This honour fell to Costa Rica, Jamaica, in its first World Cup, and Mexico, in its seventh. The eventual winners were the Mexicans who, for a second time in succession, got to the finals having played the most number of qualifying games.

The one big controversy occurred in the Asia-Africa group. It happened because, although 19 countries from the two continents applied to enter, many of them for the first time, FIFA had only allocated one place for the region in the finals. Quite understandably, this situation was regarded as wholly unfair. One by one, Algeria, Cameroon, Egypt, Ethiopia, Gabon, Ghana, Guinea, Liberia, Libya, Mali, Morocco, Nigeria, Senegal, South Korea, Sudan and the United Arab Republic all pulled out in a mass

---

World Cup Willie - A Talisman of Football in the "Swinging Sixties"

Making preparations for the 1966 World Cup, the FA sought an emblem to capture the spirit of the day and identify the tournament as England's own. They called in the services of freelance artist, Reg Hoy. Recalling images of John Bull and the British bulldog and, as he later said, "because my son's called Leo, I decided to turn this character into a lion with a Union Jack wrapped around him." Willie quickly established himself as one of the icons of the era. When asked what he thought of his creation, Hoy said: "I don't think the result's pompous. It's just to show that we're not as clapped out as people think we are... Willie is corn, but good corn." The British public obviously agreed and a mini industry developed around the mascot producing mugs, posters, key rings and the like. Willie was a money-spinner, but sadly, Hoy didn't reap the financial reward. He had worked on commission and the FA held the copyright. It was they who took the royalties, though Hoy did admit to being not too upset by this. Willie was also the subject of a song, which became one of the anthems of the year. Written by Sydney Green who had also penned the minor hit "We Love You Beatles". It was recorded by skiffle star, Lonnie Donegan and proved to be a success in the charts.

Prior to the World Cup commencing the Metropolitan Police organized a major 'clean up' of the city's West End. Their objective was to clear the clip joints and coffee bars of Soho of the con men ready to trick thousands of foreign visitors out of their money. A "clip joint" is a place where an unsuspecting punter is lured for one drink before being asked for money on the pretence that they will be introduced to a shapely girl.

Ramsey, Ráttin and the Boy from Mozambique - England 1966

Jules Rimet Trophy Goes Missing

On Sunday, 20th March 1966 the Jules Rimet Trophy was standing in a cabinet in Westminster Central Hall. It had been brought from Brazil to England in preparation for the forthcoming finals and was being displayed as part of a "Sport with Stamps" exhibition. The exhibition was closed to the public, but such valuable asset required constant surveillance and between two and four security guards were on duty at any given time. They were no deterrent to Edward Walter Betchley, a fancy goods dealer from Camberwell in South East London. He was experiencing financial difficulties and decided that Jules Rimet might just be able to help him with his predicament. Some time that Sunday, he entered the Central Hall and took the World Cup home with him.

Pickles with his owners, the Corbett family.

The loss was a great shock and embarrassment to the English football authorities, who immediately put together a reward of £6,000 for its return. Contributors included the National Sporting Club, the Gillete Company and the comedian Tommy Trinder. However, it was not the money that brought the trophy back, but the thief's own ineptitude. Bletchley decided to try to ransom the cup and made contact with Joe Mears, the Chairman of the FA and Chelsea Football Club with a demand of £15,000 for its safe return. Mears agreed, but also told the police and when Bletchley turned up to an agreed meeting, he was promptly arrested. However, he had not taken the cup with him.

On the evening of Sunday 27th March, a 26-year-old Thames lighterman called David Corbett was taking his dog for a walk in Norwood, South London. The dog was off the lead and sniffing around a tree by the driveway to a house. As Corbett said: "I was about to put the lead on Pickles, my mongrel dog, when I noticed he was sniffing at something near the path. I looked down and saw a bundle. I picked it up and saw it was wrapped in newspaper. I took the bottom off and saw a black base. I took the top off and saw gold and the words ' Brazil 1962'. I took it back indoors and to show my wife. I couldn't believe it for a few minutes, then I got into the car and took it to the police. Pickles saw it first - he found it, the little darling."

Both Corbett and Mears claimed the reward, Mears on the grounds that: "My home became a headquarters and several times the man telephoned me giving me various instructions... He has now been arrested and this is the basis of my claim." Mears eventually dropped his claim and the reward rightly went to Corbett and Pickles. Pickles also picked up a year's supply of dog meat, a medal from the National Canine Defence League and a film deal at twice the rate normally offered to dogs. Bletchley was sentenced to two years at his trial only a few days before the tournament opened. He probably watched Bobby Moore become the second Englishman to "lift" the trophy on the prison TV set.

Wembley Stadium

Wembley Stadium was built as the centrepiece for the 1924 British Empire Exhibition. Begun in 1922, using revolutionary construction techniques, the design was based on the Coliseum in Rome, with a circular design and plenty of big, wide arches. Its crowning feature was the two twin towers that rose 126 feet high and became a landmark that could be seen from miles around. The designers originally wanted the stadium to be red. It was completed just four days before the famous "White Horse" FA Cup Final between West Ham United and Bolton Wanderers. As the over-capacity crowd spilled onto the pitch a constable called George Scorey on a horse called Billy stood tall in the middle of it all and gently coaxed a good-tempered crowd away from the pitch so the game could commence. The quality of the cameras used at that time showed the horse to be white when it was in fact a grey. The first player to score at Wembley was David Jack as Bolton ran out 2-0 winners.

protest. FIFA had already excluded South Africa because of its apartheid policies and the whole embarrassing affair left only Australia and North Korea still in the contest. These two had a two-legged play-off in Phnom Penh in November 1965, which the North Koreans won easily.

Contemporary pundits found it difficult to predict a winner from the 16 teams that made up the finalists. Many felt that the World Cup would return to Europe, though few would have dared to suggest that it might end up in London. Of the South Americans, only Brazil was given any realistic chance. Neither Uruguay nor Argentina fielded teams as strong as those of the past and both were felt to be too defensively-minded to have the flair to win the cup. Some of Uruguay's best players earned their living in Argentina and had not been included in the squad to go to England. Brazil's was an ageing squad and whilst there was new talent in men like Jairzinho and Gérson, several key players had been in the 1958 side and this might work to their disadvantage. Experience, it was felt, might not be an effective substitute for youthful athleticism.

Of the European teams, both Portugal and Italy were felt to have outside chances. In Eusébio, the Portuguese had one of the world's finest attackers and Italy was reputed to have adopted a new attitude. Coach Dr Edmondo Fabbri commented: "We will not retaliate and we will not pack our defence. What we are concerned about is Italy and we will not kill football." The Italians had also gifted forwards in men like Gianni Rivera and Sandro Mazzola, but commentators still believed that they would rely on defence and that this would mitigate against eventual success. Even Fabbri himself was not optimistic. "I cannot give reasons for my lack of confidence," he had said before it all began. "It is just a feeling in my blood." Given better odds were the Soviet Union and Hungary, both of whom had strong, mobile teams, containing players of real calibre, like Igor Chislenko of the USSR and Florian Albert of Hungary. However, the favourites of most commentators were the West Germans, whose combination of youth and experience was seen as irresistible. In players such as Uwe Seeler, a goal scorer supreme, Karl-Heinz Schnellinger, "who would find a place in any world team", and Franz Beckenbauer, "their best young find since the war", the Germans were strongly tipped to go all the way.

There were some voices that carried the gauntlet for England, though not many amongst the native analysts. Edmundo Fabbri had said that he could "see no other country than England winning" and manager, Alf Ramsey, had himself predicted that his team would win, but the sentiment was not widely echoed. This was something to do with Ramsey's own personality, but he knew what he was doing, what he wanted and how to get it. A remark he once made to Jack Charlton epitomizes his philosophy. "I have an idea and a thought in my mind of the way I want the team to play, the pattern I want to play," he is quoted as saying, "so I pick the players to fit the pattern, and they are not necessarily always the best players." He was also a great motivator and knew how to get the best from his teams. He was a firm believer in team spirit and worked to instil it, giving loyalty to his players and earning it from them. "Alf was the best in the world. He was brilliant", Nobby Stiles once said.

The 1966 World Cup finals began with an opening ceremony at Wembley on 11th July, in front of the Queen and 82,000 spectators, who had paid either 12s 6d (62 ½pence) to sit or 7s 6d (37 ½pence) to stand. There was a military band and a march past of local schoolboys dressed in the colours of the sixteen finalists - the real players were at their various training camps preparing for their opening games. Apart from any that might have found their way into the crowd, the only footballers at Wembley were those of England and Uruguay, the participants in the opening game. What they served up was one of the most boring games imaginable. A simple statistic indicates Uruguayan intentions: they only had two shots on goal. England's forwards, unable to effect a breakthrough, spent "the clear summer's night bashing their heads against a powerfully knit, cleverly organized Uruguayan defensive wall." (The metaphor would appear more than once in reports on games in this tournament, though there would also be scintillating football to fascinate the well attended games.) That the English had so few chances themselves testifies to the effectiveness of Uruguay's tactics. In the second half, Bobby Charlton had one powerful shot almost go in, deflected by John Connelly, but Ladislau Mazurkiewicz saved brilliantly to deny him. He became the first overseas goalkeeper to prevent England from scoring at Wembley. Revealing his acumen as a manager, the next day Ramsey shielded his players from what he realized would be hostile press coverage by taking them down to Pinewood Film Studios, where Sean Connery was filming "You Only Live Twice", the latest James Bond movie.

Mercifully, not all the teams in 1966 were as negative as Uruguay and the 36,000 people who turned up at Hillsborough the next day saw an alto-

Going into the tournament food was a big issue. Many of the squads had their own recipes for success and had warned players off eating traditional English puddings such as plum duff and spotted dick. Uruguay based their diet on fresh English fruit, Scotch beef and a secret weapon, "Popeye Pie", which was made of spinach and eggs. The Germans came with their own chef and were only interested in small quantities English beef. The Argentinians wanted their own beef so vast quantities were airlifted to their Birmingham headquarters. The Hungarians didn't like the lamb, beef and fish that was being served at their Southport hotel so, on their request, veal, lean pork and chicken was shipped in.

The Argentinians were so anxious to get used to the UK's changeable climate that they took a 40 mile trip to Lilleshall, Shropshire, just so they could play in the rain.

The Uruguayan team was so impressed by their reception in Harlow, Essex, that they arranged to visit homes of local residents after the tournament. However, when the team turned up for training at the Harlow Sports Centre they were six practice balls short. A request went out to non-league Harlow Town who duly obliged.

On Monday 11th July Martin Wilhelm Becker of Offenbach, West Germany hanged himself during the opening game of the tournament. The police said that Becker had lost his sense of reason when his television had broken down during the match.

Ramsey, Ráttin and the Boy from Mozambique - England 1966

All roads lead to Sheffield's Mecca...

On 18th June, 48 year old Zurich window cleaner, Emil Holliger of Zurich, set off to walk to Hillsborough to watch Switzerland play West Germany. The year before he had walked the 560 miles to Amsterdam to watch Switzerland take on Holland in a qualifying match, which they drew 0-0. Pushing a pram adorned with Swiss cowbells and a white cross painted on the front, he reached the UK on 6th July, five days behind schedule and was accommodated by the Kent Police in Rochester. He reached London the next day in a state of fatigue and by 12th July he was striding down the A61 toward Sheffield. Along the road he was greeted with waves and the tooting car horns of the West German fans, some of which stopped to shake his hand. Waiting to greet him in the city centre were the Sheffield Master Window Cleaners Association who threw him a party and presented him with a giant window cleaner's leather. Unfortunately, the game itself did not go as he would have liked as his team let in five goals. Emil returned to Zurich by train a few days after the game, as he was due back at work. "People have been very good. It has been a journey I will always remember," he said on his departure.

Emil Holliger on the A2 at Cobham, Kent.

About the same time that Emil was striding out across France, an 18 year old bank clerk from Frankfurt, Rainer Ruth, set off to cycle to the same game. The Eintracht Frankfurt supporter's journey went without a hitch and he arrived in Sheffield, "as fit as fiddle", on 12th July. It had taken him eight days, but he found the last stage the most pleasant because it was all down hill. He had enough tickets to cover the possibility of West Germany reaching the final though he would not cycle to all the games. He cycled to Liverpool to see the semi-final, but took the train to the games in Birmingham and London.

gether different spectacle. The West Germans, now managed by Helmut Schön, Sepp Herberger's former assistant, had their own ideas about winning the world championship and they set out their stall against the Swiss. It was Uwe Seeler's third World Cup and Franz Beckenbauer's first, and it was the elder statesman who set up the first score. (See Uwe Seeler profile on page 195). His 16th minute shot rebounded to Siegfried Held, who lashed it into the net. The Swiss had not helped their cause by leaving out key players Jakob Kühn and Werner Leimgruber, for disciplinary reasons - both had broken the team's curfew - and four minutes later they fell further behind. This time it was Helmut Haller who did the damage. By half-time the Swiss were three behind when cute interchanging between Seeler and Beckenbauer saw the latter break through to score his first World Cup goal. "There will be few cleverer goals than that in this World Cup", commented the Times's match reporter. Two more goals in the second half, from Beckenbauer and a Haller penalty, brought an emphatic win for the Germans. The 5-0 score implies something of a rout, but it was far from that. The Swiss created enough chances of their own in this "flowing, free, open game, swinging from end to end." The difference between the two teams was that the Germans put away their chances to produce a score that rather flattered them.

The people of Liverpool turned out in force to see Brazil get their campaign started at Goodison Park that day. There was much eager anticipation, but the Brazilians did not find it easy against a resolute Bulgaria, intent on preventing the South Americans plying their craft. It was often a dirty game and particularly bruising was the

W. Germany 5 : Switzerland 0
Swiss goalkeeper Elsener saves from West Germany's Uwe Seeler.

scrap between Pelé and his marker, Zechev. Pelé was injured in this battle, but not before he had put his side in front in the 15th minute. He scored with a swerving, dipping free kick from outside the area, which goalkeeper, Naidenov, could only help on its way. Pelé had become the first man to score in three successive tournaments, though his injury meant that he was unable to take part in Brazil's next game. In spite of Bulgaria's brutal tackling, Brazil was much the better side and Garrincha, in his last tournament, sealed the victory with a second half strike.

There was a great deal of curiosity among the crowd who assembled to watch the opening game at Ayresome Park, home of Middlesbrough, to see the Soviet Union take on the strangers from North Korea. Everyone was familiar with the capabilities of the Soviets, but the Koreans were entirely unknown. They had been quietly making themselves popular with the people of the North East and their football was to win hearts and minds all over England, but not this day. They certainly "buzzed around the bigger Russian defenders, making them look square and often flatfooted", but they lacked the technical or tactical nous to get the better of their opponents. In the 30th minute, Eduard Malafeev was put through by Anatoli Banichevski to score the first and two minutes later the powerfully built Banichevski barged his way through the Korean defence to score himself. In the second half, the game continued in much the same manner, with the Koreans working hard, but the Soviet Union proving too strong and too well organized. The Soviets made the result certain late in the second half, when Malafeev, running in on the blind side of the Korean defence, latched on to a "brilliantly judged pass by Sabo" to score his second and secure the points.

The next match to be played at Wembley was the Group One game between France and Mexico on 13th July. The Mexicans had previously lost a warm up game against Tottenham Hotspur, but were full of lively invention against a disappointing French team "entirely without imagination, without great depth in defence and with little life in attack", as one reporter described them. French national football had tumbled into the doldrums since the dizzy heights of 1958 and the Mexicans had most of the initiative in this game, giving a "display of neat, intelligent and brave football." Their greatest failure was to turn advantage into goals and it was not until the 48th minute that they found the net. Enrique Borja shot and missed, but the ball rebounded to him and, under some pressure, he scored at the second attempt. They held the lead for only 12 minutes. Gerrard Hausser equalized with a shot that went in off the post to give his team a most undeserved draw.

History has identified two characteristic traits in Argentinian football, the combination of creative and technical excellence with brutal cynicism, and both were on show in their opening game against Spain at Villa Park. A goalless first half, "not entirely without its neat misses and touches of class", had seen some good, attacking play from both sides. The Argentinians were often on the look out for goals, but were equally determined to stop the Spaniards and resorted to considerable force. The Bulgarian referee, Dimiter Rumentchev, ought to have taken firmer action against the physical Argentinian tackling and that he did not only encouraged them. The nature of this defending and the almost non-stop pouring rain combined to prevent either side from scoring until mid way through the second half. The initial breakthrough was made by Argentina's centre-forward, Luís Artime, but five minutes later a headed goal

---

For the duration of the tournament the Sheffield Mounted Police wore ceremonial dress comprising old-fashioned steel helmets and carried lances.

A Swedish journalist complained about conditions for pressmen at Goodison Park when 800 journalists were crammed into a press box designed for only the local press. His report began: "This is the first report ever filed by a journalist in a mousehole. I am wedged firmly between two planks and two cigar-smoking Brazilians in yellow sombreros; and my typewriter is resting on the head of a Belgian journalist who winces every time I touch the keyboard. It means that if I turn my head I swallow a burning cigar."

The Bulgarian team was upset at having to train on an annex to the Chester City ground. In a pre-tournament visit delegates had been promised the actual ground and facilities.

The 'Eat My Own Words' Award for 1966 goes to...

The London Evening Standard. Describing their opening defeat by the USSR it said: "Although North Korea are clearly of inferior class, it took Russia half an hour to assert mastery and they lost control for long periods of the second half. Apart from inside-right, Pak Seung Zin, the forwards carry no punch and they may well leave England without a goal, while goalkeeper, Li Chan Myung, is surely the worst in the group. The Koreans would be hard pressed to survive in our second division, especially in winter conditions." A later report by Bernard Joy remarked that the Koreans "are courageous and industrious as well as fit, but they have not the qualities to match the accomplished Italians."

---

900 French supporters watched their team's opener against Mexico for free. They entered a competition based on their knowledge of sport and had won flights and tickets to the game. In the biggest French invasion of the UK since the Norman Conquest, the firm who had set up the challenge organized flights to London Gatwick from Bordeaux, Paris, Lyon, Lille, Nante and Evreux. On arrival the fans travelled by special coach to a reception at Wembley Town Hall.

brought Spain level. The match was settled not long after that with a brilliant solo effort from Ermindo Onega. His darting run split the Spanish defence wide open and, having set himself up, a "blazing, rising left-foot shot did the rest". Such goals deserve to win matches and the victory gave Argentina the points that kept them up with the Germans.

Following his team's defeat in their opening game against Portugal, the Hungarian coach said: "We were unlucky.... for the team played well and fought well, but failed to take their chances." He had a point. His forwards were responsible for a whole series of first half misses that ought to have given them the game. Instead, the Magyars went in at half-time a goal down and with an injured goalkeeper. Portugal had scored in the first minute when Antal Szentmihályi, between the Hungarian posts, failed to get to a cross and José Augusto headed in. Szentmihályi was injured shortly after and, whilst it meant that his defenders had to be alert to the dangerous Portuguese forwards, it also made it important that his forwards put away the chances they created. They did not and they were made to pay the price. The Hungarians pulled level in the 62nd minute, when Ferenc Bene found the target, but six minutes later the Portuguese punished a second goalkeeping error. Szentmihályi went for and missed a Torres cross, and the ball bounced off his chest onto Augusto's waiting head. José Torres got himself onto the score sheet in the game's last minute when he scored from Eusébio's corner.

The Portuguese had been rather fortunate at Old Trafford. At Roker Park the Italians were similarly fortuitous in their Group Four game against Chile. It was played in torrential rain and the conditions were partly responsible for Italy's ninth minute opening goal. Paolo Borison crossed the ball from the left and, as the full-back moved to clear the danger, he slipped. The goalkeeper was forced to make a hasty adjustment to guard the stumble, but was only able to palm the ball out to Sandro Mazzola, who gratefully accepted the gift. The strike had not really reflected the pattern of the match, in which the Italians were, in the words of one observer, "convincing in defence, but rather disappointing in attack." The phrase generously hides Italian negativity, but their style of play kept the busy Chilean forwards at bay and in the dying minutes of the match Borison scored his country's second to ensure the victory.

The only Group One game not to be played at Wembley was that between France and Uruguay. It was played at the White City Stadium, normally reserved for greyhounds and athletics, in pouring rain and saw the South Americans, in the first half at least, adopt a more "versatile and adventurous" style than they had against England the previous Saturday. Whilst a draw would keep them on course for qualification into the next round, a defeat might not and they went behind in the 15th minute. Manicera gave away a penalty with a callous rugby tackle on Herbet and Héctor de Bourgoing converted to give France the lead. It was hotly disputed, but it forced the Uruguayans to open up and they placed the French under considerable pressure that paid off near the end of the half. Two quick goals from Pedro Rocha and Julio Cortés gave them a 2-1 half-time lead and the opportunity to resort to more familiar tactics. The Uruguayans shut up shop in the second half and the French, willing but weak, could not break the impasse.

A similar story was played out in Sheffield that day in the game between Spain and Switzerland. The Spanish had more of the possession, but there was "little imagination in the Spanish attack" and they fell behind to a Pierre Quentin goal in the 26th minute. The Spanish needed a greater urgency and it turned to desperation the longer the game went on. There was too much over-elaboration from Spain's forwards and it gave the Swiss defence time to organize. They defended well, but eventually the Spanish persistence paid off. Spain's first was an excellent goal, a solo effort from Manuel Sanchéz, who dribbled half the length of the field through the heart of the defence to place the ball in the net. Quentin then had a goal disallowed before Amato Amancio got Spain's winner about 15 minutes from the end.

The last time Brazil had lost a World Cup game had been in 1954 and at Goodison Park on 15th July, twelve years later, they met the Hungarians again. This encounter was to be equally memorable, but for entirely different reasons. It was "a game of shimmering beauty", said one reporter and both teams seemed to want to put the past behind them. On display that night were two teams committed to the spirit of the game and the result was a spectacle of fast, imaginative and intricate football that thoroughly engrossed the knowledgeable Liverpool crowd. It sparked to life in only the third minute, when Bene "took a slanting pass from Albert, sold two dummies in a swift run, bent inward past two tackles and slid a left foot shot into the corner." It was superlative and set the standard for what was to follow. Tostão, Pelé's replacement, scored an equalizer some ten minutes later, after Lima's rebounded free kick fell to him, but the Hungarians were to stamp a convincing authority on the rest of the match. Their football combined "poetic rhythm and flow" with "a dash of gypsy fire", and Florian Albert in particular was outstanding. His performance caused one local reporter to write that if "I came home and found that Albert was in bed with my wife I'd make him a cup of coffee and a hot water bottle." He was the instigator of much of Hungary's good work and not least their second goal. His pass sent Bene on his way and the latter's cross was volleyed in by Janos Farkas. Hungary's third score came from the penalty spot after Bene had been brought down by Henrique and was taken by Kalman Mészöly. The Magyars had totally deserved their victory and the crowd had warmed to their excellence. They relayed their appreciation with chants of "Hun - gar - ee" and it made a wonderful atmosphere to accompany a brilliant game. Brazil's run of 13 games undefeated had come to an end.

The North Koreans had impressed with their enthusiasm, if not with their success against the Soviet Union, but they were about to make an indelible mark on the 1966 World Cup, beginning with an unexpected draw against Chile. For much of the game, the Koreans were "quicker into the tackle and showed better control of movement both with and without the ball." As against the Soviets, they were busy and full of energy, but, unlike the Soviets, the Chileans were unable to use their physical advantage to any telling effect. They were rather lightweight up front and it took a penalty midway through the first half to give them the lead, when Shin Yung-kyoo brought down Pedro Araya and Ruben Marcos converted. This remained the situation until two minutes from the end, by which time the Chileans thought they had done enough to avoid embarrassment. However, Pak Seung-zin picked up a poor clearance from Elías Figueroa and he ran in to score. The goal cemented the growing rapport between the Koreans and the local public and Middlesbrough crowd exploded with delight. When the final whistle went, a British sailor gave his own salute when he ran onto the pitch to shake the hands of the Korean players.

England's Group One victory over Mexico, the next day, brought their fourth World Cup win in 16 games played over 16 years. The significant statistical landmark for Mexico was that this was their 50th World Cup game, the first country to reach the half century. England's tri-

Russia 2 : Hungary 1
Hungary's Ferenc Bene (white shirt) scores their only goal.

1966 was the first tournament to have a special disciplinary committee headed by Mordy Manduro of the Netherlands Antilles. The committee suspended the Argentinian, Albrecht, after he was sent off against West Germany. Albrecht strangely jumped for joy after the FIFA decision saying: "It has taught me a lesson and I won't repeat it. It has been a lesson for the whole team. It was the first time I have been sent off."

Getting over excited at a game, one South American fan shouted himself hoarse. "I've lost my voice. I've lost my voice!" He tried to whisper to a fan next to him. "It ain't lost mate," came the reply. "It's in my right ear 'ole!"

umph was not a stylish one and the players had to spend much of the game "bashing their heads against a deep wall of plum coloured Mexican shirts and dusky legs", a "wall" that was often built from 8 or 9 "bricks". When the breakthrough came in the 38th minute, it was with a spectacular Bobby Charlton special. Martin Peters broke up a Mexican move in his own half and passed the ball to Geoff Hurst, who released Charlton on one of his devastating runs. "His thinning hair streaming in the wind, he dribbled free down the middle, jinking left then right, before suddenly unleashing a right foot thunderbolt." As he later recalled: "I just concentrated on hitting it correctly and as sweetly as I could, and it flew right in the top corner, and we were on our way." In the second half Charlton began the move that led to England's second goal. His pass sent Greaves free through the defence and his shot rebounded to Roger Hunt, who finished calmly. The win took England to top of the group and, whilst it had not been vintage football, they had at least cracked a packed defence and fans came away with more hope than they did from the Uruguay game.

The dullest games played that day were those between Argentina and West Germany and the Soviet Union against Italy. They were both grinding, defensive affairs with the former in particular noted for the viciousness of Argentina's tackling. One newspaper wrote of the Argentinians: "So long as they don't lose they do not worry whether spectators or opponents are bruised by their play." In that goalless draw, Jorge Albrecht was sent off for a series of dangerous tackles, the last straw being when he jabbed his knee into Weber's groin. The incident provoked the Argentinians into attempting to play football and their best spell came after they had been reduced to ten men. However, they were not that interested in scoring and the game yawned towards its inevitable conclusion. In Sunderland, the Italians and Soviets equally "set out not to lose" and "the game died." Italy had replaced the forward, Rivera, with an extra defender, Leoncini, signalling their intentions and it left Mazzola often alone up front, hardly in the game. Their precautions failed, however, and the match produced one ray of light to break its monotony. In the 58th minute, Malafeev ran across the edge of the Italian penalty area to make an opening for Chislenko, who hit a powerful shot low into the net. It was the only score of the game and it was sufficient to take the Soviet Union to the top of the group.

At Old Trafford, the Portuguese, who were beginning to revel in their first World Cup finals, gave the sort of performance that would take them to the semi-finals. Their forwards "showed an insatiable appetite for work" and opponents, "Bulgaria, the occasional shot apart, were easy victims, seemingly resigned to their plight." The first goal only confirmed the accuracy of this analysis. A harmless, aimless cross was sent into the Bulgarian penalty area and, with no Portuguese player anywhere near the danger area, the Bulgarians panicked and Ivan Vutzov's hurried header landed in the back of his own net. This was in only the 6th minute and it told the Portuguese that this was their game. They began to carve open the Bulgarians at will and, although they only added two more goals, it could have been many more. In the 37th minute, Simoes burst through the middle to release Eusébio to score his first World Cup goal and with eight minutes to go, a poor back pass was pounced upon by Torres. He ripped between two defenders to tap the ball home. It left the Portuguese with maximum points and worthy leaders in Group Three.

22 Men and a Bag of Wind

The penultimate set of group matches, played on 19th July, brought two more particularly soulless encounters. Against Mexico, the Uruguayans knew that they only needed a draw to get through to the next phase and they went out to make sure that they got it. Once again, the Wembley crowd suffered a pathetic fare of boring drudgery, as Uruguay shut out everything the busy Mexican forwards threw at them. The crowd, despairing of entertainment, amused themselves by cheering every Mexican attack and jeering every Uruguayan touch of the ball. It did not stop the Uruguayans having their way and up at Hillsborough, where Argentina took on Switzerland, in the first half at least, the pattern of play was almost identical. The Swiss forced the pace, but the South American defenders presented an impenetrable barrier. Argentina's only saving grace was that their defenders were not as dirty as in previous games. The second half saw some change of script when the Argentinians made some effort to go forward, even though most of the play still belonged to the Swiss. In one of these, rare sorties, Artime gave them a 52nd minute lead. The brave Swiss fought desperately to find an equalizer and forced one magnificent save out of Roma in goal, but it was not their night. It was not their tournament and their fate was sealed in the last ten minutes when Onega scored Argentina's second. The Swiss, bold but unlucky, crashed out of England 1966 having taken no points from their three matches.

That night two of the game's giants bowed out of the tournament. Brazil was one of the disappointments of the tournament and were sent packing by the Portuguese who had adopted a Brazilian approach. The Brazilian manager of Portugal, Otto Gloria, had a simple philosophy for success: "We do not know how to defend and cannot imitate teams who put a screen in front of goal. The best way to help the defence is by attacking." This Brazil team lacked the power of former sides, but the Portuguese decided to take no chances, or prisoners and combined the verve and charisma that had made them one of the tournament's favourites with a physical determination often associated with South American play. Thus "in terms of technique and ideas it was a game that was rich", but it was also full of crunching, merciless tackles, many of which were unnecessary and many of which were directed at Pelé. The difference between the two teams can be gauged in the fact that Portugal had a 2-0 lead within a quarter of an hour. Their first came when Eusébio crossed a ball that Manga, in Brazil's goal, could only push onto the head of Simoes and the provider took the second himself. A free kick was lofted into the area and Torres, "the lamppost", outjumped Brazil's defence, headed the ball square to Eusébio, who headed in. It was shortly after this that Pelé, who had been mauled all night, was taken out of the game by a cynical hack from Morais. The loss severely weakened Brazil's attack and, though they exerted considerable pressure, they could only find one reply, a 72nd minute goal from Rildo. Eusébio put the match beyond their reach five minutes from time when he found the net with a shot from a very acute angle. It was because of the rough treatment doled out to him that Pelé decided to play in no more World Cups. "I don't want to finish my life as an invalid", he said, but, happily, he later changed his mind.

Italy's demise at the hands of North Korea was seen as a national disgrace. (See Italy v N. Korea profile on page 200). One neo-Fascist deputy said that defeat by a team from Asia "humiliated millions of Italian sportsmen and injured the prestige of Italy throughout the world." The team was so worried by the reception it would receive that they tried to keep the details of their homeward journey secret. Even so, when they arrived unannounced at Genoa airport, they were pelted with tomatoes and rotten fruit. The players' cars were kicked as they drove off and the police had to intervene

Portugal 3 : Brazil 1
Brazil's goalkeeper Manga punches the ball to Simoes (right) who promptly scored in the match at Goodison Park, Liverpool.

Ramsey, Ráttin and the Boy from Mozambique - England 1966

Goalkeepers have often been made the scapegoats, as when in 1950 Moacyr Barbosa was blamed for Brazil's defeat. In 1966 the Brazilian pinned their demise on another goalkeeper, Manga. He only played once, but unfortunately made the mistake that had left Portugal with an open goal. On his return to home he was forced to leave the country and ended up playing for Nacional in Uruguay. He was a talented player, but for a long time after 1966 a mistake by any goalkeeper became known as a mangueiradas.

North Korea

Tournament preparations for the North Korean side had been long and hard. The players had been taken into the army three years previously, they could not marry, their curfew was 10pm every night and they played an international match every month. Team captain, Shin Yung-kyoo, talking about his team's chances said: "He who sweats the most will carry the day." Jean Vincent, France's centre-half in 1958, had already warned of their skill, but nobody listened to him especially the Italians. On their arrival in the North East the Koreans had been so overwhelmed by their star status that they never refused to sign autographs. Anticipating a quarter-final appearance at Goodison Park the Italians had booked themselves into a Jesuit retreat near Rainhill in Liverpool. Not expecting to get so far the North Koreans had no such accommodation booked and the English FA had to plead with the Superior to allow the Koreans to take the booking. He had been reluctant because the Koreans were Communist and atheist. Fortunately he agreed.

A Newmarket vicar, the Reverend E.J. Edmundson, stated in his church magazine that: "England should set an example to all these foreigners and cut out the girlish habit of kissing and cuddling once a goal has been scored. Now is the time for all good Englishmen to set an example and behave like men."

to protect them. Fans shouted: "Assassins, you have disgraced Italy." Giacomo Bulgarelli, injured in the game could only appologise: "All I can say is we ought to be ashamed." Questions were even asked in the Italian parliament where politicians demanded to know what the Prime Minister intended to do about it. Italy is one of the few countries where such a reaction could happen.

The final round of group games was played on 20th July and at Wembley England took on the French in front of a full house. The French were one of the disappointments of England 1966 and their cause was dealt a major blow when Robert Herbin was injured early in the game and spent the rest of it a virtual passenger. It gave the English forwards much more freedom of action and they thought they had gone ahead when Greaves put the ball in the net, but his effort was judged offside. The situation was redressed a couple of minutes later, in the 38th, when Jack Charlton's header rebounded off the bar to the feet of Geoff Hurst. The French protested that this goal was also offside, but the referee waved their complaints away. In the first fifteen minutes of the second half, the French showed more vigour than at any time in the competition and pressed the English, forcing one particularly fine save from Gordon Banks. Then they began to fade and the home team went back on the offensive. The victory was sealed in the 75th minute, but it came amid the game's major point of controversy. Nobby Stiles, whose rugged tackling had often been the subject of critical comment, had perpetrated "a bad tackle" (his own words) on Jacques Simon right in front of the royal box and the watchful eyes of the FA's officials at the match. It was while Simon lay motionless on the ground that Roger Hunt scored with a shot that keeper Aubour stopped but let slip. Again, the French protested and again the score stood, giving England a 2-0 victory and top spot in the group.

Two further developments came out of the Stiles incident. The Englishman was booked, though not by the Peruvian referee. His name was taken by a FIFA official from Northern Ireland, who was watching from the stand, one of the most unusual bookings to have happened. Then the FA put pressure on Ramsey to drop Stiles for the quarter-final against Argentina. According to Stiles's own recollections, the manager asked him in training if the tackle had been deliberate. Stiles explained that it had not been and that he had mistimed his challenge, going for the ball after the Frenchman had released it. It sounded plausible enough to Ramsey. Showing complete loyalty to his player, he refused to drop Stiles and said that he would resign if the FA insisted on it. He got his way and Stiles played in the quarter-final.

Argentina's progress had already been secured, but the second place in Group Two was still open. It would go to Spain if they could beat West Germany, who only needed a draw. The uncertainty made for a vastly entertaining game, in which each team attacked with commitment, seeking the victory that would guarantee a place in the next stage. As the game swung from end to end, the Spanish took the lead in the 23rd minute, when José Fusté struck, only for Lothar Emmerich to equalize shortly before half-time. Both men were playing their first games in the tournament. The Germans were the physically stronger of the two teams and this became decisive in the second half, when they began to get the upper hand. They had an appeal for a penalty turned down after Seeler appeared to have been tripped in the area, but their winner came soon after, some six minutes from time. Held broke down the wing and crossed low

189

into the Spanish area. Emmerich went for it, but missed and it fell to Seeler just behind him. He slid it into the net to become the second player to score in three consecutive World Cup tournaments. Pelé had beaten him by a mere eight days!

At Old Trafford, Hungary's 3-1 defeat of Bulgaria saw them through to the quarter-finals and ended what had been a miserable World Cup for the Bulgarians. It was all quite easy for the Magyars, in spite of going behind to a first half strike from George Asparoukhov, his country's only goal of the tournament. The Hungarians were not unduly worried by the set back and pressed strongly, causing numerous problems for a jittery Bulgarian defence. Their equalizer came in the last two minutes of the half, when Rákosi crossed a ball into the Bulgarian area. There appeared to be no danger, there being no Hungarian shirt near enough to cause any problem, but Ivan Davidov made a needless and hurried lunge to clear the ball and it landed in his own net. Within seconds Mészöly scored again to give Hungary a 2-1 half-time lead. The second half was largely controlled by the Magyars and in the 54th minute a Rákosi corner was headed in at the back post by Bene.

The Soviet Union had already guaranteed a place in the knock-out stage when they took on Chile in their final group game. To save their players, they fielded a weakened team and were a little fortunate to come away with a 2-1 victory that left them top of the group on maximum points. The South Americans played their best football of the tournament. They fell behind to a goal from Valeri Porkujan, one of the Soviet reserves, whose shot deceived a goalkeeper already committed to the dive, when it deflected off a defender. Undeterred, the Chileans were level within minutes when a Sánchez shot was only partially cleared by the Soviet defence and Marcos was able to steer the loose ball into the net. For much of the rest of the game the Soviets had to defend, as the Chileans pressed forwards trying to find the winner, but the Soviets stole the laurels in the game's dying minutes when Porkujan netted his second.

The quarter-final stage of the 1966 World Cup produced some very colourful games, with the Eastern European clash between the Soviet Union and Hungary being the quietest of the bunch. It was "a game won by two soft goals and lost by an unbelievable miss", with the first of these talking points coming in only the fifth minute. Gelei, the Hungarian goalkeeper, failed to hold on to a shot from Malafeev and Chislenko profited from the mistake. Early in the second half another defensive error enabled the Soviets to increase their lead. The Hungarians stood and watched as a free kick from Khusainov appeared to be going wide of the goal. Their irresolution enabled Porkujan to steel in and guide the ball in with his outstretched foot. One of the decisive factors behind the Soviet Union's lead had been the close marking they had detailed on Albert and Bene, who were not allowed to operate with any degree of freedom. It is very revealing that the one time Vasily Danilov lost his hold on Bene, the Hungarian nipped in to score. It was a goal that brought the Hungarians to life and, for the last half-hour, the Soviets had to rely on the solid defence and the brilliance of Yashin. Dominating the last third of the game, the Hungarians should at least have equalized, but Rákosi, put free in front of goal by Nagy, dragged his shot wide of the post. The Soviets clung on and went through to their first World Cup semi-final.

For the young bloods of the French team, stationed at rural Welwyn Garden City outside London, the main problem was boredom. The regime laid down by manager, Henri Guerin, was getting to his men and they wanted a trip to London to buy gifts to take home. However, their manager replied: "We have come here to play football and are not in England as tourists."

After a night spent signing 500 autographs each on postcards of a team photograph, a West German official said at their hotel in Ashbourne, Derbyshire: "We get thousands of requests for photographs and we thought this would be the best way to answer them. It saves a lot of time but it is very tiring."

One of the highlights for the Spanish team training in Birmingham was the fact that the Delta Metal Club bar had fruit machines, banned in Spain at the time.

Ramsey, Ráttin and the Boy from Mozambique - England 1966

The match between West Germany and Uruguay turned out to be a much more truculent encounter, though it did not begin that way. Things were fairly even in the first half and, with the Uruguayans seemingly shed of their negative tendencies, both teams produced attractive football. The South Americans fell behind in the 11th minute when Haller's shot took a lucky deflection to beat Mazurkiewicz, but they were not deterred and gave as good as they got for much of the half. Things began to turn sour for them shortly before the interval. A penalty appeal was turned own by Jim Finney, the English referee and they went in at the break feeling much aggrieved. This obviously festered over half-time because, when they came out to restart the game, Uruguay's Dr. Jeckyll had become Mr. Hyde. The change in temperament contributed much to their eventual demise as, first Horacio Troche was sent off for retaliation, after he had been kicked by Emmerich, and then Héctor Silva was dismissed for a foul on Haller. Unfortunately, Haller overdid the theatricals, which only added to Silva's anger and sense of injustice. He refused to leave the field and had to be persuaded off by the police. Being reduced to nine men was a deadly blow to Uruguayan confidence and morale, and they "lost heart and, eventually, interest." It allowed the Germans to turn up the pressure and three goals in the last 20 minutes, from Beckenbauer, Seeler and Haller, gives the measure of how they did it. It was an inglorious exit for the Uruguayans, but the blame for it must rest squarely on their own shoulders.

An equally bad tempered match was that between England and Argentina. Geoff Hurst once said that he thought the Argentinians were the best side in the tournament and the English showed them plenty of respect, but, supremely talented they may have been, their performance that day was blighted by a plethora of nasty fouls that were reckless and, ultimately, self-defeating. The West German referee clearly anticipated a hot game and he laid his cards out from the beginning, when he booked an Argentinian for foul play. It did not, however, calm things down. The game and the fouling continued, "a mixture of cold comfort farm, stormy weather, and the Keystone Cops", as one reporter described it. One player worse than the others was captain, Antonio Ráttin. He seemed to consider himself above the law and compounded his misdemeanours by arguing each one with the referee. Eventually, Rudolf Kreitlein could stand it no more and, in the 36th minute, ordered him from the field. What happened next was farcical. He simply refused to go. For about ten minutes his team mates buzzed and argued and threatened to walk off en masse, whilst the English players stood around in disbelief and the crowd sang "Why Are We Waiting?" It took several FIFA officials and duty police to get him off the pitch so that play could continue. When it did, tempers had hardly cooled and, by the time it was over, Hurst had almost joined Ráttin in the changing rooms, both Charltons had been booked, as had Artime, Solari, Ferreiro and Perfumo. The outcome of this dreadful catalogue of misbehaviour was decided by a lone goal in the 78th minute. Wilson took a throw in to Peters on the left and his cross to the far post was headed in by Hurst. "West Ham United, united in thought and action had done the trick for England", crooned the Times. Perhaps, Hurst's own summary gives a more revealing insight into how it had been: "With Rattin off for most of the game, we only managed to squeeze it 1-0", he said.

Watching from the sideline, the match had incensed Alf Ramsey. When it was over, he rushed on to the field to prevent his players from swapping shirts with their opponents. Later, in a TV interview, he referred to the Argentinians as "animals", though he realized that he had been tactless and retracted the remark before it caused further damage. Guillermo Stàbile, the Argentinian World Cup hero of 1930 and previous national team

England 1: Argentina 0
The Argentinian captain, Rattin, argues with the referee after being ordered off.

manager, sent Ramsey a telegram after the game. It said: "I should like to have congratulated you but such an absurd thing obliges me to send condolences in this mournful hour for world football." The rancour ran for months after the event, especially given FIFA's punishment of the Argentine players. Ráttin was banned from the next four internationals and fined £85. Ferriero and Onega were also banned from the next three games and they fined the Argentine Football Association 1000 Swiss Francs. It was also suggested that Argentina be banned from competing in the next World Cup unless they gave guarantees of good behaviour, but this was not taken up. There was a general feeling amongst the South American nations that the tournament officials and referees were biased in favour of the Europeans. The Argentinians certainly felt so and a cartoon in the Argentinian publication 'Cronica' showed World Cup Willie with skull and crossbones bandana, a patch over one eye and a wooden leg. It raged on: "Just as the English Pirates stole the Malvinas (the Falkland Islands) they made a deal with the referee to sell us out."

The most remarkable of the quarter-finals was the one that ended North Korea's World Cup (See North Korea v Portugal profile on page 202) and it was into the semi-finals and two games of totally different moods. The one between England and Portugal was a sparkling, lively meeting, whilst that between West Germany and the USSR produced yet another example of football by attrition, "a battle of dreadnoughts and heavy armour", as one commentator described it. Drab and defensive, and often physical, it was poor entertainment for the 44,000 crowd, many of whom must have wished they had stayed at home to watch the other on television. On balance, the Germans created more chances, but did not score until late in the fist half. This was despite the Soviets being disadvantaged by an injury to Sabo, which rendered him a passenger for the rest of the game. The goal came after Schnellinger robbed Chislenko in the German half and ran 30 yards before releasing a cross-field pass, from which Haller scored. Not long after, Chislenko was sent off for kicking Held and it effectively reduced the Soviets to nine men. From then on it was damage limitation, as they tightened up at the back and relied on snappy breaks to restore their honour. Their plan might have worked had not Beckenbauer, teed up by Seeler, unlashed a 25 yard thunderbolt to give the Germans a 2-0 lead. The Soviets kept the Germans out for the rest of the game and scored themselves two minutes from the end, when a Malafeev header was dropped by Tilkowski and Porkujan stabbed it into the net. He could have equalized soon after, but his header went fractionally over the bar.

"Instead of a war of destruction here was scientific, flowing football played on the ground, where it is always best." This was how the Times described the semi-final between England and Portugal, with sardonic reference to the quality of play in other games in the series. It was one of the finest semi-finals in the tournament's history, fast, skilful, sporting and friendly, and it was 22 minutes before the first foul was recorded, an obstruction by Hurst on Eusébio. There were only three fouls in the first half and this after people had predicted fireworks in the confrontation between Stiles and Eusébio. It was one of those games that could have gone either way, though the English made the first breakthrough. Wilson knocked a long pass into the Portuguese penalty area and Hunt went after it. Pereira, the goalkeeper, came out to make the save and it bounced off his knee into the path of Bobby Charlton. He stroked it into the net. This was half an hour into the match and there was no more scoring until 11 minutes from the end. George Cohen sent the ball downfield to Hurst,

Officials of the Argentinian national side took time off from their 150th Independence Day celebrations to make a presentation to a childrens spastics' charity at a children's cinema club meeting in Wolverhampton.

Whilst the Ráttin incident was happening England defender, Ray Wilson, sitting on the ball was distracted from the pushing and shoving when he glanced up at the scoreboard which had flashed the latest score from Goodison Park. It read "North Korea 3 Portugal 0". He pointed this out to Gordon Banks who said: "They've got it wrong", and they both agreed there must be a mistake.

An Argentine journalist, Osvaldo Ardizzone, cabling his report on the World Cup for his magazine in Buenos Aires, produced a masterpiece of 20,246 words. The problem was that, in 1966, it took 5 hours 40 minutes to send and, at £1 a minute, it cost his firm of £340. Once the report was compiled and pictures added it took up 32 pages of the 100 page magazine.

Ramsey, Ráttin and the Boy from Mozambique - England 1966

who held it up long enough to bring Bobby Charlton into the play. In Charlton's own words, "he just laid a beautiful ball, about a four- or five-yard ball right in front of me, on my right foot and I didn't even have to break stride, I just whipped it in." One World Cup historian has described it as "one of the finest goals ever seen at Wembley" and to watch it replayed on video confirms his opinion. The Portuguese tried to recover and, though they were awarded a penalty when Jack Charlton handled a Torres header, Eusébio's conversion was not enough. The English had reached the World Cup final and the brilliant Portuguese, with their tearful Eusébio, had to be content with the minor places. Yet they had achieved much. As one Portuguese newspaper noted in its summary: "Why tears, boys, unless they are out of emotion? You carried out your mission bravely, and we are proud of you in this defeat, as we are proud of you in your triumphs." Indeed. (See Eusébio profile on page 194 and Bobby Charlton profile on page 198).

In the light of such sentiments, the 3rd/4th play-off was an anti-climax, as if the disappointment of both sets of players was too much to bear. It was played out like a formality nobody really wanted. Even the goals appeared a little forced, as if written into the script to punctuate the tedium. The first, in the 12th minute, was a penalty taken by Eusébio, after Khurtsilava had handled the ball. It was his ninth goal and made him the tournament's leading striker. The Soviet equalizer came just before half-time, when Pereira dropped a ball at the feet of Malafeev. The spectators then had to wait until two minutes from the end before the deadlock of the second half was broken. The winner came from a well worked Portuguese move that involved three of their talented forwards. Simoes crossed the ball, the tall Augusto headed down and Torres tapped home. It gave Portugal a respectable third place, though many felt that their exciting brand of football merited more.

The 1966 final was the World Cup's 200th game and it is an injustice to both teams that it is often remembered for the controversial "did it or did it not go in" goal, rather than for the tremendous game that it was. (See England v West Germany profile on page 203 and Bobby Moore profile on page 196). It encapsulated just about everything that can be expected from a football match and was a fitting end to a tournament that was a heady mixture of the good, the bad and the plainly indifferent. At its best, the football came close to the breathtaking brilliance of 1958, but there were also many instances of the negative features that had begun to surface in 1962. For several teams the stakes were too high to risk losing and it led to some sorry games. Particularly guilty of this were the Italians and the South Americans. The tactic obviously failed in the case of Italy, but both Uruguay and Argentina were sufficiently adept at killing games to reach the quarter-finals. The brazen cynicism of these last two attracted much critical editorial comment in Britain and abroad. The one South American side which can be excepted from this detraction (Mexico is a Central American country) is Brazil. That team may have been a weaker team than previously fielded, but they at least tried to live up to their reputation and the rough treatment they received confirms the respect in which they were held. This dirty play, of which many were guilty was another feature of England 1966. It was employed to prevent teams from winning by those of lesser ambition. These aspects of the game, two sides of the same tactical coin, are to be lamented and that a player as great as Pelé should consider withdrawing from World Cup football is a bitter indictment of the whole sad scene.

Yet, the tournament was much more than the litany of villainy just described. It may have opened with a damp squib, but it ended with two pearls and there were some excellent matches in between. Games like Hungary against Brazil or England against Portugal were real classics, and for pure "Roy of the Rovers" fantasy, no team before had come close to the derring-do of the North Koreans. It would be 1990 and Cameroon before such a thing would happen again. The tournament had more than its share of drama and suspense, with the English and West Germans keeping this up until the dying minutes of the final game. Only the finals of 1950 and 1954 had been as sensational, but neither had matched its tension. Perhaps only that of 1978 has rivalled it since. Every World Cup has names that shine out above the rest, but 1966 seemed to offer a greater depth of truly outstanding stars than ever before: Banks, Beckenbauer, Charlton, Chislenko, Eusébio, Pelé, Seeler, Yashin.... the list could be made to stretch and stretch. Finally, the attendances in England were consistently the best on record. There was no stadium in England to match the Maracana, but no previous World Cup could boast, outside of its national stadium, crowds to match those who flocked into Goodison Park, Old Trafford or Hillsborough. In many respects, England 1966 was nothing less than a resounding success.

Eusébio da Silva Ferreira   Portugal

Honours: 3rd Place 1966
Played: 1966

Games 6
Goals 9

Eusébio in action against North Korea.

Whilst Benfica, Sporting Lisbon and Oporto, have reached the heights in European club competitions, the Portuguese national side has always been one of the games under-achievers. However, in 1966 the story was a little different and all because of an African known as the "Black Panther". The urchin from Mozambique, who could quite easily have spent his life selling peanuts, shining shoes or in servitude having been caught picking pockets, took one of Europe's poorer nations to a World Cup semi-final and touched the hearts of the British nation. His impact was such that they promptly added his waxwork figure to the other footballing greats in the Madam Tussaud's museum.

Born on 25th January 1942 in the shantytown of Laurenço Marques (now Maputo), Eusébio was one of the many sons of his widowed mother. Known as "Ninquém" (or "nobody"), he learned his trade kicking what passed as a ball around the streets and lots of the slums. Running with the desperation that trying to escape poverty can bring, long legs and dangling arms forcing him on, he played football with his brothers from sun-up to sundown. He only had one thing on his mind - getting paid for kicking the ball and being the best in the world. The road to success began in 1958 when he joined local side, Sporting Club of Laurenço Marques. Since Mozambique was a Portuguese colony and Laurenço Marques was a nursery club for Sporting Lisbon, it seemed he would be taken to play there. However, things did not turn out that way.

One day Benfica's Hungarian coach, Bela Guttman, was sitting in a hairdressing salon in Lisbon. In the chair next to him was the coach of the Brazilian side, São Paulo, who were touring Portugal at the time. He told Guttman of this fantastic player he had seen in Portuguese East Africa and that he thought he was worth buying. So, without further ado, Guttman flew to Mozambique and, within a week, had brought back the young Eusébio. City rivals, Sporting, went up in arms, accused Benfica of "kidnapping" their player and their anger was such that Eusébio had to be hidden away in a fishing village on the Algarve until the situation had cooled down. Guttman waited until the end of the 1960-61 season to introduce Eusébio to the side. He was on the bench during a game against Pelé's Santos in a tournament in Paris and by half-time Santos were 3-0 up and cruising. Guttman, realizing he had nothing to lose, introduced the 19 year old Eusébio and, although Santos won the game, the "nobody" from Mozambique scored a sensational hat-trick that put even Pelé in the shade. With his controversial move forgotten, Eusébio began his professional career with a bang and it was not long before he became Europe's top goal scorer, eclipsing players like Di Stefano and Puskás.

In 1961 Benfica won the Portuguese championship and were runners-up in the World Club Cup. In 1962 things got even better. Having won the European Cup five times in a row, Real Madrid were looking for a double hat trick of victories. However, the aristocrats of Spanish football were shot down when a brilliant performance by Eusébio and Benfica brought a crushing 5-3 victory. Eusébio scored twice with two blasting shots. That year Benfica won the Portuguese Cup and were again runners-up in the World Club Cup. In the fifteen years that Eusébio was at Benfica, he only failed to win major honours twice, in 1966 and in his final year, 1974. He won ten Portuguese championships, five Portuguese cups, one European Cup and was named European Footballer of the Year in 1965. In 1963 he was chosen to play for the Rest of the World team that took on England at Wembley as part of the FA's centenary celebrations.

In 1966 Europe's top marksman got the chance to pit his skills against the best in the world for his adopted nation. Using his frightening dribbling skills and lightning acceleration, which carried him around opponents and left them to stamp out the flames emitting from his heals, his football was magnificent. However, his ability brought out the darker side of defenders and he often took a fierce battering. In the quarter-finals against North Korea he produced one of the greatest individual performances of any World Cup tournament. In the 3rd/4th play-off against the USSR, Eusébio got the last of his nine World Cup goals from the penalty spot making him the leading goal scorer for the tournament. An enraptured press wrote about him with fondness and acclaim.

1966 was the only time Eusébio got to ply his trade on the world stage as Portugal failed to qualify for both Mexico and West Germany. In 1973 he was again Portuguese league and Europe's top scorer. The 46 goals in European competitions are second only to the 49 scored by Di Stefano for Real Madrid. In 1974, at the age of only 32, his first-class playing days ended with a knee injury that was so bad he was advised not to play again. He had won 64 caps and scored 48 goals, which remains a record. In the late 1970s he was tempted back into the game by the dollar and for a short while played for the Boston Minutemen, Toronto Metros-Croatia and Las Vegas Quicksilver in the North American Soccer League. However, the thrill was not the same, with every game being played like an exhibition match, and he eventually returned to Portugal to take up positions as TV pundit and assistant coach. The Portuguese public, and Benfica fans in particular, hold him with the greatest regard and his statue stands outside the entrance to the Estadio da Luz. His life story was even committed to celluloid in the film Sua Majestade o Rei (His Majesty the King). He was one of the best and most sportsmanlike players the game has ever seen. His reputation and ability was such that, in the 1960s he became as famous as Pelé and he was perhaps as good a player. The boy from the slums of Mozambique went from being nobody to a most admired and successful somebody.

Uwe Seeler   West Germany

Honours: Runner-up 1966; 3rd Place 1970;   **Games 21**
**   4th Place 1958; Quarter-finals 1962**   **Goals 9**
Played: 1958, 1962, 1966 and 1970

When the Magyar team of the 1950s broke up in the wake 1956 Hungarian Uprising, it was a West German centre-forward who inherited the guise of the "Man with the Golden Head" from Sandor Kocsis. Following the retirement of Fritz Walter, Uwe Seeler became the symbol of all that was good about West German football, until the arrival of Franz Beckenbauer. Born in Hamburg on 5th November 1936, Seeler played all his club football for the local side and had no desire to play anywhere else. He was a Hamburger heart and soul. "I'm just another fan", he said. "This team is my home." Offers came from some of Europe's biggest clubs, but he turned them down. Loyalty to Hamburg was more important than money and superstar status.

Seeler was an unlikely shape for a footballer. He was plump, slightly unsteady on his feet and, on first sight, did not appear anywhere near tall enough to be the deadly striker that he became. He was stout, with a happy, beam-

West Germany's Uwe Seeler heads for goal against Italy in the 1962 World Cup finals.

ing pink face and, like Kocsis, he had a crop of golden hair that earned him his nickname. He was usually the shortest man on the pitch and, with one of his feet bigger than the other, he was not the most graceful. However, defenders who were fooled by his appearance usually left the pitch with egg on their faces, because Seeler was the best man when it came to jumping. He was usually the fastest, too, and the power and accuracy of his heading was exceptional.

He made his World Cup debut in 1958, aged 22 at a time when West Germany were world champions and had re-established themselves after the wilderness years of the late 1940s and early 1950s. He was not the automatic choice as centre-forward, but his fine play kept him in the side for five of Germany's six games, scoring twice. The one game he missed was the 3rd/4th play-off against France. By 1962 however, he had established himself as first choice and had matured both as a player and leader. He produced some of his best ever World Cup performances in a tournament that, by German standards, was rather unsuccessful. He scored two goals in four games before they were eventually knocked out by a single Yugoslav goal in the quarter-finals. In 1966 Seeler, now 29, was moved back into the midfield to marshal the troops and attack from deep positions. The West Germans made it through to the final, but were famously thwarted by the host nation. He scored another two goals and was responsible for making several others, including a memorable one by Beckenbauer in their opening game against Switzerland. It had been his third World Cup tournament and his many admirers had witnessed more commendable performances. The honour of captaining the national side was bestowed on Seeler for the 1970 series in Mexico and he responded by leading them to yet another semi-final, ironically, knocking out England on the way. He bagged another three goals, including one against England, bringing his tally to nine in four tournaments.

Seeler was so respected by the German people that they took his first name as their chant and to shout "Uwe, Uwe" was the same as shouting "Germany, Germany". He was the archetypal West German player - determined, clinical, powerful and with a never-say-die attitude to the game. It is sad therefore, to realize that such a player never won any major honours, either at club or international level. However, he played in four World Cups and he scored in all of them. For a while also, he held the record for most appearances in World Cup final at 21 until Wladislav Zmuda of Poland equalled the record in 1986 and fellow German, Lothar Matthäus beat it in 1998.

Robert Frederick Moore   England

Honours: Winner 1966; Quarter-finals 1962 and 1970   Games 14
Played: 1962, 1966 and 1970   Goals 0

In Bobby Moore, England truly had one of the best and one of the most accomplished defenders in the world. His manager at West Ham United, Ron Greenwood, once said: "We all take Bobby too much for granted. His play is so good that we only notice him when he makes a mistake." Needless to say, mistakes were rarely part of Moore's game. He was distinguished and honest, with exceptional positional sense enabling him to read the game superbly. He had the quick thinking ability to turn defence into attack and give his forwards countless opportunities to perform. He was not the greatest header of the ball and he was never the fastest out of the blocks,

Ramsey, Ráttin and the Boy from Mozambique - England 1966

England captain Booby Moore with the Jules Rimet trophy after the 4-2 victory over West Germany.

but to compensate, he learned to use his physical presence. He was also perhaps the most measured tackler the game has known, and it was because of Bobby Moore that Brazil managed only one goal against England in the 1970 World Cup finals, their lowest score in a tournament they scored at least three in every other game.

Moore was born on 12th April 1941 at Barking. His leadership skills emerged at an early age and were developed by the England Youth Team for whom he played a record 18 times. His early talent had been nurtured as a schoolboy with Barking and Leyton Schools and with the Woodford Youth Club. At 17 he was spotted by West Ham United and was given his first outing in the senior team in September 1958 against Manchester United. That year he played for the youth team in the FA Youth Cup final. Graduating to the England U-23 side, for whom he won eight caps, he was then given a chance in the full England side in a World Cup warm-up match in 1962 against Peru. Taking over from Bobby Robson, his inclusion was something of an afterthought, but wearing the No. 4 shirt, he took his place in the defence and helped England to a 4-0 victory. He retained his place for the tournament itself and was one of the few shining lights in a series that did not go well. His World Cup debut ended in a 2-1 defeat to Hungary.

In 1963, with Jimmy Armfield temporarily out, he was made England captain in a game against Czechoslovakia in Bratislava. It was only the second time he had worn his famous No. 6 shirt and at 22 remains the youngest man ever to have captained the national side. The following year he was given the role on a permanent basis, against Uruguay at Wembley, heralding the start of three fantastic years. It began with a shock 3-1 victory over Manchester United in the FA Cup semi-final at Hillsborough, following which West Ham went on to defeat Preston North End 3-2 in the final. Moore climbed the 39 Wembley steps twice more: in 1965 to lift the European Cup-Winners Cup when they defeated 1860 Munich 2-0 and famously in 1966.

Although Moore had differences of opinion with both Ron Greenwood and Alf Ramsey, his performances on the field were impeccable. As one of two centre-backs he was solid at the heart of defence and tuned the English engine meticulously. Despite the presence of Albert, Eusébio and Bobby Chalton in 1966, Moore was quite rightly made the Players' Player of the series. In the final itself he created England's first and third goals. As he went to receive the trophy from the Queen, he noticed that she was wearing white gloves and that his hands were dirty. Ever courteous, he wiped them down his shirt before he shook the hand of his sovereign and lifted the Jules Rimet trophy.

In the New Years Honours list of 1967, Moore was awarded the OBE and was given the Freedom of London. At the 1970 series he gave what were arguably his best performances in an England shirt. The one against Brazil, in particular enhanced his reputation as the best defender in the world. But "Captain Fantastic" was unable to save his team in the quarter-final and the Germans gained revenge. During the game Moore unintentionally blasted the ball at the referee and knocked him out. Ever cool, Moore picked up the referee's whistle and stopped the game to allow him to recover. The defeat was the start of a very lean period for England who failed to qualify for the 1974 tournament and Moore who had never played in a World Cup qualifying game, made his last appearance for the national side came in 1973 when England faced Italy at Wembley. Suffering the shock of not having made it to the World Cup finals, England lost the game 1-0.

1971 was one of Moore's worst seasons in the domestic game. The Hammers travelled to Blackpool for a 3rd Round FA Cup tie in January and night before the game he went out on the town and enjoyed himself too much. The incident attracted massive publicity and the following day West Ham were unceremoniously dumped out of the cup 4-0. In consequence, Moore "missed" the next two games and was made to sit on the bench for third, the game in which he made his only league appearance as a substitute. The following season he once deputized for Bobby Ferguson in goal when the goalkeeper was knocked out in a League Cup tie at Stoke. He saved a penalty, but was beaten by the rebound. In the spring of 1974 Moore was transferred to Fulham in the Second Division. He had been at Upton Park for 16 years and had made 545 league appearances, a club record.

At the age of 36 Moore retired from the senior game, after a total of 1,000 appearances for club and country. He took up an offer from San Antonio Thunder in the NASL. Following a move to Seattle Sounders, he returned to England in 1979 to take up his first managerial post with Oxford City with Harry Redknapp as his assistant. He remained there for two years and after a year of inactivity moved to Hong Kong in 1983 to coach Eastern Athletic. On his return in June 1984 he took over at Southend United and formed a connection with the club that was to last until his untimely death nine years later. From the start things did not go well. His fame boosted expectations, but an inability to get on with players of a different generation and an inability to communicate his wishes only led to conflict. Boardroom disquiet and coaching difficulties led to Southend's relegation in 1985. Then, with two years left on his contract, three games before the end of the season and with Southend languishing in 20th place in the 4th Division, Moore resigned. He remained club president, but his days as a coach were over.

Bobby Moore OBE died of cancer on 24th February 1993 at the age of only 51. The nation had lost its greatest captain and defender. He captained the national side 90 times in ten years equalling Billy Wright's record; missed 12 of England's games between 1962 and 1973, mainly through injury and the need to try out new players; and only eight of his 108 appearances were not under the guidance of Alf Ramsey. Following England's triumph in 1966 Gordon Banks said: "He was a clinically cold professional who never put a foot wrong from the first whistle in the World Cup to the last."

Bobby Charlton   England

Honours: Winner 1966; Quarter-finals 1962 and 1970   **Games 14**
Played: 1962, 1966 and 1970   **Goals 4**

"If you can judge a person's popularity by his fame abroad there can only be one man who has truly earned the right to be called the British Footballer of the Millennium. Around the world, from Bolivia to Burkina Faso or Chile to China, you can guarantee any conversation about football in Britain will contain two words - Bobby Charlton." This is how Neale Harvey described the man in an interview with him in 1999. In it, Charlton described his own approach to the game and how he got started. His words show the importance of football to himself and to life in general. "I set off to be a footballer and I was going to be one since I can remember," he said. "My family were footballers and I felt the game was easy. I felt no difficulty in controlling and passing the ball - natural ability that I didn't really have to work on. You hope one day that you'll be a footballer and then one day you'll play for England. Maybe you will win the FA Cup, one day you will do this or one day you'll do that, but nobody could have fulfilled any dreams that they have in football more than me. It's just paradise. Football's been paradise to me since people told me what it was all about. I love watching, I love talking about it, I love the administration side and it's just so good. It gives so many people so much pleasure. People all over the world live and die by football."

He was born on 11th October 1937 at Ashington, County Durham, into a family that already boasted a fine football pedigree. His Grandfather, "Tanner" Milburn, a player of local repute with Ashington, was a great influence on his early childhood. The Milburn name was then a household name in the North East of England with George, Jim and Stan all having played for Leeds United. Jackie Milburn, Charlton's uncle, had become the most famous of them all and is still a legend on Tyneside where he played for Newcastle United and won 13 caps for England. Tanner Milburn watched brothers, Bobby and Jack, grow up and was a regular spectator at their ju-

Ramsey, Ráttin and the Boy from Mozambique - England 1966

Bobby Charlton (centre rear) with England team-mates (l-r) Brian Labone, Peter Bonetti, Norman Hunter, Bobby Moore, Alan Mullery, Alex Stepney and Martin Peters at their hotel in Mexico 1970.

nior school matches. It had been one of his uncles who had bought him his first pair of football boots, made of pig skin with thick, square toecaps. To break them in he stood in a bowl of water for an hour and then let them dry on his feet to take shape. By the age of 15 Bobby was playing excellent football and was given his chance with England Schoolboys. He promptly gave an indication of what was to come by scoring two goals on his debut against Wales Schoolboys. By the time he left school, he had 17 league clubs wanting to secure his services. He settled on Manchester United and soon became a starring member of the "Busby Babes" youth team that won the FA Youth Cup three times between 1954 and 1956. He made his full senior team debut on October 6th 1956 as a replacement for the injured Tommy Taylor and, in impressive fashion, netted twice in a 4-2 victory over Charlton Athletic. Brother Jack had already followed the family tradition by signing for Leeds United in 1952.

It was in a very much more expensive pair of boots that Charlton made his debut for England against Scotland on 19th April 1958 at Hampden Park. It was another memorable day and he scored a goal in the 4-0 victory. The most impressive aspect about Charlton's performance, though, was that it came only ten days after the Munich Air Disaster. A miracle had saved his life that day: he was flung clear still strapped to his seat and having had his shoes torn off. The tragedy had a profound effect on him, giving him a greater determination to succeed and he took a more responsible role in the Manchester United side. His rehabilitation continued a couple of weeks after his England debut, when he played centre-forward for United in the FA Cup final against Bolton Wanderers, a game they lost 2-0. In it Charlton unluckily had a shot come back off the post when Bolton were only one up. He also kept his place in the England set up for another three games, but did not make his World Cup debut in 1958. England had lost 5-0 in a pre-tournament warm-up match in Yugoslavia and Charlton was dropped. He travelled with the squad, but Bobby Robson was preferred at inside-right.

By 1962 Charlton commanded a more permanent place in the national side. His position was essentially as a deep-lying playmaker, an inside-forward, with a lethal shot that he could accomplish with either foot. His versatility also allowed him to play at left-wing or centre-forward. That World Cup saw another mediocre England performance, but Charlton took the chance to impress. He and Bobby Moore were the only two England players to shine and in one fine moment against Argentina, he produced a goal of amazing quality from the wing. In control of the left side of the pitch, Charlton charged at the Argentine defence which simply collapsed. Running at top speed, he changed feet and blasted the ball past the hapless Roma and into the net.

In such a glittering career, it is difficult to say whether the World Cup of 1966 was Charlton's finest moment. Manchester United had won the FA Cup in 1963 and the league Championship in 1965. They again won the Championship in 1967, which ultimately led to a European Cup final victory against Benfica at Wembley in 1968. In his own words Charlton reflected that: "In fact, the World Cup wasn't even on the agenda when I first started playing... My greatest memories? Yes, winning the World Cup in 1966 was a bit special. When you think about it, it takes a bit of doing. With Manchester United it was in 1968 but, funnily enough, 1966 was a bit easier than 1968. In 1966, we only won a three-week tournament! We didn't have to qualify and it was in England, but to get to the European Cup you had to win your league the year before and the whole thing takes two years which is a lot more difficult. In the World Cup it's the quality of the players you come up against that is the difference."

When England came up against Portugal in the semi-final, as Banks recalled, he "gave the performance of his life, moving with the grace of a ballet dancer and the power of a panther." The same year Charlton was named English and European Player of the year.

On 21st April 1970 at the age of 32, and just prior to the Mexico World Cup tournament, Charlton won his 100th cap against Northern Ireland at Wembley. Needless to say he scored in the 3-1 victory. He then went on to play in all four of England's games in Mexico, but was substituted in two. England's final match in the tournament was also Charlton's international swan song. He was replaced by Colin Bell, a move that some commentators believed was a mistake and blamed for the defeat. In the 17 years Charlton played in an England shirt, he captained the side twice in Bobby Moore's absence, against Romania in 1969 and Holland in 1970. His total of 106 caps took him past the record set by Billy Wright, but it didn't last long as Bobby Moore later recorded 108 caps and Peter Shilton notched up the current record of 125. However, Charlton did score a record 49 international goals.

Charlton left Manchester United in 1973, having been captain since 1968. He had made 606 senior appearances and scored 199 goals. He moved on to Preston North End for whom he appeared 38 times as a player-manager, scoring eight goals. Not all great players make the transition to management and Charlton's time at Deepdale was disappointing. He eventually resigned after a disagreement with the Board of Directors over the sale of a player and, after a spell as caretaker-manager of Wigan Athletic, serving also on the Board, he returned to Manchester United as a director, where he set up a School of Excellence to teach youngsters the game.

Bobby Charlton has now been involved in the game for over 45 years. His contribution to Manchester United and his work for his country in attempting to bring the World Cup finals back to England are more than admirable. His passion for his club and country are born out of his passion for the game. He was awarded the OBE in 1967 and was knighted in 1994.

Italy 0 : North Korea 1

Pak Doo-ik scores North Korea's first and winning goal.

Following a game that produced one of the greatest of all World Cup shocks, the British press went into purple prose to describe the occasion. "We came expecting the inevitable. We left having witnessed the impossible - or what had seemed so," went the Times. The Guardian correspondent put it this way: "Incredibly the little men from North of the 38th parallel, whose only previous success in the World Cup was two victories over Australia, beat Italy, one of the world's most expensive and complex sides." In Italy it was all so very different. The paper, Il Messagero said that it "is necessary to clean house in the Soccer world, dismissing all those responsible for the mortifying defeat," whilst La Nazione spoke of "the decadence of Italian football is but one aspect of the more sweeping decadence of our entire country." It was as if a national crisis had occurred and it was caused by an army dentist by the name of Pak Doo-ik.

The Italians had made several changes to their line up in the hope of finding the goals so far lacking. If they were to qualify, they would need these in plenty and the game certainly began brightly enough for them. For the first half-hour they dominated proceedings and created enough chances to have put the game out of their opponents' reach. At one point, Perani was put through with a splendid pass, but his shot was tame and easily dealt with. Such was the story of Italy's play. All too often their forwards were ineffectual or simply crowded out by a busy Korean defence, which moved swiftly to deny the Italians space and freedom of manoeuvre.

The game began to turn against Italy in the last quarter of the first half. With about ten minutes remaining, Bulgarelli fouled Pak Seung-zin and hurt his own knee in the process. He was forced to leave the field and his departure was decisive. He had been the lynchpin of the Italian defence and without him it lost much of its shape and composure. It presented the Koreans with an opportunity they took with aplomb. Some three minutes before the interval a Korean attack seemed to have been broken up, but the ball was only half cleared. With Rivera waiting for the ball to drop to him, he was beaten to it by Pak Seung-zin, who headed the ball forward into Italian territory. It was picked up by Im Seung-hwi, who played a quick pass to Pak Doo-ik and he slammed it past Albertosi into the Italian goal. The Middlesbrough crowd went delirious and the Italians trudged off the field a short time later in a state of some shock.

They came out for the second period in a more determined frame of mind and Facchetti, Landini and Mazzola worked tirelessly to encourage the team forward. Not long after the restart, Rivera, "with a splendid burst of individualism, flicked the ball over his head to beat one man, accelerated past two more, and sent in a superb shot which the goalkeeper almost nonchalantly fisted over the top." This was typical of many Italian attacks. Try as they might, they could not break the resolute Koreans, who were equally keen to extend their lead. They created two passable chances that might have yielded goals and at one point, in his exuberance, Han Bong-zin chased a loose ball down the right, collided with the corner flag and broke it in two. The longer the game went on the more disconsolate the Italians became. As one reporter noted, "once behind their sole hope rested with the individual brilliance of Rivera, and once he faded they looked a well beaten side." It summed it up perfectly. Italy's failure to score was not because the Koreans defended excessively, it was because their forwards were ineffective and Korea's goalkeeper, Li Chang-myung, was good. They contributed as much to their own downfall as the Koreans did. When the final whistle went, it was the Koreans who celebrated and the Italians had to plan their journey home. For them, the World Cup was over.

Since that game, much has been written about the legendary giant killing of the North Koreans of 1966 and some of this has tended towards the patronizing. Great teams do fall to little teams and the overriding point about the Koreans was that they were an unknown quantity, not a poor side. They were a "fast and fit" team, that contained some very talented players and, in Pak Seung-zin, possessed one of the hardest shots in the tournament. They were a team that believed in the virtues of attack as the way to scoring goals. "Their success," one analyst mused, was "based on three things - speed, fitness and the inherent oriental ability to learn quickly, copy and adapt." They did this well and the result was no flash in the pan. They had merely done what they were capable of doing. The Italians had not played badly. They had just not played well and lacked confidence at the crucial moments. As goalkeeper, Enrico Albertosi, said afterwards: "It was an unlucky game. If we played another 20 times we would win them all!" Perhaps the last words on the debacle should be those of Vittorio Pozzo: "It is in the head and the heart. It is their frame of mind and they do not fight. It is incomprehensible because they fought for me before the war."

North Korea 3 : Portugal 5

The 1966 North Korean team.

On 24th July, 1966 51,780 expectant football supporters crammed into Goodison Park to see the well-tuned professionals of Portugal take on a team that was relatively unknown. Portugal's own passage to this stage of the World Cup was entirely more predictable. Theirs was a team brimming with talented individuals, who blended together into a disciplined and well-oiled unit. The jewel in the Portuguese crown, undoubtedly, was Eusébio, a supremely gifted and charismatic player, sharp, quick and deadly. He was one of the stars of 1966, was instrumental to his team's progress thus far and now he faced the challenge of the unpredictable North Koreans

The match had an amazingly explosive start and, according to the Guardian: "for half an hour the Koreans shook the world let alone Portugal and the glory was all theirs." They were "clever, methodical and disrespectful," and set their stall out as early as the first minute, when a move begun by Im Seung-hwi was finished by Pak Seung-zin. His left foot drive from the edge of the area delighted the crowd and woke the Portuguese up to the fact that they were in a game of football. Some twenty minutes later, they were two goals up when Pereira, Portugal's goalkeeper, misjudged a cross and Li Dong-woo was on had to take advantage of the mistake. The crowd burst out into chants of "We Want Three" and three minutes later Yang Sung-kook duly obliged with a superb individual effort.

For the Koreans to have gone 3-0 up inside 25 minutes was more than anybody could have believed. Yet, the Portuguese appeared almost nonchalant about their situation and Korea's third goal was what they needed to pull them out of their indifference. Or, to put it more precisely, it was what was needed to awaken Eusébio to lead his team out of their predicament. As the Times reporter put it: "it was Eusébio alone, with his sixth sense for popping up exactly where he is most needed, and his immense flair for seizing the fleeting chance, who finally restored their fortunes." This said, the Koreans had a hand in their own downfall because they did not know how to close a game down. They kept trying to attack and it gave Eusébio the opportunity to weave his magic. A more experienced side would never have allowed it to happen. In the words of one reporter: "The Koreans were supposed to have evolved some plan for keeping him quiet, but they were so busy scoring goals, they forgot about Eusébio."

The turning point came after half an hour. Augusto knocked a long through ball for Eusébio to sprint on to and he scored his first. He then missed two easier chances before getting his second, three minutes before half-time. Torres was tripped from behind in the area by Oh Yoon-kyung and it was Eusébio who netted the penalty. The Portuguese were back in the game and were beginning to look the likely winners.

The second half belonged almost exclusively to Portugal, whose attacks proved sharp and incisive, and which took full advantage of the Koreans' desire to get forward whenever they could. In the 57th minute Eusébio received a pass from Simoes and levelled the scores with his hat trick. Three minutes later, he went on a solo run through the heart of the Korean defence and was brought down by Shin Yung-kyoo. He converted the penalty he had won for his fourth goal and Portugal had the lead that, once taken, they would never yield. Portugal's fifth and final goal came from a Eusébio corner. Torres, on the front post, headed it back for Augusto to score.

It had been a splendid game, epitomized by flowing, attacking football from both teams, full of excitement and incident, played out in a sporting manner, and possessing a fairy tale element to add an air of unreality to a special occasion. For a while, it looked as if Korea's dream might just happen until Eusébio stepped in to burst the bubble and return Starship Wonderland to earth. The North Koreans had come to England, played some lovely football and stolen some hearts. However, they lacked the tactical nous needed to capitalize on their sparkling achievement. Sometimes good football is not enough and a little extra is needed. Portugal had it and, to use the words of the Guardian correspondent: "In the end, however, experience and professionalism carried the day."

England 4 : West Germany 2
The World Cup Final

England's Martin Peters in a heading dual with Weber of West Germany.

An eerie atmosphere preceded this final. As the kick off hour approached an air of uneasy expectancy hung over Wembley Stadium, as over the whole country, like a leaden mantle, with the weather seeming to encapsulate the mood. There was thunder and lightening, "like some celestial orchestra playing 'The Ride of the Valkyries'... with thunderheads massing lividly, thunder shaking the giant stadium, lightening stitching the purple skies and finally the sun peeping out." "Nature imitating art", went the Daily Mirror. The parade of the players was followed by one of the most emotional renderings of "God Save the Queen" and then it all began.

Albeit unknowingly, the Germans made a tactical switch before the game that was to inhibit their style and greatly reduce their chance of victory. Franz Beckenbauer, their play maker par excellence, had been detailed to defensive duties, minding Bobby Charlton, and it weakened the German midfield. They were to sorely miss his inspiration.

With the caution of two heavy weight boxers prying and searching out each other's weaknesses, the two teams probed and tested in the early minutes of the game. Martin Peters forced one fine save out of Tilkowski in goal, but just when the game appeared about to settle into a pattern, it sprung into action and the reticence disappeared, never to return. A long diagonal cross into the England area was met by Ray Wilson. His header was weak, "probably his only serious lapse in the whole tournament", and the ball fell to the feet of Helmut Haller, whose firm shot gave the Germans the lead. The game was 12 minutes old. A lesser team might have been unnerved, but the English stuck to their task and some five minutes later, Bobby Moore was edging forwards when he was fouled by Wolfgang Overath. The free kick was quickly taken and as the ball arched into the area, Geoff Hurst backed away from his marker to give himself a free header into the goal.

It ended the scoring for the next hour, but not of the pulsating rhythm of the game. Both sets of players gave total commitment and the surprise was that there were no more goals for so long. As the Germans finished the first half strongly, Banks had to make splendid saves to deny Lothar Emmerich and Overath, and the half-time break came as a relief to give the English time to regroup. They came out refreshed and gradually began to turn the game in their favour. Moore, "the game's outstanding performer" according to the Guardian, kept things cool at the back, whilst providing a springboard from which his forwards could operate. They combined exuberance with skill and imagination, and in the 78th minute their industry got its just deserts. Alan Ball's corner found its way to Hurst, lurking just outside the penalty area, and his low shot took a cruel deflection off Horst-Dieter Höttges into the path of the unmarked Peters. He fired home gleefully. The English were in front, but knew that the next 12 minutes would test their resolve to its limit and, in the tensest of atmospheres, they steeled themselves for the onslaught. The mood was poignantly captured by one spectator: "Players were gesturing and shouting to each other. The crowd were screaming, singing, bellowing senselessly. The heart was pumping unbearably."

As the minutes, then the seconds counted down, it seemed that the task had been accomplished. Then, in injury time, Jack Charlton beat Siegfried Held to a cross to head the ball away. It looked clean, but the referee blew for a foul. Emmerich took the free kick and in a moment of confusion that saw the ball ricochet around the goal mouth, Wolfgang Weber stuck out a foot and the scores were level. It was the most deflating moment and before setting his weary team off for the extra time, Ramsey gave his inspirational and immortal exhortation: "You've beaten them once this afternoon. Now you've got to go out and do it again." "Look at them. They're finished", he said and the team went out ready to die for their boss. It was also then that their greater fitness began to tell. Stiles and Ball, in particular, worked until "they were entitled to drop" and their relentless energy galvanized the rest and contributed greatly to their ultimate victory. Ball, socks around his ankles, was like a terrier. Years later, Stiles fondly recalled his room mate's jocular exhortations and the way it motivated those around him, as his own legs appeared on the verge of giving way. At one point in the second period, Stiles tried to cross a ball, but tiredness meant that his effort "just trickled over the dead ball line, and I couldn't move. I always remember little Bally running past me and he says, 'Move you little bastard'... and he made me go, because he was everywhere that day."

It was Ball who set up England's controversial third goal. He chased a long, seemingly hopeless pass into the right corner by the flag, collected it and knocked it into the penalty area, slightly behind Hurst. As the West Ham man described it: "I had to turn on it and take a few strides to get my footing." He hit it hard against the underside of the bar and it came down, to the Germans in front of the line, to the English behind it. Hurst himself had no doubt - "it went miles in", he said. Neither had Roger Hunt, who instead of reacting to make sure the ball was in the net, simply turned, arms aloft, and moved away. The Russian linesman shared his opinion and the goal stood. It left the Germans broken and, though they did all they could to fight back, were a spent force. Hurst made certain of the result in the last minute, when Moore, "cool as ever under pressure", launched a long clearance for his forward to chase. "All I wanted to do was hit it as hard as I possibly could", said Hurst, summoning up his last reserves of energy and believing that if he missed and planted the ball in the crowd, it would waste a few valuable seconds. Instead, it steamed into the net, prompting Kenneth Wolstenholme's unforgetable words and sparking celebrations of the kind not seen in England since 1945. At the fifth attempt, "the country that gave football to the world had finally won the World Cup."

Statistics - England 1966

GROUP ONE

London, July 11th - Wembley Stadium

0 (0) ENGLAND

Banks, Cohen, Wilson, Stiles, J.Charlton, Moore, Ball, Greaves, R.Charlton, Hunt, Connelly.

0 (0) URUGUAY

Mazurkiewicz, Troche, Manicera, Ubinas, Goncálves, Caetano, Cortés, Viera, Silva, Rocha, Pérez.

Referee: Istvan Zsolt (Hungary)
Attendance: 87.148

London, July 13th - Wembley Stadium

1 (0) FRANCE

Hausser 61

Aubour, Djorkaeff, Budzinski, Artelesa, de Michele, Bosquier, Herbin, Bonnel, Combin, Gondet, Hausser.

1 (0) MEXICO

Borja 48

Calderón, Chaires, Peña, Nuñez, Hernández, Díaz, Mercado, Reyes, Borja, Fragoso, Padilla.

Referee: Menachem Ashkenasi (Israel)
Attendance: 69.237

London, July 15th - White City

2 (2) URUGUAY

Rocha 27, Cortés 32

Mazurkiewicz, Troche, Manicera, Ubinas, Goncálves, Caetano, Cortés, Viera, Sacia, Rocha, Pérez.

1 (1) FRANCE

de Bourgoing (pen)15

Aubour, Djorkaeff, Budzinski, Artelesa, de Bourgoing, Bosquier, Simon, Bonnel, Herbet, Gondet, Hausser.

Referee: Karol Galba (Czechoslovakia)
Attendance: 45.662

London, July 16th - Wembley Stadium

2 (1) ENGLAND

R.Charlton 37, Hunt 67

Banks, Cohen, Wilson, Stiles, J.Charlton, Moore, Paine, Greaves, R.Charlton, Hunt, Peters.

0 (0) MEXICO

Calderón, Chaires, Peña, Del Muro, Nuñez, Hernández, Díaz, Jauregui, Reyes, Borja, Padilla.

Referee: Concetto Lo Bello (Italy)
Attendance: 92.570

London, July 19th - Wembley Stadium

0 (0) URUGUAY

Mazurkiewicz, Troche, Manicera, Ubinas, Goncálves, Caetano, Cortés, Viera, Sacia, Rocha, Pérez.

0 (0) MEXICO

Carbajal, Chaires, Peña, Mercado, Nuñez, Hernández, Díaz, Cisneros, Reyes, Borja, Padilla.

Referee: Bertil Lööw (Sweden)
Attendance: 61.112

London, July 20th - Wembley Stadium

2 (1) ENGLAND

Hunt 38,75

Banks, Cohen, Wilson, Stiles, J.Charlton, Moore, Callaghan, Greaves, R.Charlton, Hunt, Peters.

0 (0) FRANCE

Aubour, Djorkaeff, Budzinski, Artelesa, Herbin, Bosquier, Simon, Bonnel, Herbet, Gondet, Hausser.

Referee: Arturo Maldonado Yamasaki (Peru)
Attendance: 98.270

	P	W	D	L	F	A	Pts
England	3	2	1	0	4	0	5
Uruguay	3	1	2	0	2	1	4
Mexico	3	0	2	1	1	3	2
France	3	0	1	2	2	5	1

GROUP TWO

Sheffield, July 12th - Hillsborough

5 (3) WEST GERMANY

Held 16, Haller 20,(pen)77, Beckenbauer 40,52

Tilkowski, Höttges, Schulz, Weber, Schnellinger, Beckenbauer, Haller, Brülls, Seeler, Overath, Held.

0 (0) SWITZERLAND

Elsener, Grobety, Schneiter, Tacchella, Führer, Bäni, Dürr, Odermatt, Künzli, Hosp, Schindelholz.

Referee: Hugh Phillips (Scotland)
Attendance: 36.127

Birmingham, July 13th - Villa Park

2 (0) ARGENTINA

Artime 67,78

Roma, Perfumo, Marzolini, Ferreiro, Ráttin, Albrecht, Solari, González, Artime, Onega, Mas.

1 (0) SPAIN

Pirri 72

Iribar, Sanchis, Eladio, Pirri, Gallego, Zoco, Ufarte, del Sol, Peiro, Suárez, Gento.

Referee: Dimiter Rumentchev (Bulgaria)
Attendance: 47.982

Sheffield, July 15th - Hillsborough

2 (0) SPAIN

Sanchis 57, Amancio 75

Iribar, Sanchis, Reija, Pirri, Gallego, Zoco, Amancio, del Sol, Peiro, Suárez, Gento.

1 (1) SWITZERLAND

Quentin 28

Elsener, Brodmann, Leimgruber, Armbruster, Führer, Bäni, Stierli, Gottardi, Kühn, Hosp, Quentin.

Referee: Tofik Bakhramov (Soviet Union)
Attendance: 32.028

Birmingham, July 16th - Villa Park

0 (0) ARGENTINA

Roma, Perfumo, Marzolini, Ferreiro, Ráttin, Albrecht (RED), Solari, González, Artime, Onega, Mas.

0 (0) WEST GERMANY

Tilkowski, Höttges, Schulz, Weber, Schnellinger, Beckenbauer, Haller, Brülls, Seeler, Overath, Held.

Referee: Konstantin Zecevic (Yugoslavia)
Attendance: 51.419

Sheffield, July 19th - Hillsborough

2 (0) ARGENTINA

Artime 52, Onega 81

Roma, Perfumo, Marzolini, Ferreiro, Ráttin, Calics, Solari, González, Artime, Onega, Mas.

0 (0) SWITZERLAND

Eichmann, Brodmann, Künzli, Armbruster, Führer, Bäni, Stierli, Gottardi, Kühn, Hosp, Quentin.

Referee: Joaquim Fernandes Campos (Portugal)
Attendance: 31.443

Birmingham, July 20th - Villa Park

2 (1) WEST GERMANY

Emmerich 44, Seeler 84

Tilkowski, Höttges, Schulz, Weber, Schnellinger, Beckenbauer, Emmerich, Krämer, Seeler, Overath, Held.

1 (1) SPAIN

Fusté 23

Iribar, Sanchis, Reija, Glaria, Gallego, Zoco, Amancio, Adelardo, Marcelino, Fusté, Lapetra.

Referee: Armando Marques (Brazil)
Attendance: 51.875

	P	W	D	L	F	A	Pts
W. Germany	3	2	1	0	7	1	5
Argentina	3	2	1	0	4	1	5
Spain	3	1	0	2	4	5	2
Switzerland	3	0	0	3	1	9	0

GROUP THREE

Liverpool, July 12th - Goodison Park

2 (1) BRAZIL

Pelé 15, Garrincha 63

Gilmar, D.Santos, Bellini, Altair, Paulo Henrique, Denilson, Lima, Garrincha, Pelé, Alcindo, Jairzinho.

0 (0) BULGARIA

Naidenov, Shalamanov, Vutzov, Gaganelov, Penev, Kitov, Zhechev, Yakimov, Dermendyev, Asparoukhov, Kolev.

Referee: Kurt Tschenscher (West Germany)
Attendance: 52.847

Manchester, July 13th - Old Trafford

3 (1) PORTUGAL

Augusto 1,68, Torres 90

Carvalho, Morais, Baptista, Vicente, Hilario, Graca, Coluña, Augusto, Eusébio, Torres, Simões.

1 (0) HUNGARY

Bene 62

Szentmihályi, Matrai, Kaposzta, Sovari, Mészöly, Sipos, Bene, Nagy, Albert, Farkas, Rákosi.

Referee: Leo Callaghan (Wales)
Attendance: 37.311

Liverpool, July 15th - Goodison Park

3 (1) HUNGARY

Bene 3, Farkas 64, Mészöly (pen) 72

Gelei, Matrai, Kaposzta, Szepesi, Mészöly, Sipos, Bene, Mathesz, Albert, Farkas, Rákosi.

1 (1) BRAZIL

Tostão 14

Gilmar, D.Santos, Bellini, Altair, Paulo Henrique, Gérson, Lima, Garrincha, Tostão, Alcindo, Jairzinho.

Referee: Ken Dagnall (England)
Attendance: 57.455

Manchester, July 16th - Old Trafford

3 (2) PORTUGAL

Vutzov (og)6, Eusébio 38, Torres 80

Pereira, Festa, Germano, Vicente, Hilario, Graca, Coluña, Augusto, Eusébio, Torres, Simões.

0 (0) BULGARIA

Naidenov, Shalamanov, Vutzov, Gaganelov, Penev, Zhekov, Zhechev, Yakimov, Dermendyev, Asparoukhov, Kostov.

Referee: José Maria Codesal (Uruguay)
Attendance: 33.355

Liverpool, July 19th - Goodison Park

3 (2) PORTUGAL

Simões 14, Eusébio 23,85

Pereira, Morais, Baptista, Vicente, Hilario, Graca, Coluña, Augusto, Eusébio, Torres, Simões.

1 (0) BRAZIL

Rildo 72

Manga, Fidelis, Brito, Orlando, Rildo, Denilson, Lima, Jairzinho, Silva, Pelé, Parana.

Referee: George McCabe (England)
Attendance: 62.204

Manchester, July 20th - Old Trafford

3 (2) HUNGARY

Davidov (og)43, Mészöly 45, Bene 54

Gelei, Matrai, Kaposzta, Szepesi, Mészöly, Sipos, Bene, Mathesz, Albert, Farkas, Rákosi.

1 (1) BULGARIA

Asparoukhov 14

Simeonov, Largov, Vutzov, Gaganelov, Penev, Davidov, Zhechev, Yakimov, Kotkov, Asparoukhov, Kolev.

Referee: Roberto Goicoechea (Argentina)
Attendance: 22.064

	P	W	D	L	F	A	Pts
Portugal	3	3	0	0	9	2	6
Hungary	3	2	0	1	7	5	4
Brazil	3	1	0	2	4	6	2
Bulgaria	3	0	0	3	1	8	0

GROUP FOUR

Middlesbrough, July 12th - Ayresome Park

3 (2) SOVIET UNION

Malafeev 30,88, Banichevski 32

Kavasashvili, Ponomarev, Shesterniev, Khurtsilava, Ostrovski, Sabo, Sichinava, Chislenko, Malafeev, Banichevski, Khusainov.

0 (0) NORTH KOREA

Chan-myung, Li-sup, Yung-kyoo, Zoong-sun, Bong-chil, Seung-zin, Seung-hwi, Bong-jin, Doo-ik, Ryong-woon, Seung-il.

Referee: Juan Gardeazabal Garay (Spain)
Attendance: 22.568

Sunderland, July 13th - Roker Park

2 (1) ITALY

Mazzola 9, Barison 88

Albertosi, Burgnich, Facchetti, Rosato, Salvadore, Lodetti, Perani, Bulgarelli, Mazzola, Rivera, Barison.

0 (0) CHILE

Olivares, Eyzaguirre, Cruz, Figueroa, Villanueva, Prieto, Marcos, Araya, Tobar, Fouilloux, Sánchez.

Referee: Gottfried Dienst (Switzerland)
Attendance: 30.956

Middlesbrough, July 15th - Ayresome Park

1 (1) CHILE

Marcos (pen)22

Olivares, Valentini, Cruz, Figueroa, Villanueva, Prieto, Marcos, Araya, Landa, Fouilloux, Sánchez.

1 (0) NORTH KOREA

Seung-zin 88

Chan-myung, Li-sup, Yung-kyoo, Zoong-sun, Yoon-kyung, Seung-zin, Seung-hwi, Bong-jin, Doo-ik, Dong-woon, Seung-il.

Referee: Ali Kandil (Egypt)
Attendance: 15.887

Sunderland, July 16th - Roker Park

1 (0) SOVIET UNION

Chislenko 58

Yashin, Ponomarev, Shesterniev, Khurtsilava, Voronin, Sabo, Danilov, Chislenko, Malafeev, Banichevski, Khusainov.

0 (0) ITALY

Albertosi, Burgnich, Facchetti, Rosato, Salvadore, Lodetti, Leoncini, Bulgarelli, Mazzola, Meroni, Pascutti.

Referee: Rudolf Kreitlein (West Germany)
Attendance: 31.989

Middlesbrough, July 19th - Ayresome Park

1 (1) NORTH KOREA

Doo-ik 41

Chan-myung, Yung-won, Yung-kyoo, Zoong-sun, Yoon-kyung, Seung-zin, Seung-hwi, Bong-jin, Doo-ik, Bong-hwan, Seung-kook.

0 (0) ITALY

Albertosi, Landini, Facchetti, Guarneri, Janich, Fogli, Perani, Bulgarelli, Mazzola, Rivera, Barison.

Referee: Pierre Schwinte (France)
Attendance: 18.727

Sunderland, July 20th - Roker Park

2 (1) SOVIET UNION

Porkujan 23,85

Kavasashhvili, Getmanov, Shesterniev, Afonin, Voronin, Markarov, Ostrovski, Korneyev, Metreveli, Serebrianikov, Porkujan.

1 (1) CHILE

Marcos 30

Olivares, Valentini, Cruz, Figueroa, Villanueva, Prieto, Marcos, Araya, Landa, Yavar, Sánchez.

Referee: John Adair (Northern Ireland)
Attendance: 22.590

	P	W	D	L	F	A	Pts
Soviet Union	3	3	0	0	6	1	6
North Korea	3	1	1	1	2	4	3
Italy	3	1	0	2	2	2	2
Chile	3	0	1	2	2	5	1

QUARTER-FINALS

London, July 23rd - Wembley Stadium

1 (0) ENGLAND

Hurst 78

Banks, Cohen, Wilson, Stiles, J.Charlton, Moore, Ball, Hurst, R.Charlton, Hunt, Peters.

0 (0) ARGENTINA

Roma, Ferreiro, Marzolini, Ráttin (RED), Perfumo, Albrecht, Onega, Solari, Artime, González, Mas.

Referee: Rudolf Kreitlein (West Germany)
Attendance: 90.584

Sheffield, July 23rd - Hillsborough

4 (1) WEST GERMANY

Held 11, Beckenbauer 70, Seeler 75, Haller 84

Tilkowski, Höttges, Weber, Schulz, Schnellinger, Beckenbauer, Haller, Overath, Seeler, Held, Emmerich.

0 (0) URUGUAY

Mazurkiewicz, Troche (RED), Ubinas, Goncálves, Manicera, Caetano, Salva, Rocha, Silva (RED), Cortés, Pérez.

Referee: Jim Finney (England)
Attendance: 33.751

Liverpool, July 23rd - Goodison Park

5 (2) PORTUGAL

Eusébio 27,(pen)42,55,(pen)58, Augusto 78

Pereira, Morais, Baptista, Vicente, Hilario, Graca, Coluña, Augusto, Eusébio, Torres, Simões.

3 (3) NORTH KOREA

Seung-zin 1, Dong-woon 21, Seung-kook 22

Chan-myung, Zoong-sun, Yung-kyoo, Yung-won, Yoon-kyung, Seung-zin, Seung-hwi, Bong-jin, Doo-ik, Dong-woon, Seung-kook.

Referee: Menachem Ashkenasi (Israel)
Attendance: 51.780

Sunderland, July 23rd - Roker Park

2 (1) SOVIET UNION

Chislenko 5, Porkujan 47

Yashin, Ponomarev, Shesterniev, Voronin, Danilov, Sabo, Khusainov, Chislenko, Banichevski, Malafeev, Porkujan.

1 (0) HUNGARY

Bene 50

Gelei, Matrai, Kaposzta, Mészöly, Sipos, Szepesi, Nagy, Albert, Rákosi, Bene, Farkas.

Referee: Juan Gardeazabal Garay (Spain)
Attendance: 26.844

SEMI-FINALS

Liverpool, July 25th - Goodison Park

2 (1) WEST GERMANY

Haller 44, Beckenbauer 68

Tilkowski, Lutz, Weber, Schulz, Schnellinger, Beckenbauer, Haller, Overath, Seeler, Held, Emmerich.

1 (0) SOVIET UNION

Porkujan 88

Yashin, Ponomarev, Shesterniev, Voronin, Danilov, Sabo, Khusainov, Chislenko (RED), Banichevski, Malafeev, Porkujan.

Referee: Concetto Lo Bello (Italy)
Attendance: 43.921

London, July 26th - Wembley Stadium

2 (1) ENGLAND

R.Charlton 30,79

Banks, Cohen, Wilson, Stiles, J.Charlton, Moore, Ball, Hurst, R.Charlton, Hunt, Peters.

1 (0) PORTUGAL

Eusébio (pen)82

Pereira, Festa, Baptista, Carlos, Hilario, Graca, Coluña, Augusto, Eusébio, Torres, Simoës.

Referee: Pierre Schwinte (France)
Attendance: 94.493

3RD/4TH PLACE PLAY-OFF

London, July 28th - Wembley Stadium

2 (1) PORTUGAL

Eusébio (pen)12, Torres 88

Pereira, Festa, Baptista, Carlos, Hilario, Graca, Coluña, Augusto, Eusébio, Torres, Simoës.

1 (1) SOVIET UNION

Malafeev 43

Yashin, Ponomarev, Khurtsilava, Voronin, Danilov, Korneyev, Sichinava, Metreveli, Banichevski, Malafeev, Serebrianikov.

Referee: Ken Dagnall (England)
Attendance: 87.696

FINAL

London, July 30th - Wembley Stadium

After extra time - 45 mins (1-1), 90 mins (2-2)

4 (2) ENGLAND

Hurst 18,98,120, Peters 78

Banks, Cohen, Wilson, Stiles, J.Charlton, Moore, Ball, Hurst, R.Charlton, Hunt, Peters.

2 (2) WEST GERMANY

Haller 12, Weber 90

Tilkowski, Höttges, Weber, Schulz, Schnellinger, Beckenbauer, Haller, Overath, Seeler, Held, Emmerich.

Referee: Gottfried Dienst (Switzerland)
Attendance: 96.924

QUALIFYING ROUNDS

Africa/Asia/Oceania Play-off CAF/AFC/OFC

	P	W	D	L	F	A	Pts
Korea DPR	2	2	0	0	9	2	4
Australia	2	0	0	2	2	9	0

21-11-65	Korea DPR : Australia	6:1 (1:0)
24-11-65	Australia : Korea DPR	1:3 (1:1)

Both games played in Phnom Penh

Europe - Group 1

	P	W	D	L	F	A	Pts
Belgium	4	3	0	1	11	3	6
Bulgaria	4	3	0	1	9	6	6
Israel	4	0	0	4	1	12	0

09-05-65	Belgium : Israel	1:0 (1:0)
13-06-65	Bulgaria : Israel	4:0 (2:0)
26-09-65	Bulgaria : Belgium	3:0 (2:0)
27-10-65	Belgium : Bulgaria	5:0 (1:0)
10-11-65	Israel : Belgium	0:5 (0:3)
21-11-65	Israel : Bulgaria	1:2 (0:1)

Europe - Group 1 Play-off

29-12-65	Belgium : Bulgaria	1:2 (0:2)

Played in Florence

Europe - Group 2

	P	W	D	L	F	A	Pts
Germany FR	4	3	1	0	14	2	7
Sweden	4	2	1	1	10	3	5
Cyprus	4	0	0	4	0	19	0

04-11-64	Germany FR : Sweden	1:1 (1:0)
24-04-65	Germany FR : Cyprus	5:0 (3:0)
05-05-65	Sweden : Cyprus	3:0 (1:0)
26-09-65	Sweden : Germany FR	1:2 (1:1)
07-11-65	Cyprus : Sweden	0:5 (0:4)
14-11-65	Cyprus : Germany FR	0:6 (0:2)

Europe - Group 3

	P	W	D	L	F	A	Pts
France	6	5	0	1	9	2	10
Norway	6	3	1	2	10	5	7
Yugoslavia	6	3	1	2	10	8	7
Luxembourg	6	0	0	6	6	20	0

20-09-64	Yugoslavia : Luxembourg	3:1 (2:0)
04-10-64	Luxembourg : France	0:2 (0:1)
08-11-64	Luxembourg : Norway	0:2 (0:1)
11-11-64	France : Norway	1:0 (1:0)
18-04-65	Yugoslavia : France	1:0 (0:0)
27-05-65	Norway : Luxembourg	4:2 (1:2)
16-06-65	Norway : Yugoslavia	3:0 (1:0)
15-09-65	Norway : France	0:1 (0:1)
19-09-65	Luxembourg : Yugoslavia	2:5 (1:4)
09-10-65	France : Yugoslavia	1:0 (0:0)
06-11-65	France : Luxembourg	4:1 (4:1)
07-11-65	Yugoslavia : Norway	1:1 (1:1)

Europe - Group 4

	P	W	D	L	F	A	Pts
Portugal	6	4	1	1	9	4	9
Czechoslovakia	6	3	1	2	12	4	7
Romania	6	3	0	3	9	7	6
Turkey	6	1	0	5	4	19	2

24-01-65	Portugal : Turkey	5:1 (2:1)
19-04-65	Turkey : Portugal	0:1 (0:0)
25-04-65	Czechoslovakia : Portugal	0:1 (0:1)
02-05-65	Romania : Turkey	3:0 (1:0)
30-05-65	Romania : Czechoslovakia	1:0 (1:0)
13-06-65	Portugal : Romania	2:1 (2:0)
19-09-65	Czechoslovakia : Romania	3:1 (1:1)
09-10-65	Turkey : Czechoslovakia	0:6 (0:3)
23-10-65	Turkey : Romania	2:1 (1:0)
31-10-65	Portugal : Czechoslovakia	0:0
21-11-65	Romania : Portugal	2:0 (2:0)
21-11-65	Czechoslovakia : Turkey	3:1 (2:1)

Europe - Group 5

	P	W	D	L	F	A	Pts
Switzerland	6	4	1	1	7	3	9
N. Ireland	6	3	2	1	9	5	8
Netherlands	6	2	2	2	6	4	6
Albania	6	0	1	5	2	12	1

24-05-64	Netherlands : Albania	2:0 (0:0)
14-10-64	Northern Ireland : Switzerland	1:0 (0:0)
25-10-64	Albania : Netherlands	0:2 (0:1)
14-11-64	Switzerland : Northern Ireland	2:1 (2:1)
17-03-65	Northern Ireland : Netherlands	2:1 (1:1)
07-04-65	Netherlands : Northern Ireland	0:0
11-04-65	Albania : Switzerland	0:2 (0:1)
02-05-65	Switzerland : Albania	1:0 (1:0)
07-05-65	Northern Ireland : Albania	4:1 (2:1)
17-10-65	Netherlands : Switzerland	0:0
14-11-65	Switzerland : Netherlands	2:1 (1:0)
24-11-65	Albania : Northern Ireland	1:1 (0:0)

Europe - Group 6

	P	W	D	L	F	A	Pts
Hungary	4	3	1	0	8	3	7
Germany DR	4	1	2	1	5	5	4
Austria	4	0	1	3	1	6	1

25-04-65	Austria : Germany DR	1:1 (0:0)
23-05-65	Germany DR : Hungary	1:1 (1:1)
13-06-65	Austria : Hungary	0:1 (0:1)
05-09-65	Hungary : Austria	3:0 (2:0)
09-10-65	Hungary : Germany DR	3:2 (1:1)
31-10-65	Germany DR : Austria	1:0 (1:0)

Europe - Group 7

	P	W	D	L	F	A	Pts
USSR	6	5	0	1	19	6	10
Wales	6	3	0	3	11	9	6
Greece	6	2	1	3	10	14	5
Denmark	6	1	1	4	7	18	3

21-10-64	Denmark : Wales	1:0 (0:0)
29-11-64	Greece : Denmark	4:2 (1:0)
09-12-64	Greece : Wales	2:0 (1:0)
17-03-65	Wales : Greece	4:1 (1:1)
23-05-65	USSR : Greece	3:1 (1:0)
30-05-65	USSR : Wales	2:1 (2:0)
27-06-65	USSR : Denmark	6:0 (1:0)
03-10-65	Greece : USSR	1:4 (1:2)
17-10-65	Denmark : USSR	1:3 (0:0)
27-10-65	Denmark : Greece	1:1 (1:1)
27-10-65	Wales : USSR	2:1 (1:1)
01-12-65	Wales : Denmark	4:2 (3:1)

Europe - Group 8

	P	W	D	L	F	A	Pts
Italy	6	4	1	1	17	3	9
Scotland	6	3	1	2	8	8	7
Poland	6	2	2	2	11	10	6
Finland	6	1	0	5	5	20	2

21-10-64	Scotland : Finland	3:1 (3:0)
04-11-64	Italy : Finland	6:1 (3:0)
18-04-65	Poland : Italy	0:0
23-05-65	Poland : Scotland	1:1 (0:0)
27-05-65	Finland : Scotland	1:2 (1:1)
23-06-65	Finland : Italy	0:2 (0:1)
29-09-65	Finland : Poland	2:0 (2:0)
13-10-65	Scotland : Poland	1:2 (1:0)
24-10-65	Poland : Finland	7:0 (6:0)
01-11-65	Italy : Poland	6:1 (2:0)
09-11-65	Scotland : Italy	1:0 (0:0)
07-12-65	Italy : Scotland	3:0 (1:0)

Europe - Group 9

	P	W	D	L	F	A	Pts
Spain	3	2	0	1	5	2	4
Rep. Ireland	3	1	0	2	2	5	2

05-05-65	Ireland Republic : Spain	1:0 (0:0)
27-10-65	Spain : Ireland Republic	4:1 (2:1)
10-11-65	Spain : Ireland Republic	1:0 (0:0)

Game played in Paris

Caribbean/North/Cent. America - Phase 1

Group 1

	P	W	D	L	F	A	Pts
Jamaica	4	2	1	1	5	2	5
Netherlands Antilles	4	1	2	1	2	3	4
Cuba	4	1	1	2	3	5	3

16-01-65	Jamaica : Cuba	2:0 (1:0)
20-01-65	Cuba : Netherlands Antilles	1:1 (0:0)
23-01-65	Jamaica : Netherlands Antilles	2:0 (1:0)

Games played in Kingston

30-01-65	Netherlands Antilles : Cuba	1:0 (1:0)
03-02-65	Netherlands Antilles : Jamaica	0:0
07-02-65	Cuba : Jamaica	2:1 (2:1)

Games played in Havana

Group 2

	P	W	D	L	F	A	Pts
Costa Rica	4	4	0	0	9	1	8
Surinam	4	1	0	3	8	9	2
Trinidad & Tobago	4	1	0	3	5	12	2

07-02-65	Trinidad & Tobago : Surinam	4:1 (3:1)
12-02-65	Costa Rica : Surinam	1:0 (0:0)
21-02-65	Costa Rica : Trinidad & Tobago	4:0 (1:0)
28-02-65	Surinam : Costa Rica	1:3 (0:2)
07-03-65	Trinidad & Tobago : Costa Rica	0:1 (0:1)
14-03-65	Surinam : Trinidad & Tobago	6:1 (4:1)

Group 3

	P	W	D	L	F	A	Pts
Mexico	4	3	1	0	8	2	7
United States	4	1	2	1	4	5	4
Honduras	4	0	1	3	1	6	1

28-02-65	Honduras : Mexico	0:1 (0:1)
04-03-65	Mexico : Honduras	3:0 (2:0)
07-03-65	United States : Mexico	2:2 (2:1)
12-03-65	Mexico : United States	2:0 (1:0)
17-03-65	Honduras : United States	0:1 (0:0)
21-03-65	United States : Honduras	1:1 (0:0)

Caribbean/North/Cent. America - Phase 2

Group Winners

	P	W	D	L	F	A	Pts
Mexico	4	3	1	0	12	2	7
Costa Rica	4	1	2	1	8	2	4
Jamaica	4	0	1	3	3	19	1

25-04-65	Costa Rica : Mexico	0:0
03-05-65	Jamaica : Mexico	2:3 (2:1)
07-05-65	Mexico : Jamaica	8:0 (4:0)
11-05-65	Costa Rica : Jamaica	7:0 (1:0)
16-05-65	Mexico : Costa Rica	1:0 (1:0)
22-05-65	Jamaica : Costa Rica	1:1 (1:1)

South America - Group 1

	P	W	D	L	F	A	Pts
Uruguay	4	4	0	0	11	2	8
Peru	4	2	0	2	8	6	4
Venezuela	4	0	0	4	4	15	0

16-05-65	Peru : Venezuela	1:0 (1:0)
23-05-65	Uruguay : Venezuela	5:0 (2:0)
30-05-65	Venezuela : Uruguay	1:3 (1:1)
02-06-65	Venezuela : Peru	3:6 (1:3)
06-06-65	Peru : Uruguay	0:1 (0:0)
13-06-65	Uruguay : Peru	2:1 (1:1)

South America - Group 2

	P	W	D	L	F	A	Pts
Chile	4	2	1	1	12	7	5
Ecuador	4	2	1	1	6	5	5
Colombia	4	1	0	3	4	10	2

20-07-65	Colombia : Ecuador	0:1 (0:1)
25-07-65	Ecuador : Colombia	2:0 (0:0)
01-08-65	Chile : Colombia	7:2 (4:0)
07-08-65	Colombia : Chile	2:0 (0:0)
15-08-65	Ecuador : Chile	2:2 (1:1)
22-08-65	Chile : Ecuador	3:1 (1:1)

South America - Group 2 Play-off

12-10-65	Chile : Ecuador	2:1 (2:0)

Played in Lima

South America - Group 3

	P	W	D	L	F	A	Pts
Argentina	4	3	1	0	9	2	7
Paraguay	4	1	1	2	3	5	3
Bolivia	4	1	0	3	4	9	2

25-07-65	Paraguay : Bolivia	2:0 (1:0)
01-08-65	Argentina : Paraguay	3:0 (3:0)
08-08-65	Paraguay : Argentina	0:0
17-08-65	Argentina : Bolivia	4:1 (3:0)
22-08-65	Bolivia : Paraguay	2:1 (1:1)
29-08-65	Bolivia : Argentina	1:2 (1:2)

Chapter 11

Altitude, Attitude and Artistry
The Mexico World Cup, 1970

Mexico 1970

Winners: Brazil

Runners-up: Italy

3rd Place: West Germany

4th Place: Uruguay

Total Attendance: 1,546,400

Number of Matches: 32

Being selected for your country is every footballer's dream. Or should be. It means that you are the very best in your position if only for a short period of time. The selection of the squad for the World Cup is one step higher up, because it puts you on the world stage and then to finally play in the World Cup against the greatest players in the world is the best experience ever.

I was fortunate enough to be selected to play in the 1970 World Cup - the one we lost having won in 1966. The experience of playing in Mexico in temperatures in the 90's and at altitude thousands of feet above sea level was quite a task but we had perfectly acclimatised by the start - although playing at such high temperatures is something you never get used to.

Playing against Brazil, the final winners, turned out to be a classic although we lost one nil - the Gordon Banks save and the contest between Bobby Moore and Pelé being the main features. Then, in the quarter-finals, we met West Germany, our arch rivals, and seemed to be coasting at 2-0 but eventually lost 3-2 in extra time. Sir Alf was blamed for bringing on substitutes towards the end of the game but it was just fate and the run of the ball that defeated us.

Original contribution by England's Brian Labone

The 1970s were a time of terrorism, extremism, revolution, liberation, strikes, three-day weeks, oil embargoes, ecology, full-frontal male nudity and very poor fashion sense. It was a time when the political and economic map of the world went through major upheaval. With the death of President Nasser of Egypt, who had spearheaded the Arab nations' struggle against Israel and having seen all previous political and military attempts to win back their homeland, the Palestinian Arabs adopted a more pro-active approach to their problem. 1970 became their year of air piracy and hijacks, though they didn't always get their own way. When terrorists attempted to take over an El Al Boeing 707 flight from Amsterdam to New York, the crew overcame their attackers with a steward and one guerrilla killed in the ensuing melee.

In South East Asia, President Nixon escalated the Vietnam conflict, bombing the neighbouring state of Cambodia where he claimed the Vietcong had military bases. The irony of Nixon's policy was not lost on Hollywood. Although the film of the year "MASH" depicted the lives of a medical unit in Korea, it was a satirical comment on the events in Vietnam. They were sentiments wholly in tune with the students at Kent State University where four anti-war protesters lost their lives in rioting that eclipsed anything previously seen. Add to this, the frustrations of the Black Power movement and the Women's Liberation struggle, the turmoil created led some commentators to predict the collapse of the world's "greatest" democracy.

Other trouble spots included Nigeria where the civil war that followed the cessation of Biafra came to an end amid a catastrophic famine that instigated the first mass foreign aid relief programme. Critical attention was brought to South Africa's apartheid policy when black American tennis star, Arthur Ashe, was refused a visa to enter the country to take part in a Davis Cup match. South Africa's isolation from major sporting events was virtually ensured when protestors forced the cancellation of a cricket tour of England. In Britain, Edward Heath replaced Harold Wilson in Downing Street and the discovery of North Sea oil brought the promise of untold wealth. 1970 also saw a major technological breakthrough that would revolutionize the way people lived and worked. The silicon chip had been invented in 1961, but when the Intel Corporation of the USA added housing, a monitor and a keyboard they had invented, and patented, the world's first microprocessor. A computer system

22 Men and a Bag of Wind

El Salvador and the Football War

Tension over land had been mounting for years between El Salvador and Honduras. When rioting followed both World Cup qualifying games between them in 1969, the Honduran government used it as an excuse to expel El Salvador nationals, whom it claimed were trouble makers. El Salvador fired in accusations of brutality and on 24th June declared a state of emergency. Two days later diplomatic relations were broken off and shooting began on the 4th July when El Salvador invaded with three Second World War Mustangs, an assortment of civil aeroplanes carrying hand grenades and 12,000 troops. "Fortunately, Latin American armies are ill-equipped for fighting wars... {they} are all better used to staging coups." The fighting amounted to little more than border clashes, cross-border raids and minor incursions. El Salvador, with its larger army, had the better of the fighting and the OAS eventually brokered a cease-fire in late July. By early August all El Salvador troops had evacuated Honduran territory and peace was restored.

El Salvador made it through to the World Cup finals, but their problems were not over. There was a players' strike over the lack of financial reward and then goalkeeper, Raúl Magana, wrote critically of the country's FA and was refused permission to travel. The rest of the squad threatened to pull out if he was not restored. Both issues were resolved, with the players being granted £400 for qualifying and a promise of £40 for each point gained, which may account for the phlegmatic remarks of one El Salvador delegate. "In the game it is eleven against eleven, no more. The ball is round, the field rectangular and anything can happen."

---

that used to take up a whole room was now small enough to fit into a box that could sit on a desk.

1970 also saw Oliver Reed get his tackle out and wrestle naked with Alan Bates in the film "Women in Love". The scene stretched the interpretation of the censorship laws to their limits and broke previous taboos. Full male nudity on stage and screen had arrived. However, departing the world of popular music were three of its finest exponents. Jimi Hendrix and Janis Joplin both fell victim to popularity and drugs, whilst the Beatles went their separate ways. Meanwhile, the England World Cup squad hit the top of the charts with their song "Back Home" and countless English school children pestered their parents to buy ESSO petrol so they could collect the World Cup coins showing the faces of the squad that would make the trip to join 15 other nations in the World Cup finals.

When FIFA met in Tokyo, during the 1964 Olympic Games, two countries had applied to host the 1970 World Cup finals, Argentina and Mexico. Owing to the known problems that would accompany the heat and altitude of Mexico, several European delegates had serious misgivings about taking the competition there. Notwithstanding, Mexico emerged victorious and it was in no small way due to the loyalty shown by the Mexicans to the World Cup. With the exception of that of 1938, they had entered each tournament, and had appeared in the finals in 1930 and in each one since 1950. Few countries could match this record and certainly not Argentina, whose attitude to the tournament had been very lukewarm in the years before 1958. Argentina's uncertain economy was also a worry for FIFA, who felt that it may inhibit its ability to host a successful tournament and there was the fact that Mexico had already been granted the 1968 Olympic Games. A final factor telling in Mexico's favour was the plan to build a new sports stadium, the Azteca in Mexico City.

There were 71 entrants for Mexico '70 and only the North Koreans withdrew, refusing to play Israel in the Asia-Oceania qualifying group. The rest entered the qualifying rounds, which got underway in Vienna on 19th May 1968, when Austria strode out easy 7-1 winners against Cyprus. The surprises from the European qualifying groups were the elimination of Portugal and Hungary. The Portuguese had been handicapped by an injury to Eusébio and without him they were unable to make the grade. The Hungarians, still one of Europe's stronger teams, had taken Olympic

On 23rd May the English contingent began making excuses why England would not win. FA Chairman, Dr. Andrew Stephen, stated: "From a medical point of view it is crackers to hold the World Cup in Mexico. We produced strong medical evidence at the Tokyo Congress against holding the World Cup at altitude, but we were out voted by countries like Bahrain and Kuwait. That's democracy gone mad." Others were more optimistic. Romanian captain, Cornel Dinu, thought England would thrash his team, saying: "I expect to lose by two or three goals to England." Mario Zagalo also thought "England will win. The champion is always favourite. If we get into the final we would like to meet West Germany." Italian official, Walter Mandelli, thought the same. He said that the "English are born with a determination to win. This psychological factor is true. I wish the Italian team had it. But it derives from hundreds of years of English history. They have it in all fields."

Mexico's Police Chief, General Renato Vega Amador, put his men under strict instructions to keep order and warned his commanders: "I do not want one single complaint about theft or molestation of players or tourists during the Cup." It is the custom before a major event in Mexico to round up and detain for the duration all known criminals.

The South Americans expected to encounter tough tackling from the Europeans and precautions were taken. The Peruvians were given Judo lessons "to show them how to fall without hurt", and the El Salvador players had psychotherapy to prevent retaliation. As the chairman of El Salvador's FA said: "They play very hard in Europe and more roughly than in this hemisphere. Referees in Europe only penalise bad intentions or fighting." The Swedes employed a hypnotist to help them.

The matter of referees being biased in favour of Europeans raised its head again in 1970. Jucinto de Thormes, a Brazilian sports journalist, accused the FIFA's predominantly English leadership of being the "Mafia of the Whistle". He claimed that the refereeing system that had been set up by FIFA President, Stanley Rous, and Director of Refereeing, Ken Aston, would hinder non-European players.

Before the tournament all teams had to watch a full-length feature film depicting scenes of violence that footballers had committed. It was compiled by Ken Aston to show players what would not be tolerated.

gold in Mexico, but in spite of four qualifying wins, ended up with the same number of points as Czechoslovakia. Goal difference was still not taken into account and a play-off was required in Marseille in December 1969. The Czechs ran out 4-1 winners and took the group's place in Mexico. Yugoslavia's game against Belgium in Skopje in October 1969 was that country's 50th World Cup game making them the second country to reach the half century milestone.

The big surprise in the South American groups was the elimination of Argentina, who came bottom of their group. It was won by Peru, now managed by former Brazilian star, Didí and who made it to the finals for the first time since 1930. The other South American qualifiers were Uruguay, the only country to reach the finals without conceding a goal, and Brazil, the only country to get through with a 100% record. This was a Brazilian team to match that of 1958, brilliant, compelling and charismatic. To complement existing stars, like Gérson and Pelé, there was a fantastic array of newcomers, men like Jairzinho, Rivelino and Tostão, who would set the finals alight with their individual talents and joie de sport, and who would make Brazil one of the favourites to win the tournament. To emphasize their credentials, in the six qualifying games they played, they scored 23 times and conceded only twice - and this was a team whose defence was supposed to be its weak spot. Their fourth strike in the game against Venezuela in Caracas in August, 1969 was Brazil's 100th World Cup goal and another record was created when 183,341 people crowded into the Maracana to watch the game against Paraguay on 31st August, 1969. It was the largest crowd to attend a World Cup qualifying match.

Recognizing the widening appeal of football and of the increasing number of countries from outside the two main powerhouses of the game that wanted to take part in its premier competition, FIFA had allocated three places to the CONCACAF, Africa, Asia and Oceania regions. As in previous qualifying rounds, complicated formulae were adopted to reduce the entrants down to the three finalists. In Africa, in the first phase Ghana received a bye, but the other ten competitors were paired off to play two-legged ties. Eventually, three countries emerged to play a round robin in the final phase from which Morocco won through to become the first African nation to reach the finals since Egypt in 1934.

Six countries competed in the Asia-Oceania region and a similar complex arrangement was employed to find a winner. They were placed in two sub-groups. Sub-Group One, containing Australia, Japan and South Korea played out a league system in Seoul in October, 1969. It was won by Australia, who went on to meet Rhodesia in a second phase that would decide who would reach the regional final. North Korea withdrew from Sub-Group Two leaving Israel and New Zealand to play each other over two legs to produce the other regional finalist. Out of it Australia and Israel emerged to play a two-legged final in Tel Aviv and Sydney, the first World Cup game played in Australasia, which Israel won.

The major problem of the qualifying stage came in the CONCACAF region, where the twelve entrants were placed into four sub-groups. The four group winners, El Salvador, Honduras, Haiti and the USA, were then paired off in the second phase. El Salvador defeated Honduras in football and in war and Haiti beat the USA. El Salvador then defeated Haiti to reach the finals at their first attempt and, in doing so, had played

Prior to the tournament Alf Ramsey remarked: "People say we cannot do it, that we cannot win outside England. I say we can - if we do things right." On the flight over entertainment was provided by Geoff Hurst's portable radio and Jeff Astle's portable gramophone. The team was also subjected to a playing of their hit single "Back Home". By the time the team touched down in Mexico City Ramsey's comments had changed to: "I don't say we will win, but we will be difficult to beat." Contained in their World Cup kit bag were 488 football shirts. The team also took their own food and medical equipment. Their treatment room contained a mass of equipment from ultra-sonic, short wave stuff to infrared and radiant heat machines costing £2,500. Due to an aloofness, the English did not gain many friends in Mexico. Their preparations were clinically British and they kept the media at arms length. One writer labelled the team the "Champions of Antipathy - the inaccessible." Another wrote: "If you throw tomatoes at the English, make sure they are sterilised." As the England team arrived at their hotel, Ramsey found that he did not have a room. The Mexicans, who had been staying at the hotel, were refusing to leave until they were ready. The man who eventually gave up his room for Ramsey was Billy Wright, in Mexico with the ITV television team. Two ITV commentators, Gerald Seymour and Tony Flanagan, had earlier refused to move. Ramsey's room had originally been reserved for the Italian manager whose team was sharing the hotel with England and had not yet arrived.

a record number of ten qualifying games. It was a record they shared with Morocco, who had also played ten qualifying games.

FIFA brought in a couple of rule changes for the 1970 tournament, the most important of which was the introduction of substitutes. Each team was allowed to name 13 players, two of which could be used as replacements, though they also decreed that any player designated as number 13 did not have to wear the number if he was superstitious. The second change provided for the toss of a coin to decide the outcome of quarter and semi-final matches if scores were tied after extra time had been played.

The tournament got underway with a colourful opening ceremony in the Azteca Stadium in Mexico City on 31st May. The packed house of 107,000 flag-waving, chanting fans, who made "the spirit of Mexico burst through to the surface", created a pageant of colour that shimmered and undulated all through the opening ceremony. This was conducted in searing heat and witnessed a parade of the sixteen national flags, each of which, with the exception of that of England, was cheered lustily. There had been a growing anti-English campaign developing in Mexico before the start of the tournament and it had caught the popular imagination. Some commentators put this down to jealousy caused by England being the reigning world champions, but it had also been fanned by the allegations of theft that had been levelled against Bobby Moore in Colombia. The parade was followed by speeches from the VIPs, including welcoming addresses from FIFA president, Sir Stanley Rous and President Diaz Ordaz of Mexico. The tournament was then declared open and the first game played.

It featured Mexico and the Soviet Union and, like the corresponding fixture in the 1966 World Cup, was an unmitigated bore. The Mexicans had the majority of what attacking play there was, but the Soviets "largely sulked behind thick defensive ramparts", too strong for the home side to penetrate. Lopéz, for Mexico, missed two presentable chances in the first half and Bishovets came closest for the USSR with a second half header, that he ought to have put away, but it was a game of few chances and remained scoreless. Only three noteworthy points emerged out of the tedium. One was that negative play was still in vogue. The second was the tough attitude of West German referee, Kurt Tschener, corresponding to FIFA's new directives against foul play. The last was that the first substitute in a World Cup finals game was used, when the Soviet Union brought on Pusatch to replace Shesterniev.

Before it all began there were casualties amongst the South and Central Americans. Brazil and El Salvador sacked their coaches, two Uruguayans were banned for taking drugs and Mexico dropped stars Ernesto Cisneros and Gabriel Nuñez for having nights on the town during training in Acapulco. Team captain, Gustavo Peña, appealed on their behalf, but manager, Raúl Cardenas, turned him down. "We must have discipline, because without it we haven't a team", he said.

As part of an anti-drugs strategy, the coach of any team could request the testing of any opposition player.

The Mexican authorities allocated cheap tickets so that poorer fans could see the games. The day before it began, there was rioting when fans who had been queuing for up to 48 hours were told that these tickets would not be on sale until the following day. There was fighting at two other centres selling the cheap tickets.

Altitude, Attitude and Artistry - Mexico 1970

Israel's stay in Mexico did not start well. Having a nightclub below their hotel that kept them up all night forced the Israeli team to find new accommodation. In a team of amateurs, who received out-of-pocket expenses and trained in the evenings, there was only one professional, the 23 year old David Primo, who played abroad. Coach Emanual Schaeffer hoped his team would win at least one game and optimistically stated: "As long as the ball is round there is hope." When the players saw how their counterparts from other countries were treated there was some grumbling, but Schaeffer was strict. "We had worked hard to make Mexico. It's no good sitting around enjoying the sun - we get plenty of that back home. We must work, plan and fight from now on," he said. Things remained low key in their camp and few fans visited them at their rather dull motel, unlike down the road where the Uruguayans were given star treatment and had six swimming pools.

When the England squad moved to Guadalajara in preparation for the opening match, among the fans greeting it was Paul Metcalf. He had set off for the finals in 1968 and had worked his way from New York, across Canada and down the West Coast to Mexico. There were also five fans who had driven 8,000 miles from Toronto in a converted school bus. After the tournament they planned to go to Acapulco to earn enough money to ship themselves and the bus to Australia. The eventual aim was to circle the world over the next three years.

Another team having to change hotels was Peru. On 27th May, whilst relaxing by the pool, the players had their attentions distracted by the arrival of four very shapely German girls. When coach Didí discovered that a further 20 were due to arrive the next day, he decided that the best interests of the campaign would not be served by staying put.

The Group Two series of games got underway on 2nd June and up at the Cuauhtemoc Stadium in Pueblo, the mighty Uruguayans took on the amateurs of Israel. Uruguay, now managed by Juan Hohberg, one of their stars in 1954, had lost non of their penchant for defence, though such a negative approach was hardly needed this day. They could afford to enjoy themselves and play the type of football that had gloried past Uruguayan teams. They lost Pedro Rocha early in the game with a groin strain, but it did not daunt their attacking flair and ten minutes later they went ahead when Juan Martín Mujica crossed a ball for Ildo Maneiro to head past Visoker in the Israeli goal. Vissoker, a bus driver by trade, was one of the busiest men on the field and, time after time, worked wonders to deny the constant threat posed by South American attacks. Without him, it might have been a massacre. The Uruguayans played some delightful football, with Luís Cubilla particularly menacing, but always on hand was Vissoker to spoil the party. Mujica scored his second goal five minutes into the second half, following a period when his team was camped almost exclusively in Israeli territory, but frustration mounted as they failed to turn dominance into goals. They had to settle for a 2-0 victory and hope that lack of goals might not prove decisive.

Going into the tournament, Alf Ramsey had confidently predicted a second English victory. "We do not fear any team. We are going to be champions for a second time", he had said and he had solid grounds for optimism. The addition to the squad of men like Manchester City's Colin Bell and Francis Lee, or Tottenham's Alan Mullery, gave the squad increased strength and playing dimension, and many felt, like Ramsey, that this squad could go all the way. In their first test, in the baking heat of the Jalisco Stadium in Guadalajara, they acquitted themselves well, though found it difficult to break down a Romanian team too ready to rely on dirty play and hard-nosed defence. The Romanians, with clever ball control and quick accurate passing, were more than capable of lifting their game and would have gone ahead after only five minutes had not Tataru volleyed wide. They also rattled the English crossbar later in the half. However, the English were "a studied, cool unit with scarcely a flaw in defence and always full of running up front" and gradually began to take charge as the first half went on. Bobby Charlton was unceremoniously upended in the penalty area, when Lee had put him through, but the appeal was turned down. It was typical of a referee who, in seeming disregard of FIFA's instructions, allowed the Romanians to get away with too much and England had to wait until 20 minutes into the second half before Geoff Hurst's low, left foot shot scored the game's only goal. It was a good effort and meant that Hurst had scored England's last three World Cup goals. They had been scored in two matches, with four years coming between them.

Peru's first appearance in the World Cup finals for 40 years was overshadowed by the terrible tragedy of the dreadful earthquake that had shattered the country two days previously and which claimed the lives of some 50,000 people. Most of the Peruvian squad had managed to make contact with close relatives, but the awful shock had quite clearly affected them. They played the game wearing black armbands and deserve much credit for their contribution to a vastly entertaining spectacle. It began in sombre mood, with two minutes silence, and revved up into a "pulsating match of speed and endeavour in which both sides rose above the strength-sapping obstacles of height and heat." The Bulgarians took a first half lead with the first goal of the tournament, scored by Dinko

The strange case of Bobby Moore and the missing bracelet.

In May 1970, the English squad travelled to Colombia to complete preparations for the forthcoming tournament. With them were a number of FA officials and on 25th May one of these, Dr. Andrew Stephen, received a telephone call from the head of the secret police in Bogotá inviting him to lunch. The chief added: "And please bring Mr. Moore with you." The English were preparing to leave for Mexico and there was total surprise when the two turned up for lunch and Bobby Moore was arrested, accused of stealing a diamond studded gold bracelet, valued at £600, from the Green Fire jewellery store in the Teqendama Hotel where they had been staying. According to Moore's account of the incident, he and Bobby Charlton had gone into the shop to enquire about a ring they had noticed. They left the shop, but were called back in. Moore said: "I thought the girl wanted to show me something else. But then they said the bracelet was missing. We offered to be searched and asked for them to call the police but she said it was not necessary and we thought that was the end of the matter." It was not, and the England star had to endure five days of investigation and court appearances, whilst his team mates flew on to Mexico leaving him behind. They were trying times, but Moore kept his dignity. Dr. Stephen, who stayed with him, later described his demeanour as "splendid from first to last - calm, undismayed and always with a sense of humour. I am proud of him." An example of this sense of humour came when Moore's personal guard asked him for a souvenir. Moore held out his wrists as if to be handcuffed and said that he would comply if the guard would "give me a pair of bracelets." Investigations were carried out in court, where Clara Padilla, a shop employee, said she saw Moore pocket the bracelet, as did Alvaro Suárez, who claimed to have been only three feet away when the incident occurred. Bobby Charlton was named as "accomplice to the offence" and the prosecutor asked that he be questioned in the Colombian embassy in Mexico City. Moore was even taken to the shop for an "ocular inspection" during which he was examined by the judge for his side of the story.

The case attracted a great deal of publicity and Harold Wilson was moved to send a telegram stating that: "We are all greatly concerned to hear the news about Bobby Moore." Whether or not it did any good, the case against Moore was not strong. One witness withdrew his evidence, the bracelet had not been found, Moore vehemently protested his innocence and it was not the first time that an important visitor to Bogotá had been "stung". Eventually, five days after his arrest, Moore was released after Judge Pedro Dorado declared that he did not have enough evidence "at the moment to justify a charge of theft." He was able to rejoin his team mates, but a condition of the release was that he had to report to the Colombian consul in Mexico City. He seemed to think that it was all over and he said: "I am pleased that the accusations which have been made against me have been shown to be unfounded." All went quiet until when 2nd August, the case was reopened. Moore's response was that he was "surprised this business has blown up again. I thought the whole matter was finished."

It nearly was. The case against Moore was beginning to crumble, as were the business lives of those involved. Clara Padilla was sacked and the shop owner, Danlio Rojas, closed it down at the request of the hotel. Then, the bracelet was reported as being seen offered for sale in Bogotá. Further investigations were uncovering what appeared to be a set up, either to discredit Moore personally or the England team collectively. On 13th August the police declared they were "absolutely certain about the innocence of Bobby Moore", and by 18th had "concrete evidence" that he had been framed. Two days later, after three judges had "thoroughly examined the voluminous files on the case", Moore was exonerated, though it wasn't until November 1972 that he was officially cleared. He had been one of a line of celebrities similarly framed in Colombia, most of who had paid up to avoid the scandal.

Dermendiev in the 12th minute. It was a cleverly worked goal from a free kick, which saw Christo Bonev receive the ball and play a perfectly weighted pass behind the Peruvian wall for Dermendiev to sprint on to and "hit an irresistible shot past Rubinos". Four minutes into the second half and Bulgaria's lead was doubled when Rubinos dropped a Bonev free kick into his own net. It looked all up for Peru, but they began a spirited fightback that began in the 50th minute, when Alberto Gallardo found the net. Five minutes later captain, Héctor Chumpitaz, equalized. Peru's third goal was the best, a solo effort from Téofilo Cubillas, who feinted two dummy passes, "left two defenders in a tangle, and slid the ball beyond Simeonov with contemptuous simplicity." Four decades after beginning its World Cup history, Peru had achieved its first win the final stages.

The next day, 3rd June, brought the other eight finalists into play and debutantes and part timers, El Salvador, took on Belgium in the Azteca Stadium. Playing in front of 94,000 spectators was an awesome experience for the Central Americans, but in spite of constant running and enthusiasm, they could make no headway against the stronger Europeans. The Times noted that so "supreme were the Belgians that the wonder is that they did not double their tally of goals." They had to settle for a 3-0 victory that was no reflection of the balance of play, but of the opportunities they scorned. They went ahead in the 12th minute with a 30 yard free kick from Wilfried van Moer "that stunned the crowd", he added a second

It was not just the English who wanted to be left alone. The Belgians claimed they had secret tactics that no one was allowed to see and journalists trying to get into Mexico's training sessions were arrested. Soviets reasons were more straightforward, trainer, Gavriel Katchaline, announcing that: "Everybody else is doing it, we will train alone, too." Czech trainer, Josef Marko simply said: "We don't want to be disturbed."

In a poll carried out a day before West Germany's opening match, 1470 men were asked about their wives attitudes to the tournament. 24% said they had had arguments about staying up late to watch games, 72% said their wives were "understanding" and the remaining 4% were not sure. The older wives were the most negative.

Altitude, Attitude and Artistry - Mexico 1970

Police descended on the hotel used by the 30 World Cup referees when a rumour emerged that attempts at bribery were to be made. They were given 24 hour protection and trained in deserted stadiums with doors firmly locked.

Recently captured guerrillas revealed a plot to kidnap Pelé, who received an armed guard at his Guadalajara training camp. His hotel was also placed under heavy guard and he slept in a different room each night. All the Brazilian players were insured for £83,000. The Germans were also felt to be under threat from a terrorist group, the Tumpamaros fighting for the liberation of South America, and were warned to go round in groups at all times.

Not impressed by the presence of the Brazilians in the small town of Guanajuatos near Guadalajara, a local taxi driver said: "We just don't care much for football. The town is too small to have its own team. Most people here follow baseball if they follow any sport."

The "Eat My Own Words" Award goes to...

Bernard Joy of the London Evening Standard (again!). Previewing the Czechoslovakia v Brazil match, he wrote of the Czechs: "My belief that they will bring off a surprise is backed by striker Adamac, who scored a hat trick against Brazil in Bratislava two years ago." Later, the Romanian Mercea Lusescu, told the paper: "We feel that if we can get a draw against England we will be so encouraged that we will finish higher than Brazil in the group - Brazil play old-fashioned football not like England who are the best organized in the world." Joy's response was to say that "Lusescu is typical of the new wave, highly intelligent European footballers who realize that method and teamwork will overcome individual brilliance." Both predictions were wrong!

ten minutes into the second half and the final strike was a penalty from Raoul Lambert.

The West Germans found things much tougher against the Moroccans in their Group Four encounter in Léon. The Africans were coached by the former Yugoslav goalkeeper, Blagoje Vidinic, who had moulded a very compact unit that "played with considerable skill both individually and as a team." In the 21st minute they horrified the Germans by grabbing the lead with a fine goal that ended a skilful move. Moroccan captain, Bamous, made a darting run down the middle and passed the ball out to the right-wing. The cross seemed to panic a hesitant German defence and, in their uncertainty, the ball landed at the feet of Mohamed Houmane Jarir, who stroked it into the net with ease. Shocked, the Germans immediately resumed the offensive, but the Moroccans defended well in numbers. The Germans had excellent opportunity to redeem the situation as Morocco resumed the second half without their goalkeeper. Allal Ben Kassou had allegedly not heard the referee call out the players and oddly neither the players nor the referee noticed. The second half was over a minute old before Allal took his place. Vidinic insisted that the players had not been called and angrily stated that he had "never seen such a scandal." With goalkeeper back between the posts and after a considerable period of pressure, veteran Uwe Seeler scored the equalizer in the 56th minute. He had now scored in four consecutive World Cup finals. Some 12 minutes from time, it was Germany's newest goal machine, Gerhard Müller, whose goal saved their blushes. The Germans had taken the points, but the Moroccans could look back over their performance with considerable pride, especially goalkeeper Kassou, without whose heroics the margin of victory would have been far wider. The comment made after the game by German manager, Helmut Schön, reveals both his relief and his admiration for the valiant Moroccans. "Morocco proved a very good team", he said, "I was frightened."

The Italians opened their campaign against Sweden in the Luis Desal Stadium in Toluca, at 8,000 feet, the highest of the grounds used. The first half, at least, was largely a one-sided affair. The Italians, "implacable in defence, daring and dangerous in attack" exposed "Sweden as a team without teamwork, lacking mobility and speed of movement." Their "inter-passing was electric" and they created several early chances, with Luigi Riva and Roberto Boninsegna guilty of profligacy in front of goal, before rather fortuitously taking the lead in the 15th minute. Seeing danger where there was none, the Swedes gave away an unnecessary corner and the cross was knocked out to Giacinto Facchetti. His short side pass to Angelo Domenghini was hit towards goal from outside the area. Goalkeeper, Ronnie Helström, stopped it, but then allowed it to slip under his body. Italy's best football was played in this period of the match. In the second half they fell back on defence to preserve what they had and were easily able to contain the Swedes. Domenghini's lone strike was to be his team's only goal of the group stage, a sad fact that reflects all too clearly Italy's approach to their other two matches.

The other game played that day saw Brazil take on Czechoslovakia. The Czechs, "well drilled but prosaic", began the game sprightly enough and took the lead in the 11th minute, when Ladislav Petras took advantage of a careless defence that had yet to wake up. They might have doubled their lead soon after had not Vesely blasted over the bar. This was sufficient warning for the Brazilians, now managed by Mario Zagalo, and they rose to take complete charge of the rest of the game. They put on such a wonderful display, that it caused the Times's reporter to exclaim: "Here was a different dimension of football; a different kind of magic. These Brazilians live by pure skill alone." The revival was engineered by Gérson, "who created a bonfire which was fanned by the masterly play of Pelé, Tostao, Jairzinho and the powerful shooting of Rivelino." Their equalizer came from a free kick, given when Pelé was brought down on the edge of the area. He made to take it himself, but Rivelino confounded the Czechs by swerving it into the net around the defensive wall. Pelé came close to grabbing the lead just before half-time when he tried to lob the goalkeeper from all of 60 yards and further chances were created early in the second half, one from Gérson, who hit the post with a bender of a shot. It seemed only time before the Czechs wilted under the weight of the pressure. Sure enough, some 14 minutes after the restart, Pelé took Gérson's pass on his chest, swept past three defenders and fired into the net. He had become the first player to score in four consecutive tournaments. Gérson also set up the third, when his long pass put Jairzinho free to score a goal that appeared offside. There was, however, no doubt about his next goal. He took a pass from Pelé, danced through four defenders and beat a despairing goalkeeper. The Brazilians had given the most positive display so far, a clear warning to the other finalists.

Three days later, the Soviet Union produced an equally emphatic performance to record "a victory of disarming simplicity that must have reduced every Belgian supporter to tears." The Belgians created one plausible chance in the 13th minute, which was wasted by van Moer, and for the rest of the game were forced to sit back by Soviet forwards, who "achieved mobility without effort" and "had the Belgian defence chasing shadows." The Soviets took the lead after a quarter of an hour with a long range shot from Anatoli Bishovets that skidded across the turf into the net. However, in spite of their dominance, it was ten minutes into the second half before Kakhi Asatiani registered their second with a shot that went in off the post. In the 63rd minute Bishovets followed up a brilliant run through the heart of Belgium's defence with his second and things were wrapped up 15 minutes from the end when Vitali Khmelniski steered a diving header between the posts.

Far less appealing was Italy's game against Uruguay. Both had won their opening games and both knew that they would qualify for the next stage providing they did not lose their remaining group fixtures. Here were two teams overly prone to defence and the result was a match bereft of any entertainment factor. As one reporter lamented: "We had forecast a classic.... and in a way it was - a classic bore." The Italians created only two chances in the whole game, both wasted by Riva, whilst the Uruguayans contented themselves with a few, speculative, long range efforts. It was a sorry sight for the 30,000 spectators and even Riva, after the game, admitted that it "must have been bad to watch."

In Group Three, Romania took on Czechoslovakia and they played far better than indicated by the 2-1 scoreline - or more accurately the Czechs were far worse. True, they took a 3rd minute lead when Vesely's cross was met by Petras's diving header, "a beauty under pressure", but this was virtually the Czechs' last positive move. As one reporter had it, they "snatched a quick goal, held their own for half the match and then went downhill rapidly." They managed to defend their lead into the second half, with Romania becoming increasingly dominant and Nunweiler, in particular, commanding the midfield. He set up Alexandru Neagu in the 52nd minute, to equalize with a tight-angled shot that squeezed between goalkeeper and post. He also had a hand in the second when his pass sent Neagu through on goal only for the forward to be yanked to the ground by Jan Zlocka. The penalty was put away by Florea Dumitrache for a 2-1 victory that kept the Czechs rooted to the foot of the table.

The Moroccans found their next game against Peru a much tougher operation. They held at bay the aggressive and lively Peruvians for the whole of the first half and 20 minutes of the second with a defence that was organized and resilient. However, the Peruvians always looked the more likely and they began to turn the match as their opponents tired. After the game, coach Vidinic said that two hard games in three days were too much for his amateurs. Peruvian pressure eventually forced an error from his defence when goalkeeper, Kassou failed to clear a ball effectively from his area and it fell to Téofilo Cubillas, who fired home. This was in the 65th minute and ten minutes later came the goal, a delightful solo strike from Cubillas again, that broke the Moroccan spirit. Roberto Challe scored Peru's third as the game drew to a close and gave his team a second win in the tournament and progress into the next stage. Credit, though, must go to the courageous Moroccans and the way that they had defied the odds for so long. (See Cubillas profile on page 225).

7th June saw England's classic encounter with Brazil (See England v Brazil profile on page 229and Gordon Banks profile on page 228) and a major controversy in the first half of the game between Mexico and El Salvador

Both England and Brazil had general elections going on at the time of the finals.

Ticket touts, known locally as "scalpers", sold tickets on the street at up to five times their face value. In one police action 19 were arrested, the tickets confiscated and each fined 3,000 pesos (about £100) with two weeks in gaol.

After the games between England and Brazil and Mexico and El Salvador, Guadalajara and Mexico City erupted into delirious parties. Fans chanting and dancing in the rain clogged the streets. One open-top car was seen with 26 people in and on it. Traffic cops simply gave up trying to untangle the mess. When Mexico reached the quarter-finals the partying brought chaos to Mexico City. There was one death, 70 injuries, numerous cars and a bus were stolen. Similar scenes were anticipated in Toluca for Mexico's appearance in the quarter-finals, even though the ground only held 32,000 people. Many thousands more were expected to make the short trip from Mexico City. After it, the Toluca police were relieved as the Mexicans accepted their defeat gracefully in silence and left the streets to go home to commiserate.

that threatened to disrupt the match totally. The Mexicans, seeking to please their supporters after the earlier disappointment, saw this match as the perfect opportunity to do so and went on to the offensive from the start. They dominated almost every aspect of play, though were unable to crack a defence that fought as if life depended on it. Theirs was a rugged, gritty performance and with the team playing on its nerves, tension erupted in the face of a blatant injustice as the half drew to a close. The Egyptian referee, Ali Kandil, awarded a free kick to El Salvador in their own half, but it was cheekily taken by the Mexican player, Padilla. He passed the ball to Javier Valdivia, who had no trouble cutting through an unprepared and immobile defence to score. Then, strangely, the referee allowed the goal to stand. The result was pandemonium as a wave of vehement protests exploded all over the pitch. For nearly five minutes the El Salvadorians swarmed around the referee, whilst others rolled about the floor in anguish and tears. They refused to pick the ball out of the net and place it on the centre spot. Mr Kandil had to do it himself and then they refused to kick off. In the end, the referee solved the problem by blowing for half-time, but when they came out again, the El Salvadorians were clearly broken. When, in the first minute, Valdivia wove his way through the defence to score his second, the damage was complete. Ten minutes later, Javier Frogoso netted a third and Juan Basaguren made it 4-0 in the 83rd minute. He had come on as a substitute for Lopéz, who had himself been brought on to replace Borja. Basaguren became the first substitute to replace a substitute in the World Cup finals.

Israel's first point in the World Cup finals came from a surprising 1-1 draw with Sweden in Toluca. They came out of the game with much credit and might have gained the lead had Faygenbaum taken either of the two first half chances that fell his way. The Swedes had to withstand an initial 15 minutes of Israeli pressure before beginning to exert themselves. Swedish strength began to tell in the later stages of the first half, but they could not crack a defence that was not afraid to mix in the rough stuff when needed. The Swedes responded in kind and tempers began to fray, especially when fighting broke out mid way through the second half. The Ethiopian referee, Seyoun Tarrekegn, was forced to stop the game, consult his linesman and then speak to both captains to calm things down. Before this the Swedes had taken the lead, when Axelsson broke down the right and Tom Turesson knocked in the cross. They were in front for only three minutes. Mordechai Spiegler stunned the Scandinavians with a brilliant solo run through the defence and a surprise shot from 20 yards that went in past Sven Larsson for one of the goals of the tournament.

Following their narrow escape against Morocco, the West Germans changed things round for their game against Bulgaria. In came Reinhard Libuda to add power to the attack and the ploy worked perfectly. He was nicknamed "Stan" by his team mates because of the resemblance of his style of play to that of Stanley Matthews and he showed why that afternoon. He was superb and tormented the Bulgarian defenders from the start. The Germans went on immediate attack and gave a "performance of power and purpose", but it was Bulgaria who took the lead against the run of play, the result of a defensive error. Giving away a free kick on the edge of the area, the German wall failed to line up correctly and left Sepp Maier unsighted. Asparoukhov side footed the kick to Asparuch Nikodimov, who blasted it round the wall into the net. It was merely a temporary set back and eight minutes later the irrepressible Libuda restored parity, when he sliced through the defence, "showing astonishing speed for the conditions" to unleash a shot of such power that goalkeeper, Simeonov, dropped it over his line. The referee had to consult the linesman before awarding the goal. By this stage, the Germans were running the game and in the 27th minute Libuda provided the cross from which Müller headed the lead. They scored three more in the second half, the first a Müller penalty after Libuda had been brought down, the second from Seeler and the third giving Müller his hat trick two minutes before the end. Bojil Kolev scored for Bulgaria in the last minute, but it could not disguise the crushing nature of the 5-2 victory.

El Salvador's final game was against the Soviet Union and they made a brave showing against the group's strongest team. The Soviets were below their best and "looked far from convincing in a match of few football skills." Both had their moments of attack, though El Salvador were unable to penetrate a strong Soviet defence. At the other end, in the words of the Irish Times, the Soviet forwards were "ineffective, more because of their own bad shooting than as a result of the close marking of the Central American defenders." It was not until the second half that they did what form suggested they ought to have done much earlier. In the 51st minute, Albert Shesterniev sent a long forward pass through the centre of the defence and Bishovets hammered it past Raúl Magana, who had hardly put a foot wrong until then. Bishovets struck again, in the 74th minute, latching on to a cross from Vladimir Muntian and securing a victory, which gave the Soviets the group's top spot. Much credit, though, must be given to El Salvador, who made a far stronger team look ordinary for long periods.

The game between Sweden and Uruguay should have been refereed by Brazil's Antonio De Moroes, but rumours circulated that he had taken a bribe and FIFA decided to replace him with the USA's Henry Landauer. The stories were untrue and angered the Uruguayan FA, who saw it as a slight against their national integrity. The players, however, did not allow it to upset the nature of their game. Once again, they resorted to their worst traditions and spent most of the game defending. They surrendered the initiative to the Swedes, who created several good chances without converting any. They came closest in the first half when Lief Eriksson hit the post. The pattern of play after the break remained much the same and Sweden's cause suffered a serious blow when striker, Ove Kindvall, had to go off with a knee injury. They stuck rigidly to their task and continued to chase the breakthrough that would change their fortunes. The longer the game went on, though, the more obstructive became the South Americans. As one reporter put it, "for 89 minutes the slow-motion ball dancers from Uruguay were booed and whistled for their displays of negative football." They played for time and numerous 40 yard back passes threaded their way to the goalkeeper, or they tried to slow the game down and keep possession. Eventually, fate handed out justice of a kind when, in the final minute Bo Larsson sent in the cross which substitute, Ove Grahn, headed in. The Swedes had the victory they deserved, but unfortunately needed to have won by two clear goals to have bettered Uruguay's goal difference and to get into the next stage. Instead, the South Americans yawned their way into the quarter-finals. How Sweden must have rued not hammering the Israelis.

For the first half-hour against Brazil, the Romanians "played like hypnotised rabbits caught in the glare of headlights." They allowed their opponents to dictate the pace of play and only the woodwork and some heavy tackling prevented them from being overwhelmed. In the eighth minute, Paolo Cesar crashed the ball against the underside of the bar and two minutes later, Everaldo struck the post. Yet, despite their dominance, it was 20 minutes before Brazil made anything of it. They were awarded a free kick on the edge of the area, which Tostão sent over the bar. The referee, however, had not signalled for it to be taken and ordered the ball replaced. This time Tostão jumped over the ball, leaving it to Pelé, whose well placed shot hit the mark. Three minutes later, Jairzinho made it 2-0 and the Romanians decided to make a change. Necula Raducanu had been the regular first choice keeper, but as coach Angelo Niculescu explained, he had "been taken from the list of the team nucleus for disobedience." Too many late nights had seen his place taken by Sterica Ademache. Two goals against were enough to bring him back into favour and he became the first goalkeeper to replace a goalkeeper in the World Cup finals. It also served to awaken the team from their lethargy and put some confidence into their stride. They began to play much more brightly and pulled themselves back into the reckoning. Neagu came close with two efforts, before Emerich Dembrowski crossed the ball and Dumitrache rounded two defenders before beating Felix with a left foot drive. This was ten minutes before the break and, encouraged by their success, they continued to take the game to Brazil in the second half. They were looking the better side and remained so even after Pelé struck in the 65th minute to restore the two goal advantage. Five minutes from time, Dembrowski added a second to run the Brazilians close. It was enough to put Brazil through, but Romania would have to wait on England's final group match before knowing their fate.

Altitude, Attitude and Artistry - Mexico 1970

Having been through an earlier operation for a detached retina, Tostão, offered to quit the Brazilian squad when the problem surfaced during heading practice. The coach refused his request.

The Belgian coach had to go briefly into hiding after insulting the jewel in Mexico's crown - the Azteca Stadium. "The grass is too long, and the ground is too bumpy, none of my players like the pitch", he said.

Fifteen of the Belgian squad had contracts worth £500 a game to wear a particular type of boot, three were on £1000 a game to wear another and two had contracts that involved no payment. The situation caused so much friction that some players threatened not to pass to those wearing rival boots. They even refused a compromise that the money should be pooled and divided evenly, though things were finally smoothed over.

Both West Germany and Peru had already qualified when they met in Group Four. In such circumstances many teams would simply have gone through the motions in, but whoever came second in the group would have to face Brazil and since neither wanted this they produced an entertaining match of far more chances than the final score indicated. Four goals in a 25 minute spell began in the 19th, when Müller got his first. He struck twice more in the next 20 minutes to complete his second consecutive World Cup hat trick, the first player to achieve such a feat. His tally was now seven in three games. Five minutes later, Cubillas scored for Peru and, though this was the last strike of the match, both teams continued to press in the second half. Such was the openness of the game that Müller might have had a second half hat trick and the Peruvians might have taken the lead themselves as the Germans tired in the heat. Sepp Maier played wonderfully and kept the South Americans at bay. Like Brazil, they were the only other team to go through on maximum points.

When the last round of group matches were played, there was still much at stake, as only Brazil, the Soviet Union and West Germany had places in the quarter-finals. The Mexicans needed a draw in their game against Belgium, but conscious of a need to please the crowd, went for a win. They dominated the first third of the game and took the lead with a controversial penalty awarded when Valdivia raced into the Belgian area and was challenged by Leon Jack. Jack fell whilst trying to clear the ball and the Mexican tumbled over him. As the referee pointed to the spot, the Belgians complained that their man had been fouled if anybody had. Their protests went unheeded and the kick was converted by Gustavo Peña. The Europeans rallied themselves and came back at the Mexicans. Over the next hour they created enough chances to have won the match, including one ten minutes from the end when Johannes Devrind noticed Ignacio Calderón off his line. He lobbed him quite superbly, but as the ball was heading towards the open goal, defender Mario Pérez sprinted back to hook the ball away to safety. It was a lucky escape and it had not been the first time in this tournament that fortune had smiled on the home team, which had gone further in the World Cup than any of its predecessors.

Mexico 1 : Belgium 0
Belgium goalkeepr Piot in action.

Despite having two goals disallowed in their final group game against Israel, the Italians were once again disappointing. Whilst a draw was good enough to take them through as group winners, they might have shown more ambition against a technically weaker side. Instead, they were content to play out a 0-0 draw and it was indicative of their attitude that European Footballer of the Year, Gianni Rivera, began the game on the bench, though he later came on for Domenghini. When they did show inclination to go forwards, they produced little against a hard and well organized Israeli defence. Jehoshua Schwager kept Luigi Riva quiet and Italy's other attackers disfunctioned without his inspiration. The two cancelled goals, from Bertini in the first half and Riva in the second, show what might have been had fear of losing not dictated Italian tactics. They had gone through with the second worst goal tally in the group stage, matched by only Israel and worsened only by El Salvador, who had failed to score at all.

Other teams who gave disappointing displays that day were England and Czechoslovakia. The Czechs had not had a good tournament, but England could manage only one decent first half shot when Mullery ran through the defence only for goalkeeper, Ivo Viktor, to turn it round the post. They might even have gone behind had not Jack Charlton made a timely tackle to rob Josef Adamec, who had rounded Banks and looked likely to score. It was Bobby Charlton's 105th cap, equalling Billy Wright's record, but it was only after he had been replaced by Alan Ball in the 65th minute that England began to play to potential. Even so, it took a penalty, given for hand ball and converted by Allan "Sniffer" Clarke. The English were grateful for their narrow lead, but they almost lost it eight minutes from time when the Czechs hit the bar. The Czechs were one of only two teams not to have gained a point and so dismal had been their World Cup that the manager was sacked on his return to Prague.

Israel 0 : Italy 0
Italy's Luigi Riva (right) is tackled by an Israeli defender.

England players were warned not to run for the ball if it went out of play and to pass it to feet to avoid over exertion. They were also given salt tablets, a South African potion to harden the skin against the sun, sun tan oil and refreshing drinks carried in new thermos flasks costing £9 each.

Bulgaria and Morocco were playing to avoid the wooden spoon in their final game and Bulgaria made several changes in an attempt to salvage something from their campaign. It did little good against a solid Moroccan defence. The Europeans took the lead in the first half when Dobromir Zechev stabbed a free kick into the top of the net, only to have the Moroccans equalize 15 minutes into the second. Mauhu Ghazouani, one of the best players on the pitch, let fly a surprise shot that took a fortunate deflection off a defender on its way to the goal. It was enough to secure the draw, give Morocco their first point in the World Cup finals and leave Bulgaria bottom of the group.

Morocco 1 : Bulgaria 1
Morocco goalkeeper Hazzaz punches clear from Bulgaria's Georgi Popov.

Whilst the performances and attitude of some teams in the group stages had been poor, to say the least, there had been some outstanding football played by others. However, the tournament blossomed when it reached

England's mascot, a ten-month-old Bulldog by the name of Winston, had his application for tickets turned down by the World Cup organising committee. Committee member, Enrique Ladron Guevara, said: "There are no tickets for Winston, the decision has been made by my superiors in Mexico City."

Bobby Charlton became the first non-Mexican to receive the State of Jalisco's "Sportsman of the Year" Award. The decision was made personally by State Governor, Francisco Medina Ascencio, for "setting an example his country can be proud of."

the knock-out phase. There were some tremendously exciting games, not least that between West Germany and England. The English had ambitions of retaining their championship, but the Germans were keen to avenge their defeat of four years earlier and it produced a game of high drama, which swung first one way and then the other in the heat of a Mexican afternoon. It looked to be going well for England when Mullery took a pass from Keith Newton and shot his team into a first half lead. It looked even better in the 49th minute when Martin Peters made it 2-0, but then Germany made a substitution of pivotal importance. They put on Jürgen Grabowski in place of Libuda and his fresh legs lent added pace and penetration to the German attack at the time when England's defence began to wilt in the heat.

Beckenbauer began the revival with a shot from outside the area that Peter Bonetti ought to have saved. (See Franz Beckenbauer profile on page 227). The Chelsea man, in goal because Banks had gone down to an upset stomach caused by a dodgy bottle of beer, looked to have it covered, but let it slip under his body. Ramsey then made two tactical errors that many have blamed for England's defeat. Both Bobby Charlton and Terry Cooper were tiring, but Ramsey replaced Charlton when Cooper's problem appeared worse. He then put on Norman Hunter for Peters, hoping to bolster the defence, but the move unhinged the balance of the team and the Germans took full advantage. In the 81st minute they struck again. Karl-Heinz Schnellinger lofted a high pass into the area and, with Brian Labone tired and unable to deal with the situation, Uwe Seeler equalized with a brilliant header. The game went into extra time, but by now the English were psychologically beaten. They had little more to give and realized the chips were down when Hurst had a goal disallowed. Three minutes into the second period, Grabowski crossed the ball, Löhr headed on and Gerd Müller put the world champions out. It had been a courageous showing, but the Germans had had their revenge.

A similar pattern emerged in the quarter-final between Italy and Mexico, as first Mexico dictated the pace of play and then Italy clawed their way back to take the game. Italy conceded its first goal of the tournament in the 13th minute, when Javier Frogoso deftly slipped three players before laying on the ball to José Luís González. The Italians restored parity in the 25th minute with a shot from Domenghini that deflected off Gustavo Peña, but it was not until the second half that they began to make a telling impression on the match. It was the half-time substitution of Rivera for Sandro Mazzola that made the difference and gave Italy a greater flexibility in attack. In a ten minute spell that began in the 64th minute, the Italians scored three times. Firstly, Riva's left foot shot found the target and five minutes later, Rivera extended the lead. Then both combined for Italy's last, as Riva collected the ball from his colleague, beat two defenders and slotted the ball inside the left post. By now, the Italians were in total control and playing the kind of football that followers throughout the world had hoped they would have supplied from the start.

The panache shown by Brazil in their quarter-final against Peru, explains precisely why nobody wanted to meet them. With Gérson back and "Pelé and Tostão showing the defects in Peru's defence system, and finding oceans of space in which to move", as one Irish journalist noted, "Brazil's victory was never really in doubt". Pelé revealed his early intentions, hitting the post in the fourth minute, and the Brazilians opened their account in the 11th. Tostão set up Rivelino for the first and, four minutes later, Rivelino repaid the compliment. He got the ball to Tostão, who, with all the instinct of the predator, fired home from an acute angle. The one weakness of this Brazilian team was the defence and this was highlighted when Peru's left-winger, Alberto Gallardo, scored with a narrow angled shot that Felix ought to have stopped. The goal rallied the Peruvians for their best spell of the game, though it was Pelé who came closest to scoring in the period leading up to the break with a withering long range shot that Rubinos needed two takes to stop. Early in the second half, Tostão restored Brazil's two goal lead, when Pelé's shot rebounded to him, but the Peruvians were doughty opponents and they scored again through Cubillas, following a mistake by Brito. However, the Brazilians had the last say, when a brilliant pass by Tostão split Peru's defence and Jairzinho ran in to round Rubinos and slot the ball into the empty net. (See Jairzinho profile on page 224).

Brazil 4 : Peru 2
Peru goalkeeper Rubinos saves at the feet of Brazil's Jairzinho.

Three of the quarter-finals had been thoroughbreds, but the game between Uruguay and the Soviet Union was the one that bucked the trend. The South Americans, terrified of defeat, again allowed their worst tendencies to dominate their thinking and the result was a travesty of entertainment, so frustrating for the 45,000 crowd who had paid good money to see better. With Uruguayan minds set on defence, the Soviets did most of the attacking, but were held in check at every attempt and in every way, fair or foul. A scoreless first half became a scoreless second and the match went into extra time. The heat began to take its toll on the Soviets and when Bishovets had a goal disallowed because Vitali Khmelniski had supplied the ball from an offside position, their spirits began to fail. It was pitiful reward for all their industry, typical of their poor luck, and as they faded, the Uruguayans pulled themselves into the game. The Soviet goalkeeper, Anzor Kavazashvili, had already made two superb saves to deny Ildo Maneiro and Pedro Rocha, but was unable to stop the goal which came with three minutes remaining. Uruguay had brought on Victor Esperrago in the first period of extra time and he got on to the end of Cubilla's cross to head the winner. The Soviets protested that the ball had gone out of play before it had been centred, but the referee waved aside their appeals. The goal stood and ended their World Cup so cruelly and undeservedly.

With the exception of this last game, Mexico '70 had bloomed into brilliance and the festival continued into the semi-finals, with that between Italy and West Germany producing one of the most dramatic endings the World Cup has ever seen. (See Italy v West Germany profile on page 231). Meanwhile, following the elimination of their team, the Mexican public threw their fanaticism behind Brazil, whom they had always admired and feted as the stars of the show. This was especially so at Guadalajara, where Brazil had played all of their games so far, and so it was with dismay that

Riot police had to break up a serious brawl outside the stadium prior to the Brazil-Uruguay game when unruly Brazilian fans grabbed an Uruguayan flag and the Uruguayan fans retaliated. During the game each Brazil goal was greeted with a mass of fireworks in all major Brazilian cities. Similar scenes were witnessed in Rome during the other semi-final, the biggest spontaneous outpouring of feeling since 1945. Supporters banged drums and police ignored the sounding of car horns, banned in built-up areas. Three Italians and one German died of heart attacks watching the game on television.

Altitude, Attitude and Artistry - Mexico 1970

Uruguay refused to go the post-tournament banquet to which they were invited as semi-finalsits. It was because Sir Stanley Rous was to be there.

The final was the only game East German, Rudi Glockner, had refereed in the whole tournament.

In a letter to the London Evening Standard on 7th June, Londoner J. A. Smith wrote: "Is there anyone in the country besides myself whose reaction to the subject of football is stone cold, approaching absolute zero, and who doesn't care a referee's whistle whether England wins the World Cup or not? Who, if anyone, will join me in urging that... all British professional football should be played on the moon and players, managers and club directors should stay there between games."

Brazilian captain Carlos Alberto with the Jules Rimet trophy after their 4-1 victory over Italy.

the Uruguayans learned that the semi-final would also take place there. They were still smarting from the bribery allegations and took the decision to hold the match on Brazil's "home" ground as further proof of a conspiracy to undermine their tournament. They complained vociferously, unpleasant insinuations were cast, but FIFA would not alter the venue and when the game went against them, it was through the mastery of Brazil and not the partisanship of the crowd. Uruguay's style of play had hardly won them friends, though this day they showed more mettle. They gave their opponents a fright and took the game to Brazil, whose friable defence came close to conceding the lead. Twice in the opening period of play, Felix was called upon to make saves from Morales and Fontes and twice he fumbled and nearly let the ball slip. Then, in the 19th minute, "a square, almost statuesque defence was outwitted by a sharp pass across field from Morales." It was picked up by Cubilla, who seemed to overrun the ball, taking it close to the bye line. From a tight angle, he fired at goal and "although he only half-hit his shot, it was sufficient to beat Felix", who had strayed out of position. The Uruguayans held their lead until the last moments of injury time, when Tostão "whipped in the ball from the left and Clodoaldo crashed it into the net." It was the break Brazil needed and in the second half they found their feet with the sort of up-beat display that Uruguay could not answer. Their preponderance paid dividends in the 76th minute when a brilliant move, begun by Jairzinho and involving Pelé and Tostão, was finished off by Jairzinho himself. Their third came in the last minute, scored by Rivelino and set up by Pelé. They had reached the World Cup final for the third time in the last four tournaments.

Before the final, there was the matter of the 3rd/4th play-off. After the dreadful farce that had been served up in the corresponding fixture four years earlier, many had come to doubt its value, but West Germany and Uruguay served up a match that "proved more than a little palatable", to use the Guardian's description. It was assumed the Germans were not taking it seriously when they left out Beckenbauer and replaced Maier with second choice, Wolter. Yet, German teams are not normally given to such poor attitudes and it was Uruguay, directed it seemed by some preordained script, who took their usual defensive posture and allowed the Germans to exert the pressure. They scored in the 26th minute with a goal that "was a masterpiece of planning." Libuda attacked down the right and crossed to the far post, where Seeler was lurking to head back to Müller. He deigned to go for goal himself and, instead, side tapped the ball to Overath, for the only goal of the half. After the interval, the Germans had to defend, as Uruguay at last began to play the sort of football that had won fame for previous national sides. They "mounted a series of attacks and showed a depth of imagination which should have earned them some reward." As the game drew to a close, they had the Germans hanging on, but they somehow survived to take third place by the single goal. On the balance of play of both teams over the whole tournament, it was a placing Germany deserved.

The final was a magnificent occasion (See Brazil v Italy profile on page 232) and ensured that Mexico's first World Cup had been a triumph against the expectations of those who had maintained that the conditions would be too difficult to sustain competitive football of any quality. Naturally, as with every World Cup, there were undesirable features. The ugly face of commercialism exerted its mawkish influence upon aspects of the play and organization. Notably, these were the demands of TV schedules, which resulted in some games having to be played in inhumane conditions, and the fear of losing and missing out on the rewards of success, which reduced teams like Italy and Uruguay to the most cynical (and boring) of tactics. Yet, happily, commercialism was still a developing creed and its enticement was not yet all-pervasive. There was still among many players a desire to play, win and entertain, and the notion of art for art's sake had wide currency. Maybe, the pulsating atmosphere created by the boundless enthusiasm of the Mexican public should be given much of the credit for this and certainly Mexico '70 was more the son of Sweden '58, than of either Chile '62 or England '66. For one thing, no players were sent off. The number of goals scored, whilst far below the tally for 1958, was greater than both those of 1962 and 1966. Then, there was the superlative quality of some of the football, especially though not exclusively after the group stage had ended. The number of games meriting a high entertainment quotient was far higher than in the previous two tournaments or in many of those that came later. And, of course, there were the great names. Many a team sheet resounded with players of outstanding calibre, several of whom were bowing off the World Cup stage. Among these were Pelé and Uwe Seeler, veterans of four campaigns, Bobby Charlton, Bobby Moore and Gordon Banks, though others would fight on and illuminate future tournaments. In conclusion, Mexico '70 had been the best so far.

Jair Ventura Filho (Jairzinho)   Brazil

Honours: Winner 1970; 4th Place 1974
Played: 1966, 1970 and 1974

Games 16
Goals 9

Jairzinho celebrates after scoring Brazil's 3rd goal in their 4-1 victory over Italy.

As a boy, Jairzinho had admired Garrincha and he is fittingly regarded as his natural successor on the right-wing. Like his hero, Jairzinho had an array of goals, from delicate chips to blistering shots, and a devastating speed that few defenders could deal with.

Jairzinho was born on Christmas Day in 1944 at Caxias and learned the game on the dirt pitches of the slums of Río de Janeiro. He was sharp, he was fast and he took to the game very quickly. He turned professional at the tender age of 15 with Botafogo where an injury to Garrincha gave him his chance. In those early days he played as left-wing and centre-forward. He made his international debut at the age of 20 in 1964 against Portugal in a Nations Cup tournament that included Argentina and England. He scored and was to keep his place for the next ten years. He featured in the World Cup in 1966, but made little impact in a team that failed miserably. It was a disappointment he had to overcome, but he had the heart and courage to do it.

Between 1966 and 1970 he broke his leg twice, but Mexico provided the stage on which he would shine. He scored seven goals, most of them memorable, some crucial, and, as a defence-splitting playmaker, he also provided precision passes to others. It is, though, his strike against England that most people remember. Tostão had dribbled the ball to the penalty area but had run into an imposing wall of defenders who stood solid and unyielding. However, he stepped around one, then another and then the third before releasing the ball to Pelé. Like piranhas attacking their prey, three defenders were on him in the blink of an eye. Pelé fainted to press on and the rouse worked. As the defenders dropped back, he stopped in his tracks, turned, and passed to the on-coming Jairzinho who, after rounding one Englishman, let fly with a shot that Banks had no chance of stopping. "It was the winning goal. Swaying to the rhythm of a fiesta, Brazil's attackers had tossed off seven guardians of the steel fortress, which simply melted under the breeze blowing from the south." In the semi-final against Uruguay he scored another crucial goal late in the second half. Running deep from within his own half he combined with Pelé and Tostão again, and his speed took him gracefully past the luckless Uruguayan defence. When he walked the ball into the net in the final against Italy to get Brazil's third he created a record that still stands today. He had scored in every round of the tournament including the final.

He was played out of position in Germany in 1974 and was not at his best. He scored only twice, but was one of the few highlights in a very defensive team. After the 1974 tournament, Jairzinho moved to France where he had a brief spell with Olympic Marseille. It did not work out and he returned to Rio to play for Cruzeiro. He continued to make appearances for the national side until he was 38 years old and earned more than 80 caps and scored 35 goals. At club level, the last of many fine achievements came with Cruzeiro in 1976 in the Copa Libertadores. The first leg of the final saw Cruzeiro trounce River Plate 4-1 in Belo Horizonte. However, Cruzeiro lost the second leg 2-1 in Argentina and a play-off was needed. It took place on the 30th July in Santiago. With the score finely balanced at 2-2, and with only 2 minutes to go, Jairzinho stepped up to score the third, match winning goal.

From humble streets to the top of the world, Jairzinho performed with the best. He was part of the spell that transfixed the world in 1970 and, as the cameras role on another World Championship, his goals will be replayed, and fondly remembered by those privileged to see them happen. He eventually finished his career playing for Portuguesa of Venezuela and returned home to set up and fund the small town team of São Cristováo. It was here that he was to meet a young, eager and talented 14 year old with buckteeth and a potential that must have reminded him very much of himself at that age. That boy was Ronaldo. Jairzinho became his agent and set about trying to sell Ronaldo's talents to the Brazilian big guns of Flamenco and Vasco da Gama. Both teams refused to entertain the young genius so the pair settled on Jairzinho's former club, Cruzeiro. In just 60 games Ronaldo scored 58 goals, and the rest is history.

Téofilo Cubillas Aricaga   Peru

Honours: Quarter-finals 1970   **Games 13**
Played: 1970, 1978 and 1982   **Goals 10**

Peru is more noted for its Inca history, its altitude, its llamas and its political coups than it is for its prowess on the football field. However, during the 1970s at least, they were a force to be reckoned with and, in no small part was this due to one exceptionally gifted striker, Téofilo Cubillas. All nations produce world class athletes and Peru's was Cubillas. In 1970, at he age of 21, he became a household name and, in two World Cups eight years apart, he scored ten goals.

Cubillas was born on 8th March 1949 in the poor Puente Piedra district of Lima. From an early age he watched his heroes at Alianza Lima, dreaming of becoming one himself. Pursuing those dreams, he began in the minor leagues, where his rare talent became apparent. He was fast, possessing clever close control and loved to run at defences. His intuitive reading of the game produced quick-fire passes that exploited the slimmest of situations. He was of medium build, but he always made his presence felt in or around the box. In 1965, at the age of only 16, he was given his senior debut for Alianza Lima. He was put into what was already a powerful attacking line up and it was not long before he was winning the hearts of the fans on his way to becoming the club's top scorer. It was at this time that he was given his nickname, "Nene" (Baby) by Alianza legend, Perico Léon, because of his baby face and his gleaming white smile.

On 17th July 1968 he joined the national side, then under Didí's guidance the Peruvians made it through the qualifying rounds to reach the 1970 World Cup finals. Along the way Peru had shocked the football world by eliminating Argentina on their home soil. They had won their home leg 1-0 and only needed to avoid defeat in the final group game in Argentina. A 2-2 draw took them through. The series gave Cubillas the chance to show off his skills and five goals in four games was his response. Peru had a good tournament, making it through to the quarter-finals and Cubillas was one of its undoubted stars.

After the World Cup Cubillas went back to Alianza and in 1972 became South American Player of the Year. By this time the curiosity of the top European teams had been aroused and the following year he signed for FC Basle of Switzerland for £97,000. Six months later he moved to FC Porto, this time for £2,000,000. Here he settled into a midfield role, but was still leading scorer in his first year. Unfortunately the national side was eliminated from the 1974 World Cup in a 2-1 defeat by Chile. The following year though, spearheaded by Cubillas, they roared back to win the South American Championship. They beat Brazil in the semi-final with Cubillas scoring twice over the two legs, before running out 1-0 winners against Colombia in the final. Shortly after this triumph Cubillas returned to Alianza, where he became part of a double act that became known as "La duplo de oro", or the "Golden Pair", that fronted the Alianza line up so successfully. His partner was "Cholo" Hugo Sotil and together they became the most celebrated strikers in Peruvian football history. Both had a great flair for scoring goals and in 1977 and 1978 they helped Alianza to back-to-back league titles. Real Madrid had a chance to sign the pair and the coach there admitted that he had made a big mistake in not doing do.

In 1978, Peru made it through to World Cup finals and Cubillas gave yet another sparkling display. The skill and the acceleration Cubillas had shown in the 1970 World Cup was still there and he opened his account with two superb goals against a lacklustre Scottish side. Then, after holding Holland to a 0-0 draw, they thumped Iran 4-1, with Cubillas scoring a hat trick that included two penalties. Peru topped their first round group, but they failed to perform later in the tournament and they eventually finished bottom of Group B. They conceded a total of ten goals in the second round without reply. However, for Cubillas the whole experience of the two World Cups had been a triumph and he ranked 6th highest goal scorer in tournament history.

In the 1970s the NASL was signing top players in a bid to gain national acceptance and Cubillas joined Fort Lauderdale in 1979. He joined a team that already contained George Best in a league that contained Beckenbauer and Pelé. He stayed for seven years scoring 65 goals, including a hat trick in seven minutes against Los Angeles Aztecs in 1981. In 1982 he appeared for Peru in the Spain World Cup, but it was a major disappointment. At 33 he was past his best and there were no more goals as Peru bowed out in the first round. Cubillas returned to the US before retiring in 1986. He came out of retirement briefly after a plane crash in 1987 claimed the lives of the whole of the Alianza team and he was needed as player and coach to help the club over its tragedy.

In an international career that spanned 88 games, he scored 38 goals. He was a model of control and responsibility on and off the pitch and was only ever booked once. "El Grafico", a South American soccer magazine, considered him one of the greatest of all time, a point of view that is bound to be disputed, but to Peruvians he was.

Franz Beckenbauer   West Germany

Honours: **Games 18**
Player: Winner 1974; Runner-up 1966;3rd place 1970   **Goals 5**
Manager: Winner 1990; Runner-up 1986
Played: 1966, 1970 and 1974
Manager: 1986 and 1990

Franz Beckenbauer celebrates at the end of the 1974 World Cup Final.

Franz Beckenbauer is perhaps the most successful player and manager club football has ever known and only Mario Zagalo has achieved more at international level. Wherever he went the trophies followed. He played with a style and genius that had the fans on the edges of their seats and the pitch would sizzle with the speed and daring of his play. It is the mark of great players that they transform the game and Franz Beckenbauer revolutionized the sweeper's role. After hours studying and admiring the surging runs of Giacinto Facchetti down the flanks as a modern day wing-back would, he adapted it to his position in central defence. It was devastating.

Beckenbauer was born on 11th September 1945 into a war-torn Munich. As a schoolboy he played for 1906 München before joining the Bayern Munich youth team at the age of 13. At 16 he signed on as a professional with Bayern and made his senior team debut at 18. At the time, Bayern were the less fashionable of the Munich sides and did not become part of the Bundesliga when it was formed in 1963. City rivals 1860 Munich did and it was two years before Bayern were promoted to the top flight. He was originally an outside-left, but management sensed the potential and maturity of their young find, and he was switched into midfield. It was in this position that he made his international debut aged 20 and he was to build a partnership with Helmut Schön in much the same way that Fritz Walter had with Sepp Herberger. Playing confidently, Germany sealed a 2-1 victory over Switzerland. His fourth international was the curtain raiser on what became nearly three decades of intense rivalry with Germany's greatest adversaries, England. It was a warm-up match in the run-up to the 1966 World Cup and they lost 1-0. It was one of only two defeats in Beckenbauer's first fourteen internationals. The second was the 1966 final in which he was played out of position, marking Bobby Charlton, a task he did not relish. As he later recalled: "England beat us in 1966 because Bobby Charlton was just a bit better than me."

He tasted success at club level as Bayern won the West German cup in 1966 and 1967, the European Cup-Winners Cup in 1976 and a Bündesliga championship in 1969. It was the beginning of a period of Bayern achievement that was mirrored by the national side, which saw them defeat England to reach the semi-finals in Mexico in 1970. It was at this time that Beckenbauer began experimenting with his surging runs out of defence. It added an element of surprise to his play, though Schön remained unconvinced and it was not until 1971, when Beckenbauer was captain, that it was tried at international level. Its merits became obvious in the 3-0 defeat of the USSR in the 1972 European Championship, with Beckenbauer at the heart of the victory. It resulted in him being named European Footballer of the Year. International success was quickly followed by three successive German Championships with Bayern, which were themselves followed by three European Cup triumphs against Athletico Madrid, Leeds United and St. Étienne in 1976. It was also in 1976 that Bayern beat Cruziero 2-0 to win the World Club Cup. However, Beckenbauer's greatest triumph of all came in the 1974 World Cup Final on his home ground. When he lifted the new trophy, his dream of world domination was complete.

In 1976 Beckenbauer was again named European Footballer of the Year and, by the time he accepted a $2.5 million move to New York Cosmos in 1977, he had made 103 international appearances. He remained in the NASL for four years winning three Soccer Bowl titles in 1977, 1978 and 1980, before returning to Germany for a short spell with Hamburg, helping them become runners up in the UEFA Cup. He played one final season with the Cosmos before retiring in 1984.

Surprisingly, given that he had no managerial experience, Beckenbauer was appointed national team coach and he astonishingly took what many regarded as an ordinary German team to the 1986 final. He took an even better one to Italy in 1990. Once again, he triumphed over England on the way to the title. He followed this with a move back to club football, with a spell at Olympic Marseille. It was not a happy time and in 1994 he returned to Bayern, as manager and guided them to the Bündesliga title before moving "up stairs" to become club President. All through his career Beckenbauer showed speed, vision, control and intelligence. He may have been reflective and a little introverted, but his influence on the game is undeniable. This, along with his commanding presence on the pitch, earned him his nickname, the "Kaiser" (Emperor). It was a sobriquet he richly deserved.

Gordon Banks   England

Honours: Winner 1966; Quarter-finals 1970   **Games 9**
Played: 1966 and 1970

England's Gordon Banks making his world famous save from Pelé's header watched by Terry Cooper (3), Brian Labone (5) and Bobby Moore.

Banks was born in Sheffield on 30th December 1937. His goalkeeping career began one Saturday afternoon when he went to watch local side Millspaugh play and was asked to step in when the club goalkeeper did not turn up. He later moved to Rawmarsh Welfare in the Yorkshire League and here suffered a set back surprising for one who would become the greatest goalkeeper in the world. They were defeated 12-2 in his first game and 3-1 in his second. Letting in 15 goals in two matches was too much for the Rawmarsh management and he was sacked, returning to play for Millspaugh. As he later recounted: "I was more noted for the alacrity with which I picked balls out of the net than for any stopping ability." He later played for Sheffield schoolboys and left school to become a coalman's mate, bagging coal, and then an apprentice bricklayer. He was soon spotted by a scout from League Division Three North side, Chesterfield and they took him on part-time, at £2 a game. It was 1955 and the 17 year old was about to depart for Germany to do his National Service, but not before he had a chance to shine in the Youth Cup final of 1956 against Manchester United, a game Chesterfield lost 4-3.

On his return to England, he signed full-time for Chesterfield, earning £17 a week. After only 23 games he attracted the attention of First Division Leicester City and in 1959 was snapped up for £7,000. Two years later he appeared in the FA Cup final, losing 2-0 to double winners, Spurs, and he lost again in 1963, this time going down to Manchester United. Life was not all disappointment however and he made his international debut when Alf Ramsey decided to replace Ron Springett following a 5-2 England defeat by France. The game against Scotland was also lost, but Banks now had his feet in the door and he kept it there for ten years. His next international game was against Brazil. It ended 1-1 and Banks was bamboozled by a shot from Pepe that swerved first left then right, leaving the goalkeeper stranded. He took a dressing down from Ramsey after the game that must have hit a nerve because England only lost seven more games with Banks in goal. His reputation was enhanced greatly by the 1966 World Cup, conceding only once in 433 minutes of football on the way to the final. It was against Portugal, a game he remembers fondly: "If I had to select a match from the 73 I played for England as the number one classic, it would have to be this. The football played at Wembley that evening has never in my experience been surpassed." Being beaten "was like a knife in the ribs" to such a perfectionist and he was equally scathing about Germany's equalizer in the final. "It was like being pushed off Mount Everest with just a stride to go to the top."

Within a year of the World Cup he was transferred by Leicester to Stoke City for £30,000, his old place being taken by Peter Shilton, whose early career Banks had helped. In 1968 England got to the semi-finals of the European Championships, where they were defeated 1-0 by Yugoslavia, a match he remembers less fondly. "The Yugoslavs were kicking anything and everything that moved and the referee was letting them get away with it", he later wrote. The Mexico World Cup will always be remembered for Bank's "Save of the Century", but it also marked his international swansong, against Czechoslovakia in the final group game. In 1972 he helped Stoke win the League Cup and was named Footballer of the Year, the first time a goalkeeper had won the award since Bert Trautmannn in 1956. Yet, the year was to end in tragedy when in October, as he left the Victoria Ground where he had been receiving treatment for an injury sustained in the previous game against Liverpool, his car collided with a van. He suffered severe damage to his right eye and was never able to regain full fitness. Adding insult to injury, he was fined £250 for dangerous driving.

After a year coaching the Stoke youth team coach and an attempted comeback with Scottish side Morton, he headed of to the USA to play for Fort Lauderdale Strikers in the NASL. He was one of its great attractions, though he was never sure if this was for his football or his injury. "I felt like a circus act. Roll up, roll up to see the greatest one eyed goalkeeper in the world", he said. He had been voted the NASL's most valuable goalkeeper, but left the circus in 1978 to take the position of coach to the England Youth team. In all Gordon Banks played 510 league games, 194 of which were for Stoke City and in the 73 games he played England, he lost only 9. To say that he was as safe as the Bank of England is somewhat of a misnomer as any self-respecting bank robber will say that any safe can be cracked. However, no one would argue that he was the safest goalkeeper in the world in his day.

England 0 : Brazil 1

This was one of the most anticipated games of the 1970 World Cup finals. Pairing the reigning champions with the young pretenders, it was billed as the "real" final and, in spite of conditions that were arduous in the extreme, it was a confrontation that fulfilled all expectations. Both teams combined blends of youth and experience and brimmed with exciting talent. Brazil were playing without their midfield genius, Gérson through injury and they approached the game a little more defensively than usual. There was a great deal of mutual respect between these two teams and it meant that it would be a tight game. The English met Brazilian guile and cleverness with good, solid defence. Yet, the demands of European television meant that it kicked off at noon, when temperatures and humidity in Mexico are at the worst. At a time when contemporary army manuals did not recommend that even light exercise should be undertaken in temperatures above 85° Fahrenheit, this game was played in near 100° temperatures. Further, it was a match of non-stop action, during which the English players lost, on average, half a stone in weight.

The night before the game, Brazilian and local Mexican supporters, for whom the Brazilians were big favourites, tried to faze the English players by keeping them awake. They crowded around England's team hotel sounding horns and chanting, and some even ran through the corridors. It forced several of the players to change rooms and most got little sleep. It was far from the ideal preparation for a game of such importance and played in such conditions, but it seems not to have affected the English. They came onto the pitch in good spirits and immediately took the game to Brazil. In fact they dominated proceedings for the first ten minutes, looking every bit like world champions and with Martin Peters, Alan Ball and Francis Lee contributing well. Then came the moment that proved just how dangerous the Brazilians can be and for which this match will always be remembered.

22 Men and a Bag of Wind

Bobby Moore leaves the field after the 1-0 defeat by Brazil.

Jairzinho broke past Terry Cooper and Bobby Moore and sprinted to the bye line. In Bank's own words, as "Jairzinho chipped the ball over I started back across the goal. Half way across, I was sure the ball was too high for anyone to reach, but then I saw Pelé. He seemed to climb higher and higher until he got the ball on his forehead putting everything behind it." It was "a swift, searching downward header," as another reporter noted and as the ball flashed towards goal, Pelé turned away convinced that he had scored. Banks was guarding the near post, but, in an instant and with the agility of a cougar, hurled himself the full length of the goal and "with a breathtaking one-handed save turned the ball away with his finger-tips." It was absolutely sensational and Pelé was to later recount it as the greatest save he had ever seen, a moment of pure genius from two of football's finest practitioners.

For the rest of the half, both teams probed each other warily, but neither could find a goal. Moore marshalled his troops well and Mullery was Pelé's constant shadow, giving him his most difficult game of the tournament. Similarly, the Brazilian defence kept alert to prevent the English forwards from settling into any sustained rhythm. Considering that this was a beehive match of incessant activity, surprisingly few clear scoring chances were created. Bobby Charlton forced a good save out of Felix, in Brazil's goal, Peters headed over the bar and Geoff Hurst sent a diving header straight into the arms of Brazil's custodian. At half-time, honours were even, a fair reflection of the way game had gone.

The second half began with some tantalizing play from the Brazil, "teasing, taunting triangles of progressive football," one reporter wrote, and Banks had to be at his best. He pulled off one excellent save to deny Paolo Cesar and another to deny Jairzinho. Then a flash of inspiration from Pelé saw him run past four men to set himself up, only to be denied at the last by Mullery's a perfectly timed tackle. Next it was Rivelino to test Bank's reflections with a shot that again showed his brilliance. However, he was powerless to prevent Brazil's goal, which came with half an hour of the match remaining. Rivelino began the move, sending the ball to Tostão. With some clever footwork, he beat three men before crossing to Pelé, who in turn ducked and swerved to cut through the England defence, before releasing the ball to Jairzinho. He was ten yards from the goal and his shot gave Banks no chance.

The goal did not unnerve the English, who continued to search for the equalizer, which they almost found. They were beginning to tire in the withering heat and they missed several good chances. One fell to Ball, who completely miskicked a pass from Jeff Astle, and the second fell to Astle himself, who missed an open goal after a defensive error from Everaldo let him in. They were "the greatest, and most costly misses, of the World Cup" and they denied England a result from a match to which they had contributed so valiantly. It had been a close run thing and Zagalo admitted as much. "At no moment did I think our victory was certain. Anything could have happened. Both sides had the same chances", he said afterwards. One other interview took place after the final whistle and illustrates the respect they had for each other. As Booby Moore and Pelé swapped shirts, Moore said: "See you at the Aztec Stadium", referring to the final. Pelé replied: "I think perhaps you will."

Italy 4 : West Germany 3

Italy's Luigi Riva is tackeld by West Germany's Berti Vogts.

There was an air of predictability about this game, that is until it exploded alive in its extra time. Italy, in full catenaccio defensive mind set and with star forward Rivera sitting on the bench, taking on West Germany, the masters of steamroller relentlessness, was sure to be a rugged grind of a game. That is exactly what it was for almost an hour and a half of play.

After an opening few minutes when both pestered and tested each other, the Italians took advantage of an uncharacteristic moment of indecision in the German defence. Boninsegna sent a ball through the defence intended for Riva. It was intercepted by Schulz, who had been brought in to bolster the back line, but he hesitated. "For a fraction of a second defender and attacker looked at each other, the ball in no-man's land, then Boninsegna was through in a flash for a superb ground shot" into the corner of the net. Now was the perfect opportunity for Italy to do what they set out to do and what they did best. They surrendered the midfield, shut up shop and let the Germans take the game to them. Only eight minutes of the match had gone.

The pattern of play for the rest of normal time was of periods of German pressure punctuated by Italian breakaways. The Germans played confidently, stroking the ball around purposefully and might have equalized on any number of occasions. Müller lost his marker, Cera, only to be foiled by a desperate clearance from Bertini and soon after he again got the better of the defence, only to shoot narrowly wide. Then Grabowski hit a swerving, deflected shot that produced a fine reflex save from Albertosi. Yet, the Italians had their moments too and late in the half enjoyed a five minute spell when they laid siege to the German defence. One superb move involving Riva, Domenghini and Boninsegna forced a brilliant save from Maier and moments later, Mazzola was brought down on the chalk of the area. Once more Maier had to be at his best to keep out the free kick, but he was penalized for carrying the ball too far and gave away a free kick even closer to goal. Mazzola rolled the ball to Riva, whose shot cannoned off the wall.

In the second half Mazzola was replaced by Rivera and almost immediately the Germans had their best chance of the match. Beckenbauer curled a marvelous ball around the defence, but Seeler miscued his shot and Albertosi saved easily. Single-minded and methodical, the Germans persisted with their efforts and just when it seemed that nothing would go for them, fortune smiled. Two minutes into injury time, in the dying seconds, Grabowski left Boninsegna behind on the left. He aimed a cross and Schnellinger "tearing into the area, volleyed the ball home through a crowd of defenders." It took the game into extra rime, which the Germans began as they had left off and refused to let the pressure drop. In the first few minutes Beckenbauer, in full flight, was dropped by Cera, but the referee turned down the penalty appeals. Albertosi then made a string of intuitive saves from Held, Seeler and Müller before dropping a Beckenbauer shot to Grabowski, who put the ball in the net. It was disallowed for handball, but the Germans were soon to see their efforts rewarded. Five minutes into the extra time, Seeler headed a corner into the path of Müller and, "with the Italians almost debating among themselves what to do with the ball", he pushed his team in front.

The Germans then seemed to relax and a stupid infringement gave away the free kick, which Rivera crossed for Burgnich to score. Two minutes before the break with a piece of "pure blinding skill", Domenghini broke down the right and Riva scored from his pass. The Italians were back in front, but there was more to come. Ten minutes into the second period, Müller notched his tenth of the tournament and with the game about to go to a penalty shoot-out, Rivera popped up to side-foot the ball into the net and send the jubilant Italians dramatically to their third World Cup final. It had been theatricals of the highest calibre, a finale of Wagnerian proportions, which nobody could have expected given what had gone on in the first 92 minutes of play. But this was Mexico '70 and the greatest sporting feast in the world could still produce the most delicious of dishes, even from the barest of kitchens.

Brazil 4 : Italy 1
The World Cup Final

Pelé leaps in the air as he celbrates Brazil's first goal.

For three days before this final, the people of Mexico City had been subjected to hot, sultry air, thunder, lightening and storms of tropical rain. It was as if the Aztec gods themselves were ringing out their own presage of what had every potential to be as explosive a final as any in the tournament's history. It threw together Brazil, "masterly in their ability to fashion goals from a hint, a flick or a mere intuition" and Italy, a team of flamboyant individuals, but somehow locked in a lethargy of defensive mindedness that allowed their flair to shine in patches, rather than with consistency. It was "a great confrontation between the finest attack in the world and Italy, masters of defence." Both had excellent World Cup credentials and both playing for outright possession of the Jules Rimet Trophy. It was a clash between the giants of the Old and New Worlds, fighting for the very soul of football.

The Italians did much of the first half running. On their first attack, Luigi Riva came close to opening his team's account with a 25 yard drive that tested Felix's reactions. The save set up Brazil's opening attack, which ended when Jairzinho was fouled as he threatened to break through. Over the next few minutes, both Riva and Tostão came close to scoring, but "it was Brazil, playing at a leisurely, stately pace, who drew first blood." Tostão and Everaldo combined cleverly down the left flank before Tostão crossed to the far post, where waited Pelé "erupting like a volcano, snapping his bull neck like the crack of a whip to head home violently." The goal came in the 18th minute, but did not upset the Italians who came back strongly. They pushed and harried the Brazilian defence, with Alessandro Mazzola and Giancarlo de Sisti particularly effective and providing great service to Riva, up front. The Brazilians also had their moments of pressure, with the midfield trio of Gérson, Rivelino and Clodoaldo commanding and always threatening to release the front men. It was a finely balanced game and Italy equalized fortuitously from some careless Brazilian defending eight minutes from half-time. Clodoaldo casually back-heeled a pass to nobody and Boninsegna pounced on the error. He took the ball clear of the defender Piazza, exchanged a pass with Riva, which brought Felix off his line, and then fired into the open net.

Altitude, Attitude and Artistry - Mexico 1970

The first half had been even, but the second period belonged to the South Americans, who grew stronger and more confident as time passed. Soon after the restart, Pelé chested down Gérson's pass and blasted the ball into the net, only to be adjudged offside. Not long after, Carlos Alberto stormed to the bye line and sent in a cross to Pelé, who shot just wide of the post. As Brazil took grip of the game, Italy's tackling became increasingly ferocious and they gave away a series of free kicks from which goals almost came. They were playing a dangerous game and only a fine save from Albertosi and the crossbar kept the Italians in the match. Brazil restored their lead in the 65th minute. A quick exchange of passes involving Everaldo and Jairzinho sent the ball to Gérson, unmarked some 20 metres outside Italy's goal. In a flash he turned to unleash an unstoppable rocket into the net and five minutes, he crossed from the left to Pelé on the back post. He headed down to Jairzinho, who miskicked but still found the corner of the net.

By now the Italians were being run ragged as the Brazilians "played ducks and drakes arrogantly with their foe." Bertini suffered a groin injury and was replaced with Juliano and five minutes from time Rivera came on for Boninsegna, but neither had any impact. The Brazilians had the scent of victory in their nostrils and nothing was going to shake them from it. With minutes to go, Clodoaldo, with great panache, danced his way through the centre of the field, beating four Italians, before releasing Rivelino down the left. The Italian defence was stretched to the point of ineffectiveness, as he cut in towards goal and passed the ball to Jairzinho. Combining with Pelé, they fashioned an opening for Carlos Alberto, who shot home fiercely. Minutes later, the final whistle went and Brazil became the only team to have won the World Cup three times.

A wave of emotion greeted the victory as thousands of adoring fans rushed onto the pitch to congratulate their heroes. Back in Brazil, the wild celebrations resulted in 44 deaths and 1800 injuries, caused by fireworks, falls, gunshots and traffic accidents. Among neutrals, it was a very popular result because the Brazilians had thoroughly deserved it. They had been magnificent throughout the tournament and had frequently demonstrated their complete mastery of the game of football. In the words of one reporter: "They have won because their football is a dance full of irrational surprises and Dionysiac variations." It was men and a football in total harmony, as natural and instinctive as ever it could have been. Terry Venables once wrote of their achievement: "The performance of that 1970 side, Pele, Tostao, Gerson (sic) and company, was the best I've ever seen throughout the duration of a World Cup tournament", praise indeed. The Italians had added their own touches of class to a wonderful occasion, but in the end they had been outmanoeuvred and outgunned. "The Italians began the day in hope and ended it in reverence," was the verdict of the Times.

Statistics - Mexico 1970

GROUP ONE

Mexico City, May 31st - Estadio Azteca

0 (0) MEXICO

Calderón, Vantolra, Peña, Guzman, Pérez, Hernández, Pulido, Velarde (Munguia), Valdivia, Fragoso, López.

0 (0) SOVIET UNION

Kavasashvili, Kaplichni, Lovchev, Logofet, Shesterniev (Pusatch), Asatiani, Muntian, Serebrianikov, Bishovets, Evriuzhikan, Nodija (Khmelnitski).

Referee: Kurt Tschenscher (West Germany)
Attendance: 107.000

Mexico City, June 3rd - Estadio Azteca

3 (1) BELGIUM

Van Moer 12,54, Lambert (pen)77

Piot, Heylens, Thissen, Dewalque, Dockx, Semmeling (Poleunis), Van Moer, Devrindt, Van Himst, Lambert, Puis.

0 (0) EL SALVADOR

Magana, Rivas, Mariona, Osorio, Manzano (Cortés-Mendez), Quintanilla, Vázquez, Cabezas, Rodríguez, Martínez, Aparicio.

Referee: Andrei Radulescu (Romania)
Attendance: 92.000

Mexico City, June 6th - Estadio Azteca

4 (1) SOVIET UNION

Bishovets 15,63, Asatiani 56, Khmelnitski 76

Kavasashvili, Kaplichni (Lovchev), Afonin, Shesterniev, Asatiani, Muntian, Dzodzuashvili (Kiselev), Bishovets, Evriuzhikan, Khurtisilava, Khmelnitski.

1 (0) BELGIUM

Lambert 86

Piot, Heylens, Thissen, Dewalque, Dockx, Semmeling, Van Moer, Jeck, Van Himst, Lambert, Puis.

Referee: Rudolf Scheurer (Switzerland)
Attendance: 59.000

Mexico City, June 7th - Estadio Azteca

4 (1) MEXICO

Valdivia 44,46, Fragoso 56, Basaguren 83

Calderón, Vantolra, Peña, Guzman, Pérez, González, Borja (López)(Basaguren), Munguia, Valdivia, Fragoso, Padilla.

0 (0) EL SALVADOR

Magana, Rivas, Mariona, Osorio, Cortés -Mendez (Monge), Quintanilla, Vásquez, Cabezas, Rodríguez, Martínez, Aparicio (Mendez).

Referee: Ali Kandil (Egypt/United Arab Republic)
Attendance: 103.000

Mexico City, June 10th - Estadio Azteca

2 (0) SOVIET UNION

Bishovets 51,74

Kavasashvili, Afonin, Shesterniev, Serebrianikov, Muntian, Dzodzuashvili, Kiselev (Asatiani), Bishovets, Pusatch (Evriuzhikan), Khurtisilava, Khmelnitski.

0 (0) EL SALVADOR

Magana, Rivas, Mariona, Osorio, Castro, Monge, Portillo, Vázquez, Cabezas (Aparicio), Rodríguez (Sermeno), Mendez.

Referee: Ricardo Hormazabal Díaz (Chile)
Attendance: 89.000

Mexico City, June 11th - Estadio Azteca

1 (1) MEXICO

Peña (pen)15

Calderón, Vantolra, Peña, Guzman, Pérez, González, Pulido, Munguia, Valdivia (Basaguren), Fragoso, Padilla.

0 (0) BELGIUM

Piot, Heylens, Thissen, Dewalque, Dockx, Semmeling, Van Moer, Jeck, Van Himst, Poleunis (Devrindt), Puis.

Referee: Angel Norberto Coerezza (Argentina)
Attendance: 105.000

	P	W	D	L	F	A	Pts
Soviet Union	3	2	1	0	6	1	5
Mexico	3	2	1	0	5	0	5
Belgium	3	1	0	2	4	5	2
El Salvador	3	0	0	3	0	9	0

GROUP TWO

Puebla, June 2nd - Estadio Cuauhtemoc

2 (1) URUGUAY

Maneiro 23, Mujica 50

Mazurkiewicz, Ubinas, Mujica, Montero-Castillo, Ancheta, Matosas, Cubilla, Esparrago, Maneiro, Rocha (Cortés), Losada.

0 (0) ISRAEL

Vissoker, Rosen, Daniel, Talbi (Bar), Schwager, Rosenthal, Shum, Spiegler, Spiegel, Faygenbaum, Rom (Vollach).

Referee: Bob Davidson (Scotland)
Attendance: 20.000

Toluca, June 3rd - Estadio Luis Dosal

1 (1) ITALY

Domenghini 11

Albertosi, Burgnich, Facchetti, Cera, Niccolai (Rosato), Bertini, Domenghini, Mazzola, Boninsegna, de Sisti, Riva.

0 (0) SWEDEN

Hellström, Nordquist, Grip, Svensson, Axelsson, B.Larsson (Niklasson), Grahn, Eriksson (Ejderstedt), Kindvall, Cronquist, Olsson.

Referee: Jack Taylor (England)
Attendance: 14.000

Puebla, June 6th - Estadio Cuauhtemoc

0 (0) URUGUAY

Mazurkiewicz, Ubinas, Mujica, Montero-Castillo, Ancheta, Matosas, Cubilla, Esparrago, Maneiro, Cortés, Bareño (Zubia).

0 (0) ITALY

Albertosi, Burgnich, Facchetti, Cera, Rosato, Bertini, Domenghini (Furino), Mazzola, Boninsegna, de Sisti, Riva.

Referee: Rudolf Glöckner (East Germany)
Attendance: 30.000

Toluca, June 7th - Estadio Luis Dosal

1 (0) ISRAEL

Spiegler 60

Vissoker, Rosen, Primo, Bar, Schwager, Rosenthal, Shum, Spiegler, Spiegel, Faygenbaum, Vollach (Schuruk).

1 (0) SWEDEN

Turesson 57

G.Larsson, Selander, Grip, Svensson, Axelsson, B.Larsson, Nordahl, Turesson, Kindvall, Persson (Dalsson), Olsson.

Referee: Seyoun Tarrekegn (Ethiopia)
Attendance: 9.000

Puebla, June 10th - Estadio Cuauhtemoc

0 (0) URUGUAY

Mazurkiewicz, Ubinas, Mujica, Montero-Castillo, Ancheta, Matosas, Esparrago (Fontes), Maneiro, Cortés, Zubia, Losada.

1 (0) SWEDEN

Grahn 90

G.Larsson, Selander, Grip, Svensson, Axelsson, B.Larsson, Nordquist, Eriksson, Kindvall (Turesson), Persson, Niklasson (Grahn).

Referee: Henry Landauer (United States)
Attendance: 18.000

Toluca, June 11th - Estadio Luis Dosal

0 (0) ISRAEL

Vissoker, Rosen, Bello, Primo, Bar, Schwager, Rosenthal, Shum, Spiegler, Spiegel, Faygenbaum (Rom).

0 (0) ITALY

Albertosi, Burgnich, Facchetti, Cera, Rosato, Bertini, Domenghini (Rivera), Mazzola, Boninsegna, de Sisti, Riva.

Referee: Antonio de Moraes (Brazil)
Attendance: 9.000

	P	W	D	L	F	A	Pts
Italy	3	1	2	0	1	0	4
Uruguay	3	1	1	1	2	1	3
Sweden	3	1	1	1	2	2	3
Israel	3	0	2	1	1	3	2

GROUP THREE

Guadalajara, June 2nd - Estadio Jalisco

1 (0) ENGLAND

Hurst 65

Banks, Newton (Wright), Cooper, Mullery, Labone, Moore, Lee (Osgood), Ball, R.Charlton, Hurst, Peters.

0 (0) ROMANIA

Adamache, Salmareanu, Lupescu, Dinu, Mocanu, Dumitru, Nunweiler, Dembrowski, Tataru (Neagu), Dumitrache, Lucescu.

Referee: Vital Loraux (Belgium)
Attendance: 50.000

Altitude, Attitude and Artistry - Mexico 1970

Guadalajara, June 3rd - Estadio Jalisco

4 (1) BRAZIL

Rivelino 24, Pelé 59, Jairzinho 61,81

Felix, Carlos Alberto, Piazza, Brito, Everaldo, Clodoaldo, Gérson (Paulo Cesar), Jairzinho, Tostão, Pelé, Rivelino.

1 (1) CZECHOSLOVAKIA

Petras 11

Viktor, Dobias, Migas, Horvath, Hagara, Hrdlicka (Kvašniák), Kuna, F.Vesely (B.Vesely), Petras, Adamec, Jokl.

Referee: Ramon Barreto Ruiz (Uruguay)
Attendance: 52.000

Guadalajara, June 6th - Estadio Jalisco

2 (0) ROMANIA

Neagu 52, Dumitrache (pen)75

Adamache, Salmareanu, Lupescu, Dinu, Mocanu, Dumitru (Ghergheli), Nunweiler, Dembrowski, Neagu, Dumitrache, Lucescu (Tataru).

1 (1) CZECHOSLOVAKIA

Petras 3

Vencel, Dobias, Migas, Horvath, Zlocka, Kvašniák, Kuna, B.Vesely, Petras, Jurkanin (Adamec), Jokl (F.Vesely).

Referee: Diego de Leo (Mexico)
Attendance: 56.000

Guadalajara, June 7th - Estadio Jalisco

1 (0) BRAZIL

Jairzinho 59

Felix, Carlos Alberto, Piazza, Brito, Everaldo, Clodoaldo, Paulo Cesar, Jairzinho, Tostão (Roberto), Pelé, Rivelino.

0 (0) ENGLAND

Banks, Wright, Cooper, Mullery, Labone, Moore, Lee (Astle), Ball, R.Charlton (Bell), Hurst, Peters.

Referee: Abraham Klein (Israel)
Attendance: 66.000

Guadalajara, June 10th - Estadio Jalisco

3 (2) BRAZIL

Pelé 19,67, Jairzinho 22

Felix, Carlos Alberto, Piazza, Brito, Everaldo (Marco Antonio), Clodoaldo (Edu), Paulo Cesar, Jairzinho, Tostão, Pelé, Fontana.

2 (1) ROMANIA

Dumitrache 34, Dembrowski 85

Adamache (Raducanu), Salmareanu, Lupescu, Dinu, Mocanu, Dumitru, Nunweiler, Dembrowski, Neagu, Dumitrache (Tataru), Lucescu.

Referee: Ferdinand Marschall (Austria)
Attendance: 50.000

Guadalajara, June 11th - Estadio Jalisco

1 (0) ENGLAND

Clarke (pen)49

Banks, Newton, Cooper, Mullery, J.Charlton, Moore, Clarke, Bell, R.Charlton (Ball), Astle (Osgood), Peters.

0 (0) CZECHOSLOVAKIA

Viktor, Dobias, Migas, Hrivnak, Hagara, Pollak, Kuna, F.Vesely, Petras, Adamec, Capkovic (Jokl).

Referee: René Machin (France)
Attendance: 49.000

	P	W	D	L	F	A	Pts
Brazil	3	3	0	0	8	3	6
England	3	2	0	1	2	1	4
Romania	3	1	0	2	4	5	2
Czech	3	0	0	3	2	7	0

GROUP FOUR

Leon, June 2nd - Estadio Guanajuato

3 (0) PERU

Gallardo 50, Chumpitaz 55, Cubillas 73

Rubinos, Campos (J.González), de la Torre, Chumpitaz, Fuentes, Cubillas, Mifflin, Challe, Baylon (Sotil), Leon, Gallardo.

2 (1) BULGARIA

Dermendiev 12, Bonev 49

Simeonov, Shalamanov, Dimitrov, Davidov, Aladjov, Bonev (Asparoukhov), Penev, Yakimov, Popov (Maraschliev), Jekov, Dermendiev.

Referee: Antonio Sbardella (Italy)
Attendance: 14.000

Leon, June 3rd - Estadio Guanajuato

2 (0) WEST GERMANY

Seeler 56, Müller 78

Maier, Vogts, Schulz, Fichtel, Höttges (Löhr), Haller (Grabowski), Beckenbauer, Overath, Seeler, Müller, Held.

1 (1) MOROCCO

Houmane Jarir 21

Ben Kassu, Lamrani, Benkrief, Khanoussi, Slimani, Marroufi, Bamous (Faras), El Filali, Said, Ghazouani (El Kiati), Houmane Jarir.

Referee: Laurens Van Ravens (Holland)
Attendance: 9.000

Leon, June 6th - Estadio Guanajuato

3 (0) PERU

Cubillas 65,75, Challe 67

Rubinos, P.González, de la Torre, Chumpitaz, Fuentes, Cubillas, Mifflin (Cruzado), Challe, Sotil, Leon, Gallardo (Ramírez).

0 (0) MOROCCO

Ben Kassu, Lamrani, Benkrief (Fadili), Khanoussi, Slimani, Marroufi, Bamous, El Filali, Said (Alavi), Ghazouani, Houmane Jarir.

Referee: Tofik Bakhramov (Soviet Union)
Attendance: 13.500

Leon, June 7th - Estadio Guanajuato

5 (2) WEST GERMANY

Libuda 20, Müller 27,(pen)52,88, Seeler 69

Maier, Vogts, Schnellinger, Fichtel, Höttges, Löhr (Grabowski), Beckenbauer (Weber), Overath, Seeler, Müller, Libuda.

2 (1) BULGARIA

Nikodimov 12, Kolev 89

Simeonov, Gaidarski, Zhechev, Bonev, Penev, Gaganelov (Shalamanov), Nikodimov, Kolev, Dermendiev (Mitkov), Asparoukhov, Maraschliev.

Referee: José Maria Ortíz de Mendibil (Spain)
Attendance: 12.700

Leon, June 10th - Estadio Guanajuato

3 (3) WEST GERMANY

Müller 19,26,39

Maier, Vogts, Schnellinger, Fichtel, Höttges (Patzke), Löhr, Beckenbauer, Overath, Seeler, Müller, Libuda (Grabowski).

1 (1) PERU

Cubillas 44

Rubinos, P.González, de la Torre, Chumpitaz, Fuentes, Cubillas, Mifflin, Challe (Cruzado), Sotil, Leon (Ramírez), Gallardo.

Referee: Arturo Aguilar Elizalde (Mexico)
Attendance: 18.000

Leon, June 11th - Estadio Guanajuato

1 (1) BULGARIA

Zhechev 40

Yordanov, Gaidarski, Zhechev, Yakimov (Bonev), Penev (Dimitrov), Shalamanov, Nikodimov, Kolev, Popov, Mitkov, Asparoukhov.

1 (0) MOROCCO

Ghazouani 60

Hazzaz, Benkrief, Fadili, Khanoussi, Slimani, Marroufi, Bamous (Chukri), El Filali, Said, Alavi (Faras), Ghazouani.

Referee: Antonio Saldanha Ribeiro (Portugal)
Attendance: 12.200

	P	W	D	L	F	A	Pts
West Germany	3	3	0	0	10	4	6
Peru	3	2	0	1	7	5	4
Bulgaria	3	0	1	2	5	9	1
Morocco	3	0	1	2	2	6	1

QUARTER-FINALS

Leon, June 14th - Estadio Guanajuato

After extra time - 45 mins (0-1), 90 mins (2-2)

3 (2) WEST GERMANY

Beckenbauer 69, Seeler 82, Müller 108

Maier, Schnellinger, Vogts, Fichtel, Höttges (Schulz), Beckenbauer, Overath, Seeler, Libuda (Grabowski), Müller, Löhr.

2 (2) ENGLAND

Mullery 31, Peters 49

Bonetti, Newton, Cooper, Mullery, Labone, Moore, Lee, Ball, Hurst, R.Charlton (Bell), Peters (Hunter).

Referee: Angel Norberto Coerezza (Argentina)
Attendance: 24.000

Toluca, June 14th - Estadio Luis Dosal

1 (1) MEXICO

González 13

Calderón, Vantolra, Peña, Guzman, Pérez, González (Borja), Pulido, Munguia (Díaz), Valdivia, Fragoso, Padilla.

4 (1) ITALY

Domenghini 25, Riva 64,76, Rivera 69

Albertosi, Burgnich, Cera, Rosato, Facchetti, Bertini, Mazzola, (Rivera), de Sisti, Domenghini (Gori), Boninsegna, Riva.

Referee: Rudolf Scheurer (Switzerland)
Attendance: 24.000

Guadalajara, June 14th - Estadio Jalisco

4 (2) BRAZIL

Rivelino 11, Tostão 15,52, Jairzinho 76

Felix, Carlos Alberto, Brito, Piazza, Marco Antonio, Clodoaldo, Gérson (Paulo Cesar), Jairzinho (Roberto), Tostão, Pelé, Rivelino.

2 (1) PERU

Gallardo 28, Cubillas 69

Rubinos, Campos, Fernández, Chumpitaz, Fuentes, Mifflin, Challe, Baylon (Sotil), Leon (Reyes), Cubillas, Gallardo.

Referee: Vital Loraux (Belgium)
Attendance: 54.000

Mexico City, June 14th - Estadio Azteca

After extra time - 45 mins (0-0), 90 mins (0-0)

1 (0) URUGUAY

Esparrago 117

Mazurkiewicz, Ubinas, Ancheta, Matosas, Mujica, Maneiro, Cortés, Montero-Castillo, Cubilla, Fontes (Esparrago), Morales (Gómez).

0 (0) SOVIET UNION

Kavasashvili, Afonin, Dzodzuashvili, Kaplichni, Khurtsilava (Logofet), Shesterniev, Asatiani (Kiselev), Muntian, Bishovets, Evriuzhikan, Khmelnitski.

Referee: Laurens Van Ravens (Holland)
Attendance: 45.000

SEMI-FINALS

Mexico City, June 17th - Estadio Azteca

After extra time - 45 mins (1-0), 90 mins (1-1)

4 (1) ITALY

Boninsegna 7, Burgnich 98, Riva 103, Rivera 112

Albertosi, Cera, Burgnich, Bertini, Rosato (Poletti), Facchetti, Domenghini, Mazzola (Rivera), de Sisti, Boninsegna, Riva.

3 (1) WEST GERMANY

Schnellinger 90, Müller 95,110

Maier, Schnellinger, Vogts, Patzke (Held), Schulz, Beckenbauer, Overath, Seeler, Grabowski, Müller, Löhr (Libuda).

Referee: Arturo Maldonado Yamasaki (Mexico)
Attendance: 80.000

Guadalajara, June 17th - Estadio Jalisco

3 (1) BRAZIL

Clodoaldo 45, Jairzinho 76, Rivelino 90

Felix, Carlos Alberto, Brito, Piazza, Everaldo, Clodoaldo, Gérson, Jairzinho, Tostão, Pelé, Rivelino.

1 (1) URUGUAY

Cubilla 19

Mazurkiewicz, Ubinas, Ancheta, Matosas, Mujica, Maneiro (Esparrago), Cortés, Montero-Castillo, Cubilla, Fontes, Morales.

Referee: José Maria Ortíz de Mendibil (Spain)
Attendance: 51.000

3RD/4TH PLACE PLAY-OFF

Mexico City, June 20th - Estadio Azteca

1 (1) WEST GERMANY

Overath 23

Wolter, Schnellinger (Lorenz), Vogts, Patzke, Fichtel, Weber, Overath, Seeler, Held, Müller, Libuda (Löhr).

0 (0) URUGUAY

Mazurkiewicz, Ubinas, Ancheta, Matosas, Mujica, Maneiro (Sandoval), Cortés, Montero-Castillo, Cubilla, Fontes (Esparrago), Morales.

Referee. Antonio Sbardella (Italy)
Attendance: 104.000

FINAL

Mexico City, June 21st - Estadio Azteca

4 (1) BRAZIL

Pelé 19, Gérson 65, Jairzinho 70, Carlos Alberto 86

Felix, Carlos Alberto, Brito, Piazza, Everaldo, Clodoaldo, Gérson, Jairzinho, Tostão, Pelé, Rivelino.

1 (1) ITALY

Boninsegna 37

Albertosi, Cera, Burgnich, Bertini (Juliano), Rosato, Facchetti, Domenghini, Mazzola, de Sisti, Boninsegna (Rivera), Riva.

Referee: Rudolf Glöckner (East Germany)
Attendance: 107.000

QUALIFYING ROUND

Africa Phase 1 - 1st Round

	P	W	D	L	F	A	Pts
Morocco	3	2	0	1	4	2	4
Nigeria	2	1	1	0	4	3	3
Tunisia	2	1	1	0	2	1	3
Ethiopia	2	1	0	1	5	3	2
Sudan	2	1	0	1	6	6	2
Zambia	2	1	0	1	6	6	2
Libya	2	1	0	1	3	5	2
Senegal	3	1	0	2	4	4	2
Cameroon	2	0	1	1	3	4	1
Algeria	2	0	1	1	1	2	1

27-10-68	Zambia : Sudan	4:2 (1:2)
03-11-68	Morocco : Senegal	1:0 (0:0)
08-11-68	Sudan : Zambia	4:2 a.e.t. (3:1, 1:1)
17-11-68	Algeria : Tunisia	1:2 (1:0)
07-12-68	Nigeria : Cameroon	1.1 (0.0)
22-12-68	Cameroon : Nigeria	2:3 (1:2)
29-12-68	Tunisia : Algeria	0:0
05-01-69	Senegal : Morocco	2:1 (2:1)
26-01-69	Libya : Ethiopia	2:0 (1:0)
09-02-69	Ethiopia : Libya	5:1 (2:1)
13-02-69	Morocco : Senegal	2:0 (0:0)

Africa Phase 1 - 2nd Round

	P	W	D	L	F	A	Pts
Sudan	2	1	1	0	4	2	3
Nigeria	2	1	1	0	3	2	3
Tunisia	2	0	2	0	0	0	2
Morocco	2	0	2	0	0	0	2
Ghana	2	0	1	1	2	3	1
Ethiopia	2	0	1	1	2	4	1

27-04-69	Tunisia : Morocco	0:0
04-05-69	Ethiopia : Sudan	1:1 (0:1)
10-05-69	Nigeria : Ghana	2:1 (0:1)
11-05-69	Sudan : Ethiopia	3:1 (1:0)
18-05-69	Ghana : Nigeria	1:1 (1:1)
18-05-69	Morocco : Tunisia	0:0

Africa Phase 1 - 2nd Round Play-off

| 13-06-69 | Tunisia : Morocco | 2:2 a.e.t. (2:2, 1:1) |

Played in Marseille

Africa Phase 2 - Final Matches

	P	W	D	L	F	A	Pts
Morocco	4	2	1	1	5	3	5
Nigeria	4	1	2	1	8	7	4
Sudan	4	0	3	1	5	8	3

13-09-69	Nigeria : Sudan	2:2 (2:2)
21-09-69	Morocco : Nigeria	2:1 (0:0)
03-10-69	Sudan : Nigeria	3:3 (1:0)
10-10-69	Sudan : Morocco	0:0
26-10-69	Morocco : Sudan	3:0 (1:0)
08-11-69	Nigeria : Morocco	2:0 (0:0)

Asia/Oceania Phase 1 - Group 1 AFC/OFC

	P	W	D	L	F	A	Pts
Australia	4	2	2	0	7	4	6
Korea Rep.	4	1	2	1	6	5	4
Japan	4	0	2	2	4	8	2

10-10-69	Japan : Australia	1:3 (1:1)
12-10-69	Korea Republic : Japan	2:2 (2:1)
14-10-69	Australia : Korea Republic	2:1 (1:1)
16-10-69	Australia : Japan	1:1 (1:1)
18-10-69	Japan : Korea Republic	0:2 (0:2)
20-10-69	Korea Republic : Australia	1:1 (1:1)

All games played in Seoul

Asia/Oceania Phase 1 - Group 2 AFC/OFC

	P	W	D	L	F	A	Pts
Israel	2	2	0	0	6	0	4
New Zealand	2	0	0	2	0	6	0

| 28-09-69 | Israel : New Zealand | 4:0 (0:0) |
| 01-10-69 | New Zealand : Israel | 0:2 (0:2) |

Both games played in Tel Aviv

Asia/Oceania 1st Round Play-off AFC/OFC

	P	W	D	L	F	A	Pts
Australia	3	1	2	0	4	2	4
Rhodesia	3	0	2	1	2	4	2

23-11-69	Rhodesia : Australia	1:1 (0:0)
27-11-69	Australia : Rhodesia	0:0
01-12-69	Australia : Rhodesia	3:1 (2:0)

All games played in Maputo

Asia/Oceania Phase 2 - Final Matches AFC/OFC

	P	W	D	L	F	A	Pts
Israel	2	1	1	0	2	1	3
Australia	2	0	1	1	1	2	1

| 04-12-69 | Israel : Australia | 1:0 (1:0) |
| 14-12-69 | Australia : Israel | 1:1 (0:0) |

Altitude, Attitude and Artistry - Mexico 1970

Europe - Group 1

	P	W	D	L	F	A	Pts
Romania	6	3	2	1	7	6	8
Greece	6	2	3	1	13	9	7
Switzerland	6	2	1	3	5	8	5
Portugal	6	1	2	3	8	10	4

12-10-68	Switzerland : Greece	1:0 (1:0)
27-10-68	Portugal : Romania	3:0 (2:0)
23-11-68	Romania : Switzerland	2:0 (0:0)
11-12-68	Greece : Portugal	4:2 (2:1)
16-04-69	Portugal : Switzerland	0:2 (0:2)
16-04-69	Greece : Romania	2:2 (0:0)
04-05-69	Portugal : Greece	2:2 (0:0)
14-05-69	Switzerland : Romania	0:1 (0:1)
12-10-69	Romania : Portugal	1:0 (1:0)
15-10-69	Greece : Switzerland	4:1 (3:0)
02-11-69	Switzerland : Portugal	1:1 (0:1)
16-11-69	Romania : Greece	1:1 (1:0)

Europe - Group 2

	P	W	D	L	F	A	Pts
Hungary	6	4	1	1	16	7	9
Czech	6	4	1	1	12	6	9
Denmark	6	2	1	3	6	10	5
Rep. Ireland	6	0	1	5	3	14	1

25-09-68	Denmark : Czechoslovakia	0:3 (0:2)
20-10-68	Czechoslovakia : Denmark	1:0 (0:0)
04-05-69	Ireland Rep. : Czechoslovakia	1:2 (1:0)
25-05-69	Hungary : Czechoslovakia	2:0 (1:0)
27-05-69	Denmark : Ireland Republic	2:0 (1:0)
08-06-69	Ireland Republic : Hungary	1:2 (0:1)
15-06-69	Denmark : Hungary	3:2 (2:2)
14-09-69	Czechoslovakia : Hungary	3:3 (1:2)
07-10-69	Czechoslovakia : Ireland Rep.	3:0 (3:0)
15-10-69	Ireland Republic : Denmark	1:1 (1:0)
22-10-69	Hungary : Denmark	3:0 (2:0)
05-11-69	Hungary : Ireland Republic	4:0 (1:0)

Europe - Group 2 Play-off

03-12-69	Czechoslovakia : Hungary	4:1 (1:0)

Europe - Group 3

	P	W	D	L	F	A	Pts
Italy	4	3	1	0	10	3	7
Germany DR	4	2	1	1	7	7	5
Wales	4	0	0	4	3	10	0

23-10-68	Wales : Italy	0:1 (0:1)
29-03-69	Germany DR : Italy	2:2 (1:0)
16-04-69	Germany DR : Wales	2:1 (1:0)
22-10-69	Wales : Germany DR	1:3 (0:0)
04-11-69	Italy : Wales	4:1 (1:0)
22-11-69	Italy : Germany DR	3:0 (3:0)

Europe - Group 4

	P	W	D	L	F	A	Pts
USSR	4	3	1	0	8	1	7
N. Ireland	4	2	1	1	7	3	5
Turkey	4	0	0	4	2	13	0

23-10-68	Northern Ireland : Turkey	4:1 (1:1)
11-12-68	Turkey : Northern Ireland	0:3 (0:1)
10-09-69	Northern Ireland : USSR	0:0
15-10-69	USSR : Turkey	3:0 (1:0)
22-10-69	USSR : Northern Ireland	2:0 (1:0)
16-11-69	Turkey : USSR	1:3 (1:2)

Europe - Group 5

	P	W	D	L	F	A	Pts
Sweden	4	3	0	1	12	5	6
France	4	2	0	2	6	4	4
Norway	4	1	0	3	4	13	2

09-10-68	Sweden : Norway	5:0 (1:0)
06-11-68	France : Norway	0:1 (0:0)
19-06-69	Norway : Sweden	2:5 (0:3)
10-09-69	Norway : France	1:3 (0:1)
15-10-69	Sweden : France	2:0 (1:0)
02-11-69	France : Sweden	3:0 (3:0)

Europe - Group 6

	P	W	D	L	F	A	Pts
Belgium	6	4	1	1	14	8	9
Yugoslavia	6	3	1	2	19	7	7
Spain	6	2	2	2	10	6	6
Finland	6	1	0	5	6	28	2

19-06-68	Finland : Belgium	1:2 (1:0)
25-09-68	Yugoslavia : Finland	9:1 (2:0)
09-10-68	Belgium : Finland	6:1 (3:0)
16-10-68	Belgium : Yugoslavia	3:0 (1:0)
27-10-68	Yugoslavia : Spain	0:0
11-12-68	Spain : Belgium	1:1 (0:1)
23-02-69	Belgium : Spain	2:1 (1:0)
30-04-69	Spain : Yugoslavia	2:1 (2:0)
04-06-69	Finland : Yugoslavia	1:5 (1:3)
25-06-69	Finland : Spain	2:0 (2:0)
15-10-69	Spain : Finland	6:0 (5:0)
19-10-69	Yugoslavia : Belgium	4:0 (3:0)

Europe - Group 7

	P	W	D	L	F	A	Pts
Germany FR	6	5	1	0	20	3	11
Scotland	6	3	1	2	18	7	7
Austria	6	3	0	3	12	7	6
Cyprus	6	0	0	6	2	35	0

19-05-68	Austria : Cyprus	7:1 (3:0)
13-10-68	Austria : Germany FR	0:2 (0:1)
06-11-68	Scotland : Austria	2:1 (0:1)
23-11-68	Cyprus : Germany FR	0:1 (0:0)
11-12-68	Cyprus : Scotland	0:5 (0:5)
16-04-69	Scotland : Germany FR	1:1 (0:1)
19-04-69	Cyprus : Austria	1:2 (0:1)
10-05-69	Germany FR : Austria	1:0 (1:0)
17-05-69	Scotland : Cyprus	8:0 (3:0)
21-05-69	Germany FR : Cyprus	12:0 (7:0)
22-10-69	Germany FR : Scotland	3:2 (1:1)
05-11-69	Austria : Scotland	2:0 (1:0)

Europe - Group 8

	P	W	D	L	F	A	Pts
Bulgaria	6	4	1	1	12	7	9
Poland	6	4	0	2	19	8	8
Netherlands	6	3	1	2	9	5	7
Luxembourg	6	0	0	6	4	24	0

04-09-68	Luxembourg : Netherlands	0:2 (0:1)
27-10-68	Bulgaria : Netherlands	2:0 (1:0)
26-03-69	Netherlands : Luxembourg	4:0 (2:0)
20-04-69	Poland : Luxembourg	8:1 (3:0)
23-04-69	Bulgaria : Luxembourg	2:1 (1:0)
07-05-69	Netherlands : Poland	1:0 (0:0)
15-06-69	Bulgaria : Poland	4:1 (2:1)
07-09-69	Poland : Netherlands	2:1 (0:1)
12-10-69	Luxembourg : Poland	1:5 (1:0)
22-10-69	Netherlands : Bulgaria	1:1 (1:0)
09-11-69	Poland : Bulgaria	3:0 (1:0)
07-12-69	Luxembourg : Bulgaria	1:3 (0:2)

North/Cent. America Phase 1 - Group 1

	P	W	D	L	F	A	Pts
Honduras	4	3	1	0	7	2	7
Costa Rica	4	2	1	1	7	3	5
Jamaica	4	0	0	4	2	11	0

27-11-68	Costa Rica : Jamaica	3:0 (0:0)
01-12-68	Jamaica : Costa Rica	1:3 (1:2)
05-12-68	Honduras : Jamaica	3:1 (2:0)
08-12-68	Jamaica : Honduras	0:2 (0:1)
22-12-68	Honduras : Costa Rica	1:0 (1:0)
29-12-68	Costa Rica : Honduras	1:1 (1:1)

North/Cent. America Phase 1 - Group 2

	P	W	D	L	F	A	Pts
Haiti	4	2	1	1	9	5	5
Guatemala	4	1	2	1	5	3	4
Tinidad & Tobago	4	1	1	2	4	10	3

17-11-68	Guatemala : Trinidad & Tobago	4:0 (1:0)
20-11-68	Trinidad & Tobago : Guatemala	0:0
23-11-68	Trinidad & Tobago : Haiti	0:4 (0:1)
25-11-68	Haiti : Trinidad & Tobago	2:4 (1:2)
08-12-68	Haiti : Guatemala	2:0 (2:0)
23-02-69	Guatemala : Haiti	1:1 (1:0)

North/Cent. America Phase 1 - Group 3

	P	W	D	L	F	A	Pts
El Salvador	4	3	0	1	10	5	6
Surinam	4	2	0	2	10	9	4
Netherlands Antilles	4	1	0	3	3	9	2

24-11-68	Surinam : Netherlands Antilles	6:0 (3:0)
01-12-68	El Salvador : Surinam	6:0 (1:0)
05-12-68	Netherlands Antilles : Surinam	2:0 (0:0)
12-12-68	El Salvador : Netherlands Antilles	1:0 (0:0)
15-12-68	Netherlands Antilles : El Salvador	1:2 (0:0)
22-12-68	Surinam : El Salvador	4:1 (3:1)

North/Cent. America Phase 1 - Group 4

	P	W	D	L	F	A	Pts
United States	4	3	0	1	11	6	6
Canada	4	2	1	1	8	3	5
Bermuda	4	0	1	3	2	12	1

06-10-68	Canada : Bermuda	4:0 (3:0)
13-10-68	Canada : United States	4:2 (1:1)
20-10-68	Bermuda : Canada	0:0
26-10-68	United States : Canada	1:0 (0:0)
03-11-68	United States : Bermuda	6:2 (2:1)
11-11-68	Bermuda : United States	0:2 (0:2)

North/Cent. America Phase 2 - Semi-finals

	P	W	D	L	F	A	Pts
Haiti	2	2	0	0	3	0	4
El Salvador	2	1	0	1	3	1	2
Honduras	2	1	0	1	1	3	2
United States	2	0	0	2	0	3	0

20-04-69	Haiti : United States	2:0 (1:0)
11-05-69	United States : Haiti	0:1 (0:1)
08-06-69	Honduras : El Salvador	1:0 (0:0)
15-06-69	El Salvador : Honduras	3:0 (3:0)

North/Cent. America Phase 2 - Semi-finals Play-off

27-06-69	Honduras : El Salvador	2:3 a.e.t. (2:2, 1:2)

Played in Mexico City

22 Men and a Bag of Wind

North/Cent. America Phase 2 - Final

	P	W	D	L	F	A	Pts
Haiti	2	1	0	1	4	2	2
El Salvador	2	1	0	1	2	4	2

21-09-69	Haiti : El Salvador	1:2 (0:1)
28-09-69	El Salvador : Haiti	0:3 (0:3)

North/Central America Phase 2
Final Play-off

08-10-69	Haiti : El Salvador	0:1 a.e.t. (0:0)

Played in Kingston

South America - Group 1

	P	W	D	L	F	A	Pts
Peru	4	2	1	1	7	4	5
Bolivia	4	2	0	2	5	6	4
Argentina	4	1	1	2	4	6	3

27-07-69	Bolivia : Argentina	3:1 (1:1)
03-08-69	Peru : Argentina	1:0 (0:0)
10-08-69	Bolivia : Peru	2:1 (0:0)
17-08-69	Peru : Bolivia	3:0 (2:0)
24-08-69	Argentina : Bolivia	1:0 (0:0)
31-08-69	Argentina : Peru	2:2 (0:0)

South America - Group 2

	P	W	D	L	F	A	Pts
Brazil	6	6	0	0	23	2	12
Paraguay	6	4	0	2	6	5	8
Colombia	6	1	1	4	7	12	3
Venezuela	6	0	1	5	1	18	1

27-07-69	Colombia : Venezuela	3:0 (1:0)
02-08-69	Venezuela : Colombia	1:1 (0:0)
06-08-69	Venezuela : Paraguay	0:2 (0:1)
06-08-69	Colombia : Brazil	0:2 (0:2)
10-08-69	Colombia : Paraguay	0:1 (0:0)
10-08-69	Venezuela : Brazil	0:5 (0:0)
17-08-69	Paraguay : Brazil	0:3 (0:0)
21-08-69	Paraguay : Venezuela	1:0 (1:0)
21-08-69	Brazil : Colombia	6:2 (2:1)
24-08-69	Brazil : Venezuela	6:0 (5:0)
24-08-69	Paraguay : Colombia	2:1 (1:0)
31-08-69	Brazil : Paraguay	1:0 (0:0)

South America - Group 3

	P	W	D	L	F	A	Pts
Uruguay	4	3	1	0	5	0	7
Chile	4	1	2	1	5	4	4
Ecuador	4	0	1	3	2	8	1

06-07-69	Ecuador : Uruguay	0:2 (0:1)
13-07-69	Chile : Uruguay	0:0
20-07-69	Uruguay : Ecuador	1:0 (0:0)
27-07-69	Chile : Ecuador	4:1 (0:0)
03-08-69	Ecuador : Chile	1:1 (1:0)
10-08-69	Uruguay : Chile	2:0 (1:0)

Chapter 12

Terrorism, Taylor and Total Football
The West Germany World Cup, 1974

West Germany 1974

Winners: West Germany

Runners-up: Holland

3rd Place: Poland

4th Place: Brazil

Total Attendance: 1,855,601

Number of Matches: 38

In 1974 the world was still in economic and political turmoil. Although the Vietnam War had ended with the Geneva agreement of 1973, its ramifications were still troubling American society. The US justice system was shamed when army lieutenant, William Calley, was found guilty of the murder of Vietnamese citizens in the My Lai massacre of 1968, but served only three days of a life sentence. President Nixon intervened and commuted the punishment to house arrest. It was not his only political faux pas. In 1973 he also authorised a break-in of the Democratic Party's headquarters in the Watergate building in order to discover their plans for the forthcoming presidential election and two young journalists working for the Washington Post uncovered it. Nixon's administration attempted a cover-up, but further investigation revealed that since 1968, his government had taken illegal campaign contributions, authorised telephone tapping, sold ambassadorships, lied to the press and organized the Watergate debacle. All in all, "Tricky Dicky" had been a very naughty boy. To cap this anus horribilis for the US, newspaper heiress Patti Hearst fell in love with her kidnappers, the Symbionese Liberation Army, and denounced her wealthy father as a capitalist pig. She took the "revolutionary" name, Tania, and was later found playing Bonnie and Clyde in San Francisco.

Britain was exploding in more ways than one. The Flixborough chemical works disaster killed 29 people and devastated a number of Lincolnshire villages and in Westminster the Edward Heath government prepared to do battle with the Mineworkers Union. He had already introduced decimalization and taken Britain into the EEC, but a long running series of strikes had seen the country on a three day week. Unemployment was rising rapidly toward the one million mark and inflation hit 17%, as the economy stagnated. Heath went to the polls, firmly believing public opinion would go against the miners and demanding to know "Who Rules Britain?", and lost, but all did not go well for Harold Wilson in his third term in office. His relations with the unions rested heavily on the Social Contract, which they rejected. For the first time since 1910, a second election was called in less than a year, which Wilson won with a narrow majority. Meanwhile, the troubles in Northern Ireland registered their 1000th death.

Elsewhere, dictator Augusto Pinochet's tightened grip on Chile would affect the World Cup, whilst the deaths of generals Perón and Franco brought political changes in Argentina and Spain. The latter became a democracy, but Argentina's military government stayed in place. In Portugal, 42 years of dictatorship also came to an end in the "Revolution of the Carnations" and in Ethiopia the 44 year reign of Haile Selassie was ended by a military coup. Trouble also flared in Cyprus when friction between the Greek and Turkish populations resulted in a Turkish invasion of the island

In a titanic struggle Ali beat Frazier to regain the world crown he had lost earlier in the decade. Later in the year Ali held on to the title in the epic "Rumble in the Jungle" against George Forman in Kinshasa. The music world said goodbye to Duke Ellington and the USSR deported dissident author, Alexander Solzhenitsyn. The World Cup had a new trophy and a new FIFA President. Plans for the new cup began in 1970 with the original intention of naming it in honour of Sir Stanley Rous, whose 13 year presidency was ended in 1974 by Jean Marie Faustin de Godefroid Havelange in circumstances that hinted of corruption. It was rumoured that he had bought his election by paying for the flights of the African delegates, enabling him to win by 68 votes to 52. He declared on his appointment: "I have come to sell a product named football."

A record number of 99 countries entered the qualifying tournament for the 1974 World Cup, 33 from Europe, 24 from Africa, 17 from Asia, 14 from Central and North America, 10 from South America and 2 from Oceania. Of these, Gabon, India, Jamaica, Madagascar, the Philippines, Sri Lanka, the United Arab Emirates and Venezuela withdrew before it got underway, but the game's burgeoning appeal was clear to see. With this in mind, FIFA made changes to the format of the 1974 tournament, but surprisingly these affected the finals more than the qualifying stage. The world body was slow to respond to the increasing globalization of its game and areas outside of Europe and South America remained pitifully underrepresented. As in 1970, only three places were allocated to the rest of the world, with one each going to Africa, Asia-Oceania and the CONCACAF region. It can be argued that this was a fair reflection of the balance of power in the world game, but there were many who argued that the World Cup should be exactly that. It would not be until preparations for the 1982 World Cup began that FIFA made some effort to address the situation.

The first match of the new round took place on 14th November 1970 in Valletta and saw Malta make its World Cup debut against the once-mighty Hungary in European Group One. The Hungarians ran out 2-0 winners, but it was a worthy start by the Maltese, who turned out to be the group's whipping boys. They lost all of their games, conceded 20 goals and scored only once, in their final game against Sweden. The completion of the group's fixtures left Hungary, Austria and Sweden all tied on eight points. Hungary's inferior goal difference put them in third place, but the others had identical goal differences. It required a play-off, in Gelsenkirchen in West Germany, which the Swedes won 2-1 to take their place in the finals.

The greatest surprise in the European qualifiers was the elimination of England in Group Five. The crucial match determining England's demise was a 1-1 draw with Poland at Wembley in October 1973. Having gone behind, the English equalized through a dubiously given Allan Clarke penalty and then dominated huge swathes of the game. However, they were kept out by the magnificent acrobatics of Poland's charismatic goalkeeper, Jan Tomaszewski, a man whom Brian Clough had recently described as a clown and who, by luck or judgement, stopped everything that was thrown at him. The debacle was blamed on manager, Sir Alf Ramsey and he was accused in the press of having brought on substitute, Kevin Hector, far too late to make any difference. Hector, in fact, missed the best chance of the game in the dying minutes, a header that went narrowly wide. For Ramsey, the consequence of the defeat was that he was sacked the following April and temporarily replaced by Joe Mercer, the former manager of Manchester City, before Leeds United's Don Revie was given the job on a permanent basis. It was the beginning of one of England's most unsuccessful periods ever experienced.

Of the British nations, only Scotland managed to reach the finals, having a second World Cup campaign disrupted by a change of management. In December 1972 lack of success caused Manchester United to sack their boss, Frank O'Farrell, and only days later Scotland's Tommy Docherty replaced him. Docherty had played in Scotland's first visit to the World Cup in 1954 and his successor, Willie Ormond, steered the team to their third.

When Belgium beat Scotland in a pre-tournament warm-up, Belgian coach, Raymand Goethals, was unimpressed by Scotland's performance, saying: "Scotland played like blind men." From there the Scots flew to Oslo and, after a champagne-fuelled flight, Billy Bremner and Jimmy Johnstone carried on drinking in the hotel bar. They became so drunk and disorderly they had to be removed by the manager, who threatened to send them home. They met a Norwegian side that contained only one professional, goalkeeper, Dunfermline's Geir Karlsen, who would receive £25 in gift vouchers if they won, half that if they drew and nothing if they lost. Zaïre's manager, Blagoje Vidinic, watched Scotland win, but flew back to his players in Germany and told them they had nothing to worry about. The "Champagne Charlie" image followed the Scots around doggedly. Arriving at their hotel outside Frankfurt they were treated to a traditional champagne cocktail reception. German TV flashed pictures around the world of the Scots "getting drunk again." In truth, the players only sipped a little of the cocktails and then replaced them with cups of tea.

The owners of Scottish brewery, Tennants Caledonian, flew to Oslo to negotiate bonuses for the team. The deal provided £7,500 for pictures to be used commercially; £7,500 if they qualified from their group; £10,000 if they gained 3rd or 4th place; £50,000 if they were runners-up, and £100,000 if they won. It meant it was possible to earn £115,000, whilst the management would receive £4,600 each.

Terrorism, Taylor and Total Football - West Germany 1974

Three other European nations had their qualifying tournaments disrupted by troubles, though all of different natures. Northern Ireland's campaign was plagued by the domestic problems that began to afflict the Province after civil rights protests had deteriorated into sectarian violence in 1967 between the largely Catholic nationalist community and the largely Protestant loyalists. Paramilitary organizations on both sides of the divide were drawn in, heightening the turbulence and the situation became so dire that the British army was sent in 1969 to try to restore peace. Nonetheless, the bombings and killings continued unabated and high profile events, such as World Cup matches, were considered too tempting targets for the bombers. The authorities were not prepared to take any risks and for security reasons all of Northern Ireland's "home" games were played in England. During their opening match, against Bulgaria in Sofia, George Best was sent off and his team eventually went down 3-0.

Political problems also resulted in the Soviet Union not qualifying for the finals. The Soviets had ended top of European Group Nine, above the Irish Republic and France, but FIFA had decided that the winners of this group should play-off over two legs against the winners of South American Group Three. It was an arrangement to create an extra place in the finals for teams from Asia and Africa. Chile won the South American group and played out a 0-0 draw in Moscow. However, in the meantime, a military coup in Chile had seen the left-wing President Salvador Allende overthrown and replaced by a military junta headed by General Pinochet. Allende had died in the attack on the presidential palace and in the days that followed thousands of his supporters were summarily rounded up and arrested. Many were held in the Estadio Nacional in Santiago, where numerous acts of brutality were perpetrated. Since the second leg was to be staged in the stadium, the Soviet Union refused to play, even though FIFA had decreed that it had to go ahead. When the Soviets stuck to their principles, the match and the place in Germany were awarded to Chile. The Chilean authorities had anticipated that this would happen and had arranged an alternative fixture against Santos, one of Brazil's top clubs. Santos won the game 5-0, a result that must have made very sorry reading for the Soviet players.

Yugoslavia's campaign was blighted by allegations of bribery, supposedly done to secure qualification for the finals. These proved unfounded and the Yugoslavs got to the finals through the efficacy of their football, though only just. Both they and the Spanish finished joint top of Group Seven, above Greece, on identical points and goal difference. Thus, a second European group required a play-off. It took place in Frankfurt in February 1974 and the Yugoslavs scraped a narrow 1-0 victory.

One noteworthy performance in the European qualifying competition was that of Italy, whose 5-0 victory over Luxembourg in Genoa in March 1973 was their 50th World Cup game, and who went on to become the only team to qualify without conceding a goal. Consolation, however, must go to Belgium, who also did not concede, but failed to qualify. The place from their Group Three went to Holland, whose free scoring "total" footballers notched up 24 goals in their six games, including a 9-0 defeat of Norway and an 8-1 victory over Iceland. The Icelanders, another side who played their "home" games on foreign soil, in Belgium and Holland, proved to have the leakiest defence of all 90 teams who took part in the qualifiers, letting in 29 goals in total.

In South American Group Two, Argentina and Paraguay went in to their final fixture on equal points. Both had taken maximum points from Bolivia in previous games, but the competition looked more even than it was. Argentina were the strongest team in the group and a comfortable 3-1 victory secured a place in the finals. The Uruguayans, though, were still finding it difficult to break the defensive mould in which its football had been set for the past few years. They only qualified above Colombia on goal difference because they adopted a more adventurous approach in their final game against Ecuador, the group's weakest team. They won 4-0 and Colombia, who had beaten Uruguay in Montevideo, only managed draws against Ecuador. It left them short of goals in the final assessment.

Having allocated a place in the finals for the African continent, FIFA changed the format for the qualifying tournament, adopting a two-legged knock-out system instead of a series of sub-groups. It was only when the 24 original entrants had been whittled down to three that these were put into a group to play the final round on a league basis. Trouble flared in the second round of the knock-out when crowd disturbances disrupted Nigeria's home game against Ghana, with the away side 3-2 in front. The match had to be abandoned and a FIFA disciplinary committee later disqualified the Nigerians. In the third round, Zaïre defeated Ghana and went into the final group with Morocco and Zambia. The Moroccans were unhappy with the quality of refereeing in their away match in Zaïre and refused to play the home leg. Zaïre was awarded the game, recorded as a 2-0 victory, even though they had already qualified for the finals. They had done so at the first attempt and became Black Africa's first World Cup finalists. They had also played 11 qualifying games to get to Germany, setting a new record matched only by Australia.

The Asia-Oceania zone was organizationally a much more complicated affair. Each of the entrants were placed into either Group A, whose games were all played in Seoul. South Korea and Israel emerged to play each other in the Group A final, with South Korea winning by the only goal of the match. A slightly different format was used in Group B, where only the winners of two sub-groups played off over a two-legged final. In it Australia defeated Iran 3-0 in the first game, only to be beaten 2-0 in the second. It meant that Australia won through on goal difference to meet South Korea in the zone's eventual final, played over two legs and producing two draws. The play-off took place in Hong Kong and was won by Australia, the first Oceania team to reach the World Cup finals. In doing so, they equalled Zaïre's total of games to get there. The glee of the Australians at reaching the finals, when the English had not can be gleaned from the comment of one Melbourne newspaper. "Britain, an island of 55 million Poms, will be green with envy when Australia compete in the World Cup finals," it gloated. In trying to put one over the "Old Country", the reporter made a mistake commonly committed by foreigners when discussing issues concerning Britain - only part of the island would be "green with envy". The Scots, of course, would be there too!

The biggest win in the qualifying tournament was Trinidad and Tobago's 11-1 thrashing of Antigua in November 1972 in the CONCACAF zone. This section was organized along similar lines to previous competitions, with the teams divided into six sub-groups, each of which produced one winner to go into the final round. These six played on a league basis in a mini-tournament that took place in Port au Prince, the capital of Haiti, over a 20 day period. The winners of the group were the Haitians, who suffered only one defeat in the series, in their last game against Mexico, the team most people expected to get to the finals. For the Mexicans, it was the first time they had failed to qualify since 1934, excepting 1938 when they did not enter.

Of the several changes made for the 1974 World Cup, perhaps the most obvious was the new trophy. Brazil, outright winners of the Jules Rimet Trophy, had offered to donate a new one, but FIFA decided to commission its own, which was simply named the FIFA World Cup, reverting back to the original name of the first trophy. Red cards were first introduced in 1974 and goal difference was to be used to separate teams with the same points in the groups. FIFA introduced its Fair Play Award, but the biggest change was that to the format used to organize the event. The 16 finalists were grouped into four groups, as normal, but instead of having a knock-out in the second stage, the top two teams in each were to make a further two groups of four. The winners of these groups would then meet in the final, whilst the runners up in each would play for third and fourth places. There were to be no semi-finals. The purpose of the change was to allow more games to be played, to generate more income, and it met with much criticism when announced. It was widely felt that it would reduce the excitement and quality of football in the second phase of the tournament.

Three European teams, West Germany, Italy and Bulgaria, had reached their fourth successive World Cup tournaments. Bulgarian defender, Dobromir Jetchev, was also playing his fourth series.

Argentine supporter, Carlos Tula, arrived at his team's training ground on 10th June having travelled by boat to Lisbon and hitch hiked the rest of the 9,375 miles.

Zaïre achieved a minor triumph before the tournament started when they beat North German minor league side VFB Oldenburg 5-2 in a friendly.

On 4th June Italian side, Fiorentina, completed a hat trick of victories over World Cup participants when they defeated Uruguay 2-0 in a friendly. They had already beaten Zaïre 2-1 and Argentina 2-0.

World Cup outsiders Australia arrive at Hamburg.

Terrorism, Taylor and Total Football - West Germany 1974

The World Cup and Terrorism...

A worry at any major international sporting event is that of security. The post-1945 Cold War era spawned a miasma of regional political conflicts from South America, through Africa, the Middle East and into Asia. Their impact was far more than local, as groups like the IRA, the Bader-Meinhof Gang, the PLO, ETA and Abu Nidal, to name a few, were prepared to use terrorism to further their aims. Terrorist threats had necessitated tight security at Mexico in 1970 and the atrocity committed at the 1972 Olympics meant that the authorities dared take no chance when the World Cup went to Germany in 1974. As early as April, the Bavarian Interior Ministry received warnings about possible Arab terrorist strikes and in June two Arabs were convicted of planning attacks on the West Berlin offices of El Al and a Jewish-owned nightclub amongst other targets. The head of the city's Justice Department, Horst Korber, said: "The World Cup played a role in their release. We had reports that action was planned to free them." Both were deported back to the Middle East. Two days later, a Palestinian student was arrested in Saarbrücken, where police found "concrete evidence" that attacks to disrupt the World Cup were being planned. Policing the tournament was strict and drunkards trying to get into matches were barred. There were to be no flags on poles, bottles or cans allowed into grounds.

It was not just Arabs who posed a problem. On 6th June, Haiti's World Cup squad was placed under armed police guard after an anonymous letter threatened their safety and in Munich left-wing groups, angered at General Pinochet's appalling human rights record, were planning action against the Chilean team. The security services had to be on constant alert and some of the measures taken show how seriously the threat was taken. The Post Office in Munich set up a radio screening squad to locate guided missiles, whilst riot police were posted into the hills and woods around the Olympic Stadium to prevent rocket attacks.

The World Cups of 1978 and 1982 were similarly plagued by the terrorist. In 1978 Buenos Aires went on full alert after 15 members of the Italian terrorist group, the Red Brigade, got past airport security and entered the city bent on causing mayhem and destruction. One of their targets was the Italian squad's hotel. Luckily Rome had tipped off the local authorities and the cell was apprehended before it could begin its murderous work. The 1982 tournament was threatened by the Basque separatists, ETA. Before the tournament began most ETA cells had said that they would not disrupt it, except with propaganda, but the hard-line military branch threatened a major offensive against Spanish security forces and rogue units could never be discounted. On 10th May police arrested two ETA members on reconnaissance operations checking out football grounds for possible attacks. Then, on 14th June, the day of the opening ceremony, four bombs went off in Madrid. They had been timed to go off simultaneously outside buildings owned by the Defence Ministry. Fortunately, nobody was hurt and there were no casualties when a bomb wrecked a bar five days later in Bilbao, one of the Basque ports. It was a bar frequented by English fans, though this was not the reason for the attack.

Money, then, had become a major influencing factor by 1974 and it told on the attitude of players, many of whom were making inflated demands for their services. Franz Beckenbauer had to intervene when the West Germans threatened a strike over pay and their bonuses were raised from £5,000 to £10,000, with extra payments for wearing the Adidas kit. It prompted jealousy and unrest in the Dutch camp, where a similar deal had to be negotiated. The Scots, too, were in dispute over money, with their boot manufacturers, and all were examples of how the commercial success of the game was gnawing away at the spirit that supposedly underpinned it. An entirely different attitude came from the East European teams. East German coach, Georg Buschner, proudly boasted that his team would get no bonuses as they were all amateurs and Polish boss, Kazimierz Gorski, said: "We have not even spoken about money so far. We are concentrating on getting fit."

Another unfortunate aspect of the 1974 World Cup was the need for very tight security. A repetition of the attack made by Arab terrorists against the 1972 Munich Olympic Games that killed 11 Israeli athletes was unthinkable. It was another, undesirable development as the game grew up and entered the modern era. Happily, the Germans got it right and there were no incidents, only threats, to disrupt their World Cup. In another respect, though, modern developments were of little comfort to the organizers. German weather forecasters utilised every up-to-date technique, including computer analysis of weather charts and past records, to predict when the best times to play games would be. Unhappily, they got it wrong and several games were played in appalling conditions, felt by many to have influenced the tournament's outcome.

The opening ceremony of West Germany 1974 took place on 13th June in the Wald Stadium in Frankfurt. It was, as the Guardian reported, a pageant of "music, colour, dancing, pouring rain, and the inevitable goalless draw." The 62,000 crowd cheered Pelé receiving a replica of the old trophy in honour of his three championship wins from "Unser Uwe" Seeler, who was given a copy of the new one from Pelé. The pomp was then washed away in the rain as the World Cup reverted to form and another in the series of boring opening matches. The Brazilians eschewed the verve with which they had won four years earlier and instead adopted a negative defensive style. The Yugoslavs, too, seemed to catch the mood and, whilst they were the more adventurous of the teams, they also put much into closing the game down and were often "cynically crude in stopping their opponents." With the driving rain not helping the play, it was a game of few chances. The only plausible opportunity of the first period was not created until the 42nd minute, when a cross fell to Acimovic, who was clumsily bundled over in the area. The Yugoslavs were dumfounded not to have been awarded a penalty and it was not until the second half that they fashioned another decent opening, when Oblak headed against the post. It was the last chance of the game and with the Brazilians "only showing glimpses of the carefree spontaneity of the 1970 team", there was little more to report. Many a sodden German supporter must have trudged his weary way home wondering what all the fuss was about and praying that things could only get better. From his point of view, they did.

West Germany's campaign got underway the next day in West Berlin's Olympic Stadium with a Group One game against Chile. The hosts made their customary slow start and were unimpressive against a team they might ordinarily have been expected to overcome easily. With the exception of Paul Breitner, who was lively throughout, the Germans were patchy. It was he who scored the game's only goal, and the tournament's first, in the 17th minute when he was set up by Beckenbauer and unleashed a powerful long range shot that set "an early seal on an excellent performance." From that point, the Germans were never in danger of losing the match, especially after Carlos Caszely was sent off in the 67th minute for kicking Bertie Vogts. When Rodríguez was stretchered off near the end of the game, the victory was in the bag. It was unconvincing, but a win and the Germans were happy for that.

In Hamburg that day, the other two Group One sides were making their first appearances in the World Cup finals. It was a sign of the times that the East Germans were so readily accepted in West Germany. All through the years of the Cold War, since the country had been divided in 1949 into Communist East and liberal West Germany, the West Germans had refused to recognize the existence of East Germany as a separate political entity. It had always been referred to as the "Soviet Zone", that part of Germany occupied by the Soviet Red Army, and the West Germans had shunned any diplomatic and cultural links with its neighbour on the grounds that these might prejudice the ultimate goal of political reunification. However, since the mid-1960s under the leadership of Chancellor Willy Brandt, the West Germans had been seeking to reduce East-West tensions in Europe by forging closer ties with the Soviet Union and her satellites. Implicit in this was the need to begin exchanges with East Germany and in the early 1970s both sides had entered into a series of slow and painstaking negotiations that had brought a closer understanding. At the same time, the Soviet Union and the United States had been trying to lessen the tension between them, so as to avoid the risk of a major nuclear conflagration such as had almost erupted over the 1962 Cuban Missile Crisis. The net result of both circumstances was the era known as Détente and the easing of Cold War hostilities. It meant that the East and West Germans could enter more freely and warmly into sporting competition against each other.

East Germany's game against Australia was one of pleasant surprise for the followers of southern hemisphere sport. Australia's coach, Zvonimir Rasic, had assembled a multi-national squad that far from disgraced itself in its first appearance on the main stage of international football. In the first half, they more than held their own and even, "against all expectations, dominated play for long periods." Their stubborn defence stood firm against the German attack and in Adrian Alston, they had the best player on the field. Their resistance frustrated the Germans, who had three players booked, and the 0-0 half-time score line was the least the

Yugoslav manager, Miljan Miljanic, called his team the "favourite outsiders" to win and top player, Dragan Dzajic was also convinced they would do well. Such positive thinking was due to team psychologist, Professor Voilsav Stefanovic. He made the team listen to Chopin before the opening game, saying that it "should help to make the players completely fit for the game against the Brazilians." Meanwhile, the Brazilians themselves, stationed at Hofheim, relaxed by listening to samba music. Professor Stefanovic refused to comment on the possible effects this would have.

Two men were hotly disputing the title of "Youngest Manager" at the 1974 tournament, Blagoje Vidinic at 39 years old and the Australian boss, Zvonimir Rasic, who claimed to be 38. Vidinic said of his counterpart: "I know him well, he is at least 41. He is the most handsome and may be the better coach, but I am the youngest." Rasic knew his team's chances were slim but was pleased to state: "Whether we reach the quarter-finals or not we have done better than England."

Australian goalkeeper, Jack Reilly, was a private detective, whilst Alfonso Archuneia, the Mexican referee in charge of the Scotland-Yugoslavia game, was an electrical engineer.

Zaïre travelled to Germany with a witch doctor or "Ju Ju Man". He needed the shinbones of either a man or an animal to put a hex on the Scots. These would be tied together with a leather thong. The names of the Scottish players would be written on a piece of paper, stuffed between the bones and then he would spit chewed red pepper onto them. He charged highly for his services, but was strikingly unsuccessful.

Matt McRoberts, a Scotish fan camping with four friends, was found after the Zaïre game in a Dortmund bar stripped to the waist, crying his eyes out and repeatedly uttering the phrase: "Poetry, sheer poetry."

Australians deserved. In the first half the Germans had tried to play the ball through the centre without success, but in the second they switched to using the wings and this enabled them to turn the Australians. The Germans struck first in the 58th minute, rather fortunately, when Colin Curran deflected Jürgen Sparwasser's shot into the net, though there was nothing lucky about their second goal. It came in the 72nd minute and was a "fine hooked volley" from Joachim Streich, who had got onto the end of a cross from the left. They had gone down to a better team, but the Australians could take much consolation from the manner of their defeat.

The Scots went into their opening Group Two game against Zaïre with their eyes wide open and taking no chances. There had been discipline problems in the squad, with the wilder antics of some players gaining the manager's disapproval, and both Willie Johnson and Billy Bremner had nearly been sent home. This was one reason for their caution and captain Bremner gave another when he said: "Our record against poor sides is so bad that we cannot afford to take anything for granted." Certainly, manager Ormond was prepared to pay respect to the Africans. "The Zaïre team are big, strapping lads and they run like hell", he said. It was a respect that showed in the initial tactics employed by the Scots, as they sought to slow the game down to deny Zaïre the use of their pace and strength. Yet, such patience does not come naturally to Scottish footballers and they could not long reign in their urge to go forward. It was no bad thing, because whilst they found it difficult to break Zaïre's defence when playing along the ground, they soon discovered that defence's weakness. The Zaïrians "suffered collective vertigo when the ball came at them in the air" and in Joe Jordan the Scots had a man more than capable of exploiting such hesitancy. In the 26th minute he rose to a cross, headed the ball down and Peter Lorimer, one of the hardest shots in the game, volleyed into the net. Seven minutes later, it was Jordan again "who ran through the defence like an invisible man" to get his head to Bremner's free kick. Though he headed it into the goalkeeper's hands, it was powerful enough to elicit a mishandling and the ball ended in the net. The second half saw Scotland easily the better side, but they were unable to gain further from it. The score remained 2-0. It was their first win in the World Cup finals, though it remained to be seen whether two goals would be enough should goal difference become the deciding factor.

The Group Three and Four teams came into play the following day and, in Hanover, the Dutch took on Uruguay. Although he had been the national coach only a matter of months, Holland's Rinus Michels had seen his vision of "total football", developed first at Ajax and then Barcelona, come alive in this multi-talented squad. (See Ruud Krol profile on page 255). He reckoned that a team needed at least seven world class players in order to function the way he envisaged and in men like Johan Cruyff, Johannes Neeskens, Wim Van Hanegem and Rob Rensenbrinck, to name but four, he had them in plenty. Neeskens was nicknamed the Nobby Stiles of Holland because of his hard tackling. All were versatile enough to play in a variety of positions and their flexibility added new dimensions to the dynamics of the game. Quite literally, an opposition never knew where they were coming from and it made organising resistance very problematical. The over-cautious Uruguayans described by one reporter as "much as they were four years ago, one-paced, reluctant to push men forward, and over reliant on Rocha and the ageing Cubilla for inspiration", were no match. Their only answer was a resort to brutality and such tactics rarely win games. The Dutch took the lead after seven minutes, when Johnny Rep headed in Willem Suurbier's cross, but then their "profligacy and the familiar agility of the Uruguayan goalkeeper kept the score to one goal for the next 75 minutes or so." They were 75 minutes of almost total Dutch control, with Feyenoord's Van Hanegem, known to his team mates as "the Curve", "the pulse of the Dutch performance." Meanwhile, the Uruguayans hacked and barged away in their attempt to keep their opponents quiet, but to no avail. In the 70th minute Júlio Montero-Castillo was ordered off for punching Rensenbrinck in the stomach and some three minutes from time the Dutch got their deserved second goal. Rensenbrinck drew Ladislau Mazurkiewicz out of his goal, square passed to Rep, who slotted into the undefended goal. It was Holland's first win in the World Cup finals and they had made their mark despite Uruguayan savagery. After the game, Cruyff complained: "They weren't hard, they were dirty... hard one accepts, but dirty play is dangerous."

A more open and clean game was that between Poland and Argentina, who, unlike their South American neighbours, were able to shake off their reputation of the past. Their willingness to go forward was matched by that of Poland and it made for a highly entertaining game, in which the Poles had the better of the first part, with the Argentinians staging a spirited comeback. After Mario Kempes had missed an early chance, the Poles drew first blood capitalizing on a mistake from goalkeeper, Daniel Carnivalli. He dropped a corner at the feet of Grzegorz Lato and the winger needed no second invitation. It was in the 6th minute and within two more, Lato had set up Andrzej Szarmach for the second. The Poles were soon into their stride and "played with a smooth yet fast and incisive blend", their forwards in particular buzzing like hornets. Yet, the Argentinians defended well and kept the Poles out for the rest of the half, before their own forwards started to click. In the second, they began to show what they could do, "with forwards turning in confined spaces and defenders such as the splendid Wolff weaving their way through Poland's defence." They pulled a goal back 15 minutes into the half, when Kempes set up a strike for Ramón Heredia and it began to look as if they might take something from the game. However, luck was not with them as for a second time Carnivalli and Lato combined to produce goal for Poland. Four minutes after his team had scored, Carnivalli accidentally threw the ball to Lato, who accepted the gift gracefully. It was not the end of it and, within another two minutes, Carlos Babington scored from a rebound after his first shot had been blocked. The score was now 3-2 and that is how it remained in spite of further good attack and defensive work from both teams.

It was difficult to separate Bulgaria and Sweden in their Group Three encounter in Düsseldorf and though the game ended a goalless draw, it was throughout "an absorbing tactical and technical exercise." As Gerald Sinstadt, writing for the Times, noted, "in sapping humidity, they showed enterprise, invention and a desire for goals that cannot be construed from the score line." It was Bulgaria's best performance to date in the World Cup finals and, although Sweden created marginally the better chances, a draw was a fair result. It set both teams up with a chance of making it into the next phase.

The other match played that day marked Haiti's debut in the finals in a game the Italians were expected to win easily. They did not and the part-timers from the Caribbean made a creditable fight of it, in the first half at least. Indeed, the Haitians took a shock lead just after the restart, when Emmanuel Sanon, a 23 year old student of business management, "swept fluently through the defence" to score a fine solo goal. It was the first time the Italians had conceded in 14 matches and it conjured up nightmare visions of North Korea in 1966. It was certainly an unwelcome present for goalkeeper, Dino Zoff, on his 32nd birthday and the trauma of it was enough to bring his team to its senses. Within six minutes, Gianni Rivera, now playing in his fourth World Cup, equalized and in the 66th minute Romeo Benetti grabbed the lead with a deflected shot. By now the Italians were in full flow and the Haitians dependent on the reflexes of the excellent Henri Francillon in goal. Pietro Anastasi's 78th minute strike ended the scoring and gave the Italian the win they deserved, but it had been a struggle. A sad footnote to this game created a notorious first when Haiti's Ernst Jean-Joseph later failed a drugs test and was banned from the rest of the tournament.

Having acquitted themselves with some merit against the East

Following the Uruguay game, Dutch coach, Rinus Michels, answered questions in Dutch, Spanish, German, English and French. He also had to juggle his international work with commitments to Barcelona, his club. During the tournament he flew to Spain to take charge of Barcelona's 1-1 Spanish Cup semi-final draw with Athletico Madrid before flying back to be with Holland.

The Argentineians caused controversy again as rumours circulated about late night antics. The team also refused to pose for photographs and to wear the logo of one of the team's sponsors unless they were paid.

Mario Zagalo, under fierce pressure to retain the trophy, had an enormous wooden fence built around the team's hotel to protect them from unscrupulous journalists. He feared the same treatment as had been dished out to Hilton Gosling and Vincente Feola who managed Brazil in 1966, both of whom had returned home in disgrace.

Haiti's coach, Antoine Tassy said optimistically: "Everybody remembers North Korea in 1966. We may give cause to be remembered in 1974."

The Haiti squad training in the Olympic Stadium.

Terrorism, Taylor and Total Football - West Germany 1974

Germans, on 18th June the Australians had to confront the mighty West Germans, one of the favourites for the title. It looked ominous when the Germans took the lead in the 13th minute, after Müller and Grabowski "exchanged passes at speed through the perplexed Australians" and set up Köln's Wolfgang Overath, whose left foot was "one of the truest in football when shooting at upwards of 20 yards." Müller hit the post five minutes later, but the Australians refused to cave in. They often had ten men behind the ball and "defended with admirable resilience for much of the match." However, they "were never in a position to worry the West Germans" and, though they did not make things easy, it was always going to be a damage limitation exercise. Further goals from Bernard Cullman and Müller produced a 3-0 victory, but the Germans were clearly not playing at their best. (See Gerd Müller profile on page256). Contemporary commentators were quick to note that they would have to do much better if they were to have an impact on this World Cup, especially with the Dutch winding themselves up.

Whilst the West Germans toiled against the Australians, their neighbours from across the Wall were scrapping with the Chileans. Both sides disappointed in a goalless first half, the opening period of which was played in lashing rain and which was "marred by frayed tempers and petty fouls." The Germans came close to scoring with two good shots, but the best football was played in the second half, when both teams came alive. The Germans were the first to show with a 56th minute goal from Martin Hoffman, at 19 the youngest player in the East German squad. His header came from a free kick and triggered a "magnificent second half rally" from the Chileans, who decided this was a match they had to win if they were going to make the second round. Their equalizer came some ten minutes after they had fallen behind and was a superb effort from Sergio Ahumada, who got the better of the defence to stab a low cross into the net. The game had, at last, opened up and enough opportunities were created for either team to have won it. Streich for the Germans and Figueroa for Chile, who hit the post, might have settled matters, but the best chance fell to Véliz, who fired straight at the German keeper when in the clear.

That same day, in Frankfurt, the Scots were facing their greatest challenge and acquitting themselves with distinction, if not with a victory. Before the game against Brazil, Willie Ormond was asked if he would be praying for the rain which would render the conditions more suitable to the Scots. He replied: "I'll just be praying", and maybe his prayers were answered because for the first half-hour or so, the Brazilians had the Scots on the ropes, but could not score. Rivelino had one shot marvellously saved by David Harvey in goal and a minute later Leivinho's fine volley almost broke the crossbar. Soon after, Billy Bremner, who played like a lion in the Scottish defence, managed to scoop away Jairzinho's shot before it crossed the line and it seemed impossible that they could hold out for much longer. This Brazilian team, though, was not of the same cut as its predecessors and their failure to score turned to frustration, which in turn saw them resort to foul play and give Scotland the chance to get back into the game. This they did with relish and a fiery second half performance saw them come close to winning the game themselves. At the end they had the Brazilian goal under siege as in succession Hay, Bremner, Lorimer and Jordan had chances that were well saved or missed by the narrowest of margins.

Their 0-0 draw with Brazil lifted the Scots to second place in the group, unbeaten and not having conceded a goal. However, they trailed on goal difference to Yugoslavia, whose 9-0 thrashing of Zaïre indicated just how costly was Scotland's failure to score more than twice against Zaïre. The victory was every bit as convincing as the score line suggests and "disclosed an abyss between the standards of the best in Europe and the best in Africa." The slaughter began in the sixth minute when Dusan Bajevic headed the first. When the score reached 3-0, Zaïre's Yugoslav coach Blagoje Vidinic decided to change goalkeepers in the hope of keeping the score respectable. Muamba Kazadi was replaced by Dimbi Tubilandu, the first time in the World Cup that a goalkeeper had been taken off for any reason other than injury. It was to no avail. Within seconds, Josip Katalinski had scored and Tubilandu's first touch of the ball was to pull it out of the net. Mulamba N'daye was sent off soon after for arguing with and kicking the referee, and was banned for a year by FIFA. The game was over by this point. With a 6-0 half-time lead, Yugoslavia did not need to take the second half seriously, but still scored three more to equal Hungary's 1954 record scoreline. Hong Duk-yung, South Korea's goalkeeper that day, held on to his record of having let in the most goals in the World Cup finals because Zaïre had used two. So bad did the Zaïre players feel after their mauling that they wanted to go home and it took considerable persuasion to get them to stay.

Sweden's next game, against Holland, produced another 0-0 draw, but like the first this was another "highly entertaining affair, full of wonderfully coordinated movements from Holland; countered by sharp breakaways from the Swedes." Cruyff, "the nerve centre of their football, running at, through, and around the Swedish defence with that uncanny ability he has to judge a situation" was in spellbinding form, and had Dutch play in front of goal been as faultless as their build-up, they would have won by a magnitude. As it was, their generosity when in scoring positions, some tenacious defending from Sweden and a string of saves from Helström in goal, "which ranged from the competent to the extraordinary", kept a clean sheet. The draw left Bulgaria and Uruguay needing something out of their match to keep up with the pace. Uruguay's ambitions, though, hinged on a draw and they were prepared to allow the Bulgarians to do most of the running. Christo Bonev was brilliant as his team dominated much of the game, but were unable to breach a rugged Uruguayan defence. It was not until the final 15 minutes that they made a break through and, inevitably, it was Bonev whose diving header found the target. It forced the South Americans to rethink their approach and for the last 15 minutes they attacked incessantly, trying to salvage their World Cup. Ricardo Pavoni saved the day with a long range shot that slipped under the goalkeeper's body for a draw that kept both alive, but just.

Scotland 0 : Brazil 0
Scotland's Joe Jordan (right) takes on Luis Pereira.

After Scotland's heroic draw with Brazil the British Prime Minister, who had been at the game said: "I know more about football than politics. Scotland played really well and deserved to win. I thought Peter Lorimer should have been moved to the inside-left position in the last 15 minutes." In response Willie Ormond, said: "You stick to your job and I'll stick to mine."

Star Bulgarian striker, Christo Bonev, scorer of seven goals in the qualifying competition, was reputedly married to the most beautiful girl in his home town of Plovdiv.

After Uruguayan player Luis Garisto was helped from the pitch in the game against Bulgaria an argument between players and coach ensued. The coach wanted to put on forward, Luis Cubilla, while the players wanted defender Juan Masnik. Player power ruled, but minutes later Bulgaria scored to take the lead.

Given their past records, the Group Four encounter between Argentina and Italy in Stuttgart was a surprisingly enjoyable one. Each took every opportunity to press forwards, though with Carlos Babington sparkling in midfield, the Argentinians always looked the sharper up front. Indeed, the Italian forward unit was the least effective part of the team and it was not surprising that Argentina took the lead in the 19th minute, when Babington set up René Houseman. However, their failure to score more allowed Italy a lifeline and 15 minutes later Benetti sent a harmless looking pass into the area, which Roberto Perfumo turned past his own goalkeeper. For the next 55 minutes, Argentina remained the better team and it would have been unjust had Sandro Mazzola put away the chance he had 15 minutes from the end. He shot wide, the game ended a draw, and kept both in the chase for the second phase, behind Poland.

The manner of Poland's defeat of Haiti, with a display far more ruthless than Italy or later Argentina gave against the same opposition, singled them out as one of the teams of the tournament. They were utterly remorseless, "showed a merciless superiority and were peppering the Haitian goal until the final whistle." Admittedly, the Haitians were in some disarray following Jean-Joseph's ban, but this should not detract from Poland's achievement and, had not Francillon played so well in goal, the score would have been greater than it was. The rout began in the 17th minute when Lato grabbed his first and a minute later, Kazimiercz Deyna made it 2-0. Then three in four minutes saw the Poles romp to a 5-0 half-time lead. The damage was done and there could be no recovery for Haiti. In the second half the Poles stroked the ball around with poise, occasionally letting rip to emphasize their superiority. Two more goals

Argentinians Roberto Perfumo (left) and Ruben Ayala training at Sindelfingen.

The day before the Poland-Haiti match, there were still 55,000 unsold tickets. There were 60,000 unsold for the one between Chile and East Germany. Saturation TV coverage got the blame for the low attendances at the start of the tournament. Sales of colour televisions had gone up 50% in West Germany in the first four months of the year.

It was a mistake that had Haitian Ernst Jean-Joseph sent home for using a banned stimulant. His doctor in Port au Prince had prescribed phenylmetrazin for his asthma, but he had forgotten to tell the team doctor, who would have had the prescription changed.

capped a resounding victory and left an outraged Haitian dictator, "Baby Doc" Duvalier, threatening to settle accounts when the team returned home.

The final Group one games were played on 22nd June and in Hamburg the two Germanys faced each other for the first time in a soccer international. Having taken four points already, the West Germans had qualified, but the East Germans still needed a point and their tactics reflected this. They adopted a strategy of defence and a breakaway goal if they could get one. Their ploy worked perfectly. The West Germans had most of the possession, they were "talented, they were decorative, they were occasionally very quick", but they could not score. The East Germans did, in the 80th minute, when Sparwasser picked up a long pass, "beat Vogts for pace on the outside, and drove his shot past Maier." "It was," one observer wrote, "a triumph for contemporary, breakaway football. West Germany did the running, East Germany got the goal."

East Germany's goal meant that neither Australia nor Chile could reach the second round. In torrential rain they played out a 0-0 draw with a curious incident happening near the end of the game. Australia's Raymond Richards was booked for time wasting, but Jafar Namdar, the Iranian referee, failed to notice that Richards had already been booked and should have been sent off. It was a full five minutes before a linesman pointed out the error to the referee and the Australian was asked to leave the field. Chile could not make good the advantage and Australia took their first point in the World Cup finals.

To have any chance, the Scots needed to beat Yugoslavia and they set about their task purposefully, playing deliberate, half-paced football, sticking to their shape and game plan. It left them prey to Yugoslavia's hard men, who sought to break Scotland's rhythm with a whole welter of fouls "of clear and intentional violence". Yet, the Scots never let it distract them and, having gained the upper hand, they came close to taking the lead more than once. Jordan hit one shot straight at the goalkeeper and Lorimer had another scrambled off the line before, with ten minutes to go, disaster struck. Dzajic sent in a perfectly measured cross and Stanislav Karasi "waited to shoot a superb goal." What followed was one of the most stirring ten minute spells in the history of Scottish international football as Bremner rallied his men for the final push. "With their captain now not so much a player as a flag", wrote one analyst, "they tore into the Yugoslavs in an attack that seemed to have no end, no shape, but such obvious purpose." Sadly for the Scots, that purpose was only attained in the last minute when Tommy Hutchison, on instead for Kenny Dalglish, crossed the ball for Jordan to blast the equalizer. (See Kenny Dalglish profile on page 257). It had been magnificent, but not quite enough. The Scots, unbeaten and having conceded only one goal, were cruelly eliminated, not "by Yugoslavia, a ferociously-hard team that they had mastered under an unrelenting sun... but by statistics." The Brazilians secured an uncertain 3-0 victory against Zaïre to put them above Scotland on goal difference. It was the first time a team had gone out of the World Cup finals in such a way - Italy, who went out the same way, did not complete their fixtures until the following day. After the game, the greatest Brazilian of them all paid warm tribute to the Scots and their lion-hearted captain. Bremner, Pelé said, "has been one of the few great players to stand out in this series."

The Dutch wound up their first round matches with an imperious display against Bulgaria. They got off to a flying start with a penalty scored by Neeskens after five minutes and from that point "every pass, every dovetailed switch of positions", had "a polished elegance that few teams in the world can match." Cruyff was again at the centre of things and his team "made chances in profusion but converted them with tantalising irregularity." Their second goal did not come until the final minutes of the first half, a second Neeskens penalty, and it was not until the 71st minute that Rep scored their third. It was a trait of this Dutch team that, brilliant though it undoubtedly was, goal tally rarely reflected superiority, a feature that would be ultimately costly. Another was a tendency to petulance, which had three players booked in the first half-hour, all for niggly, unnecessary fouls. Yet, this day belonged to Holland and they scored again in the 78th minute. This time it was Ruud Krol who blasted into his own net whilst trying to clear it. They even denied the Bulgarians the solace of scoring their own consolation and Holland's fourth, the best of the bunch, came less than ten minutes later. Cruyff "dropped a long, dipping centre into the gap between Bulgaria's defenders" and Theo de Jong was there to dive forward and "guide the ball into the net with a perfect header." It was Bulgaria's fourth World Cup finals in succession and they had yet to win a game.

Group Three's other game that day also brought a convincing win, for Sweden over the hugely disappointing Uruguay. The Scandinavians had been attracting little notice, but had been going about their task with quiet determination and no little competence. They were becoming more self-assured by the game and the Uruguayans fell victim to it. The first half was an even affair, with Uruguay's solid defence having the measure of Sweden's attack, but things altered in the second as the Swedes began to find ways through. Their first goal came within a minute of the restart with a strike by Ralf Edström. It was 20 minutes before they scored again, but two goals inside five minutes, from Sandberg and Edström again, were enough to end Uruguay's seventh tilt at the World Cup finals. For Pedro Rocha, veteran of four of them, it was his last World Cup game and not a happy way to bow out. Another Uruguayan who also quit the scene, though after a shorter and less distinguished career, was manager, Roberto Porta. He was so ashamed by his team's showing that he resigned when he got back to Montevideo and publicly apologized.

Argentina went into their final first round game against Haiti, uncertain of going through. They needed to win by three goals and hope that Poland defeated Italy. An early injury to Haiti's centre-half, Nazaire, made their task easier and in the 14th minute Héctor Yazalde capitalized on his opponents' discomfort with a goal he needed two stabs at to score. Three minutes later, Babington's clever chip set Yazalde free along the bye line and his pass across the goal picked out Houseman to score the second. A third goal from Ruben Ayola came some 12 minutes into the second half, but then Haiti got a goal of their own to put Argentina's progress in doubt. Mano Sanon sent in a shot that Carnivalli could only block. The Haitian was quickest to the rebound and launched it into the net "like a highly experienced professional." It was a temporary set back and three minutes later Yazalde hit his second to restore the required goal difference.

Italy knew that a draw against Poland would be good enough and reverted to past tactics to prevent defeat. Both Riva and Rivera were

Andrew McCartney was not impressed when wife, Annie, won a ticket to see Scotland play Yugoslavia. He said: "Annie doesn't know the first thing about football. She'll probably cheer if Yugoslavia score." Dave McCallan of Stenhousemuir, a 21 year old cashier, gave up his job to follow his heroes, saying, "I was pretty bored with my job anyway. I won't miss being there one minute." His mum was angry though!

The "I Got A Little Too Carried Away" Award for 1974 goes to Hugh Taylor of the Scottish Daily Record. After Scotland failed to qualify for the second round he wrote: "Yes, we're on our way home to greatness," and that heard all over Germany were "sighs of relief going up from every country left in the tournament." He went on: "Are they glad to see us pack up and go home tomorrow? Bet your life they are. For Scotland emerged with pride and purpose as the most dangerous if not the best team in this World Cup." Taylor was so nationalistic that two days before the final and 13 after Scotland had gone home, he was still claiming that Scotland had shown the way in attacking football, even though his team scored only three goals

Coach, Christo Mladenov, was a little apprehensive about returning to Bulgaria. "I think I'm going to have trouble back home. I don't exclude the possibility of being relieved of my post," he said.

Italian coach, Feruccio Valcareggi, was heavily criticized for selecting a squad of players over 30, ridiculed as a bunch of old pensioners by the press. The youngest member of the squad was the 26 year old son of a Swansea café owner, Giorgio Chinaglia. He had been substituted against Haiti and the comments he made afterwards almost saw him sent home. Following their first round failure, 500 angry fans attacked the team setting about several players and throwing missiles at the team bus. They shouted "you ought to be shot" as the coach tried to get into his private car. In Rome people burned national flags and victory banners in the streets and others simply threw their television sets out of their windows. One did not wait until the final whistle and threw his out of his window after Poland's second goal. Other fans stormed the Polish Embassy throwing bricks and tomatoes at the windows. 21 year old Franco Pera, who had been watching the game in a café, went to the toilets and slashed his wrists, but doctors managed to save his life. Returning to Italy, the team plane pulled up 250 metres from the terminal building to avoid some 4000 fans chanting "clowns".

dropped so that the back unit could be reinforced, but they were dangerous stratagies to apply against a Polish team, whose forwards were among the finest in the tournament. They were not going to restrain themselves to give satisfaction to the Italians. As they had done in previous matches, the Poles went all out for attack and presented a constant worry to a rather desperate Italian defence. Their non-stop activity reaped reward in the last six minutes of the first half when Szarmach ran a full 25 yards to plant a "powerful header into the top corner." Kasparczak had supplied the cross and a minute later he beat two defenders before sending in a cross for Deyna to drive in from the edge of the area. Finding themselves 2-0 down forced a rethink from the Italians and they came out for the second half in a more determined mood. It made for football "fought at top speed from start to finish." "From the 70th minute onwards both Zoff... and Tomaszewski... were hard put to stop a welter of shots from both sets of forwards", though only one goal came of this fervid activity. With little more than five minutes remaining, Fabio Capello found the target for Italy. It was not enough and the finalists of 1970 went out on goal difference, leaving the Poles top of the group and the only team with a 100% record.

By the end of play on 23rd June, the finalists had been reduced down to eight. Argentina, Brazil, East Germany and Holland were drawn in Group A and Poland, Sweden, West Germany and Yugoslavia made up Group B. The second round got underway with four games on 26th June, one of which was that between East Germany and Brazil. The East Germans had done well to get so far. They were, as one analyst wrote, "strong, fast, hard, with a solid manned defence", but they lacked "finesse of the highest degree" and getting to the second phase was the limit of their capability. Whilst they could beat better teams on occasions, they could never do it regularly and the Brazilians were the first to expose the deficiencies in technique and tactical awareness. It was a rather flat game in which the Brazilians always had the upper hand without showing anything special. Brazil's goal revealed the technical difference between them, a free kick awarded after Jairzinho had been brought down on the edge of the area. It was beautifully worked with Jairzinho placing himself in the German wall. He moved as the ball was struck, leaving a surprised goalkeeper "as immobile as a statue in the market square as Rivelino's low, left footed shot went past him like an arrow". They had fallen for an old trick and, although the goal stirred them to better things, they endeavoured without ever really convincing. They only went down by a single goal and it was their first defeat in 17 matches, but Brazil ought to have won by more.

A team that proved far more adept at exposing weakness were the Dutch who met Argentina. Carlos Babington had been suspended for collecting three bookings and was sorely missed by the Argentinians, but it is doubtful if he would have been able to stem the momentum gathered by a team at the top of its form. The Dutch were overpowering, with Cruyff again the midfield generator, as they "threw one player after another up field, exploiting their speed of foot - and of thought." Holland's first goal, scored in the 11th minute, was a perfect example of how to turn a defence inside out. Van Hanegem rounded the Argentine defence and coolly chipped that ball into the space behind them. Cruyff, like an electric eel, darted to gather the ball, drew out and slipped the goalkeeper, and casually placed the ball in the net. The Dutch had two more efforts cleared off the line before Krol pile-drove a second goal in the 25th minute. The Dutch were making the South Americans look ordinary and created enough chances to have sunk them without trace. It was half an hour into the second half before they got the illusive third and Cruyff added a fourth in the last minute for a victory as decisive as any. It sent due warning to those still left in the tournament.

In Group B, Poland took on the Swedes, who gave them their stiffest test so far in a "fast and closely fought" match. The Swedes were the better team in the early stages and were unlucky not to have taken the lead, though Lato also headed against the bar. He headed the Poles in front as the first half drew to close, when Gadocha's cross was nodded back to him by Szarmach, the first goal Sweden had conceded in 313 minutes of World Cup football. They had opportunity to equalize in the 63rd minute when Gorgon brought down Bayern Munich's Conny Tortensson. There was no question that it was a penalty. Tapper stepped up to take it, but Tomaszewski made a superb save to keep Poland on course.

For much of their game against Yugoslavia, West Germany, the tournament's favourites, once again failed to impress. In a sluggish game, they "were merely the better of two mediocre teams" and for the first half-hour or so "it seemed that both teams were motivated by fear of defeat than belief in victory." Passing was often too square and tentative, and neither was prepared to commit men forward. The match began to come alive in the 39th minute, when Paul Breitner latched on to "an unpromising pass by Wimmer… turned a defender and struck a drive through the narrowest of gaps past a helpless goalkeeper." It was an excellent goal, but it was not until Uli Hoeness replaced Wimmer with 25 minutes to go that the Germans began to reveal their obvious potential. He provided the cross which Müller met "with his left foot and, as the ball bounced away, hooked it in with his right." It was a wonderful exhibition of a striker's skill and it set up a final spell in which, for the first time, the West Germans played like possible world champions.

When the next games were played on 30th June, Poland took on Yugoslavia and the West Germans faced the Swedes. (See W. Germany v Sweden profile on page 262). The Yugoslavs were every bit the tough challenge the Poles expected and were unlucky not to have gained a result. A keenly contested penalty in the 25th minute, awarded when Szarmach went down in a goal mouth scramble, was put away by Deyna to give Poland the lead. The Poles could have gone further ahead shortly after when Gadocha, "like forked lightening", cut through the defence, but left himself with too narrow an angle and shot into the side netting. Yugoslavia pulled level in the last minutes of the half with a great goal from Karasi, who rounded both Zmuda and Tomaszewski before shooting hard into

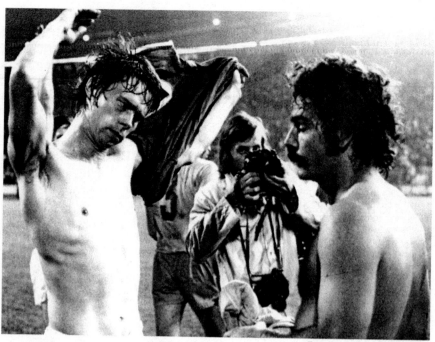

Brazil 1 : East Germany 0
East German Sparwasser (left) swaps shirts with Rivelino of Brazil.

President Tito of Yugoslavia was on an official state visit to West Germany as the second round got under way. The night before Yugoslavia took on West Germany he attended a state reception hosted by Chancellor Helmut Schmidt. During the dinner, both leaders discussed the match and Tito joked: "If the German team beat us it would be an unfriendly act since we are your guests." Tito did not attend the match itself because the German police could not guarantee his protection.

Attitudes to sex were very different. The Haitians and Argentinians had been allowed out to chance their arms with the young West German girls, while the Italians were given visits from wives and girlfriends. Sex was not an issue for the East Germans. They had not been out of their training camp for three weeks and the coach claimed: "We know other teams had problems with sex, such as the West Germans who have been in their training headquarters longer than we have. But our boys have no problem. Three weeks in camp is too short to make sex a problem. They can still stand it!" The Dutch were camped near Münster and Rinus Michels twice allowed players back to Holland to be with wives or girlfriends - "But please not both," he pleaded. When questioned about his decision, he explained: "These are men, not monks - enforced celibacy can destroy a player's concentration."

The Polish coach had moulded his coaching style on three men he regarded as masters of the game: Alf Ramsey, Feruccio Valcareggi and Helmut Schön. It was with great pleasure therefore, that he went into the game with West Germany hoping that he might complete a hat trick of victories over the teams they managed. Poland had already prevented England from qualifying for the finals and had beaten Italy in the first round. However, Schön proved to be his better and he had to settle for third place.

Angered by the decision to put an Austrian, Erich Linemayr, in charge of the match against West Germany, one Polish official admonished: "What a shocking decision to let an Austrian take charge. Austrians are Germans you know."

In a letter to the Scottish Daily Record on 27th June, E.S. of Dumfries wrote: "I realise I am in danger of being called a kill-joy but I reckon the Record headline on Tuesday, (24th June) summed it all up: 'My God, what would it have been like if we'd won!' Alright, so they came back undefeated - but, by the rules of the competition, they also came back failures. And yet here they are being feted like conquering heroes and once again the cry goes up: "Wha's like us?""

the roof of the net. There then followed a second half of virtual deadlock, with both teams showing plenty of scope, but hardly able to effect a breakthrough. It took the guile of Lato to settle things in the 62nd minute, when he met Gadocha's in-swinging corner with a forceful header. The Poles had now taken five victories from five matches and in overcoming Yugoslavia had once again revealed their fighting qualities.

The game plan adopted by East Germany for their Group A match with Holland was to man-mark Cruyff out of the play, stifle Dutch creativity and rely on solid defence to keep them out. It was a plan that had some success in the first period, during which the Dutch could not find "the fluency that had characterized their earlier play." Neeskens gave them a lead in the sixth minute, when he forced in Rep's blocked header, but for the rest of the half looked out of sorts. However, the German tactics were hardly worrying and the Dutch were a notoriously difficult side to contain for sustained periods. In the second half they began to find the space to move the ball at will through and around the perplexed Germans. There "was now a threat every time the ball was at the feet of Rep, Rensenbrinck, Neeskens and, of course, Cruyff", but in spite of their dominance, they found only one goal. It arrived in the 60th minute, when Rep headed in Cruyff's cross. It kept them on course for the final, but their inability to score more than twice against a team like East Germany, once again revealed the chink in their shining armour.

The other team making the pace in Group A was Brazil, who took on neighbours and rivals Argentina, in their first World Cup meeting. It was a "fast and exciting match", which swung like a pendulum, as both enjoyed periods of dominance. The Brazilians scored first, with a "fine ground shot" from Rivelino, just after the half-hour mark and then Argentina, who had marginally the better half, began to turn the screw in their quest for a reply. Within four minutes they drew level with a free kick from Miguel Brindisi, which caught Leão, Brazil's goalkeeper, out of position. The Brazilians were beginning to look decidedly fazed now and it showed just before half-time, when Jairzinho "missed an open goal with a wild kick." They were the better side in the second half, and though both created some good chances, it was Brazil that found the winning touch. It came just after the restart when Ze Maria, nicknamed the "Great Wall", "raced down the wing to lift a sensational pass over the defence and goalkeeper" to set Jairzinho up for an easy headed goal.

The final second phase games were played on 3rd July. West Germany took on Poland and Holland played Brazil to decide which of them would go into the final. (See W. Germany v Poland profile on page 261). Holland's was a hard, bruising contest, described by one commentator as "a sad waste of talent. It was as if Brazil had tried to hang on to their title by brute force" in "the most physical, ill-tempered match of the tournament." After a fairly even first half, the Dutch began to master the game and Neeskens opened the scoring in the 50th minute, following a neat interchange with Cruyff. It forced Brazil to greater endeavour and it opened up the game, allowing the Dutch to ply heir trade more stylishly. Finding more space in which to operate, they increased their lead 15 minutes later, when Cruyff scored a brilliant "jack-knife volley" from Krol's cross. It was the end of the scoring, but not of the rough stuff and six minutes from the end, Luís Pereira was sent off "for a vicious, scything tackle" on Neeskens. The Dutch had won their way through to their first World

Cup final against West Germany, the winners of Group B. (See Johan Cruyff profile on page 259).

The other two second round games played that day had no bearing on the outcome of the tournament. The Yugoslavs took a 27th minute lead against Sweden, but the Scandinavians made a fighting comeback to take a 2-1 victory in their best World Cup since 1958. Argentina's meeting with East Germany was a fairly lifeless occasion "in which South American flair and European efficiency cancelled each other out." Both teams scored within the first 20 minutes and the game then turned into a tepid simper, with neither prepared to force the issue, not even for the sake of entertainment. A 1-1 draw was the outcome and the 54,000 crowd could count themselves lucky to have seen two goals.

Another dull game was the 3rd/4th place play-off between Poland and Brazil. It was a "half-hearted affair between two disappointed teams." The Brazilians, who had fallen well short of the standards achieved four years earlier, had not deserved to reach the final, but the Poles had every reason to be disappointed. This was a game of few chances and Jairzinho missed one of the easiest in the first half. Inevitably, it was Lato who broke the stalemate, when 15 minutes from the end after "a magnificent burst past Alfredo, on the right-wing, he rolled his shot past Leão from a narrow angle, into the opposite corner." The Brazilians fiercely protested the goal, claiming one of the Poles had been offside. He was, but was not interfering with play and Lato had gone alone, so the referee rightly judged the goal to be legal. It was Lato's 7th goal of the tournament and Poland's 16th, making both the top scorers in West Germany 1974. This accolade, and the third place, was all the reward they got for being the stars of the event. As for Brazil, Jock Stein, the manager of Glasgow Celtic, summarized them with this remark: "A sad day. They who gave the game so much end up as just another very good, very dirty team."

With West Germany's victory over Holland (See W. Germany v Holland profile on page 263), the 1974 World Cup ended on a high note, with a thrilling and unpredictable final that had seen the triumph of the concept of "Total Football". In another shift in the balance of football power, the Old World had reasserted its supremacy in the most compelling way imaginable. The football brains of Europe had proven that they could be every bit as imaginative and that their footballers every part as skillful as the supremoes of South America. This new and dynamic brand of football was the illuminati of West Germany '74, but it was not the only one. The attendances were impressive, there were some spectacular games and there was an array of world stars on display, and not just among the Dutch and West German squads. The Argentinians, the Poles, the Scots, the Swedes and the Yugoslavs had each revealed individuals that would shine in any company. The performances of the acknowledged weaker teams had also been heartening and gave good indication of the growing strength of the world game. True, Haiti and Zaïre had been consistently outplayed and both had failed to win games, but both had been humiliated only once and this at the hands of teams that could rightly be considered to have belonged to the world's elite. On the other hand, the Australians had never been cowed and came away with their pride in tact. For all these reasons, the organizers could count the tournament a success.

On 5th July, Bob Davidson, a 45 year old company director from Airdrie, was told that he would referee the final, not to tell anyone and to thank out-going FIFA President, Stanley Rous, for supporting the decision. However, the next day, reporters told him that the final had gone to Jack Taylor of Wolverhampton. Taylor was his room-mate. Davidson was so disgusted he stormed off home. It was "the most sickening and disgraceful blow of my life," he said. "I am disgusted by this disgraceful decision so I have decided to give up football."

Third choice Dutch goalkeeper, Jan Jongbloed, came to the World Cup armed with his fishing tackle in the hope of getting a few hours by a river. However, when first and second choices Jan Beveren and Eddy Treytel were injured before it began the 33 year old, contact lens-wearing, fishing tackle shop owner from Amsterdam found himself wearing the No. 1 jersey. He played every game and conceded only three goals.

With a rather sarcastic tone to his post-final interview Helmut Schön said: "The Dutch were too quick in thinking they would be the champions. It is a pity Johan Cruyff didn't play. I told Berti Vogts that he would have had more difficulty if Cruyff had been there."

James Mitchell, a 43 year old fitter from Kirkcaldy, hated to see Scotland win because his soccer mad wife, Ann, went crazy. On 8th July he was fined £30 for grabbing his wife by the throat and punching her for celebrating too loudly following the Scotland-Yugoslavia game. He had been fined £5 for punching his wife after the 2-0 Wembley win against England in May and had then been fined a further £25 for a second offence when Scotland beat Zaïre. He told the court: "I'm ashamed of my conduct." Even stranger was the fact that Ann, proudly showing off her black eye, pleaded for leniency saying: "We'll be alright now that the World Cup is finished."

Yet, there were less desirable features of the 1974 World Cup, apart from the weather, that were beginning to exercise undue influence on the game. World Cups, like all major public events, have always required the presence of security forces to deter troublemakers, but the extraordinary measures taken to guarantee peace in 1974 were unprecedented. Then there was the pernicious hand of commercialism that revealed itself in a change of format that did not necessarily improve the entertainment factor, except in that it increased the number of games played. The second round group phase did see some excellent matches, but it also saw some dross, as teams felt more the need to avoid defeat than to go out to win. This feature of play, apparent since 1962, now happened over a longer time span. Knock-outs often bring more compelling football. Money had also threatened disruption, as players revelling in celebrity status, sought to exploit more ruthlessly their popularity. The merits or otherwise of inflated wages evoke varying opinions, but it is certain they would be alien to the minds of the game's founding fathers, as they strove to set football on its path to success over a hundred years before.

Rudolf Jozef (Ruud) Krol   Holland

Honours: Runner-up 1974 and 1978   **Games 14**
Played: 1974 and 1978   **Goals 1**

Ruud Krol (right) about to tackle Scotland's Bruce Rioch in the 1978 World Cup finals.

When "total football" arrived in the 1970s it was obvious that the stars of the Ajax and Dutch national teams would be the headline-grabbers. With Cruyff, Rensenbrink and Neeskens sparkling, it is easy to forget that every successful vehicle has to have a solid engine at its heart. For Holland and Ajax the heart who made it possible for the others to do their thing was Ruud Krol. His ability to turn defence into attack gave the teams their edge. He would use his height and build to place an imposing wall and disarm the most vociferous of forwards. He would then turn predator, spraying passes to his forwards, even going up for the kill himself.

Born in Amsterdam on 24th March 1949, the promising youngster was taken on by local team, Ruud-Wit (Red and White) at 13 and at 16 was playing in the first team. At 17 he played in an Amsterdam youth representative side and attracted the attention of several top clubs. He chose Ajax, but it was not until he was 20 that he got his first team debut in a friendly. The following season, 1969-70, he was given his chance in the league and never looked back. Under Rinus Michels and playing along side Johan Cruyff, he enjoyed great success. The club won the first of three successive European Cup victories in 1971, though a broken leg prevented his appearance in the first and he spent the night trying to get round the vastness of Wembley on a pair of crutches. In 1972 Michels moved to Barcelona. The Romanian, Stefan Kovács took his place, adapted the 4-4-3 formation Michels had developed and Ajax became even more devastating. All outfield players had to be flexible, constantly moving off the ball and aware of everyone else's position. They also had to anticipate runs from deep by the sweeper. With Krol driving from the back and Cruyff conducting the orchestra from midfield they were rarely beaten. Total football was complicated, but magnificent to watch and in 1973 a third European triumph came with victory over Juventus.

Krol made such an impression at Ajax that, after only ten first team games, he played his first international at left-back against England in November 1969. When Michels took over the national team in 1973, unsurprisingly Ajax players made up its backbone. Krol was a constant member throughout the World Cup qualifying tournament and travelled to West Germany in 1974. On their way to the final, they conceded just one goal, an own goal by Krol himself, a mistake he rectified by getting his only other World Cup goal in the 4-0 second round demolition of Argentina. Although Holland had another excellent tournament in 1978, the series provided a real nightmare moment for Krol in the final group game against Scotland. Fighting for their World Cup lives, Scotland's "Braveheart" was Archie Gemmill. He raced past Wildschut and Suurbier to come face to face with Krol's towering presence. Undaunted by a man considerably taller than himself, Gemmill slipped the ball through Krol's legs to score the goal of the tournament. In 1979, Krol won his 65th cap in FIFA's 75th Anniversary celebration match against Argentina, overtaking the Dutch record previously held by Puck van Heel, having already been appointed team captain. His total of 83 internationals is a Dutch record that has yet to be beaten.

On 26th April 1980 Krol made his 450th club appearance against Den Haag. By then his contract was up for re-negotiations and it came as a great surprise that he signed for Vancouver Whitecaps in the NASL at a time when it was in decline and its major stars were heading home. Soon after, Napoli made an offer he couldn't refuse and he returned to Europe. While in Holland he had become a very marketable commodity. He had invested money, had bought snack bars, modelled clothes and taken up interior design, but the Italians were only interested in his football. The pace of the Italian league suited him and he easily slipped into the sweeper's role. His counter-attacking moves from deep made him an extremely effective purchase and Napoli finished third in his first season. They only conceded 21 goals and were similarly tight the next, but they had problems scoring and failed to make the impact expected. When the 1982-3 and 1983-4 seasons went badly, he left for Cannes in the French second division having made 107 appearances for the Italians. By this time however, he had lost his place in the national side when Holland failed to qualify for the 1982 finals.

Krol was a fine student of the game and in 1989 felt it was time to turn professor. His first opportunity came as coach of leading Belgian side, Mechelen. However, the marriage was not a happy one and, after only half a season, with the side doing well, he was sacked. A similar story unfolded in Egypt, where he had gone in 1998 to coach top side, Zamalek. He was contracted until the end of the 1998-99 season, but differences with the Board meant that his position was never secure and after a 1-0 defeat, the only one in 11 games in charge, he was asked to leave.

Gerd Müller   West Germany

Honours: Winner 1974; 3rd 1970
Played: 1970 and 1974

Games 13
Goals 14

From humble beginnings as a 15 year old textiles worker, Gerd "der Bomber" Müller went on to become one of the most prolific goal scorers in World Cup history. In thirteen games in two World Cup finals, he amassed fourteen goals, ten of which came in the 1970 series. In all he scored 68 goals in 62 appearances for West Germany between 1966 and 1974.

Born in the Bavarian village of Zinsen on 11th November 1945, he grew up in a place with no proper football pitch. The death of his father forced him to leave school early and he became an apprentice weaver at a local textile mill. He had to travel the seven miles to Nordlingen by bus for a trial with the local side, TSV. Fortunately, they were impressed and whisked him away from a life drudgery. Playing in a pair of borrowed boots and for the first time on a proper pitch, he made his debut and scored two goals. He was overweight and it earned him the nickname "Dicker" or "Fatty", but in the next two seasons he netted 46 times and, not surprisingly, he attracted the interest of a number of larger clubs. Wilhelm Neudecker, President of Bayern Munich wanted him the most and persuaded coach, former Yugoslav international, Tchik Cajkovski, to sign the young man even though Cajkovski considered him "a bear among racehorses". Müller made his debut for Bayern against Freiburg in 1964, scoring twice in an 11-2 victory and 35 goals that season Bayern earned a much coveted place in the Bundesliga. The scoring machine had arrived. He also lost 20lb to make him a sharper, quicker and more reac-

Gerd Müller.

tive player. In his first season in the Bundesliga he scored 15 times in 33 games and played in goal once, deputizing for an injured Sepp Maier against Hamburg. In the 1966-67 season he was the league's joint top scorer with 28. He also won two German cup winners medals in 1966 and 1967 and scored eight goals on the way to winning the European Cup-Winners Cup in 1967. At 5ft 8ins, Müller was an unlikely height for a centre-forward, but his build and lightning reaction in and around the penalty area compensated for his lack of inches. Less complimentary commentators described him as "stocky", "chunky", "powerful with tree-trunk thighs", and even as "a stumpy tub". The more complementary said he had "a matchless speed of thought in the penalty area", he was "lethal, with a low centre of gravity", had "fine balance", "an agile sense of anticipation" and as "the greatest goal scorer in the modern era".

He was given his international debut on 12th October 1966, but did not appear again until April 1967 when he scored four in a 6-0 friendly victory against Albania. He did not command a regular place until 1969, a year that marked a turning point in his career. Bayern won the league for the first time with Müller scoring 30 goals. The following year he scored 38 in the league and nine of West Germany's 20 as they qualified for the 1970 World Cup finals. Although they only finished third in Mexico, he had a great time. He scored in every match except the 3rd/4th play-off, including two hat tricks in consecutive games against Bulgaria and Peru. Only two players have ever scored more goals in one tournament and through it he became European Player of the Year. After the tournament life got better as Bayern won the German cup again in 1971 and went on to win three consecutive league titles. Müller netted 106 goals in three seasons, including 40 in 1972. He scored twice in the final as West Germany won the European Championships in 1972 and in 1974 he reached the very top. Although he only scored four more World Cup goals, one of them was the all-important winner in the final from his only chance. That year Bayern won the first of three successive European Cups.

Müller retired from the international scene after the 1974 World Cup, but played on at Bayern until 1978 when he decided it was time to hang up his boots. At the age of 33 he was still the Bundesliga's top scorer with 24 goals. That year he notched up his 600th competitive goal, of which 365 had come at Bayern in 427 appearances over 14 years and is still a club record. He was tempted back to the game in 1979 when he went to play for Fort Lauderdale in the NASL for whom he scored 38 times. As time passes it is a shame that memories of the sheer beauty of Müller putting the ball in the net will fade, to be replaced by reams of statistics. These statistics are certainly impressive, but any young person with dreams of becoming a top class centre-forward should rent out videos of this great man in action for lessons on how goal scoring should be done.

Kenneth Mathieson Dalglish — **Scotland**

Played: 1974, 1978 and 1982   **Games 8**
                                                   Goals 2

It wasn't often that the great Liverpool manager, Bill Shankley, made a mistake, but when he failed to sign the 15 year old Kenny Dalglish in August 1966 after a two week trial he made a real whopper. Shankley was laying the foundations of years of success for Liverpool when the fair-haired lad turned up and was put in the B team to face Southport reserves in the Lancashire League. The match was won 1-0 but afterwards Dalglish was sent home. Eleven years later Bob Paisley rectified the situation but it cost Liverpool a record £440,000. By this time Dalglish was a massive success in Scotland

Born in Dalmarnock in the East End of Glasgow on 4th March 1951, he grew up around the docklands of Govern, under the shadow of Ibrox. It was not surprising that the young Protestant became a Rangers fan. His first

Kenny Dalglish.

forays into the game were as a goalkeeper for Millbank Primary, but he made his debut for the Under-15 Scottish Schoolboys as right-half. He scored twice in a 4-3 victory over Northern Ireland. After an unsuccessful trial with West Ham United and with his beloved Rangers showing no interest in him, Dalglish signed for Celtic in July 1967. Manager Jock Stein sent his assistant, Sean Fallon, to Dalglish's house to finalize the deal. Fallon did not envisage it taking long and took his wife and children, who waited in the car. However, it took three hours and Fallon's wife was furious when he eventually emerged. It was their wedding anniversary. Dalglish's chance in the first team came in a benefit match against Kilmarnock and he scored six of Celtic's seven goals. In 1971 he became the automatic choice and he made his international debut as a substitute against Belgium in November. It was also the year that he witnessed the first of three major tragedies when he watched from the stands as 66 supporters died when Stairway 13 collapsed at Ibrox during an Auld Firm match.

In the 1972-73 season Dalglish switched to the forward line, scored 41 goals in all competitions and began a run of 33 consecutive internationals, which started against Denmark and ended when he missed a game against Wales in 1974. As he had matured he developed his trademark style of shielding the ball, making it virtually impossible to get it from him. As David O'Leary described it: "He crouches over the ball, legs spread and elbows poking out. Whatever angle you come in from, you're liable to find his backside in your face." He was naturally in the Scotland squad that travelled to West Germany in 1974.

Celtic had been the first British team to win the European Cup and Dalglish wanted to win it himself, but did not feel that Celtic had that chance. He said that "I had to know if I could make it somewhere else. I did not want to go through the rest of my life wondering what might have been without putting myself to the test." So, in 1977 he left for Liverpool. He had won four Scottish championships, four Scottish FA Cups, one Scottish League Cup and had scored 157 goals in 292 first class games. He had also scored one of Scotland's two goals in the famous 1977 Wembley victory over England when Scottish fans invaded the pitch, taking most of it and the goal posts home with them. Paisley bought Dalglish to replace Kevin Keegan and by the time Liverpool thrashed Hamburg 6-0 in the European Super Cup, with Dalglish confidently running the game, the fans had taken the new man to their hearts. His first season at Anfield was a resounding success and ended on a personal high. He scored the only goal as Liverpool beat Brugge at Wembley to retain the European Cup. Paisley remarked that of "all the players I have played along side, managed and coached in more than 40 years at Anfield, he is the most talented."

In 1978, Dalglish travelled to Argentina tagged the most valuable player in Britain. However, with the exception of his first World Cup goal against Holland the trip was an unmitigated disaster. Ally MacLeod was sacked and replaced by Jock Stein, who promptly made Dalglish team captain, only to be replaced by Archie Gemmill four games and three defeats later. Aged 31, he travelled to Spain for his third World Cup and he was again on the score sheet as the Scots started the tournament impressively. They then hit the self-destruct button again and Dalglish was a virtual spectator as his team went down. He was chosen to go to the Mexico in 1986, but had to withdraw through injury. His final international appearance came in a 3-0 victory over Luxembourg in November 1986. He had won a record 102 caps and equalized Denis Law's scoring record of 30 goals.

That Dalglish never shone on the international stage is a mystery, but it is the reason his reputation abroad was never as great as it was at home. In 1979 Liverpool won the league and Dalglish became Player of the Year. Five more league championships and four consecutive League Cups followed. Liverpool also picked up two European Cups and Dalglish earned a second Player of the Year Award in 1983. Meanwhile, Joe Fagin had taken over from Paisley and was himself due to retire after the 1985 European Cup final against Juventus in the Heysel Stadium. Dalglish was to be his replacement, but disaster struck to spoil what should have been a proud moment. Fighting broke out between rival fans and several Italians died when a wall collapsed under the strain. Liverpool fans were held responsible and English teams were banned indefinitely from European competition. Despite the tragedy, Dalglish bounced back and in 1986 achieved a feat that had eluded all previous Liverpool managers, bringing the club's first league and cup double. He did it in style, beating Everton 3-1 in the final and was named Manager of the Year. In his second season, Liverpool won nothing, but in 1988 he rebuilt the side and rewon the title.

In 1989 came the third and worst of Dalglish's experience when 95 Liverpool fans lost their lives in the Hillsborough disaster. Although Liverpool went on to beat Everton 3-2 in the FA Cup final a month later, it was a hollow victory. The city was still paralysed with grief and in the months that followed Dalglish stood with dignity. He organized hospital visits, attended funerals and went to the homes of bereaved families. He took calls from victims' families and friends at any time of day, calmly talking to and reassuring them. In the end it got to him. Having just seen Liverpool draw 4-4 with Everton in the FA Cup fifth round, he walked into the boardroom on 20th February 1991 and twenty minutes later, without warning, he severed his links with the club. He was "a person pushed to the limit. I was putting myself under enormous pressure to be successful."

His decision to leave Liverpool had been surprising, but his decision to become manager of First Division Blackburn Rovers eight months later was more so. He was persuaded by "Uncle" Jack Walker to come and rebuild the club. In 1995, three years after they had gained promotion to the Premiership, Blackburn won their first league championship in 81 years. "King Kenny" had become only the third manager in the history of the English game to achieve the feat with more than one club. As both a player and a manager Dalglish won 14 Scottish and English league titles. It is a feat that very few will ever surpass.

Johan Cruyff   Holland

Honours: Runner-up 1974   **Games 7**
Played: 1974   **Goals 3**

Holland 4 : Bulgaria 1
Johan Cruyff (right) is challenged by Bulgaria's Kiril Iokov.

Johan Cruyff was the total footballer that epitomized Dutch "total football" of the 1970s. He was a master tactician with a gift for the game that is rarely seen. His ability was stunning, his importance immeasurable and when he got the ball something exciting was sure to happen. He was a centre-forward, but in a system in which each player was technically as good as the others and switched roles with ease, Cruyff would drop deep to confuse his opponents and pop up in any number of positions. Taking players on, he would "drag the ball behind him with his right foot, turn through 180 degrees and accelerate away outside a bemused defender." He became so popular that when he scored his final goal before retiring at the age of 37, the crowd carried him shoulder high from the ground to his home.

Born in Amsterdam on 25th April 1947, his mother was a cleaner at Ajax and persuaded the club to take on her soccer-mad ten year old son. Like all apprentices, he cleaned boots, acted as ball boy and stuck in the corner flags in on match day. He also showed a genius's temperament and it got him into trouble on more than one occasion. Growing into a gangly teenager with a slight, lanky build the club thought he looked too weak to make good. However, Vic Buckingham, the English coach, persuaded the club to give him a contract and he scored in his senior debut at the age of 17. In 1964 Rinus Michels, the man who was to change the face of Dutch football and the life of the young Cruyff, joined the club as manager. The concept of "total football" had been around since the 1950s, when it was called the "Whirl", but it was Michels who perfected the art and unleashed it in the late 1960s. Under his guidance, by 1968 Ajax had won three Dutch championships and were runners up in the European Cup that year. As the team developed, so did Cruyff into a stronger, more powerful player with superb poise, dramatic acceleration and outstanding ball control. The addition of Johan Neeskens and Ruud Krol to the side added extra dimension and they won Europe's top club prize in 1971. The 2-0 victory over Panathanaikos became the first of three successive European Cup triumphs, all orchestrated by Cruyff.

In the 1972 European Cup final, Cruyff single-handedly took on the eleven men of Internazionale and pulled them into a thousand bewildered pieces. The Italians could not reign him in and he scored both goals in a 2-0 victory. Next year's performance in the final was even more accomplished and it was said that " he inspired one of the greatest 20-minute spells in football ever seen in Belgrade as Ajax overcame another Italian outfit, Juventus." A second Footballer of the Year award followed and the cheque books began to open all over Europe. In Spain, Franco reopened the doors to foreign players and, after lengthy negotiations, Barcelona paid a record £922,300 for the Flying Dutchman, £400,000 of which went to Cruyff himself. He joined the Catalonians part way through the season and in mid-table and Cruyff made an immediate impact. By the end of the season, and via a 5-0 thrashing of arch rivals Real Madrid on their own territory, Barcelona were champions. They won the Spanish cup in 1978 and although Barcelona achieved little else with Cruyff in their side, his importance and the inspiration he had given to his fellow players cannot be underestimated. That year he achieved a third European Player of the Year award, the first player ever to do so.

His international career could not have got off to a worse start. He was given his chance as a 19 year old in 1966 against Hungary and scored the vital equalizing goal in a 2-2 draw. However, his unstable temper got him sent off in his second against Czechoslovakia. After a heated exchange with East German referee, Rudi Glockner, Cruyff appeared to strike him. Television evidence later showed that it was more of a gesture than a blow, but the result was a 12 month ban later shortened to six months. It had been a valuable lesson and ironically, his first international after the suspension was against East Germany.

Dutch preparations for the 1974 World Cup did not go smoothly. A goalless draw against Belgium and in-fighting between Ajax players and those from bitter rivals, Feyenoord, did not make qualification easy. The players were also seeking larger financial rewards for their participation. Nevertheless, they qualified for the first time since 1938 and a 4-1 pre-tournament victory over Argentina installed them as firm favourites to win the trophy. Cruyff's first task was to overcome the constant kicking he was given, which he did in style and played excellently. In the final he famously set up the opening goal, but Cruyff had to make do with a runners-up medal, when Bertie Vogts successfully extinguished his flame in the second half. Being the most skilled team in the tournament and having had an unbeaten run of 24 games ended was no conciliation.

Cruyff helped the national team get to the 1978 finals, but at the last minute decided not to travel. He quit the game altogether to pursue his business interests. There were rumours of a bust-up with management and that Cruyff had personal difficulties with the political situation in Argentina. In his 48 internationals he scored a record 33 goals. He surprised the world when he returned to club football in 1979 with the Los Angeles Aztecs in the NASL. After short spells with the Washington Diplomats and Spanish club, Lavente, he returned to Ajax in 1981 and picked up two more Dutch Championships. His next move to Feyenoord was a massive slap in the face for Ajax supporters. Feyenoord had not won the title for ten years but in 1984, with Cruyff pulling the strings, they won a League and Cup double. The following year Cruyff amazingly returned to Ajax, but this time as manager. They went on to win the European Cup-Winners Cup in 1987, but in a fit of pique, he walked away the following year. In 1988, he returned to Barcelona and in 1989 he coached them to a European Cup-Winners Cup victory over Sampdoria, defeating them again in 1992 to lift the European Cup. After winning a European Super Cup and four consecutive Spanish Championships, and recovering from a heart attack (he was a heavy smoker), Cruyff finally lost his battle of wills with an often unreasonable success-seeking Barcelona board and was sacked in 1996. He had almost walked out on the club in 1994 to become manager of Holland.

West Germany 1 : Poland 0

The Poles had been the surprise package of the World Cup, coming top of Group Four. They had played lively, entertaining football that combined solid defence with speedy, dashing forward play, a style that lived easily within the spirit of a tournament dominated by "total football". The Germans, meanwhile, had begun slowly, but had grown stronger as the tournament progressed. The prospect was for a thrilling game and it did not disappoint. "The game was a masterpiece," crooned the Guardian reporter, after what many regarded as the match of the tournament.

Its start had to be delayed for half an hour because the heavens opened and the pitch flooded. As the thunder and lightening crashed large mechanical squeegees were brought on to try to clear the water, but they failed miserably. The fire brigade had to be called in to pump the water from the pitch. Eventually, the referee declared the surface playable, but many felt that it was not and the condition of the field has been blamed for Poland's downfall. The quagmire that it had become hindered the running of the Polish forwards, who were unable to reproduce the style that had lit the tournament up. However, it suited the more methodical Germans, whose dogged and relentless determination enabled them to grind out results from even the most difficult of circumstances.

A goalless first half saw "Poland superior in almost every department," according to one commentator, and the Germans seemed unsure of how to handle their bustling forwards. In spite of the wretched conditions, both Gadocha on the left-wing and Grzegorz Lato on the right worked wonders and were constant thorns in the side of the German defence. Both were well supplied by Kazimiercz Deyna, who played majestically, and Kasparczak in mid-field. The wings were just about the only parts of the pitch upon which anything resembling passable football could be played, but even so "perfectly timed and directed passes would end abruptly with the ball stopping dead yards from the intended recipient." At one point Lato broke through, but Sepp Maier rushed out of his goal to narrow the angle and save the shot and he later flicked a Gadocha free kick over then bar. It was Maier's constant alertness that kept the Poles at bay and the scores level.

In the second half the Germans made a better show of things and it was Poland's goalkeeper, the superb Jan Tomaszewski, who had to provide the heroics. Only seven minutes into the half, a probing run into the area by Holzenbein resulted in the German being brought down by Zmuda. The normally accurate Hoeness stepped up to take the kick, but Tomaszewski dived to his right to keep the ball out, his second penalty save of the World Cup. He then made two excellent saves from Bonhof, the first from a header and the second from a free kick, as the Germans began to mount the pressure. Holzenbein also came close to scoring, but his shot climbed narrowly over the bar.

It was with fifteen minutes to go that the Germans finally made the break through. The Poles seemed to lose their concentration as Bonhof made yet another surging run from the left into the penalty area. He slipped the ball to Müller, who nippily rounded Gorgon, the aptly-named giant Polish defender, and sent an accurate shot into the corner of the net. It had been his only direct scoring chance of the game, but his predatory instincts did not let him down. The goal was a massive setback to the Poles, but they rallied strongly. They made two substitutions to try to salvage the game and it almost came off. In the dying stages of the game a shot from Deyna forced a magnificent save from Maier and it was typical of the luck that deserted the Poles that, for all their persistence and endeavour, they could not find a way through the German defence. Poland may have been the most attractive team of the finals, but the West Germans were one of the hardest to beat and Müllers's lone strike was enough to send then home team through to the final and the Poles into the 3rd/4th play-off.

West Germany 4 : Sweden 2

Played in Group B of the second phase, this match put against each other two teams of similar styles and temperaments. Whilst the Germans were regarded the stronger of the two, it was the Swedes who had been unbeaten in the first round and both had come second in their groups. The prospect was for a tight game. It eventually went to form, but not before the Swedes, who contributed greatly to a very entertaining event, had given the Düsseldorff crowd something to worry about.

The game was played in driving rain and, in spite of the appalling conditions, it was one of the best of the series. It began with 15 minutes of almost non-stop German pressure, with the home team menacing and probing a Swedish defence that was not particularly solid and with a reputation for lack of pace. The inexperienced Augustsson was playing only his second international and it appeared as if a German rout was on the cards. Yet, the Swedes held on. In goal, Helström was having an excellent game, pulling off a sequence of fine saves to deny the bustling German forwards, and, surprisingly, it was the Swedes who took the lead and stunned the packed crowd. The goal came on one of their rare incursions into German territory. Schwarzenbeck, in the German defence, failed to deal adequately with a cross. His half clearance fell to Ralf Edström, who hit a thunderous volley that easily beat Sepp Maier in goal. The worried crowd then had to spend the next 20 minutes watch their team launch a barrage of attacks against the Swedish defence without success. Beckenbauer picked up the pace of his game, to give greater urgency to the home team's cause, and he linked well with his front men, but was unable to fashion a breakthrough. The defiant Swedes, who lost Larsson through injury after half an hour, gallantly clung on and the bemused Germans went in one down at half-time, wondering what they had to do to.

Three goals with in five minutes brought the second half to life, beginning in the sixth minute. A swerving run from Uli Hoeness and some fancy footwork from Gerd Müller combined to create a chance for Wolfgang Overath, who scored with a hard low shot. Within minutes the Germans had taken the lead when a mix-up in the Swedish defence allowed Bonhof to fire home through a melee of bodies. The ball went in off the post, but two minutes later the Swedes were back on even terms when Sandberg struck to silence the crowd once again.

Following this blow, the Germans went straight on to the attack trying to snatch the initiative, but were frustrated in all of what they attempted. Then, with a little under 15 minutes from time, they decided to make a change and Grabowski came on to add weight to their onslaughts and in the hope of finding some penetration. His introduction paid immediate dividends as he raced up field to score and restore Germany's lead. With only about 12 minutes of the match remaining, it was a lead they were hardly likely squander a second time. German pressure was relentless and kept the Swedes pinned down inside their own half of the field. A fourth German goal was always a possibility and it came in the last minute of the game. Müller was pulled down in the area and the Russian referee had no hesitation about giving a penalty. It was duly converted by Hoeness to give a final 4-2 scoreline.

Undoubtedly, the Germans deserved their victory. They had dominated the midfield and their imposing attack had been in hot pursuit for most of the match, but the 4-2 result was rather flattering and fails to reflect Sweden's part in an absorbing contest. They "were outplayed for most of the game but made a gallant contribution, scoring defensive tactics and going for goal at every opportunity." Both Edström and Hellström had outstanding games, with the former's goal going down as one of the best of his career. Inevitably, though, the Germans proved just too powerful. As Gerald Sinstadt said: "In character, there was nothing to chose between these two determined teams, but in the end the superior skill of West Germany and the shrewd tactics of their manager were the decisive factors. "

West Germany 2 : Holland 1
The World Cup Final

West Germany 2 : Holland 1
Paul Breitner's 25th minute penalty beats Dutch goalkeeper Jan Jongbloed.

The 1974 final was the "total football" final, the one that placed together the finest practitioners of the concept - Holland and West Germany. Yet, they had differing interpretations of the art. The Dutch were mesmeric, colourful and showy, like a Pieter Brueghel masterpiece, whilst the Germans were more methodical. Their was less elastic, but equally ruthless. It evolved out of the catenaccio system, but was used by the Germans as a springboard for attack. Their system involved flexible players, but was achieved in a more closely define structure. The linchpin was Franz Beckenbauer, who played sweeper, but with the freedom to launch himself out of defence into attack, to set up opportunities for those in front of him. It was very effective and made this final one of the most eagerly awaited.

The match had an explosive start that suggested that the Dutch were going to run away with it. From the kick off at a walking pace, they strung together a dozen or so passes, without the Germans touching the ball. Then Cruyff picked up the ball and set off on one of his tantalizing runs, threading himself goalward through almost the whole German team. Uli Hoeness made a frantic effort to get at him, but only succeeded in bringing him down just inside the area. English referee, Jack Taylor, immediately awarded a penalty and Neeskens swept it home.

For the next twenty minutes the Germans hardly got a look in. The Dutch dominated the game, stringing together move after move with arrogant ease. Bertie Vogts was booked for repeated fouls early in the match, as his team desperately clung on, trying to halt the tide. Yet, whilst the Dutch were superior in almost every way, there were omens that should have sounded warning bells. For one, they failed to turn dominance into goals. Desperate though it was, Germany's defence held firm and Sepp Maier negated anything that got through. Vogts also held onto Cruyff like a limpet and it cramped his normally exuberant style. Holland tried to slow the game down to complete their mastery and prevent the Germans using their pace, but the Germans countered this by spreading the ball to the wings. The ploy began to open gaps in the Dutch defence and it was from wing play that the Germans got their equalizer. After 25 minutes, Bernd Holzenbein raced into the penalty area from the left and was brought down by Willem Jansen. Taylor awarded his second penalty and Paul Breitner did the rest.

The goal restored Germany's confidence and the game became more even. Beckenbauer came into his own and with Vogts continuing to keep Cruyff in check, the effectiveness of Dutch forward play was reduced considerably. Furthermore, the German used Hoeness, Holzenbein and Grabowski as double wingers to keep Willem Suurbier and Ruud Krol tied up and unable to move forward to assist the attack. The wing men fed in some fine crosses towards Müller and with Overath doing the same from midfield, the Dutch backs had to be ever alert to deny him. Both sides created good scoring chances and both might have taken the lead at various points in the match. In the 36th minute Beckenbauer tried a lob, which forced a stretching save from Jan Jongbloed and soon after Cruyff slipped Beckenbauer to feed a short pass to Neeskens, whose close range effort was saved excellently by Maier. With two minutes to go before the interval, Bonhof broke down the right. He combined with Grabowski and the ball was squared to Müller, lurking unmarked in the area. It appeared to be going away from the striker, but he had the time to drag it back and bring it under control, before flashing it into the net. The goal rattled the Dutch and Cruyff was booked for arguing with the referee as the teams walked in down the tunnel. His name joined those of Van Hanegem and Neeskens, who had been booked earlier for foul play.

The second half saw no more goals, but plenty of action. At one end Willem Rijsbergen cleared Holzenbein's shot off the line and at the other Maier produced a string of brilliant saves to keep the Dutch out. One of these was from Van Hanegem after he had ghosted past Beckenbauer to meet a Cruyff free kick and, soon after, he stopped a Neeskens free kick that appeared to be going in. Johnny Rep headed Suurbier's cross narrowly wide and it seemed as if luck had deserted the Dutch. Nothing would go in. They changed things round and replaced Rob Rensenbrinck with René van der Kerkhof. With twenty minutes to go de Jong came on for Rijsbergen who was not fully fit, but it was to no avail. Beckenbauer and Vogts stuck to their tasks magnificently and, as the game went on, the Germans grew stronger and the Dutch more frustrated. Their penetrative powers were gradually worn down by vigorous German defending. Both sides tackled hard and gave their all, but it was the Germans who edged the Dutch to claim the victory, in the first ever goalless second half in a World Cup final.

It had not been a classic and rarely "reached heights of skill achieved by the Brazilians in 1970: nor did it equal the drama of Wembley in 1966", as one reporter said, but it was gritty, determined and uncompromising. It was a "tough, brilliant and brittle battle" and could have gone either way, but the Dutch "lacked the national fervour of the Germans, who played for their fatherland rather than for bulging money bags." They were heartbroken a by the defeat, but knew that they had lost to "the only team in the competition who truly had the talent to do so." It also gave a third medal to Overath, who became the first man to collect a winner, a runner-up and a third place medal.

Statistics - West Germany 1974

GROUP ONE

Berlin, June 14th - Olympia Stadion

1 (1) WEST GERMANY

Breitner 17

Maier, Vogts, Breitner, Schwarzenbeck, Beckenbauer, Cullmann, Grabowski, Hoeness, Müller, Overath (Hölzenbein), Heynckes.

0 (0) CHILE

Vallejos, Garcia, Quintano, Arias, Figueroa, Rodríguez (Lara), Caszely (RED), Valdes (Véliz), Ahumada, Reinoso, Paez.

Referee: Dogan Babacan (Turkey)
Attendance: 83.168

Hamburg, June 14th - Volkspark Stadion

2 (0) EAST GERMANY

Curran (og)58, Streich 72

Croy, Kische, Bransch, Weise, Wätzlich, Irmscher, Pommerenke, Sparwasser, Löwe (Hoffmann), Streich, Vogel.

0 (0) AUSTRALIA

Reilly, Utjesenovic, Wilson, Schaefer, Curran, Richards, Rooney, Mackay, Warren, Alston, Buljevic.

Referee: Youssouf N'Diaye (Senegal)
Attendance: 17.000

Hamburg, June 18th - Volkspark Stadion

3 (2) WEST GERMANY

Overath 13, Cullmann 35, Müller 53

Maier, Vogts, Breitner, Schwarzenbeck, Beckenbauer, Cullmann (Wimmer), Grabowski, Hoeness, Müller, Overath, Heynckes (Hölzenbein).

0 (0) AUSTRALIA

Reilly, Utjesenovic, Wilson, Schaefer, Curran, Richards, Rooney, Mackay, Campbell (Abonyi), Alston, Buljevic (Ollerton).

Referee: Mustafa Kamel (Egypt)
Attendance: 53.300

Berlin, June 18th - Olympia Stadion

1 (0) EAST GERMANY

Hoffmann 56

Croy, Kische, Bransch, Weise, Wätzlich, Irmscher, Seguin (Kreische), Sparwasser, Hoffmann, Streich, Vogel (Ducke).

1 (0) CHILE

Ahumada 67

Vallejos, Garcia, Quintano, Arias, Figueroa, Socias (Farias), Valdes (Yavar), Ahumada, Véliz, Reinoso, Paez.

Referee: Aurelio Angonese (Italy)
Attendance: 27.300

Hamburg, June 22nd - Volkspark Stadion

0 (0) WEST GERMANY

Maier, Vogts, Breitner, Schwarzenbeck (Höttges), Beckenbauer, Cullmann, Grabowski, Hoeness, Müller, Overath (Netzer), Flohe.

1 (0) EAST GERMANY

Sparwasser 80

Croy, Kische, Bransch, Weise, Wätzlich, Irmscher (Hamann), Kurbjuweit, Kreische, Sparwasser, Hoffmann, Lauck.

Referee: Razmon Barreto Ruiz (Uruguay)
Attendance: 60.200

Berlin, June 22nd - Olympia Stadion

0 (0) AUSTRALIA

Reilly, Utjesenovic, Wilson, Schaefer, Curran (Williams), Richards (RED), Rooney, Mackay, Abonyi, Alston (Ollerton), Buljevic.

0 (0) CHILE

Vallejos, Garcia, Quintano, Arias, Figueroa, Caszely, Valdes (Farias), Ahumada, Véliz (Yavar), Reinoso, Paez.

Referee: Jafar Namdar (Iran)
Attendance: 14.000

	P	W	D	L	F	A	Pts
East Germany	3	2	1	0	4	1	5
West Germany	3	2	0	1	4	1	4
Chile	3	0	2	1	1	2	2
Australia	3	0	1	2	0	5	1

GROUP TWO

Frankfurt, June 13th - Wald Stadion

0 (0) BRAZIL

Leão, Nelinho, Luis Pereira, M.Marinho, F.Marinho, Piazza, Rivelino, Paulo Cesar Lima, Valdomiro, Jairzinho, Leivinha.

0 (0) YUGOSLAVIA

Maric, Buljan, Katalinski, Bogicevic, Hadziabdic, Muzinic, Oblak, Acimovic, Petkovic, Surjak, Dzajic.

Referee: Rudolf Scheurer (Switzerland)
Attendance: 62.000

Dortmund, June 14th - Westfalen Stadion

2 (2) SCOTLAND

Lorimer 26, Jordan 33

Harvey, Jardine, McGrain, Bremner, Holton, Blackley, Dalglish (Hutchison), Hay, Lorimer, Jordan, Law.

0 (0) ZAÏRE

Kazadi, Mwepu, Mukombo, Buhanga, Lobilo, Kilasu, Mayanga (Kembo), Mana, N'daye, Kidumu (Kibonge), Kakoko.

Referee: Kurt Schulenburg (West Germany)
Attendance: 27.000

Frankfurt, June 18th - Wald Stadion

0 (0) BRAZIL

Leão, Nelinho, Luis Pereira, M.Marinho, F.Marinho, Piazza, Rivelino, Paulo Cesar Lima, Mirandinha, Jairzinho, Leivinha (Paulo Cesar Carpegiani).

0 (0) SCOTLAND

Harvey, Jardine, McGrain, Bremner, Holton, Buchan, Dalglish, Hay, Lorimer, Jordan, Morgan.

Referee: Arie van Gemert (Holland)
Attendance: 62.000

Gelsenkirchen, June 18th - Park Stadion

9 (6) YUGOSLAVIA

Bajevic 6, 29, 81, Dzajic 13, Surjak 18, Katalinski 28, Bogicevic 34, Oblak 60, Petkovic 62

Maric, Buljan, Katalinski, Bogicevic, Hadziabdic, Bajevic, Oblak, Acimovic, Petkovic, Surjak, Dzajic.

0 (0) ZAÏRE

Kazadi (Tubilandu), Mwepu, Mukombo, Buhanga, Lobilo, Kilasu, Kembo, Mana, N'daye (RED), Kidumu, Kakoko (Mayanga).

Referee: Omar Delgado (Colombia)
Attendance: 31.700

Frankfurt, June 22nd - Wald Stadion

1 (0) SCOTLAND

Jordan 90

Harvey, Jardine, McGrain, Bremner, Holton, Buchan, Dalglish (Hutchison), Hay, Lorimer, Jordan, Morgan.

1 (0) YUGOSLAVIA

Karasi 81

Maric, Buljan, Katalinski, Bogicevic, Hadziabdic, Bajevic (Karasi), Oblak, Acimovic, Petkovic, Surjak, Dzajic.

Referee: Alfonso Gonzalez Archundia (Mexico)
Attendance: 56.000

Gelsenkirchen, June 22nd - Park Stadion

3 (1) BRAZIL

Jairzinho 12, Rivelino 67, Valdomiro 79

Leão, Nelinho, Luis Pereira, M.Marinho, F.Marinho, Piazza (Mirandinha), Rivelino, Jairzinho, Leivinha (Valdomiro), Paulo Cesar Carpegiani, Edu.

0 (0) ZAÏRE

Kazadi, Mwepu, Mukombo, Buhanga, Lobilo, Kibonge, Tshinabu (Kembo), Mana, N'tumba, Kidumu (Kilasu), Mayanga.

Referee: Nicolae Rainea (Romania)
Attendance: 36.200

	P	W	D	L	F	A	Pts
Yugoslavia	3	1	2	0	10	1	4
Brazil	3	1	2	0	3	0	4
Scotland	3	1	2	0	3	1	4
Zaire	3	0	0	3	0	14	0

GROUP THREE

Hannover, June 15th - Niedersachsen Stadion

2 (1) HOLLAND

Rep 7, 87

Jongbloed, Suurbier, Rijsbergen, Haan, Krol, Jansen, Neeskens, van Hanegem, Rep, Cruyff, Rensenbrink.

0 (0) URUGUAY

Mazurkiewicz, Jauregui, Masnik, Forlan, Pavoni, Esparrago, Montero-Castillo (RED), Rocha, Cubilla (Milar), Morena, Mantegazza.

Referee: Karoly Palotai (Hungary)
Attendance: 55.000

Düsseldorf, June 15th - Rhein Stadion

0 (0) BULGARIA

Goranov, Velitchkov, Kolev, Penev, Voinov (Mikhailov), Bonev, Denev, Panov (M.Vassilev), Nikodimov, Z.Vassilev, Ivkov.

0 (0) SWEDEN

Hellström, Olsson, Karlsson, Larsson, Andersson, Kindvall (Magnusson), Tapper, Grahn, Torstensson, Sandberg, Edström.

Referee: Edison Perz-Nuñez (Peru)
Attendance: 23.300

Dortmund, June 19th - Westfalen Stadion

0 (0) HOLLAND

Jongbloed, Suurbier, Rijsbergen, Haan, Krol, Jansen, Neeskens, van Hanegem (de Jong), Rep, Cruyff, Keizer.

0 (0) SWEDEN

Hellström, Olsson (Grip), Karlsson, Larsson, Andersson, Nordquist, Tapper (Persson), Grahn, Ejderstedt, Sandberg, Edström.

Referee: Werner Winsemann (Canada)
Attendance: 53.700

Hannover, June 19th - Niedersachsen Stadion

1 (0) BULGARIA

Bonev 75

Goranov, Velitchkov, Kolev, Penev, Voinov, Bonev, Denev, Panov, Nikodimov (Mikhailov), Z.Vassilev, Ivkov.

1 (0) URUGUAY

Pavoni 87

Mazurkiewicz, Jauregui, Milar, Forlan, Pavoni, Esparrago, Rocha, Garisto (Masnik), Morena, Mantegazza (Cardaccio), Corbo.

Referee: Jack Taylor (England)
Attendance: 13.400

Dortmund, June 23rd - Westfalen Stadion

4 (2) HOLLAND

Neeskens (pen) 5, (pen) 44, Rep 71, de Jong 87

Jongbloed, Suurbier, Rijsbergen, Haan, Krol, Jansen, Neeskens (de Jong), van Hanegem (Israël), Rep, Cruyff, Rensenbrink.

1 (0) BULGARIA

Krol (og) 78

Stoykov, Velitchkov, Kolev, Penev, Voinov, Bonev, Denev, Panov (Borisov), Stoyanov (Mikhailov), Z.Vassilev, Ivkov.

Referee: Anthony Boskovic (Australia)
Attendance: 53.300

Düsseldorf, June 23rd - Rhein Stadion

3 (0) SWEDEN

Edström 46, 78, Sandberg 74

Hellström, Grip, Karlsson, Larsson, Andersson, Nordquist, Kindvall (Torstensson), Grahn, Magnusson (Ahlström), Sandberg, Edström.

0 (0) URUGUAY

Mazurkiewicz, Jauregui, Milar, Forlan, Pavoni, Esparrago, Rocha, Garisto (Masnik), Morena, Mantegazza, Corbo (Cubilla).

Referee: Erich Linemayr (Austria)
Attendance: 28.300

	P	W	D	L	F	A	Pts
Holland	3	2	1	0	6	1	5
Sweden	3	1	2	0	3	0	4
Bulgaria	3	0	2	1	2	5	2
Uruguay	3	0	1	2	1	6	1

GROUP FOUR

Munich, June 15th - Olympia Stadion

3 (0) ITALY

Rivera 52, Benetti 66, Anastasi 78

Zoff, Spinosi, Morini, Burgnich, Facchetti, Mazzola, Capello, Rivera, Benetti, Chinaglia (Anastasi), Riva.

1 (0) HAITI

Sanon 46

Francillon, Bayonne, Jean-Joseph, Nazaire, Auguste, Antoine, Desir, Vorbe, Francois, G.Saint-Vil (Barthelemy), Sanon.

Referee: Vicente Llobregat (Venezuela)
Attendance: 53.000

Stuttgart, June 15th - Neckar Stadion

3 (2) POLAND

Lato 6, 64, Szarmach 8

Tomaszewski, Gorgon, Szymanowski, Zmuda, Musial, Kasperczak, Deyna, Maszczyk, Lato, Szarmach (Domarski), Gadocha (Cmikiewicz).

2 (0) ARGENTINA

Heredia 62, Babington 67

Carnevali, Perfumo, Wolff, Heredia, Sa, Bargas (Telch), Babington, Brindisi (Houseman), Kempes, Ayala, Balbuena.

Referee: Clive Thomas (Wales)
Attendance: 32.700

Stuttgart, June 19th - Neckar Stadion

1 (1) ARGENTINA

Houseman 19

Carnevali, Perfumo, Wolff (Glaria), Heredia, Sa, Telch, Babington, Houseman, Kempes, Ayala, Yazalde (Chazarreta).

1 (1) ITALY

Perfumo (og) 34

Zoff, Spinosi, Morini (Wilson), Burgnich, Facchetti, Mazzola, Capello, Rivera (Causio), Benetti, Anastasi, Riva.

Referee: Pavel Kasakov (Soviet Union)
Attendance: 70.100

Munich, June 19th - Olympia Stadion

7 (5) POLAND

Lato 17,87, Deyna 18, Szarmach 30,34,50, Gorgon 32

Tomaszewski, Gorgon, Szymanowski, Zmuda, Musial (Gut), Kasperczak, Deyna, Maszczyk (Cmikiewicz), Lato, Szarmach, Gadocha.

0 (0) HAITI

Francillon, Bayonne, Andre (Barthelemy), Nazaire, Auguste, Antoine, Desir, Vorbe, Francois, R.Saint-Vil (Racine), Sanon.

Referee: Suppiah Covindasamy (Singapore)
Attendance: 25.300

Munich, June 23rd - Olympia Stadion

4 (2) ARGENTINA

Yazalde 14,67, Houseman 18, Ayala 58

Carnevali, Perfumo, Wolff, Heredia, Sa, Telch, Babington, Houseman (Brindisi), Kempes (Balbuena), Ayala, Yazalde.

1 (0) HAITI

Sanon 63

Francillon, Bayonne, Ducoste, Nazaire (M.Leandre), Antoine, Desir, Vorbe, Louis, G.Saint-Vil (F.Leandre), Racine, Sanon.

Referee: Pablo Sánchez-Ibañez (Spain)
Attendance: 25.900

Stuttgart, June 23rd - Neckar Stadion

2 (2) POLAND

Szarmach 39, Deyna 44

Tomaszewski, Gorgon, Szymanowski, Zmuda, Musial, Kasperczak, Deyna, Maszczyk, Lato, Szarmach (Cmikiewicz), Gadocha.

1 (0) ITALY

Capello 85

Zoff, Spinosi, Morini, Burgnich (Wilson), Facchetti, Mazzola, Capello, Causio, Benetti, Anastasi, Chinaglia (Boninsegna).

Referee: Hans Joachim Weyland (West Germany)
Attendance: 70.100

	P	W	D	L	F	A	Pts
Poland	3	3	0	0	12	3	6
Argentina	3	1	1	1	7	5	3
Italy	3	1	1	1	6	4	3
Haiti	3	0	0	3	2	14	0

SECOND PHASE - GROUP A

Hannover, June 26th - Niedersachsen Stadion

1 (0) BRAZIL

Rivelino 61

Leão, Ze Maria, Luis Pereira, M.Marinho, F.Marinho, Paulo Cesar Carpegiani, Rivelino, Dirceu, Valdomiro, Jairzinho, Paulo Cesar Lima.

0 (0) EAST GERMANY

Croy, Kurbjuweit, Bransch, Weise, Streich, Wätzlich, Lauck (Löwe), Sparwasser, Hamann (Irmscher), Kische, Hoffmann.

Referee: Clive Thomas (Wales)
Attendance: 59.700

Gelsenkirchen, June 26th - Park Stadion

4 (2) HOLLAND

Cruyff 11,90, Krol 25, Rep 72

Jongbloed, Suurbier (Israël), Haan, Rijsbergen, Krol, Jansen, Neeskens, van Hanegem, Rep, Cruyff, Rensenbrink.

0 (0) ARGENTINA

Carnevali, Perfumo, Wolff (Glaria), Heredia, Sa, Telch, Squeo, Houseman (Kempes), Yazalde, Ayala, Balbuena.

Referee: Bob Davidson (Scotland)
Attendance: 55.000

Gelsenkirchen, June 30th - Park Stadion

2 (1) HOLLAND

Neeskens 8, Rensenbrink 60

Jongbloed, Suurbier, Haan, Rijsbergen, Krol, Jansen, Neeskens, van Hanegem, Rep, Cruyff, Rensenbrink.

0 (0) EAST GERMANY

Croy, Kurbjuweit, Bransch, Weise, Schnupase, Pommerenke, Lauck (Kreische), Sparwasser, Löwe (Ducke), Kische, Hoffmann.

Referee: Rudolf Scheurer (Switzerland)
Attendance: 69.600

Hannover, June 30th - Niedersachsen Stadion

2 (1) BRAZIL

Rivelino 31, Jairzinho 48

Leão, Ze Maria, Luis Pereira, M.Marinho, F.Marinho, Paulo Cesar Carpegiani, Rivelino, Dirceu, Valdomiro, Jairzinho, Paulo Cesar Lima.

1 (1) ARGENTINA

Brindisi 34

Carnevali, Glaria, Heredia, Sa (Carrascosa), Bargas, Squeo, Kempes (Houseman), Babington, Brindisi, Ayala, Balbuena.

Referee: Vital Loraux (Belgium)
Attendance: 39.400

Dortmund, July 3rd - Westfalen Stadion

2 (0) HOLLAND

Neeskens 50, Cruyff 65

Jongbloed, Suurbier, Haan, Rijsbergen, Krol, Jansen, Neeskens (Israël), van Hanegem, Rep, Cruyff, Rensenbrink (de Jong).

0 (0) BRAZIL

Leão, Ze Maria, Luis Pereira (RED), M.Marinho, F.Marinho, Paulo Cesar Carpegiani, Rivelino, Dirceu, Valdomiro, Jairzinho, Paulo Cesar Lima (Mirandinha).

Referee: Kurt Tschenscher (West Germany)
Attendance: 53.700

Gelsenkirchen, July 3rd - Park Stadion

1 (1) ARGENTINA

Houseman 20

Fillol, Wolff, Heredia, Carrascosa, Bargas, Telch, Kempes, Houseman, Babington, Brindisi, Ayala.

1 (1) EAST GERMANY

Streich 14

Croy, Kurbjuweit, Bransch, Weise, Schnupase, Pommerenke, Streich (Ducke), Sparwasser, Löwe (Vogel), Kische, Hoffmann.

Referee: Jack Taylor (England)
Attendance: 54.200

	P	W	D	L	F	A	Pts
Holland	3	3	0	0	8	0	6
Brazil	3	2	0	1	3	3	4
East Germany	3	0	1	2	1	4	1
Argentina	3	0	1	2	2	7	1

SECOND PHASE - GROUP B

Stuttgart, June 26th - Neckar Stadion

1 (1) POLAND

Lato 43

Tomaszewski, Szymanowski, Gorgon, Zmuda, Gut, Deyna, Kasperczak, Maszczyk, Lato, Szarmach (Kmiecik), Gadocha.

0 (0) SWEDEN

Hellström, Karlsson, Grip, Nordquist, Andersson (Augustsson), Grahn, Tapper (Ahlström), Larsson, Torstensson, Sandberg, Edström.

Referee: Ramon Barreto Ruiz (Uruguay)
Attendance: 45.000

Düsseldorf, June 26th - Rhein Stadion

2 (1) WEST GERMANY

Breitner 39, Müller 77

Maier, Vogts, Schwarzenbeck, Beckenbauer, Breitner, Bonhof, Wimmer (Hoeness), Hölzenbein (Flohe), Overath, Müller, Herzog.

0 (0) YUGOSLAVIA

Maric, Buljan, Hadziabdic, Muzinic, Katalinski, Oblak (Jerkovic), Popivoda, Acimovic, Surjak, Karasi, Dzajic (Petkovic).

Referee: Armando Marquez (Brazil)
Attendance: 67.500

Frankfurt, June 30th - Wald Stadion

2 (1) POLAND

Deyna (pen)25, Lato 62

Tomaszewski, Szymanowski, Gorgon, Zmuda, Musial,
Deyna (Domarski), Kasperczak, Maszczyk, Lato,
Szarmach (Cmikiewicz), Gadocha.

1 (1) YUGOSLAVIA

Karasi 43

Maric, Buljan, Hadziabdic, Bogicevic, Katalinski, Oblak
(Jerkovic), Bajevic, Acimovic, Surjak, Karasi, Petkovic
(V.Petrovic).

Referee: Rudolf Glöckner (East Germany)
Attendance: 53.200

Düsseldorf, June 30th - Rhein Stadion

4 (0) WEST GERMANY

Overath 50, Bonhof 51, Grabowski 77, Hoeness
(pen)89

Maier, Vogts, Schwarzenbeck, Beckenbauer, Breitner,
Bonhof, Hoeness, Hölzenbein (Flohe), Overath, Müller,
Herzog (Grabowski).

2 (1) SWEDEN

Edström 26, Sandberg 52

Hellström, Karlsson, Olsson, Nordquist, Augustsson,
Grahn, Tapper, Larsson (Ejderstedt), Torstensson,
Sandberg, Edström.

Referee: Pavel Kasakov (Soviet Union)
Attendance: 67.800

Düsseldorf, July 3rd - Rhein Stadion

2 (1) SWEDEN

Edström 30, Torstensson 86

Hellström, Karlsson, Olsson, Nordquist, Augustsson,
Grahn, Tapper, Persson, Torstensson, Sandberg,
Edström.

1 (1) YUGOSLAVIA

Surjak 27

Maric, Buljan, Hadziabdic, Bogicevic, Katalinski,
Pavlovic (Peruzovic), Dzajic, Acimovic, Surjak,
V.Petrovic (Karasi), Jerkovic.

Referee: Luis Pestarino (Argentina)
Attendance: 37.700

Frankfurt, July 3rd - Wald Stadion

1 (0) WEST GERMANY

Müller 76

Maier, Vogts, Schwarzenbeck, Beckenbauer, Breitner,
Bonhof, Hoeness, Hölzenbein, Overath, Müller,
Grabowski.

0 (0) POLAND

Tomaszewski, Szymanowski, Gorgon, Zmuda, Musial,
Deyna, Kasperczak (Cmikiewicz), Maszczyk (Kmiecik),
Lato, Domarski, Gadocha.

Referee: Erich Linemayr (Austria)
Attendance: 62.000

	P	W	D	L	F	A	Pts
West Germany	3	3	0	0	7	2	6
Poland	3	2	0	1	3	2	4
Sweden	3	1	0	2	4	6	2
Yugoslavia	3	0	0	3	2	6	0

3RD/4TH PLACE PLAY-OFF

Munich, July 6th - Olympia Stadion

1 (0) POLAND

Lato 76

Tomaszewski, Szymanowski, Gorgon, Zmuda, Musial,
Maszczyk, Deyna, Kasperczak (Cmikiewicz), Lato,
Szarmach (Kapka), Gadocha.

0 (0) BRAZIL

Leão, Ze Maria, Alfredo, M.Marinho, F.Marinho, Paulo
Cesar Carpegiani, Rivelino, Ademir (Mirandinha),
Valdomiro, Jairzinho, Dirceu.

Referee: Aurelio Angonese (Italy)
Attendance: 79.000

FINAL

Munich, July 7th - Olympia Stadion

2 (2) WEST GERMANY

Breitner (pen)25, Müller 43

Maier, Vogts, Schwarzenbeck, Beckenbauer, Breitner,
Bonhof, Hoeness, Overath, Grabowski, Müller,
Hölzenbein.

1 (1) HOLLAND

Neeskens (pen) 1

Jongbloed, Suurbier, Rijsbergen (de Jong), Haan, Krol,
Jansen, van Hanegem, Neeskens, Rep, Cruyff,
Rensenbrink (R.van der Kerkhof).

Referee: Jack Taylor (England)
Attendance: 77.833

QUALIFYING ROUNDS

Africa Phase 1 - 1st Round

	P	W	D	L	F	A	Pts
Ghana	2	2	0	0	10	1	4
Cote d' Ivoire	2	2	0	0	3	0	4
Zambia	2	1	1	0	6	1	3
Zaire	2	1	1	0	4	0	3
Nigeria	2	1	1	0	3	2	3
Morocco	2	1	1	0	2	1	3
Guinea	2	1	0	1	5	2	2
Tunisia	2	1	0	1	3	2	2
Kenya	2	1	0	1	2	1	2
Ethiopia	2	0	2	0	1	1	2
Tanzania	2	0	2	0	1	1	2
Egypt	2	1	0	1	2	3	2
Sudan	2	1	0	1	1	2	2
Algeria	2	1	0	1	2	5	2
Congo	2	0	1	1	2	3	1
Senegal	2	0	1	1	1	2	1
Togo	2	0	1	1	0	4	1
Lesotho	2	0	1	1	1	6	1
Sierra Leone	2	0	0	2	0	3	0
Republic of Dahomey	2	0	0	2	1	10	0

02-03-72	Algeria : Guinea	1:0 (0:0)
12-03-72	Guinea : Algeria	5:1 (2:0)
30-04-72	Lesotho : Zambia	0:0
04-06-72	Zambia : Lesotho	6:1 (3:1)
06-06-72	Togo : Zaire	0:0
18-06-72	Rep. of Dahomey : Ghana	0:5 (0:3)
20-06-72	Zaire : Togo	4:0 (2:0)
02-07-72	Ghana : Rep. of Dahomey	5:1 (2:0)
16-07-72	Kenya : Sudan	2:0 (1:0)
23-07-72	Sudan : Kenya	1:0 (1:0)
05-08-72	Nigeria : Congo	2:1 (1:0)
15-08-72	Congo : Nigeria	1:1 (0:1)
15-10-72	Sierra Leone : Cote d' Ivoire	0:1 (0:1)

29-10-72	Cote d' Ivoire : Sierra Leone	2:0 (1:0)
19-11-72	Morocco : Senegal	0:0
25-11-72	Tanzania : Ethiopia	1:1 (0:1)
03-12-72	Senegal : Morocco	1:2 (1:1)
03-12-72	Ethiopia : Tanzania	0:0
08-12-72	Egypt : Tunisia	2:1 (1:0)
17-12-72	Tunisia : Egypt	2:0 (1:0)

Africa Phase 1 - 1st Round Play-off

10-12-72	Ethiopia : Tanzania	3:0 (3:0)

Played in Addis Ababa

Africa Phase 1 - 2nd Round

	P	W	D	L	F	A	Pts
Kenya	2	1	1	0	5	3	3
Zambia	2	1	1	0	4	2	3
Morocco	2	1	1	0	3	1	3
Ghana	2	1	1	0	2	0	3
Cote d' Ivoire	2	1	1	0	3	2	3
Zaire	2	1	0	1	1	1	2
Cameroon	2	1	0	1	1	1	2
Tunisia	2	0	1	1	2	3	1
Mauritius	2	0	1	1	3	5	1
Ethiopia	2	0	1	1	2	4	1
Guinea	2	0	1	1	3	1	1
Nigeria	2	0	1	1	0	2	1

10-12-72	Mauritius : Kenya	1:3 (1:1)
17-12-72	Kenya : Mauritius	2:2 (0:2)
04-02-73	Cameroon : Zaire	0:1 (0:1)
10-02-73	Nigeria : Ghana	0:2
11-02-73	Guinea : Morocco	1:1 (1:1)
11-02-73	Tunisia : Cote d' Ivoire	1:1 (0:1)
22-02-73	Ghana : Nigeria	0:0
25-02-73	Cote d' Ivoire : Tunisia	2:1 (1:1)
25-02-73	Morocco : Guinea	2:0 (0:0)
25-02-73	Zaire : Cameroon	0:1 (0:1)
01-04-73	Ethiopia : Zambia	0:0
15-04-73	Zambia : Ethiopia	4:2 (0:1)

Africa Phase 2 - 2nd Round Play-off

27-02-73	Zaire : Cameroon	2:0 (1:0)

Played in Kinshasa

Africa Phase 1 - 3rd Round

	P	W	D	L	F	A	Pts
Morocco	2	1	1	0	5	2	3
Zambia	2	1	1	0	4	2	3
Zaire	2	1	0	1	4	2	2
Ghana	2	1	0	1	2	4	2
Kenya	2	0	1	1	2	4	1
Cote d'Ivoire	2	0	1	1	2	5	1

20-05-73	Cote d' Ivoire : Morocco	1:1 (0:1)
03-06-73	Morocco : Cote d' Ivoire	4:1 (2:0)
05-08-73	Ghana : Zaire	1:0 (1:0)
12-08-73	Zambia : Kenya	2:0 (1:0)
19-08-73	Zaire : Ghana	4:1 (2:0)
19-08-73	Kenya : Zambia	2:2 (0:2)

Africa Phase 2 - Final Matches

	P	W	D	L	F	A	Pts
Zaire	4	4	0	0	9	1	8
Zambia	4	1	0	3	5	6	2
Morocco	4	1	0	3	2	9	2

21-10-73	Zambia : Morocco	4:0 (2:0)
04-11-73	Zambia : Zaire	0:2 (0:2)
18-11-73	Zaire : Zambia	2:1 (1:1)
25-11-73	Morocco : Zambia	2:0 (1:0)
09-12-73	Zaire : Morocco	3:0 (0:0)
23-12-73	Morocco : Zaire	0:2

Asia/Oceania Phase 1 - Group A Preliminary Matches

	P	W	D	L	F	A	Pts
Israel	1	1	0	0	2	1	2
Hong Kong	1	1	0	0	1	0	2
South Vietnam	1	1	0	0	1	0	2
Japan	1	0	0	1	1	2	0
Thailand	1	0	0	1	0	1	0
Malaysia	1	0	0	1	0	1	0

16-05-73	Israel : Japan	2:1 (1:1)
16-05-73	Thailand : South Vietnam	0:1 (0:0)
17-05-73	Hong Kong : Malaysia	1:0 (0:0)

All games played in Seoul

Asia/Oceania Phase 1 - Group A, Subgroup 1

	P	W	D	L	F	A	Pts
Hong Kong	2	2	0	0	2	0	4
Japan	2	1	0	1	4	1	2
South Vietnam	2	0	0	2	0	5	0

15-05-73	Japan : Hong Kong	0:1 (0:0)
20-05-73	South Vietnam : Japan	0:4 (0:2)
24-05-73	Hong Kong : South Vietnam	1:0 (0:0)

All games played in Seoul

Asia/Oceania Phase 1 - Group A, Subgroup 2

	P	W	D	L	F	A	Pts
Israel	3	2	1	0	9	0	5
South Korea	3	1	2	0	4	0	4
Malaysia	3	1	1	1	2	3	3
Thailand	3	0	0	3	0	12	0

19-05-73	Israel : Malaysia	3:0 (0:0)
19-05-73	Korea Republic : Thailand	4:0 (0:0)
21-05-73	Israel : Thailand	6:0 (1:0)
21-05-73	Korea Republic : Malaysia	0:0
23-05-73	Thailand : Malaysia	0:2 (0:0)
23-05-73	Korea Republic : Israel	0:0

All games played in Seoul

Asia/Oceania Phase 1 - Group A, Semi-finals

26-05-73	Korea Republic : Hong Kong	3:1 (1:1)
26-05-73	Israel : Japan	1:0 (0:0)

Both games palyed in Seoul

Asia/Oceania Phase 1 - Group A, Final

28-05-73	Israel : Korea Republic	0:1 (0:0)

Game played in Seoul

Asia/Oceania Phase 1 - Group B, Subgroup 1

	P	W	D	L	F	A	Pts
Australia	6	3	3	0	15	6	9
Iraq	6	3	2	1	11	6	8
Indonesia	6	1	2	3	6	13	4
New Zealand	6	0	3	3	5	12	3

04-03-73	New Zealand : Australia	1:1 (0:0)

Game played in Auckland

11-03-73	Australia : Iraq	3:1 (0:0)
11-03-73	Indonesia : New Zealand	1:1 (1:0)
13-03-73	Iraq : New Zealand	2:0 (2:0)
13-03-73	Australia : Indonesia	2:1 (2:1)
16-03-73	Australia : New Zealand	3:3 (3:1)
16-03-73	Iraq : Indonesia	1:1 (1:1)

Games played in Sydney

18-03-73	Australia : Iraq	0:0
18-03-73	Indonesia : New Zealand	1:0 (1:0)

Games played in Melbourne

21-03-73	Iraq : Indonesia	3:2 (2:1)
24-03-73	Iraq : New Zealand	4:0 (3:0)
24-04-73	Australia : Indonesia	6:0 (3:0)

Games played in Sydney

Asia/Oceania Phase 1 - Group B, Subgroup 2

	P	W	D	L	F	A	Pts
Iran	6	4	1	1	7	3	9
Syria	6	3	1	2	6	6	7
Korea DPR	6	1	3	2	5	5	5
Kuwait	6	1	1	4	4	8	3

04-05-73	Iran : Korea DPR	0:0
04-05-73	Syria : Kuwait	2:1 (0:0)
06-05-73	Korea DPR : Syria	1:1 (0:0)
06-05-73	Kuwait : Iran	1:2 (0:1)
08-05-73	Syria : Iran	0:1 (0:0)
08-05-73	Korea DPR : Kuwait	0:0
11-05-73	Iran : Korea DPR	2:1 (1:0)
11-05-73	Syria : Kuwait	2:0 (1:0)
13-05-73	Korea DPR : Syria	3:0 (2:0)
13-05-73	Iran : Kuwait	2:0 (0:0)
15-05-73	Korea DPR : Kuwait	0:2 (0:1)
15-05-73	Iran : Syria	0:1 (0:1)

All games played in Teheran

Asia/Oceania Phase 1 - Group B Final

	P	W	D	L	F	A	Pts
Australia	2	1	0	1	3	2	2
Iran	2	1	0	1	2	3	2

18-08-73	Australia : Iran	3:0 (1:0)
24-08-73	Iran : Australia	2:0 (2:0)

Asia/Oceania - Final Matches

	P	W	D	L	F	A	Pts
Korea Republic	2	0	2	0	2	2	2
Australia	2	0	2	0	2	2	2

28-10-73	Australia : Korea Republic	0:0
10-11-73	Korea Republic : Australia	2:2 (2:1)

Asia/Oceania - Final Matches Play-off

13-11-73	Australia : Korea Republic	1:0 (0:0)

Played in Hong Kong

Europe - Group 1

	P	W	D	L	F	A	Pts
Sweden	6	3	2	1	15	8	8
Austria	6	3	2	1	14	7	8
Hungary	6	2	4	0	12	7	8
Malta	6	0	0	6	1	20	0

14-11-71	Malta : Hungary	0:2 (0:1)
30-04-72	Austria : Malta	4:0 (3:0)
06-05-72	Hungary : Malta	3:0 (1:0)
25-05-72	Sweden : Hungary	0:0
10-06-72	Austria : Sweden	2:0 (0:0)
15-10-72	Sweden : Malta	7:0 (5:0)
15-10-72	Austria : Hungary	2:2 (0:2)
25-11-72	Malta : Austria	0:2 (0:0)
29-04-73	Hungary : Austria	2:2 (1:2)
23-05-73	Sweden : Austria	3:2 (1:0)
13-06-73	Hungary : Sweden	3:3 (1:1)
11-11-73	Malta : Sweden	1:2

Europe - Group 1 Play-off

27-11-73	Sweden : Austria	2:1 (2:1)

Played in Gelsenkirchen

Europe - Group 2

	P	W	D	L	F	A	Pts
Italy	6	4	2	0	12	0	10
Turkey	6	2	2	2	5	3	6
Switzerland	6	2	2	2	2	4	6
Luxembourg	6	1	0	5	2	14	2

07-10-72	Luxembourg : Italy	0:4 (0:3)
21-10-72	Switzerland : Italy	0:0
22-10-72	Luxembourg : Turkey	2:0 (2:0)
10-12-72	Turkey : Luxembourg	3:0 (2:0)
13-01-73	Italy : Turkey	0:0
25-02-73	Turkey : Italy	0:1 (0:1)
31-03-73	Italy : Luxembourg	5:0 (2:0)
08-04-73	Luxembourg : Switzerland	0:1 (0:1)
09-05-73	Switzerland : Turkey	0:0
26-09-73	Switzerland : Luxembourg	1:0 (1:0)
20-10-73	Italy : Switzerland	2:0 (1:0)
18-11-73	Turkey : Switzerland	2:0 (0:0)

Europe - Group 3

	P	W	D	L	F	A	Pts
Netherlands	6	4	2	0	24	2	10
Belgium	6	4	2	0	12	0	10
Norway	6	2	0	4	9	16	4
Iceland	6	0	0	6	2	29	0

18-05-72	Belgium : Iceland	4:0 (2:0)
22-05-72	Iceland : Belgium	0:4 (0:2)
03-08-72	Norway : Iceland	4:1 (0:0)
04-10-72	Norway : Belgium	0:2 (0:0)
01-11-72	Netherlands : Norway	9:0 (1:0)
19-11-72	Belgium : Netherlands	0:0
03-08-73	Iceland : Norway	0:4 (0:1)
22-08-73	Netherlands : Iceland	5:0 (4:0)
29-08-73	Iceland : Netherlands	1:8 (1:4)
12-09-73	Norway : Netherlands	1:2 (0:1)
31-10-73	Belgium : Norway	2:0 (1:0)
18-11-73	Netherlands : Belgium	0:0

Europe - Group 4

	P	W	D	L	F	A	Pts
Germany DR	6	5	0	1	18	3	10
Romania	6	4	1	1	17	4	9
Finland	6	1	1	4	3	21	3
Albania	6	1	0	5	3	13	2

21-06-72	Finland : Albania	1:0 (1:0)
20-09-72	Finland : Romania	1:1 (0:0)
07-10-72	Germany DR : Finland	5:0 (0:0)
29-10-72	Romania : Albania	2:0 (2:0)
08-04-73	Germany DR : Albania	2:0 (0:0)
06-05-73	Albania : Romania	1:4 (0:2)
27-05-73	Romania : Germany DR	1:0 (0:0)
06-06-73	Finland : Germany DR	1:5 (0:3)
26-09-73	Germany DR : Romania	2:0 (1:0)
10-10-73	Albania : Finland	1:0 (1:0)
14-10-73	Romania : Finland	9:0 (5:0)
03-11-73	Albania : Germany DR	1:4 (1:2)

Europe - Group 5

	P	W	D	L	F	A	Pts
Poland	4	2	1	1	6	3	5
England	4	1	2	1	3	4	4
Wales	4	1	1	2	3	5	3

15-11-72	Wales : England	0:1 (0:1)
24-01-73	England : Wales	1:1 (1:1)
28-03-73	Wales : Poland	2:0 (0:0)
06-06-73	Poland : England	2:0 (1:0)
26-09-73	Poland : Wales	3:0 (2:0)
17-10-73	England : Poland	1:1 (0:0)

Europe - Group 6

	P	W	D	L	F	A	Pts
Bulgaria	6	4	2	0	13	3	10
Portugal	6	2	3	1	10	6	7
N. Ireland	6	1	3	2	5	6	5
Cyprus	6	1	0	5	1	14	2

29-03-72	Portugal : Cyprus	4:0 (2:0)
10-05-72	Cyprus : Portugal	0:1 (0:0)
18-10-72	Bulgaria : Northern Ireland	3:0 (1:0)
19-11-72	Cyprus : Bulgaria	0:4 (0:3)
14-02-73	Cyprus : Northern Ireland	1:0 (0:0)
28-03-73	Northern Ireland : Portugal	1:1 (0:1)
02-05-73	Bulgaria : Portugal	2:1 (1:0)
08-05-73	Northern Ireland : Cyprus	3:0 (3:0)
26-09-73	Northern Ireland : Bulgaria	0:0
13-10-73	Portugal : Bulgaria	2:2 (0:0)
14-11-73	Portugal : Northern Ireland	1:1 (1:0)
18-11-73	Bulgaria : Cyprus	2:0 (1:0)

Europe - Group 7

	P	W	D	L	F	A	Pts
Spain	4	2	2	0	8	5	6
Yugoslavia	4	2	2	0	7	4	6
Greece	4	0	0	4	5	11	0

19-10-72	Spain : Yugoslavia	2:2 (1:0)
18-11-72	Yugoslavia : Greece	1:0 (1:0)
17-01-73	Greece : Spain	2:3 (0:1)
21-02-73	Spain : Greece	3:1 (2:1)
21-10-73	Yugoslavia : Spain	0:0
19-12-73	Greece : Yugoslavia	2:4 (2:2)

Europe - Group 7 Play-off

13-02-74	Yugoslavia : Spain	1:0 (1:0)

Played in Frankfurt

Europe - Group 8

	P	W	D	L	F	A	Pts
Scotland	4	3	0	1	8	3	6
Czech	4	2	1	1	9	3	5
Denmark	4	0	1	3	2	13	1

18-10-72	Denmark : Scotland	1:4 (1:2)
15-11-72	Scotland : Denmark	2:0 (1:0)
02-05-73	Denmark : Czechoslovakia	1:1 (1:1)
06-06-73	Czechoslovakia : Denmark	6:0 (0:0)
26-09-73	Scotland : Czechoslovakia	2:1 (1:1)
17-10-73	Czechoslovakia : Scotland	1:0 (1:0)

Europe - Group 9

	P	W	D	L	F	A	Pts
USSR	4	3	0	1	5	2	6
Ireland Rep	4	1	1	2	4	5	3
France	4	1	1	2	3	5	3

13-10-72	France : USSR	1:0 (0:0)
18-10-72	Ireland Republic : USSR	1:2 (0:0)
15-11-72	Ireland Republic : France	2:1 (1:0)
13-05-73	USSR : Ireland Republic	1:0 (0:0)
19-05-73	France : Ireland Republic	1:1 (0:0)
26-05-73	USSR : France	2:0 (0:0)

Play-off UEFA/CONMEBOL

	P	W	D	L	F	A	Pts
Chile	2	1	1	0	2	0	3
USSR	2	0	1	1	0	2	1

26-09-73	USSR : Chile	0:0
21-11-73	Chile : USSR	2:0

Caribbean/North/Central America - Group 1

	P	W	D	L	F	A	Pts
Mexico	4	4	0	0	8	3	8
Canada	4	1	1	2	6	7	3
United States	4	0	1	3	6	10	1

20-08-72	Canada : United States	3:2 (2:0)
24-08-72	Canada : Mexico	0:1 (0:0)
29-08-72	United States : Canada	2:2 (2:1)
03-09-72	Mexico : United States	3:1 (1:0)
06-09-72	Mexico : Canada	2:1 (1:1)
10-09-72	United States : Mexico	1:2 (1:1)

Caribbean/North/Central America - Group 2

	P	W	D	L	F	A	Pts
Guatemala	2	2	0	0	2	0	4
El Salvador	2	0	0	2	0	2	0

03-12-72	Guatemala : El Salvador	1:0 (0:0)
10-12-72	El Salvador : Guatemala	0:1 (0:0)

Caribbean/North/Central America - Group 3

	P	W	D	L	F	A	Pts
Honduras	2	1	1	0	5	4	3
Costa Rica	2	0	1	1	4	5	1

03-12-72	Honduras : Costa Rica	2:1 (1:1)
10-12-72	Costa Rica : Honduras	3:3 (1:0)

Caribbean/North/Central America - Group 4

	P	W	D	L	F	A	Pts
Haiti	2	2	0	0	12	0	4
Puerto Rico	2	0	0	2	0	12	0

15-04-72	Haiti : Puerto Rico	7:0 (5:0)
23-04-72	Puerto Rico : Haiti	0:5 (0:2)

Caribbean/North/Central America - Group 5

	P	W	D	L	F	A	Pts
Trinidad & Tobago	4	3	1	0	16	4	7
Surinam	4	2	1	1	11	4	5
Antigua & Barbuda	4	0	0	4	3	22	0

10-11-72	Trin. & Tobago : Ant. & Barb.	11:1 (4:1)
19-11-72	Ant. & Barb. : Trin. & Tobago	1:2 (0:2)
28-11-72	Trin. & Tobago : Surinam	2:1 (0:0)
30-11-72	Trin. & Tobago : Surinam	1:1 (0:0)
03-12-72	Surinam : Ant. & Barb.	6:0 (2:0)
05-12-72	Ant. & Barb. : Surinam	1:3 (1:2)

Caribbean/North/Central America - Final Matches

	P	W	D	L	F	A	Pts
Haiti	5	4	0	1	8	3	8
Trinidad & Tobago	5	3	0	2	11	4	6
Mexico	5	2	2	1	10	5	6
Honduras	5	1	3	1	6	6	5
Guatemala	5	0	3	2	4	6	3
Netherlands Antilles	5	0	2	3	4	19	2

29-11-73	Honduras : Trinidad & Tobago	2:1 (1:0)
30-11-73	Mexico : Guatemala	0:0
01-12-73	Haiti : Neth. Antilles	3:0 (2:0)
03-12-73	Honduras : Mexico	1:1 (0:0)
04-12-73	Haiti : Trinidad & Tobago	2:1 (1:1)
05-12-73	Neth. Antilles : Guatemala	2:2 (1:1)
07-12-73	Honduras : Haiti	0:1
08-12-73	Mexico : Neth. Antilles	8:0 (4:0)
10-12-73	Trinidad & Tobago : Guatemala	1:0 (1:0)
12-12-73	Honduras : Neth. Antilles	2:2 (1:0)
13-12-73	Haiti : Guatemala	2:1 (1:1)
14-12-73	Trinidad & Tobago : Mexico	4:0 (2:0)
15-12-73	Guatemala : Honduras	1:1 (0:1)
17-12-73	Trin. & Tobago : Neth. Antilles	4:0 (2:0)
18-12-73	Mexico : Haiti	1:0 (1:0)

All games played in Port-au-Prince

South America - Group 1

	P	W	D	L	F	A	Pts
Uruguay	4	2	1	1	6	2	5
Colombia	4	1	3	0	3	2	5
Ecuador	4	0	2	2	3	8	2

21-06-73	Colombia : Ecuador	1:1 (1:0)
24-06-73	Colombia : Uruguay	0:0
28-06-73	Ecuador : Colombia	1:1 (1:0)
01-07-73	Ecuador : Uruguay	1:2 (1:1)
05-07-73	Uruguay : Colombia	0:1 (0:0)
08-07-73	Uruguay : Ecuador	4:0 (3:0)

South America - Group 2

	P	W	D	L	F	A	Pts
Argentina	4	3	1	0	9	2	7
Paraguay	4	2	1	1	8	5	5
Bolivia	4	0	0	4	1	11	0

02-09-73	Bolivia : Paraguay	1:2 (1:1)
09-09-73	Argentina : Bolivia	4:0 (2:0)
16-09-73	Paraguay : Argentina	1:1 (1:1)
23-09-73	Bolivia : Argentina	0:1 (0:1)
30-09-73	Paraguay : Bolivia	4:0 (3:0)
07-10-73	Argentina : Paraguay	3:1 (1:1)

South America - Group 3

	P	W	D	L	F	A	Pts
Chile	2	1	0	1	2	2	2
Peru	2	1	0	1	2	2	2

29-04-73	Peru : Chile	2:0 (1:0)
13-05-73	Chile : Peru	2:0 (0:0)

South America - Group 3 Play-off

05-08-73	Chile : Peru	2:1 (1:1)

Played in Montevideo

Chapter 13

Daniel, Super Mario and the Dutch Lions
The Argentina World Cup, 1978

Argentina 1978

Winners: Argentina

Runners-up: Holland

3rd Place: Brazil

4th Place: Italy

Total Attendance: 1,668,602

Number of Matches: 38

Little did I know that, when I left my family behind to go off to do battle in Argentina in 1978, I would still be recounting stories about this adventure twenty years on but that is the way that it has turned out, and all because I scored what was voted the 'Goal of the Competition', not because we came back victorious. Whilst I was thrilled that I managed to score at all, as I was never famed for being a prolific goal scorer, I would gladly have traded my silver salver, which was my award, for getting to the next round of the competition. Indeed, the whole experience might now be stored well into the back of my mind except that every four years, when the competition looms large again, my goal is resurrected from the annals of time and used to remind the people back home in Scotland that we can achieve good things, perhaps not quite 'great' things!!

Things could have been so different if we had not missed that penalty against Peru. They were leading 1-0 at the time and, if we had equalized at that point, I am sure we could have gone on and won but, as it turned out, they won the match 3-1. Bad start! We then played Iran in the second match which was even more of a let-down because there is no way Scotland should have failed to beat a team that was so new to the World Cup scene, but we drew 1-1 which was an exceptionally poor result.

My memories of the actual trip are very mixed. I remember the feeling of disbelief when I realised the extent of the security arrangements and wondering why this was necessary. I remember the feeling of hope within the camp that we could achieve something special and of course the extreme disappointment when we failed to reach the second round but then I never was a good loser and at that level and after all the hype it was really hard to take.

Original contribution by Scotland's Archie Gemmill

As the decade of upheaval moved into its final two years, the rollercoaster ride of political, economic and scientific change refused to end. The Vietnam War had reached its final conclusion in 1975 with the US making a "tactical" withdrawal from Saigon as the Viet Cong entered the city. Those Vietnamese who could not tolerate living under a Communist regime took to the sea in small boats trying to reach more liberal South-East Asian countries. The "Boat People" who made land were the lucky ones. Thousands of others were not. In Cambodia, the death toll inflicted by the Maoist Khmer Rouge was staggeringly worse. Pol Pot's army had forced the population out of the cities into the fields in an attempt to turn the country into a land of agricultural communes. Between two and three million of the country's pre-1975 population of seven million, those who disagreed with the policy, died as a result of his "re-education". Mao had died in 1976 and in China his successor Hua Guofeng was ousted two years later by people who wanted to modernise China's ailing economy. He was replaced by Deng Xiaoping and Hu Yaobang who introduced the "Four Modernizations", an accelerated development of industry, agriculture, defence and technology along western lines, aiming to catch up with its more prosperous neighbours. The fact that there were thousands of Communists still loyal to the ideas of Mao meant that progress was slow.

In Italy, former Prime Minister, Aldo Moro, was kidnapped and murdered by the Brigata Rossa (Red Brigade) and in Iran angry Muslims accused the Shah of showing disrespect for the laws of Islam, finally forcing him to flee the country in January 1979. In the USA, Jimmy Carter hosted the Egyptian and Israeli leaders, Anwar Sadat and Menachim Begin at Camp David and would not let them leave until they had settled their differences. The result was a peace agreement known as the "Camp David Accords". Israel promised to hand back to Egypt control of the Sinai Desert, taken after the 1967 Six Day War, but the agreement floundered because the

Palestinian question was not resolved. In Britain, three years of wage restraint lead to union action and the year ended with a series of strikes in the so-called "Winter of Discontent".

Throughout the western world disco fever took hold and John Travolta rose to prominence with the hit film "Saturday Night Fever". In Britain there was a short-lived Mods and Rockers revival, but the most striking youth culture to come out of the country's economic troubles was the Punk Rock phenomenon as disaffected youth made its statement. In the scientific world there were new discoveries for the betterment of mankind. A human sperm was introduced to an egg outside the body and the first test tube baby was conceived. Other scientific firsts were cameras with automatic focus, programmable washing machines, surrogate motherhood in cows and the use of lasers to detect fingerprints that were up to ten years old.

As the Argentina World Cup opened in Buenos Aires, the FIFA president proudly pronounced: "At last the world can see the true face of Argentina", though it was never certain up to almost the last moment that the country would host its own tournament. Ever since Uruguay had been awarded the first World Cup, jealous neighbours Argentina had been hankering after hosting a tournament of its own. Its impatience had only multiplied as first Brazil, then Chile and Mexico were all given precedence over the country that regards itself as the true home of South American football. The reasons for Argentina being overlooked were various and often to do with its own obdurate attitude, so when it was promised the 1978 World Cup by FIFA in 1966, it seemed that everything that had been wished for would come to pass. There was boundless optimism and enthusiasm in Argentina following the award, but ten years later, as the day was fast dawning, nobody could be sure if the Argentina World Cup would go ahead.

The reality was that by 1978 political and economic conditions in the country were such that influential voices not only thought that it would be impossible for the Argentinians to manage the event, but that it would be immoral for them to be allowed. In March 1976, the corrupt and ineffective, but nonetheless democratically chosen government of Isabella Péron had been overthrown in a military coup. The new dictatorship, headed by General Videla, moved decisively and ruthlessly to crush and remove its critics. Thousands were arrested, imprisoned, tortured, murdered or simply disappeared in a savage reign of political cleansing that ignored even a basic regard for human rights. The stability that the clampdown was intended to create did not materialize as those brave enough to oppose the military, denied any legal channel for their opposition, turned to violence in their struggle to restore democracy. By 1978, a state of near civil war existed between the Army and its death squads and the Mononeros, the left-wing guerrillas whose terrorist activities had even brought about the death of General Actis, the president of Argentina's World Cup Organising Committee. In the meantime, the economy slid towards collapse and inflation hit a staggering 186% during the tournament.

Out of these circumstances arose many questions. Could Argentina afford the World Cup? Could safety be guaranteed? Could FIFA risk it? Would countries go? Among others, Dutch and German players were loud in their condemnation of Argentina's appalling human rights record and were openly talking of boycotting the event, should it go ahead. Holland and Belgium were being bandied as probable alternatives. Yet, in Argentina plans were proceeding. Stadia were being rebuilt and refurbished and the wavering amber light turned fully green when the Mononeros declared that there would be no political violence for the duration of the World Cup. A cease-fire was announced because "soccer is a game of the working class" - perhaps there are some things more important than politics!

With all of this uncertainty and turmoil still in the future, the qualifying tournament kicked off on 7th March 1976 in Freetown, the capital of Sierra Leone. The African zone was organized in a way similar to that used in the previous World Cup, with the entrants paired together in a two-legged knock-out that would reduce the number down to the three required for the final group. In this opening game, Sierra Leone played Niger in a preliminary round to decide which country would go through to the first round proper. (Upper Volta and Mauritania had also to go through this process.) Sierra Leone won the home leg 5-1, lost the away leg 2-1 and went through to the first round on goal difference, only to be knocked out by Nigeria. Three countries, the Central African Republic, Sudan and Tanzania, withdrew from the first round, giving byes to their opponents, one of which was Zaïre, Africa's representative in 1974. Zaïre then withdrew at the second stage and eventually Egypt, Nigeria and Tunisia won through to the final group.

The Argentinian government made TV announcements asking to the public to be nice to visitors. They also warned maniacal taxi drivers to tidy themselves up by wearing blue or grey shirts with matching ties.

The first item on FIFA's agenda for the 30th May meeting in Buenos Aires was the question of China and Taiwan. Both claimed to be rightful representatives of China, but FIFA favoured the Beijing government, in line with most other countries. They voted to do nothing for two years, probably because Taiwan had entered, but China had not.

Although almost bankrupt, the Peruvian government found the money to send coach Calderón to Italy on a fact finding mission to see Scotland play in Verona. He got there to find a club side playing, not the national team.

Although the team had yet to display the form that it would in the finals, Tunisia ran out group winners and then almost lost its place through an ill-judged piece of team misbehaviour. Tunisia and Nigeria met in the 3rd/4th place play-off of the African Championships, a game in which Tunisia had taken the lead. Trouble flared when Nigeria equalized through a goal that the Tunisians claimed was scored after the ball had been handled. When the referee allowed the goal to stand, the Tunisian team, led by goalkeeper, Sadok Attouga, walked off the pitch in protest. Not even the appeals of coach, Abdel Majid Chetali, could persuade them to return and the match had to be abandoned. As a result, Tunisian teams were banned from international competition for two years, with ringleader Attouga receiving a personal ban of three years. It was widely expected that they would be deprived of their place in Argentina, but the African Confederation relented and the ban was not extended to the World Cup.

Following his dismissal from Manchester United, Frank O'Farrell spent a spell coaching the national team in Iran. He laid a solid foundation which his assistant and successor, Heshmat Mohajerani, built into World Cup success by taking Iran to their first World Cup finals at their second attempt. The countries of Asia-Oceania were divided into five groups, each sending one team to the group final, and out of this football labyrinth the Iranians emerged victorious, having played 11 qualifying games, the largest number played by any team to reach the 1978 finals. Only four teams played more qualifiers: Haiti, Kuwait and South Korea played 12 and Hong Kong played 13, but none of these teams qualified.

Another complicated grouping was that of the CONCACAF region. Groups One and Two, which contained three and four teams respectively, were played as round robins with both sending the two top teams into the final group. Canada and Mexico went through from Group One, whilst Guatemala and El Salvador qualified from Group Two. The teams in Group Three, however, were organized into a knock-out, with the last two teams to qualify. Haiti and Surinam won through to join up with the other four and the ultimate winner came through a series of 15 games, played over two weeks in Mexico City and Monterrey in October. As expected, Mexico finished top of the pile and achieved a notable World Cup landmark in doing so. When Victor Rangel scored their first goal in their 4-1 defeat of Haiti, it was Mexico's 150th World Cup goal and made them the third country to reach that tally, behind Brazil and Hungary, who had got there earlier in the qualifying tournament.

The South American qualifiers followed a slightly different format to that normally adopted, with the nine teams who entered being placed in three groups. Brazil, who won Group One, suffered a minor scare in their opening game against Colombia in Bogotá, when a 0-0 draw was seen as a disgrace back home. In consequence, coach Osvaldo Brandão was sacked and replaced by Claudio Coutinho, a PT university lecturer and basketball expert. There were a number of raised eyebrows at the appointment, but Coutinho proved his merit by winning the group and defeating Colombia 6-0 in the return match in Rio. Four days earlier, Brazil had beaten Paraguay in Asunción by a single goal and this was Brazil's 150th World Cup goal, making it the first country to reach that target, an achievement slightly tarnished by the fact that it was an own goal and not scored by a Brazilian. The other groups were won by Peru and Bolivia, who surprised everybody in finishing above Uruguay. The three winners then played each other in a group final, with the top two securing automatic places in Argentina. Bolivia came third and had to play Hungary over two legs to determine the last place in the finals. A 3-0 defeat in Budapest was too much of a set back and a 3-2 home defeat put Hungary into the finals.

One of the more notable stories from the European rounds was England's failure to get through for the second time in succession. Quite understandably, the man who was blamed for the catastrophe was Don Revie, the manager who quit, some would say deserted, the team half way through the campaign. It was, however, the manner of his departure that did the most damage to his reputation. England had played four games, won three of them against Finland and Luxembourg, but had lost the crucial game against Italy in Rome. In July 1977, with his squad on a summer tour of South America, Revie jumped on a plane, ostensibly to fly to Helsinki to watch Finland play Italy. On the way, he stopped off in Dubai, where he negotiated himself a lucrative, tax-free contract to manage the United Arab Emirates for four years. Back in London, he complained to the FA of the pressure he and his family were under. He asked if they would pay up the rest of his contract and give a substantial "golden handshake" for Revie "to save trouble and go." He denied he had another job to go to, but days later the story broke in the press of his defection to the Middle East. The nation was outraged, Revie slunk off to his new found wealth and Ron Greenwood was brought in to try to undo the damage. The former West Ham boss came to the job highly recommended, but was unable to realign the country's fortunes in time to reach the finals. Italy took the place by a three goal difference.

The result meant that, for a second successive tournament, Scotland was Britain's sole representative. Yet, when their campaign got off to a poor start with a 2-0 defeat in Prague against reigning European champions, Czechoslovakia, their progress to the finals looked far from certain. Critical, though, was the sending off in that game of Anton Ondrus, the Czechs' influential defender. His suspension, for the rest of the qualifying stage, severely handicapped his team and they won only one more match, against Wales in Prague. The Scots went on to win their three remaining games to finish clear group winners.

Picking up where they left off in 1974 was Poland, whose good form continued into the new tournament. They made a solid beginning, with a victory over Portugal in Oporto, and continued undefeated for the rest of their schedule. Their established stars like Lato, Deyna and Szarmach were now getting on in years, but still proved formidable. (See Grzegorz Lato profile on page 290). They scored 17 goals in six matches, conceded only four and dropped only one point, in a home draw against Portugal. The Austrians, too, refound something of the form of yesteryear, ending top of Group Three to qualify for their first finals since 1958. Manager, Helmuth Senekowitsch had done a good job and given his team a renewed sense of purpose. Like Poland, Austria also qualified without loss and took a 14 match unbeaten run to Argentina. Their 9-0 defeat of Malta was a record national victory and six of the goals were scored by Hans Krankl, "an old fashioned centre-forward with a modern mind", as one commentator wrote. He had scored 41 goals that season for his club, Austria Vienna, making him Europe's leading striker.

Before the tournament Argentine coach, César Menotti, confidently stated; "We are better than in 1974 when we reached the second stage. That was in Europe and now we are at home. We are hoping for big things." Not so the Italian press, which berated Enzo Beartzot's side, with Gianni Rivera saying they "lacked any class".

In a widely criticized deal with British American Tobacco, the Scottish team could earn £100,000 for the Sports Aid Foundation if they won the World Cup, £50,000 if they reached the semi-finals, £10,000 if they got to the quarter-finals and £2,000 for every goal they scored in the first round.

The "Eat My Own Words" Award for 1978 goes to...

a pair of Scottish optimists. Rod Stewart was so dedicated to Scotland that he cancelled a European tour to follow them to Argentina. "Football comes before money," he boasted, confident that Scotland would do well. "I wouldn't be going to Argentina if I didn't think so." Ally MacLeod agreed, though his team had not had a good pre-tournament, having scored only ten goals in ten games including a Home Nations defeat by England at Hampden. "You cannot go by form in this World Cup," he insisted.

Cable and Wireless executive, Sandy Redpath, having spent time in Argentina, gave ominous advice to travelling Scots. "Don't become involved in politics, fighting, riots, arguments, or with women. Don't discuss Peron or the police, or criticise the football. The rules are simple. If you see an excited crowed and a couple of policemen, walk away. Put a street corner between you and the trouble. Getting arrested is trouble. South American jails have four walls, a door and a window - and nothing else. If you don't have contacts outside you don't eat." Chief police officer, Senen Rosas, stated that: "It's the worst thing in the world if they hit a policeman. We will try not to fire any shots, but to arrest the man."

On 17th May, French 1st Division side Sochaux beat the Polish World Cup squad 1-0 in a friendly. Iran were beaten 3-0 by Paris St. Germain in the 3rd/4th play-off of a four-cornered tournament that also included Holland and Brugge of Belgium. Holland beat Brugge 7-1 in the final.

The Scots were given a rousing send off from Hampden Park, with a pipe band and an open bus parade around the stadium. Thousands gathered at the airport, causing Joe Jordan to exclaim: "You'd think we'd already won the cup judging by the crowds." For a time the Scots and Tunisians shared the same hotel. The Tunisians did not smoke or drink and grew puzzled by the Scots' methods and match preparations. The Tunisian manager said: "Apart from an occasional practice match, they don't seem to be doing anything in the way of training. They come out here on the terrace for a couple of hours, go and have something to eat, come out again, sit for two or three more hours, and go inside again to eat." Another official said, "They smoke and drink a lot - all sorts of alcohol, especially whisky." However, he went on to say that Scotland could win the trophy, but hedged their bets by saying that Brazil, Argentina, West Germany and Holland could also do it.

The day after their arrival, the West German team went to the Plaza San Martin in Córdoba to meet the people. A crowd was already celebrating a national hero's honour and the Germans handed out pictures, badges and autographs. "It was a lesson we learned in Léon in 1970," said Press Officer Wilfrid Gerhardt. "In the Mexico World Cup, we became the home team because we made friends with the people. England were the opposite. Alf Ramsey had too many things to do to speak to the Mexicans."

Prior to the tournament the Italian press again assaulted their national side after a series of poor results. One newspaper touted the headlines - "STAY HOME!"

Another team worthy of note was Hungary, who qualified for their seventh World Cup finals by firstly topping European Group Nine, above the Soviet Union and Greece, and then by defeating Bolivia in a two-legged play-off. Along the way, they notched a 2-1 victory over the Soviet Union in Budapest and their first goal, from Tibor Nyilasi, was Hungary's 150th in the World Cup. They became the first European country, and the second overall, to reach the century and a half, though a less fortunate 150 was reached by Luxembourg. Now fighting their tenth World Cup campaign, the third goal they conceded in their 7-1 defeat by Finland in September 1976 was their 150th goal against. It was the first time any country had conceded as many.

So, after more than two years of football, preparation, expectation, anticipation, threat and worry, Argentina got its first domestic taste of the World Cup finals on 1st June. In the imposing, colourful, noisy cauldron of heat and passion that was the Estadio Antonio Liberti "Monumental", in Buenos Aires, the first game of the series was preceded by the customary opening ceremony. To one journalist this was "another of those artificial, contrived" affairs, "in this instance graced by some pleasingly natural formation-gymnastics", whilst to another it was "a bright, autumnal afternoon of military bands, marching in pattern by youths, balloons". This reporter captured another, more sinister undertone of the occasion when he described the "inevitable black-uniformed police with their black-haired dogs." Whichever view is taken of it, the opening ceremony was a far more entertaining spectacle than the game that followed. This saw West Germany, who "performed without inspiration or authority", take on Poland. The Poles were the more enterprising of the two, but they also lacked sparkle and conviction. They created two very plausible chances in the second half, but the crowd had long since given up on the game by then. The awful state of the pitch must bear some responsibility for the dreadful football, as must the nerves that always accompany such events. Poland's stars were four years older and the Germans sorely missed Gerd Müller and Franz Beckenbauer, who was now playing for New York Cosmos in the USA and was unable to commit himself to the national cause. Excuses apart, teams ranked first and third in the world should have been able to come up with something more worthy and the jeers of the crowd, which began after only 25 minutes, were quite understandable.

A much more entertaining game took place the next day between Italy and France. France's coach, Michel Hidalgo, had been assembling a squad that contained some supremely gifted individuals, amongst whom were Michel Platini, Bernard Lacombe, Marius Trésor and Didier Six, and whilst they had yet to blend into the awesome brew they became in the 1980s, they were still capable of electrifying football. The explosive start they made to this game attests to that. With the match only seconds old, left-winger Six "raced on to a long pass from Bossis, outpaced Gentile and slung over a deep cross", which Lacombe headed home for the fastest goal of the tournament. It was the rude awakening the Italians needed and, so early in the competition, were forced out of any defensive orientation they may have had in mind. For the next period of the game they produced what must rank among the best football of the 1978 World Cup, with France featuring hardly at all. Italy's equalizer came just before the half-hour mark and was "something of a comical affair." A long cross into the French area was headed against the bar. The ball rebounded to Paolo Rossi, who shot against one of his own players before he hit the second rebound into the net. They took the lead seven minutes into the second half, when Renato Zaccarelli drove in Gentile's cross and then Italy resorted to more familiar tactics. A physical game became more so as they determined to hold on to what they had. Marco Tardelli was particularly tenacious in stifling Platini's creativity and the French could do little to advance their cause. It had been 58 years since France had beaten Italy at football.

Another exciting game, described by David Miller as "a tingling occasion", was the other Group One fixture played that day in front of a 77,000-strong phalanx of intimidation. In it the Argentinians were "given a stern examination by an uncompromising Hungarian team" that showed plenty of desire and produced some classy football. They took the lead after only ten minutes when Sandor Zambori's angled cross was only parried by Ubaldo Fillol in goal. The ball fell to Karoly Csapo, whose strike brought the night's only moment of silence from the packed house. Within five minutes Leopoldo Luque had restored parity by getting on to the end of Mario Kempes's cross and beating the despairing dive of Gujdar in Hungary's goal. It had been a dynamic opening few minutes and was sustained to the end, though Hungarian progress was often impeded by what was to prove one of the more unfortunate aspects of the tournament. The Argentinians were quite prepared to resort to foul play and referees were often prepared to let them get away with it. Portugal's Antonio Garrido was the first to display this tendency and, finding no protection from the referee, the Hungarians began to repay their hosts in kind. It made for a sour ending to a game that fell apart for the Europeans in the last ten minutes. When Daniel Bertoni fired in the winner, the Magyars complained that their goalkeeper had been fouled. Then, more out of a sense of injustice than malice, Andras Torocsik tripped Galván and was sent off. Finally, as the game drew to a close, Tibor Nyilasi also walked for running into and bundling over Alberto Tarantini. At the final whistle, seconds later, the Hungarians could look back and count themselves remarkably hard done by. (See Daniel Passarella profile on page 291)

The third game played that day brought one of the great shocks of Argentina '78, when Mexico, in their eighth finals, met Tunisia in their first. Before the tournament, the manager of the 1,000/1 rank outsiders had given his team no chance and had said that their "goal was to reach the finals. We can't expect to win anything." The Mexicans, on the other hand, had been boasting of a new, dynamic brand of football that they thought made them one of the contenders. In the first half, the match appeared to be going to form, as the Mexicans pressed forward in numbers and looked as if they might overwhelm their opponents. However, their finishing was poor. Their 1-0 half-time lead came courtesy of a fortunate penalty awarded when de la Torre's shot hit Amor Jebali on the arm. It was certainly more ball to arm than arm to ball, but Scots referee, John Gordon, saw it otherwise and Arturo Vázquez-Ayala's rather limp spot kick found the net. It also stoked up Arab passion and in the second half the Tunisians transformed their play to hit the Mexicans hard. Ten minutes after the restart, Ali Kaabi was given too much space in front of goal and equalized. In the 80th minute, Nejib Ghommidh's narrow-angled shot grabbed the lead and three minutes from time defender, Mukhtar Dhouieb made the score 3-1. In the end it had been very convincing, a point generously conceded by Mexico's coach, Antonio Roca, when he said: "I think our status was maybe overestimated by our

The French reserve goalkeeper had the unfortunate name of Dominique Dropsy. Peru's second choice goalkeeper, Juan Caceras, had to wear the number 13 shirt because FIFA overruled Peru's superstitious protestations. Their first choice keeper, Ramón Quiroga, was Argentinian by birth and had been naturalized after moving there some years before.

Alan Rough, Derek Johnstone and Sandy Jardine were arrested by Argentinian police trying to climb a security fence to get back into their hotel. They had been visiting a local casino and had forgotten their security passes. It was their first night and the guards didn't recognize them. They were asked to be more careful next time.

Brazil 1 : Sweden 1
Referee Clive Thomas nullifies Brazil's last minute goal as he signals the end of the game.

Former Brazilian coach, João Saldanha, was very critical of current team selection. "How can we win when we leave out Paulo Cesar, Luis Pesiera and Francisco Marinho? Manager Claudio Coutinho does not like these players."

Austria 2 : Spain 1
Walter Schachner launches a shot to score Austria's first goal.

own followers." The result put Tunisia on top of the group, above Poland and West Germany, which must have given them great satisfaction.

If the Tunisians had been a revelation, the Brazilians were quite the opposite in their opening game against Sweden the next day. They were stodgy and unimaginative, whilst the Swedes, through "careful tackling, and their total air of calm, controlled know-how, utterly frustrated Brazil." They dominated much of the first half and went ahead in the 37th minute, when Thomas Sjöberg got onto a clever through pass from Lennart Larrson. It was no less than they deserved, but they did not keep it for long and Brazil levelled the scores with the last kick of the half. It was a good goal, too, taken by Reinaldo, who collected a long pass into Sweden's defence and waited for Ronnie Helström, in goal, to commit himself before slotting the ball in. The Brazilians were unlucky not to go in front themselves in the second half, when Rivelino's shot deflected off a defender narrowly past the post, but it would have been an injustice. The Swedes were ahead on points, if not on goals. However, it was the Brazilians who were to end the game crying unfair. As they piled on the pressure in the dying minutes, they were awarded three corners in a row. Right-back, Nelinho, slightly delayed taking the third of them. When the ball came over, Zico headed it in, but the goal did not stand. Clive Thomas, the Welsh referee, had blown his whistle just after the kick had been taken, whilst the ball was in mid air and before it had been headed. So, Mr. Thomas, who had allowed Brazil to score with the last touch of the first half, denied them a victory with the last of the second. Afterwards, he said: "Brazil should not have wasted so much time taking the corner."

The Austrians continued the good form shown in their qualifying games when they defeated Spain 2-1 in their first match of the finals. Their tenth minute opener was one of the best goals of the tournament. A Spanish attack was broken up and a long pass was sent downfield to Walter Schachter, waiting on the half way line. He set off on a run, beat two defenders down the right, cut in and fired a brilliant, narrow-angled shot that gave little chance to Miguel Angel in goal. The Austrians squandered a clear chance to go 2-0 up only minutes later and, in the 21st minute, Spain equalized through Dani's deflected shot. The Spanish then took control of the game and had a goal disallowed for a foul on the goalkeeper, but the Austrians came back. An injury to Spain's midfield maestro, Cardenosa, and a couple of misjudged substitutions robbed them of their fluency. Austria's winner was inevitably scored by Hans Krankl in the 71st minute.

22 Men and a Bag of Wind

Iran made its debut in the World Cup finals against the powerful Dutch and, though losing 3-0, acquitted themselves well. The loss of leading striker, Hassan Rowshan, recovering from a cartilage operation, was a handicap, but their defence, well marshalled by captain, Ali Parvin, kept out the Dutch for most of the first half. The Dutch were not firing on all cylinders and, missing the influence of Cruyff, seemed content to play possession football until an opening should present itself. It came in the 38th minute when René van der Kerkhof was brought down in the area and Rob Rensenbrinck swept in his first of the night. Going ahead settled the Dutch and cured them of their hesitancy. They came out more self-assured in the second half and Rensenbrinck, slipping into the role vacated by Cruyff, proved a leader and creator of distinction. He added a second with a 62nd minute header and completed his hat trick in the 79th minute with another penalty. It all turned out very comfortable for the Netherlands, but the plucky Iranians had been far from disgraced. They took the field full of confidence in their next match, against Scotland.

The Scots opened their own account against Peru in Córdoba, fully expecting to win and, in the first 15 minutes, gave every indication that they would. They created numerous chances before taking a 15th minute lead with a goal that came from a "superb move involving Johnstone, Dalglish, Hartford, Rioch and Jordan." Bruce Rioch's shot was parried by Ramón Quiroga and the rebound was forced over the line by an ebullient Joe Jordan. Up to then, the Scots had done much good work and thoroughly merited their lead, but they suddenly wilted and allowed the Peruvians to come right back at them. It was as if they had decided that the match was already won. Roles were reversed and the Scots were swept aside as attack after attack brought chance upon chance for the South Americans. They equalized in the 42nd minute when César Cueto's powerful shot left Alan Rough standing helpless in goal. Although the Scots rallied a little in the second half, the revival was temporary and the game's defining moment came when Don Masson missed a penalty. Five minutes later the Peruvians tore through Scotland's friable defence and veteran Téofilo Cubillas lashed "a searing shot just inside the near post." By now, Peru were "producing beautiful football at breathtaking speed" and after four more minutes, they scored a third. A lovely, curving free kick by Cubillas lofted into the net and left the Scots dejected. Many have blamed Ally MacLeod's tactical misjudgement for Scotland's failure and it is hard not to agree. Peru's coach certainly indicated his own views after the match. "I would like to congratulate Scotland and Mr MacLeod for

Dutch coach, Ernst Heppel, concerned about keeping his temperamental stars content, did not train his squad very much. Their build up to the 1978 series was very relaxed.

After Iranian coach, Heshmat Mohajerani, was seen chain smoking on television there was a public outcry. He promised the Shah that he would quit and was branded a national disgrace when he didn't.

Argentine born Helenio Herrera had good advice for Ally MacLeod. The Peruvians "are not the easy opponents the Scots appear to think they are", he said. "It is true that some of their players are old and that they have not played well in recent years. But Ally MacLeod must still take the Peruvians seriously. If he does not then he will lose the game and if he loses the first game the Scots will be out of the competition.

The Scottish players were to get between £20,000 and £25,000 each if they won the tournament, whilst Umbro offered the team a further £120,000 for a victory.

Amazing Journeys

Several Scots supporters gave up their jobs to go to Argentina. Robert Stery, a 19 year old from Perth, set off on 14th April with £500 in his pocket. He had already called off his engagement saying: "I was due to get married in October. But I can't afford to do both so I broke it off to come here. I'll see her when I get back, but it will only be from a distance. She wasn't exactly delighted." He had bought a £64 air ticket to New York, was mugged in Guatemala and shared a train ride in Mexico with pigs and donkeys. By the time he reached Argentina he had £100 to last him three weeks. Jimmy Burns of Winchester set off on 20th April armed with £500 and a plane ticket to Los Angeles. He made his way to Nicaragua where, entering a bar, he was greeted by the dulcet tones of two Edinburgh lads who, seeing his kilt, called out "Hullawrerr". "It never sounded better," he said. The two were David Ednie, a fitter, and taxi driver, Brian Flemming. Both set off on 3rd April with £1000 each. They travelled to the USA, bought a car in Connecticut, abandoned it on the Mexican border and hitchhiked the rest of the way. They had £400 each left on arrival in Córdoba. "When they see you wearing the kilt they all want to congratulate you. They are the friendliest people we have met. We feel like superstars." Adrian Haren of Clydebank and Gerry Keenan of West Lothian set off on 12th March with £500 and £800 respectively. They had belongings stolen by police in Costa Rica, but received better treatment from Argentinian soldiers. "Some of the military were having a party in a house when we arrived and invited us in for drinks and dancing," said Keenan. Ralph Dargie of Crieff gave up his job at an atomic power station. Carrying £500 he had to endure the extreme heat of the Mexican desert and the extreme cold of the Andes on his way. James Blair and Ewan Robertson decided they would cycle and by 20th May were seen heading out of Lima with another 2000 miles to go.

the team they presented to us", he said. Yet he was disregarding the quality of the football given by his own players.

When the Group One games resumed again, it was a much depleted Hungarian team that took on a buoyant Italy at Mar del Plata. With two players suspended and others out injured, the Magyars were "restricted here to chasing shadows and salvaging some pride", though there was precious little of that as Roberto Bettega gave one of the finest individual attacking performances of the whole tournament. With eight Juventus players in the line up, the Italians were at ease and familiar with each other and the fact that Hungary made only a couple of decent attacks in the first half-hour gives clear indication of Italy's mood. Surprisingly, they did not score until the 34th minute, but did so from one in a series of sweeping attacks. It saw Marco Tardelli blast a shot that took a wicked deflection and was only just kept out by Meszaros, in goal. Unluckily, his block pushed the ball to Paolo Rossi, who touched it in confidently. From the restart, Bettega, who hit the bar three times, got on to the end of a long pass, beat two defenders and the score was 2-0. The Hungarians claimed that he had controlled the ball with his arm, but the referee ignored their protests. Italy's third came 15 minutes into the second half and was the result of "patient build-up and understanding" between Bettega and Benetti, whose final 18 yard drive put the game beyond Hungary. It had become a virtual one-way flow and it was only in the last 15 minutes, with Italy winding down, that Hungary made any impact. Andreas Tóth converted a consolation penalty nine minutes from time, but Italy had stylishly made it to the next stage.

Although the Argentinians "achieved a hard-fought victory in a highly skilful match" against France in Buenos Aires later that day, there was an element of luck about the way that they did it. The French were not in the least overawed by the occasion or atmosphere and, in the first half especially, played football of real quality. Inside ten minutes, Trésor headed on to the top of the net, Michel had another header well saved and Platini's free kick sailed narrowly over the bar. Juste Fontaine, Roger Piantoni and Raymond Kopa were watching from the stands and must have been impressed by the class of '78, if not by the decision that gave Argentina the lead. In the last minute of the first half, Kempes attacked into the penalty area and was confronted by the impeccable Trésor. The Frenchman timed his tackle expertly, but the ball bobbled and he lost his footing on the uneven turf. He fell backwards and flung out his arms to cushion his fall. He could not have known anything about it, but his arm seemed to touch the ball. Jean Durlach, the Swiss referee, ran to consult his linesman, stood a full 40 yards from the incident, and awarded a penalty, which Passarella converted. It was a blatant miscarriage of justice, but the French got on with it. They equalized in the 60th minute, when Dominique Rocheteau powered a shot against the bar and Platini tucked away the rebound. They had found their rhythm and had the home team under great pressure until, against the run of play, Argentina scored again. The French had been forced to replace their goalkeeper and it was whilst newcomer, Baratelli, was settling in that Luque struck. He hit a purely stunning drive on the turn from the edge of the area to top what was a superlative personal performance. It was a great goal, but only gave France 18 minutes to restore the situation. They tried bravely, with Didier Six running closest, but they could not find the telling touch and suffered further injustice in the final minutes. Six was callously hacked down in the area and Mr. Durlach hardly reacted. The final 2-1 scoreline was not what the French deserved, but was enough to see Argentina through to the next phase.

In Group Two that day, the Tunisians were back in action and establishing a reputation as the best African team to have played in the World Cup finals to date. Their 1-0 defeat at the hands of then-current world number three, Poland, was a mammoth achievement and, with a little better fortune, they might have gone one better. Twice in the first half they came close to opening the scoring, firstly when Ghoummidh had a shot parried by Tomaszewski and then when Taruk Dhiab screwed another over the bar. It was inexperience rather than lack of skill that told against them and contributed to Poland's only goal, late in the first half. The ball was crossed low into the box and a missed clearance allowed Lato to steal in and score "an easy goal." It was a blow that would have crippled many teams, but the Tunisians came out fighting and gave the Poles countless problems. At the end the Poles were left hanging on as the Tunisians buzzed around looking for the equalizer, hitting the crossbar with one effort and seeing Dhiab head wide from four yards out with only a minute to go.

The Poles had been lucky against Tunisia. Against Mexico, the West Germans refound the form that had made them world champions. They made a typically sluggish start to the game, but began to turn the screw in the 14th minute when the Köln striker, Dieter Müller, "slammed a glorious shot into the net." Some 16 minutes later, Stuttgart's Hans Müller, doubled the tally when he picked up Heinz Flohe's cross, "dribbled round a defender and hit an easy looking shot". Eight minutes before half-time, Karl-Heinz Rummenigge, restored to the team, scored the best goal of the game, "racing from well inside his own half, cutting through the Mexican defence and forcing the ball under Reyes", Mexico's keeper. Sadly, Reyes was hurt in the move and was carried off the pitch, but his replacement, Soto, fared little better. Only minutes later, the Germans went 4-0 up when Flohe's "cannonball shot" crashed into the target. The Germans emphasized their dominance with two more goals in the second half and put the dazed Mexicans early out of another World Cup finals. (See Karl-Heinz Rummenigge profile on page 287).

Of the four games played on the next day, only one produced worthwhile football. The other three were lifeless affairs, with that between Austria and Sweden being described in the Times as "played at an extraordinarily lethargic pace." A first half penalty apart, won and scored by Krankl, there was little to impress and it was a similar story when Brazil met Spain. "Too many players were happy enough to knock it around at the back and leave the creating to somebody else," as one reporter noted and with nobody able to put away the few chances that there were, a 0-0 draw ensued. It was regarded as a defeat by the Brazilian authorities and Coutinho was divested of his sole responsibility for team selection in a backroom coup. He became one of a selection committee, with responsibility for training going to an Argentine, Ruben Minelli. It was a move he fully expected if things did not go to plan.

A third game in this sequence of mediocrity was the scoreless draw between Holland and Peru played at Mendoza. The Peruvian game plan was boringly simple, but effective. They went on to the defensive, shutting their opponents out and the Dutch could not find the verve to break the tight formation. Holland hardly created a chance in the whole game and it was down to Scotland and Iran to provide the entertainment that day. After their earlier disappointment, the Scots needed a blockbuster, but their football "lacked the spirit of revival that was desperately needed." The Iranians were very well organized at the rear and were the equal of anything the Scots could create. They did create chances and in the first half any from Lou Macari, Asa Hartford, Archie Gemmill or Kenny Dalglish could have given them the lead, but there was no pattern to Scotland's play and they could not establish an effective presence on the field. When a goal came, just before half-time, it was a defensive error and not Scottish invention that provided it. Jordan challenged goalkeeper, Nasser Hedjazi, for a loose ball and centre-half, Andranik Eskandarian, intervened to protect his number one. Defender and keeper collided, tumbled and in the confusion Eskandarian stuck out a foot to clear the ball and swept it into his own net. The undeserved half-time lead ought to have provided the inspiration to go looking for more after the restart, but it was Iran that came out with bellies full of fire. They were able to smother the Scottish midfield, thwart their creativity and, with growing confidence, become more adventurous. They equalized with a little under a half-hour of play remaining, when Iraj Danaifer stole the ball from Gemmill, ran in on goal and beat Rough from a narrow angle. They might have had another only minutes later, but Rough grabbed the ball from the advancing attacker. The Scots had to press on, but poor substitutions that saw defender replace defender did nothing to bolster the attack. The draw was a triumph for Iran and a humiliation for the Scots, which left their disgruntled supporters jeering: "You only want the money," reference to the pre-tournament row over bonuses that had beset the Scottish camp.

Both the West Germans and Scots grumbled about the new style match balls. Helmut Schön complained: "My players are not happy. We've tried the ball out in three games and it has done some funny things." FIFA had provided each team with only one practice ball.

Following their disastrous defeat by West Germany, Mexican fans burned the car of captain, Arturo Vásquez-Ayala. Coach, José Antonio Roca, had planned to fly to Madrid if Mexico lost their last group game against Poland, but he relented and went home to face the music, saying: "The fans are ignorant and are not in a position to judge the play of the team in Argentina." Those fans were very angry and police had to clear away a group of stone carrying youths from the airport in Mexico City when the team returned. Team members' families were put under 24 hour police guard after threats had been made.

Following the game with Peru, Scotland's Willie Johnson tested positive for the banned substance, fencamfamine, a "psycho-motor stimulant" and normally used for fatigue and depression. He was sent home by the SFA and told that he would never play for Scotland again. He later explained that he thought he had taken anti-histamines for hay fever, but nobody had informed FIFA. On his return, he said: "I did take two pills before the game - they were prescribed by a doctor back home. They are called Reactivan and other players take them in Britain. I only take them when I am feeling low. I had hay fever almost from the time we arrived. On Friday it was so bad I came close to calling off from the game. Then I felt better, but I took two pills in the dressing room before kick-off. We were all told about drugs, about stimulants, but I didn't think there was anything wrong with these pills. I had no idea they contained any drugs, which were banned by FIFA. It turns out, too, that this drug is banned in Argentina. I had no idea of that."

Michael Bentine, of the Goons and "Potty Time", was Peruvian born and even though he had been married for 30 years to Scottish lass, Clementine, he was overjoyed at Peru's defeat of Scotland. One fan, Brian Johnstone and his new wife Anne spent their honeymoon at the World Cup.

Daniel, Super Mario and the Dutch Lions - Argentina 1978

Scotland v Iran - humiliation to end all humiliations...

Iran knew that the key to success against Scotland was to neutralize the Scots' air power and much time was spent on heading practice. Coach Heshmatt Mohajerani, a major in the police, admitted: "We know about the Scots and about their power in the air. We have heard of Joe Jordan and, therefore, we must work on heading more than anything else. It is something we are not good at." Having won the Asian Nations cup and taken the side to the Montreal Olympics in 1976, he could speak knowledgably. "We are playing for Iran and the whole of Asia," he said. "We shall not let the people down." Yet, his success that day was a tragedy for Scotland. After the game, fans hurled their scarves and flags at the departing players. Outside the ground, they waited for them and, as the team bus emerged, surrounded it, spitting and throwing stones at it. As Ally McLeod got on one fan shouted: "We've walked a million miles for f*** all." The streets of Córdoba were awash with tartan the fans no longer wanted.

So delighted was the Tunisian government with its team becoming the first Africans to win a game in the finals, it allowed them to stay on after their elimination as spectators.

Adding insult to an already wounded pride, the Scots were "asked" to move out of their HQ, the San Francisco Hotel in Mendoza, a day early because the Brazilians wanted to move in. The French press quickly followed the example set by that of Mexico and Tunisia and the headline "Eliminated by whisky" appeared in the evening paper, France-Soir. The article claimed: "They were drunk when they flew to Buenos Aires. Beer, whisky and drugs took the place of training."

Surprised that their team had made it through to the second phase, Austrian fans in Vienna took to the streets to celebrate. They walked along the wide boulevards singing the national anthem to the sound of car horns. The Sparkasse Bank paid for the players' wives and girlfriends to fly out to Buenos Aires. Hans Krankl said: "This has got to be worth two goals start in our next match."

Although purely academic, France's encounter with Hungary allowed them to bow out in style. Playing colourful, imaginative football, they were worthy 3-1 winners and marked themselves as the best team to go out at the first cut. An entirely different game was that between Italy and Argentina. Since both had qualified it is difficult to understand why it should have been so fiery. Perhaps the answer is that here were two potential finalists deciding to begin the battle of nerves a little early. The Italians laid out their stall in the first minute when Benetti deliberately let his foot drop short when stepping over Gallego and pushed his studs knowingly into the Argentinian's thigh. It was as ugly as it was unnecessary, but on hand was a referee, Israel's Abraham Klein, determined to apply the letter of the law. The result was a scrappy, stop-start game, full of unpleasant niggles and side-swipes and with the referee trying to keep the lid on a volatile situation. It was all to Klein's credit that he was firm enough to prevent the game sliding into another "battle". The players were made aware of his determination and pulled away from the more outrageous challenges that could have erupted into pure violence. On the football side, Italy had the better of the first hour and took the lead in the 67th minute with "one of the outstanding tactical goals of the tournament." Bettega and Rossi combined superbly to confound four defenders and send Bettega through to shoot past the advancing Fillol. Argentina then assumed a greater sense of urgency. They were unlucky not to win a penalty when Gallego was brought down in the area, but the Italians held on to go through as group winners on maximum points, the only team to do so. Unfortunately, Klein's approach denied him the chance to referee the final. Argentina argued that close political links between Holland and Israel cast doubts on his suitability, but the real reason lay elsewhere.

Poland clinched top spot in their group with a solid, if not altogether convincing win against Mexico, who once again bowed out of another World Cup finals without a win. Both played good football, but Poland had Zbigniew Boniek restored to the team and were able to make more of the chances they created. It told two minutes before half-time when Deyna and Lato combined superbly to set him up for his first. The Mexicans made a spirited start to the second half and were back on equal terms within seven minutes with a goal from Rangel. However, captain Deyna restored the lead inside four minutes and Boniek rounded off his day with a second strike in the 84th minute, both goals being "stunning shots from well outside the area." Another defeat completely belied Mexico's pre-tournament hype and so ashamed was their coach that he was reluctant to return home.

The West Germans needed a point to qualify when they took on Tunisia in Córdoba and it is a mark of how far German national football had declined since 1974 that they only just managed to achieve it. In an excellent advert for African football, Tunisia twice came close to finding the net in the first 15 minutes, having one shot well saved by Maier and another creeping marginally wide. Always the stronger, the Germans struggled to find any fluency and the prolific workrate of the superb Dhiab in midfield did much to disrupt their movement. They stepped up the pace of the game in the second half, but rarely threatened and when they did break through, found Mokhtar Naili firm in goal. The goalless draw was tantamount to a victory for Tunisia, whose manager recognized its significance in his post-match briefing. "The rest of the world has laughed at Africa", he said, "but now the mockery is over." The Germans were more sanguine. They were relieved that the ordeal was over and that they had crept into the second round.

Spain went into their game with Sweden needing a win to have any chance of further progress and they finally showed the form that they had often threatened, but rarely delivered. They controlled the midfield, starving Sweden's front men of service and they attacked boldly, especially down the wings. Sweden's strength, though, was their defence and for most of the game they kept the lively Spaniards at bay. Spain got the reward they deserved with a quarter of an hour remaining, when "Juanito and Cardenosa combined well" to set Juan Manuel Asensi free to beat Helström with a shot that deflected off Juanito. Had not the Swedish keeper been in such agile form, the Spanish might have won by more, but in the end it meant nothing. Their form had returned too late, for that night Brazil defeated Austria in a game that was played at half pace and had people wondering whether Austria, who had already qualified, had been bribed to go easy. The Brazilians, cumbersome and lacking in flair, won the match five minutes before half-time when the defence failed to deal with a cross from Gil and Roberto forced the ball into the net. With both content with the situation, there was little else to note.

Peru entered their final group game against Iran with qualification already secure, but it did not prevent a dashing display. They got off to a flying start when José Velásquez headed in Muñante's cross after only two minutes and they never looked back. They dominated large swathes of the game, but there was still life in the Iranians and they were unlucky not to equalize when Hassan Rowshan's shot was tipped over the bar by Quiroga. However, two goals in quick succession, both penalties and both scored by Cubillas in the 36th and 39th minutes, put the game beyond Iran. Rowshan grabbed one back before half-time to give his team a ray of hope and they came out in the second half with renewed determination. They were unable to sustain the momentum and the Peruvians gradually resumed the ascendancy. Cubillas added a fourth in the 78th minute to score the tournament's second hat trick and take his team to the top of the group. Far from disgraced, Iran went out and were soon joined by Scotland, whose victory over Holland was another case of too little too late. (See Scotland v Holland profile on page 293).

By the end of 11th June, the first round stage was over and eight teams had been eliminated. As happened in Germany, the remaining eight were placed into two further groups. Group A was made up of the winners of Groups One and Three and the runners-up from Groups Two and Four. The others went into Group B and because of Brazil's below-expected performance, both they and Argentina ended in Group B. It ensured that a final between the two South American giants, that many in FIFA had hoped to see, could not take place.

The opening games of the second phase got underway on 14th June and the Dutch finally showed their devastating potential when they met Austria. A slippery and bumpy pitch did not make it easy for either side, but the Dutch adapted best and went in front in the sixth minute. Arie Haan "floated over a dangerous cross" and Ernie Brandts had both the time and space to crash in a powerful header. Three minutes later, Rensenbrinck almost made it 2-0 with a free kick that Koncilia did well to push around the post. The Austrians then tried to make a game of it and harried to create some plausible chances, but two goals in quick succession undid their efforts. Firstly, Jansen was brought down in the area and Rensenbrinck converted the penalty, and then Rensenbrinck set up Rep, who broke free and lobbed the goalkeeper. Bravely, the Austrians tried to climb the mountain, but two shots over the bar indicated that this was not their day. In the meantime, the Dutch engine continued to throb and in the 53rd minute Rensenbrinck again set up Rep for the fourth goal. It was a vintage performance and though Obermayer grabbed an 80th minute consolation, Willy van der Kerkhof rounded off the rout two minutes later.

In Buenos Aires, the Italians met the reigning champions in a match described by one reporter as an "engrossing goalless draw." It was a game that each dominated in phases, but the impression was that this was a West German team past its best and the Italians always held the key. The early chances fell to Germany, with Fischer, Holzenbein and Bonhof coming close, but the best opportunity fell to Italy in the 38th minute. Rossi's back-heeled pass into the area was picked up by Bettega, who ran on, "dodging the tackles and the interception of Maier" and shot at the open net. Somehow, Manny Kaltz raced in to block the ball in mid air and the danger was cleared. Without success, the Italians claimed that he had handled the ball and it inspired them to a strong second half performance. For its first 20 minutes they had the Germans pinned back and relying on desperate tackling. They had two reasonable penalty appeals turned down, one from another suspected handball by Kaltz, and other chances went begging. The Germans reasserted themselves towards the end and might have had a

The "Getting a Bit Carried Away" Award for 1978 goes to...

Alex Cameron of the Scottish Daily Record. Commenting on the celebrations taking place after Argentina had beaten Poland, he said: "Having watched these such unbelievable ceremonies of object delight Lord Help Us if Argentina win the final at the River Plate Stadium in Buenos Aires on 25th June. The world may have to stop going round and let them off to show the cup to the Martians."

penalty when Fischer was brought down in the area, but a draw was a fair result and left the Dutch with a significant advantage.

Argentina needed an element of good fortune to dispose of Poland in their first Group B game. This may not have been the Poland of four years earlier, but they gave good account of themselves and ought to have had a penalty early in the match when Tarantini brought down Boniek. It was typical of their luck and, to rub it in, Kempes brilliantly headed in Bertoni's left-wing cross shortly afterwards to give his team the lead. The Poles responded positively, with both Szarmach and Boniek coming close, and a penalty given when Kempes fisted out Lato's header should have brought them back into the match. However, Deyna's spot kick was weak and Fillol saved easily. The keeper had moved early and the referee ought to have awarded a retake, but crucially he did not and the moment passed. The Poles then proceeded to miss a sequence of well made chances, with Boniek and Lato chief amongst the guilty partners, and it was this laxity that really brought Poland's downfall. In the 72nd minute, Argentina struck again, when a scintillating run from Ardíles created the opportunity for Kempes to score his second. It was all up for the Poles, but an important victory for the home team.

In the game against Brazil, Peru's hopes took an early dash when, in the fourth minute, full-back Díaz pulled a muscle and had to be replaced by Navarro. It was unsettling, but it would have taken a miracle to have stopped Dirceu's 15th minute free kick. From outside the area, he hit a sensational, swerving shot that "had it not gone in the net, it seemed it would have curved right-back on itself like a boomerang." Peru created chances, but failed to score and some 15 minutes later found themselves two behind, when Dirceu hit his second with a low shot. It was the signal for Peru to take charge of the game and the Brazilians were left hanging on as Cubillas exposed their defence time and again. Leão made some fine saves before the match began to swing in Brazil's favour again mid way through the second half. Substitute Zico wrapped the game up with a 70th minute penalty, awarded after Roberto had been brought down.

Any team of three were in with a chance of reaching the final from Group A and the Italians kept their challenge alive with an "efficient, dull victory" over Austria. The goal that provided the result they required came from a defensive error. Strasser seemed to have broken up an Italian raid, but dithered and attempted a back pass to his keeper. Rossi nipped in to steal the ball, darted into the area and scored with a diagonal shot that went in off the far post. Such a slender lead was too precious to risk. The Italians reverted to type, the "pace relaxed, midfield meshed with defence, and the Austrians were left attacking a fortress with pea-shooters." With Kreuz and Krankl effectively neutralized, Austria had little to offer up front and the match became deadlocked.

Reversing the situation in the final of four years previous, the Germans took an early lead against Holland when Bonhof drove a free kick into the area in the second minute. Goalkeeper Piet Schrijvers could only parry the ball and Rudiger Abramczik "bravely dived forwards and headed in." It began "a dramatic, full-blooded match", one of the greats of the tournament. Holland's response was all-out attack and Rensenbrinck forced a brilliant, reflex save from Maier before Haan scythed through the German defence to equalize with a thunderous drive that "had the mark of rare talent." The pace of the game continued unabated, but it was not until the 70th minute that it was graced by another goal. The Dutch defence failed to clear Beer's cross and Dieter Müller "leant down and headed in." Once more Holland had to fight to rescue the game and did so with relish. Rep hit the bar and with a little over five minutes to play, René van der Kerkhof raided from the left, evaded the tackles and swept round Kaltz to hit a wonderful, swerving shot that beat Maier and which Rüssmann's hand could only help into his own net. With both striving to find a winner, tempers frayed a little towards the end and Dirk Nanninga, on as a substitute, was sent off in the final minutes for mocking the referee as he was about to be booked. It was as stupid as it was pointless and had no bearing on the result, which kept the Dutch in the group's driving seat.

Before the game with Argentina, Brazil's coach said: "If we lose we will be lynched and I am finished. It's as bad - or as good - as that." It was no underestimation of a game that turned into one of the most volatile meetings of the tournament, as both responded to the passion that had been charging the atmosphere for hours before kick off. "Every wizened, black-shawled granny, every flag-waving two-year-old", wrote one witness, "was caught up in the great surge of nationalism which was now distilled into the vulnerable skills of 22 men and an umpire." Another wrote that the football "was almost of secondary importance", as the players clattered into each other with unconcealed relish. The first foul came after only ten seconds, when Luque charged into Batista, and it set the tone for the rest of the night. Oscar responded in kind for Brazil and the game "continued its ragged, jagged course." Amid the mini-battles, there was some pretty football, especially from Brazil, who at last found something of the rhythm they had lacked in earlier games. Fillol had to be alert to keep out some searching shots, but as it wore on, it became clear that this tense, winding game would need something exceptional to separate the protagonists, but neither would allow an opening to materialize. The second half rain could neither induce a slip nor cool the tempers and this bitty, irascible but intriguing contest ground to its inevitable, scoreless conclusion. It left Brazil still with the narrow advantage and with the Argentinians needing to beat Peru by more goals than Brazil might put past Poland in their final group games.

Poland's display against Peru that day showed that, whilst they may have lost some of their cutting edge, they were still an outfit that needed careful handling. For much of the game, their "hard-running forwards bombarded Peru's goal" and chance after chance was spurned by Deyna, Szarmach who had a first half goal disallowed, Boniek and Lato. In the 61st minute Szarmach headed Poland into the lead and it set up a tense final few minutes as Peru committed all to attack. In the heat of the moment and as it seemed Lato might break through in the last minute, "El Loco" Quiroga raced to the middle of the field to halt the danger with a rugby tackle. He was booked for his sin and it was all in vein, but it was a fine example of the colourful nature of this unconventional goalkeeper's play.

The last day of the second group stage decided who would make the final and Germany's defeat at the hands of Austria, their first such reversal since Hugo Meisl's "Wunderteam" had beaten them in 1931, ensured that they would not be there to defend their title. It also ensured that coach, Helmut Schön, retiring after the tournament, would step aside on an uncharacteristic low note, following 14 years of exemplary service in the national cause. Perhaps, the Austrians had been stung by some adverse notices they had received in the German press, because they were fired up from the start and were more than a little unlucky to go behind to Rummenigge's 19th minute opener. They controlled much of the first hour of play and drew level when Vogts deflected Walter Schachter's header into his own goal. It heralded a change in fortune and within five minutes Krankl's left foot volley put them in front. Two minutes later Holzenbein headed a second for Germany, though the Austrians pressed on. The Germans looked only spectres of the side that had straddled the world in 1974, and, as the game drew to its close, Krankl picked up the ball wide on the left. Showing what an artist he was, he beat both Rüssmann and Vogts "to push a shot past the advancing Maier for the spectacular winner." The victory meant that the Austrians could bow out of the 1978 World Cup with pride enhanced. The Germans merely bowed out.

Whilst the Austrians were teaching the Germans a lesson, a mammoth struggle was developing in Buenos Aires between Italy and the Netherlands, in the game that would determine the group's fate. Italy dominated much of the first half, but were often frustrated by the type of tactics normally associated with themselves. The Dutch were allowed to get away with much that was unethical and by half-time Italy had only a single goal lead to show for their superiority, an own goal, scored by Brandts whose attempt to knock the ball from the feet of Bettega to his goalkeeper went horribly wrong. To compound the error, he collided with his keeper, injuring him so badly he had to be replaced by Jan Jongbloed. The Italians were unable to advance their cause further and late in the half came one of the game's turning points, the booking of Bettega for a foul on Rensenbrinck. It meant that he would miss the final, should Italy get there. It sapped him of some of his determination and, as his game waned, so did his team. Then the substitution of Claudio Sala for Franco Causio distorted Italy's shape, and they were never the same force in the second half. They allowed the Dutch to come back at them and the combination of strong-arm intimidation and assured football skills proved irresistible. Brandts made amends for his first half blunder when he collected the ball some three yards outside the area and "cracked a wonderful shot past Zoff." There was no turning back and the Dutch secured their place in the final in the 75th minute when Haan received a sideways free kick and hammered a thunderous drive that screeched into the goal.

Controversially, the Group B games that would decide who would meet the Dutch in the final had been scheduled for different times. Brazil's game against Poland would have finished by the time Argentina took the field against Peru and knowing exactly what they had to do gave the host nation a decided and unfair advantage. (See Argentina v Peru profile on page 292). It was down to Brazil to score as many as they could, but it was not easy against a buoyant Poland, spurred on by the cheers of the virulently anti-Brazil partisanship of the 44,000 crowd. They had it all against them and yet took the lead in the 12th minute when Nelinho "curved a superb free kick round the Polish wall and past the diving Kukla." Zico had already retired injured and the goal roused the Poles to counter Brazilian cunning with their own sparkling energy. Yet, whilst their approach play was classy, their finishing was abysmal and it was not until the 44th minute that they equalized. Deyna broke into the area and, with three defenders closing in, squeezed the ball to Lato, who netted through the melée. The Poles continued to dominate and squander their chances into the second half, and paid the price in the 57th minute. Against the run of play, Mendonca hit a speculative shot against the bar and the ball fell nicely for Roberto to side-foot home. Five minutes later, Roberto scored his second to secure the win, but even then the Poles might have saved it had they put away the chances they made in the closing minutes. Gorgon was especially guilty, shooting wide from only two yards. It was not to be and Brazil's victory, of course, set up one of the most amazing games in World Cup history. It also set up one of the best of finals, pitting the best from the Old and New Worlds, but before it came the 3rd/4th place play-off.

Tradition had often rendered this tame and meaningless, but this game broke the dismal sequence and produced "a good and interesting match that for a period contained some of the cleverest football and the best finishing seen in the tournament." It was a largely sleepy first half of careful, efficient football that had Italy begin brightly, fade in the middle as the Brazilians took the initiative, and then finish strongly. They took the lead, somewhat against the run of play, in the 38th minute with Franco Causio's headed goal and the pace began to pick up. Both Causio and Rossi ought to have scored in those last seven minutes of the half and had they done so, there would have been no way back for Brazil. However, Brazil still had a lifeline and, when Rivelino came on as a second half substitute, the match turned emphatically in their favour. As one reporter noted, "it was a delight to see this swarthy, sinister figure take hold of the situation", and within minutes Brazil had equalized with a stunning goal that came out of nowhere. Nelinho, out on the right-wing, suddenly unleashed a shot of such velocity and swerve that it gave Zoff absolutely no chance. Within ten minutes the game was over, when Rivelino's masterful cross field pass was met by Mendonca. He knocked the ball down to Dirceu who let fly a long-range effort "of breathtaking power" to seal the win and the third place. Brazil had come good in the end, whilst the Italians, often promising much, had been found lacking at crucial moments, both in this game and in the tournament at large.

With the tense, volatile, irascible, fascinating final giving the crown to the home team (see Argentina v Holland profile on page 295 and Mario Kempes profile on page 288), the tournament that might not have been produced the only result acceptable to a nation of football fanatics. And so the "pain of over a half-century of humiliation was released in 120 minutes of vibrant football." Yet within this historian's comment can be sensed the word that more than any other sums up Argentina '78 - "pressure". It came from several quarters, appeared in different guises, but it was always present: pressure from the terraces, from the audiences back home, from the media, the press and TV, from sponsors, from players, from managers. As Helmut Schön said at the time: "The World Cups of 1958 and 1962 were garden parties compared with what is now involved... The increase in pressure seems continuous from one competition to the next. In 1966 it was already terrific, in 1970 it was worse, in 1974 still more terrible and now it is almost completely out of hand." Few were better placed to understand the reality than he.

With pressure (always in collusion with its ally, money) comes expectation, and then fear, and its effect upon the game of football is immense. It discourages players from expressing their artistry and teams their natural fluency, as caution replaces daring and games are closed down in the attempt to reduce the risk of error. In reviewing the game between Brazil and the USSR in the 1982 finals, one reporter noted that it contained more moments of invention and flair than the whole of Argentina 1978. The point is valid enough. Argentina's World Cup did contain games of class and excitement, but too often the games were examples of cool, clinical efficiency, not dull, but not charismatic either. "This is the age of the artisan", exclaimed Hungary's veteran coach, Lajos Baroti, and Argentina epitomized that notion. The pressures were too great, the prospect of failure too terrible and players tailored their games accordingly. The problem is that when teams approach their play in this frame of mind, entertainment, and sometimes even football itself, are easily sacrificed. By 1978, the World Cup had been truly shed of any innocence it had yet preserved.

Pressure is one explanation for this phenomenon, but there were others. Some of the teams appearing in the finals were clearly past their best and others did not live up to expectation. Most obvious were Germany and Brazil, their camps rent by division, and the veteran Poles. The Scots, the Spanish and the Mexicans also disappointed to a greater or lesser degree. Added to this was a quality of refereeing that was often too ready to bow to the prejudices of the crowds. Sergio Gonella's handling of the final is the oft-quoted example of the worst of this, but others, like Antonio Garrido and Jean Durlach proved too weak, ineffective or easily swayed. They allowed players to get away with acts of callous cynicism and always to the detriment of the games in question.

Yet, not all aspects of the 1978 finals were negative. Argentina had its highs as well as its lows. There seemed to be a greater element of unpredictability about the form shown by teams and the results they

After the final, Dutch manager, Ernst Heppel branded the Italian referee, Sergio Gonella, a "one-sided incompetent" and added: "It was just ridiculous. We will never have a better chance of winning the Cup. Argentina were for the cinema - just actors."

Before 1978 there had only ever been 19 0-0 draws in 48 years of World Cup football. In 1978 there were six goalless games.

gained, and it all added to the atmosphere. World Cups are always the better when supposedly more accomplished teams crash or weaker teams triumph. Certainly, the Scots stand high on the list of the unpredictables, but so too do Iran and Tunisia, whose overall performances were among the really pleasant surprises of the tournament. The notion that there are no easy games in the World Cup was beginning to have valid currency. Praise also needs to be extended to France, possibly the one team of true flair, whose early exit left a genuine question mark over the rest of the tournament and gave supporters the feeling that something worthy had been removed. Speculation on their likely impact is pointless. Argentina took the trophy and who can say they did not deserve it? They were good enough to fight their way to the final and bettered one of the best in the world when they got there. Argentina's may not have been the most memorable of World Cups, but it ended in a blaze of passion and glory, and for this alone it will never be forgotten.

Karl-Heinz Rummenigge

West Germany

Honours: Runner-up 1982 and 1986; 2nd Round 1978
Played: 1978, 1982 and 1986

Games 19
Goals 9

A dejected Karl-Heinz Rummenigge after the 1986 World Cup Final in Mexico.

Former bank clerk, Karl-Heinz Rummenigge burst onto the scene as Franz Beckenbauer's time as Germany's top player was ending and he became one of the most influential players of the 1980s. He was 18 when Bayern Munich bought him in June 1974 for £4,500, but when they sold him to Internazionale in 1984 for £2,000,000 he had become Germany's most expensive player. It is a measure of the value he had added to the Bayern team and sets him out as one of the buys of the century.

Born in Westphalia on 25th September 1955, he was playing as an amateur for Borussia Lippstadt when Bayern stepped in. Playing alongside Beckenbauer, he won the German title and the European Cup in his first season. His international call up came soon after and he was a member of the squad that travelled to Argentina. They had high hopes and although Rummenigge was not used in the first game, he was given his first taste of World Cup action in the second and proved to be a sensation, scoring two of Germany's six goals. He was included in all Germany's remaining games, but could not find the net again until he scored one of the team's two goals in the 3-2 defeat by Holland. By German standards it had been a poor tournament, but Rummenigge had established himself in attack alongside Fischer and Dieter Müller. The West Germans got back to winning ways two years later, lifting the European Nations Cup with Rummenigge playing as a deep lying forward linking midfield with attack. In the final, against a strong Belgian side, he set up the winning goal for Hrubesch and his performances earned him the Player of Tournament award. He was further honoured that year when he became European Footballer of the Year, taking it again in 1981.

His name was firmly etched on the international scene when he travelled as team captain to Spain in 1982, where a persistent knee injury dogged his play and spoiled the series for him. He could do nothing to stop the shock opening defeat by Algeria, but hit back with a vengeance in the second game when he scored a hat trick. Impaired by his knee, he was replaced by Lothar Matthäus part way through third match, played a full game against England and was again brought off in the victory over Spain. Rummenigge was left on the bench at the start of the semi-final, but came on and helped turn the game, scoring the all-important equalizer. Only half-fit, he started the final, but he was unable to keep up with the pace and was ultimately replaced.

Throughout the 1980s, the knee injury persisted, but Inter Milan kept faith with their purchase. After all, he had played 310 times for Bayern, scoring 162 goals. In 1986 he was a member of the West German team that travelled to Mexico, where the Germans made it to the final, his 19th and last appearance in the World Cup finals.

He gave a star performance and scored in the 73rd minute, but could not prevent a second consecutive defeat. By the time his international career ended, he had won 95 caps and scored 45 goals.

Rummenigge finished his club career with Swiss side, Servette, before he returned to Bayern as one of two vice-presidents. Today his concerns are more with the status of German clubs in Europe and the number of poor foreign recruits that are flooding the German league. In an interview on the web with World Soccer Page in 2000 he remarked: "We really have to watch out that we don't suffer another complete blowout in the UEFA Cup." (All Germany's representatives had gone out by the quarter-final stage that year). "Less German representatives in the European Cups will mean less revenue and mean that they will not be able to compete with the other clubs, either on a financial or sporting level. They don't come near the standard of foreigners that play in the Spanish, Italian or English leagues." His words express concerns for a game that he loves and for a nation he wants to see win the World Cup again. His pessimism was negated a little as Bayern won the European Champions League in 2001.

Mario Alberto Kempes   Argentina

Honours: Winner 1978; 2nd Round 1974 and 1982   **Games 18**
Played: 1974, 1978 and 1982   **Goals 6**

Mario Kempes is tackled by Belgium's Frank Vercauteren in 1982.

With his long hair flowing behind him, "El Matador" Kempes floated over a sea of tickertape and delighted his fans as he spun and swerved past bullish defenders to thrust a sword into the heart of opponents' goal. He was aggressive, had great balance and he was always a team player. National coach, César Luis Menotti, said after the 1978 World Cup finals: "Kempes plays consistently for the team's attack and never lets his team mates down. He is the pride of Argentina." It was mighty praise for a player who, as a boy, was rejected by one of Argentina's top teams and who made his name playing in another country.

Kempes was born on 15th July 1954 in the small town of Bell Ville in the province of Córdoba. Like so many, he learned the game in the back streets of his hometown. His father, also Mario, had played for local side Leones in the Bell Ville league and chose not to become a professional. His son was more determined. At the age of 14, Kempes joined Talleres in the Bell Ville league as a striker and, one year later, moved to Biblioteca Bell. By 1971, he had come to the attention of many of the district's bigger sides, having scored 46 goals and winning a league title in 1970. When he went for a trial with state league side Instituto Córdoba, he did not want Biblioteca to know and he used the false name Mario Aquillera. He played in a friendly against Argentinos Central and scored all four goals, but, having been rejected by Boca Juniors, he signed for Instituto in March 1972, under his real name. That year Instituto won the Córdoba championship and earned the right to play in the national league. They made their first appearance against Newell's Old Boys in October 1973 and Kempes scored his fist goal four days later against River Plate in a 3-1 defeat. In 1974 Rosario Central came in with an offer. They were looking for reinforcements to strengthen their challenge for the national title and opened negotiations with Instituto after Kempes impressed in a pre-season friendly by scoring the only goal of the game. Instituto were reluctant to sell their star player, but after two weeks of haggling Rosario came in with the cash and Kempes signed. From his first game in February 1974 to his last against Newell's in August 1976, he scored exactly 100 goals.

Having played for the national youth team and receiving positive reviews from football critics across the nation, Kempes was given his full international debut against Bolivia in 1973 at the age of 19. He was in the squad in 1974 when Argentina travelled to West Germany and played his part in all of Argentina's games, but failed to score. However, he had done enough to catch the eye of Spanish club, Valencia. They followed his progress over the next seaason and long, protracted negotiations, in which Kempes was fully involved, having taken control of his own financial affairs, a deal was struck in 1976. In his first full season he scored 24 goals, the highest in the

Spanish league for ten years. The following season he hit 28, the highest number of league goals since Di Stefano got 31 in 1957. He won three league titles and a European Cup-Winners Cup during a stay that lasted until 1980.

Undoubtedly his best year in was 1978. He was the only foreign-based player in Menotti's World Cup team and, by the end of the tournament, was its star. Wearing the number 10 shirt, he was what was needed to add the physical presence that had been lacking four years earlier. An injury to Luque meant that Menotti switched his roles, asking Kempes to join the attack from deep midfield. He failed to score in the first round, but as the second round got under way El Matador became unstoppable. Many questioned the manner of the victory over Peru that took Argentina to the final, but no one could deny a Kempes-inspired Argentina their ultimate victory. He put Argentina ahead after 38 minutes, but it was in the extra-time that his real class showed. Speaking about the tournament some years later he recalled: "Today, the 1978 World Cup is still a wonderful footballing memory for me. We had to battle though, especially in the first round, but each time we were down, we picked ourselves up again as a team. And we had tremendous understanding between ourselves. It was as if we were on another planet from everyone else. I think the secret of our success was perhaps that the Argentinian authorities let Cesar Menotti make all the decisions on his own. We didn't feel the slightest bit of pressure." Kempes finished the series as top scorer and as Player of the Tournament.

1980 brought a £1m move to River Plate and despite a serious injury suffered against Uruguay, he still scored the vital goal as they raced to the 1981 national title. Ironically, River Plate finished ahead of rivals Boca Juniors who's attack was spearheaded by the man who would eventually take over his number 10 shirt, Diego Maradona. A serious devaluation of the Argentine currency meant that River Plate could no longer afford his wages and in 1982 he moved back to Valencia. His career continued to be plagued by injury, but he was still part of the national set up as Argentina prepared to defend their title in 1982. The core of the side comprised of the veterans of 1978 reinforced by Maradona and Ramón Díaz. It was not a success. A poor start was followed by a worse second round and, by the time he was substituted against Brazil, he had failed to hit the net and his international career came to an end. He had made 18 World Cup appearances and scored six goals.

In 1984, he moved to another Spanish side, Hercules and despite accusations that he was finished, his goals kept them in the first division. The most celebrated was that scored in the last game of the season against Real Madrid in the Bernabeu to seal a 1-0 victory. There then followed a period in Austria, with Vienna and Austria Salzburg, before he returned to Spain. In April 1993 Valencia honoured him with a testimonial and Kempes scored three goals against PSV Eindhoven. By 1995 he was back in South America and was given a testimonial by Rosario Central. The Argentinian government asked him to run the Provincial School of Football along side Luque. He was now 41, but still took the field as a defender for Chilean side, Fernández Vial, playing only home games because of his commitments in Argentina. 1996 he was player-manager of Indonesia and in January of 1997 he became a manger in Albania. Political troubles, however, forced him to leave. Since then he has appeared as a TV presenter and has been linked with coaching and technical directorships in Venezuela, Argentina and Kuwait. He has also served as manager of top Bolivian side, the Strongest.

Grzegorz Lato   **Poland**

Honours: 3rd Place 1974,1982; 2nd Round 1978   **Games 20**
Played: 1974, 1978 and 1982   **Goals 10**

Grzegorz Lato (right) with Zej Szarmach.

Grzegorz Lato was often described has having "flights of fancy". Whether this refers to play that was often reckless and undisciplined or to the fact that he was also dashing and triumphant is open to debate. What is true is that those "flights of fancy" always made the game interesting. This balding, squat and stocky winger became a midfield general and was noted for his skill and excellent acceleration. His presence in the crack side of the 1970s and 80s helped to bring the most successful period in Poland's soccer history.

Born on 8th April 1950, the majority of Lato's club career was spent with Stal Mielec in Poland. It brought him two Polish league titles in 1973 and 1976, but he is more widely known for his exploits on the international battlefield. He made his international debut in 1971 against Spain and, when he played for Poland for the last time 13 years later in 1984, he had made 104 appearances and scored 46 goals. His greatest success came in the 1972 Munich Olympic Games when Poland took the gold medal and it was again in Munich two years later that he produced the most outstanding football of his career.

On their way to the finals of the 1974 World Cup, Lato hit the knock-out blow as Poland dramatically eliminated England. Yet, his place in the squad was not assured. He had impressed on a tour of the USA and Canada, and in the game against England, but it was not until Lubanski, Poland's record scorer, dropped out that Lato was given a more permanent place. He scored twice as the Poles started the tournament with an excellent, but surprising defeat of Argentina. He got another two as Poland hammered Haiti, a game before which Haitian coach, Antoine Tassy, had stated: "We will beat Poland - and I mean it. We know how to handle them. We beat Poland U23 team in Haiti recently and four of that side are in the national side now." Tassy was sacked after the tournament. Lato then scored two of Poland's second round goals and got the all-important winner in the 3rd/4th play-off to take his total for the tournament to seven. The significance of that goal is that, in the six World Cups that have taken place since, no one has managed to score more than six. In 1978, with the backbone of the 1974 side still intact and with the addition of Lubanski and Zbigniew Boniek, Poland made it to the finals, but Lato failed to produce the form of four years earlier and only scored twice.

On reaching his 30th birthday in 1980 and as a reward for services to club and country, the Communist authorities allowed him to leave Poland and he chose a more lucrative career with KCS Lokeren in the Belgian league. This was followed by a spell in Mexico with Atlante before he eventually retired from the game. This was not before he took part in his third World Cup finals in Spain. By now Lato had moved to midfield, but his influence was in no way diminished. He dictated and directed play, bringing the best out of Boniek and Szarmach in front of him. It was not an easy tournament, but with Lato driving forward whenever possible, the Poles took third place for the second time. He scored his only goal of the tournament against Peru to make him one of a small group of elite players who have reached double figures in the World Cup finals.

Daniel Alberto Passarella   Argentina

Honours:
Player: Winner 1978; 2nd Round 1982
Manager: Quarter-finals 1998
Played: 1978 and 1982
Manager 1998

Games 12
Goals 3

Daniel Passarella with the World Cup amid chaotic scenes after the 1978 final.

Daniel Passarella was the inspirational captain that drove his team to victory in the 1978 World Cup final. A powerhouse central defender, who could also play at left-back, he was noted for his ability to motivate. His surging runs into midfield were a major feature of his game and he had an extraordinarily powerful shot. Despite a lack of height his score rate, particularly with headers from corners, was second to none. He was a constant threat to opposing defences, putting them under severe pressure and in 298 appearances for River Plate he scored an unusual 99 times.

Born on 25th May 1953 at Chacabuca, Buenos Aires, the teenage Passarella played for a succession of minor clubs with little success. He was on the verge of quitting the game when his father persuaded him to persist and he signed for Sarmiento de Junin, a Division C side, where he was taken under the wing of Raúl Hernández. Hernández restored his confidence and turned him into a competent left-sided player. Successful performances in this position brought him to the attention of River Plate who signed him for a considerable 18 million pesos in January 1974. The coach there, Pipo Rossi, put great faith in the bold, adventurous Passarella and gave him his debut on the 14th April against Rosario Central. He scored his first, and the team's winning goal, on 28th July in a 3-2 victory over Argentinos Juniors. By October and aged only 21, he was team captain.

Passarella's career took off when he was given his international debut shortly after the national side had returned from their ill-fated sojourn to the 1974 World Cup finals. New coach, Menotti admired his leadership qualities and the fact that he had by now perfected his aerial ability and his thumping left foot drive. He made the 25 year old Passarella captain of the side that represented Argentina in 1978. Playing at centre-back, he never missed an opportunity to surge forward and on the 25th June "El Gran Capitán" led his men onto the pitch of his home ground, Estadio Monumental and played his best game of the tournament, launching four attacks in the first half alone. His reading of the game and constant encouragement drove his team on and, fittingly, he became the first Argentinian to lift the World Cup trophy. Menotti later called him the "Argentinian Beckenbauer". In the 30 games Argentina played before the 1982 World Cup finals Passarella top scored with 13 goals. He had another excellent tournament, showing that he was still world class, but those around him could not match him and they went out at the second stage. Aged 33, Passarella travelled to Mexico in 1986, but injury kept him sidelined and brought the curtain down on a partnership with Menotti that had been a major force. In all, he won 69 caps and scored 24 goals.

He moved to Fiorentina in Italy in 1982 and took up an offer from Internazionale shortly after the World Cup. He enjoyed a period of outstanding success, scoring 33 goals in 153 appearances in Serie A. In 1988 he moved back to River Plate where, after two seasons, he retired. They immediately installed him as coach and he led them to four Argentinian championships. In 1994, after the World Cup finals, he took over from Alfio Basile as national team coach. He was a stickler for discipline and became noted for his forthright views, particularly on homosexuality. He didn't like players to wear long hair or earrings and controversially refused to pick Claudio Caniggia and Fernando Redondo until they had theirs cut. Redondo refused and did not travel to France in 1998. Passarella led Argentina to the quarter-finals, but stepped down after the tournament. He then became coach of neighbours Uruguay in their bid to reach the 2002 World Cup finals, but stepped down complaining that he did not have his players long enough before games. When he discovered that the Nacional player, Vincente Sanchez, had gone to Chile to play a Copa Libertadores match instead of on a short European tour with the squad in February 2001, he resigned, citing "differences with the directors of Nacional," as the reason. "I want to apologise to the people of Uruguay but the way things were, I think it was necessary," he said.

Argentina 6 : Peru 0

Before the final second phase Group B game with Argentina, Peru's coach, Marcos Calderón, had declared: "We will not give in. We'll be on the pitch to beat Argentina." It was the sort of fighting talk to be expected from a World Cup manager before an important match, but the circumstances surrounding this one made his remarks all the more poignant. It was the final group game and, although Peru could not reach the final, Argentina could, but only if they won by four clear goals. So, Argentina stepped out into the cauldron of passion that was the New Rosario Stadium, knowing exactly what they had to do.

Given the enormity of the task facing them, it was no surprise to see the Argentinians going straight onto the attack and Peru's custodian, Ramón Quiroga was in early action, coming out quickly to prevent Luque getting in a shot after Passarella's neat chip put him through. Yet, it was Peru who came closest to scoring in these opening exchanges. In the fifth minute, Muñante "sped clear on the right and drew Fillol before thumping then ball off the inside of a post." The Peruvians had, it seemed, every intention of making a keen contest out of the game and it spurred Argentina into a series of frenzied attacks. For the next quarter of an hour, Peru's goal was under constant siege, but their defence clung on stubbornly to keep out the light blue waves that crashed against it. Almost inevitably, though, it began to wither. It was breached once, then twice and then it finally caved in completely.

Argentina's first goal came after 20 minutes of play and was made by a clever interchange between Passarella and Kempes. The latter "collected a pass on the edge of the Peruvian area, carved his way through the defence, and calmly placed a left foot shot past Quiroga." It was Kempes at his best and gave much encouragement to his team, but Argentina needed much more. From the kick off, they resumed their onslaught, Luque hit the post, Ortíz crashed a shot against the bar and Peru turned to increasingly desperate tackles to stem the flood. Quasada was booked in the 35th minute for a foul on Ortíz, but they somehow, miraculously, survived. They did not concede a second until two minutes before half-time. Passarella's shot had been pushed wide by a diving Quiroga and from the resulting corner, Alberto Tarantini "burst into a packed Peruvian penalty area to bullet home a great header." When the teams went in for the break, Argentina had half completed their task.

The first half had seen the home team throw everything at the job, but they had barely managed to prize the door ajar. In the second, with "an astonishing show of attacking football", they not only kicked the door in, but smashed a gaping hole in the wall as well. The inundation began in the 49th minute, when they won a free kick on the right. Bertoni lofted it into the area, "Kempes chested it down to Luque, took the return pass, and blasted the ball home." The finish was as sharp and clinical as a surgeon's scalpel and within a minute Luque had dived full length to head a fourth goal. What had begun a like a wake, now became a party, with Argentina's forwards lining up to get in on the celebration. In the 66th minute Ortíz made a sizzling solo run before teeing up René

Houseman for the fifth score and ten minutes later, Luque made the final score 6-0 with a "fantastic piece of finishing."

Such an emphatic victory caused several, especially among jealous rivals, to question the probity of the result. There were claims that Argentina's ruling military junta had bribed the Peruvians to throw the game. (There were equally improbable allegations that the Brazilians had bribed Peru to play well!) A very sharp finger of suspicion was pointed at Peru's goalkeeper, who had been born in Argentina. It is the nature of the modern game that such claims and counter-claims are bandied about. Yet, the plain fact was that, on the night, the Argentinians were simply too good, too powerful and too ruthless for a Peruvian team, whose own World Cup was effectively over. They had done well to keep the score down for as long as they did, but once Argentina began to turn the screw in the second half and the goals began to flow, Peruvian heads began to drop. There was little they could have done in the circumstances.

Argentina's supporters had no doubts about the legality of the result, nor would they have cared. The relief that greeted the win was substantial and triggered the sort of celebrations normally reserved for a victory in the final itself. Fans were out on the streets into the early hours of the morning, dancing and singing, and even police cars drove around sounding their horns and flying national flags. As one European reporter noted, even "innocent people not wearing Argentina colours were in danger of their lives.' "It was", he said, "the most ardent display of soccer loyalty I have seen anywhere."

Scotland 3 : Holland 2

Scotland 2 : Holland 3
Holland's Rene van de Kerkhof under pressure from Scotland's Martin Buchan.

When the Scots walked out on to the pitch at Mendoza on 11th June, 1978, nobody gave them a chance. Scotland's disastrous World Cup campaign would, according to the Daily Record, "go into Scottish soccer history as the most monumentally mismanaged, stupidly executed and arrogantly enacted three-game junket of all time." The hopes of Ally MacLeod's "Tartan Army" had been sunk first by a disaster and then a humiliation and now they were up against Holland, one of the most formidable football forces in the world, and needing to win by three clear goals if they were to reach the second round. It was a mountainous task. When Dutch coach, Ernst Heppel spoke before the game of facing "a team low on confidence, low on form and everything is going our way", he was not exaggerating. "I doubt even if your fighting spirit can rise high enough now to give us any serious problems", he concluded.

However, both teams had made changes in personnel that were to have important repercussions during the match and which were to ultimately affect its outcome. Dutch qualification for the next phase was by no means certain and to accomodate Johnny Rep as an extra man up front, Arie Haan was dropped, leaving Holland light in midfield. The Scots, on the other hand, had done what critics had said ought to have been done from the start and included Graeme Souness in the starting line up. His dogged tenacity, his persistence and courageous leadership qualities were to provide the drive and sense of purpose they had hitherto lacked.

Scotland's new found dynamics were very much in evidence in the opening stages, when the Dutch were prepared to lie low and allow the Scots to take the initiative. As early as the fifth minute, Souness centred the ball and, as the Dutch defence watched Jordan, Bruce Rioch stole in to head against the bar. The Scots made all the early running and the Dutch resorted to the darker side of their game, delivering some hefty tackles to try to upset Scotland's revival. One such incident, in the tenth minute, saw Johannes Neeskens lunge at Archie Gemmill, hurt himself and was stretchered off. It further unbalanced the Dutch team and three minutes later the Scots had the ball in the net. Ruud Krol mistimed a header, sending the ball backwards, and Kenny Dalglish raced in to place the ball beyond the goalkeeper. The Austrian referee, though, felt that he had used an elbow to gain an unfair advantage and disallowed it. Had it stood, it would have been no less that the Scots deserved.

So far the balance of play had been very much in Scotland's favour, but in the 34th minute disaster struck. Willy van der Kerkhof knocked a through ball to Rep, who moved swiftly in on goal, slipping Stuart Kennedy. He tried to retrieve the situation, tackled him from behind and Rep went down. It was more mistimed than it was dirty, but the referee gave the penalty and Rob Rensenbrinck hammered the Dutch into the lead. It was a serious blow. "For 10 minutes, the Scots teetered on the brink of total collapse", until just before half-time, Souness found the touch that rallied his men and "restored morale and hope with one superb cross". It was a classic ball to the far post. Jordan leaped high to head it down and Dalglish "lashed the ball into the net." Just before half-time was the perfect time to equalize and gave the Scots the interval to reassess the situation.

They came out for the second half with a renewed determination and it brought immediate dividends. Going straight onto the offensive and with Souness in the thick of things, he was hacked down by hard man Kroll and the referee pointed to the spot for the second time. Gemmill placed the ball, surveyed the situation and calmly tucked the ball into the left hand corner. Having gone in front, and brimming with confidence, the Scots embarked upon the best period of football they had yet played. The Dutch tried to take the sting out of the game by slowing it down, but the Scots just kept going at them, and behind much of it was Souness, orchestrating, encouraging and leading by example. The "timing of his passes, along with his sense of openings, complemented the scurry and bustle of Gemmill and Hartford", and the Dutch were made to look like the underdogs. "The Dutch didn't panic, but they certainly looked bothered and, at times, bewildered", under the blue onslaught. In the 68th minute, their enterprise was crowned by one of those rare moments of pure genius, a flash of intuitive adroitness that leaves a crowd wondering whether they had really witnesses what they had just seen. Dalglish was working his way forwards and, as a challenge went in, the ball broke loose to Gemmill outside the penalty area. He "wriggled his way past three white-shirted, unbelieving Dutch defenders, drew the keeper and scored with the loveliest chip you ever saw."

The Scots were now 3-1 up, firing on all fronts and suddenly the tartan dream looked a distinct possibility. For three minutes the Scottish nation lived its World Cup fantasy and the Dutch their own pang of doubt, until Johnny Rep broke through the defence and hit a 25 yard piledriver that "went past Rough like a bullet." A 3-1 scoreline might have become 4-1, but there was no way that 3-2 could become 5-2. The whole brave, fanciful, hopeless illusion was over and the Scots went out of their third successive World Cup on goal difference. At least, this time they went out with heads high, having garnered some dignity from the nightmare that had been Argentina '78.

"At least it had been a marvellous funeral", was how the Guardian began its match report. The football world had witnesses as fervid a spectacle as seen in any World Cup and were left with the same gnawing sentiments as the Dutch coach. "I was not surprised at seeing Scotland play so well", he had said. "It was just a surprise that they had not done so earlier." As the Daily Record noted: "Scotland were as good as they have been awful in the shambling games against Peru and Iran," but perhaps the last word ought to go to one of the long-suffering Scottish fans. "It was a typical Scottish performance. We seem to be the only nation that takes pride in defeat."

Argentina 3 : Holland 1
The World Cup Final

Argentina 3 : Holland 1
Mario Kempes (10) helps defend Argentina's lead.

Few World Cup finals can compete with that of 1978 for pure tension and high drama. It was a game that promised much and did not fail to satisfy. It was tough, physical football, absorbing and exciting, "an intense drama set in a theatre of sound and colour", as one reporter described it. The sparring began even before the game began, as the Dutch came out onto the field at the appointed time and had to endure an intimidating five minutes from the baying crowd before their opponents appeared. They came out to a deafening roar and a cascade of ticker tape that left both ends of the pitch looking as if it had been hit by a snow storm. It unsettled the Dutch and their discomfort deepened as the Argentinians protested about a light plastic covering that René van der Kerkhof was wearing to protect a slight injury. The referee saw nothing wrong with it, but it delayed the kick off for ten minutes, to the annoyance of the Dutch.

When the match finally got underway, it became immediately clear what sort of a game it was going to be. As if to avenge the delay, the Dutch seemed tried to unsettle their foes with a series of ruthless tackles that were designed to intimidate. For a while it worked as the Dutch took the game to Argentina. After five minutes, Arie Haan floated a delightful free kick into the Argentinian box, which Rep headed marginally wide. The home team had their moments, too, with Luque, Bertoni and the outstanding Kempes a constant threat. Early on, Kempes sent a through pass to Bertoni, which split the defence in two and brought a shot that keeper Jongbloed struggled to hold. Yet, the ferocity of Dutch tackling threatened to undo their endeavour, bringing a series of free kicks that put them under enormous pressure and which brought a caution for Krol. After several missed opportunities, the deadlock was broken on 37 minutes and fittingly, by Kempes. Ardíles began a move down the left and got the ball to Luque, whose low cross found Kempes unmarked. He reacted quickest and the ball was in the net. The Dutch should have equalized shortly before half-time, but Rensenbrinck needed too much time and his shot was saved. The Dutch went into the break one down, but knew that they had given as good as they had got. It left all to play for.

The game continued the same way in the second and the Times noted that "no previous match had been accompanied by so many bitter tackles." The Dutch had much of the better of the play, but were unable to find the equalizer and with 30 minutes remaining the hapless Rep, for whom nothing had gone right, was replaced by Dirk Nanninga, a giant brought on to add weight to the attack. "I shall come on in the last 10 minutes and I shall take a goal", is what he had been confidently telling reporters before the game. In the last fifteen minutes, the Dutch piled on the pressure, but to no avail. Shot after shot, free kick after free kick, cross after cross, were all dealt with by a resolute Argentine defence that lacked subtlety, but not commitment. René van de Kerkhof, in particular, grew increasingly menacing as time drew on and with nine minutes to go, he beat the offside trap. From the right he lofted a cross into the area and Nanninga was there to head it home. It was a terrible body blow to the Argentinians and they almost lost it when Rensenbrinck hit the post in the dying seconds, but they stood firm and the game went into extra time.

"High tackles, elbows and the boot had all been used, but neither fair nor foul means could be said to belong entirely to one team", was the verdict of the Times. "Now stamina was the key." The players may have been tired, but extra time saw no let up in the relentless nature of the football being played. It was not football for the purist, but it was hard, compelling stuff. Poortvliet was booked for a savage assault on the legs of Kempes, but it was the Argentinian who really stunned the Dutch with a piece of brilliance. Bertoni, as lively as ever, picked out Kempes just outside the penalty area. With a dazzling run, he ripped through the Dutch defence, beat three players including the goalkeeper, before slotting the ball home. It was magnificent and sent the crowd into delirium. For the Dutch it was a mortal wound they never recovered from. Their tackles became increasingly desperate and the Argentinians made the most of it. The goal that sealed the victory came four minutes from time and, inevitably, Kempes was involved. He made a dashing run down the middle and flicked the ball to Bertoni, who made a quick return. Kempes chested the ball back into the path of Bertoni and he fired it into the net.

The final whistle saw the stadium erupt into a wild frenzy of emotion. Since they had lost the 1928 Olympic football final to the Uruguayans, Argentina had been waiting for this moment. They had defeated the best of the Europeans and could be truly regarded as world masters. For the Dutch it was another bitter disappointment. They were the greatest team never to have won the World Cup and joined Czechoslovakia and Hungary in an exclusive club - of teams that had played in two World Cup finals, but had never won one.

Statistics - Argentina 1978

GROUP ONE

Mar del Plata, June 2nd
Estadio Mar del Plata

2 (1) ITALY

Rossi 29, Zaccarelli 52

Zoff, Gentile, Bellugi, Scirea, Cabrini, Benetti, Tardelli, Antognoni (Zaccarelli), Causio, Rossi, Bettega.

1 (1) FRANCE

Lacombe 1

Bertrand-Demanes, Janvion, Bossis, Rio, Trésor, Michel, Dalger, Guillou, Lacombe (Berdoll), Platini, Six (Rouyer).

Referee: Nicolae Rainea (Romania)
Attendance: 42.373

Buenos Aires, June 2nd
Estadio Monumental

2 (1) ARGENTINA

Luque 15, Bertoni 83

Fillol, Olguín, Passarella, L.Galvan, Tarantini, Ardíles, Gallego, Valencia (Alonso), Houseman (Bertoni), Luque, Kempes.

1 (1) HUNGARY

Csapo 10

Gujdar, Török (Martos), Kereki, Kocsis, J.Tóth, Nyilasi (RED), Zombori, Pinter, Csapo, Torocsik (RED), Nagy.

Referee: Antonio Garrido (Portugal)
Attendance: 77.000

Mar del Plata, June 6th
Estadio Mar del Plata

3 (2) ITALY

Rossi 34, Bettega 36, Benetti 60

Zoff, Gentile, Bellugi, Scirea, Cabrini (Cuccureddu), Benetti, Tardelli, Antognoni, Causio, Rossi, Bettega (Graziani).

1 (0) HUNGARY

A. Tóth (pen)81

Meszaros, Martos, Kereki, Kocsis, J. Tóth, Pusztai, Zombori, Pinter, Csapo, Fazekas (Halasz), Nagy (A. Tóth).

Referee: Ramon Baretto Ruiz (Uruguay)
Attendance: 32.000

Buenos Aires, June 6th
Estadio Monumental

2 (1) ARGENTINA

Passarella (pen)45, Luque 72

Fillol, Olguín, Passarella, L.Galvan, Tarantini, Ardíles, Gallego, Valencia (Alonso) (Ortíz), Houseman, Luque, Kempes.

1 (0) FRANCE

Platini 60

Bertrand-Demanes (Baratelli), Battiston, Bossis, López, Trésor, Michel, Rocheteau, Bathenay, Lacombe, Platini, Six.

Referee: Jean Dubach (Switzerland)
Attendance: 77.216

Buenos Aires, June 10th
Estadio Monumental

0 (0) ARGENTINA

Fillol, Olguín, Passarella, L.Galvan, Tarantini, Ardíles, Gallego, Valencia, Bertoni, Ortíz (Houseman), Kempes.

1 (0) ITALY

Bettega 67

Zoff, Gentile, Bellugi (Cuccureddu), Scirea, Cabrini, Benetti, Tardelli, Antognoni (Zaccarelli), Causio, Rossi, Bettega.

Referee: Abraham Klein (Israel)
Attendance: 77.260

Mar del Plata, June 10th
Estadio Mar del Plata

3 (3) FRANCE

López 22, Berdoll 37, Rocheteau 42

Dropsy, Bracci, Petit, Janvion, Berdoll, López, Trésor, Rouyver, Rocheteau (Six), Bathenay, Papi (Platini).

1 (1) HUNGARY

Zombori 41

Gujdar, Martos, Kereki, Balint, J. Tóth, Pusztai, Zombori, Pinter, Nyilasi, Torocsik, Nagy (Csapo).

Referee: Arnaldo Cesar Coelho (Brazil)
Attendance: 28.000

	P	W	D	L	F	A	Pts
Italy	3	3	0	0	6	2	6
Argentina	3	2	0	1	4	3	4
France	3	1	0	2	5	5	2
Hungary	3	0	0	3	3	8	0

Daniel, Super Mario and the Dutch Lions - Argentina 1978

GROUP TWO

Buenos Aires, June 1st
Estadio Monumental

0 (0) POLAND

Tomaszewski, Szymanowski, Makulewicz, Gorgon, Nawalka, Zmuda, Deyna, Lubanski (Boniek), Lato, Masztaler (Kasperczak), Szarmach.

0 (0) WEST GERMANY

Maier, Vogts, Rüssmann, Kaltz, Zimmermann, Bonhof, H.Müller, Flohe, Abramczik, Fischer, Beer.

Referee: Angel Coerezza (Argentina)
Attendance: 77.000

Rosario, June 2nd - Estadio Rosario

3 (0) TUNISIA

Kaabi 55, Ghommidh 80, Dhouieb 87

Naili, Dhouieb, M.Labidi, Kaabi, Jebali, Ghommidh, Lahzami (K.Labidi), Ben Rehaiem, Akid, Dhiab, R.Ben Aziza (Karoui).

1 (1) MEXICO

Vázquez-Ayala (pen)44

Reyes, Martínez, Teña, Ramos, Vázquez-Ayala, Mendizabal (Gómez), de la Torre, Cuellar, Rangel, Isiordia, Sánchez.

Referee: John Gordon (Scotland)
Attendance: 25.000

Rosario, June 6th - Estadio Rosario

1 (1) POLAND

Lato 44

Tomaszewski, Szymanowski, Makulewicz, Gorgon, Nawalka, Zmuda, Deyna, Lubanski (Boniek), Lato, Kasperczak, Szarmach (Iwan).

0 (0) TUNISIA

Naili, Dhouieb, M.Labidi, Kaabi, Gasmi, Jebali, Ghommidh, Lahzami, Ben Rehaiem, Akid, Dhiab.

Referee: Angel Martínez (Spain)
Attendance: 15.000

Cordoba, June 6th - Estadio Cordoba

6 (4) WEST GERMANY

D.Müller 14, H.Müller 30, Rummenigge 37, 73, Flohe 40, 90

Maier, Vogts, Rüssmann, Dietz, Kaltz, Bonhof, H.Müller, Flohe, Rummenigge, Fischer, D.Müller.

0 (0) MEXICO

Reyes (Soto), Martínez, Teña, Ramos, Vázquez-Ayala, Mendizabal, de la Torre, Cuellar, Rangel, López-Zarza (Lugo), Sánchez.

Referee: Faruk Bouzo (Syria)
Attendance: 46.000

Cordoba, June 10th - Estadio Cordoba

0 (0) TUNISIA

Naili, Dhouieb, M.Labidi, Kaabi, Gasmi, Jebali, Ghommidh, Lahzami, Ben Rehaiem, Akid (R.Ben Aziza), Dhiab.

0 (0) WEST GERMANY

Maier, Vogts, Rüssmann, Dietz, Kaltz, Bonhof, H.Müller, Flohe, Rummenigge, Fischer, D.Müller.

Referee: Cesar Orosco Guerrero (Peru)
Attendance: 35.000

Rosario, June 10th - Estadio Rosario

3 (1) POLAND

Boniek 43, 84, Deyna 56

Tomaszewski, Szymanowski, Rudy (Makulewicz), Gorgon, Masztaler, Zmuda, Deyna, Iwan (Lubanski), Boniek, Lato, Kasperczak.

1 (0) MEXICO

Rangel 52

Soto, Gómez, Cisneros, Cardeñas (Mendizabal), Vázquez-Ayala, de la Torre, Cuellar, Rangel, Ortega, Flores, Sánchez.

Referee: Jafar Namdar (Iran)
Attendance: 25.000

	P	W	D	L	F	A	Pts
Poland	3	2	1	0	4	1	5
West Germany	3	1	2	0	6	0	4
Tunisia	3	1	1	1	3	2	3
Mexico	3	0	0	3	2	12	0

GROUP THREE

Mar del plata, June 3rd
Estadio Mar del plata

1 (1) BRAZIL

Reinaldo 45

Leão, Amaral, Toninho, Oscar, Edinho, Cerezo (Dirceu), Zico, Rivelino, Gil (Nelinho), Reinaldo, Batista.

1 (1) SWEDEN

Sjöberg 37

Hellström, Borg, R.Andersson, Nordquist, Erlandsson, Tapper, Linderoth, L.Larsson (Edström), B.Larsson, Sjöberg, Wendt.

Referee: Clive Thomas (Wales)
Attendance: 38.000

Buenos Aires, June 3rd
Estadio José Amalfitani

2 (1) AUSTRIA

Schachner 10, Krankl 78

Koncilia, Sara, Pezzey, Obermayer, Breitenberger, Kreuz, Prohaska, Hickersberger (Weber), Schachner (Pirkner), Krankl, Jara.

1 (1) SPAIN

Dani 21

Miguel Angel, Marcelino, Migueli, Pirri, de la Cruz, San José, Asensi, Cardenosa (Leal), Rexach (Quini), Ruben Cano, Dani.

Referee: Karoly Palotai (Hungary)
Attendance: 49.317

Buenos Aires, June 7th
Estadio José Amalfitani

1 (1) AUSTRIA

Krankl (pen)43

Koncilia, Sara, Pezzey, Obermayer, Breitenberger, Kreuz, Prohaska, Hickersberger, Krieger (Weber), Krankl, Jara.

0 (0) SWEDEN

Hellström, Borg, R.Andersson, Nordquist, Erlandsson, Tapper (Torstensson), Linderoth (Edström), L.Larsson, B.Larsson, Sjöberg, Wendt.

Referee: Charles Corver (Holland)
Attendance: 46.000

Mar del Plata, June 7th
Estadio Mar del Plata

0 (0) BRAZIL

Leão, Nelinho (Gil), Amaral, Toninho, Oscar, Edinho, Cerezo, Zico (Mendonca), Dirceu, Reinaldo, Batista.

0 (0) SPAIN

Miguel Angel, Marcelino, Migueli (Biosca), Uria (Guzman), Olmo, San José, Asensi, Cardenosa, Leal, Juanito, Santillana.

Referee: Sergio Gonella (Italy)
Attendance: 40.000

Mar del Plata, June 11th
Estadio Mar del Plata

1 (1) BRAZIL

Roberto 40

Leão, Rodríguez Neto, Amaral, Toninho, Oscar, Edinho, Cerezo (Chicao), Mendonca (Zico), Dirceu, Roberto, Gil, Batista.

0 (0) AUSTRIA

Koncilia, Sara, Pezzey, Obermayer, Breitenberger, Kreuz, Prohaska, Hickersberger (Weber), Krieger (Happich), Krankl, Jara.

Referee: Robert Wurtz (France)
Attendance: 40.000

Buenos Aires, June 11th
Estadio José Amalfitani

1 (0) SPAIN

Asensi 75

Miguel Angel, Marcelino, Biosca, Uria, Olmo (Pirri), San José, Asensi, Cardenosa, Leal, Juanito, Santillana.

0 (0) SWEDEN

Hellström, Borg, R.Andersson, Nordquist, Erlandsson, Nilsson, L.Larsson, Nordin, B.Larsson, Sjöberg (Linderoth), Edström (Wendt).

Referee: Ferdinand Biwersi (West Germany)
Attendance: 48.000

	P	W	D	L	F	A	Pts
Austria	3	2	0	1	3	2	4
Brazil	3	1	2	0	2	1	4
Spain	3	1	1	1	2	2	3
Sweden	3	0	1	2	1	3	1

GROUP FOUR

Mendoza, June 3rd - Estadio Mendoza

3 (1) HOLLAND

Rensenbrink (pen)39, 62, (pen)79

Jongbloed, Suurbier, Krol, Haan, Rijsbergen, W.van der Kerkhof, Neeskens, Jansen, Rep, R.van der Kerkhof (Nanninga), Rensenbrink.

0 (0) IRAN

Hejazi, Nazari, Abdolahi, Kazerani, Eskandarian, Parvin, Ghassempour, Sadeghi, Nayebagha, Djahani, Faraki (Rowshan).

Referee: Alfonso Archundia (Mexico)
Attendance: 42.000

Cordoba, June 3rd - Estadio Cordoba

3 (1) PERU

Cueto 42, Cubillas 70,76

Quiroga, Duarte, Manzo, Chumpitaz, Díaz, Velásquez, Cueto (P.Rojas), Cubillas, Muñante, La Rosa (Sotil), Oblítas.

1 (1) SCOTLAND

Jordan 15

Rough, Kennedy, Burns, Buchan, Forsyth, Rioch (Gemmill), Masson (Macari), Hartford, Dalglish, Jordan, Johnston.

Referee: Ulf Eriksson (Sweden)
Attendance: 45.000

Mendoza, June 7th - Estadio Mendoza

0 (0) HOLLAND

Jongbloed, Suurbier, Krol, Haan, Rijsbergen, W.van der Kerkhof, Neeskens (Nanninga), Jansen, Poortvliet, R.van der Kerkhof (Rep), Rensenbrink.

0 (0) PERU

Quiroga, Duarte, Manzo, Chumpitaz, Díaz, Velásquez, Cueto, Cubillas, Muñante, La Rosa (Sotil), Oblítas.

Referee: Adolf Prokop (East Germany)
Attendance: 30.000

Cordoba, June 7th - Estadio Cordoba

1 (0) IRAN

Danaifar 77

Hejazi, Nazari, Abdolahi, Kazerani, Eskandarian, Parvin, Ghassempour, Sadeghi, Danaifar (Nayebagha), Djahani, Faraki (Rowshan).

1 (1) SCOTLAND

Eskandarian (og)43

Rough, Jardine, Burns, Buchan (Forsyth), Donachie, Gemmill, Macari, Hartford, Dalglish (Harper), Jordan, Robertson.

Referee: Youssou N'Diaye (Senegal)
Attendance: 8.000

Mendoza, June 11th - Estadio Mendoza

3 (1) SCOTLAND

Dalglish 43, Gemmill (pen)46, 67

Rough, Kennedy, Buchan, Forsyth, Donachie, Gemmill, Rioch, Hartford, Dalglish, Souness, Jordan.

2 (1) HOLLAND

Rensenbrink (pen)34, Rep 71

Jongbloed, Suurbier, Krol, Rijsbergen (Wildschut), W.van der Kerkhof, Neeskens (Boskamp), Jansen, Poortvliet, R.van der Kerkhof, Rep, Rensenbrink.

Referee: Erich Linemayr (Austria)
Attendance: 40.000

Cordoba, June 11th - Estadio Cordoba

4 (3) PERU

Velásquez 2, Cubillas 36, (pen)39, (pen)78

Quiroga, Duarte, Manzo (Leguia), Chumpitaz, Díaz, Velásquez, Cueto, Cubillas, Muñante, La Rosa (Sotil), Oblítas.

1 (1) IRAN

Rowshan 40

Hejazi, Nazari, Abdolahi, Kazerani, Allahvardi, Parvin, Ghassempour, Sadeghi, Danaifar, Faraki (Djahani), Rowshan (Fariba).

Referee: Alojzi Jarguz (Poland)
Attendance: 25.000

	P	W	D	L	F	A	Pts
Peru	3	2	1	0	7	2	5
Holland	3	1	1	1	5	3	3
Scotland	3	1	1	1	5	6	3
Iran	3	0	1	2	2	8	1

SECOND PHASE - GROUP A

**Buenos Aires, June 14th
Estadio Monumental**

0 (0) ITALY

Zoff, Gentile, Bellugi, Scirea, Cabrini, Benetti, Antognoni (Zaccarelli), Tardelli, Causio, Rossi, Bettega.

0 (0) WEST GERMANY

Maier, Vogts, Rüssmann, Zimmermann (Konopka), Dietz, Kaltz, Bonhof, Flohe (Beer), Rummenigge, Fischer, Hölzenbein.

Referee: Dusan Maksimovic (Yugoslavia)
Attendance: 60.000

Cordoba, June 14th - Estadio Cordoba

5 (3) HOLLAND

Brandts 6, Rensenbrink (pen)35, Rep 36, 53, W.van der Kerkhof 83

Schrijvers, Poortvliet, Krol, Brandts (van Kraay), Wildschut, Jansen, Haan, W.van der Kerkhof, R.van der Kerkhof (Schoenaker), Rep, Rensenbrink.

1 (0) AUSTRIA

Obermayer 80

Koncilia, Sara, Pezzey, Obermayer, Breitenberger, Hickersberger, Krieger, Prohaska, Kreuz, Krankl, Jara.

Referee: John Gordon (Scotland)
Attendance: 15.000

Cordoba, June 18th - Estadio Cordoba

2 (1) HOLLAND

Haan 26, R.van der Kerkhof 83

Schrijvers, Krol, Haan, Brandts, W.van der Kerkhof, Wildschut (Nanninga) (RED), Jansen, Poortvliet, R.van der Kerkhof, Rep, Rensenbrink.

2 (1) WEST GERMANY

Abramczik 3, D.Müller 70

Maier, Vogts, Rüssmann, Dietz, Kaltz, Bonhof, Beer, Rummenigge, Abramczik, Hölzenbein, D.Müller.

Referee: Ramon Barreto Ruiz (Uruguay)
Attendance: 46.000

**Buenos Aires, June 18th
Estadio Monumental**

1 (1) ITALY

Rossi 13

Zoff, Gentile, Bellugi (Cuccureddu), Scirea, Cabrini, Benetti, Zaccarelli, Tardelli, Causio, Rossi, Bettega (Graziani).

0 (0) AUSTRIA

Koncilia, Sara, Pezzey, Obermayer, Strässer, Hickersberger, Krieger, Prohaska, Kreuz, Krankl, Schachner (Pirkner).

Referee: Francis Rion (Belgium)
Attendance: 50.000

Buenos Aires, June 21st - Estadio Monumental

1 (1) ITALY

Brandts (og)19

Zoff, Gentile, Cuccureddu, Scirea, Cabrini, Benetti (Graziani), Zaccarelli, Tardelli, Causio (C.Sala), Rossi, Bettega.

2 (0) HOLLAND

Brandts 50, Haan 75

Schrijvers (Jongbloed), Haan, Krol, Brandts, W.van der Kerkhof, Neeskens, Jansen, Poortvliet, R.van der Kerkhof, Rep (van Kraay), Rensenbrink.

Referee: Angel Martínez (Spain)
Attendance: 70.000

Cordoba, June 21st - Estadio Cordoba

3 (0) AUSTRIA

Vogts (og)60, Krankl 67, 88

Koncilia, Sara, Pezzey, Obermayer, Strässer, Hickersberger, Krieger, Prohaska, Kreuz, Krankl, Schachner (Oberacher).

2 (1) WEST GERMANY

Rummenigge 19, Hölzenbein 72

Maier, Vogts, Rüssmann, Dietz, Kaltz, Bonhof, Beer (H.Müller), Rummenigge, Abramczik, Hölzenbein, D.Müller (Fischer).

Referee: Abraham Klein (Israel)
Attendance: 20.000

	P	W	D	L	F	A	Pts
Holland	3	2	1	0	9	4	5
Italy	3	1	1	1	2	2	3
West Germany	3	0	2	1	4	5	2
Austria	3	1	0	2	4	8	2

SECOND PHASE - GROUP B

Mendoza, June 14th - Estadio Mendoza

3 (2) BRAZIL

Dirceu 14, 27, Zico (pen)70

Leão, Toninho, Oscar, Amaral, Rodríguez Neto, Batista, Cerezo (Chicao), Dirceu, Mendonca, Gil (Zico), Roberto.

0 (0) PERU

Quiroga, Duarte, Manzo, Chumpitaz, Díaz (Navarro), Velásquez, Cueto, Cubillas, Muñante, La Rosa, Oblítas (P.Rojas).

Referee: Nicolae Rainea (Romania)
Attendance: 40.000

Rosario, June 14th - Estadio Rosario

2 (1) ARGENTINA

Kempes 15, 70

Fillol, Olguín, L.Galvan, Passarella, Tarantini, Ardíles, Gallego, Valencia (Villa), Houseman (Ortíz), Kempes, Bertoni.

0 (0) POLAND

Tomaszewski, Szymanowski, Zmuda, Kasperczak, Makulewicz, Nawalka, Deyna, Boniek, Masztaler (Mazur), Lato, Szarmach.

Referee: Ulf Eriksson (Sweden)
Attendance: 40.000

Daniel, Super Mario and the Dutch Lions - Argentina 1978

Mendoza, June 18th - Estadio Mendoza

1 (0) POLAND

Szarmach 64

Kukla, Szymanowski, Gorgon, Zmuda, Makulewicz, Nawalka, Deyna, Boniek (Lubanski), Masztaler (Kasperczak), Lato, Szarmach.

0 (0) PERU

Quiroga, Duarte, Manzo, Chumpitaz, Navarro, Quesada, Cueto, Cubillas, Muñante (P.Rojas), La Rosa (Sotil), Oblítas.

Referee: Pat Partridge (England)
Attendance: 35.000

Rosario, June 18th - Estadio Rosario

0 (0) ARGENTINA

Fillol, Olguín, L.Galvan, Passarella, Tarantini, Ardíles (Villa), Gallego, Luque, Ortíz (Alonso), Kempes, Bertoni.

0 (0) BRAZIL

Leão, Toninho, Oscar, Amaral, Rodríguez Neto (Edinho), Batista, Chicao, Dirceu, Mendonca (Zico), Gil, Roberto.

Referee: Karoly Palotai (Hungary)
Attendance: 46.000

Mendoza, June 21st - Estadio Mendoza

3 (1) BRAZIL

Nelinho 12, Roberto 57,62

Leão, Toninho, Oscar, Amaral, Nelinho, Batista, Cerezo (Rivelino), Dirceu, Zico (Mendonca), Gil, Roberto.

1 (1) POLAND

Lato 44

Kukla, Szymanowski, Gorgon, Zmuda, Makulewicz, Nawalka, Deyna, Boniek, Kasperczak (Lubanski), Lato, Szarmach.

Referee: Juan Silvagno (Chile)
Attendance: 44.000

Rosario, June 21st - Estadio Rosario

6 (2) ARGENTINA

Kempes 20,48, Tarantini 43, Luque 49, 72, Houseman 66

Fillol, Olguín, L.Galvan, Passarella, Tarantini, Larrosa, Gallego (Oviedo), Luque, Ortíz, Kempes, Bertoni (Houseman).

0 (0) PERU

Quiroga, Duarte, Manzo, Chumpitaz, R.Rojas, Quesada, Cueto, Velásquez (Gorriti) Cubillas, Muñante, Oblítas.

Referee: Robert Wurtz (France)
Attendance: 40.567

	P	W	D	L	F	A	Pts
Argentina	3	2	1	0	8	0	5
Brazil	3	2	1	0	6	1	5
Poland	3	1	0	2	2	5	2
Peru	3	0	0	3	0	10	0

3RD/4TH PLACE PLAY-OFF

Buenos Aires, June 24th - Estadio Monumental

2 (0) BRAZIL

Nelinho 63, Dirceu 65

Leão, Nelinho, Oscar, Amaral, Rodríguez Neto, Cerezo (Rivelino), Batista, Dirceu, Gil (Reinaldo), Roberto, Mendonca.

1 (1) ITALY

Causio 38

Zoff, Cuccureddu, Gentile, Scirea, Cabrini, P.Sala, Antognoni (C.Sala), Maldera, Causio, Rossi, Bettega.

Referee: Abraham Klein (Israel)
Attendance: 76.609

FINAL

Buenos Aires, June 25th - Estadio Monumental

After extra time - 45 mins (1-0), 90 mins (1-1)

3 (1) ARGENTINA

Kempes 38,105, Bertoni 115

Fillol, Olguín, L.Galvan, Passarella, Tarantini, Ardíles (Larrosa), Gallego, Kempes, Bertoni, Luque, Ortíz (Houseman).

1 (1) HOLLAND

Nanninga 80

Jongbloed, Jansen (Suurbier), Brandts, Krol, Poortvliet, Haan, W.van der Kerkhof, Neeskens, R.van der Kerkhof, Rep (Nanninga), Rensenbrink.

Referee: Sergio Gonella (Italy)
Attendance: 77.260

Qualifying Rounds

Africa - Pre-Preliminary Round

	P	W	D	L	F	A	Pts
Upper Volta	2	1	1	0	3	1	3
Sierra Leone	2	1	0	1	6	3	2
Niger	2	1	0	1	3	6	2
Mauritania	2	0	1	1	1	3	1

07-03-76	Sierra Leone : Niger	5:1 (1:1)
13-03-76	Upper Volta : Mauritania	1:1
21-03-76	Niger : Sierra Leone	2:1 (1:1)
28-03-76	Mauritania : Upper Volta	0:2 (0:1)

Africa - 1st Round

	P	W	D	L	F	A	Pts
Zambia	2	2	0	0	5	0	4
Egypt	2	2	0	0	5	1	4
Nigeria	2	1	1	0	6	2	3
Cote d' Ivoire	2	1	1	0	3	1	3
Congo	2	1	1	0	4	3	3
Togo	2	1	1	0	2	1	3
Algeria	2	1	1	0	1	0	3
Ghana	2	1	0	1	3	3	2
Guinea	2	1	0	1	3	3	2
Tunisia	2	0	2	0	2	2	2
Morocco	2	0	2	0	2	2	2
Cameroon	2	0	1	1	3	4	1
Senegal	2	0	1	1	1	2	1
Libya	2	0	1	1	0	1	1
Upper Volta	2	0	1	1	3	1	1
Sierra Leone	2	0	1	1	2	6	1
Ethiopia	2	0	0	2	1	5	0
Malawi	2	0	0	2	0	5	0

01-04-76	Algeria : Libya	1:0 (0:0)
16-04-76	Libya : Algeria	0:0

09-05-76	Zambia : Malawi	4:0 (2:0)
30-05-76	Malawi : Zambia	0:1 (0:0)
04-09-76	Upper Volta : Cote d' Ivoire	1:1 (0:1)
26-09-76	Cote d' Ivoire : Upper Volta	2:0 (2:0)
10-10-76	Ghana : Guinea	2:1 (0:0)
16-10-76	Sierra Leone : Nigeria	0:0
17-10-76	Congo : Cameroon	2:2 (0:2)
17-10-76	Togo : Senegal	1:0 (0:0)
29-10-76	Egypt : Ethiopia	3:0 (2:0)
30-10-76	Nigeria : Sierra Leone	6:2 (4:0)
31-10-76	Guinea : Ghana	2:1 (0:0)
31-10-76	Senegal : Togo	1:1 (0:0)
31-10-76	Cameroon : Congo	1:2 (1:1)
14-11-76	Ethiopia : Egypt	1:2 (1:1)
12-12-76	Morocco : Tunisia	1:1 (1:0)
09-01-77	Tunisia : Morocco	1:1 (1:0)
	4:2 penalty kicks	

Africa - 1st Round Play-off

16-01-77	Guinea : Ghana	2:0 (2:0)

Africa - 2nd Round

	P	W	D	L	F	A	Pts
Cote d' Ivoire	2	2	0	0	6	3	4
Guinea	2	2	0	0	4	1	4
Tunisia	2	1	1	0	3	1	3
Egypt	2	1	1	0	1	0	3
Zambia	2	1	0	1	4	3	2
Uganda	2	1	0	1	3	4	2
Kenya	2	0	1	1	0	1	1
Algeria	2	0	1	1	1	3	1
Congo	2	0	0	2	3	6	0
Togo	2	0	0	2	1	4	0

06-02-77	Kenya : Egypt	0:0
06-02-77	Tunisia : Algeria	2:0 (0:0)
13-02-77	Uganda : Zambia	1:0 (0:0)
13-02-77	Cote d' Ivoire : Congo	3:2 (2:1)
13-02-77	Togo : Guinea	0:2 (0:1)
27-02-77	Zambia : Uganda	4:2 a.e.t. (2:1, 2:1)
27-02-77	Egypt : Kenya	1:0 (1:0)
27-02-77	Guinea : Togo	2:1 (2:0)
27-02-77	Congo : Cote d' Ivoire	1:3 (1:2)
28-02-77	Algeria : Tunisia	1:1 (1:0)

Africa - 3rd Round

	P	W	D	L	F	A	Pts
Nigeria	2	1	1	0	6	2	3
Egypt	2	1	1	0	2	0	3
Tunisia	2	1	0	1	3	2	2
Guinea	2	1	0	1	2	3	2
Zambia	2	0	1	1	0	2	1
Cote d' Ivoire	2	0	1	1	2	6	1

05-06-77	Guinea : Tunisia	1:0 (0:0)
19-06-77	Tunisia : Guinea	3:1 (1:1)
10-07-77	Nigeria : Cote d' Ivoire	4:0 (3:0)
15-07-77	Egypt : Zambia	2:0 (1:0)
24-07-77	Cote d' Ivoire : Nigeria	2:2 (1:0)
31-07-77	Zambia : Egypt	0:0

Africa - 4th Round

	P	W	D	L	F	A	Pts
Tunisia	4	2	1	1	7	4	5
Egypt	4	2	0	2	7	11	4
Nigeria	4	1	1	2	5	4	3

25-09-77	Tunisia : Nigeria	0:0
08-10-77	Nigeria : Egypt	4:0 (1:0)
21-10-77	Egypt : Nigeria	3:1 (2:0)

12-11-77	Nigeria : Tunisia	0:1 (0:0)
25-11-77	Egypt : Tunisia	3:2 (1:0)
11-12-77	Tunisia : Egypt	4:1 (2:0)

Asia/Oceania - OFC Group Matches

	P	W	D	L	F	A	Pts
Australia	4	3	1	0	9	3	7
New Zealand	4	2	1	1	14	4	5
Chinese Taipei	4	0	0	4	1	17	0

13-03-77	Australia : Chinese Taipei	3:0 (2:0)
16-03-77	Chinese Taipei : Australia	1:2 (1:1)

Both games played in Ba.

20-03-77	New Zealand : Chinese Taipei	6:0 (4:0)
23-03-77	Chinese Taipei : New Zealand	0:6 (0:2)

Both games played in Auckland.

27-03-77	Australia : New Zealand	3:1 (0:1)
30-03-77	New Zealand : Australia	1:1 (1:1)

Asia/Oceania - AFC Phase 1, Group 1

	P	W	D	L	F	A	Pts
Hong Kong	4	2	2	0	9	5	6
Singapore	4	2	1	1	5	6	5
Malaysia	4	1	2	1	7	6	4
Indonesia	4	1	1	2	7	7	3
Thailand	4	1	0	3	8	12	2

27-02-77	Singapore : Thailand	2:0 (0:0)
28-02-77	Hong Kong : Indonesia	4:1 (0:1)
01-03-77	Malaysia : Thailand	6:4 (4:1)
02-03-77	Hong Kong : Singapore	2:2 (1:1)
03-03-77	Indonesia : Malaysia	0:0
05-03-77	Thailand : Hong Kong	1:2 (0:0)
06-03-77	Singapore : Malaysia	1:0 (1:0)
07-03-77	Thailand : Indonesia	3:2 (3:1)
08-03-77	Malaysia : Hong Kong	1:1 (1:1)
09-03-77	Indonesia : Singapore	4:0 (3:0)

All games played in Singapore.

Asia/Oceania - AFC Phase 1, Group 1 Play-off

12-03-77	Singapore : Hong Kong	0:1 (0:1)

Played in Singapore.

Asia/Oceania - AFC Phase 1, Group 2

	P	W	D	L	F	A	Pts
Korea Republic	4	2	2	0	4	1	6
Israel	4	2	1	1	5	3	5
Japan	4	0	1	3	0	5	1

27-02-77	Israel : Korea Republic	0:0
06-03-77	Israel : Japan	2:0 (1:0)
10-03-77	Japan : Israel	0:2 (0:1)
20-03-77	Korea Republic : Israel	3:1 (1:0)
26-03-77	Japan : Korea Republic	0:0
03-04-77	Korea Republic : Japan	1:0 (0:0)

Asia/Oceania - AFC Phase 1, Group 3

	P	W	D	L	F	A	Pts
Iran	4	4	0	0	8	0	8
Saudi Arabia	4	1	0	3	3	7	2
Syria	4	1	0	3	2	6	2

12-11-76	Saudi Arabia : Syria	2:0 (1:0)
26-11-76	Syria : Saudi Arabia	2:1 (1:1)
07-01-77	Saudi Arabia : Iran	0:3 (0:1)
28-01-77	Syria : Iran	0:1 (0:1)
06-04-77	Iran : Syria	2:0
22-04-77	Iran : Saudi Arabia	2:0 (1:0)

Asia/Oceania - AFC Phase 1, Group 4

	P	W	D	L	F	A	Pts
Kuwait	4	4	0	0	10	2	8
Bahrain	4	1	0	3	4	6	2
Qatar	4	1	0	3	9	2	2

11-03-77	Bahrain : Kuwait	0:2 (0:2)
13-03-77	Qatar : Bahrain	2:0 (1:0)
15-03-77	Qatar : Kuwait	0:2 (0:1)
17-03-77	Bahrain : Kuwait	1:2 (0:1)
19-03-77	Qatar : Bahrain	0:3 (0:1)
21-03-77	Qatar : Kuwait	1:4 (0:3)

All games played in Doha.

Asia/Oceania - Final Round AFC/OFC

	P	W	D	L	F	A	Pts
Iran	8	6	2	0	12	3	14
Korea Republic	8	3	4	1	12	8	10
Kuwait	8	4	1	3	13	8	9
Australia	8	3	1	4	11	8	7
Hong Kong	8	0	0	8	5	26	0

19-06-77	Hong Kong : Iran	0:2 (0:1)
26-06-77	Hong Kong : Korea Republic	0:1 (0:0)
03-07-77	Korea Republic : Iran	0:0
10-07-77	Australia : Hong Kong	3:0 (1:0)
14-08-77	Australia : Iran	0:1 (0:0)
27-08-77	Australia : Korea Republic	2:1 (0:1)
02-10-77	Hong Kong : Kuwait	1:3 (1:1)
09-10-77	Korea Republic : Kuwait	1:0 (0:0)
16-10-77	Australia : Kuwait	1:2 (0:1)
23-10-77	Korea Republic : Australia	0:0
28-10-77	Iran : Kuwait	1:0 (0:0)
30-10-77	Hong Kong : Australia	2:5 (0:3)
05-11-77	Kuwait : Korea Republic	2:2 (0:1)
11-11-77	Iran : Korea Republic	2:2 (0:1)
12-11-77	Kuwait : Hong Kong	4:0 (3:0)
18-11-77	Iran : Hong Kong	3:0 (3:0)
19-11-77	Kuwait : Australia	1:0 (0:0)
25-11-77	Iran : Australia	1:0 (0:0)
03-12-77	Kuwait : Iran	1:2 (1:0)
04-12-77	Korea Republic : Hong Kong	5:2 (2:0)

Europe - Group 1

	P	W	D	L	F	A	Pts
Poland	6	5	1	0	17	4	11
Portugal	6	4	1	1	12	6	9
Denmark	6	2	0	4	14	12	4
Cyprus	6	0	0	6	3	24	0

23-05-76	Cyprus : Denmark	1:5 (1:3)
16-10-76	Portugal : Poland	0:2 (0:0)
27-10-76	Denmark : Cyprus	5:0 (0:0)
31-10-76	Poland : Cyprus	5:0 (3:0)
17-11-76	Portugal : Denmark	1:0 (0:0)
05-12-76	Cyprus : Portugal	1:2 (0:1)
01-05-77	Denmark : Poland	1:2 (0:1)
15-05-77	Cyprus : Poland	1:3 (1:2)
21-09-77	Poland : Denmark	4:1 (2:0)
09-10-77	Denmark : Portugal	2:4 (1:2)
29-10-77	Poland : Portugal	1:1 (1:0)
16-11-77	Portugal : Cyprus	4:0 (2:0)

Europe - Group 2

	P	W	D	L	F	A	Pts
Italy	6	5	0	1	18	4	10
England	6	5	0	1	15	4	10
Finland	6	2	0	4	11	16	4
Luxembourg	6	0	0	6	2	22	0

13-06-76	Finland : England	1:4 (1:2)
22-09-76	Finland : Luxembourg	7:1 (3:0)
13-10-76	England : Finland	2:1 (1:0)
16-10-76	Luxembourg : Italy	1:4 (0:2)
17-11-76	Italy : England	2:0 (1:0)
30-03-77	England : Luxembourg	5:0 (1:0)
26-05-77	Luxembourg : Finland	0:1 (0:1)
08-06-77	Finland : Italy	0:3 (0:0)
12-10-77	Luxembourg : England	0:2 (0:1)
15-10-77	Italy : Finland	6:1 (3:0)
16-11-77	England : Italy	2:0 (1:0)
03-12-77	Italy : Luxembourg	3:0 (2:0)

Europe - Group 3

	P	W	D	L	F	A	Pts
Austria	6	4	2	0	14	2	10
Germany DR	6	3	3	0	15	4	9
Turkey	6	2	1	3	9	5	5
Malta	6	0	0	6	0	27	0

31-10-76	Turkey : Malta	4:0 (1:0)
17-11-76	Germany DR : Turkey	1:1 (1:0)
05-12-76	Malta : Austria	0:1 (0:0)
02-04-77	Malta : Germany DR	0:1 (0:0)
17-04-77	Austria : Turkey	1:0 (1:0)
30-04-77	Austria : Malta	9:0 (5:0)
24-09-77	Austria : Germany DR	1:1 (1:1)
12-10-77	Germany DR : Austria	1:1 (0:1)
29-10-77	Germany DR : Malta	9:0 (3:0)
30-10-77	Turkey : Austria	0:1 (0:0)
16-11-77	Turkey : Germany DR	1:2 (0:1)
27-11-77	Malta : Turkey	0:3 (0:2)

Europe - Group 4

	P	W	D	L	F	A	Pts
Netherlands	6	5	1	0	11	3	11
Belgium	6	3	0	3	7	6	6
N. Ireland	6	2	1	3	7	6	5
Iceland	6	1	0	5	2	12	2

05-09-76	Iceland : Belgium	0:1 (0:0)
08-09-76	Iceland : Netherlands	0:1 (0:1)
13-10-76	Netherlands : Northern Ireland	2:2 (0:1)
10-11-76	Belgium : Northern Ireland	2:0 (1:0)
26-03-77	Belgium : Netherlands	0:2 (0:1)
11-06-77	Iceland : Northern Ireland	1:0 (0:0)
31-08-77	Netherlands : Iceland	4:1 (3:0)
03-09-77	Belgium : Iceland	4:0 (2:0)
21-09-77	Northern Ireland : Iceland	2:0 (0:0)
12-10-77	Northern Ireland : Netherlands	0:1 (0:0)
26-10-77	Netherlands : Belgium	1:0 (1:0)
16-11-77	Northern Ireland : Belgium	3:0 (1:0)

Europe - Group 5

	P	W	D	L	F	A	Pts
France	4	2	1	1	7	4	5
Bulgaria	4	1	2	1	5	6	4
Ireland Rep	4	1	1	2	2	4	3

09-10-76	Bulgaria : France	2:2 (1:2)
17-11-76	France : Ireland Republic	2:0 (0:0)
30-03-77	Ireland Republic : France	1:0 (1:0)
01-06-77	Bulgaria : Ireland Republic	2:1 (1:0)
12-10-77	Ireland Republic : Bulgaria	0:0
16-11-77	France : Bulgaria	3:1 (1:0)

Daniel, Super Mario and the Dutch Lions - Argentina 1978

Europe - Group 6

	P	W	D	L	F	A	Pts
Sweden	4	3	0	1	7	4	6
Norway	4	2	0	2	3	4	4
Switzerland	4	1	0	3	3	5	2

16-06-76	Sweden : Norway	2:0 (2:0)
08-09-76	Norway : Switzerland	1:0 (0:0)
09-10-76	Switzerland : Sweden	1:2 (1:1)
08-06-77	Sweden : Switzerland	2:1 (0:0)
07-09-77	Norway : Sweden	2:1 (1:0)
30-10-77	Switzerland : Norway	1:0 (1:0)

Europe - Group 7

	P	W	D	L	F	A	Pts
Scotland	4	3	0	1	6	3	6
Czech	4	2	0	2	4	6	4
Wales	4	1	0	3	3	4	2

13-10-76	Czechoslovakia : Scotland	2:0 (0:0)
17-11-76	Scotland : Wales	1:0 (1:0)
30-03-77	Wales : Czechoslovakia	3:0 (1:0)
21-09-77	Scotland : Czechoslovakia	3:1 (2:0)
12-10-77	Wales : Scotland	0:2 (0:0)
16-11-77	Czechoslovakia : Wales	1:0 (1:0)

Europe - Group 8

	P	W	D	L	F	A	Pts
Spain	4	3	0	1	4	1	6
Romania	4	2	0	2	7	8	4
Yugoslavia	4	1	0	3	6	8	2

10-10-76	Spain : Yugoslavia	1:0 (0:0)
16-04-77	Romania : Spain	1:0 (1:0)
08-05-77	Yugoslavia : Romania	0:2 (0:2)
26-10-77	Spain : Romania	2:0 (0:0)
13-11-77	Romania : Yugoslavia	4:6 (3:2)
30-11-77	Yugoslavia : Spain	0:1 (0:0)

Europe - Group 9

	P	W	D	L	F	A	Pts
Hungary	4	2	1	1	6	4	5
USSR	4	2	0	2	5	3	4
Greece	4	1	1	2	2	6	3

09-10-76	Greece : Hungary	1:1 (0:0)
24-04-77	USSR : Greece	2:0 (1:0)
30-04-77	Hungary : USSR	2:1 (1:0)
10-05-77	Greece : USSR	1:0 (0:0)
18-05-77	USSR : Hungary	2:0 (2:0)
28-05-77	Hungary : Greece	3:0 (2:0)

Caribbean/North/Central America
Phase 1 - Extra Preliminaries

	P	W	D	L	F	A	Pts
Haiti	2	2	0	0	6	0	4
Dominican Republic	2	0	0	2	0	6	0

| 02-04-76 | Dominican Republic : Haiti | 0:3 (0:3) |
| 17-04-76 | Haiti : Dominican Republic | 3:0 (2:0) |

Caribbean/North/Central America
Phase 1 - Group 1

	P	W	D	L	F	A	Pts
Haiti	2	2	0	0	9	1	4
Cuba	2	2	0	0	5	1	4
Surinam	2	1	0	1	3	2	2
Barbados	2	1	0	1	2	2	2
Trinidad & Tobago	2	1	0	1	2	2	2
Guyana	2	1	0	1	2	3	2
Jamaica	2	0	0	2	1	5	0
Netherlands Antilles	2	0	0	2	1	9	0

04-07-76	Guyana : Surinam	2:0 (1:0)
31-07-76	Netherlands Antilles : Haiti	1:2 (0:2)
14-08-76	Haiti : Netherlands Antilles	7:0 (4:0)
15-08-76	Jamaica : Cuba	1:3 (0:1)
15-08-76	Barbados : Trinidad & Tobago	2:1 (0:0)
29-08-76	Surinam : Guyana	3:0 (2:0)
29-08-76	Cuba : Jamaica	2:0 (1:0)
31-08-76	Trinidad & Tobago : Barbados	1:0 (1:0)

Caribbean/North/Central America
Phase 1 - Group 1 Play-off

| 14-9-76 | Barbados : Trinidad & Tobago | 3:1 (1:1) |

Caribbean/North/Central America
Phase 1 - Group 2

	P	W	D	L	F	A	Pts
Trinidad & Tobago	2	0	2	0	3	3	2
Surinam	2	0	2	0	3	3	2
Cuba	2	0	2	0	2	2	2
Haiti	2	0	2	0	2	2	2

14-11-76	Surinam : Trinidad & Tobago	1:1 (1:1)
28-11-76	Trinidad & Tobago : Surinam	2:2 (1:1)
28-11-76	Cuba : Haiti	1:1 (1:0)
11-12-76	Haiti : Cuba	1:1 (0:0)

Caribbean/North/Central America
Phase 1 - Group 2 Play-offs

| 18-12-76 | Surinam : Trinidad & Tobago | 3:2 (0:1) |
| 29-12-76 | Cuba : Haiti | 0:2 (0:0) |

Caribbean/North/Central America
Phase 1 - Central Zone

	P	W	D	L	F	A	Pts
Guatemala	6	3	2	1	15	6	8
El Salvador	6	2	3	1	10	7	7
Costa Rica	6	1	4	1	8	6	6
Panama	6	1	1	4	7	21	3

04-04-76	Panama : Costa Rica	3:2 (0:1)
02-05-76	Panama : El Salvador	1:1 (0:1)
11-07-76	Costa Rica : Panama	3:0 (3:0)
01-08-76	El Salvador : Panama	4:1 (2:0)
17-09-76	Panama : Guatemala	2:4 (2:0)
26-09-76	Guatemala : Panama	7:0 (3:0)
01-12-76	El Salvador : Costa Rica	1:1 (1:0)
05-12-76	Costa Rica : Guatemala	0:0
08-12-76	Guatemala : El Salvador	3:1 (2:1)
12-12-76	Guatemala : Costa Rica	1:1 (0:0)
15-12-76	Costa Rica : El Salvador	1:1 (1:0)
19-12-76	El Salvador : Guatemala	2:0 (2:0)

Caribbean/North/Central America
Phase 1 - Northern Zone

	P	W	D	L	F	A	Pts
Mexico	4	1	2	1	3	1	4
United States	4	1	2	1	3	4	4
Canada	4	1	2	1	2	3	4

24-09-76	Canada : United States	1:1 (0:1)
03-10-76	United States : Mexico	0:0
10-10-76	Canada : Mexico	1:0 (1:0)
15-10-76	Mexico : United States	3:0 (2:0)
20-10-76	United States : Canada	2:0 (0:0)
27-10-76	Mexico : Canada	0:0

Caribbean/North/Central America
Phase 1 - Northern Zone Play-off

| 22-12-76 | Canada : United States | 3:0 (1:0) |

Played in Port-Au-Prince

Caribbean/North/Central America
Phase 2 - Final Tournament

	P	W	D	L	F	A	Pts
Mexico	5	5	0	0	20	5	10
Haiti	5	3	1	1	6	6	7
El Salvador	5	2	1	2	8	9	5
Canada	5	2	1	2	7	8	5
Guatemala	5	1	1	3	8	10	3
Surinam	5	0	0	5	6	17	0

| 08-10-77 | Guatemala : Surinam | 3:2 (2:1) |
| 08-10-77 | El Salvador : Canada | 2:1 (1:0) |

Both games played in Monterrey

09-10-77	Mexico : Haiti	4:1 (1:0)
12-10-77	Canada : Surinam	2:1 (1:1)
12-10-77	Mexico : El Salvador	3:1 (1:0)

All games played in Mexico City

| 12-10-77 | Guatemala : Haiti | 1:2 (0:2) |
| 15-10-77 | Mexico : Surinam | 8:1 (3:1) |

Both games played in Monterrey

16-10-77	Canada : Guatemala	2:1 (2:0)
16-10-77	El Salvador : Haiti	0:1 (0:1)
19-10-77	Mexico : Guatemala	2:1 (1:1)

All games played in Mexico City

20-10-77	El Salvador : Surinam	3:2 (1:0)
20-10-77	Canada : Haiti	1:1 (0:0)
22-10-77	Mexico : Canada	3:1 (2:1)

All games played in Monterrey

| 23-10-77 | Guatemala : El Salvador | 2:2 (0:1) |
| 23-10-77 | Haiti : Surinam | 1:0 (1:0) |

Both games played in Mexico City

South America - Group 1

	P	W	D	L	F	A	Pts
Brazil	4	2	2	0	8	1	6
Paraguay	4	1	2	1	3	3	4
Colombia	4	0	2	2	1	8	2

20-02-77	Colombia : Brazil	0:0
24-02-77	Colombia : Paraguay	0:1 (0:1)
06-03-77	Paraguay : Colombia	1:1 (0:0)
09-03-77	Brazil : Colombia	6:0 (4:0)
13-03-77	Paraguay : Brazil	0:1 (0:0)
20-03-77	Brazil : Paraguay	1:1 (1:0)

South America - Group 2

	P	W	D	L	F	A	Pts
Bolivia	4	3	1	0	8	3	7
Uruguay	4	1	2	1	5	4	4
Venezuela	4	0	1	3	2	8	1

09-02-77	Venezuela : Uruguay	1:1 (0:1)
27-02-77	Bolivia : Uruguay	1:0 (0:0)
06-03-77	Venezuela : Bolivia	1:3 (0:1)
13-03-77	Bolivia : Venezuela	2:0 (2:0)
17-03-77	Uruguay : Venezuela	2:0 (1:0)
27-03-77	Uruguay : Bolivia	2:2 (1:1)

South America - Group 3

	P	W	D	L	F	A	Pts
Peru	4	2	2	0	8	2	6
Chile	4	2	1	1	5	3	5
Ecuador	4	0	1	3	1	9	1

20-02-77	Ecuador : Peru	1:1 (0:1)
27-02-77	Ecuador : Chile	0:1 (0:1)
06-03-77	Chile : Peru	1:1 (1:0)
12-03-77	Peru : Ecuador	4:0 (1:0)
20-03-77	Chile : Ecuador	3:0 (2:0)
26-03-77	Peru : Chile	2:0 (0:0)

South America - Group Winners

	P	W	D	L	F	A	Pts
Brazil	2	2	0	0	9	0	4
Peru	2	1	0	1	5	1	2
Bolivia	2	0	0	2	0	13	0

10-07-77	Peru : Brazil	0:1 (0:0)
14-07-77	Brazil : Bolivia	8:0 (4:0)
17-07-77	Peru : Bolivia	5:0 (2:0)

All games played in Cali

CONMEBOL/UEFA Play-off

	P	W	D	L	F	A	Pts
Hungary	2	2	0	0	9	2	4
Bolivia	2	0	0	2	2	9	0

29-10-77	Hungary : Bolivia	6:0 (5:0)
30-11-77	Bolivia : Hungary	2:3 (1:2)

Chapter 14

Maggie, Michel and the Italian Bad Boy
The Spain World Cup, 1982

Spain 1982

Winners: Italy

Runners-up: West Germany

3rd Place: Poland

4th Place: France

Total Attendance: 2,099,214

Number of Matches: 52

My first experience of the World Cup finals was, unquestionably, amongst my best… and amongst my worst. It came in Spain in 1982 only four months after I had moved to England to join BBC Radio Sport. I had been working for the BBC in Belfast and had been doing the television commentary as Northern Ireland qualified to reach the final stages for the first time since 1958. Naturally I was anxious, despite my new position, to see the job through. I was delighted that my new employers in London were happy to take me along, albeit as a fresh and somewhat inexperienced radio commentator. I was assured I would stay in Spain for as long as Northern Ireland remained in the competition. In truth, neither of us expected them to last beyond the initial group phase.

That remained the expectation on the night of their final group match in Valencia, against the host nation. Northern Ireland had played very well to achieve two draws in their opening fixtures but few, save for the manager Billy Bingham and the more optimistic of his players, considered that they had any hope of beating Spain which is what they needed to do to qualify. Indeed, I remember sitting in the Sidi Soler Hotel on the eve of the match dreading the prospect of a thrashing from a side many believed might go on to win the World Cup itself.

I was wrong, delightfully wrong. Though faced by overwhelming odds, superior opposition, an intensively passionate home support, and overcoming the questionable sending-off of Mal Donaghy early in the second half, Northern Ireland won 1-0 with a goal from Gerry Armstrong. I was fortunate to be commentating at the time and it's one of very few commentary clips that I can bear listening to again and again. I was very proud. When the final whistle was blown, I cried at what my tiny humble nation had achieved.

I was still emotional when the person in charge of our World Cup coverage delivered his judgement. The promise was to be broken. Though Northern Ireland were to go to Madrid, I was to go home the following morning. It was a question of logistics, I suppose. Their best and most experienced people were to remain. I was in neither group at the time. There was a massive party at the team's hotel that night. Such was my huge disappointment, I couldn't bring myself to attend. I was so bitter.

In 2002, I will be commentating on my fourth successive World Cup Final. Few commentators have been as privileged as I have been and my career overflows with marvellous memories of great moments and matches in the tournament. However, I still remember with sadness that flight home in 1982… even if it's mixed in with a vision of Arconada failing to gather Billy Hamilton's cross and Gerry Armstrong shooting low into the net.

Original contribution by Alan Green of BBC Radio Five Live

The 1970's had forced new ways of thinking and a more hard faced way of conducting business. The 1980's heralded what became two decades of the enterprise culture and the two "hard faces" at the forefront of the altered economic order were Margaret Thatcher and Ronald Reagan, a former B movie actor, who many saw as a third-rate President. Their doctrine encouraged more self-reliance and saw virtue in self-interest. A way of life based on pure market forces, tacitly or not, played on people's baser instincts, on the underlying implication that people are selfish and more interested in acquisition than sharing. People, it was maintained, should be accountable for their actions. For those who had, it was a time to acquire even more, but for those who had not, it was a time to "get on your bikes" and find work. There was no such thing as society and those that could not keep up were left behind and cast onto the streets.

22 Men and a Bag of Wind

Yet, by 1982 Thatcherism was failing to deliver and Britain was slipping deeper into a recession that had started before she had come to power in 1979. Unemployment rose to a record 3,000,000 and the North in particular, suffered as its industrial heart beat with decreasing certainty. The millions of pounds made from North Sea oil however, was not used to fuel an economic revival, but to fund an ever-increasing social security bill. At the start of 1982 the government was on the brink of removal when Argentina's dictator, General Galtieri decided to up-set World Cup preparations and recover the Falkland Islands. Following the invasion of South Georgia in April, troops quickly moved on to the Falklands proper and within three hours the islands' garrison had surrendered and 1800 British citizens were under Argentinian rule. However, two months and twelve days later the Argentinians were routed by a British taskforce and later that year the British electorate thought Margaret Thatcher worth a second term. General Galtieri was ousted from power three days after the surrender.

Elsewhere, the Middle Eastern war between Iran and Iraq entered its third year and Fundamentalism was the growing force in the Islamic world. Israel, as previously agreed at Camp David, handed back the Sinai Peninsula to Egypt, but invaded Lebanon in an attempt to stop the Palestine Liberation Organisation using that country as a base from which to raid its northern territories. The USSR, having invaded in 1979, was bogged down in a war with the Afghan Mujaheddin in its own version of Vietnam, whilst in Poland civil unrest fermented by Solidarity led to the arrest of its leader, Lech Walesa. Central America was shocked by the massacre in El Salvador of over 700 villagers, half of them children, by right-wing elements determined to stamp out a left-wing insurrection and in Guatemala, General Rios Montt claimed that God was on his side as he set about the annihilation of native Indians.

Environmentally, the western world woke up to the damage being done to the planet. Phrases such as "acid rain", "greenhouse effects" and "ozone layer" entered the vocabulary and the AIDS virus, in its early days of discovery, was to dramatically change sexual behaviour. Genetic engineering was taking its first steps and in New York the Bronx jumped to the new sound of rap and hip-hop. In Italy the Pope survived a second assassination attempt and Sophia Loren went to prison for tax evasion.

Meanwhile in post-Franco Spain, the country built itself up for the emotional fervour that was to be the twelfth World Cup. FIFA had persisted with its Europe – South and Central America axis for the 1982 finals, swapping the insecurities of Argentina for those of Spain, where the threats came from the Basque separatists, ETA. The Spanish had first put themselves forwards as candidates in 1964, but had lost out to West Germany in the award

---

Poland and World Cup Defections

Qualification for the World Cup in Spain in 1982 posed something of a problem for the Polish political authorities. Diabolical mis-management by the country's Communist rulers had brought the economy to the brink of collapse. Poland was the largest single debtor nation in Europe and living standards for its working people were woefully low. Not unnaturally, the government was grossly unpopular. In 1980 the government announced a series of price rises to reduce its enormous budget deficit and the result was a wave of protest strikes and demonstrations. Unlike unrest in the past, these were directed by Solidarity, a free trade union that had sprung into existence led by shipyard electrician, Lech Walesa. The movement threatened the authority of the Party and in December 1981, General Jaruzelski assumed control of the government and imposed martial law. In the clampdown that followed, hundreds of opposition leaders, including Walesa, were imprisoned, civil rights were suspended and opponents simply disappeared.

Martial law presented the Polish authorities with many problems, one of the most embarrassing being that of people escaping to the West. By the time of the World Cup 210 sailors, 3 ambassadors and several hundred citizens already abroad had defected to the West. The government in Warsaw was keen to prevent further embarrassing losses and when about 100,000 people expressed an interest in going to Spain, it presented a real headache. The government went for damage limitation, restricting the number of places to 1,000, deciding to send the fans by sea and charging 150,000 zloties for the trip, about 18 months salary for the average Pole. This, it was hoped, would reduce the opportunity for defection. However, things did not go to plan. "Orbis", the state travel organisation, was given the task of making travel arrangements for the 819 fans lucky enough to be given permission to travel, all of them after "recommendations and backing of clubs, social organisations or factories", according to the Polish magazine, "Polityka". It did not do well: few went by sea and only about half bothered to return home.

One group of 37 travelled by bus, through Eastern Europe to Yugoslavia, where they crossed into Italy. The first to leave was a graduate, who went up to the tour guide as soon as they reached the West - such parties never travelled unaccompanied - and asked: "Can I defect now?" He was weeping when he picked up his holdall and walked off the bus. Another six supporters defected at Marseilles and the rest at least waited until they had seen the football. By the time the bus got back to Poland it had lost 19 of its passengers. Similarly, a group of 43 flew to Italy, where they were supposed to get a coach for the rest of the journey. Only 27 got back. The tour guide said that he lost two teachers, two technicians and a draughtsman when they arrived at Milan airport, a soccer coach absconded in Nîmes and the rest disappeared when the football was over.

Maggie, Michel and the Italian Bad Boy - Spain 1982

Officials at the José Rico Perez Stadium in Alicante got a security fright when they received a package marked urgent. The label said it contained nine footballs and a "bomba", an awful worry given the threat from ETA. When opened, the package was found to contain the footballs and a pump to inflate them.

In June 1982, a newspaper reported that Bolton Wanderers, who had narrowly avoided relegation to the old Second Division, had Pelé as their top choice replacement for sacked manager, George Mulhall. Club Chairman, Terry Eagle, said: "We will be looking for a big name to fill the vacancy. We want a player-manager and the first man on our list is Pelé."

of the 1974 tournament. The venue for that of 1982 was discussed during the 1966 finals and, since no one else applied, it went to Spain unopposed.

Spain has a fine tradition of football, especially at club level, and had appeared in the final stages of five World Cups before 1982, but there were many who doubted their ability to organize their own tournament. All these fears seemed justified in January 1982, when the draw to group the finalists was made in Madrid.

In a ceremony played out under the full gaze of a mass TV audience, almost everything that could have gone wrong did, to the acute embarrassment of the Spanish authorities. It began with squabbling over the seeding. All the finalists had been ranked into four tiers of seeds and FIFA's decision to put England among the top seeds, with Argentina, Brazil, Italy, Spain and West Germany, met with much criticism. This was hardly surprising given England's uninspiring recent record, the fact that the team had not qualified through the stages since 1962 and had not made it to the finals since 1970, when they got there as holders.

The names of the other three ranks of seeds were placed in three large cages, used normally to draw the winners of the Spanish lottery, with one from each rank being drawn to join the top seeds to make groups of four. After the top seeds were placed at the head of their groups, it had been decided that the teams of the third rank of seeds would be drawn. It was also decided that the four South American teams should not face each other in the first round. To ensure this, Chile and Peru were to be omitted until the first two third seeds had been drawn and placed with Argentina and Brazil. However, somebody forgot to keep them separate and they were included from the start. It was by pure chance that neither came out too soon and that it was Belgium's name that was first to be drawn. They were to be placed with Argentina to play the opening fixture, but were mistakenly placed in Italy's group. The next team out was Scotland, who should have been with Brazil, but were placed with Argentina. At this point somebody realised the mistake and the situation was rectified. Scotland was shifted to Brazil's group and Belgium placed with Argentina. The whole thing had become a farce and appeared so contrived. Then one of the cages jammed and one of the mini-footballs split open, none of which augured well for the tournament itself, especially since the format for the 1982 finals had been altered to accommodate an increased number of competing teams.

In 1974 FIFA's president, Sir Stanley Rous, offered his opinion that the World Cup would be a better balanced competition if the number of finalists was to be increased to 24. The decision to include more finalists was announced in 1978, but not if it was to be to 20 or 24. This would depend upon which number the Spanish hosts felt more able to cater for and eventually 24 was agreed. It has often been suggested that the increase was a reward to the smaller nations for their support of João Havelange in bid to become FIFA president in 1974. It did mean that a change in format was required and that adopted was a variation of that used in the previous two tournaments. The 24 teams were to be divided into six groups of four teams, to play each other once on a league basis, with the top two in each going into the second stage. Here, they would be drawn into four more groups of three teams, with the winners of these groups making up the semi-finalists. It was to prove a cumbersome and unwieldy format, which certainly did not improve the quality of the football and which FIFA used only once.

Naturally, the increased number of finalists required changes to the qualifying tournament and of the eight new places allocated, four went to Europe and the others were distributed among the South American, Asian, African and CONCACAF regions. Europe's representation was, therefore, raised to 14 teams, South America's to four and the other regions had two each.

To accommodate this increase, Europe's entrants were placed in seven groups, the first six of which were to send two teams to the finals and the last, one. Two teams qualifying from most of the groups meant that surprises were less likely, but the course of events did not flow as smoothly as anticipated. The greatest shock was Holland's failure to qualify out of Group Two. Instead, Belgium and France went through, with the latter, one of the most flamboyant teams in Europe, managing it on goal difference over the Republic of Ireland. England's passage to Spain, too, was far from easy. Defeats in Romania, Switzerland and Norway left the English relying on other results going their way and needing to beat Hungary in the group's final game at Wembley. It was, perhaps, fortunate for England that Hungary had already qualified and were not at their best. Yet, Ron Greenwood's team played with more determination and style than at any time during the competition and secured a victory, although only through Paul Mariner's lone 16th minute effort. They achieved one notable milestone on their road to the finals. The 2-1 defeat by Romania in Bucharest in October 1980 was England's 50th World Cup game, making them the first British team to reach the half century.

The stars of the European qualifying rounds were undoubtedly the West Germans, who went to Spain on a 100% record and having scored 33 goals, including a 7-0 demolition of Finland. Yugoslavia's 2-1 defeat of Greece in Athens in November 1981 also marked a statistical landmark in that country's World Cup history. The first goal they scored was their 150th in the tournament, becoming only the second European team, and the fourth in all to achieve that tally. Such are the heights of World Cup football, but some thought ought to be spared for the minnows without whom it would not be what it is. The second goal conceded by Finland in their 4-0 defeat by Bulgaria in Sofia in May 1981 was the 150th they had let in, the second country to have done so. An equally undistinguished record was achieved by Luxembourg when Italy beat them 1-0 in the last qualifying game of Group Five. It was Luxembourg's 50th World Cup game and they had yet to record a win. Two draws were all they had to show for over 45 years of endeavour.

South America's qualifying tournament was run as previously, with three groups of three countries, and threw up a couple of surprises, though not in the case of Brazil. Under new coach, Telé Santana, the Brazilians had once again assembled a squad of potential world beaters to match those of 1958 and 1970. With players of the quality of Falcão, Zico and Socrates, qualification from Group One was a straight forward affair and Brazil was the only other team to reach Spain with a 100% record. One of the teams they overcame along the way was Venezuela, whose 1-0 defeat of Bolivia in Caracas in March 1981 was their first World Cup win in 17 games stretching over four tournaments. Ecuador's victory over Paraguay in Quito in May 1981 was their first in the World Cup since the 1966 qualify-

Following Norway's defeat of England in a World Cup qualifier in Oslo in September 1981, a Norwegian radio commentator exclaimed excitedly: "We are the best in the world. We have beaten England. Lord Nelson, Lord Beaverbrook, Sir Winston Churchill, Sir Anthony Eden, Clement Atlee, Henry Cooper, Lady Diana. We have beaten them all. Maggie Thatcher can you hear me? Maggie Thatcher, your boys took one hell of a beating. Norway have beaten England at football." Ron Greenwood's phlegmatic response was: "We let them play for five minutes and they scored two goals."

Chinese workers were warned in the Shanghai Liberation Daily not to take "sickies" during the World Cup to watch television coverage, as had happened during the qualifying rounds. "A number of workers made excuses saying they were sick or that they had family problems and stayed at home. The watch word this time must be production first," the paper said.

The Argentinian team hoped for a massive following of around 15,000 supporters, but the Falklands war and the financial devastation at home meant that no more than 500 travelled.

ing stage and only their third in all, in six tournaments. The surprise of that group was that Paraguay, reigning South American champions, came bottom of a group won by Chile. The other surprise of the South American rounds was the failure of Uruguay to qualify, for the third time in succession.

As in the past, the African, CONCACAF and Asia/Oceania regions provided the most complicated routes to the finals.

Once again, the African stage was organized as a two-legged knock-out, with Liberia, Sudan, Togo and Zimbabwe all having byes into the second round, and with Egypt and Madagascar getting there because of the withdrawal of Ghana and Uganda. Egypt then secured automatic progress into the third round when opponents, Libya, withdrew, but were then narrowly defeated by Morocco. From the third round, four teams won through to the group finals, two two-legged ties producing two winners to go to Spain, Algeria and Cameroon.

The teams of the CONCACAF region were divided into Northern, Central and Caribbean zones, with two teams from each making it through to the group finals. Two of the zones were played as straight leagues, but the Caribbean zone consisted of A and B groups, both of which sent one team to the group finals. A further complication was added when Grenada and Guyana had to play a two-legged preliminary tie to decide which of them would join Cuba and Surinam in Group A. Guyana took the honour, but then failed to win any of their other games and ended up bottom of the pile. Cuba came top and went into the group finals with Haiti, Canada, Mexico, Honduras and El Salvador. The meeting of the latter two in 1969 had sparked a war, but there were to be no such problems this time. Both took their places in Spain as winners. For Honduras, it was their first qualification, whilst it was El Salvador's second visit to the finals, both at the fifth attempt.

One of the most remarkable qualifications for the finals was that of New Zealand from the Asia-Oceania region at their fourth attempt. The zone was organized on similar lines to the CONCACAF area, with four groups each sending one team to the group final. Three of the groups were straight round robins, whilst the fourth was divided into two sub groups and requiring semi-finals and a final to produce a winner. China qualified from the group and joined New Zealand, Saudi Arabia and Kuwait in the group final. To get this far, New Zealand had played eight games, six of which they had won, including a 13-0 defeat of Fiji in Auckland in August 1981, a World Cup record score. The poor Fijians had lost 10-0 to Australia in Melbourne only two days previously. The New Zealanders then had to play a further six games in the group final, where their fortunes were more mixed. A 2-2 home draw in their penultimate match against bottom of the table Saudi Arabia seemed to have ended their chances of getting to Spain since it left them needing to beat the Saudis by five clear goals in the return leg in Riyadh. Unbelievably, they did it, but ended with the same points tally as China and a play off was needed. It took place in January 1982 and goals from Steve Wooddin and Wynton Ryder earned a 2-1 victory and a place in Spain, alongside Kuwait, who had won the group. All in all, the Kiwis had played 15 qualifying games, scored 44 goals and travelled 64,000 miles to get there, all of which set new tournament records.

Politics usually rears its unwanted head at some stage during a World Cup tournament and this one had been happily free of such tribulations so far. The Spanish authorities feared the attentions of their own ETA terrorists, but it was from a totally unexpected source that the main threat to the event's smooth running came with the Falklands Crisis. The crisis was seen as an act of naked aggression by Britain and her supporters and resulted in pressure being brought to bear on FIFA to ban Argentinian participation in the World Cup.

FIFA could never contemplate not allowing the champions to defend their crown, especially in Spain where there was much pan-Hispanic support for Argentina. The threat of the British teams withdrawing in protest did not materialize and a more muted disapproval came when British broadcasters refused to cover Argentina's participation.

One of the casualties of this was that the opening ceremony and game were not screened on British television. What the public missed was a colourful display and an opening game that produced a goal, the first since 1962. The pageant unfurled on 13th June, in Barcelona's imposing Nou Camp Stadium, before a live crowd of 95,000 and an estimated world-wide TV audience of 1.3 billion people, a staggering revelation of just how far FIFA's showcase had come since those first tentative steps in Montevideo in 1930. The ceremony was as impressive as any yet seen. Witnessed by King Juan Carlos, it had the obligatory traditional dancers, a welter of Spanish flamenco, and gymnasts, "a blur of white in their criss-cross patterns." It culminated in a spectacular finale that involved 5,000 doves, 10,000 balloons, 1 million flowers and 2,000 people who came together to form a human representation of Picasso's "Dove of Peace". It was very stunning and quite moving in its own way.

The opening game barely raised itself above the ordinary, but it had more to offer than the measly morsels that had blighted previous opening days. Its greatest attraction, to the locals at least, was the much-anticipated appearance of Diego Maradona, whose £4 million pound transfer to Barcelona had recently been completed. He was making his debut on "home" territory, though his impact was less than Barcelona fans would have wanted. His team began in sprightly form, anxious that their title defence should commence in style, but the Belgians soon found their measure. They were not afraid to apply physical force to contain their technically superior opponents and were able to slow the game to a pace that suited their pedestrian approach. It frustrated the Argentinians and increased Belgium's chances of success, something they exploited more keenly than the South Americans. After a goalless first half, the Belgians capitalized on some defensive uncertainty to score the game's only goal with just over an hour of play gone. It was taken by Europe's leading scorer, Erwin Vandenbergh, who took "an interminable age to control the elusive ball but he still had time enough to beat Fillol easily before being challenged." It forced Argentina to up their pace and they might have clawed something back late in the match. Maradona hit the bar and Mario Kempes should have scored from the rebound, but he missed and Belgium held on for the win.

The next day saw Italy take on Poland in Group One and Brazil meet the USSR in Group Six. Group One was to be particularly low scoring and it began typically with an unadventurous Italy happy to share the spoils with a 0-0 draw. It was Dino Zoff's 100th international and the first time Italy

---

Before the friendly against Finland in Helsinki on 3rd June, England had played five warm-up matches and had not conceded a goal. The run came to an end when England won 4-1. Trevor Brooking, whose wife, Hilkka, was Finnish, had to get 17 tickets so that her family could see the match.

On 25th May 1982, a Brazilian supporter arrived in Paris on his way to Spain having cycled 16,250 miles to get there. His journey took him through most of South and Central America - Brazil, Uruguay, Argentina, Chile, Peru, Panama, Costa Rica, Nicaragua, Honduras, Guatamala and, finally, Mexico. He then flew to London before sailing for France to undertake the last leg of his incredible journey.

A Bangkok astrologer predicted that France, West Germany, Brazil and the USSR would all make the last four.

When Erwin Vandenbergh scored for Belgium in their 1-0 victory over holder's Argentina it was the first goal in an opening game for 20 years.

Brazil 2 : USSR 1
Oleg Blokhin - USSR.

"The Things People Say" Award I for 1982 goes to...

Peter Blackburn of the London Evening Standard. Writing about the Soviets, he said: "You virtually need a copy of Pravda to secure admission to their training hideaway in Malaga..."

had failed to win their opening game in five World Cups, but in such competitions the Italians are no respecters of traditions.

Theirs was the better first half and the second belonged to Poland, with few chances created by either team. The closest effort came ten minutes from the end, when Grzegorz Lato cleared Giancarlo Antognini's header off the line and Marco Tardelli smashed the rebound against the bar.

A better game was that played in Seville, where Brazil's showy football came up against the more directect earthiness of the Soviet Union. The Soviets made the early running, were unlucky not to have been awarded a penalty when Shengalia was brought down in the 18th minute and were well worth the lead that Andrej Bal gave them ten minutes before half-time. However, Brazilian ball mastery began to work its charm after the interval and fortunes were reversed. First to show was Socrates who, in the 75th minute, "confronted by two Soviet defenders, he shuffled to the right, accelerated, beat them both and shot high into the right corner." It was a brilliant goal and typical of the swashbuckling flamboyance of the Brazilian captain. A second piece of magic, two minutes from time, wrapped the game up, this time supplied by Eder, who "found the soul of Brazilian football with a stunning shot", as one reporter waxed.

Cameroon made their debut in the World Cup finals in Coruña on 15th June. Coached by France's former star, Jean Vincent, they were lively, inventive and unlucky not to have registered a goal against an over-cautious Peru. In the words of one who saws the match, the South Americans "started at walking pace, lost the initiative and only fleetingly managed to get back into the contest." Their's was an incomprehensible approach to the match, especially in view of their respective World Cup histories, and it served only to encourage the Africans to push forwards. Their greater sense of purpose seemed to have been rewarded when Roger Milla got the ball into the net in the first half, but he was adjudged offside. Peru picked up the pace a little in the second half, although they never seriously threatened the Cameroon goal, defended ably by captain Thomas N'Kono. He always wore the tracksuit bottoms he had been given by Germany's Sepp Maier and maybe they inspired the water board worker from Yaounde. Certainly, it was very disappointing from Peru, but very encouraging for the newcomers.

Meanwhile, in one of the most one-sided game ever seen in the World Cup finals, the Hungarians were savaging the team from El Salvador. From the time they got their first goal, in the third minute, the Hungarians virtually scored at will and had the Central Americans completely at their mercy - and little of it they showed. Tibor Nyilasi headed that strike and further scores from Gabor Pölöskei and Laszló Fazekas saw their team coast to a 3-0 half-time lead. So far, it had been torrid. The second half became a nightmare. József Tóth and Fazekas made it 5-0 before

Ramírez Zapata made himself a hero back home by pulling one back. From that point, Hungary hit with a vengeance. Laszló Kiss, on as a substitute, was the next on the score sheet and within seven more minutes had netted another two, to become the first replacement to score a hat trick in the World Cup finals. The ninth goal came from Lázár Szentes and Nyilaisi, who had begun the rout, rounded it off. The 10-1 scoreline set a new record for the World Cup finals, but it did not satisfy Kalman Mészöly, Hungary's coach, who lambasted his team for having conceded. He said his defence had "made five or six mistakes that, against Argentina, could have meant a five or six nil defeat."

Scotland 5 : New Zealand 2
New Zealand forward Stephen Wooddin celebrates New Zealand's 2nd goal.

"Scotland's peculiar habit of destroying or jeopardizing, all of the good in their football revealed itself again here", was the Times's description of their opener against New Zealand. They were up to their old tricks again. The Scots had a superb first half, hit themselves into a 3-0 lead and then almost let it slip. The first followed some brilliant work from Gordon Strachan, who ran from midfield, riding tackles and dodging defenders, before putting Kenny Dalglish away to score. It was in the 18th minute. Ten minutes later, Alan Brazil's shot was only parried by Van Hattum, in goal, and John Wark followed in to make it 2-0. Within three more minutes, Wark notched his second when he headed in Strachan's cross. The Scots were riding high and Strachan, in particular, in fine form. Then, things began to fall apart as, within 20 minutes of the second half kicking off, goals from Steve Sumner and Steve Wooddin brought the score back to 3-2.

New Zealand's first came from a defensive error, when Danny McGrain tried to back pass to Alan Rough, over hit it and it rebounded to Sumner. Their second was a pearl, as Wooddin skipped through a mesmerized defence to plant the ball in the net. The Scots needed to steady their nerves and, when John Robertson chipped a free kick in the 73rd minute, the game began to move back in their favour. Seven minutes later, Steve Archibald headed in another Strachan cross and the game was secure. New Zealand had been the 50th team to appear in the World Cup finals, but not the first to test more established opposition. The Scots would need far more care in their remaining fixtures.

By their own standards the West Germans had disappointed in recent years, but the team seemed to be coming back to form under coach, Jupp Derwall. They had won the 1980 European championships and were widely tipped to do well in Spain.

However, they were the victims of one of the great reversals of the tournament's history when they came across Algeria in Gijón on 16th June. It was a match in which they hardly lost control, but they squandered the

Preparing for the game against New Zealand, due to kick-off at 21.00, the Scots slept during the day and trained at night so the players would be at their best.

"The Things People Say" Award II for 1982 goes to...

Peter Blackman of the London Evening Standard again. Commenting on New Zealand's comeback against Scotland, he wrote: "for 10 minutes later in the match New Zealand felt as tall as Brazil. And why not?... But Scotland, for those 10 minutes, fell apart like a Lego block hit by an irate child."

When asked to give a urine sample after the game against New Zealand, Scottish player Alan Brazil, couldn't oblige because of the amount of water he had lost during the game and had to go back the following day.

West German caoch Jupp Derwall took only 19 players to Spain, his reason for leaving three at home being: "There is no point in having a few people around for more than a month only spreading gloom."

Maggie, Michel and the Italian Bad Boy - Spain 1982

many chances they created and, like many fancied teams before, it cost them.

After a goalless first half, Algeria took the lead in the 57th minute when Harald Schumacher blocked Lakhdar Belloumi's shot and the ball fell to Rabah Madjer.

Germany's response was to turn dirty in an attempt to suppress the lively Algerians and Karl-Heinz Rummenigge almost saved his country's blushes with a 68th minute equalizer. Within a minute, though, Belloumi's close range shot put Algeria back into the lead and the Germans were unable to restore their battered pride. "I still can't believe it. It's beyond my understanding", was Durwall's response to his country's shame. Incredulous the Germans may have been, but they had only themselves to blame.

Soon after kick off in England's game against France, Steve Coppell won a throw in on the right. He took it himself, Terry Butcher headed on and Bryan Robson, unmarked in the French penalty area, dispatched the ball into the net. The move took 27 seconds and was the fastest goal of the tournament. It solicited a resolute response from the French, who began to probe a fragile English defence. It was breached in the 27th minute, when Trevor Francis lost the ball and Gérard Soler was set free to round Butcher and score. For the next 40 minutes the game was evenly poised, until the English began to show their mettle in the last 25.

They grew stronger in the second half and it was the French who began to look suspect. Their increasing dominance told in the 66th minute, when Robson scored his second, heading in Francis's cross. England's third goal was set up by a magnificent 50 yard cross-field pass from Coppell. Ray Wilkins collected the ball, tapped it to Francis and his shot deflected off Marius Trésor to the feet of Paul Mariner. The Ipswich striker made no mistake and England's 3-1 victory got them off to the perfect start.

The host's campaign got off to a disastrous start against newcomers, Honduras, who "blasted Spain... and the rest of the world out of their complacency with a mighty performance." It would have been so different had Spain's early pressure been brought to bear, but in the sixth minute, in one of those rare moments that make or break football games, Gilberto Yearwood cleared a Spanish shot off his goal line. The ball was hastily cleared up field, it fell to Héctor Zelaya and, seconds later, was in the net, to the horror of the home fans. For the next 65 minutes the "hugely courageous and colourful players of Honduras led and defied the power of Spain." Inept may be one way of describing the Spanish performance, though nervous would add a little understanding to the

Spain 1 : Honduras 1
Ramon Maradiaga - Honduras.

equation. The pressure they faced was immense and given the number of chances they missed, obviously affected the players. In the end, it took a penalty to spare Spanish blushes, awarded when local favourite, Saura, was floored in the area. Roberto López-Ufarte bravely took the responsibility and scored to deny Honduras the pleasure of doing what North Korea had done in 1966 or the United States in 1950.

The weather had a decided influence on the next day's game between Chile and Austria. It had rained heavily before hand and a slippery pitch that cut easily produced "a grim uncompromising" affair that mirrored the overcast conditions. This was a match that hardly got out of first gear and, after a promising start from Chile, the better organized Austrians gradually assumed the upper hand. They took the lead in the 21st minute with a headed goal from Walter Schachter, and five minutes later Chile were awarded a penalty. Carlos Caszely missed it and with it went his team's best chance. The score remained 1-0 and Austria joined Algeria on top of the group.

The two other games played that day brought excellent results for the underdogs. In Valladolid, a very well organized and drilled Kuwait took on and defied a most disappointing Czechoslovakia, the reigning Olympic champions. The Arabs were coached by the Brazilian, Carlos Alberto (not the World Cup star), who had himself succeeded Mario Zagalo (who was the World Cup star), and the influence of both was obvious in the positive style of play the team adopted from the start. They had the Czechs under regular pressure, though fell behind to a very dubious penalty, awarded for a foul that most commentators felt was mere obstruction. Antonin Panenka fired in and the Czechs had a lead they hardly deserved. It ought to have inspired them, but they seemed devoid of any imagination and it was the Kuwaitis who continued to enjoy the best of the play. Their reward, "a ferocious, swerving drive from 25 yards" scored by Fasail Al Dakhil, came in the second half and, though they created several chances that more experienced players would have converted, victory was denied them. Instead, Kuwait had to settle for a creditable draw, when an incredible win would have been fairer.

When Northern Ireland took on a far more strongly fancied Yugoslavia, it was their first visit to the World Cup finals since 1958. That year Billy Bingham had been in the team and now he was manager. Manchester United's Norman Whiteside was also begging comparison with that earlier tournament. Aged 17 years and 41 days, he set a new record as the youngest player to appear in the finals, beating that of Pelé set in 1958. Such peripheral facts were among the most interesting features of this game, which was far from pretty. The Yugoslavs often had the best of play, but the Irish were strong and determined at the back and "deflected every ar-

Following the 1-1 draw with Spain, police were needed to restore order in Tegucigalpa, the Honduran capital when thousands of fans went onto the streets to celebrate. President Roberto Cordora sent a telegram to congratulate the team and spoke of the gallantry and pride "with which you are putting the name of this country on the sports field with a world dimension."

Yugoslavia 0 : N. Ireland 0
Norman Whiteside - N. Ireland.

row Yugoslavia had to fire." They did well to hold on for a 0-0 draw, which left all in the group on level points and with all to play for. It was a better start than the Irish could have hoped for and their joy and relief was barely disguised by the modest remarks of John McClelland after the game. "Well, it makes sure that the holiday could last a little longer", he said.

The next day saw Italy in action for the second time, against Peru, and it was situation normal. As reported in the Times, they "pushed forward gingerly from the start, scored a good goal and then sat back." Their lead came in the 19th minute and followed a skilful move involving Antognini down the left. His square pass found Bruno Conti just outside the area and Conti ducked around his marker "to fire a fierce right foot shot into the roof of the net." Defence then took priority and, as often happens when the Italians are at their cynical worse, anything goes. So negative were they that they refused even to push forwards in the last period of the first half when Peru were reduced to ten men after Duart went off temporarily with an eye injury.

In fact, they shored up their defence at half-time by taking Rossi off and replacing him with Causio. It gave Peru the best opportunity to play football and they did with some style. They were unlucky not to have been awarded a penalty when Oblitas was up-ended in the area and it was only seven minutes from the end that their finer spirit and enterprise reaped its rewards. The evergreen Cubillas rolled a free kick across the penalty area and Rubén Díaz's shot was deflected into the net off Collorati. It was a little fortunate, but the point it secured was the least that Peru deserved.

Argentina's opener had been a huge disappointment, but their second outing, against Hungary, showed just why they were reigning world champions. They went at their opponents and the Hungarians simply laid down. Maradona was in sparkling form and, had not the Hungarian goalkeeper played equally well, his team might well have been on the end of the sort of drubbing they had given to El Salvador three days earlier. It took the Argentinians 26 minutes to find the net, but by then the Magyars "were a nervous wreck". The goal was scored by Bertoni, from Passarella's free kick and, two minutes later, when another Bertoni shot was blocked, Maradona reacted quickest and "flipped the ball home with effortless efficiency." Ten minutes after half-time, Maradona struck again with a goal that was characterized by his speed, balance and deadly finishing, and four minutes later Ardíles made it 4-0. His was a rather comical goal that seemed to mirror the overall Hungarian performance. Having raced up field with the ball, he released Olguin, whose hard, low shot cannoned off the post. The ball hit the head of Hungary's keeper, who had lost sight of it and, in the confusion, Ardiles popped up and "gleefully tucked it home." Pölöskei managed a late consolation for the Europeans, but it could not disguise the manner of the defeat or the power of Argentina's football.

Argentina was not the only South American team to crush European opposition that day. In Seville, Brazil took on the Scots and, after a sluggish start that saw the Scots take the lead, they turned on the style and ran away with the game. Scotland's 18th minute lead was well merited, given the way they approached the game, and was created by the vision of Graeme Souness, whose long cross-field pass picked out Wark. He immediately played the ball to David Narey and his 22-yard shot raised the optimism of the tartan hordes dotted around the ground, intermingled with drum-beating Brazilian fans. The sporting atmosphere of the crowd was not lost on the players, but did not dampen the zeal of the Brazilian players once they had fallen behind. They picked up the pace and launched a whole "series of typically flowing attacks... (which) floundered on a retreating Scottish defence" until it was finally breached by a piece of Zico magic in the 34th minute. Alan Hansen had bundled Carezo to the ground and Zico "surveyed the wall of defenders, saw a space and a sight of the net, judged the angle and curled the ball round and over... (that defence) with such uncanny skill that poor Rough was made to look foolish." With the scores level, the Scots were still in with a chance, but the goal that changed the course of the match came three minutes into the second half, when Oscar headed in Junior's corner. It forced the Scots to press forward in search of an equalizer and they exposed themselves at the back. The Brazilians found themselves with increasing amounts of space in which to operate and the stage belonged to them. They warmed to the invitation and their third goal highlighted their "incomparable imagination." Socrates acquired the ball in the middle and he knocked it forward to Serginho, whose clever, jinking pass found Eder unmarked. Almost nonchalantly, he chipped over Rough and into the net. The Scots were being run ragged and playing for damage limitation. To their credit, their defence was broken only once more, in the 86th minute, when Falcão's long range effort crashed in to the net, but they had been thoroughly overwhelmed by the rampant Brazilians.

The next day's play brought two undistinguished displays from European teams against weaker opposition, a situation only salvaged by the more focused Soviet Union. In La Coruña, the Poles "created a wealth of scoring opportunities but then put on a demonstration of some of the worst finishing in the tournament" against Cameroon. Boniek and Lato were both guilty of blaring misses in a first half they totally dominated and their profligacy encouraged Cameroon to a bolder approach in the second. However, they too were unable to break the deadlock and a 0-0 draw was the end result.

For the Africans, this was more than creditable and after the game, Jean Vincent said: "We have shown we are a match for the best." It would have been very different had the Poles not been so generous in front of goal.

Meanwhile, at Elche, a nervous and unsure Belgium -"unsure of whether they would get what they wanted, unsure even of what they wanted", as one reporter put it - were proving quite inept against El Salvador. Admittedly, El Salvador had shored up their defence following their mauling by Hungary, but, in a game in which Belgium's goalkeeper, Bayern Munich's Jean-Marie Pfaff, had little to do, they should have done better than the single goal provided by Ludo Coeck's 25th minute free kick. Guevara Mora played brilliantly in El Salvador's goal to keep the score respectable, but this does not hide the real lack of purpose in Belgium's play and it was left to the USSR to restore some pride to Europe's football. They were far more masterful against New Zealand, especially in the second half when their opponents began to fade. New Zealand did well in a low key first half, which saw the Soviets score only once. The goal was set up by Oleg Blokhin, the son of a former sprint champion, who outpaced two defenders before crossing to Andrej Bal. His shot was blocked, but Yuri Gavrilov forced in the rebound. The play was more open after the break and some three minutes into the half, the Soviets scored again. Ramaz Shengalia completely miskicked an attempt on goal and the ball fell to Blokhin, who finished with "the most clinical of drives from the edge of the box." It was Blokhin, having an exceptional game and who "provided the decisive edge to their skillful midfield play", who sent in the cross from which the Soviets scored their third. His pass, in the 67th minute, set Sergei Baltacha free to give a final 3-0 scoreline.

When West Germany next played, on 20th June, it was with a real sense of urgency and determination. The humiliation meted out five days previously had to be firmly expunged and only a comprehensive victory would suffice. The Chileans were the victims, sacrificed on the altar of national pride, unable to find an answer to the German renewal, or to Karl-Heinz Rummenigge, whose own performance inspired his team's metamorphosis. It took him only nine minutes to register his first strike when he got on the end of Pierre Littbarski's cross and let fly a 25 yard drive that goalkeeper, Osbén, had covered, but let slip under his body. Some ten minutes into the second half and he struck again. Once more, Littbarski crossed from the right and Rummenigge headed a goal that went in off the post and the goalkeeper's body. His next was the best of the game and followed a swift exchange of passes with Felix Magath before he steered the ball into the net. That was in the 66th minute and 15 minutes later Uwe Reinders, on as a substitute, made the score 4-0. The Chileans did grab a late consolation, when Gustavo Moscoso rounded Manny Kaltz, but they had been well beaten long before. Few could have failed to appreciate the clear intentions signalled by the Germans.

The English were also in action that day, against Czechoslovakia, and whilst their victory was comfortable enough, the worrying sign was that they did not win by a wider margin. Indeed, England could easily have been 3-0 up inside ten minutes, with both Mariner and Wilkins unlucky with good efforts and further chances scorned in a goalless first half. At the interval, Robson, who had also made one blaring miss and who had picked up an injury, was replaced by Glen Hoddle. His long, thoughtful passes added a new dimension to England's team performance and gave the Czechs no end of problems.

A greater incision resulted and in the 63rd minute England took a deserved lead. Seman, the Czech goalkeeper, failed to pick up Wilkins's corner and Francis punished the mistake. Three minutes later, Mariner sent a pass into the Czech area and Jozef Barmos could only steer it into his own net. It was the only own goal of the tournament and gave England a 2-0 win that ought to have been more.

The other game played that day featured Spain and Yugoslavia and, once more, the home team appeared nervous and affected by the pressure of the occasion. They certainly failed to live up to their pre-tournament billing as one of the favourites and were often overshadowed by a Yugoslav team that rarely played to its own potential. The Yugoslavs began brightly and took the lead in the tenth minute, when Petrovic "floated in a simple free kick" and Ivan Gudelj "ran through to conquer with a scooping header." Their lead, though, lasted a mere two

Maggie, Michel and the Italian Bad Boy - Spain 1982

minutes and was ended in very controversial circumstances. When Zajec brought down Alonso, he was clearly outside the area, but the Danish referee had no hesitation in pointing to the spot. The protests having been waved away, López-Ufarte stepped up to take the kick and missed. Justice, it seemed, had been done. The referee then ordered the kick to be retaken, claiming that Pantelic had moved. The Yugoslavs were thunderstruck. This time, after more protests had been demonstrably ignored, Juanito took the kick and did score. For a while the match simmered at the edges, but after missing two good chance to restore their lead, the Yugoslavs began to fade. Their midfield play still often had the edge over that of Spain, but up front they lost their sharpness. Spain's winner came from a second half corner and was scored by the substitute, Enrique Saura, who had only been on the pitch for three minutes.

Algeria's World Cup bubble burst the next day when they met Austria in Oviedo. It was a "hard-fought match" and one in which, in the first half at least, the Africans gave good account of themselves. The Austrians appeared hesitant, as if uncertain of how to impose their authority on eager and confident opponents, as they zipped around with an assuredness belying their supposed lowly status. It disconcerted the Austrians and their frustration was heightened when they had a strong penalty appeal turned down. A 0-0 half-time scoreline was a fair reflection of the state of play, but the Algerians could not maintain their rhythm into the second half and the Europeans began to assert themselves. They took the lead in the 56th minute when Schachter latched onto a rebound and forced the ball home off the inside of the post. Eleven minutes later, Krankl's "spectacular drive" sealed a 2-0 victory that took his team to the top of the group.

The Kuwaitis were also brought fully back to earth that day when they came across France in Valladolid, in another match that had its share of controversy. The French needed a good performance to get their hopes back on track and Bernard Genghini's "swerving free kick" on the hour set them on their way. They went further ahead shortly before half-time when a through pass from Alain Giresse "was so astute that Platini... calmly walked the ball into the net." Three minutes after the break, a terrific volley from Didier Six, set up by Platini, made the score 3-0 and the French were cruising. Abdullah Al Buloushi gave Kuwait feint hope with a goal 15 minutes from the end, before refereeing idiocy cut in to disrupt what had been an enjoyable game. Giresse scored a well taken goal that was quite rightly given by Miroslav Stupar, the Soviet official.

However, the Kuwait defence had, unusually, not moved to cut out the Frenchman as he steadied himself to strike. To a man, they claimed they had stopped playing because they had heard a whistle. If they had, it must have come from the crowd and, as their protests continued, the head of the Kuwait FA, Prince Fahid al Yaber al Saber, in purple flowing robes, came down from the stand to join the remonstrations. He threatened to take his team off the pitch, a move he later denied claiming he actually asked the players to continue. The referee caved in and, to understandable French consternation, he disallowed the goal and gave a drop ball instead. It was poor judgement by the referee. The game had been held up for eight minutes and his authority had been undermined. Justice of sorts was done in the end, when a Kuwaiti goal was disallowed and Maxime Bossis netted a fourth for France. For his troubles, Prince Fahid was fined £8,000 by FIFA, a sum the oil-rich sheikh probably pulled out of his small change.

22 Men and a Bag of Wind

When Northern Ireland met Honduras in the day's third game, it was honours even as both achieved their second draws of the tournament. The 1-1 scoreline reflected well the overall balance of play and, although the Irish created marginally more chances, their boldness and conviction found no match in the accuracy of their shooting. They took an early lead when McIlroy's free kick crashed against the bar, Chris Nicholl headed the rebound onto the same piece of woodwork and Gerry Armstrong scrambled the ball in at the third attempt.

Irish hopes were for a big win after such an opening, but the Hondurans were dogged enough to defy them and mounted some cutting attacks of their own. They equalized in the 60th minute, when the Irish failed to deal with a corner and Eduardo Antonio Laing "flung himself mind and body at a vacant near post" to score a diving header. The result kept the feint hopes of both alive, but the general expectation was for the other sides in the group to qualify above them.

The dull progress of the teams in Group One was fleetingly brought to life on 22nd June, when Poland took on Peru. After withstanding an initial ten minutes of Peruvian dominance, which twice saw the South Americans denied by fine saves from Mlynarczyk in goal, Poland's midfield combination stepped up a gear. Inspired by the magnificence of Zbigniew Boniek, they took the game by the throat and never let go. He had the ball in the net in the 16th minute, but saw it disallowed, and before the half had come to a close both he and Andrzej Buncol had been denied by the woodwork. Poland had to wait until ten minutes into the second half before the power of their play began to turn to goals, their first an "angled left-foot drive" from Wlodzimierz Smolarek. Three minutes later, Boniek homed in on goal and Quiroga rushed out in an attempt to halt his progress. The Pole casually flicked the ball over the prostrate keeper and Lato raced in to shoot into the empty net. Boniek himself scored the third, in the 61st minute, side footing Buncol's free kick and seven minutes later Buncol finished off a superb move that saw the ball swept swiftly downfield, out of defence and into the net. Poland's fifth and last, taken by Wlodzimierz Ciolek on as a substitute, came 14 minutes from the end. The Peruvians were well beaten, but Guillermo La Rosa "struck a blow for their pride with a powerful drive" eight minutes from the whistle. Victory took Poland to the top of the group and assured them of a place in the second phase.

The other games played that day both produced draws. The Hungarians needed to defeat Belgium to progress further and, for a while, it looked as if they might. They had the better of the early exchanges, made several openings and then took a 28th minute lead when Jószef Varga's rising left foot shot screeched into the net. However, they had missed too many chances and falling behind spurred the Belgians to adopt a style more adventurous than had been seen in their previous outings. They hit the post in the 35th minute and drew level with a little under a quarter of an hour to go. The goal was created by Jan Ceulemans, whose strong run down the right took him past two defenders. His cross was met by Alex Czerniatynski for a goal which planted his team at the top of the group and into the second round.

Another team needing victory that day was Scotland, who faced the Soviet Union in Málaga. They gave a gritty performance, showing all their fighting qualities from the start and fully deserved the lead taken in the 15th minute, when Joe Jordan latched onto Narey's long pass. The Scots continued to take the game to the Soviets, but could not score again and, in the second half, a strong Soviet team began to assert itself more forcefully. They drew level on the hour, when Alexander Chivadze "curled a beautiful equalizer past Rough" and went ahead six minutes from time, taking advantage of a defensive error. Hansen and Willie Miller, in a rare moment of confusion, collided with each other and presented Shengelia with a clear chance on goal. The brave Scots tried manfully to salvage the situation and Graeme Souness levelled the scores with three minutes left, but it was too late. A 2-2 draw was the end result and the Scots went out of their third World Cup in succession on goal difference.

"Italy limped into the second phase" in typical style on 23rd June, with their third successive draw against Cameroon. They gave an edgy performance, marked by a decided reluctance to commit men forwards and when they got into scoring positions, the Italians were unable to make them tell. After only ten minutes, Conti missed an open goal, just one of several chances that went begging. It took them an hour to fashion a breakthrough and then they held the lead only briefly. The goal was set up by Rossi, operating on the left, whose "marvellous cross to the far post" was met by Francesco Graziani. A matter of seconds later, Milla fed a ball forwards to Gregoire M'Bida. The African appeared to be offside, but was allowed to continue his run and he placed the ball in the net. There was a much greater composure about the Cameroon's game in the second half and they created several chances, including a spectacular long range shot that Zoff did well to save. Once again, though, the Italians

Maggie, Michel and the Italian Bad Boy - Spain 1982

Following their early exit, the Yugoslav
team was welcomed home by 2,000
angry fans all shouting: "Traitors, lazy-
bones, shame." Midfielder, Safet Susic
couldn't get away from the airport as
supporters had wrecked his car.

The feast of Ramadan, when all Mos-
lems ast between sunrise and sunset,
began the day Kuwait played England.
The Kuwait team honoured their religious duties, as they had during the
1980 Olympics.

proved that they were masters of the draw and were happy to settle for it. They qualified for the next stage by virtue of having scored a single goal more than Cameroon.

Two of the tournament's other minnows, El Salvador and New Zealand, also bowed out that day. Argentina's defeat of El Salvador was much more comfortable than the 2-0 scoreline suggests and it was the Central Americans' reliance on a packed defence that prevented it being extended. Argentina's first goal, scored after 22 minutes, was the result of a hotly disputed penalty, awarded when Calderon was brought down. It was put away by Passarella, but there was no disputing their second, a well taken individual effort from Bertoni in the 53rd minute. It had been a poor match, "marred by fouls and inconsistent refereeing", and much better was that played in Seville between Brazil and New Zealand. This was New Zealand's biggest football fixture to date and they showed their appreciation of the occasion when their substitutes handed out flowers to the crowd before the kick off. It was the only impression they made as they were roundly trounced. The Brazilians were out of a different league and treated this almost as an exhibition game. They created, and missed, several early chances before Zico gave them the lead in the 29th minute, with an acrobatic bicycle kick from a Leandro cross. Two minutes later, Leandro crossed again and Zico registered his second with a "crisp right foot shot" from ten yards. (See Zico profile on page 327). Brazil's third came ten minutes into the second half when a through ball from Socrates split the defence and Falcão burst through to score. By now, the Brazilians were enjoying themselves, knocking the ball around and drawing pretty patterns on the turf. The New Zealanders had barely got out of their own half and Brazil appeared able to score at will. As expected, they scored a fourth and it came from Serginho in the 70th minute.

Chile's match with Algeria (See Algeria v Chile profile on page 329) left the progress of both dependent upon the result of the game between Austria and West Germany, whilst France's place in the second stage came courtesy of a draw against Czechoslovakia in Valladolid. After an even and goalless first half, Didier Six broke the deadlock in the 60th minute with a goal that was set up by Bernard Lacombe.

The goal woke the Czechs up to their possible elimination from the tournament and they began throwing themselves forwards in numbers. Their pressure began to tell on the French and with just over five minutes to go, Bossis brought down Ladislav Vizek, conceding a penalty, and Panenka "stepped up and confidently rammed the ball home." It was hit with an assuredness born of experience. It was the 53rd penalty of the Rapid Vienna man's career and he had yet to miss one. The equalizer spurred the Czechs and in a thrilling last five minutes that had the French on the ropes, Vizek was sent off for kicking Platini and the Czechs had a header cleared off the line. In spite of it all, the French held on and Czechoslovakia went out of the World Cup.

In the Group Five game played that day, a victory for Yugoslavia over Honduras was absolutely necessary, but would still leave their progress dependent on the result of the game between Spain and Northern Ireland. The Yugoslavs won, though it was heavy work. The Americans defended gallantly and even had the best chances of the first half. They eventually went down to a penalty, conceded in the 87th minute and awarded after Milos Serbic "had beaten off three desperate tackles as he worked his way in from the wing and was felled as he broke for goal." Vladimir Petrovic converted the spot kick and it broke the hearts of the Hondurans. According to one reporter, so overcome were the goalkeeper, Julio Arzu, and outfielder, Prudencio Norales, that "they laid down and cried like babies." Gilberto Yearwood, angered at the decision, was sent off for thumping Edhem Slijvo. It ended a bad tempered encounter in the most unfortunate circumstances.

The first round group phase ended on 25th June, and in the most controversial of circumstances, though not in the match between England and Kuwait. This produced England's least impressive performance to date and saw Glen Hoddle and Graham Rix, in particular, provide excellent service for the front men, who squandered the advantages created for them. The game's only goal came in the 27th minute, from a long clearance by goalkeeper, Peter Shilton. It was headed down by Francis to Mariner, who returned it with a subtle back heel. Francis swept forwards and shrugged off two defenders before planting the ball in the net. It was a good goal, but England's supporters were looking for something more heartening against a team supposedly vastly inferior.

Far more heroic football was seen from Northern Ireland in their game against Spain in Valencia. This was not a match for the squeamish. The home team signalled their intention of intimidating their visitors almost from the start. They were determined to secure a win and seemed prepared to go to any lengths to achieve it, so much so that one Irish reporter noted: "I've seen more sportsmanship in a Shankill Road pub-fight than was shown by the Spaniards." Spain's tackling was nasty, often brutal, but the Irish refused to cave in. Instead, they responded with fire and passion of their own and, shortly after the second half had begun, Armstrong made an incisive move and passed the ball down the right to Billy Hamilton. Luis Miguel Arconada fumbled the resulting cross and Armstrong, who had continued his run, "scored an unbelievable goal." It "fell like the clap of doom across this bowl of expectancy." As the Irish journalist quoted earlier said: "There followed the longest, most harrowing and yet most magnificent half-hour... experienced in Irish sport in recent years." Even after Mal Donaghy had been sent off for pushing José Camacho, who had just fouled him, the Irish played like lions. The Spanish launched onslaught after savage onslaught, but the Irish ship refused to sink. In Northern Ireland's greatest World Cup performance, Pat Jennings was magnificent in goal and their 1-0 victory left them sitting proudly at the top of the group. Spain also qualified, but had completely failed to live up to their pre-tournament reputation.

That the Spanish had played dirtily can be explained by the pressure of the occasion. The game between West Germany and Austria produced cynicism of the most outrageous kind - cheating is probably a more apt description. The situation was that to qualify the Germans needed to win, but if they won 1-0 both would go through at the expense of Algeria. For the first ten minutes the Germans played as if they were serious. However, when Horst Hrubesch headed in Pierre Littbarski's cross, they lost their appetite for the game. Both teams sat back and played knock-a-ball, simply going through the motions. It was as blatant as it was disgraceful, "a travesty of a football match that made a mockery of the game", and everybody knew it. Yet, there was little Scottish referee, Bob Valentine, could do. That would have to be down to FIFA. Ben Ali Sakkel, the president of Algeria's FA protested vehemently. The players had "violated the principle of sportsmanship by their lack of ambition and fighting spirit", he grumbled and complained that "their scandalous behaviour was an insult to any sportsman." FIFA, unwilling to grab a very rotten bull by the horns, did nothing. The "Great Gijón Swindle" or the "Anschluss", as it became

N. Ireland 1 : Spain 0
Sammy McIlroy and Gerry Armstrong celebrate Armstrong's winning goal.

Maggie, Michel and the Italian Bad Boy - Spain 1982

variably known, went unpunished and Algeria, conquerors of West Germany and Chile, went out to goal difference and Teutonic effrontery.

Twelve teams had now been eliminated and the twelve survivors went into the second phase, which began on 28th June with two games. In Group A, the Poles "sliced into the hitherto uncompromising Belgian defence with precision and enthusiasm" and Boniek's own contribution made the match "into one of the most exhilarating of the competition so far." It took a mere four minutes for that defence to be breached. Lato sprinted past his marker and sent the ball inside to Boniek, whose hard, low shot easily beat the goalkeeper. The Belgians gamely tried to find an answer, creating and missing some plausible chances, but when Boniek headed his team into a 28th minute two goal lead, the match was slipping from them. The Lato-Boniek combination made sure of the result in the 52nd minute. Advancing on goal and "weaving to escape three defenders, Lato spun them to distraction", and tapped the ball forwards for "Boniek to run wide of the goalkeeper to place his shot into an empty net." The hat trick rounded off his virtuoso performance.

The other game that day saw France outplay the "ponderous and lethargic" Austrians, but unlike the Poles, make little of their chances.

They missed the injured Platini's strategic vision, although Dominique Rocheteau, on as a 14th minute substitute for Lacombe, played wonderfully to keep France on top. The player who made the difference count was Genghini, who, having hit the post already, took the free kick that was awarded after Rocheteau had been fouled. His shot was misjudged by Koncilia and went in off the post. In the second half, he had the ball in the net again, to have it disallowed, and Rocheteau had a shot cleared off the line. One way or another, the Austrians kept them out and the 1-0 scoreline hardly reflected the balance of play.

Interviewed after West Germany's goalless draw with England, Uli Stielike said: "We played on the principle: 'Stop a goal at the back and God help us up front.'" It just about sums up the German attitude to a game played out as if "gripped in an iron vice of fear." Given the previous World Cup encounters between the two, it was scarcely surprising, but it did nothing for the entertainment factor in this most boring of games. The English had marginally the better of it and three good chances in the first half, which fell to Robson, Wilkins and Steve Coppell, might have given the lead. However, Germany's goal was under little pressure in the second half and Rummenigge almost stole the points in the 85th minute with a "venomous" shot that threatened "to snap the crossbar." A draw was probably a fair result and left both still in the hunt for a semi-final place.

Far more interesting was Italy's rough and tough encounter with Argentina. Two Latin temperaments, realising the importance of results and determined to give nothing away, collided to produce a "bitter but ultimately exciting game." From two sides recognized for their ability to close things down, it was always going to go the way of the one which got the tactics right. This was Italy, a fact conceded by César Menotti in his post-match briefing. "Italy surprised us by playing attacking football," he said sarcastically. "We failed to adjust to their unusual approach." Yet, the first half saw little to suggest this might be the case. Both set about upsetting the other with a stream of heavy tackles that disrupted play and kept the referee busy, taking five names in the first half hour. There were, however, signs that pointed towards the final outcome. Gentile's close attention to Maradona was denying the great man any creativity, whilst the Italians in general had the better of the kicking war. After half-time they upped the tempo and close on the hour Conti and Antognini fashioned an opening for Tardelli to score. Argentina claimed that Conti was offside when he began the run that led to the second goal, but he continued. His shot was blocked and Antonio Carbrini slotted in the rebound. The goal sparked an Argentinian revival and in the 84th minute Passarella "curled so fine and accurate a shot that Zoff did not move a muscle until the ball had passed him". The pulse of the game quickened and the final minutes were tense, with Italy defending stoically and Argentina's frustration mounting. The final blow came near the end when Americo Gallego was dismissed for foul play and Argentina's title defence virtually died with the final whistle. (See Dino Zoff profile on page 326).

Two days later, Belgium produced their best football so far against the USSR. Their approach play was crisp and tidy, but marred by poor finishing and it cost them dearly. Shortly after the restart, Gavrilov out-foxed the Belgian defence to reach the bye line. His cross went over and Khoren Oganesyan nudged his team in front.

The Belgians hit back with plenty of guts, but could not redeem the defensive slip. Their World Cup had stumbled to its end.

Meanwhile, Northern Ireland's procession continued with another feisty performance, against Austria. As the Times noted: "Their resources are slim, their talent limited but they work with an enthusiasm that is tiring to watch." The impression was reinforced by Billy Hamilton and Gerry Armstrong, who were behind much of their team's attacking momentum. They took a deserved lead on 27 minutes with a goal that was "simple, direct and typically British." Armstrong broke past two defenders to the bye line, crossed and Hamilton banged it in. The lead should have been doubled just before half-time, but Armstrong shot tamely with only the goalkeeper to beat. Austria came back with a 50th minute equalizer from Baumeister, after Schachter's shot rebounded to him and the latter had a goal disallowed six minutes later, but Reinhold Hintermaier hit a 67th minute free kick from just outside the area to take the lead. Form always suggested an Austrian victory, but form meant little to the Irish, who boldly pressed on and pulled level with 15 minutes to go. Armstrong's shot was deflected wide and Jimmy Nicholl gave chase to retrieve what appeared a lost cause. He crossed and Hamilton scored his second "with one deliberate nod of his blond head." Austria went home, but the Irish needed a good win against France in their final game.

A win was vital for both Spain and West Germany when they met in Madrid on 2nd July. The Germans began confidently and Paul Breitner supplied a precision Spain struggled to contain. Yet, despite several clear chances, they did not beak through until the 50th minute. Arconada could only block Dremmler's long range free kick and when the ball fell kindly, Littbarski needed no second invitation. It forced Spain forwards, but they left gaps at the back. They paid the price in the 75th minute when Breitner's measured pass set Littbarski free. The winger drew Arconada out of his goal and slipped the ball to Klaus Fischer to fire into an empty net. Spain responded boldly to an almost impossible task and with ten minutes to go Sánchez crossed for María Zamora to give his team a glimmer of hope and set up a barnstorming finale. In the end, though, it was too little too late and Spain's World Cup ended.

In their next game, only a win would do for Argentina, but they encountered a Brazil in buoyant mood, quite prepared to allow their rivals early possession and await a chance to pounce. Then, with just over ten minutes gone, a dazzling display of quick touch football brought a free kick. Eder curled it against the post and Zico scored. It was a mortal blow and although Argentina responded well, Brazil always had control of the game. Maradona was not able to impose himself and, without him, his colleagues could do little to threaten the unhurried Brazilians, who sprang to life in the second half. In the 67th minute Zico knocked a ball down to Falcão, whose delicate chip was headed in by Serginho. They were now on song and eight minutes from time a typically free flowing move involving five players ended with Zico setting up Junior for the third. It was all too much for Maradona, who pushed his studs into Batista's groin and was sent off. Ramón Díaz restored some pride in the last minute, but the battle of the South American giants had been a one-sided affair and sent Argentina home.

The penultimate games of the second stage saw Poland and France progress at the expense of the USSR and Northern Ireland.

The West German team were a little upset when Pelé summed them up as "a machine with Rummenigge and ten robots."

After getting to the second round the Northern Ireland team had to endure second-rate accommodation in Madrid. One player commented: "After what we have achieved we deserve better than this. Looking out of the hotel windows, the view is like something you would get in the Shankill Road."

The spectacular showdown between Brazil and Argentina on 2nd July was played in one of the smallest and oldest of the designated stadia. The organising committee had not reckoned that the round would throw up this situation. The Sarria stadium in Barcelona had a capacity of just over 40,000.

After a disappointing tournament, the Argentinian team arrived home to be greeted by absolutely no fans at all. In Brazil, hospitals were rushed off their feet dealing with a number of heart failures after their elimination.

Maggie, Michel and the Italian Bad Boy - Spain 1982

Poland's clash with the Soviets produced an angry match, but no goals, which suited the Poles enormously. The Irish, on the other hand, were mauled by a French team in which Platini and Rocheteau were outstanding. France were slow to establish their authority, during which period Martin O'Neill had a goal disallowed for off-side, but once they edged in front, they were never going to let it slip. Ireland's downfall began with a piece of pure Platini genius. In the 33rd minute he beat three defenders to reach the bye line, crossed and Giresse did the rest. So far the Irish had held on, but in the second half they were blitzed. After only three minutes Rocheteau ran from inside his own half to score a brilliant solo goal and in the 63rd minute he added another. This time it was Jean Tigana who did the damage, supplying the cross from which the goal came. The Irish were not a team to surrender supinely and some 15 minutes from the end Whiteside made a "resolute break down the left" and fired a ball into the French area. Goalkeeper, Jean-Luc Ettori failed to hold it and Armstrong headed the reply. By now, though, the match was beyond the Irish and in the 80th minute Tigana provided another centre for Giresse to score and take his team into the semi-finals. It had been a classy show from France, but the Irish deserve great credit for having gone so far. (See Platini profile on page 323).

To reach the semi-finals, England needed to beat Spain by two clear goals and although the West German coach later said that he had "cold feet until the last seconds", he was giving England's performance more credit than it deserved. They were largely uninspired in the first half, having most of the play but unable to crack a resolute defence. It was only when Trevor Brooking and Kevin Keegan replaced Graham Rix and Tony Woodcock in the second half that England created chances of any significance. Both missed chances they would normally have scored and the 0-0 draw ended England's World Cup and Ron Greenwood's reign. He handed the poison chalice to Bobby Robson.

When I look back on my career as an England player, the greatest thing was the actual honour of being chosen to represent my country. Nothing else in my career came close. The feeling never changed from the first game I played under Sir Alf to the last under Ron Greenwood in the World Cup in Spain. There's no higher achievement for an individual player and I never lost the buzz.

Not only that, but to captain your country, walking out at Wembley at the head of the team. I might only be five foot eight, but it used to make me feel ten feet tall. What a fantastic privilege! Naturally, I wanted to win the biggest prize of all - the World Cup

England captain Kevin Keegan is besieged by reporters at Bilbao airport.

– but it wasn't to be. I went to Spain in 1982 with a back injury and it went in the first training session. Had the finals been played a month earlier or a month later, there wouldn't have been a problem. But they won't delay the World Cup for anyone!

I came on as a late substitute against Spain when England were virtually out of the World Cup and it turned out to be my farewell international appearance. There were happier memories from the qualifying campaign, particularly our victory in the Nep Stadium in Budapest. Ron Greenwood had been under a lot of pressure before that game and I know he was proud of us.

Original contribution by Kevin Keegan, former England player and manager.

Against Brazil, Italy needed to win whilst a draw was sufficient for their opponents. For Italy "the urgency of the situation brought them out of their defensive abrasive character" and they attacked from the start. They took the lead in only the fifth minute when Carbrini crossed for Rossi "to enjoy vacant space and head strongly." Normally the Italians would sit back and defend, but this was too dangerous against this team and, sure enough,

Brazil drew level in the 12th minute. Zico passed the ball to Socrates and he finished a delightful solo run with a "stunning low shot" into the net. Italy were forced back onto the hunt and in the 25th minute restored their lead, courtesy of a rare Brazilian mistake. An "extraordinary, careless pass across his penalty area" by Carezo left Paolo Rossi free and the ball went in like a flash. Italy created two more good chances in the first half, failed with both and Brazil were the next to show. In the 68th minute Junior broke down the left and crossed for Falcão to power in "an enormous low drive." Yet again Italy had to go in search of a winner and it came from a corner in the 74th minute. It was headed out by Junior, but only as far as the edge of the area. A shot came in, rebounded off Socrates and Rossi forced the loose ball into the net. They had certainly done enough to deserve the lead, but almost let it slip in the dying seconds when Zoff was forced into a brilliant save. Italy's 50th World Cup win had taken them into the semi-finals. (See Paola Rossi profile on page 325).

For the first time since 1966, the semi-finals were all European affairs. The most dramatic of these, possibly of any semi-final, was undoubtedly that between France and West Germany (see West Germany v France profile on page 330), whilst in Barcelona's Nou Camp, Poland failed to find the sparkle against Italy that had illuminated past tournaments. Their talisman, Boniek, was suspended and without his inspiration, they could not contain a resurgent Italy on a mission of their own. They played Lato and Smolarek up front, but lost the game in midfield , where Italy always had men spare and were able to starve Poland's forwards of any useful service. Indeed, the Poles looked well beaten long before Rossi scored in the 22nd minute. Antognini, who supplied the cross from which the goal came, had to go off injured only minutes later and the Poles used the chance to stage a fight back. They created openings of their own, hit the post and had a decent penalty appeal rejected. Yet they seemed to lack firepower and there was always the suspicion that if Italy stepped up a gear, the match was theirs for the taking. The result was sealed in the 72nd minute when Conti ran forwards, chipped the ball over the Polish defence and Rossi was on hand to head his fifth goal in two games. The Poles were left the consolation of fighting for third place for the second time in three tournaments.

It was two crest fallen teams that took the field in Alicante to contest the minor places and the French, with a considerably weakened team had the best of the first 40 minutes. René Girard shot them into a 13th minute lead with a shot that went in off the post and within a minute Soler missed a glorious chance to put them further ahead.

However, as the half wore on, the Poles began to wrest control and in the 41st minute Boniek set up Szarmach to score with a shot that also went in off the post. They scored another three minutes later when Stefan Majewski headed in a corner and the second half was barely two minutes old before Janusz Kupcewicz added another, Poland's third in eight minutes of open play. Alain Curiol "ran on to a neat chip from Tigana" in the 73rd minute to pull a goal back, but by now there was little to suggest that France would be able to deny Poland a second spell as the world's number three. It was a sad end for France, who had been the team of the tournament and would have made worthy champions had fate smiled more benignly on them.

In Hong Kong, a resident of a tenement building was so incensed by the noise coming from fans watching the Brazil - Italy game that he cut the power supply to the building and fights broke out between knife wielding residents.

After the victory over Brazil, Paolo Rossi was promised free shoes for life by Vigevano of Milan and 1000 litres of wine from Pescara. The President, Sandro Pertini, also promised to award him the title of Commendatori, the Italian equivalent of a knighthood.

Carrying an injury that that could have kept him out for the rest of the tournament, pop music freak, Dominique Rocheteau, asked his manager if he could attend the Rolling Stones concert in Madrid on the tournament's final weekend if he was not fit enough to play in Frances's remaining fixtures. Rocheteau played in the semi-final, but missed the 3rd/4th play-off

The World Cup can be Murder

Watching the World Cup is not always safe, as the husband of Mme Claudi Trichard found to his cost in June 1982, when he put football before housework. His wife wanted him to shell peas for the evening meal, but he wanted to watch the previous night's World Cup games on television. A fierce argument ensued, the end of which came when Mme Trichard blew her husband away with the family shotgun. On 30th September, Marinko Janevski of Skopje in Yugoslavia was sentenced to eight years for the murder of his wife. Janevski, a retired policeman, had been trying to watch the live relay of the France v England match on 16th June. When his wife objected, he strangled her. In court Javenski said: "I always get excited when I watch soccer." Obviously, murdering an errant spouse can be put down to diminished responsibility during the World Cup.

After the final whistle of the final, jubilant 86-year-old Italian President, Pertini, jumped and danced for joy in the stands. Sat next to him was West German Chancellor, Helmut Schmidt who discreetly tried to look as though he didn't mind.

Italy 3 : W. Germany 1
Dino Zoff with the World Cup.

The final seemed to mirror the tournament that preceded it: much of it hardly raised itself above the level of the forgettable, but had its moments of beauty. (See Italy v West Germany profile on page 331). Perhaps the greatest criticism of Spain '82 is that it was too big for the format adopted. The increased number of teams and the decision to stick with a group system into the second round was not successful. It merely prolonged the unfortunate trend that had been increasingly prevalent in other tournaments, that of teams going into games with the limited ambition of not losing, rather than going for the win. Thus cynicism, not sportsmanship was the dominant feature. It was nourished by the inconsistent and generally poor quality of refereeing, the laxity of which at times beggared belief and brought the worst out of some players and teams.

Yet, like all World Cups. Spain had its high points. The progress and good showing of some of the smaller nations, Algeria and Northern Ireland in particular, had been wholly refreshing, as had the willingness of some teams to buck the trend and play to the spirit of the game. First among these were the wonderfully expressive French and Brazilians, though to them must be added Italy, once they had awakened to their potential. Behind such teams stand those players for whom football remains both an art and an entertainment and for whom the desire to succeed is greater than the fear of defeat. Socrates, Rocheteau and Platini are but three examples, albeit fine ones, and their presence in Spain helped the tournament rise above the mediocre.

Michel François Platini   France

Honours: 3rd 1986; 4th 1982   **Games 11**
Played: 1978, 1982, 1986   **Goals 4**

Each World Cup throws up players who rise head and shoulders above the rest. Each has a major impact on the game and each has an instinct that goes beyond talent, transcending into a beauty so clear in its precision. In the 1980s, such a player was Michel Platini, a Frenchman with the skill and daring of a Napoleon and in football terms, the mind of a Jean Paul Sartre. When Didier Deschamp raised the trophy in 1998, Platini, Chairman of the Organising Committee, realised the dream he had failed to achieve as a player, of seeing the cup come to France. It was not bad for a boy whom FC Metz had turned down on the grounds that he had "insufficient respiratory capacity".

Platini was born on 21st June 1955 in the small town of Joeuf. He was the second child of Aldo Platini, a restaurant owner of Italian extraction. Aldo was captain of the local football team, AC Joeuf and it was while he waited for his father's training sessions to end that Platini first practised shooting, dribbling and ball control. He was a small child, given the nickname "Ratz" or "Shorty" by his friends and soon realised that his strength would have to be in technical ability. Despite misgivings from club and supporters, Platini was given his debut in the Joeuf first team in the Fourth Division at the age of sixteen. Previously, he had played for Joeuf juniors, who in January 1971 made the semi-final of the Gambardella Cup to play the competition favourites, FC Metz. Metz had sent

Michel Platini is tackled by West Germany's Karl Heinze Förster and Uli Stielike in the 1982 semi-final.

along a scout and, after seeing Platini score the only goal of the game, he invited him for the ill-fated trial when he became seventeen. Platini was not deterred by the negative response of the club doctor. "I've never been very strong and I had to work harder than others to succeed", he later stated. AS Nancy were not so restrictive and took him on, though he was still at school. He played for their amateur side in the Third Division and, though he appeared as substitute once for the professional team in the First Division, it was not until 2nd May 1973 that he was given his first team debut, against Nîmes. It was a nervous match, but Nancy won 2-1 and in his next outing against Olympique de Lyon, he scored two excellent goals that secured his place for the next seven years. At 19, he was drafted into the army on national service, but soon became army team captain and scored two goals against Mauritius on his twentieth birthday.

1976 was a turning point for Platini and French football. Michel Hidalgo had been appointed national team coach and his brief was to get to the World Cup finals in 1978. He had already promised: "I'll give Platini his chance, he's very gifted", and in March 1976 did just that. Platini lined up with Maxime Bossis, Loïs Amisse, Didier Six, Henri Michel and Marius Trésor to take on Czechoslovakia in front of 50,000 fans at the Parc des Prince in Paris. With the score at 1-0 to France and 17 minutes left on the clock, the Czechs committed an obstruction on the edge of their own area. "Pass it to me and I'll put it in the net", Platini said to his captain, Michel, who, a little surprised, did as he was asked and the ball flew in under Viktor's cross bar. "It was like a dream", Platini said. Within months he had become the most popular player in France. Sponsors, press and media followed his every move and companies fought for him to endorse their products. "It's not his style to drink anything dreary. Fruité with real fruit packs more of a punch!" is probably one advert he would rather forget. The following year he scored the second goal in the 3-1 victory over Bulgaria that took France to the World Cup finals.

Platini's reputation as a skilled ball player, who could elude the most vociferous challenges and find team mates with precision passing meant it was no surprise that his appearance in the 1978 finals saw his creative ability seriously undermined by some attentive marking. In the first game against Italy, Marco Tardelli hung on to his shirt for virtually the whole game. In the second, the Argentinians were less clingy and Platini scored the equalising goal in a game the French eventually lost. 1979 saw him fulfil a childhood ambition when he signed for St. Étienne and the arrival of Patrick Battiston in 1981 created a partnership that transformed the club. They won the French league on the last day of the season, with Platini scoring both goals in a 2-0 victory over Bordeaux. The national side also defeated Holland to qualify for the 1982 World Cup with goals coming from a superb free kick from Platini and a second from Six. That tournament he led France to fourth place and was soon after transferred to Juventus for £1.2m. His new club had a poor season in 1983, but Platini did not and won the first of three consecutive European Player of the Year awards. "When you score goals with Juventus, the news travels around the world and you are really someone. And that changes your life," he later said.

In 1984 Juve won both the Italian league and European Cup-Winners Cup and his international career flourished as France won the European championships, with Platini top scoring with nine goals, including two hat-tricks against Belgium and Yugoslavia and a goal in the final as France beat Spain 2-0. He also broke the scoring record for France held by Juste Fontaine. He ended the year World Player of the Year, an honour he won the next year though this time tainted with tragedy, as Juve lifted the European Cup in 1985 amid the horrors of Heysel, with Platini's penalty sealing victory. They won Serie A again and in November he scored another two sensational goals against Yugoslavia to take France to the 1986 World Cup finals. According to Pelé, "the 1986 France - Brazil quarter-final was certainly one of the best matches in the history of the World Cup and either team could have gone through." France had reached this stage via a classic victory over Italy in which Platini had sprayed passes all over. He also scored France's first goal with a right foot lob. He then scored France's goal in the quarter-final on his 31st birthday.

When Platini retired in 1987 the pitch at the Parc des Prince in Paris was reduced by a metre on either side. The authorities figured that, with him gone, there would be no one to make such 40 metre pinpoint passes. In 72 appearances for his nation he scored 41 goals and captained "Les Bleus" 49 times. Two years later his nation called on him once again and he was made national coach. However, a poor showing at Euro'92 brought his reign to a premature end. He later remarked: "If you're not popular and you lose, you get spat on because you don't have the same ideas as other people." It overshadowed the fact that, between August 1989 and November 1991, France had gone 19 games without defeat. Four months later, Platini was appointed co-chairman of the World Cup organising committee. In 1994, he successfully lobbied FIFA to outlaw the tackle from behind and the rule that prevents goalkeepers picking the ball up from a back pass. He now travels the world as an ambassador for football and France.

Paolo Rossi   Italy

Honours: Winner 1982; 4th 1978   Games 14
Played: 1978 and 1982   Goals 9

Paolo Rossi in the 1982 World Cup Final.

Paolo Rossi went from zero to hero in the space of a few short months. For over two years he protested his innocence over match-fixing allegations and was brought back to the national side only a months and a half before Italy took part in the 1982 tournament and, despite an inauspicious start, he returned home on top of the world. Enzo Bearzot picked Rossi even though he had only played three competitive games in two years and he returned coach's faith with interest.

Born on 23rd September 1956, Rossi's early career did not go well. A persistent knee problem hindered his development and any chance of making it with Juventus was curtailed when, having played only in the junior side, he was loaned out, first to Como and then to Lanerossi Vicenza in Serie B. Coaches at both clubs saw more to the young man and under their guidance, Rossi flourished. While at Vincenza he was converted from winger to centre-forward and he scored 21 goals in his first season to help win promotion. They paid Juventus £1.5m to make his move permanent. Next reason Vincenza were relegated, but Rossi was one of the few highlights and Juventus tried to buy him back. He refused the offer and moved to Perugia for a staggering £3.5m, which almost bankrupted the club. Then, disaster struck. He was accused of taking a bribe before Perugia's game against Avellino and of involvement in match fixing organized by an underworld betting syndicate. Rossi scored both goals in a 2-2 draw, but things got worse. Perugia were relegated at the end of the season and in 1980 Rossi was banned for three years.

He had made his international debut a year before the incident and was a regular member of the Italian side that finished 4th in the 1978 World Cup. He managed three goals in the series including the winner against Austria in the second round. He also played an integral part in the goal that defeated the hosts in the first. With the Argentinian defence all at sea, Bettega threaded the ball forward to Rossi who, with his back to his team mate, deftly back-healed the ball into Bettega's path. Bettega swam around two defenders before beating Fillol with an excellent left foot drive. In 1981, while still suspended, Juventus bit the bullet and brought Rossi back to Torino for £500,000. Then, in April 1982, with only three games left of the season, he won his fight, his suspension was overturned and he was reinstated.

The admiration Bearzot had for Rossi cannot be overstated and bringing in a man who had only played three games before a major tournament was taking a big risk. Spearheading the Italian attack in Spain, Rossi failed to score in the first round and the Italians only scrapped through on goal difference. Following the victory over Argentina in the so-called "Group of Death", he was on the verge of being replaced when he failed to score, but Bearzot changed his mind and gave him a last chance. Cometh the hour, cometh the man and on a hot sunny day in Barcelona, Rossi caught fire. In a sensational game, he scored all three of Italy's goals to seal victory and a place in the semi-finals. Once lit, the fire became a blaze and he scored both goals that took Italy to the final, where he got another of the three that sunk West Germany. He had scored six to finish the as tournament's leading scorer and his comeback was further rewarded when he was named European Player of the Year. He returned home to much acclaim and the past well and truly forgotten. However, one thing he could not escape was the knee trouble that had plagued his career and in 1985 at the age of only 29, he was forced to retire.

Dino Zoff   Italy

Honours: Winner 1982; 4th 1978   **Games 17**
Played: 1974, 1978 and 1982

Goalkeepers and captains Thomas N'Kono (Cameroon) and Dino Zoff (Italy) exchange pennants before the Group 1 game in 1982.

Dino Zoff was one of the most accomplished and successful goalkeepers the game has known. He was noted for courage under fire, agility and thoughtfulness, which made him integral to the Italian defensive machine. His goal was as impenetrable as a dictator's mind to liberalism and between 1972 and 1974, Zoff remained unbeaten for a total of 1143 minutes in 12 internationals. It is a record that still stands and was only brought to an end when Haiti put one past him in the 46th minute of their 1974 World Cup match.

Born on 28th February 1942 at Mariano del Friuli in the province of Gorizia, Zoff began as a 19-year-old with Udinese, appearing four times in the 1961-62 season. His first outing, though, was a disaster as a rampant Fiorentina whacked five past him. Udinese were relegated at the end of that season, but Zoff established himself as first choice keeper in the next, when a series of fine performances attracted the attention of Mantova. They consequently signed him. They were also relegated that season, but returned to the top flight a year later and Zoff stayed there until he moved to Napoli in 1967. Having already appeared in several B internationals, he was given his full international debut in 1968 in the European Championships against Bulgaria in Naples. He made his second appearance in the semi-final, a 0-0 draw that required the toss of a coin. Italy won it and faced Yugoslavia in the final. Here Zoff conceded his first international goal, as the match ended 1-1. The Italians won the replay 2-0. His place in the national side was never secure and he alternated with Enrico Albertosi, whose greater experience saw him preferred for the 1970 World Cup. He was edged out shortly after and Zoff made the position his own.

1972 brought a move to Juventus and there he enjoyed a run of 903 minutes without conceding. He was also named runner-up at the European Player of the Year awards. His first World Cup in 1974 was a major disappointment as the Italians went out in the first round and Zoff was been beaten for the first time in thirteen games. However, there was greater success at club level and he won league and cup titles and gained a UEFA Cup winner's medal in 1977. In 1978, Italy travelled to Argentina as one of the pre-tournament favourites and, on his 68th appearance at the age of 36, scored a victory over France that put them top of their group. Hopes were further raised when they reached the semi-finals, but despite leading at half-time they were beaten by two exceptional long range drives that showed up his age. What they had done, however, was to lay the foundations for their 1982 World Cup success. With Bearzot as the master builder, the blocks fell into place and Zoff was the rock the whole construction rested on, even though he was 40 years old. He made his 100th appearance against Poland as their campaign got off to a slow start and by the time he turned out for his 104th against Brazil, Zoff was giving some of the best performances of his career. With the clock ticking away Brazil threw everything they could at him, but to no avail. Zoff showed the world that he was the best goalkeeper around, keeping the invaders at bay with every ounce of his 20 years' experience. The final itself was a far less frantic affair and, as the final whistle blew, in his trademark grey jersey and black shorts, Zoff climbed the steps to receive the World Cup. He had become the oldest man to captain a winning side and joined Giampiero Combi as only the second goalkeeper to do so.

He made his 112th and final appearance for Italy against Sweden in 1983 conceding two goals and retired altogether a few years later. Altogether, he had made a total of 644 league appearances, which included an unbroken run of 332 matches in Serie A. He took charge of the Italian Olympic side in 1988 before taking up the reigns at Juventus. He guided them to UEFA Cup success in 1990 and soon after moved to Rome to take over at Lazio. He rebuilt the side, turned them into title contenders and then became club president. In 1998, the nation called on him once more and he replaced Cesare Maldini as national coach after World Cup failure. His first task was to get Italy to the finals of European Championships in 2000. He did and though little was expected from a largely defensive side, they surprised everyone and made it to the final with some fine performances. He was only seconds away from becoming the first man to win the trophy both as a player and coach when Wiltord equalized for France in the dying seconds of normal time and in extra time France scored the winning golden goal. Undeservedly, criticism not praise greeted his return and after harsh words from AC Milan president, Silvio Berlusconi, over his tactics in the final, he resigned. "I am not criticising Berlusconi as a politician, but as a person. I don't need to take lessons in dignity from him and so I am giving up my job as national team coach," he later said. "I don't understand why someone has to undermine the work of someone else. I will reply to Berlusconi personally. It has not been easy during the last few days, because we had a few surprises, like the goal in the last minute of the final. I do not think it is right not to respect a man who has simply tried to do his job in a professional way. I've had to take decisions and I know that I'll lose out in the long run. I know what will happen. People will say I acted too hastily. I know I can't win, I've got experience of that." Given their respective records, it was very unfair.

Artur Antunes Coimbra (Zico) Brazil

Honours: 3rd Place 1978; Quarter Finals 1986 **Games 13**
Played: 1978, 1982 and 1986 **Goals 5**

Zico was a mild mannered attacking midfielder and the last to carry the sobriquet, "white Pelé", before Brazilians finally accepted that Pelé was unique. It meant he had a lot to live up to when he ought to have been accepted in his own right. He never achieved the same degree of international success, but would still light up a football field with dazzling skills, powerful runs and exceptional goals. The three World Cups he appeared in were disappointing by Brazilians standards, two being dogged by internal disputes. However, if people are asked to recall players of that era, many may recall Rivalino or Socrates, but most will remember Zico.

Zico was born in Rio de Janeiro on 3rd March 1953. He grew up surrounded by the game, with a father who played and three brothers each professionals and, like countless others, learnt his trade kicking a ball of rags around the city's beaches. He was a frail and skinny child who relied on speed and agility to keep out of trouble.

Zico in the 2-1 Brazilian victory over the USSR in 1982.

When he signed for Flamenco at the age of 15, the Paraguayan coach, Fleitas Solich, put him on a diet and course of exercise to build him up. He scored his first goal in the youth team against São Cristobal on 18th March 1970 and was given his senior debut soon after, scoring twice in fifteen outings. However, he found it difficult to adjust to the demands of the higher level and he was put back in the youth team to gain maturity and experience. By the time the season was over he had scored 20 goals in 22 outings and it not only boosted his confidence, but earned him passage back to the first team, on a more permanent basis. In 1972, he gained a place in the Brazilian Olympic team and in 1975 was given his first full international against Uruguay. It was notable because he scored the winning goal.

Zico's attraction was his versatility. He possessed determination, precision and exquisite control that was the very essence of Brazilian football and provided the essential link between midfield and front line. Brazilian football needed a boost following the debacle of the 1974 World Cup and Zico was seen as one to give it. It was strange therefore, that new coach, Claudio Coutinho, played him in a different role in Argentina to that which had brought him success at Flamenco. This was one of the problems he faced. The other was that he could not shake off an injury. The tournament started badly for Zico personally and for the team at large. With the opening game poised at 1-1 and with only seconds to go, Zico scored what he believed to be a perfectly legitimate headed winner, but which Clive Thomas controversially ruled out. Then the players fell out with Coutinho and by the end of the first round morale was desperately low. He did not feature again until the second stage when he came on as substitute to score Brazil's third and his first World Cup goal against Peru from the penalty spot. Misfortune struck after only seven minutes of the vital game against Poland when he was injured and taken off.

1979 proved to be a happier year. Fully fit and confidence high, Zico scored 89 goals that season, of which 65 came in the league and seven in internationals. He also set up a new scoring record in the Rio "Carioca" League when he netted his 254th goal. In 1981 he inspired Flamenco to South American Copa Libertadores success against Cobreloa of Chile, scoring both goals in a 2-1 home victory. After the Chileans won the away leg 1-0, he netted both goals to secure victory in the replay. That year Flamenco destroyed Liverpool in the final of the World Club Cup and he was named South American Player of the Year, an award he had won before in 1977.

The Spanish World Cup was altogether more productive for Zico. Brazil stormed the first round with the 29 year old Zico scoring three times in two games. He then scored their opener against Argentina before retiring injured after 83 minutes. It was not severe enough to keep him out of the next game, but a ragged defensive performance saw Brazil go out. He could, however, take consolation from becoming South American Player of the Year for a third time. His fine show in Spain inevitably led to offers from the big European clubs and in 1983 he signed for Udinese for £2.5m. He had scored 690 goals for Flamenco, won three Brazilian and six Rio State championships. He did not experience the same level of success at Udinese and, although scoring 19 goals in his first season, his second was riddled by injury and he returned to Flamenco. An operation on his knee brought some, if not permanent relief and he travelled with the national side to Mexico in 1986 after his cause had been boosted by a hat trick in a friendly with Yugoslavia. His appearances at the tournament were sporadic, but when he played, he was impressive. At 33 he had lost his pace, but not his vision or dexterity. Unfortunately, his World Cup finale against France ended in disappointment. He had already missed one penalty in the game, but had the composure to put it aside and scored in the penalty shoot out that eliminated Brazil.

Following a spell as Brazilian Minister of Sport in 1990, Zico went to Kashima Antlers in Japan. His love of the game and the lure of the Yen drew him to attempt to rekindle his career. Along with a number of other big names from around the world Zico's presence was vital for the credibility and progress of the newly formed J League. He remained there a number of years, delighting the fans with flashes of brilliance before returning home.

Algeria 3 : Chile 2

Chile's Moscoso is tackled by Algeria's Merzekane in the 1982 Group 2 match.

When Algeria took the field for their Group Two game with Chile, they knew they had every chance of becoming the first African nation to make it through to the second round of the World Cup. They had taken much confidence from their previous matches, whereas Chile, playing their 50th World Cup game, had yet to make any impression.

The Algerians showed great tactical awareness in the opening period of the match and cleverly "drew the Chilean sting for the first hour with a well-organized defence, scoring 3 times with quick breakaways", as the reporter from the Irish Times noted. They opened their account in the eighth minute with a move started and finished by Salah Assad. Tedj Bensaoula supplied some classy footwork to feed the ball to Assad, who swept it into the net. With 31 minutes on the clock Assad struck again. This time he was set on his way with a through pass from Bourebbou and his shot took a deflection off Figueroa before beating Osbén in Chile's goal. Four minutes later Bensaoula made it 3-0 with a fine low shot from just inside the area.

With such a commanding lead, it looked all up for Chile, who had had little chance so far to display the canny Latin flair that many had expected of them. They looked dispirited and dreadfully out of sorts, as they were outplayed and outgunned in the first half. Things began to move in their favour after they brought on Juan Carlos Letelier for Carlos Caszely in a 59th minute substitution. Within a minute, the Chileans were on the attack, Patricio Yáñez fell in the area and the Guatemalan referee judged that he had been brought down by the defender Kourichi. It seemed a harsh decision and one that clearly upset Algeria, but a penalty was awarded and emphatically swept in by Miguel Niera. It was now the turn of the Africans to feel the cosh, as Chile, sensing that there might be something in it for them, picked up their game. Having given so much in the first half, the Algerians understandably began to tire and, as Chilean pressure began to mount, they wilted under the onslaught. Suddenly they looked disjointed and decidedly vulnerable.

It was time for desperate defence. As if to affirm the altered circumstances, Gustavo Moscoso fired a shot narrowly over the bar and minutes later Letelier picked up the ball. His run took him past three defenders before he unleashed his shot into the Algerian net. The pressure mounted as Chile went in search of an equalizer and Algeria fought with every sinew to keep them out. It gave the match a nerve-racking ending and somehow the Algerians held on. The score remained at 3-2 with the place in the next stage still seemingly open to them.

Algeria's fate, though, was not to be of their own making. The group's final game took place the next day between West Germany and Austria. The Germans were still smarting from their earlier defeat by Algeria and the Austrians knew that they could afford a 3-0 defeat. It ended 1-0 to the Germans, both having seemingly to go for damage limitation and see both of them through. So Algeria exited the World Cup the victim of one of its greatest travesties.

West Germany 3 : France 3

The Times described this semi-final as "the most dramatic tie in the history of the competition" and it is difficult to contradict the judgement. Here were two teams of entirely different character. The Germans, forceful, compelling and doggedly disciplined, had not been beaten by European opposition in the nearly four years that Jupp Derwall had been in charge. Their plan to extend this run was to suffocate the French of their creative life blood and to do it Karl-Heinz and Bernd Förster would man mark Rocheteau and Six, whilst Dremmler would look after Platini. The rest of the German backs, Stielike, Kaltz and Briegel, were to keep watchful eyes on the free roving French forwards, because this was the major difference between the sides. The French were wily practitioners, gifted and subtly cunning. They were not easily contained, even by the most rigid of defences.

The French generally had the best of the opening exchanges with an inventiveness that rivalled any. "Whenever the Germans thought they had the French under control, another blue shirt would squeeze through into open territory" and the Germans were in danger. Behind much of it was Giresse, excellent throughout, who totally outplayed his opposite, Breitner, and was able to pick out his front runners with his intelligent pin-point passes. Yet, the Germans were the first to show. Breitner sent a pass to release Fischer, who exposed French defensive frailties as he ran in on goal. Ettori got down to block his advance with his knees, but the ball fell to Littbarski to score with a precise low shot. It was in the 17th minute and ten minutes later Giresse floated a free kick into the penalty area. Bernd Förster failed to deal with it and in the confusion floored Rocheteau "in a manner more in keeping with the rules governing the oval ball." Platini stepped up to take the penalty, kissed the ball as he placed it and sent Schumacher the wrong way. For the rest of the half the French were always the livelier, but lacked the penetration to make their flair tell against a defence more than adequately marshalled by Stielike.

The second half saw much of the same. The French, often with four or five men up front, buzzed like hornets and sprayed passes across the park with gay abandon. They came close to scoring on the hour, but then came the incident for which this game will always be remembered. Battiston, who had replaced the injured Genghini only ten minutes before, latched on to a perfectly weighted through ball. As he homed in on goal Schumacher raced out and perpetrated "a moment of cruelty, a dramatically ferocious act with intent to kill", as Le Monde described the incident. Kicking Battiston full in the face, the Frenchman went down unable to breath and it was ten minutes before medical staff could carry him off to receive oxygen in the dressing room. In another instance of refereeing madness, not only did Schumacher stay on the field, but no penalty was given. It was scandalous and knocked the French out of their rhythm. The Germans now had the chance to finish the job and came close on several occasions. Great saves from Ettori kept out Dremmler and Briegel, and Fischer and Littbarski both missed a ball that bounced tantalisingly across the French goalmouth. Ettori then could only parry a Breitner shot and as Hrubesch, recently on for Magath, charged in to score, he was denied by a last ditch challenge from Tigana. Rocheteau should then have scored after Amoros had sidestepped Kaltz to set him up and in the 90th minute Amoros made space for himself and hit the bar with his shot. It took a match most neutrals wanted France to win into extra time.

Things could not have got off to a better start for the French. Moments after it began, Giresse sent over a nicely weighted free kick, found Trésor in space and the ball was volleyed impressively into the net. Six minutes later, Giresse finished off a move that he himself had started and at 3-1 France seemed to have the game sewn up. Soon after, the Germans gambled on a half fit Rummenigge, on for Breigel, and it paid almost instant dividends. Not long after, Littbarski crossed and the new man flicked the ball into the net. Even now, few would have bet against France making the final, but in the 102nd minute a cross came over to the French back post. Hrubesch headed it back across the face of the goal and Fischer levelled the scores with a masterful overhead kick. It was heartbreaking and the French just could not muster the wherewithal to mount a final telling challenge. A game the French deserved to have won was to be decided on the lottery of a penalty shoot out.

Even then the drama was not over. First Giresse, Kaltz, Amoros, Breitner and then Rocheteau dispatched their shots cleanly. Up stepped Stielike, a man who had all but died to keep his team in the match, and Ettori judged his kick correctly. He sank to his knees, head in hands, in exhausted despair. Six then had his saved and Littbarski pulled things level. Both Platini and Rummenigge blasted the next kicks home and it went down to sudden death. The tension at this point was absolutely unbearable, for players and spectators alike. Max Bossis sent in the next kick and this time it was Schumacher's turn to anticipate correctly. Bravely, Hrubesch marched out of the knot of players, placed the ball and calmly sent West Germany through to the final.

For such a great team to have gone out of the World Cup under such calamitous and unjust circumstances was the bitterest moment in the history of French football. Coach Hiladago tried to put on a brave face in his post match interview, but was unable to hide his extreme disappointment. "This defeat, it is necessary to accept it," he said, "but it will be hard for the players. It will be hard for us all and we will have to take time to get over it." Patrick Battiston was discharged from hospital the next day and fortunately, two broken teeth was all the lasting damage he suffered. Realising the magnitude of his assault, Schumacher was quick to apologise and did so with genuine contrition. He offered to visit Battiston in his home to show his sincerity – and to pay to have the two teeth capped.

Italy 3 : West Germany 1
The World Cup Final

Marco Tardelli scores the 2nd Italian goal.

This was described by the Daily Telegraph reporter as "one of the worst finals in history until the last half hour" and few would have disagreed with his judgement. The Italians were without the injured Giancarlo Antognini and brought in the defender Bergoni as his replacement. He was given the job of marking Rummenigge, whilst Gentile was detailed to cover Littbarski and it set the tone of the game. Both went out to stop the other from playing and were prepared to use any means to this end. Tardelli and Dremmler often "clattered into each other with a ferocity which was, at times, disturbing", in the words of the Irish Times, and it was a particularly brutal tackle from Dremmler in the eighth minute that put Francesco Graziani out of the game with an injured shoulder, Altobelli coming on in his place. Dremmler then became the subject of heavy retaliatory challenges from the Italians, the Germans responded in kind and "there were times when one wondered why the ball had been taken on to the pitch", said another commentator. The Brazilian referee was content to let them get on with it and the result was that it got worse. He only showed his yellow card once in the first half and this was for a relatively innocuous tackle from Conti.

One of the defining moments of the first half came at its mid point. Briegel and Conti went up together to get to a cross and Conti went down. The referee viewed it as Briegel having given the Italian a shove and duly awarded a penalty. It seemed a harsh decision, but justice had its way as Antonio Carbrini dragged the ball wide with his left foot and became the first man to miss a penalty in a World Cup final. It was certainly a savage blow to Italy and they struggled to come to terms with it over the rest of the half. So far the game had produced little, but the Italians revealed telltale signs of what was to come. Their defence had been sound with Gentile and Bergoni patrolling the flanks and Scirea solid in the middle, leaving Zoff "able to dictate without any real stress in goal." Furthermore Oriali, "flipping in and out of the game in moments of rich skill", was gradually winning the midfield battle with Breitner and in the second half it began to come together.

In the 56th minute Cabrini crossed the ball and Paolo Rossi's diving header found the target with his sixth goal of the tournament. Its effect was to lift the burden from Italian shoulders and the change was electric. They had a scare in the 55th minute when Zoff could only parry Briegel's swerving cross and Cabrini and Collovati cleared the danger as Fischer steadied himself to shoot, but this apart Italy came into their own. Their attacks became fluid and incisive and not even Germany's continued use of strong arm tactics could dent their ardour. In the 69th minute, in a move that involved seven Italian players, Scirea's low cross was met by Tardelli, who "executed the perfect finish with a long, languorous flick of his left boot." The Germans were reeling and a change was necessary. They had already replaced Dremmler with Hrubesch and soon after Italy's second goal, Hansi Müller came on for Rummenigge, who was clearly not fully fit. The Germans had to take risks if they were to salvage anything from the game and they paid the price in the 81st minute. With Stielike out of position and complaining to the referee about one of his decisions, Collovati's perceptive clearance freed Conti. Running some 50 yards, Conti released the ball to Altobelli, who avoided Schumacher's last gasp tackle and placed it in the net. At 3-0 and ten minutes to go the game was as good as won.

The Germans tried to engineer a comeback and Breitner volleyed a goal from Kaltz's pass in the 83rd minute, but it was all too late. So confident were the Italians that for the last two minutes of time Enzo Bearzot sent on Causio in place of Altobelli. It was a touching piece of sentimentality to thus reward his veteran campaigner for his years of loyal service. Minutes later the final whistle went and Italy became the second team to win the World Cup three times, a victory they so richly merited in the end. The point was conceded by Jupp Derwall after the game when he said: "The way they played in the second half they deserved to win. We never found our strength". Uli Stielike, though, had a different opinion. "The referee clearly cheated us and if you don't believe it you saw another game", he grumbled. Somehow it just didn't ring true.

Statistics - Spain 1982

1st PHASE - GROUP ONE

Vigo, June 14th - Estadio Balaidos

0 (0) ITALY

Zoff, Gentile, Collovati, Scirea, Cabrini, Antognoni, Marini , Tardelli, Conti, Graziani, Rossi.

0 (0) POLAND

Mlynarczyk, Janas, Jalocha, Matysik, Zmuda, Majewski, Smolarek, Buncol, Lato, Iwan (Kusto), Boniek.

Referee: Michel Vautrot (France)
Attendance: 33.000

La Coruña, June 15th - Estadio Riazor

0 (0) CAMEROON

N'Kono, Kaham, Kunde, Onana, N'djeya, M'Bom, Abega, M'Bida, Aoudou, N'guea (Bahoken), Milla, (Tokoto).

0 (0) PERU

Quiroga, Duarte, Díaz, Salguero, Olaechea, Leguia (Barbadillo), Cueto, Velásquez, Oblitas, Cubillas (La Rosa), Uribe.

Referee: Franz Wohrer (Austria)
Attendance: 11.000

Vigo, June 18th - Estadio Balaidos

1 (1) ITALY

Conti 19

Zoff, Gentile, Collovati, Scirea, Cabrini, Antognoni, Marini, Tardelli, Conti, Graziani, Rossi (Causio).

1 (0) PERU

Díaz 84

Quiroga, Duarte, Díaz, Salguero, Olaechea, Barbadillo (La Rosa), Cueto, Velásquez, Oblitas, Cubillas, Uribe (Leguia).

Referee: Walter Eschweiler (West Germany)
Attendance: 25.000

La Coruña, June 19th - Estadio Riazor

0 (0) CAMEROON

N'Kono, Kaham, Kunde, Onana, N'djeya, M'Bom, Abega, M'Bida, Aoudou, N'guea (Tokoto), Milla.

0 (0) POLAND

Mlynarczyk, Janas, Jalocha, Matysik, Zmuda, Majewski, Smolarek, Buncol (Szarmach), Lato, Palasz (Kusto), Boniek.

Referee: Alexis Ponnet (Belgium)
Attendance: 19.000

La Coruña, June 22nd - Estadio Riazor

5 (0) POLAND

Smolarek 55, Lato 58, Boniek 61, Buncol 68, Ciolek 76

Mlynarczyk, Janas, Jalocha (Dziuba), Matysik, Zmuda, Majewski, Smolarek (Ciolek), Buncol, Lato, Kupcewicz, Boniek.

1 (0) PERU

La Rosa 83

Quiroga, Duarte, Díaz, Salguero, Olaechea, La Rosa, Cueto, Velásquez, Oblitas (Barbadillo), Cubillas (Uribe), Leguia.

Referee: Mario Rubio Vázquez (Mexico)
Attendance: 25.000

Vigo, June 23rd - Estadio Balaidos

1 (0) ITALY

Graziani 60

Zoff, Gentile, Collovati, Scirea, Cabrini, Antognoni, Oriali, Tardelli, Conti, Graziani, Rossi.

1 (0) CAMEROON

M'Bida 61

N'Kono, Kaham, Kunde, Onana, N'djeya, M'Bom, Abega, M'Bida, Aoudou, Tokoto, Milla.

Referee: Bogdan Dotchev (Bulgaria)
Attendance: 20.000

	P	W	D	L	F	A	Pts
Poland	3	1	2	0	5	1	4
Italy	3	0	3	0	2	2	3
Cameroon	3	0	3	0	1	1	3
Peru	3	0	2	1	2	6	2

Maggie, Michel and the Italian Bad Boy - Spain 1982

1st PHASE - GROUP TWO

Gijon, June 16th - Estadio El Molinon

2 (0) ALGERIA

Madjer 54, Belloumi 69

Cerbah, Merzekane, Kourichi, Guendouz, Dahleb, Mansouri, Fergani, Belloumi, Madjer (Larbes), Zidane (Bensaoula), Assad.

1 (0) WEST GERMANY

Rummenigge 68

Schumacher, Kaltz, K-H Förster, Stielike, Briegel, Dremmler, Breitner, Magath (Fischer), Littbarski, Hrubesch, Rummenigge.

Referee: Ravoredo Enrique Labo (Peru)
Attendance: 42.000

Oviedo, June 17th - Estadio Carlos Tartiere

1 (1) AUSTRIA

Schachner 21

Koncilia, Krauss, Obermayer, Pezzey, Degeorgi (Baumeister), Hattenberger, Prohaska, Hintermaier, Schachner, Krankl, Weber (Jurtin).

0 (0) CHILE

Osbén, Garrido, Valenzuela, Figueroa, Bigorra, Dubo, Yañez, Neira (Rojas), Bonvallet, Caszely, Moscoso (Gamboa).

Referee: Juan Daniel Cardellino (Uruguay)
Attendance: 22.500

Gijon, June 20th - Estadio El Molinon

1 (0) CHILE

Moscoso 89

Osbén, Garrido, Valenzuela, Figueroa, Bigorra, Dubo, Yañez, Bonvallet, Soto (Letelier), Moscoso, Gamboa (Neira).

4 (1) WEST GERMANY

Rummenigge 9, 56, 66, Reinders 81

Schumacher, Kaltz, K-H Förster, Stielike, Briegel, Dremmler, Breitner (Matthäus), Magath, Littbarski (Reinders), Hrubesch, Rummenigge.

Referee: Bruno Galler (Switzerland)
Attendance: 42.000

Oviedo, June 21st - Estadio Carlos Tartiere

2 (0) AUSTRIA

Schachner 56, Krankl 67

Koncilia, Krauss, Obermayer, Pezzey, Degeorgi, Hattenberger, Prohaska (Weber), Hintermaier, Schachner, Krankl, Baumeister (Welzl).

0 (0) ALGERIA

Cerbah, Merzekane, Kourichi, Guendouz, Dahleb (Tlemcani), Mansouri, Fergani, Belloumi (Bensaoula), Madjer, Zidane, Assad.

Referee: Tony Boskovic (Australia)
Attendance: 22.000

Oviedo, June 24th - Estadio Estadio Carlos Tartiere

3 (3) ALGERIA

Assad 8, 30, Bensaoula 34

Cerbah, Merzekane, Kourichi, Guendouz, Bourrebou (Yahi), Mansouri (Dahleb), Fergani, Madjer, Larbes, Bensaoula, Assad.

2 (0) CHILE

Neira (pen)60, Letelier 74

Osbén, Gallindo, Valenzuela, Figueroa, Bigorra, Dubo, Yañez, Bonvallet (Soto), Caszely (Letelier), Moscoso, Neira.

Referee: Romulo Mendez (Guatemala)
Attendance: 16.000

Vigo, June 23rd - Estadio Balaidos

1 (1) WEST GERMANY

Hrubesch 11

Schumacher, Kaltz, K-H Förster, Stielike, Briegel, Dremmler, Breitner, Magath, Littbarski, Hrubesch (Fischer), Rummenigge (Matthäus).

0 (0) AUSTRIA

Koncilia, Krauss, Obermayer, Pezzey, Degeorgi, Hattenberger, Prohaska, Hintermaier, Schachner, Krankl, Weber.

Referee: Bob Valentine (Scotland)
Attendance: 41.000

	P	W	D	L	F	A	Pts
W. Germany	3	2	0	1	6	3	4
Austria	3	2	0	1	3	1	4
Algeria	3	2	0	1	5	5	4
Chile	3	0	0	3	3	8	0

1st PHASE - GROUP THREE

Barcelona, June 13th - Estadio Nou Camp

1 (0) BELGIUM

Van den Bergh 62

Pfaff, Gerets, Millecamps, Baecke, De Schrijver, Coeck, Vercauteren, Van der smissen, Van den Bergh, Czerniatynski, Ceulemans.

0 (0) ARGENTINA

Fillol, Olguin, Galvan, Passarella, Tarantini, Ardiles, Maradona, Gallego, Bertoni, Díaz (Valdano), Kempes.

Referee: Vojtech Christov (Czechoslovakia)
Attendance: 95.000

Elche, June 15th - Nuevo Estadio

10 (3) HUNGARY

Nyilasi 3, 83, Pölöskei 11, Fazekas 23, 54, Tóth 50, Kiss 70, 73, 78, Szentes 71

Meszaros, Balint, Martos, Garaba, Tóth, Müller (Szentes), Nyilasi, Sallai, Fazekas, Torocsik (Kiss), Pölöskei.

1 (0) EL SALVADOR

Ramirez Zapata 64

Guevara Mora, Castillo, Cruz Jovel, Rodríguez, Recinos, Huezo, Rugamas (Ramirez Zapata), Ventura, Rivas, Hernández, González.

Referee: Ebrahim Al Doy (Bahrain)
Attendance: 23.000

Alicante, June 18th - Estadio Josè Rico Perez

4 (2) ARGENTINA

Bertoni 26, Maradona 28, 55, Ardiles 60

Fillol, Olguin, Galvan, Passarella, Tarantini (Barbas), Ardiles, Maradona, Gallego, Bertoni, Valdano (Calderon), Kempes.

1 (0) HUNGARY

Pölöskei 76

Meszaros, Balint, Martos (Fazekas), Garaba, Tóth, Rab, Nyilasi, Sallai, Varga, Kiss (Szentes), Pölöskei.

Referee: Belaid Lacarne (Algeria)
Attendance: 32.093

Elche, June 19th - Nuevo Estadio

1 (1) BELGIUM

Coeck 25

Pfaff, Gerets, Millecamps, Baecke, Meeuws, Coeck, Vercauteren, Van der smissen (Van der Elst), Van den Bergh, Czerniatynski, Ceulemans (Van Moer).

0 (0) EL SALVADOR

Guevara Mora, Osorto (Díaz Arevalo), Cruz Jovel, Rodríguez, Recinos, Fagoaga, Ramirez Zapata, Ventura, Rivas, Huezo, González.

Referee: Malcolm Moffat (Ireland)
Attendance: 15.000

Elche, June 22nd - Nuevo Estadio

1 (0) BELGIUM

Czerniatynski 76

Pfaff, Gerets (Plessers), Millecamps, Baecke, Meeuws, Coeck, Vercauteren, Van der smissen (Van Moer), Van den Bergh, Czerniatynski, Ceulemans.

1 (1) HUNGARY

Varga 28

Meszaros, Kerekes, Martos, Fazekas, Garaba, Tóth, Müller (Sallai), Nyilasi, Torocsik, Varga, Kiss (Csongradi), Pölöskei.

Referee: Clive White (England)
Attendance: 37.000

Alicante, June 23rd - Estadio José Rico Perez

2 (1) ARGENTINA

Passarella (pen)23, Bertoni 52

Fillol, Olguin, Galvan, Passarella, Tarantini, Ardiles, Maradona, Gallego, Bertoni (Díaz), Calderon (Santamaria), Kempes.

0 (0) EL SALVADOR

Guevara Mora, Osorto (Díaz Arevalo), Cruz Jovel, Rodríguez, Recinos, Rugamas, Ramirez Zapata, Ventura (Alfaro), Rivas, Huezo, González.

Referee: Luis Barrancos (Bolivia)
Attendance: 32.000

	P	W	D	L	F	A	Pts
Belgium	3	2	1	0	3	1	5
Argentina	3	2	0	1	6	2	4
Hungary	3	1	1	1	12	6	3
El Salvador	3	0	0	3	1	13	0

1st PHASE - GROUP FOUR

Bilbao, June 16th - Estadio San Mamés

3 (1) ENGLAND

Robson 1, 66, Mariner 82

Shilton, Butcher, Mills, Sansom (Neal), Thompson, Coppell, Robson, Wilkins, Francis, Mariner, Rix.

1 (1) FRANCE

Soler 25

Ettori, Battiston, Bossis, Trésor, López, Larios (Tigana), Girard, Giresse, Rocheteau (Six), Platini, Soler.

Referee: Antonio Garrido (Portugal)
Attendance: 44.172

Valladolid, June 17th - Nueva Estadio José Zorilla

1 (1) CZECHOSLOVAKIA

Panenka (pen) 21

Hruska, Barmos, Jurkemic, Fiala, Kukucka, Panenka (Bicovsky), Berger, Kriz, Janecka (Petrzela), Nehoda, Vizek.

1 (0) KUWAIT

Al Dakhil 58

Al Tarabulsi, Naeem Saed, Ma'Yoof, Mubarak, Jasem, Al Bouloushi, Al Houti, Ahmed Karam (Kameel), Al Anbari, Yaqoub, Al Dakhil.

Referee: Benjamin Dwomoh (Ghana)
Attendance: 25.000

Bilbao, June 20th - Estadio San Mamés

2 (0) ENGLAND

Francis 63, Barmos (og) 66

Shilton, Butcher, Mills, Sansom, Thompson, Coppell, Robson (Hoddle), Wilkins, Francis, Mariner, Rix.

0 (0) CZECHOSLOVAKIA

Seman (Stromsik), Barmos, Jurkemic, Fiala, Radimec, Chaloupka, Berger, Vojacek, Janecka (Masny), Nehoda, Vizek.

Referee: Charles Corver (Holland)
Attendance: 41.123

Valladolid, June 21st - Nuevo Estadio José Zorilla

4 (2) FRANCE

Genghini 30, Platini 42, Six 48, Bossis 90

Ettori, Amoros, Bossis, Trésor, Janvion (López), Genghini, Giresse, Six, Platini (Girard), Lacombe, Soler.

1 (0) KUWAIT

Al Bouloushi 75

Al Tarabulsi, Naeem Saed, Ma'Yoof, Mubarak, Jasem (Al Shemmari), Al Bouloushi, Al Houti, Ahmed Karam (Kameel), Al Anbari, Yaqoub, Al Dakhil.

Referee: Miroslav Stupar (Soviet Union)
Attendance: 30.034

Valladolid, June 24th - Nuevo Estadio José Zorilla

1 (0) CZECHOSLOVAKIA

Panenka (pen) 84

Stromsik, Barmos, Kriz (Masny), Fiala, Radimec, Stambacher, Bicovsky, Vojacek, Janecka (Panenka), Nehoda, Vizek (RED).

1 (0) FRANCE

Six 66

Ettori, Amoros, Bossis, Trésor, Janvion, Genghini, Giresse, Six, Platini, Lacombe (Couriol), Soler (Girard).

Referee: Paolo Casarin (Italy)
Attendance: 25.000

Bilbao, June 25th - Estadio San Mamés

1 (1) ENGLAND

Francis 27

Shilton, Foster, Mills, Neal, Thompson, Coppell, Hoddle, Wilkins, Francis, Mariner, Rix.

0 (0) KUWAIT

Al Tarabulsi, Naeem Saed, Ma'Yoof, Mubarak, Jasem (Al Shemmari), Al Bouloushi, Al Houti, Kameel, Al Anbari, Al Suwaayed, Al Dakhil.

Referee: Gilberto Aristizabal (Colombia)
Attendance: 39.700

	P	W	D	L	F	A	Pts
England	3	3	0	0	6	1	6
France	3	1	1	1	6	5	3
Czech'vakia	3	0	2	1	6	4	2
Kuwait	3	0	1	2	6	6	1

1st PHASE - GROUP FIVE

Valencia, June 16th - Estadio Luis Casanova

1 (1) HONDURAS

Zelaya 7

Arzu, Gutierrez, Villegas, Costly, Bulñes, Maradiaga, Yearwood, Zelaya, Norales (Caballero), Betancourt, Figueroa.

1 (0) SPAIN

López -Ufarte (pen) 65

Arconada, Camacho, Tendillo, Alexanco, Gordillo, Joaquin (Sánchez), Alonso, Zamora, Juanito (Saura), Satrustegui, López -Ufarte.

Referee: Arturo Ithurralde (Argentina)
Attendance: 49.562

Zaragoza, June 17th - Estadio La Romereda

0 (0) NORTHERN IRELAND

Jennings, J.Nicholl, C.Nicholl, McClelland, Donaghy, McIlroy, O'Neill, McCreery, Armstrong, Hamilton, Whiteside.

0 (0) YUGOSLAVIA

Pantelic, Zajec, Jovanovic, Stojkovic, Hrstic, Slijvo, Gudelj, Surjak, Petrovic, Vujovic, Susic.

Referee: Erik Fredriksson (Sweden)
Attendance: 25.000

Valencia, June 20th - Estadio Luis Casanova

2 (1) SPAIN

Juanito (pen) 12, Saura 66

Arconada, Camacho, Tendillo, Alexanco, Gordillo, Sánchez (Saura), Alonso, Zamora, Juanito, Satrustegui (Quini), López-Ufarte.

1 (1) YUGOSLAVIA

Gudelj 10

Pantelic, Zajec, Jovanovic (Halilhodzic), Stojkovic, Krmpotic, Slijvo, Gudelj, Surjak, Petrovic (Sestic), Susic.

Referee: Henning Lund-Sørensen (Denmark)
Attendance: 48.000

Zaragoza, June 21st - Estadio La Romereda

1 (0) HONDURAS

Laing 61

Arzu, Gutierrez, Villegas, Costly, Cruz, Maradiaga, Yearwood, Zelaya, Norales (Laing), Betancourt, Figueroa.

1 (1) NORTHERN IRELAND

Armstrong 2

Jennings, J.Nicholl, C.Nicholl, McClelland, Donaghy, McIlroy, O'Neill (Healy), McCreery, Armstrong, Hamilton, Whiteside (Brotherston).

Referee: Sun Cham Tan (Hong Kong)
Attendance: 15.000

Zaragoza, June 24th - Estadio La Romereda

1 (0) YUGOSLAVIA

Petrovic (pen) 87

Pantelic, Zajec, Jovanovic (Halilhodzic), Stojkovic, Krmpotic, Slijvo, Gudelj, Surjak, Petrovic, Vujovic (Sestic), Susic.

0 (0) HONDURAS

Arzu, Drummond, Villegas, Costly, Cruz (Laing), Maradiaga, Yearwood (RED), Zelaya, Bulñes, Betancourt, Figueroa.

Referee: Gastón Castro (Chile)
Attendance: 25.000

Valencia, June 25th - Estadio Luis Casanova

1 (0) NORTHERN IRELAND

Armstrong 46

Jennings, J.Nicholl, C.Nicholl, McClelland, Donaghy (RED), McIlroy (Cassidy), O'Neill, McCreery, Armstrong, Hamilton, Whiteside (Nelson).

0 (0) SPAIN

Arconada, Camacho, Tendillo, Alexanco, Gordillo, Sánchez, Alonso, Saura, Juanito, Satrustegui (Quini), López-Ufarte (Gallego).

Referee: Hector Ortiz (Paraguay)
Attendance: 49.562

	P	W	D	L	F	A	Pts
N. Ireland	3	1	2	0	2	1	4
Spain	3	1	1	1	3	3	3
Yugoslavia	3	1	1	1	2	2	3
Honduras	3	0	2	1	2	3	2

1st PHASE - GROUP SIX

Seville, June 14th - Estadio Sánchez Pizjuan

2 (0) BRAZIL

Socrates 75, Eder 88

Valdir Perez, Leandro, Oscar, Luizinho, Junior, Socrates, Dirceu (Paulo Isidoro), Zico, Falcão, Serginho, Eder.

1 (1) SOVIET UNION

Bal 33

Dassajev, Sulakvelidze, Chivadze, Baltacha, Demianenko, Bessonov, Gavrilov (Susloparov), Bal, Daraselia, Shengelia (Andreyev), Blokhin.

Referee: Augusto Lamo Castillo (Spain)
Attendance: 68.000

Malaga, June 15th - Estadio La Rosaleda

5 (3) SCOTLAND

Dalglish 18, Wark 29, 32, Robertson 73, Archibald 80

Rough, McGrain, Hansen, Evans, Gray, Souness, Strachan (Narey), Dalglish, Wark, Brazil (Archibald), Robertson.

2 (0) NEW ZEALAND

Sumner 55, Wooddin 65

Van Hattum, Hill, Malcolmson (Cole), Elrick, Almond (Herbert), Sumner, McKay, Cresswell, Boath, Rufer, Wooddin.

Referee: David Socha (United States)
Attendance: 36.000

Seville, June 18th - Estadio Benito Villamarin

4 (1) BRAZIL

Zico 33, Oscar 48, Eder 64, Falcão 86

Valdir Perez, Leandro, Oscar, Luizinho, Junior, Socrates, Cerezo, Zico, Falcão, Serginho (Paulo Isidoro), Eder.

1 (1) SCOTLAND

Narey 18

Rough, Miller, Hansen, Hartford (McLeish), Gray, Souness, Strachan (Dalglish), Narey, Wark, Archibald, Robertson.

Referee: Luis Siles Calderón (Costa Rica)
Attendance: 47.379

Malaga, June 19th - Estadio La Rosaleda

3 (1) SOVIET UNION

Gavrilov 24, Blokhin 48, Baltacha 69

Dassajev, Sulakvelidze, Chivadze, Baltacha, Demianenko, Bessonov, Gavrilov (Rodionov), Bal, Daraselia (Oganesian), Shengelia, Blokhin.

0 (0) NEW ZEALAND

Van Hattum, Dods, Cole, Elrick, Herbert, Sumner, McKay, Cresswell, Boath, Rufer, Wooddin.

Referee: Yousef El Ghoul (Syria)
Attendance: 19.000

Malaga, June 22nd - Estadio La Rosaleda

2 (1) SCOTLAND

Jordan 15, Souness 87

Rough, Miller, Hansen, Jordan (Brazil), Gray, Souness, Strachan (McGrain), Narey, Wark, Archibald, Robertson.

2 (0) SOVIET UNION

Chivadze 60, Shengelia 84

Dassajev, Sulakvelidze, Chivadze, Baltacha, Demianenko, Bessonov, Gavrilov, Bal, Borovsky, Shengelia (Andreyev), Blokhin.

Referee: Nicolae Rainea (Romania)
Attendance: 45.000

Seville, June 23rd - Estadio Benito Villamarin

4 (2) BRAZIL

Zico 29, 31, Falcão 55, Serginho 70

Valdir Perez, Leandro, Oscar (Edinho), Luizinho, Junior, Socrates, Cerezo, Zico, Falcão, Serginho (Paulo Isidoro), Eder.

0 (0) NEW ZEALAND

Van Hattum, Dods, Almond, Elrick, Herbert, Sumner, McKay, Cresswell (Cole), Boath, Rufer (B.Turner), Wooddin.

Referee: Damar Matovinovic (Yugoslavia)
Attendance: 43.000

	P	W	D	L	F	A	Pts
Brazil	3	3	0	0	10	2	6
USSR	3	1	1	1	6	4	3
Scotland	3	1	1	1	8	8	3
N. Zealand	3	0	0	3	2	12	0

2nd PHASE - GROUP A

Barcelona, June 28th - Estadio Nou Camp

3 (2) POLAND

Boniek 4, 26, 52

Mlynarczyk, Dziuba, Majewski, Zmuda, Janas, Lato, Buncol, Matysik, Kupcewicz (Ciolek), Boniek, Smolarek.

0 (0) BELGIUM

Custers, Renquin, Millecamps, Meeuws, Plessers (Baecke), Van Moer (Van der Elst), Coeck, Vercauteren, Ceulemans, Van den Bergh, Czerniatynski.

Referee: Luis Siles Calderon (Costa Rica)
Attendance: 65.000

Barcelona, July 1st - Estadio Nou Camp

1 (0) SOVIET UNION

Oganesian 49

Dassajev, Borovsky, Chivadze, Baltacha, Demianenko, Bessonov, Bal (Daraselia), Gavrilov, Shengelia (Rodionov), Oganesian, Blokhin.

0 (0) BELGIUM

Munaron, Renquin, Millecamps, Meeuws, De Schrijver (M.Millecamps), Verheyen, Van der Smissen (Czerniatynski), Coeck, Vercauteren, Ceulemans, Van den Bergh.

Referee: Michel Vautrot (France)
Attendance: 45.000

Barcelona, July 4th - Estadio Nou Camp

0 (0) POLAND

Mlynarczyk, Dziuba, Majewski, Zmuda, Janas, Lato, Buncol, Matysik, Kupcewicz (Ciolek), Boniek, Smolarek.

0 (0) SOVIET UNION

Dassajev, Borovsky, Chivadze, Baltacha, Demianenko, Bessonov, Sulakvelidze, Gavrilov (Daraselia), Shengelia (Andreyev), Oganesian, Blokhin.

Referee: Bob Valentine (Scotland)
Attendance: 65.000

	P	W	D	L	F	A	Pts
Poland	2	1	1	0	3	0	3
USSR	2	1	1	0	1	0	3
Belgium	2	0	0	2	0	4	0

2nd PHASE - GROUP B

Madrid, June 29th - Estadio Santiago Bernabeu

0 (0) ENGLAND

Shilton, Butcher, Mills, Thompson, Sansom, Coppell, Robson, Wilkins, Francis (Woodcock), Mariner, Rix.

0 (0) WEST GERMANY

Schumacher, Kaltz, K-H Förster, Stielike, Briegel, Dremmler, B.Förster, Breitner, H.Muller (Fischer), Reinders (Littbarski), Rummenigge.

Referee: Arnaldo Cesar Coelho (Brazil)
Attendance: 75.000

Madrid, July 2nd - Estadio Santiago Bernabeu

2 (0) WEST GERMANY

Littbarski 50, Fischer 75

Schumacher, Kaltz, K-H Förster, Stielike, Briegel, Dremmler, B.Förster, Breitner, Fischer, Littbarski, Rummenigge (Reinders).

1 (0) SPAIN

Zamora 81

Arconada, Urquiaga, Tendillo, Alexanco, Gordillo, Camacho, Alonso, Zamora, Juanito (López-Ufarte), Quini (Sánchez), Santillana.

Referee: Paolo Casarin (Italy)
Attendance: 90.089

Madrid, July 5th - Estadio Santiago Bernabeu

0 (0) ENGLAND

Shilton, Butcher, Mills, Thompson, Sansom, Robson, Wilkins, Francis, Woodcock (Keegan), Mariner, Rix (Brooking).

0 (0) SPAIN

Arconada, Urquiaga, Tendillo (Maceda), Alexanco, Gordillo, Saura (Uralde), Alonso, Zamora, Camacho, Satrustegui, Santillana.

Referee: Alexis Ponnet (Belgium)
Attendance: 75.000

	P	W	D	L	F	A	Pts
W. Germany	2	1	1	0	2	1	3
England	2	0	2	0	0	0	2
Spain	2	0	1	1	1	2	1

2nd PHASE - GROUP C

Barcelona, June 29th - Estadio Sarria

2 (0) ITALY

Tardelli 55, Cabrini 68

Zoff, Gentile, Cabrini, Collovati, Scirea, Tardelli, Antognoni, Oriali (Marini), Conti, Rossi (Altobelli), Graziani.

1 (0) ARGENTINA

Passarella 83

Fillol, Olguin, Galvan, Passarella, Tarantini, Gallego (RED), Ardiles, Maradona, Bertoni, Díaz (Calderon), Kempes (Valencia).

Referee: Nicolae Rainea (Romania)
Attendance: 43.000

Barcelona, July 2nd - Estadio Sarria

3 (1) BRAZIL

Zico 12, Serginho 67, Junior 72

Valdir Perez, Leandro (Edevaldo), Oscar, Luizinho, Junior, Cerezo, Zico (Batista), Falcão, Serginho, Socrates, Eder.

1 (0) ARGENTINA

Díaz 89

Fillol, Olguin, Galvan, Passarella, Tarantini, Barbas, Ardiles, Maradona (RED), Bertoni (Santamaria), Calderon, Kempes (Díaz).

Referee: Mario Rubio Vázquez (Mexico)
Attendance: 44.000

Barcelona, July 5th - Estadio Sarria

3 (2) ITALY

Rossi 5,25,75

Zoff, Gentile, Cabrini, Collovati (Bergomi), Scirea, Tardelli (Marini), Antognoni, Oriali, Conti, Rossi, Graziani.

2 (1) BRAZIL

Socrates 12, Falcão 68

Valdir Perez, Leandro, Oscar, Luizinho, Junior, Cerezo, Zico, Falcão, Serginho (Paulo Isidoro), Socrates, Eder.

Referee: Abraham Klein (Israel)
Attendance: 44.000

	P	W	D	L	F	A	Pts
Italy	2	2	0	0	5	3	4
Brazil	2	1	0	1	5	4	2
Argentina	2	0	0	2	2	5	0

2nd PHASE - GROUP D

Madrid, June 28th - Estadio Vicente Calderon

1 (1) FRANCE

Genghini 39

Ettori, Battiston, Janvion, Trésor, Bossis, Giresse, Tigana, Genghini (Girard), Soler, Lacombe (Rocheteau), Six.

0 (0) AUSTRIA

Koncilia, Krauss, Obermayer, Pezzey, Degeorgi (Baumeister), Prohaska, Hintermaier, Hattenberger, Schachner, Jara (Welzl), Krankl.

Referee: Karoly Palotai (Hungary)
Attendance: 37.000

Madrid, July 1st - Estadio Vicente Calderon

2 (0) AUSTRIA

Pezzey 50, Hintermaier 67

Koncilia, Krauss, Obermayer, Pezzey, Baumeister, Prohaska, Pregersbauer (Hintermaier), Pichler, Schachner, Hagmayr (Welzl), Jurtin.

2 (1) NORTHERN IRELAND

Hamilton 27, 74

Platt, J.Nicholl, C.Nicholl, McIlroy, Nelson, O'Neill, McClelland, Armstrong, Hamilton, Whiteside (Brotherston), McCreery.

Referee: Adolf Prokop (East Germany)
Attendance: 20.000

Madrid, July 4th - Estadio Vicente Calderon

4 (1) FRANCE

Giresse 33, 80, Rocheteau 47,63

Ettori, Amoros, Janvion, Trésor, Bossis, Giresse, Tigana, Genghini, Soler (Six), Platini, Rocheteau (Couriol).

1 (0) NORTHERN IRELAND

Armstrong 75

Jennings, J.Nicholl, C.Nicholl, McIlroy, Donaghy, O'Neill, McClelland, Armstrong, Hamilton, Whiteside, McCreery (J.O'Neill).

Referee: Alojzi Jarguz (Poland)
Attendance: 37.000

	P	W	D	L	F	A	Pts
France	2	2	0	0	5	1	4
Austria	2	0	1	1	2	3	1
N. Ireland	2	0	1	1	3	6	1

SEMI-FINALS

Barcelona, July 8th - Estadio Nou Camp

2 (1) ITALY

Rossi 22,72

Zoff, Cabrini, Collovati, Bergomi, Scirea, Antognoni (Marini), Conti, Oriali, Tardelli, Rossi, Graziani (Altobelli).

0 (0) POLAND

Mlynarczyk, Dziuba, Zmuda, Janas, Majewski, Matysik, Kupcewicz, Buncol, Lato, Ciolek (Palasz), Smolarek (Kusto).

Referee: Juan Daniel Cardellino (Uruguay)
Attendance: 50.000

Seville, July 8th - Estadio Sánchez Pizjuan

After extra time & penalty shoot-out - 45 mins (1-1), 90 mins (1-1), 120 mins (3-3)

8 (5)(3) WEST GERMANY

Littbarski 17, Rummenigge 102, Fischer 108

Schumacher, Kaltz, K-H Förster, Stielike, Briegel (Rummenigge), B.Förster, Dremmler, Breitner, Littbarski, Magath (Hrubesch), Fischer.

7 (4)(3) FRANCE

Platini (pen)26, Trésor 92, Giresse 98

Ettori, Amoros, Janvion, Bossis, Tigana, Trésor, Genghini (Battiston)(López), Giresse, Platini, Rocheteau, Six.

Penalty shoot-out - France started to shoot

FRANCE	4		GERMANY	5
Giresse	Goal		Kaltz	Goal
Amoros	Goal		Breitner	Goal
Rocheteau	Goal		Stielike	Miss
Six	Miss		Littbarski	Goal
Platini	Goal		Rummenigge	Goal
Bossis	Miss		Hrubesch	Goal

Referee: Charles Corver (Holland)
Attendance: 63.000

3RD/4TH PLACE PLAY-OFF

Alicante, July 10th - Estadio José Rico Perez

2 (1) FRANCE

Girard 13, Couriol 73

Castaneda, Amoros, Mahut, Trésor, Janvion (López), Girard, Larios, Tigana (Six), Couriol, Soler, Bellone.

3 (2) POLAND

Szarmach 41, Majewski 44, Kupcewicz 46

Mlynarczyk, Dziuba, Zmuda, Janas, Majewski, Matysik (Wojcicki), Kupcewicz, Buncol, Lato, Boniek, Szarmach.

Referee: Antonio Garrido (Portugal)
Attendance: 28.000

FINAL

Madrid, July 11th - Estadio Santiago Bernabeu

3 (0) ITALY

Rossi 56, Tardelli 68, Altobelli 80

Zoff, Cabrini, Scirea, Gentile, Collovati, Oriali, Bergomi, Tardelli, Conti, Rossi, Graziani (Altobelli)(Causio).

1 (0) WEST GERMANY

Breitner 82

Schumacher, Kaltz, Stielike, K-H Förster, B.Förster, Dremmler (Hrubesch), Breitner, Briegel, Littbarski, Fischer, Rummenigge (H.Müller).

Referee: Arnaldo Cesar Coelho (Brazil)
Attendance: 90.000

Maggie, Michel and the Italian Bad Boy - Spain 1982

QUALIFYING ROUNDS

Africa - 1st Round

	P	W	D	L	F	A	Pts
Zaire	2	2	0	0	7	3	4
Zambia	2	1	1	1	4	0	3
Cameroon	2	1	1	1	4	1	3
Algeria	2	1	1	1	5	3	3
Guinea	2	1	1	1	4	2	3
Libya	2	1	1	1	2	1	3
Morocco	2	1	1	1	1	0	3
Tanzania	2	1	0	0	6	3	2
Nigeria	2	1	0	0	2	2	2
Tunisia	2	1	0	0	2	2	2
Niger	2	0	2	2	1	1	2
Somalia	2	0	2	2	1	1	2
Kenya	2	1	0	0	3	6	2
Gambia	2	0	1	1	1	2	1
Senegal	2	0	1	1	0	1	1
Sierra Leone	2	0	1	1	3	5	1
Lesotho	2	0	1	1	2	4	1
Malawi	2	0	1	1	1	4	1
Ethiopia	2	0	1	1	0	4	1
Mozambique	2	0	0	0	3	7	0

08-05-80	Libya : Gambia	2:1 (1:0)
18-05-80	Ethiopia : Zambia	0:0
31-05-80	Sierra Leone : Algeria	2:2 (0:0)
01-06-80	Zambia : Ethiopia	4:0 (2:0)
13-06-80	Algeria : Sierra Leone	3:1 (1:0)
22-06-80	Guinea : Lesotho	3:1 (1:1)
22-06-80	Senegal : Morocco	0:1 (0:1)
29-06-80	Tunisia : Nigeria	2:0 (1:0)
29-06-80	Cameroon : Malawi	3:0 (1:0)
05-07-80	Kenya : Tanzania	3:1 (1:1)
06-07-80	Morocco : Senegal	0:0
06-07-80	Gambia : Libya	0:0
06-07-80	Lesotho : Guinea	1:1 (0:1)
12-07-80	Nigeria : Tunisia	2:0 (1:0)
13-07-80	Zaire : Mozambique	5:2 (1:1)
16-07-80	Niger : Somalia	0:0
19-07-80	Tanzania : Kenya	5:0 (1:0)
20-07-80	Malawi : Cameroon	1:1 (0:0)
27-07-80	Mozambique : Zaire	1:2 (0:2)
27-07-80	Somalia : Niger	1:1 (0:1)

Africa - 2nd Round

	P	W	D	L	F	A	Pts
Nigeria	2	1	1	0	3	1	3
Algeria	2	1	1	0	3	1	3
Zaire	2	1	1	0	4	3	3
Guinea	2	1	1	0	1	0	3
Cameroon	2	1	0	1	2	1	2
Niger	2	1	0	1	2	2	2
Togo	2	1	0	1	2	2	2
Zambia	2	1	0	1	2	2	2
Morocco	2	1	0	1	2	2	2
Zimbabwe	2	1	0	1	1	2	2
Madagascar	2	0	1	1	3	4	1
Liberia	2	0	1	1	0	1	1
Sudan	2	0	1	1	1	3	1
Tanzania	2	0	1	1	1	3	1

12-10-80	Cameroon : Zimbabwe	2:0 (0:0)
16-11-80	Zimbabwe : Cameroon	1:0 (1:0)
16-11-80	Morocco : Zambia	2:0 (2:0)
16-11-80	Madagascar : Zaire	1:1 (1:1)
30-11-80	Zambia : Morocco	2:0 (0:0)
06-12-80	Nigeria : Tanzania	1:1 (1:0)
07-12-80	Liberia : Guinea	0:0
12-12-80	Algeria : Sudan	2:0 (2:0)

14-12-80	Niger : Togo	0:1 (0:0)
20-12-80	Tanzania : Nigeria	0:2 (0:1)
21-12-80	Zaire : Madagascar	3:2 (2:2)
21-12-80	Guinea : Liberia	1:0 (1:0)
28-12-80	Sudan : Algeria	1:1 (0:0)
28-12-80	Togo : Niger	1:2 (0:0)

Africa - 3rd Round

	P	W	D	L	F	A	Pts
Nigeria	2	1	1	0	2	1	3
Morocco	2	1	1	0	1	0	3
Cameroon	2	1	0	1	6	2	2
Algeria	2	1	0	1	4	1	2
Niger	2	1	0	1	1	4	2
Zaire	2	1	0	1	2	6	2
Guinea	2	0	1	1	1	2	1
Egypt	2	0	1	1	0	1	1

12-04-81	Guinea : Nigeria	1:1 (0:1)
12-04-81	Zaire : Cameroon	1:0 (1:0)
25-04-81	Nigeria : Guinea	1:0 (0:0)
26-04-81	Cameroon : Zaire	6:1 (3:0)
26-04-81	Morocco : Egypt	1:0 (1:0)
01-05-81	Algeria : Niger	4:0 (1:0)
08-05-81	Egypt : Morocco	0:0
31-05-81	Niger : Algeria	1:0 (0:0)

Africa - Final Round

	P	W	D	L	F	A	Pts
Algeria	2	2	0	0	4	1	4
Cameroon	2	2	0	0	4	1	4
Nigeria	2	0	0	2	1	4	0
Morocco	2	0	0	2	1	4	0

10-10-81	Nigeria : Algeria	0:2 (0:2)
30-10-81	Algeria : Nigeria	2:1 (1:1)
15-11-81	Morocco : Cameroon	0:2 (0:2)
29-11-81	Cameroon : Morocco	2:1 (1:1)

Asia/Oceania - Phase 1/Group 1

	P	W	D	L	F	A	Pts
New Zealand	8	6	2	0	31	3	14
Australia	8	4	2	2	22	9	10
Indonesia	8	2	2	4	5	14	6
Ch. Talpei	8	1	3	4	5	8	5
Fiji	8	1	3	4	6	35	5

25-04-81	New Zealand : Australia	3:3 (2:3)
03-05-81	Fiji : New Zealand	0:4 (0:3)
07-05-81	Chinese Taipei : New Zealand	0:0
11-05-81	Indonesia : New Zealand	0:2 (0:1)
16-05-81	Australia : New Zealand	0:2 (0:1)
20-05-81	Australia : Indonesia	2:0 (2:0)
23-05-81	New Zealand : Indonesia	5:0 (2:0)
30-05-81	New Zealand : Chinese Taipei	2:0 (1:0)
31-05-81	Fiji : Indonesia	0:0
06-06-81	Fiji : Chinese Taipei	2:1 (1:0)
10-06-81	Australia : Chinese Taipei	3:2 (1:0)
15-06-81	Indonesia : Chinese Taipei	1:0 (0:0)
28-06-81	Chinese Taipei : Indonesia	2:0 (2:0)
26-07-81	Fiji : Australia	1:4 (0:4)
04-08-81	Fiji : Chinese Taipei	0:0
10-08-81	Indonesia : Fiji	3:3 (3:1)
14-08-81	Australia : Fiji	10:0 (3:0)
16-08-81	New Zealand : Fiji	13:0 (7:0)
30-08-81	Indonesia : Australia	1:0 (0:0)
06-09-81	Chinese Taipei : Australia	0:0

Asia/Oceania - Phase 1/Group 2

	P	W	D	L	F	A	Pts
Saudi Arabia	4	4	0	0	5	0	8
Iraq	4	3	0	1	5	2	6
Qatar	4	2	0	2	5	3	4
Bahrain	4	1	0	3	1	6	2
Syria	4	0	0	4	2	7	0

18-03-81	Qatar : Iraq	0:1 (0:0)
19-03-81	Syria : Bahrain	0:1 (0:0)
21-03-81	Iraq : Saudi Arabia	0:1 (0:0)
22-03-81	Qatar : Bahrain	3:0 (2:0)
24-03-81	Syria : Saudi Arabia	0:2 (0:0)
25-03-81	Iraq : Bahrain	2:0 (1:0)
27-03-81	Qatar : Syria	2:1 (1:1)
28-03-81	Bahrain : Saudi Arabia	0:1 (0:0)
30-03-81	Iraq : Syria	2:1 (1:0)
31-03-81	Qatar : Saudi Arabia	0:1 (0:0)

All games played in Riyadh.

Asia/Oceania - Phase 1/Group 3

	P	W	D	L	F	A	Pts
Kuwait	3	3	0	0	12	0	6
Korea Rep.	3	2	0	1	7	4	4
Malaysia	3	0	1	2	3	8	1
Thailand	3	0	1	2	3	13	1

21-04-81	Korea Republic : Malaysia	2:1 (1:1)
22-04-81	Kuwait : Thailand	6:0 (4:0)
24-04-81	Korea Republic : Thailand	5:1 (2:1)
25-04-81	Kuwait : Malaysia	4:0 (2:0)
27-04-81	Malaysia : Thailand	2:2 (0:0)
29-04-81	Kuwait : Korea Republic	2:0 (0:0)

All games played in Kuwait City.

Asia/Oceania - Phase 1/Group 4
Preliminary Round

	P	W	D	L	F	A	Pts
Korea DPR	1	1	0	0	3	0	2
China PR	1	1	0	0	1	0	2
Japan	1	1	0	0	1	0	2
Hong Kong	1	0	0	1	0	1	0
Singapore	1	0	0	1	0	1	0
Macao	1	0	0	1	0	3	0

21-12-80	Hong Kong : China PR	0:1 (0:0)
22-12-80	Korea DPR : Macao	3:0 (2:0)
22-12-80	Singapore : Japan	0:1 (0:1)

All games played in Hong Kong.

Asia/Oceania - Phase 1/Group 4
Subgroup A

	P	W	D	L	F	A	Pts
China PR	2	2	0	0	4	0	4
Japan	2	1	0	1	3	1	2
Macao	2	0	0	2	0	6	0

24-12-80	China PR : Macao	3:0 (2:0)
26-12-80	China PR : Japan	1:0 (1:0)
28-12-80	Japan : Macao	3:0 (0:0)

All games played in Hong Kong.

Asia/Oceania - Phase 1/Group 4
Subgroup B

	P	W	D	L	F	A	Pts
Korea DPR	2	1	1	0	3	2	3
Hong Kong	2	0	2	0	3	3	2
Singapore	2	0	1	1	1	2	1

24-12-80	Hong Kong : Singapore	1:1 (0:0)
26-12-80	Singapore : Korea DPR	0:1 (0:1)
28-12-80	Hong Kong : Korea DPR	2:2 (1:2)

All games played in Hong Kong.

Asia/Oceania - Phase 1/Group 4
Semi-Finals

30-12-80	Korea DPR : Japan	1:0 (0:0)
31-12-80	Hong Kong : China PR	0:0
	4:5 penalty kicks

Both games played in Hong Kong.

Asia/Oceania - Phase 1/Group 4 Final

04-01-81	Korea DPR : China PR	2:4 a.e.t.
		(2:2, 1:1)

Game played in Hong Kong.

Asia/Oceania - Phase 2 Final Matches

	P	W	D	L	F	A	Pts
Kuwait	6	4	1	1	8	6	9
New Zealand	6	2	3	1	11	6	7
China PR	6	3	1	2	9	4	7
Saudi Arabia	6	0	1	5	4	16	1

24-09-81	China PR : New Zealand	0:0
03-10-81	New Zealand : China PR	1:0 (1:0)
10-10-81	New Zealand : Kuwait	1:2 (1:0)
18-10-81	China PR : Kuwait	3:0 (2:0)
04-11-81	Saudi Arabia : Kuwait	0:1 (0:0)
12-11-81	Saudi Arabia : China PR	2:4 (2:0)
19-11-81	China PR : Saudi Arabia	2:0 (2:0)
28-11-81	New Zealand : Saudi Arabia	2:2 (2:1)
30-11-81	Kuwait : China PR	1:0 (1:0)
07-12-81	Kuwait : Saudi Arabia	2:0 (1:0)
14-12-81	Kuwait : New Zealand	2:2 (1:0)
19-12-81	Saudi Arabia : New Zealand	0:5 (0:5)

Asia/Oceania - Final Matches Play Off

10-01-82	China PR : New Zealand	1:2 (0:1)

Game played in Singapore.

Europe - Group 1

	P	W	D	L	F	A	Pts
Germany FR	8	8	0	0	33	3	16
Austria	8	5	1	2	16	6	11
Bulgaria	8	4	1	3	11	10	9
Albania	8	1	0	7	4	22	2
Finland	8	1	0	7	4	27	2

04-06-80	Finland : Bulgaria	0:2 (0:1)
03-09-80	Albania : Finland	2:0 (2:0)
24-09-80	Finland : Austria	0:2 (0:1)
19-10-80	Bulgaria : Albania	2:1 (1:0)
15-11-80	Austria : Albania	5:0 (3:0)
03-12-80	Bulgaria : Germany FR	1:3 (0:2)
06-12-80	Albania : Austria	0:1 (0:1)
01-04-81	Albania : Germany FR	0:2 (0:1)
29-04-81	Germany FR : Austria	2:0 (2:0)
13-05-81	Bulgaria : Finland	4:0 (1:0)
24-05-81	Finland : Germany FR	0:4 (0:3)
28-05-81	Austria : Bulgaria	2:0 (1:0)
17-06-81	Austria : Finland	5:1 (2:0)
02-09-81	Finland : Albania	2:1 (0:0)
23-09-81	Germany FR : Finland	7:1 (2:1)
14-10-81	Albania : Bulgaria	0:2 (0:0)
14-10-81	Austria : Germany FR	1:3 (1:2)
11-11-81	Bulgaria : Austria	0:0
18-11-81	Germany FR : Albania	8:0 (5:0)
22-11-81	Germany FR : Bulgaria	4:0 (1:0)

Europe - Group 2

	P	W	D	L	F	A	Pts
Belgium	8	5	1	2	12	9	11
France	8	5	0	3	20	8	10
Rep. Ireland	8	4	2	2	17	11	10
Netherlands	8	4	1	3	11	7	9
Cyprus	8	0	0	8	4	29	0

26-03-80	Cyprus : Ireland Republic	2:3 (1:3)
10-09-80	Ireland Republic : Netherlands	2:1 (0:0)
11-10-80	Cyprus : France	0:7 (0:4)
15-10-80	Ireland Republic : Belgium	1:1 (1:1)
28-10-80	France : Ireland Republic	2:0 (1:0)
19-11-80	Ireland Republic : Cyprus	6:0 (4:0)
19-11-80	Belgium : Netherlands	1:0 (0:0)
21-12-80	Cyprus : Belgium	0:2 (0:1)
18-02-81	Belgium : Cyprus	3:2 (2:1)
22-02-81	Netherlands : Cyprus	3:0 (1:0)
25-03-81	Netherlands : France	1:0 (0:0)
25-03-81	Belgium : Ireland Republic	1:0 (0:0)
29-04-81	Cyprus : Netherlands	0:1 (0:1)
29-04-81	France : Belgium	3:2 (3:1)
09-09-81	Belgium : France	2:0 (1:0)
09-09-81	Netherlands : Ireland Republic	2:2 (1:1)
14-10-81	Ireland Republic : France	3:2 (3:1)
14-10-81	Netherlands : Belgium	3:0 (2:0)
18-11-81	France : Netherlands	2:0 (1:0)
05-12-81	France : Cyprus	4:0 (2:0)

Europe - Group 3

	P	W	D	L	F	A	Pts
USSR	8	6	2	0	20	2	14
Czechoslovakia	8	4	2	2	15	6	10
Wales	8	4	2	2	12	7	10
Iceland	8	2	2	4	10	21	6
Turkey	8	0	0	8	1	22	0

02-06-80	Iceland : Wales	0:4 (0:1)
03-09-80	Iceland : USSR	1:2 (0:1)
24-09-80	Turkey : Iceland	1:3 (0:1)
15-10-80	USSR : Iceland	5:0 (2:0)
15-10-80	Wales : Turkey	4:0 (2:0)
19-11-80	Wales : Czechoslovakia	1:0 (1:0)
03-12-80	Czechoslovakia : Turkey	2:0 (2:0)
25-03-81	Turkey : Wales	0:1 (0:0)
15-04-81	Turkey : Czechoslovakia	0:3 (0:0)
27-05-81	Czechoslovakia : Iceland	6:1 (2:0)
30-05-81	Wales : USSR	0:0
09-09-81	Czechoslovakia : Wales	2:0 (1:0)
09-09-81	Iceland : Turkey	2:0 (1:0)
23-09-81	USSR : Turkey	4:0 (3:0)
23-09-81	Iceland : Czechoslovakia	1:1 (1:0)
07-10-81	Turkey : USSR	0:3 (0:2)
14-10-81	Wales : Iceland	2:2 (1:0)
28-10-81	USSR : Czechoslovakia	2:0 (1:0)
18-11-81	USSR : Wales	3:0 (2:0)
29-11-81	Czechoslovakia : USSR	1:1 (1:1)

Europe - Group 4

	P	W	D	L	F	A	Pts
Hungary	8	4	2	2	13	8	10
England	8	4	1	3	13	8	9
Romania	8	2	4	2	5	5	8
Switzerland	8	2	3	3	9	12	7
Norway	8	2	2	4	8	15	6

10-09-80	England : Norway	4:0 (1:0)
24-09-80	Norway : Romania	1:1 (1:1)
15-10-80	Romania : England	2:1 (1:0)
29-10-80	Switzerland : Norway	1:2 (0:1)
19-11-80	England : Switzerland	2:1 (2:0)
28-04-81	Switzerland : Hungary	2:2 (1:1)
29-04-81	England : Romania	0:0
13-05-81	Hungary : Romania	1:0 (1:0)
20-05-81	Norway : Hungary	1:2 (0:0)
30-05-81	Switzerland : England	2:1 (2:0)
03-06-81	Romania : Norway	1:0 (0:0)
06-06-81	Hungary : England	1:3 (1:1)
17-06-81	Norway : Switzerland	1:1 (0:0)
09-09-81	Norway : England	2:1 (2:1)
23-09-81	Romania : Hungary	0:0
10-10-81	Romania : Switzerland	1:2 (0:0)
14-10-81	Hungary : Switzerland	3:0 (1:0)
31-10-81	Hungary : Norway	4:1 (1:1)
11-11-81	Switzerland : Romania	0:0
18-11-81	England : Hungary	1:0 (1:0)

Europe - Group 5

	P	W	D	L	F	A	Pts
Yugoslavia	8	6	1	1	22	7	13
Italy	8	5	2	1	12	5	12
Denmark	8	4	0	4	14	11	8
Greece	8	3	1	4	10	13	7
Luxembourg	8	0	0	8	1	23	0

10-09-80	Luxembourg : Yugoslavia	0:5 (0:0)
27-09-80	Yugoslavia : Denmark	2:1 (2:1)
11-10-80	Luxembourg : Italy	0:2 (0:1)
15-10-80	Denmark : Greece	0:1 (0:0)
01-11-80	Italy : Denmark	2:0 (1:0)
15-11-80	Italy : Yugoslavia	2:0 (1:0)
19-11-80	Denmark : Luxembourg	4:0 (2:0)
06-12-80	Greece : Italy	0:2 (0:1)
28-01-81	Greece : Luxembourg	2:0 (2:0)
11-03-81	Luxembourg : Greece	0:2 (0:1)
29-04-81	Yugoslavia : Greece	5:1 (3:0)
01-05-81	Luxembourg : Denmark	1:2 (1:0)
03-06-81	Denmark : Italy	3:1 (0:0)
09-09-81	Denmark : Yugoslavia	1:2 (0:0)
14-10-81	Greece : Denmark	2:3 (0:2)
17-10-81	Yugoslavia : Italy	1:1 (1:1)
14-11-81	Italy : Greece	1:1 (1:0)
21-11-81	Yugoslavia : Luxembourg	5:0 (2:0)
29-11-81	Greece : Yugoslavia	1:2 (1:2)
05-12-81	Italy : Luxembourg	1:0 (1:0)

Europe - Group 6

	P	W	D	L	F	A	Pts
Scotland	8	4	3	1	9	4	11
N. Ireland	8	3	3	2	6	3	9
Sweden	8	3	2	3	7	8	8
Portugal	8	3	1	4	8	11	7
Israel	8	1	3	4	6	10	5

26-03-80	Israel : Northern Ireland	0:0
18-06-80	Sweden : Israel	1:1 (1:0)
10-09-80	Sweden : Scotland	0:1 (0:0)

15-10-80	Northern Ireland : Sweden	3:0 (3:0)
15-10-80	Scotland : Portugal	0:0
12-11-80	Israel : Sweden	0:0
19-11-80	Portugal : Northern Ireland	1:0 (0:0)
17-12-80	Portugal : Israel	3:0 (2:0)
25-02-81	Israel : Scotland	0:1 (0:0)
25-03-81	Scotland : Northern Ireland	1:1 (0:0)
28-04-81	Scotland : Israel	3:1 (2:0)
29-04-81	Northern Ireland : Portugal	1:0 (0:0)
03-06-81	Sweden : Northern Ireland	1:0 (0:0)
24-06-81	Sweden : Portugal	3:0 (1:0)
09-09-81	Scotland : Sweden	2:0 (1:0)
14-10-81	Northern Ireland : Scotland	0:0
14-10-81	Portugal : Sweden	1:2 (0:1)
28-10-81	Israel : Portugal	4:1 (4:1)
18-11-81	Portugal : Scotland	2:1 (1:1)
18-11-81	Northern Ireland : Israel	1:0 (1:0)

Europe - Group 7

	P	W	D	L	F	A	Pts
Poland	4	4	0	0	12	2	8
Germany DR	4	2	0	2	9	6	4
Malta	4	0	0	4	2	15	0

07-12-80	Malta : Poland	0:2 (0:0)
04-04-81	Malta : Germany DR	1:2 (1:2)
02-05-81	Poland : Germany DR	1:0 (0:0)
10-10-81	Germany DR : Poland	2:3 (0:2)
11-11-81	Germany DR : Malta	5:1 (2:1)
15-11-81	Poland : Malta	6:0 (1:0)

North/Central America - Pre-Group Matches

	P	W	D	L	F	A	Pts
Guyana	2	2	0	0	8	4	4
Grenada	2	0	0	2	4	8	0

| 30-03-80 | Guyana : Grenada | 5:2 (2:2) |
| 13-04-80 | Grenada : Guyana | 2:3 (0:2) |

North/Central America - Phase 1/Group A

	P	W	D	L	F	A	Pts
Cuba	4	3	1	0	7	0	7
Surinam	4	2	1	1	5	3	5
Guyana	4	0	0	4	0	9	0

17-08-80	Cuba : Surinam	3:0 (0:0)
07-09-80	Surinam : Cuba	0:0
28-09-80	Guyana : Surinam	0:1 (0:1
12-10-80	Surinam : Guyana	4:0 (2:0)
09-11-80	Cuba : Guyana	1:0 (1:0)
30-11-80	Guyana : Cuba	0:3 (0:3)

North/Central America - Phase 1/Group B

	P	W	D	L	F	A	Pts
Haiti	4	2	1	1	4	2	5
Trinidad & Tobago	4	1	2	1	1	2	4
Netherlands Antilles	4	0	3	1	1	2	3

01-08-80	Haiti : Trinidad & Tobago	2:0 (0:0)
17-08-80	Trinidad & Tobago : Haiti	1:0 (0:0)
12-09-80	Haiti : Netherlands Antilles	1:0 (0:0)
09-11-80	Trin. & Tobago : Neth. Antilles	0:0
29-11-80	Neth. Antilles : Trin. & Tobago	0:0
12-12-80	Netherlands Antilles : Haiti	1:1 (0:1)

North/Central America - Phase 1/Central Zone

	P	W	D	L	F	A	Pts
Honduras	8	5	2	1	15	5	12
El Salvador	8	5	2	1	12	5	12
Guatemala	8	3	3	2	10	2	9
Costa Rica	8	1	4	3	6	10	6
Panama	8	0	1	7	3	24	1

02-07-80	Panama : Guatemala	0:2 (0:1)
30-07-80	Panama : Honduras	0:2 (0:1)
10-08-80	Panama : Costa Rica	1:1 (1:0)
24-08-80	Panama : El Salvador	1:3 (0:1)
01-10-80	Costa Rica : Honduras	2:3 (0:2)
05-10-80	El Salvador : Panama	4:1 (2:1)
12-10-80	Guatemala : Costa Rica	0:0
26-10-80	Honduras : Guatemala	0:0
26-10-80	El Salvador : Costa Rica	2:0
05-11-80	Costa Rica : Panama	2:0 (1:0)
09-11-80	Guatemala : El Salvador	0:0
16-11-80	Honduras : Costa Rica	1:1 (0:1)
16-11-80	Guatemala : Panama	5:0 (2:0)
23-11-80	El Salvador : Honduras	2:1 (1:0)
26-11-80	Costa Rica : Guatemala	0:3 (0:1)
30-11-80	Honduras : El Salvador	2:0 (1:0)
07-12-80	Guatemala : Honduras	0:1 (0:0)
10-12-80	Costa Rica : El Salvador	0:0
14-12-80	Honduras : Panama	5:0 (3:0)
21-12-80	El Salvador : Guatemala	1:0 (0:0)

North/Central America - Phase 1/Nothern Zone

	P	W	D	L	F	A	Pts
Canada	4	1	3	0	4	3	5
Mexico	4	1	2	1	8	5	4
USA	4	1	1	2	4	8	3

18-10-80	Canada : Mexico	1:1 (1:0)
25-10-80	United States : Canada	0:0
01-11-80	Canada : United States	2:1 (2:0)
09-11-80	Mexico : United States	5:1 (4:0)
16-11-80	Mexico : Canada	1:1 (0:0)
23-11-80	United States : Mexico	2:1 (1:1)

North/Central America - Phase 2/Final Tournament

	P	W	D	L	F	A	Pts
Honduras	5	3	2	0	8	1	8
El Salvador	5	2	2	1	2	1	6
Mexico	5	1	3	1	6	3	5
Canada	5	1	3	1	6	6	5
Cuba	5	1	2	2	4	8	4
Haiti	5	0	2	3	2	9	2

01-11-81	Mexico : Cuba	4:0 (2:0)
02-11-81	Canada : El Salvador	1:0 (0:0)
03-11-81	Honduras : Haiti	4:0 (2:0)
06-11-81	Canada : Haiti	1:1 (0:1)
06-11-81	Mexico : El Salvador	0:1 (0:0)
08-11-81	Honduras : Cuba	2:0 (1:0)
11-11-81	Cuba : El Salvador	0:0
11-11-81	Haiti : Mexico	1:1 (0:0)
12-11-81	Honduras : Canada	2:1 (2:1)
15-11-81	Haiti : Cuba	0:2 (0:0)
15-11-81	Mexico : Canada	1:1 (1:0)
16-11-81	Honduras : El Salvador	0:0
19-11-81	El Salvador : Haiti	1:0 (1:0)
21-11-81	Cuba : Canada	2:2 (1:0)

| 22-11-81 | Honduras : Mexico | 0:0 |

All games played in Tegucigalpa.

South America - Group 1

	P	W	D	L	F	A	Pts
Brazil	4	4	0	0	11	2	8
Bolivia	4	1	0	3	5	6	2
Venezuela	4	1	0	3	1	9	2

08-02-81	Venezuela : Brazil	0:1 (0:0)
15-02-81	Bolivia : Venezuela	3:0 (1:0)
22-02-81	Bolivia : Brazil	1:2 (1:1)
15-03-81	Venezuela : Bolivia	1:0 (1:0)
22-03-81	Brazil : Bolivia	3:1 (1:0)
29-03-81	Brazil : Venezuela	5:0 (1:0)

South America - Group 2

	P	W	D	L	F	A	Pts
Peru	4	2	2	0	5	2	6
Uruguay	4	1	2	1	5	5	4
Colombia	4	0	2	2	4	7	2

26-07-81	Colombia : Peru	1:1 (0:0)
09-08-81	Uruguay : Colombia	3:2 (1:1)
16-08-81	Peru : Colombia	2:0 (1:0)
23-08-81	Uruguay : Peru	1:2 (0:2)
06-09-81	Peru : Uruguay	0:0
13-09-81	Colombia : Uruguay	1:1 (1:1)

South America - Group 3

	P	W	D	L	F	A	Pts
Chile	4	3	1	0	6	0	7
Ecuador	4	1	1	2	2	5	3
Paraguay	4	1	0	3	3	6	2

17-05-81	Ecuador : Paraguay	1:0 (0:0)
24-05-81	Ecuador : Chile	0:0
31-05-81	Paraguay : Ecuador	3:1 (0:0)
07-06-81	Paraguay : Chile	0:1 (0:0)
14-06-81	Chile : Ecuador	2:0 (1:0)
21-06-81	Chile : Paraguay	3:0 (3:0)

Chapter 15

Glasnost, Nuclear Fallout and the Hand of God
The Mexico World Cup, 1986

Mexico 1986

Winners: Argentina

Runners-up: West Germany

3rd Place: France

4th Place: Poland

Total Attendance: 2,391,103

Number of Matches: 52

By the mid point of the 1980s, as Western economies were hurtling towards the boom that would characterize the second half of the decade, years of stagnation and economic decline in the USSR and Eastern Europe meant the beginning of the end of Communism. In a speech of February 1986, recently appointed President Gorbachev of the USSR attacked the wasted years of the Brezhnev era, blaming corruption, lazy workers and inefficient management for his country's decline. Heralding a period of unprecedented reform, he called for "perestroika", or reconstruction, and "glasnost", or openness, terms that would soon enter the Oxford English Dictionary. The extent of the USSR's fall was starkly illustrated in April when neglect, poor design and human error led to the explosion at the Chernobyl nuclear power plant on the outskirts of Kiev. It caused a radiation cloud to spread across the whole of Europe, as far as Great Britain, with Scandinavia and Poland taking the brunt of the radioactive dust. Fortunately, the number of casualties in the immediate vicinity was minimized because the explosion happened at night while most people were indoors and strong winds raised the dust high into the atmosphere.

With the US refusing to help their ally, Philippine dictator, Ferdinand Marcos, was ousted by people power. When the newly elected President Aquino's forces entered his apartments, they fond a fortune in clothes, shoes and jewellery, amassed by his wife, Imelda. 1986 also saw the end of "Baby Doc" Duvalier in Haiti, but in Cuba Castro looked as strong as ever, despite rumours of his impending downfall coming out of Miami. Elsewhere, Ronald Reagan continued to impose his values on the rest of the world. His forces had already visited Central America and Grenada and in the early hours of 15th April, it was Libya's turn. Blaming Colonel Gadaffi for terrorist attacks on Americans abroad, Reagan ordered his bombers to attack Tripoli and Benghazi. Several civilian sites were hit and one of Colonel Gadaffi's daughters was killed. Yet he did not have it all his own way. At home the Irangate scandal, in which his administration were accused of illegally selling arms to Iran, reached its climax, but Reagan was saved from impeachment when Colonel Oliver North, of his national security staff, admitted responsibility for the sordid affair. Scandal also dogged the Thatcher government in Britain with both Michael Heseltine and Leon Brittan resigning over the Westland Helicopters debacle. In both instances, neither Thatcher nor Reagan claimed to know anything about the matters.

As a sign of things to come, it was reported that book sales in Britain and the US had been falling since 1980 and, with the advance of television and computer games, the "couch potato" was born. The face of European travel was soon to be irreversibly changed when it was announced that work on the Channel Tunnel between Folkestone and Frethun in France was to start. A new anti-leukaemia drug came onto the market, nine moons were discovered around Neptune and it was confirmed that there were holes in the ozone layer. On 28th January the space shuttle, Challenger, exploded only 73 seconds after take-off from Cape Canaveral, killing all seven astronauts. The world said goodbye to sculptor Henry Moore, jazzman Benny Goodman, author Simone de Beauvoir, whilst the Sun said goodbye to Page Three girl, Samantha Fox. On 6th June she announced her retirement and the paper carried an "In Loving Memory" picture to mark the momentous event. Meanwhile and somewhat controversially, Mexico was preparing for its second World Cup tournament.

The 1986 World Cup finals were originally awarded to Colombia. However, with cocaine-related violence on the increase and its economy in rapid decline, it could no longer afford it and the offer was declined in 1982. Brazil, Mexico, Canada and the USA all stepped in with offers to act as replacement, but the latter two, lacking sound

World Cup pedigrees, were not taken seriously. With a Brazilian president of FIFA, that country's bid was regarded as the strongest. Inexplicably, though, Brazil withdrew its name and the award went to Mexico unopposed. The decision was not greeted with wholesale approval and there were many who questioned Mexico's own ability to meet the costs of hosting a second tournament, given the severe economic difficulties it was facing. Unemployment levels were calamitous and the government had been unable to repay its international debts. Then, as if this was not bad enough, a terrible earthquake struck in 1985, killing some 25,000 people and causing widespread devastation to Mexico City and several coastal regions. FIFA began to consider finding an alternative, but the Mexican authorities insisted that none of their designated grounds had been damaged and plans were allowed to proceed.

The European qualifying tournament was organized on similar lines to those for the 1982 finals. Four of the groups sent two teams to Mexico and places were guaranteed for the winners of the other three groups. The runners up in these went into play-offs, with two playing each other and the third meeting the winner of the Oceania-Israel group. It all got underway in May 1984 in Nicosia, when Cyprus went down 2-1 to Austria, and produced no major upsets. Belgium and Holland were the two second placed teams that had to play-off against each other and, since both won their home ties, the result went to Belgium on the away goals rule. Scotland was the third country that needed to play-off for its place in Mexico. When West Germany suffered a home defeat against Portugal in October 1985, it was the first World Cup qualifying game the Germans had lost. Both teams got through the group, in which Malta gained its first World Cup point, in April 1985 in a goalless draw with Czechoslovakia. Hungary achieved a significant landmark when defeating Cyprus in the same month. Their second goal in the 2-0 victory was Hungary's 200th World Cup goal, making it the second country to reach that total. Luxembourg set less desirable records in the 5-0 home defeat at the hands of East Germany in November 1984. They became the first country to suffer 50 World Cup defeats and East Germany's fourth goal was the 200th they had conceded, the first country to let in so many.

An element of controversy emerged from Group Three, from which England and Northern Ireland qualified. England's passage was booked with a 5-0 defeat of Turkey at Wembley in October 1985, a game in which Gary Lineker scored a hat trick, but the Irish and the Romanians were in hot pursuit for the group's second place. Jimmy Quinn had given the Irish a real boost, when his goal gave his team a 1-0 victory in Bucharest on the same day. However, it would all be decided on 13th November, in the group's last games when England would entertain the Irish at Wembley and Romania would meet Turkey in Izmir. The Romanians won their game, but cried foul when they were pipped at the post by the Irish, whose goalless draw gave them the point they needed. The Romanians felt that the English had given the Irish a helping hand, but it was the hands of Pat Jennings that the Irish really had to thank. Despite not having played a league game for over a year, the veteran had a magnificent game to stop everything the English could throw at him. Having beaten Romania twice, the Irish deserved their place. England qualified as the only undefeated European team.

The Canadian FA had hoped to finance part of their trip to Mexico by staging a friendly against England at the 60,000 seater, synthetically surfaced BC Place Dome in Vancouver, where the Expo '86 exhibition was being held. With the presence of large numbers of Europeans there, the game was expected to be a sell-out. However, Bobby Robson refused to play on Astroturf, fearing there would be too many injures and insisted it be played on grass. The only venue available was a 15,000 seater stadium, which did not generate the needed income.

West German carpenter, Kurt Meier of Bielefeld, had promised to take his wife, Helga, on a cruise for their silver wedding anniversary to make up for his lack of attention over 25 years of watching football. He had saved £4,000 but in a change of heart, fixed himself up with a flight to Mexico instead. When Helga found out she demanded that he chose either football or her. They were divorced soon after.

Following an ill-tempered friendly between Uruguay and Mexico both teams were fined $5,000 after fighting broke out at the end of a game Mexico won 1-0. There was also trouble in a warm-up between Belgium and Mexican club side, Puma, when Nico Claesen's right knee was injured in a bad challenge from Puma's keeper, Sousa. In the resulting fight, Sousa injured Eric Gerets, kicking him on the thigh.

The Origins of the World Cup

Scotland's progress to the finals was marred very tragically in September 1985 by the death of their charismatic manager, Jock Stein. As boss of Glasgow Celtic between 1965 and 1978, Stein had made himself the most successful manager in British club football and had a short spell at Leeds United before becoming Scotland's manager, taking over from Ally MacLeod following Scotland's poor showing in Argentina. His team were playing Wales at Ninian Park in Cardiff, in a World Cup qualifier, and he had just seen Davie Cooper equalize for Scotland with a late penalty in a 1-1 draw that was vital to their hopes. As the teams left the field, Stein suffered a fatal heart attack and collapsed in the tunnel. He was 62 years old. It was a fitting tribute to this remarkable man that the Scots went on to qualify for Mexico by overcoming Australia in a two-legged play-off.

The three South American groups produced three winners that went straight to Mexico, whilst the four other teams best placed in those groups went into a play-off for the continent's fourth place. There were no surprises as the region's big powers, Argentina, Brazil and Uruguay all topped their respective groups, with Brazil reaching its own significant milestone on the way. The second goal scored in their 2-0 defeat of Paraguay in June 1985 in Asunción was its 200th World Cup goal. Brazil had become the third, and the first non-European team to reach that landmark. The Paraguayans came second in the group and went into the play-off. They overcame Colombia in the semi-final and Chile in the final to reach their first World Cup finals since 1958.

The countries of the CONCACAF region were organized into three groups and played two-legged knock-outs to determine the teams that would go into Round Two. Here they were divided into three groups of three, played on a league basis, with the winners of each going into the group final. They were Costa Rica, Honduras and Canada, managed by Tony Waiters. The former England goalkeeper had fashioned a useful side and it won through to Canada's first appearance in the World Cup finals.

Another complicated qualifying grouping was that which decided who would be Asia's two representatives. In the first round, the countries were placed in eight groups, numbered 1A to 4B, each of which sent one team into the second round. There were fireworks in Group 4A, where Brunei, in its first World Cup, received a mauling. In two successive games over four days in February 1985 the team was beaten 8-0, against Hong Kong and China, and they finished bottom of the group, having scored two goals and conceded 29 in six matches. The Chinese deserve some sympathy for scoring 23 goals and failing to get through to Round Two. There were riots in Beijing following China's 2-1 defeat by Hong Kong in the Workers' Stadium in May 1985. It was the group's last game and both had to win to progress to the next stage. The 80,000 crowd jeered Hong Kong throughout the match and the visitors needed police protection after it, as Chinese fans went on the rampage. They turned on foreign visitors to the city and smashed up the cars of diplomats and foreign correspondents. It took hundreds of police, wielding batons, to restore calm. Their victory took Hong Kong into the next phase, where the eight teams were paired off in a two-legged knock-out. Four of them made it into the semi-finals and from these South Korea, the region's strongest team, and Iraq emerged to take their places in Mexico.

The strength of football in the countries north of the Sahara compared with that in the rest of the continent was clearly demonstrated in Africa's qualifying tournament. As in previous years this was organized as a knock-out, with each tie taking place over two legs, and for the first round the countries were grouped into zones. This reduced the entrants down to the 16 teams needed for a continental knock-out. Of the eight teams that made it to the quarter-final stage, five were north African, as were all of the semi-finalists. Eventually, Algeria and Morocco won through to the finals, defeating Tunisia and Libya respectively.

The only region that did not guarantee a place in the finals was the Oceania Group, in which Israel and Taiwan also competed. The Taiwanese proved to be the group's "whipping boys", conceding 36 goals and scoring only once, in a 5-1 defeat at the hands of New Zealand in October 1985. It was the greatest number of goals given away in the tournament and ensured that Taiwan took bottom spot in the group. Top of the table was Australia, who won the right to meet Scotland in a play-off to decide which would become the last team to qualify. The first leg, played in Glasgow in November, 1985, ended 2-0 in Scotland's favour, with both goals coming from West Ham's Frank McAvennie on his international debut. The second took place in Melbourne two weeks later and was a goalless draw. It was enough to take the Scots to the finals, having made the longest journey of any team to qualify.

The format adopted for the expanded 1982 finals had not been satisfactory and changes were made for the second stage of the 1986 tournament. The second phase group system was abandoned in favour of a straight knock-out and in the hope that it would improve the quality of the football. Its effect was to turn the World Cup into "a juggernaut of a competition", to use the words of one historian, that needed two weeks and 36 games to eliminate a mere eight teams, only a third of those that took part. Another important change was the decision that the final games in the group stage should be played simultaneously. This was to avoid the unsavoury situation that had occurred in Spain when West Germany and Austria seemed to contrive a 1-0 German victory that ensured that both made it through to the next round.

One other organizational feature of the 1986 finals deserves some mention. The growth of commercialism and the vast sums of money generated had long been gaining a decisive influence and not always beneficial on the development of the World Cup. It reached new heights in Mexico and concerned the rights to broadcast the event, an enormously lucrative award. These were given to the TV and radio company, Televisa Mexicana, whose president, Amilio Azcarraga, was a close friend of João Havelange. Furthermore Guillermo Cañedo, another of the company's executives, was FIFA's vice-president and president of the World Cup Organizing Committee. Whilst the words "corruption" and "nepotism" may be a little strong, there was certainly an aroma of "jobs for the boys" about the way the matter was handled and it attracted much criticism. It was made worse by the mess the company made of broadcasting the matches, several of which went out without commentary and raising objections about the poor quality of some of the camera work. A member of the European Broadcasting Union described it as "the biggest disaster in the history of sports broadcasting" and was scandalous considering the 49 million Swiss francs paid to Televisa by the EBU.

The opening ceremony took place on 31st May and was, in the words of one observer, "a muddled shambles, a swirl of flamenco skirts and musicians around the perimeter of the pitch and overrun by photographers." The last remark was reference to the antics of too many pressmen anxious to capture the atmosphere for their audiences back home and which threatened to get out of hand. The poignant moment came during the speeches of the VIPs. One after the other, Cañeda, Havelange and Mexico's president, Miguel de la Madrid, were booed, as the crowd vented their anger at the commercial exploitation of their World Cup. They were also expressing their anger at Madrid's record. His government was riddled with corruption, accused of trafficking drugs and presided over a massive increase in unemployment, which caused thousands to illegally cross the border into the USA to avoid hardship. In one way, the authorities were mindful of these problems and had set up huge screens in public places so that games could be viewed without having to pay for tickets.

For the duration of the World Cup, the steel works in Monterrey was to be closed down to avoid unnecessary smog and to give its workers a chance to watch the games. However, it was later announced that the works would close for good with the loss of 5,000 jobs, adding to the already high unemployment rate. As the economic crisis deepened, there were demonstrations across the country and banners carried the slogan "Queremos Frijoles No Goles!", meaning "We want beans not goals".

The Azteca Stadium was built in 1968 to host the Olympic Games. It holds 100,000 people, is 7,400 feet above sea level and temperatures on the pitch can reach up to 100 degrees Fahrenheit. It is home to four Mexican teams, including top sides, America and Cruz Azul.

As the tournament was getting under way, so was campaigning for the forthcoming Spanish general election. To avoid any conflict and maximize potential audiences, the political parties organized their broadcasts around the World Cup television coverage.

Glamour at the opening ceremony

Glasnost, Nuclear Fallout and the Hand of God - Mexico 1986

The opening ceremony was followed by the opening game and for the second time in succession there were goals. This Group A clash between Bulgaria and Italy was "a match of absorbing if hardly explosive quality", as both sides felt the nerves of the occasion and the Italians, in particular, being too ready to fall back on defence rather than risk defeat. They had not had a good run in to the World Cup and the Bulgarian squad had not been together long enough to feel fully confident. Given such circumstances, a tentative game was to be expected, but it proved better than many opening games before it. The Bulgarians, their play described as "plodding unimagination", had much of the early ball only to see their attacks flounder against a packed defence and " the rocks of the usual cynical professional foul outside the area." Italy picked up the pace a little as the first half went on and took the lead in the 43rd minute through Alessandro Altobelli. In the second, they created many more chances and could have had the game sown up, but their overall lack of ambition saw them spurned and it was Bulgaria who scored next. The equalizer came five minutes from the end and was "an absolutely stunning header" by Nasko Sirakov. On the balance of play a draw was fair and both were happy to settle for it. It had not been a classic, but a great improvement on other openers.

The next day saw two games, one involving one of the World Cup's least experienced sides and one involving its most. At Léon, new comers Canada took on one of Europe's classiest teams and for more than 70 minutes did a heroic containing act. Canadian defending may have been rugged and lacking in finesse, but it was effective and stifled French creativity. Indeed, the North Americans had the two best chances of the first half, but the French created the most. The only goal came 17 minutes from the end and it was the boot of Jean-Pierre Papin that spared Gallic blushes. Meanwhile, the spectators at the game between Brazil and Spain saw two teams play "without adventure or risk." The Brazilians, once again under Telé Santana, in his second spell, looked far from convincing. That their national anthem was not played before the kick off may have unsettled them, but a more likely explanation is the aggression of Spain's tackling, designed to put the Brazilians off their stride. That it took just four minutes for the name of Spain's Julio Alberto to get into the referee's notebook for a foul on Edinho testifies to the rigour of their defence. It resulted in a goalless first half, though both had goals disallowed in the second. In the 55th minute, Miguel González of Real Madrid hit the bar with a shot and the ball seemed to come down over the goal line. The Spanish thought so, but the Australian referee and American linesman were badly placed and felt unable to award the "goal". Five minutes later, Socrates saw his strike discounted for a handball offence. The game was settled in the 63rd minute, when Careca's shot rebounded off the bar and Socrates headed in. Brazil had their first win, but they would need to perform with greater alacrity if they were to make an impression on this tournament.

Argentina came into action on 2nd June against South Korea and there was speculation about whether another giant killing act might be on the cards. It was not. The Koreans disappointed, "were naïve, constantly misjudged the flight and pace of the ball in an amateurish way" and were too quickly into the foul. Maradona was subjected too some particular maltreatment, though it did not prevent a star performance from the maestro. He had a hand in all three Argentine goals, beginning after five minutes when he was brought down just outside the area. The resulting free kick rebounded off the wall to him. He passed to Jorge Valdano and the South Americans were one ahead. They scored a second from a free kick, as Maradona "curled the ball in a wicked arc high over the defence" to be headed in by Oscar Ruggeri. The game was 17 minutes old and already won. Argentina slowed things down and waited until the second half for their third. Maradona "wriggled clear on the right, swung the ball low across the goal mouth" and Valdano tapped in his second. Park Chang-sun reduced the deficit with a 25 yard shot 15 minutes from time, but his team had been well beaten.

The Soviet Union got their campaign off to a breathtaking start by demolishing Hungary at Irapuato. They had one of the more physical teams in the competition and it told after just two minutes. A free kick taken on the right bobbled dangerously in the goalmouth of an uncertain Hungarian defence and Pavel Yakovenko rammed the ball home with a left foot shot. Two minutes later Sergei Aleinikov's 25 yard drive made it 2-0 and before 30 minutes were up a penalty made and scored by Igor Belanov gave them an unassailable lead. The Soviets struck again in the 66th minute when Yakovenko's magnificent through ball split the Magyar defence in two and Ivan Yaremchuk virtually walked the ball past the goalkeeper, Peter Disztl. The unfortunate last man had been nicknamed "Mr No Nerves" by Hungary's press because of his unflappable temperament. He was far from this today and eight minutes later his goal was breached again. The goal was accredited to Yaremchuk, but it took a hefty deflection off a defender on its way in. In the 78th minute Yevtushenko lofted a penalty over the bar, though amends were made in the next minute when substitute Sergei Radionov fired in Aleinikov's pass. The 6-0 score was Hungary's heaviest World Cup defeat and put a real dent in their confidence.

Following the Group F game between Morocco and Poland, a French journalist asked José Faria, Morocco's Brazilian coach, if people should be expected to pay to see games as this. The reply was sadly altogether typical of attitudes prevalent in football at the time. "Sometimes you have to close the game up for your own protection," he was told and the coach added that if he had wanted to see beautiful football he should have gone to see Hungary and the USSR. It summed up the game admirably. If there is any credit it goes to Morocco for keeping out a Polish team that was far below its best and created few chances. Mlnarczyk, the Polish keeper who played in Portugal, made one fine save in the first half and Poland hit the post in the second, but this was a game of little incident and the journalist's question was totally justified.

Competition in Group B began on 3rd June with the game between Mexico and Belgium. The pitch had been made slippery by heavy rain, but it did not unduly affect the outcome, a narrow 2-1 victory to the hosts. Mexico always had the slight edge and took the lead in the 12th minute when Tomás Boy's free kick was headed in by Fernando Quirate and such was the joy generated that Hugo Sánchez, described as "arguably the most popular man in Mexico", kicked the ball into the crowd and was promptly booked. It was the right decision, but given the horrendous sins that went unpunished in a World Cup noted for bad refereeing, it was harsh. He more than made up for his indiscretion in the 38th minute when he headed in a corner and Belgium pulled one back on the stroke of half-time when Pablo Larios, Mexico's keeper, misjudged a long throw and Erwin Vandenbergh headed in. The game slowed down after the

Optimism's flame burned brightly for the South Korean manager, Kim Jung nam, who was sure his team would be a "big surprise" in the finals. "Fame doesn't win games," he stated, referring to other group members. He also pointed out that his team had "extraordinary speed and co-ordinated play." In the end, they were thumped by Argentina, but drew with Bulgaria and gave Italy a real scare.

Diego Maradona's attitude toward South Korea before their midday first round opener was clear. "If they run and run they will collapse after 20 minutes," he said.

Soviet manager, Valeri Lobonovski, had been in the job only three weeks when the World Cup started. He had been drafted in from Dinamo Kiev, where he had enjoyed major success, winning the European Cup-Winners Cup. Eight Dinamo players appeared in their first game, though goalkeeper Dasayev almost did not. Five hours before kick off he was in hospital with food poisoning.

Northern Ireland midfielder, Mark Caughey, was a Detective Constable with the Royal Ulster Constabulary.

On 3rd June, around 3,000 England fans quickly sobered up when confronted by the Mexican army in a show of force before England's opening game against Portugal. Some were so drunk they could hardly stand.

Portugal's preparations had been endangered when players demanded $4,000 a match, $60 a day pocket money and free passes to home internationals for life, backing their demands with a threat to boycott training. It was much more than was on offer and the Portuguese FA was on the point of sending the players home when national president, Mario Soares, intervened to solve the crisis. "The prestige of Portugal is at stake," he said.

When Mexican journalist, Miquel Hirsch criticized the West Germans once too often, Franz Beckenbauer angrily retorted that he was "so small, you can hardly see him." They later made up.

break and whilst Mexico remained the better team, the Belgians came closest to scoring. Jan Ceulemans missed a glorious last minute chance and Mexico had only their fourth win in nine World Cup tournaments.

By only day four, the poor quality of refereeing had made itself abundantly obvious and it was exposed further when Algeria met Northern Ireland. Violent is the only word to describe some of the play, especially from Algeria, who sometimes spat at the Irish and the Soviet referee did little to reign in the brutality. Despite all, the Irish made most of the early running and went ahead in the fifth minute, after Brighton's Steve Penney was crudely bundled down outside the penalty area and Norman Whiteside's free kick deflected into the net. They then created enough chances to have won the game, had a header cleared off the line with the goalkeeper beaten and then fate contrived to deny them. Tactical misjudgement in the second half, when the Irish tried to defend their lead, gave Algeria a way back. The Irish had rarely had success with such a ploy and in the 58th minute Djamel Zidane's 25 yard shot levelled the scores. The Irish then lost all sense of direction and the game drifted to a draw.

Portugal's game plan for their first game was to stifle England's midfield, prevent them from scoring and hope for a breakaway. They adopted a five man midfield that crowded any creativity out of the game and the result was tedium. England's situation was not helped by the fact that when the forwards got in with a chance, they let them slip. In the tenth minute Gary Lineker was brought down when through on goal and moments later Bryan Robson narrowly missed with a header. The best chance fell in the 25th minute when Hoddle's free kick found Mark Hateley free in front of goal, only for the AC Milan striker to fluff the shot. There were fewer chances in the second half and Portugal pinched the result 15 minutes from the end with their only serious chance of the match. Diamantino slipped Kenny Sansom sent over a cross that evaded everybody and fell conveniently to Carlos Manuel, who tapped in under little pressure. It was the first World Cup goal Peter Shilton had let in since 1982 and his 499 minute unbeaten run broke the record held by Sepp Maier. It was the only interesting statistic to come out of this game.

Iraq made its debut in the finals the next day and by common consent acquitted themselves well. In players like Hussein Saeed, an "elegant forward", they had men of genuine quality and they gave Paraguay no end of problems in the first half. Their game began to fall apart in the last ten minjutes of the half when two set backs disturbed their concentration. Firstly, Julio César Romero, "Romerito" to his many fans, beautifully lobbed goalkeeper Raad Hammoudi to put his team in front. Then, in the dying seconds, Iraq won a corner. Ahmed Amaiesh Rhadi headed what he thought was the equalizer, only to turn and find that the referee had blown time before the ball had crossed the line. Their protests were to no avail and it was a dispirited team that lined up after the break. They allowed Paraguay to dominate the play and it was careless finishing that prevented the South Americans adding to their score.

Group E's opening game produced a crunching, brutal contest between West Germany and Uruguay, which the Czech referee did little to soften and which set the tone for what became known as the "Group of Death". Uruguay took an early lead when Antonio Alzamendi latched onto an unguarded back pass from Thomas Berthold. His shot crashed against the crossbar, bounced back onto the line and was given. Not for the first time did the Germans feel aggrieved by such a decision and, their sense of injustice rekindled, their response was a series of withering attacks. The Uruguayans resorted to a packed defence and ferocious tackling to hold onto what they had. The Germans brought on Littbarski and Rummenigge to increase their firepower and the final frenzied 25 minutes were a virtual non-stop German barrage. That they scored only once is testament to Uruguayan stubbornness and the virtuosity of goalkeeper Fernando Alvez, who flung himself everywhere to frustrate the German onslaught. The equalizer came with six minutes remaining, from Klaus Allofs who powered in an angled drive from outside the penalty area. It was scant reward for such a bruising encounter. It may have been an exhibition of savagery, but the game produced one sporting touch. When one of the Germans went down injured, the Uruguayans kicked the ball into touch to allow him to receive treatment. The Germans acknowledged the gesture by throwing the ball back to them. It was the first instance in the World Cup of this now common practice.

Denmark made their debut in the finals that day against Scotland in a game that "for 90 minutes ran on a knife edge." For the first 15 minutes the Danes powered forwards and tore the Scots ragged, but unable to force a breakthrough, slowed the game down. As would be expected from a side managed by Alex Ferguson, the Scots were a disciplined and well balanced unit and the change of pace allowed their greater composure to show through. They created the better first half chances, with Arsenal's Charlie Nicholas and Dundee United's Richard Gough coming closest. Six minutes before the break, Nicholas was viciously hacked down by Klaus Berggreen, as he threatened to break through and had to leave the pitch with torn ligaments. Berggreen should have gone off, but in another instance of awful refereeing, a free kick was the only decision. Afterwards and typical of the cynicism that was spoiling the football, Berggreen said: "It was a professional foul. I had to do it". It was not the game's turning point, but it reduced the potency of Scotland's attack. The game was won in the 51st minute when a superb pass from Frank Arnesen split the Scottish defence and sent Preben Elkjaer-Larsson through to score. Roy Aitken later had a goal disallowed for offside and MvAvennie came close, but they could not retrieve the game and another Scottish World Cup got off to a poor start.

"It looked like a sparring match in which both contestants were under strict orders not to inflict much damage", was how the Times described next day's game between Italy and Argentina. Both scored in the first half. Italy's strike came from a hotly disputed penalty awarded when José Luis Brown's clearance hit a fellow defender on the arm and was converted by Altobelli. Maradona hit back in the 34th minute after he gathered a long through pass, jinked past his marker and fired in from a narrow angle. It was an excellent goal, crowning an exquisite performance, though tempers almost erupted as the half drew to its close. They cooled in the second when both teams settled for the draw, though Carbrini and Conti both came close to snatching a winner for Italy. It remained, however, a game of "some superbly studious football and finishing of the highest order," and pundits noted that here were two sides capable of going all the way.

The game between South Korea and Bulgaria may have been played in torrential rain, but it did not dampen the enthusiasm of the Koreans nor

Frank Sheeran, a Scots fan from Windsor, nicknamed "Spotty the Ball", was told by his doctor that he was suffering from a nervous reaction to the excitement of watching the World Cup. He first suffered as he watched his team play Denmark. Then, although on medication, the complaint came back whilst watching Northern Ireland play Spain. He could, however, watch England with little difficulty: "I haven't been affected during England's games - but the way they're playing it's not surprising", he said.

John Saddler of the Sun, writing about Maradona, commented: "But against the modest, almost apologetic footballers of South Korea in a comfortable 3-1 victory for Argentina, he shamed the reputation of the South Americans. Such was the level of play-acting displayed by Argentina's captain in a match they were never in danger of losing. He rolled, twisted and writhed in mock agony every time he was challenged by Korean players hardly built like hatchet men ...most of all I don't want to see the cheats prosper."

prevent them gaining their first point in the World Cup finals. Plamen Getov put the Europeans in front in the 11th minute when he saw goalkeeper, Oh Yun-kyo, off his line and "coolly lobbed the ball in", but the Koreans more than held their own and created enough chances to have won. They hit the post with one shot before Kim Jong-boo set up the 68th minute equalizer with a neat piece of footwork. It had been good, all round entertainment.

Another superb game served up that day featured France and the USSR, "a dazzling encounter between rare subtlety and organized power - touched with class." In one of the few examples of good refereeing this tournament, Brazilian Romualdo Arppi Filho, was quick to stamp on early signs of naughtiness and the players settled to play football. With both fully committed to attack, both could have profited from the excellent creativity on show and Platini came especially close in the first half, hitting a 20 yard free kick against the post. The crowd had to wait until the 53rd minute for the first goal, but it was worth the wait. Vasily Rats hit a 30 yard rocket through a crowd of players for one of the strikes of the tournament. Some superb Soviet play deserved a goal, but the French had hardly been second best and equalized in the in the 61st minute with another piece of Gallic cunning. A "peerless chip into open space by Giresse" found Fernández storming through and he needed no second invitation. This was a see-saw, end to end contest that either could have won, but defeat would have been a travesty for either and the draw was the fairest result.

When the Canadians took on Hungary the next day, they went down as much to inexperience as poor play. The Magyars grabbed a second minute lead when Marton Esterhazy of AEK Athens took advantage of slack defending and for the next 70 minutes Canada showed lively invention against a team clearly still suffering from their earlier mauling. They could have drawn level on numerous occasions, but in pressing forwards exposed themselves to a counter charge and it was from such a move that Hungary's second goal came. Racing into the area, Kiprich fired his shot straight at Tino Lettieri, in Canada's goal, and the ball bounced out to Lajos Détári who slotted in the easy chance. Canada fought on, but time was against them and when Mike Sweeney was sent off for pulling back Gyorgy Bognar, it ended any hope of a revival. Hungary had their win, but it had been far from convincing.

The other games played that day brought below par performances from established teams against supposedly inferior opposition. The English had a particularly poor first half against Morocco and hardly created a scoring opportunity. Things got worse as half-time loomed when they lost captain and vice-captain in the space of four minutes. In one of few effective attacks, Bryan Robson challenged Mustafa Merry for the ball, fell badly and dislocated his shoulder for the third time in his career. He was replaced by Aston Villa's Steve Hodge and then Ray Wilkins threw the ball at the referee in disgust at a poor decision and was sent off, the first Englishman dismissed in the World Cup finals. In the second half the ten men played with greater credit than the eleven had done, but could not break a tight defence and had to settle for a point. Brazil also failed to impress against a buoyant, confident Algeria looking to add another scalp to its belt. A disallowed goal and a free kick against the post was all that Brazil had to show for their first half superiority. It was hardly vintage Brazil and could easily have been worse if any of three good chances had gone in, as Algeria began the second period strongly. One of these was desperately cleared off the line by a Brazilian defender, but Brazil had more fortune than England and in the 66th minute "Algeria handed them victory after a fearful defensive blunder." The defence froze as Muller crossed the ball, the danger was not cleared and Careca was left with the simplest of chances. It was enough to see them through to the next round, but two goals in two games was a worry for their fans.

The next day's meeting between Mexico and Paraguay was another game marred by ill-discipline and incompetent refereeing. It began with Mexico taking a second minute lead when Raúl Servin broke down the left and crossed for Luís Flores to chest down and bang in amid very casual defending. It "raised the din from 110,000 Mexicans through the highest decibel barrier imaginable", as the fans anticipated a glorious victory. However, two Latin temperaments boiled over in the heat and a total of 77 fouls committed prevented the early promise being fulfilled. In a stop-start affair, Mexico edged the first half and Paraguay the second. The inevitable equalizer came in the 84th minute as Romerito launched himself bravely between the central defenders to head in superbly Cañete's cross. Mexico had a perfect opportunity to win the game when they gained a last minute penalty for a foul on Sánchez as he broke for goal. He decided to take it himself but hit it badly and it was saved by Roberto Fernández. The local hero became villain as his team had to settle for a draw.

Spain had chance to avenge their 1982 defeat when they met Northern Ireland in Guadalajara that day. They began in a way that indicated that they were going to take it, a sprint start that had Emilio Butragueño, the "little vulture", reacting fastest to a low pass through a square Irish defence to record the tournament's fastest strike. It was a classic coup that took just 63 seconds and 16 minutes later they capitalized on sloppier defending to go two up. This time Butragueño began the move from which Julio Salinas "swept home a masterful volley." So far Spain had been the better team and the Irish only settled when two goals in arrears. They showed more zest in the second half and reduced the deficit two minutes after the restart. Gallego tried to break up their first assault by back heading to Zubizarreta, but the goalkeeper sliced the clearance. (See Zubizarreta profile on page 359). It went out to Colin Clark, facing the wrong way and his instinctive backward header found the target. It inspired the Irish to press and battle, but the Spanish defence was organized and resilient. With Brazil still to face, defeat seriously dented Irish hopes of making round two.

The poor quality of football and low scoring on offer in Group F had led locals to dub it the "Group of the Sleeping" and the game between Poland and Portugal gave no cause to reassess. The Portuguese showed more zest than in previous games and Zbigniew Boniek played well for Poland, but it took until the 63rd minute for

---

An interview with Northern Ireland's Sammy McIlroy

What do you remember about beating Spain in 1982?

We were always the underdogs, but it was a tag we didn't mind having. The ground was full an hour and a half before kick-off and as we walk out of the tunnel the noise was deafening and the atmosphere was electric. When Armstrong scored it silenced the crowed and after that the Spanish were in our hands. They retaliated physically, something we were expecting and we could handle it. Afterwards, as we relaxed at our hotel, journalists put empty beer cans and bottles all over the tables and took pictures of them. They printed them the next day, making out that Spain had lost to the boozy Irish, but it wasn't true.

What about the second round?

We began with a good performance against Austria, but then we came across the French. Had the disallowed goal been allowed to stand we might have had a chance, but the French we magnificent. They were classy.

Was there a feeling of rivalry when you had to play Spain again in 1986?

Yes, the Spanish had revenge on their minds, but with players like Goicoechea and Butragueño they were a much better outfit this time round. By then the damage had already been done when we let ourselves down against Algeria in a game we had to win. The last match against Brazil was a hell of a game. They were just too good and seemed to keep the ball just for fun. After the tournament the Northern Ireland squad was broken up and players retired. Billy Bingham started to rebuild. We always felt like underdogs in the big competitions, but we didn't let it bother us.

Now you are Northern Ireland's manager, what are your thoughts on the recent 2002 qualifying campaign?

With a combination of injuries, withdrawals and suspensions, it has been a real problem. Kids have had to be thrown who are still learning the game and their lack of experience meant that we found it difficult to get back into games when we went behind. France are definitely the favourites for the World Cup itself, but England are certainly coming on.

Glasnost, Nuclear Fallout and the Hand of God - Mexico 1986

Wlodzimierz Smolarek scored the game's only goal. Poland then shut the match down and since the Portuguese had not the wit to affect a break, it yawned its way to an inevitable end.

Iraq's next outing brought another spirited performance and they were unlucky to go down to a Belgian side, who on paper were much stronger. Belgium rushed to a 2-0 lead, as first Vincenzo Scifo scored with a fine shot and then, on 20 minutes, Nico Claesen tucked away a penalty given for a foul on Frank Vercauteren. They then had to struggle desperately to hold back a fiery Iraqi team that threw everything, including caution into the cause. Tempers frayed in the passion and five Iraqis were booked, but not even the 52nd minute sending off of Basil Hanna, only minutes after he had forced a magnificent save out of Pfaff in Belgium's goal, could dent heir ardour. They pulled a goal back in the 58th minute through Ahmed Amaiesh and though they had the Belgians hanging on grimly at the end, they could not find an equalizer. Following the game Iraq's Samir Mahmoud was found guilty of spitting at the referee and was suspended indefinitely, whilst midfielders Hanna and Haris Hassan received two match bans for insulting him.

The day's other games saw Denmark's battling performance against Uruguay (See Denmark v Uruguay profile on page 364) and the Scots throw their all at West Germany in a grim attempt to get their World Cup back on track. This was a relentless game played in searing heat that caused some players to lose 7lbs in weight. The Germans showed first with two good chances in the opening minutes, one of which hit the post, but Scottish World Cups often see indomitable resolution arise from improbable situations. With a little over 15 minutes gone, Steve Nichol threaded a long ball through to Roy Aitken and his short pass "found Strachan running round the outside to beat Schumacher from an acute angle." It set Scottish hearts pounding, but "World Cup disasters have followed Scotland like a faithful dog", as one pundit noted, and inevitably the Germans drew level five minutes later. Littbarski set Allofs free down the left and Jim Leighton came out and misjudged his cross, leaving Rudi Völler free to chip into the empty net. The Scots had looked good so far, but the Germans drew strength and purpose from the goal and they took the lead five minutes into the second half. It came from another defensive error as Dundee United's David Narey missed his tackle on Völler, probing into the area. The ball was switched and Allofs scored. The next 30 minutes were dominated by Germany and Leighton showed gritty determination to keep them out and allow the Scots to mount a mini revival in the last ten minutes. It came to nothing, but at least the Scots had gone down fighting.

The competition in Group C came to a close on 9th June, when France and the Soviet Union confirmed their places in the next phase. The USSR fielded virtually a reserve team against Canada and made things more difficult than they should have. It took them 58 minutes to find the initial breakthrough, from Oleg Blokhin's close range effort and it was not until 15 minutes from time that Alexander Zavonov made the match secure. In Léon against Hungary, on the other hand, after "a casual start, the French gave us some delicious one-touch stuff in the burning heat, lobbing the ball from man to man like handball players." For 30 minutes they did little of note, "standing round like so many Mexican goatherds" and Hungary did most of the attacking. The French, however, were rarely stale when Platini was on the field and when the game was halted so that Jean-Pierre Papin could receive treatment, he held an impromptu time out in the centre circle. It did the trick and soon after a long cross from the right into Hungary's area was headed in by Yannick Stopyra to give France a slender half-time lead. The start of the second half brought a Hungarian revival, which saw Détári hit the bar and several other chances come close before France reasserted themselves. In the 62nd minute Rocheteau began the move from which Tigana extended the lead and six minutes from time the outstanding Platini set up Rocheteau to give France a 3-0 victory.

The next day had two games bring the competition in Group A to an end, with that between Argentina and Bulgaria being described in the Guardian as "largely a dire match… redeemed only by fleeting moments of Maradona magic." After Cucuiffo's "far-post cross was crashed home by Valdano's head" in the third minute to give Argentina the lead, there followed 75 minutes of the dullest football in World Cup history. Bulgaria seemed content to hold the score down and Argentina hardly exerted themselves. The game's only other moment came in the 75th minute when Jorge Burruchaga headed in Maradona's cross to see his team into the next round. By a quirk of fate, Bulgaria also went into the next round as one of the best third placed teams, thought they had not won a game. It was their fifth appearance in the finals and they had yet to register any victory at all.

Italy secured their passage into the second round with a 3-2 victory over South Korea that was far more convincing than the scoreline suggests. It was another bad tempered game, with three booked from each side, and once Altobelli had given Italy an 18th minute lead, they never looked like losing. Yet, there was a nonchalance about their play that better opposition might have exploited. Altobelli crashed a penalty against the post in the 28th minute, but despite a period of sustained pressure from Italy, it was the Koreans who equalized with a "stunning right foot shot from 25 yards" from Choi Soon-ho on the hour. It was typical of the lack of urgency shown by the Italians and it was not until the 73rd minute that Altobelli restored their lead with a free kick. Ten minutes later, he "combined neatly with Di Napoli to slice open the Korean defence" and lash in a shot, given by FIFA as an own goal by Cho Kwang-rae. At 3-1, the Koreans should have been dead and buried, but they were not and came back with a last minute goal from Hu Jung-mo.

Three teams went through from Group B on 11th June, Belgium and Paraguay courtesy of a hard-fought and totally entertaining draw played out in Toluca. It was end-to-end stuff, with the Belgians producing their best football so far and could have gone ahead with any of three good chances in the first ten minutes. They had to wait until the 31st minute before they did, when Ceulemans set up Vercauteren who lobbed the out rushing goalkeeper. (See Jan Ceulemans profile on page 358). Pfaff was himself beaten by a lob five minutes later, but Renquin scurried back to clear off the line and, despite numerous chances, Paraguay did not equalize until the 50th minute, when Roberto Cabañas pounced onto a poorly judged back pass. Danny Veyt put Belgium back in front ten minutes later. Scifo then curled a brilliant free kick into the net only to find that it was indirect and with a quarter of an hour remaining Cabañas beat the offside trap to level the scores again. It was enough to see both through, with Belgium as one of the best third placed teams, where they were joined by Mexico, who took top spot in the group with a narrow win over Iraq. Again the Iraqis defended stubbornly to keep out a welter of Mexican attacks as the ball was rarely out of their half in the first period. However, with Sánchez suspended, the home team lacked punch up front and it was not until the 54th minute that they made a breakthrough. Manuel Negrete floated over "a harmless looking free kick" and Quirate ran on to head in. Iraq bowed out of the finals without a win, but they had far from disgraced themselves and left Mexico with more admirers than detractors.

The places from Group F were also decided that day and England, who had put themselves in a make or break situation, finally produced a display against Poland worthy of the name to secure one of them. With Wilkins and Robson unavailable, Bobby Robson was forced to make the changes many had been urging from the start. Chris Waddle was dropped so that Peter Beardsley could partner Lineker up front and Peter Reid and Steve Hodge came in to bolster the midfield. "The new formation clicked." Hoddle found the freedom he needed to thread his intelligent passes and keep the front men well served and it took just eight minutes for Lineker to net his first. Hoddle began the move, Gary Stevens provided the cross and Lineker did the rest. Five minutes later, Hodge provided the cross from which Lineker netted his second and Hodge himself got in on the act only for his strike to be disallowed. For the first time England looked like match winners and when Lineker added a third, the game was beyond the Poles. The pace dropped in the second half, but the Poles lacked the ability to get back into the game. The win put England in second place and the Poles also went through as one of the best third place teams. (See Gary Lineker profile on page 362). Top spot went to Morocco, the surprise of the group, who secured a thoroughly

A nurse at Southmead Hospital in Bristol set up a portable television in the delivery room so that Phil Stone would not miss England's match with Poland when his wife was about to give birth. They called the boy Samuel John Monterrey Stone. Obsessed with Diego Maradona, Janiece Harris officially changed her name to Jandiego Janiece Jennifer Dorothy Arsenal Maradona for £3, whilst Mark Haynes of Bristol had his name changed to Karl-Heinz Rummenigge. "I had talked about the switch for a long time," he confessed.

merited victory over Portugal. The Europeans started the game confidently enough and might have taken the lead in the 15th minute, but Morocco grew stronger the longer it went on and took the lead in the 18th minute with a 25 yard shot from Abdelrazak Khairi. The Portuguese were sliding into mediocrity and in the 27th minute Khairi grabbed another. In the second half, Krimau put away Timoumi's cross and though Diamentino grabbed a consolation ten minutes from time, it could not prevent Portugal being dumped out of the tournament by a team few had given a prayer to before it began.

When Northern Ireland met Brazil on 12th June, it was Pat Jennings's 41st birthday and his 119th cap. There would be no birthday present, though, as his team made the tactical error of trying to defend to secure a draw that might have seen them through. Brazil came out to play their best football of the tournament and left the Irish "battle plan shot to pieces within 15 minutes", the time it took Brazil to crack the defence. The goal came as Muller's cross was "met perfectly by Careca who, holding off O'Neill, blasted the ball through Jennings's hands from five yards." Brazil struck again in the 41st minute with "a piece of vintage Brazilian power and accuracy." Branco set up Josimar whose shot from 35 yards had Jennings "beaten from the moment it left his left boot." It forced the Irish onto the offensive, but they were always chasing a lost cause and three minutes from time the substitute Zico back-heeled a ball to Careca to score his third of the series.

Spain joined Brazil in the next round with a victory in a game that caused one British journalist to bemoan that the "only consistent feature of this tie was the gross surplus of Algerian aggression." Their behaviour was shameful, but the Spanish were prepared to pay like with like and their opening goal came indirectly from a piece of retaliation. Adoni Goicoechea, the "Butcher of Bilbao", repaid one foul with an over zealous challenge on Drid, Algeria's keeper, which left him injured. He was unable to deal with Spain's next attack when Salinas set up Ramón Calderé to score "a goal of stunning simplicity" in the 18th minute. Drid was replaced soon after and from then on, perhaps incensed by the violence of their opponents, Spain did most of the attacking. They scored a second in the 68th minute, when Eloy Olaya Preendes set up Calderé and three minutes later Eloy struck himself to make it 3-0. Algerian discipline then fell completely apart and it did much credit to Spain that "they held on to both their composure and their temper" in the face of disgraceful provocation. Mr Tokada, the Japanese referee did nothing to stem the brutality and even refused to award a penalty when Butragueño was blatantly hacked down in the area. The only protection Spain received was when he blew his whistle to end the travesty.

The fate of Group E was decided on 13th June and at Querétaro Denmark and West Germany spread a "glorious feast" before the 36,000 crowd. It was a game of little significance, since both had already qualified, but the group winner would remain in Querétaro and the Danes decided they liked it there. They went for all out attack and showed "how dangerous and unpredictable the wild spirit of adventure can be." John Sivebeck and Lerby both came close with early efforts and Laudrup had the ball in the net only for it to be denied for offside. Having soaked up the pressure, the Germans hit back and dominated the next phase of play, also seeing several chances spurned, including a shot from Andreas Brehme that hit the bar. The first half advantage finally went Denmark's way when Jasper Olsen put away a penalty given when his unrelated namesake, Morten, was brought down. The quality of the second half was the same as the first, with both playing clever football and, like the first, was edged by the Danes with a "picture goal to match their performance." Just after the hour, Arnesen broke free on the right. He sent in a perfect pass which John Eriksen had only to tap in, but his glory was tainted in the 88th minute when Arnesen was sent off for taking a swing at Lothar Matthäus.

To progress further, Scotland had to beat Uruguay in their last game and they were given the best of chances when, in the first minute, José Batista was sent off for an assault on Strachan. It meant that Uruguay resorted to form and were guilty of some callous acts of thuggery and time wasting, unpunished by weak refereeing and which the Scots had not the power to overcome. Yet, this does not tell the whole story. The South Americans also revealed some of their best style and their "manipulation of the ball at times made Scotland look naive amateurs." They were, in the words of one reporter, "brilliant, yet temperamentally deranged", as they "simultaneously illuminate and corrupt the game." Meanwhile, the Scots struggled, mismanaged the ball and wasted possession, time and effort. In the 18th minute Liverpool's Steve Nichol had only to put the ball in the net, but with the goalkeeper well beaten, he shot weakly and gave him time to recover. It was typical of their lack of purpose and the goalless draw saw Uruguay through as one of the best third placed teams. Afterwards, Alex Ferguson ranted: "If this is the World Cup, I am glad we are going home." FIFA fined the Uruguayans and threatened to expel them if they played like that again.

The knock-out stage of Mexico '86 began two days later, on 15th June, when Mexico made the quarter-finals for the second time in their history. It was at the expense of a Bulgarian side that "looked technically more competent", but whose attitude was too casual, especially in front of goal. The Mexicans had more of the possession and forwards that were prepared to take their chances. Bulgaria had let several openings slip before Negrete snatched the lead in the 35th minute with a spectacular effort, "twisting to hit a left-foot volley at almost shoulder height". It gave Mexico an edge they never lost. Roared on by a packed and incredibly passionate crowd, whose noise level was among the loudest of any World Cup game, they were sure at the back and steady up front. Bulgaria was always second best and the result was made sure when Servin headed in Negrete's corner.

A much better game was that between Belgium and the USSR. It was a superb end-to-end contest, full of free and open play, goalmouth incident and a result that was in doubt until the very end. It began with a flurry of attacks from both sides during which Belanov ended a solo run with a "spectacular 20-yard shot" that whistled into the top corner of the net. The game then settled into a quiet period that lasted into he second half, before springing to life in its final quarter. A period of sustained Belgian pressure brought a goal for Scifo and in the 70th minute Ceulemans failed to deal with Zavarov's cross and Belanov squeezed his side in front under the body of the goalkeeper. The Belgians levelled again six minutes later and this time Ceulemans did the right thing, gathering a long through ball and hitting it on the turn. Radionov almost snatched it in the last minute, but his shot hit the bar and the game went into extra time. Here, Belgium edged in front with a goal from Anderlecht's Stéphane Demol and in the second period Nico Claesen headed them further in front. Belanov then scored from the penalty spot and Pfaff pulled off an impossible finger tip save to deny Yevtushenko a late equalizer. It had been wonderful fare, but sympathy should go to Belanov who became the first player since Ernst Willimowski in 1938 to score three goals in a game in the finals and finish on the losing side.

The Poles dominated the opening exchanges of their match against Brazil on 16th June and might have taken a two goal lead inside ten minutes. In their first attack, Josimar misheaded a cross against his own post and watched in relief as it rolled harmlessly into his goalkeeper's arms. Ten minutes later, the woodwork denied Poland again and the warning was enough to fire life into Brazil. From that moment the game belonged exclusively to them and they stamped their authority in the 28th minute, when Careca won a penalty. Socrates elected to take it, took two paces and "arrogantly hooked the ball into the top corner." The Poles tired in the second half and Brazil turned the screw ever more tightly. In the 52nd minute Josimar atoned for his earlier blunder, disdainfully slipping through the Polish defence for a solo goal and 24 minutes later, a cool back-heel from Careca found Edinho, who "calmly took the ball around the goalkeeper and a defender" to score. Four minutes later, Zico was dropped in the area and Careca tucked away the game's second penalty. Zmuda came on shortly afterwards, equalling Uwe Seeler's record of 21 appearances in the finals, but he could make no difference. The Poles had been well beaten.

The day's other game was the 400th of the finals and featured two adversaries who had not met in the competition since the 1930 final.

After Mexico's opening victory, 25,000 delighted fans crammed into Mexico City's main plaza. After bottles and paving stones were thrown at passing cars, 250 riot police waded in and 200 fans were injured and 200 arrested. It was witnessed by Scots fan Andrew Johnson from Leith, who said: "The police didn't care who they walloped and there was bodies everywhere. Skulls were smashed open and there was blood all over the place." In the hysteria that followed the second round victory over Bulgaria, two men shot each other in an argument over Hugo Sánchez, eleven people died falling out of cars and buses and three others were shot.

Maradona had many nicknames during the World Cup, two of the more complementary being "Little Tank" and the "One Who Shoots Like A Bazooka".

The "Eat My Own Words" Award for 1986 goes to...

Mark Ellis of the Sun who wrote: "I have to confess my tip to win the World Cup is Uruguay." The Uruguayans scraped into the second round having not won a game, scored only two goals and conceded eight.

There were problems in the West German camp over the team captaincy. Franz Beckenbauer had to step in after Harold Schumacher, who had been captain when Karl-Heinz Rummenigge was injured, was reluctant to give it up.

Glasnost, Nuclear Fallout and the Hand of God - Mexico 1986

After England beat Paraguay, 5,000 ecstatic England fans chanted "Bring on the Argies - we want another war." In response, Maradona made an appeal to the supporters saying: "When we go on the pitch we take a ball, not a gun. The supporters must forget politics." Argentina had still not recognized the UK's sovereignty over the Falkland Islands and diplomatic relations had not been restored. 7,500 police and armed servicemen patrolled the game, backed up by helicopter gunships and armoured cars. There was a rumour that 500 Argentinian fans calling themselves the "Barras Bravas", or "Fighting Men", would try to provoke trouble.

In their article seductively called "Turn off your telly and turn on your man", the Sun dished out advice on how a girl could lure her man away from the football and into bed. The first rule was to: "Fiddle with his aerial if you want some interference off the screen as well as on. But don't get caught at it in the living room. He might send you off for an early bath." Tip number seven was: "Once you have got him where you want him in the bedroom bring him a tray of drinks. Then accidentally spill a glass of beer all over his pyjama bottoms so you can make him take them off. Then you can mop him up in the way he likes best."

Before Brazil's quarter-final with France, Pelé announced: "The Pope is Polish - but God is most definitely a Brazilian."

France's goalkeeping hero, Jöel Bats, had suffered cancer five years earlier and had taken six months out of the game to get cured.

Argentina against Uruguay had the potential to turn nasty, but was well handled by Italian referee, Luigi Agnolin, and whilst it was hard fought, it was never violent. In an even first half, Maradona was the difference between the two sides, ever busy, seeking out Uruguay's weaknesses, setting up his team mates or having a go himself. He "showed how to play a real team game", said coach, Carlos Bilardo, after the game and he came close to scoring on several occasions, hitting one free kick against the bar. Argentina took the lead in the 41st minute, when Valdano pulled the keeper out of position and passed to Pablo Pasculli, who "easily slammed the ball into the empty goal from 10 yards." It gave them the psychological edge that kept them the better team. A thunderstorm broke out that made the pitch slippery and prevented them putting away the chances they set up. They had to settle for a 1-0 victory, not that it worried them. It had been a long time coming, but they had finally taken revenge for that afternoon in Montevideo 56 years before.

France met Italy next day in confident mood and their meticulous, majestic football ran as smooth as an antique clock. At the rear, the full-backs linked ingenuously with the midfield, where Platini was in a class of his own," not so much in the match as above it, wielding a superior intelligence and peerless touch" to provide a mosaic of options for his front men. He was ably abetted by Luis Fernández, "the ugly duckling of French football", a man of absolute dependability and full of heart for the big occasion. France, "calm, assured masters from the start", did not overwhelm Italy, but never allowed them to settle into any pattern. It was one-sidedness without arrogance and when Platini opened the scoring in the 14th minute, the result was never in doubt. Rocheteau was the provider and he set up Stopyra for France's second, a narrow angled shot in the 57th minute. It ended 2-0, but it was the magnificence of France's football, not the goal tally that made others take note, something that could not be said about West Germany, who struggled woefully against Morocco. Afterwards Beckenbauer said that "Morocco played more backwards than forwards and it made it very difficult for us" and whilst his remark reveals the defensive nature of Morocco's plan, it hides the inadequacy with which the Germans tried to counter it. They did much of the attacking, but could not put away the few chances they created. Morocco's keeper, Ezaki Badau, known usually as Zaki, made an exceptional save to deny Germany in the last minute of the first half and it was not until the last minute of the second that the result was secured. The Germans were awarded a free kick 30 yards out and Matthäus hit it before the Moroccans were ready. It was a fortuitous way of getting through, but Morocco had never looked like scoring and it was, on balance, a fair result.

England began their second round game against Paraguay nervously and took half an hour to settle down. They might have gone behind in this period had not two fine saves from Shilton denied Cañete, but the English grew in composure as the match went on and "assumed control in midfield where the less disciplined Paraguayans were outnumbered and eventually overrun." Just after the half-hour a Hoddle cross seemed to elude everybody. It was turned back by Hodge and Lineker prodded it in. It steadied the nerves and as England tightened their grip on the game, Paraguay turned physical. They also lost much of their sharpness and the game swung in England's favour. Lineker hit a fierce volley that the goalkeeper did well to turn over and ten minutes into the second half

Beardsley added a second. Another Lineker goal in the 72nd minute rounded off what had become a good English performance.

So far the Danes had been one of the real joys of the tournament, but they came unstuck against Spain in the second round. When Jasper Olsen converted a 33rd minute penalty, after Berggreen had been brought down, there was no hint of what was to come, but two minutes before the break, a howling back pass across his own goal by the same Olsen allowed Butragueño in for the easiest of equalizers and the game changed completely. A revitalized Spain turned on the style in a second half that turned into the "Butragueño Show". In the 56th minute he headed in Victor's cross and 12 minutes later his solo run produced the penalty from which Goicoechea scored. Butragueño added another, his hat trick, in the 80th minute and he won another penalty in the last minute, which he took himself to become the first man since Eusébio in 1966 to score four in match in the finals.

The quarter-finals took place over two days, with France and Brazil producing the best of the games played on 21st June. It was "a classic tussle that swung from end to end throughout, almost with the rapidity of ice hockey" and which left both sets of players drained at the end. It began with a period of French pressure, but Brazil took the lead in the 18th minute with a move of pure flamboyance - " a ripple of passes between Socrates, Branco and Josimar, a first time exchange between Junior and Muller and a final thrust by Junior sending Careca through a stricken French rearguard." It was superlative and Muller almost extended the lead on the half-hour with a shot that hit the post. Yet, the French were far from overawed and hit back just before half-time when Platini "stole through unnoticed, and with all the calm of a training stint in a deserted stadium, tapped into the net" Rocheteau's cross. It was honours even and that is how it remained through the second half and extra time. Both threw all at each other, but both were unable to break the other's resolve. Observers described it as the best game they had ever seen. It was pulsating, unrelenting football, made greater by the severe conditions it was played under and the tragedy was that such a marvellous game had to be decided by penalties. Hearts seemed to stop as Socrates, intelligent, educated, elegant, stepped up and saw his shot saved by Jöel Bats. Stopyra netted his and the French held the advantage until the fourth kick, when Platini showed that all people are fallible and missed his effort. Josimar then strode up to take Brazil's fifth and smashed it against the post. It was 3-3 with one kick to go. Under massive pressure, Fernández steadied himself and sent France into the semi-finals. It was cruel, but it had been sensational.

An entirely different match was that between West Germany and Mexico, a " scrappy, ill-tempered affair" that had eight players booked and two sent off, Berthold for Germany and Aquirre for Mexico. Both teams struggled in the withering heat, but 90 minutes of normal time and 30 of extra time could produce not a single goal. The penalty shoot-out allowed Germany's greater self control to win through, as Allofs, Brehme, Matthäus and Littbarski all succeeded, whilst only Negrete scored for the hosts. It put the Germans into the semi-finals for a record eighth time.

The next day saw England take on Argentina (See England v Argentina profile on page 365) and Belgium become the least expected of the semi-finalists. They had, "like a top weight handicapper with no form to

---

A group of 20 women from Crawley formed their own protest group "Wives Against Mexico" (WAM) in response to the lack of attention from their men. They organized nights out and theatre trips.

The West German reserve goalkeeper watched his team's quarter-final on television in an airport lounge because he had been sent home for insubordination.

One legged English fan, Terry Exelby found himself in the hands of the FBI and facing a one-year jail sentence or a £600 fine after being arrested following his flight from London to Houston on route to Mexico. He had got drunk and become abusive toward the flight crew, allegedly pushing or punching a stewardess. Four Scots were also taken into custody before being sent home.

Before the semi-final with West Germany, Patrick Battiston, vowed to keep clear of the keeper who had put him out of football for six months four years earlier. "Certainly I don't intend to get within 40 yards of him if I can help it," he said.

Even though Argentina won, Daniel Passarella, was not impressed by quality of football. "It's the worst playing standard I've seen," he said.

show of late, but plenty of class", rather crept up unnoticed. They were "a curious force, a mixture of enormous but dissident talent, constantly at odds with one another" and they did the necessary against Spain, defending stoutly for much of the game and hitting out when allowed. They were pinned back for the first half-hour, during which Butragueño had a penalty appeal denied, and took the lead in the 34th minute, when Ceulemans's brave diving header connected with Vercauteren's cross. Almost immediately, Zubizarreta pulled off a superb save to keep out Veyt and for the rest of the match Spain did most of the attacking without success. It was not until the last five minutes that Antonio Señor saved the situation with a 25 yard free kick that was deflected past Pfaff. The game went into extra time and with nobody able to force the issue, it became the third quarter-final to be decided by penalties. Both scored with their first four shots, but Eloy missed with his and Belgium went through, to their best ever World Cup placing.

In their semi-final, the Belgians were undone by their failure to hold on to Maradona tightly enough. As coach, Guy Thys, said afterwards: "We were organized until the second half when he escaped more often and he punished us twice." The game was not high on quality football and, with Maradona under close attention, there was little to note in the first half. Valdano handled the ball into the net, but this referee was not fooled and it did not stand. The important touches came in the second. In the 51st minute, Maradona gathered Enrique's cross and dribbled past two defenders to score his first. Ten minutes later he struck again, this time taking on and beating three defenders before firing into the net, two superb goals that took Argentina into the final. (See Maradona profile on page 361).

Before the semi-final between France and West Germany, French supporters hanged an effigy of Schumacher behind his goal in memory of the infamous incident of 1982. That encounter had proved a classic. This was much flatter, with neither showing much flair. The French had not recovered from their epic with Brazil and "the fire that had scorched so many opponents had burned out. The Germans seemed to anticipate this and set themselves to giving nothing away. They were "stronger, faster and, from their opening foul after only 20 seconds, comprehensively more intimidating." France struggled against such a rugged approach and went behind after eight minutes from Brehme's free kick. Their best patch followed, but with Platini tightly marked and unable to make an impression, they failed to shine. They showed greater urgency in the second half when a spate of attacks provided a grandstand finish, but could make none of them count. The result was sealed with Völler's breakaway goal in the last minute and yet another great French side was left to contemplate the minor places.

The penultimate game of Mexico '86 was between two very disappointed teams, the attitude of which can be gauged from remarks made beforehand. "It is not important", said the Belgian coach. "I am not very concerned about it." France's Maxime Bossis was even more pointed. "It's a match which should not be played. There's a lack of motivation when you have passed so close", he said. The French fielded a weakened team, partly through injury and tiredness and partly because Platini was left out at his own request. Not surprisingly, Belgium made the best early showing and went ahead in the tenth minute with a goal from Ceulemans. Jean-Marc Ferreri grabbed an equalizer in the 27th minute and Papin gave France the lead just before the break. The Belgians were unlucky to be behind and Claesen duly levelled the scores in the 73rd minute, to take the game into an extra time nobody wanted. In it, France's fresher legs proved decisive and a goal in each period, the first from Genghini and the other from a last minute penalty won and converted by Manuel Amoros, gave France another third place.

With the final providing one of the tournament's better games, the 1986 World Cup ended on a high note. (See Argentina v West Germany profile on page 366). Yet, it had been a tournament that encapsulated all that was good and bad about the world of football. The undisguised commercial exploitation of the people's game to line the already bulging pockets of a chosen few was shameful enough, but the insidious effects of such dealings were not confined to those who occupied football's inner sanctums. They spread damagingly wider into the heart of the game and nowhere was this more obvious than on the pitches of Mexico '86. It is unfair to criticize players for using their art to emulate those that govern them, but instances of players writhing in agony at the merest contact, of time wasting, of stonewall defences and of thuggery were all examples of footballers trying to gain advantage by unethical means. They happened because the desire to attain the glittering prizes that await the victor were far stronger than the desire to uphold a more nobler tradition. When Maradona spoke of the "hand of God", he was mistaking virtue for greed and should more appropriately have referred to the "hand of Mammon".

It was, however, only one, albeit large aspect that rendered the tournament unsatisfactory. It had been unwieldy, a fact that would have been palatable had the quality of football been higher, but when teams set out not to lose and use unfair tactics to do it, then something important is lost to the game - its spirit. It is up to those in charge to do something about it, but there were flaws in the two tiers of officialdom in a position to have taken decisive action. On the lower level and with a few exceptions, the referees were not of a calibre needed to control players and their tantrums. Mexico '86 contained some of the most inconsistent and at times absurd refereeing seen to date and the football suffered accordingly. In the first round in particular there were some atrocious games. Then on a higher level, the game's administrators were every bit a part of the financial merry-go-round and therefore hardly likely to seek the fundamental shift in the direction of the game's development that might have brought improvement.

To give the impression that all was rotten would be wrong. No aspect of human endeavour is absolutely corrupt and Mexico '86 had much to recommend it. Few nations seem to take to World Cups like the Mexicans and their enthusiasm is contagious, often inspiring players to give their best. There was some exceptional football. The French stood out as beacons, but similarly illuminating were the Spanish, the Soviets and the Belgians, once they got going. The progress of the lesser teams was also commendable. None were outclassed and, whilst Algeria may have been spoilers, Canada and Iraq won friends for their efforts. In getting to the second round, Morocco showed how far football had travelled outside its traditional bases. It took the eventual finalists to stop them. Amid the droll, there were some outstanding games and fine individual performances. Among the French several stand out as purveyors of the grandest traditions and ethics of the game and would grace any World Cup "best team". Put them besides men like Laudrup, Elkjaer, Romerito and Negrete and they would make a mighty complement. However, one man towers above this World Cup like no other. He hit the headlines for cheating, but Maradona's contribution cannot be dismissed so lightly or so inaccurately. It was pure magic.

Jan Ceulemans   Belgium

Honours: 4th 1986   **Games 15**
Played: 1982, 1986 and 1990   **Goals 4**

A dejected Jan Ceulemans after the 2-0 semi-final defeat by Argentina.

Belgian football, although generally sound, has never been noted for setting the world alight. However, in a decade now referred to as its the golden age, when players like Pfaff, Gerets, Vercauteren, Scifo and Claesen became household names, their football rose above the ordinary and making it tick was Jan Ceulemans, first as a striker and then in midfield. Ceulemans was born on 28th February 1957 and began his career as an 18 year old for his hometown club, SK Lierse, making his debut in 1975 against Winterslag. In the summer of 1978, he moved to FC Brugge for a record domestic transfer fee of £250,000 and was to remain at the club for the rest of his career. He won two Belgian cups and three domestic league titles, the first of which came in 1980 when he scored 29 of Brugge's 76 goals, winning him the Belgian Footballer of the Year award.

1980 was also the year he played in attack for the national side that reached the final of the European Championships. He scored the goal that brought a 1-1 draw with England in the first game and, having beaten Spain in the second, the Belgians drew against Italy to take them to their first, and only, final in major international championships against West Germany. They fell behind and came back through a controversial penalty, but then an inch perfect corner in the last minute from Rummenigge was headed home by Hrubesch to give victory to the Germans. Ceulemans's performances attracted the attention of Europe's top clubs and the following year he was offered the chance to join AC Milan. However, not wanting her son to go too far away, Ceulemans's mother asked him to stay at home and he did. It was a decision he never regretted, however strange it seemed at the time.

1982 saw the first Belgian qualification for World Cup finals since 1970, at the expense Holland. It was sweet revenge because the Dutch had been responsible for eliminating Belgium at the same stage in 1974 and 1978. In light of recent performances, Belgium figured as a good outside bet for the trophy and, with Ceulemans in fine form, they were expected to score goals. They started well, beating the reigning champions and got through to the second phase at the head of their group. However, this was the pinnacle of their endeavours as two defeats saw them finish bottom of their group. Ceulemans had played well, but had failed to score. The European Championship campaign of 1984 started in much in the same way. They qualified for the finals in France at the head of their second round group with some fine performances. Here they followed an opening victory against Yugoslavia with a 5-0 defeat by France. In the next game against Denmark, Ceulemans scored the opening goal as Belgium went into a 2-0 lead, but a stirring second-half performance saw the Danes score three times to end Belgium's tournament.

Qualification for the 1986 World Cup finals again saw Belgium take revenge for past failures against Holland. The side had been strengthened by the inclusion of Enzo Scifo and Nico Claesen and expectations were high. However, they did not shine and by the end of the first round they had to rely on results from others going their way. They had managed five goals, but Ceulemans had still not broken his World Cup duck. When he finally did, it came in controversial fashion and heralded the start of his team's finest ever World Cup run. In the second round the Belgians faced the fast attacking style of the Soviets and punished it with some fine counter-attacks of their own. With the score at 2-1 against and with only 15 minutes to play, the game was turned on its head when Ceulemans scored the equalizer. It had looked offside but the referee let it stand and the game went into extra-time. Here it swung Belgium's way and, despite a Belanov hat trick, they triumphed. In the quarter-final, he was aware of the threat posed by Butragueño, saying: "Butragueño is a marvellous striker but he needs space to operate. We need to deny him that." They did and it was Ceulemans's flying header that put them in the lead, but it was Pfaff's penalty shout-out save that took them to the semi-finals. It was their misfortune to be drawn against a Maradona-inspired Argentina and a double strike from the world's best player ended Belgian dreams. In the 3rd/4th play-off, Ceulemans's third World Cup goal was not enough, but they had gone further than any Belgian team before or since and Ceulemans had emerged as one of the tournaments finest players.

By 1990, the 33 year old Ceulemans, now playing a midfield role, was still an integral part of the Belgian national side. In Italy they progressed relatively smoothly into the second round with Ceulemans dictating matters from the centre and scoring once more against Uruguay. Then, in a second phase game that looked as though it was going to penalties, Platt's last minute goal for England sent them out. The Belgian Player of the Year Award he received when he got home was little consolation. His career came to a premature end in 1991 when a severe knee injury forced him to quit. He had scored 26 times for his country in a record 96 appearances, but not wanting to leave the game altogether, he became coach with second division side, Alost, taking them into Belgium's top flight and, in 1994-95, earning them a place in Europe.

Andoni Zubizarreta   Spain

Honours: Quarter-finals 1986 and 1994   **Games 16**
Played: 1986, 1990, 1994 and 1998

Not since 1950 had the Spanish achieved more than a first round knock in the World Cup, but in 1986 two players were introduced into the side and made a real difference. One was the prolific striker Butragueño and the other was Andoni Zubizarreta. Zubizarreta was one of the best of a long line of good Spanish goalkeepers from the Basque region that includes Carmelo, Iribar, Artola and Arconada. He was not the best penalty saver in the world, he was sometimes vulnerable in one-on-one situations and he was sometimes clumsy at clearing the ball, but he was strong in the air and he was a fine shot stopper. So much so that, in 1986, Barcelona paid £1.2m for him, a world record for a goalkeeper at the time. The 1998 Spanish World Cup manager, Javier Clemente, once said: "I leave it until as late as possible to tell my players the team - with the exception of Zubi. I tell him the night before." Even at the age of 36, he was the natural first choice for the Spanish side that travelled to France, although some would now claim his selection was a mistake.

Zubizarreta was born on 23rd October 1961 at Vitoria in Northern Spain. His mother always claimed that her roots lay in the nearby town of Aretxabaleta and there he was brought up. It was also where he passed his formative years playing for the local side. Once a team outing to Zarautz coincided with a visit by Athletico Bilbao with his goalkeeper hero, Iribar. The young Zubizarreta requested an autographed photograph, little knowing that in a few years he would take Iribar's place in both the Bilbao and national sides. At the age of 17, he signed for the Deportivo Alavés, a team with high ambitions, but never the talent to carry it off. "They were regarded as the Barcelona of the second division," Zubizarreta explained. "They always aspired to rise to the first division, but they never obtained it." At the end of the 1980-81 season, he got his big break when he was asked to sign for Bilbao, although his first season was interrupted by military service. His initial months there were fundamental to his future development, not least because it was at Bilbao that he first teamed up with coach, Javier Clemente. Under Clemente's guidance he gained in confidence and made it to the first team, starting a record run in the top flight that lasted for over 550 games. His first appearance was on 19th September 1981 against Athletico Madrid, a game won 2-0 thanks in no small part to the performance of their goalkeeper. Zubizarreta and Bilbao went on to win league championships in 1983 and a Spanish double in 1984. They would have brought home the title in 1985 had there not been a players' strike that year.

1985 was also the year he made his international debut as a substitute for Arconada in a 3-1 victory over Finland on 23rd January and was still in goal when Spain went to the World Cup in 1986 in Mexico. The quarter-final against Belgium became a battle of goalkeepers as it went to a penalty shoot-out, in which Zubizarreta came off worst and Spain went out. Penalty shoot-outs are always a lottery, but Zubizarreta's inability to stop them was very evident. Spain had, however, progressed past the second round for the first time since 1950.

After the disillusionment of the World Cup, Zubizarreta found himself the target of a very tempting transfer request from Barcelona. He had just signed an extension to his contract with Bilbao in June that year and the club did not want to part with their star player. He had to go to the directors to persuade them to let him go. They did and it was the greatest and most lucrative step of his career. In 1989 Barcelona, having acquired the services of Johan Cruyff as manager, hit a rich vein of form that saw them win the Spanish championships four times in five years, two Spanish cups, a European Champions cup, a Cup-winners cup and a European Super Cup. Barcelona also reached the Cup-winners Cup final in 1991, but were defeated by Manchester United, a game Zubizarreta missed through suspension.

At the 1990 World Cup, Spain began with a draw and two victories, which put them top of their group and into the second round, where it was their misfortune to come up against a Yugoslavia team inspired by the magnificent of Stojkovic, whose first goal was an unbelievable dummy. At the 1994 tournament, Zubizarreta was replaced by Canizares for the first game, but played in the others as Spain finished the group phase in second place. Lighting struck again, this time in the form of Roberto Baggio. As the game raced toward extra time, the little Italian found himself unmarked and bearing down on Zubizarreta's goal. He skilfully rounded the stranded keeper, looked to have gone too wide to score, but put the ball in the net. This defeat was not the only misfortune to face him that year. Following a European Champions Cup defeat by Milan, he was given a free transfer and left Barcelona under a cloud of disappointment. Cruyff wanted to rejuvenate the team and the defeat offered the perfect excuse to offload his goalkeeper. However, a move to Valencia rejuvenated him and he kept his place in the national side.

By the time of the 1998 World Cup, he had played over 100 times for Spain, though he will not remember France with any fondness. His dreadful mistake against Nigeria, when he seemed to accidentally push the ball into his own net, almost certainly cost Spain the game and was crucial in sending them home. It must have doubly hurt when, in the game against Paraguay he saw Chilavert, his opposite number, make the save of the tournament to deny a rare shot from Raúl. When it was over, Zubizarreta held a press conference from his hotel in Vineuil-Saint-Firmin, saying: "I come before you here today to say farewell to football. Farewell to football fields, concentration, injuries, criticism. I thank all those who have helped me to understand this sport through a gesture, a word or a phrase. I also wish to thank my family, my friends and my wife, all of whom have always been there when I was at my lowest. Javier (Clemente), thank you for believing in me and supporting me through the hard times. Football is a very tough sport but it has brought me joy... I am proud to have managed my football career in the way I have done. My time is over, I must leave. Thank you." The record 123 appearances he made for Spain is perhaps the best testament to his ability.

Diego Armando Maradona   Argentina

Honours: Winner 1986; Runner-up 1990   **Games 21**
Played: 1982, 1986, 1990 and 1994   **Goals 8**

Diego Maradona.

Diego Maradona will often be remembered for the infamous 'Hand of God' incident, but he should be better remembered for a divinely inspired left foot. He was the most exciting and gifted player of his generation and one of the greatest ever. Born on 30th October 1960 in a poor suburb of Lanus in the province of Buenos Aires, he was one of eight children of a factory worker. He showed an aptitude for football from an early age and at seven made an appearance on Argentinian TV juggling oranges with his feet. He later entertained crowds at professional matches, juggling balls during half-time breaks, often non-stop. At the age of nine, he started playing for the junior team, Estrella Roja before founding his own team with a group of friends. Los Cebollitas (The Little Onions) were so impressive they were signed en-mass by Argentinos Juniors in 1970. He made his debut as a 15 year old substitute in October 1976 against Talleres from Cordoba and played his first full game a week later. His international debut came in February 1977, as a substitute for René Houseman in a friendly against Hungary. However, although he made the preparatory squad of 25 for the 1978 World Cup, César Menotti felt he was too immature and dropped him on the eve of the tournament. Maradona was so incensed he did not talk to Menotti for a month. A peace was brokered and he led Argentina to victory in the 1979 World Youth Cup in Japan.

In 1981, he moved to top league side, Boca Juniors, for a world record £1m and they duly won the league. He was also part of the national team that went to Spain in 1982, where he was on the receiving end of some particularly brutal treatment from hatchet-men defenders. Against Brazil in the second phase, he was so provoked he was sent off for a particularly gruesome retaliatory lunge at Batista. Following the series, he moved to Barcelona for a world record fee, but it was not a happy time for the effervescent Argentinian. He scored 22 goals in 36 games, but his temperament did not fit and Spanish defenders seemed hell-bent on making his stay a painful on. In one notorious tackle in September 1983, Andoni Goicoechea hacked him down and left him needing leg-pins to restore the damage. It is rumoured that Goicoechea still has the boot he wore on display in a glass case in his living room. In 1984, the coach at Barcelona, Terry Venables, rescued his career and sold him to Napoli, where he enjoyed a change of fortune. The Italians had struggled to raise the world record £5m, but within weeks the club had sold 70,000 season tickets. He proved to be a great success and the Napoli fans adored him for seven glorious years. Their reward was two league titles in 1987 and 1990, and a UEFA cup success in 1989.

Perhaps, the pinnacle of his career came in 1986 in the World Cup finals. The Argentina side was not the best ever fielded, but the genius of Maradona ultimately made the telling difference. As Franz Beckenbauer said: "In 1986 there were moments when he reached the level of Pelé." Following a second round triumph over Uruguay, Argentina faced England in the quarter-finals. The game became notorious for the "Hand of God" goal, but its finest moment was his brilliant second. He did it again against Belgium in the semi-final and in the final he showed he could create as well as he could score with a brilliant pass to set up Burruchaga for the winner.

In 1987, the success continued at club level, but cracks were beginning to appear in his make-up. Facing a number of personal problems, he began to fall to the temptation offered by the seedier, more corrupt side of life in Naples and things began to turn sour. At the end of a lacklustre 1990-1991 season, he tested positively for cocaine and was banned for 15 months, first from Italian and then from world football. Although he had captained Argentina to the final of the World Cup the year before, his performances there had also been uninspired and his team lost their crown to the Germans. He became unfit and overweight, and rarely produced the sparkle that had hallmarked his earlier career. The fact that Argentina had defeated Italy on penalties in Naples made it worse.

He returned to Argentina, but was arrested soon after for taking cocaine and was ordered by a judge to quit the habit under medical supervision. Napoli wanted him to return after serving his ban, but he refused and instead joined Seville in Spain in 1992. It proved to be a disaster and he returned to Argentina and Newell's Old Boys in 1993. They sacked him the following year for missing training. 1994, however, was the year of the World Cup finals and pressure was building in Argentina for Maradona to be recalled to the national side despite his misdemeanours. He did much to get himself fit and when Argentina played Greece in their opening game the 33 year old looked a new man. He showed flashes of past greatness and few who saw the game could forget his celebrations when he scored what was to be his last goal for his nation. He ran to the cameras with a face that screamed both pride and defiance. Days later, he failed a dope test and was on his way home. His international career was over, as was Argentina's World Cup only two games later. In 1997, he made a brief comeback with Boca Juniors, but again failed a drug test after only his second game, ironically against Argentinos Juniors, and bowed out for good. In 1999, Maradona sought help for his addictions in Cuba where he was diagnosed as suffering from a heart condition brought about by years of drug and alcohol abuse. It was an unfortunate way to end a career, but it cannot detract from the spectacular contribution he made to world football and the pleasure he gave to millions.

Gary Lineker   England

Honours: 4th 1990; Quarter-finals 1986   Games 12
Played: 1986 and 1990   Goals 10

Gary Lineker takes on Paraguay's Rogelio Delgado in England's 3-0 victory.

Gary Lineker was the "nice guy" of world football, never booked nor sent off. From humble beginnings as a weedy 5'6" schoolboy, he became a World Cup hero, a national treasure and, if it wasn't for a fluffed penalty, he would have equalled Bobby Charlton's England record of 49 goals. He was born in Leicester on 30th November 1960, though it was a quirk of fate that led him to football. As he later explained: "My family were living just outside Leicester when I took my 11-Plus. The school I was allocated to didn't play football. They played rugby instead. My father decided it wouldn't do and chose to move. It took them a while to find somewhere else to live, so I stayed with my grandparents who lived in Leicester itself for six months so I could start at a football-playing school. At the time I thought it was a ludicrous decision, but with hindsight it was a marvellous thing for him to do."

That so slight a boy was never bullied at school was because he kept scoring goals for the school team and could run quicker than anyone else. He joined Leicester City at the age of 17, but at only 9 stones, his build remained a concern for the next two years during which time he reached a respectable 5' 10" and put on weight. He was given his senior debut in the 1978-79 season, scoring one goal in seven outings, but it would be another three seasons before he could hold the centre-forward's position regularly. Then over the next four years, he finished the club's top scorer with 17 goals from 39 appearances in 1981-82 and then with 26, 22 and 24 goals respectively. It was inevitable that the England hierarchy would take a look and in May 1984 he came on as a substitute against Scotland. Three more appearances as substitute followed before he was included from the start. He scored six goals in his first ten internationals. In 1985 an £800,00 move took him to Everton. Leicester had wanted £1m, but a tribunal settled the fee. In his first season there he scored

Glasnost, Nuclear Fallout and the Hand of God - Mexico 1986

30 goals, helping them to second place in the First Division, an FA Cup final and was named Player of the Year. His ability to get in behind defenders and his speed and agility getting away from them made him a marked man, so it was to his amazing credit and a mark of his professionalism and temperament that he never retaliated. Lineker was always in control of his emotions and saw no need to argue with referees. Getting on with the game was what mattered.

Although his critics were not convinced, he was in the squad that travelled to the 1986 World Cup. Bobby Robson confirmed his place in the number 10 position and he took the field as England faced Portugal in their opening group game. By the time they played Poland in the last they needed a miracle to keep them in the tournament. They had employed a 4-3-3 system with Lineker paired with Mark Hateley, but Robson was forced to resort to a 4-4-2 system with remarkable effect for both England and its striker. As Lineker later explained: "It was a game that changed my life... If I hadn't scored that first goal we'd have all gone home probably. I would have perhaps never played for England again. Scoring that goal we went on, (I) scored six, top scorer. Everything was different. I was known throughout the world. Without a shadow of a doubt it was the watershed moment of my career." He became a national hero and was named British Football Writers Association and PFA Footballer of the Year. His performance revived interest in the national side and wetted the appetite of Barcelona, who paid £2.75m for him. He slotted into the Spanish league with little problem and, although they only finished second behind Real Madrid in his first season, his ability to score goals impressed the local faithful and they took him to their hearts. He scored all four goals as England beat Spain 4-2 in a Madrid friendly in February 1987 and at the end of the season was runner up at the European Footballer of the Year Awards. The arrival of Johan Cruyff as coach at Barcelona and a bout of jaundice in 1988 meant that his career in Spain waned. He was played out of position on the wide right and, although winning the European Cup-Winners Cup in 1989, he was soon on the move again. Tottenham Hotspur came in with a £1.25m bid for him to end his unhappiness. Spurs had also acquired Paul Gascoigne and the pair sparkled together. In 1991, despite Gascoigne's notorious lunge and consequent injury in the FA Cup semi-final, Tottenham went on to beat Nottingham Forest 2-1 in the final.

Prime Minister, Margaret Thatcher, asked England to pull out of the 1990 World Cup because of the poor behaviour of England supporters abroad. However, the request was ignored and the team travelled, despite a run of poor form. With the press more interested in what was going on off the pitch, the England team retreated into their headquarters and would speak to no one. The stand off solidified team spirits, which were in no small part enhanced by Lineker's professionalism and Paul Gascoigne's antics. It took Lineker only eight minutes to make an impact when he scored against Ireland and, with only 15 minutes to go he once more became the nations saviour with two penalties against Cameroon. Of the first, he said: "PENALTY! I saw the ref.; straight away he's pointing to the spot. I thought 'Yes! We're back in the game.' Then, all of a sudden it dawned: 'I've got to take this.'" He scored and it "was a relief, but then again 10 or 15 minutes later there's another one." Again he put it away and England went into the semi-final for the first time in 24 years. Of the goal against Germany, he later said: "People ask you what you feel like when you score a goal like that. Well, I always say 'What did you feel like when that goal went in?' It was probably the same, but at the time perhaps just that bit more." It was as far as they got, but Lineker had become only the eighth player to score 10 goals in the final stages.

By 1992 Graham Taylor took over as England coach and Lineker began to lose confidence in the direction the side was moving in. Several of the players who had given the team dimension were either injured or not selected for the Euro '92 championships and matters came to a head in the game against tournament hosts, Sweden, at the quarter-final stage. With the game poised at 1-1, Taylor brought Lineker off the pitch and ended his international career. Brolin put England out of the tournament and Taylor became "public enemy number one". Lineker later said: "He made a decision and perversely it affected him a lot more than it did me. He got all the criticism and I hardly got any." In his 80 games for England Lineker scored 48 goals, one short of Bobby Charlton's record, which many feel he would have broken had he been given the chance. Following his retirement from the English game, he was tempted to join a number of other world greats to help get the J League off the ground in Japan and, in the colours of Nagoya Grampus 8, he proved a fine ambassador for the game. He has since taken up a career in broadcasting and now heads the BBC's football team. Needless to say, he employs the same professional and calm manner as front man for Match of the Day as he did throughout his playing days.

Denmark 6 : Uruguay 1

One of the entertainers of the 1986 finals in their first appearance were the Danes. They arrived in Mexico relatively unknown, outside Europe at least, were sent home on the back of a crushing defeat, but in between played some deliciously appealing football. They hit the competition untainted by the cynicism that riddled so many supposedly better teams and approached their football with an almost child-like naïvety that was as uplifting as it was pleasing to watch. They had sent notice of their credentials via the qualifying tournament, in which they topped their group and scored a total of 17 goals, but had now to secure their reputation in the main event itself. A narrow 1-0 victory over Scotland in their opening game did not seem that impressive, but their football had at times been sublime. They were winding themselves up and waiting to give somebody a taste of their exuberance.

The football played by Uruguay came from an altogether different cast. At times they could turn on the style in the way that only South Americans can, but they were too willing to slip into a slough of brutal beastliness, which would see them kick, maul and generally intimidate their opponents in order to hang on to any narrow advantage they had gleaned for themselves. This approach had been all too obvious in their previous game against West Germany, when having gone in front, they sought to hack the Europeans back into their own half every time they advanced into Uruguayan territory. In this they had been abetted by some dreadful refereeing and now it was the turn of Denmark to step into the gladiatorial arena. Few expected the impish, but inexperienced Danes to stand steady against the skulduggery they would surely experience.

How differently it all turned out as "Denmark set the 1986 World Cup aflame... with a marvellous and ultimately remorseless display of fast, imaginative football." They were anything but intimidated and responded to Uruguayan negativity with a disdain that bordered on impudence. The show began to warm up in the tenth minute with a move begun on the right by Michael Laudrup, who "cleverly made space for himself just outside the penalty area." His work was made dangerous "by the strength and timing of Elkjaer's run on the left." He tore through Uruguay's defence and, when Laudrup sent the ball into his path, he scored "with a crisp low shot." Uruguay's response was typical. Only moments later Laudrup was kicked by Miguel Bossio, whose name went into the referee's notebook, but it was "going to take more than spoiling fouls to curb the sheer ebullience of Denmark's play." They continued to punch holes in the South American defence and the Uruguayans began to lose their heads. In the 19th minute Bossio tripped Frank Arnesen. It was totally unnecessary, as the play was up near the half way line and in a completely harmless area and resulted in him being sent off. It did his team's cause no end of harm.

The Uruguayans had one good goal attempt soon after, when Enzo Francescoli's powerful shot, through a crowd of players, was tipped wide by Rasmussen. It was their best effort of the half, but was very much against the run of play. Six minutes before half-time, Laudrup whipped his way through the defence to reach the bye line. He pulled the ball back and Elkjaer was unlucky to see his shot sail over the bar. Two minutes later, though, his efforts brought greater success. Sören Lerby broke free and continued his run as he sent he ball wide to Elkjaer. The pass was returned and he struck the ball into the net. The Danes were cruising comfortably, but on the stroke of half-time, Francescoli was body checked in the area and won a penalty. The decision seemed a little harsh and obstruction with an indirect free kick might have been a more correct interpretation. However, it gave Uruguay an opportunity to restore something in a game that was drifting away from them and Francescoli converted the kick himself to bring the half-time score to 2-1.

In the second half, a game that had been bubbling away nicely erupted like a volcano and the Uruguayans were roasted by the brilliance and expressive mobility of Laudrup and Elkjaer. In the 52nd minute, "Laudrup collected the ball some 20 yards from goal and accelerated past a defender and the goalkeeper" to score one of the best individual goals of the tournament. Soon after, Da Silva chopped down Betelsen and he had to be replaced by Jan Mölby, but it did not affect Denmark's rhythm. When Laudrup wriggled his was through the defence in the 68th minute, he panicked Alvez into coming out of his goal to dive at his feet. The keeper failed to gather the ball, which fell to Elkjaer and the score rose to 4-1. The Danes were now enjoying themselves and their plight forced the Uruguayans to push themselves forwards in order to limit the damage. It was, however, too late and left them fatally exposed at the back, a situation relished by Denmark's forwards. In the 79th minute Elkjaer collected the ball in his own half and ran half the length of the field to secure his hat trick and four minutes later,

Jasper Olsen, on for Laudrup, popped to stamp his own mark on the game and bring the final score to 6-1 to Denmark.

It had been a thoroughly adroit performance from the Danes. Morten Olsen explained his team's performance this way: "We play the way we like to. Laudrup and Elkjaer consider Italian league football as work. This is their hobby." In the cloudy vista of Mexico '86 this was refreshing and needed. They would provide a further gem before making their Viking funeral exit, but few other teams sought to emulate their example and the tournament made its dreary progress without them.

Match 2 - England 1 : Argentina 2

This was one of the most eagerly awaited quarter-finals in World Cup history, especially in Argentina where football fans felt they had two scores to settle, one going back 20 years and one of more recent origin. Many of those fans blamed and had not forgiven the English players and football authorities for what they saw as contriving to get their captain, Antonio Ráttin, sent off when the teams had met at the corresponding stage in the 1966 tournament. Ungentlemanly conduct was seen by many in Argentina as simply part of the game and they saw nothing amiss in Ráttin's behaviour in 1966, just as they were to see nothing wrong with Maradona's chicanery on this day. The second issue was, of course, Argentina's defeat by the British in the Falklands War of 1982.

Maradona beats Englands Peter Shilton with the infamous "Hand of God".

The build-up to the game was, understandably, highly charged and on match day, as the Times's reporter noted, "the tension, stretched out in the unforgiving mid-day sun, crackled like strips of bacon in a huge frying pan." The security forces were out in numbers to separate the rival fans and were able to keep trouble to a few minor skirmishes. Happily, the atmosphere surrounding the pitch did not spill over onto it. The occasion began in a sporting vein, with each England player receiving a pennant from the Argentinians and neither set of players had any intentions of letting other, non-sporting concerns disrupt the play. Football was to be the deciding factor. It was, therefore, a relatively good natured match and, one blaring exception apart, was evenly handled by the Tunisian referee. One of the few incidents of foul play came early, in the tenth minute when Terry Fenwick made a rash challenge on Maradona. He was booked for the offence and his punishment served notice to the others to behave themselves, which they generally did.

The first half was largely played out in midfield. England's defensive priority was, obviously, to neutralize the threat posed by Maradona, but they decided not to risk the inflexibility of a man-to-man approach. Instead, they concentrated on blocking his supply to and from those around him, a ploy that was largely successful. It prevented him from seeing much of the ball, limited his ability to mount his surging runs and meant that his attempts on goal were mainly from free kicks, which gave Shilton the minimum of trouble. Peter Beardsley had one early chance, created when Nery Pumpido chased out of his goal to tackle a through pass from Hoddle. The Argentinian lost his footing and the ball fell nicely for Beardsley, who fired his shot into the side netting, but there were few clear-cut scoring opportunities created by either team. Argentina's defence went for the man-to-man marking of Lineker and Beardsley to keep them quiet and blunt the potency of England's attack. The 0-0 half-time scoreline was a reasonable reflection of the balance of play, though one note of menace was that as the half neared its end, Maradona was increasingly breaking free of his shackles. In the last ten minutes especially, his influence was perceptibly growing and with it the expectations of the ranks of Argentinian supporters.

The first half had been a sparring contest. The teams had probed and poked each other without inflicting serious damage, but the match assumed a more earnest appearance in the second half, beginning in the 51st minute with the goal that brought this game's infamy. The move was begun by Maradona himself, whose pass brought Jorge Valdano into the play. He was quickly challenged by Steve Hodge, who sought to avert the danger with a back pass to his goalkeeper. However, he miskicked and the ball sliced into the air. With Maradona charging forwards, Shilton came out of his goal to gather the ball, but before he could do so, the Argentine launched himself into the fray. He raised his arm and knocked the ball into the net. As the referee signalled the goal, Shilton, who had plainly seen what had happened, angrily confronted him. Unfortunately, the referee's line of vision had not been so clear and he had assumed what many others did on first take, that it was legal. The other man who knew the truth was dancing in celebration and only later, euphemistically and blasphemously, acknowledged his guilt with his notorious remark: "It was a little bit of Maradona's head, a little bit the hand of God."

Five minutes later the other side of Maradona was seen, with a "goal of such dazzling beauty that it will be remembered forever by those privileged enough to witness it." With the English still in a state of shock, "like a man who has had his wallet stolen", said one Italian journalist, he picked the ball up in his own half and wide on the right. He then, "accelerating as swiftly as a bird on the wing, swayed and swerved his way past Sansom, Butcher, Fenwick and finally Shilton with effortless ease." He had left "three English defenders lying on the ground like broken dolls" before he slipped the ball into the net. It was one of the greatest pieces of individual artistry ever seen in a World Cup match and alone was worthy of the victory.

Now the game really boiled over. Maradona had come into his own and the English defence "and the whole stadium itself trembled in expectation whenever he was on the run, either twisting and weaving with the ball attached securely to his remarkable left foot or merely gliding smoothly into position." Up to this point, the English had put little pressure on the Argentine defence, but the situation forced them to it and the result was a transformation that left people wondering what the outcome might have been had they been more adventurous from the start. First, Waddle was brought on in place of Reid, a change that did not have the radical effect required. Ten minutes later, Barnes was brought on for Trevor Steven. Good wing play was what the English had needed all along and Barnes was able to provide the impetus to launch a last-ditch assault on Argentina's goal. Hoddle had a free kick well saved by Pumpido, but soon after, in the 81st minute, Barnes's loping run down the left took him to the bye line. He crossed the ball neatly and Lineker headed in. Six minutes later, a similar move brought another cross from Barnes, but this time Lineker just failed to connect. As the English pressed, "boldly and bravely", time was running out and three minutes after Lineker had almost equalized, the referee called time.

It had been a game of epic qualities, in the second half at least, that turned on a piece of fraudulence, but was won by a moment of genius. When asked for his thoughts on that first goal, Pelé said that it "is certain that if the Argentines or Uruguayans had been in the same spot as the English, they would have trampled the referee." The English response was more phlegmatic. They picked themselves up, got on with it and almost turned the situation round. Of that first goal, England's coach, Bobby Robson, said that he did not "expect decisions like that at World Cup level." Of the second, he remarked that it was "a brilliant goal. I didn't like it, but I had to admire it." The whole world admired it, as it declaimed the first. There was nothing left but to be philosophical in defeat. As the football correspondent of the Guardian said "few could dispute that the winners had given a thoroughly professional performance and on balance deserved their place in the last four."

Argentina 3 : West Germany 2
The World Cup Final

In reaching the final, the characteristics displayed by these two teams had been entirely different. Argentina's progress had not been entirely clean, but there had been flair and improvisation that had at times dazzled. The Germans had won through "by dour defending and dogged persistence." Both sets of traits were to be seen in

West Germany's Ditmar Jakobs (left) clashes with Argentina's Jorge Valdano.

the final itself and in this lay the key to the game's outcome. Germany's plan was to give Matthäus the job of keeping Maradona quiet and it proved costly in more than one way. Firstly, it seemed to concede the myth that this Argentina was Maradona and ten other journeymen, which it was definitely not. Secondly, Maradona was always capable of slipping even the tightest marker and thirdly it denied the Germans Matthäus's own creativity, which greatly hampered their game. Matthäus later admitted that using him to "mark Maradona was a big mistake, I think... I concentrated on Maradona, but we neglected our own game. When we were 2-0 down we changed our system. Karl-Heinz Forster was put on Maradona, I was freed, we got back to 2-2. Then we made a dumb mistake and lost." His remarks sum up this game admirably.

Indeed, it was largely won in midfield, where Burruchaga and his colleagues were exceptional. "Their ability to pressurise the Germans whenever possession was lost, fall back to broaden the defensive barrier, then break out swiftly and incisively once the ball had been regained enabled them to take a grip on the game which West Germany seldom challenged." Maradona himself was content to play a cameo, though none the less pivotal role - he "stayed in the engine room... checking on the gauges and pistons and giving a less spectacular though no less valuable performance", wrote the Guardian correspondent. He was booked in the 19th minute for throwing a tantrum when the referee had ordered a German free kick to be retaken because his defence had not retreated sufficiently. Three minutes later, Matthäus was booked for a crude tackle on his mark, an incident that led to the first goal. Burruchaga's free kick from the right swung away from Schumacher. The keeper was left punching at the air as José Luis Brown headed "the simplest of goals."

The Germans typically came back and Rummenigge missed one easy chance to equalize, but it was Argentina who drew the next blood and Maradona was again key. He turned tightly in the centre circle, exposing the Germans on the left. His pass found Enrique who in turn set Valdano free down the wing. As he raced forwards, he "calmly drew Schumacher off his line and slipped the ball past him inside the far post." Clearly it was not working for the Germans. They had already brought on Völler for the ineffective Allofs and they then replaced Magath with Hoeness. It enabled them to get more men forwards and it brought almost immediate reward. Their three man attack hit the Argentinians with "formidable stamina and strength" and in the 73rd minute Brehme took a corner from the left. It was met by Völler at the near post, who headed on for Rummenigge to score. Less than ten minutes later a similar move drew the Germans level. This time Brehme's corner was headed on by Berthold at the back post and Völler supplied the finish.

German celebrations were hardly over when Maradona provided the touch that won the game. He let go "a beautiful little pass" across the half way line that enabled Burruchaga to slip the offside trap. He ran in to score a goal that gave Schumacher no chance. Later the German goalkeeper said that his team lost "because I was so bad." He was being absolutely unfair to himself. The Germans lost because Argentina were the better team, applied more astute tactics and had greater ability to exploit situations as they arose. It had been "their most accomplished all-round performance of this tournament" and that is why they won.

Statistics - Mexico 1986

GROUP A

Mexico City, May 31st - Estadio Azteca

1 (1) ITALY

Altobelli 43

Galli, Bergomi, Vierchowod, Scirea, Cabrini, De Napoli, Bagni, Di Gennaro, Conti (Vialli), Galderisi, Altobelli.

1 (0) BULGARIA

Sirakov 85

Mikhailov, Zdravkov, Dimitrov, Arabov, A.Markov, Sadkov, Sirakov, Getov, Gospodinov (Yeliazkov), Iskrenov (Kostadinov), Mladenov.

Referee: Erik Fredriksson (Sweden)
Attendance: 95.000

Mexico City, June 2nd - Estadio Olimpico '68

3 (2) ARGENTINA

Valdano 5,46, Ruggeri 17

Pumpido, Clausen, Brown, Ruggeri, Garre, Giusti, Batista (Olarticoechea), Burruchaga, Pasculli (Tapia), Maradona, Valdano.

1 (0) SOUTH KOREA

Park Chang-sun 75

Oh Yung-kyo, Park Kyung-hoon, Jung Yong-hwan, Cho Min-kook, Kim Yong-se (Byun Byung-Joo), Huh Jung-moo, Kim Pyung-suk (Cho Kwang-rae), Park Chang-sun, Kim Joo-sung, Choi Soon-hoo, Cha Bum-keun.

Referee: Victoriano Sánchez Arminio (Spain)
Attendance: 60.000

Puebla, June 5th - Estadio Cuauhtemoc

1 (1) ARGENTINA

Maradona 34

Pumpido, Cuciuffo, Brown, Ruggeri, Garre, Giusti, Batista (Olarticoechea), Burruchaga, Borghi (Enrique), Maradona, Valdano.

1 (1) ITALY

Altobelli (pen) 5

Galli, Bergomi, Vierchowod, Scirea, Cabrini, De Napoli (Baresi), Bagni, Di Gennaro, Conti (Vialli), Galderisi, Altobelli.

Referee: Jan Keizer (Holland)
Attendance: 32.000

Mexico City, June 5th - Estadio Olimpico '68

1 (1) BULGARIA

Getov 11

Mikhailov, Zdravkov, Dimitrov, Arabov, Petrov, Sadkov, Sirakov, Getov (Yeliazkov), Gospodinov, Iskrenov (Kostadinov), Mladenov.

1 (0) SOUTH KOREA

Huh Jong-boo 68

Oh Yung-kyo, Park Kyung-hoon, Jung Yong-hwan, Cho Young-jeung, Huh Jung-moo, Cho Kwang-rae (Choe Min-kook), Park Chang-sun, No Soo-jin (Kim Jong-boo), Byun Byung-joo, Kim Joo-sung, Cha Bum-keun.

Referee: Fallaj Al-Shanar (Saudi Arabia)
Attendance: 45.000

Mexico City, June 10th - Estadio Olimpico '68

2 (1) ARGENTINA

Valdano 3, Burruchaga 78

Pumpido, Cuciuffo, Brown, Ruggeri, Garre, Giusti, Batista (Olarticoechea), Burruchaga, Borghi (Enrique), Maradona, Valdano.

0 (0) BULGARIA

Mikhailov, A.Markov, Dimitrov, Petrov, Sadkov, Sirakov (Zdravkov), Getov, Yeliazkov, Yordanov, P.Markov, Mladenov (Velitchkov).

Referee: Morera Berny Ulloa (Costa Rica)
Attendance: 65.000

Puebla, June 10th - Estadio Cuauhtemoc

2 (0) SOUTH KOREA

Choi Soon-ho 61, Huh Jung-moo 89

Oh Yung-kyo, Park Kyung-hoon, Jung Yong-hwan, Cho Young-jeung, Huh Jung-moo, Cho Kwang-rae, Choi Soon-ho, Park Chang-sun, Byun Byung-joo (Kim Jong-boo), Kim Joo-sung (Chung Jong-soo), Cha Bum-keun.

3 (1) ITALY

Altobelli 18, 73, Cho Kwang-rae (og) 82

Galli, Collovati, Vierchowod, Scirea, Cabrini, De Napoli, Bagni (Baresi), Di Gennaro, Conti, Galderisi (Vialli), Altobelli.

Referee: David Socha (United States)
Attendance: 20.000

	P	W	D	L	F	A	Pts
Argentina	3	2	1	0	6	2	5
Italy	3	1	2	0	5	4	4
Bulgaria	3	0	2	1	2	4	2
South Korea	3	0	1	2	4	7	1

GROUP B

Mexico City, June 3rd - Estadio Azteca

2 (2) MEXICO

Quirarte 23, Sánchez 38

Larios, Trejo, Felix Cruz, Quirarte, Servin, Aguirre, Negrete, Muños, Boy (España), Flores (Javier Cruz), Sánchez.

1 (1) BELGIUM

Van den Bergh 44

Pfaff, Gerets, Broos, F.Van Der Elst, De Wolf, Vercauteren, Vandereycken, Scifo, Ceulemans, Van Den Bergh (Demol), Desmet (Claesen).

Referee: Carlos Esposito (Argentina)
Attendance: 110.000

Toluca, June 4th - Estadio Bombonera

1 (1) PARAGUAY

Romero 35

Fernández, Torales, Zabala, Schettina, Delgado, Nuñez, Ferreira, Romero, Cabañas, Cañete, Mendoza (Guasch).

0 (0) IRAQ

Hammoudi, Allawi, Samir, Nadhum, Ghanim, Haris (Abdul), Natik, Basil (Basim), Hussein, Rhadi, Said.

Referee: Edwin Pikon-Ackong (Mauritius)
Attendance: 24.000

Mexico City, June 7th - Estadio Azteca

1 (1) MEXICO

Flores 2

Larios, Trejo, Felix Cruz, Quirarte, Servin, Aguirre, Negrete, Muños, Boy (España), Flores (Javier Cruz), Sánchez.

1 (0) PARAGUAY

Romero 84

Fernández, Torales (Hicks), Zabala, Schettina, Delgado, Nuñez, Ferreira, Romero, Cabañas, Cañete, Mendoza (Guasch).

Referee: George Courtney (England)
Attendance: 114.600

Toluca, June 8th - Estadio Bombonera

2 (2) BELGIUM

Scifo 15, Claesen (pen)20

Pfaff, Gerets, Demol (Grün), F.Van Der Elst, De Wolf, Vercauteren, Vandereycken, Scifo (Clijsters), Ceulemans, Desmet, Claesen.

1 (0) IRAQ

Rhadi 58

Hammoudi, Allawi, Samir, Nadhum, Ghanim, Haris, Natik, Basil(RED), Hussein, Rhadi, Saddam (Abdul).

Referee: Palacio Jesus Díaz (Colombia)
Attendance: 20.000

Toluca, June 11th - Estadio Bombonera

2 (1) BELGIUM

Vercauteren 31, Veyt 60

Pfaff, Broos, Demol, Grün (L.Van Der Elst), Renquin, Vercauteren, Vervoort, Scifo, Ceulemans, Veyt, Claesen.

2 (0) PARAGUAY

Cabañas 50, 76

Fernández, Torales, Zabala, Delgado, Nuñez, Ferreira, Romero, Cabañas, Cañete, Mendoza (Hicks), Guasch.

Referee: Bogdan Dotchev (Bulgaria)
Attendance: 16.000

Mexico City, June 11th - Estadio Azteca

1 (0) MEXICO

Quirarte 54

Larios, Amador (Dominguez), Felix Cruz, Quirarte, Servin, Aguirre, Negrete, Boy, España, Flores, De los Cobos (Javier Cruz).

0 (0) IRAQ

Fattah, Allawi, Ibrahim, Nadhum, Ghanim, Basim, Natik (Abdul), Ainid (Shaker), Hussein, Rhadi, Saddam.

Referee: Zoran Petrovic (Yugoslavia)
Attendance: 103.762

	P	W	D	L	F	A	Pts
Mexico	3	2	1	0	4	2	5
Paraguay	3	1	2	0	4	3	4
Belgium	3	1	1	1	5	5	3
Iraq	3	0	0	3	1	4	0

Statistics - Mexico 1986

GROUP C

Leon, June 1st - Estadio Nou Camp

1 (0) FRANCE

Papin 78

Bats, Amoros, Battiston, Bossis, Tusseau, Fernández, Tigana, Platini, Giresse, Papin, Rocheteau (Stopyra).

0 (0) CANADA

Dolan, Lenarduzzi, Samuel, Bridge, Wilson, Ragan, James (Segota), Norman, Sweeney (Lowery), Valentine, Vrablic.

Referee: Hernan Silva Arce (Chile)
Attendance: 35.748

Irapuato, June 2nd - Estadio Irapuato

6 (3) SOVIET UNION

Yakovenko 2, Aleinikov 4, Belanov (pen)23, Yaremchuk 66, 74, Rodionov 79

Dassajev, Larionov, Bessonov, Kuznetsov, Demianenko, Yaremchuk, Aleinikov, Yakovenko (Yevtushenko), Rats, Belanov (Rodionov), Zavarov.

0 (0) HUNGARY

Disztl, Sallai, Garaba, Peter (Dajka), Kardos, Bognar, Nagy, Detari, Roth (Burcsa), Kiprich, Esterhazy.

Referee: Luigi Agnolin (Italy)
Attendance: 16.600

Leon, June 5th - Estadio Nou Camp

1 (0) FRANCE

Fernández 61

Bats, Amoros, Battiston, Bossis, Ayache, Fernández, Tigana, Platini, Giresse (Vercruysse), Papin (Bellone), Stopyra.

1 (0) SOVIET UNION

Rats 53

Dassajev, Larionov, Bessonov, Kuznetsov, Demianenko, Yaremchuk, Aleinikov, Yakovenko (Rodionov), Rats, Belanov, Zavarov (Blokhin).

Referee: Romualdo Arppi Filho (Brazil)
Attendance: 36.540

Irapuato, June 6th - Estadio Irapuato

2 (1) HUNGARY

Esterhazy 2, Detari 75

Szendrei, Sallai, Garaba, Varga, Kardos, Bognar, Nagy (Dajka), Detari, Burcsa (Roth), Kiprich, Esterhazy.

0 (0) CANADA

Lettieri, Lenarduzzi, Samuel, Bridge, Wilson (Sweeney) (RED), Ragan, James (Segota), Norman, Valentine, Gray, Vrablic.

Referee: Jamal Al-Sharif (Syria)
Attendance: 13.800

Leon, June 9th - Estadio Nou Camp

3 (1) FRANCE

Stopyra 41, Tigana 62, Rocheteau 84

Bats, Amoros, Battiston, Bossis, Ayache, Fernández, Tigana, Platini, Giresse, Papin (Rocheteau), Stopyra (Ferreri).

0 (0) HUNGARY

Disztl, Sallai, Garaba, Varga, Kardos, Roth, Detari, Hannich (Nagy), Dajka, Kovacs (Bognar), Esterhazy.

Referee: Carlos Antonio Silva Valente (Portugal)
Attendance: 31.420

Irapuato, June 9th - Estadio Irapuato

2 (0) SOVIET UNION

Blokhin 58, Zavarov 75

Chanov, Morozov, Bubnov, Kuznetsov, Bal, Aleinikov, Litovchenko, Rodionov, Yevtushenko, Protasov (Belanov), Blokhin (Zavarov).

0 (0) CANADA

Lettieri, Lenarduzzi, Samuel, Bridge, Wilson, Ragan, James (Segota), Norman, Valentine, Gray (Pakos), Mitchell.

Referee: Idriss Traore (Mali)
Attendance: 14.200

	P	W	D	L	F	A	Pts
Soviet Union	3	2	1	0	9	1	5
France	3	2	1	0	5	1	5
Hungary	3	1	0	2	2	9	2
Canada	3	0	0	3	0	5	0

GROUP D

Guadalajara, June 1st - Estadio Jalisco

1 (0) BRAZIL

Socrates 60

Carlos, Branco, Edinho, Julio Cesar, Edson, Junior (Falcão), Socrates, Alemão, Elzo, Casagrande (Müller), Careca.

0 (0) SPAIN

Zubizarreta, Tomas, Maceda, Goicoechea, Camacho, Víctor, Michel, Francisco (Señor), Julio Alberto, Butragueño, Salinas.

Referee: Chris Bambridge (Australia)
Attendance: 65.000

Guadalajara, June 3rd - Estadio Trez de Marzo

1 (0) ALGERIA

Zidane 58

El Hadi, Medjadi, Kourichi, Guendouz, Mansouri, Kaci-Saïd, Ben Mabrouk, Maroc, Madjer (Harkouk), Zidane (Belloumi), Assad.

1 (1) NORTHERN IRELAND

Whiteside 6

Jennings, J.Nicholl, O'Neill, McDonald, Donaghy, Penney (Stewart), McIlroy, McCreery, Worthington, Hamilton, Whiteside (Clarke).

Referee: Valeri Butenko (Soviet Union)
Attendance: 22.000

Guadalajara, June 6th - Estadio Jalisco

1 (0) BRAZIL

Careca 66

Carlos, Branco, Edinho, Julio Cesar, Edson (Falcão), Junior, Socrates, Alemão, Elzo, Casagrande (Müller), Careca.

0 (0) ALGERIA

Drid, Medjadi, Megharia, Guendouz, Mansouri, Kaci-Saïd, Ben Mabrouk, Madjer, Menad, Belloumi (Zidane), Assad (Bensaoula).

Referee: Romulo Mendez Molina (Guatemala)
Attendance: 48.000

Guadalajara, June 7th - Estadio Trez de Marzo

2 (2) SPAIN

Butragueño 2, Salinas 18

Zubizarreta, Tomas, Gallego, Goicoechea, Camacho, Víctor, Michel, Francisco, Gordillo (Caldere), Butragueño, Salinas (Señor).

1 (0) NORTHERN IRELAND

Clarke 47

Jennings, J.Nicholl, O'Neill, McDonald, Donaghy, Penney (Stewart), McIlroy, McCreery, Worthington (Hamilton), Whiteside, Clarke.

Referee: Horst Brummeier (Austria)
Attendance: 28.000

Guadalajara, June 12th - Estadio Jalisco

3 (2) BRAZIL

Careca 15, 87, Josimar 41

Carlos, Branco, Edinho, Julio Cesar, Josimar, Junior, Socrates (Zico), Alemão, Elzo, Müller (Casagrande), Careca.

0 (0) NORTHERN IRELAND

Jennings, J.Nicholl, O'Neill, McDonald, Donaghy, Stewart, McIlroy, McCreery, Campbell (Armstrong), Whiteside (Hamilton), Clarke.

Referee: Sigfried Kirschen (East Germany)
Attendance: 51.000

Guadalajara, June 12th - Estadio Trez de Marzo

3 (1) SPAIN

Calderé 18, 68, Eloy 71

Zubizarreta, Tomas, Gallego, Goicoechea, Camacho, Víctor, Michel (Señor), Francisco, Caldere, Butragueño (Eloy), Salinas.

0 (0) ALGERIA

Drid (El Hadi), Kourichi, Megharia, Guendouz, Mansouri, Kaci-Saïd, Zidane (Menad), Madjer, Harkouk, Maroc, Belloumi.

Referee: Shizuo Takada (Japan)
Attendance: 28.000

	P	W	D	L	F	A	Pts
Brazil	3	3	0	0	5	0	6
Spain	3	2	0	1	5	2	4
N. Ireland	3	0	1	2	2	6	1
Algeria	3	0	1	2	1	5	1

GROUP E

Queretaro, June 4th - Estadio La Corregidora

1 (0) WEST GERMANY

Allofs 84

Schumacher, Berthold, K-H Förster, Eder, Briegel, Matthäus (Rummenigge), Magath, Brehme (Littbarski), Augenthaler, Völler, Allofs.

1 (1) URUGUAY

Alzamendi 4

Alvez, Diogo, Acevedo, Gutiérrez, Batista, Bossio, Barrios (Saralegui), Santin, Francescoli, Alzamendi (Ramos), Da Silva.

Referee: Vojtech Christov (Czechoslovakia)
Attendance: 30.500

**Nezahualcoyotl, June 4th -
Estadio Neza '86**

1 (0) DENMARK

Elkjær-Larsen 58

Rasmussen, Busk, M.Olsen, Nielsen, Lerby, J.Olsen (Mølby), Berggren, Bertelsen, Arnesen (Sivebaek), Laudrup, Elkjær-Larsen.

0 (0) SCOTLAND

Leighton, Gough, Malpas, McLeish, Miller, Souness, Aitken, Nicol, Nicholas, Strachan (Bannon), Sturrock (McAvennie).

Referee: Lajos Nemeth (Hungary)
Attendance: 18.000

**Queretaro, June 8th -
Estadio La Corregidora**

2 (1) WEST GERMANY

Völler 22, Allofs 50

Schumacher, Berthold, K-H Förster, Eder, Briegel (Jakobs), Matthäus, Magath, Littbarski (Rummenigge), Augenthaler, Völler, Allofs.

1 (1) SCOTLAND

Strachan 17

Leighton, Gough, Malpas, Narey, Miller, Souness, Aitken, Nicol (McAvennie), Strachan, Bannon (Cooper), Archibald.

Referee: Ioan Igna (Romania)
Attendance: 30.000

**Nezahualcoyotl, June 8th -
Estadio Neza '86**

6 (2) DENMARK

Elkjær-Larsen 10, 68, 80, Lerby 41, Laudrup 52, J.Olsen 88

Rasmussen, Busk, M.Olsen, Nielsen, Lerby, Andersen, Berggren, Bertelsen (Mølby), Arnesen, Laudrup (J.Olsen), Elkjær-Larsen.

1 (1) URUGUAY

Francescoli (pen)45

Alvez, Diogo, Acevedo, Gutiérrez, Batista, Bossio (RED), Saralegui, Santin (Salazar), Francescoli, Alzamendi (Ramos), Da Silva.

Referee: Antonio Ramírez Marquez (Mexico)
Attendance: 26.500

**Queretaro, June 13th -
Estadio La Corregidora**

2 (1) DENMARK

J.Olsen (pen)43, Eriksen 63

Høgh, Busk, M.Olsen, Sivebaek, Lerby, Andersen, Mølby, Arnesen (RED), Laudrup, J.Olsen (Simonsen), Elkjær-Larsen (Eriksen).

0 (0) WEST GERMANY

Schumacher, Berthold, K-H Förster (Rummenigge), Eder, Herget, Jakobs, Matthäus, Rolff (Littbarski), Brehme, Völler, Allofs.

Referee: Alexis Ponnet (Belgium)
Attendance: 36.000

**Nezahualcoyotl, June 13th -
Estadio Neza '86**

0 (0) SCOTLAND

Leighton, Gough, Albiston, Narey, Miller, McStay, Aitken, Nicol (Cooper), Strachan, Sharp, Sturrock (Nicholas).

0 (0) URUGUAY

Alvez, Diogo, Acevedo, Gutiérrez, Batista (RED), Pereya, Barrios, Santin, Francescoli (Alzamendi), Ramos (Saralegui), Cabrera.

Referee: Joël Quiniou (France)
Attendance: 20.000

	P	W	D	L	F	A	Pts
Denmark	3	3	0	0	9	1	6
West Germany	3	1	1	1	3	4	3
Uruguay	3	0	2	1	2	7	2
Scotland	3	0	1	2	1	3	1

Denmark and West Germany qualified, as well as Uruguay who managed to go through with their poor record as one of the four best third placed teams. Scotland was eliminated

GROUP F

**Monterrey, June 2nd -
Estadio Universitario**

0 (0) MOROCCO

Zaki, Khalifi, El Biaz, Bouyahyaoui, Lamriss, Dolmy, El Haddaoui (Souleymani), Timoumi (Khairi), Mustapha Merry, Bouderbala, Krimau.

0 (0) POLAND

Mlynarczyk, Kubicki (Przybys), Wojcicki, Majewski, Ostrowski, Matysik, Buncol, Komornicki, Boniek, Smolarek, Dziekanowski (Urban).

Referee: José Luis Martínez (Uruguay)
Attendance: 19.000

**Monterrey, June 3rd -
Estadio Tecnologico**

1 (0) PORTUGAL

Carlos Manuel 75

Bento, Alvaro, Frederico, Oliveira, Inacio, Diamantino (José Antonio), Pacheco, André, Sousa, Carlos Manuel, Gomes (Futre).

0 (0) ENGLAND

Shilton, G.M.Stevens, Fenwick, Butcher, Sansom, Hoddle, Robson (Hodge), Wilkins, Waddle (Beardsley), Hateley, Lineker.

Referee: Volker Roth (West Germany)
Attendance: 23.000

**Monterrey, June 6th -
Estadio Tecnologico**

0 (0) ENGLAND

Shilton, G.M.Stevens, Fenwick, Butcher, Sansom, Hoddle, Robson (Hodge), Wilkins (RED), Waddle, Hateley (G.A.Stevens), Lineker.

0 (0) MOROCCO

Zaki, Khalifi, El Biaz, Bouyahyaoui, Lamriss (Oudani), Dolmy, Timoumi, Khairi, Mustapha Merry (Souleymani), Bouderbala, Krimau.

Referee: Gabriel González (Paraguay)
Attendance: 20.200

**Monterrey, June 7th -
Estadio Universitario**

1 (0) POLAND

Smolarek 63

Mlynarczyk, Pawlak, Wojcicki, Majewski, Ostrowski, Matysik, Komornicki (Karas), Boniek, Smolarek (Zgutczynski), Dziekanowski, Urban.

0 (0) PORTUGAL

Damas, Alvaro, Frederico, Oliveira, Inacio, Diamantino, Pacheco, André (J.Magalhães), Sousa, Carlos Manuel, Gomes (Futre).

Referee: Ali Bennaceur (Tunisia)
Attendance: 19.915

**Monterrey, June 11th -
Estadio Universitario**

3 (3) ENGLAND

Lineker 8, 13, 36

Shilton, G.M.Stevens, Fenwick, Butcher, Sansom, Hoddle, Steven, Hodge, Reid, Beardsley (Waddle), Lineker (Dixon).

0 (0) POLAND

Mlynarczyk, Pawlak, Wojcicki, Majewski, Ostrowski, Matysik (Buncol), Komornicki (Karas), Boniek, Smolarek, Dziekanowski, Urban.

Referee: André Daina (Switzerland)
Attendance: 22.700

**Monterrey, June 11th -
Estadio Tecnologico**

3 (2) MOROCCO

Khairi 18, 27, Krimau 63

Zaki, Khalifi, El Biaz, Bouyahyaoui, Lamriss, Dolmy, El Haddaoui (Souleymani), Timoumi, Khairi, Bouderbala, Krimau.

1 (0) PORTUGAL

Diamantino 80

Damas, Alvaro (Aguas), Frederico, Oliveira, Inacio, Pacheco, J.Magalhães, Sousa (Diamantino), Carlos Manuel, Gomes, Futre.

Referee: Alan Snoddy (Northern Ireland)
Attendance: 23.980

	P	W	D	L	F	A	Pts
Morocco	3	1	2	0	3	1	4
England	3	1	1	1	3	1	3
Poland	3	1	1	1	1	3	3
Portugal	3	1	0	2	2	4	2

SECOND ROUND

Mexico City, June 15th - Estadio Azteca

2 (1) MEXICO

Negrete 35, Servin 60

Larios, Amador, Quirarte, Felix Cruz, Servin, Muñoz, Negrete, España, Boy (De los Cobos), Aguirre, Sánchez.

0 (0) BULGARIA

Mikhailov, Zdravkov, Arabov, Petrov, Dimitrov, Sadkov, Yordanov, Kostadinov, Gospodinov, Paschev (Iskrenov), Getov (Sirakov).

Referee: Romualdo Arppi Filho (Brazil)
Attendance: 114.580

Leon, June 15th - Estadio Nou Camp

After extra time - 45 mins (0-1), 90 mins (2-2)

4 (2) BELGIUM

Scifo 54, Ceulemans 75, Demol 102, Claesen 108

Pfaff, Grün (Clijsters), Gerets (L.Van Der Elst), Renquin, Vervoort, Scifo, Demol, Ceulemans, Vercauteren, Claesen, Veyt.

3 (2) SOVIET UNION

Belanov 27, 70, (pen)111

Dassajev, Bessonov, Demianenko, Kuznetsov, Bal, Zavarov (Rodionov), Aleinikov, Yakovenko (Yevtushenko), Yaremchuk, Belanov, Rats.

Referee: Erik Fredriksson (Sweden)
Attendance: 32.277

Guadalajara, June 16th - Estadio Jalisco

4 (1) BRAZIL

Socrates (pen)30, Josimar 55, Edinho 78, Careca (pen)82

Carlos, Josimar, Julio Cesar, Edinho, Branco, Elzo, Alemão, Socrates (Zico), Junior, Careca, Müller (Silas).

0 (0) POLAND

Mlynarczyk, Przybys (Furtok), Ostrowski, Tarasiewicz, Karas, Wojcicki, Majewski, Urban (Zmuda), Boniek, Dziekanowski, Smolarek.

Referee: Volker Roth (West Germany)
Attendance: 45.000

Puebla, June 16th - Estadio Cuauhtemoc

1 (1) ARGENTINA

Pasculli 41

Pumpido, Cuciuffo, Ruggeri, Brown, Garre, Giusti, Batista (Olarticoechea), Burruchaga, Pasculli, Maradona, Valdano.

0 (0) URUGUAY

Alvez, Gutiérrez, Acevedo (Paz), Rivero, Santin, Ramos, Bossio, Barrios, Pereira, Cabrera (Da Silva), Francescoli.

Referee: Luigi Agnolin (Italy)
Attendance: 26.000

Mexico City, June 17th - Estadio Olimpico '68

2 (1) FRANCE

Platini 14, Stopyra 57

Bats, Ayache, Battiston, Bossis, Amoros, Giresse, Tigana, Fernández (Tusseau), Platini (Ferreri), Rocheteau, Stopyra.

0 (0) ITALY

Galli, Bergomi, Vierchowod, Scirea, Cabrini, Baresi (Di Gennaro), De Napoli, Bagni, Conti, Altobelli, Galderisi (Vialli).

Referee: Carlos Esposito (Argentina)
Attendance: 70.000

Monterrey, June 17th - Estadio Universitario

1 (0) WEST GERMANY

Matthäus 87

Schumacher, Berthold, K-H Förster, Jakobs, Briegel, Eder, Matthäus, Magath, Rummenigge, Allofs, Völler (Littbarski).

0 (0) MOROCCO

Zaki, Khalifi, Bouyahyaoui, Oudani, Lamriss, Dolmy, El Haddaoui, Bouderbala, Timoumi, Khairi, Krimau.

Referee: Zoran Petrovic (Yugoslavia)
Attendance: 19.800

Mexico City, June 18th - Estadio Azteca

3 (1) ENGLAND

Lineker 32, 72, Beardsley 55

Shilton, G.M.Stevens, Martin, Butcher, Sansom, Steven, Reid (G.A.Stevens), Hoddle, Hodge, Lineker, Beardsley (Hateley).

0 (0) PARAGUAY

Fernández, Torales (Guasch), Schettina, Delgado, Zabala, Cañete, Romero, Nuñez, Ferreira, Cabañas, Mendoza.

Referee: Jamal Al-Sharif (Syria)
Attendance: 98.728

Queretaro, June 18th - Estadio La Corregidora

5 (1) SPAIN

Butragueño 43, 56, 80, (pen)90, Goicoechea (pen)69

Zubizarreta, Tomas, Gallego, Goicoechea, Camacho, Julio Alberto, Víctor, Michel (Francisco), Caldere, Butragueño, Salinas (Eloy).

1 (1) DENMARK

J.Olsen (pen)33

Høgh, Busk, M.Olsen, Nielsen, Andersen (Eriksen), Berggren, J.Olsen (Mølby), Bertelsen, Lerby, Laudrup, Elkjær-Larsen.

Referee: Jan Keizer (Holland)
Attendance: 38.500

QUARTER-FINALS

Guadalajara, June 21st - Estadio Jalisco

5 (4)(1) FRANCE

Platini 41

Bats, Battiston, Amoros, Bossis, Tusseau, Giresse (Ferreri), Tigana, Platini, Fernández, Stopyra, Rocheteau (Bellone).

4 (3)(1) BRAZIL

Careca 18

Carlos, Josimar, Julio Cesar, Edinho, Branco, Alemão, Socrates, Junior (Silas), Elzo, Müller (Zico), Careca.

After extra time & penalty shoot-out - 45 mins (1-1), 90 mins (1-1), 120 mins (1-1)

Penalty shoot-out - Brazil started to shoot.

BRAZIL	3	FRANCE	4
Socrates	Miss	Stopyra	Goal
Alemão	Goal	Amoros	Goal
Zico	Goal	Bellone	Goal
Branco	Goal	Platini	Miss
Julio Cesar	Goal	Fernández	Miss

Referee: Ioan Igna (Romania)
Attendance: 65.777

Monterrey, June 21st - Estadio Universitario

4 (4)(0) WEST GERMANY

Schumacher, Berthold (RED), K-H Förster, Jakobs, Briegel, Brehme, Eder (Littbarski), Matthäus, Magath, Allofs, Rummenigge (Hoeness).

1 (1)(0) MEXICO

Larios, Servin, Felix Cruz, Quirarte, Amador (Javier Cruz), Muñoz, Aguirre (RED), Negrete, España, Boy (De los Cobos), Sánchez.

After extra time & penalty shoot-out - 45 mins (0-0), 90 mins (0-0), 120 mins (0-0)

Penalty shoot-out - West Germany started to shoot.

W. GERMANY	4	MEXICO	1
Allofs	Goal	Negrete	Goal
Brehme	Goal	Quirarte	Miss
Matthäus	Goal	Servin	Miss
Littbarski	Goal		

Referee: Palacio Jesus Díaz (Colombia)
Attendance: 44.386

Mexico City, June 22nd - Estadio Azteca

2 (0) ARGENTINA

Maradona 51,55

Pumpido, Cuciuffo, Brown, Ruggeri, Olarticoechea, Batista, Giusti, Burruchaga (Tapia), Enrique, Valdano, Maradona.

1 (0) ENGLAND

Lineker 81

Shilton, G.M.Stevens, Butcher, Fenwick, Sansom, Hoddle, Steven (Barnes), Reid (Waddle), Hodge, Lineker, Beardsley.

Referee: Ali Bennaceur (Tunisia)
Attendance: 114.580

Puebla, June 22nd - Estadio Cuauhtemoc

6 (5)(1) BELGIUM

Ceulemans 34

Pfaff, Gerets, Renquin, Demol, Vervoort, Vercauteren (L.Van der Elst), Scifo, Grün, Ceulemans, Claesen, Veyt (Broos).

5 (4)(1) SPAIN

Señor 85

Zubizarreta, Tomas (Señor), Gallego, Chendo, Camacho, Julio Alberto, Víctor, Michel, Caldere, Butragueño, Salinas (Eloy).

After extra time & penalty shoot-out - 45 mins (1-0), 90 mins (1-1), 120 mins (1-1)

Penalty shoot-out - Spain started to shoot.

SPAIN	4	BELGIUM	5
Señor	Goal	Claesen	Goal
Eloy	Miss	Scifo	Goal
Chendo	Goal	Broos	Goal
Butragueño	Goal	Vervoot	Goal
Víctor	Goal	L.van der Elst	Goal

Referee: Sigfried Kirschen (East Germany)
Attendance: 45.000

SEMI-FINALS

Guadalajara, June 25th - Estadio Jalisco

2 (1) WEST GERMANY

Brehme 9, Völler 90

Schumacher, Brehme, K-H Förster, Jakobs, Briegel, Eder, Matthäus, Magath, Rolff, Allofs, Rummenigge (Völler).

0 (0) FRANCE

Bats, Ayache, Battiston, Bossis, Amoros, Tigana, Giresse (Vercruysse), Platini, Fernández, Stopyra, Bellone (Xuereb).

Referee: Luigi Agnolin (Italy)
Attendance: 45.000

Mexico City, June 25th - Estadio Azteca

2 (0) ARGENTINA

Maradona 51,61

Pumpido, Cuciuffo, Ruggeri, Brown, Olarticoechea, Giusti, Enrique, Batista, Burruchaga (Bochini), Maradona, Valdano.

0 (0) BELGIUM

Pfaff, Gerets, Grün, Demol, Renquin (Desmet), Vervoort, Scifo, Vercauteren, Ceulemans, Claesen, Veyt.

Referee: Antonio Ramírez Marquez (Mexico)
Attendance: 110.420

3RD/4TH PLACE PLAY-OFF

Puebla, June 28th - Estadio Cuauhtemoc

4 (2) FRANCE

Ferreri 26, Papin 42, Genghini 103, Amoros (pen)108

Rust, Le Roux (Bossis), Battiston, Bibard, Amoros, Tigana (Tusseau), Genghini, Vercruysse, Ferreri, Bellone, Papin.

2 (2) BELGIUM

Ceulemans 10, Claesen 72

Pfaff, Gerets, Grün, Demol, Renquin (F.Van der Elst), Vervoort, Scifo (L.Van der Elst), Mommens, Ceulemans, Claesen, Veyt.

After extra time - 45 mins (2-1), 90 mins (2-2)

Referee: George Courtney (England)
Attendance: 21.000

FINAL

Mexico City, June 29th - Estadio Azteca

3 (1) ARGENTINA

Brown 21, Valdano 55, Burruchaga 84

Pumpido, Cuciuffo, Brown, Ruggeri, Olarticoechea, Batista, Giusti, Enrique, Burruchaga (Trobbiani), Maradona, Valdano.

2 (0) WEST GERMANY

Rummenigge 73, Völler 81

Schumacher, Brehme, K-H Förster, Jakobs, Briegel, Eder, Matthäus, Magath (Hoeness), Berthold, Allofs (Völler), Rummenigge.

Referee: Romualdo Arppi Filho (Brazil)
Attendance: 114.590

QUALIFYING ROUNDS

Africa - 1st Round

	P	W	D	L	F	A	Pts
Tunisia	2	2	0	0	6	0	4
Malawi	2	2	0	0	5	0	4
Morocco	2	2	0	0	5	0	4
Nigeria	2	2	0	0	4	0	4
Kenya	2	1	1	0	5	4	3
Egypt	2	1	1	0	2	1	3
Cote d' Ivoire	2	1	0	1	6	3	2
Zambia	2	1	0	1	3	1	2
Sudan	2	0	2	0	1	1	2
Tanzania	2	0	2	0	1	1	2
Angola	2	1	0	1	1	1	2
Senegal	2	1	0	1	1	1	2
Uganda	2	1	0	1	1	3	2
Gambia	2	1	0	1	3	6	2
Ethiopia	2	0	1	1	4	5	1
Zimbabwe	2	0	1	1	1	2	1
Liberia	2	0	0	2	0	4	0
Sierra Leone	2	0	0	2	0	5	0
Mauritius	2	0	0	2	0	5	0
Benin	2	0	0	2	0	6	0

30-06-84	Sierra Leone : Morocco	0:1 (0:0)
01-07-84	Angola : Senegal	1:0 (0:0)
15-07-84	Mauritius : Malawi	0:1 (0:1)
15-07-84	Morocco : Sierra Leone	4:0 (1:0)
15-07-84	Senegal : Angola	1:0 a.e.t (1:0, 1:0) 3:4 penalty kicks
28-07-84	Malawi : Mauritius	4:0 (1:0)
29-07-84	Zambia : Uganda	3:0 (1:0)
25-08-84	Uganda : Zambia	1:0 (0:0)
28-08-84	Egypt : Zimbabwe	1:0 (1:0)
30-09-84	Zimbabwe : Egypt	1:1 (1:1)
13-10-84	Kenya : Ethiopia	2:1 (1:1)
13-10-84	Tanzania : Sudan	1:1 (1:0)
20-10-84	Nigeria : Liberia	3:0 (2:0)
21-10-84	Cote d' Ivoire : Gambia	4:0 (0:0)
27-10-84	Sudan : Tanzania	0:0
28-10-84	Ethiopia : Kenya	3:3 (2:0)
28-10-84	Benin : Tunisia	0:2 (0:0)
04-11-84	Liberia : Nigeria	0:1 (0:1)
04-11-84	Gambia : Cote d' Ivoire	3:2 (1:1)
13-11-84	Tunisia : Benin	4:0 (2:0)

Africa - 2nd Round

	P	W	D	L	F	A	Pts
Nigeria	2	2	0	0	6	1	4
Libya	2	1	1	0	4	0	3
Zambia	2	1	1	0	5	2	3
Ghana	2	1	1	0	2	0	3
Morocco	2	1	1	0	2	0	3
Algeria	2	1	1	0	3	2	3
Tunisia	2	1	0	1	2	1	2
Madagascar	2	1	0	1	1	1	2
Egypt	2	1	0	1	1	1	2
Guinea	2	1	0	1	1	2	2
Angola	2	0	1	1	2	3	1
Malawi	2	0	1	1	0	2	1
Cote d' Ivoire	2	0	1	1	0	2	1
Cameroon	2	0	1	1	2	5	1
Sudan	2	0	1	1	0	4	1
Kenya	2	0	0	2	1	6	0

10-02-85	Guinea : Tunisia	1:0 (1:0)
22-02-85	Sudan : Libya	0:0
24-02-85	Tunisia : Guinea	2:0 (1:0)
08-03-85	Libya : Sudan	4:0 (0:0)
31-03-85	Angola : Algeria	0:0
05-04-85	Egypt : Madagascar	1:0 (0:0)

06-04-85	Kenya : Nigeria	0:3 (0:2)
07-04-85	Morocco : Malawi	2:0 (1:0)
07-04-85	Zambia : Cameroon	4:1 (4:0)
07-04-85	Cote d' Ivoire : Ghana	0:0
19-04-85	Algeria : Angola	3:2 (2:0)
20-04-85	Nigeria : Kenya	3:1 (2:1)
21-04-85	Cameroon : Zambia	1:1 (1:1)
21-04-85	Madagascar : Egypt	1:0 a.e.t (1:0, 0:0) 2:3 penalty kicks
21-04-85	Malawi : Morocco	0:0
21-04-85	Ghana : Cote d' Ivoire	2:0 (0:0)

Africa - 3rd Round

	P	W	D	L	F	A	Pts
Algeria	2	2	0	0	3	0	4
Morocco	2	1	1	0	2	0	3
Libya	2	1	1	0	2	0	3
Tunisia	2	1	0	1	2	1	2
Nigeria	2	1	0	1	1	2	2
Ghana	2	0	1	1	0	2	1
Egypt	2	0	1	1	0	2	1
Zambia	2	0	0	2	0	3	0

06-07-85	Nigeria : Tunisia	1:0 (0:0)
12-07-85	Egypt : Morocco	0:0
13-07-85	Algeria : Zambia	2:0 (1:0)
14-07-85	Ghana : Libya	0:0
20-07-85	Tunisia : Nigeria	2:0 (2:0)
26-07-85	Libya : Ghana	2:0 (1:0)
28-07-85	Morocco : Egypt	2:0 (1:0)
28-07-85	Zambia : Algeria	0:1 (0:0)

Africa - 4th Round

	P	W	D	L	F	A	Pts
Algeria	2	2	0	0	7	1	4
Morocco	2	1	0	1	3	1	2
Libya	2	1	0	1	1	3	2
Tunisia	2	0	0	2	1	7	0

06-10-85	Morocco : Libya	3:0 (1:0)
06-10-85	Tunisia : Algeria	1:4 (1:2)
18-10-85	Libya : Morocco	1:0 (1:0)
18-10-85	Algeria : Tunisia	3:0 (2:0)

Asia Phase 1 - 1st Round, Group 1A

	P	W	D	L	F	A	Pts
United Arab Emirates	2	1	1	0	1	0	3
Saudi Arabia	2	0	1	1	0	1	1

12-04-85	Saudi Arabia : UAE	0:0
19-04-85	UAE : Saudi Arabia	1:0 (1:0)

Asia Phase 1 - 1st Round, Group 1B

	P	W	D	L	F	A	Pts
Iraq	4	3	0	1	7	6	6
Qatar	4	2	0	2	6	3	4
Jordan	4	1	0	3	3	7	2

15-03-85	Jordan : Qatar	1:0 (0:0)
29-03-85	Jordan : Iraq	2:3 (0:1)
05-04-85	Qatar : Iraq	3:0 (1:0)
12-04-85	Qatar : Jordan	2:0 (0:0)
19-04-85	Iraq : Jordan	2:0 (0:0)
05-05-85	Iraq : Qatar	2:1 (1:1)

Asia Phase 1 - 1st Round, Group 2A

	P	W	D	L	F	A	Pts
Syria	4	3	1	0	5	0	7
Kuwait	4	2	1	1	8	2	5
Yemen	4	0	0	4	1	12	0

22-03-85	Syria : Kuwait	1:0 (1:0)
29-03-85	Yemen : Syria	0:1 (0:0)
05-04-85	Kuwait : Yemen	5:0 (1:0)
12-04-85	Kuwait : Syria	0:0
19-04-85	Syria : Yemen	3:0 (2:0)
26-04-85	Yemen : Kuwait	1:3 (0:2)

Asia Phase 1 - 1st Round, Group 2B

	P	W	D	L	F	A	Pts
Bahrain	2	1	1	0	7	4	3
Yemen DR	2	0	1	1	4	7	1

29-03-85	Yemen DR : Bahrain	1:4 (0:2)
12-04-85	Bahrain : Yemen DR	3:3 (0:1)

Asia Phase 1 - 1st Round, Group 3A

	P	W	D	L	F	A	Pts
Korea Republic	4	3	0	1	8	1	6
Malaysia	4	2	1	1	6	2	5
Nepal	4	0	1	3	0	11	1

02-03-85	Nepal : Korea Republic	0:2 (0:1)
10-03-85	Malaysia : Korea Republic	1:0 (0:0)
16-03-85	Nepal : Malaysia	0:0
31-03-85	Malaysia : Nepal	5:0 (5:0)
06-04-85	Korea Republic : Nepal	4:0 (3:0)
19-05-85	Korea Republic : Malaysia	2:0 (2:0)

Asia Phase 1 - 1st Round, Group 3B

	P	W	D	L	F	A	Pts
Indonesia	6	4	1	1	8	4	9
India	6	2	3	1	7	6	7
Thailand	6	1	2	3	4	4	4
Bangladesh	6	2	0	4	5	10	4

15-03-85	Indonesia : Thailand	1:0 (0:0)
18-03-85	Indonesia : Bangladesh	2:0 (0:0)
21-03-85	Indonesia : India	2:1 (1:1)
23-03-85	Thailand : Bangladesh	3:0 (1:0)
26-03-85	Thailand : India	0:0
29-03-85	Thailand : Indonesia	0:1 (0:1)
30-03-85	Bangladesh : India	1:2 (1:1)
02-04-85	Bangladesh : Indonesia	2:1 (0:1)
05-04-85	Bangladesh : Thailand	1:0 (0:0)
06-04-85	India : Indonesia	1:1 (0:1)
09-04-85	India : Thailand	1:1 (1:0)
12-04-85	India : Bangladesh	2:1 (1:1)

Asia Phase 1 - 1st Round, Group 4A

	P	W	D	L	F	A	Pts
Hong Kong	6	5	1	0	19	2	11
China PR	6	4	1	1	23	2	9
Macao	6	2	0	4	4	15	4
Brunei Darussalam	6	0	0	6	2	29	0

17-02-85	Macao : Brunei Darussalam	2:0 (0:0)
17-02-85	Hong Kong : China PR	0:0
20-02-85	Macao : China PR	0:4 (0:1)
23-02-85	Hong Kong : Brunei Darussalam	8:0 (3:0)
26-02-85	China PR : Brunei Darussalam	8:0 (4:0)
01-03-85	Brunei Darussalam : China PR	0:4 (0:2)
06-04-85	Brunei Darussalam : Hong Kong	1:5 (1:3)
13-04-85	Brunei Darussalam : Macao	1:2 (0:0)
20-04-85	Macao : Hong Kong	0:2 (0:0)
04-05-85	Hong Kong : Macao	2:0 (0:0)

12-05-85	China PR : Macao	6:0 (3:0)
19-05-85	China PR : Hong Kong	1:2 (1:1)

Asia Phase 1 - 1st Round, Group 4B

	P	W	D	L	F	A	Pts
Japan	4	3	1	0	9	1	7
Korea DPR	4	1	2	1	3	2	4
Singapore	4	0	1	3	2	11	1

19-01-85	Singapore : Korea DPR	1:1 (1:0)
23-02-85	Singapore : Japan	1:3 (1:1)
21-03-85	Japan : Korea DPR	1:0 (1:0)
30-04-85	Korea DPR : Japan	0:0
18-05-85	Japan : Singapore	5:0 (0:0)
25-05-85	Korea DPR : Singapore	2:0 (2:0)

Asia Phase 2 - 2nd Round

	P	W	D	L	F	A	Pts
Korea Republic	2	2	0	0	6	1	4
Japan	2	2	0	0	5	1	4
Syria	2	1	1	0	2	1	3
United Arab Emirates	2	1	0	1	4	4	2
Iraq	2	1	0	1	4	4	2
Bahrain	2	0	1	1	1	2	1
Hong Kong	2	0	0	2	1	5	0
Indonesia	2	0	0	2	1	6	0

21-07-85	Korea Republic : Indonesia	2:0 (0:0)
30-07-85	Indonesia : Korea Republic	1:4 (0:3)
11-08-85	Japan : Hong Kong	3:0 (2:0)
06-09-85	Bahrain : Syria	1:1 (1:0)
20-09-85	Syria : Bahrain	1:0 (1:0)
20-09-85	United Arab Emirates : Iraq	2:3 (1:1)
22-09-85	Hong Kong : Japan	1:2 (0:1)
27-09-85	Iraq : United Arab Emirates	1:2 (0:1)

Asia Phase 3 - 3rd Round

	P	W	D	L	F	A	Pts
Korea Republic	2	2	0	0	3	1	4
Iraq	2	1	1	0	3	1	3
Syria	2	0	1	1	1	3	1
Japan	2	0	0	2	1	3	0

26-10-85	Japan : Korea Republic	1:2 (1:2)
03-11-85	Korea Republic : Japan	1:0 (0:0)
15-11-85	Syria : Iraq	0:0
29-11-85	Iraq : Syria	3:1 (1:0)

Europe - Group 1

	P	W	D	L	F	A	Pts
Poland	6	3	2	1	10	6	8
Belgium	6	3	2	1	7	3	8
Albania	6	1	2	3	6	9	4
Greece	6	1	2	3	5	10	4

17-10-84	Poland : Greece	3:1 (0:1)
17-10-84	Belgium : Albania	3:1 (0:0)
31-10-84	Poland : Albania	2:2 (1:0)
19-12-84	Greece : Belgium	0:0
22-12-84	Albania : Belgium	2:0 (0:0)
27-02-85	Greece : Albania	2:0 (2:0)
27-03-85	Belgium : Greece	2:0 (0:0)
01-05-85	Belgium : Poland	2:0 (1:0)
19-05-85	Greece : Poland	1:4 (0:1)
30-05-85	Albania : Poland	0:1 (0:1)
11-09-85	Poland : Belgium	0:0
30-10-85	Albania : Greece	1:1 (1:0)

Europe - Group 2

	P	W	D	L	F	A	Pts
Germany FR	8	5	2	1	22	9	12
Portugal	8	5	0	3	12	10	10
Sweden	8	4	1	3	14	9	9
Czech	8	3	2	3	11	12	8
Malta	8	0	1	7	6	25	1

23-05-84	Sweden : Malta	4:0 (2:0)
12-09-84	Sweden : Portugal	0:1 (0:0)
14-10-84	Portugal : Czechoslovakia	2:1 (1:1)
17-10-84	Germany FR : Sweden	2:0 (0:0)
31-10-84	Czechoslovakia : Malta	4:0 (2:0)
14-11-84	Portugal : Sweden	1:3 (1:3)
16-12-84	Malta : Germany FR	2:3 (1:1)
10-02-85	Malta : Portugal	1:3 (0:2)
24-02-85	Portugal : Germany FR	1:2 (0:2)
27-03-85	Germany FR : Malta	6:0 (5:0)
21-04-85	Malta : Czechoslovakia	0:0
30-04-85	Czechoslovakia : Germany FR	1:5 (0:4)
05-06-85	Sweden : Czechoslovakia	2:0 (0:0)
25-09-85	Sweden : Germany FR	2:2 (0:2)
25-09-85	Czechoslovakia : Portugal	1:0 (1:0)
12-10-85	Portugal : Malta	3:2 (1:0)
16-10-85	Czechoslovakia : Sweden	2:1 (1:1)
16-10-85	Germany FR : Portugal	0:1 (0:0)
17-11-85	Malta : Sweden	1:2 (0:1)
17-11-85	Germany FR : Czechoslovakia	2:2 (1:0)

Europe - Group 3

	P	W	D	L	F	A	Pts
England	8	4	4	0	21	2	12
N. Ireland	8	4	2	2	8	5	10
Romania	8	3	3	2	12	7	9
Finland	8	3	2	3	7	12	8
Turkey	8	0	1	7	2	24	1

27-05-84	Finland : Northern Ireland	1:0 (0:0)
12-09-84	Northern Ireland : Romania	3:2 (1:1)
17-10-84	England : Finland	5:0 (2:0)
31-10-84	Turkey : Finland	1:2 (1:1)
14-11-84	Northern Ireland : Finland	2:1 (1:1)
14-11-84	Turkey : England	0:8 (0:3)
27-02-85	Northern Ireland : England	0:1 (0:0)
03-04-85	Romania : Turkey	3:0 (3:0)
01-05-85	Northern Ireland : Turkey	2:0 (1:0)
01-05-85	Romania : England	0:0
22-05-85	Finland : England	1:1 (1:0)
06-06-85	Finland : Romania	1:1 (1:1)
28-08-85	Romania : Finland	2:0 (1:0)
11-09-85	Turkey : Northern Ireland	0:0
11-09-85	England : Romania	1:1 (1:0)
25-09-85	Finland : Turkey	1:0 (1:0)
16-10-85	England : Turkey	5:0 (4:0)
16-10-85	Romania : Northern Ireland	0:1 (0:1)
13-11-85	England : Northern Ireland	0:0
13-11-85	Turkey : Romania	1:3 (0:2)

Europe - Group 4

	P	W	D	L	F	A	Pts
France	8	5	1	2	15	4	11
Bulgaria	8	5	1	2	13	5	11
Germany DR	8	5	0	3	16	9	10
Yugoslavia	8	3	2	3	7	8	8
Luxembourg	8	0	0	8	2	27	0

29-09-84	Yugoslavia : Bulgaria	0:0
13-10-84	Luxembourg : France	0:4 (0:4)
20-10-84	Germany DR : Yugoslavia	2:3 (1:1)
17-11-84	Luxembourg : Germany DR	0:5 (0:0)

Date	Match	Score
21-11-84	France : Bulgaria	1:0 (0:0)
05-12-84	Bulgaria : Luxembourg	4:0 (2:0)
08-12-84	France : Germany DR	2:0 (1:0)
27-03-85	Yugoslavia : Luxembourg	1:0 (1:0)
03-04-85	Yugoslavia : France	0:0
06-04-85	Bulgaria : Germany DR	1:0 (0:0)
01-05-85	Luxembourg : Yugoslavia	0:1 (0:0)
02-05-85	Bulgaria : France	2:0 (1:0)
18-05-85	Germany DR : Luxembourg	3:1 (3:0)
01-06-85	Bulgaria : Yugoslavia	2:1 (1:1)
11-09-85	Germany DR : France	2:0 (0:0)
25-09-85	Luxembourg : Bulgaria	1:3 (0:3)
28-09-85	Yugoslavia : Germany DR	1:2 (0:0)
30-10-85	France : Luxembourg	6:0 (4:0)
16-11-85	Germany DR : Bulgaria	2:1 (2:1)
16-11-85	France : Yugoslavia	2:0 (1:0)

Europe - Group 5

	P	W	D	L	F	A	Pts
Hungary	6	5	0	1	12	4	10
Netherlands	6	3	1	2	11	5	7
Austria	6	3	1	2	9	8	7
Cyprus	6	0	0	6	3	18	0

Date	Match	Score
02-05-84	Cyprus : Austria	1:2 (0:1)
26-09-84	Hungary : Austria	3:1 (0:1)
17-10-84	Netherlands : Hungary	1:2 (1:1)
14-11-84	Austria : Netherlands	1:0 (1:0)
17-11-84	Cyprus : Hungary	1:2 (1:0)
23-12-84	Cyprus : Netherlands	0:1 (0:0)
27-02-85	Netherlands : Cyprus	7:1 (3:1)
03-04-85	Hungary : Cyprus	2:0 (0:0)
17-04-85	Austria : Hungary	0:3 (0:2)
01-05-85	Netherlands : Austria	1:1 (1:0)
07-05-85	Austria : Cyprus	4:0 (2:0)
14-05-85	Hungary : Netherlands	0:1 (0:0)

Europe - Group 1-5 Play-offs

	P	W	D	L	F	A	Pts
Netherlands	2	1	0	1	2	2	2
Belgium	2	1	0	1	2	2	2

Date	Match	Score
16-10-85	Belgium : Netherlands	1:0 (1:0)
20-11-85	Netherlands : Belgium	2:1 (0:0)

Europe - Group 6

	P	W	D	L	F	A	Pts
Denmark	8	5	1	2	17	6	11
USSR	8	4	2	2	13	8	10
Switzerland	8	2	4	2	5	10	8
Ireland Rep	8	2	2	4	5	10	6
Norway	8	1	3	4	4	10	5

Date	Match	Score
12-09-84	Norway : Switzerland	0:1 (0:1)
12-09-84	Ireland Republic : USSR	1:0 (0:0)
26-09-84	Denmark : Norway	1:0 (0:0)
10-10-84	Norway : USSR	1:1 (0:0)
17-10-84	Norway : Ireland Republic	1:0 (1:0)
17-10-84	Switzerland : Denmark	1:0 (1:0)
14-11-84	Denmark : Ireland Republic	3:0 (1:0)
17-04-85	Switzerland : USSR	2:2 (1:1)
01-05-85	Ireland Republic : Norway	0:0
02-05-85	USSR : Switzerland	4:0 (4:0)
02-06-85	Ireland Republic : Switzerland	3:0 (2:0)
05-06-85	Denmark : USSR	4:2 (2:1)
11-09-85	Switzerland : Ireland Republic	0:0
25-09-85	USSR : Denmark	1:0 (0:0)
09-10-85	Denmark : Switzerland	0:0
16-10-85	Norway : Denmark	1:5 (1:0)
16-10-85	USSR : Ireland Republic	2:0 (0:0)

Date	Match	Score
30-10-85	USSR : Norway	1:0 (0:0)
13-11-85	Switzerland : Norway	1:1 (0:1)
13-11-85	Ireland Republic : Denmark	1:4 (1:1)

Europe - Group 7

	P	W	D	L	F	A	Pts
Spain	6	4	0	2	9	8	8
Scotland	6	3	1	2	8	4	7
Wales	6	3	1	2	7	6	7
Iceland	6	1	0	5	4	10	2

Date	Match	Score
12-09-84	Iceland : Wales	1:0 (0:0)
17-10-84	Spain : Wales	3:0 (1:0)
17-10-84	Scotland : Iceland	3:0 (2:0)
14-11-84	Scotland : Spain	3:1 (2:0)
14-11-84	Wales : Iceland	2:1 (1:0)
27-02-85	Spain : Scotland	1:0 (0:0)
27-03-85	Scotland : Wales	0:1 (0:1)
30-04-85	Wales : Spain	3:0 (1:0)
28-05-85	Iceland : Scotland	0:1 (0:0)
12-06-85	Iceland : Spain	1:2 (1:0)
10-09-85	Wales : Scotland	1:1 (1:0)
25-09-85	Spain : Iceland	2:1 (1:1)

Caribbean/North/Cent. America - 1st Round

	P	W	D	L	F	A	Pts
El Salvador	2	2	0	0	8	0	4
Honduras	2	2	0	0	4	0	4
United States	2	1	1	0	4	0	3
Surinam	2	1	1	0	2	1	3
Haiti	2	1	0	1	5	2	2
Antigua and Barbuda	2	1	0	1	2	5	2
Guyana	2	0	1	1	1	2	1
Netherlands Antilles	2	0	1	1	0	4	1
Panama	2	0	0	2	0	4	0
Puerto Rico	2	0	0	2	0	8	0

Date	Match	Score
15-06-84	Panama : Honduras	0:3 (0:2)
24-06-84	Honduras : Panama	1:0 (0:0)
29-07-84	El Salvador : Puerto Rico	5:0 (4:0)
04-08-84	Antigua and Barbuda : Haiti	0:4 (0:0)
05-08-84	Puerto Rico : El Salvador	0:3 (0:2)
07-08-84	Haiti : Antigua and Barbuda	1:2 (1:1)
15-08-84	Surinam : Guyana	1:0 (1:0)
29-08-84	Guyana : Surinam	1:1 (1:0)
29-09-84	Netherlands Antilles : USA	0:0
06-10-84	USA : Netherlands Antilles	4:0 (0:0)

Caribbean/North/Cent. America - 2nd Round, Group 1

	P	W	D	L	F	A	Pts
Honduras	4	2	2	0	5	3	6
El Salvador	4	2	1	1	7	2	5
Surinam	4	0	1	3	2	9	1

Date	Match	Score
24-02-85	Surinam : El Salvador	0:3 (0:1)
27-02-85	El Salvador : Surinam	3:0 (0:0)
03-03-85	Surinam : Honduras	1:1 (1:1)
06-03-85	Honduras : Surinam	2:1 (1:0)
10-03-85	El Salvador : Honduras	1:2 (0:1)
14-03-85	Honduras : El Salvador	0:0

Caribbean/North/Cent. America - 2nd Round, Group 2

	P	W	D	L	F	A	Pts
Canada	4	3	1	0	7	2	7
Guatemala	4	2	1	1	7	3	5
Haiti	4	0	0	4	0	9	0

Date	Match	Score
13-04-85	Canada : Haiti	2:0 (2:0)
20-04-85	Canada : Guatemala	2:1 (2:0)
26-04-85	Haiti : Guatemala	0:1 (0:0)
05-05-85	Guatemala : Canada	1:1 (0:1)
08-05-85	Haiti : Canada	0:2 (0:1)
15-05-85	Guatemala : Haiti	4:0 (1:0)

Caribbean/North/Cent. America - 2nd Round, Group 3

	P	W	D	L	F	A	Pts
Costa Rica	4	2	2	0	6	2	6
United States	4	2	1	1	4	3	5
Trinidad & Tobago	4	0	1	3	2	7	1

Date	Match	Score
24-04-85	Trinidad & Tobago : Costa Rica	0:3 (0:1)
28-04-85	Costa Rica : Trinidad & Tobago	1:1 (0:1)
15-05-85	Trinidad & Tobago : USA	1:2 (1:1)
19-05-85	USA : Trinidad & Tobago	1:0 (1:0)
26-05-85	Costa Rica : USA	1:1 (1:1)
31-05-85	United States : Costa Rica	0:1 (0:0)

Caribbean/North/Cent. America - 3rd Round

	P	W	D	L	F	A	Pts
Canada	4	2	2	0	4	2	6
Honduras	4	1	1	2	6	6	3
Costa Rica	4	0	3	1	4	6	3

Date	Match	Score
11-08-85	Costa Rica : Honduras	2:2 (1:2)
17-08-85	Canada : Costa Rica	1:1 (0:1)
25-08-85	Honduras : Canada	0:1 (0:0)
01-09-85	Costa Rica : Canada	0:0
08-09-85	Honduras : Costa Rica	3:1 (1:1)
14-09-85	Canada : Honduras	2:1 (1:0)

Oceania - Group Matches

	P	W	D	L	F	A	Pts
Australia	6	4	2	0	20	2	10
Israel	6	3	1	2	17	6	7
New Zealand	6	3	1	2	13	7	7
Chinese Taipei	6	0	0	6	1	36	0

Date	Match	Score
03-09-85	Israel : Chinese Taipei	6:0 (3:0)
08-09-85	Chinese Taipei : Israel	0:5 (0:2)
Both matches played in Tel Aviv		
21-09-85	New Zealand : Australia	0:0
05-10-85	New Zealand : Chinese Taipei	5:1 (3:1)
08-10-85	Israel : Australia	1:2 (0:0)
12-10-85	Chinese Taipei : New Zealand	0:5 (0:2)
Match played in Christchurch		
20-10-85	Australia : Israel	1:1 (1:0)
23-10-85	AAustralia : Chinese Taipei	7:0 (2:0)
26-10-85	New Zealand : Israel	3:1 (2:1)
27-10-85	Chinese Taipei : Australia	0:8 (0:1)
Match played in Sydney		
03-11-85	Australia : New Zealand	2:0 (1:0)
10-11-85	Israel : New Zealand	3:0 (0:0)

OFC/UEFA Play-off

	P	W	D	L	F	A	Pts
Scotland	2	1	1	0	2	0	3
Australia	2	0	1	1	0	2	1

20-11-85	Scotland : Australia	2:0 (0:0)
04-12-85	Australia : Scotland	0:0

South America - Group 1

	P	W	D	L	F	A	Pts
Argentina	6	4	1	1	12	6	9
Peru	6	3	2	1	8	4	8
Colombia	6	2	2	2	6	6	6
Venezuela	6	0	1	5	5	15	1

26-05-85	Venezuela : Argentina	2:3 (1:2)
26-05-85	Colombia : Peru	1:0 (1:0)
02-06-85	Venezuela : Peru	0:1 (0:0)
02-06-85	Colombia : Argentina	1:3 (0:1)
09-06-85	Peru : Colombia	0:0
09-06-85	Argentina : Venezuela	3:0 (1:0)
16-06-85	Argentina : Colombia	1:0 (1:0)
16-06-85	Peru : Venezuela	4:1 (2:1)
23-06-85	Peru : Argentina	1:0 (1:0)
23-06-85	Venezuela : Colombia	2:2 (1:1)
30-06-85	Argentina : Peru	2:2 (1:2)
30-06-85	Colombia : Venezuela	2:0 (2:0)

South America - Group 2

	P	W	D	L	F	A	Pts
Uruguay	4	3	0	1	6	4	6
Chile	4	2	1	1	10	5	5
Ecuador	4	0	1	3	4	11	1

03-03-85	Ecuador : Chile	1:1 (1:1)
10-03-85	Uruguay : Ecuador	2:1 (1:0)
17-03-85	Chile : Ecuador	6:2 (4:2)
24-03-85	Chile : Uruguay	2:0 (1:0)
31-03-85	Ecuador : Uruguay	0:2 (0:0)
07-04-85	Uruguay : Chile	2:1 (1:1)

South America - Group 3

	P	W	D	L	F	A	Pts
Brazil	4	2	2	0	6	2	6
Paraguay	4	1	2	1	5	4	4
Bolivia	4	0	2	2	2	7	2

26-05-85	Bolivia : Paraguay	1:1 (1:0)
02-06-85	Bolivia : Brazil	0:2 (0:0)
09-06-85	Paraguay : Bolivia	3:0 (2:0)
16-06-85	Paraguay : Brazil	0:2 (0:1)
23-06-85	Brazil : Paraguay	1:1 (1:1)
30-06-85	Brazil : Bolivia	1:1 (1:0)

South America - 2nd Round

	P	W	D	L	F	A	Pts
Chile	2	2	0	0	5	2	4
Paraguay	2	1	0	1	4	2	2
Colombia	2	1	0	1	2	4	2
Peru	2	0	0	2	2	5	0

27-10-85	Chile : Peru	4:2 (3:1)
27-10-85	Paraguay : Colombia	3:0 (1:0)
03-11-85	Colombia : Paraguay	2:1 (0:0)
03-11-85	Peru : Chile	0:1 (0:0)

South America - 3rd Round

	P	W	D	L	F	A	Pts
Paraguay	2	1	1	0	5	2	3
Chile	2	0	1	1	2	5	1

10-11-85	Paraguay : Chile	3:0 (1:0)
17-11-85	Chile : Paraguay	2:2 (1:2)

Chapter 16

Freedom, Change and the Tears of a Clown Prince
The Italian World Cup, 1990

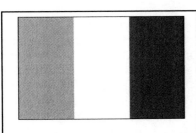

Italy 1990

Winners: West Germany

Runners-up: Argentina

3rd Place: Italy

4th Place: England

Total Attendance: 2,514,962

Number of Matches: 52

As the world spun into the final decade of the century, technology was fast turning the planet into one vast market place - "globalization" was the new economic order. The Asian Tigers succeeded in filling homes with electrical goods and mobile phones the size of house bricks were the plaything of those who could afford them. Sadam Hussain, attempting to take back land he believed belonged to Iraq, marched his troops into neighbouring Kuwait and was thrown out again by a US-led coalition. It was not Kuwait that was being protected, but the black gold under its soil. Ironically, once Saddam's army was back over the border, the coalition stopped its pursuit and the dictator still sits in his palace threatening disruption. The most monumental of the world's changes had started the year before in Eastern Europe. The Berlin Wall had come down, East and West Germany were re-united after the dark days of Communism and the new democracies on the Danube opened their doors to the west and its conglomerates. In Poland Lech Walesa, the leader of Solidarity, was released from prison and became the country's leader. Another sign of the times came when McDonalds moved into Moscow in 1990. Yet there was a cost. The Romanians reacted to years of repression by executing former leader, Nicolae Ceausescu, and both Yugoslavia and the USSR began to split into their component parts. In Peru, Fujimori rode into Lima on a tractor bringing democracy and on 11th February at around 3.00pm, Nelson Mandela was released from captivity after 27 years in jail - Apartheid was also coming to an end.

In the United Kingdom hard times were around the corner. Disastrously, the country was to enter the European Exchange Rate Mechanism and its deepest recession since the World Cup began. People took to the streets in protest at the injustice of the Poll Tax, riots followed, cars and buildings were burnt and the police routed. It was also the end for Margaret Thatcher, dumped by the Conservative Party in November. Also having a riot were the youth in the Rave phenomenon. After the mechanized pop of the late 1980s had dulled down the charts, the new craze hit the scene. In the dark corners of public houses, the urban pop guerrilla found out about the night's rave, tickets would be purchased and by midnight a field in the local area would be jumping to the sound of Acid House. The nation's youth bopped until they dropped fuelled by the music and whatever illicit substance they could lay their hands on. Farmers, residents and police alike suffered many sleepless nights.

In the USA, George Bush replaced Ronald Reagan, Panama was invaded yet again and the rest of the world was subjected to Teenage Mutant Ninja Turtles and Vanilla Ice. The Australians were filling our airways with numerous sunny soap operas and Kylie Minogue and Jason Donovan were never far from our ears. The world said goodbye to Jim Henson, Terry Thomas and Max Wall. Rita said goodbye to Alan Bradley in Coronation Street and the City said farewell to the flash money-obsessed 20-somethings known as "the Yuppie".

Four countries applied to host the 1990 World Cup finals. By the time the decision was made in May 1984, England and Greece had withdrawn their bids leaving only Italy and the Soviet Union in the running. Politically, the latter had done much to ruin its international prestige. The country's ageing and increasingly infirm leadership was losing its ability to control and direct affairs, and was becoming steadily more intractable and hardline. The 1979 invasion of Afghanistan had been widely condemned and in 1983 it had shot sown a South Korean passenger airliner that had accidentally strayed into Soviet airspace, killing all the passengers on board. It provided ample ammunition for the slick propaganda machine of rabidly anti-Soviet Ronald Reagan, who leapt on any opportunity to damage the standing of his ideological enemy. When the Soviets announced they were boycotting the 1984 Los Angeles Olympics, in retaliation for Washington's boycott of the 1980 Moscow Olympics, it was one move too many. FIFA announced that Italy was to become the second country to be given another World Cup.

This was the first tournament for which the number of countries applying to enter fell. Many smaller nations, opting for realism rather than optimism, decided that they had no chance of making the finals and that it was cheaper simply not to enter. With only two places on offer for both the African and Asian regions, their attitude was understandable. Then, of the 109 who did enter, Bahrain, India, Lesotho, Rwanda, South Yemen and Togo subsequently withdrew and it left 102 countries to compete for the 22 places on offer.

In this series, the CONCACAF region provided the first game when Trinidad and Tobago secured a 4-0 away win against Guyana in Georgetown on 17th April 1988. It was a first round game, a round in which the region's lesser nations were paired together in two-legged knock-outs to decide out which would go through to meet the stronger sides in the second round. This was also a round of two-legged knock-outs from which emerged five teams to go into Round Three, organized as a league. Mexico had been one of the favourites to qualify for Italy, but had made a blunder in fielding over-age players in the under-20 World Youth Cup in 1988. For this, they had been banned from international competition for two years, including the 1988 Seoul Olympics and the 1990 World Cup. It left the CONCACAF final group more open than had been expected and of the five teams involved, Costa Rica, Trinidad and Tobago and the USA established themselves as clear front runners. The first to complete their quota of eight games was Costa Rica, amassing 11 points from five wins and a draw. It was enough to secure top spot, but the second place was not determined until the group's final game, won by the USA by a single goal to take them to the finals for the first time since 1950. Unusually, Trinidad and Tobago had played 12 games, including the first and last of the qualifying tournament.

Guatemala and El Salvador were the other two teams to make it into the third round league, but "due to the domestic situation" in El Salvador, the games which had been scheduled to be played in November, were cancelled. The problem was a flare up in that country's long-running civil war. The left-wing, Marxist guerrilla Farbundo Marti's National Liberation Front mounted another offensive aimed at overthrowing the US-backed right-wing administration of president Alfredo Cristiani. It was a particularly brutal conflict, in which acts of terrorism perpetuated by the guerrillas were countered by state-sponsored atrocities committed by the so-called death squads, and between them they were responsible for the deaths of some 75,000 people. It was said that this latest round of violence was the result of the arrival in guerrilla hands of 1,500 AK47 rifles, supposedly a gift from Cuba's Communist leader, Fidel Castro.

Politics had frequently intervened to disrupt World Cup competitions, but only occasionally had blatant cheating done so. One of the worst instances of such conduct was witnessed in the qualifying matches in South America's Group Three. In this, Venezuela had proved to be the poor relations, losing all four of their games and conceding 17 goals in the process. The group's all-important game was its last between Brazil and Chile, played in Río on 3rd September 1989. They went into the match on equal points, having each won two games and having drawn against each other. Goal difference meant that Chile had to win by two goals to qualify. It was going Brazil's way, with the home team winning 1-0 when, in the 66th minute, a spectator threw a flare onto the pitch. It landed in the Chilean goalmouth and the goalkeeper, Roberto Rojas, collapsed, writhing in agony and claiming to have been injured and blinded by the missile. The Chilean medical staff who rushed out to administer treatment agreed that Rojas was too badly shaken to continue the game, a position upheld by Chilean FA officials. He was carried off bleeding and the game was abandoned. Only later did TV coverage reveal that the flare had landed away from the goalkeeper, that it had not hit him and that it had all been a sham, an attempt to get Brazil disqualified. His wound had been self-inflicted. Rojas was subsequently banned for life, along with several of the officials who had connived in his deceit. The game was awarded as a 2-0 victory to Brazil, Chile's FA was fined $100,000 and its team banned from the 1990 and 1994 World Cups. Uruguay, who won through from Group One, joined Argentina and Brazil. Colombia came top of Group Two, but it only secured them the right to meet the winner of the Oceania region in a two-legged play-off for a place in the finals. Thus they met Israel and a 1-0 victory in Bogotá was followed by a goalless away draw to ensure that South America had four teams in the finals.

The European qualifying tournament was organized along lines similar to those used for the 1986 World Cup. The entrants were divided into seven groups, four of which sent two teams to the finals and three of which sent

Freedom, Change and the Tears of a Clown Prince - Italy 1990

The "Eat My Own Words" Award for 1990 goes to...

Alex Montgomery of the Sun for his comments on England's "dismal" 1-1 draw in a warm-up match with Tunisia. "Bobby Robson has exactly one week to stop this humiliation turning into a World Cup disaster. To do this he must cut off what, to him, will be the equivalent of his right arm and axe Terry Butcher for the opening game against the Republic of Ireland." The back page of the paper was ringed with the words "World Cup Crisis". The appalling pre-tournament "witch hunt" for Butcher was due in part to an accusation that he had head butted Fahed Dermeich in the game. It was little wonder the England team stopped talking to the press altogether.

one. Of these three groups, the best two runners up also went through to make up Europe's complement of 14 teams. There were no major surprises, though France and Poland both failed to get through. The Poles had qualified for the previous four tournaments and the French, now under the stewardship of Michel Platini, missed out by only a single point. Their team was being rebuilt and could look back to a 1-1 draw with Cyprus in Nicosia was the result that did the damage, giving them third place in the group behind Yugoslavia and Scotland, who set a British record for their fifth successive visit to the finals. The point gained by Cyprus against France was the only one gained from eight matches.

Cyprus may have lost seven games, but they were not Europe's leakiest defence. Not for the first time this dubious distinction fell to Luxembourg, who conceded 22 goals in their campaign of seven defeats and a draw. The highest winning margin from the European rounds was Denmark's 7-1 defeat of Greece in Copenhagen in May 1989. The Danes, though, despite once again producing some fine football, failed to make it to Italy. They finished second in Group One, behind Romania, but did not have a goal difference good enough to see them through as one of the two best placed runners up. These two spots were taken by England, the only team to qualify without conceding a goal, and West Germany, who came second to Holland in Group Four. The Germans' first goal in their 2-1 victory over Wales in Cologne in November 1989, scored by Rudi Völler was that country's 250th World Cup goal, the first time that that tally had been reached. One new comer to the finals from Europe was Eire, whose 3-0 victory over neighbours, Northern Ireland, in October 1989 gave them the points they needed, though the Irish made doubly sure with a 2-0 victory in Malta a month later. It had been their 13th tilt at the tournament, going back to 1933.

Disaster marred the African qualifying tournament. In this, the weaker teams played each other in a first round of two-legged knock-outs, to determine which would progress to meet the other entrants in the second round. The 15 teams who got this far were divided into four groups, each of which sent one country into the third and final round where they were paired off to play over two legs, with the two winners going to Italy. The tragedy occurred in the Group C match between Nigeria and Angola in Lagos on 12th August 1989. The game attracted much local interest and such were the crowds that thronged to see it that the 80,000 capacity was exceeded by some 20,000. The resulting crush killed seven fans and 24 year old Nigerian international, Sam Okwaraji, who collapsed and died. The Nigerians won the game 1-0, but lost their final group game against Cameroon by the same margin. It left Cameroon as group champions and put them into the third round, where two victories over Tunisia took them to the finals. The other final round qualifier pitted Egypt against Algeria and a 1-0 victory in Cairo, followed by a goalless draw, was sufficient to steer the Egyptians to the finals for the first time since 1934.

The Asian entrants were divided into six groups, organized on roughly geographical lines, each group sending one team to the second round to play each other in a group final. The "whipping boys" of the first round and of the whole tournament were Nepal, who conceded 28 goals in six games, including a 9-0 defeat by South Korea in Seoul and a 7-0 away defeat by Singapore. It was Nepal's second entry into the World Cup and so far their ten games had seen them let in 37 goals, whilst they had yet to score.

Possibly the most unfortunate team not to qualify was China, especially in view of their near miss and goal scoring exploits in the previous tournament. The Chinese must have felt that they were in with a real chance when they qualified for the second round out of Group Five, albeit on goal difference over Iran. South Korea was the strongest team in the final group and became its eventual winners, but when China defeated North Korea in October 1989 and the United Arab Emirates could only draw with South Korea a few days later, it meant that the second spot would go to China if they could defeat Qatar in their final match. It took place in Singapore on 28th October 1989 and, with four minutes to go, the Chinese had only to hold on to their 1-0 lead. Inexplicably, they conceded two late goals and could only manage fourth place in the group, behind Qatar. The second place was taken by the UAE, who therefore qualified for their first appearance in the finals.

The opening ceremony of Italy '90 took place on 8th June in Milan's imposing Giuseppe Meazza Stadium, the home of Inter-Milan. It was a grand affair, attended by over 73,000 fans and watched by an estimated TV audience of 500 million, and featured a parade of women in the national costumes of the 24 finalists. Its most remarkable feature, though, was the singing of Luciano Pavarotti, beamed to the ground from Milan's famous opera house, La Scala. This transmission had been a bold and moving innovation, but sadly the football in the tournament that followed rarely raised itself to such lofty heights. In terms of the quality of football, the 1990 World Cup was the worst ever, and the elements that were responsible for the degeneration could be easily detected in the opening game. The unpleasant aftertaste, though, was quickly disguised by the great shock produced by the result.

The expectation was that Argentina would destroy Cameroon. Yet, the Africans were the only country in Italy to have never been beaten in the finals and, whilst this record came from only one previous appearance, it still stood and they were to show the same doughty determination and lack of respect as they had in 1982. Their play contained two notable elements: fast, bold and imaginative attack, and bruising defence. Both were apparent in equal measure in the opening phase of play, during which Benjamin Massing was booked in the ninth minute for clattering Maradona from behind and Victor Akem Ndip soon after for a foul that left stud marks on the same player's shoulder. They also had the best of the play, though Argentina should have taken the lead in the 16th minute, when an unmarked José Basualdo headed wide in front of goal. Poor shooting accounted for the failure of Cameroon to go ahead themselves. Following a goalless first half, the fireworks started to go off in the second, beginning in the 60th minute with the sending off of André Kana Biyik for bringing down substitute Claudio Caniggia. Its effect was to stir the Cameroon players up and five minutes later they took the unlikeliest of leads. Pumpido was left uncovered at a cross, but François Oman Biyik's "harmless-looking header from the edge of the goal area" should have caused him no problems. Instead, it screwed through the goalkeeper's hands and into the net. It gave the Argentinians real distress and they were unable to respond. Cameroon continued to press, even after Massing had been sent off for a nasty challenge on Caniggia and they had been reduced to nine men. They held on for one of the most amazing victories in World Cup history.

A doctor on a "free love" commune in India had an unusual recommendation to avoid player violence. "Let everyone close their eyes and then scream and shout without touching each other for 10 minutes to release all their pent-up violence," he prescribed.

Before the tournament started, it was rumoured that Maradona was suffering from in-growing toenails. He had a special carbon protector fitted over his infected toe so he could play through the pain.

FIFA took up a very firm stance in their drive to rid the game of foul play. A player could be fined up to £12,000 for two yellow cards or a sending off. A second booking in group games could cost £2,000, £4,000 in the second round and £6,000 from the semi-finals onward. A red card could double the amount. Players from Cameroon or Costa Rica had probably never seen such amounts of money.

Cameroon's Russian manager, Valeri Napomniachi, spoke to his team via an interpreter.

The Pope had to cut short a visit to Italian school children when he was told the Italy-Austria match was about to start and the children wanted to see it. Its 26 million viewers was the highest ever audience for a programme broadcast in Italy. When Italy played the USA the Pope had to bring forward the yearly Corpus Domini by an hour.

Freedom, Change and the Tears of a Clown Prince - Italy 1990

The referee that day was highly criticized for what some commentators took to be an over-zealous use of the sanctions available to him. Yet, he was only following orders. At long last, FIFA had recognized the malaise that had crept into the game, the violence and the cynicism and had belatedly decided to do something about it. Referees had been instructed to clamp down on unruly players and the effect was a clash between players and officials that resulted in a record 16 players dismissed and 164 cautioned. Such were the depths to which things had fallen.

The hosts came into action the next day with a match against Austria in Rome's Olympic Stadium. There was much expected of this Italy team and pundits believed they could do well if they could garner the right mental approach. They began in some style. "Seldom, if ever, has a nation staging the World Cup given such an impressive opening display", wrote one reporter. The Italians were full of mobility and invention in midfield, were slick and speedy up front and solid at the rear. The chances they created were legion, but one after another were squandered in one of the greatest acts of profligacy seen at this level. Indeed, Napoli's Andrea Carnevale "kept dropping chances like a child with a melting ice-cream on a hot day." Their fans had to wait until the 78th minute before their team converted superiority into a score. Gianluca Vialli crossed the ball and "Toto" Schillaci took the game with a "solid, finely directed header."

The opening game in Group B had produced a shock of earthquake proportions. The result of the group's second game was also unexpected and saw the Soviet Union go down to Romania, a team not much fancied before the tournament. Based on previous form, the Soviets were expected to be one of the stronger sides, but they failed to live up the achievements of 1986. The Romanians, on the other hand, played with a carefree zest that might be expected from the players of country relieved at their recent release from a brutal dictatorship. "Back-heeling and flicking their way round the Stadia San Nicola, this was a team that really looked the part", though it was not until late in the first half that they got the upper hand. Play had been even up to then and the Soviets had been denied the lead on several occasions by a string of fine saves from Silviu Lung in the goal. Yet, the Romanians were always more imaginative and, in the 41st minute, Marius Lacatus sent a "ripping shot between keeper and post" to take the lead. The football was end-to-end in the second half, but Romania always looked in charge and they scored a second with a 54th minute penalty awarded for a hand ball that seemed to have been committed outside the area. Lacatus was unconcerned by such niceties. He tucked the ball away to give his team their first victory in the finals for 20 years.

The third game that day featured Colombia against the United Arab Emirates. Before the tournament, the UAE's Brazilian coach, Carlos Alberto Parreira had declared that it had been "a miracle that we have qualified", and they were lucky to keep Colombia to a 2-0 final score. The South Americans had had their preparations disrupted by the country's rising tide of drug-related violence. The league programme had been suspended because of a spate of murders, kidnappings and death threats, and coach Francisco Maturana had himself been threatened by drug gangs. Nevertheless, the Colombians had some very talented individuals and only a series of sometimes embarrassing misses prevented them from taking the lead they deserved. In fact, their profligacy was almost punished just before half-time when Ali Thani Jumaa raced onto Andreas Escobar's careless back pass and Higuita, the goalkeeper, had to rush out to block his effort. Similarly, Adnan Khamees Al Talyani broke through and almost scored early in the second half, but Higuita dived at his feet to save the situation. Realism was restored to the proceedings in the 50th minute when "a clever one-two by Leonel Alvarez" sprung the offside trap, enabling him to send over the cross that Bernardo Redin headed in strongly and Carlos Valderrama made the result secure in the 87th minute with a goal coming at the end of a dinking solo run.

When the USA made their appearance on 10th June they were found to be "short of technical skill and tactically naive", and they were made to pay by a more professional Czechoslovakia. The Americans had a good opening quarter of an hour, went behind in the 26th minute and then fell apart. Czechoslovakia's first goal came when Tomás Skuhravy sprinted ahead of a static defence to get onto Lubomir Moravcik's through ball and finish "nothing less than comfortably." Michael Bílek, Czechoslovakia's Footballer of the Year, added a second from the penalty spot, after Ivan Hasek had been tripped, and Hasek headed in a corner five minutes into the second half to make it 3-0. A controversial decision then harmed the American cause fatally. Eric Wynalda was sent off for pushing one of the Czechs at a throw in, though he claimed that the Czech had stamped on his foot. Reduced to ten men, the Americans produced their best football of the match and in the 53rd minute Paul Caligiuri pulled a goal back, though their purple patch did not last long. Skuhravy netted his second 15 minutes later and another penalty ought to have made the score 5-1. However, Tony Meola saved Bílek's shot and it was not until injury time that Milan Luhovy's strike brought that final scoreline.

Franz Beckenbauer reckoned that his West German squad was the finest set of players he had ever worked with and they showed why when they came across Yugoslavia in Group D's second game. They were their usual slow starters and allowed the Yugoslavs plenty of possession in the opening phase of play, but they took control from the instant Lothar Matthäus gave them a 28th minute lead. The captain latched on to Stefan Reuter's "top spin chip" and drilled his shot angrily past the goalkeeper. It seemed to relieve them of their nerves and they began to mount the pressure that produced their second goal, scored when Jürgen Klinsmann headed in Andreas Brehme's cross. Davor Jozic, Yugoslavia's Cesena-based striker, outjumped Klinsmann in the 55th minute to reduce the deficit, but the goal came against the flow of play and eight minutes later Matthäus's solo run took him past three defenders before he netted with a 20 yard shot. Germany's fourth and final goal came from a goalkeeping error. Brehme's shot should have presented no worries for Tomislav Ivkovic, but the keeper fumbled and juggled the ball over his shoulder into the path of Rudi Völler. It had been a thoroughly convincing performance from the Germans and it delighted the local Inter-Milan fans, cheering their heroes Klinsmann and Brehme.

The competition in Group C began that day with a game between Brazil and Sweden. The style of play adopted by coach, Sebastião Lazaroni, had a greater degree of rigidity and discipline than previous Brazilian teams had employed and had met with criticism at home. "He has limited our characteristic flair", was the verdict of Socrates and this new approach was in clear evidence in the opening exchanges against the Swedes. They were cautious and hesitant and it suited the Swedes, whose own game plan was reliance on defence to contain the Brazilians. It worked for long periods of the game, but attempting to contain Brazil's natural instincts can be a dangerous ploy and in the 40th minute Sweden came unstuck. A magnificent through pass from Branco sent Careca on his way, he feinted to send keeper Thomas Ravelli the wrong way and planted the ball into an empty net for a half-time lead. In the first minutes of the second Tomas Brolin came close to equalizing, but Brazil were the next to register. "Muller ripped through to the line, pulled the ball back and another feint by Careca... left him with an open goal", again. The Swedes now had to go all out and the final phase of the match was frantic as they launched attack after attack. They pulled one back, when Brolin, "twisting past a slowly reacting Mozer, scored low in the corner", but it was all they got.

The tournament was only three days old and had already thrown up surprises. On the fourth it provided another of mighty proportions. In Group C, Scotland took on Costa Rica in Genoa and, despite controlling the vast majority of play, were unable to find the net. In the first half, "with Aitken in inspirational mood and McCall impressively busy", the flow of the game was virtually all one way. The Costa Ricans had one decent chance, in the sixth minute, when Juan Cayasso slipped past Alex McLeish and shot narrowly wide, but after that the Scots were hardly troubled. They were plagued by a combination of bad luck and a lack of imagination that saw every opportunity spurned. Five minutes before half-time, Roy Aitken chipped the ball into the area, Mo Johnston headed

The USA players were so well mannered, they addressed referees as "Sir".

Before the tournament, Franz Beckenbauer said: "Winning the World Cup means nothing to me. For me personally this World Cup has no importance but I want it for the team."

Sweden's Klaus Ingusson was a lumberjack.

down to Richard Gough and the Rangers man shot powerfully, only to see a superb fingertip save from Gabelo Conajo deny his effort. The half finished scoreless, but the Scots paid dearly for their lack of firepower four minutes after the restart. In a rare Central American attack, a back-heel from Claudio Jara took out Scotland's defence and left Cayasso with a chance he could not miss. Jim Leighton managed to get a hand to the ball, but could not keep it out. Yet again in a World Cup game, the Scots were forced into desperate attack against inferior opposition and yet again they were unable to make superiority pay. As manager, Andy Roxburgh, said after another humiliation, his team "hammered into them non-stop, we just could not finish."

The other two representatives from the British Isles were in action that night, when they met each other in Caligiuri in Sardinia. The match took place in dreadful conditions of torrential rain and high winds, and it made playing football very difficult. Neither team was able to produce their best form. England went in front in the eighth minute, when Chris Waddle, then with Marseille, crossed the ball and Tottenham's Gary Lineker chested it down and guided it into the net with an out-stretched leg that just made contact. It was only the third goal that the Irish had conceded in 14 internationals. Thereafter, England became "disjointed and unconvincing", as the quality of the game deteriorated. The Irish were just as purposeless in a game that swirled in the wind. England's next best chance came on the hour after Waddle collided with Blackburn's Kevin Moran, giving rise to a half decent penalty shout that the referee would have nothing to do with. With no one looking like scoring again, the England manager sent on Steve McMahon to try to tighten things at the back. However, in the 70th minute, when the Liverpool man "had scarcely shaken the nerves out of his legs", he lost control of the ball on the edge of the area. Kevin Sheedy pounced and equalized with a left foot shot. It was an unfortunate climax to Peter Shilton's 119th international, but gave the Irish "a great 1-1 win", as they later described it. Bobby Robson was less up beat. Referring to his substitution, he said: "I sent him on to save the game. Instead, he cost us it."

There were no other worldly experiences when Belgium took on South Korea in Group E's opening game on 12th June. As the reporter from the Times said of the Koreans: "They began the match with a huddle to demonstrate their solidarity, and instantly fell apart under a colossal initial hammering." They were quickly thrust back on improvized defence as in the initial ten minutes, first Marc Degryse hit the post and then Enzo Scifo forced a marvellous reflex save out of Choi In-young. With Belgium pressing heavily, the Koreans relied on breaks as their principle hope of taking something from the game, and the remarkable thing was not that the Belgians failed to score, but that the Koreans kept them out so long. It was a battered, though valiant South Korea who trudged in after a goalless first half. However, they could not be expected to hold out indefinitely and they were prized open eight minutes after the restart. A long through pass from Scifo to Degryse enticed the goalkeeper out to ward away the danger and he was beaten with "one of the highest lobs seen in serious football." It was heartbreaking for the Koreans, but they could not find a reply and in the 64th minute, Michel De Wolf "hit a straight-forward blaster" to take the game 2-0. For the Belgians it had been workmanlike; for the Koreans, a minor success.

The Group F game played that day witnesses another great shock as Egypt "handed out a lesson to the acknowledged masters of improvisation and flair." The Dutch were poor that day, though to apportion this as the sole reason for the result would be to denigrate the Egyptians. They were well organized, skilful, much more willing to take risks than their opponents and they created by far the better chances. Two of the game's biggest names, Ruud Gullit and Marco Van Basten had only one strike apiece in the first 45 minutes of play. The goalless first half was a great credit to Egypt and they were unlucky to concede the lead in the 59th minute. Against the run of play, Van Basten crossed, Frank Rijkaard miskicked and the ball fell to Willem Kieft, who "stabbed home a thoroughly ill-deserved goal." The Dutch then had to rely on the good offices of goalkeeper, Hans van Breukelen, to maintain their stolen advantage, but justice was restored with seven minutes to go. As Hossam Hassan broke free, he was pulled back by Erwin Koeman. The offence had occurred outside the area and he fell inside it, but the Spanish referee gave the penalty. It was converted by Magdy Abed El Ghani, to complete an exceptional piece of work from his team mates.

The game between Argentina and the Soviet Union, played on 13th June, was one that both had to win to keep alive realistic hopes of making the second round. The first half was largely even and saw the Argentinians do most of the attacking without looking particularly dangerous. They had a bad start, seeing goalkeeper Pumpido carried off with a broken leg following a collision with team mate Julio Olarticoechea. He was replaced by Sergio Goycoechea and a moment later their luck was reversed with a major piece of fortune. Igor Kuznetsov got his head to a corner, directed it well, but before the ball crossed the line, Maradona handled it out. It was a blatant infringement and should have been severely punished by a referee who was standing only yards away. He claimed not to have seen the incident, a dereliction that was censured by FIFA when he was sent home. The Argentinians had got away with it and they compounded their luck in the 27th minute. Maradona's corner was redirected by Olarticoechea and Pedro Troglio headed it in. The game further swung their way in the last minute of the first half, when Vladimir Bessanov was sent off for pulling Caniggia's shirt. Most teams would have buckled, but the ten-man Soviets upped their game in the second half. Often the better team, they were unable to break down a well organized defence and, as they tired, lost the game in the 79th minute. Jorge Burruchaga intercepted Kuznetsov's poor back pass and his goal gave a final score of 2-0.

The only worthwhile conclusion to be drawn from the game between Spain and Uruguay was that it was awful, so much so that both teams were jeered off at half-time. It was "a bout of shadow boxing." Neither side showed any ambition and the few openings created were scorned in cavalier manner, Emilio Butragueño and Antonio Alzamendi being particularly guilty in this respect. The attitude on display was all too clearly exemplified 20 minutes from the end, when the Spanish played a back pass to their goalkeeper from inside Uruguay's half. It was dire and to make matters worse, the players added tetchiness to their repertoire of misdemeanour. They "hacked irritably at each others' ankles, ran into each other with expressions of bewilderment, or dived pathetically to the ground in football's equivalent of what ornithologists call 'the broken wing display'." When the referee blew his whistle to end the drudgery, he did everybody concerned a favour.

Diego Maradona had a dig at the Italians, saying: "They are telling everyone they are going to win the World Cup. They talk too much - they should shut up. It's better to let the football do the talking."

Uruguayan players were banned from having sex before and during the tournament, 77 days celebate should they make the final. Sergio Martínez was not put off stating that: "The World Cup is every four years. We can have sex the rest of our lives." The Argentinians were only warned not to have sex a few days before each game and went much further in the tournament. After Cameroon's second victory they were given a day off to spend with their wives. Coach, Valeri Nepomniachi, said, "If a man is in discomfort for long it can affect his work."

Italian fan, Dante Molfetti, was so sure his side would beat the USA he threatened to change his nationality, his name to John Wayne and work for a month without pay if they lost.

Freedom, Change and the Tears of a Clown Prince - Italy 1990

The next day's game between Italy and the United States was widely billed as the greatest mismatch of World Cup history (shades of 1950). When, in the 11th minute, "Vialli laid off with classical delicacy, Giannini picked up and charged between two men" to score a marvellous opener, the predicted massacre seemed about to unfold. However, past American teams have refused to lie down and be mauled, and this team was no different. They had tightened up since the Czechs had wreaked such havoc, particularly at the back where they often had nine men to thwart Italian artistry. The hosts employed every trick and "played sumptuous stuff: skilled, balanced, intuitive, a delight to the eye", but were checked on every account. Vialli missed a penalty to compound the frustration, watching his shot rebound tantalizingly off the post, and in the second half Bruce Murray almost produced the shock that would have caused mass hysteria. Walter Zenga could only parry his shot and as the keeper went down to smother the ball, it eluded him. His embarassment was spared by Riccardo Ferri and a last-ditch, off the line clearance. The hosts had to settle for a 1-0 victory that was more a triumph for the Americans than for Italy.

In a similar vein, though with more success, the Cameroon's dance with destiny continued its inexorable progress against Romania. Both teams had caught the popular imagination, though there was little evidence of why in a lifeless first 75 minutes that should have seen Romania edge in front. That they did not was down to Thomas N'Kono, who produced two brilliant saves, one to keep out Gheorghe Hagi's withering 30 yard free kick and a second to turn away Lacatus's diving header. The game sprung to life in a final quarter of an hour that saw the Africans sieze the initiative and it was the enigmatic Roger Milla, brought out of retirement by popular demand and at 38 the oldest man in the tournament, who did the damage. In the 76th minute, he leaped for a cross with Ioan Andone. Both men fell, but Milla was quickest to his feet to stab the ball into the net and set the record as the oldest player to score in the finals. (See Roger Milla profile on page 398). Ten minutes later, he did it again, with a fine shot that finished a powerful run into the area. A minute later, substitute Gavrila Balint restored some equity, scoring with a close range shot, but it was all too late. Cameroon held on to become the first team into the next stage and the first from Africa to get so far.

Yugoslavia and Colombia, two of the potentially more attractive teams in the competition, came together in the day's third game and both entertained by degrees. The Colombians had marginally the better of an uninspiring first half, in which the Yugoslavs appeared nervous and reticent and which produced only one clear-cut chance for either team. This pattern was repeated in the first part of the second half, with the reluctant Yugoslavs maintaining their defensive stranglehold, until the match sprung to life in the 73rd minute. The change of pace was prompted by Davor Jozic, who "chested down a high cross and volleyed fiercely" into the net and awakened his team from their back-footed lethargy. In the final quarter of an hour they pulled the South Americans apart with an exhibition of incisive, quick-fire football that was a treat to watch. They did not score again, but should have done. Safet Susic hit the post and Hadzibevic missed a penalty, awarded when Luis Carlos Perea handled a cross.

George Smith, the Scottish referee in charge of Czechoslovakia's meeting with Austria on 15th June, clearly believed that "football is a man's game and that real men are defenders." Since it was a game both felt they needed to win, and since Smith was prepared to tolerate a physical element in the tackling, it meant that "both sides went at each other like rabid dogs." The result was "a thoroughly jolly game of football", hard and sometimes dirty, but always entertaining. The Czechs were the better team, with their vibrant interchanges, confidence and creativity, though the Austrians defended solidly and had five men booked for going beyond what even Mr. Smith deemed acceptable. It was low scoring and inevitably, the goal that broke the deadlock came from a free kick, given after Jozef Chovanec intercepted a careless back pass and homed in on the Austrian goal. Klaus Lindenberger, "the silliest-looking goalkeeper in the competition with a costume of purple and yellow stripes", charged out and brought his assailant down. Chovanec was stretchered off, but Bílek converted the resultant penalty. Austria's Gerhard Rodex, the "Blond Rocket", was later presented with a chance to level the scores, but he fluffed his effort and the narrow win virtually ensured Czechoslovakia a place in the second round.

Costa Rica and Cameroon had both ensured glory for the underdog in this tournament. There was to be no such heroics from the United Arab Emirates, who found the West Germans in relentless mood when they met in Milan's San Siro Stadium, the Germans' adopted home ground. The match was played amid a massive thunder and lightening storm that provided "a Wagnerian backcloth to the destruction of the Arab outsiders" that was destined from the minute the match kicked off. As the German steamroller bore down mercilessly on the hapless defence, the only surprise was that it did not crack earlier than it did. The Germans had three good chances in the first five minutes and Völler himself four in the first 11, including a glorious opening set up by Klinsmann. Inability to score was frustrating, but "there was no panic. They just kept doing the same thing, and maintained the same pressure until they did score." The dam was finally breached in the 35th minute, when Völler put away Klinsmann's cross and four minutes later, Klinsmann himself jumped to head in Stefan Reuter's centre. The floodgates were now open and, apart from one moment at the start of the second half, when Khalid Ismail Mubarak's strike gave a brief glimmer of a fairytale come back, the Germans were untroubled. Further goals from Matthäus, Uwe Bein with a 20 yard shot and Völler again, brought an emphatic 5-1 victory that put the Germans firmly into the second round. It was a fitting result to celebrate West Germany's 250th World Cup game.

Another potential massacre was Brazil's encounter with Costa Rica the following day and with the Brazilians quickly establishing absolute dominance, it seemed very likely. Their midfield "sent wonderful imaginative balls into space" and, up front, "Careca and Muller made space, laid off, got into great positions, but failed again and again to score." The Costa Ricans had decided that this was a game they could not win and set out with damage limitation in mind. They defended deeply in numbers to frustrate their opponents and were largely successful. The Brazilians rattled the woodwork four times and goalkeeper Taffarel had virtually nothing to do, but his team could manage only a single, first half goal. It came in the 33rd minute, when Mozer's flicked on header was driven forcefully goalward by Muller. Even then, it needed a deflection off Mauricio Montero before it found the net.

Group C's other teams were also in action that day and the Scots, putting behind them their recent debacle, responded to the encouragement of their magnificent, vociferous fans to raise their game against Sweden. It was, as Andy Roxburgh later said, "the most remarkable environment in which to play football" and his team quickly stamped their authority on the game. They took the lead in the tenth minute, when a corner was headed back by David MacPherson and Stuart McCall diverted the ball into the net, his first international goal. From then on, they never looked out of contention and their search for a second goal brought success in the 83rd minute. Alex McLeish and Robert Fleck combined cutely to release Aitken, "romping across the Swedish goalmouth", where he was tripped by Sheffield Wednesday's Roland Nilsson. Mo Johnston converted the spot kick for a lead that seemed unassailable with seven minutes to go. However, Glenn Strömberg's 85th minute reply set up a maelstrom final five minutes, which had the Scots pushed back and defending unflinchingly. They held on and collected the points they deserved, but their further progress would depend upon their final group game, against Brazil.

When England came out for their second group game, there was an unusual disposition about the way they lined up. In a ploy that could have been catastrophic, Bobby Robson had decided to adopt the sweeper system, so common in continental Europe, but hardly used at all in Britain. It was a game the English were not expected to win, but the gamble paid off and the team took to the new system as if they had been born to it, giving their best World Cup performance in many a game.

Wishing to watch his team in style, Sheikh Zayed bin Sultan Al Nahiyai hired seven helicopters to take his party to see the United Arab Emirates play West Germany. The pre-match meal was prepared by his personal chefs from the Abu Dhabi Sheraton flown over to Modena where he was staying.

When Mubarak of the UAE scored his country's first goal in the World Cup finals, he was awarded a Rolls Royce, as promised by a car company back home. He said: "It is the greatest goal in my life and worth the other 100 I have scored."

Threatening to fly home if he wasn't at least a substitute against Costa Rica, Brazil's forward Renato complained: "I didn't come to Italy as a tourist."

Freedom, Change and the Tears of a Clown Prince - Italy 1990

When asked about facing two of the world's top strikers, Marco van Basten and Ruud Guillit, Terry Butcher said: "I'm more worried about my wife's Access bill at home."

Football fanatic Chris Bridges named his new-born daughter after the wives and girlfriends of the England squad. Her name was Julie, Sarah, Sandra, Wendy, Heather, Rita, Sara, Sandra, Karen, Maxine, Denise, Shelly, Sue, Michelle, Rachel, Julie, Suzie Bridges. They were the partners of McMahon, Wright, Stevens, Parker, Dorigo, Butcher, Woods, Beardsley, Steven, Walker, Robson, Webb, Shilton, Lineker, Platt, Bull and Barnes in that order. A boy would have been named after the squad itself.

Roland Woods, publican of the Old Inn in north Devon, ceremoniously smashed up his television with an axe when customers asked if they could watch the tournament, declaring his pub, a "football free zone" and a potential haven for wives and girlfriends wishing to avoid the football. In Ireland, Guinness sales went up 25% after the draw with England.

The pressure was plainly telling on Jack Charlton. "I'm not enjoying it," he said. "It's all the hassle and work and sitting around." His remark came during a tempestuous press conference, out of which he stormed when Eammon Dunphy, an ex-Republic star who had slated the team's performance on television, tried to ask a question. "You're not allowed to ask a question - you're not a proper journalist. End of story," Chalton blasted. "If he stays, I go. I don't want to answer questions from him." He later said: "Dunphy is a bitter little man - I don't like him." When Chalton accused the Egyptians of being "time wasting spoilers", the Egyptians hit back. Dr Ahmed El Mokedem, an England based economist who had financed his team's trip, said about Irish football: "It's terrible. We don't enjoy that sort of thing. We might as well go to the pub and get pissed and decide it that way. No team has managed to escape this contagious crap."

They played with a sense of direction missing against the Irish and Paul Gascoigne especially was inspired. The Dutch were outplayed in almost every department and England came close to scoring on several occasions, Barnes, Lineker and Robson being guilty of early misses. Lineker had the ball in the net in the 50th minute, but the Yugoslav referee adjudged him to have handled and it did not count. Similarly, Stuart Pearce's "goal" from a free kick was disallowed because it had been given as indirect. A goalless draw was the final result, but, as one reporter noted, the English "collected significantly more than a point from their enthralling moral victory." England's supremacy was later acknowledged by Ruud Gullit. "We were lucky to draw", he said.

South Korea took on Spain the next day and were undone by a hat trick from Real Madrid's Míchel that all but ended their interest in the tournament. It was a game in which the Koreans had much of the possession, but could do little with it against an opposition who, whilst rarely playing to potential, was physically stronger, tactically more proficient and who always looked dangerous when moving forwards. Míchel was the greatest difference between the two sides and he struck first in the 22nd minute, volleying in Francisco Villarroya's cross. The Koreans restored parity shortly before the break, when Choi Soon-ho tapped a free kick to Hwang Bo-kwan and he "blasted a shot high into the top left-hand corner" from 25 yards. However, an upset was never likely and in the 62nd minute Míchel fired a 22 yard free kick over the wall and between the posts. Going behind again stimulated the Koreans into a more urgent approach, but the game would not turn in their favour. In the 81st minute, Julio Salinas headed the ball on and Míchel wove his way through the Korean defence for a solo goal that put the result beyond reach.

The steady progress of Belgian national football since the days when most observers regarded it as sterile and boring was clear to see against Uruguay, (See Belgium v Uruguay profile on page 402), a rare treat in this blandest of World Cups, but when Egypt and Eire met the general course was resumed. This was another dire game, in which the Egyptians employed every time wasting and spoiling trick available to prevent the Irish from scoring. Whilst Packie Bonner in the Irish goal had virtually nothing to do, his team mates lacked the flair to take something from a match in which they were always the better team, but unable to get control of. Ray Houghton and Steve Staunton both shot wide the game's clearest openings, but such were the negative aspects of Egypt's play that, when asked for his thoughts in the post-match press conference, coach Jack Charlton replied: "What match? I didn't think we played a match today."

The competition in Group B was the first to reach its conclusion with two matches played simultaneously on 18th June. The Soviet Union had a mathematical chance of progress into the next round when they took the field, but were dependent on the result of the game between Argentina and Romania. They knew they faced a daunting task against Cameroon and they took to the job superbly with a display that finally did justice to the talent at their disposal. Quite simply, they made the team that had caught everyone's imagination look less than ordinary. They missed several chances before Oleg Protasov beat both the goalkeeper and the defence to slide in a cross from the right and less than ten minutes later, Sergei Aleinikov crashed a shot against the bar. The ball fell loose to Andrei Zygmantovich and he made no mistake from six yards out. The

Soviets scored twice more in the second half, through Alexander Zavanov and Igor Dobravolsky, but it had all come too late. The other result had not gone their way, but at least they exited the tournament on the back of a thumping victory. It was the last ever appearance in the World Cup of the Soviet Union, which had ceased to exist as a country by the time the next came round. Cameroon went marching into the next round as group winners.

That other Group B game was "a strange, savage, skilful, petulant and sometimes bizarre match", in which both showed the best and worst aspects of the game of football, with Maradona leading the misbehaviour, arguing the toss and play acting to get players booked whenever opportunity presented. Yet, there was also some fine open and attacking football of which the Romanians had the better, but some quite steely defence prevented either from opening the scoring. The Romanians fell behind in the 60th minute, somewhat against the run of play, when Pedro Monzon headed in Maradona's corner, but Romania's response was swift. They realized that the goal could put them out of the tournament and within five minutes, Lacatus's "charging, flickering run" had provided the cross from which Balint headed the equalizer. Thereafter, the pace of the game slowed considerably as it was realized that a draw was sufficient to see both into the next round.

Italy's final group game against Czechoslovakia was the first time these two had met in the World Cup since the final of 1934. Both had already done enough to go on, but the Italians wanted to win to ensure that they played their next round game in Rome. It meant that what could have been a dull, meaningless encounter, was good entertainment with both playing quality football. If anything, the Italians tried too hard and with a combination of nerves and over-elaboration, made things difficult for themselves. They took the lead in the 11th minute through Schillaci's header, "not a goal of classic beauty, but of classic appetite," as one journalist described it. Yet, they did not have it all their own way. The Czechs did all that they could to try to spoil the Italian dream and might have levelled the scores on numerous occasions, most notably with a headed goal in the second half that was ruled offside. The Italians then had a goal of their own disallowed for a handling offence and were lucky not to have had Berti, the culprit, sent off for blatant cheating. However, there was nothing wrong with the goal that wrapped things up. With ten minutes remaining, Roberto Baggio in his first outing in the tournament, exchanged a quick one-two with Maldini, "went through two men, beat a third and undid the goalkeeper with a sweet shot at the near post."

Group A's other game was a meaningless encounter, but proved to be bad-tempered and undisciplined, "littered with late tackling and ferocious challenges." It was as if Austria and the USA were seeking to take out previous disappointments on each other and amid the unpleasantness, eight players were booked and one sent off. The man dismissed was Austria's Peter Artner, for a dangerous two-footed tackle on Peter Vermes in the 34th minute. The incident had little noticeable impact on the course of the match, in which the Austrians were always the classier team and largely kept at bay by the outstanding goalkeeping of Tony Meola. His guard was finally broken in the 51st minute and it was an excellent individual run, half the length of the pitch, by Andreas Ogris that did it. Rodex added a second 12 minutes later and, in the 82nd minute, Murray got one back when he finished off Tab Ramos's weaving run down the left with a goal that went under Lindenberger's legs. Both teams duly bowed out of the finals, though the Americans with slightly more honour than the Austrians.

The fate of the teams in Group D was also decided that day, with games between Colombia and West Germany and Yugoslavia against the UAE. In Milan, the Colombians, a contradictory mixture of "exhilarating play and shabby behaviour", alternately thrilled with their tight control and speedy man-to-man passes and appalled with their play acting and feigned injuries. At one time, Valderrama lay motionless for a full three minutes after a seemingly innocuous challenge and gave referee Alan Snoddy an unenviable dilemma. He allowed play to proceed before giving way to the bluff and had the Colombian stretchered off. He made a miraculous recovery and in no time was running as if nothing had happened, which of course it hadn't, but it was typical of the chicanery that went on in this game as in others. In spite of this, the Colombians were the better team for most of the game and created opportunity enough to have won it. However, as is often the case, the Germans came good at the end and both Matthäus and Völler came close to scoring before the latter eventually did with only a couple of minutes to go. They thought it was enough, but in the last seconds of injury time, Valderrama gave the perfect through pass for Freddy Rincón to chase and score between Bodo Illgner's legs. The draw saw both into the next round in top and third places in the group.

Freedom, Change and the Tears of a Clown Prince - Italy 1990

Second place went to Yugoslavia, who cruised to their 50th World Cup victory in convincing style. An opening eight minutes of devastating football saw them race to a two goal lead as first Susic headed in Refic Sabanadzovic's cross for his 50th international goal and then Darko Pancev added a second four minutes later. Content that the game was already won, the Yugoslavs slowed it down and it allowed the Arabs to get back into the game with a headed goal from Thani Jumaa mid way through the first half, but they were not about to let it go. They picked up the pace again and soon after the restart, Zlatko Vujovic chested a ball down for Pancev to score his second. Robert Prosinecki added a fourth in injury time and the rout was complete.

Already out of the competition, the Swedes sought to take something from their disappointing World Cup when they took on Costa Rica on 20th June and they duly dominated the first half. They went ahead in the 31st minute, when Johnny Ekström followed in Stefan Schwarz's free kick that goalkeeper, Gabelo Conejo, had only parried and things continued to go their way until Hernán Medford came on as a 62nd minute substitute. His impact was almost immediate and only an excellent save from Ravelli denied him an equalizer. The Costa Ricans, though, were buoyed by his presence and in the 75th minute, Roger Flores headed in Cayasso's free kick to level the scores. The match swung wildly in the last quarter of an hour as both teams pressed for a winner, but it was the Costa Ricans who took the result three minutes from time. A headed clearance from Alexander Guimaraes landed in the heart of the Swedish defence and Medford ran a full 40 yards to pick up the ball and score. They had done magnificently to come from behind and their victory earned them second place in the group behind Brazil.

The Scots knew none of this when they took the field against Brazil in Turin. What they did know was that only a win would do, but strangely for the best part of an hour they struggled to find the passion with which to seriously challenge their opponents. Even with Brazil nowhere near their best, the Scots hardly troubled Taffarel's goal in a drab first half. Scotland's best chance came in the 65th minute, when Ally McCoist broke down the left to win a corner. McCall's cross was met powerfully by Johnston, but his header was hacked away by Branco on the line. It was only in the final few minutes that the game discovered any life and only after Muller had given Brazil the lead in the 82nd minute. Realizing that they were about to exit their fifth successive World Cup, the Scots went gamely in search of an equalizer. Johnston forced a brilliant save from Taffarel in the last minute, but the talisman eluded them and the final whistle signalled the end of their participation in Italia '90.

The group stage of the tournament was completed on 21st June with the last games in Groups E and F. The best of the crop was Spain's encounter with Belgium, an open, flowing game despite the fact that both had already qualified. To their credit, both decided that they wanted to win and, after a sluggish opening 20 minutes, the pace of the game picked up. Andoni Zubizarreta made a string of excellent first half saves to keep the Belgians out and it was from one of these in the 26th minute that Butragueño set up a counter-attack. Breaking free, he fed the ball to Salinas, who wriggled into the penalty area and was brought down by Preud'homme. Míchel converted the penalty, but the Belgians were quick to reply. Three minutes later, they won a free kick and Patrick Vervoort blasted it "straight into the net as if it had been attached there by an unusually strong piece of elastic." Spain regained the lead in the 39th minute, when Alberto Górriz headed in Míchel's corner 'with massive emphasis" and, although this was the last of the scoring, there was still plenty to entertain the crowd. Both goalkeepers performed superbly throughout the second half, though the biggest talking point came when Scifo crashed a 61st minute penalty against the post, leaving Spain as group winners.

If it had been one the best game's of the group, that between Uruguay and South Korea was undoubtedly the worst and possibly of the whole tournament. It was "sterile and grey" and both "looked set to bow out of the World Cup with barely a whimper." There were only two incidents of note. Yoon Deuk-yeo was sent off in the 72nd minute for time wasting, ridiculous in the circumstances, and Daniel Fonseca snatched an injury time winner. Unfortunately, it kept Uruguay in the competition as one of the four best placed third teams and sent the Scots out. Almost equally as bad was that between England and Egypt. Every game in the group had been drawn and another would greatly enhance Egypt's prospects of making the next round. To get it they went for time wasting and a massed and dirty defence, a ploy the English found almost impossible to counter. Inexplicably, Robson abandoned the sweeper system, so successful against Holland, and his flat back four formation robbed his team of the flexibility that might have made a difference. Only Gascoigne showed any sparkle. He "painted flashes of colour across a largely drab canvas" and unsurprisingly he set up the game's only goal. In the 55th minute Des Walker was fouled, Gascoigne floated over the free kick and Derby County's Mark Wright rose to head his first international goal. It put England top of the group and Egypt deservedly out.

Group F's other game produced a predictable draw, although the unfancied Irish worked tirelessly to get more from it. They fell behind in the tenth minute when Ruud Gullit received Koeman's free kick and "after a quick transfer of passes with Kieft, glided serenely between two Irish defenders to beat Bonner from an acute angle." It was vintage finishing from the man who was a constant threat to the Irish, but his team mates were less spirited and he lacked the support needed to inflict further damage. Being less troubled at the back than they might have expected enabled Charlton's men to apply their own attacking prowess. Soon after going behind, John Aldridge was unlucky to have a headed goal disallowed for an infringement and they equalized in the 71st minute when Niall Quinn headed in Packie Bonner's long clearance. They both finished the group with identical records and lots had to be drawn to determine which would take second spot. The Irish drew correctly, though both went into the second round.

With the cumbersome drudgery of the group stage over, what many regarded as the competition proper began on 23rd June. The eight games of round two took place over four days and the first featured the surprise survivors. In Naples, Cameroon took on Colombia and triumphed with a combination of skill and steel. For the first part of the match, the Africans defended heavily to keep at bay a Colombian team that had the better of the play. They came closest late in the half when Rincón hit the post, but were unable to fashion a breakthrough. The play was more even in the second half, but with neither scoring, extra time was required, where the greater fitness of the Africans and some eccentric Colombian goalkeeping proved decisive. Roger Milla had come on as a second half substitute and it was his instinct for goal that took his team further than any African had gone before. The second period had hardly begun when he received a pass from Oman Biyik and swept past two defenders into the area. René Higuita had strayed too far off his line and had left a gap at the near post into which Milla pushed his shot. Three minutes later the goalkeeper was caught in possession trying to exchange passes with his full-back and Milla stole the ball to score into the empty net. Redin pulled a goal back four minutes from the end, but it came too late.

Like Cameroon, Costa Rica had played beyond themselves to reach the second round, but in the World Cup's 450th game, the greater experience and power of Czechoslovakia overcame raw enthusiasm. In Tomás Skuhravy, the Czechs had an old-fashioned centre-forward capable of dominating defences with his size and strength, and he headed in Moravcik's free kick to take an 11th minute lead. Going behind so early might have killed the game, especially had a second Czech strike not been disallowed, but the Central Americans battled bravely and for long stretches more than held their own. They drew level ten minutes into the second half with a well headed goal from Ronald Gonzáles, the youngest player in the tournament, and the game remained finely poised until Skuhravy headed the Czechs in front again. The result was never more in doubt. Czechoslovakia's defence was too canny to allow another breach and, as the Costa Ricans were forced to abandon caution, the risk of a counter-punch became greater. Two more goals, a Kubic free kick and a third headed goal from Skuhravy eight minutes from time, took the fight out of Costa Rica and ensured Czechoslovakia's passage into the quarter-finals.

Egyptian striker and current world record holder for the most international caps, Hossam Hassan, said of his expected clash with Terry Butcher: "I'm going to give him a game that he'll remember for all the wrong reasons. Butcher is slow - I'm quick. It's as simple as that. He may have the experience, but I'm younger and fitter." Butcher didn't play.

It was estimated that 50 million Egyptians watched their game with England. Head of the Egyptian Football Federation, Mohammed Elsiajey, said that it was the biggest match in Egyptian history and that: "They may not all understand football, but everyone is very proud that Egypt are doing so well." After the game, Egyptian civil servant, Abdel Al Sayed, hanged himself at his home in Damiette. The suicide note read: "My life came to an end when Egypt's match with England ended."

Freedom, Change and the Tears of a Clown Prince - Italy 1990

After fans whistled during the playing of the Argentinian national anthem before the game with Brazil, Maradona seethed: "I let most things pass but not whistling during a national anthem. Fans are becoming barbarians."

In a phone-in conducted by the Sun the overwhelming choice of eventual winner was West Germany, with 75% of the vote. England got 10%. Oddly, adding the percentages gained by each team - West Germany 75%, Italy 12%, England 10% Brazil 7%, Holland 3% and Cameroon 1% - comes to 108.

The Dutch postal service prematurely printed a million stamps with the words "Netherlands Football World Champions 1990". It cost £100,000.

Having had a few to drink, David Monaghan decided to try his luck with an Italian girl in a bar in Bologna. Reacting badly, the locals chased him from the bar and running into the road, Monaghan looked left instead of right, was hit by an oncoming car and lost his life.

The next day brought another sample of South America's classic encounter, Argentina against Brazil, and whilst the latter "should have, and could have, won with embarrassing ease", they were let down by an all-too-familiar failing. Their approach play was often exemplary and reduced the Argentinians, Maradona included, to the role of bit players, but "the accuracy of Brazil's final touch was in complete contrast to the rest of their measured play." Dunga, Alemão and Muller all hit the post in the first half and at times, Maradona was left looking like "a spoiled school child", moaning, contesting every decision given against his team and overreacting at each hint of physical contact. Yet, disreputable though his demeanour often was, he was still capable of flashes of his former glory and one such magical moment provided the sparkle that turned the game on its head. He picked up the ball near the half way line and ran at the defence. Recognizing the possibilities in an instant, he dragged the defenders away to the right, creating space for Caniggia, whom he released to score the game's only goal. When Brazil's Ricardo Gomes was sent off soon after, there was no way back. As Maradona later said, they "had made use of the first opening we made" to inflict their first ever World Cup defeat on their old rivals. After the final whistle, he revealed another side to his paradoxical personality. Whilst his team mates celebrated, Maradona's first act was to go to console his Napoli colleague, Careca, who was naturally distraught.

The most exciting match of the round also put together old adversaries, West Germany and Holland in a game that was "by turns brilliant and nasty": brilliant because of the majestic football served up by both and nasty through the undertones of bad feeling that generated a truculence that at times declined into thuggery. The worst example of this was a confrontation between Rijkaard and Völler that began to fester in the 20th minute when Rijkaard fouled him and was booked. Völler then had his own name taken for complaining too loudly that he had been spat at. Moments later, Völler landed a hefty challenge on the Dutch goalkeeper, to which Rijkaard took offence. As the two men reared up to each other, the referee saw no choice but to send both off. It did not settle things down, but between the kicking and tripping, some exceptional football was played, with both producing a plethora of chances. By the time that the first goal came, in the 50th minute, the Germans had broken Holland's earlier mastery and when Guido Buchwald centred the ball, Klinsmann fired it in. He hit the post fifteen minutes later and ten minutes after that Brehme curled a shot around the defence and beyond the goalkeeper. A Dutch penalty pulled one back, but it was not enough. Afterwards, Rijkaard was suspended for three games, Völler missed the quarter-final and both were fined £8,300. (See Jürgen Klinsmann profile on page 399).

Holland 1 : West Germany 2
Holland's Frank Rijkaard and West German Rudi Voller are both sent off.

22 Men and a Bag of Wind

The next day's game between Eire and Romania was a hard-fought and even battle, the outcome of which was decided more by mental toughness than by fleetness of foot. Romania played the cleverer football, but with Lacatus suspended, Hagi could not find his best form. Meanwhile, the Irish were unforgiving and they shadowed, covered, blocked, tackled and intercepted passes with grim single-mindedness, leaving Romania like "a Ferrari stuck in a traffic jam - all power but nowhere to go." It was not pretty, but it was effective and, as time went on the Irish assumed a limited control of the game without posing much threat themselves. It remained scoreless throughout extra time and needed the first penalty shoot-out of the competition. The coolest nerves would win and, having hectored and harried throughout, the psychological edge had fallen to the Irish. Having had four successful kicks each, Daniel Timofte strode forward to take Romania's fifth. Bonner read it all the way and, in the words of Roddy Doyle, "dived to the left and parried the ball and got up quickly and jumped into the air, his arms up, one leg slightly lifted." David O'Leary converted his kick to send the jubilant Irish into the quarter-finals at the first attempt. In one small corner of the world at least, Jack Charlton could do no wrong.

Romania 0 : Republic of Ireland 0 (aet)
Ireland's David O'Leary scores the match winning penalty.

Following his penalty save against Romania, a bust was made of Packie Bonner and a sports centre named after him.

Predictably, defence was the commanding feature in the game between Italy and Uruguay. After an initial flurry in which Schillaci had three good chances to open his account, the South Americans settled and the pattern of play was established. The Italians attacked, Uruguay defended and hoped that long balls pumped from the back would give their speedy forwards something to chase. The plan seemed to have fallen apart after a quarter of an hour, when Roberto Baggio hit a free kick into the net, but the referee disallowed it claiming the kick had been indirect. So, the Uruguayans stuck to their task until the final third of the game, when in the 67th minute, Aldo Serena teed up Schillaci to hit a wonderful 20 yard shot into the net. It gave Uruguay no option but to press for the equalizer and leave themselves vulnerable at the back. Four minutes from the end, the Italians won a free kick outside the area. Giannini floated the ball over and Serena,

Italy 2 : Uruguay 0
Uruguay's Jose Pintos is tackled by Italy's Paolo Maldini.

In 1990 the Sun published an article entitled "10 Ways to Woo Your Man" suggesting ways women could tempt their men away from the television. In it a number of suggestions were identical to ones made in a similar article in 1986. Tip number one read: "Turn on the candle light, soft music and slip into a sexy number. He'll gasp for extra time." Number ten was: "Bring him a shaken six-pack. When he gets covered in froth, help him out of his wet trousers." A very similar suggestion had appeared in the 1986 article. It is also rare to see six packs in Britain as most cans of beer are sold in fours.

"as serene as you like", headed Italy into the next stage.

Next day Yugoslavia and Spain provided another dreary defensive occasion, in which the Spanish created the better chances, but still contrived to lose. Scoring opportunities were few and so when Butragueño pulled his shot wide in the opening minutes and later crashed a header against the bar, it was to be costly. The Yugoslavs had shown little ambition, but took the lead in the 77th minute. Vujovic was the provider and Stojkovic "killed the cross, waited for one Spanish body to slide by and then stabbed the ball in past Zubizarreta." It was undeserved and the Spaniards felt further aggrieved only minutes later when Salinas was brought down in the area and the referee turned down their penalty appeal. It fired them up and within two minutes Martín Vásquez knocked the ball into the area, where Salinas was lurking to tap it in and take the game into extra time. Here, a second piece of opportunism, a well hit free kick from Stojkovic two minutes after the restart won the game and, press as they might, the Spanish could not find the shot that would have given them justice.

The Belgians could also look to missed opportunities to explain their defeat by England. They played with a greater technical competence and dominated the early exchanges with bright, imaginative formations that forced many mistakes from an uncertain English defence. Yet, the nearest they came was when Ceulemans turned Wright and hit the post. England improved later in the half, but were also unable to put away their chances. John Barnes fumbled a shot in front of goal with only Preud'homme to beat and, when he got the ball into the net, he was ruled offside. Scifo hit the post in a second half that saw even fewer chances and it went to extra time. A further 30 minutes could not separate them, but in injury time and with penalties looming, Gascoigne won a free kick in the Belgian half. He took it quickly, lofted the ball into the area, where it fell to David Platt. In a flash, he swivelled and volleyed into the net for the first and most important goal of his international career.

The first quarter-finals were played on 30th June and the best was Italy's narrow defeat of the Irish. It was a game of passion and commitment, especially from the Irish, who never accepted their underdog tag and harried the home team relentlessly. They constantly denied Italy the freedom of movement they needed and often forced them back to find the space needed to go forwards. It was a superb display of containment, but rarely produced the scoring opportunities that might have won the game. Quinn, and in the second half Tony Cascarino, often found themselves alone up front and presenting a rather muted threat, though had Quinn put away the header McGrath's cross provided for him in the 24th minute, a greater self-belief

England 1 : Belgium 0
David Platt scores England's last minute goal.

might have underpinned their endeavour. He could not direct it wide enough of Walter Zenga and it was saved easily. The Irish paid for their lack of punch 13 minutes later, when Bonner could only parry Roberto Donadoni's shot. Uncharacteristically, he stumbled as he tried to extinguish the danger and Schillaci turned the ball in from an acute angle. He came close in the second half with a free kick that rattled the bar and rebounded on the line, but no goal was given and a single goal sent Italy into the semi-finals and the Irish to a hero's welcome in Dublin.

Much more ponderous was the game between Yugoslavia and Argentina, whose approach "as usual, was excessively cautious." The South Americans preferred to remain on the back foot and to let the Europeans try to work their way through their well-drilled defence. Even after Sabanadzovic had been sent off for tripping Maradona and the Yugoslavs had to be cautious, they were still the more adventurous side. The three best chances fell to Yugoslavia, but were missed and with 120 minutes of open play producing no goals, it was decided by penalties. Despite Maradona missing his kick, Argentina won. They had not so much marched into the semi-finals as crawled there.

The best of the quarter-finals were undoubtedly those played the following day. England took on Cameroon (see England v Cameroon profile on page 403) and against Czechoslovakia, West Germany gave an "awesome performance... that will reverberate all the way to Rome." Theirs was football of steel, clinical, methodical and utterly ruthless, and it was great credit to the Czechs that they did not buckle under the weight. They were able to launch some penetrating assaults of their own, but too often found themselves striving against the odds to resist the German sledgehammer. Hasek cleared off the line twice, goalkeeper Stéjskal pulled off some superb saves and the German barrage was kept to single first half strike. It came in the 25th minute when Klinsmann, "displaying all the pent-up fury of a wild horse", surged between two defenders and was brought down. Matthäus converted the penalty, though they could never sit safely on one goal and the second half saw further German pressure. (See Lothar Matthäus profile on page 401). Lubomir Moravcik was sent off in the 65th minute to add to Czechoslovakia's defensive worries, and the Germans should have had another penalty, when Uwe Bein was brought down, but somehow the Czechs held on to go out by the one goal.

For the semi-final against Italy, the Argentinians transformed themselves "from the self-pitying side of previous rounds into one determined not to surrender its crown" and they were prepared to use any means, fair or foul, to accomplish this end. It was a tense, gritty game, the tone of which was set after only eight seconds when Riccardo Ferri kicked Burruchaga. However, this was an Argentinian team adept at winning wars of attrition and, having gone behind to Schillaci's opportunist strike in the 17th minute, they composed themselves to come back at the

---

Hooliganism

Hooliganism was always going to be a problem in 1990 and with Holland and England in the same group, the Calgliari police geared up for the worst. Unrepentant hooligan Paul Scarrott, top of the FA's blacklist, claimed he had smuggled tear gas into Italy to use on rival fans. He boasted: "The police here know who I am but they are scared of me and haven't got the bottle to use their guns. They will never stop me - I am the world's No. 1 yob. We are after the Dutch and we are going to give them a right good kicking." He was deported on the 6th June before the tournament began having entered the country on a false passport. In another incident, police fired over the heads of 40 German supporters on the rampage near Lake Garda

Before the game with Holland, English fans arranged a march through the town and said to be leading it was Chris Wright, later accused of inciting the 2,000 England fans to riot. Wright, a 40 year-old Crystal Palace fan nicknamed the "Pratt in the Hat" because he always wore a top hat in Palace colours, had already been banned from the ground for bad behaviour. The riot started when the police blocked the route of the march, tear gas was thrown and there were several arrests and deportations. In his defence, Wright said: "I am most angry about being accused of causing the riot because my wife, Brenda, was upset by the press reports. I am no hooligan. I have no criminal convictions and have never been in trouble with the police. I've even been put forward as a Justice of the Peace." He had a history of militancy and was an official of he NGA Union in the 1970s and 80s. He had twice been a losing Labour candidate in the 1983 and 1987 elections. Many were unhappy with their convictions and claimed that it was mainly innocents who had been punished. On their arrival at Gatwick Airport many tried to hide their identities with football magazines or deportation papers. Some had been given no opportunity to retrieve luggage before being marched to the aircraft, causing one British Transport policeman to remark: "No one deserves to be kicked out with no luggage, passport or money. They look like the walking tramps of Europe."

Trouble also flared up across Britain. Twice fans in Bedford went on the rampage after watching England games in local pubs. Whilst England fans in Italy behaved themselves after the quarter-final victory, back home violence was widespread. Across the south east fans smashed windows and fought running battles with police. In the riots that followed the semi-final, one woman and two men lost their lives. Kathleen Penfold, a 62 year old landlady from Brighton, had gone outside to inspect the damage done to her property and suffered a heart attack. Paul Butler from Ashford was killed by a high speed police patrol car on its way to a riot.

Freedom, Change and the Tears of a Clown Prince - Italy 1990

Cameroon's unexpected progress had unusual consequences. Fern Osbourne, jumped up to celebrate their first goal against Colombia, hit her head on a low beam in the kitchen of her Kent farm house and ended up in hospital. In Cameroon, a monkey ended up in the celebration food pot when it was accidentally run over by jubilant supporters, though with only one television for every 500 people, watching games there was difficult. Mongo Essoube, the Minister for Youth and Sport in Cameroon, a country widely known as the "Armpit of Africa", was convinced they could win against England: "It is part of our national diplomatic plan to win," he said. "It shows what our country can do. We have amateur leagues and the children often have to make their football out of old car tyres or tapping rubber trees, but we have something that is maybe lacking among the youth of other countries. We have enthusiasm." The popular belief was they would win

A training ground fight between Maradona, his relatives and security staff broke out after his brother, Raúl, who had taken one of his Ferraris for a spin, was refused entry to the ground on his return. Raúl had no driving licence or identification and security staff were accused of trying to wind Maradona up and that they had stopped his brother out of spite.

When it was realized that England's semi-final coincided with the opening performance of a Rolling Stones' tour at Wembley Stadium and a Frank Sinatra concert at Wembley Arena, thousands phoned to see if they could change their tickets for another night. They were told no.

Following a very violent thunderstorm that ruined many people's sets before the semi-final, television hire shops in West Germany run out as panic set in amongst the public

After England's demise, Bobby Robson commented: "Nobody beat us, did they? Sad, it was very sad. Ironic too. It was probably the best performance of my time and we saved it right until the very end, that's all chaps. I'm sorry we're not there."

comparatively young and inexperienced Italians. It was the deliberate pressure they brought to bear, through the power of their football and the raffish nature of their challenges, which undid Italy. The weight of the occasion and the nervousness of the crowd were too much. When Caniggia headed in Olarticoechea's cross in the 67th minute, the writing was on the wall. Even the sending off of Ricardo Giusti for an unpleasant tussle with Baggio could not upset their purpose. A second successive Argentina game went to penalties and with the scores at 3-3, Goycoechea saved Donadoni's kick. Italy's dream now lay at Maradona's feet and his successful punt duly shattered it to put Argentina into another final.

In the first 40 minutes of their semi-final against West Germany, England outplayed their adversaries "to an astonishing degree." They were cunning, agile and colourful in their approach, though "the product of their dominance was disproportionately meagre." Their failure to score allowed the Germans to assert themselves. They grew menacingly stronger as the half progressed and began the second on top. Klaus Augenthaler brought an excellent save from Shilton before Andreas Brehme's free kick deflected cruelly off Parker and into the net. So far it had been a splendid game of football, played in a wonderfully sporting manner, but the goal lifted it "on to an even higher plane and it stirred the imagination of Gascoigne in particular." He created three good chances in an inspired five minute spell and England's resurgence brought reward in the 80th minute. Parker's cross into the area caused confusion in the German ranks, they were unable to clear and Lineker stabbed the ball into the net. This second semi-final went into extra time, in which both Waddle and Buchwald hit the post, but since neither could fashion a break, penalties were needed. Lineker, Brehme, Beardsley, Matthäus, Platt and Riedle all scored, but Pearce's shot was saved. Thon then made it 4-3 to Germany and Waddle strode forward to take the most pressured kick of his career. Sadly, he blasted it over the bar and set up a re-run of the 1986 final.

When England met Italy for the 3rd/4th play-off on 3rd July, it was Bobby Robson's last game in charge and Peter Shilton's 125th and final appearance for his country. (See Bobby Robson profile on page 396). Both had announced their decisions to quit after the tournament and both, despite the controversy that often surrounded Robson's time in charge, had served their nation well. The match itself was "played in a predictably generous and amicable spirit" and was pleasantly entertaining, though the large crowd had to wait until the 67th minute for the first goal. Unusually, it came from a mistake by Shilton, robbed by Baggio when trying to play the ball out to his defender. Baggio passed the ball to Schillaci and, under considerable pressure, scored from the return pass. England's predictable response came in the 81st minute, when Platt headed in Tony Dorigo's cross and five minutes later Parker brought down Schillaci to set up the penalty from which he won the game. It was his sixth strike and made him top scorer. Berti had a goal disallowed in injury time and when it was all over, both teams did a lap of honour to complete the sporting atmosphere - after all, England had won FIFA's Fair Play award.

"If the finals of the World Cup are supposed to be football's showcase then the 1990 tournament in Italy was an unmitigated disaster." So began one survey of the event and, after the most boring of finals, it is difficult not to concur. (See West Germany v Argentina profile on page 405). The decline in the game's morality, in evidence since the 1960s, had reached its nadir as fear and greed became the two most influential factors determining its course. They led to some of the most shameful behaviour and some of the most wearisome games in 60 years of World Cup football. It was abetted by inconsistent and at times overzealous refereeing. Beyond doubt, there were great stars on display, but few reached their potential. Maradona, the greatest of them all, was a shadow of the man who had dazzled the audiences of 1986. Similarly the Dutch, who had won the 1988 European Championships so radiantly, were witless in comparison. Three draws and a defeat was puerile form from a team of such talent. Other statistics bear sorry testament to this fall from grace. On average, three players were booked each game and one sent off every three. Of course, it is possible to argue that this was because of FIFA's tougher stance, but players have to sin before referees can punish and the real reason for so many cards being brandished was the disreputable attitude of some of the players. The 52 games produced a paltry 115 goals, at an average of 2.21 per game, the lowest ever recorded and of the last seven matches (the 3rd/4th play-off excluded), only two were decided in open play. The rest were won by penalties or shoot-outs. It really was poor and in the words of the historian just quoted: "Football had become a travesty of itself."

It is not easy to find something positive to say about Italy '90, but if anything emerges from the mire it is the progress of some of the lesser teams. With the odd exception, they did not allow themselves to be contaminated by the dearth going on around them. Simply getting to the finals is a great motivator for teams who would not normally expect to get there and mention has to be made of Cameroon and Costa Rica and their exceptional performances in going as far as they did. The English, too, charmed with Gascoigne's tears and fair play. Otherwise, it is best to consign Italia '90 to the bootbag of history.

England's Paul Gascoigne applauds the crowd after the semi-final defeat by West Germany.

The referee for the final, Mexico's Edgardo Codesal, was a doctor.

Robert William Robson   England

Honours: **Games 3**
Player: Quarter-finals 1962   **Goals 0**
Manager: Quarter-finals 1986; Semi-finals 1990
Played: 1958 and 1962
Manager: 1986 and 1990

"Nurturing and empathetic, but ruthless in his judgement and resolve, Robson's managerial style has been a unique blend of the paternal and the professional. His unquenchable passion for the game and genuine affection for each subsequent generation of young stars are unmistakable." This is how Alex Hankin described the most successful English manager since Alf Ramsey in a review of Robson's autobiography, "An Englishman Abroad". Not even a brush with cancer could dampen the enthusiasm of a man who, even though he achieved little major successes as a player, certainly did as a manager. Robson is now one of the most respected characters in the game.

Born on 18th February 1933 at Sacriston in County Durham, he was an ardent Newcastle United supporter and played for Langley Park Juniors in the inside-forward position. On leaving school, he followed his father down the mines while continuing to play as an amateur for Langley, but in May 1950, Fulham signed him. He made 152 appearances for the club, scoring 68 goals before they turned down a record £25,000 bid from Newcastle and sold him to West Bromwich Albion. Not long after, he made his England debut and was in the squad that

Freedom, Change and the Tears of a Clown Prince - Italy 1990

Bobby Robson after England's 1-0 victory over Belgium.

travelled to Sweden in 1958, playing all three games. Along side Johnny Haynes, he became an integral part of England's midfield as Walter Winterbottom gave up the WM formation in favour of 4-2-4. However, by 1962, though in the squad, he had lost his place to Bobby Charlton and his England playing career was over. In August that year, he rejoined Fulham after 239 appearances and 56 goals for West Brom. Over the next five years he played 193 games for Fulham, but managed only nine goals.

Retiring from playing in 1967, he made an unorthodox move to Canada to manage Vancouver Whitecaps, but five months later he was installed as manager of Fulham. He lasted 10 months before a run of poor results got him the sack in November 1968. The following year, Ipswich Town took a chance, resurrected his career and he never looked back. Ipswich were languishing in the Second Division, but within three and a half seasons they were challenging at the top of the First. In 1978, they defeated Arsenal in the FA Cup final and a third and two second places in the league followed. The crowning glory came in 1981 when Ipswich beat AZ Alkmaar in the final of the UEFA Cup. He was now recognized as the best manager in the country and it was only natural that he was chosen to take over from Ron Greenwood after the 1982 World Cup finals. He was intelligent, romantic, but pragmatic, and had an ability to spot and develop talented, but somewhat temperamental, young players, a skill he showed when he persuaded Barcelona to sign the up-and-coming Ronaldo. In an interview on BBC television in 2000 he reflected: "The greatest job you can ever have I think, is to be football manager of your national team. I knew it was the most important job in football, it's certainly the most prestigious. But it had its headaches!"

He got off to an awful start. A defeat by Denmark prevented England qualifying for the 1984 European Championship and going down 2-0 to the USSR in 1984 at Wembley had the crowd chanting: "What a load of rubbish". It was a tour of Brazil that brought a change of fortune and got the press off his back. With John Barnes helping England to a 2-0 victory with what Robson described as "one of the greatest goals I've ever seen in my life," a rejuvenated England strolled to the 1986 World Cup finals, where he experienced the whole set of emotions from anger to joy and despair. Of the "Hand of God" goal, he later said: "I saw the whole incident. It was as clear as a bell to me. It was only maybe two or three seconds before I realised he (the referee) was actually walking away from the situation toward the centre spot. I said to Don Howe: 'Don, I don't think he's seen the hand ball, I think he's given a goal' and Don said: 'What, what, what?'... He kept walking away to the centre circle and I said: 'Look, he hasn't seen it Don,' and it was an unbelievable state of mind that I was in."

Following a disappointing European Championships in 1988 when England lost all three of their matches, Robson took his men off to Italy. He thought his was team one of the strongest in years, with Gascoigne adding that creative dimension, but the nation remained pessimistic. The team was plagued by the reputaion of its supporters, but reaching the semi-final was England's biggest game in 24 years. Recalling it, he later said: "Under all those circumstances, the hype of the game, the importance of the game, where it was, the situation. I think England played that night one of the best games they'd played for 25 years. The team of '90 was the best team we've had in England since Sir Alf's 1966 heroes." It was no idle boast. He left his successor the finest legacy any new manager could want. Under Robson's guidance, England played 95 games. They won 47, drew 30 and lost only 18.

Robson left the England set-up to become manager of PSV Eindhoven. The Dutch press were scathing about the appointment and the fans sceptical at having an Englishman at their club. However, in his first two seasons, Robson brought them the Dutch title. In 1993, he moved to Portugal to take over at Sporting Lisbon. Relations here were not always smooth and having led them to 25 wins, 12 draws and 8 defeats he upped sticks again to take over at Porto. Things here were much better and in his four seasons there he won a Portuguese cup and a league title. It was in Portugal that he was diagnosed as having cancer of the mouth in 1995, but he was not deterred and, after one more season, was tempted at the third time of asking into the hottest seat in Spain, at Barcelona. It was a bold move. The club were awaiting the arrival of Louis Van Gaal from Holland and he was only wanted as a one year stopgap. There was some criticism, as he changed the system round to one that was less attractive than the fans were used to, but it brought success. In 1997, Barcelona finished second in the league, won the domestic Copa del Rey and the European Cup-Winners Cup beating Paris St. Germain 1-0 in Rotterdam. On more than one occasion, Ronaldo was responsible for saving his neck. With the arrival of Van Gaal, he moved to back to PSV in 1998 on a short-term contract. Thirty-four games later, including 17 victories, he found himself on the sidelines again. Back home, Newcastle United had made a turbulent start to the 1999-2000 season and coach, Ruud Gullit, was about to part company. The temptation to manage the club he supported as a boy was too great and in September 1999 he came home. He took the club to the FA Cup final in his first season and saved them from an embarrassing fight against relegation.

Roger Milla   Cameroon

Honours: Quarter-finals 1990   **Games 10 (7 as substitute)**
Played: 1982, 1990 and 1994   **Goals 5**

Roger Milla pictured in 1982.

Cameroon made their first tilt at the World Cup in 1982, but their greatest impact came in 1990. One of the most endearing images they left behind was of a 38 year old player with a wide beaming grin and a gap in his front teeth charging at goal, scoring and celebrating his triumph by dancing a samba around the corner flag. The leader of the pride was Roger Milla. Born on May 20th 1952 at Yaoundé, he was the son of a railway worker. His father probably adopted the German name Muller, but Roger changed it to Milla to make it sound more African. He cut his teeth playing for Éclair Douala before moving on to Léopards of Douala. He then moved to his hometown club of Tonnerre Yaoundé where he won league and cup titles and an African Cup-Winners Cup medal in 1975. Next year he won the first of his two African Footballer of the Year Awards, a second coming in 1990. It was inevitable that he would attract the attention of French clubs and in 1977 he moved to Valenciennes. In 12 years of playing for several French sides there was some success and he gained respect, but he was never a star. A move to Monaco brought him a French cup winner's medal in 1980 and he earned another with Bastia in 1981. He also won the French Second Division title with St. Etienne, but this was the extent of his achievements. When asked why some Africans are such nonentities at their European clubs in an interview with Simon Kuper for his book "Football against the Enemy", he replied: "Because when Africans arrive in Europe they are taken for monkeys. The clubs must give the players confidence." After scoring 152 goals in the French league Milla "retired" to the French Réunion Islands in the Indian Ocean and it was here, whilst playing Indian Ocean league football for Saint Pierre, he was tempted back to play for Cameroon again at Italia '90.

Milla had been long established as an international footballer when Cameroon first qualified for the 1982 World Cup finals. He played well in all three games, but inexperience and a lack of goals saw the team out after the first round. He had 81 full caps when he was plucked from obscurity to play once again in Italy. The decision was in no small part influenced by Cameroon President, Paul Biya, and what transpired finally dispelled any illusion that African football was inferior to that of Europe or South America, a fact later confirmed when Nigeria won the Olympic gold medal in 1996. If any one player is to be credited with putting African football on the map, it was Roger Milla and he fully appreciated the effect it had. "It brought me a great deal, in terms of football thinking and technique, and it opened up the world for me as well as other talented African players like George Weah, Abedi Pele and others. In turn, we have helped make Africa better known across the globe," he said in an interview with African Soccer Magazine in 1999. He later said his most endearing memory of the 1990 finals was of Biya shaking hands with other heads of state after they defeated Argentina. "Do you appreciate that?" he said in France Football Magazine. "An African head of state who leaves as the victor, and who greets with a smile the defeated heads of state! It's thanks to football that a small country could become great."

After the tournament it was rumoured that not all Milla's team mates had been happy to have him in the side and certainly some of his antics since have not always enhanced his reputation. François Omam Biyik remarked that: "We played, but Milla won." In response Milla said: "Omam Biyik has understood nothing. It was not the manager or the minister who chose me to play in the World Cup, it was the people. I accept the verdict of public opinion, relayed to me by the head of state, President Biya, who ordered the minister to send me to Italy. I did it all for them, for the young lads. If I had done it for me, I would have descended upon the Champs-Elysées in an open-top car and say, 'I am the greatest.'" The following year he travelled the world appearing in exhibition games and looking for the contract that would make him rich. It was often reported that he had signed for a club, but the deal would break down because of his excessive wage demands. Once he was offered a contract with Cape Town Hellenic, but he asked for 65 times the amount that other players received, the South Africans decided a younger player was a better bet. He would charge for interviews, refused to play against England at Wembley in 1991 because the English FA would not pay an appearance fee and, when a Nigerian chief gave him an award that was meant to go to a different person each year, he refused to give it back. The chief had to have a new one made. By 1993 Milla was back in Yaoundé and was appointed financial and administrative director of the national side, a position created for him by President Biya. When asked what he did, he replied: "I administer the team, I call the national team for training camps, I prepare water, balls, kit and so on for their practices, I prepare the fees for the training camps… I like the job because it keeps me in contact with my old comrades in the national team." It also enabled him to keep fit in case he was needed in 1994 and it gave him a chance to organize events. He once invited 120 pygmies to play in a tournament to raise funds for their education and health and formed them into teams with names like Bee-sting of Lomie and Ants of Salapoumbe. He kept them locked up before kick-off, but only 50 supporters turned up, most to hurl abuse. The tournament was a disaster and he lasted only a few months before being made redundant.

Cameroon never really exploited his knowledge of the game and once the state felt they had got what they wanted from him they discarded him. He was recalled for the 1994 World Cup finals and, at the age of 42, became the oldest player to score in the finals, getting the only goal in a 6-1 drubbing by Russia. However, there has been no compensation and it was the state that benefited more from Milla's popularity than he ever did. Today, he lives a quiet life as a youth trainer for his former club, Montpelier in France and makes the odd appearance around the world. He may not have had as an illustrious career as Beckenbauer or Pelé, but the World Cup needs characters like Roger Milla and in 1990 he certainly set the tournament alight. He also gave middle-aged men an icon they could look to for inspiration. In 1999 he was made African Player of the Century.

Jürgen Klinsmann   West Germany/Germany

Honours: Winner 1990; Quarter-finals 1994 and 1998   **Games 17**
Played: 1990, 1994 and 1998   **Goals 11**

Jürgen Klinsmann was the "gentleman" of German football. He was a prolific scorer, played top class football in several countries, was cultured and articulate, had a knowledge of several languages and, like the "gentleman" of English football, Gary Lineker, he was treated shabbily at the end of his international career. Having played 108 times for his country, leading them to European Championship victory in 1996, he was refused an official farewell match by the German Football Federation on his retirement after the 1998 World Cup. Speaking in 1999, he remarked: "The reaction of the German Federation left me speechless. It's not so much the fact that

22 Men and a Bag of Wind

Jürgen Klinsmann takes on Holland's van Aerle in West Germany's 2-1 victory.

they don't want to do it, but the way they went about it. The President couldn't even call me up directly, I had to find out through a third party." "I am and bitterly disappointed," he told the German Sports Agency and in reply, the DFB Vice-President, Franz Beckenbauer, would only say: "There will be no more farewell games for internationals." Lothar Matthäus, on the other hand, was not treated so badly.

Born on 30th July 1964 at Göppingen, Klinsmann served his apprenticeship with minor West German league clubs Gingen and Geislingen before taking up his first professional appointment with second division Stuttgart Kickers in 1982. In his second season with the club he became the division's top scorer prompting VfB Stuttgart, who had just finished the season as champions and were looking to strengthen their position, to take him on. His first real taste of success came in 1988 when he was the league's top scorer with 19 goals and was voted German Player of the Year. By now he was a full international and it was as such that he experienced his first real taste of disappointment, when West Germany lost to Holland on home ground in the 1988 European Championships. The following year Stuttgart reached the final of the UEFA Cup against Napoli, but he did not feature in the first leg as Stuttgart went down 2-1. He scored Stuttgart's first goal in the home leg, but they could only manage a 3-3 draw. At the end of the season, he joined fellow countrymen, Matthäus and Brehme, at Internazionale and went on to win the Serie A title in his first season. He adapted quickly to his new surroundings and his calm nature meant the culture of Italian life posed no problems.

By the time West Germany went to the 1990 World Cup finals, he had built a reputation as a top class international striker and he did not disappoint. Playing five of his seven World Cup games on his club's home ground in Milan he opened his account in the 63rd minute of a victory over Yugoslavia. He got another against the UAE and then produced the finest performance of his international career as Germany exacted revenge on Holland for the earlier Euro '88 defeat, opening the scoring after 50 minutes. Following his World Cup triumph, Internazionale went on to win the UEFA Cup in 1991 and in 1992 he moved to Monaco in another multi-million pound deal that netted him a large cut of the fee. However, after only two seasons in the French league that brought no reward, he was on the move again, this time to England. In a sensational capture, Tottenham Hotspur's chairman, Alan Sugar, brought "Jürgen the German" to White Hart Lane. He became an instant star, finished the 1994-95 season with 29 goals and the English Player of the Year Award. However, his first stay had an acrimonious end when Klinsmann and Sugar fell out over Klinsmann's intentions to depart the club. More than a little annoyed, Sugar famously announced that he would not wash his car with Klinsmann's shirt. He went to Bayern Munich in 1995 and helped them to UEFA Cup success, scoring 15 goals on the way.

In the opening round of the 1994 World Cup, Klinsmann was the only light in an ageing German side. He scored four goals including two against South Korea, but when an Hristo Stoichkov-inspired Bulgaria sealed their fate in the quarter-finals, the Germans went out at their earliest stage since 1962. Klinsmann left the pitch in tears, but there had been a degree of personal success. He had brought his World Cup goal tally to eight and finished second highest scorer in the tournament. In 1996, and in the absence of Lothar Matthäus, he captained Germany to European Championship success in England, when the Germans beat the Czech Republic with the first Golden Goal in a major championship final.

Following a spell with Sampdoria, he made up with Sugar and returned to Spurs in 1998, then languishing at the bottom of the Premiership. The fans accepted him back, Spurs were rejuvenated and Klinsmann was a hero once again. In the penultimate game of the season they trounced Wimbledon 6-2 with Klinsmann scoring four of the goals. His reason for returning to North London was to gain regular first team football and a place in the German squad for the 1998 World Cup. It was rumoured that he had a clause built into his contract that prevented him being dropped from the first team. In France, he scored an impressive, well-controlled goal against the USA to make him the 17th player to score in three World Cups, but in the next game against Yugoslavia, he was injured two minutes from time and had to be stretchered off. He recovered for the next to score his tenth World Cup goal. As team captain, he believed Germany had a chance and said: "We are capable of moving up a gear, and we can beat any team here." In the second round, Mexico had been on the verge of a major upset, winning 1-0 when Klinsmann pounced on a mistake by Lara to slide the ball past the goalkeeper to equalize and become the joint 4th highest scorer in World Cup competitions. The defeat by Croatia in the quarter-final, closed the door on his international career. He also decided to quit altogether. Speaking the day after the match he said: "I don't know if I'm going to go on at all. I need to take a holiday and spend time with my family. A new stage of my life is beginning. I want to be there for my son and my wife." It was a real shock. He was only 34.

Lothar Matthäus   West Germany/Germany

Honours: Winner 1990; Runner-up 1986/1982);   **Games 25 (record)**
Quarter-finals 1994/1998   **Goals 6**
Played: 1982, 1986, 1990, 1994, 1998 (joint record)

Lothat Matthäus (left) and Rudi Voller celebrate West Germany's 1990 World Cup final victory over Argentina.

When Hossom Hassan of Egypt took the field against Zambia in January 2001 he broke the record for the highest number of international caps held by Lothar Matthäus for only a few months. However, one record Hassan will never beat is Matthäus's record for the number of games played in World Cup finals. Matthäus might have missed his opportunity to emulate Franz Beckenbauer when he was kept out of the 1996 European Championships winning side through injury, but, like Beckenbauer, he has been a World Cup winner and runner-up.

Born on 21st March 1961 at Erlangen, as a teenager his parents insisted that he at least train for a "proper job" and he served as an apprentice in design and decoration before taking up football full-time. It seems inevitable that the young Matthäus would do something in the game, as his father, mother and brother all worked at the local Puma factory manufacturing football boots. His playing career started with FC Herzogenaurach. Then, at the age of 18, the year he received a drink-driving ban, he moved to Borussia Mönchengladbach, one of Europe's top clubs. In five years with the club he showed the ability and understanding to become a great midfielder, who could create and score goals. His reputation grew and his hard work was rewarded when he was called into the West German national squad for the European Championships in 1980. He made his first full international appearance in the group stages. West Germany won the tournament, but Matthäus did not feature in the final. He was still in the squad when the Germans travelled to Spain to take part in the World Cup in 1982, but made just two appearances as a substitute in Round One and did not qualify for a runner's-up medal when Germany lost the final. During the series he had caused an almighty row with coach, Jupp Derwall, for breaking the team curfew.

In 1984, Matthäus moved to Bayern Munich who were fast re-establishing themselves as West Germany's premier club. The 1984-85 season began a run of three consecutive league titles. Bayern also won the West German Cup in 1986 and were beaten finalists in the 1987 European Cup, going down 2-1 to FC Porto. He was now a regular fixture in the national side and was one of the few commanding presences as West Germany failed to impress in the opening round of the 1986 World Cup. In the second round he again played well, scoring the only goal of the game to take his side through to a quarter-final against the hosts. In the final, he was given the task of suppressing the mercurial talents of Maradona, but it proved to be beyond his abilities.

He was clearly delighted with his 1988 move to Internazionale, for a fee of £2.5m. "It was the best decision I have ever made," he said. "I've improved my game because the Italian league is the strongest in the world." Inter won the Serie A title in 1989 and the UEFA Cup in 1991 with Matthäus scoring one of Inter's two goals in the home leg of the final. By Italia '90, Matthäus was national team captain. His surging runs had brought him three goals in the first round as they cruised into the second to face old adversaries, Holland. He got a fourth from the penalty spot in the quarter-final against Czechoslovakia and again contributed from the spot in the penalty shoot-out that took them past England in the semi-final. In the final he again faced Maradona's Argentina, determined not to let the same thing happen and later to claim that he would have done anything to avoid another defeat. The Germans dominated the final and Matthäus became the third West German captain to lift the trophy. The same year he was named West German and European Player of the Year.

Early in 1992 Matthäus was transferred back to Bayern, but was not fit enough to take part in that year's European Championships when Germany lost the final to Denmark. However, the following season, fully fit once again, Bayern won the UEFA Cup, beating Bordeaux in the final and the German title in 1994. He was now playing as a sweeper, a position he held in the national side that went to the USA. In the quarter-final, he put the Germans ahead from the penalty spot, but a late double blow from Bulgaria sent them crashing. Everyone expected that his World Cup odyssey was over. An Achilles tendon injury kept him out of the game for most of the 1995-96 season, and this and a public row with Jürgen Klinsmann over the national team captaincy kept him out of Germany's triumph in Euro '96. He helped Bayern to another German title in 1997 and was a German Cup winner in 1998, but he had been away from the international set for some time when he was surprisingly called up to take the place of the injured Matthias Sammer at the 1998 World Cup finals. He started the tournament on the bench, but then came on as a substitute to make a record breaking 22nd appearance in the finals against Yugoslavia. Three more matches as a first choice followed to bring his total to 25. Croatia dumped Germany out at the quarter-final stage, but as the team headed home, Matthäus could hold his head up high as one of the few who had acquitted themselves well.

In 1999, aged of 37, he won a world record breaking 144th cap in February when Germany were defeated 2-1 by Holland and helped Bayern to the final of the European Champions League, where they lost to a last gasp goal from Manchester United. He was also named German Footballer of the Year for the second time and decided to end his career in the lucrative US Major League, joining New York Metro Stars in March 2000. He was recalled to the national side for Euro 2000 in Belgium and Holland and played in all three of Germany's games, but it was a tournament too far. He looked tired and off the pace and it was a disastrous campaign. He had however, earned himself three more international caps and in 2001 he played his final and 150th international before hanging up his international boots for good.

Belgium 3 : Uruguay 1

One of the finest games of Italy '90 was undoubtedly the Group E clash between Belgium and Uruguay. It was a match of breathtaking, relentless football, "tenaciously fought between teams equal in technique and tactical subtlety", that saw Belgium claw their way to a 3-0 lead and bravely defend it amid the most testing of Uruguayan pressure. It was a game that had reporters reaching for the thesaurus to find ways of relating the skills on display.

Belgium's first goal, in the 15th minute, was a "thrilling passing movement", described by the Times's correspondent as "without doubt the most clinically schemed and executed" goal of the tournament so far. It began when Ceulemans sent Bruno Versavel away down the left flank. He held the ball long enough for de Wolf to overlap and he crossed high into the penalty area, where Clijsters rose majestically above the defence to send "a pulverising header" into the net. It was a goal that left the Uruguayans standing there "hands on hips, looking at each other in awe." Eight minutes later they went 2-0 up with an equally impressive strike from Enzo Scifo. Receiving the ball from Van der Elst 30 yards out, he "let fly with a vicious shot, which curled low out of the reach of the despairing Alvarez." As it travelled goalwards, the ball rarely raised a foot above the ground.

Uruguay were shell shocked, but they picked themselves up and hit back with a determination as powerful as anything so far shown by their opponents. Throwing caution to the wind, for the rest of the half "Belgium reeled under a wave of cutting attacks that failed only in their finishing thrust." José Herrera came close with two headers in quick succession, both from free kicks by Alzamendi. He could not get enough power on his first and his second followed a rare mistake by Preud'homme, who misjudged the cross, and let him in. Gerets, however, did enough to put him off his stride and he placed the ball narrowly wide. Nelson Gutiérrez also had a header sail tantalizingly over the bar from Ruben Paz's free kick and there were times when "Francescoli was almost untouchable as he ghosted his way past tackle after tackle." Yet Uruguay could not score and Preud'homme himself was a lion saving his team on countless occasions when lesser players would have buckled under the sheer weight of the pressure. The Belgians held on, but some of their defending was crude, to say the least. Uruguay were unlucky not to get a penalty when Grun brought down Sosa and both he and Gerets were booked before Gerets was sent off, four minutes before half-time, for a lunging two-footed tackle on Paz. The Belgians were grateful for the half-time whistle and the opportunity to draw breath and review the situation.

Soon after the restart came the moment that won the match. In the 47th minute, Ceulemans broke through "a gaping hole in the defence" and shot powerfully into the net from 18 yards. It was a cruel blow and hardly deserved, but Uruguay's response was manful. They simply continued to pile on the pressure and once more put Belgium's goal under sustained assault. It was a remarkably illustrious showing and never once did Uruguay let their play slide into nastiness, as so often in the past, testament to the attitude instilled in his players by coach, Oscar Tabárez. Carlos Aguilera, on as a substitute, had three clear scoring opportunities, but was unable to beat the acrobatic Preud'homme and Paz broke through the defence only to be denied at point blank range by the goalkeeper's legs. As the game wore on there came the increasing realization that it was not going to be Uruguay's night, but they still had one last sting in their tail. In the 63rd minute Bengeochea came on and eight minutes later grabbed a lone, but thoroughly merited consolation and the match ended at 3-1 to the Europeans.

It had been an epic and titanic struggle, a match that contained all that is commendable about world football. Apart from Gerets's unseemly misadventure, it had been a collection of gems. The Belgians had gained a "highly creditable victory" somewhat against the odds and it was down to "their finishing power on the night, to their determination, which was as severe in the second half with ten men as it was before they had scored, and to the agility of Preud'homme in goal." There was certainly no discredit to defeated Uruguay.

England 3 : Cameroon 2

England's quarter-final tie with Cameroon should have been, on paper at least, a mere stride along England's progress, but it turned into one of the greatest escapes in their World Cup history. The Africans had taken some notable scalps and played some superb football on their way to the last eight. Yet they had also displayed some bewildering tactical inexperience and naïvety and this was the key to their downfall against the English.

Both teams began cautiously, but it soon became clear that the English were the team with the problems. Cameroon strength lay in two areas. One was their flexibility and "the speed with which they can transform a typically nonchalant and languid move at the back into a threatening attack." The other was their defensive qualities. Not only were they very physical and rugged in the tackle, they also "dropped behind the ball whenever they lost possession." It gave them a great unpredictability and it was not long before they had the English defence in trouble. In only the 13th minute, Louis-Paul Mfede crossed the ball, Des Walker misjudged it and the ball fell to Oman Biyik in a scoring position. Fortunately for the English, he decided to go for power, not accuracy and Shilton blocked his shot. The ball sprang out to Mfede who pushed his shot wide. It was a sign of things to come, as Cameroon front men frequently made Terry Butcher look uncomfortable. More than once was he rescued by Walker and Wright.

The English took the lead with a superb goal against the run of play in the 26th minute. Butcher chipped the ball beyond defender Stephen Tataw Eta for Stuart Pearce to run on to. Looking up, he saw David Platt stealing in

England 3 : Cameroon 2
Gary Lineker scores his second penalty to seal an English victory.

unnoticed at the far post and "released a perfect cross which Platt met with a powerful downward header." It was a goal "of rich quality", but it did not unsettle the Africans. They came back with tenacity and power and twice before half-time came close to scoring themselves. One time Thomas Libiih headed narrowly over the bar from Mfede's cross and Oman Biyik's "control let him down a few minutes later when he was in the clear." Somehow the English held on and were relieved to meet the half-time interval 1-0 in front.

The game was transformed after the break by the arrival of Roger Milla. He was now 38, but his impact was dramatic. In the 61st minute, he twisted and turned in the England area, was brought down when Gascoigne hit the panic button and Emmanuel Kunde hit home the subsequent penalty. Five minutes later, Milla avoided the attentions of Gascoigne and Butcher and released Eugene Ekeke Ebelle, only recently on as a substitute. He was able to lift the ball over the advancing Shilton and England were behind. For the next part of the game the English floundered and could find no response. Gascoigne was often crowded out in midfield, Waddle was trapped on the touchline and Lineker "found Cameroon were prepared to use whatever methods necessary to halt him." With the English in disarray, Cameroon pressed to put the game beyond their reach. Pearce blocked Cyrille Makanaky's shot and Shilton made two reflex saves before Lineker restored his country's pride. In the 83rd minute he spun away from Kunde and the defender's inexperience showed as he brought him down. Lineker dusted himself down before dispatching the penalty into the net. In the dying minutes Wright was injured in his struggle to contain Milla. With England having already made two changes, he was forced to stay on the field with impaired vision and had to play with his head heavily bandaged. He needed six stitches and ensured that the extra time Lineker had won would not be easy.

In the extra time, Cameroon sought to take advantage of England's patched up defence and came close on several occasions to winning the game. Trevor Steven, covering for the struggling Butcher, played heroically to prevent the goal that was threatened. He twice cleared off his line as the Africans poured into the gaps left by England's desperate defenders. Lineker finally won the game in circumstances similar to those that had saved his team earlier. Gascoigne provided the through ball and as he ran on he was brought down by goalkeeper N'Kono. Once more he steadied to take the spot kick and fired England into the semi-finals.

It had been a magnificent occasion and England deserved as much credit for pulling "it out of the fire", as Bobby Robson later described it, as Cameroon did for putting them in the mess. Afterwards Milla gave his views: "I am obviously disappointed that we didn't win after playing so well, but the game will be the greatest souvenir of my career. It was fantastic. We were so close to reaching the semi-finals. Good luck to England."

West Germany 1 : Argentina 0
The World Cup Final

Argentina's Troglio argues with the referee as team-mate Dezotti is sent off.

Beginning his report of this game, David Miller of the Times wrote: "Once again Argentina have demeaned football." His comment echoed what all impartial commentators had to say about the worst final ever seen and about those who the commentators blamed for the appalling spectacle. That Argentina fielded a team that had five regulars missing, four through suspension, was indicative of the approach to the whole tournament of a team that had collected 21 yellow cards and had three men sent off on the way to the final. The Germans themselves had hardly sparkled and had won through by sheer dogged, though colourless persistence and determination. The omens were less than promising as the mechanical and unimaginative took on the negative and petulant.

Argentina laid out their stall from the start and it took only six minutes for them to collect their first booking, Dezotti being shown the yellow card for a foul just outside the area on Littbarski. This apart, there is little more to say about a first half that was characterized by tedium and misbehaviour. It was played largely in the Argentinian half of the field, as the Germans dominated possession, but lacked the versatility to break a defence that had one purpose in mind - to get to the final whistle without conceding! There could be little doubt that the Germans would extract their revenge for the defeat of four years previous. The only question was when they would affect their breakthrough.

Perhaps one reason for Argentina's poor showing was the performance of their talisman, Maradona. He was virtually marked out of the game by Buchwald. So tight were his shackles that he rarely showed any of the spark that had characterized his career so far and he remained "a lonely spectator, unprovided and unsupported." Without his inspiration, the rest of his team mates were functionless, like a body deprived of its brain, and Illgner's goal was mostly unmolested.

The second half was more interesting, though not because of the quality of the football. This showed a marginal improvement, but was for the most part a monotonous repetition of the first half. Early in the half Littbarski beat three men on the edge of the penalty area and grazed the post with his shot. Both Berthold and Völler missed clear-cut chances and on the hour Augenthaler advanced into the area, was brought down by Goycoechea, but was given no penalty.

Argentina had replaced Ruggeri with Monzon in an attempt to shore up their defence and in the 65th minute he committed the offence that was to turn boring into farcical. With a particularly crude and late challenge after Klinsmann had broken down the right, he sent the German flying through the air and was rightly sent off. He became the first man ever to be sent off in a World Cup final and it did nothing to calm Argentinian nerves. With six minutes remaining Völler went down under a challenge from Sensini and the referee awarded a penalty. It was a little dubious given the nature of the game and certainly Argentina felt so. Troglio was booked for the strength of his protests, but the penalty stood and was duly converted by Brehme. As Miller noted in his report: "The only good thing that could be said about the match is that Brehme's penalty... ensured that Argentina lost and that the watching sporting world would not have to endure more extra time or a penalty lottery."

Going behind at last forced Argentina out of their negative mind set. They threw everything into attack and it gave the game an explosive ending. With two minutes left, the ball went out for an Argentinian throw in. Jürgen Kohler tried to prevent Dezotti from getting to it in a clear attempt at time wasting. The Argentinian grabbed him by the neck and flung him to the ground. He was sent off and there is every ground for arguing that Kohler should have walked too, if not for the time wasting, then at least for the unsporting way that he milked the incident. In the ensuing fury of protest Maradona was booked and he later refused to shake the hand of FIFA's president during the presentation ceremony. It gave a very sour ending to what had been a sour occasion. To quote the Times again, Argentina had transformed "potentially the brightest of nights into a display first of excessive caution, then of physical brutality and eventually of pathetic petulance." In the words of Beckenbauer, now the first man to captain and manage a World Cup winning team, they "tried to destroy the game, playing a very, very negative match." He was always the gentleman!

Statistics - Italy 1990

GROUP A

Rome, June 9th - Stadio Olimpico

1 (0) ITALY

Schillaci 78

Zenga, Baresi, Bergomi, Ferri, Maldini, Ancelotti (De Agostini), De Napoli, Giannini, Donadoni, Carnevale (Schillaci), Vialli.

0 (0) AUSTRIA

Lindenberger, Russ, Pecl, Aigner, Streiter, Schötell, Linzmaier (Hörtnagl), Artner (Zsak), Herzog, Polster, Ogris.

Referee: José Ramiz Wright (Brazil)
Attendance: 72.303

Florence, June 10th - Stadio Communale

5 (2) CZECHOSLOVAKIA

Skuhravy 25, 78, Bilek (pen)39, Hasek 50, Luhovy 90

Stejskal, Straka, Kadlec, Kocian, Hasek, Kubic, Bilek, Chovanec, Moravcik (Weiss), Skuhravy, Knoflicek (Luhovy).

1 (0) UNITED STATES

Caligiuri 61

Meola, Trittschuh, Windischmann, Armstrong, Wynalda (RED), Caligiuri, Ramos, Harkes, Stollmeyer (Balboa), Murray (Sullivan), Vermes.

Referee: Kurt Röthlisberger (Switzerland)
Attendance: 33.266

Rome, June 14th - Stadio Olimpico

1 (1) ITALY

Giannini 11

Zenga, Baresi, Bergomi, Ferri, Maldini, Berti, De Napoli, Giannini, Donadoni, Carnevale (Schillaci), Vialli.

0 (0) UNITED STATES

Meola, Doyle, Banks (Stollmeyer), Windischmann, Armstrong, Balboa, Caligiuri, Ramos, Harkes, Murray (Sullivan), Vermes.

Referee: Edgardo Codesal Mendez (Mexico)
Attendance: 73.423

Florence, June 15th - Stadio Communale

1 (1) CZECHOSLOVAKIA

Bilek (pen)30

Stejskal, Kadlec, Kocian, Hasek, Kubic, Bilek, Chovanec (Bielik), Moravcik, Nemecek, Skuhravy, Knoflicek (Weiss).

0 (0) AUSTRIA

Lindenberger, Pfeffer, Pecl, Aigner, Russ (Streiter), Schötell (Ogris), Hörtnagl, Zsak, Herzog, Rodax, Polster.

Referee: George Smith (Scotland)
Attendance: 38.962

Rome, June 19th - Stadio Olimpico

2 (1) ITALY

Schillaci 10, Baggio 78

Zenga, Baresi, Bergomi, Ferri, Maldini, Berti, De Napoli (Vierchowod), Giannini, Donadoni (De Agostini), Baggio, Schillaci.

0 (0) CZECHOSLOVAKIA

Stejskal, Kadlec, Kinier, Hasek, Bilek, Chovanec, Moravcik, Nemecek (Bielik), Skuhravy, Knoflicek, Weiss (Griga).

Referee: Joël Quiniou (France)
Attendance: 73.303

Florence, June 19th - Stadio Communale

2 (0) AUSTRIA

Ogris 51, Rodax 63

Lindenberger, Pfeffer, Pecl, Aigner, Streiter, Artner (RED), Ogris, Zsak, Herzog, Rodax (Glatzmeyer), Polster (Reisinger).

1 (0) UNITED STATES

Murray 82

Meola, Doyle, Banks (Wynalda), Windischmann, Armstrong, Balboa, Caligiuri (Bliss), Ramos, Harkes, Murray, Vermes.

Referee: Jamal Al-Sharif (Syria)
Attendance: 34.857

	P	W	D	L	F	A	Pts
Italy	3	3	0	0	4	0	6
Czech	3	2	0	1	6	3	4
Austria	3	1	0	2	2	3	2
United States	3	0	0	3	2	8	0

GROUP B

Milan, June 8th - Stadio Giuseppe Meazza (San Siro)

1 (0) CAMEROON

Omam-Biyik 65

N'Kono, Ebwelle, Massing (RED), Kunde, N'Dip, Tataw, M'Bouh, Kana-Biyik (RED), Makanaky (Milla), M'Fede (Libiih), Omam-Biyik.

0 (0) ARGENTINA

Pumpido, Simon, Ruggeri (Caniggia), Fabbri, Sensini (Calderón), Lorenzo, Batista, Burruchaga, Basualdo, Maradona, Balbo.

Referee: Michel Vautrot (France)
Attendance: 73.780

Bari, June 9th - Stadio Della Vittoria

2 (1) ROMANIA

Lacatus 41, (pen)54

Lung, Rednic, Klein, Andone, G.Popescu, Rotariu, Sabau, Timofte, Lupescu, Lacatus (Dumitrescu), Raducioiu (Balint).

0 (0) SOVIET UNION

Dassajev, Bessonov, Khidiatullin, Kuznetsov, Gorlukovich, Rats, Aleinikov, Litovchenko (Yaremchuk), Zavarov, Protasov, Dobrovolsky (Borodyuk).

Referee: Juan Daniel Cardellino (Uruguay)
Attendance: 42.960

Naples, June 13th - Stadio San Paolo

2 (1) ARGENTINA

Troglio 27, Burruchaga 79

Pumpido (Goycoechea), Simon, Olarticoechea, Serrizuela, Monzon (Lorenzo), Batista, Burruchaga, Caniggia, Basualdo, Maradona, Troglio.

0 (0) SOVIET UNION

Uvarov, Bessonov (RED), Khidiatullin, Kuznetsov, Gorlukovich, Aleinikov, Zygmantovich, Shalimov, Zavarov (Liuty), Protasov (Litovchenko), Dobrovolsky.

Referee: Erik Fredriksson (Sweden)
Attendance: 55.759

Bari, June 14th - Stadio Della Vittoria

2 (0) CAMEROON

Milla 76,86

N'Kono, Ebwelle, Onana, Kunde (Pagal), N'Dip, Tataw, M'Bouh, Makanaky, M'Fede, Maboang (Milla), Omam-Biyik.

1 (0) ROMANIA

Balint 87

Lung, Rednic, Klein, Andone, G.Popescu, Rotariu, Sabau, Timofte, Hagi (Dumitrescu), Lacatus, Raducioiu (Balint).

Referee: Hernan Arce Silva (Chile)
Attendance: 38.687

Bari, June 18th - Stadio Della Vittoria

4 (2) SOVIET UNION

Protasov 21, Zygmantovich 29, Zavarov 52, Dobrovolsky 63

Uvarov, Demianenko, Khidiatullin, Kuznetsov, Gorlukovich, Aleinikov, Zygmantovich, Shalimov (Zavarov), Protasov, Litovchenko (Yaremchuk), Dobrovolsky.

0 (0) CAMEROON

N'Kono, Ebwelle, Onana, Kunde (Milla), N'Dip, Tataw, M'Bouh, Makanaky (Pagal), M'Fede, Kana-Biyik, Omam-Biyik.

Referee: José Ramiz Wright
Attendance: 37.307

Naples, June 18th - Stadio San Paolo

1 (0) ARGENTINA

Monzon 60

Goycoechea, Simon, Olarticoechea, Serrizuela, Monzon, Batista, Burruchaga (Dezotti), Caniggia, Basualdo, Maradona, Troglio (Giusti).

1 (0) ROMANIA

Balint 65

Lung, Rednic, Klein, Andone, G.Popescu, Rotariu, Sabau (Mateut), Hagi, Lacatus, Lupescu, Balint (Lupu).

Referee: Carlos Antonio Silva Valente (Portugal)
Attendance: 52.733

	P	W	D	L	F	A	Pts
Cameroon	3	2	0	1	3	5	4
Romania	3	1	1	1	4	3	3
Argentina	3	1	1	1	3	2	3
Soviet Union	3	1	0	2	4	4	2

GROUP C

Turin, June 10th - Stadio Delle Alpi

2 (1) BRAZIL

Careca 40, 62

Taffarel, Jorginho, Ricardo Gomes, Branco, Mozer, Mauro Galvao, Dunga, Alemão, Valdo (Silas), Careca, Müller.

1 (0) SWEDEN

Brolin 79

Ravelli, R.Nilsson, Larsson, Ljung (Strömberg), Schwarz, Ingesson, Limpar, J.Nilsson, Thern, Brolin, Magnusson (Petterson).

Referee: Tullio Lanese (Italy)
Attendance: 62.628

Genoa, June 11th - Stadio Luigi Ferraris

1 (0) COSTA RICA

Cayasso 50

Conejo, Flores, González, Montero, Chavez, Chavarria, Ramírez, Gómez, Cayasso, Marchena, C.Jara (Medford).

0 (0) SCOTLAND

Leighton, Gough (McKimmie), McLeish, McPherson, Malpas, Aitken, McStay, Bett (McCoist), McCall, Johnston, McInally.

Referee: Juan Carlos Loustau (Argentina)
Attendance: 30.867

Turin, June 16th - Stadio Delle Alpi

1 (1) BRAZIL

Müller 33

Taffarel, Jorginho, Ricardo Gomes, Branco, Mozer, Mauro Galvao, Dunga, Alemão, Valdo (Silas), Careca (Bebeto), Müller.

0 (0) COSTA RICA

Conejo, Flores, González, Montero, Chavez, Chavarria, Ramírez, Gómez, Cayasso (Guimaraes), Marchena, C.Jara (Mayers).

Referee: Naji Jouini (Tunisia)
Attendance: 58.007

Genoa, June 16th - Stadio Luigi Ferraris

2 (1) SCOTLAND

McCall 10, Johnston (pen)83

Leighton, Levein, MacLeod, McLeish, McPherson, Malpas, Aitken, Durie (McStay), McCall, Johnston, Fleck (McCoist).

1 (0) SWEDEN

Strömberg 85

Ravelli, R.Nilsson, Larsson (Strömberg), Hysén, Schwarz, Ingesson, Limpar, J.Nilsson, Thern, Brolin, Petterson (Ekström).

Referee: Carlos Maciel (Paraguay)
Attendance: 31.823

Genoa, June 20th - Stadio Luigi Ferraris

2 (0) COSTA RICA

Flores 75, Medford 87

Conejo, Flores, González, Montero, Chavez, Chavarria (Guimaraes), Ramírez, Gómez (Medford), Cayasso, Marchena, C.Jara.

1 (1) SWEDEN

Ekström 31

Ravelli, R.Nilsson, Larsson, Hysén, Schwarz, Strömberg (Engquist), Ingesson, J.Nilsson, Brolin (Gren), Petterson, Ekström.

Referee: Zoran Petrovic (Yugoslavia)
Attendance: 30.223

Turin, June 20th - Stadio Delle Alpi

1 (0) BRAZIL

Müller 82

Taffarel, Jorginho, Ricardo Gomes, Branco, Ricardo Rocha, Mauro Galvao, Dunga, Alemão, Valdo, Careca, Romario (Müller).

0 (0) SCOTLAND

Leighton, McKimmie, MacLeod (Gillespie), McLeish, McPherson, Malpas, Aitken, McStay, McCall, Johnston, McCoist (Fleck).

Referee: Helmut Kohl (Austria)
Attendance: 62.502

	P	W	D	L	F	A	Pts
Brazil	3	3	0	0	4	1	6
Costa Rica	3	2	0	1	3	2	4
Scotland	3	1	0	2	2	3	2
Sweden	3	0	0	3	3	6	0

GROUP D

Bologna, June 9th - Stadio Renato Dall'Ara

2 (0) COLOMBIA

Redin 50, Valderrama 87

Higuita, Herrera, Perea, Escobar, Gildardo Gómez, Alvarez, Gabriel Gómez, Valderrama, Redin, Iguaran (Estrada), Rincón.

0 (0) UNITED ARAB EMIRATES

Faraj, E.M.Abdulrahman (Ali Sultan), I.M.Abdulrahman, Y.H.Mohamed, K.G.Mubarak, Abdullah, N.K.Mubarak, Abbas, Jumaa, F.K.Mubarak (Bilal), Al Talyani.

Referee: George Courtney (England)
Attendance: 30.791

Milan, June 10th - Stadio Giuseppe Meazza (San Siro)

4 (2) WEST GERMANY

Matthäus 28,63, Klinsmann 40, Völler 70

Illgner, Reuter, Brehme, Augenthaler, Buchwald, Berthold, Hässler (Littbarski), Matthäus, Bein (Möller), Völler, Klinsmann.

1 (0) YUGOSLAVIA

Jozic 55

Ivkovic, Spasic, Vulic, Hadzibegic, Jozic, Susic (Prosinecki), Baljic, Stojkovic, Katanec, Vujovic, Savicevic (Brnovic).

Referee: Peter Mikkelsen (Denmark)
Attendance: 74.765

Bologna, June 14th - Stadio Renato Dall'Ara

1 (0) YUGOSLAVIA

Jozic 73

Ivkovic, Spasic, Stanojkovic, Hadzibegic, Jozic, Susic,Stojkovic, Katanec (Jarni), Vujovic (Pancev), Sabanadzovic, Brnovic.

0 (0) COLOMBIA

Higuita, Herrera, Perea, Escobar, Gildardo Gómez, Alvarez, Gabriel Gómez, Valderrama, Redin (Estrada), Iguaran, Rincón (Hernández).

Referee: Luigi Agnolin (Italy)
Attendance: 32.257

Milan, June 15th - Stadio Giuseppe Meazza (San Siro)

5 (2) WEST GERMANY

Völler 35, 74, Klinsmann 37, Matthäus 47, Bein 58

Illgner, Reuter, Brehme, Augenthaler, Buchwald, Berthold (Littbarski), Hässler, Matthäus, Bein, Völler, Klinsmann (Riedle).

1 (0) UNITED ARAB EMIRATES

K.I.Mubarak 46

Faraj, E.M.Abdulrahman, I.M.Abdulrahman (Al Haddad), Y.H.Mohamed, K.G.Mubarak, Abdullah, N.K.Mubarak, Abbas, K.I.Mubarak (Hussain), Jumaa, Al Talyani.

Referee: Alexei Spirin (Soviet Union)
Attendance: 71.167

Milan, June 19th - Stadio Giuseppe Meazza (San Siro)

1 (0) COLOMBIA

Rincón 92

Higuita, Herrera, Perea, Escobar, Gildardo Gómez, Alvarez, Gabriel Gómez, Valderrama, Fajardo, Estrada, Rincón.

1 (0) WEST GERMANY

Littbarski 89

Illgner, Reuter, Pflügler, Augenthaler, Buchwald, Berthold, Hässler (Thon), Matthäus, Bein (Littbarski), Völler, Klinsmann.

Referee: Alan Snoddy (Northern Ireland)
Attendance: 72.510

**Bologna, June 19th -
Stadio Renato Dall'Ara**

4 (2) YUGOSLAVIA

Susic 4, Pancev 8, 46, Prosinecki 90

Ivkovic, Spasic, Stanojkovic, Hadzibegic, Jozic, Susic, Stojkovic, Pancev, Vujovic (Vulic), Sabanadzovic (Prosinecki) Brnovic.

1 (1) UNITED ARAB EMIRATES

Jumaa 23

Faraj, E.M.Abdulrahman, I.M.Abdulrahman, Al Haddad, Y.H.Mohamed, K.G.Mubarak (RED), N.K.Mubarak (Ali Sultan), Abbas, K.I.Mubarak, Jumaa (F.K.Mubarak), Al Talyani.

Referee: Shizuo Takada (Japan)
Attendance: 27.833

	P	W	D	L	F	A	Pts
West Germany	3	2	1	0	10	3	5
Yugoslavia	3	2	0	1	6	5	4
Colombia	3	1	1	1	3	2	3
United Arab Emirates	3	0	0	3	2	11	0

GROUP E

**Verona, June 12th -
Stadio Marc Antonio Bentegodi**

2 (0) BELGIUM

Degryse 52, De Wolf 64

Preud'homme, Gerets, Clijsters, Demol, De Wolf, Versavel, Van Der Elst, Scifo, Degryse, Emmers, Van Der Linden (Ceulemans).

0 (0) SOUTH KOREA

Choi In-young, Hong Myung-bo, Gu Sang-bum, Choi Hang-kee, Chung Young-hwan, Park Kyung-joon, Noh Jung-yoon (Lee Tae-ho), Kim Joo-sung, Lee Young-jin (Cho Min-kook), Hwang Seon-hong, Choi Soon-ho.

Referee: Vincent Mauro (United States)
Attendance: 32.486

Udine, June 13th - Stadio Friuli

0 (0) SPAIN

Zubizarreta, Chendo, Andrinua, Sanchis, Jimenez, Michel, Roberto, Villaroya (Paz), Vázquez, Butragueño, Manolo (Gorriz).

0 (0) URUGUAY

Alvez, Herrera, Gutiérrez, De Leon, Dominguez, Perdomo, Francescoli, Paz, Pereira (Correa), Alzamendi (Aguilera), Sosa.

Referee: Helmut Kohl (Austria)
Attendance: 35.713

Udine, June 17th - Stadio Friuli

3 (1) SPAIN

Michel 24, 62, 81

Zubizarreta, Chendo, Andrinua, Sanchis, Michel, Roberto (Bakero), Villaroya, Vázquez, Butragueño (Gómez), Salinas, Gorriz.

1 (1) SOUTH KOREA

Hwang Bo-kwan 43

Choi In-young, Hong Myung-bo, Gu Sang-bum, Choi Hang-kee, Yoon Deuk-yeo, Park Kyung-joon (Chung Jong-soo), Chung Hae-won (Noh Jung-yoon), KimJoo-sung, Hwang Bo-kwan, Byun Byung-joo, Choi Soon-ho.

Referee: Elias Guerrero (Ecuador)
Attendance: 32.733

**Verona, June 17th -
Stadio Marc Antonio Bentegodi**

3 (2) BELGIUM

Clijsters 15, Scifo 23, Ceulemans 47

Preud'homme, Gerets (RED), Clijsters (Emmers), Demol, De Wolf, Versavel (Vervoort), Van Der Elst, Scifo, Degryse, Grün, Ceulemans.

1 (0) URUGUAY

Bengoechea 72

Alvez, Herrera, Gutiérrez, De Leon, Dominguez, Perdomo, Francescoli, Paz, Ostolaza (Bengoechea), Alzamendi (Aguilera), Sosa.

Referee: Sigfried Kirschen (East Germany)
Attendance: 33.759

**Verona, June 21st -
Stadio Marc Antonio Bentegodi**

2 (2) SPAIN

Michel (pen)27, Gorriz 39

Zubizarreta, Chendo, Andrinua, Sanchis, Michel, Roberto, Villaroya, Vázquez, Butragueño (Alcorta), Salinas (Pardeza), Gorriz.

1 (1) BELGIUM

Vervoort 30

Preud'homme, Staelens (Van der Linden), Albert, Emmers (Plovie), Demol, De Wolf, Vervoort, Van Der Elst, Scifo, Degryse, Ceulemans.

Referee: Juan Carlos Loustau (Argentina)
Attendance: 35.950

Udine, June 21st - Stadio Friuli

1 (0) URUGUAY

Fonseca 92

Alvez, Herrera, Gutiérrez, De Leon, Dominguez, Perdomo, Francescoli, Paz, Ostolaza (Aguilera), Martínez, Sosa (Fonseca).

0 (0) SOUTH KOREA

Choi In-young, Hong Myung-bo, Choi Hang-kee, Yoon Deuk-yeo (RED), Park Kyung-joon, Lee Heung-sil, Kim Joo-sung, Chung Jong-soo, Hwang Bo-kwan (Chung Hae-won), Byun Byung-joo (Hwang Sun-hong), Choi Soon-ho.

Referee: Tullio Lanese (Italy)
Attendance: 29.039

	P	W	D	L	F	A	Pts
Spain	3	2	1	0	5	2	5
Belgium	3	2	0	1	6	3	4
Uruguay	3	1	1	1	2	3	3
South Korea	3	0	0	3	1	6	0

GROUP F

Cagliari, June 11th - Stadio Sant' Elia

1 (1) ENGLAND

Lineker 8

Shilton, Stevens, Pearce, Walker, Butcher, Robson, Waddle, Gascoigne, Barnes, Lineker (Bull), Beardsley (McMahon).

1 (0) IRELAND

Sheedy 72

Bonner, Morris, Staunton, McCarthy, Moran, McGrath, Houghton, Townsend, Aldridge (McLoughlin), Cascarino, Sheedy.

Referee: Aron Schmidhuber (West Germany)
Attendance: 35.238

**Palermo, June 12th -
Stadio Della Favorita**

1 (0) EGYPT

Abdelghani (pen)82

Shobeir, I.Hassan, Yassein, H.Ramzy, A.Ramzy (Tolba), Yakan, Youssef, Abdelghani, H.Hassan, Abdelhamid (Abdelrahman), El Kass.

1 (0) HOLLAND

Kieft 58

van Breukelen, van Aerle, Rijkaard, R.Koeman, van Tiggelen, Rutjes, Wouters, E.Koeman (Witschge), Vanenburg (Kieft), van Basten, Gullit.

Referee: Emilio Soriano Aladren (Spain)
Attendance: 33.288

Cagliari, June 16th - Stadio Sant' Elia

0 (0) ENGLAND

Shilton, Parker, Pearce, Walker, Butcher, Wright, Robson (Platt), Waddle (Bull), Gascoigne, Barnes, Lineker.

0 (0) HOLLAND

van Breukelen, van Aerle, Rijkaard, R.Koeman, van Tiggelen, Wouters, Witschge, Van't Schip (Kieft), Gillhaus, van Basten, Gullit.

Referee: Zoran Petrovic (YugoslaviaAtt)
endance: 35.267

**Palermo, June 17th -
Stadio Della Favorita**

0 (0) EGYPT

Shobeir, I.Hassan, Yassein, H.Ramzy, Tolba (Abouzeid), Yakan, Youssef, Abdelghani, H.Hassan, Oraby, El Kass (Abdelhamid).

0 (0) IRELAND

Bonner, Morris, Staunton, McCarthy, Moran, McGrath, Houghton, Townsend, Aldridge (McLoughlin), Cascarino (Quinn), Sheedy.

Referee: Marcel van Langenhove (Belgium)
Attendance: 33.288

Cagliari, June 21st - Stadio Sant' Elia

1 (0) ENGLAND

Wright 58

Shilton, Parker, Pearce, Walker, Wright, McMahon, Waddle (Platt), Gascoigne, Barnes, Lineker, Bull (Beardsley).

0 (0) EGYPT

Shobeir, I.Hassan, Yassein, H.Ramzy, A.Ramzy, Yakan, Youssef, Abdelghani, H.Hassan, El Kass (Soliman), Abdelhamid (Abdelrahman).

Referee: Kurt Röthlisberger (Switzerland)
Attendance: 34.959

**Palermo, June 21st -
Stadio Della Favorita**

1 (1) HOLLAND

Gullit 10

van Breukelen, van Aerle, Rijkaard, R.Koeman, van Tiggelen, Wouters, Witschge (Fraser), Kieft (van Loen), Gillhaus, van Basten, Gullit.

1 (0) IRELAND

Quinn 71

Bonner, Morris, Staunton, McCarthy, Moran, McGrath, Houghton, Townsend, Aldridge (Cascarino), Quinn, Sheedy (Whelan).

Referee: Michel Vautrot (France)
Attendance: 33.288

	P	W	D	L	F	A	Pts
England	3	1	2	0	2	1	4
Ireland	3	0	3	0	2	3	3
Holland	3	0	3	0	2	2	3
Egypt	3	0	2	1	1	2	2

SECOND ROUND

Naples, June 23rd - Stadio San Paolo

2 (0) CAMEROON

Milla 106, 109

N'Kono, Ebwelle, Onana, N'Dip, Tataw, Kana-Biyik, M'Bouh, M'Fede (Milla), Maboang, Makanaky (Djonkep), Omam-Biyik.

1 (0) COLOMBIA

Redin 116

Higuita, Herrera, Perea, Escobar, Gildardo Gómez, Gabriel Gómez (Redin), Alvarez, Valderrama, Rincón, Fajardo (Iguaran), Estrada.

After extra time - 45 mins (0-0), 90 mins (0-0), 120 mins 2-1

Referee: Tullio Lanese (Italy)
Attendance: 50.026

Bari, June 23rd - Stadio Della Vittoria

4 (1) CZECHOSLOVAKIA

Skuhravy 11, 62, 82, Kubic 78

Stejskal, Kadlec, Kocian, Chovanec, Hasek, Bilek, Kubic, Moravcik, Straka, Skuhravy, Knoflicek.

1 (0) COSTA RICA

González 55

Barrantes, Flores, Montero, Obando (Medford), Chavez, González, Chavarria (Guimaraes), Marchena, Cayasso, Ramírez, C.Jara.

Referee: Sigfried Kirschen (East Germany)
Attendance: 47.673

Turin, June 24th - Stadio Delle Alpi

1 (0) ARGENTINA

Caniggia 81

Goycoechea, Simon, Ruggeri, Monzon, Olarticoechea, Giusti, Troglio (Calderón), Caniggia, Basualdo, Burruchaga, Maradona.

0 (0) BRAZIL

Taffarel, Mauro Galvao (Renato), Ricardo Gomes (RED), Ricardo Rocha, Jorginho, Valdo, Dunga, Alemão (Silas), Branco, Careca, Müller.

Referee: Joël Quiniou (France)
Attendance: 61.381

Milan, June 24th - Stadio Giuseppe Meazza (San Siro)

2 (0) WEST GERMANY

Klinsmann 50, Brehme 84

Illgner, Reuter, Brehme, Kohler, Augenthaler, Buchwald, Berthold, Littbarski, Völler (RED), Matthäus, Klinsmann (Riedle).

1 (0) HOLLAND

R.Koeman (pen) 88

van Breukelen, van Aerle (Kieft), Rijkaard (RED), R.Koeman, van Tiggelen, Wouters, Witschge (Gillhaus), Winter, Van't Schip, van Basten, Gullit.

Referee: Juan Carlos Loustau (Argentina)
Attendance: 74.559

Genoa, June 25th - Stadio Luigi Ferraris

5 (0)(0) IRELAND

Bonner, Morris, Staunton (O'Leary), McCarthy, Moran, McGrath, Houghton, Townsend, Aldridge (Cascarino), Sheedy, Quinn.

4 (0)(0) ROMANIA

Lung, Rednic, Klein, Andone, G.Popescu, Rotariu, Sabau (Timofte), Hagi, Lupescu, Raducioiu (Lupu), Balint.

After extra time & penalty shoot-out - 90 mins (0-0), 120 min (0-0)

Penalty shoot-out - Romania started to shoot.

ROMANIA	4	IRELAND	5
Hagi	Goal	Sheedy	Goal
Lupu	Goal	Houghton	Goal
Rotariu	Goal	Townsend	Goal
Lupescu	Goal	Cascarino	Goal
Timofte	Miss	O'Leary	Goal

Referee: José Ramiz Wright (Brazil)
Attendance: 31.818

Rome, June 25th - Stadio Olimpico

2 (0) ITALY

Schillaci 65, Serena 83

Zenga, Baresi, Bergomi, De Agostini, Ferri, Maldini, Berti (Serena), De Napoli, Giannini, Baggio (Vierchowod), Schillaci.

0 (0) URUGUAY

Alvez, Gutiérrez, De Leon, Dominguez, Pintos, Perdomo, Ostolaza (Alzamendi), Francescoli, Pereira, Aguilera (Sosa), Fonseca.

Referee: George Courtney (England)
Attendance: 73.303

Verona, June 26th - Stadio Marc Antonio Bentegodi

2 (1) YUGOSLAVIA

Stojkovic 77, 92

Ivkovic, Spasic, Hadzibegic, Jozic, Brnovic Susic, Stojkovic, Katanec (Vulic), Sabanadzovic, Pancev (Savicevic), Vujovic,

1 (1) SPAIN

Salinas 83

Zubizarreta, Chendo, Villaroya, Gorriz, Andrinua (Jimenez), Sanchis, Roberto, Vázquez, Butragueño (Rafael Paz), Michel, Salinas.

After extra time - 45 mins (0-0), 90 mins (1-1)

Referee: Aron Schmidhuber (West Germany)
Attendance: 35.500

Bologna, June 26th - Stadio Marc Antonio Bentegodi

1 (0) ENGLAND

Platt 119

Shilton, Pearce, Walker, Butcher, Parker, Wright, Waddle, McMahon (Platt), Gascoigne, Lineker, Barnes (Bull).

0 (0) BELGIUM

Proud'homme, Gerets, Clijsters, Demol, Grün, De Wolf, Van der Elst, Scifo, Versavel (Vervoort), Degryse (Claesen), Ceulemans.

After extra time - 45 mins (0-0), 90 mins (0-0)

Referee: Peter Mikkelsen (Denmark)
Attendance: 34.520

QUARTER-FINALS

Florence, June 30th - Stadio Communale

3 (0)(0) ARGENTINA

Goycoechea, Ruggeri, Simon, Olarticoechea (Troglio), Serrizuela, Giusti, Burruchaga, Basualdo, Calderón (Dezotti), Caniggia, Maradona.

2 (0)(0) YUGOSLAVIA

Ivkovic, Spasic, Hadzibegic, Jozic, Vulic, Sabanadzovic (RED) Brnovic, Susic, (Savicevic), Stojkovic, Prosinecki, Vujovic,

After extra time & penalty shoot-out - 90 mins (0-0), 120 mins (0-0)

Penalty shoot-out - Argentina started to shoot.

ARGENTINA	3	YUGOSLAVIA	2
Serrizuela	Goal	Stojkovic	Miss
Burruchaga	Goal	Prosinecki	Goal
Maradona	Miss	Savicevic	Goal
Troglio	Miss	Brnovic	Miss
Dezotti	Goal	Hadzibegic	Miss

Referee: Kurt Röthlisberger (Switzerland)
Attendance: 38.971

Rome, June 30th - Stadio Olimpico

1 (1) ITALY

Schillaci 37

Zenga, Baresi, Bergomi, De Agostini, Ferri, Maldini, Donadoni, De Napoli, Giannini (Ancelotti), Baggio (Serena), Schillaci.

0 (0) IRELAND

Bonner, Morris, Staunton, McCarthy, Moran, McGrath, Houghton, Townsend, Aldridge (Sheridan), Sheedy, Quinn (Cascarino).

Referee: Carlos Antonio Silva Valente (Portugal)
Attendance: 73.303

Milan, July 1st - Stadio Giuseppe Meazza (San Siro)

1 (1) WEST GERMANY

Matthäus (pen) 24

Illgner, Brehme, Kohler, Augenthaler, Buchwald, Berthold, Littbarski, Bein (Möller), Matthäus, Klinsmann, Riedle.

0 (0) CZECHOSLOVAKIA

Stejskal, Kadlec, Kocian, Chovanec, Hasek, Bilek (Nemecek), Kubic (Griga), Moravcik (RED), Straka, Skuhravy, Knoflicek.

Referee: Helmut Kohl (Austria)
Attendance: 73.347

Naples, July 1st - Stadio San Paolo

After extra time - 45 mins (1-0), 90 mins (2-2)

3 (2) ENGLAND

Platt 25, Lineker (pen)82, (pen)105

Shilton, Pearce, Walker, Butcher (Steven), Parker, Wright, Waddle, Platt, Gascoigne, Lineker, Barnes (Beardsley).

2 (2) CAMEROON

Kunde (pen)62, Ekeke 65

N'Kono, Ebwelle, Massing, Kunde, Tataw, Pagal, Libiih, M'Fede (Ekeke), Maboang (Milla), Makanaky, Omam-Biyik.

Referee: Edgardo Codesal Mendez (Mexico)
Attendance: 55.205

SEMI-FINALS

Naples, July 3rd - Stadio San Paolo

5 (4)(1) ARGENTINA

Caniggia 67

Goycoechea, Ruggeri, Simon, Olarticoechea, Serrizuela, Giusti (RED), Burruchaga, Basualdo (Batista), Calderón (Troglio), Caniggia, Maradona.

4 (3)(1) ITALY

Schillaci 17

Zenga, Baresi, Bergomi, De Agostini, Ferri, Maldini, Donadoni, De Napoli, Giannini (Baggio), Vialli (Serena), Schillaci.

After extra time & penalty shoot-out - 90 mins (1-1), 120 mins(1-1).

Penalty shoot-out - Italy started to shoot.

ITALY	3	ARGENTINA	4
Baresi	Goal	Serrizuela	Goal
Baggio	Goal	Burruchaga	Goal
De Agostini	Goal	Olarticoechea	Goal
Donadoni	Miss	Maradona	Goal
Serena	Miss		

Referee: Michel Vautrot
Attendance: 59.978

Turin, July 4th - Stadio Delle Alpi

5 (1) WEST GERMANY

Brehme 59

Illgner, Brehme, Kohler, Augenthaler, Buchwald, Berthold, Hässler (Reuter), Thon, Matthäus, Klinsmann, Völler (Riedle).

4 (1) ENGLAND

Lineker 80

Shilton, Pearce, Walker, Butcher (Steven), Parker, Wright, Waddle, Platt, Gascoigne, Lineker, Beardsley.

After extra time & penalty shoot-out - 90 mins (1-1), 120 mins (1-1).

Penalty shoot-out - England started to shoot.

ENGLAND	3	W. GERMANY	4
Lineker	Goal	Brehme	Goal
Beardsley	Goal	Matthäus	Goal
Platt	Goal	Riedle	Goal
Pearce	Miss	Thon	Goal
Waddle	Miss		

Referee: José Ramiz Wright (Brazil)
Attendance: 62.628

3RD/4TH PLACE PLAY-OFF

Bari, July 7th - Stadio Della Vittoria

2 (0) ITALY

Baggio 70, Schillaci (pen)85

Zenga, Baresi, Bergomi, De Agostini (Berti), Ferrara, Maldini, Vierchowod, Giannini (Ferri), Ancelotti, Baggio, Schillaci.

1 (0) ENGLAND

Platt 80

Shilton, Stevens, Walker, Steven, Parker, Wright (Waddle), McMahon (Webb), Platt, Dorigo, Lineker, Beardsley.

Referee: Joël Quiniou (France)
Attendance: 51.426

FINAL

Rome, July 8th - Stadio Olimpico

1 (0) WEST GERMANY

Brehme (pen)85

Illgner, Brehme, Kohler, Augenthaler, Buchwald, Berthold, (Reuter), Hässler, Littbarski, Matthäus, Klinsmann, Völler.

0 (0) ARGENTINA

Goycoechea, Ruggeri (Monzon) (RED), Simon, Lorenzo, Serrizuela, Sensini, Burruchaga (Calderón), Basualdo, Troglio, Dezotti (RED), Maradona.

Referee: Edgardo Codesal Mendez (Mexico)
Attendance: 73.603

QUALIFYING ROUNDS

Africa - 1st Round, Group 1

16-07-88	Uganda : Malawi	1:0 (0:0)
30-07-88	Malawi : Uganda	3:1 (2:0)
07-08-88	Angola : Sudan	0:0
11-11-88	Sudan : Angola	1:2 (1:0)

Africa - 1st Round, Group 2

	P	W	D	L	F	A	Pts
Liberia	2	1	1	0	2	0	3
Tunisia	2	1	0	1	5	3	2
Libya	2	1	0	1	3	2	2
Burkina Faso	2	1	0	1	2	3	2
Guinea	2	1	0	1	3	5	2
Ghana	2	0	1	1	0	2	1

03-06-88	Libya : Burkina Faso	3:0 (3:0)
03-07-88	Burkina Faso : Libya	2:0 (0:0)
05-08-88	Tunisia : Guinea	5:0 (2:0)
07-08-88	Ghana : Liberia	0:0
21-08-88	Guinea : Tunisia	3:0 (1:0)
21-08-88	Liberia : Ghana	2:0 (1:0)

Africa - 2nd Round, Group A

	P	W	D	L	F	A	Pts
Algeria	4	3	1	0	6	1	7
Cote d' Ivoire	4	1	2	1	5	1	4
Zimbabwe	4	0	1	3	1	10	1

06-01-89	Algeria : Zimbabwe	3:0 (2:0)
22-01-89	Zimbabwe : Cote d' Ivoire	0:0
11-06-89	Cote d' Ivoire : Algeria	0:0
25-06-89	Zimbabwe : Algeria	1:2 (0:1)
13-08-89	Cote d' Ivoire : Zimbabwe	5:0 (1:0)
25-08-89	Algeria : Cote d' Ivoire	1:0 (0:0)

Africa - 2nd Round, Group B

	P	W	D	L	F	A	Pts
Egypt	6	3	2	1	6	2	8
Liberia	6	2	2	2	2	3	6
Malawi	6	1	3	2	3	4	5
Kenya	6	1	3	2	2	4	5

06-01-89	Egypt : Liberia	2:0 (2:0)
07-01-89	Kenya : Malawi	1:1 (0:1)
21-01-89	Malawi : Egypt	1:1 (0:0)
22-01-89	Liberia : Kenya	0:0
10-06-89	Kenya : Egypt	0:0
11-06-89	Liberia : Malawi	1:0 (1:0)
24-06-89	Malawi : Kenya	1:0 (0:0)
25-06-89	Liberia : Egypt	1:0 (1:0)
11-08-89	Egypt : Malawi	1:0 (1:0)
12-08-89	Kenya : Liberia	1:0 (1:0)

25-08-89	Egypt : Kenya	2:0 (0:0)
26-08-89	Malawi : Liberia	0:0

Africa - 2nd Round, Group C

	P	W	D	L	F	A	Pts
Cameroon	6	4	1	1	9	6	9
Nigeria	6	3	1	2	7	5	7
Angola	6	1	2	3	6	7	4
Gabon	6	2	0	4	5	9	4

07-01-89	Nigeria : Gabon	1:0 (1:0)
08-01-89	Cameroon : Angola	1:1 (0:1)
22-01-89	Angola : Nigeria	2:2 (1:0)
22-01-89	Gabon : Cameroon	1:3 (1:2)
10-06-89	Nigeria : Cameroon	2:0 (1:0)
11-06-89	Angola : Gabon	2:0 (2:0)
25-06-89	Gabon : Nigeria	2:1 (2:0)
25-06-89	Angola : Cameroon	1:2 (1:0)
12-08-89	Nigeria : Angola	1:0 (1:0)
13-08-89	Cameroon : Gabon	2:1 (2:0)
27-08-89	Gabon : Angola	1:0 (1:0)
27-08-89	Cameroon : Nigeria	1:0 (1:0)

Africa - 2nd Round, Group D

	P	W	D	L	F	A	Pts
Tunisia	6	3	1	2	5	5	7
Zambia	6	3	0	3	7	6	6
Zaire	6	2	2	2	7	7	6
Morocco	6	1	3	2	4	5	5

08-01-89	Zaire : Tunisia	3:1 (2:1)
08-01-89	Morocco : Zambia	1:0 (1:0)
22-01-89	Zambia : Zaire	4:2 (2:1)
22-01-89	Tunisia : Morocco	2:1 (2:1)
11-06-89	Zaire : Morocco	0:0
11-06-89	Zambia : Tunisia	1:0 (0:0)
25-06-89	Tunisia : Zaire	1:0 (0:0)
25-06-89	Zambia : Morocco	2:1 (1:0)
13-08-89	Morocco : Tunisia	0:0
13-08-89	Zaire : Zambia	1:0 (1:0)
27-08-89	Tunisia : Zambia	1:0 (0:0)
27-08-89	Morocco : Zaire	1:1 (0:0)

Africa - 3rd Round

	P	W	D	L	F	A	Pts
Cameroon	2	2	0	0	3	0	4
Egypt	2	1	1	0	1	0	3
Algeria	2	0	1	1	0	1	1
Tunisia	2	0	0	2	0	3	0

08-10-89	Algeria : Egypt	0:0
08-10-89	Cameroon : Tunisia	2:0 (0:0)
17-11-89	Egypt : Algeria	1:0 (1:0)
19-11-89	Tunisia : Cameroon	0:1 (0:1)

Asia - 1st Round, Group 1

	P	W	D	L	F	A	Pts
Qatar	6	3	3	0	8	3	9
Iraq	6	3	2	1	11	5	8
Jordan	6	2	1	3	5	7	5
Oman	6	0	2	4	2	11	2

06-01-89	Qatar : Jordan	1:0 (1:0)
06-01-89	Oman : Iraq	1:1 (1:1)
13-01-89	Jordan : Iraq	0:1 (0:0)
13-01-89	Oman : Qatar	0:0
20-01-89	Jordan : Oman	2:0 (2:0)
20-01-89	Qatar : Iraq	1:0 (0:0)
27-01-89	Iraq : Oman	3:1 (1:0)
27-01-89	Jordan : Qatar	1:1 (0:0)
03-02-89	Qatar : Oman	3:0 (1:0)

03-02-89	Iraq : Jordan	4:0 (2:0)
10-02-89	Oman : Jordan	0:2 (0:0)
10-02-89	Iraq : Qatar	2:2 (1:1)

Asia - 1st Round, Group 2

	P	W	D	L	F	A	Pts
Saudi Arabia	4	3	1	0	7	4	7
Syria	4	2	1	1	7	5	5
Yemen	4	0	0	4	0	5	0

10-03-89	Yemen : Syria	0:1 (0:1)
15-03-89	Saudi Arabia : Syria	5:4 (2:1)
20-03-89	Yemen : Saudi Arabia	0:1 (0:0)
25-03-89	Syria : Yemen	2:0 (1:0)
30-03-89	Syria : Saudi Arabia	0:0
05-04-89	Saudi Arabia : Yemen	1:0 (1:0)

Asia - 1st Round, Group 3

	P	W	D	L	F	A	Pts
United Arab Emirates	4	3	0	1	12	4	6
Kuwait	4	3	0	1	6	3	6
Pakistan	4	0	0	4	1	12	0

06-01-89	Pakistan : Kuwait	0:1 (0:0)
13-01-89	Kuwait : United Arab Emirates	3:2 (1:0)
20-01-89	United Arab Emirates : Pakistan	5:0 (2:0)
27-01-89	Kuwait : Pakistan	2:0 (1:0)
03-02-89	United Arab Emirates : Kuwait	1:0 (0:0)
10-02-89	Pakistan : United Arab Emirates	1:4 (0:3)

Asia - 1st Round, Group 4

	P	W	D	L	F	A	Pts
Korea Republic	6	6	0	0	25	0	12
Malaysia	6	3	1	2	8	8	7
Singapore	6	2	1	3	12	9	5
Nepal	6	0	0	6	0	28	0

23-05-89	Singapore : Korea Republic	0:3 (0:2)
23-05-89	Malaysia : Nepal	2:0 (0:0)
25-05-89	Korea Republic : Nepal	9:0 (5:0)
25-05-89	Malaysia : Singapore	1:0 (0:0)
27-05-89	Korea Republic : Malaysia	3:0 (2:0)
27-05-89	Singapore : Nepal	3:0 (2:0)

All games played in Seoul

03-06-89	Singapore : Malaysia	2:2 (2:1)
03-06-89	Korea Republic : Nepal	4:0 (3:0)
05-06-89	Singapore : Nepal	7:0 (4:0)
05-06-89	Malaysia : Korea Republic	0:3 (0:3)
07-06-89	Malaysia : Nepal	3:0 (1:0)
07-06-89	Singapore : Korea Republic	0:3 (0:1)

All games played in Singapore

Asia - 1st Round, Group 5

	P	W	D	L	F	A	Pts
China PR	6	5	0	1	13	3	10
Iran	6	5	0	1	12	5	10
Bangladesh	6	1	0	5	4	9	2
Thailand	6	1	0	5	2	14	2

19-02-89	Thailand : Bangladesh	1:0 (0:0)
23-02-89	Thailand : Iran	0:3 (0:2)
23-02-89	China PR : Bangladesh	2:0 (0:0)
27-02-89	Bangladesh : Iran	1:2 (0:1)
28-02-89	Thailand : China PR	0:3 (0:0)
04-03-89	Bangladesh : China PR	0:2 (0:1)
08-03-89	Bangladesh : Thailand	3:1 (2:0)
17-03-89	Iran : Bangladesh	1:0 (0:0)
30-05-89	Iran : Thailand	3:0 (2:0)
15-07-89	China PR : Iran	2:0 (0:0)
22-07-89	Iran : China PR	3:2 (3:0)
26-07-89	China PR : Thailand	2:0 (2:0)

Asia - 1st Round, Group 6

	P	W	D	L	F	A	Pts
Korea DPR	6	4	1	1	11	5	9
Japan	6	2	3	1	7	3	7
Indonesia	6	1	3	2	5	10	5
Hong Kong	6	0	3	3	5	10	3

21-05-89	Indonesia : Korea DPR	0:0
22-05-89	Hong Kong : Japan	0:0
27-05-89	Hong Kong : Korea DPR	1:2 (0:2)
28-05-89	Indonesia : Japan	0:0
04-06-89	Japan : Korea DPR	2:1 (0:0)
04-06-89	Hong Kong : Indonesia	1:1 (1:0)
11-06-89	Japan : Indonesia	5:0 (4:0)
18-06-89	Japan : Hong Kong	0:0
25-06-89	Indonesia : Hong Kong	3:2 (0:1)
25-06-89	Korea DPR : Japan	2:0 (1:0)
02-07-89	Korea DPR : Hong Kong	4:1 (2:1)
09-07-89	Korea DPR : Indonesia	2:1 (1:0)

Final Matches

	P	W	D	L	F	A	Pts
Korea Republic	5	3	2	0	5	1	8
United Arab Emirates	5	1	4	0	4	3	6
Qatar	5	1	3	1	4	5	5
China PR	5	2	0	3	5	6	4
Saudi Arabia	5	1	2	2	4	5	4
Korea DPR	5	1	1	3	2	4	3

12-10-89	China PR : Saudi Arabia	2:1 (0:1)
12-10-89	UAE : Korea DPR	0:0
13-10-89	Korea Republic : Qatar	0:0
16-10-89	Korea Republic : Korea DPR	1:0 (1:0)
16-10-89	Qatar : Saudi Arabia	1:1 (0:1)
17-10-89	China PR : UAE	1:2 (0:0)
20-10-89	China PR : Korea Republic	0:1 (0:0)
20-10-89	Korea DPR : Qatar	2:0 (2:0)
21-10-89	Saudi Arabia : UAE	0:0
24-10-89	UAE : Qatar	1:1 (1:1)
24-10-89	Korea DPR : China PR	0:1 (0:0)
25-10-89	Saudi Arabia : Korea Republic	0:2 (0:1)
28-10-89	Saudi Arabia : Korea DPR	2:0 (1:0)
28-10-89	Qatar : China PR	2:1 (0:0)
28-10-89	UAE : Korea Republic	1:1 (1:1)

All games played in Singapore

Europe - Group 1

	P	W	D	L	F	A	Pts
Romania	6	4	1	1	10	5	9
Denmark	6	3	2	1	15	6	8
Greece	6	1	2	3	3	15	4
Bulgaria	6	1	1	4	6	8	3

19-10-88	Greece : Denmark	1:1 (1:0)
19-10-88	Bulgaria : Romania	1:3 (1:1)
02-11-88	Denmark : Bulgaria	1:1 (1:1)
02-11-88	Romania : Greece	3:0 (2:0)
26-04-89	Bulgaria : Denmark	0:2 (0:1)
26-04-89	Greece : Romania	0:0
17-05-89	Denmark : Greece	7:1 (2:1)
17-05-89	Romania : Bulgaria	1:0 (1:0)
11-10-89	Bulgaria : Greece	4:0 (0:0)
11-10-89	Denmark : Romania	3:0 (2:0)
15-11-89	Romania : Denmark	3:1 (2:1)
15-11-89	Greece : Bulgaria	1:0 (0:0)

Europe - Group 2

	P	W	D	L	F	A	Pts
Sweden	6	4	2	0	9	3	10
England	6	3	3	0	10	0	9
Poland	6	2	1	3	4	8	5
Albania	6	0	0	6	3	15	0

19-10-88	Poland : Albania	1:0 (0:0)
19-10-88	England : Sweden	0:0
05-11-88	Albania : Sweden	1:2 (1:0)
08-03-89	Albania : England	0:2 (0:1)
26-04-89	England : Albania	5:0 (2:0)
07-05-89	Sweden : Poland	2:1 (0:0)
03-06-89	England : Poland	3:0 (1:0)
06-09-89	Sweden : England	0:0
08-10-89	Sweden : Albania	3:1 (1:1)
11-10-89	Poland : England	0:0
25-10-89	Poland : Sweden	0:2 (0:1)
15-11-89	Albania : Poland	1:2 (0:1)

Europe - Group 3

	P	W	D	L	F	A	Pts
USSR	8	4	3	1	11	4	11
Austria	8	3	3	2	9	9	9
Turkey	8	3	1	4	12	10	7
Germany DR	8	3	1	4	9	13	7
Iceland	8	1	4	3	6	11	6

31-08-88	Iceland : USSR	1:1 (1:0)
12-10-88	Turkey : Iceland	1:1 (0:0)
19-10-88	USSR : Austria	2:0 (0:0)
19-10-88	Germany DR : Iceland	2:0 (1:0)
02-11-88	Austria : Turkey	3:2 (2:0)
30-11-88	Turkey : Germany DR	3:1 (1:0)
12-04-89	Germany DR : Turkey	0:2 (0:1)
26-04-89	USSR : Germany DR	3:0 (3:0)
10-05-89	Turkey : USSR	0:1 (0:1)
20-05-89	Germany DR : Austria	1:1 (0:1)
31-05-89	USSR : Iceland	1:1 (0:0)
14-06-89	Iceland : Austria	0:0
23-08-89	Austria : Iceland	2:1 (0:0)
06-09-89	Iceland : Germany DR	0:3 (0:0)
06-09-89	Austria : USSR	0:0
20-09-89	Iceland : Turkey	2:1 (0:0)
08-10-89	Germany DR : USSR	2:1 (0:0)
25-10-89	Turkey : Austria	3:0 (1:0)
15-11-89	USSR : Turkey	2:0 (0:0)
15-11-89	Austria : Germany DR	3:0 (2:0)

Europe - Group 4

	P	W	D	L	F	A	Pts
Netherlands	6	4	2	0	8	2	10
Germany FR	6	3	3	0	13	3	9
Finland	6	1	1	4	4	16	3
Wales	6	0	2	4	4	8	2

31-08-88	Finland : Germany FR	0:4 (0:2)
14-09-88	Netherlands : Wales	1:0 (0:0)
19-10-88	Wales : Finland	2:2 (2:2)
19-10-88	Germany FR : Netherlands	0:0
26-04-89	Netherlands : Germany FR	1:1 (0:0)
31-05-89	Finland : Netherlands	0:1 (0:0)
31-05-89	Wales : Germany FR	0:0
06-09-89	Finland : Wales	1:0 (0:0)
04-10-89	Germany FR : Finland	6:1 (1:0)
11-10-89	Wales : Netherlands	1:2 (0:1)
15-11-89	Netherlands : Finland	3:0 (0:0)
15-11-89	Germany FR : Wales	2:1 (1:1)

Europe - Group 5

	P	W	D	L	F	A	Pts
Yugoslavia	8	6	2	0	16	6	14
Scotland	8	4	2	2	12	12	10
France	8	3	3	2	10	7	9
Norway	8	2	2	4	10	9	6
Cyprus	8	0	1	7	6	20	1

14-09-88	Norway : Scotland	1:2 (1:1)
28-09-88	France : Norway	1:0 (0:0)
19-10-88	Scotland : Yugoslavia	1:1 (1:1)
22-10-88	Cyprus : France	1:1 (0:1)
02-11-88	Cyprus : Norway	0:3 (0:0)
19-11-88	Yugoslavia : France	3:2 (1:1)
11-12-88	Yugoslavia : Cyprus	4:0 (3:0)
08-02-89	Cyprus : Scotland	2:3 (1:1)
08-03-89	Scotland : France	2:0 (1:0)
26-04-89	Scotland : Cyprus	2:1 (1:0)
29-04-89	France : Yugoslavia	0:0
21-05-89	Norway : Cyprus	3:1 (3:1)
14-06-89	Norway : Yugoslavia	1:2 (0:1)
05-09-89	Norway : France	1:1 (0:1)
06-09-89	Yugoslavia : Scotland	3:1 (1:0)
11-10-89	Yugoslavia : Norway	1:0 (1:0)
11-10-89	France : Scotland	3:0 (1:0)
28-10-89	Cyprus : Yugoslavia	1:2 (1:1)
15-11-89	Scotland : Norway	1:1 (1:0)
18-11-89	France : Cyprus	2:0 (1:0)

Europe - Group 6

	P	W	D	L	F	A	Pts
Spain	8	6	1	1	20	3	13
Ireland Rep	8	5	2	1	10	2	12
Hungary	8	2	4	2	8	12	8
N. Ireland	8	2	1	5	6	12	5
Malta	8	0	2	6	3	18	2

21-05-88	N. Ireland : Malta	3:0 (3:0)
14-09-88	N. Ireland : Ireland Republic	0:0
19-10-88	Hungary : N. Ireland	1:0 (0:0)
16-11-88	Spain : Ireland Republic	2:0 (0:0)
11-12-88	Malta : Hungary	2:2 (0:1)
21-12-88	Spain : N. Ireland	4:0 (1:0)
22-01-89	Malta : Spain	0:2 (0:1)
08-02-89	N. Ireland : Spain	0:2 (0:1)
08-03-89	Hungary : Ireland Republic	0:0
23-03-89	Spain : Malta	4:0 (1:0)
12-04-89	Hungary : Malta	1:1 (0:1)
26-04-89	Malta : N. Ireland	0:2 (0:0)
26-04-89	Ireland Republic : Spain	1:0 (1:0)
28-05-89	Ireland Republic : Malta	2:0 (1:0)
04-06-89	Ireland Republic : Hungary	2:0 (1:0)
06-09-89	N. Ireland : Hungary	1:2 (0:2)
11-10-89	Hungary : Spain	2:2 (1:2)
11-10-89	Ireland Republic : N. Ireland	3:0 (1:0)
15-11-89	Spain : Hungary	4:0 (1:0)
15-11-89	Malta : Ireland Republic	0:2 (0:1)

Europe - Group 7

	P	W	D	L	F	A	Pts
Belgium	8	4	4	0	15	5	12
Czech	8	5	2	1	13	3	12
Portugal	8	4	2	2	11	8	10
Switzerland	8	2	1	5	10	14	5
Luxembourg	8	0	1	7	3	22	1

21-09-88	Luxembourg : Switzerland	1:4 (0:3)
18-10-88	Luxembourg : Czechoslovakia	0:2 (0:1)
19-10-88	Belgium : Switzerland	1:0 (1:0)
16-11-88	Portugal : Luxembourg	1:0 (1:0)
16-11-88	Czechoslovakia : Belgium	0:0
15-02-89	Portugal : Belgium	1:1 (0:0)
26-04-89	Portugal : Switzerland	3:1 (0:0)
29-04-89	Belgium : Czechoslovakia	2:1 (1:1)
09-05-89	Czechoslovakia : Luxembourg	4:0 (1:0)
01-06-89	Luxembourg : Belgium	0:5 (0:1)
07-06-89	Switzerland : Czechoslovakia	0:1 (0:1)
06-09-89	Belgium : Portugal	3:0 (1:0)
20-09-89	Switzerland : Portugal	1:2 (1:0)
06-10-89	Czechoslovakia : Portugal	2:1 (1:0)
11-10-89	Luxembourg : Portugal	0:3 (0:1)
11-10-89	Switzerland : Belgium	2:2 (0:0)
25-10-89	Czechoslovakia : Switzerland	3:0 (1:0)
25-10-89	Belgium : Luxembourg	1:1 (0:0)
15-11-89	Portugal : Czechoslovakia	0:0
15-11-89	Switzerland : Luxembourg	2:1 (0:1)

Caribbean/North/Cent. America - 1st Round

	P	W	D	L	F	A	Pts
Trinidad & Tobago	2	2	0	0	5	0	4
Netherlands Antilles	2	2	0	0	4	1	4
Jamaica	2	2	0	0	3	1	4
Costa Rica	2	1	1	0	3	1	3
Guatemala	2	1	1	0	2	1	3
Cuba	2	0	1	1	1	2	1
Panama	2	0	1	1	1	3	1
Puerto Rico	2	0	0	2	1	3	0
Antigua and Barbuda	2	0	0	2	1	4	0
Guyana	2	0	0	2	0	5	0

17-04-88	Guyana : Trinidad & Tobago	0:4 (0:2)
30-04-88	Cuba : Guatemala	0:1 (0:1)
08-05-88	Trinidad & Tobago : Guyana	1:0 (0:0)
12-05-88	Jamaica : Puerto Rico	1:0 (1:0)
15-05-88	Guatemala : Cuba	1:1 (0:1)
29-05-88	Puerto Rico : Jamaica	1:2 (0:1)
19-06-88	Antigua & Barbuda : N. Antilles	0:1 (0:0)
17-07-88	Costa Rica : Panama	1:1 (1:1)
29-07-88	N. Antilles : Antigua & Barbuda	3:1 a.e.t. (0:1, 0:1)
31-07-88	Panama : Costa Rica	0:2 (0:1)

Caribbean/North/Cent. America - 2nd Round

	P	W	D	L	F	A	Pts
El Salvador	2	2	0	0	6	0	4
United States	2	1	1	0	5	1	3
Guatemala	2	1	0	1	3	3	2
Canada	2	1	0	1	3	3	2
Trinidad & Tobago	2	0	2	0	1	1	2
Honduras	2	0	2	0	1	1	2
Jamaica	2	0	1	1	1	5	1
Netherlands Antilles	2	0	0	2	0	6	0

24-07-88	Jamaica : United States	0:0
13-08-88	United States : Jamaica	5:1 (1:0)
01-10-88	Netherlands Antilles : El Salvador	0:1 (0:0)
09-10-88	Guatemala : Canada	1:0 (1:0)
15-10-88	Canada : Guatemala	3:2 (0:2)
16-10-88	El Salvador : Netherlands Antilles	5:0 (2:0)
30-10-88	Trinidad & Tobago : Honduras	0:0
13-11-88	Honduras : Trinidad & Tobago	1:1 (0:0)

Caribbean/North/Cent. America - 3rd Round

	P	W	D	L	F	A	Pts
Costa Rica	8	5	1	2	10	6	11
United States	8	4	3	1	6	3	11
Trinidad & Tobago	8	3	3	2	7	5	9
Guatemala	6	1	1	4	4	7	3
El Salvador	6	0	2	4	2	8	2

19-03-89	Guatemala : Costa Rica	1:0 (1:0)
02-04-89	Costa Rica : Guatemala	2:1 (1:0)
16-04-89	Costa Rica : United States	1:0 (1:0)
30-04-89	USA : Costa Rica	1:0 (0:0)
13-05-89	USA : Trinidad & Tobago	1:1 (1:0)
28-05-89	Trinidad & Tobago : Costa Rica	1:1 (0:0)
11-06-89	Costa Rica : Trinidad & Tobago	1:0 (1:0)
17-06-89	USA : Guatemala	2:1 (1:1)
25-06-89	El Salvador : Costa Rica	2:4 (1:1)
16-07-89	Costa Rica : El Salvador	1:0 (1:0)
30-07-89	Trinidad & Tobago : El Salvador	2:0 (1:0)
13-08-89	El Salvador : Trinidad & Tobago	0:0
20-08-89	Guatemala : Trinidad & Tobago	0:1 (0:0)
03-09-89	Trinidad & Tobago : Guatemala	2:1 (1:1)
17-09-89	El Salvador : USA	0:1 (0:0)
08-10-89	Guatemala : USA	0:0
05-11-89	United States : El Salvador	0:0
19-11-89	Trinidad & Tobago : USA	0:1 (0:1)

Oceania - 1st Round, Group 1

	P	W	D	L	F	A	Pts
New Zealand	2	2	0	0	8	1	4
Chinese Taipei	2	0	0	2	1	8	0

11-12-88	Chinese Taipei : New Zealand	0:4 (0:2)
15-12-88	New Zealand : Chinese Taipei	4:1 (3:0)

Both games played in New Zealand

Oceania - 1st Round, Group 2

	P	W	D	L	F	A	Pts
Australia	2	1	0	1	5	2	2
Fiji	2	1	0	1	2	5	2

26-11-88	Fiji : Australia	1:0 (0:0)
03-12-88	Australia : Fiji	5:1 (2:0)

Oceania - 2nd Round

	P	W	D	L	F	A	Pts
Israel	4	1	3	0	5	4	5
Australia	4	1	2	1	6	5	4
New Zealand	4	1	1	2	5	7	3

05-03-89	Israel : New Zealand	1:0 (1:0)
12-03-89	Australia : New Zealand	4:1 (2:0)
19-03-89	Israel : Australia	1:1 (0:0)
02-04-89	New Zealand : Australia	2:0 (1:0)
09-04-89	New Zealand : Israel	2:2 (2:2)
16-04-89	Australia : Israel	1:1 (0:1)

OFC/CONMEBOL Play-off

	P	W	D	L	F	A	Pts
Colombia	2	1	1	0	1	0	3
Israel	2	0	1	1	0	1	1

15-10-89	Colombia : Israel	1:0 (0:0)
30-10-89	Israel : Colombia	0:0

South America - Group 1

	P	W	D	L	F	A	Pts
Uruguay	4	3	0	1	7	2	6
Bolivia	4	3	0	1	6	5	6
Peru	4	0	0	4	2	8	0

20-08-89	Bolivia : Peru	2:1 (1:1)
27-08-89	Peru : Uruguay	0:2 (0:0)
03-09-89	Bolivia : Uruguay	2:1 (1:0)
10-09-89	Peru : Bolivia	1:2 (0:0)
17-09-89	Uruguay : Bolivia	2:0 (2:0)
24-09-89	Uruguay : Peru	2:0 (1:0)

South America - Group 2

	P	W	D	L	F	A	Pts
Colombia	4	2	1	1	5	3	5
Paraguay	4	2	0	2	6	7	4
Ecuador	4	1	1	2	4	5	3

20-08-89	Colombia : Ecuador	2:0 (1:0)
27-08-89	Paraguay : Colombia	2:1 (0:0)
03-09-89	Ecuador : Colombia	0:0
10-09-89	Paraguay : Ecuador	2:1 (1:0)
17-09-89	Colombia : Paraguay	2:1 (1:0)
24-09-89	Ecuador : Paraguay	3:1 (1:1)

South America - Group 3

	P	W	D	L	F	A	Pts
Brazil	4	3	1	0	13	1	7
Chile	4	2	1	1	9	4	5
Venezuela	4	0	0	4	1	18	0

30-07-89	Venezuela : Brazil	0:4 (0:1)
06-08-89	Venezuela : Chile	1:3 (0:2)
13-08-89	Chile : Brazil	1:1 (0:0)
20-08-89	Brazil : Venezuela	6:0 (4:0)
27-08-89	Chile : Venezuela	5:0 (3:0)
03-09-89	Brazil : Chile	2:0

Chapter 17

Razzmatazz, Romario and the Divine Ponytail
The USA World Cup, 1994

USA 1994

Winners: Brazil

Runners-up: Italy

3rd Place: Sweden

4th Place: Bulgaria

Total Attendance: 3,574,491

Number of Matches: 52

Midway through the 1990s there was still little evidence that, despite advances in technology and medicine, mankind would ever treat each other with humanity. The year opened on a conciliatory note when the British and Irish Prime Ministers signed an historic declaration that brought the prospect of peace to Northern Ireland. Sinn Fein were to be allowed to join the peace talks if the IRA renounced violence forever and a ceasefire was called. Ironically, on 2nd June, 25 of the UK's top terrorist experts were killed in an helicopter crash. In the Middle East, PLO leader Yasir Arafat crossed from Egypt into the Gaza Strip after 27 years in exile, whilst in South Africa, there was a new constitution and Nelson Mandela's African National Congress were elected to government on 10th May. The country's first black president hoped he could unite all South Africans: "Let there be justice for all. Let there be peace for all. Let there be work, bread and salt for all. The time for the healing of wounds has come," he announced. His election campaign had been marred by violence as rival Zulu and ANC supporters clashed with loss of life. However, that violence paled into insignificance alongside the genocide taking place to the north in Rwanda. Here, in two April weeks, over 100,000 people were slaughtered following the death of President Habyarimana. Disease, starvation and rape followed murder as Hutu massacred Tutsi and, by the time the atrocities ended, countless thousands had lost their lives. In Europe, NATO attempting to keep the peace in Yugoslavia finally got involved in February when a US F-16 fighter shot down four Serbian planes after one of their more vicious bombing raids.

Great Britain was permanently linked to the continent when the Channel Tunnel was opened after eight years of construction and 31 miles of engineering genius gave British booze-cruisers access to cheap wine, beer and cigarettes. The most farcical event of the year was the trial of O J Simpson in the USA. In April, he was charged with the murder of his wife, Nicole and her friend, Ronald Goldman. The televised show-trial was played out like a soap opera in front of a worldwide audience but, in the event, all it was to prove was that that was just what the American judicial system had become. Black opinion was pitted against white, jurors were replaced and after nine months of evidence it took the ten women and two men only four hours to find O J not guilty. The whole case had hung on a pair of gloves from Bloomindales.

The world said goodbye to Jackie Onassis and Burt Lancaster. Ayrton Senna lost his life in a Formula One car crash in San Marino the day after Roland Ratzenberg had lost his in practice on the same stretch of track. Denis Potter lost his fight against cancer, Kurt Cobain lost his fight against drug addiction and went to his own Nirvana, and Henry Mancini left us with some of the most beautiful scores ever written, including the unforgettable "Moon River". The world's longest serving ruler, Kim Il Sung, also passed away, aged 82. He had been the only president North Korea had ever known.

Brazil, Chile, Morocco and the United States each applied to host the 1994 tournament, but Chile quickly dropped out. A FIFA visit to Brazil resulted in that country's bid being declined. Economic worries, a rising crime rate in the major conurbations, administrative chaos and stadia in dire need of major refurbishment gave the impression that a tournament held there would not go smoothly (as in 1950). Morocco pressed its bid with some determination, but could only boast two first class stadia and it seemed unlikely that there would be time or money to build others. The facilities in the USA, on the other hand, were superb and FIFA was keen to advance the game there, where it was already gaining popularity with the young, if not with the media. The choice, then, seemed obvious and was announced in Berne in 1988, timed to coincide with 4th July Independence Day celebrations. The Moroccans were furious and claimed with justification that commercial and not sporting considerations lay behind the award, but FIFA had cast its die. The World Cup circus had moved away from South America or Europe for the first time and blessed with its presence the Americans declared that: "soccer is the game of the future and always will be." The public seemed more interested in American football and base-ball, England would not be there, but there was some consolation when England's women beat the USA 38-23 in the Rugby World Cup Final.

It was later decided to make changes in the balance of places allocated for the finals, to redress the unfair bias favouring Europe and South America. An extra place was given to Africa, raising its representation to three, and Europe had its number reduced from 14 to 13 (Germany as reigning champions and 12 others). There were also changes in the allocation of places to the American continent. The USA gained an automatic place as host nation and four other places were reserved for the rest of the Americas, three for South America and one for CONCACAF. A series of play-offs involved the second best placed CONCACAF team meeting the winner of the Oceania group with the winner of this playing the second best placed team in South America's Group A for the remaining place in the finals. Argentina ultimately emerged triumphant from this arrangement, raising the American representation to six.

The full qualifying tournament began in the CONCACAF region with arrangements even more complicated than usual. The Caribbean teams were divided geographically into north and south zones and involved pre-preliminary and preliminary rounds before six teams emerged to go into Round One. Here they were joined by six teams from Central America and divided into two groups of six to play two-legged ties and further reduce them to the six that went into Round Two. Mexico and Canada came into the competition at this stage and the eight teams in Round Two were divided into two groups of four, the top two in each making it into the final round group of four. The top team in this final group gained automatic qualification for the USA, whilst its second placed team went into a play-off against the winner of the Oceania group.

The first game of the qualifying tournament was a pre-preliminary round match between the Dominican Republic and Puerto Rico in March 1992. A draw and a win over the two legs saw Puerto Rico into the preliminary round, where they were eliminated, but St Vincent, who contested the other pre-preliminary round made it through to Round Two. Here, they found the competition all too tough and lost all six of their matches, finishing bottom of the group and having conceded 29 goals to 2 scored, including an 11-0 thrashing by Mexico. The four teams that won through to the region's final round were Mexico, Canada, El Salvador and Honduras, with the Mexicans securing the automatic place in the USA as group champions. On the way they reached some significant milestones in their World Cup story: the third goal scored in the 3-2 victory over Costa Rica in November 1992 was their 200th World Cup goal; the win over St Vincent in December 1992 was their 100th World Cup game; and the 4-0 defeat of Canada in April 1993 was their 50th World Cup win. The Canadians took second place in the region's final group and went into the play-off with Australia, the Oceania winner. Scores were tied after two legs and it required a penalty shoot-out to put Australia into the play-off with Argentina, where they were narrowly defeated.

The USA World Cup was the first to be staged in a country without a professional football league, it was the first World Cup to have matches played indoors, it was the first time three substitutes would be allowed, it was the first all squad members not in the starting 11 would be available as substitutes, it was the first finals to be played without a British nation since the Football Association rejoined FIFA, it was the first time since 1982 that all the previous winners were not involved and it was the first time that first round yellow cards would not be carried forward to the second round.

According to eminent Israeli scientist, Dr Alexander Olshietsky, twenty minutes of dribbling the ball can use up as much energy as having sex. He drew up a timetable recommending when players should stop having sex before games: for forwards it was six days, midfielders four days and defenders and goalkeepers three days if they wanted to remain at peak fitness.

Razzmatazz, Romario and the Divine Ponytail - USA 1994

The entrants from South America were divided into two groups of four and five and the competition began in July 1993 with a surprising 0-0 draw between Ecuador and Brazil in Group B. The Brazilians then lost their first ever World Cup qualifier, a 2-0 away defeat by Bolivia and the mighty Brazilian steamroller was looking decidedly frail. They picked themselves up with a 5-1 win over Venezuela and ended top of the group, having scored a 250th World Cup goal with the second in their defeat of Uruguay in September 1993. The second automatic place from Group B went to Bolivia, giving them their first appearance in the finals since 1950. There was no place for Uruguay. The biggest upset in South America was the failure of Argentina to secure automatic qualification. Colombia finished top of Group A and had Paraguay beaten Peru in the last game of the group, they would have taken second spot, putting Argentina out. However, that game ended in a 2-2 draw and so gave Argentina the chance to take the long route to the finals, via a uninspiring 0-0 draw in Australia and a 1-0 victory in Buenos Aires.

In the Oceania region, the six entrants were divided into two groups of three, won by Australia and New Zealand respectively. The final was a two-legged play-off and with Australia securing a 4-0 aggregate victory, it was they who went on to meet Canada and ultimately Argentina.

The growing number of teams from Africa wishing to enter necessitated changes to its qualifying tournament. The 28 countries, including South Africa, allowed back after the abandonment of apartheid and introduction of majority rule, were divided into nine groups for the first round stage. Each of these sent one team into the second round, arranged as three groups of three, the winners of each taking Africa's places in the finals. The competition in Group B of the second round was marred by a terrible tragedy when the twin-engine De Havilland Buffalo carrying the Zambian team on its way to an away game against Senegal crashed into the sea only minutes after take off from the airport at Libreville, Gabon's capital, on 27th April 1993. All passengers were killed, including 18 members of the soccer squad. The 150,000 crowd who lined the streets of Lusaka to see the team buried together outside the National Stadium was testament to the nation's grief. To Zambia's great credit, a new, inexperienced squad was assembled, captained by Kalusha Bwalaya, who had not been picked to play against Senegal. They did remarkably well and missed a place in the USA by a single point. A draw in the final game against Morocco would have sufficed, but they went down 1-0 and ensured Morocco's third appearance in the finals. Africa's other places were taken by Nigeria and Cameroon.

A similar structure was used for Asia's qualifying tournament. The 27 competitors were divided into six groups, each sending one team into Round Two, and to reduce the amount of travelling, group fixtures were played in mini-tournaments, each lasting about a week. There were some notoriously leaky defences among the Asian teams, with first timers Sri Lanka letting in 26 goals, Pakistan 36 and Macao 46 with only one scored. When Taiwan went down 7-1 to Oman in its last group game, it was its 100th goal conceded in only five tournaments. Much more illustrious were Saudi Arabia, who qualified for the finals undefeated. Japan were only seconds away from becoming the other qualifier. They needed to win their last Round Two game against Iraq, but conceded a goal in the dying seconds to level the scores at 2-2. It gave South Korea the second spot and the place in the USA.

The region most affected by political considerations was Europe, where the changes that had swept Eastern Europe in the wake of the collapse of Communism and the break up of the Soviet Union between 1989 and 1991, made their mark on the World Cup. Once Mikhail Gorbachev had relaxed Moscow's iron grip, the Communist governments of Eastern Europe fell one by one in 1989 and Germany was able to compete as a unified country for the first time since 1938. Gorbachev also admitted that Stalin's occupation of Estonia, Latvia and Lithuania in 1940 had been illegal. They became the first republics to leave the decaying Soviet empire and, like Germany, competed for the first time since 1938. When a hardline Communist attempt to restore the old order in August 1991 was defeated by Boris Yeltsin, the other constituent republics of the Soviet Union also broke away, though too late to register for the 1994 tournament. Russia inherited the Soviet Union's entry, competing for the first time under that name, but it brought objection from the Ukraine, who quite rightly argued that many former Soviet players had been supplied by that republic. A compromise was reached whereby Ukrainian players could play for Russia, but they would compete as separate countries in future tournaments.

1993 also saw the two constituent parts of Czechoslovakia separate into two independent countries. They had entered as one, but failed to qualify, coming third in Group 4 behind Romania and Belgium. The 0-0 away draw with Belgium in November 1993 was Czechoslovakia's last international match, ending a World Cup tradition that went back to 1933 and included two appearances in the final itself. Another Eastern European country with a long World Cup history was barred from competing. Civil war had erupted in Yugoslavia in 1991, when the federated republics of Slovenia, Croatia and the then Bosnia-Herzegovina attempted to gain their independence and were resisted by the central Yugoslav authorities, dominated by Slobodan Milosevic's Serbia. The brutal atrocities that came to be known as ethnic cleansing were particularly, though by no means exclusively, associated with the Serbs and resulted in UN sanctions against Yugoslavia. They included a ban on sporting links and Yugoslavia's omission was Greece's fortune. They made it to the finals for the first time, undefeated out of Group Five.

Among the European teams who failed to qualify were Denmark, England and France. The Danes were reigning European champions, but were eliminated by a goal from Fernando Hierro in a 1-0 defeat by Spain in Seville in November 1993. England could only manage third place in Group Two, behind Holland and surprise package, group-topping Norway. Managed by Egil Olsen, who later spent time with Wimbledon, Norway kicked off its campaign with a 10-0 defeat of San Marino and followed with home wins and away draws against both England and Holland. They lost only once, away to Turkey, but by then qualification had been secured. France's elimination came via careless home defeats by Israel and Bulgaria in their final group games. Against Israel in October 1993, they were 2-1 up with seven minutes to go, but conceded two late goals to give Israel their first ever win on European soil. Similarly, three weeks later when a draw would have been sufficient, a goal from Emil Kostadinov in injury time gave Bulgaria the 2-1 victory that took themselves and Sweden to the USA.

Among the statistical milestones reached during the European qualifying matches, France played its 100th World Cup game, against Sweden in August 1993, and Sweden celebrated its 50th victory against Finland in October. Both England and Italy scored their 200th competition goals, against San Marino and Estonia respectively, whilst Italy played its 100th game against Switzerland and England gained its 50th victory against Turkey in March 1993. Malta's away win against Estonia was the island's first World Cup victory, whilst Iceland came third in Group Five, above Hungary and Luxembourg and for the first time scored more goals than were conceded. Luxembourg also conceded its 250th goal, though the European "whipping boys" were first-timers, the Faroe Islands, who let in 38, and San Marino, whose 46 goals against equaled Macao's tally for the tournament's worst defence.

The format that had been used in 1990 was maintained for 1994, but FIFA was anxious to avoid the criticism that had followed Italia '90 and several changes were made to the rules. To try to induce attacking play, three points for a win was introduced at the group stage. Later, and more controversially, tackling from behind became a sending off offence and referees were instructed to give more latitude to attacking players in offside situations. There was good intention in both, but the changes ought to have been given longer for trial, testing and interpretation before being applied. A further ruling said that injured players had to leave the field, to avoid time wasting. They led to referees making mistakes, but there can be no doubt that their effects were beneficial. The quality of football seen in the USA was much higher than in 1990 and came closer to the spirit of Mexico '70.

Dutch superstar, Ruud Gullit, had refused to play for his country because he didn't get on with the national coach, Dick Advocaat.

On the present World Cup trophy there are seventeen spaces for the winner's names. Any team that wants to get their name on it will have to do so by 2038.

Iranian television companies covered up pictures of the "half-naked" US cheerleaders to avoid offending religious leaders.

Razzmatazz, Romario and the Divine Ponytail - USA 1994

The "Eat My Own Words" Award for 1994 goes to...

Jimmy Greaves. In his column in the Sun on 18th June he said about the Irish: "The last time Jack Chalton went to the World Cup he got an audience with the Pope. This time, unfortunately, I think even divine intervention will not prevent him catching the first plane home when the group matches end on June 28th. To have Italy as his opening game must be Jack's worst nightmare. Result: Italy 3 points, Ireland nil." After the match headlines in the Italian press read "Legendary Fiasco" (La Stampa) and "What a Sacchhi Disaster" (Gazzetta Sportiva).

The USA's draw with Switzerland gave them their first World Cup point since beating England in 1950. Before the match Eric Wynalda suffered an allergic reaction to something he had eaten and was sick.

The 1994 World Cup finals were impeccably organized. Few nations can match the Americans for showbiz razzmatazz and sense of occasion, and both were plentiful in the opening ceremony that took place on Soldier Field, Chicago on 17th June. It was a spectacular array of colour and noise, involving 576 dancers representing the various nations of the world, 2,000 local volunteers and Diana Ross, who stumbled on the way to kicking a ball goalwards. She regained her composure, but still fired her second attempt wide. President Bill Clinton and João Havelange supplied the welcoming addresses, though missing from the event was the mascot, "Shooter" the dog. The Disney Corporation, whose creation he was, had severed its association with the event and the company brought in to take its place decided not to use him "because we think he's stupid."

The game that followed between Germany and Bolivia scarcely mirrored the glitz that preceded it, but it had its moments and at least produced the victory required by US sporting audiences, for whom a draw is something of an enigma and to be avoided wherever possible. The searing heat resulted in slow, deliberate football and an hour of stalemate before Jürgen Klinsmann's decider "came like a drop of water on a parched tongue." A long through ball caught the defence off guard. It was chested down by Thomas Hässler and, as Carlos Trucco came off his line to deal with the danger, the ball fell to Klinsmann for the easiest of chances. Bolivia tried to mount a comeback, but could not break German resolve and when 78th minute substitute Marco "El Diabolo" Etcheverry lived up to his name and was sent off for retaliation, it was all up for the South Americans. Germany became the first champions to win an opening game since 1974.

The heat also played a part in the other Group C match played that day and contributed to the first upset of the tournament. As expected Spain dominated the play against South Korea, but were unable to make it tell. The first half sending off of captain Miguel Nadal did not help. A second half reorganization that had Guerrero brought on in midfield seemed to provide the answer as Spain rushed to a two goal lead within seven minutes of the restart. Both strikes, by Julio Salinas and Antonio Goikoetxea, were set up by the substitute and victory appeared secure until the heat took its toll in the last ten minutes. The Spanish began to wilt in temperatures that topped 40° C and two goals in the last six minutes, from Hong Myong-bo and substitute Seo Jung-won brought South Korea an unexpected draw. The point was only the second they had achieved in the World Cup finals.

Three games featured the next day and produced a crop of interesting results, among them the Irish Republic's unexpected conquering of Italy in Group E. (See Italy v Republic of Ireland profile on page 435). In Detroit in Group A Roy Hodgson's Switzerland proved "the more accomplished of two ordinary teams", but could only manage a draw against the hosts. A Georges Bregy free kick gave Switzerland the lead, but Eric Wynalda's free kick just before half-time restored parity, a strike he later described as "the best goal of my life." The Swiss were left to rue a succession of missed opportunities, as were Colombia who went down 3-1 to Romania. The South Americans dominated the early exchanges with their precision control and close passing, but went behind to Florin Raducioiu's crisp and powerful 16th minute strike. In spite of their obvious technical superiority, the Colombians went further behind in the 34th minute when

Gheorghe Hagi lobbed the goalkeeper. Adolfo Valencia pulled a goal back just before half-time, but the Romanian defence held firm before considerable second half pressure. Bogdan Stelea was unbeatable in goal and when Raducioiu grabbed his second late in the half, Romania had pulled off an unlikely victory. Significantly, Hagi had scored one goal and had set up the other two.

The next day saw three European teams struggle to grind out results against what was regarded as weaker opposition. In Washington Norway gave a performance of "tenacity and sheer Scandinavian will-power" against a Mexican team full of invention and trickery, but lacking the decisive cutting edge. Resisting stubbornly Mexico's pressure, Norway were unlucky not to have registered a goal earlier than they did as Jan Age Fjortoft had one goal disallowed and a penalty appeal turned down when his shot hit the hand of a defender. Their winner came late in the game, when Kjetil Rekdal took advantage of Fjortoft's good approach work, whereas Belgium's winner against Morocco in Group F came early. Anderlecht's Luc Nilis crossed in the 11th minute and Marc Degryse jumped high to head the ball home. Thereafter, the Belgians had to dig deep to keep out a vibrant Morocco that regularly threatened to upset the show. A Moroccan shot hit the bar in the closing stages of the first half and Preud'homme did well to keep out a 70th minute header. They held on to take the three points, something the Swedes were unable to do in their Group B meeting with Cameroon. The Africans came close to taking a first minute lead, but generally began nervously and the Swedes went in front in the 9th minute with a headed goal by Roger Ljung. Cameroon gradually found their composure and in the 30th minute Marc Vivien Foe blocked a Swedish clearance out of defence. He fed the ball to David Embe, who pushed the ball over the line for the equalizer. There was a hint of offside, but he was given the benefit of the doubt. Two minutes after the restart Rigobert Song floated in a free kick and a defensive error allowed Oman Biyik, "moving with mind and feet at top speed", to nip in and grab the lead. It was now the Swedes that had to find something extra as it began to look as if Cameroon would extend the World Cup tradition they had been acquiring over recent years. Their blushes were spared some 15 minutes from the end when a shot rebounded off the bar and Martin Dahlin was on hand to level the scores.

Russia's preparation for the finals had been far from satisfactory, with internal squabbling and several key players refusing to take part, so it was hardly surprising that they struggled in their Group B game with Brazil the next day. They held their own for some 20 minutes, but once the Brazilians found their rhythm the outcome was never in doubt. They opened the scoring in the 26th minute, when Romario tucked in Bebeto's curling cross, and it was only an outstanding display from Chelsea's Dmitri Kharine that kept the result respectable. He was beaten only once more, a penalty eight minutes into the second half given when Romario was brought down and converted by Rai.

A second game that day saw the Dutch give a stuttering performance against unfancied Saudi Arabia, who were beaten "not for skill, but for physical strength, experience and late opportunism." Indeed, for periods of the match the Saudis looked the better team and took a deserved lead in the 19th minute from Faud Amin's "majestic header." However, Dutch physical play gradually wore their opponents down and five minutes after the restart Wim Jonk equalized with a 25 yard shot that bent cruelly to

Colombian Faustino Asprilla, was confident that his team would win the World Cup easily. "I want to rule the world - and this is my chance," he said. "I want to finish top scorer and believe I, and the team, are as ready as we'll ever be." They went home in disgrace.

On 18th June, terrorists burst into a tiny bar in Loughhinisland, County Down in Northern Ireland carrying AK47 rifles. The 23 locals in the tiny bar were watching Ireland beat Italy and had no where to run to when they opened fire. Six people died. The Ulster Volunteer Force tried to cover up the mistake by claiming that a Republican meeting was taking place there.

When Belgium played Morocco the ball was in play for 56 minutes and 27 seconds making it the longest game of the first round.

The Cameroon team was split over the inclusion of 42 year old Roger Milla in the squad, there at the behest of President Biya, because some team mates thought he was past it. Milla thought differently: "I'm in reasonable condition," he said. "I play tennis throughout the week and football with the locals at weekends." Biya also had to head off a potential player strike before their final group game when the players demanded far more in back pay than the £430,000, which had arrived at their hotel before the match with Brazil to settle an earlier grumble. He promised to raise the amount to £800,000, but it was not before goalkeeper, Joseph Antoine Bell, accused of leading the whole affair, walked out on the team.

Majed Abdullah of Saudi Arabia was known as the "Desert Pelé". According to Saudi records he had scored 118 goals in 168 international games.

In an analysis of their ability to dive, the Sun had Diego Maradona beating Jürgen Klinsmann by 48 points to 47. Criteria included persuasive talent, whingeing and play-acting.

"The man-to-man marking on Batistuta and Caniggia allowed the Argentine midfield a great deal of real estate." - Quote from the New York Times on 22nd June on the match with Greece.

The US authorities had clamped down on Nigerians entering the country after their presidential elections had been cancelled. It meant that the team's plane was delayed in Lagos because the aircrew had not yet obtained their entry visas. The team was followed everywhere by a band of supporters known as the "Drummers from Hell", banging their drums to drown out opposition fans. Their leader, the Chairman of Nigeria's official fan club, Dr Rafiu Oladipo, stood with his back to the play to conduct his drummers and keep control. "I have to see them, to do what we are here to do," he said. "Only once in a while can I turn my back and see the action. It really is quite a sacrifice."

When a television crew upset the Romanians by forcing their way into Gheorghe Hagi's room for an interview, a huge row ensued and the press were banned from hotel.

Blamed for his part in Colombia's early exit and for his own-goal against the USA, Andres Escobar was shot dead in the early hours of 2nd July out side the Restaurante el Indio in Medellin, Colombia. Confronted by three men and a woman hurling insults about his mistake, Escobar replied in kind. Two of the men drew guns and shot him 12 times. "All of a sudden, we heard gunfire, and then Escobar was on the ground, groaning and clutching his chest," a witness said. It was rumoured at the time, that a number of illegal gambling organizations that had lost a lot of money were responsible for his assassination. Humberto Castro later confessed to the murder and was sentenced to 43 years. The Colombian authorities now maintain that the murder was the result of an argument caused when Escobar parked his car badly.

beat the goalkeeper at the last. They won the game late after keeper Muhammed Al Deayea misjudged a cross and Gaston Taument headed into an open goal. After the match Saudi defender Mohamed Al Jawad said: "We proved that Arabic countries can play this game very well." Having seen two European neighbours struggle against Arab sides in the group, he had a point.

The next day Germany went behind to a vibrant Spain, who were the better team in the first half. Goikoetxea put Spain ahead in the 14th minute, but the Germans battled back in the second half. They created more chances, whilst never fully convincing and only managed a single goal to secure the draw that kept them top of Group C. It came early in the half, when Klinsmann headed down Hässler's free kick, a goal that Stefan Effenberg may have got a final touch to. Argentina, on the other hand, had little difficulty overcoming Greece in Group D. Maradona's return from a drugs ban revived the morale of the squad and his team gave a scintillating display in Boston's pouring rain. Batistuta gave them the lead after only 87 seconds, running freely from the half way line to stroke the ball past an over-awed Antonis Minou in goal. He scored twice more, late in each half, and Maradona grabbed a goal in the 59th minute for an easy 4-0 victory.

Later that day the other first-time finalists in Group D had a much happier day. Nigeria went ahead with a 21st minute strike from Yekini and then had to hold firm as Bulgaria came back at them. Hristo Stoichkov appeared to have equalized with a sharp free kick soon after, but it was inexplicably disallowed and Daniel Amokachi extended Nigeria's lead shortly before the break. Neither team performed particularly well in the second period and the game was made secure with a third Nigerian goal, this time from Amunike.

When Switzerland took the field against Romania in Detroit the next day they looked an altogether better team than they had against the USA. The Romanians had the best of the opening exchanges, but Sutter stole the lead in the 16th minute with a "fierce shot from the edge of the penalty area", only minutes after having a shot disallowed. Hagi equalized with a typical rocket volley 20 minutes later, but the Swiss stepped up the pace in the second half. Stephane Chapuisat restored the lead in the 52nd minute and after having a goal disallowed themselves, Romania lost their composure. Adrian Knup and Bregy both netted in a seven minute spell to make the score 4-1 and when Romanian substitute, Ion Vladoiu, was sent off for a wicked foul on Christophe Ohrel, their misery was complete. FIFA banned Vladoiu for three matches and his own team mates asked him to leave the tournament because of his conduct on and off the pitch.

Later the USA added to Colombia's woes with a fantastic giant killing victory. The Colombians were clearly upset by the withdrawal of Gabriel Gómez from the line up, the result of a death threat delivered two hours before kick off, but their bright opening hid their uncertainty. Although Earnie Stewart missed an early chance to give USA the lead, Colombia responded with football "built on impulse, on telepathy of passing, of quick explosive bursts out of languid inertia." It seemed they might win handsomely. Yet the hosts had had moments of their own and they took the lead in the 33rd minute when John Harkes sent a speculative ball into the area which the unfortunate Andres Escobar turned into his own net. It was a telling blow, to which Colombia could find little in response. Five minutes into the second half, Tab Ramos chipped the ball over the defence and Stewart ran on to atone for his earlier miss. Valencia scored a breakaway in the final minute, but the result virtually ended Colombia's World Cup, gave the USA a famous victory and left the rest of the group wide open.

The next day saw Italy face the Norwegians desperate for a win to get their campaign back on track. The cause was not helped when in the 21st minute, Mykland burst clear of the

Colombian fans with a print of Andres Escobar calling for peace at the 1998 World Cup finals.

defence and forced goalkeeper Gianluca Pagliuca to charge out to stop him. He handled the ball and was duly sent off, the first goalkeeper to be dismissed in the World Cup finals. Surprisingly, it was Roberto Baggio who was sacrificed so that the replacement keeper, Luca Marchegiani, could be brought on. Norway launched a series of direct attacks trying to make good their advantage, but were unable to make them tell. Italy suffered a second setback early in the second half, when Franco Baresi had to go off injured, but in the 69th minute, Dino Baggio headed in a free kick to grab a lead. Further injuries to Paolo Maldini and Giuseppe Signori reduced them to virtual passengers, Oyvind Leonhardsen had a late goal disallowed for a handball offence and it was a very depleted team that struggled to the final whistle and an improbable victory. Later, South Korea's good showing continued with a second draw, this time against Bolivia. Their forwards proved more than a handful and gave the South

> In a Bangladeshi prison, inmates went on hunger strike because the guards wouldn't let them watch the World Cup. They took up food again when the authorities relented and ate whilst watching a match.

Americans all sorts of problems. They created the better openings, but were let down by poor finishing. Bolivia had Luis Cristaldo sent off near the end for a bad tackle on Kim Pan-keun and could count themselves fortunate for a point gained.

Brazil became the first team to qualify for the second phase when they disposed of Cameroon in Palo Alto on 24th June. Cameroon, who had earlier threatened to boycott the match because they had not been paid their bonuses, had a surprisingly good first half until the 39th minute, when a pass from Dunga was "chopped as if by radar into

Brazil 3 : Cameroon 0
Cameroon's Omam Biyick (left) takes on the Brazilian defence.

the stride of Romario." He was tightly marked, but drew the goalkeeper and skilfully placed the ball into the net. It set the Brazilians up to take control of the second half and further goals from Marcio Santos, with "a

In response to Jack Charlton's fine and touchline ban the Irish public raised a staggering £150,000 to help him pay it. Unfortunately, the rules stated that the Irish FA could not accept the money and ever pragmatic Charlton said: "I'll pay the fine out of my own pocket - then the rest can be turned over to charity."

Hundreds of Maradona fans in Bangladesh marched through the streets of Dhaka demanding their hero's reinstatement and shouts of "Dhaka will burn if Maradona is not allowed to play", could be heard. A court in the country ordered the FIFA President to stand trial when one fan accused him of causing mental anguish.

powerful, stooping header from six yards", and Bebeto gave them a comfortable victory. Cameroon took two unlikely records from the match, the first in the 66th minute when Rigobert Song, aged 17, became the youngest player sent off in the finals and the second soon after when Roger Milla came on as a substitute. At 42 he became the oldest man to make such an appearance.

Later, Sweden virtually ended Russia's hopes of further progress with a 3-1 victory and Mexico brought the Irish down to earth, defeating them 2-1 in Group E. Sweden's display was plucky and opportunistic, especially as they fell behind to a fourth minute Salenko penalty. They equalized from another penalty, given when Dahlin was brought down and which Brolin converted, and they took advantage of the sending off of Gorlukovich in the second half. They controlled the last third of the game and won it with two Dahlin strikes. Against Mexico the Irish lacked the drive and imagination that had been seen against Italy. They clearly suffered in the heat and most of the first half was played on Irish territory. They missed a good early chance when Motherwell's Tommy Coyne sent Terry Phelan's cross wide and later when Andy Townsend's header was well saved, but it was virtually all Mexico. They took the lead in the 43rd minute when Luis Garcia hit a low 25 yard drive. He added a second in the 66th minute and soon after Jack Charlton found himself in trouble with the FIFA officials over a substitution that he felt was being unnecessarily delayed. Coming on top of the regular complaints he had made about what he saw as an inadequate supply of water for the players to drink during the matches, it was all too much for FIFA. Charlton received a £10,000 fine and a touchline ban. His team ignored his antics, fought back and in the 83rd minute John Aldridge headed in Jason McAteer's centre for a goal that had great significance for the group's final outcome.

Of the three games played the next day, the two in Group F were brimming with significance. Saudi Arabia's meeting with Morocco was the first ever all-Arab game in the history of the finals, whilst the other was the much anticipated clash between Belgium and Holland. In the first, the Moroccans played the better football, but went behind to a seventh minute penalty from Sami Al Jaber. Despite their dominance, Morocco could find only one goal, when Chaouch found the net in the 26th minute and Amin regained the lead on the stroke of half-time. For most of the second half the Saudis played off the back foot, but they somehow survived to take all the points. In Orlando the European rivals served up a "slow jog punctuated by explosive moments." It was an end to end thriller, with Bergkamp "a joy to watch" and Rijkaard masterful in the middle, but the hero of the day was Michel Preud'homme in the Belgian goal. He flung himself everywhere to deny Holland's forwards and keep the game open. Its result was decided in the 65th minute when Anderlecht's Phillipe Albert drove a low shot into the net and gave Belgium their 50th World cup victory in their 100th game. The third of the day's games saw Argentina progress into the next round courtesy of a 2-1 win over Nigeria, though not before Saisia had given the Africans a shock eighth minute lead. The South Americans then fought back gamely and Caniggia's two first half replies spared their blushes, though not for long. Maradona, who had played well, was given a post-match drugs test and traces of five prohibited substances were found in his urine. His subsequent departure was a sad finale to a wonderful career.

22 Men and a Bag of Wind

The final games in Group A, on 26th June, featured Romania against the hosts and Colombia against Switzerland. The Americans played with plenty of heart and passion, but could make little impression against a well organized Romanian defence. They made early chances, with John Harkes hitting the post, but once Petrescu had given his side the lead in the 18th minute, the Americans were always struggling. Romania simply closed it down and settled for the narrow win. The Colombians decided they had to win their game and played as if they meant it. They dominated much of the play with sweeping attacks and beguiling interchanges and took a deserved lead just before half-time through a headed goal from Hermán Gaviria. Lozano added a second late in the second half, but it was too little and too late. The three points from the victory was not enough. Colombia went out of the tournament and the other three progressed into the next stage.

The day's other game was between Bulgaria and Greece. It was Bulgaria's 18th game in the finals and it brought their first victory. It was a hard-fought affair that saw eight players booked and "rarely pretty to watch", but the Greeks were largely outclassed. Two penalties by Hristo Stoichkov in the sixth and 56th minutes, and a strike from Yordan Lechkov ten minutes later put the game beyond Greece. The strangest goal came in injury time when the Greek goalkeeper dived to save a free kick that was going wide. He kept it in play and substitute Daniel Borimorov pounced to put it in the net.

The competition in Group C came to a close the next day with two highly entertaining encounters. In Chicago a lifeless first half was punctuated only by Guardiola's 19th minute penalty to give Spain a lead against Bolivia. However, the match sprang to life in the second with Latin football at its best, "lazy in the sunshine, but full of disguise and inventive passing", as one reporter noted. Caminero made it 2-0 with a well taken goal from a difficult angle, but Bolivia's response was immediate. From the kick off they drove forwards and replied with a 30 yard deflected shot from Erwin Sánchez. It was Bolivia's first ever goal in the World Cup finals and it opened up a game that both went out to win. It was secured in the 71st minute when Caminero chested down Ferrer's long through pass, turned and fired it majestically into the net. It took Spain into the next stage, where they were joined by Germany, victors in an equally exciting 3-2 meeting with South Korea in Dallas. This game appeared to be going to plan as the Germans rushed to a 3-0 first half lead, the goals coming from Klinsmann twice and Riedle. The Koreans changed things round at the start of the second period and the Germans made the mistake of sitting back. The Koreans seized the opportunity and in the 52nd minute Hwang Sun-hong scored with a delightful little flick. Nine minutes later Hong Myong-bo pulled another back with a crisp 30 yard shot and the game was suddenly looking very different. With his team tiring in the heat, Vogts replaced the injured Matthäus with Möller and tried to bolster his defence. Yet the Koreans kept coming and it was only the acrobatics of Illgner in goal that saved his team and sent them into the second round.

The final games in Groups B and E took place on 28th June and produced one win and three draws. The victory was one of the most convincing in recent World Cup history and saw Russia take apart Cameroon by a 6-1 margin. Oleg Salenko was the man of the day with a tally of five, including a first half hat trick begun in the 15th minute. Cameroon attempted to come straight back and Oman Biyik hit the bar soon after, but two more Salenko strikes, one a penalty late in the half, put the game beyond the Africans. Milla was brought on at half-time and within two minutes had got one back. However, two more Salenko goals and one from substitute Radchenko put Cameroon out of the tournament. It had been a good display, but sadly for the Russians it was not enough. They also went out. The qualifiers from the group were Brazil and Sweden, who fought out a tense 1-1 draw in the sixth meeting between these two sides in the finals, another record. The Swedes went all out for victory and gave their opponents no end of trouble. They went ahead in the 23rd minute when Brolin's pass was chested down by Kennet Andersson. He beat Mauro Silva and "struck the ball with stunning power and accuracy" to beat Taffarel. Romario equalized early in the second half with a brilliant solo effort that beat three defenders with his "astonishing pace and low slung balance" and after both seemed content with the draw that was sufficient for the further progress of both.

In one of the dullest of the series in New York, the Norwegians found it difficult to break their defensive frame of mind and were far too cautious in their approach against Ireland. Only as they realized that a draw was probably not going to be sufficient did they begin to push and by then it was too late. The game ended goalless, unlike the other between Italy and Mexico in Washington. Both set out to win and both attacked with conviction. Roberto Baggio saw a decent long range effort go wide in the sixth minute and soon after Pierluigi Casiraghi miscued a shot from a good position. Italy took the lead three minutes into the second half when substitute Daniele Massaro found the target, but Mexico equalized in the 58th minute with a scorching 25 yard shot from

Marcelino Bernal. With the match bringing a 1-1 scoreline, it meant that all four teams finished with four points. They also had identical goal differences and it had to be decided on goals scored. Here Norway had the worst record, having only netted once, and it was they who departed. The other three went through.

In Group F the next day, Holland struggled against Morocco. The Africans had nothing to loose and upset the Dutch with their physical play that brought four bookings in the first 30 minutes. Bergkamp put the Dutch ahead in the 43rd minute, taking advantage of a clumsy collision between the Moroccan goalkeeper and two of his defenders, but Hassan Nadar equalized within three minutes of the restart. It was not until the 78th minute, with Bergkamp turning provider, that substitute Bryan Roy's goal made sure of the points. Meanwhile, in Washington the Belgians were having a torrid time against Saudi Arabia. Saeed Owairan gave the Arabs a shock lead in the fifth minute with a brilliant solo goal that saw him gather the ball in his own half and beat four defenders before firing a smart shot past Preud'homme. The rest of the game was a procession of Belgian attacks, but "a mixture of stubborn defence and occasional luck" enabled the Saudis to hold out for a famous victory. The final group table had Holland, Saudi Arabia and Belgium on six points apiece and all three went through. Bottom spot went to Morocco.

Nigeria's 2-0 victory over Greece the next day took them to the top of Group D. They gave their "least convincing performance to date", though were rarely troubled and won the game with goals scored at the end of each half, Finidi George grabbing the first and Amokachi the second. The group's other game saw a totally dispirited Argentina go down to Bulgaria. The Maradona drugs scandal had ripped team morale apart and when Caniggia limped off after 25 minutes, their misery was compounded. Stoichkov put Bulgaria ahead in the 61st minute and, although Argentina rallied a little, their hearts were not in it and Sirakov's "emphatic header" in injury time gave Bulgaria a 2-0 win. Afterwards, coach Alfio Basile spoke of their talisman. "We really missed him very much, both on and off the field", he said. "He is a fundamental player for our team." The result meant that, as in Group F the final table had three teams on six points and they all qualified. Only Greece went out, having joined Morocco as the only other team not to gain any points.

The knock-out stage of USA '94 began on 2nd July with Germany taking on Belgium and Spain meeting Switzerland. In the German line up for his first start of the tournament was Rudi Völler, who had retired from international football in 1992, but had been brought back for the World Cup. The game brought three goals in the first ten minutes and Völler played a part in each. He scored the first after five minutes, from Matthäus's pass, and two minutes later it was his mistake that led to Grun's equalizer. Three minutes later he provided the pass from which Klinsmann restored Germany's lead with a "fierce left-foot shot." Völler headed his second from a corner in the 39th minute and with a 3-1 lead the Germans were content to defend in the second half. The Belgians enjoyed much of the possession, but were unable to make it tell until the 90th minute when Albert's strike made the score 3-2. Following the match, Swiss referee, Kurt Röthlisberger, was dismissed from the tournament when he admitted his decision to refuse Belgium a penalty was wrong.

22 Men and a Bag of Wind

The match between Spain and Switzerland was a bad tempered affair of "little beauty or excitement." For much of the game the Swiss attack was the more lively, with Chapuisat in particular playing well, but they could create little of merit. When they did, Zubizarreta stood like a rock to deny them. It was Spain, whose attack was always more vibrant and fluid, that stole the lead with a cheeky goal. Chapuisat had been floored by a hefty tackle by Nadal and as the Swiss argued for a foul, Hierro ran through to score. Much of the rest of the game was bruising stuff, with Spain seeking virtue in defence and the Swiss trying to break them down. The match was made safe with 16 minutes to go when Luis Enrique got a second and to be absolutely sure, Aitor Beguiristáin converted a penalty in the 87th minute.

The next day saw Argentina bow out with a 3-2 defeat by Romania (See Romania v Argentina profile on page 436 and Gheorghe Hagi profile on page 432) and Saudi Arabia's brave tilt at the world championship end at the hands of Sweden. It took the Scandinavians only six minutes to crack the Arab defence, when Kennet Andersson's lobbed pass dropped behind the back line and Martin Dahlin ran on to head in. They should have added more before half-time, such were the chances they created, but it was not until the 51st minute that they scored again, this time through Andersson. Five minutes before the end Al Gashiyan's exquisite turn and strike gave the Saudis feint hope of a revival, but they lacked real power up front. Andersson, having been set up by Dahlin's flick, completed the job with another goal in the 88th minute.

On Independence Day the USA took on mighty Brazil in San Francisco. However, it was a game of little passion and had no fairytale, though the Americans gave their guests a scare early in the first half. In the 12th minute Dooley chased onto a through pass from Ramos. He appeared offside, but was allowed to run on and his shot skimmed across the goal line to be missed by Taffarel's dive. It was also missed by Alexi Lalas and the danger was cleared. It was just about their only chance of a match the Americans spent much of camped in their own half. Even so, Brazil were strangely subdued and made little of their dominance and possession. They were reduced to ten men shortly before half-time when Leonardo savagely elbowed Ramos in the face and was sent off. Unfortunately Ramos also had to go off with a fracture to the left parietal lobe-temple bone. The match was eventually won in the 74th minute and followed a sublime piece of skill from Romario. He "accelerated with hypnotic grace" and pulled three defenders with him before stabbing the ball to Bebeto, who scored "from a forbidding angle." Later, Clavijo was sent off, picking up a second yellow card for a foul on Romario and the game was all over.

The Irish also went out of the tournament that day, the result of "two basic errors that cost us", as Jack Charlton later explained. Unusually they were defensive errors, the first in the 11th minute when Terry Phelan miscued a header towards his own goal. Marc Overmars sprinted onto the loose ball and set up Bergkamp for the opening goal. The Dutch then gradually assumed control and, though the Irish showed plenty of fight and spirit, they could make little impression. Bergkamp and Wim Jonk were in inspirational form and only determined defence from Babb and McGrath kept them at bay. The Dutch went 2-0 up in the 41st minute, when Jonk easily got past Sheridan and shot from 25 yards. Packie Bonner seemed to have it covered, but it squirmed out of his arms and into the net. The Irish tried to make a game of it and in the 53rd minute Houghton headed narrowly over the bar from Staunton's cross, but the Dutch were too good to let it go. Whilst there were many to praise Irish efforts, not all saw virtue in Charlton's achievements at USA '94 and there were several quick to highlight what were seen as negative aspects of Irish play. Continuing his feud with the Irish boss, Eamon Dunphy later said: "At a tournament notable for its quality, Ireland stood out like beggars at the banquet."

The next day Nigeria came close to doing "a North Korea" on Italy in their game in Boston. They took the lead in the 27th minute when Maldini reacted too slowly to George's corner. The ball bounced off him to Amunike who scored with "a clever flick off the outside of his left foot." However, their inexperience and tactical naïvety showed as they clumsily tried to defend the lead and allowed Italy back into it. When Gianfranco Zola, on as a 63rd minute substitute, was rather harshly sent off for a second bookable

Holland 2 : Ireland 0
Holland's Dennis Bergkamp (left) clashes
with Ireland's Paul McGrath.

Dutch defender, Stan Valckx, had a reputation for being a drinker. "It all started when I was a kid," he claimed. I was hyperactive as a child and my mum used to give me a drink at night to make me sleep. At the time I didn't realise it was laced with cherry brandy."

When Roberto Baggio scored from the penalty spot against Nigeria he broke the record for the highest number of penalties awarded in a single tournament. The previous highest had been 11 at Italia '90.

When the elbow of Mauro Tassotti broke Luis Enrique's nose in an incident the referee didn't see, the Italian was fined £10,000 and given an eight match ban, a record for World Cup finals. Enrique later said: "If FIFA had not acted I would have lost faith in the campaign for fair play." Tassotti never played for his country again.

offence 16 minutes from the end, the Italians were incensed and the more assertive side of Italian football came to the fore. They pressed for an equalizer and were rewarded with two minutes to go, Roberto Baggio grabbing the all-important score. Italy were the better team in the extra time that ensued and the Nigerian defending grew increasingly more desperate. They cracked in the 102nd minute when Benarrivo was brought down in the area and Baggio converted the penalty. It had been close, often reckless and crude, but it put Italy into the quarter-finals. (See Roberto Baggio profile on page 433).

The last game of the second phase involved Mexico and Bulgaria and turned into something of a farce as the Syrian referee was plainly not up to the task. He punished things he ought to have left alone and allowed clear offences to go unremarked. It gave an air of uncertainty to a game in which both scored early goals. Bulgaria took an early lead when Stoichkov latched on to a superb pass from Yordanov and "hammered an unstoppable shot" into the net. Ten minutes later, Alves went down in the area and Alberto Garcia Aspe scored from the resulting penalty. For the next 100 minutes of normal and extra time the game remained deadlocked and so became the first game of the series to go to a penalty shoot-out, which Bulgaria won 3-1.

The first of the quarter-finals took place on 9th July. For the first time since 1958 there were seven European teams involved at this stage with, significantly, Brazil as the other. They faced Holland in Dallas and it was a hard-fought, sometimes tetchy duel. Holland's game plan was to frustrate Brazil and any means, fair or foul, were used to this end. They smothered the midfield and kept men behind the ball so much that they created only one passable chance in the first hour of play, by which time they were 2-0 down. In the 52nd minute Romario masterly rammed in Bebeto's cross and ten minutes later Branco set Bebeto free to score. The Dutch protested loudly that the goal should not stand because Romario had been in an offside position. However, he had not been interfering with play and was walking back in an attempt to get on side so the referee, quite rightly, allowed the goal. It fired up the Dutch and within two minutes Bergkamp had reduced the deficit. In the 76th minute Taffarel hesitated at a corner, Winter headed in and the complexion of the game had changed completely. It was now finely balanced and might have gone either way. Eventually, Branco won it in the 81st minute when his 30 yard free kick soared into the net.

Italy faced Spain in the day's other match and were given a stern test. As one reporter wrote: "Spain were everything Italy were not - well organized, purposeful, knowing what they were doing." They did much of the attacking and Caminero might have given them a lead before Dino Baggio put them behind with a 25 yard shot, having received the ball from Donadoni. The Italians then enjoyed their best spell of the match before Spain once again became dominant in the second half. They equalized in the 59th minute through a deflected goal from Caminero and should have taken the lead in the 82nd minute when Salinas found himself through on goal with only Pagliuca to beat. However, his shot was tame and was saved by the keeper's legs. Italy's winner came from a breakaway two minutes from time. Signori played Roberto Baggio in behind the defence and he coolly rounded the goalkeeper to score.

22 Men and a Bag of Wind

The next day Germany took on Bulgaria, but failed to turn strength and tactical superiority into victory. Indeed, Bulgaria were the better team for the first 15 minutes and might have taken the lead when Balakov hit a shot against the post after Illgner had blocked an earlier attempt. The Germans, though, gradually assumed control with typically relentless football and their reward came three minutes into the second half. Klinsmann was brought down by Lechkov and Matthäus converted the penalty. For the next 25 minutes "there was the appearance of men against boys", as Bulgaria struggled to halt the flow. Völler appeared to have made the result safe in the 73rd minute when he almost netted a rebound from Möller's shot, but somehow Bulgaria clawed their way back into it. In the 76th minute they were awarded a free kick and Stoichkov cleverly curled the ball over the wall and into the net, leaving Illgner stranded. Then, two minutes later, Yankov crossed the ball and Lechkov steered a diving header into the net. It had all been so unexpected, but it put Bulgaria in the semi-finals for the first time. (See Hristo Stoichkov profile on page 429).

In the fourth quarter-final, Romania went out to stifle Sweden's front men and for much of the game were highly successful. It did not make for pretty football and it took 30 minutes before Romania launched their first serious attack on Sweden's goal. Yet it came marvellously to life in the final 15 minutes. Ingessen rolled a free kick to Brolin in yards of space for Sweden's first goal in the 78th minute and ten minutes later Hagi's free kick spun off a defender to Raducioiu, who made no mistake with the goal at his mercy. It called for extra time and Romania stole the advantage in the 101st minute when Patrik Andersson failed to clear a free kick and Raducioiu netted his second. When Stefan Schwarz was sent off two minutes later, there seemed no way back, but the game had another twist. In the final minute, Roland Nilsson launched the ball into the area and Kennet Andersson headed powerfully to take the match to a penalty shoot-out, which Sweden won 5-4.

Both semi-finals took place on 13th July and in the first of these, against Bulgaria, the Italians "at last put on their style". The occasion seemed to over awe the Bulgarians and, with Roberto Baggio in scintillating style, Italy dominated from the start. In the 21st minute he collected a throw in and beat two defenders to score a magical opener. Albertini hit the bar twice before Baggio netted his second in the 26th minute. The Bulgarians came back late in the first half, but could not score and the second half was a largely defensive affair, a ploy at which Italy are masters and 2-0 remained the final score.

Despite dominating vast swathes of their game against Sweden, the Brazilians were well below their best. They had much in their favour and dominated huge swathes of the game, especially after Sweden had Thern sent off in the 63rd minute and they began to tire in the withering heat, but it was not until the 80th minute that they made their advantage tell. Romario breached Sweden's dogged defence with the only goal of the game and set up a repeat of the 1970 final.

The 3rd/4th place play-off on 16th July was as one-sided an affair as any in the past and had been won by half-time. The Bulgarians had already peaked and could find little against a Swedish team disappointed by the semi-final and determined to go home with something. Brolin blazed them into the lead in the eighth minute and further strikes from Mild,

Bulgaria 2 : Germany 1
Germany's Jürgen Klinsmann on his knees in despair after the shock defeat.

Following her son's goal against Germany the mother of Hristo Stoichkov had to be taken to hospital when she collapsed.

With the score at 1-0 to Germany in their quarter-final, Martin Wagner was knocked out following a clash of heads. When he came round the score was 2-1. "Who got our second?" he asked, not knowing Bulgaria had won the game.

Following his team's victory over Bulgaria, jubilant Italian fan, Geatano Diomede, lost his balance while hanging out of a car window and was knocked over when he fell into on-coming traffic in Bari.

Brazil 1 : Sweden 0
Romario of Brazil (centre) takes on the Swedish defence.

Not one to hide his light under a bushel, Brazilian Bebeto's final comments were emphatic. "Forget the penalties," he said. Look back at the tournament. Who played the best football? Who always attacked? Who entertained the public? It was Brazil. My country has waited since 1970 for this moment. This is the best team since then. We are good for football. We are the best."

Larsson and Kennet Andersson gave them a 4-0 half-time advantage. Understandably, they eased off in the second half, but the shell shocked Bulgarians had no stomach to make a fight of it. It ended 4-0, but it was no fair reflection of Bulgaria's overall contribution to this World Cup.

The final, which took place on 17th July in Los Angeles, was sadly one of the most disappointing games of the tournament and completely failed to live up to the spirit of USA '94. It took a penalty shoot-out before "beauty beat the beast", as one historian headlined the final and, though it was not the ending FIFA would have scripted for its showpiece, it must be the merits of the whole tournament, and not its ending, that should be taken into account when passing judgement on the 15th World Cup. (See Brazil v Italy profile on page 436 and Dunga profile on page 431). It had been one of the best final tournaments ever and some commentators have suggested that it eclipsed even that of 1970. It was well organized, as one would expect from the USA, and more importantly it was well attended. Average crowds of 68,592 were far higher than FIFA could have predicted and even though a common joke was that the American public hardly knew that it was taking place, it aroused sufficient interest to make it a success and raise the profile of the game inside the United States. The crowds were well behaved and the games mostly played in a sporting manner that allowed teams and individuals to shine. The changes made to the rules only facilitated this aspect. It also produced its share of pleasant surprises with some of the lesser football nations going farther than they might have expected. If it had weaknesses, they were that TV schedules meant that some of the games were played in sapping conditions and that some teams had to travel vast distances to meet their schedules, which adversely affected performance. All-in-all, though, this was a tournament in which the good far outweighed the bad and was an undoubted success.

Hristo Stoichkov — Bulgaria

Honours: 4th 1994
Played: 1994 and 1998

Games 10
Goals 6

Stoichkov became a player many loved to see, not only because he was such so accomplished, but also because he was unpredictable. At times he would produce flashes of brilliance that were a pleasure, like the magnificent free kick that brought Bulgaria level in the quarter-final of the 1994 World Cup. At others he would be petulant and get sent-off for some cynical act or piece of chicanery.

Born at Plovdiv on 8th February 1966, the son of a former employee of the Ministry of Defence, he began as a 10 year old with local side, Maritza Plovdiv, serving a five-year apprenticeship as a number five before moving to lo-

Hristo Stoichkov (right).

cal rivals, Juri Gagarin Plovdiv for a year in 1981. In 1982 he was moved to Hebros Harmanli, a small town on the Turkish boarder, to do his national service and he played for the local side for two years. The move got him noticed by the army team, CSKA Sofia, the biggest club in the country, and in 1984 he signed as a professional. Six years with CSKA brought unprecedented levels of success, but had not the Bulgarian FA been lenient his career would have come to an inglorious end. In 1985, CSKA reached the final of the Bulgarian Cup to face local rivals, Levski Sofia. They won, but a mass brawl followed and Stoichkov and Mihailov of Levski both received life bans for their parts in it. Stoichkov's was later reduced to one year and the "Bitch", as he became known, resumed his career. Over the next four years, CSKA dominated the Bulgarian league and cup, winning three of each and in 1990 Stoichkov scored 38 goals to become joint winner of the European Golden Boot with Hugo Sánchez of Real Madrid. It did not go unnoticed by the manager of Barcelona, Johan Cruyff, who paid £2.5m for the Bulgarian star, a sum that, in post-communist Bulgaria, could probably have bankrolled the government.

From the start he didn't get on with Cruyff who wanted to play him in midfield. He also received a two month ban for his on-pitch conduct, but he quickly became a firm favourite of the Barcelona faithful. The sniping between coach and star player didn't get in the way of club success, and between 1991 and 1994 Barcelona dominated Spanish football. They won four consecutive Spanish titles and the European Cup and Super Cup in 1992. Stoichkov scored over 100 goals in this period and was recognized as one of the finest players in Europe. Yet, it did not bring personal reward and he was furious when Roberto Baggio was chosen above him for the European Player of the Year Award in 1993. He did not understand the decision, but it ignited a passion that was to carry him to greater things.

The 1994 World Cup began disastrously with a defeat to Nigeria. However, Bulgarian heads did not go down and they bounced back to their first ever victory in the finals, showing the flair and resilience that had previously knocked out France in the qualifying tournament, with Stoichkov scoring twice from the penalty spot. He scored again in their next, victorious outing and they eased through to the second round for the first time. A penalty shoot-out then saw them through to the quarter-finals to face the reigning champions. His team was 1-0 down with only 15 minutes to go when a superb curling free kick showed that he was the one of the best players in Europe. Another penalty in the semi-final made him joint top scorer with Oleg Salenko, but it was Italy who triumphed. Despondent, Stoichkov later claimed that the French referee had overlooked two other penalty claims effectively handing the game to Italy.

He received the recognition he craved when he became European Player of the Year in 1994. By now relations with Cruyff had broken down completely and in 1995 he was transferred to Parma in Italy. The discipline of the Italian game did not suit his temperament and by the end of the 1996 season he was back at Barcelona. That year he scored all three of Bulgaria's goals in Euro '96, but they could not prevent a first round exit. In 1997 he won a Spanish Cup medal, but his second spell at the club was not happy and in the spring of 1998 he was loaned to CSKA Sofia. He played in the 1998 World Cup finals, but a tired and ageing Bulgaria went out early, having scored one goal and gained one point. The final humiliation came when he was substituted in his last World Cup game, the 6-1 defeat by Spain. After the tournament, he became a football mercenary, making two appearances for Al-Nasar of Saudi Arabia, earning himself £130,000 and helping them to the 1998 Asian Cup. He then spent a year in Japan with Kashiwa Reysol before joining Chicago Fire in the USA. In June 2000, he hung up his international boots after playing 17 years for his country and scoring 37 goals. He now spends his time playing for Chicago and watching and analysing matches with his one time idol, then nemesis, and now good friend, Johan Cruyff when in Europe. He is very concerned for the future of the game in Bulgaria, but knows where the rebuild needs to start. "The revival of junior soccer could give a boost," he says. "But it is hard. Unfortunately, only a handful of clubs work to develop junior soccer. I have always said, soccer is a simple game - but for clever people." True words from Bulgaria's finest player.

Carlos Caetano Bledorn Verri (Dunga)　　　　　　**Brazil**

Honours: Winner 1994; Runner-up 1998　　　　　　**Games 18**
Played: 1990, 1994 and 1998　　　　　　　　　　　　　**Goals 0**

Carlos Caetano Bledorn Verri (Dunga).

Dunga was unlike other Brazilians. He was technically accomplished and he could hit accurate 40-yard pinpoint cross-field passes with the best, but what made him different was the way he commanded the midfield. He played in the more regimented and mechanical style of a Beckenbauer or Matthäus than with the finesse of a Socrates or the creativity of a Didí. It never endeared him to a discerning Brazilian public, but when, as team captain, he raised the World Cup in 1994, even the most vigorous of his critics were silenced. He was mouthy, bossy and distracting to opponents, but was also organized and an excellent motivator. Throughout his career he was hailed as hero and villain, acclaimed and pilloried, but his commitment was never questioned.

Born on 31st October 1963 at Porto Alegre, Dunga made his first forays into the professional game with Vasco Da Gama. He combined technical skill with old-fashioned hard work, grit and endeavor, which always impressed his coaches. He was also courageous and hard hitting. It brought him to the attention of the Europeans and first Pisa then Fiorentina and Pescara in Italy and VfB Stuttgart in Germany benefited before he made the decision to wind up his career in Japan's J-League with Jubilo Iwata. However, Dunga's story is not a tale of league success, of which there was some. It is a tale of three very different World Cup tournaments.

He made his first appearance in the blue and gold as a member of the Brazilian side that played in the 1984 Olympic Games and his full international debut was as a substitute in the 1987 friendly goalless draw against England at Wembley. By 1990, he had made his mark and his performances so impressed the national coach, Sebastião Lazaroni, he announced that a new era was dawning in Brazilian football, the "Dunga Era" and that his World Cup team would be "Dunga and ten more". However, it did not go down well with fans, who preferred a more charismatic player like Careca or Bebeto as the public face of Brazilian football. The 1990 World Cup started well enough for the Brazilians, going into Round Two as group leaders. However, a catalogue of missed chances and a moment of brilliance by Maradona saw Brazil down and out. Dunga took most of the criticism that was inevitably heaped on the team by the fanatical Brazilian press. The "Dunga Era" became synonymous with a type of football that Brazilians found hard to swallow. It was uninteresting and lacked creativity and excitement and his style became an object of ridicule.

It is a mark of his toughness and determination that the little player with spiky hair bounced back to lead his nation to World Cup triumph. He never lost the faith of his managers and coaches who admired the skill and value to the side supporters could nor would not accept. "I am strong mentally, very strong, and that is more important than anything," he said. "How many very talented players have done badly in a World Cup because they were not strong mentally. I'm not trying to build myself up out of vanity. I am also very aware of what I'm not. But I know exactly who I am and what I can give." At the 1994 World Cup finals coach Carlos Perriera felt that his tactical know-how should play an essential part in his strategy and it paid off. The pressure on the Brazilians was enormous, but, with Dunga dictating and Romario sparkling, they made it to a final that saw Italy buckle in an exhilarating penalty shoot-out. Dunga became the fourth Brazilian captain to lift the world trophy and the first for 24 years. "It was victory or exile and nothing in between," he said. "That's why I was so emotional when I held the cup moments after victory. For Brazil, we must try to win always. I know how much it hurts to lose and how joyful it is to win, so I want always to continue being a winner." His critics had been made to eat humble pie.

Dunga's philosophy was always that it is more joyful to win than lose and that is why his club career was successful. Age and experience also brought perspective to his leadership skills and even though he was playing in what some regarded as a footballing backwater in the J-League, he was captain of the Brazilian side that beat Bolivia 1-0 in the 1997 Copa America. He was still there when they travelled to France in 1998 when Brazil again made it to the final. There it fell apart and they suffered their greatest ever defeat in a World Cup finals. Following it, Dunga retired from the international scene. "Nobody likes to leave, if it were possible I would like to continue doing this for eternity," he said. "Despite the problems and the pressures, it's always been an enormous pleasure to put on the Brazil shirt. It is a great thrill. There's no description for what I feel at that moment when the national anthem plays. A phase in my life is coming to an end. I hope I have left good memories." It is an honourable statement from an honourable man who indeed left good memories.

Gheorghe Hagi   Romania

Honours: Quarter-finals 1994   **Games 12**
Played: 1990, 1994 and 1998   **Goals 3**

Gheorghe Hagi pictured setting up Romania's first goal in the 1998 World Cup match against England.

Like Hristo Stoichkov, Gheorghe Hagi was vibrant, volatile, technically brilliant, a dead ball specialist and prone to fits of pique. By 1994, he had earned the title the "Maradona of the Carpathians" and at the World Cup that year he was acclaimed as the best midfielder in the tournament. Born on 5th February 1965 at Constanta, Hagi's rise to the top was rapid. By the age of 15 he was a youth international, had earned his first professional contract with Farul Constanta and at 17 was playing at the top level with Sportul Studentesc. He made his full international debut on 10th August 1983 in a 0-0 draw with Norway aged 18 and one year older scored his first international goal in September 1984 against Northern Ireland in a World Cup qualifier. That year he played in the European Championships, when Romania went out at the group stage. Yet, it was clear he would become one of the star players in the league and in 1985 became its top scorer with 20 goals. He did it again the next year with 31 goals, six of which came in one game. Then, with the help of Valentin Ceaucescu, son of all-powerful President Nicolae, the army team, Steaua Bucharest, virtually kidnapped him from Sportul paying no transfer fee. Success was instant. A Hagi goal defeated Dinamo Kiev in the European Super Cup in 1986 and Steaua won the domestic double in three consecutive years between 1987 and 1989.

With the fall of Communism in 1989, Romanian clubs found it difficult to hold on to their best players. It was not long before Real Madrid took him to Spain, but his limited experience of Western European football meant that he made few first team appearances. Yet 1990 saw him in the Romanian squad that went to the World Cup finals. He came on as a substitute in the defeat by Cameroon, but played the whole game against Argentina that put Romania into the second round. He played in the defeat by the Republic of Ireland, but what the tournament had done was give a glimpse of the potential of the Romanian side containing men like Hagi, Popescu, Lupescu, Dumitrescu and Raducioiu, the backbone of what became a very attractive national side.

In 1993 he was transferred to Brescia in Italy and had a relatively successful first season, but it was the USA World Cup that confirmed him as a great player. He was tipped as one of the players to watch and by the time he went home, was world famous. It got off to a flying start and after 34 minutes of their opening match, Hagi launched a long-range drive that put his side 2-0 up. He scored another against the Swiss and they made the second round again with a narrow defeat of the hosts. Against Argentina, the match of the tournament, Hagi scored the winner. His success saw him snapped up by Barcelona and he had two years there before Galatasaray of Turkey paid $6m to secure his services. The local press ridiculed the move, complaining that he was too old and a waste of money. By the end of 1997, they were eating their words as his mercurial talents inspired the team to the Turkish title. He became a local hero. In 1998 he took part in his third World Cup finals, though by now he could produce only fleeting moments of magic and was more prone to shooting his mouth off than shooting at goal.

The year 2000 brought mixed fortunes. On the domestic front, his club won the double and the UEFA Cup, beating Arsenal on penalties. Internationally, Euro 2000 was a disaster. His former pace had been replaced by a more considered approach that belied his 35 years, but he had a growing reputation for petulance and two bookings in the first two games had him sidelined for the 3-2 victory over England that took Romania through to the quarter-finals against Italy, where he went one worse. He received one caution for stamping on Antonio Conte's ankle, causing him ligament damage and to miss the rest of the tournament. In the 59th minute, under pressure from Gianluca Zambrotta, he took a dive in the penalty area and was promptly sent off. It was a very disappointing end to his international career. He had played 125 internationals and had scored 34 goals. He has since made the headlines for all the wrong reasons, receiving a hefty ban in Turkey for spitting at a referee in March 2001. However, it should not detract from the fact that he is the best player Romania has produced and, for a while in the 1990s, was the best in the world. He is now coach of the Romanian national team.

Roberto Baggio   Italy

Honours: Runner-up 1994; 3rd Place 1990;   **Games 16**
Quarter-finals 1998   **Goals 9**
Played: 1990, 1994 and 1998

Roberto Baggio celebrates Italy's 2-1 semi-final victory over Bulgaria.

One of eight children, Baggio was born on 18th February 1967 at Caldogno near Vicenza in northern Italy. As a boy he took little interest in schoolwork, doing enough to get by, and much preferred to ride his motorcycle and play football. At the age of nine he was taken on by his local club, Caldogno, where his ability to score developed quickly and, when he hit six of Caldogno's seven against Leva in 1982 a Vicenza scout had no doubt that the prolific 15 year old should be playing at his club. To this day Baggio still claims the Leva game was the best he ever played. Vicenza, then in the Italian 3rd Division, paid $500 for him, but in his first two seasons, he made only twelve first team appearances and managed only one goal. At end of the 1984-85 season it all changed and he became a permanent fixture in the Vicenza team. He played 34 league and cup games, scoring 14 goals which helped Vicenza into Serie B. Then, on 3rd May 1985 he was sold to Fiorentina in Serie A.

It was not until 21st September 1986 that he made his debut against Sampdoria, but a knee operation in December meant that he made only five first team appearances that season. The surgery proved successful and in May 1987 he scored his first top flight goal against Napoli. 1987 was significant for Baggio for three reasons. Firstly, at the start of the 1987-88 season he secured his place in the first team and played 34 times scoring seven goals. Secondly, he converted to Buddhism and finally he unleashed his trademark ponytail on the world. He then married his long time girlfriend, Andreina. Azeglio Vicini gave him his first international cap in November 1988 against Holland and he topped the season with 24 goals in 40 appearances. His tally included nine in ten Italian cup games. The 1989-90 season proved the biggest in his career so far, as he scored 17 goals in 32 Serie A appearances and led his club into UEFA Cup for the first time. They made it to the final, against Juventus, but lost the away leg 3-1 and could only manage a 0-0 home draw. Juventus were on the lookout for a player to replace the departing Michel Platini and it was after the final that Juventus made Fiorentina an offer they couldn't refuse. When the news spread that the "Divin Cordino" (Divine Ponytail) was on his way to their bitter rivals supporters took to the streets in protest and it took two days before riot police settled the city down. Baggio was so emotionally shaken by the reaction, his form suffered and when he refused to take a penalty against his old club in their first post-sale meeting, he was taken off. The Fiorentines had known what the rest of the world was about to find out. Roberto Baggio was the best.

Although in the squad for Italia '90, he did not make his first World Cup appearance until the 3rd game. Italy had won the first two matches, but had scored only twice and Vicini was desperate to improve the team's fire-power. So he was brought on to partner Toto Schillaci up front against Czechoslovakia, the toughest challenge so far and in the 78th minute, he launched a solo run that finished with one of the finest goals of the tournament. The double act with Schillaci lasted until the semi-final when he was replaced by Vialli in a move that backfired. Realizing the mistake, he was sent on as a substitute, but too late in the game. He scored in the penalty shoot-out, but Argentina triumphed. He scored in the 3rd/4th place match, but it was scant consolation.

By 1993, Baggio had become one of the most consistent players in Serie A. He was joint second top scorer in the league in both 1992 and 1993, the year that Juventus secured their third UEFA Cup success. He scored twice in the away leg against Borussia Dortmund as Juve ran out 6-1 aggregate winners. He was recognized as the best in the world when he won the World Player of the Year Award. He scored his 100th Serie A goal in October, netted 17 goals in 32 appearances and saw the birth of his second child. With the 1994 World Cup approaching he was in buoyant mood and, as with Paolo Rossi in 1982, the Italian people had a hero they could believe in. It was no mistake that the "Azzurri" team that went to the USA was built around him. There it took a while to get going and it was not until the second round that he came into his own. With his side trailing 1-0 to Nigeria, he struck in the 88th minute to drag his team out of the jaws of defeat and then he scored the penalty in extra time that took Italy into the last eight. Against Spain, with scores tied with only two minutes to go and a tired Italian side not relishing the prospect of another 30 minutes, he netted mightily once again to spare them. The semi-final was more straightforward and Baggio hammered two spectacular strikes in five first half minutes to seal Bulgaria's fate. Unfortunately, he picked up a thigh injury and was doubtful for the final, but not wanting to let people down, he chose to play. He came close on a couple of occasions, though it was not enough to prevent defeat in the penalty shoot-out. The pictures of his dejection that flashed around the world as he put Italy's final penalty high and wide are not ones he remembers fondly.

Although Juventus secured the domestic double and were runners-up in the UEFA Cup in 1995, Baggio's career took a turn for the worse. He moved to AC Milan at the end of the season, where he picked up a second successive Serie A title, but was used mainly as a substitute. Arrigo Sacchi dropped him from the international side that travelled to England for Euro '96 and after another season spent mainly on the bench and the arrival of Sacchi at the club, Baggio signed for Bologna on 18th July 1997. The move revived his fortunes. Out went the ponytail and the appointment of Cesare Maldini as national coach meant he was once again picked for international duty at the last minute as they travelled to France for the World Cup. He might have started the tournament on the bench had not the "new Baggio", Alessandro Del Piero, been injured, but he got his chance and had another good tournament. He bravely scored from the spot in the 2-2 draw with Chile and hit the 90th minute winner against Austria when he came on as a substitute. His next appearance was as a substitute against France in the quarter-finals and he scored in the penalty shoot-out that put Italy out of its third successive World Cup that way. His next move was to the melting pot that is Internazionale, but it did not work out and, after two seasons and few first team appearances, he went to Brescia in 2000.

Italy 0 : Republic of Ireland 1

Ireland set up a defensive wall against an Italian free-kick.
Pictured (l-r) are Roy Keane, Ray Houghton, John Sheridan and Andy Townsend.

The build up to this game saw the largest ever one day transatlantic airlift of Irish people. Twenty planes took the supporters to New York to join the thousands that were already there and it prompted one immigration official to ask: "Are there any Irish left in Ireland?" What those supporters witnessed was one of the greatest World Cup performance by an Irish team and fitting revenge for their dismissal from the previous World Cup by Italy. In the words of one reporter: "Ireland were magnificent, Italy poor, and sometimes verging on the shambolic."

The conditions did not favour Eire. The game was played in intense heat of over 90° and 74% humidity, but much of the crowd was squarely behind the Irish, prompting the Irish Times reporter to declare that it was "perhaps the only occasion that Italians have ever been outshouted in the New York area." The crowd erupted in the 12th minute when Ray Houghton gave them the lead. Dennis Irwin sent a cross into the penalty area and Franco Baresi, under pressure from Tommy Coyne, misjudged his clearance and headed the ball into Houghton's path. The "rest, from an Irish view point, was sheer perfection." Running along the edge of the area, he chested the ball to control it, "looked up to see Pagliuca in no man's land and with the precision of a Jack Nicklaus wedge shot, looped the ball over the goalkeeper's head into an unprotected net."

The goal stunned the Italians and they failed to respond to the set back with any cohesiveness in the first half. As to be expected, the Irish were thrown back and forced to defend, but they did so with aplomb and amazing courage and spirit. It seems unfair to single out individuals from what was a terrific team effort, but Houghton and Terry Phelan were peerless in their non-stop running, Paul McGrath "embarked on another display to enthral" and in midfield Roy Keane "was sharp and unsparing in the tackle." Against such a powerhouse of determination, Italy found no answer and failed to create a chance of note in the first half. Roberto Baggio often found himself alone up front and hardly able to challenge Packie Bonner's goal.

The second half picked up where the first had left off. Once again Ireland's defence was called into action and were not found lacking. When "the Italians were in full cry for an equalizer" Phil Babb effected one marvellous tackle to keep out Dino Baggio and soon after Irwin timed a challenge immaculately to deny the same player. Bonner had to be constantly vigilant and pulled off one particularly fine save to stop Signori's shot. As time wore on, as the heat began to get to both sets of players and as desperation crept into the Italian game, the waves of attack that had floundered so often against the rocks of Irish defence began to lessen in intensity. The pressure eased, the match became a little scrappy and, growing more confident, the Irish began to threaten themselves. In the 71st minute Keane made a brilliant run that tore through Italy's defence and set up John Sheridan, but his shot crashed against the bar. Late in the game shots from Houghton and Andy Townsend forced excellent saves out of Pagliuca, but with neither side able to make further inroads, the match ended 1-0 to the Irish.

It had been a far from classic encounter and the football had not been top drawer, but it had much to recommend it. It was certainly passionate and invoked all the best qualities from the Irish players. They had had to dig very deep to find the strength and composure needed to stand firm against the odds, and that they did so was every credit to those players and to the fighting qualities instilled within them by coach, Jack Charlton.

Romania 3 : Argentina 2

One of the best games of the marvellous tournament that was USA '94 was the second round meeting between Romania and Argentina in Los Angeles. From two teams both with reputations for volatility, this was "high on quality, low on rancour" and aided by some intelligent refereeing from an Italian official prepared to let the game flow and stop it for only major offences. The result was a classic encounter of free flowing, end to end football from teams both possessing players of exceptional quality. Indeed, the first half-hour "flowed with more intent on accurate passing, more cunning and movement off the ball" than from any teams in the tournament so far.

The match began with a period of intense Argentinian pressure which could have seen them 3-0 up inside ten minutes had not Abel Balbo missed his chances. In the first minute Belodedici cleared weakly and Balbo forced a fine save out of Prunea with his flash shot and seconds later the goalkeeper had more work to do as Balbo shot fiercely, having been supplied by Sensini. Yet it was Romania that took the lead, against the run of play in the 11th minute. Selymes was fouled by Caceres and Ilie Dumitrescu from 30 yards scored "a craftsman's goal" with the free kick. The goalkeeper had strayed a mere two yards off his line, but the curve of the shot deceived him totally.

Four minutes later, the scores were even. Daniel Ortega, who had "the nerve and the verve to dance among the yellow Romanian shirts as if balance was his by God's will", slipped the ball to Batistuta. With a clever back heel, he turned Prodan, his marker, and forced the Romanian into conceding a penalty, from which he scored himself. From their next attack, Romania scored again. "With an exquisite angled pass from the right", Hagi found Dumitrescu who matched "the perfection of the pass with anticipation on the run" to slot the ball into the net from close range. The game had developed into a tight and evenly matched affair, with thrills at both ends. Twice Popescu had goalbound shots blocked and twice Ortega set up Balbo, but both his header and his shot could not find the target. At the interval the score was still 2-1.

The Argentinians forced much of the pace in the second half, with Ortega the midfield orchestrator of much of their play. Batistuta brought an excellent save out of Prunea and minutes later Redondo went down in the area, though no penalty was given. Despite their pressure, it was Romania that scored again. In the 58th minute and returning the earlier favour, Dumitrescu found Hagi "with a lovely pass... that simply demanded to be converted." Hagi duly responded with a right foot shot into the net. It was a mortal blow, but Argentina's spirit would not be dampened. They immediately resumed the charge and with 15 minutes remaining Prunea fumbled Caceres's 20 yard shot. The ball fell to Balbo, who was rushing to score, "a predator sweeping the ball into the roof of the net." With the score now at 3-2, it set up a lively final quarter of an hour. Both teams pushed and probed, Argentina did most of the attacking desperate as they were to rescue the game. However, time and fortune had run out for the South Americans. They were unable to breach Romania's back line and they held out for a famous victory in a much celebrated match.

Brazil 3 : Italy 2
The World Cup Final

Possibly the most disappointing game of the 1994 World Cup tournament was the final itself, in which the defensive qualities of both combatants emerged to the fore. Neither was able to find the freedom of movement of earlier games and the result was 120 minutes of stalemate. Surprisingly, the Italians brought back the AC Milan veteran defender, Franco Baresi, only three weeks after having keyhole surgery to a damaged cartilage and he had a hero's game. So too did Paolo Maldini, who began in central defence but who switched to his favoured left-back position when Mussi had to go off in the first half and was replaced by Apolloni. Similarly the stars of Brazil's team were its central defenders, Aldair and Marcio Santos.

The nature of this game was indicated early on when Mazinho floored Berti with a hefty challenge and was booked. Pagliuca was the busier of the two goalkeepers as Brazil created and missed a series of early scoring

Brazil's captain Dunga receives the World Cup trophy from U.S. Vice President Al Gore.

chances. In the 12th minute Romario was especially guilty when, unmarked, he placed his header straight into the goal-keeper's arms. Then Italy created a great chance with Baresi setting Daniele Massaro on a goalward run with a masterful pass to split the Brazilian defence. The move was broken up by a last ditch dive at the Italian's feet from Taffarel. After 20 minutes, Jorginho was forced to retire with injury and his replacement, Cafú, went on to provide innumerable opportunities for his front men which Romario and Bebeto uncharacteristically spurned. In the 25th minute Pagliuca scrambled clear a scorching free kick from Branco at the second attempt and later in the game he pulled off fine saves to deny Branco again, Romario and Bebeto.

However, in this game real scoring chances were few and far between and it was not until the 75th minute that either keeper was severely tested. Mauro Silva let fly and Pagliuca fumbled the save. He allowed the ball to slip through his arms and to his relief it rebounded off the post into his arms. It was the last scoring chance of the 90 minutes and the game was dragged into extra time. On three minutes both Bebeto and Romario missed easy chances within seconds of each other "when scoring seemed the easier option" and then Roberto Baggio had a shot tipped over the bar. At the half way point the referee tried to get an immediate turn round, but he was ignored as the players trooped to the bye line to quench their thirsts. The Brazilians then brought on Viola for Zinho in an attempt to widen their options and instil a little pace into the game. He instigated some interesting moves, but without reward and the game drew to its inevitable conclusion.

For the first time a World Cup final had to be decided by a penalty shoot-out. Baresi stepped up to take the first kick. He had only recently received treatment for cramp and he blasted his shot high over the bar. Marcio Santos took Brazil's first shot, but he hit it weakly and it was easily saved by Pagliuca. Albertini, Romario, Evani and Branco each scored with the next four kicks and Massaro elected to take Italy's fourth. He too hit it poorly and his attempt was well saved by Taffarel, who played his football with the Italian club, Reggiana. The captain, Dunga, made no mistake with his shot and Italy's survival depended on the normally dependable boot of Roberto Baggio. To his absolute horror, he lofted it over the bar and Brazil were world champions. It was an unsatisfactory ending to a poor game, but there can be no doubt that the best team had won - just.

Statistics - USA 1994

GROUP A

Detroit, June 18th - Pontiac Silverdome

1 (1) UNITED STATES

Wynalda 45

Meola, Kooiman, Lalas, Balboa, Caligiuri, Ramos, Dooley, Harkes, Sorber, Stewart (Jones), Wynalda (Wegerle).

1 (1) SWITZERLAND

Bregy 39

Pascolo, Hottiger, Herr, Geiger, Quentin, Ohrel, Sforza (Wyss), Bregy, Bickel (Subiat), Sutter, Chapuisat.

Referee: Lamolina (Argentina)
Attendance: 73.425

Los Angeles, June 18th - Rose Bowl

1 (1) COLOMBIA

Valencia 43

Cordoba, Escobar, Herrera, Pérez, Perea, Alvarez, Valderrama, Gómez, Rincón, Valencia, Asprilla.

3 (2) ROMANIA

Raducioiu 16, 89, Hagi 34

Stelea, Petrescu, Belodedici, Popescu, Prodan, Mihali, Lupescu, Munteanu, Hagi, Dumitrescu (Selymes), Raducioiu (Papura).

Referee: Al-Sharif (Syria)
Attendance: 91.856

Detroit, June 22nd - Pontiac Silverdome

4 (1) SWITZERLAND

Sutter 16, Chapuisat 53, Knup 66, 72

Pascolo, Hottiger, Herr, Geiger, Quentin, Ohrel (Sylvestre), Sforza, Bregy, Knup, Sutter (Bickel), Chapuisat.

1 (1) ROMANIA

Hagi 36

Stelea, Petrescu, Belodedici, Popescu, Prodan, Mihali, Lupescu (Panduru), Munteanu, Hagi, Dumitrescu (Vladiou) (RED), Raducioiu.

Referee: Jouini (Tunisia)
Attendance: 61.428

Los Angeles, June 22nd - Rose Bowl

2 (1) UNITED STATES

Escobar (og)33, Stewart 50

Meola, Clavijo, Lalas, Balboa, Caligiuri, Ramos, Dooley, Harkes, Sorber, Stewart (Jones), Wynalda (Wegerle).

1 (0) COLOMBIA

Valencia 89

Cordoba, Escobar, Herrera, Pérez, Perea, Alvarez, Valderrama, Gaviria, Rincón, De Avila (Valencia), Asprilla (Valenciano).

Referee: Baldas (Italy)
Attendance: 93.194

San Francisco, June 26th - Stanford Stadium

2 (1) COLOMBIA

Gaviria 44, Lozano 89

Cordoba, Escobar, Herrera, Pérez, Mendoza, Alvarez, Valderrama, Gaviria (Lozano), Rincón, Valencia (De Avila), Asprilla.

0 (0) SWITZERLAND

Pascolo, Hottiger, Herr, Geiger, Quentin, Ohrel, Sforza, Bregy, Knup (Subiat), Sutter (Grassi), Chapuisat.

Referee: Mikkelsen (Denmark)
Attendance: 83.769

Los Angeles, June 26th - Rose Bowl

1 (1) ROMANIA

Petrescu 16

Prunea, Petrescu, Belodedici (Mihali), Popescu, Prodan, Selimenes, Lupescu, Munteanu, Hagi, Dumitrescu, Raducioiu (Galca).

0 (0) UNITED STATES

Meola, Clavijo, Lalas, Balboa, Caligiuri, Ramos (Jones), Dooley, Harkes, Sorber (Wegerle), Stewart, Wynalda.

Referee: van der Ende (Holland)
Attendance: 93.869

	P	W	D	L	F	A	Pts
Romania	3	2	0	1	5	5	6
Switzerland	3	1	1	1	5	4	4
United States	3	1	1	1	3	3	4
Colombia	3	1	0	2	4	5	3

GROUP B

Los Angeles, June 19th - Rose Bowl

2 (1) SWEDEN

Ljung 7, Dahlin 74

Ravelli, R.Nilsson, P.Andersson, Björklund, Ljung, Schwarz, Blomquist (Larsson), Thern, Ingesson (K.Andersson), Brolin, Dahlin.

2 (1) CAMEROON

Embe 29, Omam-Biyik 46

Bell, Tataw, Song, Kalla, Agbo, Mbouh, Libiih, Foe, Mfede (Maboang), Embe (Mouyeme), Omam-Biyik.

Referee: Tejada (Peru)
Attendance: 70.000

San Francisco, June 20th - Stanford Stadium

2 (1) BRAZIL

Romario 26, Rai (pen)53

Taffarel, Jorginho, Marcio Santos, Ricardo Rocha (Aldair), Leonardo, Dunga (Mazinho), Zinho, Mauro Silva, Rai, Romario, Bebeto.

0 (0) RUSSIA

Kharine, Ternavski, Gorlokovich, Kuznetsov, Tsymbalar, Nikiforov, Khlestov, Karpine, Piartnitski, Radchenko (Borodiuk), Yuran (Salenko).

Referee: Lim Kee Chong (Mauritius)
Attendance: 81.061

San Francisco, June 24th - Stanford Stadium

3 (1) BRAZIL

Romario 38, Marcio Santos 64, Bebeto 72

Taffarel, Jorginho, Marcio Santos, Aldair, Leonardo, Dunga, Zinho (P.Sergio), Mauro Silva, Rai (Müller), Romario, Bebeto.

0 (0) CAMEROON

Bell, Tataw, Song (RED), Kalla, Agbo, Mbouh, Libiih, Foe, Mfede (Maboang), Embe (Milla), Omam-Biyik.

Referee: Brizio (Mexico)
Attendance: 85.000

Detroit, June 24th - Pontiac Silverdome

3 (1) SWEDEN

Brolin (pen)38, Dahlin 59, 81

Ravelli, R.Nilsson, P.Andersson, Björklund (Erlingmark), Ljung, Schwarz, Thern, Ingesson, K.Andersson (Larsson), Brolin, Dahlin.

1 (1) RUSSIA

Salenko (pen) 3

Kharine, Onopko, Gorlokovich (RED), Kuznetsov, Popov (Karpine), Nikiforov, Khlestov, Radchenko, Borodiuk (Galiamine), Mostovoi, Salenko.

Referee: Quiniou (France)
Attendance: 71.258

San Francisco, June 28th - Stanford Stadium

6 (3) RUSSIA

Salenko 16, 41,(pen) 45, 73, 75, Radchenko 82

Cherchesov, Onopko, Ternavski, Tetradze, Karpine, Nikiforov, Khlestov, Korneyev (Radchenko), Lediakov (Bestchastnykh), Tsymbalar, Salenko.

1 (0) CAMEROON

Milla 47

Songo, Tataw, N'dip Akem, Kalla, Agbo, Kana-Biyik, Libiih, Foe, Mfede (Milla), Embe (Tchami), Omam-Biyik.

Referee: Al-Sharif (Syria)
Attendance: 74.914

Detroit, June 28th - Pontiac Silverdome

1 (1) SWEDEN

K.Andersson 21

Ravelli, R.Nilsson, P.Andersson, Kåmark, Ljung, Schwarz, Thern, Ingesson, K.Andersson, Larsson (Blomquist), Brolin.

1 (0) BRAZIL

Romario 47

Taffarel, Jorginho, Marcio Santos, Aldair, Leonardo, Dunga, Zinho, Mauro Silva (Mazinho), Rai (P.Sergio), Romario, Bebeto.

Referee: Puhl (Hungary)
Attendance: 77.217

	P	W	D	L	F	A	Pts
Brazil	3	2	1	0	6	1	7
Sweden	3	1	2	0	6	4	5
Russia	3	1	0	2	7	6	3
Cameroon	3	0	1	2	3	11	1

GROUP C

Chicago, June 17th - Soldier Field

1 (0) GERMANY

Klinsmann 61

Illgner, Kohler, Matthäus, Berthold, Brehme, Hässler (Strunz), Effenberg, Sammer, Möller, Riedle (Basler), Klinsmann.

0 (0) BOLIVIA

Trucco, Borja, Quinteros, Rimba, Sandy, Cristaldo, Soria, Melgar, Sánchez, Baldivieso (Moreno), Ramallo (Etcheverry) (RED).

Referee: Brizio (Mexico)
Attendance: 63.117

Dallas, June 17th - Cotton Bowl

2 (0) SOUTH KOREA

Myung-bo 85, Jung-won 89

Choi In-young, Kim Pan-keun, Park Jung-bae, Hong Myung-bo, Shin Hong-gi, Lee Young-jin, Choi Young-il, Kim Joo-sung (Seo Jung-won), Noh Jung-Yoon (Ha Seok-ju), Ko Jeong-woon, Hwang Sun-hong.

2 (0) SPAIN

Salinas 51, Goicoechea 56

Canizares, Ferrer, Alkorta, Abelardo, Nadal (RED), Sergi, Hierro, Luis Enrique, Goicoechea, Salinas (Felipe), Guerrero (Caminero).

Referee: Peter Mikkelsen (Denmark)
Attendance: 56.247

Chicago, June 21st - Soldier Field

1 (0) GERMANY

Klinsmann 48

Illgner, Kohler, Matthäus, Berthold, Brehme, Hässler, Strunz, Effenberg, Sammer, Möller (Völler), Klinsmann.

1 (1) SPAIN

Goicoechea 14

Zubizarreta, Ferrer, Alkorta, Abelardo, Guardiola (Camarasa), Sergi, Hierro, Luis Enrique, Goicoechea (Bakero), Salinas, Caminero.

Referee: Cavani (Uruguay)
Attendance: 63.113

Boston, June 23rd - Foxboro Stadium

0 (0) SOUTH KOREA

Choi In-young, Kim Pan-keun, Park Jung-bae, Hong Myung-bo, Shin Hong-gi, Lee Young-jin, Kim Joo-sung, Seo Jung-Yoon (Choi Young-il), Ko Jeong-woon, Noh Jung-yoon (Ha Seok-ju), Hwang Sun-hong.

0 (0) BOLIVIA

Trucco, Borja, Quinteros, Rimba, Sandy, Cristaldo (RED), Soria, Melgar, Sánchez, Baldivieso, Ramallo (Peña).

Referee: Leslie Mottram (Scotland)
Attendance: 53.456

Chicago, June 27th - Soldier Field

3 (1) SPAIN

Guardiola (pen)19, Caminero 66, 71

Zubizarreta, Ferrer, Voro, Abelardo, Guardiola (Bakero), Sergi, Minabres (Hierro), Goicoechea, Guerrero, Salinas, Caminero.

1 (0) BOLIVIA

Sánchez 67

Trucco, Borja, Rimba, Sandy, Peña, Soria (Castillo), Melgar, Socuro, Sánchez, Ramos (Moreno), Ramallo.

Referee: Badilla (Czech Republic)
Attendance: 63.089

Dallas, June 27th - Cotton Bowl

3 (3) GERMANY

Klinsmann 11,35, Riedle 18

Illgner, Kohler, Matthäus (Möller), Berthold, Brehme, Hässler, Buchwald, Effenberg (Helmer), Sammer, Riedle, Klinsmann.

2 (0) SOUTH KOREA

Sun-hong 52, Myung-bo 63

Choi In-young (Lee Woon-jae), Kim Pan-keun, Park Jung-bae, Hong Myung-bo, Shin Hong-gi, Lee Young-jin (Chung Son-chung), Kim Joo-sung, Choi Young-il, Ko Jeong-woon, Cho Jin-ho (Seo Jung-woh), Hwang Sun-hong.

Referee: Joel Quiniou (France)
Attendance: 63.998

	P	W	D	L	F	A	Pts
Germany	3	2	1	0	5	3	7
Spain	3	1	2	0	6	4	5
South Korea	3	0	2	1	4	5	2
Bolivia	3	0	1	2	1	4	1

GROUP D

Boston, June 21st - Foxboro Stadium

4 (2) ARGENTINA

Batistuta 1, 44, (pen)89, Maradona 60

Islas, Sensini, Caceres, Ruggeri, Chamot, Simeone, Redondo, Maradona (Ortega), Balbo (Mancuso), Caniggia, Batistuta.

0 (0) GREECE

Minou, Manolas, Apostolakis, Kolitsidakis, Kalitzakis, Kofidis, Tsalouhidis, Nioplias, Tsiantakis (Marangos), Saravakos, Machlas (Mitropoulos).

Referee: Angeles (United States)
Attendance: 53.486

Dallas, June 21st - Cotton Bowl

3 (2) NIGERIA

Yekini 21, Amokachi 43, Amunike 55

Rufai, Eguavon, Uchechukwu, Nwanu, Iroha, Oliseh, Siasia (Adepoju), Amokachi, Finidi (Ezeugo), Yekini, Amunike.

0 (0) BULGARIA

Mihailov, Kremenljev, Ivanov, Houbtchev, Tzvetanov, Yankov, Letchkov (Sirakov), Borimirov (Yordanov), Balakov, Stoichkov, Kostadinov.

Referee: Badilla (Czech Republic)
Attendance: 44.132

Boston, June 25th - Foxboro Stadium

2 (2) ARGENTINA

Caniggia 22, 29

Islas, Sensini (Díaz), Caceres, Ruggeri, Chamot, Simeone, Redondo, Maradona, Balbo (Mancuso), Caniggia, Batistuta.

1 (1) NIGERIA

Siasia 8

Rufai, Eguavon, Uchechukwu, Nwanu, Emenalo, Oliseh (Okocha), Siasia (Adepoju), Amokachi, Finidi, Yekini, Amunike.

Referee: Karlsson (Sweden)
Attendance: 61.000

Chicago, June 26th - Soldier Field

4 (1) BULGARIA

Stoichkov (pen)5, (pen)55, Letchkov 66, Borimirov 89

Mihailov, Kremenljev, Ivanov, Houbtchev, Tzvetanov (Kiriakov), Yankov, Letchkov, Sirakov, Balakov, Stoichkov, Kostadinov (Borimirov).

0 (0) GREECE

Afmatzidis, Karataidis, Apostolakis, Karagiannis, Kalitzakis, Kofidis, Hantzidis (Mitropoulos), Nioplias, Marangos, Alexoudis (Dimitriadis), Machlas.

Referee: Bujsaim (United Arab Emirates)
Attendance: 63.160

Boston, June 30th - Foxboro Stadium

2 (1) NIGERIA

Finidi 45, Amokachi 90

Rufai, Keshi, Uchechukwu, Nwanu, Emenalo, Oliseh, Siasia, Amokachi, Finidi (Adepoju), Yekini (Okocha), Amunike.

0 (0) GREECE

Karkamanis, Alexiou, Karagiannis, Kalitzakis, Kofidis, Hantzidis, Mitropoulos (Tsiantakis), Nioplias, Tsalouhidis, Alexandris, Machlas (Dimitriadis).

Referee: Mottram (Scotland)
Attendance: 53.001

Dallas, June 30th - Cotton Bowl

2 (0) BULGARIA

Stoichkov 61, Sirakov 90

Mihailov, Kremenljev, Ivanov, Houbtchev, Tzvetanov (RED), Yankov, Letchkov (Borimirov), Sirakov, Balakov, Stoichkov, Kostadinov (Kiriakov).

0 (0) ARGENTINA

Islas, Díaz, Caceres, Ruggeri, Chamot, Simeone, Redondo, Rodríguez (Bello), Balbo, Caniggia (Ortega), Batistuta.

Referee: Jouini (Tunisia)
Attendance: 63.988

	P	W	D	L	F	A	Pts
Nigeria	3	2	0	1	6	2	6
Bulgaria	3	2	0	1	6	3	6
Argentina	3	2	0	1	6	3	6
Greece	3	0	0	3	0	10	0

GROUP E

New York, June 18th - Giants Stadium

1 (1) IRELAND

Houghton 12

Bonner, Irwin, McGrath, Babb, Phelan, Sheridan, Keane, Townsend, Staunton, Houghton (McAteer), Coyne (Aldridge).

0 (0) ITALY

Pagliuca, Tassotti, Costacurta, Baresi, Maldini, Albertini, D.Baggio, Donadoni, Evani (Massaro), R.Baggio, Signori (Berti).

Referee: van der Ende (Holland)
Attendance: 73.511

Washington DC, June 19th - RFK Memorial Stadium

1 (0) NORWAY

Rekdal 85

Thorstvedt, Håland, Bratseth, Berg, Bjørnebye, Flo, Mykland (Rekdal), Leonhardsen, Bohinen, Fjørtoft, Jakobsen (Halle).

0 (0) MEXICO

Campos, Suárez, Ramírez Perales, Gutiérrez (Bernal), R. Ramírez, Ambriz, Del Olmo, L.Garcia, Valdez (Galindo), Sánchez, Alves Zague.

Referee: Puhl (Hungary)
Attendance: 52.395

New York, June 23rd - Giants Stadium

1 (0) ITALY

D.Baggio 69

Pagliuca (RED), Benarrivo, Costacurta, Baresi (Apolloni), Maldini, Albertini, D.Baggio, Berti, R.Baggio (Marchegiani), Casiraghi (Massaro), Signori.

0 (0) NORWAY

Thorstvedt, Håland, Bratseth, Berg, Bjørnebye, Flo, Mykland (Rekdal), Leonhardsen, Bohinen, Fjørtoft, Rushfeldt (Jakobsen).

Referee: Krug (Germany)
Attendance: 74.624

Orlando, June 24th - Citrus Bowl

2 (1) MEXICO

L.Garcia 44, 66

Campos, Suárez, Ramírez Perales, Bernal, J. Rodríguez (Salvador), Ambriz, Del Olmo, L.Garcia, Garcia Aspe, Hermosillo (Gutiérrez), Alves Zague.

1 (0) IRELAND

Aldridge 84

Bonner, Irwin, McGrath, Babb, Phelan, Sheridan, Keane, Townsend, Staunton (Aldridge), Houghton, Coyne (McAteer).

Referee: Röthlisberger (Switzerland)
Attendance: 68.000

New York, June 28th - Giants Stadium

0 (0) IRELAND

Bonner, G.Kelly, McGrath, Babb, Sheridan, Keane, Townsend, Staunton, Houghton, McAteer, Aldridge (D.Kelly).

0 (0) NORWAY

Thorstvedt, Halle (Jakobsen), Bratseth, Johnsen, Berg, Bjørnebye, Flo, Mykland, Rekdal, Leonhardsen (Bohinen), Sørloth.

Referee: Torres (Colombia)
Attendance: 76.322

Washington DC, June 28th - RFK Memorial Stadium

1 (0) ITALY

Massaro 48

Marchegiani, Benarrivo, Costacurta, Apolloni, Maldini, Albertini, D.Baggio (Donadoni), Berti, R.Baggio, Casiraghi (Massaro), Signori.

1 (0) MEXICO

Bernal 58

Campos, Suárez, Ramírez Perales, Bernal, J.Rodríguez, Ambriz, Del Olmo, L.Garcia (Chavez), Garcia Aspe, Hermosillo, Alves Zague.

Referee: Lamolina (Argentina)
Attendance: 53.186

	P	W	D	L	F	A	Pts
Mexico	3	1	1	1	3	3	4
Ireland	3	1	1	1	2	2	4
Italy	3	1	1	1	2	2	4
Norway	3	1	1	1	1	1	4

GROUP F

Orlando, June 19th - Citrus Bowl

1 (1) BELGIUM

Degryse 11

Preud'homme, Smidts, Grün, De Wolf, Staelens, Van der Elst, Scifo, Boffin (Borkelmans), Degryse, Nilis (Emmers), Weber.

0 (0) MOROCCO

Azmi (Alaoui), Nacer, El Hadrioui, Triki, Naybet, El Hadaoui (Bahja), Hadji, Azzouzi, Hababi, Daoudi, Chaouch (Samadi).

Referee: Cadena (Colombia)
Attendance: 60.190

Washington DC, June 20th - RFK Memorial Stadium

2 (0) HOLLAND

Jonk 50, Taument 86

De Goey, Van Gobbel, Rijkaard, Koeman, F.de Boer, Jonk, Bergkamp, Wouters, Overmars, R.de Boer, Roy (Taument).

1 (1) SAUDI ARABIA

Amin 19

Al Deayea, Madani, Al Jebreen, Al Khlawi, Al Kawad, Al Dosari, Amin, Al Bishi, Owairan (Saleh), Al Muwallid, Abdullah (Falatah).

Referee: Vega (Spain)
Attendance: 50.535

Orlando, June 25th - Citrus Bowl

1 (0) BELGIUM

Albert 65

Preud'homme, Albert, Grün (Smidts), De Wolf, Staelens, Van de Elst, Scifo, Borkelmans, Degryse, Emmers (Medved), Weber.

0 (0) HOLLAND

De Goey, Valckx, Rijkaard, Koeman, F.de Boer, Jonk, Bergkamp, Wouters, Roy, R.de Boer (Witschge), Taument (Overmars).

Referee: Marsiglia (Brazil)
Attendance: 61.200

New York, June 25th - Giants Stadium

2 (2) SAUDI ARABIA

Al Jaber (pen)8, Amin 45

Al Deayea, Madani, Al Jebreen, Al Khlawi, Al Anazi (Zebermawi), Abdel-Jawad, Amin, Al Owairan, Al Muwallid, Al Jaber (Al Ghesheyan).

1 (1) MOROCCO

Chaouch 27

Azmi, El Kahlej, El Hadrioui, Triki, Naybet, Abdellah (El Ghrissi), Bahja, Azzouzi, Hababi (Hadji), Daoudi, Chaouch.

Referee: Don (England)
Attendance: 72.404

Orlando, June 29th - Citrus Bowl

2 (1) HOLLAND

Bergkamp 42, Roy 79

De Goey, Valckx, Koeman, F.de Boer, Jonk (Roy), Bergkamp, Wouters, Winter, Witschge, Overmars (Taument), Van Vossen.

1 (0) MOROCCO

Nader 46

Alaoui, El Kahlej, El Hadrioui, Triki, Samadi, Neqrouz, Bouyboud (Hadji), Bahja, Azzouzi (Daoudi), Hababi, Nader.

Referee: Tejada (Peru)
Attendance: 60.578

Washington DC, June 29th - RFK Memorial Stadium

1 (1) SAUDI ARABIA

Owairan 5

Al Deayea, Zebermawi, Al Khlawi, Madani, Al Jawad, Owairan (Al Dosari), Al Bishi, Al Jebreen, Saleh, M.Abdullah (Muwallid), Falatah.

0 (0) BELGIUM

Preud'homme, Albert, Smidts, De Wolf, Staelens, Van der Elst, Boffin, Scifo, Degryse (Nilis), Medved, Wilmots (Weber).

Referee: Krug (Germany)
Attendance: 52.959

	P	W	D	L	F	A	Pts
Holland	3	2	0	1	4	3	6
Saudi Arabia	3	2	0	1	4	3	6
Belgium	3	2	0	1	2	1	6
Morocco	3	0	0	3	2	5	0

SECOND ROUND

Chicago, July 2nd - Soldier Field

3 (3) GERMANY

Völler 5, 39, Klinsmann 10

Illgner, Matthäus (Brehme), Kohler, Berthold, Helmer, Hässler, Buchwald, Sammer, Wagner, Völler, Klinsmann (Kuntz).

2 (1) BELGIUM

Grün 7, Albert 90

Preud'homme, Albert, De Wolf, Grün, Smidts (Boffin), Staelens, Van der Elst, Scifo, Emmers, Nilis (Czerniatynski), Weber.

Referee: Röthlisberger (Switzerland)
Attendance: 60.246

Razzmatazz, Romario and the Divine Ponytail - USA 1994

Washington, July 2nd - RFK Memorial Stadium

3 (1) SPAIN

Hierro 15, Luis Enrique 73, Beguiristain (pen)86

Zubizarreta, Nadal, Ferrer, Abelardo, Alkorta, Sergi, Goicoechea (Beguiristain), Hierro (Otero), Bakero, Camarasa, Luis Enrique.

0 (0) SWITZERLAND

Pascolo, Hottiger, Herr, Geiger, Quentin (Studer), Ohrel (Subiat), Bregy, Sforza, Bickel, Knup, Chapuisat.

Referee: van der Ende (Holland)
Attendance: 56.500

Dallas, July 3rd - Cotton Bowl

3 (1) SWEDEN

Dahlin 5, K.Andersson 50, 87

Ravelli, Nilsson, P.Andersson, Björklund (Kåmark), Ljung, Schwarz, Thern (Mild), Ingesson, Brolin, Dahlin, K.Andersson.

1 (0) SAUDI ARABIA

Al Gheshayan 85

Al Deayea, Zebermawi, Madani, Al Khlawi, Abdel-Jawad (Al Gheshayan), Amin, Saleh, Al Bishi (Al Muwallid), Owairan, Al Jaber, Falatah.

Referee: Marsiglia (Brazil)
Attendance: 60.277

Los Angeles, July 3rd - Rose Bowl

3 (2) ROMANIA

Dumitrescu 9, 17, Hagi 57

Prunea, Petrescu, Prodan, Belodedici, Lupescu, Popescu, Munteanu, Mihali, Selymes, Hagi (Galca), Dumitrescu (Papura).

2 (1) ARGENTINA

Batistuta (pen)15, Balbo 74

Islas, Sensini (Bello), Ruggeri, Caceres, Chamot, Basualdo, Simeone, Ortega, Redondo, Balbo, Batistuta.

Referee: Pairetto (Italy)
Attendance: 90.469

Orlando, July 4th - Citrus Bowl

2 (2) HOLLAND

Bergkamp 10, Jonk 40

De Goey, Koeman, Valckx, F.de Boer, Witschge (Numan), Rijkaard, Jonk, Winter, Overmars, Bergkamp, Van Vossen (Roy).

0 (0) IRELAND

Bonner, G.Kelly, McGrath, Babb, Phelan, Houghton, Keane, Townsend, Sheridan, Staunton (McAteer), Coyne (Cascarino).

Referee: Mikkelsen (Denmark)
Attendance: 61.355

San Francisco, July 4th - Stanford Stadium

1 (0) BRAZIL

Bebeto 73

Taffarel, Jorginho, Marcio Santos, Aldair, Leonardo (RED), Mazinho, Zinho (Cafu), Mauro Silva, Dunga, Bebeto, Romario.

0 (0) UNITED STATES

Meola, Clavijo (RED), Balboa, Lalas, Caligiuri, Jones, Dooley, Pérez (Wegerle), Sorber, Ramos (Wynalda), Stewart.

Referee: Quiniou (France)
Attendance: 84.147

Boston, July 5th - Foxboro Stadium

After extra time - 45 mins (0-1), 90 mins (1-1)

2 (1) ITALY

R.Baggio 89, (pen)103

Marchegiani, Mussi, Costacurta, Maldini, Benarrivo, Berti (D.Baggio), Albertini, Donadoni, Signori (Zola) (RED), R.Baggio, Massaro.

1 (1) NIGERIA

Amunike 26

Rufai, Eguavon, Nwanu, Uchechukwu, Emenalo, Oliseh, Finidi, Okocha, Amokachi (Adepoju), Yekini, Amunike (Oliha).

Referee: Brizio (Mexico)
Attendance: 54.367

New York, July 5th - Giants Stadium

4 (3)(1) BULGARIA

Stoichkov 7

Mihailov, Kremenljev (RED), Kiriakov, Houbtchev, Balakov, Letchkov, Sirakov (Guentchev), Borimirov, Yordanov, Kostadinov (Mihtarski), Stoichkov.

2 (1)(1) MEXICO

Garcia Aspe (pen)18

Campos, Suárez, Ramírez Perales, Ambriz, R. Ramírez, Bernal, Garcia Aspe, Galindo, Rodríguez, L.Garcia (RED), Alves Zague.

After extra time & penalty shoot-out - 45 mins (1-1), 90 mins (1-1), 120 mins (1-1)

Penalty shoot-out - Mexico started to shoot.

MEXICO	1	BULGARIA	3
Garcia Aspe	Miss	Balakov	Miss
Bernal	Miss	Guentchev	Goal
Rodrigues	Miss	Borimirov	Goal
Suárez	Goal	Letchkov	Goal

Referee: Al-Sharif (Syria)
Attendance: 71.030

QUARTER-FINALS

Boston, July 9th - Foxboro Stadium

2 (1) ITALY

D.Baggio 26, R.Baggio 88

Pagliuca, Tassotti, Costacurta, Maldini, Benarrivo, Conte (Berti), D.Baggio, Albertini (Signori), Donadoni, R.Baggio, Massaro.

1 (0) SPAIN

Caminero 59

Zubizarreta, Nadal, Ferrer, Abelardo, Alkorta, Sergi (Salinas), Goicoechea, Otero, Bakero (Hierro), Caminero, Luis Enrique.

Referee: Puhl (Hungary)
Attendance: 53.400

Dallas, July 9th - Cotton Bowl

3 (0) BRAZIL

Romario 52, Bebeto 62, Branco 81

Taffarel, Jorginho, Marcio Santos, Aldair, Branco (Cafu), Mazinho (Rai), Zinho, Mauro Silva, Dunga, Bebeto, Romario.

2 (0) HOLLAND

Bergkamp 64, Winter 76

De Goey, Koeman, Valckx, Wouters, Witschge, Rijkaard (R.de Boer), Jonk, Winter, Overmars, Bergkamp, Van Vossen (Roy).

Referee: Badilla (Czech Republic)
Attendance: 63.998

New York, July 10th - Giants Stadium

2 (0) BULGARIA

Stoichkov 76, Letchkov 78

Mihailov, Yankov, Kiriakov, Houbtchev, Balakov, Letchkov, Sirakov, Ivanov, Tzvetanov, Kostadinov (Guentchev), Stoichkov (Yordanov).

1 (0) GERMANY

Matthäus (pen)48

Illgner, Matthäus, Kohler, Berthold, Helmer, Hässler (Brehme), Buchwald, Möller, Wagner (Strunz), Völler, Klinsmann.

Referee: Torres (Colombia)
Attendance: 72.416

San Francisco, July 10th - Stanford Stadium

7 (5)(2) SWEDEN

Brolin 78, K.Andersson 115

Ravelli, Nilsson, P.Andersson, Björklund (Kåmark), Ljung, Schwarz (RED), Mild, Ingesson, Brolin, Dahlin (Larsson), K.Andersson.

6 (4)(2) ROMANIA

Raducioiu 88, 100

Prunea, Petrescu, Prodan, Belodedici, Lupescu, Popescu, Munteanu (Panduru), Selymes, Hagi, Dumitrescu, Raducioiu.

After extra time & penalty shoot-out - 45 mins (0-0), 90 mins (1-1), 120 mins (2-2)

Penalty shoot-out - Sweden started to shoot.

SWEDEN	5	ROMANIA	4
Mild	Miss	Raducioiu	Goal
K.Andersson	Goal	Hagi	Goal
Brolin	Goal	Lupescu	Goal
Ingesson	Goal	Petrescu	Miss
Nilsson	Goal	Dumitrescu	Goal
Larsson	Goal	Belodedici	Miss

Referee: Don (England)
Attendance: 83.500

SEMI-FINALS

New York, July 13th - Giants Stadium

2 (2) ITALY

R.Baggio 20,25

Pagliuca, Mussi, Costacurta, Maldini, Benarrivo, Berti, D.Baggio (Conte), Albertini, Donadoni, R.Baggio (Signori), Casiraghi.

1 (1) BULGARIA

Stoichkov (pen)42

Mihailov, Yankov, Kiriakov, Houbtchev, Balakov, Letchkov, Sirakov, Ivanov, Tzvetanov, Kostadinov (Yordanov), Stoichkov (Guentchev).

Referee: Quiniou (France)
Attendance: 77.194

Los Angeles, July 13th - Rose Bowl

1 (0) BRAZIL

Romario 80

Taffarel, Jorginho, Marcio Santos, Aldair, Branco, Mazinho (Rai), Zinho, Mauro Silva, Dunga, Bebeto, Romario.

0 (0) SWEDEN

Ravelli, Nilsson, P.Andersson, Björklund, Ljung, Thern (RED), Mild, Ingesson, Brolin, Dahlin (Rehn), K.Andersson.

Referee: Torres (Colombia)
Attendance: 93.000

3RD/4TH PLACE PLAY-OFF

Los Angeles, July 16th - Rose Bowl

4 (4) SWEDEN

Brolin 8, Mild 30, Larsson 37, K.Andersson 39

Ravelli, Nilsson, P.Andersson, Björklund, Kåmark, Schwarz, Mild, Ingesson, Brolin, Larsson (Limpar), K.Andersson.

0 (0) BULGARIA

Mihailov (Nikolov), Yankov, Kiriakov, Houbtchev, Balakov, Letchkov, Sirakov, Ivanov (Kremenljev), Tzvetanov, Kostadinov (Yordanov), Stoichkov.

Referee: Bujsaim (United Arab Emirates)
Attendance: 83.716

FINAL

Los Angeles, July 17th - Rose Bowl

3 (0) BRAZIL

Taffarel, Jorginho (Cafu), Marcio Santos, Aldair, Branco, Mazinho, Zinho (Viola), Mauro Silva, Dunga, Bebeto, Romario.

2 (0) ITALY

Pagliuca, Mussi (Apolloni), Baresi, Maldini, Benarrivo, Berti, D.Baggio (Evani), Albertini, Donadoni, R.Baggio, Massaro.

After extra time & penalty shoot-out - 45 mins (0-0), 90 mins (0-0), 120 mins (0-0)

Penalty shoot-out - Italy started to shoot.

ITALY	2	BRAZIL	3
Baresi	Miss	Branco	Goal
Albertini	Goal	Romario	Goal
Evani	Goal	M. Santos	Miss
Massaro	Miss	Dunga	Goal
R.Baggio	Miss		

Referee: Puhl (Hungary)
Attendance: 94.194

QUALIFYING ROUNDS

Africa - 1st Round, Group A

	P	W	D	L	F	A	Pts
Algeria	4	2	1	1	5	4	5
Ghana	4	2	0	2	4	3	4
Burundi	4	1	1	2	2	4	3

09-10-92	Algeria : Burundi	3:1 (1:0)
25-10-92	Burundi : Ghana	1:0 (0:0)
20-12-92	Ghana : Algeria	2:0 (1:0)
17-01-93	Burundi : Algeria	0:0
31-01-93	Ghana : Burundi	1:0 (1:0)
26-02-93	Algeria : Ghana	2:1 (0:1)

Africa - 1st Round, Group B

	P	W	D	L	F	A	Pts
Cameroon	4	2	2	0	7	1	6
Swaziland	3	1	1	1	5	3	3
Zaire	3	0	1	2	1	3	1

18-10-92	Cameroon : Swaziland	5:0 (2:0)
25-10-92	Swaziland : Zaire	1:0 (0:0)
10-01-93	Zaire : Cameroon	1:2 (0:0)
17-01-93	Swaziland : Cameroon	0:0
01-03-93	Cameroon : Zaire	0:0

Africa - 1st Round, Group C

	P	W	D	L	F	A	Pts
Zimbabwe	6	4	2	0	8	4	10
Egypt	6	3	2	1	9	3	8
Angola	5	1	2	2	3	4	4
Togo	5	0	0	5	2	11	0

09-10-92	Zimbabwe : Togo	1:0
11-10-92	Egypt : Angola	1:0 (0:0)
25-10-92	Togo : Egypt	1:4 (0:2)
20-12-92	Zimbabwe : Egypt	2:1 (1:0)
10-01-93	Angola : Zimbabwe	1:1 (0:1)
17-01-93	Togo : Zimbabwe	1:2 (0:0)
18-01-93	Angola : Egypt	0:0
31-01-93	Egypt : Togo	3:0 (0:0)
31-01-93	Zimbabwe : Angola	2:1 (1:1)
28-02-93	Togo : Angola	0:1 (0:0)
15-04-93	Egypt : Zimbabwe	0:0

Africa - 1st Round, Group D

	P	W	D	L	F	A	Pts
Nigeria	4	3	1	0	7	0	7
South Africa	4	2	1	1	2	4	5
Congo	4	0	0	4	0	5	0

10-10-92	Nigeria : South Africa	4:0 (1:0)
24-10-92	South Africa : Congo	1:0 (1:0)
20-12-92	Congo : Nigeria	0:1 (0:1)
16-01-93	South Africa : Nigeria	0:0
31-01-93	Congo : South Africa	0:1 (0:0)
27-02-93	Nigeria : Congo	2:0 (1:0)

Africa - 1st Round, Group E

	P	W	D	L	F	A	Pts
Cote d' Ivoire	4	2	2	0	7	0	6
Niger	4	2	1	1	3	2	5
Botswana	4	0	1	3	1	9	1

11-10-92	Cote d' Ivoire : Botswana	6:0 (3:0)
25-10-92	Niger : Cote d' Ivoire	0:0
20-12-92	Botswana : Niger	0:1 (0:0)
17-01-93	Botswana : Cote d' Ivoire	0:0
31-01-93	Cote d' Ivoire : Niger	1:0 (0:0)
28-02-93	Niger : Botswana	2:1 (1:1)

Africa - 1st Round, Group F

	P	W	D	L	F	A	Pts
Morocco	6	4	2	0	13	1	10
Tunisia	6	3	3	0	14	2	9
Ethiopia	6	1	1	4	3	11	3
Benin	6	1	0	5	3	19	2

11-10-92	Tunisia : Benin	5:1 (3:1)
11-10-92	Morocco : Ethiopia	5:0 (4:0)
25-10-92	Benin : Morocco	0:1 (0:0)
25-10-92	Ethiopia : Tunisia	0:0
20-12-92	Ethiopia : Benin	3:1 (2:1)
20-12-92	Tunisia : Morocco	1:1 (1:0)
17-01-93	Benin : Tunisia	0:5 (0:4)
17-01-93	Ethiopia : Morocco	0:1 (0:1)
31-01-93	Tunisia : Ethiopia	3:0 (1:0)
31-01-93	Morocco : Benin	5:0 (3:0)
28-02-93	Morocco : Tunisia	0:0
28-02-93	Benin : Ethiopia	1:0 (0:0)

Africa - 1st Round, Group G

	P	W	D	L	F	A	Pts
Senegal	4	3	0	1	10	4	6
Gabon	4	2	1	1	7	5	5
Mozambique	4	0	1	3	3	11	1

11-10-92	Gabon : Mozambique	3:1 (2:1)
25-10-92	Mozambique : Senegal	0:1 (0:0)
20-12-92	Gabon : Senegal	3:2 (1:1)
17-01-93	Mozambique : Gabon	1:1 (0:1)
30-01-93	Senegal : Mozambique	6:1 (3:1)
27-02-93	Senegal : Gabon	1:0 (1:0)

Africa - 1st Round, Group H

	P	W	D	L	F	A	Pts
Zambia	4	3	0	1	11	3	6
Madagascar	4	3	0	1	7	3	6
Namibia	4	0	0	4	0	12	0

11-10-92	Madagascar : Namibia	3:0 (2:0)
25-10-92	Namibia : Zambia	0:4 (0:4)
20-12-92	Madagascar : Zambia	2:0 (0:0)
17-01-93	Namibia : Madagascar	0:1 (0:1)
31-01-93	Zambia : Namibia	4:0 (2:0)
28-02-93	Zambia : Madagascar	3:1 (1:0)

Africa - 1st Round, Group I

	P	W	D	L	F	A	Pts
Guinea	2	1	0	1	4	2	2
Kenya	2	1	0	1	2	4	2

20-12-92	Guinea : Kenya	4:0 (0:0)
27-02-93	Kenya : Guinea	2:0 (1:0)

Africa - 2nd Round, Group A

	P	W	D	L	F	A	Pts
Nigeria	4	2	1	1	10	5	5
Cote d' Ivoire	4	2	1	1	5	6	5
Algeria	4	0	2	2	3	7	2

16-04-93	Algeria : Cote d' Ivoire	1:1 (1:1)
02-05-93	Cote d' Ivoire : Nigeria	2:1 (0:1)
03-07-93	Nigeria : Algeria	4:1 (3:1)
18-07-93	Cote d' Ivoire : Algeria	1:0 (0:0)
25-09-93	Nigeria : Cote d' Ivoire	4:1 (3:1)
08-10-93	Algeria : Nigeria	1:1 (0:1)

Africa - 2nd Round, Group B

	P	W	D	L	F	A	Pts
Morocco	4	3	0	1	6	3	6
Zambia	4	2	1	1	6	2	5
Senegal	4	0	1	3	1	8	1

18-04-93	Morocco : Senegal	1:0 (0:0)
04-07-93	Zambia : Morocco	2:1 (0:1)
17-07-93	Senegal : Morocco	1:3 (0:1)
07-08-93	Senegal : Zambia	0:0
26-09-93	Zambia : Senegal	4:0 (1:0)
10-10-93	Morocco : Zambia	1:0 (0:0)

Africa - 2nd Round, Group C

	P	W	D	L	F	A	Pts
Cameroon	4	3	0	1	7	3	6
Zimbabwe	4	2	0	2	3	6	4
Guinea	4	1	0	3	4	5	2

18-04-93	Cameroon : Guinea	3:1 (1:0)
02-05-93	Guinea : Zimbabwe	3:0 (2:0)
04-07-93	Zimbabwe : Cameroon	1:0 (1:0)
18-07-93	Guinea : Cameroon	0:1 (0:1)
26-09-93	Zimbabwe : Guinea	1:0 (1:0)
10-10-93	Cameroon : Zimbabwe	3:1 (3:1)

Razzmatazz, Romario and the Divine Ponytail - USA 1994

Asia - Group A

	P	W	D	L	F	A	Pts
Iraq	8	6	1	1	28	4	13
China PR	8	6	0	2	18	4	12
Yemen	8	3	2	3	12	13	8
Jordan	8	2	3	3	12	15	7
Pakistan	8	0	0	8	2	36	0

22-05-93	Jordan : Yemen	1:1 (0:0)
22-05-93	Pakistan : China PR	0:5 (0:1)
24-05-93	Yemen : Pakistan	5:1 (1:1)
24-05-93	Jordan : Iraq	1:1 (1:0)
26-05-93	Yemen : Iraq	1:6 (1:3)
26-05-93	Jordan : China PR	0:3 (0:0)
28-05-93	Pakistan : Iraq	0:8 (0:4)
28-05-93	Yemen : China PR	1:0 (0:0)
30-05-93	Iraq : China PR	1:0 (0:0)
30-05-93	Jordan : Pakistan	3:1 (1:0)

All games played in Irbed

12-06-93	China PR : Pakistan	3:0 (0:0)
12-06-93	Yemen : Jordan	1:1 (0:0)
14-06-93	Pakistan : Yemen	0:3 (0:1)
14-06-93	Iraq : Jordan	4:0 (3:0)
16-06-93	China PR : Jordan	4:1 (1:0)
16-06-93	Iraq : Yemen	3:0 (0:0)
18-06-93	Iraq : Pakistan	4:0 (2:0)
18-06-93	China PR : Yemen	1:0 (0:0)
20-06-93	Pakistan : Jordan	0:5 (0:4)
20-06-93	China PR : Iraq	2:1 (0:0)

All games played in Chengdu

Asia - Group B

	P	W	D	L	F	A	Pts
Iran	6	3	3	0	15	2	9
Syria	6	3	3	0	14	4	9
Oman	6	2	2	2	10	5	6
Chinese Taipei	6	0	0	6	3	31	0

23-06-93	Iran : Oman	0:0
23-06-93	Chinese Taipei : Syria	0:2 (0:2)
25-06-93	Iran : Chinese Taipei	6:0 (3:0)
25-06-93	Oman : Syria	0:0
27-06-93	Iran : Syria	1:1 (0:0)
27-06-93	Oman : Chinese Taipei	2:1 (2:0)

All games played in Teheran

02-07-93	Syria : Chinese Taipei	8:1 (6:1)
02-07-93	Oman : Iran	0:1 (0:1)
04-07-93	Chinese Taipei : Iran	0:6 (0:4)
04-07-93	Syria : Oman	2:1 (0:1)
06-07-93	Chinese Taipei : Oman	1:7 (0:3)
06-07-93	Syria : Iran	1:1 (0:1)

All games played in Damascus

Asia - Group C

	P	W	D	L	F	A	Pts
Korea DPR	8	7	1	0	19	6	15
Qatar	8	5	1	2	22	8	11
Singapore	8	5	0	3	12	12	10
Indonesia	8	1	0	7	6	19	2
Vietnam SR	8	1	0	7	4	18	2

09-04-93	Korea DPR : Vietnam SR	3:0 (1:0)
09-04-93	Qatar : Indonesia	3:1 (0:0)
11-04-93	Qatar : Vietnam SR	4:0 (2:0)
11-04-93	Korea DPR : Singapore	2:1 (0:1)
13-04-93	Vietnam SR : Singapore	2:3 (1:2)
13-04-93	Korea DPR : Indonesia	4:0 (2:0)
16-04-93	Qatar : Singapore	4:1 (0:0)
16-04-93	Vietnam SR : Indonesia	1:0 (0:0)
18-04-93	Qatar : Korea DPR	1:2 (0:0)

18-04-93	Indonesia : Singapore	0:2 (0:0)

All games played in Doha

24-04-93	Indonesia : Qatar	1:4 (1:1)
24-04-93	Vietnam SR : Korea DPR	0:1 (0:0)
26-04-93	Singapore : Korea DPR	1:3 (0:2)
26-04-93	Vietnam SR : Qatar	0:4 (0:2)
28-04-93	Indonesia : Korea DPR	1:2 (1:1)
28-04-93	Singapore : Vietnam SR	1:0 (0:0)
30-04-93	Indonesia : Vietnam SR	2:1 (0:1)
30-04-93	Singapore : Qatar	1:0 (0:0)
02-05-93	Singapore : Indonesia	2:1 (0:0)
02-05-93	Korea DPR : Qatar	2:2 (1:1)

All games played in Singapore

Asia - Group D

	P	W	D	L	F	A	Pts
Korea Republic	8	7	1	0	23	1	15
Bahrain	8	3	3	2	9	6	9
Lebanon	8	2	4	2	8	9	8
Hong Kong	8	2	1	5	9	19	5
India	8	1	1	6	8	22	3

07-05-93	Lebanon : India	2:2 (1:0)
07-05-93	Hong Kong : Bahrain	2:1 (1:1)
09-05-93	Bahrain : Korea Republic	0:0
09-05-93	Lebanon : Hong Kong	2:2 (1:2)
11-05-93	Lebanon : Korea Republic	0:1 (0:1)
11-05-93	India : Hong Kong	1:2 (0:1)
13-05-93	Lebanon : Bahrain	0:0
13-05-93	India : Korea Republic	0:3 (0:1)
15-05-93	Hong Kong : Korea Republic	0:3 (0:1)
15-05-93	Bahrain : India	2:1 (2:0)

All games played in Beirut

05-06-93	Bahrain : Lebanon	0:0
05-06-93	Korea Republic : Hong Kong	4:1 (1:1)
07-06-93	India : Bahrain	0:3 (0:1)
07-06-93	Korea Republic : Lebanon	2:0 (1:0)
09-06-93	Korea Republic : India	7:0 (4:0)
09-06-93	Hong Kong : Lebanon	1:2 (1:1)
11-06-93	India : Lebanon	1:2 (1:1)
11-06-93	Bahrain : Hong Kong	3:0 (1:0)
13-06-93	Hong Kong : India	1:3 (1:0)
13-06-93	Korea Republic : Bahrain	3:0 (0:0)

All games played in Seoul

Asia - Group E

	P	W	D	L	F	A	Pts
Saudi Arabia	6	4	2	0	20	1	10
Kuwait	6	3	2	1	21	4	8
Malaysia	6	2	2	2	16	7	6
Macao	6	0	0	6	1	46	0

01-05-93	Malaysia : Kuwait	1:1 (0:1)
01-05-93	Macao : Saudi Arabia	0:6 (0:3)
03-05-93	Malaysia : Saudi Arabia	1:1 (1:0)
03-05-93	Macao : Kuwait	1:10 (0:2)
05-05-93	Kuwait : Saudi Arabia	0:0
05-05-93	Malaysia : Macao	9:0 (4:0)

All games played in Kuala Lumpur

14-05-93	Saudi Arabia : Macao	8:0 (5:0)
14-05-93	Kuwait : Malaysia	2:0 (0:0)
16-05-93	Saudi Arabia : Malaysia	3:0 (1:0)
16-05-93	Kuwait : Macao	8:0 (2:0)
18-05-93	Macao : Malaysia	0:5 (0:2)
18-05-93	Saudi Arabia : Kuwait	2:0 (1:0)

All games played in Taif

Asia - Group F

	P	W	D	L	F	A	Pts
Japan	8	7	1	0	28	2	15
United Arab Emirates	8	6	1	1	19	4	13
Thailand	8	4	0	4	13	7	8
Bangladesh	8	2	0	6	7	28	4
Sri Lanka	8	0	0	8	0	26	0

08-04-93	Japan : Thailand	1:0 (1:0)
08-04-93	Sri Lanka : UAE	0:4 (0:2)
11-04-93	Japan : Bangladesh	8:0 (3:0)
11-04-93	Thailand : Sri Lanka	1:0 (0:0)
13-04-93	UAE : Thailand	1:0 (0:0)
13-04-93	Sri Lanka : Bangladesh	0:1 (0:0)
15-04-93	Japan : Sri Lanka	5:0 (3:0)
15-04-93	UAE : Bangladesh	1:0 (0:0)
18-04-93	Japan : United Arab Emirates	2:0 (1:0)
18-04-93	Thailand : Bangladesh	4:1 (2:0)

All games played in Japan

28-04-93	Thailand : Japan	0:1 (0:0)
28-04-93	UAE : Sri Lanka	3:0 (1:0)
30-04-93	Bangladesh : Japan	1:4 (1:3)
30-04-93	Thailand : UAE	1:2 (0:1)
03-05-93	Bangladesh : UAE	0:7 (0:4)
03-05-93	Sri Lanka : Thailand	0:3 (0:2)
05-05-93	Bangladesh : Thailand	1:4 (0:2)
05-05-93	Sri Lanka : Japan	0:6 (0:2)
07-05-93	UAE : Japan	1:1 (0:0)
07-05-93	Bangladesh : Sri Lanka	3:0 (1:0)

All games played in Dubai and Al Ain City

Asia - 2nd Round

	P	W	D	L	F	A	Pts
Saudi Arabia	5	2	3	0	8	6	7
Korea Republic	5	2	1	9	4	6	
Japan	5	2	2	1	7	4	6
Iraq	5	1	3	1	9	9	5
Iran	5	2	0	3	8	11	4
Korea DPR	5	1	0	4	5	12	2

15-10-93	Saudi Arabia : Japan	0:0
15-10-93	Korea DPR : Iraq	3:2 (0:1)
16-10-93	Iran : Korea Republic	0:3 (0:1)
18-10-93	Korea DPR : Saudi Arabia	1:2 (0:0)
18-10-93	Japan : Iran	1:2 (0:1)
19-10-93	Iraq : Korea Republic	2:2 (1:1)
21-10-93	Korea DPR : Japan	0:3 (0:1)
22-10-93	Iran : Iraq	1:2 (1:2)
22-10-93	Korea Republic : Saudi Arabia	1:1 (1:1)
24-10-93	Iraq : Saudi Arabia	1:1 (1:1)
25-10-93	Japan : Korea Republic	1:0 (0:0)
25-10-93	Iran : Korea DPR	2:1 (0:1)
28-10-93	Korea Republic : Korea DPR	3:0 (0:0)
28-10-93	Iraq : Japan	2:2 (0:1)
28-10-93	Saudi Arabia : Iran	4:3 (2:1)

All games played in Doha

Europe - Group 1

	P	W	D	L	F	A	Pts
Italy	10	7	2	1	22	7	16
Switzerland	10	6	3	1	23	6	15
Portugal	10	6	2	2	18	5	14
Scotland	10	4	3	3	14	13	11
Malta	10	1	1	8	3	23	3
Estonia	10	0	1	9	1	27	1

16-08-92	Estonia : Switzerland	0:6 (0:2)
09-09-92	Switzerland : Scotland	3:1 (1:1)
14-10-92	Italy : Switzerland	2:2 (0:2)
14-10-92	Scotland : Portugal	0:0

25-10-92	Malta : Estonia	0:0
18-11-92	Switzerland : Malta	3:0 (2:0)
18-11-92	Scotland : Italy	0:0
19-12-92	Malta : Italy	1:2 (0:0)
24-01-93	Malta : Portugal	0:1 (0:0)
17-02-93	Scotland : Malta	3:0 (1:0)
24-02-93	Portugal : Italy	1:3 (0:2)
24-03-93	Italy : Malta	6:1 (2:0)
31-03-93	Switzerland : Portugal	1:1 (1:1)
14-04-93	Italy : Estonia	2:0 (1:0)
17-04-93	Malta : Switzerland	0:2 (0:1)
28-04-93	Portugal : Scotland	5:0 (2:0)
01-05-93	Switzerland : Italy	1:0 (0:0)
12-05-93	Estonia : Malta	0:1 (0:1)
19-05-93	Estonia : Scotland	0:3 (0:1)
02-06-93	Scotland : Estonia	3:1 (2:0)
19-06-93	Portugal : Malta	4:0 (3:0)
05-09-93	Estonia : Portugal	0:2 (0:0)
08-09-93	Scotland : Switzerland	1:1 (0:0)
22-09-93	Estonia : Italy	0:3 (0:1)
13-10-93	Italy : Scotland	3:1 (2:1)
13-10-93	Portugal : Switzerland	1:0 (1:0)
10-11-93	Portugal : Estonia	3:0 (2:0)
17-11-93	Switzerland : Estonia	4:0 (3:0)
17-11-93	Italy : Portugal	1:0 (0:0)
17-11-93	Malta : Scotland	0:2 (0:1)

Europe - Group 2

	P	W	D	L	F	A	Pts
Norway	10	7	2	1	25	5	16
Netherlands	10	6	3	1	29	9	15
England	10	5	3	2	26	9	13
Poland	10	3	2	5	10	15	8
Turkey	10	3	1	6	11	19	7
San Marino	10	0	1	9	2	46	1

09-09-92	Norway : San Marino	10:0 (4:0)
23-09-92	Norway : Netherlands	2:1 (1:1)
23-09-92	Poland : Turkey	1:0 (1:0)
07-10-92	San Marino : Norway	0:2 (0:2)
14-10-92	England : Norway	1:1 (0:0)
14-10-92	Netherlands : Poland	2:2 (1:2)
28-10-92	Turkey : San Marino	4:1 (1:0)
18-11-92	England : Turkey	4:0 (2:0)
16-12-92	Turkey : Netherlands	1:3 (0:0)
17-02-93	England : San Marino	6:0 (2:0)
24-02-93	Netherlands : Turkey	3:1 (2:1)
10-03-93	San Marino : Turkey	0:0
24-03-93	Netherlands : San Marino	6:0 (2:0)
31-03-93	Turkey : England	0:2 (0:2)
28-04-93	Poland : San Marino	1:0 (0:0)
28-04-93	Norway : Turkey	3:1 (2:0)
28-04-93	England : Netherlands	2:2 (2:1)
19-05-93	San Marino : Poland	0:3 (0:0)
29-05-93	Poland : England	1:1 (1:0)
02-06-93	Norway : England	2:0 (1:0)
09-06-93	Netherlands : Norway	0:0
08-09-93	England : Poland	3:0 (1:0)
22-09-93	Norway : Poland	1:0 (0:0)
22-09-93	San Marino : Netherlands	0:7 (0:3)
13-10-93	Netherlands : England	2:0 (0:0)
13-10-93	Poland : Norway	0:3 (0:0)
27-10-93	Turkey : Poland	2:1 (0:1)
10-11-93	Turkey : Norway	2:1 (2:0)
17-11-93	San Marino : England	1:7 (1:3)
17-11-93	Poland : Netherlands	1:3 (1:1)

Europe - Group 3

	P	W	D	L	F	A	Pts
Spain	12	8	3	1	27	4	19
Ireland Rep	12	7	4	1	19	6	18
Denmark	12	7	4	1	15	2	18
N Ireland	12	5	3	4	14	13	13
Lithuania	12	2	3	7	8	21	7
Latvia	12	0	5	7	4	21	5
Albania	12	1	2	9	6	26	4

22-04-92	Spain : Albania	3:0 (1:0)
28-04-92	N.Ireland : Lithuania	2:2 (2:1)
26-05-92	Ireland Republic : Albania	2:0 (0:0)
03-06-92	Albania : Lithuania	1:0 (0:0)
12-08-92	Latvia : Lithuania	1:2 (1:0)
26-08-92	Latvia : Denmark	0:0
09-09-92	Ireland Republic : Latvia	4:0 (1:0)
09-09-92	N.Ireland : Albania	3:0 (3:0)
23-09-92	Lithuania : Denmark	0:0
23-09-92	Latvia : Spain	0:0
14-10-92	Denmark : Ireland Republic	0:0
14-10-92	N.Ireland : Spain	0:0
28-10-92	Lithuania : Latvia	1:1 (0:1)
11-11-92	Albania : Latvia	1:1 (0:1)
18-11-92	N.Ireland : Denmark	0:1 (0:0)
18-11-92	Spain : Ireland Republic	0:0
16-12-92	Spain : Latvia	5:0 (0:0)
17-02-93	Albania : N.Ireland	1:2 (0:2)
24-02-93	Spain : Lithuania	5:0 (3:0)
31-03-93	Denmark : Spain	1:0 (1:0)
31-03-93	Ireland Republic : N.Ireland	3:0 (3:0)
14-04-93	Denmark : Latvia	2:0 (0:0)
14-04-93	Lithuania : Albania	3:1 (3:0)
28-04-93	Ireland Republic : Denmark	1:1 (0:1)
28-04-93	Spain : N.Ireland	3:1 (3:1)
15-05-93	Latvia : Albania	0:0
25-05-93	Lithuania : N.Ireland	0:1 (0:1)
26-05-93	Albania : Ireland Republic	1:2 (1:1)
02-06-93	Latvia : N.Ireland	1:2 (0:2)
02-06-93	Denmark : Albania	4:0 (4:0)
02-06-93	Lithuania : Spain	0:2 (0:0)
09-06-93	Latvia : Ireland Republic	0:2 (0:2)
16-06-93	Lithuania : Ireland Republic	0:1 (0:1)
25-08-93	Denmark : Lithuania	4:0 (1:0)
08-09-93	Albania : Denmark	0:1 (0:0)
08-09-93	Ireland Republic : Lithuania	2:0 (2:0)
08-09-93	N.Ireland : Latvia	2:0 (1:0)
22-09-93	Albania : Spain	1:5 (1:3)
13-10-93	Denmark : N.Ireland	1:0 (0:0)
13-10-93	Ireland Republic : Spain	1:3 (0:3)
17-11-93	Spain : Denmark	1:0 (0:0)
17-11-93	N.Ireland : Ireland Republic	1:1 (0:0)

Europe - Group 4

	P	W	D	L	F	A	Pts
Romania	10	7	1	2	29	12	15
Belgium	10	7	1	2	16	5	15
Czech	10	4	5	1	21	9	13
Wales	10	5	2	3	19	12	12
Cyprus	10	2	1	7	8	18	5
Faroe Islands	10	0	0	10	1	38	0

22-04-92	Belgium : Cyprus	1:0 (1:0)
06-05-92	Romania : Faroe Islands	7:0 (5:0)
20-05-92	Romania : Wales	5:1 (5:0)
03-06-92	Faroe Islands : Belgium	0:3 (0:1)
16-06-92	Faroe Islands : Cyprus	0:2 (0:1)
02-09-92	Czechoslovakia : Belgium	1:2 (0:1)
09-09-92	Wales : Faroe Islands	6:0 (3:0)
23-09-92	Czechoslovakia : Faroe Islands	4:0 (1:0)
14-10-92	Cyprus : Wales	0:1 (0:0)
14-10-92	Belgium : Romania	1:0 (1:0)
14-11-92	Romania : Czechoslovakia	1:1 (0:0)
18-11-92	Belgium : Wales	2:0 (0:0)
29-11-92	Cyprus : Romania	1:4 (1:2)
13-02-93	Cyprus : Belgium	0:3 (0:1)
24-03-93	Cyprus : Czechoslovakia	1:1 (0:1)
31-03-93	Wales : Belgium	2:0 (2:0)
14-04-93	Romania : Cyprus	2:1 (1:1)
25-04-93	Cyprus : Faroe Islands	3:1 (2:0)
28-04-93	Czechoslovakia : Wales	1:1 (1:1)
22-05-93	Belgium : Faroe Islands	3:0 (1:0)
02-06-93	Czechoslovakia : Romania	5:2 (2:1)
06-06-93	Faroe Islands : Wales	0:3 (0:2)
16-06-93	Faroe Islands : Czechoslovakia	0:3 (0:3)
08-09-93	Faroe Islands : Romania	0:4 (0:1)
08-09-93	Wales : Czechoslovakia	2:2 (2:1)
13-10-93	Romania : Belgium	2:1 (0:0)
13-10-93	Wales : Cyprus	2:0 (0:0)
27-10-93	Czechoslovakia : Cyprus	3:0 (2:0)
17-11-93	Wales : Romania	1:2 (0:1)
17-11-93	Belgium : Czechoslovakia	0:0

Europe - Group 5

	P	W	D	L	F	A	Pts
Greece	8	6	2	0	10	2	14
Russia	8	5	2	1	15	4	12
Iceland	8	3	2	3	7	6	8
Hungary	8	2	1	5	6	11	5
Luxembourg	8	0	1	7	2	17	1

13-05-92	Greece : Iceland	1:0 (1:0)
03-06-92	Hungary : Iceland	1:2 (1:0)
09-09-92	Luxembourg : Hungary	0:3 (0:1)
07-10-92	Iceland : Greece	0:1 (0:0)
14-10-92	Russia : Iceland	1:0 (0:0)
28-10-92	Russia : Luxembourg	2:0 (2:0)
11-11-92	Greece : Hungary	0:0
17-02-93	Greece : Luxembourg	2:0 (1:0)
31-03-93	Hungary : Greece	0:1 (0:0)
14-04-93	Luxembourg : Russia	0:4 (0:1)
28-04-93	Russia : Hungary	3:0 (0:0)
20-05-93	Luxembourg : Iceland	1:1 (0:1)
23-05-93	Russia : Greece	1:1 (0:1)
02-06-93	Iceland : Russia	1:1 (1:1)
16-06-93	Iceland : Hungary	2:0 (1:0)
08-09-93	Iceland : Luxembourg	1:0 (0:0)
08-09-93	Hungary : Russia	1:3 (1:1)
12-10-93	Luxembourg : Greece	1:3 (1:0)
27-10-93	Hungary : Luxembourg	1:0 (1:0)
17-11-93	Greece : Russia	1:0 (0:0)

Europe - Group 6

	P	W	D	L	F	A	Pts
Sweden	10	6	3	1	19	8	15
Bulgaria	10	6	2	2	19	10	14
France	10	6	1	3	17	10	13
Austria	10	3	2	5	15	16	8
Finland	10	2	1	7	9	18	5
Israel	10	1	3	6	10	27	5

14-05-92	Finland : Bulgaria	0:3 (0:0)
09-09-92	Bulgaria : France	2:0 (2:0)
09-09-92	Finland : Sweden	0:1 (0:0)
07-10-92	Sweden : Bulgaria	2:0 (0:0)
14-10-92	France : Austria	2:0 (1:0)
28-10-92	Austria : Israel	5:2 (2:0)
11-11-92	Israel : Sweden	1:3 (1:1)

14-11-92	France : Finland	2:1 (2:0)
02-12-92	Israel : Bulgaria	0:2 (0:0)
17-02-93	Israel : France	0:4 (0:1)
27-03-93	Austria : France	0:1 (0:0)
14-04-93	Austria : Bulgaria	3:1 (2:0)
28-04-93	Bulgaria : Finland	2:0 (2:0)
28-04-93	France : Sweden	2:1 (1:1)
12-05-93	Bulgaria : Israel	2:2 (1:0)
13-05-93	Finland : Austria	3:1 (2:0)
19-05-93	Sweden : Austria	1:0 (0:0)
02-06-93	Sweden : Israel	5:0 (2:0)
16-06-93	Finland : Israel	0:0
22-08-93	Sweden : France	1:1 (0:0)
25-08-93	Austria : Finland	3:0 (2:0)
08-09-93	Bulgaria : Sweden	1:1 (1:1)
08-09-93	Finland : France	0:2 (0:0)
13-10-93	France : Israel	2:3 (2:1)
13-10-93	Bulgaria : Austria	4:1 (2:0)
13-10-93	Sweden : Finland	3:2 (2:1)
27-10-93	Israel : Austria	1:1 (1:1)
10-11-93	Israel : Finland	1:3 (0:0)
10-11-93	Austria : Sweden	1:1 (0:0)
17-11-93	France : Bulgaria	1:2 (1:1)

Caribbean/North/Cent. America
Pre-preliminary - Caribbean Zone

	P	W	D	L	F	A	Pts
Puerto Rico	2	1	1	0	3	2	3
St Vincent / Grenadines	2	1	0	1	3	2	2
St Lucia	2	1	0	1	2	3	2
Dominican Rep	2	0	1	1	2	3	1

21-03-92 Dominican Republic : Puerto Rico 1:2 (0:1)
22-03-92 St Lucia : St Vincent/Grenadines 1:0 (1:0)
28-03-92 Puerto Rico : Dominican Republic 1:1 (1:1)
29-03-92 St Vincent/Grenadines : St Lucia 3:1 (1:1)

Caribbean/North/Cent. America
Preliminary Round - North

	P	W	D	L	F	A	Pts
Jamaica	2	2	0	0	3	1	4
Haiti	2	1	0	1	2	2	2
Bermuda	2	1	0	1	2	2	2
Puerto Rico	2	0	0	2	1	3	0

26-04-92 Bermuda : Haiti 1:0 (0:0)
23-05-92 Jamaica : Puerto Rico 2:1 (0:1)
24-05-92 Haiti : Bermuda 2:1 (1:1)
30-05-92 Puerto Rico : Jamaica 0:1 (0:1)

Caribbean/North/Cent. America
Preliminary Round - South

	P	W	D	L	F	A	Pts
Trinidad & Tobago	2	2	0	0	5	1	4
Antigua and Barbuda	2	1	1	0	4	1	3
Surinam	2	1	1	0	3	2	3
Guyana	2	0	1	1	2	3	1
Netherlands Antilles	2	0	1	1	1	4	1
Barbados	2	0	0	2	1	5	0

19-04-92 N. Antilles : Antigua & Barbuda 1:1 (1:1)
19-04-92 Barbados : Trinidad & Tobago 1:2 (0:1)
26-04-92 Antigua & Barbuda : N. Antilles 3:0 (1:0)
26-04-92 Guyana : Surinam 1:2 (0:1)
24-05-92 Surinam : Guyana 1:1 (1:1)
31-05-92 Trinidad & Tobago : Barbados 3:0 (0:0)

Caribbean/North/Cent. America
1st Round - Caribbean Zone

	P	W	D	L	F	A	Pts
Bermuda	2	2	0	0	5	1	4
Jamaica	2	1	1	0	3	2	3
St Vincent / Grenadines	2	1	1	0	2	1	3
Trinidad & Tobago	2	0	1	1	2	3	1
Surinam	2	0	1	1	1	2	1
Antigua and Barbuda	2	0	0	2	1	5	0

14-06-92 Antigua and Barbuda : Bermuda 0:3 (0:1)
04-07-92 Bermuda : Antigua and Barbuda 2:1 (1:1)
05-07-92 Trinidad & Tobago : Jamaica 1:2 (0:0)
02-08-92 Surinam : St Vincent/Grenadines 0:0
16-08-92 Jamaica : Trinidad & Tobago 1:1 (1:1)
30-08-92 St Vincent/Grenadines : Surinam 2:1 (0:1)

Caribbean/North/Cent. America
1st Round - Central Zone

	P	W	D	L	F	A	Pts
El Salvador	2	2	0	0	10	1	4
Honduras	2	1	1	0	2	0	3
Costa Rica	2	1	0	1	5	2	2
Panama	2	1	0	1	2	5	2
Guatemala	2	0	1	1	0	2	1
Nicaragua	2	0	0	2	1	10	0

19-07-92 Nicaragua : El Salvador 0:5 (0:3)
19-07-92 Guatemala : Honduras 0:0
23-07-92 El Salvador : Nicaragua 5:1 (2:0)
26-07-92 Honduras : Guatemala 2:0 (0:0)
16-08-92 Panama : Costa Rica 1:0 (1:0)
23-08-92 Costa Rica : Panama 5:1 (4:0)

Caribbean/North/Cent. America
2nd Round - Group A

	P	W	D	L	F	A	Pts
Mexico	6	4	1	1	22	3	9
Honduras	6	4	1	1	14	6	9
Costa Rica	6	3	0	3	11	9	6
St Vincent / Grenadines	6	0	0	6	0	29	0

08-11-92 Costa Rica : Honduras 2:3 (2:0)
08-11-92 St Vin./Grenadines : Mexico 0:4 (0:1)
15-11-92 St Vin./Grenadines : Costa Rica 0:1 (0:0)
15-11-92 Mexico : Honduras 2:0 (1:0)
22-11-92 Mexico : Costa Rica 4:0 (0:0)
22-11-92 St Vin./Grenadines : Honduras 0:4 (0:2)
28-11-92 Honduras : St Vin./Grenadines 4:0 (3:0)
29-11-92 Costa Rica : Mexico 2:0 (0:0)
05-12-92 Honduras : Costa Rica 2:1 (1:0)
06-12-92 Mexico : St Vin./Grenadines 11:0 (6:0)
13-12-92 Costa Rica : St Vin./Grenadines 5:0 (2:0)
13-12-92 Honduras : Mexico 1:1 (0:0)

Caribbean/North/Cent. America
2nd Round - Group B

	P	W	D	L	F	A	Pts
El Salvador	6	4	1	1	12	6	9
Canada	6	2	3	1	9	7	7
Jamaica	6	1	2	3	6	9	4
Bermuda	6	1	2	3	7	12	4

18-10-92 Bermuda : El Salvador 1:0 (0:0)
18-10-92 Jamaica : Canada 1:1 (0:0)
25-10-92 Bermuda : Jamaica 1:1 (0:0)
25-10-92 El Salvador : Canada 1:1 (1:0)
01-11-92 El Salvador : Bermuda 4:1 (2:0)
01-11-92 Canada : Jamaica 1:0 (0:0)

08-11-92	Canada : El Salvador	2:3 (1:1)
08-11-92	Jamaica : Bermuda	3:2 (2:0)
15-11-92	Canada : Bermuda	4:2 (3:0)
22-11-92	Jamaica : El Salvador	0:2 (0:1)
06-12-92	El Salvador : Jamaica	2:1 (1:1)
06-12-92	Bermuda : Canada	0:0

Caribbean/North/Cent. America
3rd Round

	P	W	D	L	F	A	Pts
Mexico	6	5	0	1	17	5	10
Canada	6	3	1	2	10	10	7
El Salvador	6	2	0	4	6	11	4
Honduras	6	1	1	4	7	14	3

04-04-93 El Salvador : Mexico 2:1 (1:0)
04-04-93 Honduras : Canada 2:2 (1:1)
11-04-93 Mexico : Honduras 3:0 (1:0)
11-04-93 Canada : El Salvador 2:0 (2:0)
18-04-93 Canada : Honduras 3:1 (0:1)
18-04-93 Mexico : El Salvador 3:1 (1:0)
25-04-93 Honduras : El Salvador 2:0 (1:0)
25-04-93 Mexico : Canada 4:0 (2:0)
02-05-93 El Salvador : Canada 1:2 (0:1)
02-05-93 Honduras : Mexico 1:4 (0:2)
09-05-93 El Salvador : Honduras 2:1 (2:0)
09-05-93 Canada : Mexico 1:2 (1:1)

Oceania - 1st Round, Group 1

	P	W	D	L	F	A	Pts
Australia	4	4	0	0	13	2	8
Tahiti	4	1	1	2	5	8	3
Solomon Islands	4	0	1	3	5	13	1

17-07-92 Solomon Islands : Tahiti 1:1 (0:0)
04-09-92 Solomon Islands : Australia 1:2 (0:1)
11-09-92 Tahiti : Australia 0:3 (0:2)
20-09-92 Australia : Tahiti 2:0 (1:0)
26-09-92 Australia : Solomon Islands 6:1 (1:1)
09-10-92 Tahiti : Solomon Islands 4:2 (3:0)

Oceania - 1st Round, Group 2

	P	W	D	L	F	A	Pts
New Zealand	4	3	1	0	15	1	7
Fiji	4	2	1	1	6	3	5
Vanuatu	4	0	0	4	1	18	0

07-06-92 New Zealand : Fiji 3:0 (2:0)
27-06-92 Vanuatu : New Zealand 1:4 (1:2)
01-07-92 New Zealand : Vanuatu 8:0 (3:0)
12-09-92 Fiji : Vanuatu 3:0 (0:0)
19-09-92 Fiji : New Zealand 0:0
26-09-92 Vanuatu : Fiji 0:3 (0:2)

Oceania - 2nd Round

	P	W	D	L	F	A	Pts
Australia	2	2	0	0	4	0	4
New Zealand	2	0	0	2	0	4	0

30-05-93 New Zealand : Australia 0:1 (0:0)
06-06-93 Australia : New Zealand 3:0 (2:0)

OFC/CONCACAF Play-off

	P	W	D	L	F	A	Pts
Canada	2	1	0	1	3	3	2
Australia	2	1	0	1	3	3	2

31-07-93 Canada : Australia 2:1 (0:1)
15-08-93 Australia : Canada 2:1 a.e.t.
4:1 penalty kicks (2:1, 1:0)

OFC/CONMEBOL Play-off

31-10-93	Australia : Argentina	1:1 (1:1)
17-11-93	Argentina : Australia	1:0 (0:0)

South America - Group A

	P	W	D	L	F	A	Pts
Colombia	6	4	2	0	13	2	10
Argentina	6	3	1	2	7	9	7
Paraguay	6	1	4	1	6	7	6
Peru	6	0	1	5	4	12	1

01-08-93	Colombia : Paraguay	0:0
01-08-93	Peru : Argentina	0:1 (0:1)
08-08-93	Peru : Colombia	0:1 (0:1)
08-08-93	Paraguay : Argentina	1:3 (1:1)
15-08-93	Colombia : Argentina	2:1 (1:0)
15-08-93	Paraguay : Peru	2:1 (2:1)
22-08-93	Argentina : Peru	2:1 (2:0)
22-08-93	Paraguay : Colombia	1:1 (0:1)
29-08-93	Colombia : Peru	4:0 (2:0)
29-08-93	Argentina : Paraguay	0:0
05-09-93	Argentina : Colombia	0:5 (0:1)
05-09-93	Peru : Paraguay	2:2 (1:0)

South America - Group B

	P	W	D	L	F	A	Pts
Brazil	8	5	2	1	20	4	12
Bolivia	8	5	1	2	22	11	11
Uruguay	8	4	2	2	10	7	10
Ecuador	8	1	3	4	7	7	5
Venezuela	8	1	0	7	4	34	2

18-07-93	Ecuador : Brazil	0:0
18-07-93	Venezuela : Bolivia	1:7 (1:3)
25-07-93	Venezuela : Uruguay	0:1 (0:0)
25-07-93	Bolivia : Brazil	2:0 (0:0)
01-08-93	Venezuela : Brazil	1:5 (0:1)
01-08-93	Uruguay : Ecuador	0:0
08-08-93	Ecuador : Venezuela	5:0 (2:0)
08-08-93	Bolivia : Uruguay	3:1 (0:0)
15-08-93	Bolivia : Ecuador	1:0 (1:0)
15-08-93	Uruguay : Brazil	1:1 (0:1)
22-08-93	Bolivia : Venezuela	7:0 (1:0)
22-08-93	Brazil : Ecuador	2:0 (1:0)
29-08-93	Brazil : Bolivia	6:0 (5:0)
29-08-93	Uruguay : Venezuela	4:0 (3:0)
05-09-93	Ecuador : Uruguay	0:1 (0:0)
05-09-93	Brazil : Venezuela	4:0 (3:0)
12-09-93	Uruguay : Bolivia	2:1 (2:1)
12-09-93	Venezuela : Ecuador	2:1 (1:1)
19-09-93	Brazil : Uruguay	2:0 (0:0)
19-09-93	Ecuador : Bolivia	1:1 (0:1)

Chapter 18

Reggae, Ronaldo and a French Revolution
The France World Cup, 1998

France 1998

Winners: France

Runners-up: Brazil

3rd Place: Croatia

4th Place: Holland

Total Attendance: 2,711,908

Number of Matches: 64

My greatest World Cup memory is of trying to get back from the Stade de France on the night after France won the Cup in 1998. We were in a bus besieged by thousands of fans singing the national anthem and chanting the names of Petit and Zidane. When we eventually got as near to the centre of town and our hotel as possible, we walked down the Champs Elysees watching in awe and amazement as two million Frenchmen and women celebrated long into the night. We'd booked a restaurant table for midnight…got there at two…and they were happy to serve until everyone dropped from exhaustion just before five. One of those evenings that you know you were very privileged to share in a nation's triumph.

Original contribution by John Inverdale of the BBC

With only three years to go before the third post-Christ millennium, sleaze, gloss and personality (or lack of) was the new driving forces behind a world that seemed to have lost sight of the need for substance. It was the face rather than the intellect that mattered. The year started with a major sex scandal that rocked the United States, as Monica Lewinsky's allegations of her 18 month affair with President Bill Clinton became public knowledge. Clinton categorically stated in a rather emotional outburst under oath: "I did not have sexual relations with that woman", but evidence told a different story and Clinton was forced to make a public apology. Elsewhere in the country, Karla Faye became the first woman to be executed in Texas since 1863 having spent 14 years on death row for murder. The US's third school shoot-out in five months happened in Arkansas when an 11 year old and a 13 year old from the West Side Middle School in Jonesboro killed four schoolgirls and a teacher during a hoax fire alarm.

Eight years after the Gulf War, Saddam Hussain was still in power in Iraq and still causing problems. A UN Special Commission wanted access to his weapons sites, but by the time he capitulated on 17th February he had hidden his weapons of mass destruction. In Europe, the Yugoslavian crisis flared again when the Kosovan Liberation Army hit back against the tyranny of Slobodan Milosevic and his attempts to ethnically cleanse the province of its Albanian population. Many of those involved have yet to be brought to justice, but deposed Serbian President, Milosovic, is now standing trial for war crimes in The Hague. North Korean people were starving, prompting intervention from the south hoping ultimately to bring unity to the peninsula. In Rwanda, 22 people were executed for their part in the Tutsi massacres four years earlier and the Vatican finally admitted that it could have done more to help the Jews escape Nazi persecution. Nick Leason's illegal trading brought Barings Bank to its knees and when financial markets across the world took a dive, the Japanese economy went into recession taking the other Asian Tigers with it. The biggest fear was that the emerging Chinese market economy would be sucked into the turmoil.

In Britain, 18 years of Conservative rule had come to an end when Tony Blair's New Labour swept to power on 2nd May 1997 with one of the biggest majorities ever and immediately faced the problem of what to put inside the ill-fated Millennium Dome, a project conceived by an all-party group under Tory rule. 1998 was the first time the Winter Olympics and the World Cup would be held in the same year. Evidence of vast amounts of frozen water was found on Mars, the film "Titanic" won 11 Oscars and Geri Halliwell quit the Spice Girls. The world said goodbye to Sonny Bono and Michael Hutchence of INXS died in a freak accident after suffering depression. Carl Perkins hung up his Blue Suede Shoes at the age of 65 and Frank Sinatra died at 82, leaving

$200m in his will. Also taking her final bow was the "First Lady" of country music, Tammy Wynette, Linda McCartney lost her fight against breast cancer and Pol Pot died in his jungle hideout in Cambodia.

As the summer arrived, all eyes turned to La Belle France. A massive 172 teams entered the qualifying tournament of the 16th World Cup, 49 of them from Europe, 38 from Africa, 36 from Asia, 30 from the CONCACAF region, 10 from Oceania and 9 from South America. With hosts, France, and reigning champions, Brazil, it made a grand total of 174 participants. A small number of countries declined to take part or withdrew, among them North Korea and Libya, but this was more than compensated by the array of new nations anxious to be part of football's great occasion.

The tournament kicked off on the tiny Caribbean island of Dominica, but it was in Europe and Asia that the arrival of the new nations had the greatest impact. Here, the momentous events that had swept across Eastern Europe in 1989 and the early 1990s, ending the Cold War and breaking up the Soviet Union and the Yugoslavian Federation, at last had their impact. The qualifying groups for both regions were swelled with the names of former Soviet and Yugoslav republics, though only Yugoslavia and Croatia made it through to the finals.

The European rounds, in which England, Holland, Hungary, Spain, Switzerland and Yugoslavia each played their 100th World Cup games and Belgium scored its 200th World Cup goal, produced no major surprises. An emotional and resilient 0-0 draw in Rome in October 1997, which saw a valiant England take everything Italy could throw at them, put the English safely through to the finals at the head of the group and left Italy needing to face Russia in a play-off. A narrow 1-0 victory in November in Rome, following a draw in Moscow, saved Italian blushes and took them undefeated to France. Elsewhere Germany, Norway, Romania and Spain progressed to the finals without losing, with Romania scoring 37 goals in the high-scoring Group 8. Scotland got through as the best runner-up, though Eire narrowly missed out, going down 2-1 to Belgium in Brussels in a November play-off. In the other play-offs Croatia saw off Ukraine, but the biggest shock was the massacre of the once mighty Hungary at the hands of Yugoslavia, allowed back in after having been forced to miss the 1994 tournament. Yugoslavia was only the rump of the country that had taken part in previous World Cups, Serbia and Montenegro remaining in the federation, but it had proved a free-scoring side in the group round and did so again in the play-off. A 7-1 humiliation of Hungary in Budapest in October, with Aston Villa's Savo Milosevic hitting the last, was followed by an equally emphatic 5-0 win in Belgrade in November. They had scored 41 goals in their 12 qualifying matches, though sympathy ought to be extended to first-timers Liechtenstein, who conceded 52 goals in their 10 games, and San Marino, who conceded 42 in 8 games. The latter had now conceded 88 goals in 2 tournaments over 18 games.

As with Europe, Asia's qualifying tournament followed a group format with the winners of the ten groups going into the second round. Of the new nations, only Kazakhstan and Uzbekistan won through to the second round, where the teams were divided into two groups of five. Saudi Arabia and South Korea came top of these and thereby secured automatic places in France, whilst Iran and Japan as runners up had to play-off for the third automatic place. Japan duly won, leaving Iran to play-off against Australia, the winner of the Oceania group. Both legs produced draws, but Iran took it on the away goals rule. It had meant that they had played 17 games to get to the finals and had scored 57 goals on the way, including 17-0 and 9-0 victories against the Maldives, who conceded 57 times in total. Iran's 6th against the Maldives in their second meeting was its 100th World Cup goal. Another notable first in the Asia region was Nepal's first World Cup goal in its opening 1-1 draw against Macao in Group 4 in March 1997.

No automatic place was allocated to the Oceania region. Here the smaller island states were divided into Polynesian and Melanesian groups, the winners of each meeting in a two-legged play-off for a place in Round 2. Having secured this honour, the Solomon Islands joined the five more established teams of the region, which were also divided into two groups, won by Australia and New Zealand respectively. An aggregate 5-0 score in the final round play-off saw Australia through to its meeting with Iran.

Far less complicated was the South American grouping, in which the competitors played each other in a round robin group, with automatic qualification going to the top four giving the continent five places in the finals. These were taken by Argentina, Paraguay, Colombia and Chile. Argentina's 1-1 draw with Colombia in November 1997 was its 100th World Cup game, but the real surprise of the series was the poor showing of

Reggae, Ronaldo and a French Revolution - France 1998

Dropping Paul Gascoigne meant that no England player had previous World Cup experience. Gascoigne was left out because Glen Hoddle was not impressed by his late night drinking binges and considered him unfit. When told the news, Gascoigne fired a barrage of four letter words at the coach and was so angry when he walked out of England's training camp he forgot to take his luggage.

Thirty four police were injured, a Scots fan was stabbed and 30 arrests were made when the official opening parade in Paris descended into a riot, as drunken fans began fighting amongst themselves.

Arriving in high spirits, thousands of Scots supporters headed for Paris with kilts flying and bagpipes blaring. "We're here for the football, the beer and the girlies," one announced. Their good-natured partying made them popular with the hosts.

Jim Leighton became the first Scottish player to take part in four World Cups when he played against Brazil.

Uruguay, who could only win six of their 16 matches. It left them third from the bottom of the table, above Bolivia and Venezuela, the region's ultimate "whipping boys", who conceded 41 goals in total and did not secure a single victory.

Of the African teams Cameroon, Egypt, Morocco and Nigeria were allocated automatic places in the tournament's second round, whilst the rest of the entrants played off over two legs to reach that stage. The 20 teams that competed in the second round were divided into five groups of four with a place in the finals going to the five eventual group winners, Nigeria, Tunisia, South Africa, Cameroon and Morocco. The second strike in their final game against Gabon in August 1997 was Morocco's 100th World Cup goal.

The most complicated format in the qualifying tournament was that adopted for the CONCACAF region. The Caribbean teams competed over three rounds of two-legged ties, with the weaker teams entering Round One and the more established sides coming in for the second round. Round Three whittled them down to four for the region's semi-final round. Four Central American countries played one round, with two of them reaching the semi-finals. At this stage the region's six strongest nations came in and these 12 teams were divided into three groups of four. Of them the top two in each group made the final round, a round robin and eventually, 20 months after it had begun, Mexico, the USA and Jamaica secured the region's three places in France. The Jamaican "Reggae Boyz" had played 18 matches to get there, the most by any team, whilst Mexico had played 16 games. The 1st goal scored by Mexico in their 4-0 defeat of Canada in the opening game of the final round had been their 250th World Cup goal.

Changes were made to the rules for France '98. In an attempt to keep the football exciting and ensure results, FIFA introduced the "golden goal" tie-breaker in extra-time in the knock-out stage. It had been seen previously in other tournaments, notably in the European Championships in England in 1996, but it was the first time it had been used in the World Cup. They also introduced the display board, used by the fourth official to indicate at the end of each half how much injury time was to be played. Both were much praised by match commentators.

The finals themselves kicked off on 10th June. After the opening ceremony in which a "sea of Brazilian gold and Scottish tartan washed around the Stade de France", fans were treated to an exhibition of flowing fast football in a match that presaged the event as a whole. For the Scots in their 100th World Cup game, it was disappointment as usual, though they could count themselves unlucky. They went behind to a 4th minute strike from César Sampaio, who got behind Craig Burley to force Bebeto's corner into the net off his shoulder, but made a strong recovery. Two fine first half saves from Jim Leighton, at 39 the oldest man in the tournament, seemed to raise Scotland's confidence and towards the end of the half they forced a series of corners. From one of these, a defensive header looped towards Kevin Gallacher, who was held back trying to get to it. Monaco's John Collins slammed in the resulting penalty. Gallacher came close to snatching the lead ten minutes into the second half, but his cross was deflected wide. Although the Scots were having much the better of the play, they lost the game 17 minutes from time when Dunga crossed the ball. It was picked up by Cafú whose shot was parried, hit Tommy Boyd and went into the net for an unfortunate own goal.

The second Group A game saw Morocco take on Norway. After surviving an initial onslaught, the Africans took the game to Norway and often "cut them open with superior invention and possession." Twice they took the lead, through Hadji in the 38th minute and Abeljili Hadda in the 59th with "another impressive goal", but twice they conceded an equalizer. The first was an own goal as Chippo headed into his own net and the second a header from Dan Eggen, securing a draw that put Brazil at the top of the group and Scotland at its foot.

The competition in Group B got underway the following day and produced two draws. In Bordeaux Italy met Chile, controlled the early part of the game and took the lead in the 10th minute with a goal from Christian Vieri, who latched on to a through ball from Maldini. However they let things slip, and instead of opening the floodgates, fell behind to goals on either side of the interval, both from Marcelo Salas. His first was from a corner and the second a powerful header from Pedro Reyes's cross. This unsettled the Italians, who surrendered the initiative and lost their shape. They equalized five minutes from time with a fortuitous penalty awarded when Roberto Baggio's shot hit the hand of Ronaldo Fuentes. He took it himself and became the first Italian to score in three separate tournaments. Meanwhile, in Toulouse, "plodding, ponderous" Austria, playing its 100th World Cup game, "showed a shameful lack of ambition" against Cameroon and could also count themselves lucky to come away with a point. It had all been very tedious until Pierre Njanka broke down the left in the 78th minute and "hit a rasping rising drive into the top corner", but in injury time the indomitable Toni Polster popped up to score a simple equalizer that his team hardly deserved.

In one of three games played the next day, Paraguay and Bulgaria played out a lifeless 0-0 draw in a match noted only for the first sending off of the tournament, the dismissal of Anatoly Nankov in the 88th minute for a second yellow card. The Bulgarians were now an ageing unit, but Paraguay's defensive tactics particularly in the first half, did nothing to improve the poor quality of play. In Lens, took place what was probably the most boring match of the tournament between Denmark and Saudi Arabia. The Arabs were coached by Carlos Alberto Parreira, who had now gained the distinction of having guided four different sides to the finals. His team, though, were less inspirational and seemed only to want to spoil the game. They hardly troubled Peter Schmeichel's goal and the Danes were themselves guilty of some dreadful misses. It was not until the 69th minute that they finally made the breakthrough. Brian Laudrupp's cross beat the off-side trap and found Marc Rieper unmarked to head into the

Italian striker, Christian Vieri, was brought up in Australia, played cricket and Aussie Rules as a youth and didn't kick a football at a competitive level until he was sixteen. His Italian born father had been a professional footballer and had finished his career with Canberra, but it wasn't until Vieri saw the 1990 World Cup that he decided to play the game full-time. In 1997, aged 22, he was sold to Atletico Madrid by Juventus for £12m.

Italy's victory over Cameroon was their biggest winning margin since 1970.

It was feared that Islamic fundamentalists would attack the World Cup finals on 12th July after Italian police intercepted coded telephone conversations between terrorist groups in an operation code-named "Sure Ball".

Mimi Spencer in the London Evening Standard advised girls: "Sit in a darkened room with 15 footie fans and a job-lot of strong larger. You'll love it by the time the final swings around." She was referring to her university experiences.

France 3 : South Africa 0
The South African team before their first ever game in the World Cup finals.

Brazilian coach, Mario Zagalo, placed an unprecedented sex ban on his players so they could concentrate on the football. It was the first time in living memory that it had been done. Both Chilean coach, Nelson Acosta and Philippe Troussier of South Africa did the same, though the latter offered his players a night with their wives if they got to the quarter-finals. "By that stage of the competition the players will have beaten teams like France, Spain and Bulgaria, and endured almost a month of abstinence. I reckon they and their wives will deserve a treat," he said.

The "Eat My Own Words" Award I for 1998 goes to...

Alan Fettis of Northern Ireland. Following his team's 4-0 pre-tournament demolition by Spain, he said: "They could do really well in France."

A "Rude Name" World Cup team could have included Zlatko Yankov of Bulgaria, Cha Bum-keun, the South Korean coach, Francisco Arce of Paraguay, Johan de Kock of Holland, Stefan Kuntz and Uwe Fuchs of Germany and López Ufarte of Spain.

Believing he had been unfairly provoked into elbowing Belgian Lorenzo Staelens, Patrick Kluivert complained: "Staelens shouted something to do with my private life. Believe me, it was below the belt."

After the game with Argentina, Japanese fans placed their rubbish in plastic backs and bowed to stewards on their way out of the ground.

Walter Boyd, described as Jamaica's Paul Gascoigne, was a surprise inclusion in their squad. He had not played for his country since the start of the year, having been dropped for not attending the nation's prestigious annual Sportsman and Sportswoman of the Year Awards in February.

net. By far the pick of the trio was France's 3-0 defeat of South Africa in windy Toulouse. In their first finals, the South Africans were strong, but lacking in creativity. France, on the other hand, were "passionate, brave and stern", their attacks "sweeping and vivacious" and they went in front after 35 minutes when substitute Christophe Dugarry glanced in Zidane's corner. He had a second effort disallowed in the 54th minute and it was not until the 78th that France turned their dominance into more goals. Firstly, Dugarry beat two defenders to set up Youri Djorkaeff with a shot that Issa turned into his own net and in the final minute Henry, "twisting and turning like an eel" scored a tremendous third to secure the result.

The first upset of the tournament came the next day. Spain dominated the early stages of their game against Nigeria and Raúl headed against the bar before Hierro opened their account with a 21st minute free kick. Going behind pricked the Nigerians into action and four minutes later they drew level when Adepoju headed in a corner. Spain switched to employing a back four for the second half to give them greater flexibility and it paid dividends when two minutes after the restart Raúl scored with a magnificent left foot volley. Once more, though, the Nigerians proved equal to the task. In the 73rd minute a seemingly harmless shot from Lawal was parried into his own net by Zubizarreta, winning his 124th cap, and five minutes later Hierro failed to deal adequately with a long throw in and Sunday Oliseh of Ajax fired in the winner from 30 yards. It had been an impressive and thoroughly deserved opening victory for Nigeria, especially since Spain were one of the favourites to win the trophy.

A second upset seemed on the cards when Ha Seok-ju put South Korea ahead in the 28th minute with a rather fortunate free kick against Mexico in Lyon, but he ruined his team's chance of a first win in the finals a minute later when he was sent off for a dangerous tackle from behind. Although they defended "bravely, resourcefully and energetically", the odds were stacked against the Koreans. They began to tire in the second half and after substitute Pelaez put away Ramírez's corner in the 51st minute, Mexico took a grip on the match. In the 74th minute, Ramírez crossed from the left and Hernández had plenty of time to control the ball and score. Then, to emphasize their dominance, he rammed in Blanco's square pass with a low right foot shot to give them a comfortable 3-1 win. Another defensive performance was that of Belgium in their 120th meeting with old rivals Holland. Neither team impressed and, though both created half-chances, there was little to enthral the crowd. Jap Stam, arguably Holland's best player on the night, forced a fine save out of Filip de Wilde in goal in the 75th minute, but the only other point of interest was the sending off of Patrick Kluivert six minutes later for elbowing Lorenzo Staelens, a decision that was certainly assisted by the Belgian's histrionics.

Croatia, Jamaica and Japan all made their debuts in the World Cup finals in Group H the next day, with Japan facing the stiffest challenge against Argentina. They acquitted themselves well and "buzzed around their South American opponents, harassing and irritating them into uncharacteristic errors", especially in the first period of play. Yet, Japan lacked finesse and, after a lively first 20 minutes, Argentina took a grip on the game. Though they only scored once, they were never troubled. The goal came in the 28th minute when Diego Simeone's through ball was flicked on by Ortega and Batistuta put it away. (See Batistuta profile on page 465). Similarly, Croatia had little difficulty in dispatching Jamaica. Mario

Stanic put them in front from a rebound in the 27th minute, after Derby County's Igor Stimac had fired against the bar. Robbie Earle headed an equalizer just before half time to give Jamaica some hope, but Croatia controlled the second half. In the 53rd minute Robert Prosinecki's cross completely deceived Warren Barrett, the Jamaican keeper, landing in the net and some 16 minutes later Davor Suker put the game out of reach with a deflected shot. In between these games, Yugoslavia took on Iran in Group F in St Etienne. It was a slow game, dominated by the defences. Yugoslavia played the better football, but seemed to lack urgency and were unable to crack Iran until the 72nd minute when Sinisa Mihajlovic curled a 30 yard free kick around the Iranian wall for the only score of the game. After it, the scorer admitted how difficult Iran had made things. "They defended very well and we were very lucky to get the goal," he said.

England came into action Monday 15th June and, after a nervous start, saw off Tunisia "with an effectiveness that suggested that they were playing well within themselves." By the half-hour mark the English were beginning to assert an authority and Paul Scholes gave note of this, heading Graeme Le Saux's cross powerfully to force a fine save out of El-Quaer. Both Sheringham and Scholes should have scored before Alan Shearer finally headed Le Saux's free kick home in the 42nd minute. From that moment there was little threat to the result and England created enough chances to have won comfortably. However, it was not until late in the second period that Scholes made absolutely certain with a curling 20 yard shot from Paul Ince's flick on.

The two other winning teams that day were Romania and Germany, but neither with the same ease as England. In Group G, Romania were largely the better team, especially in the first half when Colombia insisted on playing Faustino Asprilla alone up front. They took the lead when Adrian Ilie took advantage of a defensive error just before half-time, but had to defend well to keep it in the second when the South Americans brought on Adolfo Valencia to assist Asprilla. Colombia began to look more threatening and created several openings. It was to no effect and Romania held on without "exerting themselves to the full." Similarly, the Germans were rarely troubled against the USA in Paris, though their own performance was uninspired. The ageing German team featured no forwards younger than 30 and many felt they were too old to do much in this World Cup. The USA could provide no real test of the mettle of Berti Vogts's veterans and the result was never in doubt after Andreas Möller headed a ninth minute lead, from Olaf Thon's corner which Klinsmann had helped on its way. Oliver Bierhof missed a clear chance half way through the first half, but it was his cross that provided Klinsmann's 65th minute strike that made the game safe. He chested the ball down, wrong-footed Dooley and fired a rising shot past Keller. The Germans were "not rampant, just tidy and efficient", as one commentator noted.

Scotland's fans belted out their national anthem before the clash with Norway on 16th June in Bordeaux and knowing that a defeat would end their chances, the team responded with passion. Christian Dailly might have given them an early lead, heading John Collins's cross wide, and they were denied a solid penalty appeal, but the Norwegians played a packed midfield and the Scots could not find a goal to match their possession. Yet, as one commentator noted, even "when functioning with apparent smoothness... there tends to be a glitch in Scotland's displays" and, sure enough, they went behind to a Harvard Flo goal just after

After Warren Barrett saved a ferocious Croatian shot with his groin, Ron Atkinson, commenting for ITV, said: "Now he knows how our batsmen have felt for the last 20 years."

Part of England's back room staff was faith healer, Eileen Drewery, a close friend of the coach.

Before the game in Marseille, drunken English supporters threw bottles at opposing and the Tunisians replied with drink cans and firecrackers. Trouble had started the previous day when a group of flag-waving, drum beating Tunisians had had to run the gauntlet of bottle and glass throwing England fans as they walked through the Vieux Port area of the city. In one incident, England fans attacked an organ grinder and forced his monkey to drink a bottle of wine. Chaos reigned as Marseille supporters, resident Tunisians and riot police joined in. CS gas was used and the police gained control at 2am, ten hours after the fighting begun, ending one of the most obnoxious nights in World Cup history.

Before he could be selected for the USA, the Spanish-speaking Tab Ramos had to pass a citizenship exam by writing a sentence in English. He wrote: "Have a nice day" and passed easily.

Scotland's team headquarters were near a mental institution that once housed Vincent van Gogh.

Unrest in the Brazilian team took hold as early as the 12th June when it was reported that Zagalo was rowing with Zico, the assistant coach forced on him by the BFA, and Edmundo caused havoc when he was left on the bench for the opener.

half-time when the defence showed hesitancy in dealing with Riseth's cross. Once again they found themselves in need of inspiration and in Craig Burley they found it. He ran on to a through pass to equalize in the 67th minute, though it was the only reward for all their endeavour. The game ended 1-1 and Scotland's further progress would depend on their final match against Morocco, who were routed by Brazil in the second game played that day. Despite having a Bebeto goal disallowed, Brazil took an early lead when Ronaldo sprinted onto Rivaldo's clever chip and they never let go their grip on the match. Once they found their rhythm, they were irresistible and just before half-time Bebeto "slipped a neat ball to the marauding Cafú" and his cross was side footed in by Rivaldo. In the 50th minute Ronaldo ran at a confused defence and selflessly slipped the ball to Bebeto to score and thereafter Brazil played "footballing frippery that bewitched the crowd and the opposition." It left Zagalo singing his team's praises. "We played a more joyful, happy, efficient game here tonight", he declared and few would disagree.

The next day saw Chile battle out a dour 1-1 draw against Austria. As the Times's reporter noted: "Here were two teams in the crawler lane of the World Cup. Chile can be fast and flash, but they were stuck behind Austria's bumper." Salas scored in the 70th minute from a free kick, but substitute Vastic grabbed an equalizer in injury time to force the group's third draw in three games. It needed Italian guile and a solid performance against Cameroon to break the sequence. The Africans spent much of the early part of the game seemingly in awe of the Italians and paid for it when di Biagio's headed goal gave Italy a first half lead. At times Cameroon tackling had been vicious and just before half-time Raymond Nkongo was sent off for a two-footed assault on di Biagio. They could count themselves lucky that he was the only dismissal, but it sealed their fate. They came back with a brief 15 minute spell that had Italy reeling, but then tired and handed the game over. The Italians missed several good chances before Vieri capped what ultimately was an easy victory with late strikes in the 75th and 89th minutes.

The next day should have seen a similarly comfortable victory for Denmark against South Africa and it seemed to be on the cards after Allan Nielsen fired them into a lead in the 16th minute. However, they let too many chances go and in the second half made the mistake of trying to sit on their lead. The price was paid when Benni McCarthy got behind two defenders to equalize in the 52nd minute. The referee, John Rendón of Colombia, then went card crazy and three dismissals in the last half-hour totally disrupted the flow of play. Firstly, Miklos Molnar walked for stamping on an opponent. He was followed by South Africa's Alfred Phiri and Denmark's Martin Wieghorst in the 77th and 78th minutes respectively. In consequence the game remained deadlocked and South Africa's World Cup had all but ended.

Profligacy was not a charge that could be levelled against the French, who gave a superb display against Saudi Arabia that evening. The sending off of Al-Khilaiwi for scything down Lizarazu after 20 minutes only added in-evitability to the result. France's cause was not helped when Dugarry was carried off injured and replaced by David Trézéguet and they could only manage one first half goal from Henry. However they sprang to life in the second half and the replacement headed his team further in front in the 68th minute after the goalkeeper had dropped Thuram's cross. Two minutes later Zidane was sent off for stamping on Faud Amin, but even this blow could not upset the French. Two goals in the final 15 minutes gave them a deserved 4-0 win and top spot in the group. (See Zinedine Zidane profile on page 462).

Paraguay's José Luis Chilavert.

On 19th June, Nigeria took on Bulgaria and gave "a delightful performance, a compound of loose-limbed athleticism, sublime technique and enthralling enterprise." For most of the game they totally outplayed their opponents, with Daniel Amokachi and Finidi George often beguiling Bulgaria's defence. It was Amokachi's pass that set up Victor Ikpelsa for the goal that won the game in the 27th minute, but they were left holding on at the end as Bulgaria staged a spirited come-back in the final few minutes. Far less inspiring was Spain's meeting with Paraguay. The Spanish were strangely nervous and did not mount a serious challenge for the first 20 minutes, Chilavert commanding in Paraguay's goal and just about the only noteworthy statistic was that Zubizarreta won his 125th cap to equal Peter

Shilton's record for goalkeeping appearances. Inevitably the game ended goalless.

The next day witnessed three excellent games in what was becoming an intriguing competition. Firstly the footballers of Japan and Croatia "sweated buckets in the savage heat and yelled and screamed and begged as chance after chance disappeared into the clear blue yonder." The main difference between the teams was Davor Suker, a class above the rest, and it was his 77th minute strike that settled the match. Later Belgium and Mexico battled out a 2-2 draw, also in blistering heat in Bordeaux. The Mexicans began the better side, but seemed to lose confidence when Pavel Pardo was sent off after half an hour for a tackle that was mistimed rather than malicious. The Belgians took advantage and Marc Wilmots put them in a great position with goals on either side of the interval. However, when Gert Verheyen gave away a penalty and was sent off in the 56th minute, Garcia Aspen was able to pull one back and the game took another twist. Seven minutes later Cuauktemoc Blanco equalized to retrieve another match in which the referee's influence was more than decisive. That evening the Dutch, inspired by the magnificent Bergkamp and Davids, demolished South Korea. It was credit to the Asians that they kept a clean sheet until he 38th minute, but once Bergkamp wrong-footed the defence to set up Cocu the rest was inevitable. Four minutes later Bergkamp was again pivotal in creating a goal for Marc Overmars and in the 71st minute he got one himself with a scintillating piece of footwork that totally foxed his markers. Two more goals from Pierre van Hooijdonk and Ronald de Boer completed the 5-0 rout.

In winning their previous world titles the Germans had always beaten Yugoslavia on the way to the final. This time their football was not good enough, though they did stage a typically battling come-back. The Yugoslavs were rampant for the first hour of the game and inside ten minutes of the second half had a comfortable two goal lead, Stankovic and Stojkovic being the hit men. So angered was German coach Bertie Vogts at his team's lacklustre display that he brought on Lothar Matthäus at half-time. He was now 37 years old and his arrival gave him the distinction of becoming only the second player to appear in five World Cups. It was also his record-breaking 22nd game in the finals. It seemed to do the trick and with 17 minutes to go Michael Tarnat deflected a 30 yard free kick into the net off Sinisa Mihajlovic. Seven minutes later Oliver Bierhof headed the equalizer from a corner and he might have won the game shortly after when he headed against the bar. Earning a draw was more than the Germans deserved, though it was testament to their dauntless spirit.

The next day saw Iran's much anticipated clash with the USA (See Iran v USA profile on page 467) and the "Reggae Boyz" against Argentina. Jamaica acquitted themselves well in the first half, when they played some cultured football and conceded only once, when Ortega "danced past an infinity of defenders" to score. The game's turning point came in injury time in the first half, when Derby County's Darryl Powell was sent off for a second yellow card. From then on it was all Argentina. In the 55th minute a quick one-two with López brought another goal for Ortega and a ten minute hat trick from Batistuta completed the rout. His first was a low right foot shot in the 73rd minute and his second came six minutes later when Simeone set him up. His third came from a penalty awarded after Ortega had been brought down and was put away in the 83rd minute.

South Korea 0 : Holland 5
Marc Overmars of Holland (left) and South Korea's Young Il-choi.

When the Iranians discovered that the Kappa logo was a naked man and woman sitting back-to-back they turned down a very lucrative kit deal and went with Puma.

The prostitutes in Bangkok, caught up in World Cup fever, took to wearing football shirts.

Disturbed by the loss of Asprilla, the Colombians started to complain about money. They were unhappy about the £280,000 the team had been given between them and demanded the same amount if they got through to the next round.

Not only were England players banned from too much sun bathing, they were also barred from reading the Sun. It meant some players only found out about Stan Collymore hitting Ulrika Jonsson in a Paris bar when they were asked to comment.

Hungarian referee, Laszlo Vagner, was a soldier.

The "Eat My Own Words" Award II for 1998 goes to...

Henri Michel, Morocco's French coach, who said before his team's clash with Brazil: "Brazil will not have an easy time getting past our strong, tactical team." The headline in the London Evening Standard the following day read: "Brazilian smoke beats Moroccan bludgeon".

Scotland players found the choice of referee for their game against Morocco strange. "It would be fair to say we were surprised to have an Arab referee," said Kevin Gallacher. "Craig (Burley) was sent off when it seemed to us that the Moroccan players surrounded the referee and got him to change a yellow card to red one. Yet there were several challenges on us that could have brought cards."

South Africans Brendan Augustine and Naughty Mokoena were both sent home for breaking the team's curfew to spend an evening at a nightclub in Vichy.

Following Colombia's defeat by Romania, Asprilla had walked out of the squad in anger at the way he had been played and after a very public row with coach, Dario Gómez. The damage it did to the morale of his team mates was plain to see when they played Tunisia on 22nd June. They were disjointed, indisciplined and incoherent and though they created many chances, they only put one away. In the 84th minute Valderrama sent a telling pass into the heart of Tunisia's defence and Leider Preciado latched on to it to score a "goal of such certainty, such beauty and such quality" that it alone deserved the result. England's performance against Romania later that day certainly did not merit victory. Hoddle had been forced to change things round in the wake of an injury to Ince and it did not come off. The defence was frail, Sheringham ineffectual up front and it was no surprise when Moldovan chested down Hagi's cross to sweep the ball past Seaman soon after half-time. The English rallied a little, but hardly looked like scoring until Owen replaced Sheringham with a little over a quarter of an hour to go. Within minutes he had levelled the score and seemed to have mastered a great escape. It was not to be and in the 90th minute Dan Petrescu shot low through Seaman's legs to secure the win that saw his team into the second round.

Both Italy and Chile had to battle hard to get into the knock-out stage against Austria and Cameroon respectively. The Austrians proved stubborn opponents and their defence was not breached until the 49th minute when Vieri headed a goal. It had been a sterile first half, but Inzaghi replaced Vieri in the second half and the Italians began to show more enterprise. Yet it was not until the 90th minute that Roberto Baggio worked a sublime exchange with Inzaghi to grab a second goal, but a last gasp penalty allowed Andreas Hertzog to make it 2-1. In Nantes, Chile took a 21st minute lead through José Sierra, but Cameroon refused to lie down. Although their cause was severely dented when Song was sent off early in the second half for elbowing Salas - he was 21 years old and had become the first player to be sent off in two tournaments - Mboma headed an equalizer in the 56th minute. In a game full of incident, Etame was then sent off for violent play and Oman Biyik had a seemingly good goal disallowed. The final whistle provoked riots in Cameroon, but the draw was enough to put Chile into the next round.

It was the match between Brazil and Norway in Marseille that proved decisive in Group A. Norway defended for much of the game and went behind in the 78th minute to a headed goal from Bebeto. They then showed great fighting qualities to pull of an incredible result. Five minutes after going behind, Torre Andre Flo got the better of Junior Baiano to equalize and five minutes after that a mid-air collision between Bjorneby and Junior Baiano brought a penalty that should never have been. It was converted by Rekdal. Meanwhile, in St Etienne Scotland's World Cup was drawing to its miserable climax as first Bassir in the first half and Hadda in the second gave Morocco a 2-0 lead. The dismissal of Burley in the 52nd minute for a tackle from behind sealed Scotland's fate and five minutes from time Bassir's second strike, deflected off Colin Hendry, seemed to put the Africans into the next round. However, only minutes before, Tore Andre Flo had equalized for Norway. A draw in this game would still have seen Morocco through above Norway, but Rekdal's penalty sent them home. The Moroccans heard the heartbreaking news as they filed off the field.

22 Men and a Bag of Wind

The final games in Group C took place the following day. Taking on Saudi Arabia, South Africa had a mathematical chance of qualification but needed a win and a favourable result in the other game. They got neither. They took the lead through a Shaun Bartlett goal, but three further penalty strikes saw the game end 2-2. It gave South Africa only two points and they could not catch Denmark, who went through despite being beaten 2-1 by France in Lyon in a very entertaining game. France went ahead in the 13th minute when Trézéguet was brought down and Djorkaeff converted the penalty. Michael Laudrupp equalized shortly before half-time with another spot kick, but the French were playing well. They created a host of chances in the second half, but hit the target only once. Viera's shot was blocked and Emmanuel Petit knocked in the rebound. The French had now won all three games and were looking serious contenders for the championship

Brazil 1 : Norway 2
Norway's Torre Andre Flo fends off Brazilian's Ronaldo and Junior Baiano.

In Group D Nigeria had already qualified, but the second place was still up for grabs. Knowing this, Spain set about Bulgaria with gusto. They scored after six minutes when Luis Enrique, in devastating form, was bought down and Hierro converted the penalty. He scored himself 12 minutes later and early in the second half Francisco Morientes made it 3-0. Kostadinov grabbed one back in the 56th minute, but it was mere consolation. Another Morientes goal and two more from Kiko in the final three minutes gave Spain a 6-1 victory, but their fate lay in Toulouse where Paraguay were facing a weakened Nigeria. This was the decisive factor, though the South Americans showed plenty of spirit and went ahead in the first minute when Ayala headed in Arce's free kick. The next period of play belonged to Nigeria, who equalized through Oruma in the 11th minute. Paraguay began to look more forceful after the break and exploited the frailties of Nigeria's defence with goals from Benitez on the hour and an angled drive from Cardozo four minutes from time. The result meant that Paraguay qualified with a point advantage over Spain.

The next day brought the conclusion to affairs in Groups E and F. In the first Belgium needed to beat South Korea and began the match as if they were going to win handsomely. In the fifth minute Scifo had a powerful shot well saved and they took the lead in the sixth when Nilis drove in from a corner. However, this Belgian team lacked both conviction and ruthlessness and they allowed the Koreans to play themselves back into the game. You Sang-chui equalized in the 70th minute and the Belgians went out whatever the score in the game between Holland and Mexico. Here, the Dutch "began exquisitely, strolling as if this were a training encounter, passing the ball with a sureness and invention that few in this decade can equal." Bergkamp set up Phillip Cocu in the fourth minute and in the 18th Ronnie de Boer beat three men to score a second. The Mexicans were looking ragged, but the Dutch, who controlled things for 70 minutes, eased off too much. When Wim Jonk, their midfield play-maker was replaced by Aron Winter, the Mexicans seized the chance. In an eventful final 15 minutes, Ricardo Pelaez headed a goal back, Ramón Ramírez was sent off and Luiz Hernández equalized in the last minute. It gave Mexico the point needed to get into the next round.

In Group F both Germany and Yugoslavia faced the group's weakest teams and though both won to go through, neither did so convincingly. In Montpellier Germany gave a robust performance that stifled rather than overran Iran, who played well within themselves, but were unable to crack a resolute German defence. The Germans became more aggressive in the second half and two goals won the match. The first came in the 50th minute Bierhof headed in Hässler's cross and the second came eight minutes later when Klinsmann scored a rebound after Bierhof's shot came out off the post. Meanwhile in Nantes the Americans played their best football of the tournament and came close to scaring Yugoslavia. They changed tactics away from the long ball that had not worked in previous games, hit the post in the opening seconds, but went behind in the fourth minute when Slobodan Komljenovic headed in Mihajlovic's powerful free kick. Their heads never fell, they made some confident forays and the Yugoslavs had to be wary throughout to keep their lead.

When Romania took the field against Tunisia the next day, they appeared with their hair dyed gold, the result of a bet with coach Anghel Iordanescu. They had already qualified and seemed not to take the game seriously.

Reggae, Ronaldo and a French Revolution - France 1998

The England team was banned from having breakfast cereal because Glen Hoddle said that milk was difficult to digest.

An anagram of Graeme Le Saux is "A Male Sex Urge". Gareth Southgate can be turned into "Huge Tart Hostage".

Having put his prized World Cup ticket in what he thought was an out-of-the-way place, secure from his two sons, Keith Boundy of Enfield was looking forward to seeing England play Colombia. However, with a couple of days to go, he received a phone call from his wife asking him to come home. To his horror he found that his youngest son, Isaac, had found the ticket, cut it up and used it in a football collage he was making. "The thing I used in my drawing was something to do with football," Isaac explained. "I cut it up and stuck it on some card and I thought it looked really good." His father managed to remain calm and later said: "When Isaac looked at me and proudly showed off his work, I just didn't have the heart to get angry with him. He knew something was wrong and that he'd upset me, because I was so quiet." Fortunately, the FA replaced the ticket.

When César Sampaio scored his first goal against Chile he had his eyes closed.

A Brazilian team doctor believed Ronaldo was overweight.

Consequently, they struggled against the Africans and fell behind to a tenth minute penalty converted by Skander Souayah. At half-time they realized that England were 2-0 up against Colombia and that if things stayed that way they faced a possible next round game against Argentina, who were themselves beating Croatia 1-0. It stirred things up, changes were made and Moldovan, who had only been on the field for five minutes, notched an equalizer in the 72nd minute. In going into a 2-0 half-time lead England showed much more commitment than in previous matches. Anderton, Beckham and Owen were all included from the start and it gave the team a greater vibrancy. Anderton opened the scoring in the 20th minute with a fierce volley after Owen cross had been headed out weakly and ten minutes later Ince, surging forwards, was fouled. Beckham lined up the free kick and floated it over the wall for his first international goal. The result took England into the second round and another fateful meeting with Argentina, there courtesy of Hector Pineda's volleyed goal in their narrow victory over Croatia. The other game in Group H saw Jamaica and Japan play with pride and commitment and Jamaica pick up its first win in the finals. Theodore Whitman put them ahead in the 39th minute, when he got onto a pass into the area from Marcus Gayle. They scored a second, beautifully worked goal in the 54th minute, but it aroused Japan to action. A series of positive attacks created several openings before Masashi Nakayama pulled one back in the 75th minute. It was all they could get and Japan left the tournament the only team not to gain a point.

With the group stage now complete, the opening games of the knock-out were played over the next four days, beginning on Saturday 27th June with Italy against Norway and Brazil versus Chile. In the first the Italians gave a typically robust performance, using muscle to prevent Norway settling to their preferred pattern of play. With the Norwegians lacking penetrative flair, Vieri's instinctive 18th minute strike was enough to settle the affair. An altogether greater spectacle was the second encounter, a match full of South American eloquence and eventually won by Brazil's power. Two goals from free kicks from César Sampaio, the first an 11th minute header and the second a side foot in the 27th began the scoring. Just before half-time Ronaldo's powerful run was clumsily stopped by Chile's goalkeeper and he scored the resulting penalty to give Brazil an unassailable lead. Chile, though, refused to bow to the inevitable. In the 68th minute they were rewarded when Taffarel could only flick Zamorano's header as far as Salas. He took the chance well, but Chile's hope lasted a mere two minutes. Ronaldo ran in to score beneath the goalkeeper for a 4-1 scoreline and a step closer to the final.

The next day saw the home team face Paraguay, "equivalent to a two-stroke lawnmower being put into a race against a Ferrari" as one journalist described it. Yet Zidane was not in the driver's seat and the French missed his creativity. They had a frustrating day against a team that had come to defend and spoil. Henry hit the post in the 39th minute, but it was about the sum total of his team's achievement for 114 minutes of normal and extra time. Then, as the game neared a penalty shoot-out, Laurent Blanc popped up to score the first ever golden goal in the World Cup. It put France into the quarter-finals and, significantly, it took a defender to do it.

Far more emphatic was Denmark's dismissal of Nigeria. They made an explosive start with PSV Eindhoven's Peter Moller was set up by Brian

Laudrupp to score after only three minutes of his first appearance in the finals. Nine minutes later he had a shot blocked, but Brian Laudrupp followed in to make it 2-0. The Nigerians were being made to look a definite second best and only the goalkeeper kept the score respectable. They gamely tried to fight back, but could make no real headway against a well marshalled defence and 15 minutes after the restart the game slipped further from them. Sand, who had replaced Moller only 16 seconds earlier, scored a third and in the 76th minute Helveg added a fourth.

Denmark 4 : Nigeria 1
Denmark goalkeeper Peter Schmeichel celebrates his team's second goal.

Babangida got a consolation soon after, but the game was all over by then.

Germany and Holland got into the quarter-finals the next day, but only just. In Montpellier, Germany had marginally the better of a goalless first half in which Bierhof headed against the bar, but in the second Mexico began to use their pace against the German veterans. Within two minutes Hernández skipped past two defenders to grab the lead and the Mexicans continued to worry the Germans until, in the 75th minute, Klinsmann benefited from Lara's mishit clearance to equalize. It sapped Mexico's confidence and four minutes from time Bierhof made amends for his first half miss, by heading the winner from Kirsten's cross.

"It drives me crazy... when they are ahead they stop being alert", was Dutch coach Gus Hiddinck's reaction at seeing his team almost go out to Yugoslavia. For the first period of the game they probed without dominating and made a break through in the 37th minute when Bergkamp's diagonal run got him onto Frank de Boer's long pass. He beat his defender and scored at the near post for his 35th international goal equalling, the Dutch record set by Faas Wilkes in the 1950s. The Yugoslavs came back strongly and four minutes after half-time Komljenovic headed the equalizer from Stojkovic's free kick. They should have gone in front two minutes later when Stam was adjudged to have fouled Jugovic and conceded a penalty. However Mijatovic crashed his kick against the bar and the Dutch could breath freely. They duly picked up the pace and Davids fired in a 20 yard injury time winner to keep Dutch hopes alive.

The next day brought the eagerly awaited tie between England and Argentina, and England's heroic exit, (See England v Argentina profile on page 468 and David Beckham profile on page 461) but before that Romania gave a surprisingly lifeless display against Balkan rivals Croatia. Their best player was Bogdan Stelea, who made save after save to keep out the lively Croats. Yet, it was at the end of the first half, when Romania played their only effective football of the game, that Croatia scored the only goal. It came from a contentious penalty, given as a result of a collision and calmly put away by Suker. As was noted in the Times, Croatia "may have only won by a single goal, but they won by a distance."

When Denmark beat Nigeria in the Stade de France, officials breathed a huge sigh of relief because it was the first time any team had won a game using dressing room B since the stadium had been opened in January. France were due to use it when they played Italy.

At 6 feet 3 inches, Argentinian Juan Sebastian Veron's nickname was the "Little Wizard".

Croatioan coach, Miroslav Blazevic, known as "Atilla" because of his strict regime, wore a white scarf and a Gendarme's hat throughout the tournament for luck.

Reggae, Ronaldo and a French Revolution - France 1998

The first of the quarter-finals was played on 3rd July and was an untidy, defensive and scrappy meeting between France and Italy. The Italians in particular lacked attacking ambition and the French were only marginally better and lacked striking power. It was as if advancing so far on home soil inhibited their style. Both Baggio and Djorkaeff might have scored in extra time, but neither did and it needed penalties to separate them. With the score lying at 4-3 to France, both having one miss, Luigi di Biagio stepped up to take the tenth kick. He crashed it against the bar, Italy went out and coach Cesare Maldini was left lamenting: "We must be cursed."

A much more exciting spectacle came that evening when Brazil took on Denmark in Nantes. In a see-saw game that saw Brazil tested to the end, first and early blood went to Denmark when Udinese's Martin Jorgensen hit a powerful shot from just inside the area. It stung Brazil who drew level in the 11th minute, Ronaldo setting up Bebeto who slipped a challenge and hit a low shot into the net. By now the Brazilians were purring sweetly and in the 26th minute they took the lead, this time Ronaldo providing the chance for Rivaldo. It was then Denmark's turn to stage a come back and they missed several chances before Brian Laudrupp found space early in the second half to equalize. Rivaldo restored Brazil's lead on the hour with a withering shot and the rest of the game was nip and tuck as both pressed and harried without further success. Brazil went into the semi-finals 3-2 winners of one of the best games of the series.

Two days later Holland met Argentina determined to avenge their defeat in the 1978 final. The Argentinians were suffering from their marathon against England, but both produced a match of drama, incident and arguably the goal of the tournament. Bergkamp proved the difference between them and stamped an early mark, stooping to head Ronald de Boer's cross into Kluivert's path to chip the first score. Argentina came back five minutes later when López beat Stam to find the equalizer and the rest of the half saw both attack keenly to carve chances without scoring. The game seemed to swing in Argentina's favour in the 77th minute when Arthur Numan was sent off for a second yellow card, but ten minutes later Ortega foolishly head butted Holland's goalkeeper and also went off. It gave Holland their chance and it was brilliantly taken by Bergkamp in the 90th minute. He deftly controlled a 50 yard long pass from Frank de Boer, side stepped Roberto Ayala and planted a volley into the net in one sweet movement.

That evening Germany played the better football in their quarter-final against Croatia until Christian Wörns was sent off in the 40th minute for a crude rather than malicious body check on Suker. The game was goalless until then and it proved the turning point. Within minutes Jarni gave Croatia a half-time lead and they came out for the second in a more composed frame of mind. Growing German desperation revealed itself in some torrid tackling that might have elicited a stronger response from the Norwegian referee and in the 80th minute Vlaovic extended Croatia's lead with a shot from outside the area. Five minutes later Suker made it 3-0 and Croatia marched into the semi-finals in their first appearance in the World Cup finals, only eight years after gaining independence.

In the first of the semi-finals Holland "took Brazil to the very edge, exposing their defensive frailties for all to see" and unusually the South Americans had to look to their goalkeeper, not their strongest position, to see them into the final. The Dutch were often the better team, with Davids exceptional in midfield, but Bergkamp was strangely subdued and it denied them the sharpness up front that might have produced a result. The second half was only seconds old when Ronaldo beat Cocu to Rivaldo's through pass and slotted the ball under Van der Sar's legs. Eight minutes later Taffarel saved point blank from Frank de Boer, but the Brazilians were dominating and it was against the run of play that Ronald de Boer provided the cross, which Kluivert headed powerfully into the net in the 87th minute to take the game into extra time. Here chances came and went and Holland's hero was undoubtedly Frank de Boer who twice saved the day, clearing one ball off the line and taking the match to penalties. After both had scored twice, Taffarel saved kicks from Cocu and Ronald de Boer and Brazil went through to the final with a 4-2 scoreline.

The next day France dominated the first half against Croatia without scoring and inside the first minute of the second, Suker swept onto a through ball from Asanovic to put them behind. The villain had been defender Lilian Thuram, who had played the Croat on side. However, he quickly made amends when he dispossessed Zvonimir Boban on the edge of the Croatian area, played a speedy one-two with Djorkaeff and equalized. It was his first international goal in 37 appearances and it enabled France to resume their attacking posture. In the 70th minute he struck again. He took the ball from Jarni and, showing all the poise of a striker, hit low into the net. It won the game, but celebrations were somewhat muted after Blanc was sent off in the 75th minute. He stupidly pushed Slaven Bilic in the face, but it was undoubtedly Bilic's overreaction that got him dismissed.

Blanc's dismissal meant he would miss the final and it had a notable effect on the atmosphere in the Parc des Princes on the day of the third place play-off. Thousands turned up to watch this traditionally meaningless game simply to deride Bilic and throughout he was booed and jeered at his every move. Even the Dutch supporters joyfully joined in. As a football event, this proved to have a higher entertainment factor than most previous fixtures. Croatia saw status in coming third in the world and played to achieve it. It gave impetus to the Dutch and made for a competitive match in which Holland saw enjoy most of the possession, but Croatia made skillful use of the counter attack, especially down the right where injury had weakened the Dutch. It was from there that Jarni cut in to provide Prosinecki, who cleverly twisted away from Numan to score a 13th minute opener. Holland's reply came eight minutes later with a fantastically swerving shot from Zenden, which began its flight

> Describing Emmanuel Petit, a knowledgeable CNN reporter in the USA said: "Sensitivity to others is second nature to this rugged midfielder. Not only does he pick and scatter blades of grass before every game in honour of his late brother, but when CNN asked him about Croatia he said: 'It would be nice for the Croatian people to have something good happen to them after all their suffering.' That is Emmanuel Petit. A player with a small name and a big heart."

> The arm badge depicting the check design on Croatian kits is the same as that worn by those Croats who supported the Nazis in World War Two, banned until 1990.

> On a night when a million people took to the streets of Paris to celebrate their team's victory, one French woman, seemingly out of control, ploughed her black Volkswagen Golf into supporters injuring 60, ten seriously, at the Arc de Triomphe. The angry crowd set upon her before police could rescue her from the mess she had caused. Rumours spread that she was drunk, but it is more likely that she had simply panicked when revellers surrounded her car.

French supporters celebrate on the Champs Elysees after France defeated Croatia 2-1 in their semi-final.

heading for the goalkeeper's left and ended by beating him on the right. Overall, the Dutch lacked ruthlessness and were sloppy up front. The only other goal came in the 35th minute, a low shot from Suker to give him his sixth of the tournament and the Golden Boot award. (See Davor Suker profile on page 464). It also ensured third place for Croatia, a very worthy achievement indeed in its first World Cup campaign.

The showpiece final took place the following day in the Stade de France and what a final it turned out to be. (See France v Brazil profile on page 469). Beginning in the strangest of circumstances and ending in France's fairytale victory, it surely put the finishing touch to what had been a masterpiece of a tournament. From Scotland's brave if unsuccessful stance against Brazil to the final itself, France '98 thrilled with its quality. There were bad games, but remarkably few. The competition was tight and few teams could be treated lightly, final proof that since its early inception in 1930, FIFA's game had truly gone global. There was drama, jinx, highs, lows and brilliant goals. There were superlative players and tremendous matches. In fact, the only marring factors were the overreactions of some players to physical contact, sadly a feature of the modern game, and the disgraceful behaviour of some supporters, the English and Germans particularly, though not exclusively. They brought disrepute, but not enough to spoil the overall effect. Those who witnessed the final could not help but feel a glow of satisfaction and look forwards in anticipation of the next.

David Robert Joseph Beckham   England

David Beckham.

Honours: Second round 1998   Games 3
Played: 1998   Goals 1

Not since George Best graced Old Trafford has Manchester United produced a player of such star quality. In Best's day United did not know how to handle the pressures that elevated him to the same dizzy heights as the Beatles, but today the United machinery has kept David Beckham's feet firmly on the ground. He has not embraced the excesses of superstardom even though he and wife, Victoria Adams, are never far from the pages of the tabloid newspapers or OK Magazine. Being possibly the best player England has produced and married to one of the most famous celebrities of the 21st century he has to expect it. In October 2000, Beckham gave an insight into what it means to be the phenomenon known as "Posh and Becks." "We get phoned up about stories every day. Some you just laugh at and others are hurtful, saying things that are so not true. There was a story saying me and Victoria were arguing because she was spending so much time doing her new single. Which is a load of crap. I don't know whether they are trying to get to us or make people not like us but it is things like that that upset us!" It is undeniable that Beckham's talent is sublime and his influence immense. "Beckham thrills me," Johan Cruyff once said. "He is one of the elite players in Europe. He is truly gifted."

Born in Leytonstone, London on 2nd May 1975, he grew up as a Manchester United fan with the dream of one day playing for them. His father, Ted, regularly made the trek to Old Trafford with his son and encouraged his interest. At the age of 11 he won the Bobby Charlton Soccer Skills Award and never looked back. It was presented to him on the Old Trafford pitch on a match day and included a trip to the Nou Camp Stadium in Barcelona. "If you stuck a girl or a ball in front of David he'd pick up the ball," his former P.E. teacher, John Bullock, once remarked. His first forays into the professional game were at the Tottenham Hotspur School of Excellence. He also tried out for Leyton Orient, but the dream of playing for the Red Devils was too strong and, on 8th July 1991, he became a trainee at Old Trafford.

Manchester United won the 1992 FA Youth Cup with a team that included several of the names that now provide the backbone of the most successful English club in history. It was proof that their youth policy was working. The philosophy instilled into those youngsters was of hard work and team spirit. "Me, Gary (Neville), Phil (Neville),

Scholesy (Paul Scholes), Butty (Nicky Butt), Giggsy (Ryan Giggs), we were brought up to work hard at our game and we knew the rewards in front of us if we did," he said. "We had to go back in the afternoons and some of us went back in the evenings to work with the kids who were coming up when we were apprentices." He still goes back in the afternoons to practice free kicks, usually with bare feet.

He made his first team debut as a 17 year old substitute on 23rd September 1992 in the Rumbelows Cup against Brighton and then had to wait until September 1994 before he got another chance, against Port Vale in the League Cup. Two months later, he scored his first senior goal in the 4-0 victory over Galatasaray in the European Champions League. He was loaned to Preston North End in March 1995 to "toughen him up", but was recalled after a month to make his first league appearance at home to Leeds. "Although the 19 year old Beckham did well on his Premiership debut," the Guardian wrote, "he could not be expected to provide the service that Cole has come to expect from Kanchelskis." However, when he fooled the Wimbledon goalkeeper, Neil Sullivan, on the first day of the 1996 season with a lobbed shot from inside his own half he was catapulted into the limelight. That season he came of age, United won the domestic title again and they made the semi-finals of the European Cup. He had a superb season and his fellow professionals voted him PFA Young Player of the Year.

Glen Hoddle, England manager after 1996, was a major fan and he made his senior international debut, against Moldova on 1st September 1996. He was also a member of the England team that made it to the World Cup finals in France in 1998 and his versatility meant that he could be played both in midfield and as a wing back. He scored his first international goal when he delivered a delightful free kick safely into the net against Columbia. Then, with the score at 2-2 against Argentina in Round Two, came the incident that temporarily ruined his reputation and helped put England out. The level of abuse hurled at him could easily have forced a move abroad, with offers from Italy and Spain, but he stayed put and has become a better man for it. "I had a lot go on after the World Cup. Victoria was away on tour and I was in the house, the old house in Manchester, on my own. But all that stuff definitely made me a stronger person. Made me change the way I thought about things and people. A lot of good came out, not that I want it to happen again but looking back, it was good for me in a weird way." 1999 was a momentous year. Manchester United won the domestic double and the European Champions League; he finished runner-up to Rivaldo at the 1999 World Player of the Year awards: and he married his sweetheart in the summer. Not long after their first child, Brooklyn, was born. He has Brooklyn's name on the tongue of his football boots, a new pair of which he has for almost every game.

Beckham might not use his left foot much and he is not the best tackler, but there is no one to beat his ability to send over pin-point crosses and passes. He is a dead-ball specialist to compare with any of the greats. He is not a saint and his career has seen controversy. There was the time he was accused of diving against Rapid Vienna at Old Trafford and then trying to get the defender booked. He has been accused of mooning at Southampton fans, which he denies, and there was the infamous two-fingered incident aimed at booing England fans as he left the pitch at the end of the 3-2 defeat Portugal at Euro 2000. However, even the most ardent United hater has to agree that Beckham has something special, as recognized by him coming second in the 2001 World Player of the Year awards. Only time will tell if he can achieve true greatness, but he is certainly on the road to it.

Zinedine Yazid Zidane   France

Honours: Winner 1998   **Games 5**
Played: 1998   **Goals 2**

Zinedine Zidane is regarded as the best midfielder in the world and one off the most successful at international and club level. From an early age he was making the headlines, and for the right reasons, unlike Eric Cantona who he replaced as the top talent in French football. He is hard working, dedicated and has the ability to dictate a game, rising to the occasion without pause, and all this from a man for whom football wasn't the first choice in his life.

Reggae, Ronaldo and a French Revolution - France 1998

Zinedine Zidane (centre) with French team-mates Christophe Dugarry (left) and Bixente Lizarazu.

Born on 23rd June 1972 at Marseille, Zidane is the son of Algerian immigrants and a Muslim. His first taste of the game came when he joined local amateur club, US Saint-Henri. He then moved to Septemes Sports Olympiques where he started in the Under 11s side and stayed until he was 14. At the end of the 1986 season he was asked to attend a three day course at the regional sports centre (CREPS) in Aix-en-Provence and it was here that his life took a dramatic turn for the better. Jean Verraud, a scout from AS Cannes, spotted him and persuaded the management of Cannes to take him on a week's trial. He stayed six weeks and came to realize that, having trained with professionals, he too could make it in the game. His first team debut came in May 1989. "I played my first game in the First Division. I played against Nante at La Beaujoire Stadium against Marcel Desailly and Didier Dechamp's team. I was seventeen and from then on football became my only real passion," he says. In 1991, he earned himself a Renault Clio as a reward for scoring his first professional goal and by the end of the season Cannes had qualified for the UEFA Cup by finishing fourth in the league. Now 20 years old he was voted Young Player of the Year, though next season, they were knocked out of Europe early and relegated to the Second Division. Not wanting to play outside the top flight, Zidane accepted an offer from Bordeaux.

His wife, Veronique, moved with him and at his new club he met and began a partnership with Christophe Dugarry, now his best friend. He also scored ten goals in his first season. "I spent four wonderful seasons even if I must admit I had a hard time in the first six months," he says. "I really made a step forward after those four seasons in Bordeaux. The results were not always that good but I have excellent memories from that time. Each year, we qualified for the UEFA Cup. The last season, 1995-96 was brilliant as we qualified to UEFA Cup through the Intertoto and went to the final." Unfortunately, they lost to Bayern Munich, but by now Juventus had noticed him and at the end of the 1995-96 season, he signed for the Turin club. He has always been philosophical about his career and gives the impression that every move was been carefully considered and made to benefit to his career. "At twenty-four, when you have already played in the UEFA Cup and with your national team, you want to experience something new. It was for me the opportunity to make a step forward and get new experience. It was Italy and Juventus. I couldn't have made a better choice." He matured and developed his skills and almost from the start won titles and recognition. Juventus won the Serie A title in 1997 and 1998 and reached consecutive European Champions League finals in both 1997 and 1998 losing out to Borussia Dortmund and Real Madrid respectively. However, next season Juventus struggled to find form in the league and were dumped out of the Champions' League and the UEFA Cup by November 2000. Having been beaten 3-1 at home by Hamburg in the Champions' League in a game in which both Zidane and Edgar Davids were sent off, they then lost to Panathanikos in Greece and went out.

Zidane's international career started in spectacular fashion in 1994 when he was 22. He came on as a 63rd minute substitute, replacing Corentin Martins, in a match France were losing 2-0 to Czechoslovakia. By the end of the game they had drawn 2-2 and Zidane got both goals to save the game. His performance made it impossible for him to be overlooked for future games. Having played 57 league and European games in 1995-96 he did not perform to his best at the 1996 European Championships, but it was a different story at the 1998 World Cup and the European Championships in 2000. In the World Cup the French public were expectant, but the national team nervous. "We had been expecting this moment, and it suddenly arrived. After a few weeks of preparation, we arrived at Stade Vélodrome to play against the Bafana Bafana (*South Africa*). The first fifteen minutes were quite difficult to manage, but luckily enough Christophe Dugarry scored the first goal, and we all sighed with relief." In France's second game, with the team 2-0 up against Saudi Arabia, he "touched" an opponent lying on the ground with his foot and was sent off. It brought a two match ban. France defeated Denmark to go into the second round, but they did not look sharp without their playmaker. It was the same in the next game, won in extra time and which he described as "the hardest game of the World Cup. From a personal point of view, I suffered from staying on the bench for the second and last game… My worries proved to be well founded, as the score did not change during regular time." The final became an exhibition of his ability and, having been told by the manager, Aimee Jaquet, that Brazil were weak on corners, the French exploited it and Zidane scored twice from corners. He became a national hero and at the end of the year was named World Player of the Year.

France confirmed themselves as the world's best by winning the 2000 European Championships, with Zidane sparkling again. He was outstanding, leading France's midfield in a way that brought new meaning to the role. Unlike the individualism Platini brought to the position, Zidane went about his business for the greater good of all and was always prepared to forsake the limelight. In the final, switching roles from attacking midfield supporting Thierry Henry to deep midfield when France appeared to be losing the impetus, served to confuse the Italians and secured the result. His performance was such that it led Pelé to remark that "Zidane is even better now than two years ago. The extra experience of winning a World Cup has given him even more confidence to be able to dictate a game as well as star in it." Zidane remains philosophical about the business of football. "I knew what to expect and I am aware of the greatness I am experiencing today. But I won't live that way my whole life. There is a time in your life when you want to concentrate on the ones you love and stop thinking about your career. I am happy to live this life to the full. But, when comes the time, I will chose to do something else." In July 2001 he moved to Real Madrid for a world record £47.2m.

Davor Suker   Croatia

Davor Suker.

Honours: 3rd Place 1998
Played: 1998

Games 7
Goals 6

Davor Suker may not be on many people's list of instantly recognisable world class players and his club career has been erratic, but in 1998 he showed the world just how fine and outstanding a goal scorer he was. In all but one of the games he played at the France World Cup he scored to earn himself the tournament's Golden Boot Award. A quiet, unassuming man, he goes about his business with an air of confidence and an eye for the target that has brought many goals and the respect of fellow professionals.

Born on New Year's Day in 1968 at Osijek in Croatia, he played for the local team as a young man, where he first came to prominence. His goal scoring and skill earned him a place in the Yugoslav Youth team and, at the age of 19, he travelled to the World Youth Cup in 1987. The following season he became top scorer in the Yugoslavian league with 18 goals, showing the instinct and ability, particularly of his left foot, to create chances out of nothing. Defenders began to realize that having Suker in their 18 yard box was a very dangerous thing. It earned him a place in the Yugoslav squad that went to Italia '90, but he did not feature in the tournament.

When civil war broke out in Yugoslavia, Suker declared himself for Croatia. When life got back to normal, he moved to FC Zagreb and here he came to the attention of the Spanish in Seville. In 1991, they put him into the spotlight of the Primera Liga and he spent five good years in Andalucia, proving that, as a goal scoring commodity, he could hold his own with the best. Real Madrid made him an offer and, in 1996, he found it difficult to resist the step up in his career. He became an instant success and scored a hat full of goals in his first season to help Real to the Spanish title in 1997. However, with Mijatovic, Morientis and Raúl joining the squad, competition for places was great and Suker found it difficult to command a regular first team place the following year, in which he was used mainly as a substitute. He featured in Real's successful Champions League campaign in 1998, but was only a 90th minute substitute in the final. It was imperative that Real won the game, as their league form that year had been so poor they had slipped out of the automatic qualification places.

By the time Croatia went to the 1998 World Cup, Suker was already a permanent fixture in the side having scored an incredible 35 goals in 41 appearances. Twelve of these had come in the country's 10 qualifying games for the 1996 European Championships, which made him top goal scorer. At the Euro '96 finals, he scored two of Croatia's three goals against Denmark in the first round, including a sublime chip over the head of Peter Schmeichel. He got a third to square the quarter-final with Germany, but they eventually lost 2-1. He also established himself as a defender of the team's commercial rights, negotiating with the Croatian FA and potential sponsors in the interests of the players. Like Bulgaria in 1994, Croatia was the surprise package of the 1998 World Cup series, at least to most onlookers. The squad included names such as Jarni, Stanic, Boban, Bilic and Asanovic, all of whom were very talented individuals. The tournament started well with two victories and two goals for Suker. Then, in the head-to-head with Argentina to decide who won Group H, the Argentinians triumphed and it was also the only game of the series in which Suker did not score. A 45th minute Suker penalty took them into the quarter-finals where he netted Croatia's third to send Germany crashing. However, although he silenced the Stade de France in the semi-final, the French dared not lose. Contenting themselves with a 3rd/4th place play-off against Holland, it was inevitably Suker who scored the winner to bring his total to six for the tournament. What Croatia had achieved as a nation that had only been in existence for a few years, was remarkable.

By July 1999, Suker had had enough of playing a bit part at Real Madrid and he accepted a £3.5m move to Arsenal with Nicolas Anelka going the other way. He settled quickly in North London and scored twice on his debut against Aston Villa. However, lightning seemed to strike twice and, in a squad that also included Henry, Bergkamp and Kanu, he once again found himself on the sidelines. In all, he scored 11 goals for Arsenal in 39 appearances,, 24 of which had been as a substitute. So, in June 2000, he accepted a free transfer to West Ham United and became an instant hit. With his new team trailing 2-0 at home to Manchester United at the start of the 2000-01 season Paolo Di Canio pulled one back from the penalty spot before Suker levelled the match with a magnificent header. An injury limited the number of appearances he made that season. With his career coming to an end, it seems likely he will move into coaching. He has taken a great interest in the young Croatian players coming through and is now, professionally and financially, helping Mario Carevic at Hadjuk Split and the 16 year old Niko Kranjcar at FC Zagreb. Having already given so much to the game, the Croatian Player of the Century wants to keep on giving.

Gabriel Omar Batistuta   Argentina

Honours: Quarter-finals 1998; 2nd Round 1994   **Games 9**
Played: 1994 and 1998   **Goals 8**

The opening sentences of Batistuta's official web page reads: "Gabriel Omar Batistuta is, was and forever will remain in history as one of the best strikers in the world. He is rich, handsome, famous, envied by men and desired by women." Now, this is making some large presumptions, especially since whether he forever will be one of the best strikers the world has known is a matter of opinion. What is true, is that in the past few years he has been one of the most prolific. In 75 international appearances he has scored 54 goals including a creditable eight in nine World Cup appearances. In the Italian Serie A he broke a 30 year old record when he scored on 11 consecutive weekends in 1996 and has also been the league's top scorer. Not at all bad for a man who was referred to as "il gordo", or the "fat one" when he was a child.

Batistuta was born on 1st February 1969 in the small town of Avellaneda near Reconquista. The oldest of four children - he has three sisters - this "beautiful, happy, chubby child" spent his youth fishing or playing ball and later chasing Irina, the girl he married when he was 21. His early experiences of football were played out on a piece of dirt ground the locals called "il lombrico", or the "earthworm". However, his favourite sport was basketball and it wasn't until he saw Mario Kempes in the 1978 World Cup that he considered a career in football. "Football never appealed to me. It was something you did in the street with your friends to pass the time away,"

Gabriel Batistuta.

he says. "I never thought it would change my life. Then I was inspired by Kempes. The moment I saw him play with those surging runs I wanted to be like him." Even then it was still only by chance that a representative of Newell's Old Boys of Rosario saw him playing and literally picked him up, took him home to see his father and signed him as a youth player. He was just short of his 17th birthday.

Throughout his career he has suffered the cruelties of the cut-throat business that football is. Obstacles have been put in his way, there have been personality clashes and a need to deal with a constant drive to prove himself. However, his persistence and an incredibly competitive nature took him to the top and have been an inspiration to the players he works with. When he arrived at Newell's he met Marcelo Bielsa, who would become his international coach and who gave him his debut as a substitute in September 1988 in a league game Newell's lost 1-0 to San Martin. His full debut came when regular striker, Gabrich, got injured. It was in the semi-final of the Copa Libertadores against San Lorenz, "Bati" had a fantastic game and the next day was headline news. Newell's won the home leg of the final against Nacional of Uruguay but lost the away leg. Unfortunately, there was jealousy at the attention he received after games, especially from Daniel Passarella, and it had a detrimental effect on his career. One critic, Sivori, carried on his attacks for years and has only recently changed his mind.

In 1989, Batistuta was loaned to Deportivo Italiano of Buenos Aires so he could travel with them to the Viareggio Tournament in Italy that year. He had a good time, scoring a hat trick in one game, but Deportivo were eliminated by Juventus when he missed the crucial penalty in the shoot-out. It was on his 20th birthday. Back home he moved to River Plate, but the arrival of Passarella as coach saw his career take a dive. In his first season he played 17 games and scored four goals. After Passarella came, he didn't play at all. His form and temper suffered, and by June 1990 he had had enough. He moved to Boca Juniors and, with the arrival of Oscar Tabárez as coach, his prospects improved. The goals started to come and Boca started to win. They won the Argentine title and were runner-up in the Copa Libertadores that year.

While playing in the 1991 Copa America for Argentina, he was first seen by the Fiorentina Vice-President, Vittorio Cecchi Gori. Gori like the look of him and the deal was done. He found it difficult at first, but when he scored against Juventus in February 1992 "Batigol" found a place in the hearts of the Fiorentina fans. The following season they were relegated, but he stayed and Fioretina dominated Serie B, going straight back up. Claudio Ranieri was appointed coach and in the 1995-96 season "Firenze" finished third in Serie A and Batistuta was the league's top score with 26 goals. They also won the Italian Cup, the Super Cup and a place in European competition. The "tifosi viola" presented him with a life sized bronze statue of himself. Batistuta scored five goals in the opening two games of the 1997-98 season and in the next the most successful Italian coach, Giovanni Trapattoni, arrived. By February 1999, Fiorentina were at the top of the table, but then Batistuta injured his knee, was sidelined for a month and the team faltered, finishing third.

Batistuta's international career began with a friendly against Brazil on 27th March 1991. Part of a team that also included Goicoechea and Caniggia in the early 1990s they played 33 internationals without defeat and won the Copa America in both 1991 and 1993. In 1991 he was the competition's top scorer with six goals in six games and scored both goals against Mexico in the 1993 final. After their opening game against Greece in the 1994 World Cup, he said: "I have never scored a hat trick for my country and to do it in our first World Cup match is the greatest experience of my life." He then scored a 15th minute penalty in the game against Bulgaria, but things turned sour and Batistuta was one of the few Argentinian players who could walk away with his head up. After it, Passarella was installed as national team coach and although Argentina did not do well under his early tutelage, for Batistuta it could not have been worse. He was dropped altogether, didn't play for almost a year and played little part in Argentina's qualification for the 1998 World Cup. Passarella then strangely recalled him for the finals where he showed his undoubted quality, scoring the winner against Japan, a hat trick against Jamaica and the first against England in Round Two before he was replaced by Crespo in the second half. He had proved himself once again and finished the tournament as its second highest scorer with five goals.

Following the departure of Trapattoni from Fiorentina and a series of unfulfilled promises from Vittorio Gori, now club president, "the Archangel" decided it was time to move. At 31, many commentators thought AS Roma were mad to pay £22m for him in July 2000, but he has proved them wrong and is now playing with renewed determination. Injury dogged his first season, but he continues to relish the challenge. "In Roma," he says, "the pressure is off me. I am no longer the captain who has to try to make up for the shortcomings of his club. At Roma, things are organized properly, they don't change from hour to hour. Roma cannot help me win the World Cup but they can give me the league title and, after that, European success. I'm in the final years of my career but that's not to say that I don't still have time to win something." Roma won the Italian league in 2001.

Iran 2 : USA 1

Iran 2 : U.S.A. 1
Iran's Mehdi Mahdavikia is tackled by U.S.A.'s Tom Dooley.

Ever since the 1979 Iranian Revolution that overthrew the Shah and resulted in several hundred Americans stationed in Iran being held hostage for 444 days by Revolutionary Guards, these two countries have been ideological enemies. Iran's flirtation with pro-Palestinian and Middle East terrorists and frequent outbursts against the decadence of western society in the years since have kept the quarrel simmering. On their part, the USA's support for Saddam Hussein in the Iran-Iraq War in the 1980s did the same. It all added distinct political overtones to this match and meant that security in the ground was heavy and very obvious. Before the game Iranian coach, Jalal Talebi, revealed the rivalry when he said: "If we are going to die, we will die standing. We will fight to the last." Fortunately, the game itself remained above any but sporting considerations and the biggest sign that there was anything different about it came from the Iranian supporters. They vocalized their passion and filled the stadium "with a shrill, piercing noise as they urged on their side."

Both teams began the match knowing that defeat would put them out of the tournament and this was what dictated the pace of play. Both also adopted contrasting tactics and styles of play: Iran playing "the ball from foot to foot; fresh, articulate, co-ordinated", as one reporter noted, whilst the USA had a more direct approach, relying on the power of Brian McBride to head them an advantage. It was a ploy that almost paid immediate dividends as in the third minute Claudio Reyna sent a free kick into the Iranian area and McBride crashed a header against the bar. The Americans hit the woodwork three times in the first 32 minutes, but they also should have lost goalkeeper, Kasey Keller, whose reckless dive at the feet of Khazadad Azizi sent the Iranian sprawling. Both sides created plausible chances. Half way through the first half, Karim Bagheri's 25 yard free kick narrowly sailed over Keller's crossbar and Reyna also came close with a free kick that hit the post. Yet, with the Americans playing the long ball game and Iran supplying the cleverer football, matters were fairly even for most of the half, until Iran stole the advantage in the 40th minute. During a counter attack, the Iranians broke down the right and the cross found Hamid Estili unmarked in the area. He fired home with a powerful header and "instigated the type of noise seldom witnessed at any gathering, political or sporting."

Going in front seemed to fire up Iranian players and supporters alike and in "the second half the fervour was every bit as exhilarating, if often provocative." The Americans were forced to think in terms of attack, but Iran were the better organized and always able to cope with their blunted efforts. Iran held the key and often presented the greater threat. They came close to extending their lead soon after the restart when Ali Daei crossed the ball to Mehdi Mahdavikia, whose shot went wide, and midway through the half Keller made a good save to deny Javad Zarincheh. The USA were clearly the weaker of the teams, but were not ineffective. Reyna had a shot cleared off the line in a desperate last-ditch defensive ruck and Tom Dooley headed narrowly wide when it appeared he would equalize. So the game threaded and swung, with the Iranians containing the heavier American forwards and hitting back with sharp, piercing breakaway attacks. The result was all but sealed in the 84th minute with a superb piece of play that typified the differences between the two teams. The Americans, conscious of the need to go forwards, left themselves exposed at the back and this was cruelly exposed when Daei sent a clever little through pass into the heart of the American half which allowed Mahdavikia to run on from the half way line. He tore through the American ranks and beat Keller " with a marvellous shot." Once again the score was greeted with a cacophonic wail, but it was not all over yet. The Americans went onto immediate attack in the hope of saving their honour and the game. In the frantic final minutes they threw what they could at a defence that appeared ready to buckle and in the 87th minute it did. As if following a script, the USA's single response came from McBride's head, but not soon enough to give anything but slight consolation to his team's late rally. Minutes later the referee blew his whistle and signal a very emotional and historic victory for the men from Iran.

England 2 : Argentina 2

Argentina 2 : England 2 (4-3 on penalties)
Argentina's Javier Zanetti celebrates after scoring Argentina's second goal, a finely worked free-kick.

The football tradition between these two nations may not be a long one, but it is rich and replete with political and sporting controversy. Games between them are amongst the most eagerly awaited in any tournament. The sense of anticipation and expectation in both countries is heavy, even among those who don't normally follow football. They are tense, fervent, nationalistic affairs, always with the potential for explosion, and this was no different. Nobody who saw it could have remained unmoved by each savage twist of its rakish tail and by the tension that wore like a lead mantle until its final kick. The "most dramatic, possibly the most exciting of the championship", wrote one commentator; a "nerve-shredding encounter", wrote another. It was draining for player and spectator alike, raw, unforgiving emotion - international football at its very best.

It took only five minutes to burst into life. Diego Simeone honed in on goal, David Seaman came out to challenge, Simeone went down and the referee gave a penalty. It was questionable and seemed legitimate, but Simeone milked the occasion and it swung the referee. Batistuta stepped up and dispatched it into the net. The England players merely picked themselves up and got on with it. Five minutes later, Scholes's header released Owen and as he rounded Roberto Ayala, he was brought down and the referee awarded his second penalty, this time hammered in by Shearer. Nobody could have expected a better start and in the 16th minute there was a third goal. Beckham chipped a ball into space for Owen to chase, and "with a sensational run and finish" he "slipped past Chamot and Ayala and then rifled a rising shot past the bemused Roa" in goal. By now, as the Daily Telegraph reported, Argentina "were rattled, struggling under a white blanket thrown by Tony Adams and his defenders." England's midfield sweated relentlessly to control the flow of the play and as if to emphasize their mastery, Shearer's header found Scholes on the back post, but he scuffed his shot wide.

It all seemed to be going England's way until two incidents, on either side of half-time, swung the advantage to Argentina. Just before the break they won a free kick outside the area. The defence prepared for a shot from Batistuta, but instead Juan Veron slipped "a slide rule pass" to Javier Zanetti and his shot beat Seaman. It was the perfect time to equalize and two minutes after the restart Beckham stood in the centre circle waiting to receive the ball. He was bundled to the ground by Simeone and a free kick was rightly given. Stupidly, as he lay on the ground, Beckham flicked his right leg and caught the Argentine on the calf. It was innocuous enough, but again Simeone ladled on the histrionics and Beckham was sent off for retaliation. Simeone was shown the yellow card. "I am not denying it cost us the game", was Glen Hoddle's assessment and it certainly gave Argentina an impetus they had previously lacked. As they forced the pace of play, it was "back to the wall stuff" for England, who provided "almost one of the greatest stories English football has ever told." It was totally gripping and absolutely magnificent as England's ten men held back and continually frustrated Argentina's fury. "The heart thrilled at the resolve of Tony Adams and swelled at the application of Alan Shearer." Paul Ince "played as if he were three men" and the others, Owen, Batty, Campbell among them, gave what must rank as the greatest England performance since 1966. True, Argentina created chances, as when Ariel Ortega ran into the box and was stopped by Adams, but England too had their moments. Owen broke through only to shoot wide and Campbell headed the ball into the net to produce the biggest cheer of the night, but Shearer was judged off-side and his effort did not count. For most of that second half and for the whole of extra time it was the same breathtaking story. Both Adams and Veron had chances in the extra time to have won the match, but it was always against the English. Somehow, and deservedly the three lions held on and forced the match into a penalty shoot-out.

The English had one great disadvantage going into the penalties. Beckham, their dead ball specialist, was missing. First up was Argentina's Berti and he made no mistake. Neither did the ice-cool Shearer with his kick. Both Crespo and Ince missed with theirs and the next four were dispatched by Veron, Merson, Gallardo and Owen. Ayala was the next to find the net and with the score 3-2 to Argentina, David Batty strode forwards. He had never taken a penalty kick before and it speaks volumes for the man's bravery that he opted to do so on that fiery night. Of course, he missed, but no blame could be attached to him or to Ince after the battling performance both had just given. One set of supporters stood heartbroken, the other ecstatic and both were left to contemplate the enormity of what had just happened. "It was the story of the weakness of one man and the almost superhuman strength of the ten he left behind", was how the Times summarised it. "Never outplayed, never outfought, never outsung," was the verdict of another reporter. "The whole country can be incredibly proud of the way the England team played. They showed the English spirit at its very best", was Tony Blair's assessment. They were all correct, but each ignored Argentina's contribution to a thoroughly absorbing occasion. They, too, showed the steely resolve needed to overcome the pressures of the evening - and they won!

France 3 : Brazil 0
The World Cup Final

Before the final, French coach Aimé Jacquet declared: "It will be an honour to challenge the masters of the game for their title." His team were as good as his words, especially in the first half when they played as well as any that have lifted the World Cup. The final was a grand affair, but it began in the strangest of circumstances. When the team sheets were handed out to the press before the kick off, Brazil's did not include Ronaldo's name. What happened is unclear, but he appears to have had a fit and was taken to hospital. In his place was Edmundo, nicknamed the "Animal". At the last minute Ronaldo was reinstated and Edmundo was naturally displeased. There were rumours of arguments and even fights in Brazil's dressing room, but whatever the truth, when play began the South Americans were not at their best and it allowed the French to dictate the course of play.

Almost immediately, France went onto the attack and Stephane Guivarc'h missed two good chances in the first three minutes. It was not to be his night as he went on to miss a succession of chances. In these opening exchanges "Brazil looked a team in disarray" and "Ronaldo appeared even more lugubrious than usual and hardly had a touch in the first half." France did most of the running and in the seventh minute Zidane came close to opening the scoring with a free kick that was going in, but was diverted wide off Djorkaeff's shoulder. Rivaldo forced one good save out of Barthez, before Zidane, who "presumably decided he had to do it himself", gave his team the reward their hard work deserved. In the 28th minute, Petit floated a corner over from the right and

F.I.F.A. President Sepp Blatter (left) with losing finalist Ronaldo of Brazil.

Zidane "stepping away from Ronaldo and leaping ahead of Leonardo, met it with a centre-forward's header", to use the words of the Independent. With confidence reinforced, the French continued to sweep forwards and Brazil's incursions into their half were momentary. In a procession of attacks, Djorkaeff's piercing run set himself up with an excellent chance, but shot tamely, Petit saw a rasping volley deflected wide by Junior Baiano and Guivarc'h had a shot saved when he ought to have scored. In the 40th minute, Bebeto was given a chance, but he headed into the arms of Barthez and "then France took over again." The surprise was that their second goal came as late as it did and it was in injury time at the end of the half that Zidane struck again. This time the corner came from the left, supplied by Djorkaeff, and Dunga was the beaten defender as the header powered into the net.

Brazil made a change at the start of the second half, putting on Denilson in place of Leonardo and giving instruction to allow the full-backs to rove forwards. The difference was obvious as Brazil began to take the game to France. In the 56th minute Ronaldo got on the end of Roberto Carlos's cross, but needed too much time with the shot, allowing Barthez to make a very good save. Minutes later Roberto Carlos took a throw-in and found Bebeto, who beat the goalkeeper with his shot. It was cleared off the line by a lunging slide from Desailly. Soon after that, Lebouef's long ball was headed too casually back to his keeper by Cafú and Guivarc'h pounced. However, ten yards in front of goal, he shot wildly over the bar and Brazil were left with a lifeline. They were handed another only a minute later when Desailly, who had already been booked earlier in the half, foolishly and clumsily lunged at Cafú and was sent off. It began a desperate final period of play, as a revived Brazil forced the French onto the back foot. Jacquet tried to shore up his defences by pulling Petit back to centre-half and sent on Viera to replace Djoerkaeff and Brazil tried to strengthen their attack by bringing in Edmundo. One of his first acts was to shout abuse at Rivaldo for sportingly putting the ball out of play so that Zidane could receive treatment.

Of the ploys, that of France proved the more successful. In the final 15 minutes Brazil launched attack after attack, but all floundered on the Gallic barricades erected before them. It may have been desperate at times, but it was effective and it was France that had the last say. Breaking out of jail in injury time, the French surged gleefully forwards, accepting any respite that came their way. Viera took hold of the ball and threaded it carefully to Petit who "rolled the ball inside the far post to start France's biggest party since Liberation." It was all bitterly disappointing for Brazil and their distinguished coach. Undoubtedly, the pre-match goings-on upset the concentration of his players, but they were decidedly second best for much of the game, often made to look ordinary by one of the best French teams ever assembled. France '98 had been a wonderful tournament and one its highlights had been the French. When Didier Deschamps lifted the trophy, it was a proud moment for the nation who gave the world its World Cup. It was also one they thoroughly deserved.

Statistics - France 1998

GROUP A

Saint-Denis, June 10th - Stade de France

2 (1) BRAZIL

C.Sampaio 4, Boyd (og)73

Taffarel, Cafu, Aldair, J.Baiano, R.Carlos, C.Sampaio, Giovanni (Leonardo), Dunga, Rivaldo, Ronaldo, Bebeto (Denilson).

1 (1) SCOTLAND

Collins (pen) 38

Leighton, Boyd, Calderwood, Hendry, Dailly (T.McKinlay), Lambert, Burley, Collins, Jackson (B.McKinlay), Gallacher, Durie.

Referee: J.M. Garcia Aranda (Spain)
Attendance: 80.000

Montpellier, June 10th - Stade de la Mosson

2 (1) NORWAY

Chippo (og) 45, Eggen 81

Grodås, Berg, Eggen, Johnsen, Bjørnebye, H.Flo (Solbakken), Mykland, Rekdal, Leonhardsen, Solskjær (Riseth), T.A.Flo.

2 (1) MOROCCO

Hadji 39, Hadda 59

Benzekri, Saber, Rossi, Naybet, El Hadrioui, Hadji, Chiba, El Khalej (Azzouzi), Chippo (Amzine), Bassir, Hadda (El Khattabi).

Referee: P. Un-Prasert (Thailand)
Attendance: 29.750

Bordeaux, June 16th - Stade Lescure

1 (0) SCOTLAND

Burley 66

Leighton, Boyd, Calderwood (Weir), Hendry, Burley, Collins, Dailly, Lambert, Durie, Gallacher, Jackson (McNamara).

1 (0) NORWAY

H.Flo 46

Grodås, Berg (Halle), Bjørnebye, Eggen, Johnsen, Strand, Rekdal, Solbakken, H.Flo (J.I.Jakobsen), T.A.Flo, Riseth (Østenstad).

Referee: L.Vagner (Hungary)
Attendance: 30.236

Nantes, June 16th - Stade de la Beajoire

3 (2) BRAZIL

Ronaldo 9, Rivaldo 45, Bebeto 50

Taffarel, Cafu, Aldair, J.Baiano, R.Carlos, C.Sampaio (Doriva), Dunga, Leonardo, Rivaldo (Denilson), Bebeto (Edmundo), Ronaldo.

0 (0) MOROCCO

Benzekri, Saber (Abrami), Rossi, El Hadrioui, Naybet, Hadji, Chiba (Amzine), Chippo, El Khalej, Hadda (El Khattabi), Bassir.

Referee: N.Levnikov (Russia)
Attendance: 33.266

Saint-Etienne, June 23rd - Stade Geoffroy Guichard

3 (1) MOROCCO

Bassir 22,85, Hadda 47

Benzekri, Saber (Rossi), Triki, Naybet, Abrami, Hadji, Amzine (Azzouzi), El Khalej, Chippo (Sellami), Bassir, Hadda.

0 (0) SCOTLAND

Leighton, Dailly, Hendry, Weir, Boyd, Burley (RED), Collins, McNamara (T.McKinlay), Lambert, Durie (Booth), Gallacher.

Referee: A.M. Bujsaim (United Arab Emirates)
Attendance: 36.000

Marseille, June 23rd - Stade Velodrome

2 (0) NORWAY

T.A.Flo 83, Rekdal (pen)89

Grodås, Bjørnebye, Berg, Johnsen, Strand (Mykland), Eggen, Leonhardsen, Rekdal, T.A.Flo, Riseth (J.Flo), H.Flo (Solskjær).

1 (0) BRAZIL

Bebeto 78

Taffarel, Cafu, J.Baiano, R.Carlos, Goncalves, Dunga, Denilson, Leonardo, Rivaldo, Ronaldo, Bebeto.

Referee: E. Baharmast (United States)
Attendance: 60.000

	P	W	D	L	F	A	Pts
Brazil	3	2	0	1	6	3	6
Norway	3	1	2	0	5	4	5
Morocco	3	1	1	1	5	5	4
Scotland	3	0	1	2	2	6	1

GROUP B

Toulouse, June 11th - Stadium Municipal

1 (0) CAMEROON

Njanka 77

Songo'o, Wome, Song, Kalla N'Kongo, Njanka, N'Do, Omam Biyik (Tchami), Angibeau, M'Boma, Simo (Olembe), Ipoua (Job).

1 (0) AUSTRIA

Polster 90

Konsel, Schöttel, Pfeffer, Feiersinger, Pfeifenberger (Stöger), Herzog (Vastic), Cerny (Haas), Wetl, Mählich, Kühbauer, Polster.

Referee: E. González Chavez (Paraguay)
Attendance: 33.460

Bordeaux, June 11th - Stade Lescure

2 (1) ITALY

Vieri 10, R.Baggio (pen)85

Pagliuca, Costacurta, Maldini, Nesta, Cannavaro, Di Livio (Chiesa), Di Matteo (Di Biagio), Albertini, D.Baggio, Vieri (Inzaghi), R.Baggio.

2 (1) CHILE

Salas 45,50

Tapia, Rojas, Fuentes, Margas (Ramírez P), Reyes, Acuña (Cornejo), Estay (Sierra), Parraguez, Villarroel, Zamorano, Salas.

Referee: L.O. Bouchardeau (Nigeria)
Attendance: 31.800

Saint-Etienne, June 17th - Stade Geoffroy Guichard

1 (0) CHILE

Salas 70

Tapia, Fuentes, Rojas, Margas, Reyes, Parraguez, Acuña, Villarroel (Castañeda), Estay (Sierra), Zamorano, Salas.

1 (0) AUSTRIA

Vastic 90

Konsel, Schöttel, Pfeffer, Feiersinger, Haas (Vastic), Pfeifenberger, Cerny (Schopp), Wetl, Mählich, Kühbauer (Herzog), Polster.

Referee: G.M.A. Ghandour (Egypt)
Attendance: 30.392

Montpellier, June 17th - Stade de la Mosson

3 (1) ITALY

Di Biagio 8, Vieri 75,89

Pagliuca, Maldini, Cannavaro, Costacurta, Nesta, Albertini (Di Matteo), D.Baggio, Di Biagio, Moriero (Di Livio), R.Baggio (Del Piero), Vieri.

0 (0) CAMEROON

Songo'o, Wome, Song, Kalla N'Kongo (RED), Njanka, Omam Biyik (Tchami), Angibeau, M'Boma (Eto'o), N'Do, Ipoua (Job), Olembe.

Referee: E. Lennie (Australia)
Attendance: 35.000

Saint-Denis, June 23rd - Stade de France

2 (0) ITALY

Vieri 48, R.Baggio 90

Pagliuca, Costacurta, Cannavaro, Nesta (Bergomi), Maldini, Moriero, Di Biagio, D.Baggio, Pessotto, Vieri (Inzaghi), Del Piero (R.Baggio).

1 (0) AUSTRIA

Herzog (pen)91

Konsel, Feiersinger, Schöttel, Pfeffer, Reinmayr, Kühbauer (Stöger), Pfeifenberger (Herzog), Mählich, Wetl, Vastic, Polster (Haas).

Referee: P. Durkin (England)
Attendance: 80.000

Nantes, June 23rd - Stade de la Beajoire

1 (1) CHILE

Sierra 21

Tapia, Reyes, Fuentes, Margas, Villarroel (Cornejo), Acuña, Sierra (Estay), Parraguez, Rojas (Ramírez P), Zamorano, Salas.

1 (0) CAMEROON

M'Boma 56

Songo'o, Njanka, Song (RED), Pensee, N'Do (Etame) (RED), Olembe (Angibeau), M'Boma, Mahouve, Wome, Omam-Biyik, Job (Tchami).

Referee: L. Vagner (Hungary)
Attendance: 39.500

	P	W	D	L	F	A	Pts
Italy	3	2	1	0	7	3	7
Chile	3	0	3	0	4	4	3
Austria	3	0	2	1	3	4	2
Cameroon	3	0	2	1	2	5	2

GROUP C

Lens, June 12th - Stade Felix Bollaert

1 (0) DENMARK

Rieper 68

Schmeichel, Rieper, Høgh, Colding, Schjønberg, Helveg, Wieghorst (Nielsen), Jørgensen (Frandsen), M.Laudrup, B.Laudrup (Heintze), Sand.

0 (0) SAUDI ARABIA

Al Deayea, Al Jahani, Al Khilaiwi, Zubromawi, Sulimani, Amin (Saleh), S.Owairan (Al Dosari), Al Muwalid, Al Owairan, Al Shahrani, Al Jaber (Al Thyniyan).

Referee: J.A. Castrilli (Argentina)
Attendance: 38.140

Marseille, June 12th - Stade Velodrome

3 (1) FRANCE

Dugarry 35, Issa (og)78, Henry 90

Barthez, Blanc, Desailly, Lizarazu, Thuram, Deschamps, Djorkaeff (Trezeguet), Petit (Boghossian), Zidane, Henry, Guivarc'h (Dugarry).

0 (0) SOUTH AFRICA

Vonk, Fish, Issa, Jackson, Nyathi, Radebe, Fortune, Augustine (Mkhalele), Masinga, McCarthy (Bartlett), Moshoeu.

Referee: M. Rezende de Freitas (Brazil)
Attendance: 55.077

Saint-Denis, June 18th - Stade de France

4 (1) FRANCE

Henry 36,77, Trezeguet 68, Lizarazu 85

Barthez, Lizarazu, Blanc, Desailly, Thuram, Deschamps, Boghossian, Zidane (RED), Diomede (Djorkaeff), Henry (Pires), Dugarry (Trezeguet).

0 (0) SAUDI ARABIA

Al Deayea, Al Jahni (Al Dosari), Al Khilaiwi (RED), Zubromawi, Sulimani, Amin, S.Owairan (Al Harbi) (Al Mowalad), Dossari, Saleh, Al Jaber, Al Shahrani.

Referee: A. Brizio Carter (Mexico)
Attendance: 80.000

Toulouse, June 18th - Stadium Municipal

1 (0) SOUTH AFRICA

McCarthy 52

Vonk, Fish, Issa, Nyathi (Buckley), Radebe, Fortune, Mkhalele, Moshoeu, Augustine (Phiri) (RED), Bartlett (Masinga), McCarthy.

1 (1) DENMARK

Nielsen 13

Schmeichel, Colding, Høgh, Rieper, Helveg, Jørgensen, Nielsen, Schjønberg (Wieghorst) (RED), B.Laudrup, M.Laudrup (Molnar) (RED), Sand (Heintze).

Referee: J.J. Toro Rendon (Colombia)
Attendance: 37.500

Lyon, June 24th - Stade de Gerland

2 (1) FRANCE

Djorkaeff (pen)12, Petit 56

Barthez, Karembeu, Leboeuf, Desailly, Candela, Petit (Boghossian), Vieira, Pires (Henry), Djorkaeff, Trezeguet (Guivarc'h), Diomede.

1 (1) DENMARK

M.Laudrup (pen)42

Schmeichel, Laursen (Colding), Rieper, Høgh, Heintze, Jørgensen (Sand), Helveg, Nielsen, Schjønberg, B.Laudrup (Tøfting), M.Laudrup.

Referee: P. Collina (Italy)
Attendance: 44.000

Bordeaux, June 24th - Stade Lescure

2 (1) SOUTH AFRICA

Bartlett 18,(pen)90

Vonk, Issa, Fish, Radebe, Nyathi, Mkhalele, Moshoeu, Jackson (Buckley), Fortune (Khumalo), McCarthy (Sikhosana), Bartlett.

2 (1) SAUDI ARABIA

Al-Jaber (pen)45, Al-Thyniyan (pen)73

Al Deayea, Al Jahani, Zubromawi, Sulaimani, Amin, Al Owairan, Al Temiyat, Saleh, Al Jaber, Al Mehallel (Al Sharani), Al Thunyan (Al Harbi).

Referee: M.F. Sánchez Yanten (Chile)
Attendance: 35.200

	P	W	D	L	F	A	Pts
France	3	3	0	0	9	1	9
Denmark	3	1	1	1	3	3	4
South Africa	3	0	2	1	3	6	2
Saudi Arabia	3	0	1	2	2	7	1

GROUP D

Montpellier, June 12th - Stade de la Mosson

0 (0) PARAGUAY

Chilavert, Gamarra, Ayala, Sarabia, Acuña, Paredes, Benitez, Enciso, Morales (Caniza), Cardozo (C. Ramírez), Campos (Yegros).

0 (0) BULGARIA

Zdravkov, Kischichev, Ivanov, Petkov, Yankov, Balakov, Iliev (Borimirov), Nankov (RED), Iordanov, Stoitchkov, Penev (Kostadinov).

Referee: R. Al-Zeid (Saudi Arabia)
Attendance: 27.650

Nantes, June 13th - Stade de la Beaujoire

3 (1) NIGERIA

Adepoju 24, Lawal 73, Oliseh 79

Rufai, Oparaku (Yekini), West, Uche, Babayaro, Ikpeba (Babangida), Oliseh, Lawal (Okpara), Okocha, Adepoju, Finidi.

2 (1) SPAIN

Hierro 21, Raul 47

Zubizarreta, Ferrer (Amor), Alkorta, Sergi, Campo, Nadal (Celades), Hierro, Luis Enrique, Raul, Alfonso (Etxeberria), Kiko.

Referee: E. Baharmast (United States)
Attendance: 33.257

Paris, June 19th - Parc des Princes

1 (1) NIGERIA

Ikpeba 27

Rufai, Babayaro, Uche, West, Finidi (Babangida), Adepoju, Okocha, Lawal, Oliseh, Ikpeba (Yekini), Amokachi (Kanu).

0 (0) BULGARIA

Zdravkov, Kischischev, Ivanov, Petkov, Guentchev, Hristov (Borimirov), Yankov (Batchev), Balakov, Iliev (Penev), Kostadinov, Stoitchkov.

Referee: M.F. Sánchez Yanten (Chile)
Attendance: 49.300

Saint-Etienne, June 19th - Stade Geoffroy Guichard

0 (0) SPAIN

Zubizarreta, Alkorta, Abelardo (Celades), Sergi, Aguilera, Hierro, Amor, Luis Enrique, Pizzi (Morientes), Raul (Kiko), Etxeberria.

0 (0) PARAGUAY

Chilavert, Arce, Gamarra, Ayala, Sarabia, Caniza, Acuña (Yegros), Benitez, Enciso, Rojas (C. Ramírez), Campos (Paredes).

Referee: I. McLeod (South Africa)
Attendance: 36.000

Lens, June 24th - Stade Felix-Bollaert

6 (2) SPAIN

Hierro (pen)6, L.Enrique 18, Morientes 53,81, Kiko 88,90

Zubizarreta, Aguilera, Alkorta, Nadal, Sergi, Etxeberria (Raul), Amor, Hierro, Luis Enrique (Guerrero), Morientes, Alfonso (Kiko).

1 (0) BULGARIA

Kostadinov 56

Zdravkov, Kischichev, Ivanov, Jordanov, Gintchev, Nankov (Penev), Balakov (Hristov), Borimirov, Batchev, Kostadinov, Stoitchkov (Iliev).

Referee: M. van der Ende (Holland)
Attendance: 41.275

Toulouse, June 24th - Stadium Municipal

3 (1) PARAGUAY

Ayala 1, Benitez 59, Cardozo 86

Chilavert, Sarabia, Ayala, Gamarra, Arce, Enciso, Benitez (Acuña), Paredes, Caniza (Yegros), Cardozo, Brizuela (Rojas).

1 (1) NIGERIA

Oruma 11

Rufai, Eguavoen, Iroha, Uche, West, Babangida, Oliseh (Okpara), Oruma (Finidi), Lawal, Kanu, Yekini.

Referee: P. Un-Prasert (Thailand)
Attendance: 35.000

	P	W	D	L	F	A	Pts
Nigeria	3	2	0	1	5	5	6
Paraguay	3	1	2	0	3	1	5
Spain	3	1	1	1	8	4	4
Bulgaria	3	0	1	2	1	7	1

GROUP E

Saint-Denis, June 13th - Stade de France

0 (0) HOLLAND

Van der Sar, Stam, F.de Boer, Numan, Winter, Seedorf (Zenden), R.de Boer (Jonk), Cocu, Overmars, Kluivert (RED), Hasselbaink (Bergkamp).

0 (0) BELGIUM

de Wilde, Crasson (Deflandre), Staelens, Borkelmans, Verstraeten, Van der Elst, Wilmots, Clement, Boffin, Oliveira (M.Mpenza), Nilis.

Referee: P. Collina (Italy)
Attendance: 75.000

Lyon, June 13th - Stade de Gerland

3 (0) MEXICO

Pelaez 51, Hernández 75,84

Campos, Suárez, Davino, Pardo, Ramírez, Garcia Aspe (Bernal), Ordiales (Pelaez), Lara, Luna (Arellano), Hernández, Blanco.

1 (1) SOUTH KOREA

S.J.Ha 28

Kim Byung-ji, Kim Tae-young, Hong Myung-bo, Lee Min-sung, Ko Jong-soo (Seo Jung-won), Lee Sang-yoon, Ha Seok-ju (RED), Yoo Sang-Chul, Kim Do-keun (Choi Sung-yong), Noh Jung-yoon (Jang Hyung-seok), Kim Do-hoon.

Referee: G. Benkö (Austria)
Attendance: 39.133

Marseille, June 20th - Stade Velodrome

5 (2) HOLLAND

Cocu 37, Overmars 41, Bergkamp 71, van Hooijdonk 79, R.de Boer 83

van der Sar, Winter, Stam, F.de Boer, Numan (Bogarde), R.de Boer (Zenden), Jonk, Davids, Overmars, Cocu, Bergkamp (van Hooijdonk).

0 (0) SOUTH KOREA

Kim Byung-ji, Choi Young-il, Lee Min-sung, Hong Myung-bo, Choi Sung-yong (Kim Tae-young), Yoo Sang-Chul, Lee Sang-yoon, Kim Do-hoon (Ko Jong-soo), Choi Yong-soo, Seo Jung-won (Lee Dong-gook).

Referee: R. Wojcik (Poland)
Attendance: 60.000

Bordeaux, June 20th - Stade Lescure

2 (1) BELGIUM

Wilmots 43,48

De Wilde, Deflandre, Staelens, Vidovic, Borkelmans, Van der Elst (De Boeck), Wilmots, Scifo, Boffin (Verheyen) (RED), Oliveira, Nilis (M.Mpenza).

2 (0) MEXICO

Garcia Aspe (pen)56, Blanco 62

Campos, Suárez, Sánchez, Davino, Pardo (RED), Blanco, Garcia Aspe (Lara), Ordiales (Villa), Ramírez, Hernández, Palencia (Arellano).

Referee: H. Dallas (Scotland)
Attendance: 36.500

Paris, June 25th - Parc des Princes

1 (1) BELGIUM

Nilis 7

Walle, Borkelmans, Clement (L.Mpenza), Deflandre, Staelens, Vidovic, Scifo (Van der Elst), van Kerckhoven, Nilis, Oliveira (M.Mpenza), Wilmots.

1 (0) SOUTH KOREA

Yoo Sang-chul 70

Kim Byung-ji, Kim Tae-young, Lee Min-sung, Hong Myung-bo, Lee Sang-hun (Jang Hyung-seok), Ha Seok-ju, Kim Do-keun (Ko Jong-soo), Seo Jung-won, Choi Sung-yong (Lee Lim-saeng), Yoo Sang-Chul, Choi Yong-soo.

Referee: M. Rezende de Freitas (Brazil)
Attendance: 48.764

Saint-Etienne, June 25th - Stade Geoffroy Guichard

2 (2) HOLLAND

Cocu 4, R.de Boer 19

van der Sar, Reiziger, Stam, F.de Boer, Numan (Bogarde), Jonk (Winter), R.de Boer, Cocu, Davids, Bergkamp (Hasselbaink), Overmars.

2 (0) MEXICO

Pelaez 75, Hernández 93

Campos, Suárez, Sánchez (Pelaez), Davino, Carmona, Villa, Ramírez (RED), Garcia Aspe, Blanco, Hernández, Luna (Arellano).

Referee: R. Al-Zeid (Saudi Arabia)
Attendance: 35.211

	P	W	D	L	F	A	Pts
Holland	3	1	2	0	7	2	5
Mexico	3	1	2	0	7	5	5
Belgium	3	0	3	0	3	3	3
South Korea	3	0	1	2	2	9	1

GROUP F

Saint-Etienne, June 14th - Stade Geoffroy Guichard

1 (0) YUGOSLAVIA

Mihajlovic 73

Kralj, Mirkovic, Djorovic, Mihajlovic, Petrovic, Jokanovic, Brnovic (Stankovic), Jugovic, Stojkovic (Kovacevic), Mijatovic, Milosevic (Ognjenovic).

0 (0) IRAN

Nakisa, Khakpour, Pashazadeh, Mahdavikia, Bagheri, Estili (Mansourian), Mohammadkhani, Zarincheh, Minavand Chal, Daei, Azizi.

Referee: A. Tejada Noriega (Peru)
Attendance: 30.392

Paris, June 15th - Parc des Princes

2 (1) GERMANY

Möller 9, Klinsmann 65

Köpke, Wörns, Kohler, Thon, Reuter (Ziege), Heinrich, Möller (Babbel), Hässler (Hamann), Jeremies, Klinsmann, Bierhoff.

0 (0) UNITED STATES

Keller, Pope, Regis, Burns (Hejduk), Dooley, Stewart, Jones, Deering (Ramos), Maisonneuve, Reyna, Wynalda (Wegerle).

Referee: S. Belqola (Morocco)
Attendance: 43.815

Lens, June 21st - Stade Felix-Bollaert

2 (0) GERMANY

Mihajlovic (og)73, Bierhoff 79

Köpke, Wörns, Kohler, Thon, Heinrich, Möller (Kirsten), Jeremies, Hamann (Matthäus), Ziege (Tarnat), Klinsmann, Bierhoff.

2 (1) YUGOSLAVIA

Mijatovic 13, Stojkovic 54

Kralj, Mihajlovic, Komljenovic, Djorovic, Petrovic (Stevic), Jokanovic, Stojkovic, Stankovic (Govedarrica), Jugovic, Kovacevic (Ognjenovic), Mijatovic.

Referee: K.M. Nielsen (Denmark)
Attendance: 41.275

Lyon, June 21st - Stade de Gerland

2 (1) IRAN

Estili 40, Mahdavikia 84

Abedzadeh, Mahdavikia, Khakpour, Bagheri, Estili, Daei, Azizi (Mansourian), Mohammadkhani (Peyravani), Zarincheh (Sadavi Sad), Pashazadeh, Minavand.

1 (0) UNITED STATES

McBride 87

Keller, Hejduk, Pope, Dooley (Maisonneuve), Regis, Wegerle (Radosavljevik), Moore, Ramos (Stewart), Jones, McBride, Reyna.

Referee: U. Meier (Switzerland)
Attendance: 44.000

Montpellier, June 25th - Stade de la Mosson

2 (0) GERMANY

Bierhoff 51, Klinsmann 58

Köpke, Wörns, Matthäus, Helmer, Thon (Ziege), Heinrich, Tarnat (Hamann), Hässler (Kirsten), Kohler, Bierhoff, Klinsmann.

0 (0) IRAN

Abedzadeh, Khakpour, Pashazadeh, Mohammadkhani, Bagheri, Estili, Chal, Mahdavikia, Zarincheh (Mohammadi), Azizi, Daei.

Referee: E. González Chavez (Paraguay)
Attendance: 35.158

Nantes, June 25th - Stade de la Beajoire

1 (1) YUGOSLAVIA

Komljenovic 4

Kralj, Djorovic, Komljenovic, Petrovic, Jokanovic, Jugovic, Stojkovic (Savicevic), Stankovic (Brnovic), Mihajlovic, Mijatovic (Ognjenovic), Milosevic.

0 (0) UNITED STATES

Friedel, Hejduk (Wynalda), Dooley (Balboa), Regis, Jones, Maisonneuve, Reyna, Burns, Stewart, Moore (Radosavljevik), McBride.

Referee: G.M.A. Ghandour (Egypt)
Attendance: 38.645

	P	W	D	L	F	A	Pts
Germany	3	2	1	0	6	2	7
Yugoslavia	3	2	1	0	4	2	7
Iran	3	1	0	2	2	4	3
United States	3	0	0	3	1	5	0

GROUP G

Lyon, June 15th - Stade de Gerland

1 (1) ROMANIA

Ilie 45

Stelea, Petrescu, Gi.Popescu, Cibotariu, Galca, Munteanu, Hagi (Marinescu), Ga.Popescu (Stanga), Filipescu, Moldovan (Niculescu), Ilie.

0 (0) COLOMBIA

Mondragon, Palacios, Santa, Bermudez, Cabrera, Serna, Lozano, Valderrama, Rincón, Asprilla (Preciado), Aristizabal (Valencia).

Referee: A-Y Lim Kee Chong (Mauritius)
Attendance: 37.572

Marseille, June 15th - Stade Velodrome

2 (1) ENGLAND

Shearer 42, Scholes 90

Seaman, Campbell, Le Saux, Adams, Southgate, Ince, Batty, Scholes, Anderton, Shearer, Sheringham (Owen).

0 (0) TUNISIA

El Ouaer, Clayton, Badra, S.Trabelsi, Boukadida, H.Trabelsi (Thabet), Godhbane, Chihi, Souayah (Baya), Sellimi, Ben Slimane (Ben Younes).

Referee: M. Okada (Japan)
Attendance: 54.587

Montpellier, June 22nd - Stade de la Mosson

1 (0) COLOMBIA

Preciado 83

Mondragon, Cabrera, Bermudez, Palacios, Santa, Serna (Bolano), Lozano, Valderrama, Rincón (Aristizabal), De Avila, Valencia (Preciado).

0 (0) TUNISIA

El Ouaer, Thabet (Godhbane), Chouchane, S.Trabelsi, Clayton, Bouazizi, Chihi, Souayah, Baya (Ahmed), Sellimi (Ben Younes), Slimane.

Referee: B. Heynemann (Germany)
Attendance: 33.782

Toulouse, June 22nd - Stadium Municipal

2 (0) ROMANIA

Moldovan 47, Petrescu 90

Stelea, Gi.Popescu, Petrescu, Cibotariu, Filipescu, Munteanu, Hagi (Stinga) (Marinescu), Galca, Ga.Popescu, Moldovan (Lacatus), Ilie.

1 (0) ENGLAND

Owen 79

Seaman, Neville, Adams, Campbell, Anderton, Batty, Ince (Beckham), Scholes, Le Saux, Sheringham (Owen), Shearer.

Referee: M. Batta (France)
Attendance: 35.602

Saint-Denis, June 26th - Stade de France

1 (0) ROMANIA

Moldovan 72

Stelea, Petrescu, Dulca (Gi.Popescu), Dobos, Cibotariu, Galca, Munteanu, Hagi, Marinescu, Dumitrescu (Moldovan), Lacatus (Ilie).

1 (1) TUNISIA

Souayah (pen)10

El Ouaer, H.Trabelsi, Boukadida, Chouchane, Beya, Godhbane (Thabet), Bouazizi, Chihi, Souayah (Ben Younes), Adel, Slimane (Jelassi).

Referee: E. Lennie (Australia)
Attendance: 79.869

Lens, June 26th - Stade Felix-Bollaert

2 (2) ENGLAND

Anderton 20, Beckham 30

Seaman, Neville, Campbell, Adams, Le Saux, Anderton (Lee), Ince (Batty), Scholes (McManaman), Beckham, Shearer, Owen.

0 (0) COLOMBIA

Mondragon, Palacios, Bermudez, Cabrera, Moreno, Serna (Aristizabal), Lozano, Valderrama, Rincón, De Avila (Valencia), Preciado (Ricard).

Referee: A.P. Brizio Carter (Mexico)
Attendance: 35.000

	P	W	D	L	F	A	Pts
Romania	3	2	1	0	4	2	7
England	3	2	0	1	5	2	6
Colombia	3	1	0	2	1	3	3
Tunisia	3	0	1	2	1	4	1

GROUP H

Lens, June 14th - Stade Felix-Bollaert

3 (1) CROATIA

Stanic 27, Prosinecki 53, Suker 69

Ladic, Soldo, Jarni, Simic (Vlaovic), Stimac, Bilic, Boban, Stanic, Asanovic, Prosinecki, Suker.

1 (1) JAMAICA

Earle 45

Barrett, Goodison, Gardener, Sinclair, Simpson, Cargill (Powell), Whitmore, Earle (Williams), Lowe, Burton, Hall (Boyd).

Referee: V. Melo Pereira (Portugal)
Attendance: 38.058

Toulouse, June 14th - Stadium Municipal

1 (1) ARGENTINA

Batistuta 28

Roa, Ayala, Sensini (Chamot), Zanetti, Vivas, Almeyda, Simeone, Veron, Ortega, López (Balbo), Batistuta.

0 (0) JAPAN

Kawaguchi, Narahashi, Ihara, Nakanishi, Akita, Soma (Hirano), Nanami, Nakata, Yamaguchi, Jo, Nakayama (Lopes).

Referee: M. van der Ende (Holland)
Attendance: 33.400

Nantes, June 20th - Stade de la Beajoire

1 (0) CROATIA

Suker 77

Ladic, Soldo, Stimac (Vlaovic), Bilic, Jarni, Simic, Jurcic, Asanovic, Prosinecki (Mari), Stanic (Tudor), Suker.

0 (0) JAPAN

Kawaguchi, Narahashi (Morishima), Akita, Ihara, Soma, Nakanishi, Nanami (Lopes), Nakata, Yamaguchi, Jo, Nakayama (Okano).

Referee: R. Ramdhan (Trinidad & Tobago)
Attendance: 40.000

Paris, June 21st - Parc des Princes

5 (1) ARGENTINA

Ortega 32,55, Batistuta 73,79,(pen)83

Roa, Ayala, Chamot, Sensini (Vivas), Zanetti, Almeyda, Simeone (Pineda), Ortega, Veron, López (Gallardo), Batistuta.

0 (0) JAMAICA

Barrett, Goodison, Gardener, Sinclair, Malcolm (Boyd), Dawes, Simpson, Whitmore (Earle), Powell (RED), Burton (Cargill), Hall.

Referee: R. Pedersen (Norway)
Attendance: 49.300

Lyon, June 26th - Stade de Gerland

2 (1) JAMAICA

Whitmore 39,54

Lawrence, Malcolm, Sinclair, Goodison, Lowe, Whitmore, Simpson (Earle), Dawes, Gardener, Hall (Boyd), Gayle (Burton).

1 (0) JAPAN

Nakayama 75

Kawaguchi, Ihara, Omura (Hirano), Akita, Narahashi, Nakata, Nanami (Ono), Yamaguchi, Soma, Jo (Lopes), Nakayama.

Referee: G. Benkö (Austria)
Attendance: 43.000

Bordeaux, June 26th - Stade Lescure

1 (1) ARGENTINA

Pineda 36

Roa, Ayala, Vivas, Paz, Zanetti (Simeone), Almeyda, Veron, Ortega (López), Pineda, Batistuta, Gallardo (Berti).

0 (0) CROATIA

Ladic, Soldo, Simic, Bilic, Maric (Vlaovic), Prosinecki (Stimac), Asanovic, Boban, Jarni, Stanic, Suker.

Referee: S. Belqola (Morocco)
Attendance: 34.500

	P	W	D	L	F	A	Pts
Argentina	3	3	0	0	7	0	9
Croatia	3	2	0	1	4	2	6
Jamaica	3	1	0	2	3	9	3
Japan	3	0	0	3	1	4	0

SECOND ROUND

Marseille, June 27th - Stade Velodrome

1 (1) ITALY

Vieri 18

Pagliuca, Costacurta, Bergomi, Cannavaro, Moriero, D.Baggio, Di Biagio, Albertini (Pessotto), Maldini, Del Piero (Chiesa), Vieri.

0 (0) NORWAY

Grodås, Berg, Eggen, Johnsen, Bjørnebye, H.Flo (Solskjær), Mykland, Rekdal, Leonhardsen (Strand)(Solbakken), Riseth, T.A.Flo.

Referee: B. Heynemann (Germany)
Attendance: 57.183

Paris, June 27th - Parc de Princes

4 (3) BRAZIL

C.Sampaio 11,27, Ronaldo (pen)45,70

Taffarel, Cafu, J.Baiano, R.Carlos, Aldair (Goncalves), C.Sampaio, Dunga, Rivaldo, Leonardo, Ronaldo, Bebeto (Denilson).

1 (0) CHILE

Salas 68

Tapia, Fuentes, Margas, Reyes, Ramírez (Estay), Aros, Cornejo, Acuña (Mussri), Sierra (Vega), Zamorano, Salas.

Referee: M. Batta (France)
Attendance: 47.694

Reggae, Ronaldo and a French Revolution - France 1998

Lens, June 28th - Stade Felix-Bollaert

1 (0) FRANCE

Blanc 113

Barthez, Thuram, Blanc, Desailly, Lizarazu, Deschamps, Petit (Boghossian), Djorkaeff, Henry (Pires), Diomede (Guivarc'h), Trezeguet.

0 (0) PARAGUAY

Chilavert, Arce, Gamarra, Ayala, Sarabia, Acuña, Enciso, Paredes (Caniza), Benitez, Campos (Yegros), Cardozo (Rojas).

After golden goal

Referee: A. Bujsaim (United Arab Emirates)
Attendance: 35.200

Saint-Denis, June 28th - Stade de France

4 (2) DENMARK

Möller 3, B.Laudrup 12, Sand 59, Helveg 76

Schmeichel, Rieper, Høgh, Heintze, Colding, Jørgensen, Helveg, Nielsen, M.Laudrup (Frandsen), B.Laudrup (Wieghorst), Möller (Sand).

1 (0) NIGERIA

Babangida 77

Rufai, Babayaro, Uche, West, Finidi, Adepoju, Okocha, Lawal (Babangida), Oliseh, Ikpeba, Kanu (Yekini).

Referee: U. Meier (Switzerland)
Attendance: 79.740

Montpellier, June 29th - Stade de la Mosson

2 (0) GERMANY

Klinsmann 75, Bierhoff 86

Köpke, Matthäus, Wörns, Babbel, Heinrich (Möller), Hamann, Helmer (Ziege), Tarnat, Hässler (Kirsten), Klinsmann, Bierhoff.

1 (0) MEXICO

Hernández 47

Campos, Pardo, Davino, Suárez, Villa, Garcia Aspe (Pelaez), Lara, Bernal (Carmona), Palencia (Arellano), Blanco, Hernández.

Referee: M. Melo Pereira (Portugal)
Attendance: 35.500

Toulouse, June 29th - Stadium Municipal

2 (1) HOLLAND

Bergkamp 38, Davids 91

van der Sar, Reiziger, Stam, F.de Boer, Numan, R.de Boer, Seedorf, Davids, Overmars, Bergkamp, Cocu.

1 (0) YUGOSLAVIA

Komljenovic 49

Kralj, Mirkovic, Djorovic, Mihajlovic (Saveljic), Komljenovic, Petrovic, Jokanovic, Stojkovic (Savicevic), Brnovic, Jugovic, Mijatovic.

Referee: J. Garcia Aranda (Spain)
Attendance: 35.000

Bordeaux, June 30th - Stade Lescure

1 (1) CROATIA

Suker (pen)45

Ladic, Stimac, Bilic, Jarni, Simic, Asanovic, Boban, Stanic (Tudor), Jurcic, Suker, Vlaovic (Krpan).

0 (0) ROMANIA

Stelea, Petrescu (Marinescu), Gh.Popescu, Ciobotariu, Galca, Munteanu, Hagi (Craioveanu), Ga.Popescu (Niculescu), Filipescu, Moldovan, Ilie.

Referee: J.A. Castrilli (Argentina)
Attendance: 36.500

Saint-Etienne, June 30th - Stade Geoffroy Guichard

6 (4)(2) ARGENTINA

Batistuta (pen)6, Zanetti 45

Roa, Ayala, Chamot, Vivas, Zanetti, Almeyda, Simeone (Berti), Ortega, Veron, López (Gallardo), Batistuta (Crespo).

5 (3)(2) ENGLAND

Shearer (pen)10, Owen 16

Seaman, Campbell, Le Saux (Southgate), Adams, Neville, Ince, Beckham (RED), Anderton (Batty), Scholes (Merson), Shearer, Owen.

After extra time & penalty shoot-out - 45 mins (2-2), 90 mins (2-2), 120 mins (2-2)

Penalty shoot-out - Argentina started to shoot.

ARGENTINA	4	ENGLAND	3
Berti	Goal	Shearer	Goal
Crespo	Miss	Ince	Miss
Veron	Goal	Merson	Goal
Gallardo	Goal	Owen	Goal
Ayala	Goal	Batty	Miss

Referee: K.M. Nielsen (Denmark)
Attendance: 36.000

QUARTER-FINALS

Saint-Denis, July 3rd - Stade de France

4 (0) FRANCE

Barthez, Lizarazu, Blanc, Desailly, Thuram, Djorkaeff, Deschamps, Zidane, Petit, Karembeu (Henry), Guivarc'h (Trezeguet).

3 (0) ITALY

Pagliuca, Bergomi, Maldini, Cannavaro, Costacurta, Pessotto (Di Livio), D.Baggio (Albertini), Di Biagio, Moriero, Del Piero (R.Baggio), Vieri.

After extra time & penalty shoot-out - 45 mins (0-0), 90 mins (0-0), 120 mins (0-0)

Penalty shoot-out - France started to shoot.

FRANCE	4	ITALY	3
Zidane	Goal	R. Baggio	Goal
Lizarazu	Miss	Albertini	Miss
Trezeguet	Goal	Costacurta	Goal
Henry	Goal	Vieri	Goal
Blanc	Goal	Di Biagio	Miss

Referee: H. Dallas (Scotland)
Attendance: 77.000

Nantes, July 3rd - Stade de la Beajoire

3 (2) BRAZIL

Bebeto 11, Rivaldo 27,60

Taffarel, Cafu, J.Baiano, R.Carlos, Aldair, C.Sampaio, Dunga, Rivaldo (Ze Roberto), Leonardo (Emerson), Ronaldo, Bebeto (Denilson).

2 (1) DENMARK

Jørgensen 2, B.Laudrup 50

Schmeichel, Rieper, Høgh, Heintze, Colding, Helveg (Schjønberg), Nielsen (Tøfting), Jørgensen, M.Laudrup, B.Laudrup, Møller (Sand).

Referee: G. Ghandour (Egypt)
Attendance: 35.500

Marseille, July 4th - Stade Velodrome

2 (1) HOLLAND

Kluivert 12, Bergkamp 89

van der Sar, Reiziger, Stam, F.de Boer, Numan (RED), Jonk, R.de Boer (Overmars), Cocu, Davids, Bergkamp, Kluivert.

1 (1) ARGENTINA

López 17

Roa, Ayala, Chamot (Balbo), Sensini, Zanetti, Almeyda (Pineda), Simeone, Ortega (RED), Veron, López, Batistuta.

Referee: A. Brizio Carter (Mexico)
Attendance: 55.000

Lyon, July 4th - Stade de Gerland

3 (1) CROATIA

Jarni 45, Vlaovic 80, Suker 85

Ladic, Stimac, Bilic, Simic, Jarni, Soldo, Asanovic, Boban, Stanic, Suker, Vlaovic (Maric).

0 (0) GERMANY

Köpke, Wörns (RED), Kohler, Matthäus, Heinrich, Hässler (Kirsten), Jeremies, Hamann (Marschall), Tarnat, Klinsmann, Bierhoff.

Referee: R. Pedersen (Norway)
Attendance: 39.000

SEMI-FINALS

Marseille, July 7th - Stade Velodrome

5 (1) BRAZIL

Ronaldo 46

Taffarel, Aldair, J.Baiano, R.Carlos, Ze Carlos, C.Sampaio, Dunga, Rivaldo, Leonardo (Emerson), Ronaldo, Bebeto (Denilson).

3 (1) HOLLAND

Kluivert 87

van der Sar, Reiziger (Winter), Stam, F.de Boer, Jonk (Seedorf), R.de Boer, Cocu, Davids, Bergkamp, Kluivert, Zenden (van Hooijdonk).

After extra time & penalty shoot-out - 45 mins (0-0), 90 mins (1-1), 120 mins (1-1)

Penalty shoot-out - Brazil started to shoot.

BRAZIL	4	HOLLAND	2
Ronaldo	Goal	F. de Boer	Goal
Rivaldo	Goal	Bergkamp	Goal
Emerson	Goal	Cocu	Miss
Dunga	Goal	R. de Boer	Miss

Referee: A. Bujsaim (United Arab Emirates)
Attendance: 54.000

Saint-Denis, July 8th - Stade de France

2 (0) FRANCE

Thuram 47,69

Barthez, Lizarazu, Blanc (RED), Desailly, Thuram, Djorkaeff (Leboeuf), Deschamps, Zidane, Petit, Karembeu (Henry), Guivarc'h (Trezeguet).

1 (0) CROATIA

Suker 46

Ladic, Soldo, Jarni, Simic, Stimac, Bilic, Boban (Maric), Stanic (Prosinecki), Asanovic, Vlaovic, Suker.

Referee: J.M. Garcia Aranda (Spain)
Attendance: 76.000

3RD/4TH PLACE PLAY-OFF

Paris, July 11th - Parc des Princes

2 (2) CROATIA

Prosinecki 13, Suker 35

Ladic, Stimac, Bilic, Soldo, Jarni, Asanovic, Prosinecki (Vlaovic), Boban (Tudor), Stanic, Jurcic, Suker.

1 (1) HOLLAND

Zenden 21

van der Sar, Stam, F.de Boer, Numan, Jonk, Seedorf, Cocu (Overmars), Davids, Bergkamp (van Hooijdonk), Kluivert, Zenden.

E. González Chavez (Paraguay)
Attendance: 45.500

FINAL

Saint-Denis, July 12th - Stade de France

3 (2) FRANCE

Zidane 27,45, Petit 90

Barthez, Lizarazu, Leboeuf, Desailly (RED), Thuram, Djorkaeff (Vieira), Deschamps, Zidane, Petit, Karembeu (Boghossian), Guivarc'h (Dugarry).

0 (0) BRAZIL

Taffarel, Cafu, Aldair, J.Baiano, R.Carlos, C.Sampaio (Edmundo), Dunga, Rivaldo, Leonardo (Denilson), Bebeto, Ronaldo.

Referee: S. Belqola (Morocco)
Attendance: 80.000

QUALIFYING ROUNDS

Africa - 1st Round

31-05-96	Mauritania : Burkina Faso	0:0
16-06-96	Burkina Faso : Mauritania	2:0 (1:0)
01-06-96	Namibia : Mozambique	2:0 (1:0)
16-06-96	Mozambique : Namibia	1:1 (1:0)
01-06-96	Malawi : South Africa	0:1 (0:1)
15-06-96	South Africa : Malawi	3:0 (3:0)
01-06-96	Uganda : Angola	0:2 (0:1)
16-06-96	Angola : Uganda	3:1 (2:1)
01-06-96	Guinea-Bissau : Guinea	3:2 (2:0)
16-06-96	Guinea : Guinea-Bissau	3:1 (1:0)
01-06-96	Gambia : Liberia	2:1 (1:1)
23-06-96	Liberia : Gambia	4:0 (1:0)
02-06-96	Swaziland : Gabon	0:1 (0:1)
16-06-96	Gabon : Swaziland	2:0 (1:0)
02-06-96	Burundi : Sierra Leone	1:0 (0:0)
16-06-96	Sierra Leone : Burundi	0:1 (0:1)
02-06-96	Madagascar : Zimbabwe	1:2 (1:0)
16-06-96	Zimbabwe : Madagascar	2:2 (0:1)
02-06-96	Congo : Cote d' Ivoire	2:0 (1:0)
16-06-96	Cote d' Ivoire : Congo	1:1 (1:0)
02-06-96	Mauritius : Zaire	1:5 (0:2)
16-06-96	Zaire : Mauritius	2:0 (1:0)
02-06-96	Rwanda : Tunisia	1:3 (0:1)
16-06-96	Tunisia : Rwanda	2:0 (1:0)
02-06-96	Kenya : Algeria	3:1 (0:0)
14-06-96	Algeria : Kenya	1:0 (1:0)
02-06-96	Togo : Senegal	2:1 (1:0)
15-06-96	Senegal : Togo	1:1 (1:0)
01-06-96	Sudan : Zambia	2:0 (1:0)
16-06-96	Zambia : Sudan	3:0 (2:0)
08-06-96	Tanzania : Ghana	0:0
17-06-96	Ghana : Tanzania	2:1 (0:0)

Africa - 2nd Round, Group 1

	P	W	D	L	F	A	Pts
Nigeria	6	4	1	1	10	4	13
Guinea	6	4	0	2	10	5	12
Kenya	6	3	1	2	11	12	10
Burkina Faso	6	0	0	6	7	17	0

09-11-96	Nigeria : Burkina Faso	2:0 (0:0)
10-11-96	Guinea : Kenya	3:1 (2:1)
12-01-97	Kenya : Nigeria	1:1 (1:0)
12-01-97	Burkina Faso : Guinea	0:2 (0:2)
05-04-97	Nigeria : Guinea	2:1 (0:0)
06-04-97	Kenya : Burkina Faso	4:3 (0:2)
27-04-97	Burkina Faso : Nigeria	1:2 (0:1)
27-04-97	Kenya : Guinea	1:0 (1:0)
07-06-97	Nigeria : Kenya	3:0 (2:0)
08-06-97	Guinea : Burkina Faso	3:1 (2:1)
16-08-97	Burkina Faso : Kenya	2:4 (1:2)
17-08-97	Guinea : Nigeria	1:0 (0:0)

Africa - 2nd Round, Group 2

	P	W	D	L	F	A	Pts
Tunisia	6	5	1	0	10	1	16
Egypt	6	3	1	2	15	5	10
Liberia	6	1	1	4	2	10	4
Namibia	6	1	1	4	6	17	4

08-06-96	Liberia : Namibia	1:2 (1:1)
08-11-96	Egypt : Namibia	7:1 (4:1)
10-11-96	Liberia : Tunisia	0:1 (0:0)
11-01-97	Namibia : Liberia	0:0
12-01-97	Tunisia : Egypt	1:0 (1:0)
06-04-97	Liberia : Egypt	1:0 (1:0)
06-04-97	Namibia : Tunisia	1:2 (0:1)
26-04-97	Namibia : Egypt	2:3 (0:0)
27-04-97	Tunisia : Liberia	2:0 (0:0)
08-06-97	Egypt : Tunisia	0:0
17-08-97	Tunisia : Namibia	4:0 (2:0)
17-08-97	Egypt : Liberia	5:0 (2:0)

Africa - 2nd Round, Group 3

	P	W	D	L	F	A	Pts
South Africa	6	4	1	1	7	3	13
Congo	6	3	1	2	5	5	10
Zambia	6	2	2	2	7	6	8
Zaire	6	0	2	4	4	9	2

09-11-96	South Africa : Zaire	1:0 (0:0)
10-11-96	Congo : Zambia	1:0 (0:0)
11-01-97	Zambia : South Africa	0:0
12-01-97	Zaire : Congo	1:1 (1:1)
06-04-97	Congo : South Africa	2:0 (0:0)
09-04-97	Zaire : Zambia	2:2 (1:1)
27-04-97	Zambia : Congo	3:0 (1:0)
27-04-97	Zaire : South Africa	1:2 (1:1)
08-06-97	South Africa : Zambia	3:0 (2:0)
08-06-97	Congo : Zaire	1:0 (0:0)
16-08-97	Zambia : Zaire	2:0 (1:0)
16-08-97	South Africa : Congo	1:0 (1:0)

Africa - 2nd Round, Group 4

	P	W	D	L	F	A	Pts
Cameroon	6	4	2	0	10	4	14
Angola	6	2	4	0	7	4	10
Zimbabwe	6	1	1	4	6	7	4
Togo	6	1	1	4	6	14	4

10-11-96	Angola : Zimbabwe	2:1 (1:0)
10-11-96	Togo : Cameroon	2:4 (0:2)
12-01-97	Zimbabwe : Togo	3:0 (2:0)
12-01-97	Cameroon : Angola	0:0
06-04-97	Angola : Togo	3:1 (2:1)
06-04-97	Cameroon : Zimbabwe	1:0 (0:0)
27-04-97	Zimbabwe : Angola	0:0
27-04-97	Cameroon : Togo	2:0 (0:0)
08-06-97	Angola : Cameroon	1:1 (0:0)
08-06-97	Togo : Zimbabwe	2:1 (2:0)
17-08-97	Togo : Angola	1:1 (0:1)
17-08-97	Zimbabwe : Cameroon	1:2 (0:0)

Africa - 2nd Round, Group 5

	P	W	D	L	F	A	Pts
Morocco	6	5	1	0	14	2	16
Sierra Leone	5	2	1	2	4	6	7
Ghana	6	1	3	2	7	7	6
Gabon	5	0	1	4	1	11	1

09-11-96	Morocco : Sierra Leone	4:0 (1:0)
10-11-96	Gabon : Ghana	1:1 (0:0)
11-01-97	Sierra Leone : Gabon	1:0 (1:0)
12-01-97	Ghana : Morocco	2:2 (0:1)
05-04-97	Sierra Leone : Ghana	1:1 (0:1)
06-04-97	Gabon : Morocco	0:4 (0:4)
26-04-97	Sierra Leone : Morocco	0:1 (0:1)
27-04-97	Ghana : Gabon	3:0 (1:0)
07-06-97	Morocco : Ghana	1:0 (0:0)
16-08-97	Morocco : Gabon	2:0 (2:0)
17-08-97	Ghana : Sierra Leone	0:2 (0:1)

Asia - 1st Round, Group 1

	P	W	D	L	F	A	Pts
Saudi Arabia	6	5	1	0	18	1	16
Malaysia	6	3	2	1	5	3	11
Chinese Taipei	6	1	1	4	4	13	4
Bangladesh	6	1	0	5	4	14	3

16-03-97	Chinese Taipei : Saudi Arabia	0:2 (0:2)
16-03-97	Malaysia : Bangladesh	2:0 (1:0)
18-03-97	Malaysia : Saudi Arabia	0:0
18-03-97	Bangladesh : Chinese Taipei	1:3 (0:0)
20-03-97	Bangladesh : Saudi Arabia	1:4 (1:2)
20-03-97	Malaysia : Chinese Taipei	2:0 (2:0)
All games played in Kuala Lumpur		
27-03-97	Chinese Taipei : Malaysia	0:0
27-03-97	Saudi Arabia : Bangladesh	3:0 (2:0)
29-03-97	Saudi Arabia : Malaysia	3:0 (0:0)
29-03-97	Chinese Taipei : Bangladesh	1:2 (0:1)
31-03-97	Bangladesh : Malaysia	0:1 (0:1)
31-03-97	Saudi Arabia : Chinese Taipei	6:0 (4:0)
All games played in Jeddah		

Asia - 1st Round, Group 2

	P	W	D	L	F	A	Pts
Iran	6	5	1	0	39	3	16
Kyrgyzstan	5	3	0	2	12	11	9
Syria	5	2	1	2	27	5	7
Maldives	6	0	0	6	0	59	0

02-06-97	Maldives : Iran	0:17 (0:6)
02-06-97	Syria : Kyrgyzstan	Abandoned
04-06-97	Kyrgyzstan : Iran	0:7 (0:1)
04-06-97	Syria : Maldives	12:0 (7:0)
06-06-97	Kyrgyzstan : Maldives	3:0 (3:0)
06-06-97	Syria : Iran	0:1
All games played in Damascus		
09-06-97	Maldives : Syria	0:12 (0:1)
09-06-97	Iran : Kyrgyzstan	3:1 (1:0)
11-06-97	Kyrgyzstan : Syria	2:1 (1:0)
11-06-97	Iran : Maldives	9:0 (7:0)
13-06-97	Maldives : Kyrgyzstan	0:6 (0:3)
13-06-97	Iran : Syria	2:2 (2:2)
All games played in Tehran		

Asia - 1st Round, Group 3

	P	W	D	L	F	A	Pts
United Arab Emirates	4	3	1	0	7	1	10
Jordan	4	1	1	2	4	4	4
Bahrain	4	1	0	3	3	9	3

08-04-97	Jordan : United Arab Emirates	0:0

Played in Bahrain

11-04-97	Bahrain : United Arab Emirates	1:2 (0:1)
14-04-97	Bahrain : Jordan	1:0 (1:0)

Both games palyed in Manama

19-04-97	Jordan : Bahrain	4:1 (2:1)
22-04-97	United Arab Emirates : Bahrain	3:0 (1:0)
26-04-97	United Arab Emirates : Jordan	2:0 (1:0)

All games played in Sharjah

Asia - 1st Round, Group 4

	P	W	D	L	F	A	Pts
Japan	6	5	1	0	31	1	16
Oman	6	4	1	1	14	2	13
Macao	6	1	1	4	3	28	4
Nepal	6	0	1	5	2	19	1

23-03-97	Nepal : Macao	1:1 (1:1)
23-03-97	Oman : Japan	0:1 (0:1)
25-03-97	Macao : Japan	0:10 (0:3)
25-03-97	Oman : Nepal	1:0 (1:0)
27-03-97	Nepal : Japan	0:6 (0:1)
27-03-97	Oman : Macao	4:0 (2:0)

All games played in Muscat

22-06-97	Nepal : Oman	0:6 (0:3)
22-06-97	Japan : Macao	10:0 (6:0)
25-06-97	Macao : Oman	0:2 (0:1)
25-06-97	apan : Nepal	3:0 (1:0)
28-06-97	Macao : Nepal	2:1 (0:1)
28-06-97	Japan : Oman	1:1 (1:0)

All games played in Tokyo

Asia - 1st Round, Group 5

	P	W	D	L	F	A	Pts
Uzbekistan	6	5	1	0	20	3	16
Yemen	6	2	2	2	10	7	8
Indonesia	6	1	4	1	11	6	7
Cambodia	6	0	1	5	2	27	1

06-04-97	Indonesia : Cambodia	8:0 (6:0)
13-04-97	Indonesia : Yemen	0:0
20-04-97	Cambodia : Yemen	0:1 (0:1)
27-04-97	Cambodia : Indonesia	1:1 (0:0)
09-05-97	Yemen : Uzbekistan	0:1 (0:1)
16-05-97	Yemen : Cambodia	7:0 (3:0)
25-05-97	Uzbekistan : Cambodia	6:0 (4:0)
01-06-97	Indonesia : Uzbekistan	1:1 (1:0)
13-06-97	Yemen : Indonesia	1:1 (1:0)
20-06-97	Uzbekistan : Indonesia	3:0 (2:0)
29-06-97	Cambodia : Uzbekistan	1:4 (1:3)
24-08-97	Uzbekistan : Yemen	5:1 (1:1)

Asia - 1st Round, Group 6

	P	W	D	L	F	A	Pts
Korea Republic	4	3	1	0	9	1	10
Thailand	4	1	1	2	5	6	4
Hong Kong	4	1	0	3	3	10	3

23-02-97	Hong Kong : Korea Republic	0:2 (0:0)
02-03-97	Thailand : Korea Republic	1:3 (0:1)
09-03-97	Thailand : Hong Kong	2:0 (1:0)
30-03-97	Hong Kong : Thailand	3:2 (1:1)
28-05-97	Korea Republic : Hong Kong	4:0 (2:0)
01-06-97	Korea Republic : Thailand	0:0

Asia - 1st Round, Group 7

	P	W	D	L	F	A	Pts
Kuwait	4	4	0	0	10	1	12
Lebanon	4	1	1	2	4	7	4
Singapore	4	0	1	3	2	8	1

13-04-97	Lebanon : Singapore	1:1 (0:0)
26-04-97	Singapore : Kuwait	0:1 (0:1)
08-05-97	Kuwait : Lebanon	2:0 (1:0)
24-05-97	Singapore : Lebanon	1:2 (0:1)
05-06-97	Kuwait : Singapore	4:0 (3:0)
22-06-97	Lebanon : Kuwait	1:3 (0:2)

Asia - 1st Round, Group 8

	P	W	D	L	F	A	Pts
China PR	6	5	1	0	13	2	16
Tajikistan	6	4	1	1	15	2	13
Turkmenistan	6	2	0	4	8	13	6
Vietnam SR	6	0	0	6	2	21	0

04-05-97	Tajikistan : Vietnam SR	4:0 (2:0)
04-05-97	Turkmenistan : China PR	1:4 (0:2)
11-05-97	Turkmenistan : Vietnam SR	2:1 (1:0)
11-05-97	Tajikistan : China PR	0:1 (0:0)
25-05-97	Turkmenistan : Tajikistan	1:2 (1:1)
25-05-97	Vietnam SR : China PR	1:3 (1:3)
01-06-97	Vietnam SR : Tajikistan	0:4 (0:2)
01-06-97	China PR : Turkmenistan	1:0 (0:0)
08-06-97	Vietnam SR : Turkmenistan	0:4 (0:2)
08-06-97	China PR : Tajikistan	0:0
22-06-97	Tajikistan : Turkmenistan	5:0 (4:0)
22-06-97	China PR : Vietnam SR	4:0 (2:0)

Asia - 1st Round, Group 9

	P	W	D	L	F	A	Pts
Kazakhstan	4	4	0	0	15	2	12
Iraq	4	2	0	2	14	8	6
Pakistan	4	0	0	4	3	22	0

11-05-97	Kazakhstan : Pakistan	3:0 (1:0)
23-05-97	Pakistan : Iraq	2:6 (1:2)
06-06-97	Iraq : Kazakhstan	1:2 (1:1)
11-06-97	Pakistan : Kazakhstan	0:7 (0:3)
20-06-97	Iraq : Pakistan	6:1 (2:0)
29-06-97	Kazakhstan : Iraq	3:1 (2:0)

Asia - 1st Round, Group 10

	P	W	D	L	F	A	Pts
Qatar	3	3	0	0	14	0	9
Sri Lanka	3	1	1	1	4	4	4
India	3	1	1	1	3	7	4
Philippines	3	0	0	3	0	10	0

20-09-96	Qatar : Sri Lanka	3:0 (1:0)
21-09-96	India : Philippines	2:0 (0:0)
23-09-96	Qatar : Philippines	5:0 (5:0)
24-09-96	Sri Lanka : India	1:1 (1:1)
26-09-96	Philippines : Sri Lanka	0:3 (0:1)
27-09-96	Qatar : India	6:0 (3:0)

All games played in Doha

Asia - 2nd Round, Group A

	P	W	D	L	F	A	Pts
Saudi Arabia	8	4	2	2	8	6	14
Iran	8	3	3	2	13	8	12
China PR	8	3	2	3	11	14	11
Qatar	8	3	1	4	7	10	10
Kuwait	8	2	2	4	7	8	8

13-09-97	China PR : Iran	2:4 (1:0)
14-09-97	Saudi Arabia : Kuwait	2:1 (1:1)
19-09-97	Iran : Saudi Arabia	1:1 (0:1)

19-09-97	Qatar : Kuwait	0:2 (0:1)
26-09-97	Qatar : China PR	1:1 (1:0)
26-09-97	Kuwait : Iran	1:1 (1:0)
03-10-97	China PR : Saudi Arabia	1:0 (0:0)
03-10-97	Iran : Qatar	3:0 (2:0)
10-10-97	Kuwait : China PR	1:2 (1:1)
11-10-97	Saudi Arabia : Qatar	1:0 (0:0)
17-10-97	Iran : China PR	4:1 (2:0)
17-10-97	Kuwait : Saudi Arabia	2:1 (0:1)
24-10-97	Kuwait : Qatar	0:1 (0:1)
24-10-97	Saudi Arabia : Iran	1:0 (0:0)
31-10-97	Iran : Kuwait	0:0
31-10-97	China PR : Qatar	2:3 (1:1)
06-11-97	Saudi Arabia : China PR	1:1 (1:1)
07-11-97	Qatar : Iran	2:0 (1:0)
12-11-97	Qatar : Saudi Arabia	0:1
12-11-97	China PR : Kuwait	1:0 (1:0)

Asia - 2nd Round, Group B

	P	W	D	L	F	A	Pts
Korea Republic	8	6	1	1	19	7	19
Japan	8	3	4	1	17	9	13
United Arab Emirates	8	2	3	3	9	12	9
Uzbekistan	8	1	3	4	13	18	6
Kazakhstan	8	1	3	4	7	19	6

06-09-97	Korea Republic : Kazakhstan	3:0 (1:0)
07-09-97	Japan : Uzbekistan	6:3 (4:0)
12-09-97	UAE : Kazakhstan	4:0 (1:0)
12-09-97	Korea Republic : Uzbekistan	2:1 (1:0)
19-09-97	UAE : Japan	0:0
20-09-97	Kazakhstan : Uzbekistan	1:1 (0:0)
27-09-97	Uzbekistan : UAE	2:3 (1:0)
28-09-97	Japan : Korea Republic	1:2 (1:0)
04-10-97	Kazakhstan : Japan	1:1 (0:1)
04-10-97	Korea Republic : UAE	3:0 (1:0)
11-10-97	Kazakhstan : Korea Republic	1:1 (0:1)
11-10-97	Uzbekistan : Japan	1:1 (1:0)
18-10-97	Kazakhstan : UAE	3:0 (0:0)
18-10-97	Uzbekistan : Korea Republic	1:5 (0:3)
25-10-97	Uzbekistan : Kazakhstan	4:0 (3:0)
26-10-97	Japan : UAE	1:1 (1:1)
01-11-97	Korea Republic : Japan	0:2 (0:2)
02-11-97	UAE : Uzbekistan	0:0
08-11-97	Japan : Kazakhstan	5:1 (3:0)
09-11-97	UAE : Korea Republic	1:3 (0:2)

Asia - Play-off

16-11-97	Japan : Iran	3:2 a.e.t. (2:2, 1:0)

Played in Johor Bahru

Europe - Group 1

	P	W	D	L	F	A	Pts
Denmark	8	5	2	1	14	6	17
Croatia	8	4	3	1	17	12	15
Greece	8	4	2	2	11	4	14
Bosnia-Herzegovina	8	3	0	5	9	14	9
Slovenia	8	0	1	7	5	20	1

24-04-96	Greece : Slovenia	2:0 (0:0)
01-09-96	Greece : Bosnia-Herzegovina	3:0 (1:0)
01-09-96	Slovenia : Denmark	0:2 (0:0)
08-10-96	Bosnia-Herzegovina : Croatia	1:4 (1:2)
09-10-96	Denmark : Greece	2:1 (1:1)
10-11-96	Slovenia : Bosnia-Herzegovina	1:2 (1:2)
10-11-96	Croatia : Greece	1:1 (1:1)

29-03-97	Croatia : Denmark	1:1 (0:0)
02-04-97	Bosnia-Herzegovina : Greece	0:1 (0:0)
02-04-97	Croatia : Slovenia	3:3 (2:1)
30-04-97	Denmark : Slovenia	4:0 (2:0)
30-04-97	Greece : Croatia	0:1 (0:0)
08-06-97	Denmark : Bosnia-Herzegovina	2:0 (0:0)
20-08-97	Bosnia-Herzegovina : Denmark	3:0 (3:0)
06-09-97	Croatia : Bosnia-Herzegovina	3:2 (2:1)
06-09-97	Slovenia : Greece	0:3 (0:0)
10-09-97	Denmark : Croatia	3:1 (3:1)
10-09-97	Bosnia-Herzegovina : Slovenia	1:0 (1:0)
11-10-97	Slovenia : Croatia	1:3 (0:2)
11-10-97	Greece : Denmark	0:0

Europe - Group 2

	P	W	D	L	F	A	Pts
England	8	6	1	1	15	2	19
Italy	8	5	3	0	11	1	18
Poland	8	3	1	4	10	12	10
Georgia	8	3	1	4	7	9	10
Moldova	8	0	0	8	2	21	0

01-09-96	Moldova : England	0:3 (0:2)
05-10-96	Moldova : Italy	1:3 (1:1)
09-10-96	Italy : Georgia	1:0 (1:0)
09-10-96	England : Poland	2:1 (2:1)
09-11-96	Georgia : England	0:2 (0:2)
10-11-96	Poland : Moldova	2:1 (1:0)
12-02-97	England : Italy	0:1 (0:1)
29-03-97	Italy : Moldova	3:0 (2:0)
02-04-97	Poland : Italy	0:0
30-04-97	England : Georgia	2:0 (1:0)
30-04-97	Italy : Poland	3:0 (2:0)
31-05-97	Poland : England	0:2 (0:1)
07-06-97	Georgia : Moldova	2:0 (1:0)
14-06-97	Poland : Georgia	4:1 (2:1)
10-09-97	England : Moldova	4:0 (1:0)
10-09-97	Georgia : Italy	0:0
24-09-97	Moldova : Georgia	0:1 (0:1)
07-10-97	Moldova : Poland	0:3 (0:1)
11-10-97	Georgia : Poland	3:0 (0:0)
11-10-97	Italy : England	0:0

Europe - Group 3

	P	W	D	L	F	A	Pts
Norway	8	6	2	0	21	2	20
Hungary	8	3	3	2	10	8	12
Finland	8	3	2	3	11	12	11
Switzerland	8	3	1	4	11	12	10
Azerbaijan	8	1	0	7	3	22	3

02-06-96	Norway : Azerbaijan	5:0 (2:0)
31-08-96	Azerbaijan : Switzerland	1:0 (1:0)
01-09-96	Hungary : Finland	1:0 (1:0)
06-10-96	Finland : Switzerland	2:3 (1:2)
09-10-96	Norway : Hungary	3:0 (0:0)
10-11-96	Switzerland : Norway	0:1 (0:1)
10-11-96	Azerbaijan : Hungary	0:3 (0:1)
02-04-97	Azerbaijan : Finland	1:2 (0:1)
30-04-97	Norway : Finland	1:1 (0:0)
30-04-97	Switzerland : Hungary	1:0 (0:0)
08-06-97	Finland : Azerbaijan	3:0 (0:0)
08-06-97	Hungary : Norway	1:1 (1:1)
20-08-97	Hungary : Switzerland	1:1 (0:0)
20-08-97	Finland : Norway	0:4 (0:2)
06-09-97	Azerbaijan : Norway	0:1 (0:1)
06-09-97	Switzerland : Finland	1:2 (0:1)
10-09-97	Hungary : Azerbaijan	3:1 (2:0)
10-09-97	Norway : Switzerland	5:0 (0:0)
11-10-97	Finland : Hungary	1:1 (0:0)
11-10-97	Switzerland : Azerbaijan	5:0 (3:0)

Europe - Group 4

	P	W	D	L	F	A	Pts
Austria	10	8	1	1	17	4	25
Scotland	10	7	2	1	15	3	23
Sweden	10	7	0	3	16	9	21
Latvia	10	3	1	6	10	14	10
Estonia	10	1	1	8	4	16	4
Belarus	10	1	1	8	5	21	4

01-06-96	Sweden : Belarus	5:1 (2:0)
31-08-96	Belarus : Estonia	1:0 (1:0)
31-08-96	Austria : Scotland	0:0
01-09-96	Latvia : Sweden	1:2 (0:2)
05-10-96	Estonia : Belarus	1:0 (0:0)
05-10-96	Latvia : Scotland	0:2 (0:1)
09-10-96	Belarus : Latvia	1:1 (0:1)
09-10-96	Sweden : Austria	0:1 (0:1)
09-11-96	Austria : Latvia	2:1 (1:1)
10-11-96	Scotland : Sweden	1:0 (1:0)
11-02-97	Estonia : Scotland	0:0
29-03-97	Scotland : Estonia	2:0 (1:0)
02-04-97	Scotland : Austria	2:0 (1:0)
30-04-97	Latvia : Belarus	2:0 (1:0)
30-04-97	Sweden : Scotland	2:1 (1:0)
30-04-97	Austria : Estonia	2:1 (1:0)
18-05-97	Estonia : Latvia	1:3 (1:0)
08-06-97	Belarus : Scotland	0:1 (0:0)
08-06-97	Latvia : Austria	1:3 (0:0)
08-06-97	Estonia : Sweden	2:3 (0:1)
20-08-97	Estonia : Austria	0:3 (0:0)
20-08-97	Belarus : Sweden	1:2 (1:0)
06-09-97	Latvia : Estonia	1:0 (1:0)
06-09-97	Austria : Sweden	1:0 (0:0)
07-09-97	Scotland : Belarus	4:1 (1:0)
10-09-97	Sweden : Latvia	1:0 (0:0)
10-09-97	Belarus : Austria	0:1 (0:0)
11-10-97	Scotland : Latvia	2:0 (1:0)
11-10-97	Austria : Belarus	4:0 (4:0)
11-10-97	Sweden : Estonia	1:0 (1:0)

Europe - Group 5

	P	W	D	L	F	A	Pts
Bulgaria	8	6	0	2	18	9	18
Russia	8	5	2	1	19	5	17
Israel	8	4	1	3	9	7	13
Cyprus	8	3	1	4	10	15	10
Luxembourg	8	0	0	8	2	22	0

01-09-96	Israel : Bulgaria	2:1 (1:1)
01-09-96	Russia : Cyprus	4:0 (2:0)
08-10-96	Luxemburg : Bulgaria	1:2 (1:2)
09-10-96	Israel : Russia	1:1 (0:0)
10-11-96	Luxembourg : Russia	0:4 (0:2)
10-11-96	Cyprus : Israel	2:0 (1:0)
14-12-96	Cyprus : Bulgaria	1:3 (1:2)
15-12-96	Israel : Luxembourg	1:0 (1:0)
29-03-97	Cyprus : Russia	1:1 (1:1)
31-03-97	Luxembourg : Israel	0:3 (0:1)
02-04-97	Bulgaria : Cyprus	4:1 (3:0)
30-04-97	Israel : Cyprus	2:0 (1:0)
30-04-97	Russia : Luxembourg	3:0 (1:0)
08-06-97	Bulgaria : Luxembourg	4:0 (1:0)
08-06-97	Russia : Israel	2:0 (2:0)
20-08-97	Bulgaria : Israel	1:0 (0:0)
07-09-97	Luxemburg : Cyprus	1:3 (1:1)
10-09-97	Bulgaria : Russia	1:0 (0:0)
11-10-97	Cyprus : Luxembourg	2:0 (0:0)
11-10-97	Russia : Bulgaria	4:2 (2:0)

Europe - Group 6

	P	W	D	L	F	A	Pts
Spain	10	8	2	0	26	6	26
Yugoslavia	10	7	2	1	29	7	23
Czech Rep	10	5	1	4	16	6	16
Slovakia	10	5	1	4	18	14	16
Faroe Islands	10	2	0	8	10	31	6
Malta	10	0	0	10	2	37	0

24-04-96	Yugoslavia : Faroe Islands	3:1 (3:0)
02-06-96	Yugoslavia : Malta	6:0 (3:0)
31-08-96	Faroe Islands : Slovakia	1:2 (0:1)
04-09-96	Faroe Islands : Spain	2:6 (0:1)
18-09-96	Czech Republic : Malta	6:0 (2:0)
22-09-96	Slovakia : Malta	6:0 (3:0)
06-10-96	Faroe Islands : Yugoslavia	1:8 (1:5)
09-10-96	Czech Republic : Spain	0:0
23-10-96	Slovakia : Faroe Islands	3:0 (2:0)
10-11-96	Yugoslavia : Czech Republic	1:0 (1:0)
13-11-96	Spain : Slovakia	4:1 (1:1)
14-12-96	Spain : Yugoslavia	2:0 (2:0)
18-12-96	Malta : Spain	0:3 (0:3)
12-02-97	Spain : Malta	4:0 (2:0)
31-03-97	Malta : Slovakia	0:2 (0:2)
02-04-97	Czech Republic : Yugoslavia	1:2 (1:0)
30-04-97	Malta : Faroe Islands	1:2 (1:0)
30-04-97	Yugoslavia : Spain	1:1 (0:1)
08-06-97	Faroe Islands : Malta	2:1 (2:0)
08-06-97	Yugoslavia : Slovakia	2:0 (1:0)
08-06-97	Spain : Czech Republic	1:0 (1:0)
20-08-97	Czech Republic : Faroe Islands	2:0 (2:0)
24-08-97	Slovakia : Czech Republic	2:1 (1:1)
06-09-97	Faroe Islands : Czech Republic	0:2 (0:2)
10-09-97	Slovakia : Yugoslavia	1:1 (0:0)
24-09-97	Malta : Czech Republic	0:1 (0:1)
24-09-97	Slovakia : Spain	1:2 (0:0)
11-10-97	Malta : Yugoslavia	0:5 (0:3)
11-10-97	Spain : Faroe Islands	3:1 (2:1)
11-10-97	Czech Republic : Slovakia	3:0 (0:0)

Europe - Group 7

	P	W	D	L	F	A	Pts
Netherlands	8	6	1	1	26	4	19
Belgium	8	6	0	2	20	11	18
Turkey	8	4	2	2	21	9	14
Wales	8	2	1	5	20	21	7
San Marino	8	0	0	8	0	42	0

02-06-96	San Marino : Wales	0:5 (0:3)
31-08-96	Wales : San Marino	6:0 (4:0)
31-08-96	Belgium : Turkey	2:1 (2:0)
05-10-96	Wales : Netherlands	1:3 (1:0)
09-10-96	San Marino : Belgium	0:3 (0:2)
09-11-96	Netherlands : Wales	7:1 (4:1)
10-11-96	Turkey : San Marino	7:0 (2:0)
14-12-96	Wales : Turkey	0:0
14-12-96	Belgium : Netherlands	0:3 (0:2)
29-03-97	Wales : Belgium	1:2 (0:2)
29-03-97	Netherlands : San Marino	4:0 (1:0)
02-04-97	Turkey : Netherlands	1:0 (0:0)
30-04-97	Turkey : Belgium	1:3 (1:3)
30-04-97	San Marino : Netherlands	0:6 (0:1)
07-06-97	Belgium : San Marino	6:0 (5:0)
20-08-97	Turkey : Wales	6:4 (3:3)
06-09-97	Netherlands : Belgium	3:1 (1:0)
10-09-97	San Marino : Turkey	0:5 (0:2)
11-10-97	Belgium : Wales	3:2 (3:0)
11-10-97	Netherlands : Turkey	0:0

Reggae, Ronaldo and a French Revolution - France 1998

Europe - Group 8

	P	W	D	L	F	A	Pts
Romania	10	9	1	0	37	4	28
Ireland Rep	10	5	3	2	22	8	18
Lithuania	10	5	2	3	11	8	17
Macedonia FYR	10	4	1	5	22	18	13
Iceland	10	2	3	5	11	16	9
Liechtenstein	10	0	0	10	3	52	0

24-04-96	Macedonia FYR : Liechtenstein	3:0 (1:0)
01-06-96	Iceland : Macedonia FYR	1:1 (0:0)
31-08-96	Liechtenstein : Ireland Republic	0:5 (0:4)
31-08-96	Romania : Lithuania	3:0 (1:0)
05-10-96	Lithuania : Iceland	2:0 (1:0)
09-10-96	Lithuania : Liechtenstein	2:1 (1:0)
09-10-96	Iceland : Romania	0:4 (0:1)
09-10-96	Ireland Republic : Macedonia FYR	3:0 (1:0)
09-11-96	Liechtenstein : Macedonia FYR	1:11 (0:6)
10-11-96	Ireland Republic : Iceland	0:0
14-12-96	Macedonia FYR : Romania	0:3 (0:2)
29-03-97	Romania : Liechtenstein	8:0 (3:0)
02-04-97	Macedonia FYR : Ireland Republic	3:2 (2:1)
02-04-97	Lithuania : Romania	0:1 (0:1)
30-04-97	Liechtenstein : Lithuania	0:2 (0:0)
30-04-97	Romania : Ireland Republic	1:0 (1:0)
21-05-97	Ireland Republic : Liechtenstein	5:0 (3:0)
07-06-97	Macedonia FYR : Iceland	1:0 (0:0)
11-06-97	Iceland : Lithuania	0:0
20-08-97	Liechtenstein : Iceland	0:4 (0:2)
20-08-97	Ireland Republic : Lithuania	0:0
20-08-97	Romania : Macedonia FYR	4:2 (2:0)
06-09-97	Iceland : Ireland Republic	2:4 (1:1)
06-09-97	Liechtenstein : Romania	1:8 (0:6)
06-09-97	Lithuania : Macedonia FYR	2:0 (1:0)
10-09-97	Romania : Iceland	4:0 (2:0)
10-09-97	Lithuania : Ireland Republic	1:2 (0:1)
11-10-97	Iceland : Liechtenstein	4:0 (0:0)
11-10-97	Ireland Republic : Romania	1:1 (0:0)
11-10-97	Macedonia FYR : Lithuania	1:2 (1:0)

Europe - Group 9

	P	W	D	L	F	A	Pts
Germany	10	6	4	0	23	9	22
Ukraine	10	6	2	2	10	6	20
Portugal	10	5	4	1	12	4	19
Armenia	10	1	5	4	8	17	8
N Ireland	10	1	4	5	6	10	7
Albania	10	1	1	8	7	20	4

31-08-96	Northern Ireland : Ukraine	0:1 (0:0)
31-08-96	Armenia : Portugal	0:0
05-10-96	Northern Ireland : Armenia	1:1 (1:1)
05-10-96	Ukraine : Portugal	2:1 (1:0)
09-10-96	Albania : Portugal	0:3 (0:1)
09-10-96	Armenia : Germany	1:5 (0:3)
09-11-96	Albania : Armenia	1:1 (0:0)
09-11-96	Germany : Northern Ireland	1:1 (1:1)
09-11-96	Portugal : Ukraine	1:0 (0:0)
14-12-96	Northern Ireland : Albania	2:0 (2:0)
14-12-96	Portugal : Germany	0:0
29-03-97	Northern Ireland : Portugal	0:0
29-03-97	Albania : Ukraine	0:1 (0:1)
02-04-97	Ukraine : Northern Ireland	2:1 (1:1)
02-04-97	Albania : Germany	2:3 (0:0)
30-04-97	Armenia : Northern Ireland	0:0
30-04-97	Germany : Ukraine	2:0 (0:0)
07-05-97	Ukraine : Armenia	1:1 (1:0)
07-06-97	Ukraine : Germany	0:0

07-06-97	Portugal : Albania	2:0 (1:0)
20-08-97	Ukraine : Albania	1:0 (0:0)
20-08-97	Northern Ireland : Germany	1:3 (0:0)
20-08-97	Portugal : Armenia	3:1 (2:0)
06-09-97	Armenia : Albania	3:0 (0:0)
06-09-97	Germany : Portugal	1:1 (0:0)
10-09-97	Albania : Northern Ireland	1:0 (0:0)
10-09-97	Germany : Armenia	4:0 (0:0)
11-10-97	Portugal : Northern Ireland	1:0 (1:0)
11-10-97	Germany : Albania	4:3 (0:0)
11-10-97	Armenia : Ukraine	0:2 (0:1)

Europe - Play-offs

29-10-97	Croatia : Ukraine	2:0 (1:0)
29-10-97	Ireland Republic : Belgium	1:1 (1:1)
29-10-97	Hungary : Yugoslavia	1:7 (0:5)
29-10-97	Russia : Italy	1:1 (0:0)
15-11-97	Yugoslavia : Hungary	5:0 (3:0)
15-11-97	Ukraine : Croatia	1:1 (1:1)
15-11-97	Belgium : Ireland Republic	2:1 (1:0)
15-11-97	Italy : Russia	1:0 (0:0)

Caribbean/North/Cent. America
Carribbean Zone - 1st Round

24-03-96	Dominican Republic : Aruba	3:2 (1:0)
31-03-96	Aruba : Dominican Republic	1:3 (1:1)
29-03-96	Guyana : Grenada	1:2 (1:0)
07-04-96	Grenada : Guyana	6:0 (2:0)
10-03-96	Dominica : Antigua and Barbuda	3:3 (2:2)
31-03-96	Antigua and Barbuda : Dominica	1:3 (0:1)

Caribbean/North/Cent. America
Carribbean Zone - 2nd Round

04-05-96	Dominican Republic : N.Antilles	2:1 (1:1)
11-05-96	N. Antilles : Dominican Republic	0:0
12-05-96	Haiti : Grenada	6:1 (2:0)
18-05-96	Grenada : Haiti	0:1 (0:0)
12-05-96	Cayman Islands : Cuba	0:1 (0:1)
14-05-96	Cuba : Cayman Islands	5:0 (1:0)
Game played in Grand Cayman		
05-05-96	St Kitts & Nevis : St Lucia	5:1 (4:0)
19-05-96	St Lucia : St Kitts & Nevis	0:1 (0:0)
04-05-96	Puerto Rico : St Vin/Grenadines	1:2 (0:1)
12-05-96	St Vin/Grenadines : Puerto Rico	7:0 (5:0)
14-05-96	Dominica : Barbados	0:1 (0:0)
19-05-96	Barbados : Dominica	1:0 (0:0)
31-03-96	Surinam : Jamaica	0:1 (0:0)
21-04-96	Jamaica : Surinam	1:0 (0:0)

Caribbean/North/Cent. America
Carribbean Zone - 3rd Round

10-06-96	Cuba : Haiti	6:1 (2:0)
30-06-96	Haiti : Cuba	1:1 (1:0)
23-06-96	St Kitts & Nevis : St Vin/Gren	2:2 (1:2)
30-06-96	St Vin/Gren : St Kitts & Nevis	0:0
23-06-96	Barbados : Jamaica	0:1 (0:0)
30-06-96	Jamaica : Barbados	2:0 (1:0)
15-06-96	Dominican Rep : Trin & Tobago	1:4 (0:2)
23-06-96	Trin & Tobago : Dominican Rep	8:0 (6:0)

Caribbean/North/Cent. America
Central American Zone

05-05-96	Nicaragua : Guatemala	0:1 (0:1)
10-05-96	Guatemala : Nicaragua	2:1 (0:0)

02-06-96	Belize : Panama	1:2 (1:0)
09-06-96	Panama : Belize	4:1 (1:0)

Caribbean/North/Cent. America
Semi-final Round - Group 1

	P	W	D	L	F	A	Pts
United States	6	4	1	1	10	5	13
Costa Rica	6	4	0	2	9	5	12
Guatemala	6	2	2	2	6	9	8
Trinidad & Tobago	6	0	1	5	3	9	1

01-09-96	Trinidad & Tobago : Costa Rica	0:1 (0:0)
06-10-96	Trinidad & Tobago : Guatemala	1:1 (1:1)
03-11-96	USA : Guatemala	2:0 (0:0)
10-11-96	USA : Trinidad & Tobago	2:0 (0:0)
17-11-96	Costa Rica : Guatemala	3:0 (0:0)
24-11-96	Trinidad & Tobago : USA	0:1 (0:1)
24-11-96	Guatemala : Costa Rica	1:0 (0:0)
01-12-96	Costa Rica : USA	2:1 (1:0)
08-12-96	Guatemala : Trinidad & Tobago	2:1 (1:1)
14-12-96	USA : Costa Rica	2:1 (1:0)
21-12-96	Costa Rica : Trinidad & Tobago	2:1 (1:1)
21-12-96	Guatemala : USA	2:2 (2:1)

Caribbean/North/Cent. America
Semi-final Round - Group 2

	P	W	D	L	F	A	Pts
Canada	6	5	1	0	10	1	16
El Salvador	6	3	1	2	12	6	10
Panama	6	1	2	3	8	11	5
Cuba	6	1	0	5	4	16	3

30-08-96	Canada : Panama	3:1 (2:0)
08-09-96	Cuba : El Salvador	0:5 (0:1)
22-09-96	Cuba : Panama	3:1 (1:0)
06-10-96	Panama : El Salvador	1:1 (1:0)
10-10-96	Canada : Cuba	2:0 (1:0)
13-10-96	Cuba : Canada	0:2 (0:1)
27-10-96	Panama : Canada	0:0
03-11-96	Canada : El Salvador	1:0 (0:0)
10-11-96	El Salvador : Panama	3:2 (1:1)
01-12-96	El Salvador : Cuba	3:0 (2:0)
15-12-96	Panama : Cuba	3:1 (1:0)
15-12-96	El Salvador : Canada	0:2 (0:0)

Caribbean/North/Cent. America
Semi-final Round - Group 3

	P	W	D	L	F	A	Pts
Jamaica	6	4	1	1	12	3	13
Mexico	6	4	0	2	14	6	12
Honduras	6	3	1	2	18	11	10
St Vincent / Grenadines	6	0	0	6	6	30	0

15-09-96	St Vincent/Grenadines : Mexico	0:3 (0:1)
15-09-96	Jamaica : Honduras	3:0 (2:0)
21-09-96	Honduras : Mexico	2:1 (0:0)
23-09-96	St Vincent/Grenadines : Jamaica	1:2 (0:2)
13-10-96	St Vincent/Grenadines : Honduras	1:4 (0:3)
16-10-96	Mexico : Jamaica	2:1 (1:0)
26-10-96	Honduras : Jamaica	0:0
30-10-96	Mexico : St Vincent/Grenadines	5:1 (2:0)
06-11-96	Mexico : Honduras	3:1 (3:0)
10-11-96	Jamaica : St Vincent/Grenadines	5:0 (2:0)
17-11-96	Honduras : St Vincent/Grenadines	11:3 (5:1)
17-11-96	Jamaica : Mexico	1:0 (0:0)

Caribbean/North/Cent. America Final Round

	P	W	D	L	F	A	Pts
Mexico	10	4	6	0	23	7	18
United States	10	4	5	1	17	9	17
Jamaica	10	3	5	2	7	12	14
Costa Rica	10	3	3	4	13	12	12
El Salvador	10	2	4	4	11	16	10
Canada	10	1	3	6	5	20	6

02-03-97	Mexico : Canada	4:0 (0:0)
02-03-97	Jamaica : United States	0:0
16-03-97	Costa Rica : Mexico	0:0
16-03-97	United States : Canada	3:0 (2:0)
23-03-97	Costa Rica : United States	3:2 (2:1)
06-04-97	Canada : El Salvador	0:0
13-04-97	Mexico : Jamaica	6:0 (3:0)
20-04-97	United States : Mexico	2:2 (1:2)
27-04-97	Canada : Jamaica	0:0
04-05-97	El Salvador : Costa Rica	2:1 (1:0)
11-05-97	Costa Rica : Jamaica	3:1 (1:0)
18-05-97	Jamaica : El Salvador	1:0 (1:0)
01-06-97	Canada : Costa Rica	1:0 (0:0)
08-06-97	El Salvador : Mexico	0:1 (0:0)
29-06-97	El Salvador : United States	1:1 (0:0)
10-08-97	Costa Rica : El Salvador	0:0
07-09-97	United States : Costa Rica	1:0 (0:0)
07-09-97	Jamaica : Canada	1:0 (0:0)
14-09-97	El Salvador : Canada	4:1 (1:1)
14-09-97	Jamaica : Costa Rica	1:0 (0:0)
03-10-97	United States : Jamaica	1:1 (0:0)
05-10-97	Mexico : El Salvador	5:0 (3:0)
12-10-97	Canada : Mexico	2:2 (0:1)
02-11-97	Mexico : United States	0:0
09-11-97	Mexico : Costa Rica	3:3 (2:0)
09-11-97	Canada : United States	0:3 (0:1)
09-11-97	El Salvador : Jamaica	2:2 (0:0)
16-11-97	Costa Rica : Canada	3:1 (2:0)
16-11-97	Jamaica : Mexico	0:0
16-11-97	United States : El Salvador	4:2 (2:0)

Oceania - 1st Round Melanesian Group

	P	W	D	L	F	A	Pts
Papua New Guinea	2	1	1	0	3	2	4
Solomon Islands	2	0	2	0	2	2	2
Vanuatu	2	0	1	1	2	3	1

16-09-96	Papua New Guinea : Sol. Islands	1:1 (1:0)
18-09-96	Solomon Islands : Vanuatu	1:1 (1:1)
20-09-96	Papua New Guinea : Vanuatu	2:1 (0:1)

All games played in Papua new Guinea

Oceania - 1st Round Polynesian Group

	P	W	D	L	F	A	Pts
Tonga	2	2	0	0	3	0	6
Samoa	2	1	0	1	2	2	3
Cook Islands	2	0	0	2	1	4	0

11-11-96	Tonga : Cook Islands	2:0 (1:0)
13-11-96	Samoa : Cook Islands	2:1 (2:0)
15-11-96	Tonga : Samoa	1:0 (1:0)

All games played in Tonga

Oceania - 2nd Round, Group 1

	P	W	D	L	F	A	Pts
Australia	4	4	0	0	26	2	12
Solomon Islands	6	3	1	2	20	21	10
Tahiti	4	0	1	3	2	12	1
Tonga	2	0	0	2	0	13	0

15-02-97	Tonga : Solomon Islands	0:4 (0:1)

Played in Nuku ' alofa

01-03-97	Solomon Islands : Tonga	9:0 (4:0)

Played in Honiara

11-06-97	Australia : Solomon Islands	13:0 (4:0)
13-06-97	Australia : Tahiti	5:0 (2:0)
15-06-97	Solomon Islands : Tahiti	4:1 (2:0)
17-06-97	Solomon Islands : Australia	2:6 (0:3)
19-06-97	Tahiti : Australia	0:2 (0:1)
21-06-97	Tahiti : Solomon Islands	1:1 (1:1)

All games played in Sydney

Oceania - 2nd Round, Group 2

	P	W	D	L	F	A	Pts
New Zealand	4	3	0	1	13	1	9
Fiji	4	2	0	2	4	7	6
Papua New Guinea	4	1	0	3	2	11	3

31-05-97	Papua New Guinea : N. Zealand	1:0 (1:0)
07-06-97	Fiji : New Zealand	0:1 (0:0)
11-06-97	N. Zealand : Papua New Guinea	7:0 (5:0)
15-06-97	Fiji : Papua New Guinea	3:1 (1:0)
18-06-97	N. Zealand : Fiji	5:0 (1:0)
21-06-97	Papua New Guinea : Fiji	0:1 (0:1)

OFC Play-off

28-06-97	New Zealand : Australia	0:3 (0:2)
05-07-97	Australia : New Zealand	2:0 (1:0)

OFC/AFC Play-off

22-11-97	Iran : Australia	1:1 (1:1)
29-11-97	Australia : Iran	2:2 (2:0)

South America - Final Table

	P	W	D	L	F	A	Pts
Argentina	16	8	6	2	23	13	30
Paraguay	16	9	2	5	21	14	29
Colombia	16	8	4	4	23	15	28
Chile	16	7	4	5	32	18	25
Peru	16	7	4	5	19	20	25
Ecuador	16	6	3	7	22	21	21
Uruguay	16	6	3	7	18	21	21
Bolivia	16	4	5	7	18	21	17
Venezuela	16	0	3	13	8	41	3

24-04-96	Venezuela : Uruguay	0:2 (0:0)
24-04-96	Ecuador : Peru	4:1 (0:0)
24-04-96	Colombia : Paraguay	1:0 (0:0)
24-04-96	Argentina : Bolivia	3:1 (2:1)
02-06-96	Ecuador : Argentina	2:0 (0:0)
02-06-96	Uruguay : Paraguay	0:2 (0:1)
02-06-96	Peru : Colombia	1:1 (0:0)
02-06-96	Venezuela : Chile	1:1 (1:1)
06-07-96	Chile : Ecuador	4:1 (1:0)
07-07-96	Colombia : Uruguay	3:1 (2:0)
07-07-96	Peru : Argentina	0:0
07-07-96	Bolivia : Venezuela	6:1 (2:0)
01-09-96	Ecuador : Venezuela	1:0 (1:0)
01-09-96	Bolivia : Peru	0:0
01-09-96	Colombia : Chile	4:1 (3:0)
01-09-96	Argentina : Paraguay	1:1 (1:1)
08-10-96	Uruguay : Bolivia	1:0 (0:0)
09-10-96	Ecuador : Colombia	0:1 (0:0)
09-10-96	Venezuela : Argentina	2:5 (1:1)
09-10-96	Paraguay : Chile	2:1 (1:1)
10-11-96	Bolivia : Colombia	2:2 (2:1)
10-11-96	Peru : Venezuela	4:1 (2:0)
10-11-96	Paraguay : Ecuador	1:0 (1:0)
12-11-96	Chile : Uruguay	1:0 (0:0)
15-12-96	Bolivia : Paraguay	0:0
15-12-96	Venezuela : Colombia	0:2 (0:1)
15-12-96	Argentina : Chile	1:1 (0:0)
15-12-96	Uruguay : Peru	2:0 (2:0)
12-01-97	Venezuela : Paraguay	0:2 (0:1)
12-01-97	Bolivia : Ecuador	2:0 (2:0)
12-01-97	Peru : Chile	2:1 (2:0)
12-01-97	Uruguay : Argentina	0:0
12-02-97	Ecuador : Uruguay	4:0 (2:0)
12-02-97	Bolivia : Chile	1:1 (1:1)
12-02-97	Colombia : Argentina	0:1 (0:1)
12-02-97	Paraguay : Peru	2:1 (2:1)
02-04-97	Bolivia : Argentina	2:1 (1:1)
02-04-97	Peru : Ecuador	1:1 (0:0)
02-04-97	Uruguay : Venezuela	3:1 (1:0)
02-04-97	Paraguay : Colombia	2:1 (1:1)
30-04-97	Colombia : Peru	0:1 (0:0)
30-04-97	Paraguay : Uruguay	3:1 (1:0)
30-04-97	Argentina : Ecuador	2:1 (2:0)
30-04-97	Chile : Venezuela	6:0 (3:0)
08-06-97	Ecuador : Chile	1:1 (1:0)
08-06-97	Uruguay : Colombia	1:1 (1:0)
08-06-97	Venezuela : Bolivia	1:1 (0:0)
08-06-97	Argentina : Peru	2:0 (1:0)
05-07-97	Chile : Colombia	4:1 (3:0)
06-07-97	Paraguay : Argentina	1:2 (0:2)
06-07-97	Peru : Bolivia	2:1 (1:0)
06-07-97	Venezuela : Ecuador	1:1 (0:1)
20-07-97	Bolivia : Uruguay	1:0 (0:0)
20-07-97	Colombia : Ecuador	1:0 (0:0)
20-07-97	Argentina : Venezuela	2:0 (1:0)
20-07-97	Chile : Paraguay	2:1 (1:0)
20-08-97	Ecuador : Paraguay	2:1 (0:1)
20-08-97	Venezuela : Peru	0:3 (0:1)
20-08-97	Uruguay : Chile	1:0 (1:0)
20-08-97	Colombia : Bolivia	3:0 (2:0)
10-09-97	Chile : Argentina	1:2 (1:1)
10-09-97	Peru : Uruguay	2:1 (0:1)
10-09-97	Colombia : Venezuela	1:0 (0:0)
10-09-97	Paraguay : Bolivia	2:1 (2:0)
12-10-97	Ecuador : Bolivia	1:0 (1:0)
12-10-97	Paraguay : Venezuela	1:0 (0:0)
12-10-97	Argentina : Uruguay	0:0
12-10-97	Chile : Peru	4:0 (1:0)
16-11-97	Peru : Paraguay	1:0 (1:0)
16-11-97	Chile : Bolivia	3:0 (2:0)
16-11-97	Uruguay : Ecuador	5:3 (2:1)
16-11-97	Argentina : Colombia	1:1 (0:1)

Chapter 19

The Qualifying Story
Korea/Japan 2002

It is a privilege to play for my Country and I feel very proud to play for my country. I feel very happy, but I didn't know I scored the first goal until after the game finished. I thank God for giving me the opportunity to score the first goal in the World Cup 2002. It is a great honour to go into the history book and it will be a great honour for the national team of Trinidad and Tobago to make it to the World Cup 2002 in Japan.

Original contribution by Trinidad and Tobago's Marvin Andrews

As the sun rose on January 1st 2001 a new millennium dawned. What people expect is hard to tell, but Britain will want to forget the debacle that was its millennium celebrations. The Americans discharged masses of tickertape and the Australians showed us how it should be done - twice, when they repeated the celebrations at the end of 2001. They also showed how sporting events should be organized when, in September 2000, they produced the most spectacular Olympic Games. The sporting prowess on show was breathtaking and having Kylie Minogue sing "Dancing Queen" was a sign of Australia's increasing national self-confidence. Only days later the Paralympians produced 14 days of the most outstanding bravery and achievement.

In 2000 Fidel Castro again embarrassed the USA taking Elian Gonzáles back to his father in Cuba despite the best efforts of opponents. The American presidential election came to a farcical conclusion in the courts of Florida and in Britain the shine seemed to be coming off Tony Blair. "Education, education, education" became "spin, spin, spin", but his lead in the polls was such that a historic second period in office was assured in the June election that had to be delayed as disaster struck the farming community with Foot and Mouth following Mad Cow Disease. Elsewhere, the Middle East crisis simmered away and was brought into stark relief in the most appalling way when terrorists crashed hijacked planes into New York's World Trade Center and the Pentagon. The subsequent attacks against Taliban and Osama Bin Laden positions in Afghanistan are only the immediate consequences of an outrage that has brought great insecurity and potential danger from any number of sources.

It wasn't all bad news. In February 2001 Ellen MacArthur showed great bravery to become the youngest sailor to circumnavigate the globe and mans' ingenuity was celebrated with the 10th anniversary of the Hubble Space Telescope. The world has said "hello" to the Euro, Harry Potter and mobile phones became part of everyday life. England won a cricket test series, Steve Redgrave won his fifth Olympic Gold in Sydney and two suspects in the Lockerbie air disaster went on trial. Saying "goodbye" were sporting legends Sir Stanley Matthews and Don Bradman. Jill Dando was murdered at home, Kirsty MacColl was killed on holiday in Mexico and Damilola Taylor and Victoria Climbié were children who met tragic ends.

AFRICA

Of the 197 nations who entered this World Cup, by 1st December 2001 there were 29 left to join the co-hosts and France when the tournament kicks off on 31st May 2002. The qualifying tournament for the 2002 World Cup began in the Football Confederation, on 4th March 2000 with a match between Trinidad and Tobago and the Dutch Antilles, but the first region to complete was Africa. Here the 50 entrants, including nine first timers, were paired off to play each other over two legs in the first round and the winners placed in five groups of five for the places available. The first games took place on 7th April 2000, one of them involving Tunisia, whose 2-1 defeat of Mauritania set them on the road to the finals. On their way they scored 34 goals, the highest in the region, and the last of them, in their final group game against the Democratic Republic of Congo, was their 125th World Cup goal. They became the second African country to reach that landmark, having been pipped by Nigeria, winners of Group B, who reached it two weeks earlier with the last strike in a 4-0 defeat of Sudan. Cameroon were easy winners of Group A, losing only once, and this was despite having to endure four changes of coach and playing their home games on one of the worst pitches in Africa. It will be the Indomitable Lions' fifth visit to the finals, a new record for an African nation. In the same group was Togo, who achieved two unlucky 13s and ended their tournament with a set of balanced statistics. In all they played ten games, won three, lost three and drew four, scoring 13 and conceding 13. Other qualifiers were South Africa from Group E, going to their second successive finals, and Senegal, who qualified for the first time at the eighth attempt going back to 1970. Definite bad boys of the region, at least to FIFA, were Guinea, whose government fired its football federation. FIFA demanded a reinstatement and expelled them when the government refused. Oddly the team was doing well, having won two and drawn the other of the three group games they had played before they were removed. They were the only team in the group that might have provided a challenge to South Africa.

South Africa's progress to the finals was marred by a terrible tragedy during the away match against Zimbabwe. Whilst being treated for injury after scoring his second goal, Delron Buckley was hit on the head by a plastic bottle thrown from a group of home supporters. Police responded by firing tear gas into all sections of the 60,000 crowd who panicked and stampeded. In the chaos, 13 people were crushed to death and players and supporters collapsed on the pitch, eyes streaming and coughing blood. Once outside the ground, fans were again confronted by tear gas and some started throwing stones at police. President Robert Mugabe blamed supporters of the opposition Movement for Democratic Change, who in turn blamed the police for over-reacting. The referee abandoned the match and awarded a 2-0 victory to South Africa, a decision upheld by FIFA.

Introduced from Britain, football has been played in South Africa since the late 19th century and an FA was set up in 1892. Popular among the black population, football has been held back through the political domination of the whites, for whom rugby and cricket were the preferred sports. The country's first league was won by Orlando Pirates in 1970 and the first cup competition by Wits University in 1978, but the existence of apartheid meant that football remained a backwater sport. FIFA expelled South Africa from the 1966 World Cup and banned them from later competitions until majority rule was introduced. They were readmitted in July 1992 and won their first international against Cameroon that month. Football has gone from strength to strength since and in 1996 South Africa won the African Nations Cup, becoming the first southern African nation to reach the World Cup finals in 1998. Known as "Bafana Bafana", meaning the "Boys", several of the players who featured in France '98 are still around. Among them are Eric Tinkler of Barnsley, Lucas Radebe of Leeds and Quinton Fortune of Manchester United. Other players who add sparkle to the side include Benni McCarthy, Delron Buckley and Phil Masinga.

It is said that Georges Goethe, a photographer from Sierra Leone, first introduced football into Cameroon, giving displays of ball juggling after work in the streets of Douala in the 1920s. The game spread, but as in most African countries in colonial times, progress was initially slow. The first cup competition was won by Oryx Douala in 1956, but it was not until after independence in 1960 that serious national organization happened. That year an FA was set up and in 1962 affiliated to FIFA. Oryx became first league winners in 1961 and revealed the progress of Cameroon football by winning the first African Champions Cup in 1964. Cameroon entered and withdrew from the 1966 World Cup, but the game was

---

Moacyr Barbosa - Brazil

On 7th April 2000 Moacir Barbosa died of an heart attack aged 79. Not many people outside Brazil will remember him, but in certain parts of South America he will never be forgotten or forgiven. He was born on 27th March 1921 at Campinas in the state of São Paulo. He served his time playing locally, before spending 14 years with Vasco da Gama. He became the first black goalkeeper to represent Brazil and appeared in the 1950 World Cup "final", a match every Brazilian expected to win. With the score at 1-1 and ten minutes to go, Barbosa misjudged Gigghia's goalward ball and to this day the Brazilian public have never forgiven him. He was made the scapegoat and his career went down hill. As much as twenty years later, visiting a market, a woman recognized him and said to her boy: "Look at him son. He is the man that made all of Brazil cry." Later still, in 1993 as Zagalo prepared his squad for the World Cup, he had Barbosa turned away from the camp for fear he would bring bad luck. "Under Brazilian law the maximum sentence is 30 years. But my imprisonment has been for 50 years," he said on his 79th birthday. He had a sad end. Clotilde, his wife of 50 years, died in 1997. There were no children and he lived alone with little contact from relatives. One good friend helped out and when Vasco heard of his plight, they gave a monthly £700 grant so he could live in his own flat. At times he would cry and say: "I am not guilty. There were 11 of us."

There is still much sensitivity in Korea about Japan's former occupation and it is unlikely that Emperor Akihito of Japan will travel there during the World Cup.

South Korea managed only 3rd place at the 2000 Asian Cup in Lebanon and coach Hu Jung-mo was dismissed. He was replaced Gus Hiddink, who coached Holland in France '98, whose main brief is ensure they do better than Japan.

Reflecting the cost of living in Japan, the price of tickets for the World Cup is "completely out of the reach of the ordinary fan," as Malcolm Clarke, Chairman of the English Supporters Association complained. "I think the prices are outrageous, they even make the Premier League look like the height of generosity." Tickets are in three categories, with the "behind the goal" C seats the cheapest at £40 for a group game and £200 for the final. About half of the tickets are in the A category, priced between £100 and £500 for the final. In France '98 over half of all tickets cost £25 with the highest priced ticket for the final at £295. FIFA were unmoved by complaints: "The organizers have to make money," a spokesman said. "Japan has 130 million people and they have the money to buy tickets. They are football mad. Japan is the most expensive country in the world and you have to accept that." To that, Mr. Clarke replied: "We think that's appalling. The market might bear the price but it doesn't justify it." Tickets went on sale in February 2001, but those wishing to buy over the Internet needed patience as the site kept breaking down. There was also a row between the hosts over which name would appear first. The official name of the tournament is 2002 FIFA World Cup Korea/Japan, but Japan wanted its name first on tickets sold there.

Guatemala's goalkeeper, Edgar "El Gato" Estrada received telephoned death threats from fans blaming him for elimination from the qualifying tournament. They were defeated 5-2 by Costa Rica in a play-off required because both had finished the semi-final round exactly level.

When FIFA posted the world rankings before the draw for the 2002 tournament there were 202 nations on the list. Head of the table was Brazil, France in second place and the Czech Republic in third. Germany were 5th, England 11th, Scotland 23rd, Ireland 36th, Northern Ireland 80th and Wales 93rd. Montserrat and Anguilla were joint 201st. American Samoa, who had once been as high as 193rd, and Guam were ranked 198th and 200th respectively. One nation was not on the list. Afghanistan have been affiliated to FIFA since 1948 and played in the Olympics that year, but have yet to play a World Cup game.

gaining a surer footing and it was in the late 1970s that Cameroon football began to have its international impact. Cameroon clubs won the African Champions Cup in 1979 and 1980, they made their first World Cup finals in 1982 and won the African Nations Cup in 1984 and 1988. They won it again in 2000 and added the Olympic title. The current squad, widely regarded as being the strongest so far, is captained by West Ham's Rigobert Song, and includes the current African Player of the Year Patrick Mboma of Parma, Marc-Vivien Foe of Lyon and Middlesbrough's Joseph-Desire Job.

Organized football has a much longer tradition in Nigeria, whose FA and cup competition go back to 1945, when the country was still in British hands. The first cup winners were Marine, who along with Lagos Railways, dominated club football in those early years. Nigeria joined FIFA in 1959, the year before independence, entered and then withdrew from the 1966 World Cup and were disqualified from the 1974 tournament following trouble in a match against Ghana. However, since then Nigerian football has grown in prestige. A league was set up and won by Mighty Jets in 1972, and international success came in 1980 with the African Nations Cup. In 1985 they became the first Africans to win a FIFA world tournament when they beat West Germany in the final of the under-17 World Cup. The "Green Eaglets" won it again in 1993, took the African Nations Cup in 1994 and defeated Argentina to lift the Olympic title in 1996, the first African nation to do so. They had beaten Brazil in the semi-final. Among the current crop of players that should ensure a satisfactory showing in 2002 include Arsenal's Nwankwo Kanu, Finidi George of Ipswich Town, Sunday Oliseh and Taribo West.

The surprise of the African tournament was the qualification of Senegal, which until recently has had no football history of any note. An FA was set up in 1960, the year of independence, and the first cup competition was won by Espoir St. Louis in 1961. Senegal joined FIFA in 1962 and withdrew from the 1966 World Cup. They have entered every subsequent tournament. The first league champions were ASC Dairaf in 1970 and since then football had made steady progress, seen by the emergence of Arsenal's Patrick Viera, who was born in Senegal though plays for France. There are some talented individuals in the squad and in Ousseinoh Diouf they have a goal scorer of repute. He scored two hat tricks in the qualifying games, against Algeria and Namibia, and will be ably backed by regulars such as goalkeeper Tony Silva, Khalilou Fudiya, who has played for several French and Belgian clubs, and Henri Camara.

2002 will see Tunisia's third visit to the World Cup finals, a country that has played organized football much longer than some European countries, introduced there by French settlers and administrators. League and cup competitions were first won in 1921, by Racing Club and Avant Garde respectively. It was not long before the Arabs took up the sport and since gaining independence in 1956 Tunisian football has steadily grown in stature. The FA was set up in 1957, joined FIFA in 1960 and entered their first World Cup in 1962. Qualification for the finals did not happen until 1978 when they defeated Mexico to become the first Africans to win a match at that level. Several of the current squad have experience of the finals, playing in France '98, including regular goal scorer Zoubeir Baya, who has played professionally for Freiberg in the German league. Among other players of note are Ziad Jaziri, another talented goal getter, and Sirajeddine Chihi. Goalkeeper, Chokri El-ouaer has recently ended a year long ban for mutilating himself during African Champions League match against Ghana's Hearts of Oak. He claimed his bloodied head was the result of being hit by a missile from the crowd, but he had cut himself in an attempt to get the match abandoned hoping that his club, Esperance Tunis, would be awarded the match by default.

OCEANIA

The only region not guaranteed a place in the 2002 finals was Oceania. Here the ten entrants were placed in two groups, with the Group 1 matches being played in April 2001 in Coff's Harbour and the Group 2 games in Aukland in June. They were won by New Zealand and Australia, who then won the two-legged play-off, only to lose to Uruguay for the last place in the finals. Yet they created the sensation of the group stage and set a new record by scoring 73 goals, one of which was their 200th in the World Cup. In November 2000 Iran's victory over Guam had set a new international scoring record, but six months later Australia hammered in 22 against Tonga to better it. Two days later, on 11th April, they did it again against American Samoa, the tiny Pacific islands colonized respectively over the past 100 years both by Germany and the USA. They must have felt they were in a war when hit by the Soceroos that day. The problem began when FIFA ruled that their players must have American passports, which meant that all first team players, with the exception of goalkeeper Nicky Salapu, could not go to Australia for the qualifying tournament. The under-20 team, who could have deputized were sitting exams, and they had to go with a patched-up team with an average age of 19 and including two 15 year olds. They were no match for an Australian side that, although not at full strength without several of the big names from the Premiership, had enough seasoned pros to take the Samoans apart. They scored the first after ten minutes and the rest of the game was a rout. By half-time they were leading 16-0 and they put away another 15 in the second half, with Archie Thompson setting his own record. Before the game Samoa's devoutly Christian coach, Tunoa Lui, said: "We are asking the Lord to help keep the score down." They had only won one previous international and were ranked 203rd in the world. Overall, they were "whipping boys" of the group, scoring none and conceding 57.

SOUTH AMERICA

The Conmebol qualifying tournament was the simplest of all the regions, being a straight round robin with automatic places going to the top four countries and the fifth having to play-off against the winners of the Oceania region. First to qualify were Argentina, who showed impressive form and whose second goal against Chile in March 2000 was their 200th in the World Cup. Brazil's tournament was disrupted by three changes of coach as Wanderleyt Luxemburgo was replaced by former international Emerson Leão, in turn replaced by Luiz Filipe "Big Phil" Scolari in 2001. They also faced possible elimination after it was discovered that they knowingly fielded overage players in the 1995 and 1999 under-17 World Cups. In December 1999 FIFA decided that a ban would only apply to youth tournaments and Brazil was spared the humiliation of missing a World Cup. They went on to add another first to their famous history in October 2001 when they reached 300 World Cup goals in a 6-1 demolition of Venezuela. Venezuela's victory over Bolivia in June 2000 was only that country's third World Cup triumph in 56 games and nine tournaments. Achieving 100 World Cup goals were Peru, against Chile in March

The preliminary draw for the 2002 tournament took place at the Tokyo International Forum, an impressive building designed by Uruguayan architect, Rafael Viñoly, containing four halls, an information centre, an exhibition hall and conference rooms. It stands on the site of the old Tokyo Metropolitan Government offices, is close to the Imperial Palace and Tokyo Station, in the Ginza shopping district.

FIFA rules allow British players to play for any country that operates inside British jurisdiction. The Cayman Islands consequently made offers to 24 British players to help them qualify for the 2002 World Cup. They received 22 positive replies from players keen to be in the World Cup, far more than needed. "I thought that maybe I would get one out of every three players," said overseas representative, Barry McIntosh. Among those who played for the islands were Wayne Allison of Tranmere Rovers, Ged Brannan of Motherwell, David Barnett of Lincoln City, Martin O'Connor of Birmingham City, Dwayne Plummer of Bristol City, Barry Hayles of Fulham, Neville Roach of Southend United and Neil Sharp of Boreham Wood. They lost to Cuba in the first round.

Kenny Hughes, who has played amateur football for Slough Town, Windsor and Eton and Burnham, represented Anguilla in their first ever World Cup match. He scored their first World Cup goal in the first leg against the Bahamas, but when his money ran out he had to come home and missed the next. He was later offered a professional contract to play in the Bahamas.

The two Malaysian goalkeepers Kamarulzaman Hassan and Azim Azram Abdul Aziz, and striker Khalid Jamlus, stayed out too late at disco and were dropped before the tournament began, throwing preparations into turmoil.

After drawing the vital qualifying game against Algeria, which put them out, Egypt asked FIFA if it could be replayed, claiming intimidation from an hostile Algerian crowd.

2000, and Colombia, against Venezuela in April 2001. Uruguay's game against Venezuela in July 2000 was that nation's 100th World Cup game.

Argentina's performance in the qualifying tournament has been as solid as any, befitting a country with such an illustrious football tradition. British residents in Buenos Aires first introduced the game there in the 1860s. Descriptions exist of locals being intrigued watching them play on the sea front and in 1891 Alexander Hutton, an Englishman, organised a league first won by St Andrews. He became president of the first Argentinian FA in 1893, but it was not long before the locals were playing the game themselves. Progress was rapid and Argentina emerged as a major force in South American football. They won the first unofficial South American championship in 1910, were runners up to Uruguay in a second unofficial staging in 1916 and won it for the first time in 1921. They burst onto the world stage at the 1928 Olympics, adopted professionalism in 1931, when Boca Juniors won the first professional league, and have remained pre-eminent since. Estudiantes de La Plata famously beat Manchester United in the World Club Cup in 1968. The ease with which they qualified for the 2002 finals is testament to the strength of the current squad, many of whom play abroad. Recognized goalscorers include Gabriel Batistuta, Juan Veron, Manchester United's record signing, and Lazio's Hernan Crespo. Diego Simeone and Kily Gonzáles are both players of repute, whilst less well known is the very talented Esteban Cambiasso. They certainly look like being one of the major forces in the summer.

Another team to perform powerfully is Paraguay, whose opening match in the finals against South Africa will be its 100th World Cup game. There has been organized football there since 1906, when Guarani won the league, but Olimpia have emerged as the most successful club. They got to the final of the first Copa Libertadores in 1960, when they were narrowly beaten by Peñarol, and won it in 1979 and 1990. Internationally, Paraguay has lived in the shadows of its neighbours, but there have been moments of success, some of it outstanding. It joined FIFA in 1921 and the next year was beaten into second place in the South American championship by Brazil in a play-off. They have often come second or third, but did not win it until 1953. A second title came in 1979. The most famous player is goalkeeper Chilavert, now with Strasbourg and the only Paraguayan to win the South American Player of the Year Award, though the current line up is among the strongest ever fielded. The lively Nelson Cuevas, who plays in Argentina, is a thrilling prospect and in defence Celso Ayala works tirelessly for the cause. Juan Daniel Caceres is a defender who has hit rich form recently, as had Miguel Caceres up front. Also likely to feature is Newcastle's Diego Gavilan.

Traditionally, Ecuador has been one of South America's weaker teams, having never before qualified for any international competition. An FA was established in 1925 and affiliated to FIFA the following year, but no league competition was established until Emelec won it in1957. Between 1938 and 1975 Ecuador won only eight internationals, but recent signs have been encouraging. In 1990, club side Barcelona got to the final of the Copa Libertadores, beating River Plate in the semi-final and losing narrowly to Olimpia of Paraguay over two legs. In 1993, Ecuador came fourth in the Copa America, as the South American Championship is now called. They failed to make the quarter-finals in this year's championship, but coach, Hernan Dario Gómez, who was recently shot in the town of

Before their first ever World Cup match, the Yugoslav coach of the Seychelles, Vojo Gardasevic, said: "We will play our heart out today and we will not fly the white flag. Our opponents are the favourites on paper, but they will have to sweat if they are to beat us. We have a lot of respect for them but we are not afraid to take them on." A capacity 6,000 crowd saw a 1-1 draw against Namibia.

Before the home tie against Paraguay, the Brazilian coach told his side: "Shoot, shoot, Chilavert has 400 kilos of fat." Roberto Carlos continually insulted the Paraguayan goalkeeper throughout the game and Chilavert attacked him in the centre circle when it ended and police had to intervene. "Chilavert assaulted me, he spat at me," Carlos raged. "He was angry because he lost and he's at the end of his career." "I've always been a big guy," responded Chilavert, "but I'm not too fat to keep playing."

After a brawl in a Prague lap-dancing bar called the Nancy, in which a doorman received a gashed eye and bruising, five Northern Irish players were arrested, spent a night in police cells and missed the plane home. The incident followed a 3-1 defeat and prompted the Irish FA to review their liberal approach to off field behaviour.

Guayaquil, resigned from the job and was then persuaded back, has built up a useful squad. He has a more than useful strike pair in Agustin Delgado and Ivan Kaviedes. Alex Aguinaga is the playmaker and in Edison Mendez and Jorge Guagua have two young players of real potential. They will not be overawed by the World Cup.

Brazil's passage to the finals may not have been easy, but they remain the most famous football nation, with a colourful history stretching back into the 19th century. Its FA was set up in 1914 and affiliated to FIFA in 1923. Sheer size prevented the emergence of a national league, but regional competition has been strong. São Paulo Athletic Club won the first São Paulo State Championship in 1903 and that in Rio was won by Fluminense in 1906, though fully national competitions did not happen until much later. It was in 1959 that Bahia won the first national cup and it was not until 1971 that Athletico Mineiro took the first national championship. Producing a regular crop of outstanding players, Brazilian clubs have enjoyed considerable international success. Vasco da Gama won an initial South American championship organized by Chile's Colo Colo in 1948 and Palmeiros made it to the second Copa Libertadores final in 1962, when they narrowly lost to Peñarol. Santos won the title in 1963, the year after they defeated Benfica in the World Club Cup. The national team has featured regularly in the South American Championship, but with surprisingly little success. Brazil came third in its second, unofficial running in 1916 and took the title in 1919, but there have only been three victories since. The World Cup has been Brazil's stage and despite their collapse in France '98 and recent difficulties, they will be one of the teams to look out for in 2002. Home-based stars like Vasco's Romario and Flamenco's prolific striker, Edilson, are complemented by an array of European-based talent. Italy-based Cafú in defence and Emerson in midfield, will dovetail with Roberto Carlos and Rivaldo, who play in Spain, to make a potentially explosive mix. And, of course, there remains Ronaldo - if he goes.

In the end, Uruguay's 3-0 victory over Australia to reach the finals for the first time since 1990 proved all too easy and ended an uncertain run that saw coach, Daniel Passarella, quit. It is a nation that, like Brazil and Argentina, considers itself the spiritual home of football and where, according to Galeano, there is nobody "who does not consider himself a PhD in football's tactics and strategy". It is an attitude that comes from a long and proud association with the game that goes back into the 19th century. An FA was founded in 1900, the third oldest on the continent, and an amateur league was competed for and won by Peñarol that same year. The first professional league happened in the 1930s and was won again by Peñarol in 1932, who also won the first two stagings of the Copa Libertadores in 1960 and 1961. By this time the glory days of Uruguay's national team had been and gone. Uruguay came second in the first, unofficial South American Championship in 1910, and came first when it took place again in 1916. The first official championship happened in 1917 and was won by Uruguay, but it was in the 1920s that it established itself as the world's greatest football nation. It affiliated to FIFA in 1923 and then took the 1924 Olympics by storm. Further success at the Olympics in 1828 and the World Cup in 1930 effectively meant that the tiny nation were world champions for a decade. Though they declined to enter the next World Cups, success in 1950 only confirmed their pre-eminence. However, Uruguayan football has witnessed a sad decline since and teams have often been more noted for brutality than for their football, but there

The mascots for the World Cup are Nik, Kaz and Ato, aliens from a spiky-headed race known as the Spheriks (spheres), who live in Atmozone and play a version of football called Atmonall. They were dreamed up by Interbrand Co., a London-based company. The English were responsible for the first World Cup mascot, World Cup Willie. Since then there have been Juanito, an urchin boy in a sombrero in 1970, Tip and Tap the West German boys in 1974 and the Argentine Gauchito, in 1978. Spain 1982 had an orange, Naranjito, Mexico 1986 a chilli-pepper called Pique and at Italia '90 there was the headless creation, Ciao. The USA had Shooter the dog, later dropped, and France had Footix the cockerel.

Following Iraq's failure to reach the World Cup finals several high-ranking members of their football federation resigned. One of the few who didn't was the IFF president who just happens to be the son of Saddam Hussain.

has been a revival lately and the current team possesses some gifted individuals. The star of the line up is playmaker, Alvaro Recoba, known popularly as "El Chino", and a man who inspires those around him. Among these colleagues are talented defender, Alejandro Lemba, Richard Morales, the hero against Australia, and Peñarol's Daniel Rodríguez in midfield, whilst up front are noted goal scorers Nicolas Olivera and Malaga's Dario Silva.

ASIA

39 countries entered Asia's qualifying tournament. They were placed in ten groups for the first round and the winners of each were divided into two groups for the second round. The winners of these went automatically to the finals, whilst the two runners up played each other in a play-off to decide who would meet one of the European runners up for a place in the finals. Out of it China and Saudi Arabia gained automatic places, with Iran beating the UAE for the play-off against the Irish Republic. Teams who made their debuts were Mongolia, Laos, who conceded 40 goals and Guam, who let in 35 without reply in only two games. Palestine also made its first appearance in the World Cup since 1938, when it was a British controlled mandate. It did well to achieve second place in its group, but sympathy must go to Syria, whose 40 goals in the first round was the highest at that stage and still not enough to get them into the next. Only the Saudis scored more, with 47, the highest of any of the finalists and Pakistan achieved its first World Cup point in a 3-3 draw against Sri Lanka in May 2001.

2002 will be the first time there have been co-hosts and both claim automatic places. Both have long football histories, the sport getting to Japan through contacts with European nations, especially England, with whom Japan was allied after 1902. An FA was established in 1921 and the first cup competition was won that year by Tokyo FC. Affiliation to FIFA came in 1929 and a year later a national team shared the title at the Far Eastern Games with a 3-3 draw with China. A notable victory over Sweden occurred in the Berlin Olympics, but football was never a major sport in these early years. FIFA membership lapsed between 1945 and 1950 and though international soccer resumed thereafter, Japan gaining third place at the Asian Games in 1951, progress was slow before the 1960s. Kunishige Kamamoto, regarded as the finest Japanese player to date, inspired Japan to third place at the 1968 Olympics, taking some notable scalps on the way and bringing an offer from Germany. He refused to go, knowing that it would lead to a decline in football's popularity, but the game still lagged far behind baseball in the public conscience. It received a boost in the 1970s when the exploits of Yasuhiko Okudera of club Furukawa Denko, cup winners in 1977, accepted an offer from the Bundesliga. Japanese TV began showing German games, albeit in an unusual format with one half showed one week and the second half the next, but the game was being exposed. It began to take off in the 1990s. Japan won the Asian Championship in 1992 and amid massive publicity the J-League was launched in May 1993. Corporate sponsorship enabled players like Zico and Gary Lineker to be brought in to maintain its profile. Qualification for the 1998 finals and the performances of men like Hidetoshi Nakata showed how far the game has progressed. Indeed, French coach Philippe Troussier reckons Japan are one of the top 20 nations in the world and winning the 2002 Asian Cup seems to confirm his opinion. They usually play with a back three in which Ryuzo Moioka is the lynch pin and Yuji Nakazawa provides the pace. The key to their success is midfield where Nakata still shines and Shunsuke Nakamura's ball skills add an unpredictability to proceedings. In Naohito Takahara Japan have a striker of strength, pace and with an eye for goal.

Whilst Korea as a whole has had a chequered history, out of it has emerged the region's strongest football power. The united country lost its independence when Japan began to impose a protectorate in 1905 and it was whilst under Japan's dominion that the Korean FA was set up in 1928. It was not until 1948 that the association was affiliated to FIFA, by which time a separate North Korean FA existed to mirror the country's division into the Communist north and a nominally democratic south. It was far from democratic and suffered three years of terrible war between 1950 and 1953, but emerged from the trauma to send a team to the 1954 World Cup, the first Asian side since 1938 and the first independent Asian nation ever. They won Asian Championships in 1956 and 1960 and in 1970 won the first of their three gold medals at the Asian Games. In March 1985 a 2-0 away victory over Nepal began the most successful World Cup run of any Asian country. Seven wins and one defeat later they qualified for the finals in Mexico and have made it to every subsequent finals since. In that 1985 side was Cha Bum-keun, possibly Korea's most famous player, who featured in the Bundesliga and scored a crucial goal for Bayer Leverkusen in their 1988 UEFA Cup triumph against Español of Spain. He managed the side that went to France in 1998. It was undoubtedly this proud record and their success with the 1988 Olympic Games that brought the honour of co-hosting the current tournament and it is a side that mixes youth with experience that they will field in it. Goalkeeper Lee Woon-jae is strong and agile and has some able defenders in front of him, most notably the combative Lee Lim-saeng, one of the survivors from 1998. Midfield drive is provided by Lee Young-pyo and free kick specialist Park Ji-sung, whilst the pin-up of the squad, Korea's most popular sportsman and one with European experience with Werder Bremen is Lee Dong-gook.

China has been knocking on the door of the World Cup finals since the late 1980s and finally they have made it. It is a country with a longer football history than most would expect, but the game's progress has been hindered by war and political troubles. A Chinese team took part in the first international played in Asia when they played the Philippines in the Far Eastern Games in 1913 and the FA was established in 1924. There was also a rudimentary league, first won by the Hong Kong outfit South China in 1926, but by then the country was heading into the political troubles that would eventually deteriorate into civil war. With a Japanese invasion in 1931 to complicate matters, it is little surprising that the league was not contended in 1932 or from 1934-1946. Tung Hwa and East China was the collective name of the players who won the title in 1947, on the league's resumption, but trouble was not long away. The success of the Communists in 1949 led to a dispute with Taiwan over who should represent China and in 1958 China walked out of FIFA, leaving Taiwan to compete in the World Cup qualifying tournament. They returned to the fold in 1979 and entered the qualifying tournament for 1982. Two years later they achieved runners up spot in the Asian Cup, but it has remained the pinnacle of their achievement. There can be no doubting the passion the Chinese have for the game and the game has taken enormous strides over the past few years. Whilst there is a rawness and inexperience about the team, there is also some considerable talent. Defender Fan Zhiyi has had experience in the English game with Crystal Palace and striker Qi Hong has been a regular goal scorer. Impresive throughout the qualifying tournament has been midfielder Sun Jihai, ably supported by Hao Haidang.

This will be Saudi Arabia's third visit to the World Cup finals in the last four tournaments, a fine tribute to the pace of development of football there. A football federation has been in existence and affiliated to FIFA since 1959, and a cup competition is a year older, being first won by Al Wehda in 1958, but it was in the 1970s that the game began to climb steeply out of the backwoods. Oil wealth enabled vast sums of money to be pumped into developing an infrastructure and foreign experience to be brought in to forge a direction. With a club structure more firmly in place and league was set up and won by Al Hilal in 1977. A vast new stadium was built in Riyadh to match the growing confidence and international honours followed soon after with Asian Championship titles coming in 1984 and 1988. Six years later Saudi Arabia made it to the second round of the World Cup finals in their first visit, with returns in 1998 and 2002. The current line up contains some experienced campaigners and will not be awed by the company. The seemingly ever-present Mohammed Babkr in goal provides a reassuring presence at the back, whilst the midfield bustles with talent. Sami Al Jaber has been playing club football with Wolves and Ahmed Dukhi Al Dossary and Khamis Al Owairan, both of the Al Hilal club, provide imagination and drive. Al Wehda's Obeid Al Dossary is a man with a keen eye for goal and can trouble any defender.

EUROPE

Europe's qualifying tournament was a simple group format, with the teams being divided into nine groups. The winners went straight to the finals, whilst the runners-up and Asia's third placed team were paired off in two-legged play-offs for the other places. Croatia made it to the finals for the second time in two attempts, whilst the highest scorers of the stage were Portugal with 33 goals, providing an impressive goal difference that put them above the Irish Republic to clinch Group Two's top spot. The surprise elimination of the group was that of Holland, who went out despite being Europe's second highest scorers with 30, among which was their 250th World Cup goal against Andorra in October 2001. Also reaching the same landmark were Italy with the final strike in a 4-0 defeat of Lithuania in March and Yugoslavia with their second against Luxembourg in October. When Luxembourg went down 3-0 to Switzerland in September, the first conceded made them the first country to let in 300 World Cup goals, though the region's "whipping boys" proved to be Andorra in their first tournament. Only Liechtenstein failed to score at all - they have now let in 75 goals in two tournaments - and San Marino took its first World Cup point with a 1-1 draw with Latvia in April 2001.

Undoubtedly, the thorniest qualification was that of England, whose challenge got off to a disastrous start with a 1-0 defeat by Germany in October 2000, the saddest possible way to end Wembley's tradition in international football. Coming hot on the heels of a shambolic performance in Euro 2000, it was a painfully poignant low point in Kevin Keegan's time in charge that had begun so promisingly with a 3-1 defeat of Poland on the same turf some 19 months before. Most commentators agreed that Keegan was out of his depth and he resigned. A temporary management was put in place for the match with Finland four days later, but it soon became clear that the target was Sven Goran Eriksson, whose contract at Lazio was due to end. His appointment brought immediate dividends as he went on to engineer five victories in his first five games and an astounding 5-1 victory over Germany in Munich in September 2001, the highest point in England's history since 1966. Nervousness hallmarked England's final two games, but with Germany gaining only a draw against Finland in their final outing, David Beckham's dramatic last-ditch free kick against Greece at Old Trafford secured England's unlikely passage to the finals. In that build up, injury has forced various changes in line up, but some outstanding young talent has emerged to show real promise. Ashley Cole and Rio Ferdinand have both benefited from recent experiences and have the potential to become world-class players, as has Steven Gerard in midfield. Waiting in the wings to join him is Bayern Munich's enigmatic Owen Hargreaves and Blackburn's David Dunn, and in David Beckham and Michael Owen, England have two of the most exciting players in the game.

One of the undoubted favourites for the 2002 title are reigning World and European champions, France. Yet, surprisingly, football was slow to catch on in a country where rugby held sway into the early 20th century. The oldest club was Le Havre, founded in 1872, and it did not have a soccer section until 1892. The early progress of the game was quite anarchic, with several organizations springing up to claim responsibility for it and it was not until the FFF was established after the First World War that some semblance of organization was imposed. A cup competition was played and won by Olympique de Pantin in 1918, but no league existed until the 1930s as football authorities argued about the legality of professionalism. It was finally allowed and Olympique Lille became the first champions in 1933. There have been three glory periods in French football, the first in the 1950s when Stade de Reims dominated the domestic scene, winning five championships between 1953 and 1962 and with the national squad performing heroically in 1958. Reims also reached two European Cup finals, in 1956 and 1959, further than any French side until St Etienne did it in 1976. French football hit a low in the 1960s, but began to revive in the 1980s when Michel Hidalgo rebuilt the national to achieve fourth and third places in 1982 and 1986 and the European Championship in 1984. Club football also revived with Marseille reaching the European Cup final in 1991 and winning it in 1993. Paris Saint-Germain also won the Cup-Winners Cup in 1996 and were runners up a year later. This latter period has been the third of France's glory times, with arguably the greatest of all national teams. The team that performed so brilliantly in 1998 and at Euro 2000 forms the basis of the side will compete in 2002. It is full of charm and vision and not a little eccentricity. At the back is the incomparable Fabien Barthez, defended by stalwarts of the calibre of Bayern Munich's Bixente Lizarazu and Lilian Thuram, but it is in midfield that the team shines. Real Madrid's Zidane and Arsenal's Viera are sublime in their vision and majestic in their execution, whilst Thierry Henry is one the most feared and respected attackers in the game.

Football in Russia has mirrored the country's political past, but has a long and often proud tradition. The Russian FA was set up in 1912, but the game was already over 30 years old by then. It quickly became popular among students and in the military academies and a league was established in Moscow in 1901. Regional leagues sprang up across the Czar's domains over the next few years and there was confidence enough to enter a national team for the 1912 Olympics, against which Gottfried Fuchs equaled the international scoring record that stood until 2001. The turmoil that followed the 1917 revolutions gave little opportunity for sporting development, though Stalin saw clearly the propaganda value of a game of popular appeal and it was in the 1930s that a more structured approach was adopted and some of the country's better known clubs set up. The Soviet league and cup were first won in 1936 by Dinamo Moscow and Lokomotiv respectively. Moscow teams dominated the league until 1961, when Dinamo Kiev took the title, though Zenit Leningrad took the cup in 1944. In 1945 Dinamo Moscow thrilled British crowds with a goodwill tour that saw them draw 2-2 with Chelsea, hammer Cardiff City 10-1, beat an Arsenal side that guested Stan Matthews and Mortensen and then draw a very physical match against Rangers. During the Cold War that followed, Soviet teams took little part in international sport, but the death of Stalin brought an end to the isolation and the USSR won the gold medal at the 1956 Olympics. They won the first European Championship in 1960 and have been three times runners up since. Soviet clubs also emerged onto the European scene at roughly the same time and in 1975 Dinamo Kiev won the Cup-Winners Cup. The collapse of Communism in 1990 saw the Soviet Union enter the 1992 European Championship as the Commonwealth of Independent States, but since then Russia has re-emerged as a nation in its own right. Theirs has been a qualifying tournament noted more for steadiness than fireworks, but Yegor Titov and Vladimir Beschastnykh, both of Spartak Moscow, have been regularly finding the target. Defender Dmitri Khokhlov and goalkeeper Rouslan Nigmatullin have both been catching the eye with efficient performances.

22 Men and a Bag of Wind

Like Russia, Portugal has a long and proud football history, with the game being introduced there by the British and the first official club game being played as early as 1888. Benfica was founded in 1904, an initial league in 1909 and the FA in 1914, though fully organised competition came later with a cup competition won by FC Porto in 1922. Portugal affiliated to FIFA in 1923 and a first league championship was won, also by Porto, in 1935. That Portuguese club football has always done better than its national side is seen in the fact that clubs have had their name on international trophies whilst the national team, though coming close, has not. The 1960s was one of the finest decades for Portuguese football, with Benfica taking the European Cup in 1961 and 1962, reaching two other finals, second spot in the World Club Cup in 1961 and with Sporting taking the European Cup-Winners Cup in 1964. It was also the decade that the national team reached its highest World Cup placing in its first finals. Since then the national teams have often flattered to deceive. They reached the semi-finals of the European Championship in 1984, but the current squad of players is one of the finest ever assembled. It is based around the crop that won the Under-20 World Youth Cup in 1989 and 1991. Among those who featured in either or both of those victories were Jorge Couto, João Pinto, Milan's Rui Costa and Real Madrid's Luis Figo, the 2001 World Player of the Year, all men who took Portugal to the semi-finals of the 2000 European Championships. When they play alongside men like Inter's Sergio Conceicao and Nuno Gomes, the blend is truly potent.

Denmark has one of the oldest traditions of football outside the UK, with recorded matches going back as far as the 1870s and an international record as old as the 1896 Olympics. Denmark was one of FIFA's founding members and continued to play in the Olympics until the issue of professionalism caused their withdrawal in 1924. The continuation of amateur status long after the first league title was won by KB Kobenhavn in 1913 was one of the chief bars on the game's development. Yet the power of Danish football in those early years is clearly seen in the case of Nils Middleboe, England's first overseas player, who played for Chelsea from 1913 to 1920. A cup competition was won by AGF Aarhus in 1955 and it was soon after that Danish football began to slowly emerge from the backwaters. The bronze medal was won at the 1960 Rome Olympics and in 1964 they came third in the European Championships. Further progress was made in the 1980s when, under the coach Sepp Piontek, the "Danish Dynamite" made it to the semi-finals of the European Championships in 1984 and to their first World Cup finals in 1986. This was a team based on the attacking prowess of men like Brian Laudrup, but once new coach Richard Moller Nielsen added a reliable defence, the improvement was obvious and Denmark achieved its greatest moment with the European title in 1992 with a victory over Germany. Since then the highest achievement has been the quarter-final defeat by Brazil in 1998, but after the ignominy of Euro 2000, it has been a revitalized Danish team that took the field for the recent qualifiers. In Schalke's Ebbe Sand they have one of Europe's most prolific goal scorers and whilst Jon Tomasson of Feyenoord and Dennis Rommedahl may not have the same consistency, they present an attack that will need some watching. Everton's Thomas Gravesen is a midfielder of talent.

Another country with a long football history is Sweden. The league championship was first won in 1896 by Orgryte, Sweden was a founder member of FIFA and has a long record of participation in the Olympic Games going back to 1908. For much of its history, Swedish football was played at only amateur status, but it was still able to set a fine tradition. Third place was achieved at the 1938 World Cup finals and whilst the rest of Europe fretted over World War Two, neutral Sweden set up a domestic cup competition that was won by Helsingborg in 1941. The continuation of domestic football during the war may have been a factor in Sweden's only major international title to date, the 1948 Olympic gold medal, but there has been much since to distinguish its football. Coach George Raynor's achievements of the 1950s were outstanding, beginning with a third place at the 1950 World Cup and finishing with the glory of 1958. The exploits of 1974 apart, the next years were modest in comparison for the national team, whilst club football enjoyed greater success. Malmö reached the final of the European Cup in 1979, being piped by Brian Clough's Nottingham Forest and IFK Gothenburg have proved Sweden's doughtiest campaigners, winning the UEFA Cup in 1982 and 1987 and getting to the semi-final of the European Cup in 1986. IFK have made several appearances in the Champions League since, getting to the quarter-finals in 1994, but by then the national team had enjoyed a mini-revival, attaining third place at the 1994 World Cup. Performance at Euro 2000 was disappointing and much more is expected from a squad that is unbeaten in the qualifying stage and led by the excellent Henrik Larsson up front. Other players of pedigree include Kennet Andersson, now with Fenerbahçe, and Arsenal's mercurial Freddie Ljungberg.

Although football has been played there since the start of the 20th century, until 1919 the territory that makes up Poland was divided between Russia, Germany and Austria-Hungary. When the country was reconstituted after World War One, an FA was immediately set up and affiliated to FIFA two years later in 1923. A loose championship was won by Cracovia in 1921 and the first running of the Polish cup was won by Wisla Krakow in 1926, but those early years were years of war and internal disturbance and organized football was difficult to establish. The first national league was won by Wisla in 1927, though a cup competition was not resumed until Unia Chorzow won it in 1951. By then, following the war time Nazi occupation, the league had been resumed and won by Polonia Warsaw in 1946 and the Communists were in power. Under the Communists football hardly flourished until Gornik Zabrze broke briefly onto the European scene in 1970, to be beaten by Manchester City in the final of the European Cup-Winners Cup. It was the only time a Polish club made any impact abroad until Legia Warsaw made the semi-finals of the Cup-Winners Cup in 1991 and the quarter-finals of the Champions League in 1996. At the defensive heart of that Gornik side was Jerzy Gorgon, who played a significant part in the glory years of Polish international football that followed, beginning in 1972 when two goals against Hungary from another stalwart of those years, Kazimiercz Deyna, gave them the Olympic title. In four visits to the World Cup finals in a row, the Poles achieved two third place spots, though since 1986 times have been lean. The present outfit shows much more of the promise of the past. Liverpool's Jerzy Dudek has developed a fine reputation and in front of him Kaiserslautern's Tomasz Klos is a sound defender. Radoslaw Kaluzny is a regular scorer, whilst undoubted pride of the attack is the "Black Pearl", Nigerian-born Emmanuel Olisadebe, who plies his craft with Panathinaikos.

Although Croatia has existed only a short time, it has built itself a formidable reputation as a football nation. When its FA was set up in 1912 it was still part of the Austro-Hungarian Empire. In 1919 it was incorporated in to the Kingdom of Yugoslavia, where the spirit of Croatian football revealed itself in the fact that in the years before the Second World War Croatian teams won the Yugoslav league ten out of 17 times, the first of these champions being Gradanski Zagreb in 1923. When the Nazis gave Croatia a brief spell of independence during World War Two, a separate league operated for the first time and was each time won by Gradinski. After the war, Croatia once more became part of Yugoslavia and its teams continued to thrive in the reconstituted federal league and new cup competition. Europe, too, proved fertile ground for the Croats with Dinamo Zagreb reaching the semi-final of the Cup-Winners Cup in 1961, the semi-final of the Fairs Cup in 1966 and winning it in 1967 and Hadjuk Split reaching the last four of the Cup-Winners Cup in 1973 and the UEFA Cup in 1984. However, it has been since independence that the impact has come. Domestically, Croatia Zagreb and Hadjuk have ruled the roost, the latter reaching the Champions League quarter-finals in 1994, whilst the national team reached a similar stage at Euro '96, its first international tournament. In France '98 it did even better and it has now achieved its second World Cup qualification at its second attempt. National pride alone should ensure a reasonable showing, especially when combined with skill and determination. Croatia has both in plenty. Several of the current squad are well known to the English game, with Alen Boksic playing at Middlesbrough and Bosko Balaban at Aston Villa. Both are noted strikers, whilst Robert Posinecki, now of Portsmouth, has wide experience. Real Madrid's Robert Jarni is a dogged defender.

In 1898 Genoa won a tournament that contained only four teams and was played out in a single day. Doing so, it became Italy's first league champions. Italy's FA joined FIFA in 1905 and in 1912 took part its first international tournament, being put out of the Stockholm Olympics by Finland in the preliminary round. It was poor fare, but from such humble beginnings has grown one of the mightiest football pedigrees of any country. By the 1930s Vittorio Pozzo had forged one of the greatest international teams, winning two World Cups and the 1936 Olympics, and Bologna was able to challenge the stranglehold of the central Europeans on club football when it captured the Mitropa Cup in 1935. After the Second World War, the game went from strength to strength to flower in the late 1950s and 1960s. AC Milan reached the final of the European Cup in 1958, winning it in 1963 and Internazionale followed in 1964 and 1965. From then it was not until 1970 that an Italian team failed to reach at least the semi-finals, though surprisingly Juventus did not win the cup until the Heysel Stadium disaster of 1985. Fiorentina reached the first two finals of the Cup-Winners Cup, which Milan won in 1968, and Roma won the Fairs Cup in 1961. Club success has been regular ever since, though the national team has not quite had the success fans demand. The European title came after a replay in 1968 and the World Cup in 1982, but on only three further occasions have the team featured in the minor places: second in the World Cup in 1994, third in the European championships in 1980 and second in 2000. As with previous World Cup squads, the current line up is brimming with talented individuals, but there is always the potential to slip up. Goalkeeper Francesco Toldo has a considerable reputation and in Roma's Francesco Totti and Alessandro Del Piero of Juventus, Italy have two of the best strikers in the world. Paolo Maldini and midfielder Filippo Inzaghi are both men who can turn a game with one crisp, clever ball.

22 Men and a Bag of Wind

Spain is another country whose club success has not been matched by its international team. Football has been played there since the late 19th century and a first organized cup competition was won by Vizcaya Bilbao in 1903. There were Spanish representatives at FIFA's inaugural meeting, though an FA was not set up until 1913. By the time that Barcelona won the first league title in 1929, Spain had made its first inauspicious forays into international competition in the Olympic games of the 1920s. Though they became the first team from outside the UK to beat England in 1929, Spanish football made little impact before the Second World War. It was in the 1950s that Spanish club football became the force it remains, when Real Madrid won the first five European Cups between 1956 and 1960, adding the World Club Cup by defeating Peñarol in 1960. With Barcelona and Valencia taking three out the first four Fairs Cup titles between 1958 and 1962 (the competition was not an annual event then) and Athletico Madrid the Cup-Winners Cup in 1962, Spanish clubs were the dominant force in Europe at the time. It would have been virtually impossible to maintain such a strangle hold on European competitions, given the growing strength of football in other countries, but Spanish clubs continue to remain one of the standards by which others judge themselves. The national team has been unable to match this proud tradition. It has come first and second in the European Championship in 1964 and 1984 respectively, but has only managed fourth place in the World Cup in 1950. Much will be expected of the present squad and it will do well if it the team performance matches the cumulative potential of the individuals in it. Sergi, Gaizka Mendieta and Luis Enrique are players who can set the world alight with their intuitive and sublime skills, whilst up front Raúl and Pedro Munitis of Real Madrid can wreak havoc with the best defenders.

Although undefeated, qualification came through the European play-offs for Slovenia, a country that has had an FA since 1920, but which has only recently enjoyed independence. Its football made little telling impact on the domestic Yugoslav competitions and it is only since independence that its national identity has been able to shine through. It joined FIFA in 1992, the year that Olimpija Ljubljana became its first league champions and Branik Maribor won its first cup competition, though its clubs have yet to make an impact internationally. A more accurate gauge of the growing strength of its football has been the gradual emergence of its national team, keen like its neighbour, Croatia, to establish itself. Early forays in competition brought lean results, in the qualifying stages of Euro '96 and France '98, though it did make the finals of Euro 2000, where a thrilling 3-3 draw with rivals Yugoslavia showed what its players are capable of. Overcoming Romania to reach the current finals is also testament to a team that coach, Srecko Katanec, has moulded well. Its star is Benfica's striker Zlatko Zahovic, whose goals have been crucial, but in men like midfielders Ales Ceh and Miran Pavlin the Slovenes have solid performers. Milenko Acimovic, is another who played with consistency throughout their run in.

One of the trickiest qualification play-offs was that of the Irish Republic over Iran, whose Islamic authorities had to bend the rule that barred women from the stadium to allow 300 traveling Irish girls in. It was there to protect the modesty of women from the bad language used by men at matches, but since the Irish would not understand Farsi, they could not be offended by the swearing. The 1-0 defeat was enough to ensure a third appearance in the finals for a nation with the longest World Cup history of any in the British Isles. Football is long established in Ireland, but its separate identity only came after independence from Britain in 1921. A separate FA was set up that year, league and cup competitions set up and won by St James Gate in 1922 and affiliation to FIFA came in 1923. The Free State, as it was known then, was still bound by legal ties to the British Crown, a situation much resented by some section of Irish opinion, and any opportunity to show its independence was used. So, when Britain did not enter the 1924 Olympic Games, an Irish team did and got to the quarter-finals. Similarly, the Irish have entered every World Cup since 1934. The Republic has also provided a long string of professionals to grace the English, Scottish and other leagues, but it only emerged as a force in international football after the appointment of Jack Charlton as coach. He led them to the 1988 European Championship and the World Cup finals in 1990, when they reached the quarter-finals, and 1994. That year he was replaced by Mick McCarthy and the team has since been rebuilt. Its mainstay is undoubtedly Roy Keane, but its talent does not end there. Shay Given has matured into a superb goalkeeper and Blackburn's Damien Duff and Leed's Robbie Keane are both players who can turn a game. Consistently solid are men like Matt Holland and Mark Kinsella and there will be few who relish the prospect of meeting the Irish.

Turkey's play-off qualification is another step along a road that has since the country take remarkable strides in recent years. It also has a long football history, though in the early years of the last century football had to be played in secret to avoid the disapproving interference of the Moslem authorities. The Young Turk Revolt of 1908 brought to power a government with a more modern outlook and football could emerge from the shadows. It was in these years that the several of the clubs that dominate the present domestic scene were established. This trend continued under the government of Kemal Attaturk in the 1920s and an FA was set up and affiliated to FIFA in 1923, in time for Turkey to take part in its first international competition, the 1924 Olympic Games. That was the year that Besiktas became the first national championship, but it was not until 1960 that the league was put on a proper footing and a host of foreign coaches brought in to develop the game. A cup competition followed in 1963, won by Galatasaray. Turkey competed in the 1954 World Cup finals, but its greatest contribution to international football has been recent. Galatasaray reached the semi-final stage of the 1994 European Cup and Turkish teams have featured consistently since, whilst the national team got to the finals of Euro '96, and progressed to the quarter-finals in 2000. The current team is built around a very solid set of players of proven value and experience, among whom are goalkeeper, Rüstü Reçber of Fenerbahçe Tugay Kerimoglu and Alpay Ozalan, who both play in the English league. Muzzy Izzet is another well known in England, whilst Inter's Hakan Süker is a prolific goal scorer.

Germany's recent international football has had its low points, but its defeat of Ukraine to get to the finals show the folly of writing off a country with such a massive history. Its FA was founded in 1900 and became a founder member of FIFA, by when regional leagues had been set up with a play-off system to decide the national champions. The honour first went to VfB Leipzig in 1903. A cup competition was not launched until the Nazis were in power and its first winner was Nurnberg. Eintracht Frankfurt reached the final of the European Cup in 1960, but it was after the formation of the Bundesliga in 1963 (first won by IFC Köln in 1964) that German clubs have been able to assert themselves in Europe. Borussia Dortmund beat Liverpool in the 1966 European Cup-Winners Cup and in 1974 Bayern Munich became Grmany's first European champions. Bayern won the title again in the next two seasons and won the World Club Cup in 1976. Success has been regular since. The national team's progress has followed a similar pattern. It first entered international competition in 1912, when Gottfried Fuch's marvelous performance took his team to the semi-final of the consolation tournament, but times were relatively lean until the country was divided after World War Two. Having missed the World Cups of 1930 and 1950, the triumph of 1954 was the beginning of a success that has set Germany aside as one of the great football nations. It took its first European Championship in 1972 and has won it twice since and been second once. The 2000 European campaign was a disaster by German standards, but the team has shown great fortitude to get to the 2002 finals. There can be no doubting the class of some of its members. Bayern's Oliver Kahn is a fearless goalkeeper, whilst Liverpool's Dietmar Hamann and Thomas Linke are both defenders of quality. Mehmet Scholl and Carsten Jancker are both men with proven goal scoring records and Michael Ballack is a promising young talent. Altogether, German teams have competed in the World Cup under four different names and have notched 199 games between them. Of these they have lost only 39 and have scored 458 goals.

Belgium is another country with a long football past, with an FA founded in 1895 and being a founder member of FIFA. It has had a league competition since FC Liège won it in 1896 and a cup competition was first won by Racing CB in 1912. One of the oldest international fixtures outside the UK is that between Belgium and France, which goes back to 1904, a 3-3 draw, though it was not until 1920 that Belgium first competed in the Olympic Games. The game's development was held up by the lack of professionalism and it was not until the 1950s that any significant progress was made. Standard Liège got to the semi-final of the European Cup in 1962 and Brugge went one better in 1978, though no Belgian side has won it yet. More successful have been forays into the Cup-Winners Cup, which Anderlecht won twice and came second once between 1976 and 1978. Anderlecht also won the Fairs Cup in 1970. The national team has won no major honours, though it came third in the European Championships in 1972 and second in 1980. Its best World Cup placing was fourth in 1986, but this is Belgium's sixth successive visit to the finals and if the players reach their potential they can do well. Two of the squad's Schalke players, Emile Mpenza and "Mr 1,000 Volts" Marc Wilmots, are both men with tremendous pedigrees and Wesley Sonck of Racing Ghent is a young striker who is receiving critical acclaim in Belgium. Eric Deflandre is a steady defender and Geert de Vlieger a goalkeeper of note.

CARIBBEAN, NORTH AND CENTRAL AMERICA

The Football Confederation provided the most complicated qualifying tournament of all the regions. In the preliminary phase, the six smaller Central American states were divided into two groups, the winners of which went into the semi-final round and the runners up into inter-zone play-offs. Meanwhile the Caribbean entrants were put in three groups to play two-legged knock outs. The eventual winners of each group went into the semi-final whilst the runners up also went into the inter-zone play-offs. Canada came in at this stage to join those runners up in three play-offs. Costa Rica, Jamaica, Mexico and the USA had automatic places in the semi-finals, where the eight survivors from the earlier stages joined them. They were divided into three groups and the top two teams in each went into the final round, a round robin sending the top three to the finals. The region provided the first game of the tournament and in it Marvin Andrews scored its first goal, which was also the first World Cup goal of the new millennium. Tragedy blighted Jamaica's progress, when Steve Malcolm, winner of 76 caps, was killed in a car crash near Montego Bay following a friendly against Bulgaria in 2001. Hull City's Theodore Whitmore was injured in the same accident. The players were then finger printed and had to pay £100 bond before they were allowed to enter Mexico for their game in the final round, the Mexican authorities being fearful of possible Yardie problems. More fortuitously, the 1-1 draw with Honduras in April 2001 stretched an unbeaten home run to 50 games. Mexico's own 20 year unbeaten home run in the World Cup came to an end in June 2001 with a 2-1 defeat by Costa Rica, but they did score their 300th World Cup goal in a 4-0 home victory over Jamaica in March. The USA's home game against Honduras in September was that country's 100th World Cup game.

Much has already been said about the USA's World Cup past, a country that has known club football since 1862 when the Boston club, Oneida, became the oldest outside England. A Soccer Federation was established and affiliated to FIFA in 1913 and a national cup competition was staged and won by New York's Brooklyn Field Club in 1914. Entry into its first international tournament came in 1924 when a team was sent to the Olympic Games. A 2-0 defeat of Estonia saw them into the second round, where a hat trick from Uruguay's Pedro Petrone sunk them. Disaster struck in Amsterdam four years later, when they had the misfortune to come across a rampant Argentina in the first round and went down 11-2. Despite brief sparkles in 1930 and 1950, football at both club and international levels went downstairs for a while and the USA did not have an international team to send to the inaugural North American Championship in 1947. Instead they were represented by Ponta Delgada of Fall River, Massachusetts and roundly trounced. Club football began a revival in 1967 when the North American Soccer League was set up. Backed by huge corporate sponsorship, it was able to attract some of the biggest names from Europe and South America until its collapse in the 1980s. It was replaced by regional soccer leagues and it was not until 1996 that a nationwide league was reconvened, with Major League Soccer, won first by DC United. By this time American international soccer was more firmly established. Coach Bora Milutinovic steered the side to its first international success in 1991 with a penalty shoot-out victory over Honduras in the CONCACAF Championship and Steve Sampson took them to the semi-finals of the Copa America in 1995. Since then, third place in the CONCACAF Championship in 1996, reaching the final in the competition in 1998, after beating Brazil in the semi-final, and qualification for the 1998 World Cup show the steady progress of the national side. Sampson resigned as coach following failure in 1998, but new coach Bruce Arena, the man behind DC United's success, has seen qualification for a fourth finals series in succession to confirm the recent trend. The success has been based around the sturdy midfield play of captain Claudio Reyna, arguable the only world-class player in the squad. Yet, there is solidity in other areas, from Kasey Keller and Blackburn's Brad Friedel in goal, through Carlos Llamosa and Jeff Agoos in defence, to the goal scoring talents of Earnie Stewart and Joe-Max Moore up front.

Costa Rica will be making its second appearance in the World Cup finals, a surprising statistic considering that they have been one of the region's stronger sides. There has been a football federation since 1921, the year of its affiliation to FIFA, and its international football has flourished, at least regionally, since the 1940s. Costa Rica won ten CONCACAF Championship titles between 1941 and 1989, with success being enjoyed at club level as well. In 1986 Liga Deportiva Alajuelense became the first side from the tiny republic to win the CONCACAF Champions Cup and further titles came in 1994 with CS Cartagines and 1995 with Deportivo Saprissa. Bora Milutinovic was the inspiration behind Costa Rica's progress into the second round of the World Cup in 1990 and their good standing meant that they did not enter the qualifying tournament for 2002 until its semi-final stage. Here it began badly with a 2-1 defeat by Barbados, who went on to lose all their other games, but a change of management steadied the ship. Out went one Brazilian, Gilson Nunez, in came another, Alexander Guimaraes, and the team began to realize its latent potential. The unorthodox goal scoring exploits of Manchester City's Paulo Wanchope have been instrumental in its success, but this is far from being a one-man show. Between the posts is the eccentric, but talented Erick Lonnis and propping up the defence is captain, Gilberto Martínez, a man with a keen eye for the game. The heart of the team is a midfield that combines the hard work of Mauricio Solis and Ronald Gómez with the skill of Roy Myers and Wilmer López. Still around and still troubling defences is Hernán Medford, a veteran of the 1990 squad.

The real powerhouse of Central American football has been Mexico, where there has been organized football since Orizaba Athletic Club first won the championship in 1903. A cup competition soon followed, won by Pachuca Athletic club in 1908. A FA was formed in 1927 and affiliated to FIFA in 1929, though a Mexican team did compete in the 1928 Olympic Games, going down 7-1 to Spain in the first round and 3-1 to Chile in the consolation tournament. International football in the region between the 1930s and 1950s did not benefit from the existence of rival football authorities jealously guarding their own patches and Mexico suffered the consequences. It was after the Caribbean, North and Central American federations came together to form CONCACAF in the early 1960s that affairs became more settled and Mexican football could reveal its merits. Guadalajara won the first CONCACAF Champions Cup in 1962 and Monterrey won the second staging of the CONCACAF Cup-Winners Cup in 1993, with Necaxa taking it in 1994. On the international scene, Mexico has done well in local competitions and won both stagings of the North American Championships in the 1940s. It did not feature in the placings in the first CONCACAF Championship in 1963, but won the title in its second in 1965. Mexican clubs and national teams have regularly done well since and in 1993 Mexico was invited to compete in the Copa America, when it took second place losing in the final to Argentina. Only twice since 1950 has Mexico failed to qualify for the World Cup finals and whilst there has been much swapping and changing in the qualifying tournament, they will field some doughty campaigners. Defender Claudio Suárez, nicknamed the "Emperor", has a wide local following, whilst Luis Hernández and Alberto Aspe in midfield have solid reputations. Players to watch up front include Victor Ruiz and the striker Jared Borguetti.

THE DRAW

The Draw for the 2002 World Cup finals took place in Busan, in South Korea, on 1st December 2001. The ceremony attempted to present a pageant of colour and glamour to raise the excitement and set the tone of the coming tournament, but a mixture of western opera, oriental pop music and traditional culture rendered it a curious affair. The formality that often accompanies official events in Japan and Korea was very much in evidence and the nervousness of the presenters and VIPs made it feel as if everyone concerned expected something to go wrong. It didn't, though the draw itself was made long and drawn out by the rules imposed by FIFA in its attempt to limit the possibilities and maximize its appeal, such as that which said China had to play in Korea.

Group A: (Korea):   FRANCE - SENEGAL - URUGUAY - DENMARK

Group B: (Korea):   SPAIN - SLOVENIA - PARAGUAY - SOUTH AFRICA

Group C: (Korea):   BRAZIL - TURKEY - CHINA - COSTA RICA

Group D: (Korea):   SOUTH KOREA - POLAND - USA - PORTUGAL

Group E: (Japan):   GERMANY - SAUDI ARABIA - REPUBLIC OF IRELAND - CAMEROON

Group F: (Japan):   ARGENTINA - NIGERIA - ENGLAND - SWEDEN

Group G: (Japan):   ITALY - ECUADOR - CROATIA - MEXICO

Group H: (Japan):   JAPAN - BELGIUM - RUSSIA - TUNISIA

Statistics - Korea/Japan 2002

QUALIFYING ROUNDS

Africa - 1st Round

08/04/00	Guinea-Bissau : Togo	0:0
23/04/00	Togo : Guinea-Bissau	3:0 (1:0)
07/04/00	Mauritania : Tunisia	1:2 (0:0)
22/04/00	Tunisia : Mauritania	3:0 (2:0)
09/04/00	Benin : Senegal	1:1 (1:1)
23/04/00	Senegal : Benin	1:0 (0:0)
09/04/00	Gambia : Morocco	0:1 (0:0)
22/04/00	Morocco : Gambia	2:0 (2:0)
09/04/00	Cape Verde Islands : Algeria	0:0
21/04/00	Algeria : Cape Verde Islands	2:0 (2:0)
08/04/00	Botswana : Zambia	0:1 (0:0)
22/04/00	Zambia : Botswana	1:0 (0:0)
09/04/00	Sudan : Mozambique	1:0
23/04/00	Mozambique : Sudan	2:1
09/04/00	Lesotho : South Africa	0:2 (0:1)
22/04/00	South Africa : Lesotho	1:0 (0:0)
08/04/00	Madagascar : Gabon	2:0 (1:0)
22/04/00	Gabon : Madagascar	1:0 (1:0)
09/04/00	Swaziland : Angola	0:1 (0:0)
23/04/00	Angola : Swaziland	7:1 (4:0)
08/04/00	São Tomé e Prín. : Sierra Leone	2:0 (1:0)
22/04/00	Sierra Leone : São Tomé e Prín.	4:0 (2:0)
09/04/00	Rwanda : Côte d'Ivoire	2:2 (0:1)
23/04/00	Côte d'Ivoire : Rwanda	2:0 (1:0)
09/04/00	Libya : Mali	3:0 (1:0)
23/04/00	Mali : Libya	3:1 (0:1)
09/04/00	Central African Rep. : Zimbabwe	0:1 (0:1)
23/04/00	Zimbabwe : Central African Rep.	3:1
09/04/00	Equatorial Guinea : Congo	1:3 (1:2)
23/04/00	Congo : Equatorial Guinea	2:1
19/04/00	Somalia : Cameroon	0:3 (0:3)
23/04/00	Cameroon : Somalia	3:0 (2:0)
07/04/00	Djibouti : Congo DR	1:1 (1:0)
23/04/00	Congo DR : Djibouti	9:1
20/04/00	Mauritius : Egypt	0:2 (0:1)
23/04/00	Egypt : Mauritius	4:2
09/04/00	Eritrea : Nigeria	0:0
22/04/00	Nigeria : Eritrea	4:0 (2:0)
08/04/00	Seychelles : Namibia	1:1 (1:1)
22/04/00	Namibia : Seychelles	3:0 (2:0)
08/04/00	Uganda : Guinea	4:4 (0:1)
23/04/00	Guinea : Uganda	3:0 (0:0)
09/04/00	Ethiopia : Burkina Faso	2:1 (0:0)
23/04/00	Burkina Faso : Ethiopia	3:0 (3:0)
08/04/00	Malawi : Kenya	2:0 (0:0)
22/04/00	Kenya : Malawi	0:0
08/04/00	Tanzania : Ghana	0:1 (0:1)
23/04/00	Ghana : Tanzania	3:2 (2:1)
09/04/00	Chad : Liberia	0:1
23/04/00	Liberia : Chad	0:0

Africa - 2nd Round, Group A

	P	W	D	L	F	A	Pts
Cameroon	8	6	1	1	14	4	19
Angola	8	3	4	1	11	9	13
Zambia	8	3	2	3	14	11	11
Togo	8	2	3	3	10	13	9
Libya	8	0	2	6	7	19	2

18/06/00	Angola : Zambia	2:1 (0:1)
18/06/00	Libya : Cameroon	0:3 (0:1)
08/07/00	Zambia : Togo	2:0 (1:0)
09/07/00	Cameroon : Angola	3:0 (1:0)
28/01/01	Angola : Libya	3:1 (0:1)
28/01/01	Togo : Cameroon	0:2 (0:0)
23/02/01	Libya : Togo	3:3 (2:2)
25/02/01	Cameroon : Zambia	1:0 (1:0)
10/03/01	Zambia : Libya	2:0 (2:0)
11/03/01	Togo : Angola	1:1 (0:0)
21/04/01	Zambia : Angola	1:1 (1:0)
22/04/01	Cameroon : Libya	1:0 (0:0)
06/05/01	Angola : Cameroon	2:0 (0:0)
06/05/01	Togo : Zambia	3:2 (0:1)
29/06/01	Libya : Angola	1:1 (1:0)
01/07/01	Cameroon : Togo	2:0 (1:0)
14/07/01	Zambia : Cameroon	2:2 (0:0)
15/07/01	Togo : Libya	2:0 (2:0)
27/07/01	Libya : Zambia	2:4 (2:0)
29/07/01	Angola : Togo	1:1 (1:1)

Africa - 2nd Round, Group B

	P	W	D	L	F	A	Pts
Nigeria	8	5	1	2	15	3	16
Liberia	8	5	0	3	10	8	15
Sudan	8	4	0	4	8	10	12
Ghana	8	3	2	3	10	9	11
Sierra Leone	8	1	1	6	2	15	4

17/06/00	Nigeria : Sierra Leone	2:0 (2:0)
18/06/00	Sudan : Liberia	2:0 (0:0)
09/07/00	Liberia : Nigeria	2:1 (1:1)
09/07/00	Ghana : Sierra Leone	5:0 (1:0)
27/01/01	Nigeria : Sudan	3:0 (0:0)
28/01/01	Ghana : Liberia	1:3 (0:1)
25/02/01	Liberia : Sierra Leone	1:0 (0:0)
25/02/01	Sudan : Ghana	1:0 (0:0)
10/03/01	Sierra Leone : Sudan	0:2 (0:2)
11/03/01	Ghana : Nigeria	0:0
21/04/01	Sierra Leone : Nigeria	1:0 (1:0)
22/04/01	Liberia : Sudan	2:0 (1:0)
05/05/01	Nigeria : Liberia	2:0 (1:0)
05/05/01	Sierra Leone : Ghana	1:1 (0:1)
01/07/01	Liberia : Ghana	1:2 (1:1)
01/07/01	Sudan : Nigeria	0:4 (0:1)
14/07/01	Sierra Leone : Liberia	0:1 (0:0)
15/07/01	Ghana : Sudan	1:0 (1:0)
29/07/01	Nigeria : Ghana	3:0 (3:0)
29/07/01	Sudan : Sierra Leone	3:0 (2:0)

Africa - 2nd Round, Group C

	P	W	D	L	F	A	Pts
Senegal	8	4	3	1	14	2	15
Morocco	8	4	3	1	8	3	15
Egypt	8	3	4	1	16	7	13
Algeria	8	2	2	4	11	14	8
Namibia	8	0	2	6	3	26	2

16/06/00	Algeria : Senegal	1:1 (1:1)
17/06/00	Namibia : Morocco	0:0
09/07/00	Senegal : Egypt	0:0
09/07/00	Morocco : Algeria	2:1 (0:1)
26/01/01	Algeria : Namibia	1:0 (1:0)
28/01/01	Egypt : Morocco	0:0
24/02/01	Namibia : Egypt	1:1 (0:0)
24/02/01	Morocco : Senegal	0:0
10/03/01	Senegal : Namibia	4:0 (2:0)
11/03/01	Egypt : Algeria	5:2 (3:2)
21/04/01	Senegal : Algeria	3:0 (1:0)
21/04/01	Morocco : Namibia	3:0 (0:0)
04/05/01	Algeria : Morocco	1:2 (1:1)
06/05/01	Egypt : Senegal	1:0 (0:0)
30/06/01	Namibia : Algeria	0:4 (0:3)
30/06/01	Morocco : Egypt	1:0 (1:0)
13/07/01	Egypt : Namibia	8:2 (5:0)
14/07/01	Senegal : Morocco	1:0 (1:0)
21/07/01	Algeria : Egypt	1:1 (0:0)
21/07/01	Namibia : Senegal	0:5 (0:3)

Africa - 2nd Round, Group D

	P	W	D	L	F	A	Pts
Tunisia	8	6	2	0	23	4	20
Cote d' Ivoire	8	4	3	1	18	8	15
Congo DR	8	3	1	4	7	16	10
Madagascar	8	2	0	6	15	15	6
Congo	8	1	2	5	5	15	5

17/06/00	Madagascar : Congo DR	3:0 (1:0)
18/06/00	Côte d'Ivoire : Tunisia	2:2 (1:2)
08/07/00	Tunisia : Madagascar	1:0 (1:0)
09/07/00	Congo DR : Congo	2:0 (1:0)
28/01/01	Madagascar : Côte d'Ivoire	1:3 (0:1)
28/01/01	Congo : Tunisia	1:2 (1:1)
25/02/01	Tunisia : Congo DR	6:0 (3:0)
10/03/01	Congo DR : Côte d'Ivoire	1:2 (0:2)
22/04/01	Congo DR : Madagascar	1:0 (1:0)
22/04/01	Côte d'Ivoire : Congo	2:0 (1:0)
28/04/01	Congo : Madagascar	2:0 (1:0)
05/05/01	Madagascar : Tunisia	0:2 (0:0)
06/05/01	Congo : Congo DR	1:1 (0:0)
20/05/01	Tunisia : Côte d'Ivoire	1:1 (0:1)
01/07/01	Côte d'Ivoire : Madagascar	6:0 (2:0)
01/07/01	Tunisia : Congo	6:0 (3:0)
15/07/01	Congo : Côte d'Ivoire	1:1 (0:0)
15/07/01	Congo DR : Tunisia	0:3 (0:1)
29/07/01	Madagascar : Congo	1:0 (0:0)
29/07/01	Côte d'Ivoire : Congo DR	1:2 (0:1)

Africa - 2nd Round, Group E

	P	W	D	L	F	A	Pts
South Africa	6	5	1	0	10	3	16
Zimbabwe	7	4	0	3	7	8	12
Guinea	3	2	1	0	7	3	7
Burkina Faso	7	1	2	4	9	11	5
Malawi	7	0	2	5	5	13	2

17/06/00	Malawi : Burkina Faso	1:1 (1:1)
18/06/00	Guinea : Zimbabwe	3:0 (1:0)
09/07/00	Zimbabwe : South Africa	0:2 (0:1)
09/07/00	Burkina Faso : Guinea	2:3 (1:2)
27/01/01	South Africa : Burkina Faso	1:0 (1:0)
28/01/01	Guinea : Malawi	1:1 (1:0)

Having failed to get the executive body reinstated by the deadline imposed by FIFA (18 March 2001), the Football Association of Guinea was officially suspended and eliminated from the 2002 FIFA World Cup™.

24/02/01	Burkina Faso : Zimbabwe	1:2 (1:2)
25/02/01	Malawi : South Africa	1:2 (0:1)
11/03/01	Zimbabwe : Malawi	2:0 (1:0)
21/04/01	Burkina Faso : Malawi	4:2 (1:1)
05/05/01	South Africa : Zimbabwe	2:1 (2:0)
01/07/01	Burkina Faso : South Africa	1:1 (0:1)
14/07/01	South Africa : Malawi	2:0 (1:0)
15/07/01	Zimbabwe : Burkina Faso	1:0 (1:0)
28/07/01	Malawi : Zimbabwe	0:1 (0:0)

Asia - Group 1

	P	W	D	L	F	A	Pts
Oman	6	5	1	0	33	3	16
Syria	6	4	1	1	40	6	13
Laos	6	1	1	4	3	40	4
Philippines	6	0	1	5	2	29	1

30/04/01	Syria : Philippines	12:0 (5:0)
30/04/01	Oman : Laos	12:0 (8:0)
04/05/01	Philippines : Syria	1:5
04/05/01	Laos : Oman	0:7 (0:5)
07/05/01	Syria : Laos	11:0 (4:0)
07/05/01	Oman : Philippines	7:0 (3:0)
11/05/01	Laos : Syria	0:9 (0:3)
11/05/01	Philippines : Oman	0:2 (0:1)
18/05/01	Syria : Oman	3:3 (1:1)
19/05/01	Laos : Philippines	2:0
25/05/01	Oman : Syria	2:0 (1:0)
26/05/01	Philippines : Laos	1:1 (1:0)

Asia - Group 2

	P	W	D	L	F	A	Pts
Iran	2	2	0	0	21	0	6
Tajikistan	2	1	0	1	16	2	3
Guam	2	0	0	2	0	35	0

24/11/00	Iran : Guam	19:0 (8:0)
26/11/00	Tajikistan : Guam	16:0 (7:0)
28/11/00	Iran : Tajikistan	2:0 (0:0)

Asia - Group 3

	P	W	D	L	F	A	Pts
Qatar	6	5	1	0	14	3	16
Palestine	6	2	1	3	8	9	7
Malaysia	6	2	1	3	8	11	7
Hong Kong	6	1	1	4	3	10	4

04/03/01	Qatar : Malaysia	5:1 (2:1)
04/03/01	Hong Kong : Palestine	1:1 (0:0)
08/03/01	Palestine : Qatar	1:2 (0:1)
08/03/01	Malaysia : Hong Kong	2:0 (0:0)
11/03/01	Palestine : Malaysia	1:0 (1:0)
11/03/01	Qatar : Hong Kong	2:0 (1:0)
20/03/01	Palestine : Hong Kong	1:0 (0:0)
20/03/01	Malaysia : Qatar	0:0 (0:0)
23/03/01	Qatar : Palestine	2:1 (2:1)
23/03/01	Hong Kong : Malaysia	2:1 (1:0)
25/03/01	Hong Kong : Qatar	0:3 (0:1)
25/03/01	Malaysia : Palestine	4:3 (1:2)

Asia - Group 4

	P	W	D	L	F	A	Pts
Bahrain	6	5	0	1	9	4	15
Kuwait	6	4	1	1	9	3	13
Kyrgyzstan	6	1	1	4	3	9	4
Singapore	6	0	2	4	3	8	2

03/02/01	Bahrain : Kuwait	1:2 (0:0)
03/02/01	Singapore : Kyrgyzstan	0:1 (0:0)
06/02/01	Bahrain : Kyrgyzstan	1:0 (0:0)
06/02/01	Kuwait : Singapore	1:1 (0:0)
09/02/01	Kyrgyzstan : Kuwait	0:3 (0:0)
09/02/01	Singapore : Bahrain	1:2 (0:2)
21/02/01	Kyrgyzstan : Bahrain	1:2 (1:1)
21/02/01	Singapore : Kuwait	0:1 (0:0)
24/02/01	Kuwait : Kyrgyzstan	2:0 (1:0)
24/02/01	Bahrain : Singapore	2:0 (2:0)
27/02/01	Kyrgyzstan : Singapore	1:1 (0:0)
27/02/01	Kuwait : Bahrain	0:1 (0:0)

Asia - Group 5

	P	W	D	L	F	A	Pts
Thailand	6	5	1	0	20	5	16
Lebanon	6	4	1	1	26	5	13
Sri Lanka	6	1	1	4	8	20	4
Pakistan	6	0	1	5	5	29	1

13/05/01	Thailand : Sri Lanka	4:2 (1:1)
13/05/01	Lebanon : Pakistan	6:0 (2:0)
15/05/01	Thailand : Pakistan	3:0 (1:0)
15/05/01	Lebanon : Sri Lanka	4:0 (1:0)
17/05/01	Pakistan : Sri Lanka	3:3 (0:1)
17/05/01	Lebanon : Thailand	1:2 (1:2)
26/05/01	Pakistan : Lebanon	1:8 (1:4)
26/05/01	Sri Lanka : Thailand	0:3 (0:1)
28/05/01	Sri Lanka : Lebanon	0:5 (0:2)
28/05/01	Pakistan : Thailand	0:6 (0:1)
30/05/01	Sri Lanka : Pakistan	3:1 (2:1)
30/05/01	Thailand : Lebanon	2:2 (0:1)

Asia - Group 6

	P	W	D	L	F	A	Pts
Iraq	6	4	2	0	28	5	14
Kazakhstan	6	4	2	0	20	2	14
Nepal	6	2	0	4	13	25	6
Macao	6	0	0	6	2	31	0

12/04/01	Nepal : Kazakhstan	0:6 (0:3)
12/04/01	Iraq : Macao	8:0 (4:0)
14/04/01	Kazakhstan : Macao	3:0 (1:0)
14/04/01	Nepal : Iraq	1:9 (1:5)
16/04/01	Nepal : Macao	4:1 (2:1)
16/04/01	Kazakhstan : Iraq	1:1 (1:1)
21/04/01	Kazakhstan : Nepal	4:0 (1:0)
21/04/01	Macao : Iraq	0:5 (0:1)
23/04/01	Macao : Kazakhstan	0:5 (0:0)
23/04/01	Iraq : Nepal	4:2 (3:1)
25/04/01	Macao : Nepal	1:6 (0:1)
25/04/01	Iraq : Kazakhstan	1:1 (1:1)

Asia - Group 7

	P	W	D	L	F	A	Pts
Uzbekistan	6	4	2	0	20	5	14
Turkmenistan	6	4	0	2	12	7	12
Jordan	6	2	2	2	12	7	8
Chinese Taipei	6	0	0	6	0	25	0

23/04/01	Turkmenistan : Jordan	2:0 (0:0)
23/04/01	Uzbekistan : Chinese Taipei	7:0 (5:0)
25/04/01	Chinese Taipei : Jordan	0:2 (0:1)
25/04/01	Uzbekistan : Turkmenistan	1:0 (0:0)
27/04/01	Chinese Taipei : Turkmenistan	0:5 (0:2)
27/04/01	Uzbekistan : Jordan	2:2 (0:2)
03/05/01	Jordan : Chinese Taipei	6:0 (1:0)
03/05/01	Turkmenistan : Uzbekistan	2:5 (2:2)
05/05/01	Chinese Taipei : Uzbekistan	0:4 (0:1)
05/05/01	Jordan : Turkmenistan	1:2 (1:1)
07/05/01	Turkmenistan : Chinese Taipei	1:0 (1:0)
07/05/01	Jordan : Uzbekistan	1:1 (0:0)

Asia - Group 8

	P	W	D	L	F	A	Pts
United Arab Emirates	6	4	0	2	21	5	12
Yemen	6	3	2	1	14	8	11
India	6	3	2	1	11	5	11
Brunei Darussalam	6	0	0	6	0	28	0

07/04/01	Brunei Darussalam : Yemen	0:5 (0:1)
08/04/01	India : UAE	1:0 (0:0)
14/04/01	Brunei Darussalam : UAE	0:12 (0:5)
15/04/01	India : Yemen	1:1 (0:1)
26/04/01	UAE : India	1:0 (0:0)
27/04/01	Yemen : Brunei Darussalam	1:0 (0:0)
04/05/01	UAE : Brunei Darussalam	4:0 (1:0)
04/05/01	Yemen : India	3:3 (2:2)
11/05/01	Yemen : UAE	2:1 (0:1)
12/05/01	Brunei Darussalam : India	0:1 (0:0)
18/05/01	UAE : Yemen	3:2 (2:1)
20/05/01	India : Brunei Darussalam	5:0 (3:0)

Asia - Group 9

	P	W	D	L	F	A	Pts
China PR	6	6	0	0	25	3	18
Indonesia	6	4	0	2	16	7	12
Maldives Rep	6	1	1	4	8	19	4
Cambodia	6	0	1	5	2	22	1

01/04/01	Maldives Republic : Cambodia	6:0 (1:0)
08/04/01	Indonesia : Maldives Republic	5:0 (2:0)
15/04/01	Cambodia : Maldives Republic	1:1 (0:0)
22/04/01	Indonesia : Cambodia	6:0 (2:0)
22/04/01	China PR : Maldives Republic	10:1 (4:0)
28/04/01	Maldives Republic : China PR	0:1 (0:1)
29/04/01	Cambodia : Indonesia	0:2 (0:0)
06/05/01	Cambodia : China PR	0:4 (0:2)
06/05/01	Maldives Republic : Indonesia	0:2 (0:1)
13/05/01	China PR : Indonesia	5:1 (0:1)
20/05/01	China PR : Cambodia	3:1 (2:1)
27/05/01	Indonesia : China PR	0:2 (0:1)

Asia - Group 10

	P	W	D	L	F	A	Pts
Saudi Arabia	6	6	0	0	30	0	18
Vietnam SR	6	3	1	2	9	9	10
Bangladesh	6	1	2	3	5	15	5
Mongolia	6	0	1	5	2	22	1

08/02/01	Vietnam SR : Bangladesh	0:0 (0:0)
08/02/01	Saudi Arabia : Mongolia	6:0 (4:0)

22 Men and a Bag of Wind

10/02/01	Mongolia : Vietnam SR	0:1 (0:1)
10/02/01	Bangladesh : Saudi Arabia	0:3 (0:1)
12/02/01	Mongolia : Bangladesh	0:3 (0:1)
12/02/01	Saudi Arabia : Vietnam SR	5:0 (2:0)
15/02/01	Mongolia : Saudi Arabia	0:6 (0:4)
15/02/01	Bangladesh : Vietnam SR	0:4 (0:0)
17/02/01	Vietnam SR : Mongolia	4:0 (3:0)
17/02/01	Saudi Arabia : Bangladesh	6:0 (6:0)
19/02/01	Bangladesh : Mongolia	2:2 (1:1)
19/02/01	Vietnam SR : Saudi Arabia	0:4 (0:1)

Asia - 2nd Round, Group A

	P	W	D	L	F	A	Pts
Saudi Arabia	8	5	2	1	17	8	17
Iran	8	4	3	1	10	7	15
Bahrain	8	2	4	2	8	9	10
Iraq	8	2	1	5	9	10	7
Thailand	8	0	4	4	5	15	4

17/08/01	Iraq : Thailand	4:0 (1:0)
17/08/01	Saudi Arabia : Bahrain	1:1 (0:1)
23/08/01	Bahrain : Iraq	2:0 (0:0)
24/08/01	Iran : Saudi Arabia	2:0 (0:0)
31/08/01	Saudi Arabia : Iraq	1:0 (1:0)
01/09/01	Thailand : Iran	0:0
06/09/01	Bahrain : Thailand	1:1 (1:0)
07/09/01	Iraq : Iran	1:2 (1:1)
14/09/01	Iran : Bahrain	0:0
15/09/01	Thailand : Saudi Arabia	1:3 (1:0)
21/09/01	Bahrain : Saudi Arabia	0:4 (0:3)
22/09/01	Thailand : Iraq	1:1 (1:0)
28/09/01	Iraq : Bahrain	1:0 (1:0)
28/09/01	Saudi Arabia : Iran	2:2 (1:1)
05/10/01	Iran : Thailand	1:0 (1:0)
05/10/01	Iraq : Saudi Arabia	1:2 (1:1)
12/10/01	Iran : Iraq	2:1 (1:0)
16/10/01	Thailand : Bahrain	1:1 (1:0)
21/10/01	Bahrain : Iran	3:1 (2:0)
21/10/01	Saudi Arabia : Thailand	4:1 (1:0)

Asia - 2nd Round, Group B

	P	W	D	L	F	A	Pts
China PR	8	6	1	1	13	2	19
United Arab Emirates	8	3	2	3	10	11	11
Uzbekistan	8	3	1	4	13	14	10
Qatar	8	2	3	3	10	10	9
Oman	8	1	3	4	7	16	6

16/08/01	Qatar : Oman	0:0 (0:0)
17/08/01	United Arab Emirates : Uzbekistan	4:1 (3:1)
25/08/01	China PR : United Arab Emirates	3:0 (3:0)
26/08/01	Uzbekistan : Qatar	2:1 (1:0)
31/08/01	United Arab Emirates : Qatar	0:2 (0:0)
31/08/01	Oman : China PR	0:2 (0:0)
07/09/01	Qatar : China PR	1:1 (1:0)
08/09/01	Uzbekistan : Oman	5:0 (2:0)
14/09/01	Oman : United Arab Emirates	1:1 (0:1)
15/09/01	China PR : Uzbekistan	2:0 (0:0)
21/09/01	Oman : Qatar	0:3 (0:2)
22/09/01	Uzbekistan : United Arab Emirates	0:1 (0:1)
27/09/01	United Arab Emirates : China PR	0:1 (0:1)
28/09/01	Qatar : Uzbekistan	2:2 (1:1)
04/10/01	Qatar : United Arab Emirates	1:2 (0:1)
07/10/01	China PR : Oman	1:0 (1:0)
13/10/01	Oman : Uzbekistan	4:2 (0:2)
13/10/01	China PR : Qatar	3:0 (2:0)
19/10/01	United Arab Emirates : Oman	2:2 (1:2)
19/10/01	Uzbekistan : China PR	1:0 (0:0)

Asia - 3rd Round AFC

25/10/01	Iran : United Arab Emirates	1:0 (1:0)
31/10/01	United Arab Emirates : Iran	0:3 (0:1)

Europe - Group 1

	P	W	D	L	F	A	Pts
Russia	10	7	2	1	18	5	23
Slovenia	10	5	5	0	17	9	20
Yugoslavia	10	5	4	1	22	8	19
Switzerland	10	4	2	4	18	12	14
Faroe Islands	10	2	1	7	6	23	7
Luxembourg	10	0	0	10	4	28	0

02/09/00	Switzerland : Russia	0:1 (0:0)
03/09/00	Faroe Islands : Slovenia	2:2 (0:1)
03/09/00	Luxembourg : Yugoslavia	0:2 (0:2)
07/10/00	Switzerland : Faroe Islands	5:1 (4:1)
07/10/00	Luxembourg : Slovenia	1:2 (0:2)
11/10/00	Russia : Luxembourg	3:0 (1:0)
11/10/00	Slovenia : Switzerland	2:2 (1:1)
24/03/01	Luxembourg : Faroe Islands	0:2 (0:0)
24/03/01	Russia : Slovenia	1:1 (1:1)
24/03/01	Yugoslavia : Switzerland	1:1 (0:0)
28/03/01	Russia : Faroe Islands	1:0 (1:0)
28/03/01	Switzerland : Luxembourg	5:0 (2:0)
28/03/01	Slovenia : Yugoslavia	1:1 (0:1)
25/04/01	Yugoslavia : Russia	0:1 (0:0)
02/06/01	Russia : Yugoslavia	1:1 (1:1)
02/06/01	Faroe Islands : Switzerland	0:1 (0:0)
02/06/01	Slovenia : Luxembourg	2:0 (1:0)
06/06/01	Faroe Islands : Yugoslavia	0:6 (0:2)
06/06/01	Luxembourg : Russia	1:2 (0:1)
06/06/01	Switzerland : Slovenia	0:1 (0:0)
15/08/01	Yugoslavia : Faroe Islands	2:0 (1:0)
01/09/01	Faroe Islands : Luxembourg	1:0 (0:0)
01/09/01	Switzerland : Yugoslavia	1:2 (1:1)
01/09/01	Slovenia : Russia	2:1 (0:0)
05/09/01	Faroe Islands : Russia	0:3 (0:2)
05/09/01	Yugoslavia : Slovenia	1:1 (0:1)
05/09/01	Luxembourg : Switzerland	0:3 (0:1)
06/10/01	Yugoslavia : Luxembourg	6:2 (1:1)
06/10/01	Slovenia : Faroe Islands	3:0 (2:0)
06/10/01	Russia : Switzerland	4:0 (3:0)

Europe - Group 2

	P	W	D	L	F	A	Pts
Portugal	10	7	3	0	33	7	24
Ireland Rep	10	7	3	0	23	5	24
Netherlands	10	6	2	2	30	9	20
Estonia	10	2	2	6	10	26	8
Cyprus	10	2	2	6	13	31	8
Andorra	10	0	0	10	5	36	0

16/08/00	Estonia : Andorra	1:0 (0:0)
02/09/00	Andorra : Cyprus	2:3 (1:1)
02/09/00	Netherlands : Ireland Republic	2:2 (0:1)
03/09/00	Estonia : Portugal	1:3 (0:1)
07/10/00	Andorra : Estonia	1:2 (0:0)
07/10/00	Cyprus : Netherlands	0:4 (0:0)
07/10/00	Portugal : Ireland Republic	1:1 (1:0)
11/10/00	Ireland Republic : Estonia	2:0 (1:0)
11/10/00	Netherlands : Portugal	0:2 (0:2)
15/11/00	Cyprus : Andorra	5:0 (3:0)
28/02/01	Portugal : Andorra	3:0 (2:0)
24/03/01	Cyprus : Ireland Republic	0:4 (0:2)
24/03/01	Andorra : Netherlands	0:5 (0:2)
28/03/01	Andorra : Ireland Republic	0:3 (0:1)
28/03/01	Cyprus : Estonia	2:2 (0:0)

Europe - Group 3

	P	W	D	L	F	A	Pts
Denmark	10	6	4	0	22	6	22
Czech Rep	10	6	2	2	20	8	20
Bulgaria	10	5	2	3	14	15	17
Iceland	10	4	1	5	14	20	13
N Ireland	10	3	2	5	11	12	11
Malta	10	0	1	9	4	24	1

02/09/00	Northern Ireland : Malta	1:0 (0:0)
02/09/00	Iceland : Denmark	1:2 (1:1)
02/09/00	Bulgaria : Czech Republic	0:1 (0:0)
07/10/00	Northern Ireland : Denmark	1:1 (1:0)
07/10/00	Czech Republic : Iceland	4:0 (3:0)
07/10/00	Bulgaria : Malta	3:0 (1:0)
11/10/00	Malta : Czech Republic	0:0
11/10/00	Denmark : Bulgaria	1:1 (0:0)
11/10/00	Iceland : Northern Ireland	1:0 (0:0)
24/03/01	Northern Ireland : Czech Republic	0:1 (0:1)
24/03/01	Bulgaria : Iceland	2:1 (1:1)
24/03/01	Malta : Denmark	0:5 (0:1)
28/03/01	Bulgaria : Northern Ireland	4:3 (2:1)
28/03/01	Czech Republic : Denmark	0:0 (0:0)
25/04/01	Malta : Iceland	1:4 (1:2)
02/06/01	Northern Ireland : Bulgaria	0:1 (0:0)
02/06/01	Iceland : Malta	3:0 (2:0)
02/06/01	Denmark : Czech Republic	2:1 (1:1)
06/06/01	Czech Republic : Northern Ireland	3:1 (1:1)
06/06/01	Iceland : Bulgaria	1:1 (1:0)
06/06/01	Denmark : Malta	2:1 (1:1)
01/09/01	Iceland : Czech Republic	3:1 (1:0)
01/09/01	Denmark : Northern Ireland	1:1 (1:0)
01/09/01	Malta : Bulgaria	0:2 (0:0)
05/09/01	Czech Republic : Malta	3:2 (2:1)
05/09/01	Bulgaria : Denmark	0:2 (0:0)
05/09/01	Northern Ireland : Iceland	3:0 (0:0)
06/10/01	Malta : Northern Ireland	0:1 (0:0)
06/10/01	Czech Republic : Bulgaria	6:0 (3:0)
06/10/01	Denmark : Iceland	6:0 (4:0)

Europe - Group 4

	P	W	D	L	F	A	Pts
Sweden	10	8	2	0	20	3	26
Turkey	10	6	3	1	18	8	21
Slovakia	10	5	2	3	16	9	17
Macedonia FYR	10	1	4	5	11	18	7
Moldova	10	1	3	6	6	20	6
Azerbaijan	10	1	2	7	4	17	5

02/09/00	Turkey : Moldova	2:0 (1:0)
02/09/00	Azerbaijan : Sweden	0:1 (0:1)
03/09/00	Slovakia : Macedonia FYR	2:0 (1:0)
06/10/00	Macedonia FYR : Azerbaijan	3:0 (2:0)

Europe - Group 3

07/10/00	Sweden : Turkey	1:1 (0:0)
07/10/00	Moldova : Slovakia	0:1 (0:0)
11/10/00	Azerbaijan : Turkey	0:1 (0:0)
11/10/00	Moldova : Macedonia FYR	0:0
11/10/00	Slovakia : Sweden	0:0
24/03/01	Sweden : Macedonia FYR	1:0 (1:0)
24/03/01	Azerbaijan : Moldova	0:0
24/03/01	Turkey : Slovakia	1:1 (0:0)
28/03/01	Slovakia : Azerbaijan	3:1 (2:1)
28/03/01	Macedonia FYR : Turkey	1:2 (1:0)
28/03/01	Moldova : Sweden	0:2 (0:0)
02/06/01	Sweden : Slovakia	2:0 (1:0)
02/06/01	Macedonia FYR : Moldova	2:2 (1:1)
02/06/01	Turkey : Azerbaijan	3:0 (3:0)
06/06/01	Azerbaijan : Slovakia	2:0 (1:0)
06/06/01	Sweden : Moldova	6:0 (1:0)
06/06/01	Turkey : Macedonia FYR	3:3 (1:2)
01/09/01	Moldova : Azerbaijan	2:0 (1:0)
01/09/01	Slovakia : Turkey	0:1 (0:1)
01/09/01	Macedonia FYR : Sweden	1:2 (0:2)
05/09/01	Azerbaijan : Macedonia FYR	1:1 (0:1)
05/09/01	Slovakia : Moldova	4:2 (0:1)
05/09/01	Turkey : Sweden	1:2 (0:0)
06/10/01	Moldova : Turkey	0:3 (0:1)
07/10/01	Sweden : Azerbaijan	3:0 (0:0)
07/10/01	Macedonia FYR : Slovakia	0:5 (0:1)

Europe - Group 5

	P	W	D	L	F	A	Pts
Poland	10	6	3	1	21	11	21
Ukraine	10	4	5	1	13	8	17
Belarus	10	4	3	3	12	11	15
Norway	10	2	4	4	12	14	10
Wales	10	1	6	3	10	12	9
Armenia	10	0	5	5	7	19	5

02/09/00	Norway : Armenia	0:0
02/09/00	Belarus : Wales	2:1 (1:0)
02/09/00	Ukraine : Poland	1:3 (1:2)
07/10/00	Wales : Norway	1:1 (0:0)
07/10/00	Armenia : Ukraine	2:3 (2:1)
07/10/00	Poland : Belarus	3:1 (1:1)
11/10/00	Belarus : Armenia	2:1 (2:0)
11/10/00	Norway : Ukraine	0:1 (0:1)
11/10/00	Poland : Wales	0:0
24/03/01	Norway : Poland	2:3 (0:2)
24/03/01	Ukraine : Belarus	0:0
24/03/01	Armenia : Wales	2:2 (1:1)
28/03/01	Poland : Armenia	4:0 (2:0)
28/03/01	Wales : Ukraine	1:1 (1:0)
28/03/01	Belarus : Norway	2:1 (1:0)
02/06/01	Wales : Poland	1:2 (1:1)
02/06/01	Ukraine : Norway	0:0
02/06/01	Armenia : Belarus	0:0
06/06/01	Norway : Belarus	1:1 (0:1)
06/06/01	Ukraine : Wales	1:1 (1:0)
06/06/01	Armenia : Poland	1:1 (1:1)
01/09/01	Wales : Armenia	0:0
01/09/01	Poland : Norway	3:0 (1:0)
01/09/01	Belarus : Ukraine	0:2 (0:1)
05/09/01	Ukraine : Armenia	3:0 (1:0)
05/09/01	Norway : Wales	3:2 (1:2)
05/09/01	Belarus : Poland	4:1 (1:0)
06/10/01	Wales : Belarus	1:0 (0:0)
06/10/01	Poland : Ukraine	1:1 (1:0)
06/10/01	Armenia : Norway	1:4 (0:0)

Europe - Group 6

	P	W	D	L	F	A	Pts
Croatia	8	5	3	0	15	2	18
Belgium	8	5	2	1	25	6	17
Scotland	8	4	3	1	12	6	15
Latvia	8	1	1	6	5	16	4
San Marino	8	0	1	7	3	30	1

02/09/00	Latvia : Scotland	0:1 (0:0)
02/09/00	Belgium : Croatia	0:0
07/10/00	San Marino : Scotland	0:2 (0:0)
07/10/00	Latvia : Belgium	0:4 (0:2)
11/10/00	Croatia : Scotland	1:1 (1:1)
15/11/00	San Marino : Latvia	0:1 (0:1)
28/02/01	Belgium : San Marino	10:1 (3:0)
24/03/01	Scotland : Belgium	2:2 (2:0)
24/03/01	Croatia : Latvia	4:1 (3:0)
28/03/01	Scotland : San Marino	4:0 (3:0)
25/04/01	Latvia : San Marino	1:1 (1:0)
02/06/01	Belgium : Latvia	3:1 (2:0)
02/06/01	Croatia : San Marino	4:0 (2:0)
06/06/01	Latvia : Croatia	0:1 (0:1)
06/06/01	San Marino : Belgium	1:4 (1:1)
01/09/01	Scotland : Croatia	0:0
05/09/01	San Marino : Croatia	0:4 (0:1)
05/09/01	Belgium : Scotland	2:0 (1:0)
06/10/01	Scotland : Latvia	2:1 (1:1)
06/10/01	Croatia : Belgium	1:0 (0:0)

Europe - Group 7

	P	W	D	L	F	A	Pts
Spain	8	6	2	0	21	4	20
Austria	8	4	3	1	10	8	15
Israel	8	3	3	2	11	7	12
Bosnia-Herzegovina	8	2	2	4	12	12	8
Liechtenstein	8	0	0	8	0	23	0

02/09/00	Bosnia-Herzegovina : Spain	1:2 (1:1)
03/09/00	Israel : Liechtenstein	2:0 (1:0)
07/10/00	Liechtenstein : Austria	0:1 (0:1)
07/10/00	Spain : Israel	2:0 (1:0)
11/10/00	Israel : Bosnia-Herzegovina	3:1 (1:0)
11/10/00	Austria : Spain	1:1 (1:1)
24/03/01	Bosnia-Herzegovina : Austria	1:1 (1:0)
24/03/01	Spain : Liechtenstein	5:0 (2:0)
28/03/01	Liechtenstein : Bosnia-Herzegovina	0:3 (0:1)
28/03/01	Austria : Israel	2:1 (2:1)
25/04/01	Austria : Liechtenstein	2:0 (1:0)
02/06/01	Liechtenstein : Israel	0:3 (0:3)
02/06/01	Spain : Bosnia-Herzegovina	4:1 (1:1)
06/06/01	Israel : Spain	1:1 (1:0)
01/09/01	Bosnia-Herzegovina : Israel	0:0
01/09/01	Spain : Austria	4:0 (1:0)
05/09/01	Liechtenstein : Spain	0:2 (0:1)
05/09/01	Austria : Bosnia-Herzegovina	2:0 (1:0)
07/10/01	Bosnia-Herzegovina : Liechtenstein	5:0 (2:0)
27/10/01	Israel : Austria	1:1 (0:0)

Europe - Group 8

	P	W	D	L	F	A	Pts
Italy	8	6	2	0	16	3	20
Romania	8	5	1	2	10	7	16
Georgia	8	3	1	4	12	12	10
Hungary	8	2	2	4	14	13	8
Lithuania	8	0	2	6	3	20	2

03/09/00	Romania : Lithuania	1:0 (0:0)
03/09/00	Hungary : Italy	2:2 (1:2)
07/10/00	Lithuania : Georgia	0:4 (0:2)

07/10/00	Italy : Romania	3:0 (3:0)
11/10/00	Lithuania : Hungary	1:6 (0:2)
11/10/00	Italy : Georgia	2:0 (0:0)
24/03/01	Hungary : Lithuania	1:1 (0:0)
24/03/01	Romania : Italy	0:2 (0:2)
28/03/01	Georgia : Romania	0:2 (0:0)
28/03/01	Italy : Lithuania	4:0 (1:0)
02/06/01	Romania : Hungary	2:0 (1:0)
02/06/01	Georgia : Italy	1:2 (0:1)
06/06/01	Lithuania : Romania	1:2 (0:1)
06/06/01	Hungary : Georgia	4:1 (2:0)
01/09/01	Lithuania : Italy	0:0
01/09/01	Georgia : Hungary	3:1 (1:1)
05/09/01	Hungary : Romania	0:2 (0:2)
05/09/01	Georgia : Lithuania	2:0 (0:0)
06/10/01	Italy : Hungary	1:0 (1:0)
06/10/01	Romania : Georgia	1:1 (0:0)

Europe - Group 9

	P	W	D	L	F	A	Pts
England	8	5	2	1	16	6	17
Germany	8	5	2	1	14	10	17
Finland	8	3	3	2	12	7	12
Greece	8	2	1	5	7	17	7
Albania	8	1	0	7	5	14	3

02/09/00	Finland : Albania	2:1 (1:0)
02/09/00	Germany : Greece	2:0 (1:0)
07/10/00	England : Germany	0:1 (0:1)
07/10/00	Greece : Finland	1:0 (0:0)
11/10/00	Finland : England	0:0
11/10/00	Albania : Greece	2:0 (0:0)
24/03/01	England : Finland	2:1 (1:1)
24/03/01	Germany : Albania	2:1 (0:0)
28/03/01	Albania : England	1:3 (0:0)
28/03/01	Greece : Germany	2:4 (2:2)
02/06/01	Finland : Germany	2:2 (2:0)
02/06/01	Greece : Albania	1:0 (0:0)
06/06/01	Albania : Germany	0:2 (0:1)
06/06/01	Greece : England	0:2 (0:0)
01/09/01	Albania : Finland	0:2 (0:0)
01/09/01	Germany : England	1:5 (1:2)
05/09/01	Finland : Greece	5:1 (4:1)
05/09/01	England : Albania	2:0 (1:0)
06/10/01	England : Greece	2:2 (0:1)
06/10/01	Germany : Finland	0:0

Europe - 2nd Round

10/11/01	Ukraine : Germany	1:1 (1:1)
10/11/01	Slovenia : Romania	2:1 (1:1)
10/11/01	Belgium : Czech Republic	1:0 (1:0)
10/11/01	Austria : Turkey	0:1 (0:0)
14/11/01	Romania : Slovenia	1:1 (0:0)
14/11/01	Czech Republic : Belgium	0:1 (0:0)
14/11/01	Germany : Ukraine	4:1 (3:0)
14/11/01	Turkey : Austria	5:0 (3:0)

UEFA/AFC Play-offs

| 10/11/01 | Ireland Republic : Iran | 2:0 (1:0) |
| 15/11/01 | Iran : Ireland Republic | 1:0 (0:0) |

Caribbean/North/Cent. America Preliminary - Caribbean 1

05/03/00	Cuba : Cayman Islands	4:0 (1:0)
19/03/00	Cayman Islands : Cuba	0:0
05/03/00	St. Lucia : Surinam	1:0 (0:0)

19/03/00	Surinam : St. Lucia	1:0 a.e.t.
	(1:0, 0:0) 3:1 penalty kicks	
11/03/00	Aruba : Puerto Rico	4:2 (0:2)
18/03/00	Puerto Rico : Aruba	2:2 (2:2)
05/03/00	Barbados : Grenada	2:2 (1:0)
18/03/00	Grenada : Barbados	2:3 a.e.t.
		(2:2, 1:2)

Caribbean/North/Cent. America
2nd Round - Caribbean 1

02/04/00	Cuba : Surinam	1:0 (1:0)
16/04/00	Surinam : Cuba	0:0
01/04/00	Aruba : Barbados	1:3 (0:2)
16/04/00	Barbados : Aruba	4:0 (1:0)

Caribbean/North/Cent. America
3rd Round - Caribbean 1

07/05/00	Cuba : Barbados	1:1 (1:1)
21/05/00	Barbados : Cuba	1:1 (0:0)
	5:4 penalty kicks	

Caribbean/North/Cent. America
Preliminary - Caribbean 2

05/03/00	St. Vin./Gren. : US Virgin Islands	9:0 (5:0)
19/03/00	US Virgin Islands : St. Vin./Gren.	1:5 (0:3)
18/03/00	St. Kitts & Nevis : Turks & Caicos	8:0 (2:0)
21/03/00	Turks & Caicos : St. Kitts & Nevis	0:6 (0:2)
05/03/00	British Virgin Islands : Bermuda	1:5 (0:2)
19/03/00	Bermuda : British Virgin Islands	9:0 (2:0)

Guyana suspended by FIFA; Antigua and Barbuda went through to the second round.

Caribbean/North/Cent. America
2nd Round - Caribbean 2

16/04/00	St. Vin./Gren. : St. Kitts & Nevis	1:0 (0:0)
22/04/00	St. Kitts & Nevis : St. Vin./Gren.	1:2 (0:1)
16/04/00	Antigua and Barbuda : Bermuda	0:0
23/04/00	Bermuda : Antigua and Barbuda	1:1

Caribbean/North/Cent. America
3rd Round - Caribbean 2

07/05/00	Ant. & Barbuda : St. Vin./Gren.	2:1 (1:0)
21/05/00	St. Vin./Gren. : Ant. & Barbuda	4:0 (1:0)

Caribbean/North/Cent. America
Preliminary - Caribbean 3

04/03/00	Trinidad & Tobago : Neth. Antilles	5:0 (2:0)
18/03/00	Neth. Antilles : Trinidad & Tobago	1:1 (1:0)
05/03/00	Dom. Republic : Montserrat	3:0 (3:0)
19/03/00	Montserrat : Dom. Rep	1:3 (0:1)
11/03/00	Haiti : Dominica	4:0 (3:0)
19/03/00	Dominica : Haiti	1:3 (1:0)
05/03/00	Anguilla : Bahamas	1:3 (0:3)
19/03/00	Bahamas : Anguilla	2:1 (1:1)

Caribbean/North/Cent. America
2nd Round - Caribbean 3

02/04/00	Trinidad & Tobago : Dom. Rep.	3:0 (0:0)
16/04/00	Dom. Rep. : Trinidad & Tobago	0:1 (0:0)
01/04/00	Haiti : Bahamas	9:0 (6:0)
16/04/00	Bahamas : Haiti	0:4 (0:3)

Caribbean/North/Cent. America
3rd Round - Caribbean 3

07/05/00	Trinidad and Tobago : Haiti	3:1 (1:0)
19/05/00	Haiti : Trinidad and Tobago	1:1 (0:1)

Caribbean/North/Cent. America
Preliminary - Cent. American Zone
Group A

05/03/00	El Salvador : Belize	5:0 (2:0)
19/03/00	Belize : Guatemala	1:2 (1:1)
02/04/00	Guatemala : El Salvador	0:1 (0:0)
16/04/00	Belize : El Salvador	1:3 (0:1)
07/05/00	El Salvador : Guatemala	1:1 (1:1)
19/05/00	Guatemala : Belize	0:0

Caribbean/North/Cent. America
Preliminary - Cent. American Zone
Group B

04/03/00	Honduras : Nicaragua	3:0 (2:0)
19/03/00	Nicaragua : Panama	0:2 (0:1)
02/04/00	Panama : Honduras	1:0 (0:0)
16/04/00	Nicaragua : Honduras	0:1 (0:0)
07/05/00	Honduras : Panama	3:1
21/05/00	Panama : Nicaragua	4:0

Caribbean/North/Cent. America
Caribbean/Central American Play-offs

04/06/00	Cuba : Canada	0:1 (0:1)
11/06/00	Canada : Cuba	0:0
11/06/00	Antigua and Barbuda : Guatemala	0:1 (0:1)
18/06/00	Guatemala : Antigua and Barbuda	8:1 (4:0)
03/06/00	Honduras : Haiti	4:0 (2:0)
17/06/00	Haiti : Honduras	1:3 (0:1)

Caribbean/North/Cent. America
Semi-finals - Group C

	P	W	D	L	F	A	Pts
Trinidad & Tobago	6	5	0	1	14	7	15
Mexico	6	4	1	1	17	2	13
Canada	6	1	2	3	1	8	5
Panama	6	0	1	5	1	16	1

16/07/00	Canada : Trinidad and Tobago	0:2 (0:1)
16/07/00	Panama : Mexico	0:1 (0:0)
23/07/00	Panama : Canada	0:0 (0:0)
23/07/00	Trinidad and Tobago : Mexico	1:0 (0:0)
15/08/00	Mexico : Canada	2:0 (0:0)
16/08/00	Trinidad and Tobago : Panama	6:0 (3:0)
03/09/00	Mexico : Panama	7:1 (3:0)
03/09/00	Trinidad and Tobago : Canada	4:0 (2:0)
08/10/00	Mexico : Trinidad and Tobago	7:0 (4:0)
09/10/00	Canada : Panama	1:0 (0:0)
15/11/00	Panama : Trinidad and Tobago	0:1 (0:1)
15/11/00	Canada : Mexico	0:0

Caribbean/North/Cent. America
Semi-finals - Group D

	P	W	D	L	F	A	Pts
Honduras	6	5	0	1	25	5	15
Jamaica	6	4	0	2	7	4	12
El Salvador	6	3	0	3	13	13	9
St Vincent / Grenadines	6	0	0	6	2	25	0

16/07/00	El Salvador : Honduras	2:5 (1:3)
16/07/00	St. Vin./Gren.s : Jamaica	0:1 (0:1)
23/07/00	El Salvador : St. Vin./Gren.	7:1 (2:1)
23/07/00	Jamaica : Honduras	3:1 (1:1)
16/08/00	Jamaica : El Salvador	1:0 (1:0)
16/08/00	Honduras : St. Vin./Gren.	6:0 (3:0)
02/09/00	Honduras : El Salvador	5:0 (2:0)
03/09/00	Jamaica : St. Vin./Gren.	2:0 (1:0)
08/10/00	St. Vin./Gren. : El Salvador	1:2 (0:1)
08/10/00	Honduras : Jamaica	1:0 (0:0)
14/11/00	St. Vin./Gren. : Honduras	0:7 (0:2)
15/11/00	El Salvador : Jamaica	2:0 (2:0)

Caribbean/North/Cent. America
Semi-finals - Group E

	P	W	D	L	F	A	Pts
United States	6	3	2	1	14	3	11
Costa Rica	6	3	1	2	9	6	10
Guatemala	6	3	1	2	9	6	10
Barbados	6	1	0	5	3	20	3

16/07/00	Guatemala : United States	1:1 (0:1)
16/07/00	Barbados : Costa Rica	2:1 (0:0)
22/07/00	Guatemala : Barbados	2:0 (1:0)
23/07/00	Costa Rica : United States	2:1 (1:0)
15/08/00	Costa Rica : Guatemala	2:1 (1:0)
16/08/00	United States : Barbados	7:0 (3:0)
03/09/00	Costa Rica : Barbados	3:0 (2:0)
03/09/00	United States : Guatemala	1:0 (0:0)
08/10/00	Barbados : Guatemala	1:3 (1:2)
11/10/00	United States : Costa Rica	0:0
15/11/00	Guatemala : Costa Rica	2:1 (0:0)
15/11/00	Barbados : United States	0:4 (0:0)

Caribbean/North/Cent. America
Semi-finals - Play-off for Group E

06/01/01	Costa Rica : Guatemala	5:2 (2:1)

Played in Miami

Caribbean/North/Cent. America
Finals

	P	W	D	L	F	A	Pts
Costa Rica	10	7	2	1	17	7	23
Mexico	10	5	2	3	16	9	17
United States	10	5	2	3	11	8	17
Honduras	10	4	2	4	17	17	14
Jamaica	10	2	2	6	7	14	8
Trinidad & Tobago	10	1	2	7	5	18	5

28/02/01	Jamaica : Trinidad and Tobago	1:0 (1:0)
28/02/01	USA : Mexico	2:0 (0:0)
28/02/01	Costa Rica : Honduras	2:2 (0:1)
25/03/01	Mexico : Jamaica	4:0 (2:0)
28/03/01	Honduras : USA	1:2 (0:1)
28/03/01	Costa Rica : Trinidad and Tobago	3:0 (0:0)
25/04/01	Trinidad and Tobago : Mexico	1:1 (1:0)
25/04/01	USA : Costa Rica	1:0 (0:0)
25/04/01	Jamaica : Honduras	1:1 (0:0)
16/06/01	Mexico : Costa Rica	1:2 (1:0)
16/06/01	Jamaica : USA	0:0
16/06/01	Trinidad and Tobago : Honduras	2:4 (0:2)
20/06/01	Honduras : Mexico	3:1 (1:0)
20/06/01	USA : Trinidad and Tobago	2:0 (2:0)
20/06/01	Costa Rica : Jamaica	2:1 (2:1)
30/06/01	Trinidad and Tobago : Jamaica	1:2 (1:1)
01/07/01	Mexico : USA	1:0 (1:0)
01/07/01	Honduras : Costa Rica	2:3 (2:2)
01/09/01	USA : Honduras	2:3 (1:1)
01/09/01	Trinidad and Tobago : Costa Rica	0:2 (0:2)
02/09/01	Jamaica : Mexico	1:2 (1:0)

The Qualifying Story - Korea/Japan 2002

05/09/01	Honduras : Jamaica	1:0 (0:0)
05/09/01	Costa Rica :USA	2:0 (1:0)
05/09/01	Mexico : Trinidad and Tobago	3:0 (2:0)
07/10/01	Honduras : Trinidad and Tobago	0:1 (0:0)
07/10/01	Costa Rica : Mexico	0:0
07/10/01	USA : Jamaica	2:1 (1:1)
11/11/01	Mexico : Honduras	3:0 (0:0)
11/11/01	Jamaica : Costa Rica	0:1 (0:1)
11/11/01	Trinidad and Tobago : USA	0:0

Oceania - Group 1

	P	W	D	L	F	A	Pts
Australia	4	4	0	0	66	0	12
Fiji	4	3	0	1	27	4	9
Tonga	4	2	0	2	7	30	6
Samoa	4	1	0	3	9	18	3
American Samoa	4	0	0	4	0	57	0

07/04/01	Samoa : Tonga	0:1 (0:0)
07/04/01	Fiji : American Samoa	13:0 (8:0)
09/04/01	Tonga : Australia	0:22 (0:10)
09/04/01	American Samoa : Samoa	0:8 (0:3)
11/04/01	Samoa : Fiji	1:6 (1:3)
11/04/01	Australia : American Samoa	31:0 (16:0)
14/04/01	Fiji : Australia	0:2 (0:1)
14/04/01	American Samoa : Tonga	0:5 (0:2)
16/04/01	Australia : Samoa	11:0 (3:0)
16/04/01	Tonga : Fiji	1:8 (0:4)

Oceania - Group 2

	P	W	D	L	F	A	Pts
New Zealand	4	4	0	0	19	1	12
Tahiti	4	3	0	1	14	6	9
Solomon Islands	4	2	0	2	17	10	6
Vanuatu	4	1	0	3	11	21	3
Cook Islands	4	0	0	4	2	25	0

04/06/01	Vanuatu : Tahiti	1:6 (0:3)
04/06/01	Solomon Islands : Cook Islands	9:1 (3:1)
06/06/01	Tahiti : New Zealand	0:5 (0:1)
06/06/01	Cook Islands : Vanuatu	1:8 (1:3)
08/06/01	Vanuatu : Solomon Islands	2:7 (1:1)
08/06/01	New Zealand : Cook Islands	2:0 (0:0)
11/06/01	Solomon Islands : New Zealand	1:5 (0:2)
11/06/01	Cook Islands : Tahiti	0:6 (0:3)
13/06/01	New Zealand : Vanuatu	7:0 (5:0)
13/06/01	Tahiti : Solomon Islands	2:0 (1:0)

Oceania - Play-off

20/06/01	New Zealand : Australia	0:2 (0:1)
24/06/01	Australia : New Zealand	4:1 (2:1)

South America

	P	W	D	L	F	A	Pts
Argentina	18	13	4	1	42	15	43
Ecuador	18	9	4	5	23	20	31
Brazil	18	9	3	6	31	17	30
Paraguay	18	9	3	6	29	23	30
Uruguay	18	7	6	5	19	13	27
Colombia	18	7	6	5	20	15	27
Bolivia	18	4	6	8	21	33	18
Peru	18	4	4	10	14	25	16
Venezuela	18	5	1	12	18	44	16
Chile	18	3	3	12	15	27	12

28/03/00	Colombia : Brazil	0:0
29/03/00	Ecuador : Venezuela	2:0 (1:0)
29/03/00	Uruguay : Bolivia	1:0 (1:0)
29/03/00	Peru : Paraguay	2:0 (0:0)
29/03/00	Argentina : Chile	4:1 (2:1)
26/04/00	Bolivia : Colombia	1:1 (1:1)
26/04/00	Paraguay : Uruguay	1:0 (1:0)
26/04/00	Venezuela : Argentina	0:4 (0:2)
26/04/00	Chile : Peru	1:1 (1:1)
26/04/00	Brazil : Ecuador	3:2 (2:1)
03/06/00	Uruguay : Chile	2:1 (2:1)
03/06/00	Paraguay : Ecuador	3:1 (2:0)
04/06/00	Argentina : Bolivia	1:0 (0:0)
04/06/00	Peru : Brazil	0:1 (0:1)
04/06/00	Colombia : Venezuela	3:0 (2:0)
28/06/00	Venezuela : Bolivia	4:2 (2:0)
28/06/00	Brazil : Uruguay	1:1 (0:1)
29/06/00	Ecuador : Peru	2:1 (1:0)
29/06/00	Chile : Paraguay	3:1 (2:0)
29/06/00	Colombia : Argentina	1:3 (1:2)
18/07/00	Uruguay : Venezuela	3:1 (1:1)
18/07/00	Paraguay : Brazil	2:1 (1:0)
19/07/00	Bolivia : Chile	1:0 (0:0)
19/07/00	Argentina : Ecuador	2:0 (1:0)
19/07/00	Peru : Colombia	0:1 (0:0)
25/07/00	Ecuador : Colombia	0:0
25/07/00	Venezuela : Chile	0:2 (0:0)
26/07/00	Uruguay : Peru	0:0
26/07/00	Brazil : Argentina	3:1 (2:1)
27/07/00	Bolivia : Paraguay	0:0
15/08/00	Colombia : Uruguay	1:0 (0:0)
15/08/00	Chile : Brazil	3:0 (2:0)
16/08/00	Ecuador : Bolivia	2:0 (1:0)
16/08/00	Argentina : Paraguay	1:1 (0:0)
16/08/00	Peru : Venezuela	1:0 (0:0)
02/09/00	Paraguay : Venezuela	3:0 (3:0)
02/09/00	Chile : Colombia	0:1 (0:0)
03/09/00	Uruguay : Ecuador	4:0 (2:0)
03/09/00	Peru : Argentina	1:2 (0:2)
03/09/00	Brazil : Bolivia	5:0 (1:0)
07/10/00	Colombia : Paraguay	0:2 (0:1)
08/10/00	Venezuela : Brazil	0:6 (0:5)
08/10/00	Bolivia : Peru	1:0 (1:0)
08/10/00	Ecuador : Chile	1:0 (0:0)
08/10/00	Argentina : Uruguay	2:1 (2:0)
15/11/00	Brazil : Colombia	1:0 (0:0)
15/11/00	Bolivia : Uruguay	0:0
15/11/00	Venezuela : Ecuador	1:2 (0:2)
15/11/00	Paraguay : Peru	5:1 (3:0)
15/11/00	Chile : Argentina	0:2 (0:1)
27/03/01	Colombia : Bolivia	2:0 (0:0)
27/03/01	Peru : Chile	3:1 (0:0)
28/03/01	Ecuador : Brazil	1:0 (0:0)
28/03/01	Uruguay : Paraguay	0:1 (0:0)
28/03/01	Argentina : Venezuela	5:0 (2:0)
24/04/01	Ecuador : Paraguay	2:1 (1:1)
24/04/01	Venezuela : Colombia	2:2 (1:0)
24/04/01	Chile : Uruguay	0:1 (0:1)
25/04/01	Bolivia : Argentina	3:3 (1:1)
25/04/01	Brazil : Peru	1:1 (0:0)
02/06/01	Peru : Ecuador	1:2 (1:1)
02/06/01	Paraguay : Chile	1:0 (0:0)
03/06/01	Argentina : Colombia	3:0 (3:0)
03/06/01	Bolivia : Venezuela	5:0 (3:0)
01/07/01	Uruguay : Brazil	1:0 (1:0)
14/08/01	Venezuela : Uruguay	2:0 (0:0)
14/08/01	Chile : Bolivia	2:2 (1:1)
15/08/01	Ecuador : Argentina	0:2 (0:2)
15/08/01	Brazil : Paraguay	2:0 (1:0)
16/08/01	Colombia : Peru	0:1 (0:0)
04/09/01	Chile : Venezuela	0:2 (0:0)
04/09/01	Peru : Uruguay	0:2 (0:2)
05/09/01	Paraguay : Bolivia	5:1 (2:1)
05/09/01	Argentina : Brazil	2:1 (0:1)
05/09/01	Colombia : Ecuador	0:0
06/10/01	Bolivia : Ecuador	1:5 (0:2)
06/10/01	Venezuela : Peru	3:0 (0:0)
07/10/01	Uruguay : Colombia	1:1 (1:0)
07/10/01	Brazil : Chile	2:0 (0:0)
07/10/01	Paraguay : Argentina	2:2 (0:0)
07/11/01	Ecuador : Uruguay	1:1 (0:1)
07/11/01	Colombia : Chile	3:1 (1:1)
07/11/01	Bolivia : Brazil	3:1 (1:1)
08/11/01	Argentina : Peru	2:0 (0:0)
08/11/01	Venezuela : Paraguay	3:1 (3:1)
14/11/01	Peru : Bolivia	1:1 (1:0)
14/11/01	Uruguay : Argentina	1:1 (1:1)
14/11/01	Paraguay : Colombia	0:4 (0:2)
14/11/01	Chile : Ecuador	0:0 (0:0)
14/11/01	Brazil : Venezuela	3:0 (3:0)

CONMEBOL/OFC Play-off

20/11/01	Australia v Uruguay	1:0 (0:0)
25/11/01	Uruguay v Australia	3:0 (1:0)

Appendices

Appendix One - The Cambridge Rules (1848)

1. This Club shall be called the University Foot Ball Club.

2. At the commencement of play, the ball shall be kicked off from the middle of the ground; after every goal there shall be a kick-off in the same way or manner.

3. After a goal, the losing side shall kick off; the sides changing goals unless a previous arrangement be made to the contrary.

4. The ball is out when it has passed the line of the flag-post on either side of the ground, in which case it shall be thrown in straight.

5. The ball is "behind" when it has passed the goal on either side of it.

6. When the ball is behind, it shall be brought forward at the place where it left the ground not more than ten paces, and kicked off.

7. Goal is when the ball is kicked through the flag-posts and under the string.

8. When a player catches the ball directly from the foot, he may kick it as he can without running with it. In no other case may the ball be touched with the hands, except to stop it.

9. If the ball has passed a player and has come from the direction of his own goal, he may not touch it till the other side have kicked it, unless there are more than three of the other side before him. No player is allowed to loiter between the ball and the adversaries' goal.

10. In no case is holding a player, pushing with the hands or tripping up allowed. Any player may prevent another from getting to the ball by any means consistent with this rule.

11. Every match shall be decided by a majority of goals.

Appendix Two - The Sheffield Club Rules (1857)

1. The kick from the middle must be a place kick.

2. Kick Out must not be more than 25 yards out of goal.

3. Fair Catch is a catch from any player provided the ball has not touched the ground or has not been thrown from touch and is entitled to a free-kick.

4. Charging is fair in case of a place kick (with the exception of a kick-off as soon as a player offers to kick) but he may always draw back unless he has actually touched the ball with his foot.

5. Pushing with the hands is allowed but no hacking or tripping up is fair under any circumstances whatever.

6. No player may be held or pulled over.

7. It is not lawful to take the ball off the ground (except in touch) for any purpose whatever.

8. The ball may be pushed or hit with the hand, but holding the ball except in the case of a free kick is altogether disallowed.

9. A goal must be kicked but not from touch nor by a free kick from a catch.

10. A ball in touch is dead, consequently the side that touches it down must bring it to the edge of the touch and throw it straight out from touch.

11. Each player must provide himself with a red and dark blue flannel cap, one colour to be worn by each side.

Appendix Three - The Uppingham School Rules (1862)

1. A goal is scored whenever the ball is forced through the goal and under the bar, except it be thrown by the hand.

2. Hands may be used only to stop a ball and place it on the ground before the feet.

3. Kicks must be aimed only at the ball.

4. A player may not kick the ball whilst in the air.

5. No tripping up or heel kicking allowed.

6. Whenever a ball is kicked beyond the side flags, it must be returned by the player who kicked it, from the spot it passed the flag-line in a straight line towards the middle of the ground.

7. When a ball is kicked behind he line of goal, it shall be kicked off from that line by one of the side whose goal it is.

8. No player may stand within six paces of the kicker when he is kicking off.

9. A player is out of play immediately he is in front of the ball and must return behind the ball as soon as possible. If the ball is kicked by his own side past a player, he may not touch it, or advance, until one of the other side has first kicked it, or one of his own side, having followed it up, has been able, when in front of him, to kick it.

10. No charging is allowed when a player is out of play - i.e. immediately the ball is behind him.

Appendix Four - The Football Association Rules (1863)

1. The maximum length of the ground shall be 200 yards, the maximum breadth shall be 100 yards, the length and breadth shall be marked off with flags; and the goal shall be defined by two upright posts, eight yards apart, with out any tape or bar across them.

2. A toss for goal shall take place, and the game shall be commenced by a place kick from the centre of the ground by the side losing the toss for goals; the other side shall not approach within 10 yards of the ball until it is kicked off.

3. After a goal is won, the losing side shall be entitled to kick off, and the two sides shall change goals after each goal is won.

4. A goal shall be won when the ball passes between the goal-posts or over the space between the goal-posts (at whatever height), not being thrown, knocked on, or carried.

5. When the ball is in touch, the first player who touches it shall throw it from the point on the boundary line where it left the ground in a direction at right angles with the boundary line, and the ball shall not be in play until it has touched the ground.

6. When a player has kicked the ball, any one of the same side who is nearer to the opponent's goal line is out of play and may not touch the ball himself, nor in any way whatever prevent any other player from doing so, until he is in play; but no player is out of play when the ball is kicked off from behind the goal line.

7. In case the ball goes behind the goal line, if a player on the side to whom the goal belongs first touches the ball, one of his side shall be entitled to a free kick from the goal line at the point opposite the place where the ball shall be touched. If a player of the opposite side first touches the ball, one of his side shall be entitled to free kick at the goal only from a point 15 yards outside the goal line, opposite the place where the ball is touched, the opposing side standing within their goal line until he has had his kick.

8. If a player makes a fair catch, he shall be entitled to a free kick, providing he claims it by making a mark with his heel at once; and in order to take such a kick he may go back as far as he pleases, and no player on the opposite side shall advance beyond his mark until he has kicked.

9. No player shall run with the ball.

10. Neither tripping nor hacking shall be allowed, and no player shall use his hands to hold or push his adversary.

11. A player shall not be allowed to throw the ball or pass it to another with his hands.

12. No player shall be allowed to take the ball from the ground with his hands under any pretext whatever while it is play.

13. No player shall be allowed to wear projecting nails, iron plates, or gutta percha on the soles or heels of his boots.

Bibliography

General Works

Bryon Butler, *The Official Illustrated History of the FA Cup* (Headline Book Publishing, London, 1996)

Bryon Butler, *The Official History of the Football Association* (Queen Anne Press, 1991)

Jack Rollin, *The World Cup 1930-1990, Sixty Glorious Years of Soccer's Premier Event* (Guinness Publishing Limited, Enfield, 1990)

Eduardo Galeano, *Football in Sun and Shadow* (Fourth Estate Limited, London, 1997)

Glenn Moore (ed.), *The Concise Encyclopedia of World Football* (Colour Library Direct, Godalming, 1998)

Pete Davies, *Twenty-two Men in Funny Shorts, The Intelligent Fan's Guide to Soccer and World Cup '94* (Random House, 1994)

David Miller, *World Cup, The Argentina Story* (Frederick Warne Limited, London, 1978)

World Cup Cock Ups, The Extraordinary Facts and Funny Stories from the 1930-1998 World Cups (Chameleon Books, London, 998)

Nicholas Keith and Norman Fox, *World Cup '82, A Complete Guide* (Park Lane Press, London, 1982)

Elizabeth Campling, *Portrait of a Decade, The 1980s* (B. T. Batsford Limited, London, 1990)

Simon Kupper, *Football Against the Enemy* (Orion Books Limited, London, 1994)

Stephen F. Kelly, *Back Page Football* (MacDonald, Queen Anne, 1988)

Terry Venables, *The Best Game in the World* (Arrow Books, 1997)

Ian Buchan, *British Olympians, A Hundred Years of Gold Medals* (Guiness, 1991)

Guy Oliver, *The Guiness Book of World Football* (Guy Oliver, 1992)

Norman Barrett, *The Daily Telegraph Football Chronicle* (Carlton Books, 1996)

Roger Taylor and Andrew Ward, *Kicking and Screaming, An Oral History of Football in England* (Robson Books, 1995)

Norman S. Barrett, *Purnell's Encyclopedia of Association Football* (Purnell books, 1972)

Shakespeare's England, Volume Two (Oxford University Press, 1916)

John Robinson, *Soccer - The World Cup, 1930-1998* (Soccer Books Ltd., 1998)

Chris Nawrat and Steve Hutchings, *The Sunday Times Illustrated History of Football* (Reed International Books, 1994)

The Victorian County History of Derbyshire

Ian Morrison, *The World Cup: A Complete Guide* (Breedon Books, 1990)

Frank Nicklis, *The Ultimate World Cup Fact and Quiz Book* (Stopwatch Publishing, 1998)

Newspapers

The Times (London), The Observer (London), The Daily and Sunday Telegraphs (London), The Independent and Independent on Sunday (London), The Guardian (Manchester/London), The Daily Mail (London), The Sun (London), The Daily Herald (London), London Evening Standard, The Sheffield Star, The Daily Record (Glasgow), Liverpool Echo, The Daily Express (London), Athletic News (London), Le Figaro (Paris), Gazeta Polska (Warsaw), The Irish Times (Dublin), Le Monde (Paris), Le Monde Illustré (Paris), Neue Freie Press (Vienna), The New York Times, The News of the World (London), The Sporting Chronicle (Manchester), The Standard and River Plate News (Buenos Aires), The Sunday Mail (Glasgow), The Sunday Post (Glasgow), Le Temps (Paris), La Tribuna (Rome).

Magazines

The Observer Sports Monthly, World Soccer, Football World, Time Magazine

Web Sites

www.fifa.com

www.worldcuparchive.com

www.geocities.com

www.the-afs.com

www.cc.columbia.edu

www.hcm.fpt.vn

www.quark.lu.se

www.platini.com

www.football.nationwide.co.uk

www.sportinglife.com

www.sportscheduler.co.sz/AfSocMag

www.fortunecity.com

www.washingtonpost.com

www.canoe.com

www.risc.uni-linz.ac.at

www.soccerindex.com

Index

Index

Index

Index